Children in Context

To FHM

With love always, TKM

Children in Context

A Topical Approach

Tara L. Kuther

Western Connecticut State University, USA

FOR INFORMATION:

2455 Teller Road
Thousand Oaks, California 91320
E-mail: order@sagepub.com

1 Oliver's Yard
55 City Road
London, EC1Y 1SP
United Kingdom

Unit No. 323-333, Third Floor, F-Block
International Trade Tower
Nehru Place, New Delhi – 110 019
India

18 Cross Street #10-10/11/12
China Square Central
Singapore 048423

Acquisitions Editor: Adeline Grout
Content Development Editor: Emma Newsom
Production Editor: Neelu Sahu
Copy Editor: Deanna Noga
Typesetter: diacriTech
Cover Designer: Scott Van Atta
Marketing Manager: Victoria Velasquez

Copyright © 2026 by Sage.

All rights reserved. Except as permitted by U.S. copyright law, no part of this work may be reproduced or distributed in any form or by any means, or stored in a database or retrieval system, without permission in writing from the publisher.

All third party trademarks referenced or depicted herein are included solely for the purpose of illustration and are the property of their respective owners. Reference to these trademarks in no way indicates any relationship with, or endorsement by, the trademark owner.

Printed in the United States of America

Library of Congress Cataloging-in-Publication Data

Names: Kuther, Tara L., author.

Title: Children in context : a tropical approach / Tara L. Kuther, Western Connecticut State University, USA.

Description: Thousand Oaks, California : Sage, [2026] | Includes bibliographical references and index. | Summary: "In the topically organized Children in Context, award-winning author Tara L. Kuther emphasizes three core themes of child development: the importance of context, the relevance of research, and the applied value of developmental science. Examining child development by using real-life contexts, including gender, race and ethnicity, and socioeconomic status, the text engages students with current data, relatable examples, and cross-cultural stories. Students will come away with an understanding of these themes that they can immediately apply to their own lives and future careers"—Provided by publisher.

Identifiers: LCCN 2024044788 | ISBN 9781544334189 (paperback) | ISBN 9781544334172 | ISBN 9781544334158 (epub) | ISBN 9781544334165 (epub) | ISBN 9781544334196 (pdf)

Subjects: LCSH: Child development.

Classification: LCC HQ767.9 .K865 2026 | DDC 305.231—dc23/eng/20241202

LC record available at https://lccn.loc.gov/2024044788

This book is printed on acid-free paper.

25 26 27 28 29 10 9 8 7 6 5 4 3 2 1

BRIEF CONTENTS

Preface	xxi
Acknowledgments	xxv
About the Author	xxvii

PART 1 FOUNDATIONS OF CHILD DEVELOPMENT   1
Chapter 1   Introduction to Child Development: Themes, Theories, and Research   3

PART 2 PHYSICAL DEVELOPMENT AND HEALTH   41
Chapter 2   Biological and Environmental Foundations of Development   43
Chapter 3   The Prenatal Period, Birth, and the Newborn   71
Chapter 4   Brain, Perception, and Motor Development   103
Chapter 5   Physical Development and Health   135

PART 3 COGNITIVE DEVELOPMENT   171
Chapter 6   Cognitive Change: Cognitive-Developmental and Sociocultural Approaches   173
Chapter 7   Information Processing Theory   203
Chapter 8   Intelligence   233
Chapter 9   Language Development   257

PART 4 SOCIOEMOTIONAL DEVELOPMENT   287
Chapter 10   Emotional Development   289
Chapter 11   Self, Identity, and Personality   319
Chapter 12   Moral Development   345
Chapter 13   Gender   371

PART 5 CONTEXTS OF DEVELOPMENT   401
Chapter 14   Families   403
Chapter 15   Contexts of Development   431

Glossary	465
References	475
Author Index	627
Subject Index	649

Instructors,
what if your students...

...truly enjoyed their reading?

...were better prepared for class?

...felt invested in their learning?

"Interactive, engaging, and simple to use."
—Alyssa Salazar, Student
University of North Texas

Choose to use this textbook on the Vantage learning platform

See why you'll love Vantage at
collegepublishing.sagepub.com/vantage

Sage Vantage
engage. learn. soar.

Sage Vantage is not available for purchase outside of the United States.

DETAILED CONTENTS

Preface	xxi
Acknowledgments	xxv
About the Author	xxvii

PART 1   FOUNDATIONS OF CHILD DEVELOPMENT   1

Chapter 1   Introduction to Child Development: Themes, Theories, and Research   3

Understanding Development	4
Why Study Children?	4
Periods of Development	5
Prenatal period (conception to birth)	5
Infancy and toddlerhood (Birth to about 2 years)	5
Early childhood (about 2 to about 6 years)	5
Middle childhood (about 6 to about 11 years)	5
Adolescence (about 11 to about 18 years)	5
Developmental Domains	6
Context	6
Sociohistorical Context	7
Cultural Context	7
Core Concepts in Developmental Science	8
Nature and Nurture: How do biology and environment influence development?	8
The Active Child: How do children influence their own development?	9
Continuities and Discontinuities: In what ways is development continuous and discontinuous?	9
Theories of Child Development	11
Psychoanalytic Theories	11
Freud's Psychosexual Theory	11
Erikson's Psychosocial Theory	11
Behaviorist and Social Learning Theories	13
Pavlov's Classical Conditioning	13
Skinner's Operant Conditioning	14
Bandura's Social Cognitive Theory	14
Cognitive Theories	15
Piaget's Cognitive-Developmental Theory	15
Information Processing Theory	16
Vygotsky's Sociocultural Theory	17
Systems Theories	17
Bronfenbrenner's Bioecological Systems Theory	17
Thelen's Dynamic Systems Theory	19
Ethology and Evolutionary Developmental Theory	20
Research in Child Development	22
The Scientific Method	22
Methods of Data Collection	23
Observational Measures	23
Self-Report Measures	24
Physiological Measures	25
Research Designs	27
Case Study	27
Correlational Research	27

Experimental Research	27
Developmental Research Designs	28
Cross-Sectional Research	28
Longitudinal Research	28
Sequential Research	29
Applied Developmental Science, Ethics, and Intersectionality	30
Research Ethics	31
Help and Not Harm Participants	31
Responsibility to Participants and Society	31
Be Honest and Fair to Participants	31
Respect Participant Autonomy	31
Intersectionality and Development	32
Apply Your Knowledge	33
Chapter Summary	34
Key Terms	35
Careers in Child Development: Foundations of Development	36

PART 2 PHYSICAL DEVELOPMENT AND HEALTH 41

Chapter 2 Biological and Environmental Foundations of Development 43

Genetic Foundations of Development	44
Genetics	44
Cell Reproduction	44
Sex Determination	45
Genes Shared by Twins	45
Patterns of Genetic Inheritance	46
Dominant-Recessive Inheritance	46
Incomplete Dominance	48
Genomic Imprinting	48
Polygenic Inheritance	48
Chromosomal and Genetic Abnormalities	49
Genetic Disorders	49
Dominant-Recessive Disorders	49
X-Linked Disorders	50
Chromosomal Abnormalities	51
Down Syndrome	51
Sex Chromosome Abnormalities	52
Mutation	53
Reproductive Technology and Genetic Disorders	54
Genetic Counseling	54
Assisted Reproductive Technology	54
Artificial Insemination	55
In Vitro Fertilization	55
Surrogacy	56
Adoption	56
Prenatal Diagnosis	57
Methods of Prenatal Diagnosis	57
Prenatal Treatment of Genetic Disorders	59
Heredity and Environment Interactions	59
Behavior Genetics	59
Behavior Genetics Research Methods	60
Heritability and Personal Characteristics	60
Nonshared Environment	61
Gene-Environment Interactions	61
Range of Reaction	62

	Gene-Environment Correlation	63
	Gene-Environment (G x E) Interactions	64
	Epigenetic Framework	66
	Epigenetic Processes in Animals	66
	Epigenetic Processes in People	66
Apply Your Knowledge		67
Chapter Summary		68
Key Terms		69

Chapter 3 The Prenatal Period, Birth, and the Newborn — 71

Prenatal Development — 72
- Conception — 72
- Germinal Period (0 to 2 Weeks) — 73
- Embryonic Period (3 to 8 Weeks) — 74
- Fetal Period (9 Weeks to Birth) — 75

Environmental Influences on Prenatal Development — 77
- Principles of Teratology — 77
  - Critical Periods — 77
  - Dose — 77
  - Individual Differences — 78
  - Complicated Effects — 78
- Types of Teratogens — 78
  - Prescription and Nonprescription Drugs — 79
  - Alcohol — 79
  - Cigarette Use and E-Cigarette Use — 80
  - Marijuana — 80
  - Cocaine — 81
  - Opioids — 81
  - Environmental Hazards — 81
- Contextual Influences on Prenatal Substance Use and Perinatal Outcomes — 81
  - Racial Disparities in Addressing Maternal Substance Use — 82
  - Teratogen-Context Interactions — 82

The Prenatal Environment and Prenatal Care — 83
- Maternal Nutrition — 83
- Maternal Illness — 84
- Maternal Emotional Well-Being — 85
- Maternal Age — 85
- Paternal Characteristics and Prenatal Development — 86
- Prenatal Care — 87
  - Barriers to Prenatal Care — 87
  - Race, Ethnicity, and Prenatal Care — 87

Childbirth — 89
- Labor — 89
- Medication During Delivery — 91
- Cesarean Delivery — 91
- Natural Childbirth — 91
- Home Birth — 91
- Cultural Childbirth Practices — 92
- Newborn Health Screening — 92
- Low Birth Weight and Preterm Infants — 93
  - Characteristics of Low Birth Weight Infants — 93
  - Race, SES, and Low Birth Weight — 94
  - Caring for Low Birth Weight Infants — 94

The Newborn — 95
- Perceptual Capacities — 95

States of Arousal	96
Reflexes	97
Early Learning Capacities	97
Habituation	97
Classical Conditioning	98
Operant Conditioning	99
Apply Your Knowledge	100
Chapter Summary	101
Key Terms	102

Chapter 4   Brain, Perception, and Motor Development   103

Processes of Brain Development	104
The Neuron	104
Neurogenesis	105
Synaptogenesis and Pruning	106
Myelination	107
The Cerebral Cortex	107
Lateralization	108
Brain Development	109
Infancy	109
Experience-Expectant Brain Development	109
Experience-Dependent Brain Development	109
Childhood	111
Growth and Plasticity	111
Gray and White Matter	111
Adolescence	112
Volume Changes	112
Differences in Timing	112
Reward Sensitivity	114
Motor Development	114
Gross Motor Development	114
Infancy	115
Childhood	116
Fine Motor Development	117
Infancy	117
Childhood	117
Motor Development as a Dynamic System	118
Biological Influences on Motor Development	119
Practice and Motor Development	119
Cultural Styles of Interaction and Motor Development	120
Dynamic Systems Theory	121
Physical Maturation and Integrated Abilities	122
Goal-Directed Behavior	122
Social and Cultural Context	123
Sensory and Perceptual Development	124
Methods for Studying Infant Perception	124
Vision	125
Newborn Visual Processing	125
Face Perception	126
Color Vision	126
Depth Perception	127
Visual Impairment	128
Hearing	128
Touch	128
Smell and Taste	129

Detailed Contents **xi**

Intermodal Perception	129
Infant-Context Interactions and Perceptual Development	130
Apply Your Knowledge	131
Chapter Summary	131
Key Terms	133

Chapter 5 Physical Development and Health 135

Body Growth in Infancy and Childhood	136
Patterns of Growth	136
Growth in Infancy	137
Growth in Childhood	138
Nutrition and Growth	138
Breastfeeding	138
Childhood Food Preferences	139
Malnutrition	139
Marasmus, Kwashiorkor, and Growth Stunting	140
Malnutrition and Brain Development	140
Physical Activity	142
Sleep	142
Infancy	142
Childhood	143
Body Growth and Maturation in Adolescence	144
Puberty	144
Growth Spurt	144
Secondary Sex Characteristics	145
Primary Sex Characteristics	145
Biological and Contextual Influences on Pubertal Timing	146
Genetics	146
Weight and Nutrition	146
Stress	147
Secular Trend	147
Pubertal Timing and Socioemotional Development	147
Physical Activity	148
Sleep	149
Threats to Infants and Children's Health	150
Injuries and Mortality	150
Infancy	150
Childhood	152
COVID-19 and Children	153
Childhood Asthma	153
Childhood Obesity	153
Child Abuse	155
Threats to Adolescent Health	157
Injuries and Mortality	157
Eating Disorders	158
Anorexia Nervosa, Bulimia Nervosa, and Binge Eating Disorder	158
Prevalence of Eating Disorders	159
Influences and Treatment	159
Alcohol and Substance Use	159
Cigarette and E-Cigarette Use	161
Depression and Suicide	161
Risk Factors for Depression and Suicide	162
COVID-19, Depression, and Suicide	163
Suicide Prevention	163
Apply Your Knowledge	164

Chapter Summary	165
Key Terms	166
Careers in Child Development: Physical Development and Health	166

PART 3 COGNITIVE DEVELOPMENT — 171

Chapter 6 Cognitive Change: Cognitive-Developmental and Sociocultural Approaches — 173

Piaget's Theory: Sensorimotor Reasoning in Infancy	174
Processes of Cognitive Development	174
Assimilation and Accommodation	175
Equilibration	175
Sensorimotor Reasoning	176
Substage 1: Reflexes (Birth to 1 Month)	176
Substage 2: Primary Circular Reactions (1 to 4 Months)	176
Substage 3: Secondary Circular Reactions (4 to 8 Months)	176
Substage 4: Coordination of Secondary Circular Reactions (8 to 12 Months)	177
Substage 5: Tertiary Circular Reactions (12 to 18 Months)	177
Substage 6: Mental Representation (18 to 24 Months)	178
Evaluating Piaget's Theory: Underestimating Infants	179
Violation-of-Expectation Tasks	179
Simple Tasks	181
A-Not-B Tasks	181
Deferred Imitation Tasks	182
Core Knowledge Theory	182
Preoperational Reasoning in Early Childhood	183
Characteristics of Preoperational Reasoning	184
Egocentrism	184
Animism	184
Centration	185
Irreversibility	185
Evaluating Piaget's Theory: Underestimating Young Children	186
Egocentrism and Animism	187
Reversibility and the Appearance-Reality Distinction	187
Preoperational Reasoning and Education	187
Concrete Operational Reasoning in Middle Childhood	188
Characteristics of Concrete Operational Reasoning	188
Classification	188
Conservation	189
Evaluating Piaget's Theory: Context, Culture, and Concrete Operational Reasoning	190
Schooling and Language	190
Familiarity and Contextual Demands	190
Concrete Operational Reasoning and Education	191
Formal Operational Reasoning in Adolescence	192
Characteristics of Formal Operational Reasoning	192
Evaluating Formal Operational Reasoning	192
Opportunities to Apply Formal Operational Reasoning	192
Limited Use of Formal Operational Reasoning	193
Variability in Formal Operational Reasoning	194
Social Cognition in Adolescence	194
Perspective Taking	194
Adolescent Egocentrism	194
Vygotsky's Sociocultural Theory	195
Cultural Tools	196
Guided Participation and Scaffolding	196

Zone of Proximal Development	197
Private Speech	198
Evaluating Vygotsky's Sociocultural Theory	198
Apply Your Knowledge	199
Chapter Summary	200
Key Terms	202

Chapter 7 Information Processing Theory — 203

Information Processing Theory	204
Information Processing Assumptions	204
Mental Stores	205
Sensory Memory	205
Working Memory	205
Long-Term Memory	206
What Develops	206
Attention	207
Types of Attention	207
Infancy	207
Childhood	209
Developmental Changes	210
Attention-Deficit/Hyperactivity Disorder	210
Adolescence	210
Implications for Education and Parenting	211
Working Memory and Executive Function	212
Infancy	212
Childhood	213
Planning	213
Inhibitory Control	213
Adolescence	214
Exposure to Poverty and Executive Function	214
Implications for Education and Parenting	215
Long-Term Memory	216
Infancy	217
Deferred Imitation	217
Childhood Amnesia	217
Childhood	218
Autobiographical Memory	218
Memory Strategies	219
Knowledge and Experience	220
Memory Suggestibility	220
Adolescence	221
Implications for Education and Parenting	221
Thinking	222
Infancy	222
Habituation Tasks	223
Sequential Touching Tasks	223
Childhood	223
Theory of Mind	223
Context, Culture, and Theory of Mind	224
Metacognition	226
Adolescence	226
Metacognition	226
Decision Making	227
Implications for Education and Parenting	228
Apply Your Knowledge	229

Chapter Summary	229
Key Terms	231

Chapter 8 Intelligence — 233

- Approaches to Understanding Intelligence — 234
  - Psychometric Approach — 234
  - Information Processing and Intelligence — 235
  - Neurological Development and Intelligence — 235
  - Triarchic Theory of Intelligence — 236
  - Multiple Intelligences — 237
  - Emotional Intelligence — 238
- Measuring Intelligence — 239
  - Group Administered Tests — 239
  - Individually Administered Tests — 240
    - Bayley Scales of Infant Development — 240
    - Stanford-Binet Test — 241
    - Weschler Tests — 242
  - Stability and Change in Intelligence in Childhood and Adolescence — 243
- Contextual Influences on Intelligence — 244
  - Sociohistorical Context and IQ — 244
  - Socioeconomic Status and IQ — 245
  - Group Differences and the Majority Culture — 245
  - Stereotypes and IQ — 246
  - Reducing Cultural Bias in IQ Tests — 246
- Neurodevelopmental Conditions — 247
  - Autism Spectrum Disorders — 248
  - Specific Learning Disorder — 249
  - Sensory Processing Disorder — 250
  - Intellectual Disability — 251
  - Context and Disability: Race and SES — 252
  - Giftedness — 253
- Apply Your Knowledge — 254
- Chapter Summary — 255
- Key Terms — 256

Chapter 9 Language Development — 257

- Foundations of Language — 258
  - Language and Development — 258
  - Components of Language — 259
    - Phonology — 259
    - Morphology — 259
    - Syntax — 259
    - Semantics — 260
    - Pragmatics — 260
  - Language Development in Infancy and Toddlerhood — 261
    - Early Preferences for Speech Sounds — 261
    - Prelinguistic Communication — 262
    - Putting Words Together — 262
      - First Words — 262
      - Learning Words — 263
      - Two-Word Utterances — 264
    - Infant Gesture — 265
    - Language Development in Bilingual Infants — 265
    - Language Development in Deaf Infants — 266

Language Development In Childhood And Adolescence	267
Early Childhood	267
Vocabulary	267
Syntax and Pragmatics	268
Bilingual Language Learning	268
School-Age Children and Adolescents	270
Vocabulary	270
Grammar	270
Pragmatics	271
Bilingual Language Learning	271
Explanations for Language Development	273
Learning Theory	273
Nativist Theory	274
Interactionist Theory	274
Biological Influences	275
Environmental Influences	275
Contextual Influences on Language Development	276
Exposure to Infant-Directed Speech	276
Socioeconomic Status and Language Development	277
Apply Your Knowledge	280
Summary	280
Key Terms	281
Careers in Child Development: Cognitive Development	282

PART 4   SOCIOEMOTIONAL DEVELOPMENT   287

Chapter 10   Emotional Development   289

Emotional Experience	290
Infants' Emotional Experience	290
Primary Emotions	290
Self-Conscious Emotions	292
Recognizing Others' Emotions	292
Stranger Wariness	293
Children's Emotional Experience	294
Understanding Others' Emotions	294
Social Interaction and Emotional Understanding	295
Masks and Emotion Recognition	295
Adolescents' Emotional Experience	296
Emotional Regulation	297
Infancy	297
Managing Emotions	297
Caregiver Sensitivity	298
Dynamic Caregiver-Infant Interactions	299
Childhood	299
Strategies	299
Emotional Display Rules	300
Cultural Socialization	300
Adolescence	301
Temperament	302
Styles of Temperament	302
Context and Goodness of Fit	304
Infant Temperament	304
Caregiver Temperament and Expectations	305
Experience and Goodness of Fit	305
Cultural Differences in Temperament	306

Attachment ... 307
- What Is Attachment? ... 307
- Bowlby's Ethological Theory of Attachment ... 307
  - Infants' Signals and Adults' Responses ... 307
  - Phases of Attachment ... 308
- Ainsworth's Strange Situation and Attachment Classifications ... 309
- Secure Base and Internal Working Models ... 310
- Influences on Attachment ... 311
  - Sensitive Caregiving ... 311
  - Caregiver Depression ... 311
  - Father-Infant Attachment ... 312
- Stability of Attachment ... 313
- Cultural Variations in Attachment Classifications ... 313
- Attachment in Childhood and Adolescence ... 315

Apply Your Knowledge ... 316

Chapter Summary ... 317

Key Terms ... 318

Chapter 11 Self, Identity, and Personality ... 319

Self-concept ... 320
- Infancy ... 320
  - Self-Awareness ... 320
  - Self-Recognition ... 321
  - Emerging Self-Concept ... 322
- Childhood ... 322
- Adolescence ... 323

Self-esteem ... 324
- Early Childhood ... 324
- Middle Childhood ... 324
- Adolescence ... 325
  - Shifts in Self-Esteem ... 325
  - Racial and Ethnic Differences ... 325
  - Self-Esteem and Adjustment ... 326
  - Contextual Influences on Self-Esteem ... 326

Identity ... 327
- Psychosocial Moratorium ... 327
- Identity Status ... 328
- Domains of Identity ... 329
- Influences on Identity Development ... 330
- Outcomes Associated With Identity Development ... 331

Ethnic-racial Identity ... 331
- Infancy ... 332
- Childhood ... 332
- Ethnic-Racial Identity in Adolescence ... 333
- Influences on Ethnic-Racial Identity ... 334
  - Parents ... 334
  - Peers ... 335
  - Teachers and Schools ... 336
- Discrimination and Ethnic-Racial Identity ... 336

Achievement Motivation ... 337
- Mastery Motivation ... 337
- Achievement Motivation ... 338
  - Achievement Attributions ... 338
  - Mindset ... 338
  - Goals ... 338

Mastery Orientation and Helpless Orientation	339
Contextual Influences on Achievement Motivation	339
Parents	339
Teachers	340
Peers	341
Apply Your Knowledge	341
Chapter Summary	342
Key Terms	343

Chapter 12 Moral Development — 345

Moral Reasoning	346
Reasoning About Rules: Piaget's Theory	346
Reasoning About Justice: Kohlberg's Theory	347
Developmental Changes in Moral Reasoning	349
Influences on Moral Reasoning	349
Gender and Moral Reasoning	350
Culture and Moral Reasoning	350
Moral Reasoning and Behavior	350
Children's Conceptions of Moral, Social, and Personal Issues	351
Young Children	351
Older Children	351
Culture	352
Prosocial Behavior	353
Helping	353
Sharing	354
Developmental Changes	354
Prosocial Behavior in Adolescence	355
Prosocial Behavior and Adjustment	355
Influences on Prosocial Behavior	355
Biological Influences	356
Family Influences	356
Peer Influences	357
Cultural Context	358
Aggression and Antisocial Behavior	359
Aggression	359
Bullying	360
Children Who Bully	360
Children who are Bullied	361
Bullying Intervention	362
Delinquency	363
Religion and Spirituality	364
Religiosity in Childhood	364
Religiosity in Adolescence	364
Religious Socialization	365
Religiosity and Adjustment	366
Apply Your Knowledge	367
Chapter Summary	367
Key Terms	369

Chapter 13 Gender — 371

Sex Differences and Gender Stereotypes	372
Gender Stereotypes	372
Sex Differences	373
Physical Abilities	373

Cognitive Abilities	374
Similarities and Differences in Socioemotional Abilities	375
Gender Typing	**375**
Biological Explanations	376
Evolution	376
Genes	376
Hormones	376
Cognitive Explanations	376
Cognitive Developmental Theory	376
Gender Schema Theory	377
Contextual Explanations	378
Parents	378
Peers	379
Media	380
Reducing Gender Stereotyping	380
Gender Identity in Childhood and Adolescence	**382**
Dimensions of Gender Identity	382
Felt Gender Typicality	382
Gender Contentedness	382
Felt Pressure to Conform to Gender Roles	383
Gender Typing and Sexual Orientation	383
Gender Identity in Adolescence	384
Gender Identity	384
Gender Intensification	384
Transgender Identity	**385**
Childhood	386
Adolescence	386
Adjustment	387
Gender Affirming Support	387
Gender-Affirming Health Care	388
Sexual Activity in Adolescence	**389**
Prevalence of Sexual Activity	389
Lesbian, Gay, and Bisexual Adolescents	390
Parents, Peers, and Adolescent Sexual Activity	392
Contraceptive Use	392
Adolescent Pregnancy	392
Outcomes of Adolescent Pregnancy	393
Supports for Adolescent Parents	393
Sexuality Education	393
Apply Your Knowledge	**394**
Chapter Summary	**395**
Key Terms	**396**
Careers in Child Development: Socioemotional Development	**396**

PART 5   CONTEXTS OF DEVELOPMENT   401

Chapter 14   Families   403

The Family as a System	404
Changing Child	404
Changing Parent	405
Siblings	406
Childhood	406
Adolescence	406
Only Children	407

Parenting	408
Parenting Styles	409
Authoritarian Parenting Style	409
Permissive Parenting Style	410
Uninvolved Parenting Style	410
Authoritative Parenting Style	411
Discipline	411
Physical Punishment	411
Inductive Discipline	412
Culture, Context, and Parenting	413
Cross Cultural Comparisons	413
North American Children	414
Parent-Adolescent Relationships	414
Conflict	415
Monitoring	416
Family Constellations	416
Same-Sex Parented Families	417
One-Parent Families	418
Cohabiting Families	419
Divorced and Divorcing Families	419
Blended Families	420
Adoptive Families	421
Adoption and Child Outcomes	421
Transracial Adoption	422
Grandparent-Headed Families	422
Challenges for Families	423
Parental Incarceration	423
Parental Deployment	424
Migrant Families	425
COVID-19 and Families	426
Family System	426
Racial Disparities	426
Apply Your Knowledge	428
Chapter Summary	428
Key Terms	430
Chapter 15 Contexts of Development	**431**
Children's Play	432
Play and Cognitive Development	432
Social Development and Early Friendships	433
Sociodramatic Play	433
Rough-and-Tumble Play	434
Imaginary Companions	434
Culture and Play	435
Peer Relationships	436
Friendship	436
Who are children's and adolescents' friends?	436
Friendship Qualities	437
Friendship Stability	437
Peer Acceptance, Popularity, and Rejection	438
Cliques and Crowds	439
Peer Conformity	440
School	442

Educational Approaches	442
Early Childhood Education Interventions	443
Children's Access to Digital Technology	444
Educating Children With Special Needs	445
School Transitions	446
Connections With Teachers	446
Racial and Ethnic Differences	447
Contextual Influences on Academic Achievement	447
Parents	447
Peers	447
Teachers	448
Schools	448
Media	448
Screen Media Use in Infancy	449
Screen Media Use in Childhood and Adolescence	449
Media Violence	450
Television	450
Video Games	451
Social Media and Adolescent Development	452
Adolescents' Views of Social Media	452
Effects of Social Media	452
Social Media and Development	452
Risk and Resilience	453
Exposure to Early Life Stress	453
Foster Care	454
Neighborhood and Community Violence	455
War and Terror	456
Resilience	457
Apply Your Knowledge	458
Chapter Summary	459
Key Terms	461
Careers in Child Development: Contexts of Development	461

Glossary	**465**
References	**475**
Author Index	**627**
Subject Index	**649**

PREFACE

Thirty years ago, I taught my first undergraduate course in child development. In the following decades, I've interacted with thousands of students in over 100 course sections. *Children in Context: A Topical Approach* is the result of my in-class and out-of-class discussions with my students about the nature of development. Students often find child development inherently interesting as they have observed and experienced many of the topics we discuss. Sharing observations and personal experiences is fun and engaging. But sometimes our individual experiences and observations don't completely match the theoretical and research conclusions we discuss. How do we make sense of the differences? In class and in this text, I adopt a contextual perspective to help students understand variability in development and make sense of the growing body of findings in child and adolescent development. My goal in writing this text is to explain the sophisticated interactions that constitute development in a comprehensive yet concise way.

THEMES: CONTEXT AND APPLICATION

Children in Context: A Topical Approach focuses on three key themes for understanding child development: the centrality of context, the applied value of developmental science, and the relevance of intersectionality for understanding development. These themes are highlighted throughout the text and in critical thinking features. An accessible writing style helps students grasp these complex issues, and the text is firmly grounded in classic and cutting-edge science.

Contextual Perspective

The most central tenet of development is that it occurs in context. It is the result of dynamic transactions among individuals, their physical, cognitive, and socioemotional capacities, and the web of interacting contexts in which they are immersed, including family, peers, school, neighborhood, society, culture, and history. *Children in Context: A Topical Approach* discusses these processes, emphasizing how individual factors combine with the people, places, circumstances, and time in which children live to influence development. A contextual approach can provide the backstory to development and help us understand why children vary.

This contextual theme is infused throughout the text and highlighted in critical thinking questions at the end of each section. Thinking in Context items ask students to consider a range of developmental issues, including the impact of biological factors, applying developmental theory and themes, applying Bronfenbrenner's bioecological theory to address real-world problems, and the role of culture in development. Thinking in Context items also highlight the ways in which race, ethnicity, gender, and socioeconomic status (SES) overlap to determine developmental opportunities and outcomes.

Applied Emphasis

The field of developmental science is unique because so much of its content has immediate relevance to our daily lives. Students may wonder: Do the first 3 years shape the brain for a lifetime of experiences? Can we teach babies to communicate through sign language? Is learning more than one language beneficial to children? What does it mean to be a transgender child? Developmental science is increasingly applied to influence social policy. For example, why vaccinate infants? Can we outlaw bullying? Research in child and adolescent development can inform our understanding of each of these topics. Moreover, these topics fascinate students because they illustrate clear-cut examples of why developmental science matters.

Application is integrated throughout the text, including Thinking in Context items that ask students to apply the course content by generating examples, designing research studies, and explaining the material to different audiences and contexts. Each chapter closes with an Apply Your Knowledge case that invites students to consider how the content may be applied to a realistic scenario.

Intersectionality and Development

A contextual and applied perspective highlights the role of intersectionality in development. Diverse identities and experiences accompany race, ethnicity, gender, sexual orientation, SES, and other social category memberships. Inequities are experienced as racism, sexism, classism, heterosexism, and more, and shape children's and families' lived experiences, opportunities, and developmental outcomes. Until recently, people of color have either been excluded from research studies or grouped as *minorities*, masking differences and contributing to a sense of invisibility among people of color. I examine development through an intersectional lens whenever possible.

Examples of intersectional and diversity, equity, and inclusion-related content in *Children in Context: A Topical Approach* include examining racial, ethnic, gender, sexual orientation, and SES differences and interactions in:

- Individuals' experiences of pregnancy and prenatal development, including access to reproductive technology and prenatal care, birth outcomes, barriers to breastfeeding, adolescent pregnancy, and reporting and criminal sanctions for drug use in pregnant women.

- Children's physical development and health, such as socioeconomic influences on brain development and health, including growth, activity, and nutrition, and illnesses, injuries, and mortality, as well as COVID-19 experiences and outcomes. Persistent problems such as food insecurity and exposure to stress and trauma influence brain development, stress reactivity, and pubertal timing and play a role in mental health, including rates of eating disorders, depression, and suicide.

- Cognitive and language development, such as facial perception and the other race-face effect, diagnoses of neurodevelopmental disabilities, rates and forms of child-directed speech, influences and outcomes of bilingualism, and even gene-IQ correlations.

- Socioemotional development, such as emotional regulation and the sense of self, including self-concept, self-esteem, and identity. Ethnic-racial identity is a major heading in Chapter 11, including children's understanding of race, perception of skin color, ethnic socialization, experiences with discrimination, and overall adjustment. Transgender identity is a major heading in Chapter 13, which examines transgender identity in childhood and adolescence, adjustment, and gender-affirming care, as well as developmental transitions, risks, and supports for LGBTQ+ adolescents.

- Children's social contexts, including family formations, such as one-parent, cohabitating, adoptive, and foster families, parenting styles, and the effects of different family experiences, such as parental incarceration, parental deployment, and immigration. Contextual stressors that vary with intersectional factors include exposure to early life stress, neighborhood and community violence, war and terror, and experiences during the COVID-19 pandemic.

Current Research

Child development instructors face the challenge of covering the growing mass of research findings within the confines of a single semester. *Children in Context: A Topical Approach* integrates recently published and classic findings. Rather than present an exhaustive review of current work simply for the sake of including recent references, I carefully select the most relevant findings. I integrate cutting-edge and classic research to present a unified story of what is currently known in developmental science.

Accessible Writing Style

Having taught undergraduate students at a regional public university for 30 years, I write in a style intended to engage diverse readers like my own students. My day-to-day classroom experiences have helped me keep college students' interests and abilities at the forefront. Unlike many textbook authors, I teach four classes each semester. I taught my first online course in 2002, well before the COVID-19 pandemic. My daily exposure to multiple classes and many students helps keep me grounded in college students' ever-changing concerns and interests.

My institution is embedded in a diverse community in which about 40 languages are spoken. My students are similarly diverse in background, race, ethnicity, and SES. Some live on campus, but at least three-quarters of students commute. Most of my students are age 18 to 24, but my classes also include many adults over the age of 24. Many are veterans, a rapidly increasing population at my institution with unique perspectives and needs.

I attempt to write in the same voice as I teach, carefully structuring sections to build explanations and integrating content with examples that are relevant to students. My experience teaching 12 courses during the COVID-19 pandemic in the Spring of 2020 and the 2020–2021 academic year reinforced (for me) the importance of accessible, concise textbooks. Like many faculty, I was able to record only so many videos for my asynchronous classes, so I relied heavily on my text, asynchronous discussion posts, and, for the classes where available, Vantage, which enabled students to read the text interactively. I believe that accessible and engaging course materials can make a difference in students' learning despite difficult circumstances.

PEDAGOGICAL FEATURES

Each year I teach two to four sections of child development. I regularly use my own text in class, and students' responses, learning, and especially their questions guide my writing. Current and former students worked with me in preparing this text. I have many opportunities to try new examples and activities. I believe that what works in my classroom will be helpful to readers and instructors. I use the pedagogical elements of *Children in Context: A Topical Approach* in my own classes and modify them based on my experiences.

Critical Thinking Questions

As noted previously, Thinking in Context critical thinking questions appear at the end of each main section of the chapter. The items encourage readers to compare concepts, apply theoretical perspectives, and consider applications of the research findings presented.

Case-Based Application

Each chapter closes with a case scenario, Applying Your Knowledge, followed by in-depth questions that require students to apply their understanding to address a particular situation or problem.

Learning Objectives and Summaries

Core learning objectives are listed at the beginning of each chapter. The end-of-chapter summary returns to each learning objective, recapping the key concepts presented in the chapter related to that objective.

Careers in Child Development

It is an understatement to say that my students are interested in careers—what they will do after college. Students often don't know where to begin in considering possible careers. The Careers in Child Development feature highlights over 30 careers that are related to or benefit from an understanding of child development. Beginning with a discussion of transferrable skills and fields, this feature is organized by developmental domain and appears at the end of each Part: Physical Development and Health, Cognitive Development, Socioemotional Development, and Contexts of Development.

Organization

Children in Context: A Topical Approach is organized into 15 topical chapters, within five units, that depict the wide range of developments that occur over childhood. Part 1, Foundations of Child and Adolescent Development, includes Chapter 1, which combines developmental theory and research design within a single chapter. I chose this approach because, given limited class time, many instructors do not cover stand-alone research chapters. The streamlined approach combines comprehensive coverage of methods of data collection, research design, developmental designs (such as sequential designs), and ethical issues in research with full coverage of the major theories in developmental psychology. Chapter 2 presents the biological foundations of development, including patterns of genetic inheritance, gene-environment interactions, and epigenetics.

Part 2, Physical Development and Health, includes Chapter 3, which describes prenatal development and birth, from conception to the newborn. I chose to present prenatal development, birth, and the newborn as a single chapter (rather than birth and the newborn as a stand-alone chapter) to reflect continuity in the perinatal period. Chapter 4 examines perceptual and motor development, and Chapter 5 presents physical development and health.

Part 3, Cognitive Development, presents cognition from constructivist (Chapter 6) and information processing (Chapter 7) perspectives. Chapter 8 examines intelligence, as well as neurodevelopmental conditions such as autism spectrum and learning disorders. Chapter 9 presents language development, including development in bilingual language learners.

Part 4 examines Socioemotional Development, specifically emotional development (Chapter 10), the developing sense of self, including ethnic-racial identity (Chapter 11), and moral development (Chapter 12). Chapter 13 focuses on gender development, with extended coverage of children who identify as transgender. The final two chapters, Part 5, focus on contexts of development. Chapter 14 examines the family context, and Chapter 15 focuses on peer, school, neighborhood, and media contexts.

In sum, *Children in Context* contains 15 chapters that correspond to the 15 weeks of the typical college semester.

Resources

This text includes an array of resources designed to save instructors time and to keep students engaged. To learn more, visit sagepub.com or contact your SAGE representative at sagepub.com/findmyrep.

ACKNOWLEDGMENTS

This book has benefitted from the input of many bright, enthusiastic, and generous people. I am fortunate to work with a talented team at SAGE and am grateful for their support. I thank Adeline Grout for her steadfast encouragement and guidance. Emma Newsom provided invaluable support in brainstorming, figures, and photos, ultimately moving this project forward. Thank you! I thank Reid Hester for bringing me to the SAGE family and Lara Parra for her support. Michele Sordi first encouraged me to write a great big book, and I am forever grateful for her confidence.

I thank my students for asking the questions and engaging in the discussions that inform these pages. I am especially appreciative of those who have shared their feedback and helped me improve this book. Thank you to the many instructors who have reviewed and provided feedback on these chapters.

Finally, I thank my family, especially my parents, for their unwavering support: Howdy neighbors! Most of all, I thank my husband, Fred, for his love, encouragement, optimism, and puppy-wrangling skills.

SAGE wishes to thank the following reviewers for their valuable contributions to the development of this manuscript:

Melissa Barnett, University Of Arizona

Charlene Chester, Morgan State University

Li Huang, Tuskegee University

Rosa Li, University of North Carolina-Chapel Hill

Barbara McPherson, California State University-San Marcos

Jennifer Morey, Virginia Peninsula Community College

Sherri Restauri, Coastal Carolina University

Michael Sheridan, SUNY at Buffalo

Nancy Smuckler, University of Wisconsin-Milwaukee

Jodi Swanson, Arizona State University

Dimple Vadgama, Texas Woman's University

Theah Vasquez-O'Brien, Eastern Connecticut State University

ABOUT THE AUTHOR

Tara L. Kuther is professor of psychology at Western Connecticut State University where she has taught courses in child, adolescent, and adult development since 1996. She earned her PhD in developmental psychology at Fordham University. Dr. Kuther is fellow of the Society for the Teaching of Psychology (APA, Division 2), has served in various capacities in the Society for the Teaching of Psychology and Society for Research on Adolescence, and is the former chair of the Teaching Committee for the Society for Research in Child Development. Her research interests include social cognition and risky activity in adolescence and adulthood. She is the award-winning author of *Lifespan Development: Lives in Context*, other developmental psychology texts, as well as books to promote student professional development and help them succeed in college and afterward.

PART 1
FOUNDATIONS OF CHILD DEVELOPMENT

AJ_Watt/istock

1 INTRODUCTION TO CHILD DEVELOPMENT: THEMES, THEORIES, AND RESEARCH

> **LEARNING OBJECTIVES**
>
> 1.1 Describe developmental periods, developmental domains, and the contexts in which development takes place.
>
> 1.2 Explain the nature-nurture debate, how children are active in their development, and how development reflects continuous and discontinuous change.
>
> 1.3 Summarize five categories of theories about child development.
>
> 1.4 Examine the methods and research designs used to study child development.
>
> 1.5 Discuss the field of applied developmental science, scientists' obligation to conduct ethical research, and the role of intersectionality in development.

It was a sunny day. I looked up at the bright sky as I leaned back in my stroller and used two hands to pull my hat down onto my head. The simplest of events, but it is one of my first memories. How old was I? Probably on the brink of early childhood.

What is your first memory? Is it similarly vague? What were you doing? Where were you? Who was nearby? How have you changed in the time since that early memory? Are there ways in which you remain the same? How is your experience similar to and different from other children's experiences? What contributes to these differences?

Why do some children thrive and others struggle? How do the people children interact with and the places they live influence them? How can parents, teachers, and other adults help children? These are some of the questions we consider in this book as we examine the nature of child development, its importance, how it is studied, and how scientific findings can be applied to help children and their families.

UNDERSTANDING DEVELOPMENT

> 1.1 Describe developmental periods, developmental domains, and the contexts in which development takes place.

People undergo innumerable changes as they grow from infants to children and from children to adolescents. **Development** refers to the processes of growth and change, as well as the ways in which we stay the same over time. **Developmental science** is the study of human development at all points in life, from conception to death. In this book, we examine child development. However, individuals undergo complex changes at every period in life, beginning before birth and continuing throughout adulthood. We therefore begin our study of development by considering the question: Why study children?

Why Study Children?

Perhaps the most obvious reason to study children is to promote their development. Parents and caregivers, teachers, researchers, and policymakers approach this goal with different concerns. Parents and caregivers may seek information about physical development, such as the process of pregnancy, patterns of growth, and how children learn to crawl and walk. They may also wonder when children learn language. How do they think? Do caregivers and infants form strong emotional bonds, and how does that help children develop? What is effective discipline? How can caregivers direct children's behavior?

Teachers rely on an understanding of child development to create classroom plans and assignments that match children's abilities. How can educators balance challenging children with supporting their emotional development? School administrators, including principals and school boards, ask questions such as: Should schools focus on physical and emotional development? Should recess and unstructured play be part of the school day?

Through scientific studies, researchers work to answer these questions. They examine developmental processes that influence all aspects of children's functioning. Most researchers narrow their study to specific areas of development, such as thinking or emotional development. Some researchers work in laboratory settings. Others study children in their homes, schools, and communities. Some study children's adjustment. How does adversity, such as living in homes and communities in poverty, exposure to violence, and experiencing discrimination, affect development? Researchers often apply their findings to help children by creating interventions and making recommendations to parents, teachers, and policymakers.

Policymakers are individuals who create and shape **social policy**, local, state, or federal governments' plans and actions to support or improve the residents' welfare. Policymakers turn to researchers for accurate scientific information about child development. What nutritional and health behaviors promote healthy birthweight? How is poverty related to children's brain development? How are race and socioeconomic status related to children's exposure to developmental risks, such as poverty and toxins? How is health care access related to children and families' health and well-being? How can policies address these risks, anticipate other risks, and promote children's development?

Studying children can also help us understand ourselves. What abilities are inborn? How do our childhood experiences influence us? How have factors such as race, socioeconomic status, gender, language, and religion influenced our development? Throughout this book we examine interactions among demographic factors, including race, socioeconomic status, and gender, because they shape our experiences and who we become.

Periods of Development

One of the challenges of studying infants and children is that they develop and change so quickly. A great many changes occur over just a few years. Researchers divide the time between conception and adulthood into a series of periods. Each developmental period is characterized by a predictable pattern of physical, cognitive, and social abilities.

Prenatal period (conception to birth)

After conception, a single cell is formed. It multiplies repeatedly, and all the structures and organs in the body at birth originate from this single cell.

Infancy and toddlerhood (Birth to about 2 years)

Newborns' senses and early learning abilities enable them to adapt to the world. Dramatic changes occur in physical growth as well as motor, perceptual, and intellectual abilities. Infants begin to use language, and emotional bonds form with caregivers. Infancy comprises the first year of life; toddlerhood spans the second.

Early childhood (about 2 to about 6 years)

Children's muscles strengthen and they become more coordinated as they move out of toddlerhood. As thinking, language, and self-regulation improve, children establish ties with peers and engage in make-believe play.

Middle childhood (about 6 to about 11 years)

As children enter school, their memory and reasoning improve and they learn academic skills, such as reading, writing, and arithmetic. As children advance cognitively and gain social experience, their self-understanding and self-control improves; friendships develop and deepen, and peer group memberships become more important.

Adolescence (about 11 to about 18 years)

With puberty, adolescents become physically and sexually mature. Their thinking becomes more complex and abstract. Adolescents spend more time with peers, and friendships become more important. They are driven to learn about themselves, become independent from their parents, and define their values and goals.

Developmental Domains

Children grow and change in many ways. These changes are grouped into three **developmental domains** or types of development. *Physical development* includes the most visible set of changes: body maturation and growth, such as body size, proportion, appearance, health, and perceptual abilities. *Cognitive development* refers to the maturation of thought processes and how we become aware of the world around us, learn, and solve problems. *Socioemotional development* includes changes in emotions, social abilities, self-understanding, and interpersonal relationships with family and friends.

Developmental domains overlap and interact. For example, the onset of walking precedes advances in language development in infants in the United States and China (He et al., 2015; Lüke et al., 2019). Babies who walk tend to spend more time interacting with caregivers; they can initiate interactions with caregivers, such as by bringing objects to them (West & Iverson, 2021). They also evoke more verbal responses and warnings from caregivers as they interact with items and explore their environment. Therefore, walking, physical development, influences language and social development (Kobaş et al., 2023). Figure 1.1 illustrates how the three domains of development interact, a central principle of development.

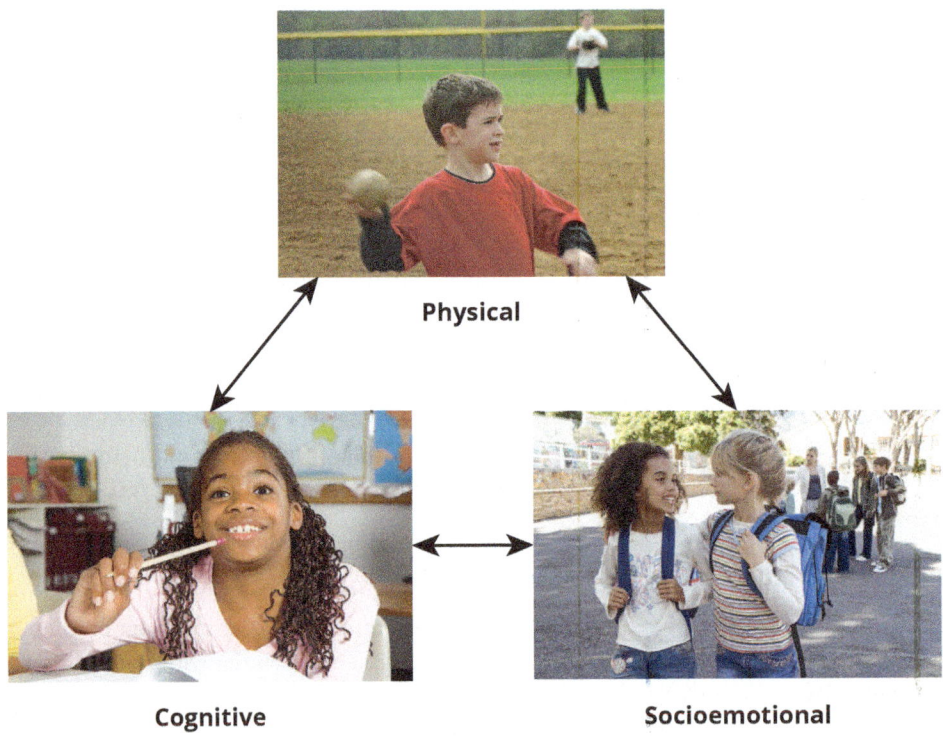

FIGURE 1.1 ■ Developmental Domains

Physical development influences learning, which influences children's interactions with others. Relationships with others help children learn and offer opportunities for growth and physical development through play.

Essentials/istock; Signature/istock; Jupiter/Pixland; istock

Context

Where did you grow up? Describe your childhood neighborhood. Did you play in a park or playground? Ride your bike outside? What was your elementary school like? Did you have access to technology such as tablets and computers? Did you learn to touch type in school? How large is your family? What were some of your family traditions? What holidays did you celebrate? Did you share family meals often? Your responses to these questions reveal aspects of your context.

Generally, context refers to where and when a person develops. Context includes all aspects of the physical and social environments in which we are immersed. Our context also includes intangible characteristics that are not visible to the naked eye, such as values, customs, ideals, and culture. Were you encouraged to be assertive and actively question the adults around you, or were you expected to be quiet and avoid confrontation? What values shaped your parents' childrearing practices and your own values? How did your family's economic status affect your development? These questions examine a critical context for our development, namely home and family. However, we are embedded in many more contexts that influence us, and that we influence, such as our peer group, school, neighborhood or community, and culture (Osher et al., 2021).

Sociohistorical Context

Our development is not just influenced by our surroundings, but also the time period in which we live and its unique historical circumstances, known as sociohistorical context. Historical events and trends, including wars, epidemics, advances in science and technology, and economic shifts such as periods of recession or prosperity influence our development (Baltes, 1987). Contextual influences tied to specific historical eras explain why a generation of people born at the same time, called a cohort, is similar in ways that people born at other times are different. Adults who were children during the Great Depression and World War II are similar in some ways that make them different from later cohorts; they tend to have particularly strong views on the importance of the family, civic mindedness, and social connection (Bühler & Nikitin, 2020; Rogler, 2002). The same is true for children of the 1960s who grew up during the Vietnam War, children of the 1990s who experienced rapid changes in technology, and so on. How might today's historical circumstance influence children?

The COVID-19 pandemic, which began in 2020, illustrates the influence of sociohistorical context. Children, adolescents, and adults donned face coverings and avoided close contact with other people, often including extended family and friends. School closures during the pandemic posed risks to children's and adolescents' academic and social development as well as their mental health (Mazrekaj & De Witte, 2023; R. S. Mistry et al., 2022). Even relatively temporary changes, such as these, are contextual influences that shape our world and our development. The effect of historical events on development depends in part on when they occur in a person's life—and experience can leave indelible marks on children's and adolescents' development (Bühler & Nikitin, 2020; Elder et al., 2015).

Sociohistorical influences, such as the COVID-19 pandemic, contribute to cohort, or generational, differences in development.

Halfpoint Images/Getty Images

Cultural Context

Culture, the set of customs, knowledge, attitudes, and values shared by members of a group, is learned early in life through interactions with group members, such as family (Markus & Kitayama, 1991). The culture in which we are immersed influences all our contexts and includes the processes we use to understand and interact with group members (Jones & Mistry, 2019).

Developmental scientists have only recently recognized the importance of culture. Most classic theories and research on development are based on Western samples because researchers once believed that the processes of human development were universal. Yet these studies often yielded narrow views of human development that did not consider the variety of cultural settings in which people live. In some cases, developmental differences in children of other cultural groups were considered abnormal rather than the result of different contextual circumstances (Packer & Cole, 2020).

We now know that development varies dramatically with cultural context—and that these differences are not deficiencies or abnormalities (McCoy, 2022). The cultural context in which individuals live influences the timing and expression of many aspects of development, even physical developments, such as walking, long thought to be a matter of biological maturation (Amir & McAuliffe, 2020). In Uganda, infants begin to walk at about 10 months of age, in France at about 15 months, and in the United States at about 12 months. These differences are influenced by parenting practices that vary by culture. African parents tend to handle infants in ways that stimulate walking, by playing games that allow infants to practice jumping and walking skills (Hopkins & Westra, 1989; Super, 1981). Applying principles of development derived from Western samples to children of other cultures can yield misleading conclusions about children's abilities (Keller, 2017; J. G. Miller et al., 2020). Culture is inherent in all domains of development and is a contributor to the context in which we are embedded, transmitting values, attitudes, and ideas that shape our thoughts, beliefs, and behaviors.

Our development plays out within the contexts in which we live, a theme that we return to throughout this book.

THINKING IN CONTEXT 1.1

1. Identify personal examples of physical, cognitive, and socioemotional development. What changes have you experienced in each of these areas over your childhood? How have these abilities influenced one another?
2. Describe the multiple contexts in which you were raised. Consider your home, school, and neighborhood. Did you spend time at a friend's or relative's home? How might have your experiences in these places influenced your physical, cognitive, and socioemotional development? Provide examples.
3. In what ways have your abilities—physical, cognitive, or socioemotional—influenced aspects of your context, the people and places around you?

CORE CONCEPTS IN DEVELOPMENTAL SCIENCE

1.2 Explain the nature-nurture debate, how children are active in their development, and how development reflects continuous and discontinuous change.

What causes development? What path does development take? What role do children play in their development? Developmental scientists hold different views about these basic questions about child development. The following sections examine each of these questions.

Nature and Nurture: How do biology and environment influence development?

Perhaps the oldest question about development concerns its origin. Often referred to as the **nature-nurture debate**, researchers once asked whether development is most influenced by biological factors (*nature*) or environmental factors (*nurture*). Explanations that rely on biology point to inborn genetic traits and maturational processes as causes of developmental change. Most infants crawl at roughly the same age, suggesting a maturational trend supporting the role of biology in development (Payne & Isaacs, 2020). In contrast, proponents of environmental explanations view children as molded by the physical and social environment in which they are raised. From this perspective, children tend to walk at about the same time because they experience similar environmental circumstances and parenting practices.

While the nature-nurture debate seems to present biology and environment as alternative explanations for development, most scientists generally agree that *both* biology and environment contribute to development. The question is *how* do biology and environment work together to influence child development (Bjorklund, 2018; Lickliter & Witherington, 2017)? For example, walking is heavily influenced by physical maturation, but experiences and environmental conditions can speed up or slow down the process. Although most infants begin to walk at about the same time, infants who experience malnutrition may walk later than well-nourished infants, and those who are given practice making stepping or jumping movements may walk earlier (Cavagnari et al., 2023; Siekerman et al., 2015).

The Active Child: How do children influence their own development?

Children are influenced by the physical and social contexts in which they live, but they also play a role in influencing their development by interacting with and changing those contexts (Elder et al., 2015). Baby Mickey smiles at each adult he passes by as his mother pushes his stroller in the park. Adults often respond with smiles, use baby talk, and make faces. Baby Mickey's actions, even simple smiles, influence adults, bringing them into close contact and one-on-one interactions that create opportunities for him to learn. Infants and children contribute to their own development by engaging the world around them, thinking, being curious, and interacting with people, objects, and their environment (Lerner et al., 2014). Even without awareness, children interact with and influence the people and things around them, creating experiences that influence their physical, cognitive, and emotional development. That is, they play an active role in influencing their own development.

Infants influence their own development by smiling at adults, making adults more likely to smile, use "baby talk," and play with them in response.

monkeybusinessimages/istock

Infants and children actively influence others and their environment through their behavior and also through their characteristics, such as temperament and appearance. For instance, infants born prematurely often have unique characteristics and needs, such as environmental sensitivity and physical disabilities, that can influence their relationships with caregivers and the care they receive (Green et al., 2021).

Continuities and Discontinuities: In what ways is development continuous and discontinuous?

Some aspects of development unfold slowly and gradually over time, demonstrating **continuous change**. Children slowly gain experience and learn strategies to become quicker at problem solving (Siegler, 2016). Others are best described as **discontinuous change**, characterized by abrupt change. Infants' vocabulary shows a *burst* of growth, and puberty quickly transforms children's bodies into more adult-like adolescent bodies (Manotas et al., 2022; Samuelson, 2021). As shown in Figure 1.2, a discontinuous view of development emphasizes sudden transformation, whereas a continuous view emphasizes gradual and steady changes.

It was once believed that development was either continuous or discontinuous, but not both. Today, scientists agree that development includes both continuity and discontinuity (Bornstein et al., 2017). Whether a particular developmental change appears continuous or discontinuous depends in part on our point of view. Consider physical growth. We often think of increases in height as involving a slow and steady process; each month, an infant is taller than the prior month, illustrating continuous change. However, as shown in Figure 1.3, when researchers measured infants' height every day, they discovered that infants have growth days and nongrowth days, days in which they show rapid change in height interspersed with days in which there is no change in height, illustrating discontinuous change (Lampl et al., 2001). In this example, monthly measurements of infant height suggest gradual increases, but daily measurements show spurts of growth, each lasting 24 hours or less. Thus, whether a given phenomenon, such as height, is described as continuous or discontinuous can vary depending on perspective. Most developmental scientists agree that some aspects of development are best described as continuous and others as discontinuous (P. H. Miller, 2016).

FIGURE 1.2 ■ Continuous and Discontinuous Change

Discontinuous change

Continuous change

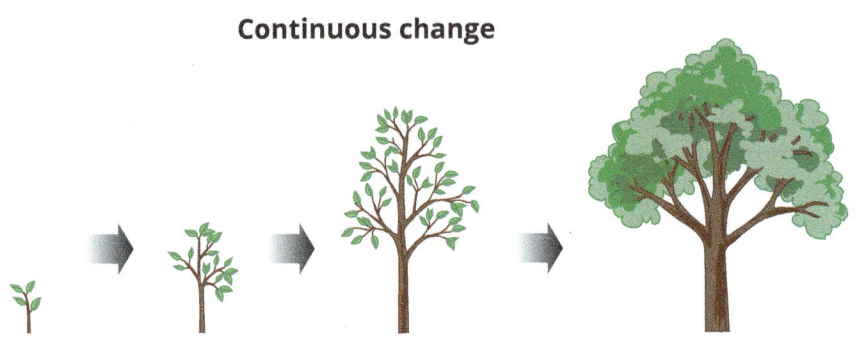

FIGURE 1.3 ■ Infant Growth: A Continuous or Discontinuous Process

Infant's growth occurs in a random series of roughly 1-centimeter spurts in height that occur in 24 hours or less. The overall pattern of growth entails increases in height, but whether the growth appears to be continuous or discontinuous depends on our point of view.

Adapted from Lampl, M., Veldhuis, J. D., & Johnson, M. L. (1992). Saltation and stasis: A model of human growth. *Science, 258*, 801–803.

THINKING IN CONTEXT 1.2

1. Consider your own traits and abilities. Which might be influenced by nature, biology? Nurture, environment? Give an example of a trait or ability that might be influenced by both nature and nurture.

2. Can you identify ways in your physical, cognitive, or socioemotional abilities have changed very gradually over the years? Were there other times in which you showed abrupt change, such as physical growth, strength and coordination, thinking abilities, or social skills? In other words, in what ways is your development characterized by continuity? Discontinuity?
3. Give an example of how you played an active role in your own development. Identify how your childhood traits and actions may have influenced others and your environment and, in turn, how they influenced you.

THEORIES OF CHILD DEVELOPMENT

1.3 Summarize five categories of theories about child development.

How do children grow and change? Why do children act the way they do? What developmental changes are most important? To answer these questions developmental scientists observe children's behavior and construct theories to explain what they see. A **theory** is a way of organizing a set of observations or facts into a comprehensive explanation of how something works. Theories are important tools for compiling and interpreting the growing body of research in developmental science as well as determining gaps in our knowledge and making predictions about what is not yet known.

An effective theory generates a specific **hypothesis**, or proposed explanation for a given phenomenon, that can be tested by research, as described later in this chapter. A good theory is *falsifiable* or capable of generating hypotheses that can be tested. As scientists conduct research and learn more about a topic, they modify their theories, then test new hypotheses derived from those theories, and so on. Next, we examine several prominent theories of child development, which are summarized at the end of this section, in Table 1.3.

Psychoanalytic Theories

An early, now classic, set of theories poses that children's development is driven by powerful inner forces. **Psychoanalytic theories** explain development as the result of the interplay of inner drives, memories, and conflicts we are unaware of and cannot control. These inner forces influence our behavior throughout our lives. Psychoanalytic theories emerged and were most popular during the early to mid-1900s.

Freud's Psychosexual Theory

The *father* of psychoanalytic theory, Sigmund Freud (1856–1939), believed that unconscious sexual and aggressive impulses drive our behavior. He described development as the progression through a series of *psychosexual stages*, periods in which unconscious sexual impulses focus on different parts of the body, making stimulation to those parts a source of pleasure (summarized in Table 1.1). Freud believed that the resolution of each stage and, ultimately, the adult personality, is based on how parents gratify children's needs.

Perhaps unsurprisingly, psychosexual stage framework's emphasis on childhood sexuality is unpopular and not widely accepted (Westen, 1998). Notably, Freud did not study children; his theory grew from his work with female psychotherapy patients (Crane, 2017). Some of Freud's ideas, such as the notion of unconscious processes of which we are unaware and the importance of early family experience, especially the parent-child relationship, have permeated popular culture (Bargh, 2013). However, Freud's theory, including unconscious drives and psychosexual stages, is not falsifiable because its parts cannot be directly observed and tested (Miller, 2016). How can we study unconscious drives, for instance, when we are not aware of them?

Erikson's Psychosocial Theory

Erik Erikson (1902–1994) was influenced by Freud, but he placed less emphasis on unconscious motivators of development. Erikson instead focused on interactions between the individual and their social world, including society, and culture. Over their lifetimes, according to Erikson, people progress through eight *psychosocial stages* that include changes in how they understand and interact with others, as well as changes in how they understand themselves and their roles as members of society (Erikson, 1950). Each stage presents a unique developmental task, which Erikson referred to as a crisis or conflict that must be resolved. How well individuals address the crisis determines their ability to deal with the demands made by the next stage of development. The first developmental task or crisis is for infants to develop a sense of trust (versus mistrust) in others. The resolution of this stage influences their progress in the next stage, developing a sense of autonomy, or the ability to be independent and guide their own behavior, and the outcome of each stage influences the following stages.

Regardless of their success in resolving a crisis of a given stage, children are driven by maturation and social expectations to the next psychosocial stage. No crisis is ever fully resolved, and unresolved crises are revisited throughout life. Although it is never too late, resolving a crisis from a previous stage becomes more challenging given the demands and crises of current psychosocial stages.

Erikson's psychosocial theory views development as life-long, well beyond childhood. Unlike Freud, Erikson studied children, including larger and more diverse samples than Freud, and emphasized the role of the social world, including society and culture. Largely viewed as unfalsifiable, Erikson's theory is criticized as difficult to test. Yet it has nonetheless sparked research on specific stages, such as identity development during adolescence (Crane, 2017). We revisit Erikson's theory throughout this book.

TABLE 1.1	Psychoanalytic Theories of Development				
Approximate Age	**Freud's Psychosexual Theory**		**Erikson's Psychosocial Theory**		
0 to 18 months	Oral	Basic drives focus on the mouth, tongue, and gums. Feeding and weaning influence personality development. Freud believed that failure to meet oral needs influences adult habits centering on the mouth, such as fingernail biting, overeating, smoking, or excessive drinking.	Trust vs. Mistrust	Infants learn to trust that others will fulfill their basic needs (nourishment, warmth, comfort) or to lack confidence that their needs will be met.
18 months to 3 years	Anal	Basic drives are oriented toward the anus, and toilet training is an important influence on personality development. If caregivers are too demanding, pushing the child before they are ready, or too lax, children may develop control issues such as a need to impose extreme order and cleanliness on their environment or extreme messiness and disorder.	Autonomy vs. Shame and Doubt	Toddlers learn to be self-sufficient and independent through toilet training, feeding, walking, talking, and exploring or to lack confidence in their own abilities and doubt themselves.
3 to 6 years	Phallic	In Freud's most controversial stage, basic drives shift to the genitals. The child develops a romantic desire for the other-sex parent and a sense of hostility and fear of the same-sex parent. The conflict between the child's desires and fears arouses anxiety and discomfort. It is resolved by pushing the desires into the subconscious and spending time with the same-sex parent and adopting their behaviors and roles, adopting societal expectations and values. Failure to resolve this conflict may result in guilt and a lack of conscience.	Initiative vs. Guilt	Young children become inquisitive, ambitious, and eager for responsibility or experience overwhelming guilt for their curiosity and overstepping boundaries.

Approximate Age	Freud's Psychosexual Theory		Erikson's Psychosocial Theory	
6 years to puberty	Latency	This is not a stage but a time of calm between stages when the child develops talents and skills and focuses on school, sports, and friendships.	Industry vs. Inferiority	Children learn to be hardworking, competent, and productive by mastering new skills in school, friendships, and home life or experience difficulty, leading to feelings of inadequacy and incompetence.
Adolescence	Genital	With the physical changes of early adolescence, the basic drives again become oriented toward the genitals. The person becomes concerned with developing mature adult sexual interests and sexual satisfaction in adult relationships throughout life.	Identity vs. Role Confusion	Adolescents search for a sense of self by experimenting with roles. They also look for answers to the question, "Who am I?" regarding career, sexual, and political roles or remain confused about who they are and their place in the world.
Early adulthood			Intimacy vs. Isolation	Young adults seek companionship and a close relationship with another person or experience isolation and self-absorption through difficulty developing intimate relationships and sharing with others.
Middle adulthood			Generativity vs. Stagnation	Adults contribute to, establish, and guide the next generation through work, creative activities, and parenting or stagnate, remaining emotionally impoverished and concerned about themselves.
Late adulthood			Integrity vs. Despair	Older adults look back at life to make sense of it, accept mistakes, and view life as meaningful and productive or feel despair over goals never reached and fear of death.

Behaviorist and Social Learning Theories

In contrast with psychoanalytic theory's emphasis on the unconscious, which cannot be observed or falsified by research, scientists who study **behaviorism** examine only observable behavior—what can be seen. Thoughts and emotion cannot be seen or objectively verified; therefore behaviorists believe they cannot be studied. Central to behaviorism is the belief that all behavior is controlled by the environment. Consider this famous quote from John Watson (1925), a founder of behaviorism:

> Give me a dozen healthy infants, well formed, and my own specified world to bring them up in and I'll guarantee to take any one at random and train him to become any type of specialist I might select—doctor, lawyer, artist, merchant, chief, and yes, even beggar-man and thief, regardless of his talents, penchants, tendencies, abilities, vocations, and race of his ancestors. (p. 82)

By controlling an infant's physical and social environment, Watson believed he could control the child's destiny. Behaviorist theory is also known as *learning theory* because it emphasizes how people and animals learn new behaviors and develop through environmental shaping. Classical and operant conditioning are two forms of behaviorist learning; social cognitive theory integrates behaviorist theory and cognitive theories.

Pavlov's Classical Conditioning

Classical conditioning is a form of learning in which a person or animal comes to associate environmental stimuli with physiological responses. Ivan Pavlov (1849–1936), a Russian physiologist,

Ivan Pavlov (1849–1936) discovered classical conditioning when he noticed that dogs naturally salivate when they taste food, but they also salivate in response to various sights and sounds that they associate with food.

Sovfoto/Contributor/Getty Images

discovered the principles of classical conditioning when he noticed that dogs naturally salivate when they taste food, but they also salivate in response to various sights and sounds that they encounter before tasting food, such as their bowl clattering or their owner opening the food cupboard. Pavlov tested his observation by pairing the sound of a tone with the dog's' food; the dogs heard the tone, then received their food. Soon the tone itself began to elicit the dogs' salivation.

Through classical conditioning, a neutral stimulus (in this example, the sound of the tone) comes to elicit a response originally produced by another stimulus (food). Many fears, as well as other emotional associations, are the result of classical conditioning. For example, some children may fear a trip to the doctor's office because they associate the doctor's office with the discomfort they felt while receiving a vaccination shot. Classical conditioning applies to involuntary physiological and emotional responses only, yet it is a cornerstone of psychological theory. A second behaviorist theory, operant conditioning, accounts for voluntary, nonphysiological responses.

Skinner's Operant Conditioning

Perhaps it is human nature to notice that the consequences of our behavior influence our future behavior. A child praised for setting the dinner table may be more likely to spontaneously set the table in the future. One scolded for writing on a wall with crayon may be less likely to do so. These two examples illustrate the basic tenet of B. F. Skinner's (1905–1990) theory of **operant conditioning**, which holds that behavior becomes either more or less probable depending on its consequences. According to Skinner, a behavior followed by a rewarding or pleasant outcome, called **reinforcement**, will be more likely to recur. One followed by an aversive or unpleasant outcome, called **punishment**, will be less likely to recur.

Operant conditioning explains much about human behavior, including how children learn skills and habits. Behaviorist ideas about operant conditioning are woven into the fabric of North American culture and are often applied to understand parenting and parent-child interactions (Troutman, 2015). Developmental scientists, however, tend to disagree with operant conditioning's emphasis on only external events (reinforcing and punishing consequences) over internal events (thoughts and emotions) as influences on behavior and development (Crane, 2017). That is, controlling children's environments can influence their development, but recall that children play an active role in influencing their development. Children think and act of their accord. A child can devise new ideas and learn independently, without reinforcement or punishment.

Bandura's Social Cognitive Theory

Like B. F. Skinner, Albert Bandura (1925–2021) viewed the environment as an important influence on behavior. Bandura also believed that thoughts and emotions contribute to behavior and development. Children actively process information—they think and feel emotion—and their thoughts and feelings influence their behavior. Moreover, children are active in their development; they are not passively molded by their physical and social environments. Bandura's **social cognitive theory** explains children's development as the result of interactions among their physical and social environment, their cognition and personal characteristics, and behavior, a concept he called **reciprocal determinism** (see Figure 1.4; Bandura, 2011, 2018).

Bandura argues that children's thoughts and characteristics determine their behavior and the environments they seek. Children who are athletically inclined (cognitive/personal characteristic) tend to play sports (behavior) and seek out environments that support their interests, such as athletic teams.

Environments (athletic teams), in turn, influence children's thoughts and personal characteristics (interest in athletics) and behaviors (playing sports). The complex interplay among person, behavior, and physical and social environment underlies much of what we discuss throughout this book.

One of Bandura's most enduring ideas about development is that children learn by observing and imitating others, referred to as **observational learning** (Bandura, 2010). Specifically, children learn by observing the consequences of others' actions. Children who observe violence rewarded, such as a child grabbing another child's toy and getting to play with it, may imitate what they see and use aggressive means to take other children's toys. Alternatively, a child might be less likely to imitate a child who takes another child's toy if the aggressor is scolded by a teacher. Observational learning is one of the most powerful ways in which we learn. We do not need to experience punishment or reinforcement to change our behavior (Bandura, 2012). We can learn by observing and thinking about the potential consequences of our actions. Our thoughts and emotions about the consequences of our behavior influence our future behavior.

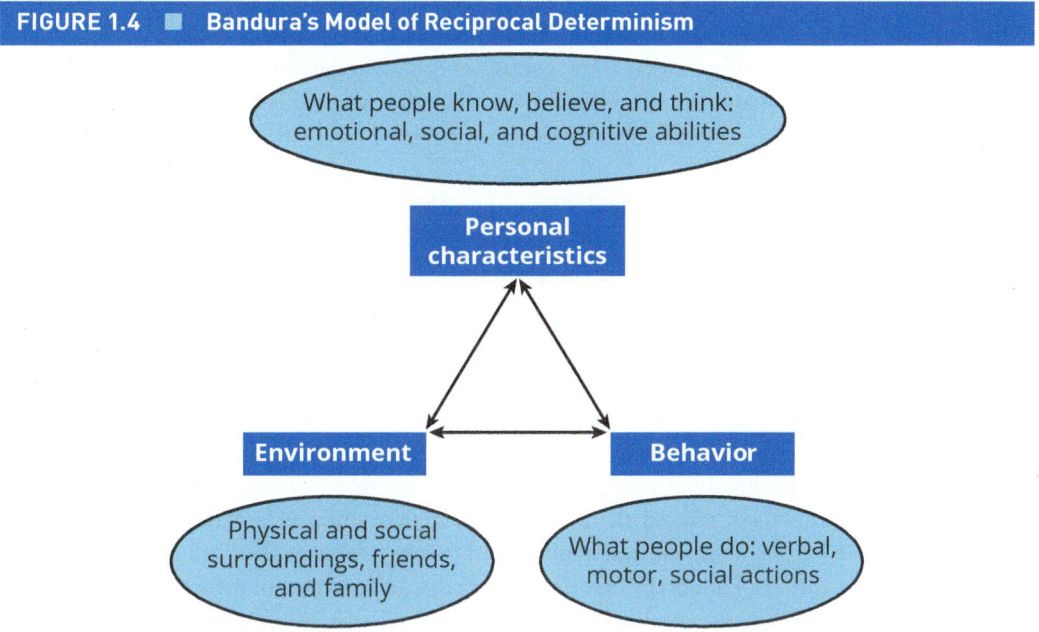

FIGURE 1.4 ■ Bandura's Model of Reciprocal Determinism

Cognitive Theories

Thinking changes with development. Developmental scientists agree the infants, children, and adolescents have different cognitive capacities, but they offer varying explanations for these differences. Some view cognition as developing in spurts and others as gradual increases in abilities.

Piaget's Cognitive-Developmental Theory

The first to systematically examine infants' and children's thinking was Swiss scholar Jean Piaget (1896–1980), who believed that cognition is at the center of child development because it influences all behavior. According to Piaget's **cognitive-developmental theory**, children actively explore their world and are driven to learn by interacting with the world around them, organizing what they learn into **cognitive schemas**, or concepts and ways of interacting with the world. Through their exploration, such as grasping, touching, and interacting with objects, children construct and refine their cognitive schemas, thereby contributing to their own cognitive development.

Piaget proposed that children's drive to explore and understand the world—to construct more sophisticated cognitive schemas—propels them through four stages of cognitive development, as shown in Table 1.2.

TABLE 1.2 ■ Piaget's Stages of Cognitive Development

Stage	Approximate Age	Description
Sensorimotor	Birth to 2 years	Infants understand the world and think using only their senses and motor skills, by watching, listening, touching, and tasting.
Preoperations	2 to 6 years	Preschoolers explore the world using their own thoughts as guides and develop the language skills to communicate their thoughts to others. Despite these advances, their thinking is characterized by several errors in logic.
Concrete Operations	7 to 11 years	School-aged children become able to solve everyday, logical problems. Their thinking is not yet fully mature because they can apply it only to tangible problems and tied to specific substances.
Formal Operations	12 years to adulthood	Adolescents and adults can reason logically and abstractly about possibilities, imagined instances and events, and hypothetical concepts.

Piaget's cognitive-developmental theory transformed the field of developmental psychology and remains one of the most widely cited developmental theories. It was the first to consider *how* infants and children think and to view people as active contributors to their development. In addition, Piaget's concept of cognitive stages and the suggestion that children's reasoning is limited by their stage has implications for education—specifically, the idea that effective instruction must match the child's developmental level.

Some critics of cognitive-developmental theory argue that Piaget focused too heavily on cognition and ignored emotional and social factors in development (Crane, 2017). Others believe that Piaget neglected the influence of contextual factors by assuming that cognitive-developmental stages are universal, that all children everywhere progress through the stages in unvarying sequence. Some cognitive theorists believe that cognitive development is not a discontinuous series of stages but instead is a continuous process of gaining skills in manipulating information (Birney & Sternberg, 2011).

Information Processing Theory

In contrast with Piaget's stage theory, cognitive development is viewed as continuous in **information processing theory**. This theory likens the mind to a computer where information is received, processed and organized, stored, recalled, and manipulated to solve problems (Halford & Andrews, 2011; Wickens & Carswell, 2021). Unlike the theories we have discussed so far, information processing theory isn't attributed to a single theorist but is made up of numerous theories, each emphasizing a different aspect of thinking (Conte & Richards, 2021; Eggen, 2020; Winne, 2021). Some theories focus on how people perceive, attend to, and absorb information. Others examine how people store information, create memories, and remember information. Still others examine problem-solving skills, such as how people approach and solve problems in school, the workplace, and in everyday life. For example, a researcher might give a 5-year-old child a toy maze with a dog, cat, and a mouse who must find their way through to reach a bone, a fish, and a piece of cheese (Klahr, 1985). How does the child approach this task? What strategies do they use? How quickly do they respond? How do they explain their thinking? Finally, how does their process and performance differ from those of children older and younger than them?

Information processing theorists believe that children are born with the ability to process information. The mental processes of noticing, taking in, manipulating, storing, and retrieving information change gradually over infancy and childhood (Klahr & Wallace, 2022). Development is continuous, influenced by brain development, and includes improvements in efficiency and speed (Gibb, 2020). Through experience and interaction with others, children learn new ways of managing and manipulating information.

Information processing theory offers a detailed view of how children think, which permits scientists to make specific predictions about behavior and performance that can be tested. Indeed, information processing theory has generated a great many research studies and has garnered much empirical support (Halford & Andrews, 2011; Wickens & Carswell, 2021). Critics of information processing theory argue that a computer model cannot capture the complexity of the human mind and people's unique cognitive abilities. In addition, findings from laboratory research may not extend to everyday contexts in which people must adapt to changing circumstances and challenges to attention (Miller, 2016).

Vygotsky's Sociocultural Theory

Writing at the same time as Piaget, Russian scholar Lev Vygotsky (1896–1934) emphasized the importance of culture in cognition. Recall that culture refers to the beliefs, values, customs, and skills of a group; it is a product of people's interactions in everyday settings (Markus & Hamedani, 2020). Vygotsky's (1978) **sociocultural theory** examines how culture and its tools (such as language) are transmitted from one generation to the next through social interaction.

Children interact with adults and more experienced peers as they talk, play, and work alongside them. Through these formal and informal social contacts, children learn about their culture and acquire cultural tools, including a culture's language, which transmits ways of thinking. Vygotsky believed that acquiring language is a critical milestone for children because it enables children to participate in culturally valued activities, have more sophisticated dialogues with others, and adopt attitudes and perspectives valued by their community (Daniels, 2017). By participating in cooperative dialogues and receiving guidance from adults and more expert peers, children adopt their culture's perspectives and practices, learning to think and behave as members of their group (Rogoff, 2016). Over time, children apply these ways of thinking to guide their own actions, thus requiring less assistance from adults and peers (Daniels, 2017; Rogoff et al., 2014).

Vygotsky's sociocultural theory holds important implications for understanding cognitive development. Like Piaget, Vygotsky emphasized that children actively participate in their development by engaging with the world around them. However, Vygotsky placed greater emphasis than Piaget on the cultural context in influencing people's development. He viewed cognitive development as a social process that relies on interactions with adults, more mature peers, and other members of their culture. Critics of Vygotsky's theory argue that it overemphasizes context and undervalues the roles of biological factors and children's own influence on their development (Crane, 2017). We revisit Vygotsky's ideas about the roles of culture, language, and thought in Chapter 8.

Systems Theories

Many theories examine a specific aspect of development, such as cognition, the sense of self, and environmental determinants of behavior. Systems theories take a broader approach, considering all parts of the individual and the many contexts in which they are embedded, such as home, school, peer group, and so on. A system is a set of interacting parts that are interconnected and work together as a network. We are composed of multiple interacting systems that make up the physical, cognitive, and socioemotional developments that we have discussed so far. We are also embedded in systems, or contexts. People take an active role in their development by interacting with people, objects, and settings—and they are also influenced by these factors. These interactions take place all throughout our lives, changing over time. The two predominant systems theories are the bioecological systems theory and dynamic systems theory.

Bronfenbrenner's Bioecological Systems Theory

Similar to other developmental theorists, Urie Bronfenbrenner (1917–2005) believed that children influence their own development. He also emphasized the importance of context in development. Bronfenbrenner proposed that all individuals are embedded in, or surrounded by, a series of contexts: home, school, neighborhood, culture, and society. As shown in Figure 1.5, contexts are organized into a series of systems in which individuals are embedded and that interact with one another and the person to influence development. Bronfenbrenner's **bioecological systems theory** explains development as the result of the ongoing interactions among biological, cognitive, and psychological changes in children and their changing context (Bronfenbrenner & Morris, 2006). The bioecological systems theory thus offers a comprehensive perspective on the role of context as an influence on development.

Ontogenetic development. At the center of the bioecological system is the individual. **Ontogenetic development** refers to the changes that take place within the individual over their lifetime, including biological, cognitive, and socioemotional changes, which influence each other. Physical development, such as brain maturation, may influence children's cognitive development, such as reasoning and the ability to consider other people's perspectives. These changes might influence social development, specifically the ability to have more complex and intimate friendships, which can influence cognitive development, as children learn from each other. In this way the various forms of development interact. Ontogenetic development is not only influenced by but also influences the many contexts in which children are embedded (Bronfenbrenner & Morris, 2006).

Microsystem. Perhaps the most visible context of the bioecological system is the **microsystem**, the innermost layer. It includes a child's interactions with the immediate physical and social environment surrounding the child, such as family, peers, and school. Because the microsystem includes the child, it has an immediate and direct influence on their development—and children affect it. Interactions with friends, family, and teachers (all part of the microsystem) can influence (and are influenced by) children's sense of self-esteem, social skills, and emotional development (ontogenetic development).

Mesosystem. Microsystem factors naturally interact. Experiences in the home (one microsystem factor) influence those at school (another microsystem factor). Encouragement and support for reading at home, for instance, can influence the child's experiences in the classroom. These interactions comprise the **mesosystem**, which refers to the relations among microsystems, connections among contexts, such as home, peer group, school, work, and neighborhood. Like the microsystem, the mesosystem has a direct influence on children (and is influenced by children) because they participate in it.

Exosystem. The **exosystem** consists of settings that affect children but in which they do not participate. A parent's experiences at work can influence their children's home environment. Promotions, raises, long work hours, stressful interactions, and lengthy commutes can influence parents' interactions with family members and the emotional climate at home. The availability of funding for schools, another exosystem factor, indirectly affects children by influencing the availability of classroom resources. Exosystem factors trickle down to influence children's interactions in the mesosystem and microsystem.

Macrosystem. The **macrosystem** is the greater sociocultural context in which the microsystem, mesosystem, and exosystem are embedded. It includes cultural values, legal and political practices, and other elements of society at large. The macrosystem indirectly influences children because it affects each of the other contextual levels. Cultural beliefs about the value of education (macrosystem) influence funding decisions made at national and local levels (exosystem), as well as what happens in the classroom and in the home (mesosystem and microsystem).

Chronosystem. By its very nature, the bioecological system is always shifting because individuals and their contexts interact dynamically and perpetually, resulting in a constant state of change. The final element of the bioecological system is the **chronosystem**, which refers to the passing of time. The historical time in which children live influences their development. Large scale social changes, such as those that accompany war, natural disasters, and epidemics, can influence each level of the bioecological system. Neighborhood resources may change over time with changes in local policies and funding. Children's relationships with parents, friends, and teachers change over time—and their microsystems and mesosystems change dynamically.

Evaluating Bronfenbrenner's bioecological systems theory. Recently, bioecological systems theory has been criticized for its vague explanation of development, especially the role of culture (Vélez-Agosto et al., 2017). Situated in the macrosystem, culture is said to influence development through the interdependence of the systems. Today's developmental scientists believe that culture is not just a macrosystem factor. Culture refers to *all* the processes used by people as they make meaning or think through interactions with group members (J. Mistry et al., 2016; Varnum & Grossmann, 2017). Critics argue that since culture is manifested in our daily interactions and activities, it is inherent in each bioecological level, not just the macrosystem as Bronfenbrenner believed (Vélez-Agosto et al., 2017).

A second criticism arises from the sheer complexity of the bioecological system and its attention to patterns and dynamic interactions. We can never measure and account for all the potential individual and contextual influences on development at once, making it difficult to devise research studies to test the validity of the model. In contrast, proponents of bioecological theory argue that rather than conducting large studies to test all the model's components at once, smaller studies can examine each component over time (Jaeger, 2016; Tudge et al., 2016, 2022). In any case, bioecological theory remains an important contribution toward explaining children's development and is a theory that we consider throughout this book.

FIGURE 1.5 ■ Bronfenbrenner's Bioecological Systems Theory

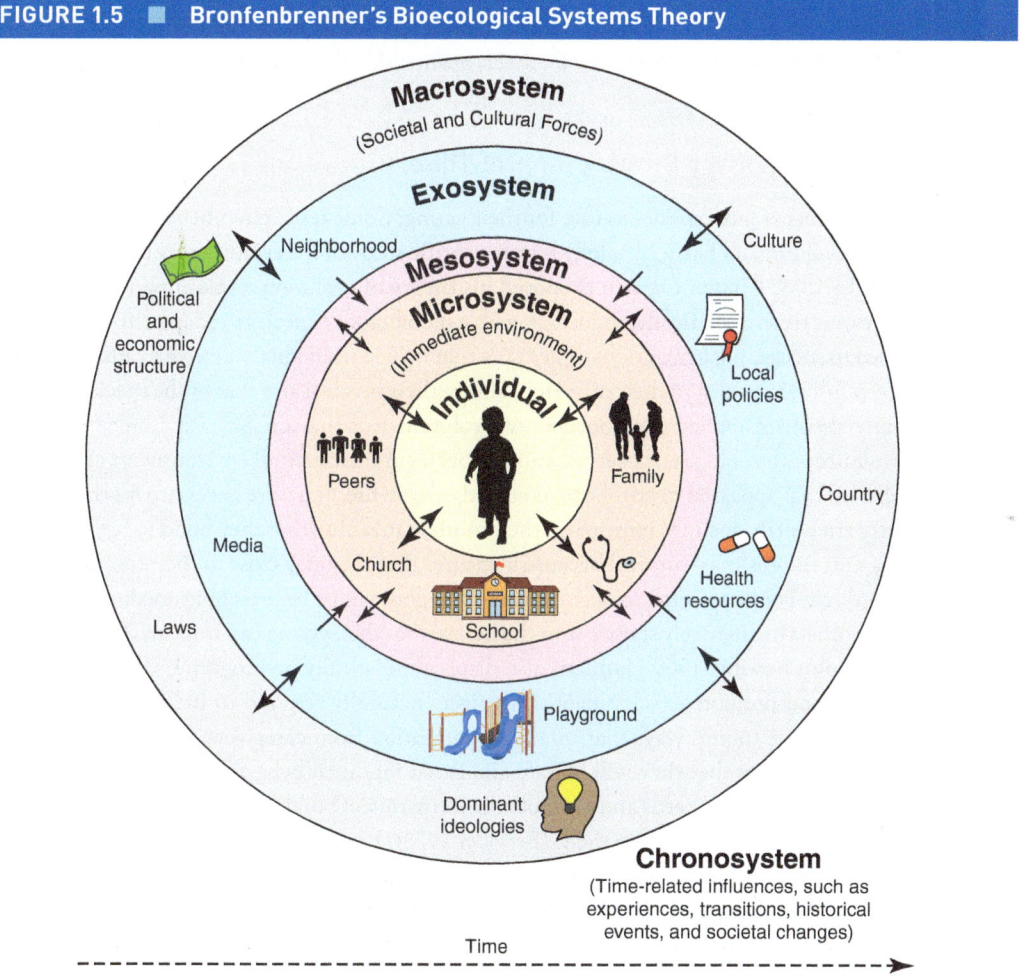

Adapted from Bronfenbrenner, U., & Morris, P. A. (2006). The bioecological model of human development. In R. M. Lerner & W. Damon (Eds.), *Handbook of child psychology: Theoretical models of human development* (Vol. 1, pp. 793–828). John Wiley & Sons.

Thelen's Dynamic Systems Theory

As we have discussed, developmental scientists generally agree that development is influenced by the interaction of biology and environment—and that children influence their development through their interactions with their context. These important ideas are reflected in Esther Thelen's (1995, 2000) **dynamic systems theory**, which emphasizes interactions between biological maturation, environmental circumstances and constraints, and individuals' drive to engage the world. Collectively these are an integrated system that is constantly changing, resulting in developmental change and the emergence of new abilities in children.

Dynamic systems theory places children at the center of their development. Children direct and advance their own development because they are motivated to obtain objects, interact with others, understand their experience, and control their environment. Each child's physical characteristics are unique. Their environmental circumstances are also unique, affording specific opportunities and constraints for movement and learning. Therefore, children's behavior and development are the result of their motivation to master their unique environment, capitalizing on opportunities, and adapting to constraints. Infants' desire to reach objects and master their environment drives them to crawl, but how they crawl and the timeframe in which crawling unfolds varies with their physical abilities and their specific environment, such as whether they live in a home with carpeting (which might make crawling easier) or slippery floors (which might make it more difficult).

Thelen described dynamic systems theory with motor development in mind. Theorists are now applying it to understand children's cognitive and emotional development as well as the nature of development itself (Adolph, 2020; Perone et al., 2021; Sosnowska et al., 2020). We explore this theory in Chapter 4.

Ethology and Evolutionary Developmental Theory

What motivates parents of most species to care for their young? Some researchers believe that caregiving behaviors have an evolutionary basis. **Ethology** is the scientific study of the evolutionary basis of behavior (Bateson, 2015). In 1859, Charles Darwin proposed his theory of evolution, explaining that all species adapt and evolve over time. Specifically, traits that enable members of a species to adapt, thrive, and mate tend to be passed to succeeding generations. The traits that helped individuals survive to adulthood and reproduce successfully are passed to their offspring, aiding their survival and that of the species.

Several early theorists applied the concepts of evolution to behavior. Konrad Lorenz and Kiko Tinbergen, two European zoologists, observed animal species in their natural environments and noticed patterns of behavior that appeared to be inborn, emerged early in life, and were necessary for the animals' survival. Shortly after birth, goslings imprint on their mother, meaning that they bond to her and follow her. Imprinting aids the goslings' survival because it ensures that they stay close to their mother, get fed, and remain protected. For imprinting to occur, the mother goose must be present immediately after the goslings hatch; mothers instinctively stay close to the nest so that their young can imprint (Lorenz, 1952).

According to John Bowlby (1969), humans also display biologically preprogrammed behaviors that have survival value and promote development. Caregivers naturally respond to infants' cues. Crying, smiling, and grasping are inborn ways that infants get attention from caregivers, bring caregivers into physical contact, and ensure that they will be safe and cared for. Such behaviors have adaptive significance because they meet infants' needs and promote the formation of bonds with caregivers who then feel a strong desire and obligation to care for them (Bowlby, 1973). In this way innate biological drives and behaviors work together with experience to influence adaptation and ultimately an individual's survival.

Another theory, **evolutionary developmental theory**, also applies principles of evolution to understand development; however, this approach emphasizes the interactive influence of genetic and environmental mechanisms in development (Bjorklund & Hart, 2022; Blasi, 2020). You may have wondered whether you—your abilities, personality, and competencies—result from your genes or from the physical and social environment in which you were raised. Evolutionary developmental scientists explain that this is the wrong question to ask because genes and context interact in an ever-changing way so that it is impossible to isolate the contributions of each to development (Blasi, 2020).

Evolutionary developmental theorists view children as active in their development, influencing their contexts, responding to the demands for adaptation posed by their contexts, and constantly interacting with and adapting to the world around them (see Table 1.3). In this way, children's genetic factors and biological predispositions interact with their physical and social environment to influence development. Ultimately, Darwinian natural selection determines what genes and traits are passed from adults to the next generation (Bjorklund, 2020; Witherington & Lickliter, 2016).

Most developmental scientists appreciate the contributions of evolutionary developmental theory because the relevance of both biological and contextual factors to human development is indisputable (DelGiudice, 2018; Frankenhuis & Tiokhin, 2018; Legare et al., 2018). We examine the interactive effect of genes and environment in Chapter 2.

TABLE 1.3 Comparing Theories of Child Development

Theory	How do biology and environment influence development?	How do children influence their own development?	In what ways is development continuous and discontinuous?
Freud's psychosexual theory	*Greater emphasis on biology*: People are driven by inborn drives, but the extent to which the drives are satisfied influences developmental outcomes.	*Children are passive*: People are driven by inborn instincts and are not active participants in their development.	*Discontinuous*: Stages
Erikson's psychosocial theory	*Both biology and environment*: Biological and social forces propel children through the stages, and social and psychosocial influences determine the outcome of each stage.	*Children are active*: Children interact with their social world to resolve psychosocial tasks.	*Discontinuous*: Stages
Behaviorist theory	*Environment*: Environmental influences shape behavior.	*Children are passive*: Children are shaped and molded by their environment.	*Continuous*: Gradual process of learning new behaviors
Bandura's social learning theory	*Both biology and environment*: Inborn characteristics and the physical and social environment influence behavior.	*Children are active*: Children are influenced by the environment and also play an active role in their development through reciprocal determinism.	*Continuous*: Gradual process of learning new behaviors
Piaget's cognitive-developmental theory	*Both biology and environment*: An inborn ability to learn coupled with brain development leads children to interact with the world. Opportunities provided by the physical and social environment influence development.	*Children are active*: Children actively interact with the world to create their own schemas.	*Discontinuous*: Stages
Information processing theory	*Both biology and environment*: Children are born with processing capacities that develop through maturation and environmental influences.	*Children are active*: Children attend to, process, and store information.	*Continuous*: Gradual increase of skills and capacities
Vygotsky's sociocultural theory	*Both biology and environment*: Children learn through interactions with more skilled members of their culture; capacities are influenced by genes, brain development, and maturation.	*Children are active*: Children actively interact with members of their culture.	*Continuous*: Continuous interactions with others lead to developing new reasoning capacities and skills.
Bronfenbrenner's bioecological systems theory	*Both biology and environment*: Children's inborn and biological characteristics interact with an ever-changing context to influence behavior.	*Children are active*: Children interact with their contexts, being influenced by their contexts but also determining what kinds of physical and social environments are created and how they change.	*Continuous*: People constantly change through their interactions with the contexts in which they are embedded.

(Continued)

TABLE 1.3 ■ Comparing Theories of Child Development (Continued)			
Theory	How do biology and environment influence development?	How do children influence their own development?	In what ways is development continuous and discontinuous?
Dynamic systems theory	*Both biology and environment*: Developmental domains, maturation, and environment form an integrated system.	*Children are active*: Children's goal-oriented behavior influences their development.	*Continuous*: New developmental achievements are the result of systematic skill-building.
Ethology and evolutionary developmental theory	*Both biology and environment*: Genetic programs and biological predispositions interact with the physical and social environment to influence development, and Darwinian natural selection determines what genes and traits are passed on to the next generation.	*Children are active*: Children interact with their physical and social environment.	*Both continuous and discontinuous*: People gradually grow and change throughout life, but there are sensitive periods in which specific experiences and developments must occur.

THINKING IN CONTEXT 1.3

"Babies naturally bond to their caregivers. It's inborn," Chloe explains. "No," Dedra counters, "at birth they don't know who their caregivers are! Bonding comes with experience."

1. Consider the following theoretical perspectives: Erik Erikson's psychosocial theory, behaviorism, Bandura's social learning theory, Piaget's cognitive developmental theory, and evolutionary developmental theory. Which theories align with Chloe's argument? Which fit(s) Dedra's? Explain your choices.
2. Considering bioecological systems theory, what microsystem and mesosystem factors influence the parent-child bond? What role might exosystem and macrosystem factors take?

RESEARCH IN CHILD DEVELOPMENT

1.4 Examine the methods and research designs used to study child development.

Developmental scientists create theories, such as those we have discussed, to organize their observations of how children behave in various settings and circumstances. Theories guide these scientists as they ask and answer questions about how people grow and change over childhood and throughout their lives. Theories suggest new hypotheses to test in research studies. In turn, research findings are used to modify theories.

The Scientific Method

The **scientific method** refers to a process of asking and answering questions through systematic observation to gather and summarize information and draw conclusions. It is an organized way of formulating questions, finding answers, and communicating research discoveries. Its basic steps are as follows:

1. Identify the research question or problem to be studied and formulate the hypothesis, or proposed explanation, to be tested.
2. Gather information to address the research question.

3. Summarize the information gathered and determine whether the hypothesis is refuted or shown to be false.

4. Interpret the summarized information, consider the findings in light of prior research studies, and share findings with the scientific community and world at large.

This 4-step process seems straightforward and linear. In practice, it is often more complicated. Frequently research studies raise as many questions as they answer—and sometimes more. Unexpected findings can prompt new studies. Researchers may repeat an experiment (called a *replication*) to see whether the results are the same as previous ones. Sometimes analyses reveal flaws in data collection methods or research design, prompting a revised study. Experts may also disagree on the interpretation of a study, leading to new hypotheses and studies. For these reasons, scientists often say the scientific method is *messy*.

Methods of Data Collection

All research involves gathering data, information, about the topic of interest—Step 2 in the scientific method. How can we gather data about children? Should we simply talk with them? Watch them as they play? Hook them up to machines that measure physiological activity such as heart rate or brain waves? Developmental scientists use a variety of different methods, summarized in Table 1.4 and discussed next.

Observational Measures

Some developmental scientists collect data by watching and recording children's behavior. Developmental scientists employ two types of observational measures: naturalistic observation and structured observation.

Naturalistic observation. Scientists who use **naturalistic observation** observe and record behavior in natural, real-world settings. For example, Salo et al. (2018) observed 12-month-old infants playing with their parents. They recorded infants' gestures and how often they participated with parents in paying attention to or interacting with an object (such as a toy). One year later, infants who used more gestures and engaged in more joint attention, especially responses to parents' efforts to direct their attention, showed more advanced language development; they understood and produced more words.

Naturalistic observation can reveal patterns of behavior in everyday settings, such as whether a particular event or behavior typically precedes another. Such observations can help researchers determine which behaviors are important to study. A scientist who studies bullying by observing children's play may notice that some victims act aggressively *before* a bullying encounter (Kamper-DeMarco & Ostrov, 2017). The scientist may then decide to examine aggression in victims not only after a bullying incident but also beforehand.

A challenge of using naturalistic observation is that sometimes the presence of an observer causes those being observed to behave unnaturally. This is known as *participant reactivity*. One way of reducing the effect of participant reactivity is to conduct multiple observations so that the children get used to the observer and return to their normal behavior. Another promising method of minimizing participant reactivity is to use an *electronically activated voice recorder* (EAR) (Carey et al., 2020; Mehl, 2017). Participants carry the EAR as they go about their daily lives. The EAR captures segments of audio information over time: hours, days, or even weeks. It records a log of people's activities as they naturally unfold. The EAR minimizes participant reactivity because the participant is unaware of exactly when the EAR is recording. Researchers who study child trauma use EAR to sample conversations between parents and children to understand how parent-child interactions influence children's adjustment and how the family environment can aid children's recovery from trauma (Alisic et al., 2016; Vasileva et al., 2022).

Naturalistic observation is a useful way of studying events and behaviors that are common. Some behaviors and events are difficult to observe or occur infrequently, however, requiring a researcher to observe for very long periods of time to obtain data on the behavior of interest. For this reason, many researchers make structured observations.

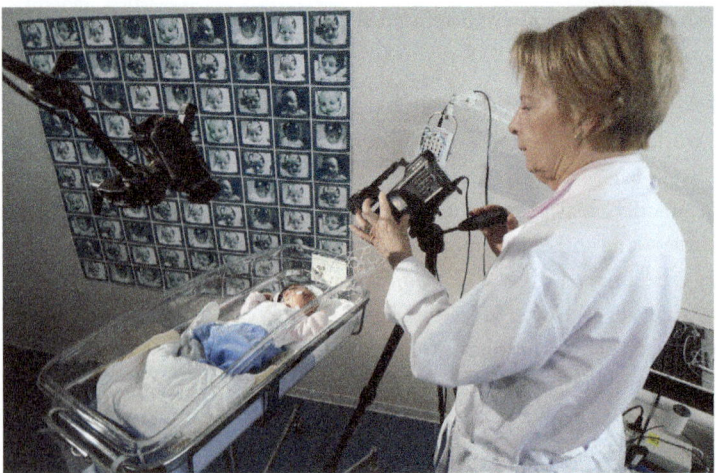

This researcher is using a video camera to observe and record the facial expressions a newborn baby makes while it sleeps.

Thierry Berrod, Mona Lisa Production/Science Source

Structured observation. Observing and recording behaviors displayed in a controlled environment, a situation constructed by the experimenter, is known as **structured observation**. Children might be observed in a laboratory setting as they play with another child or complete a puzzle-solving task. The challenges of identifying and categorizing which behaviors to record are similar to those involved in naturalistic observation. However, the laboratory environment permits researchers to exert more control over the situation than is possible in natural settings. In addition to cataloguing observable behaviors, researchers can use technology to measure biological functions such as heart rate, brain waves, and blood pressure. One disadvantage to conducting structured observations, of course, is that people do not always behave in laboratory settings as they do in real life.

Self-Report Measures

Interviews and questionnaires are known as *self-report measures* because participants, such as children and parents under study, answer questions about their experiences, attitudes, opinions, beliefs, and behavior. Interviews are one-on-one conversations that can take place in person, over the phone, or over videoconferencing.

In an **open-ended interview** a trained interviewer uses a conversational style that encourages children to expand their responses. The scientist begins with a question and then follows up with prompts to better understand the child's reasoning (McConaughy & Whitcomb, 2022). Interviewers may vary the order of questions, probe, and ask additional questions based on each child's responses. Cognitive-developmental theorist Jean Piaget adopted this approach to study children's thinking. Consider this dialogue between Piaget (1929) and a 6-year-old child:

You know what a dream is?

When you are asleep and you see something.

Where does it come from?

The sky.

Can you see it?

No! Yes, when you're asleep

Could I see it if I was there?

No.

Why not?

Because it is in front of us. . . . When you are asleep you dream and you see them, but when you aren't asleep you don't see them.

In open-ended interviews children can explain their thoughts thoroughly and in their own words, but the flexibility of these interviews also poses challenges. When questions are phrased differently for each child, responses may not capture real differences in how children think about a given topic and instead may reflect differences in how the questions were posed and followed up by the interviewer.

In contrast, a **structured interview** poses the same set of questions in the same order to each child. Structured interviews are less flexible than open-ended interviews. All participants receive the same set of questions so differences in responses are more likely to reflect true differences among participants and not merely differences in the manner of interviewing. Evans et al. (2002) used a structured interview to examine North American children's beliefs about magic. Children between the ages of 3 and 8 were asked the following set of questions:

What is magic? Who can do magic?

Is it possible to have special powers? Who has special powers?

Does someone have to learn to do magic? Where have you seen magic? (p. 49).

After compiling and analyzing the children's responses, as well as administering several cognitive tasks, the researchers concluded that even older children who can think logically and perform concrete operations may display magical beliefs.

To collect data from large samples of people, scientists may develop and use **questionnaires**, also called surveys, made up of sets of questions, typically multiple choice. Questionnaires can be administered in person, online, or by telephone, email, or postal mail. Questionnaires are popular data collection methods because they are easy to use and enable scientists to collect information from many people quickly, inexpensively, and anonymously (people can respond without sharing their name). The Monitoring the Future Study, for instance, is an annual survey of 50,000 8th-, 10th-, and 12th-grade students that collects information about their behaviors, attitudes, and values concerning drug and alcohol use (Miech et al., 2024). This anonymous survey permits scientists to gather an enormous amount of data while protecting the adolescent participants from the consequences of sharing personal information that they might not otherwise reveal.

Despite these benefits, questionnaires rely on children's ability to read and understand questions and provide responses. It is not until late childhood, and more often adolescence, that questionnaires become feasible sources of data.

A challenge of self-report measures, both survey and interview, is that sometimes people give socially desirable answers rather than sharing their true feelings. They respond in ways that reflect how they would like themselves to be perceived or give answers they believe researchers want to hear. A fifth-grade student might sometimes peek at other students' tests but might not report this behavior when completing a survey about cheating. Their survey responses might instead match the person they aspire to be or the behaviors they believe a teacher expects—that is, someone who does not cheat on exams. Self-report data, then, may not always reflect children's true understanding, attitudes, or behavior. Also, people are not always fully aware of their feelings and may not provide useful insight into their thoughts and behavior through self-report measures (Newell & Shanks, 2014).

Physiological Measures

Physiological measures are increasingly used in developmental research because cognition, emotion, and behavior have physiological indicators. When speaking in public, such as when you give a class presentation, do you feel your heart beat more rapidly or your palms grow sweaty? Increases in heart rate and perspiration are physiological measures of anxiety that might be measured by researchers. Other researchers might measure cortisol, a hormone triggered by the experience of stress (Simons et al., 2017).

Eye movements and pupil dilation can indicate attention and interest. Researchers studying children's acquisition of a second language might measure children's eye movements to track their attention and determine whether a child connects a new word with an object or concept (Dussias & Miller, 2022). Pupil dilation can be used as a measure of infants' interest and of attention and processing in older children (Köster & Hepach, 2024; Selezneva & Wetzel, 2022).

Physiological measures of brain activity are a particularly promising source of data. Several tools are used to study the brain. **Electroencephalography (EEG)** measures electrical activity patterns produced by the brain via electrodes placed on the scalp. Researchers study fluctuations in activity that occur when participants are presented with stimuli or when they sleep. EEG simply measures electrical activity but cannot provide information about the location of that activity or the brain structures that are the source of brain activity.

Computerized tomography (CT) compiles multiple x-ray images to create a 3-D picture of a person's brain, including brain structures, bone, brain vasculature, and tissue (Withers et al., 2021). CT scans can provide researchers with information about the density of brain structures to illustrate how the thickness of the cortex changes with development. Recording multiple x-ray images, however, exposes research participants to higher levels of radiation than a single x-ray (Rehani & Nacouzi, 2020).

Positron emission tomography (PET) involves injecting a small dose of radioactive material into the participant's blood stream to monitor the flow of blood (Gellman, 2020). Because blood flows more readily to active areas of the brain, PET scans allow researchers to identify what parts of the brain are active as participants view stimuli and solve problems.

Functional magnetic resonance imaging (fMRI) uses a powerful magnet and radio waves to measure blood oxygen level (Moriguchi, 2020). Active areas of the brain require more oxygen-rich blood, which fMRI can detect, enabling researchers to determine what parts of the brain are active as individuals complete cognitive tasks. fMRI images are much more detailed than PET scans and do not rely on radioactive molecules that can only be administered a few times before becoming unsafe.

Diffusion tensor imaging (DTI) uses an MRI machine to track how water molecules move in and around the fibers connecting different parts of the brain (Lope-Piedrafita, 2018). DTI gauges the thickness and density of the brain's connections, permitting researchers to measure the brain's white matter and determine changes that occur with development.

An advantage of physiological measures is they do not rely on verbal reports and generally cannot be faked. On the other hand, although physiological responses can be recorded, they may be difficult to interpret. Excitement and anger may both cause an increase in heart rate.

TABLE 1.4 ■ Data Collection Methods

	Advantage	Disadvantage
Observational Measures		
Naturalistic observation	Gathers data on everyday behavior in a natural environment as behaviors occur.	The observer's presence may influence the children's behavior. No control over the observational environment.
Structured observation	Observation in a controlled setting.	May not reflect real-life reactions and behavior.
Self-Report Measures		
Open-ended interview	Gather a large amount of information quickly and inexpensively.	Nonstandardized questions. Characteristics of the interviewer may influence participant responses.
Structured interview	Gather a large amount of information quickly and inexpensively.	Characteristics of the interviewer may influence children's responses.
Questionnaire	Gather data from a large sample more quickly and inexpensively than by interview methods.	Some participants may respond in socially desirable or inaccurate ways.
Physiological Measures		
Electroencephalography (EEG)	Measures electrical activity patterns produced by the brain.	Does not provide information about the brain structures that are the source of brain activity.
Computerized tomography (CT scan)	Provides images of brain structures, bone, brain vasculature, and tissue.	Exposes participants to low levels of radiation.
Positron emission tomography (PET)	Illustrates activity in specific parts of the brain as participants complete cognitive tasks.	Exposes participants to low levels of radiation
Functional magnetic resonance imaging (fMRI)	Illustrates activity in specific parts of the brain as participants complete cognitive tasks. More detailed images than PET scans and do not rely on radiation.	Expensive and requires participants to be completely still during the scan.
Diffusion tensor imaging (DTI)	Measures the thickness and density of brain connections. Less expensive than fMRI.	Requires participants to be completely still during the scan.

Research Designs

Conducting research entails determining a question, deciding what information to collect, and choosing a research design—a technique for conducting the research study. Developmental scientists employ several types of designs, summarized in Table 1.5.

Case Study

A child with unique experiences, abilities, or disorders might prompt a developmental scientist to conduct a **case study**, which is an in-depth examination of a single person (or small group of individuals). Intended to provide a rich description of a person's life and influences on their development, a case study is conducted by gathering information from many sources, including observations, interviews, and conversations with family, friends, and others who know the individual. It may include samples or interpretations of a person's writing, such as poetry or journal entries, artwork, and other creations. Conclusions drawn from a case study may shed light on a specific person's development but may not be generalized or applied to others. Case studies can be a source of hypotheses to examine in large scale research.

Correlational Research

Are children with high self-esteem more likely to excel at school? Do infants who walk early relative to their peers also have a larger vocabulary than other infants? Is screen time related to adolescents' social skills? All these questions can be studied with **correlational research**, which examines relationships among measured characteristics, behaviors, and events.

For example, scientists examined the relationship between physical fitness and cognitive performance in children and found that children with a higher aerobic capacity scored higher on tests of attention and concentration achievement tests than did those with poorer aerobic capacity (González-Fernández et al., 2023). Notice, however, that this correlation does not tell us *why* physical fitness was associated with cognitive performance. Correlational research cannot answer this question because it simply describes relationships that exist among variables; it does not enable us to reach conclusions about the causes of those relationships. It is likely that other variables influence both the child's physical fitness and cognitive performance, such as general health. Correlational studies do not yield information about the causes of behavior—for that we need an experiment.

Experimental Research

Scientists who seek to test hypotheses about *causal* relationships, such as whether media exposure influences behavior or whether hearing particular types of music influences mood, conduct an **experiment**. An experiment is a procedure that uses control to determine causal relationships among variables. Specifically, one or more variables thought to influence a behavior of interest are changed, or manipulated, while other variables are held constant. Researchers can then examine how the changing variable influences the behavior under study. If the behavior changes as the variable changes, this suggests that the variable caused the change in the behavior.

Gentile et al. (2017) examined the effect of playing violent videogames on children's physiological stress and aggressive thoughts. Children were randomly assigned to play a violent videogame (*Superman*) or a nonviolent videogame (*Finding Nemo*) for 25 minutes in the researchers' lab. The researchers measured physiological stress as indicated by heart rate and cortisol levels before and after the children played the videogame. Children also filled out a word completion task that the researchers used to measure the frequency of aggressive thoughts. The researchers found that children who played violent videogames showed higher levels of physiological stress and aggressive thoughts than did the children who played nonviolent videogames. They concluded that the type of videogame changed children's stress reactions and aggressive thoughts.

Let's take a closer look at the components of this experiment. Conducting an experiment requires choosing at least one **dependent variable**, the behavior under study (in this case two behaviors: physiological stress, indicated by heart rate and cortisol, and aggressive thoughts) and at least one **independent variable**, the factor proposed to change the behavior under study (type of videogame). The independent variable is manipulated or varied systematically by the researcher during the experiment (a child plays with a violent or a nonviolent videogame). Specifically, this manipulation is administered to one or more *experimental groups*, or test groups (children who are asked to play a violent videogame). The *control group* is treated just like the experimental group except that it is not exposed to the independent variable (children who play a nonviolent videogame). After the independent variable is manipulated, if the experimental and control groups differ on the dependent variables (levels of physiological stress and aggressive thoughts are different in the two groups), it is concluded that the independent variable *caused* the change in the dependent variables. That is, a cause-and-effect relationship has been demonstrated.

A procedure called **random assignment** is critical to drawing conclusions from experiments. When participants are randomly assigned to groups, each participant has an equal chance of being assigned to the experimental group and the control group. Random assignment ensures that the groups are as equal as possible in all preexisting characteristics (e.g., age, ethnicity, and gender). Random assignment makes it less likely that preexisting differences between the groups are the cause of any observed differences in the outcomes of the experimental and control groups.

The type of experiment described here is good for identifying the impact of various interventions in the short term, but experimental research relies on experimenters' exerting control over variables. Developmental scientists frequently study problems, such as influences on academic achievement, that cannot be controlled. In these instances correlational research can shed light on relationships among variables. In addition, developmental scientists are interested in how people change over time. For this kind of study, researchers must carefully consider age and use specialized research designs.

Developmental Research Designs

Do children outgrow shyness? Are infants' bonds with their parents associated with their peer relationships in adolescence? These challenging questions require developmental scientists to examine relationships among variables over time. There are several approaches to examining developmental change.

Cross-Sectional Research

A **cross-sectional research study** compares groups of children of different ages at a single point in time. To examine how vocabulary improves in elementary school, a researcher might measure the vocabulary size of children in first, third, and fifth grade. The resulting comparison describes how the vocabulary of first-grade children differs from older children in Grades 3 and 5. But are these changes in vocabulary age-related or developmental change? In a cross-sectional research study, we will not know how the first graders' vocabulary changes over the next few years because this type of study does not follow children over time; it compares the current first graders to current third and fifth graders.

The conclusions researchers can draw about development are limited in a cross-sectional study because participants differ in both age and cohort. A cohort is a group of people of the same age who are exposed to similar historical events and cultural and societal influences. In this example, although the first- and fifth-grade children may attend the same school, they are different ages and different cohorts with potentially different experiences. Suppose the elementary school adopted a new language curriculum, leading the first-grade children to be taught by a new, improved curriculum, whereas the fifth graders received the old curriculum. Any differences in vocabulary may be not only due to age but also to different experiences.

Longitudinal Research

In contrast with a cross-sectional study, which examines children just once, a **longitudinal research study** follows the same group of children over time. By repeatedly examining a set of children, we can describe how they change and the circumstances that surround their development. We can witness development unfolding. Returning to the previous example, a developmental scientist using longitudinal research would measure children's vocabulary size in first grade, then follow up 2 years later in third grade, and then 2 years later in fifth grade. This longitudinal study would take 4 years to complete.

Because longitudinal research follows children over time, scientists can study the first graders' vocabulary progression throughout elementary school. However, longitudinal research studies only one cohort or age group over time. Are the observed findings due to developmental change or are they specific to the children studied? Because only one cohort is assessed, it is not possible to determine whether the observed changes are developmental age-related changes or those that are unique to the cohort examined.

Sequential Research

Sequential research combines the best features of cross-sectional and longitudinal research by assessing multiple cohorts over time, enabling scientists to disentangle the effects of cohort and age (see Figure 1.6). Consider the vocabulary study of children in Grades 1, 3, and 5 once more. A sequential design would begin by measuring vocabulary in first-, third-, and fifth-grade children. Two years later, the first graders are in third grade; the third graders are now in fifth grade; and the fifth graders, now in seventh grade, have presumably graduated from the elementary school and are no longer under study. Next, a new group of first-grade children are introduced to the study. Unique to the sequential design is the addition of new participants at various points throughout the study. The pattern continues. Two years later, that new set of first graders are now in third grade; the original first graders are in fifth grade; the original third graders are in seventh and have aged out of the study; and a new group of first-grade children are introduced to the study, and so on.

The sequential design combines cross-sectional and longitudinal designs to provide information about age, cohort, and age-related change. The cross-sectional data (comparisons of first, third, and fifth graders from a given year) provide information about age differences, meaning how the age groups differ from one another. The longitudinal data captures age-related change, meaning how the group of first graders develop throughout elementary school, because the participants are followed biannually. Because several cohorts are examined at once, the effect of cohort can be studied and conclusions about age-related developmental changes can be drawn. The sequential design is complex, but it permits human development researchers to disentangle the effects of age and cohort and answer questions about developmental change.

FIGURE 1.6 ■ Developmental Designs

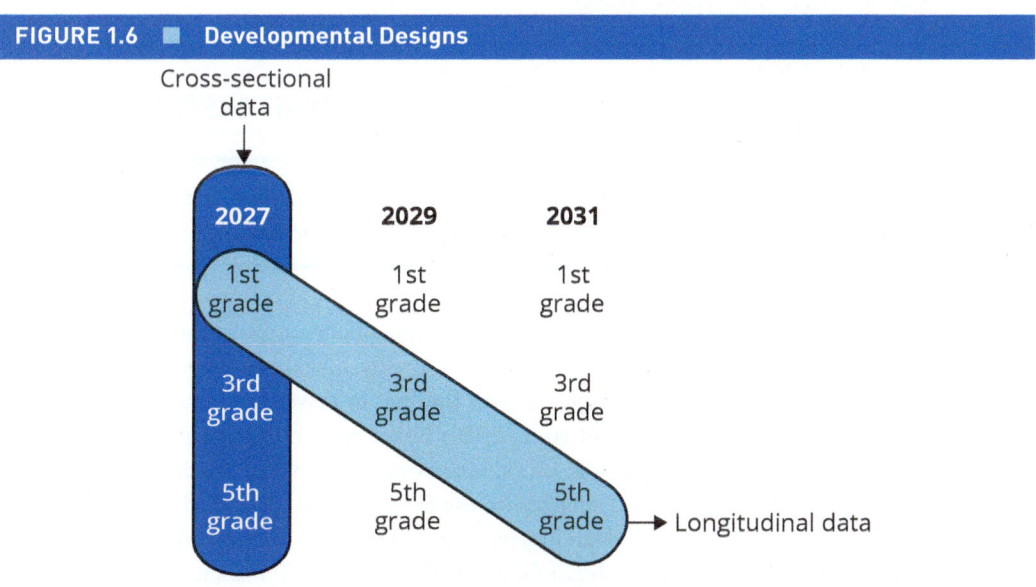

Adapted from Kim, J.-S., & Böckenholt, U. (2000). Modeling stage-sequential change in ordered categorical responses. *Psychological Methods, 5*(3), 380–400.

TABLE 1.5	Comparing Research Designs	
Design	**Strengths**	**Limitations**
Research Designs		
Case study	Provides a rich description of an individual.	Conclusions may not be generalized to other individuals.
Correlational	Permits the analysis of relationships among variables as they exist in the real world.	Cannot determine cause-and-effect relations.
Experimental	Permits a determination of cause-and-effect relationships.	Data collected in artificial environments may not represent behavior in real-world environments.
Developmental Research Designs		
Cross-sectional	More efficient and less costly than the longitudinal design. Permits the determination of age differences.	Does not permit inferences regarding age change. Confounds age and cohort.
Longitudinal	Permits the determination of age-related changes in a sample of participants assessed for a period of time.	Time consuming and expensive. Participant attrition may limit conclusions. Cohort-related changes may limit the generalizability of conclusions.
Sequential	Permits thorough analyses of developmental change. Simultaneous longitudinal and cross-sectional comparisons reveal age differences and age change, as well as cohort effects.	Time consuming, expensive, and complicated data collection and analysis.

THINKING IN CONTEXT 1.4

Paulo is interested in determining whether screen time is related to children's physical activity.

1. How might Paulo gather information to address this hypothesis? How might Paulo measure children's physical fitness? Screen time?
2. What are some of the challenges of measuring behaviors such as these?
3. What kind of research design should Paulo use? What are the advantages and disadvantages of this design?
4. Suppose Paulo wanted to know how children's use of screens changes over elementary school. What kind of study might Paulo choose?

APPLIED DEVELOPMENTAL SCIENCE, ETHICS, AND INTERSECTIONALITY

1.5 Discuss the field of applied developmental science, scientists' obligation to conduct ethical research, and the role of intersectionality in development.

Throughout this book our discussions of child development exemplify **applied developmental science**. Applied developmental science is a field of study that examines the lifelong developmental interactions among individuals and their contexts and applies these findings to prevent and intervene in problems and promote positive development (Barbot et al., 2020; Fisher et al., 2013; Lerner, 2012). Applied developmental scientists study pressing social issues, such as ways to promote the development of preterm infants, the impact of children's and adolescents' use of screens and social media, the juvenile justice system, and ways to help children and families manage the stress that accompanied the COVID-19 pandemic (C. Brown et al., 2023; Fernández de Gamarra-Oca et al., 2021; Hassinger-Das et al., 2020; Odgers et al., 2020; Shorer & Leibovich, 2022). Working to enhance the life chances of diverse groups of individuals, families, and communities requires a multidisciplinary approach that combines the expertise of scientists from many fields, such as human development, psychology, medicine, biology, anthropology, and more. This work poses unique ethical challenges.

Research Ethics

Suppose a researcher wanted to determine the effects of malnutrition on development or the effects of bullying on emotional development. Would it be possible to design a study in which some kindergarteners are deprived of food or some children are exposed to bullying? Of course not. These studies violate the basic ethical principles that guide developmental scientists' work. Developmental scientists must balance conducting scientifically sound research with protecting their participants' rights and welfare. Specifically, developmental scientists must (1) help and not harm participants, (2) be responsible to participants and society, (3) be honest and fair, and (4) respect participants' autonomy (American Psychological Association, 2010).

Help and Not Harm Participants

Researchers are obligated to protect and help the children, families, and communities in their work. They must maximize the benefits for participants and minimize the potential harms of their research. Participating in research must never pose threats to children and families beyond those they might encounter in everyday life. Researchers also have the responsibility to aid individuals for example, by directing a distressed adolescent toward helpful resources.

Responsibility to Participants and Society

Responsible scientists adhere to professional standards of conduct, clarify their obligations and roles to others, and avoid conflicts of interest. Psychologists who conduct research with children and parents must explain their role as scientists and that they are not counselors. They must help participants understand they are simply gathering information from them rather than conducting therapy.

Researchers' responsibility extends beyond their participants to society at large. Research findings often gain media attention. Scientists must work to ensure that their findings are accurately portrayed. This is admittedly difficult, but scientists must attempt to foresee ways in which their results may be misinterpreted and correct any misinterpretations that occur (Lilienfeld, 2002; Society for Research in Child Development, 2021).

Be Honest and Fair to Participants

Developmental scientists must be honest with participants. They must be mindful and attempt to keep the promises they make to children and families. Honesty can take the form of **debriefing** or informing participants about the purpose and results of their research after the study is completed. Researchers are also obligated to treat their participants fairly. **Justice** requires ensuring that the risks and benefits of research participation are spread equitably across individuals and groups. Every participant should have access to the contributions and benefits of research. When a treatment or intervention under study is found to be successful, all participants must be allowed to benefit from it.

Respect Participant Autonomy

Perhaps the most important principle of research ethics is respect for autonomy. Scientists have a special obligation to respect participants' **autonomy**, their ability to make and implement decisions. Ethical codes of conduct require that researchers protect adult participants' autonomy by obtaining **informed consent**—adults' informed, rational, and voluntary agreement to participate. Soliciting informed consent requires providing the individuals under study with information about the research study, answering questions, and ensuring that they understand that they are free to decide not to participate in the research study.

Respecting children's autonomy is more complicated because they are not capable of making judgments and asserting themselves. Parents provide parental permission for their minor children to participate in research because researchers (and lawmakers) assume that minors cannot meet the rational criteria of informed consent (Remien & Kanchan, 2022). Although children cannot provide informed consent, researchers respect their growing capacities for decision making in ways appropriate to their age by seeking **child assent**, children's agreement to participate (Tait & Geisser, 2017; Weisleder, 2020).

For toddlers and young children, obtaining assent may involve simply asking if they want to play with the researcher (H. R. Brown et al., 2017). As children age, and their cognitive and social development increases, they can better understand the nature of science and engage meaningfully in decisions about research participation. Discussions about research participation should be tailored to children's development, including offering more detailed information and seeking more comprehensive assent as children grow older (Gaches, 2021). Moreover, seeking assent has the benefit of helping children learn how to make decisions and participate in decision making within safe contexts (Weisleder, 2020).

Intersectionality and Development

Children's opportunities and outcomes vary with their personal characteristics and contexts—and the opportunities that accompany each. **Intersectionality** refers to the dynamic interrelations of social categories with which people identify, such as gender, race and ethnicity, sexual orientation, socioeconomic status, immigration status, and ability, as well as the interwoven systems of power and privilege that accompany social category membership (Crenshaw, 1989). Inequities in power, opportunity, privilege, and disadvantage accompany some social categories and are experienced as racism, sexism, classism, heterosexism, and more, to shape individuals' lived experiences (Azmitia et al., 2023; Iruka et al., 2022; Santos & Toomey, 2018).

Parents provide informed consent for a child to participate in research. Researchers respect children's developing autonomy by seeking assent, the children's willingness to participate.

Phynart Studio/ Getty Images

All people are members of multiple intertwined social categories, including gender, race, and sexual orientation. Individuals' understanding and experience of each category is influenced by their membership in other categories. Children and adolescents' experience of gender may be filtered through the lens of their membership in another social category, such as ethnicity. Latina girls' views of themselves and their worlds may be quite different from those of Latino boys as well as those of girls of other ethnicities, such as Black and white girls. In this example the intersection of ethnicity and gender combine to influence girls' self-understanding and experience. Power and opportunity are enmeshed with social categories, such as ethnicity and gender. Latina girls' views of themselves reflect not simply their gender and ethnicity, but the relative power ascribed girls and persons of color in U.S. society.

The effects of social category membership are not experienced universally, but vary with context (Ghavami et al., 2016; Stein et al., 2023). Intersectionality is inherently tied to context. Social categories such as gender, race, and sexual orientation may be more salient and meaningful in some contexts and at some times than others, creating distinct experiences for subgroup members with implications for development (Crenshaw, 1989; Mathews et al., 2020). For instance, intersecting expectations about race and gender may uniquely shape the experience of Black boys in classroom settings, how they are perceived and treated, that is unique from those experienced by boys of other races and ethnicities and the experiences of Black girls—with implications for their academic performance, development, and long-term outcomes (Cooper et al., 2022; Iruka et al., 2022). Likewise, Black boys' classroom experiences might vary with context, whether rural, suburban, or urban, and part of the United States, such as the North, South, Midwest, and coasts.

Applied developmental scientists study systemic inequities in children's and families' opportunities (Alegría et al., 2023; Elenbaas et al., 2020). They seek to promote equity and social justice, the basic human right of children to have access to experiences and resources that maximize their potential for growth, health, and happiness (Killen et al., 2021; Smith & Smith Lee, 2019). Equity and social justice involve recognizing and addressing these disparities and the complex factors that contribute to them.

Intersectionality is an emerging approach in developmental science with a small but rapidly growing body of research that recognizes the many ways that gender, ethnicity and race, sexual orientation, socioeconomic status, and disability interact to influence development (Godfrey & Burson, 2018; Grzanka, 2020). Throughout this book we examine development through an intersectional lens whenever possible.

> **THINKING IN CONTEXT 1.5**
>
> 1. Suppose, as part of your research, you wanted to interview children in first and seventh grade. What ethical principles are most relevant to your work in studying school children? What challenges do you anticipate in conducting this work? How might your considerations vary with children's age?
> 2. Consider the social categories of which you are a member. What is your race and ethnicity? Gender? Sexual orientation? Skin color? Socioeconomic status? Did your parents attend college? Do you speak more than one language? What is your first language? Where do you live—city, suburb, rural area? Are you able-bodied? These are just a few categories on which people vary.
>   a. Consider the differences in status that might accompany each of these categories. Are some responses "dominant" or representative of the majority culture, or most people?
>   b. Can you identify other social categories?
>   c. How do the categories to which you belong intersect or interact? To what extent are these important to you? To what extent have they influenced your experience?

APPLY YOUR KNOWLEDGE

In school, at recess, 9-year-old Christiano taunts his classmate, Josh, "Chicken! What are you afraid of? Everything!" He shoves Josh, who quietly walks away, head down and sniffling. This happens several times each week. Christiano and Josh's classmates usually notice and most watch. Some laugh at the funny things Christiano says or when Josh trips as he slinks away and hopes that Christiano will leave him alone.

After school Christiano walks home alone. He usually takes the long way, walking around the block to avoid the older kids who hang out outside the convenience store on the corner. The older kids are friends with Christiano's brother, and they often tease Christiano—especially when his brother his there. Sometimes the kids take Christiano's hat and laugh when he tries to retrieve it. No one in the neighborhood seems to notice. Christiano thinks it's because no one cares.

Christiano returns to an empty home. After entering he quickly and quietly walks through his home to be sure that it's empty. His mother always reminds him to be sure that it's safe before settling in. He feels silly but also a little bit nervous as he looks around. You can't be too careful, he thinks to himself. Afterward Christiano locks the door and makes a snack.

Christiano's mother usually doesn't get home from work until 7 p.m. Christiano knows he should do his homework like his mother says, but what's the point when he keeps getting Ds and Fs? Instead Christiano plays video games. He likes to pretend that he's in the game, running, leaping, and shooting at the bad guys. Christiano wants to be strong and tough so that nobody messes with him. "Not like that weakling Josh," he thinks.

1. Describe Christiano's behavior and interactions at school, in his neighborhood, and at home.
2. How might behaviorist and social learning theorists explain Christiano's behavior at school? In his neighborhood? At home?
3. How might Erikson explain Christiano's development and behavior?

4. Consider Christiano's development and behavior from the perspective of Bronfenbrenner's bioecological theory. Specifically:

5. Identify macrosystem influences on Christiano's behavior.

6. Discuss the interactions among mesosystem factors that might influence Christiano.

7. Give examples of exosystem factors and discuss how might they influence Christiano's behavior and development.

8. How might the macrosystem affect Christiano?

CHAPTER SUMMARY

1.1 Describe developmental periods, developmental domains, and the contexts in which development takes place.

Development begins at conception and progresses from the prenatal period through infancy, early childhood, middle childhood, adolescence, and into adulthood. Each period is characterized by a predictable pattern of functioning across three developmental domains (physical, cognitive, and socioemotional development) that unfold across a variety of contexts in which the developing person interacts, such as home, school, and peer group.

1.2 Explain the nature-nurture debate, how children are active in their development, and how development reflects continuous and discontinuous change.

Developmental scientists examine three fundamental questions about how development proceeds and its influences. First, how do biology (nature) and environment (nurture) influence development? Second, how do children play an active role in their own development, interacting with and influencing the world around them? Finally, in what ways is developmental change continuous, characterized by slow and gradual change, or discontinuous, characterized by sudden and abrupt change? Most developmental scientists agree that development reflects the interactions of nature and nurture, children influence their own development, and some aspects of development appear continuous and others discontinuous.

1.3 Summarize five categories of theories about child development.

Psychoanalytic theories include Freud's psychosexual theory, which explains personality development as progressing through a series of psychosexual stages during childhood, and Erikson's psychosocial theory, in which people move through eight stages of psychosocial development across the lifespan. Behaviorist and social cognitive theories emphasize environmental influences on behavior, specifically, classical conditioning and operant conditioning, as well as observational learning. Cognitive theories include Piaget's cognitive-developmental theory, information processing theory, and Vygotsky's sociocultural theory. Piaget describes cognitive development as an active process proceeding through four stages. Information processing theorists study the steps involved in cognition: perceiving and attending, representing, encoding, retrieving, and problem solving. Vygotsky's sociocultural theory examines the importance of culture and context in cognition. Systems theories include both Bronfenbrenner's bioecological model and Thelen's dynamic systems theory. Bronfenbrenner's bioecological model explains development as a function of the ongoing reciprocal interaction among biological and psychological changes in the person and their changing context. Dynamic systems theory views children's developmental capacities, goals, and context as an integrated system that influences the development of new abilities. Finally, ethology and evolutionary developmental psychology integrate Darwinian principles of evolution and scientific knowledge about the interactive influence of genetic and environmental mechanisms.

1.4 Examine the methods and research designs used to study child development.

A case study is an in-depth examination of an individual. Interviews and questionnaires are called self-report measures because they ask the persons under study questions about their own experiences, attitudes, opinions, beliefs, and behavior. Observational measures are methods that scientists use to collect and organize information based on watching and monitoring people's behavior. Physiological measures gather the body's physiological responses as data. Scientists use correlational research to describe relations among measured characteristics, behaviors, and events. To test hypotheses about causal relationships among variables, scientists employ experimental research. Developmental designs include cross-sectional research, which compares groups of people at different ages simultaneously, and longitudinal research, which studies one group of participants at many points in time. Cross-sequential research combines the best features of cross-sectional and longitudinal designs by assessing multiple cohorts over time.

1.5 Discuss the field of applied developmental science, scientists' obligation to conduct ethical research, and the role of intersectionality in development.

Applied developmental science examines the lifelong interactions among individuals and their contexts and applies these findings to prevent and intervene in problems and promote positive development in people of all ages. Developmental scientists conduct ethical research by working to help and not harm their participants and taking responsibility to ensure that others understand their role and the scope of their research findings. Developmental scientists must be honest and fair to their participants, debriefing them and ensuring that risks and benefits are justly distributed. They must respect participants' autonomy by seeking informed consent and child assent. Children's experiences and access to support and opportunity vary dramatically with intersectionality, the dynamic interrelations of social categories, such as gender, race and ethnicity, sexual orientation, socioeconomic status, immigration status, and disabilities. These experiences are shaped by context and systemic inequities. By recognizing the diverse ways in which children's experiences vary due to their membership in multiple social categories, applied developmental scientists are better equipped to identify and address disparities in power, privilege, and opportunity. This, in turn, can help promote equity and social justice for all children.

KEY TERMS

applied developmental science
autonomy
behaviorism
bioecological systems theory
case study
child assent
chronosystem
classical conditioning
cognitive schemas
cognitive-developmental theory
cohort
Computerized tomography (CT scan)
context
continuous change
correlational research
cross-sectional research
culture
debriefing

dependent variable
development
developmental domains
developmental science
Diffusion tensor imaging (DTI)
discontinuous change
dynamic systems theory
Electroencephalography (EEG)
ethology
evolutionary developmental theory
exosystem
experiment
Functional magnetic resonance imaging (fMRI)
hypothesis
independent variable
information processing theory
informed consent
intersectionality

justice
longitudinal research
macrosystem
mesosystem
microsystem
naturalistic observation
nature-nurture debate
observational learning
ontogenetic development
open-ended interview
operant conditioning
Positron emission tomography (PET)
psychoanalytic theory
punishment
random assignment
reciprocal determinism
reinforcement
scientific method
sequential research
social cognitive theory
social policy
sociocultural theory
sociohistorical context
structured interview
structured observation
theory
questionnaires

CAREERS IN CHILD DEVELOPMENT: FOUNDATIONS OF DEVELOPMENT

Developmental science is a multidisciplinary field, integrating findings from many disciplines and settings. In this feature that appears at the end of each major part of this book, we explore some of the diverse career opportunities for students interested in child development. Students with interest in child development select many college majors, such as human development and family studies, psychology, social work, education, nursing, and more. Besides a grounding in developmental science, these fields hold in common training in transferable skills that are valuable in a range of employment settings.

Transferrable Skills

Just as it sounds, transferable skills are those that can *transfer* to and be applied in a variety of settings. Employers value transferable skills because they can be adapted and used in many contexts. In fact, the top five attributes that employers look for in potential employees are not tied to any one major (Table 1.6). Instead, they all involve transferable skills, including problem solving, analytical/quantitative abilities, teamwork, and a strong work ethic. These are skills that students of all disciplines who study child development have the opportunity to hone. Let's take a closer look at some of these transferable skills.

TABLE 1.6 ■ Top 5 Key Attributes Employers Prefer in Applicants

Desired Attribute	Percentage of Employers Endorsing
Problem-solving skills	86
Analytical/quantitative skills	78
Ability to work in a team	76
Communication skills (written)	73
Strong work ethic	71

Source: National Association of College and Employers. (2022). *The attributes employers want to see on college students' resumes.* https://www.naceweb.org/about-us/press/the-attributes-employers-want-to-see-on-college-students-resumes/

Perhaps not surprisingly, the skill employers view as more valuable is *problem solving*. Individuals who are successful at problem solving can gather and synthesize information from various sources. They learn to weigh multiple sources of information, determine the degree of support for each position, and generate solutions based on the information at hand. Effective problem solving relies on *analytical skills*. Exposure to diverse perspectives and ideas about human development trains students to think flexibly and to accept some ambiguity because solutions to complex problems are often not clear-cut.

Students in child development fields learn *teamwork skills* in coursework and placements. For example, nursing, psychology, and human development and family studies students may work together as lab members. Education students may collaborate on group projects, such as designing curricula, and social work students may get hands-on experience working with others in field placements. These valuable experiences foster the ability to effectively work with teams, a skill coveted by employers of all fields.

Students in child development and family studies, psychology, social work, education, and nursing take coursework relevant to their discipline, but success in each of these fields requires a *strong work ethic* and good *communication skills*. Succeeding in challenging courses like anatomy and physiology, research methods, and statistics require dedication and consistent work. Oral and written communication skills are developed not only in coursework but also in field and practicum experiences when students learn to communicate with children, adolescents, adults, and supervisors.

Each transferrable skill contributes to an individual's ability to be versatile, adaptable, and collaborative in the workplace. Skilled problem solvers, communicators, and team workers foster a productive work environment, enabling employees to tackle complex tasks and efficiently work together.

Child Development Career Fields

As we consider career opportunities in child development, we organize them into several areas: education; health care and nursing; counseling, psychology, and social work; and research and advocacy.

EDUCATION

Perhaps the most obvious career for students passionate about child development is that of an educator or teacher. Educators who work with young children include *early childhood educators* and *preschool teachers*. For older children and adolescents there are *elementary* and *high school teachers*. Some educators specialize in working with children with specific developmental needs (*special education teachers*). Others focus on teaching English as a Second Language (*ESL teachers*) and work with children, adolescents, and adults. Becoming a teacher requires a bachelor's degree and certification.

The education field also includes administrative careers, overseeing educational programs and educators. *Preschool and childcare center directors* collaborate with early childhood educators to develop educational plans for young children, supervise staff, prepare budgets, and manage all aspects of the program. *Elementary, middle, and high school principals* supervise all school operations, including teachers, personnel, curricula, and daily school activities, and promote a safe and productive learning environment.

HEALTH CARE AND NURSING

An understanding of child development is invaluable to those working in healthcare settings. Nurses of various specialties can benefit from developmental knowledge. Examples of nurses specializing in developmental science include *pediatric nurses* who work with infants, children, and adolescents. *Neonatal nurses* care for infants born preterm, have low birth weight, or suffer health problems from birth until they are discharged from the hospital. A *nurse midwife* provides gynecological care focusing on pregnancy, labor, and delivery.

All physicians must learn about human development during their medical education, but only some specialize in working with specific age groups. *Obstetrician-gynecologists* are physicians who concentrate on female reproductive health, pregnancy, and childbirth. *Pediatricians* treat infants, children, and adolescents. To specialize, physicians must complete additional training, often a fellowship after earning their medical degree and obtaining licensure.

Allied health is a field of health care that assists, facilitates, or complements the work of nurses, physicians, and other health care specialists. *Recreational therapists* assess clients and provide recreational activities to children and adolescents with physical or emotional disabilities in a variety of medical and community settings. *Physical therapists* design and provide treatments and interventions for individuals suffering pain, loss of mobility, or other physical disabilities. *Occupational therapists* help patients with physical, developmental, or psychological impairments, helping them develop, recover, and maintain skills needed for independent daily living and activity. Physical therapists and occupational therapists require graduate degrees, while *assistant physical therapists* and *assistant occupational therapists* can be hired with specialized associate degrees and certifications.

Other allied healthcare specialists include *speech-language pathologists*, who assess, diagnose, and treat speech, language, and social communication disorders in children, adolescents, and adults. A speech-language pathologist must earn a graduate degree. Depending on the U.S. state, assistant speech-language pathologists may be hired with associate or bachelor's degrees with specialized coursework and certification. *Child life specialists* typically work in hospital settings, helping children and families adjust to a child's hospitalization by educating and supporting families in the physically and emotionally demanding process of caring for hospitalized or disabled children. An entry-level position as a child life specialist requires a bachelor's degree and certification.

Knowledge about health and development is also needed to become a health educator.

Health educators design and implement educational programs (classes, promotional pamphlets, community activities) to educate individuals and communities about healthy lifestyles and wellness.

Social Work, Psychology, and Counseling

Children and adolescents have different communication needs and abilities compared to adults; these abilities undergo significant changes as they develop. Professionals who work closely with children must understand how their abilities change over time.

Social workers help people improve their lives by identifying needed resources (such as housing or food stamps) and providing guidance. *Clinical social workers* also conduct therapy and implement counseling treatments with individuals and families. Entry-level social workers require a bachelor's degree, whereas clinical social workers must earn a graduate degree and obtain licensure.

There are various types of counselors, generally requiring master's degrees. *Mental health counselors* assist people in managing and overcoming mental and emotional disorders. *School counselors* help elementary, middle, and high school students develop skills to enhance personal, social, and academic growth. *Marriage and family therapists* focus on the family system and treat individuals, couples, and families to help people overcome problems with family and relationships. *Substance use counselors* help people with addictions, helping them recover and modify behaviors through individual and group therapy sessions.

Applied behavior analysts apply scientific principles of learning to modify children and adolescents' behavior to improve social, communication, academic, and adaptive skills. They teach parents, teachers, and support professionals how to implement behavioral procedures, skills, and interventions. A position as an applied behavior analyst requires a graduate degree. *Assistant behavior analysts* support the work of applied behavior analysts. They assist in gathering data or information about clients, monitoring client progress and maintaining records, and administering assessments and treatment under the supervision of the applied behavior analysts.

Psychologists are doctoral-level mental health professionals. *Clinical psychologists* and *counseling psychologists* conduct therapy with children, adolescents, adults, and families. Clinical psychologists specialize in treating mental disorders, and counseling psychologists emphasize helping people adjust to life changes. *School psychologists* work within school settings, assessing individuals' learning and mental health needs, collaborating with parents, teachers, and school administrators, designing interventions to improve students' well-being, and counseling students. Depending on their training, *applied developmental psychologists* may assess and treat children, adolescents, and adults and design and evaluate intervention programs to address problems and enhance the development of people of all ages.

Research and Advocacy

Developmental scientists also work in educational and clinical research settings, such as universities, research institutions, and hospitals. These researchers design and conduct studies to investigate various aspects of child and adolescent development, ranging from cognitive, emotional, social, and physical development to the impact of environmental factors on developmental outcomes. Their research can inform educational policies, parenting practices, clinical interventions, and the development of new assessment tools.

Developmental scientists design and conduct research on social problems and apply their findings to advocate for children, adolescents, and families. They are employed at social service agencies, nonprofits, think tanks, and government agencies. They conduct research to gather information about social problems and policies; assess and improve programs for children, youth, and families; and write reports and other documents to inform policymakers and the public. Some work as program directors and administrators for these programs, while others assess programs. Developmental scientists can contribute to policy development at the local, state, or national level by advising on creating and implementing policies that support the well-being of children, adolescents, and families.

Some developmental scientists head nonprofit organizations as *foundation directors*. They develop goals and strategies in line with the foundation's mission statement and oversee all activities within an organization, including program delivery, program evaluation, finance, and staffing. Other developmental scientists work as *grant writers*, submitting proposals to fund programs. Organizations that award grants to others have *grant directors* who oversee the funding process by analyzing grant proposals, communicating with applicants, and determining which proposals are suitable for funding. Developmental scientists who work for the government might evaluate government-supported social media–based health initiatives, such as those targeting distracted driving, or educational initiatives, such as the effects of providing free kindergarten to children.

Although developmental scientists generally have doctoral degrees in human development, psychology, or a related field, many individuals with bachelor's and master's degrees work alongside them as research associates, project coordinators, or research assistants, depending on their level of education and experience.

Expertise in child development is also needed in business and industry settings to help companies design materials, such as toys, products, and media, that cater to people's needs and abilities. They might determine the developmental appropriateness of toys and provide insight into children's abilities or examine children's and parents' reactions to particular toys, advertising, and promotional techniques. Others might provide developmental and educational advice to creators of children's media, such as by interpreting research on children's attention spans to inform creative guidelines for television programs such as *Sesame Street*.

We discuss many of the previously discussed job titles in upcoming Careers in Child Development profiles. For additional information on careers, consult *The Occupational Outlook Handbook*, published by the U.S. Bureau of the Census (https://www.bls.gov/ooh/).

PART 2
PHYSICAL DEVELOPMENT AND HEALTH

video1/istock

2 BIOLOGICAL AND ENVIRONMENTAL FOUNDATIONS OF DEVELOPMENT

> **LEARNING OBJECTIVES**
>
> **2.1** Discuss the genetic foundations of development and patterns of genetic inheritance.
>
> **2.2** Identify examples of genetic disorders and chromosomal abnormalities.
>
> **2.3** Explain the choices of reproductive technology and prenatal diagnostic methods available to individuals and couples.
>
> **2.4** Examine interactions among heredity and environment, including behavior genetics, gene-environment correlations and interactions, and the epigenetic framework.

"Diego is your brother?" Alejandra's new friend asked, surprised. "He's so tall and you're . . ." "Not? I know. We look totally different. He's tall, dark, and brooding, with deep brown eyes and hair. And I'm just short and pale. Everyone wonders where I got my blond hair and blue eyes from—no one in my family looks quite like me," Alejandra said. "Diego and I are different in other ways, too. I'm outgoing and he's a homebody. He's into video games and hanging out at home. I play sports and am in the school play."

How can two people who have the same parents and live in the same home be so different? In this chapter, we discuss the process of genetic inheritance and principles that can help us understand how members of a family can share a great many similarities and also many differences.

GENETIC FOUNDATIONS OF DEVELOPMENT

> **2.1** Discuss the genetic foundations of development and patterns of genetic inheritance.

We are born with a hereditary "blueprint" that influences our development, including our appearance, physical characteristics, health, and even personality. This blueprint is inherited from our biological parents.

Genetics

Our body is composed of trillions of cells that make up all our tissues and organs. At the center of each cell is a nucleus containing 23 matching pairs of rod-shaped structures called **chromosomes** (Finegold, 2021). Each chromosome holds the basic units of heredity, known as **genes**, composed of stretches of **deoxyribonucleic acid (DNA)**, a complex molecule shaped like a twisted ladder or staircase. Genes carry the plan for creating all the traits that organisms carry. The human genome, or full set of human genes, consists of about 20,000 to 25,000 genes that influence all genetic characteristics (Taneri et al., 2020).

Much of our genetic material is not exclusive to humans. Although every species has a different genome, we share some genes with all organisms, from bacteria to primates. We share nearly 99% of our DNA with our closest genetic relative, the chimpanzee. There is even less genetic variation among humans. People around the world share 99.9% of their genes (Lewis, 2024). Although all humans share the same basic genome, every person has a slightly different code, making them genetically unique from other humans.

Cell Reproduction

Cell reproduction in humans occurs through two processes: mitosis and meiosis. Most cells in the human body reproduce through **mitosis**, in which DNA replicates itself, duplicating its chromosomes and resulting in genetically identical new cells (Sadler, 2023). **Gametes**, sex cells specialized for reproduction, replicate through a different process, called **meiosis**. During meiosis the 46 chromosomes duplicate and undergo a process called *crossing over*. The chromosome pairs align, and DNA segments cross over, moving from one member of the pair to the other, essentially *mixing up* the DNA segments to create unique combinations of genes (Padiath, 2023). The resulting gametes (sperm in males and ova in females) consist of only 23 single, unpaired chromosomes. Each gamete has a unique genetic profile, and it is estimated that individuals can produce millions of genetically different gametes (Brooker, 2022). When humans breed, ova and sperm join to create a **zygote**, or fertilized egg. The zygote contains 46 chromosomes, forming 23 pairs with half of each pair from the biological mother and half from the biological father.

Sex Determination

A single pair of chromosomes, known as sex chromosomes, determines whether a zygote will develop into a male or female. Twenty-two of the 23 pairs of inherited chromosomes are matched pairs (see Figure 2.1). They contain similar genes in almost identical positions and sequence. The 23rd pair of chromosomes are not identical because they are sex chromosomes that specify the genetic sex of the individual. In females, sex chromosomes consist of two large X-shaped chromosomes (XX). Males' sex chromosomes consist of one large X-shaped chromosome and one much smaller Y-shaped chromosome (XY).

| FIGURE 2.1 | Chromosomes |

Because females have two X sex chromosomes, all their ova contain one X sex chromosome. A male's sex chromosome pair is composed of one X and one Y chromosome; therefore, half of the sperm males produce contain an X chromosome and half contain a Y. The Y chromosome contains genetic instructions that will cause the fetus to develop male reproductive organs. Thus, whether the fetus develops into a male or female is determined by which sperm fertilizes the ovum. If the ovum is fertilized by a Y sperm, the fetus will develop male reproductive organs, and if the ovum is fertilized by an X sperm, it will develop female reproductive organs (see Figure 2.2).

Genes Shared by Twins

Siblings who share the same biological parents inherit chromosomes from each parent. Despite this genetic similarity, siblings are often quite different from one another. Siblings who share the same womb at the same time are known as twins. Twins occur in about 1 out of every 33 births in the United States (Martin et al., 2018).

The majority of naturally conceived twins (over 70%) are **dizygotic (DZ) twins**, or fraternal twins, created when a woman releases more than one ovum and each is fertilized by a different sperm (Gill et al., 2022). Like siblings who are not twins, DZ twins share about one half of their genes and most differ in

FIGURE 2.2 ■ Sex Determination

Males carry both X and Y chromosomes while females carry two X chromosomes. When offspring inherit X chromosomes from both biological parents, they develop female reproductive organs. Offspring that inherit both X and Y chromosomes develop male reproductive organs.

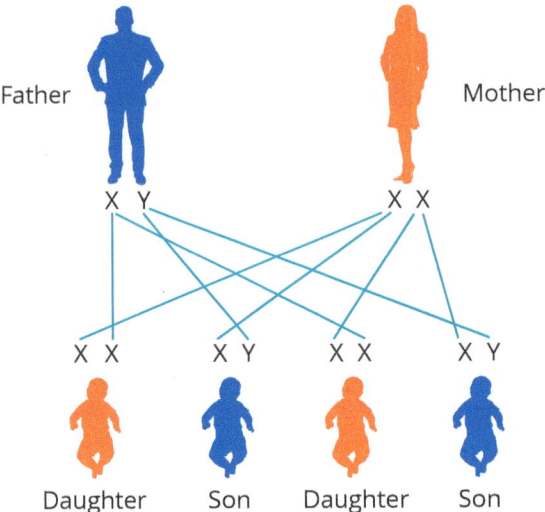

appearance, including hair color, eye color, and height. In about half of fraternal twin pairs, one twin is a boy and the other a girl. DZ twins tend to run in families, suggesting a genetic component that controls the tendency for a woman to release more than one ovum each month (Hazel et al., 2020). Rates of DZ twins increase with maternal age and with each subsequent birth and have also been more common in pregnancies that result from in vitro fertilization where more than one embryo is transferred to the uterus (Gill et al., 2022; Pison et al., 2015). Since the 1980s, the rate of twinning has increased by one third worldwide, especially in wealthy nations where medically assisted reproduction, in vitro fertilization has become common (Monden et al., 2021). Twinning rates peaked in the U.S. in 2014 and declined 4% through 2020 (Osterman et al., 2023).

Monozygotic (MZ) twins, or identical twins, originate from the same zygote, sharing the same **genotype**, or set of genetic instructions for all physical and psychological characteristics. MZ twins occur when the zygote splits into two distinct separate but identical cells that develop into two infants. MZ twins are estimated to occur in about 3% of births in the United States (De Paepe, 2022). The causes of MZ twinning are not well understood (McNamara et al., 2016). Rates of MZ twins are not related to maternal age or the number of births, but in vitro fertilization increases the likelihood of MZ twins (Busnelli et al., 2019; Dallagiovanna et al., 2021).

Patterns of Genetic Inheritance

Genes combine in many ways to influence our **phenotype**, the characteristics that we display, such as hair color, health and propensities for specific diseases and disorders, and even personality. Traits and characteristics are inherited through several patterns.

Monozygotic, or identical, twins share 100% of their DNA.
Ray Evans/Alamy Stock Photo

Dominant-Recessive Inheritance

Lynn has red hair while her brother, Jim, does not—and neither do their parents. How did Lynn end up with red hair? Some traits, like hair color, are passed through **dominant-recessive inheritance** (Lakhani et al., 2023; Plomin, 2019). As we have discussed, each person has 23 pairs of chromosomes, half inherited from the biological mother and half from the biological father. Some genes, like those for nonred hair, are *dominant* and are always expressed or displayed, regardless of the gene they are paired with. Other genes, such as for red hair, are *recessive* and are only expressed if paired with another recessive gene.

Suppose two biological parents each carry a dominant gene for nonred hair (symbolized by N in Figure 2.3) and a recessive gene for red hair (r). Since dominant genes override recessive genes, both parents will have nonred hair (phenotype). When children inherit a dominant nonred hair gene (N) they will show the phenotype for nonred hair, regardless of whether they have a second nonred hair gene (N) or a recessive red hair gene (r). The red hair phenotype can result only from inheriting two recessive genes (rr), one from each parent. Several characteristics are passed through dominant-recessive inheritance (see Table 2.1).

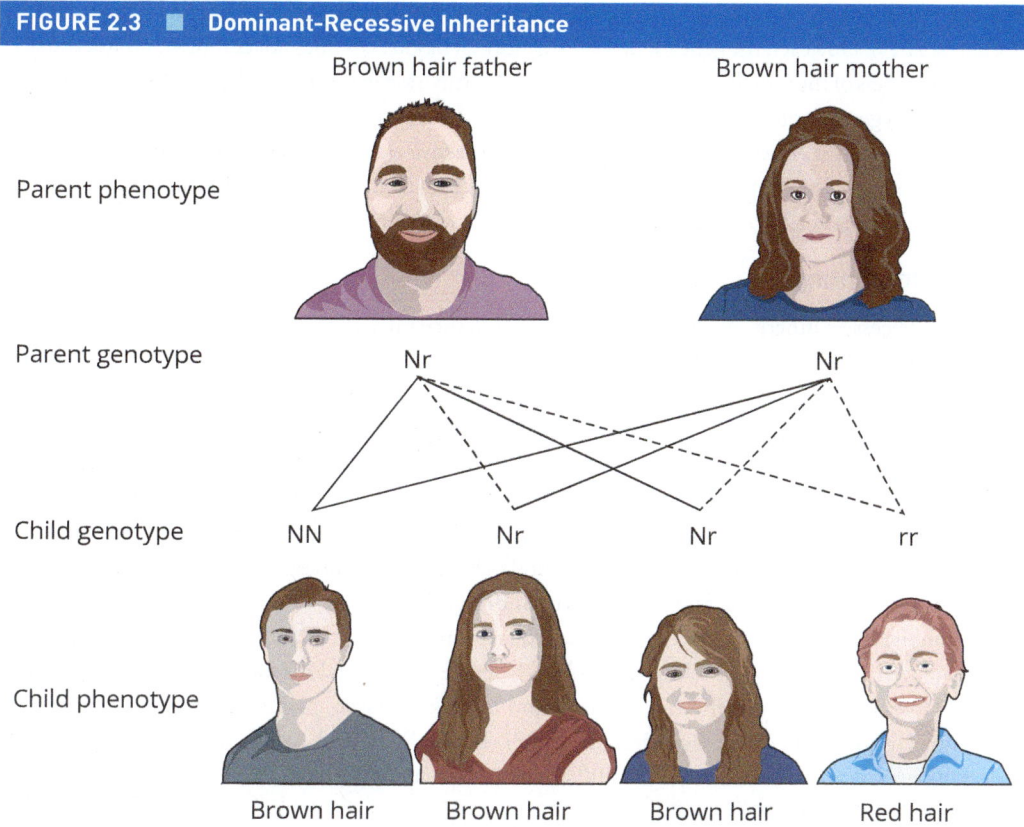

FIGURE 2.3 ■ Dominant-Recessive Inheritance

TABLE 2.1 ■ Dominant and Recessive Characteristics	
Dominant Trait	**Recessive Trait**
Dark hair	Light hair
Curly hair	Straight hair
Hair	Baldness
Freckles	No freckles
Widow's peak hairline	Straight hair line
Facial dimples	No dimples
Brown eyes	Blue, green, hazel eyes

Source: McKusick-Nathans Institute of Genetic Medicine. 2020. *OMIM - Online Mendelian Inheritance in Man.* Johns Hopkins University School of Medicine. http://www.omim.org/about

Incomplete Dominance

In most cases, dominant-recessive inheritance is an oversimplified explanation for patterns of genetic inheritance. **Incomplete dominance** is a genetic inheritance pattern in which both genes jointly influence the characteristic (Lakhani et al., 2023). For example, consider blood type. Neither the genes for blood type A nor those for type B dominate each other. A person with one gene for blood type A and one for blood type B will express both and have blood type AB.

Sometimes a gene is stronger than but does not completely dominate another gene. In this case some, but not all, characteristics of the recessive gene appear. The gene that causes **sickle cell anemia** is recessive. Individuals who inherit two of these genes develop the disorder, in which red blood cells become crescent, or sickle, shaped. Cells that are sickle-shaped cannot distribute oxygen effectively throughout the circulatory system and can cause inflammation and damage the blood vessels (Ware et al., 2017). People who carry only one recessive sickle cell gene do not develop full-blown sickle cell anemia (Chakravorty & Williams, 2015). However, the gene for developing normal blood cells does not completely mask the sickle cell gene. Carriers of the trait for sickle cell anemia tend to function well but may show some symptoms such as reduced oxygen distribution throughout the body and exhaustion after exercise (Xu & Thein, 2019). About 5% of African American newborns carry the recessive sickle cell gene (Ojodu et al., 2014). The sickle cell gene is also common in Latino populations but relatively uncommon in white and Asian Americans (Valle et al., 2022). Sickle cell anemia is discussed later in this chapter.

Genomic Imprinting

Dominant-recessive inheritance and incomplete dominance inheritance account for over 1,000 human traits (Finegold, 2021). But a few traits are determined by **genomic imprinting**, in which the expression of a gene is determined by whether it is inherited from the biological mother or father (Hubert & Demars, 2022; Thamban et al., 2020) Prader-Willi syndrome and Angelman syndrome, for instance, are both caused by an abnormality in the 15th chromosome (Volkmar, 2021). Individuals who acquire the chromosome 15 abnormality from the biological father develop Prader-Willi syndrome, a set of specific physical and behavioral characteristics including insatiable hunger, which usually leads to obesity, short stature, mild to moderate developmental delays, and psychological problems, such as temper outbursts, obsessive behaviors, and anxiety (M. G. Butler et al., 2019; L. Schwartz et al., 2021).

When the abnormal chromosome 15 arises from the mother, individuals instead develop Angelman syndrome, characterized by developmental delays, severe intellectual disability, severe speech impairment, problems with movement and balance, and hyperactivity coupled with a characteristic happy demeanor (Dagli et al., 2021; Roche et al., 2022). Prader-Willi and Angelman syndromes are rare, occurring on average in 1 in 15,000–30,000 births (Volkmar, 2021).

Polygenic Inheritance

Despite the simple examples used in our discussion of inheritance this far, most traits result from the interaction of many genes, known as **polygenic inheritance** (Armstrong-Carter et al., 2021). Hereditary influences act in complex ways and researchers cannot trace most characteristics to only one or two genes. Examples of polygenic traits include height, intelligence, personality, and susceptibility to certain forms of cancer (Flint et al., 2020). As the number of genes that contribute to a trait increases, so does the range of possible phenotypes. Genetic propensities interact with environmental influences to produce a wide range of individual differences in human traits. Patterns of genetic inheritance are summarized in Table 2.2.

TABLE 2.2 ■ Summary: Patterns of Genetic Inheritance	
Inheritance Pattern	**Description**
Dominant-recessive inheritance	Genes that are dominant are always expressed, regardless of the gene they are paired with. Recessive genes are expressed only if paired with another recessive gene.
Incomplete dominance	Both genes influence the characteristic, and aspects of both genes appear.
Polygenic inheritance	Polygenic traits are the result of interactions among many genes.
Genomic imprinting	The expression of a gene is determined by whether it is inherited from the mother or the father.

> **THINKING IN CONTEXT 2.1**
>
> 1. From an evolutionary developmental perspective (see Chapter 1), why are some characteristics dominant and others recessive? Is it adaptive for some traits to dominate over others? Why or why not?
> 2. Consider your own physical characteristics, such as hair and eye color. Are they examples of recessive traits or dominant ones? Which of your traits are likely polygenic?

CHROMOSOMAL AND GENETIC ABNORMALITIES

> 2.2 Identify examples of genetic disorders and chromosomal abnormalities.

Just as many traits and characteristics are products of genetic inheritance, so are many disorders and diseases. Other disorders result from chromosomal abnormalities. Some hereditary and chromosomal abnormalities are diagnosed before birth. Others are evident at birth or can be detected as an infant begins to develop. Some abnormalities are discovered only after many years—or not at all.

Genetic Disorders

Inherited genetic disorders and abnormalities are passed from biological parents to offspring through the inheritance processes that we have discussed. These include well-known conditions as sickle cell anemia, as well as others that are rare.

Dominant-Recessive Disorders

Some genetic disorders are inherited through dominant-recessive patterns (see Table 2.3). Recall that in dominant-recessive inheritance, dominant genes are always expressed regardless of the gene they are paired with, and recessive genes are expressed only if paired with another recessive gene. Few severe disorders are inherited through dominant inheritance because most disorders develop early in life. Children who inherit the dominant version of the gene often do not reach reproductive age to pass it to the next generation. One exception is Huntington's disease, a fatal disease in which the central nervous system deteriorates (Ghosh & Tabrizi, 2018; McKusick-Nathans Institute of Genetic Medicine, 2020). Individuals with the gene for Huntington's show typical functioning in childhood, adolescence, and early adulthood. Symptoms of Huntington's disease do not appear until age 35 or later. By then, many affected individuals have already had children, and one half of those children, on average, will inherit the dominant Huntington's gene.

Phenylketonuria (PKU) is a common recessive disorder that prevents the body from producing an enzyme that breaks down phenylalanine, an amino acid, from proteins (McKusick-Nathans Institute of Genetic Medicine, 2020). Without treatment, the phenylalanine builds up quickly to toxic levels that damage the central nervous system, leading to intellectual disability by 1 year of age. The United States and Canada require all newborns to be screened for PKU (Camp et al., 2014).

PKU illustrates how genes interact with the environment to produce developmental outcomes. Intellectual disability results from the interaction of the genetic predisposition for PKU and exposure to phenylalanine in the diet (Blau, 2016). Infants with PKU are placed on a diet low in phenylalanine, though it is difficult to remove nearly all phenylalanine from the diet. When children with PKU maintain a strict diet, they usually score in the average range on measures of intelligence, though often lower than children without PKU (Hofman et al., 2018; Romani et al., 2017). Some cognitive and psychological problems may appear in childhood and persist into adulthood, including poor attention, planning skills, and emotional regulation, as well as depression and anxiety (Christ et al., 2020; Romani et al., 2022; Spronsen et al., 2021).

TABLE 2.3 ■ Conditions Inherited Through Dominant-Recessive Inheritance

Condition	Occurrence	Mode of Inheritance	Description	Treatment
Huntington disease	1 in 20,000	Dominant	Degenerative brain disorder that affects muscular coordination and cognition.	No cure. Appears in adulthood, after age 35. Death typically occurs 10 to 20 years after onset.
Cystic fibrosis	1 in 2,000–2,500	Recessive	An overproduction of thick, sticky mucus clogs the lungs and digestive system, leading to respiratory infections, problems with digestion, and a short lifespan.	Therapy to loosen and drain mucus, diet, gene replacement therapy.
Phenylketonuria (PKU)	1 in 10,000–15,000	Recessive	Inability to digest phenylalanine that, if untreated, results in neurological damage and death.	Diet
Sickle cell anemia	1 in 500 African Americans	Recessive	Sickling of red blood cells leads to inefficient distribution of oxygen throughout the body that leads to organ damage and respiratory infections.	No cure. Blood transfusions, treatment of infections, bone marrow transplant(s). Death typically occurs by middle age.
Tay-Sachs disease	1 in 3,600 to 4,000 descendants of Central and Eastern European Jews	Recessive	Degenerative brain disease	No cure. Death typically occurs by age 4.

Source: McKusick-Nathans Institute of Genetic Medicine. 2020.

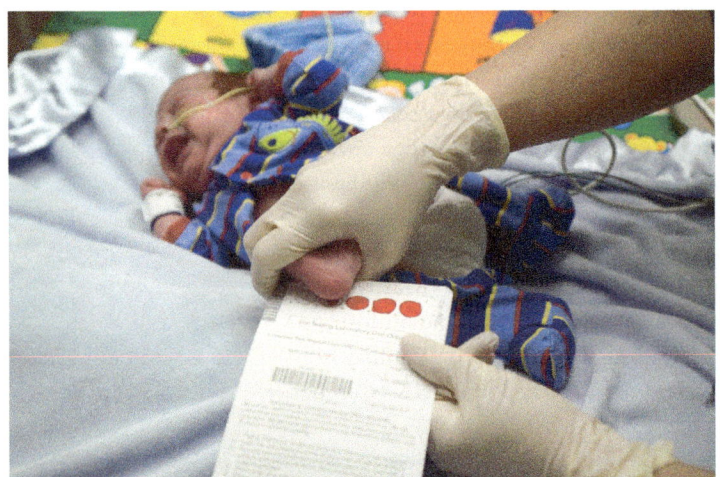

A newborn's blood is tested for phenylketonuria (PKU), a genetic disorder in which the body lacks the enzyme that breaks down phenylalanine. Without treatment, the phenylalanine builds up to toxic levels and can damage the central nervous system.

Marmaduke St. John/Alamy Stock Photo

X-Linked Disorders

A special instance of the dominant-recessive pattern occurs with genes that are located on the 23rd pair of chromosomes, the sex chromosomes (Shah et al., 2017). Some recessive genetic disorders, like the gene for red-green colorblindness, are carried on the X sex chromosome (see Table 2.4). Recall that females have two X chromosomes; as a result, a recessive gene located on one X chromosome will be masked by a dominant gene on the other X chromosome. But males carry an X and Y sex chromosome. Because they have only one X chromosome, any recessive genes on their X chromosome are expressed. Females are thereby less likely to display X-linked genetic disorders because both of their X chromosomes must carry the recessive genetic disorder for it to be displayed. A female carrier has a 50/50 chance of transmitting the gene to each child.

Fragile X syndrome is an example of a dominant-recessive disorder carried on the X chromosome (Salcedo-Arellano et al., 2020). Because the gene is dominant, it need appear on only one X chromosome to be displayed by both males and females. Fragile X syndrome is the most common form of inherited intellectual disability, and individuals with fragile X syndrome tend to display severe difficulties with executive function (Hagerman & Hagerman, 2022; Schmitt et al., 2019). Cardiac abnormalities are common as well as several behavioral mannerisms, including poor eye contact and repetitive behaviors such as hand flapping, hand biting, and mimicking others, behaviors common in individuals with autistic spectrum disorders (Salcedo-Arellano et al., 2020). Fragile X syndrome is often diagnosed along with autism; about 40%–60% of boys and 16%–20% of girls with fragile X syndrome are estimated to meet the diagnostic criteria for autism (Bagni & Zukin, 2019; Kaufmann et al., 2017).

Hemophilia, a condition in which the blood does not clot normally, is recessive disease inherited through genes on the X sex chromosome (McKusick-Nathans Institute of Genetic Medicine, 2020; Pipe et al., 2022). As with fragile X syndrome, males with the hemophilia gene display the disorder because the Y chromosome does not have the corresponding genetic information to counter the gene. Females who inherit the gene for hemophilia typically do not show the disorder unless they inherit the gene from both parents, because the dominant gene on their second X chromosome promotes normal blood clotting (d'Oiron, 2019). Females, therefore, can carry the gene for hemophilia without exhibiting the disorder.

TABLE 2.4 ■ Diseases Acquired Through X-Linked Inheritance

Syndrome/Disease	Occurrence	Description	Treatment
Color blindness	1 in 12 males	Difficulty distinguishing red from green; less commonly difficulty distinguishing blue from green	No cure
Duchenne muscular dystrophy	1 in 3,500 males	Weakness and wasting of limb and trunk muscles; progresses slowly but will affect all voluntary muscles	Physical therapy, exercise, body braces; survival rare beyond late 20s
Fragile X syndrome	1 in 4,000 males and 1 in 8,000 females	Cognitive impairment; attention problems; anxiety; unstable mood; long face; large ears; flat feet; and hyper extensible joints, especially fingers	No cure
Hemophilia	1 in 3,000–7,000 males	Blood disorder in which the blood does not clot	Blood transfusions

Source: McKusick-Nathans Institute of Genetic Medicine. 2020.

Chromosomal Abnormalities

Not all inborn disorders or conditions are the result of genetic inheritance. Chromosomal abnormalities are the result of errors during cell reproduction, meiosis or mitosis, or damage caused afterward.

Down Syndrome

Occurring in about 1 of 1,500 births, trisomy 21, more commonly called Down syndrome, occurs when a third chromosome appears alongside the 21st pair of chromosomes (Akhtar & Bokhari, 2024). Down syndrome is associated with marked physical, health, and cognitive attributes, including a short, stocky build, and often a round face, almond-shaped eyes, and a flattened nose. Children with Down syndrome tend to show delays in physical and motor development relative to other children, and health problems, such as congenital heart abnormalities, vision impairments, poor hearing, and immune system deficiencies (Antonarakis et al., 2020; Bull, 2020).

Down syndrome is the most common genetic cause of intellectual disability, but children vary in their abilities (Santoro et al., 2021). Generally, children with Down syndrome show greater strengths in nonverbal learning and memory relative to their verbal skills. Expressive language (what children can say) is delayed relative to comprehension (what they can understand). Infants and children who participate in early intervention and receive sensitive caregiving and encouragement to explore their environment show positive outcomes, especially in the motor, social, and emotion areas of functioning (Antonarakis et al., 2020; Bull, 2020).

Advances in medicine have addressed many of the physical health problems associated with Down syndrome so that today, the average life expectancy is 60 years of age, as compared with about 25 during the 1980s (National Association for Down Syndrome, 2020). Many individuals live into their 70s and 80s. However, Down syndrome is associated with premature aging and an accelerated decline of cognitive functioning (Hithersay et al., 2017). Individuals with Down syndrome are more likely than other adults to show signs of Alzheimer's disease (a form or dementia) very early (Fortea et al., 2021; Tramutola et al., 2020). This is an example of how disorders and illnesses can be influenced by multiple genes and complex contextual interactions; in this case, Down syndrome and Alzheimer's disease share genetic markers (Handen, 2020; Lee et al., 2017).

Sex Chromosome Abnormalities

Some abnormalities occur in the 23rd pair of chromosomes, the sex chromosomes. These abnormalities result from either a missing sex chromosome or an additional sex chromosome. Given their different genetic makeup, sex chromosome abnormalities yield different effects in males and females (see Table 2.5)

One of the most common sex chromosome abnormalities is **Klinefelter syndrome**, in which males are born with an extra X chromosome (XXY) (McKusick-Nathans Institute of Genetic Medicine, 2020). Symptoms range in severity but most men are unaware of the disorder unless they are tested for infertility (Bird & Hurren, 2016; Gravholt et al., 2018). Symptoms in severe cases include a high-pitched voice, feminine body shape, breast enlargement, and infertility. Many boys and men with Klinefelter syndrome have short stature, a tendency to be overweight, and language and short-term memory impairments that can interfere with learning (Bonomi et al., 2017; G. Butler et al., 2023). Dyslexia, a learning disorder affecting reading comprehension, is diagnosed in half of all boys and men with Kleinfelter syndrome (Skakkebæk et al., 2021). As adults, men with Klinefelter syndrome are at risk for a variety of disorders that are more common in women, such as osteoporosis (Grande et al., 2023).

A second type of sex chromosome abnormality experienced by men is XYY syndrome, or **Jacob's syndrome**, a condition that causes men to produce high levels of testosterone (McKusick-Nathans Institute of Genetic Medicine, 2020; Pappas et al., 2017). Boys with Jacob's syndrome commonly show behavioral problems, delayed speech and language development, tall stature, and mild learning difficulties (Sood & Fuentes, 2022). Most males are not diagnosed unless they experience fertility problems (Zhang et al., 2020). The prevalence of XYY syndrome is uncertain given that most men go undiagnosed.

Women are susceptible to a different set of sex chromosome abnormalities. About 1 in 1,000 girls are born with three X chromosomes, known as **triple X syndrome** (McKusick-Nathans Institute of Genetic Medicine, 2020; Wigby et al., 2016). Triple X syndrome goes largely unnoticed. Girls with the syndrome tend to be taller than other children and taller than predicted by parents' heights. Triple X syndrome is associated with delayed language and motor skills, difficulty learning, and symptoms of attention-deficit/hyperactivity disorder and autism spectrum disorder (Freilinger et al., 2018; Otter et al., 2023). Because many cases of triple X syndrome go unnoticed, little is known about the syndrome.

The sex chromosome abnormality known as **Turner syndrome** occurs when a girl is born with only one X sex chromosome (McKusick-Nathans Institute of Genetic Medicine, 2020). Girls with Turner syndrome show abnormal growth, irregularities in ovary development, delayed puberty, and infertility (Davis et al., 2020; Gravholt et al., 2023). Turner syndrome is typically diagnosed in middle adolescence, at about age 15, but many cases remain undiagnosed (Gravholt et al., 2023). Children with Turner syndrome may show difficulty with visual-spatial reasoning, attention, motor skills, math skills, and executive functioning (Baker et al., 2020; Mauger et al., 2018). They are also prone to social difficulties, anxiety, and depression (Hutaff-Lee et al., 2019; Morris et al., 2020). If diagnosed early, regular injections of human growth hormones can increase stature and promote reproductive development (Isojima & Yokoya, 2023; Klein et al., 2020). As adults, women with Turner syndrome tend to be short in stature, have webbed necks (extra folds of skin), and are prone to health conditions affecting the heart as well as diabetes, autoimmune disorders, and early osteoporosis (Gravholt et al., 2023).

TABLE 2.5		Sex Chromosome Abnormalities		
Female Genotype	**Syndrome**	**Description**		**Prevalence**
XO	Turner	Abnormal growth patterns, delayed puberty, lack of prominent female secondary sex characteristics, and infertility. Short adult stature, webbing around their neck.		1 in 2,500 females
XXX	Triple-X	Taller than average height, by about an inch, with unusually long legs and slender torsos; normal development of sexual characteristics and fertility. Because many cases go undiagnosed, little is known.		Unknown
Male Genotype	**Syndrome**	**Description**		**Prevalence**
XXY	Klinefelter	High-pitched voice, short stature, feminine body shape, and infertility. Increased risk for osteoporosis and other disorders that are more common in women.		1 in 1,000 males
XYY	Jacob's	High levels of testosterone. Because many cases go undiagnosed, little is known.		Unknown

Source: McKusick-Nathans Institute of Genetic Medicine. 2020.

Mutation

Like chromosomal abnormalities, mutations are inborn characteristics that are not inherited. **Mutations** are sudden changes and abnormalities in the structure of genes that occur spontaneously, without apparent cause. Mutations may also be triggered by exposure to environmental toxins such as radiation and agricultural chemicals in food. A mutation may involve only one gene or many. It is estimated that as many as one half of all conceptions include mutated chromosomes (Taneri et al., 2020). Most mutations are fatal—the developing organism often dies very soon after conception, often before the woman knows she is pregnant (Sadler, 2023).

Sometimes mutations are beneficial. This is especially true if the mutation is induced by stressors in the environment and provides an adaptive advantage to the individual. The gene that causes sickle cell anemia (discussed earlier in this chapter) is a mutation that originated in areas where malaria is widespread, such as Africa, and serves a protective role against malaria (Esoh & Wonkam, 2021; Kavanagh et al., 2022). Children who inherited a single sickle cell gene were more resistant to malarial infection and more likely to survive and pass it along to their offspring (Gong et al., 2013; Uyoga et al., 2019). Though its advantages may outweigh its harm in places where malaria is common, the sickle cell gene has no benefit for individuals who live in places where malaria is not a risk. As we have discussed, sickle cell anemia poses serious health risks, including a reduced lifespan of about 54 years in North America (Kavanagh et al., 2022).

It may perpetuate racial disparities in health and wealth as African Americans are disproportionately likely to inherit sickle cell anemia and to lack consistent access to health care and economic resources needed to thrive with a chronic illness (Graf et al., 2022).

The sickle cell trait is becoming less common in places in the world where malaria is uncommon. For example, only 8%–10% of African Americans are carriers, compared with as many as 40% of Black Africans in some African countries (Tebbi, 2022). Therefore, the developmental implications of genotypes—and mutations—are context-specific, posing benefits in some contexts and risks in others.

THINKING IN CONTEXT 2.2

1. Give advice to prospective parents. Explain how genetic and chromosomal disorders are transmitted. What, if anything, can parents do to reduce the risks? Why?
2. Recall from Chapter 1 that most developmental scientists agree that nature and nurture interact to influence development. Choose a genetic or chromosomal disorder discussed in this section and explain how it illustrates the interaction of genes and context.

REPRODUCTIVE TECHNOLOGY AND GENETIC DISORDERS

> **2.3** Explain the choices of reproductive technology and prenatal diagnostic methods available to individuals and couples.

Although genetic inheritance may seem like a random roll of the dice, we can predict the likelihood of many genetic disorders before conception. Advances in technology enable individuals and couples to learn about the risk for genetic abnormalities, detect abnormalities, and often prevent them.

Genetic Counseling

Genetic risks can be detected. DNA tests coupled with **genetic counseling** can help individuals and couples understand the risk of conceiving a child with genetic or chromosomal abnormalities (Im et al., 2023). Candidates for genetic counseling include individuals and couples whose relatives have a genetic condition, women over the age of 35, and couples from the same ethnic group who might share recessive genetic disorders. Genetic testing can also help couples who have had difficulty conceiving or recurrent miscarriage determine whether chromosomal abnormalities carried by ova or sperm have played a part (Poornima et al., 2020; Softness et al., 2020).

Through interviews with a couple, a genetic counselor constructs a family history of heritable disorders for both prospective biological parents. If members of either parent's family have a genetic disorder or are at risk for a genetic disorder, blood tests may be carried out to detect the presence of dominant and recessive genes and chromosomal abnormalities. The tests determine whether each parent is a carrier for recessive disorders, such as Huntington's disease and estimate the likelihood that a child may be affected by a genetic disorder (Caceres et al., 2022). The genetic counselor interprets the results and helps the parents understand genetic concepts by tailoring the explanation to match the parents' knowledge (Abacan et al., 2019).

Once prospective parents learn about the risk of conceiving a child with a disorder, they can determine how to proceed—whether it is to attempt to conceive a child naturally or to use reproductive technology that can test for abnormalities at conception. Given advances in our knowledge of genetic disorders and ability to screen for them, the American College of Obstetricians and Gynecologists (2024) recommends that genetic counseling should be available to all prospective parents. Others argue that abnormalities are rare and that so few would be discovered that universal screening is of little utility (Larion et al., 2016). Whether to seek genetic counseling is a personal decision for prospective parents based on their history, view of their risks, and their values.

Assisted Reproductive Technology

About 2.3% of infants in the United States are conceived through **assisted reproductive technology (ART)**, alternative methods of conception that rely on medical technology (Centers for Disease Control, 2024). As noted above, some individuals and couples at risk for bearing children with genetic or chromosomal abnormalities seek ART, as do some couples experiencing infertility, which is defined as the inability to conceive naturally after 1 year of unprotected intercourse (Carson & Kallen, 2021). About 15% to 20% of couples in the United States experience infertility (about 25% of couples in developing countries) (Cox et al., 2022; Rezaeiyeh et al., 2022). Other candidates for ART include single adults and same-sex couples who wish to conceive.

There are racial, ethnic, and socioeconomic disparities in the use of ART. White, Asian-American, college-educated, and high socioeconomic status women are more likely to give birth via ART than Black and Hispanic women (Ebeh & Jahanfar, 2021; Tierney & Cai, 2019). Black women are less likely to use ART. Those who do, tend to use it later in life than women of other races and are more likely to experience poor outcomes related to later use (Butts, 2021; Lisonkova et al., 2022). Race and ethnicity are interwoven with socioeconomic status and disparities in health care in the United States—including reproductive health and access to reproductive technology (Dieke et al., 2017; Shirazi & Rosinger, 2021), which can take several forms, including artificial insemination, in vitro fertilization, and surrogacy (see Figure 2.4).

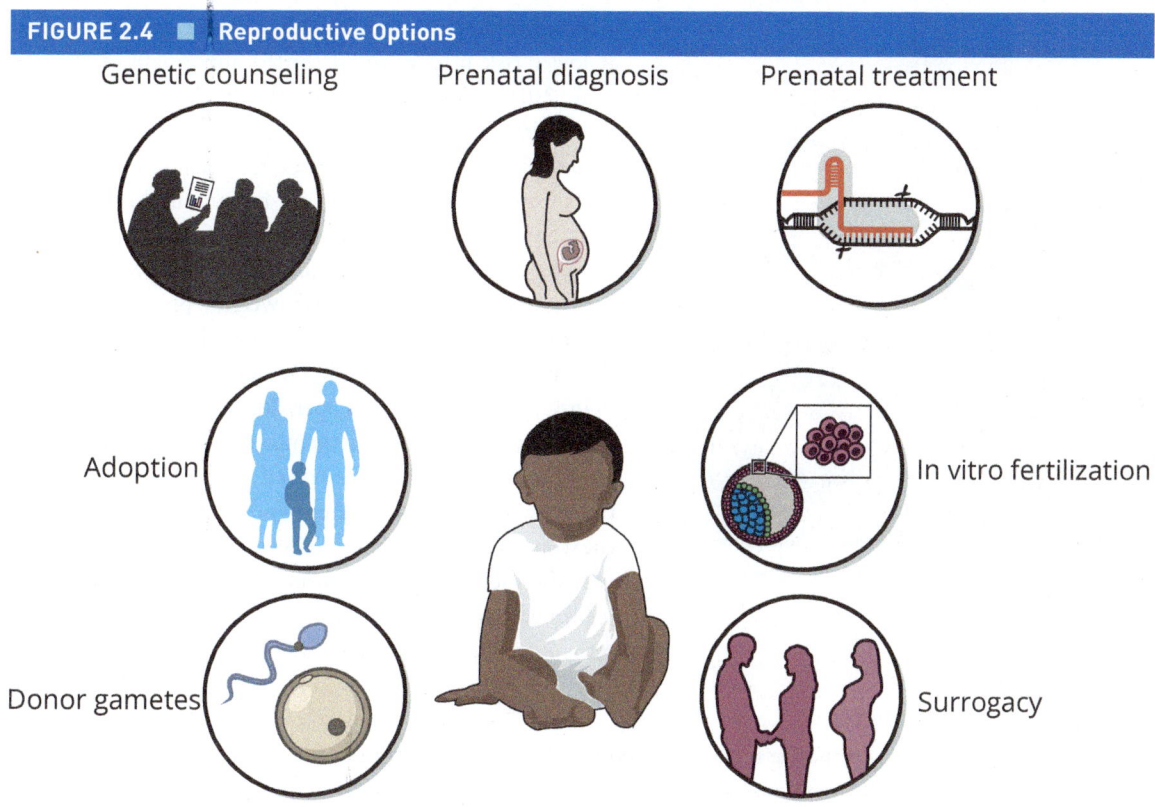

FIGURE 2.4 ■ Reproductive Options

Source: Adapted from Turocy, J., Adashi, E. Y., & Egli, D. (2021). Heritable human genome editing: Research progress, ethical considerations, and hurdles to clinical practice. *Cell, 184*(6), 1561–1574.

Artificial Insemination

The simplest, least invasive type of alternative conception is **artificial insemination**, the insertion of sperm from a partner or donor into a woman. Artificial insemination is the least expensive alternative method of conception, but the success rate is low, usually requiring multiple cycles. The cost of the procedure ranges from about $300 to $1,000 per cycle (Harris, 2020). Women and couples who seek donor sperm may also expect to pay about $700 to $1,000 per vial.

In Vitro Fertilization

In contrast to artificial insemination, where conception occurs inside of the women's body, **in vitro fertilization** initiates conception outside of the body. A woman is prescribed hormones to stimulate the maturation of several ova, which are surgically removed. The ova are placed in a dish and sperm are added in the hope that one or more ova will be fertilized and the resulting zygote will begin to divide. After several cell divisions, the cluster of cells are placed in the woman's uterus where, if all goes well, they will implant and begin to divide, resulting in pregnancy.

The success rate of in vitro fertilization is about 50% and varies with the mother's age and whether the ova are from the patient or donated (Centers for Disease Control, 2024). For instance, the percentage of embryo transfers resulting in live births from patients who use their own eggs is 45% for 35–37-year-old women, 40% in 38–40-year-old women, and 24% in women over age 40. In vitro fertilization is expensive, costing an average of over $12,400 per trial, not including medication, and often requires multiple cycles, posing a financial burden too great for women and couples of low socioeconomic status (Asch & Marmor, 2020; Teoh & Maheshwari, 2014).

Controlling for maternal age, infants conceived by in vitro fertilization show no differences in growth, health, development, or cognitive function relative to infants conceived without assistance (Farhi et al., 2019; Wang et al., 2021). Because in vitro fertilization permits cells to be screened for genetic problems prior to implantation, in vitro infants are at lower risk of congenital (birth) abnormalities (Fauser et al., 2014). However, over one third of births from artificial insemination include more than one infant (twins or even triplets), either because the zygote that was transferred splits (resulting in MZ twins) or because multiple zygotes are transferred to increase the odds of success (resulting in DZ twins) (Sunderam et al., 2019). Multiple gestations increase the risk for low birth weight, prematurity, and other poor outcomes (Sullivan-Pyke et al., 2017).

Intravaginal culture (IVC) is a less expensive alternative to in vitro fertilization (Cooper, 2022). In IVC the ova and sperm are placed in a tiny incubator that is placed inside the woman's vagina. After several rounds of cell duplication, the incubator is removed and the cells are placed in the woman's uterus, similar to in vitro fertilization. IVC is a more financially accessible form of ART, but its availability is limited, and research is just beginning to examine long-term outcomes associated with IVC (Kaye et al., 2022).

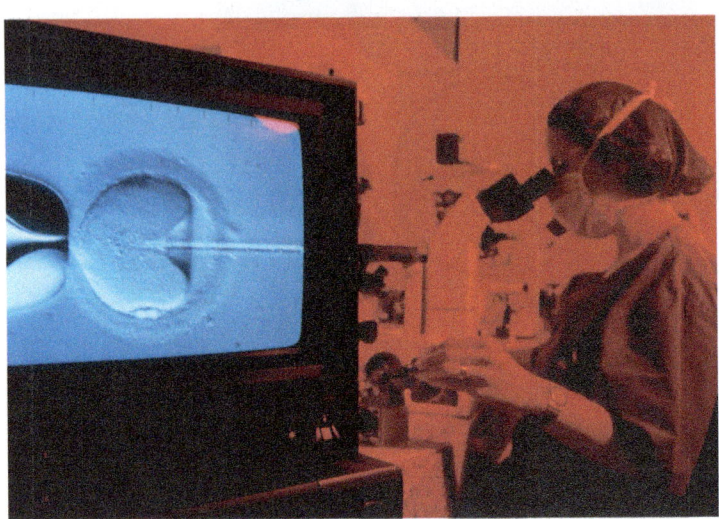

In vitro fertilization is a form of reproductive technology in which an ovum is fertilized outside of the womb.

Mauro Fermariello/Science Source

Surrogacy

Surrogacy is an alternative form of reproduction in which a woman (the surrogate) is impregnated and carries a fetus to term and agrees to turn the baby over to another person or couple who will raise it. Single parents, same-sex couples, and couples in which one or both members are infertile are those most likely to choose surrogacy. Sometimes the surrogate carries a zygote composed of one or both couple's gametes. Other times, the ova, sperm, or zygote are donated. Despite several highly publicized cases of surrogate mothers deciding not to relinquish the infant, most surrogacies are successful.

Roughly 3,000 babies are born through surrogacy in the United States each year (Beitsch, 2017). Longitudinal research suggests no psychological differences through age 14 between children born through surrogacy compared with other methods, including children born to gay father and lesbian mother families (Carone et al., 2018, 2020; Golombok, 2013; Golombok et al., 2017). In addition, mothers of children who were the product of surrogates do not differ from those conceived using other methods, and surrogate mothers show no negative effects (Jadva et al., 2015; Söderström-Anttila et al., 2015).

We have seen that reproductive technology is expensive. Surrogacy is often prohibitively expensive for most prospective parents, limiting its access to high socioeconomic status parents. Prospective parents pay for the surrogate's medical care, attorney, travel expenses, health care, and more, which can amount to $100,000 or more (Caron, 2020). Finally, surrogacy may pose ethical issues. Carrying a fetus to term poses physical and mental health risks to the surrogate. Relinquishing a newborn is difficult, even with planning, posing emotional risks to the surrogate. The financial incentives to surrogate a fetus are substantial. Although paying a surrogate is illegal in many U.S. states, women are often compensated for the physical and emotional burden of surrogating a fetus (Caron, 2020). A surrogate tends to receive at least $30,000 to $55,000 to carry a fetus, sums that may be difficult for some marginalized women to resist (Harrison, 2017).

Adoption

Another reproductive option for prospective parents is **adoption**. Adoptive parents typically undergo extensive screening to ensure that they can provide a home that is safe, nurturing, and stimulating to children. Many prospective parents endure lengthy waiting times to receive children. The ability to provide a suitable home is linked with socioeconomic status, and adoption itself can cost tens of thousands of dollars, therefore it is not surprising that adoptive children tend to be raised by parents with higher levels of education and income than other children (Drozd et al., 2018; Family Equality, n.d.).

Children's experiences prior to adoption, especially neglect and maltreatment, and their developmental status at the time of adoption influence their short- and long-term adjustment (Blake et al., 2022; Hornfeck et al., 2019). Adopted children tend to experience greater stress prenatally, early in life, prior to adoption, and during the adoption process that influences their long-term adjustment after adoption (Pace et al., 2022; Wiley, 2017).

The quality of adoptive parent-child relationships influences children's outcomes and the long-term effects of preadoption adversity (Farr & Grotevant, 2019). Children who develop a close bond with adoptive parents tend to show better emotional understanding and regulation, social competence, and also self-esteem (Drozd et al., 2018; Schoemaker et al., 2020). This is true also of children who have experienced emotional neglect, regardless of the child's age at adoption (Brodzinsky et al., 2022; Paine et al., 2021). Once the effects of early adversity are considered, adoptees from childhood through middle adulthood do not differ from their nonadopted peers in distress or internalizing problems, such as anxiety and depression (Brown et al., 2019; Sehmi et al., 2020).

Prenatal Diagnosis

Prenatal testing is a routine procedure that enables physicians to examine a fetus and determine its health. Prenatal testing is especially important and recommended when genetic counseling has determined a risk for genetic abnormalities, when the woman is older than age 35, when both parents are members of an ethnicity at risk for particular genetic disorders, or when fetal development appears abnormal (Krstić & Običan, 2020). Technology has advanced rapidly, equipping professionals with an array of tools to assess the health of the fetus.

Methods of Prenatal Diagnosis

The most widespread and routine diagnostic procedure is **ultrasound**, in which high-frequency sound waves are directed at the mother's abdomen to provide clear images of the womb represented on a video monitor. Ultrasound enables physicians to observe the fetus, measure fetal growth, judge gestational age, determine the sex of the fetus, detect multiple pregnancies (twins, triplets, etc.), and detect physical abnormalities. Many abnormalities can be observed, such as cardiac malformations, cleft palate, and microencephaly (small head size). At least 80% of women in the United States receive at least one prenatal ultrasound scan (Sadler, 2023). Three to four screenings over the duration of pregnancy are common to evaluate fetal development. Repeated ultrasound of the fetus does not appear to affect growth and development (Abramowicz, 2019; Stephenson, 2005)

Amniocentesis is a prenatal diagnostic procedure in which a small sample of the amniotic fluid that surrounds the fetus is extracted from the mother's uterus through a long, hollow needle that is guided by ultrasound as it is inserted into the mother's abdomen (Odibo, 2015). The amniotic fluid contains fetal cells, which are then grown in a laboratory dish to create enough cells for genetic analysis. Genetic analysis is then performed to detect genetic and chromosomal anomalies. Amniocentesis is safe, posing no additional risks to the fetus than other procedures (Homola & Zimmer, 2019; Likar et al., 2020). Despite its safety, many women find the procedure stressful, even if they are provided with information about what to expect (Mojahed et al., 2021).

Amniocentesis is recommended for women aged 35 and over, especially if the woman and partner are both known carriers of genetic diseases or when other prenatal tests suggest abnormalities (Vink & Quinn, 2018a). Usually, amniocentesis is conducted between the 15th and 18th week of pregnancy. Conducted any earlier, an amniocentesis may increase the risk of miscarriage (Akolekar et al., 2015).

Chorionic villus sampling (CVS) also samples fetal genetic material and can be conducted earlier than amniocentesis, between 9 and 12 weeks of pregnancy (Vink & Quinn, 2018b). CVS requires studying a small amount of tissue from the chorion, part of the membrane surrounding the fetus. The tissue sample is obtained through a long needle inserted either abdominally or vaginally, depending on the location of the fetus. CVS is relatively painless, poses few risks to the fetus, and, like amniocentesis, has a diagnostic success rate of over 99% (Likar et al., 2020; Salomon et al., 2019). CVS should not be conducted prior to 10 weeks gestation because some studies suggest an increased risk of limb defects and miscarriages (Jones & Montero, 2021).

Fetal MRI applies MRI technology to image the fetus' body and diagnose abnormalities (Aertsen et al., 2020). It is often used as a follow-up to ultrasound imaging to provide more detailed views of any suspected abnormalities. Fetal MRI can detect abnormalities throughout the body, including the central nervous system (Masselli et al., 2020). MRI is safe for mother and fetus in the second and third trimesters but is expensive and has limited availability in some areas (Patenaude et al., 2014).

Noninvasive prenatal testing (NIPT) screens the mother's blood to detect chromosomal abnormalities. Cell-free fetal DNA (chromosome fragments that result from the breakdown of fetal cells) circulates in maternal blood in small concentrations that can be detected and studied by sampling the mother's blood (Alberry et al., 2021; Hartwig et al., 2017). Testing can be done as early as 9 weeks (Ravitsky et al., 2021). Given that the test involves drawing blood from the mother, there is no risk to the fetus.

NIPT can provide accurate sex determination, but NIPT cannot detect as many chromosomal abnormalities as amniocentesis or CVS and is less accurate because fetal DNA is not sampled (Samura, 2020; Villela et al., 2019). Currently, NIPT produces a high rate of false positive results, incorrectly identifying nonexistent anomalies (Johnston et al., 2022). However, researchers have identified the entire genome sequence using NIPT, suggesting that NIPT may eventually be as effective as other, more invasive techniques (Alberry et al., 2021).

In consultation with their obstetrician, pregnant women and their partners should carefully weigh the risks and benefits of any procedure designed to monitor prenatal development. Table 2.6 summarizes methods of prenatal diagnosis.

TABLE 2.6 ■ Methods of Prenatal Diagnosis

	Explanation	Advantages	Disadvantages
Ultrasound	High-frequency sound waves directed at the mother's abdomen provide clear images of the womb viewed on a video monitor.	Can measure fetal growth, reveal the sex of the fetus, and determine physical abnormalities in the fetus.	Many abnormalities are not easily observed.
Amniocentesis	A small sample of the amniotic fluid that surrounds the fetus and contains fetal cells is extracted from the mother's uterus through a long, hollow needle inserted into the mother's abdomen. The fetal cells are grown in a laboratory and analyzed for genetic abnormalities	Thorough analysis of the fetus' genotype with 100% diagnostic success rate.	Safe, but greater risk to the fetus than ultrasound. If conducted before the 15th week of pregnancy, it may increase the risk of miscarriage.
Chorionic villus sampling (CVS)	A small sample of tissue from the chorion, part of the membrane surrounding the fetus, is obtained through a long needle inserted either abdominally or vaginally, depending on the location of the fetus. The sample is tested for genetic abnormalities.	Thorough analysis of the fetus' genotype with 100% diagnostic success rate. Can be conducted earlier than amniocentesis, between 10 and 12 weeks.	It may pose a higher rate of spontaneous abortion and limb abnormalities when conducted prior to 10 weeks' gestation.
Fetal MRI	Uses a magnetic scanner to record detailed images of fetal organs and structures.	Provides detailed and accurate images.	It is expensive. At present there is no evidence to suggest that it is harmful to the fetus.
Noninvasive prenatal testing (NIPT)	Cell-free fetal DNA are examined by drawing blood from the mother.	There is no risk to the fetus. It can diagnose several chromosomal abnormalities.	It cannot yet detect all abnormalities. It may be less accurate than other methods.

Sources: Akolekar et al., 2015; Chan et al., 2013; Gregg et al., 2013; Odibo, 2015; Shahbazian et al., 2012; Shim et al., 2014; Theodora et al., 2016

Prenatal Treatment of Genetic Disorders

What happens when a genetic or chromosomal abnormality is found? Advances in genetics and in medicine have led to therapies that can be administered prenatally to reduce the effects of many genetic abnormalities. **Fetoscopy** is a technique in which a small camera is inserted through a small incision on the mother's abdomen or cervix and placed into the amniotic sac that encases the fetus. The camera is used to examine the fetus and facilitate procedures performed on the fetus during pregnancy. Risks of fetoscopy include infection, rupture of the amniotic sac, premature labor, and fetal death. When serious abnormalities are suspected, fetoscopy permits a visual assessment of the fetus, which aids in diagnosis and treatment. Hormones and other drugs, as well as blood transfusions, can be given to the fetus by inserting a needle into the uterus (Kurtz, 2023). Surgeons rely on the images provided by fetoscopy to surgically repair defects of the heart, lungs, urinary tract, and other areas prior to birth (Ahmad et al., 2023; Peiro & Scorletti, 2019).

Gene therapy is becoming increasingly available, in which genetic material that may be missing or abnormal is injected into fetal cells. These cells reproduce and replace those containing the abnormal gene (Peranteau & Flake, 2020). Similar to gene therapy, stem cell therapy involves delivering stem cells (which can reproduce into any type of cell) into the umbilical cord that connects the fetus to the mother (O'Connell et al., 2020). These therapies have successfully treated heritable disorders in animals (Neff, 2019). In human fetuses, gene and stem cell therapies are currently applied to treat severe conditions that may cause death or lifelong disabilities (Kiani et al., 2020; Rytting et al., 2022). However, prenatal use of these therapies is new, and there is much to learn. Gene and stem cell therapies are expensive and not widely available, posing economic and social barriers to members of marginalized groups (Turocy et al., 2021). In addition, the long-term effects of these therapies on mothers' and children's physical, cognitive, and socioemotional development and development are not known (Hendriks et al., 2022).

> **THINKING IN CONTEXT 2.3**
>
> 1. Compare and contrast reproductive options for a woman in her mid-30s who wishes to conceive a child without a partner. What are the pros and cons of each option? What considerations do you deem most important in choosing an option?
> 2. What information would you give to a person considering becoming pregnant about prenatal diagnosis? How would you explain the various options, including their advantages and disadvantages? What would you suggest?

HEREDITY AND ENVIRONMENT INTERACTIONS

> 2.4 Examine interactions among heredity and environment, including behavior genetics, gene-environment correlations and interactions, and the epigenetic framework.

Our genotype, inherited from our biological parents, influences all our traits, from hair and eye color to personality, health, and behavior. However, genes do not work alone. The traits and characteristics we display, our phenotype, result from interactions among our genotype and our experiences.

Behavior Genetics

Behavior genetics is the study of how genetic and environmental variations influence the phenotypes people show, including traits, characteristics, abilities, and behavior (Harden, 2021). All traits, even those with a strong genetic component, such as height, are modified by environmental influences (Jelenkovic et al., 2016; Plomin, 2019). For example, healthy nutrition (an environmental factor) can promote children's growth in height, and malnutrition can stunt growth.

Behavior Genetics Research Methods

Behavior geneticists attempt to tease apart the role of biology and environment in development. They estimate the *heritability* of various traits, the degree to which variation among people is due to genetic differences. The remaining variation is assumed to be the result of environmental influences and experiences. Heritability research therefore examines the contributions of both the genotype and the role of experience in determining phenotypes, the traits that people show (Barry et al., 2023; Fowler-Finn & Boutwell, 2019). Methods that behavior geneticists to examine hereditary influences on behavior include selective breeding, twin, and adoption studies.

Selective breeding studies. Through selective breeding, researchers modify the genetic makeup of animals in a laboratory setting to study the contribution of heredity to attributes and behavior. Mice can be bred to very physically active or very sedentary by mating highly active mice only with other highly active mice or, similarly, breeding mice with very low levels of activity with each other. Over subsequent generations, mice bred for high levels of activity become many times more active than those bred for low levels of activity (N. L. Schwartz et al., 2018). Selective breeding in rats, mice, and other animals such as chickens has revealed genetic contributions to many traits and characteristics, such as aggressiveness, emotionality, sex drive, and even maze learning (Bubac et al., 2020).

Unlike animals, people cannot be bred. Behavior geneticists who study humans must rely on observing natural variations in hereditary and environmental influences. Family members share varying amounts of genes and environmental experiences. Behavior geneticists study siblings, especially twins and adopted siblings, to compare people who live together and share varying degrees of relatedness (Friedman et al., 2021; York, 2020).

Twin studies. Twin studies compare identical and fraternal twins to estimate how much of a trait or behavior is attributable to genes. Recall that identical (MZ) twins share 100% of their genes because they originated from the same zygote. Like all nontwin siblings, fraternal (DZ) twins share 50% of their genes because they are the result of two different ova fertilized by two different sperm, and therefore two genetically different zygotes. If a given attribute is influenced by genes, identical twins should be more similar than fraternal twins because identical twins share 100% of their genes, whereas fraternal twins share about half.

Adoption studies. Whereas twin studies examine biologically related persons, adoption studies compare the degree of similarity between people who are not biologically related but share an environment. Some studies compare adopted children to their biological parents, with whom they share genes (50% with each parent) but no environment, and to their adoptive parents with whom they share an environment but not genes (Friedman et al., 2021; York, 2020). If the adopted children share similarities with their biological parents, even though they were not raised by them, it suggests that the similarities are genetic. The similarities are influenced by the environment if the children are more like their adoptive parents.

Observations of adoptive siblings also shed light on the extent to which attributes and behaviors are influenced by the environment. The degree to which two genetically unrelated adopted children reared together are similar speaks to the role of environment. Likewise, comparisons of identical twins who are reared in the same home with other sets of twins who were separated and reared in different environments also illustrate environmental contributions to phenotypes. If identical twins reared together are more similar than those reared apart, an environmental influence can be inferred.

Heritability and Personal Characteristics

Twin and adoption studies have suggested that genes contribute to many traits, such as sociability, temperament, emotionality, and susceptibility to various conditions such as obesity, heart disease, cancer, anxiety, poor mental health, and a propensity to be physically aggressive (Ask et al., 2021; Bralten et al., 2019; Isen et al., 2022; Loos & Yeo, 2022; Morneau-Vaillancourt et al., 2019).

Identical twins consistently have more similar intelligence scores than do fraternal twins (Plomin, 2019). A classic study of intelligence in over 10,000 twin pairs showed a correlation coefficient of .86

for identical and .60 for fraternal twins (Plomin & Spinath, 2004). Recall from Chapter 1 that correlational research examines relationships among variables. Correlations range from 0 to 1, with higher scores indicating a stronger relationship between the two variables. Table 2.7 summarizes the results of comparisons of intelligence scores from individuals who share different genetic relationships with each other. Notice that correlations rise not only with genetic relatedness but also when kin live together, supporting the role of environment. Notice that even identical twins who share 100% of their genes are not 100% alike. Those differences are due to the influence of environmental factors unique to each sibling.

TABLE 2.7 ■ Average Correlation of Intelligence Scores From Family Studies for Related and Unrelated Kin Reared Together or Apart

Type of Kin	Reared Together	Reared Apart
MZ twins (100% shared genes)	.85	.74
DZ twins (50% shared genes)	.59	.52
Siblings (50% shared genes)	.46	.24
Biological parent/child (50% shared genes)	.41	.22
Half-siblings (25% shared genes)	.31	—
Unrelated (adopted) siblings (0% shared genes)*	.34	—
Nonbiological parent/child (0% shared genes)*	.20	—

Notes: *Estimated correlation for individuals sharing neither genes nor environment = .0; MZ = monozygotic; DZ = dizygotic.

Source: Adapted from Bouchard & McGue, 1981 and Devlin, B., Daniels, M., & Roeder, K. (1997). The heritability of IQ. *Nature, 388*(6641), Article 6641. https://doi.org/10.1038/41319

Nonshared Environment

Siblings may be raised in the same house, by the same parents, and thereby share an environment and many everyday experiences. Despite this **shared environment,** siblings, even twins, are often very different in personality, interests, and competencies. In addition to heredity, behavior geneticists point to environmental factors, specifically the nonshared environment, as a contributor to differences among siblings (Hetherington et al., 2013).

The nonshared environment refers to experiences that are unique to a particular child. Even with the same parents and in the same home, siblings are often treated differently. The oldest sibling often has a very different parenting and family experience than the youngest child. With each child, parents gain experience and knowledge about child development and rearing, which might influence their confidence and parenting. In addition, parents' interactions are influenced by children's personalities, leading to unique experiences for each child. A shy child might elicit different reactions from parents than a very outgoing child. We examine the ways that children evoke reactions in their environment later in this chapter.

Even twins who share the womb and a birthday have a nonshared environment—different friends, activities, teachers, and interactions with parents that are influenced by their unique personality and characteristics. The nonshared environment contributes to many of the differences we see among siblings and interacts with genetics to influence children's development.

Gene-Environment Interactions

At 6 feet 2 inches in height, 16-year-old Deondre towers over his 5-foot-tall mother and is substantially taller than his father, who is 5 feet 11 inches. Why is Deondre so much taller than his biological parents? Shared genes account for only part of the story of development. As we have discussed, genes and the environment work together in complex ways to determine our characteristics, behavior, development, and health (Morgan et al., 2020; Ritz et al., 2017). **Gene-environment interactions** refer to the dynamic interplay between our genes and our environment. Several principles illustrate these interactions and can help us account for differences among family members.

Range of Reaction

The effects of the environment varies with the genetic makeup of the individual (Briley et al., 2019). Everyone has a different genetic makeup and therefore responds to the environment in a unique way. In addition, any one genotype can be expressed in a variety of phenotypes. There is a **range of reaction**, a wide range of potential expressions of a genetic trait, depending on environmental opportunities and constraints (see Figure 2.5; Gottlieb, 2007).

Consider height. Height is largely a function of genetics, yet an individual may show a range of sizes depending on environment and behavior (Jelenkovic et al., 2016; Thompson, 2021). Children born to two very tall parents may have the genes to be tall. But unless they have adequate nutrition, they will not fulfill their genetic potential for height. In societies where nutrition has improved dramatically over a generation, it is common for children to tower over their parents. Enhanced environmental opportunities, in this case nutrition, enable the children to meet their genetic potential for height.

Therefore, a person's genetic makeup sets boundaries on the range of possible developmental outcomes; the environment influences where, within that range, the phenotype will fall (Manuck & McCaffery, 2014; Morgan et al., 2020). Gene-environment interactions are complex and often difficult to predict, partly because individuals vary in their sensitivity to environmental stimuli. Children's genetic makeup can make them more sensitive to environmental stimuli, or to particular stimuli, than other children (Briley et al., 2019; Harden, 2021).

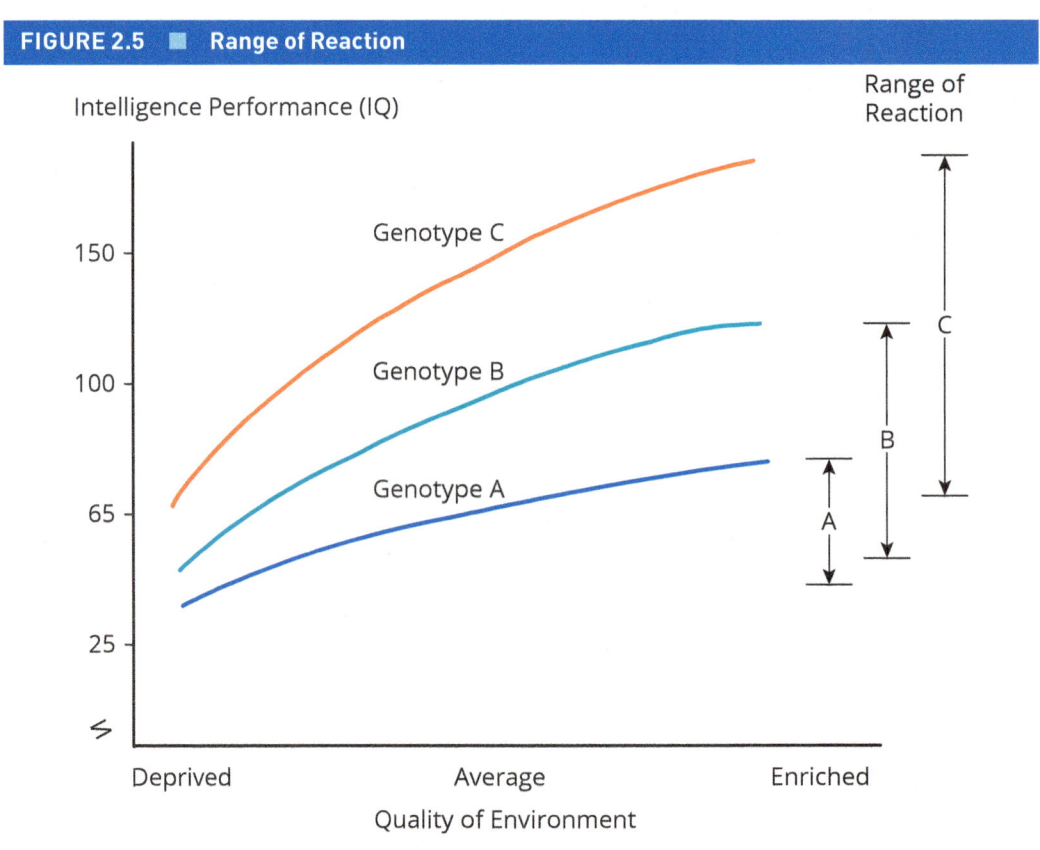

FIGURE 2.5 ■ Range of Reaction

Adapted from Gottlieb, G. (2007). Probabilistic epigenesis. *Developmental Science, 10*(1), 1–11.

Some traits have a narrow reaction range, with a very small array of phenotypes or outcomes. This is known as **canalization**. Canalized traits are biologically programmed, and only powerful environmental forces can change their developmental path (Posadas & Carthew, 2014; Takahashi, 2019).

For example, infants follow an age-related sequence of motor development, from crawling, to walking, to running, suggesting that motor development is a canalized trait. Around the world, most infants walk at about 12 months of age. Generally, only extreme experiences, such as severe deprivation, can prevent this developmental sequence from occurring (Adolph & Franchak, 2017). We examine the role of experience in motor development in Chapter 4.

Gene-Environment Correlation

Heredity and environment each contribute to development. Not only do they interact, but environmental factors often support hereditary traits (Briley et al., 2019; Scarr & McCartney, 1983). **Gene-environment correlation** refers to the finding that many genetically influenced traits tend to be associated with environmental factors that promote their development (Saltz, 2019). That is, genetic traits often influence children's behavior, which is then supported or encouraged by the environment (Knafo & Jaffee, 2013). There are three types of gene-environment correlations: passive, evocative, and active.

Passive gene-environment correlation. Adults naturally create home environments that support their own preferences. Because parents are genetically similar to their children, the homes they create may also correspond to their child's genotype—an example of a *passive gene-environment correlation* (Wilkinson et al., 2013). Parents might provide genes that predispose a child to develop music ability and create a home environment that supports the development of music ability, such as by playing music in the home and owning musical instruments (Corrigall & Schellenberg, 2015; see Figure 2.6). This is a passive gene-environment correlation because the environment just happens to support the child's abilities. This type of gene-environment correlation tends to occur early in life because parents create rearing environments for their infants and young children.

Evocative gene-environment correlation. People naturally evoke responses from others and the environment, just as the environment and the actions of others evoke responses from the individual. In an *evocative gene-environment correlation*, a child's genetic traits (e.g., personality characteristics including openness to experience) influence the social and physical environment, which shape development in ways that support the genetic trait (Pieters et al., 2015; Saltz, 2019).

Active, happy infants tend to receive more adult attention than do passive or moody infants (Deater-Deckard & O'Connor, 2000), and even among infant twins reared in the same family, the more outgoing and happy twin receives more positive attention than does the more subdued twin (Deater-Deckard, 2001). Why? Babies who are cheerful and smile often influence their social world by evoking smiles and affection from others, including their parents, which in turn support the tendency to be cheerful (Klahr et al., 2013). In this way, the child's trait leads them to behave in ways that influence the physical and social environment to support the genetic trait. To return to the music example, a child with a genetic trait for musical talent will evoke adult approval when the child plays music; this environmental support, in turn, encourages further development of the child's musical trait.

Active gene-environment correlation. Children also take a hands-on role in shaping their development. As children grow older, they have increasing freedom in choosing their own activities and environments. An *active gene-environment correlation* occurs when the child creates experiences and seeks environments that correspond to and support their genetic predisposition. The child with a genetic trait for interest and ability in music seeks experiences and environments that support that trait, such as friends with similar interests and after-school music classes (Corrigall & Schellenberg, 2015). This tendency to actively seek out experiences and environments compatible and supportive of our genetic tendencies is called **niche picking** (Saltz, 2019; Scarr & McCartney, 1983).

Developmental shifts in gene-environmental correlations. The strength of passive, evocative, and active gene-environment correlations changes with development, as shown in Figure 2.7 (Lynch, 2016; Scarr, 1992). Passive gene-environment correlations are common at birth as caregivers determine infants' experiences. Correlations between their genotype and environment tend to occur because their environments are made by genetically similar parents (Armstrong-Carter et al., 2021). Evocative

FIGURE 2.6 ■ Gene-Environment Correlation

The availability of instruments in the home corresponds to the child's musical abilities, and she begins to play piano (passive gene-environment correlation). As she plays piano, she evokes positive responses in others, increasing her interest in music (evocative gene-environment correlation). Over time, she seeks opportunities to play, such as performing in front of an audience (niche picking) and may obtain additional instruments, further supporting her musical abilities.

AJ_Watt/istock; Fancy/Veer/Corbis/Getty Images; SA2RN/Getty Images

gene-environment correlations also occur from birth, as infants' inborn traits and tendencies influence others, evoking responses that support their own genetic predispositions.

In contrast, active gene-environment correlations take place as children grow older and more independent. As they become increasingly capable of controlling parts of their environment, they engage in niche picking by choosing their own interests and activities, shaping their own development. Niche picking contributes to the differences we see in siblings, including fraternal twins, as they grow older. Interestingly, identical twins tend to become more similar over time, perhaps because they are increasingly able to select the environments that best fit their genetic propensities (contributing to a shared environment). As adults, identical twins—even those reared apart—tend to become alike in attitudes, personality, cognitive ability, strength, mental health, and preferences, and they tend to select similar spouses and best friends (McGue & Christensen, 2013; Plomin & Von Stumm, 2018; York, 2020).

Gene-Environment (G x E) Interactions

Despite our growing understanding of genetic influences on behavior, phenotypes (the traits people ultimately show) are often unpredictable (Flint et al., 2020). Not only do the effects of genes vary with environmental influences, but not all genotypes respond to environmental influences in the same way (Fowler-Finn & Boutwell, 2019; Harden, 2021).

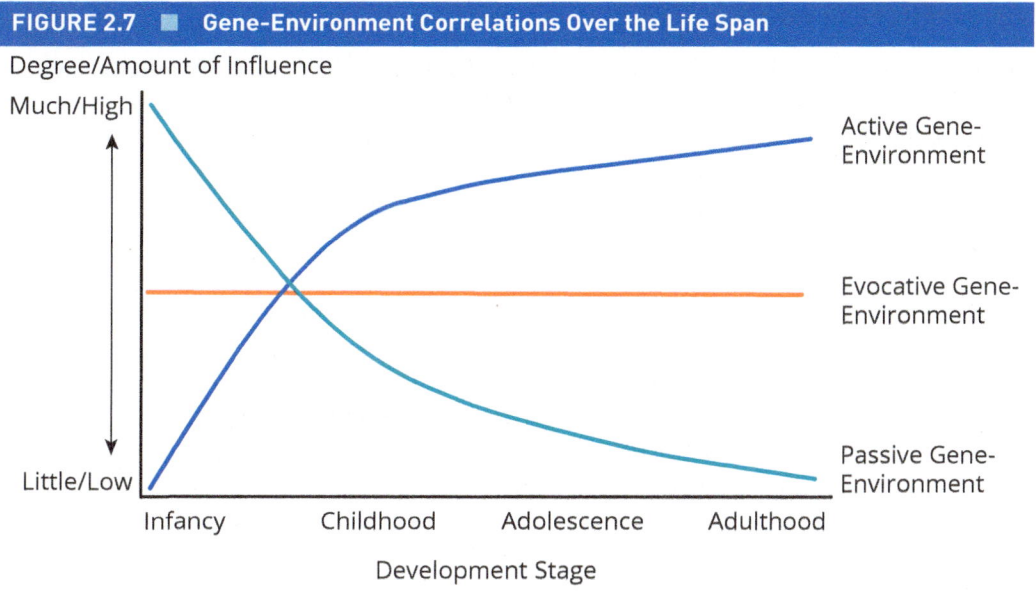

FIGURE 2.7 ■ Gene-Environment Correlations Over the Life Span

In a classic longitudinal study, boys who experienced trauma and abuse tended to show developmental and behavioral problems (Caspi et al., 2002). Their adaptation varied depending on the presence of a gene that controls monoamine oxidase A (MAOA), an enzyme that regulates specific chemicals in the brain. Maltreated boys were about twice as likely to develop problems with aggression, violence, and to even be convicted of a violent crime—but only if they carried the low-MAOA gene. Maltreated boys who carried the high-MAOA gene were no more likely to become violent than nonmaltreated boys. In addition, the presence of the low-MAOA gene itself was not associated with violence, but it predicted violence only for boys who experience abuse early in life. These findings have been replicated in another 30-year longitudinal study of boys (Fergusson et al., 2011) as well as a meta-analysis of 27 studies (Byrd & Manuck, 2014).

Similar findings of a MAOA gene x environment interaction in which low MAOA, but not high MAOA, predicts negative outcomes in response to childhood adversity have been extended to include other mental health outcomes such as antisocial personality disorder and depression (Dash et al., 2023; Manuck & McCaffery, 2014; Mariz et al., 2022). Many of these studies have examined only males. Females show a more mixed pattern, with some studies showing that girls display the MAOA gene x environment interaction on emotional reactivity and aggression but to a much lesser extent than boys, whereas other studies suggest no relationship (Byrd et al., 2018). Other genes interact with the environment in similar ways. For example, the 5-HTTLPR gene interacts with environmental factors to influence parenting sensitivity, depression, stress, and responses to trauma (Baião et al., 2020; Li et al., 2013).

Just as some genes increase our susceptibility to environmental risks, others might increase our sensitivity to, and therefore the effectiveness of, environmental interventions (Bakermans-Kranenburg & van IJzendoorn, 2015; Chhangur et al., 2017). The effects of genes vary with environmental influences and not all genotypes respond to environmental influences in the same way (Fowler-Finn & Boutwell, 2019). Moreover, most human traits, such as intelligence, are influenced by multiple genes, each of which have multiple variants that can each interact with the environment in different ways (Armstrong-Carter et al., 2021; Briley et al., 2019; Plomin et al., 2016).

We have learned a great deal about how our genes and environments work together to influence our development. However, it is worth noting that these conclusions pertain to populations, large groups of people, and not to specific individuals. Conclusions from behavior genetic research cannot predict individual behavior (Turkheimer, 2019). In addition, behavior genetic research, like many other areas of research, is based on samples that are not diverse. Ethnically diverse samples and those of low socioeconomic status are underrepresented in behavior genetics research, limiting the conclusions that we can draw (Sirugo et al., 2019). Although we have learned much about behavior genetics, the genetics of most traits still poorly understood (Brandes et al., 2022).

Epigenetic Framework

By now it is clear that development is the product of a dynamic interaction of biological and contextual forces. Recently scientists have determined that environmental factors do not simply interact with genes to determine people's traits. Environmental factors can determine *how* genes are expressed through a process known as **epigenetics** (Carlberg & Molnar, 2019; von Lüpke, 2021). The epigenome is a molecule that stretches along the length of DNA and provides instructions to genes, determining how they are expressed, whether they are turned on or off. The epigenome carries the instructions that determine what each cell in your body will become, whether heart cell, muscle cell, or brain cell. Those instructions are carried out by directing genes to turn on and off (O'Donnell & Meaney, 2020).

At birth, each cell in our body turns on only a fraction of its genes. The epigenome instructs genes to be turned on and off over the course of development and also in response to the environment (Paro et al., 2021). Epigenetic mechanisms determine how genetic instructions are carried out to determine the phenotype, the characteristics shown (Pinel et al., 2018). Environmental factors such as toxins, injuries, crowding, diet, and responsive parenting can influence the expression of genetic traits through epigenetic mechanisms (O'Donnell & Meaney, 2020). These processes were first discovered in animals.

Epigenetic Processes in Animals

One of the earliest examples of epigenetics is the case of agouti mice, which carry the agouti gene. Mice that carry the agouti gene have yellow fur, are extremely round and obese, and are prone to diabetes and cancer. When agouti mice breed, most of the offspring are identical to the parents—yellow, obese, and susceptible to life-shortening disease. A groundbreaking study showed that yellow agouti mice can produce offspring that look very different (Waterland & Jirtle, 2003). The mice in this photo both carry the agouti gene, yet they look very different; the brown mouse is slender, is lean, has a low risk of developing diabetes and cancer, and is likely to live well into old age. Why are these mice so different? Epigenetics. In the case of the yellow and brown mice, the phenotype of the brown mouse has been altered, but the DNA remains the same. Both carry the agouti gene, but in the yellow mouse, the agouti gene is turned on all the time. In the brown mouse, it is turned off.

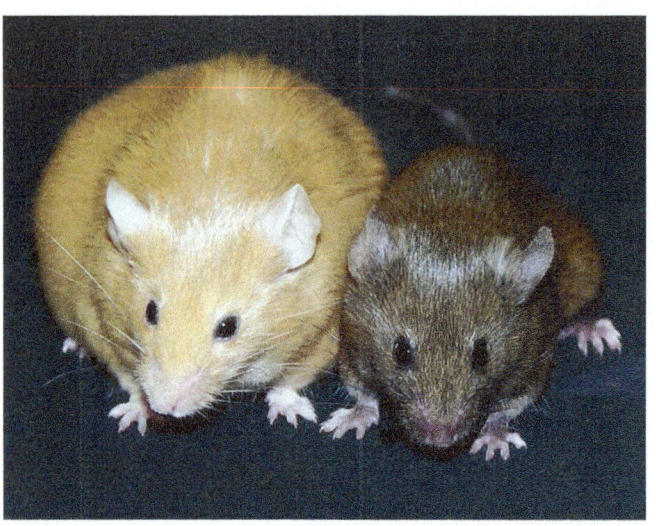

These two mice are genetically identical. Both carry the agouti gene, but it is turned on all the time in the yellow mouse and turned off in the brown mouse.
Randy Jirtle and Dana Dolinoy, CC BY 3.0

How is the agouti gene turned on or off? An environmental factor: The pregnant female's diet, specifically the presence of chemical clusters that attach to, or mark, the gene, determines the offspring's phenotype (Waterland & Jirtle, 2003). These chemical clusters are found in many foods such as onions, garlic, beets, soy, and the nutrients in prenatal vitamins. Yellow agouti mothers that were fed a diet high in these chemical clusters passed along the agouti gene to their offspring, but the presence of epigenetic marks (the chemical clusters) turned it off. The offspring looked radically different from the mothers (brown instead of yellow) and were healthier (lean, not susceptible to disease) even though they carried the gene.

Epigenetic Processes in People

Epigenetic processes also influence human development. Just as in animals, the human epigenome can be influenced by the environment before birth. The epigenome can even be transmitted from one generation to the next through epigenetic marks passed on ova and sperm (Ghai & Kader, 2022; Legoff et al., 2019). This means that what you eat and do today could affect the epigenome of your descendants, including the development, characteristics, and health of your children, grandchildren, and great-grandchildren (Breton et al., 2021; Ghai & Kader, 2022; Grover & Jenkins, 2020).

The epigenome is also influenced by our experiences after birth. Early exposure to trauma and adversity can reprogram children's development, leading to accelerated aging (Kim et al., 2023; Raffington et al., 2021). The quality of maternal caregiving predicts epigenetic changes linked with socioemotional development and adjustment to adversity (Mariani Wigley et al., 2022; Provenzi et al., 2020). Experiences can place epigenetic marks on genes that influence our physical, cognitive, and socioemotional competencies, including physical and mental health (Manczak et al., 2021; O'Donnell & Meaney, 2020; Raffington et al., 2023).

To date most epigenetic research focuses on exposure to adversity, but epigenetic processes operate for all people, at all ages, and in all environments. Interactions between heredity and environment change throughout development as does the role we play in constructing environments that support our genotypes, influence our epigenome, and determine who we become (Lickliter & Witherington, 2017).

THINKING IN CONTEXT 2.4

1. Suppose you wanted to determine the influence of genetics and environment on a characteristic, such as intelligence, body weight, or athletic ability.
    a. What kind of study would you conduct? Consider twin and adoption study methods.
    b. What would you measure? Choose one aspect (intelligence, body weight, or athletic ability), and explain how you would study it in groups of people.
    c. Considering your design and measure, how would you determine the degree to which the characteristic is influenced by genes and environment?
    d. What are the challenges of conducting research such as this?
2. Give a personal example of a passive gene-environment correlation, evocative gene-environment correlation, and active-gene environment correlation. Which types of gene-environment correlations do you most commonly encounter?

APPLY YOUR KNOWLEDGE

Sitting in her doctor's office, Zinnia tells Dr. Rasheed, "I want to have a baby. I have no partner, but I'm ready. I'm 37 and financially stable. It's time. What are my options?" Dr. Rasheed replies, "There are a number of choices. It's a matter of figuring out what's right for you. In addition to a full examination to assess your health, we will seek assistance from a genetic counselor to determine the risk for genetic disorders. This information can help you decide among reproductive options."

1. Identify three ways that genetic disorders are passed. Why does Dr. Rasheed advise genetic testing?

2. What are some of the reproductive options available to Zinnia? What are some of the advantages and disadvantages to each option? Which option do you suggest for Zinnia? Why?

After much deliberation, Zinnia decided to pursue in vitro fertilization using a sperm donor. Soon Zinnia was delighted to learn that she was pregnant—with twins!

1. What types of prenatal screening tests might Zinnia experience? Discuss some of the advantages and disadvantages of each.

2. Do you expect Zinnia to carry identical or fraternal twins? Why?

3. Describe the portions of genetics and environment you expect the twins to share. Discuss the nonshared environment and examples of experiences that the twins may not share.

CHAPTER SUMMARY

2.1 Discuss the genetic foundations of development and patterns of genetic inheritance.

Genes are composed of stretches of deoxyribonucleic acid (DNA). Most cells in the human body reproduce through mitosis, but sex cells reproduce by meiosis, creating gametes with 23 single, unpaired chromosomes. Some genes are passed through dominant-recessive inheritance, in which some genes are dominant and will always be expressed, and others are recessive and will only be expressed if paired with another recessive gene. Other patterns include incomplete dominance, in which both genes are shown, and genomic imprinting, in which the expression of a gene is determined by whether it is inherited from the biological mother or father. Most traits are polygenic, the result of interactions among many genes.

2.2 Identify examples of genetic disorders and chromosomal abnormalities.

Genetic disorders carried through dominant-recessive inheritance include PKU, a recessive disorder, and Huntington's disease, carried by a dominant gene. Some recessive genetic disorders, like the gene for hemophilia, are carried on the X chromosome. Males are more likely to be affected by X-linked genetic disorders. Fragile X syndrome is an example of a dominant-recessive disorder carried on the X chromosome. Other X-linked genetic disorders include Klinefelter syndrome, Jacob's syndrome, triple X syndrome, and Turner syndrome. Some disorders, such as trisomy 21, known as Down syndrome, are the result of chromosomal abnormalities. Others result from mutations.

2.3 Explain the choices of reproductive technology and prenatal diagnostic methods available to individuals and couples.

Artificial insemination, the simplest ART, involves inserting sperm into a woman. In vitro fertilization involves fertilizing ova with sperm outside the body and implanting the resulting cluster of cells in the woman's uterus. Surrogacy involves a woman (the surrogate) carrying a fetus to term for another person or couple who will raise it. There are many options for monitoring fetal health. Ultrasound enables physicians to observe the fetus, measure fetal growth, judge gestational age, and determine physical abnormalities in the fetus. Fetal MRI applies MRI technology to image the fetus' body and diagnose malformations and is often used as a follow-up to ultrasound imaging. Amniocentesis involves extracting a small sample of the amniotic fluid that surrounds the fetus, then growing and analyzing it. Chorionic villus sampling (CVS) also samples genetic material and can be conducted earlier than amniocentesis. Noninvasive prenatal testing (NIPT) screens the mother's blood to detect chromosomal abnormalities but is not as accurate as amniocentesis and CVS. Fetoscopy involves inserting a camera into the womb to examine the fetus and perform procedures, including surgery, during pregnancy.

2.4 Examine interactions among heredity and environment, including behavior genetics, gene-environment correlations and interactions, and the epigenetic framework.

Behavior genetics is the field of study that examines how genes and experience combine to influence the diversity of human traits, abilities, and behaviors. Heritability research examines the contributions of the genotype in determining phenotypes but also provides information on the role of experience through three types of studies: selective breeding studies, family studies, and adoption studies. Genetics contribute to many traits, such as intellectual ability, sociability, anxiety, agreeableness, activity level, obesity, and susceptibility to various illnesses. Passive, evocative, and active gene-environment correlations illustrate how traits often are supported by both our genes and environment. Reaction range refers to the idea that there is a range of potential expressions of a genetic trait, depending on environmental opportunities and constraints. Some traits illustrate canalization and require extreme changes in the environment to alter their course. People's genes and environment interact in complex ways such that the effects of experience may vary with a person's genes. The epigenetic framework is a model for understanding the dynamic ongoing interactions between heredity and environment whereby the epigenome's instructions to turn genes on and off throughout development are influenced by the environment.

KEY TERMS

adoption
amniocentesis
artificial insemination
assisted reproductive technology (ART)
behavior genetics
canalization
chorionic villus sampling (CVS)
chromosome
deoxyribonucleic acid (DNA)
dizygotic (DZ) twin
dominant–recessive inheritance
Down syndrome
epigenetics
fetal MRI
fetoscopy
fragile X syndrome
gamete
gene
gene–environment correlation
gene–environment interactions
genetic counseling
genomic imprinting
genotype

hemophilia
in vitro fertilization
incomplete dominance
Jacob's syndrome
Klinefelter syndrome
meiosis
mitosis
monozygotic (MZ) twin
mutation
niche-picking
noninvasive prenatal testing (NIPT)
nonshared environment
phenotype
phenylketonuria (PKU)
polygenic inheritance
range of reaction
sickle cell anemia
surrogacy
Triple X syndrome
Turner syndrome
ultrasound
zygote

FatCamera/istock

3 THE PRENATAL PERIOD, BIRTH, AND THE NEWBORN

> **LEARNING OBJECTIVES**
>
> **3.1** Describe the three periods of prenatal development.
>
> **3.2** Examine the effects of teratogens on prenatal development.
>
> **3.3** Consider ways in which parental characteristics and behaviors influence prenatal development.
>
> **3.4** Discuss the process of childbirth and the experience of low birth weight infants
>
> **3.5** Discuss newborns' ability to sense and learn about the world.

"Your tummy is round like a ball!" 3-year-old Mika exclaimed. "Do you remember why?" asked Lena. "Maybe?" Mika questioned. "There's someone in here, in my tummy," Lena said. "My brother?" asked Mika. "Yes," Lena smiled, "your little brother is growing quickly, making Mommy's tummy really big and round, like a ball. He will be born soon. Will you help me take care of him?" "Yes!" Mika said. As Mika observed, women's bodies change dramatically during pregnancy. In this chapter we explore prenatal development, how individuals develop before birth.

PRENATAL DEVELOPMENT

> **3.1** Describe the three periods of prenatal development.

Prenatal development begins with fertilization, the union of sperm and ovum. Over the next 38 weeks, the resulting zygote transforms from a single cell to a **neonate**, a newborn.

Conception

Fertilization is possible only during a short window of time each month. Women ovulate on average about every 28 days (roughly 10 to 16 days after their last menstrual period), beginning the possibility of conception. An ovum bursts from one of the two ovaries into the long, thin fallopian tube that leads to the uterus (see Figure 3.1). The ovum is the largest cell in the human body. At about 100 microns in diameter (.004 inches), the ovum is just visible to the human eye (about the size of the period on a printed page).

Over several days, the ovum travels down the fallopian tube toward the uterus. The corpus luteum, the spot on the ovary from which the ovum was released, secretes hormones that cause the lining of the uterus to thicken in preparation for the fertilized ovum (Sadler, 2023). If fertilization does not occur, the uterus lining is shed about 2 weeks later through menstruation.

Males' testes produce millions of sperm each day. Sperm are the smallest human body cell, up to only 5 microns long, or about .0002 inches in length. Sperm contain a pointed head packed with 23 chromosomes' worth of genetic material and a long tail. During ejaculation, about 360 million, and as many as 500 million, sperm are released, bathed in a protective fluid called semen (K. L. Moore et al., 2021). After entering the female's vagina, sperm travel through the cervix into the uterus and onward to the fallopian tubes, where an ovum may be present. Sperm are guided toward the ovum by temperature, tracking the heat of an expectant ovum (Lottero-Leconte et al., 2017). The female's reproductive fluid attracts viable and healthy sperm, which aids in conception because defective sperm do not reach the ovum (Cattelan et al., 2023; Soto-Heras et al., 2023). In the presence of an ovum, sperm become hyperactivated, they swim even more vigorously, and the sperm's head releases enzymes to help it penetrate the protective layers of the ovum (Bianchi & Wright, 2016). As soon as one sperm penetrates the ovum, a chemical reaction makes the ovum's membrane impermeable to other sperm.

Perhaps surprisingly, relatively few sperm reach the ovum. Some sperm get tangled up with other sperm, some travel up the wrong fallopian tube, and others do not swim vigorously enough to reach the ovum. On average, only about 300 of the hundreds of millions of sperm released reach the ovum, if one is present (Miller, 2024). Sperm that travel up the fallopian tube can live up to 6 days, able to fertilize a

FIGURE 3.1 ■ Female Reproductive System

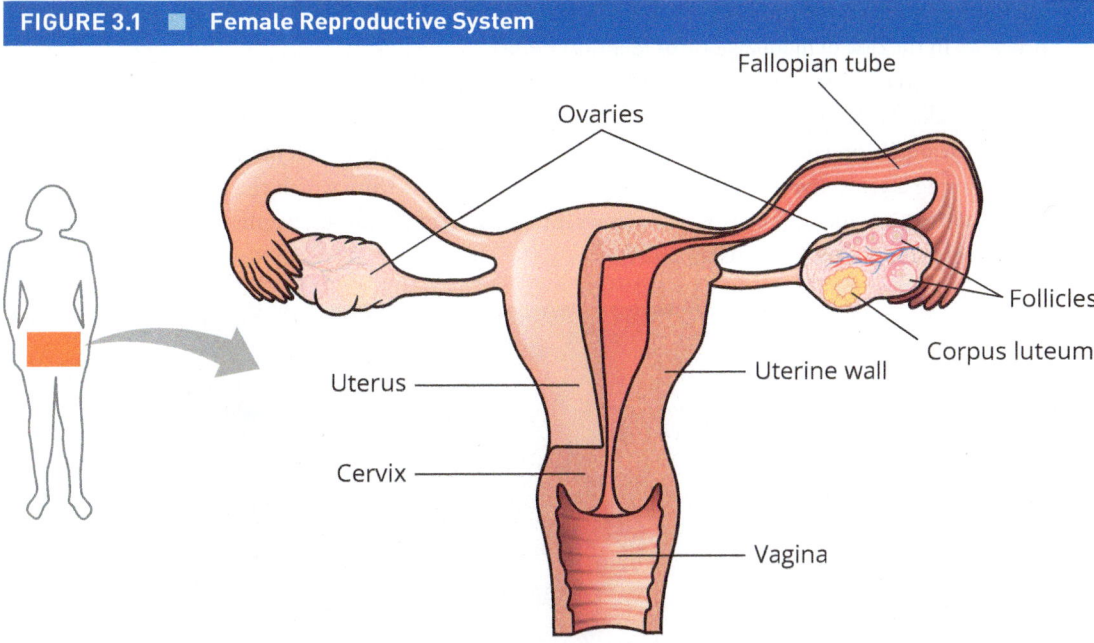

yet-unreleased ovum. But the ovum remains viable and can be fertilized for about only a day after being released into the fallopian tube.

When a sperm penetrates the ovum, its tail falls off, and the sperm's genetic contents merge with that of the ovum. The newly formed zygote contains 46 chromosomes, half from the ovum and half from the sperm. After fertilization, the zygote rapidly transforms into a multicelled organism. Prenatal development takes place over three developmental periods: (1) the germinal period, (2) the embryonic period, and (3) the fetal period.

Germinal Period (0 to 2 Weeks)

The **germinal period**, also known as the period of the zygote, is characterized by cell division. About 30 hours after conception, as it travels down the fallopian tube, the zygote splits down the middle, forming two identical cells (Carlson, 2024). This process is called cleavage, and it continues at a rapid pace. The two cells each split to form four cells, then eight, and so on (see Figure 3.2). Each resulting cell is

FIGURE 3.2 ■ The Germinal Period

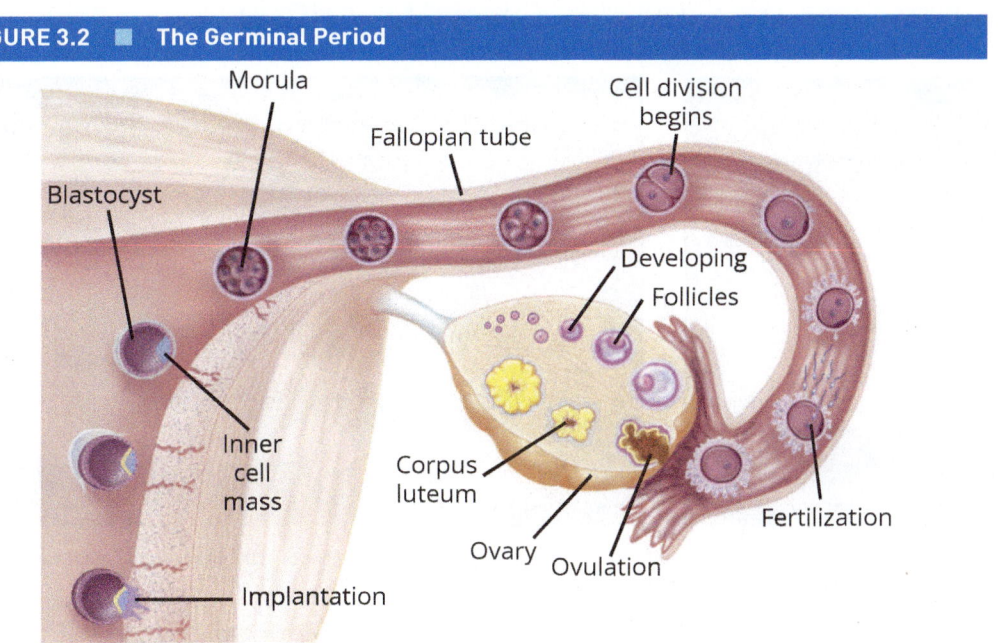

identical until about the third set of cell divisions. Any of these cells may become a person (and sometimes do, in the case of monozygotic or identical twins).

Cell differentiation begins roughly 72 hours after fertilization when the organism consists of about 16 to 32 cells. Differentiation means that the cells begin to specialize and are no longer identical. By Day 4, the organism consists of about 60 to 70 cells formed into a **blastocyst**, a fluid-filled sphere of cells forming a protective circle around an inner cluster of cells from which the embryo will develop. **Implantation**, in which the blastocyst burrows into the wall of the uterus, begins at about Day 6 and is complete by about Day 11 (Carlson, 2024).

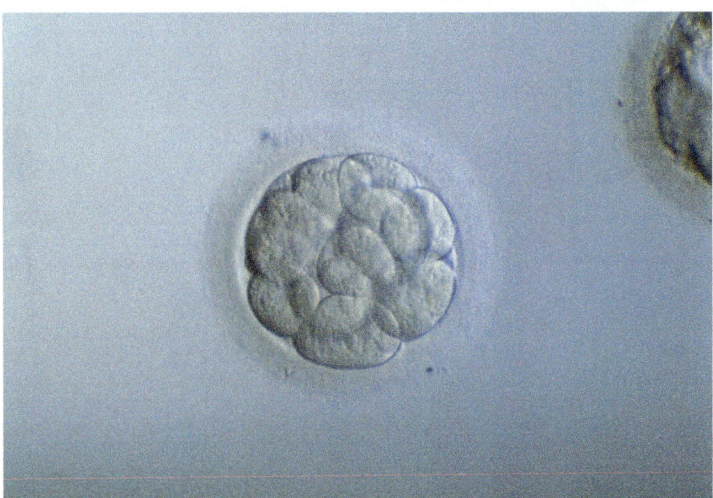

This ball of cells, known as a morula, is formed at about 3 days after conception. Each of these cells is identical. Differentiation has not yet begun.

Pascal Goetgheluck/Science Source

Embryonic Period (3 to 8 Weeks)

After implantation, the developing organism is called an **embryo** All the organs and major body systems form during the embryonic period, making it the most rapid period of structural development in the lifespan. The mass of cells composing the *embryonic disk* forms layers, which will develop into all the body's major organs. The *ectoderm*, the upper layer, will become skin, nails, hair, teeth, sensory organs, and the nervous system. The *endoderm*, the lower layer, will become the digestive system, liver, lungs, pancreas, salivary glands, and respiratory system. The middle layer, the *mesoderm*, forms later and will become muscles, the skeleton, the circulatory system, and internal organs.

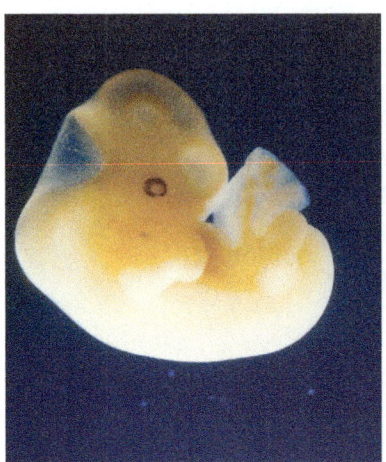 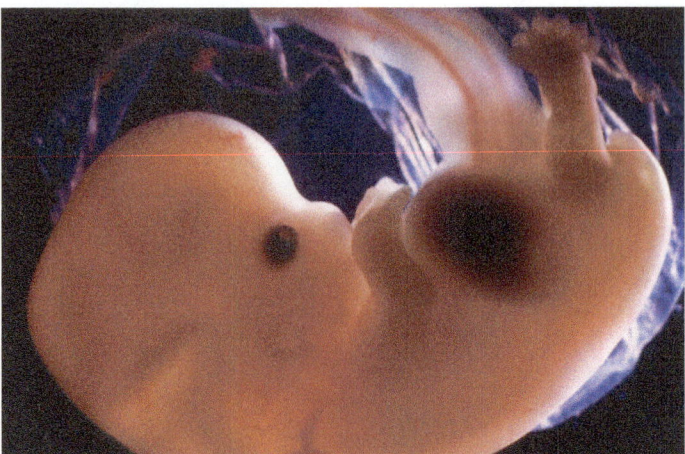

Development proceeds very quickly during the embryonic period. Note the dramatic changes in the head, limbs, and torso from the 5th week (left) to the 7th week (right) of prenatal development.

Professor Pietro M. Motta/Science Source; Petit Format/Science Source

Support structures form that protect the embryo, provide nourishment, and remove wastes. The **amnion**, a membrane that holds amniotic fluid, surrounds the embryo, providing temperature regulation, cushioning, and protection from shocks. The **placenta**, a principal organ of exchange between the mother and embryo, also begins to form. It contains tissue from both the mother and embryo and, once formed, it will act as a filter, enabling the exchange of nutrients, oxygen, and wastes through the umbilical cord. The placenta is also a protective barrier, preventing some toxins from entering the embryo's bloodstream as well as keeping the mother and embryo's bloodstreams separate. Still, many toxins can pass through the placenta, including drugs and chemicals such as alcohol, cannabis, and opioids, as we discuss later.

About 22 days after conception the ectoderm folds to form the **neural tube**, which will develop into the central nervous system (brain and spinal cord) (Webster et al., 2018). By this point, the head can be distinguished. A blood vessel that will become the heart begins to pulse, and blood begins to circulate throughout the body. Arm buds appear during Days 26 and 27, followed by leg buds on Days 28 through 30 (Sadler, 2023). The brain develops rapidly and the head grows faster than the other parts of the body during the 5th week of development. The eyes, ears, nose, and mouth begin to form during the 6th week. Upper arms, forearms, palms, legs, and feet appear. The embryo shows reflex responses to touch.

During the 7th week, webbed fingers and toes are apparent; they separate completely by the end of the 8th week. A ridge called the *indifferent gonad* appears; it will develop into the male or female genitals, depending on the fetus's sex chromosomes (Carlson, 2024). The Y chromosome of the male embryo instructs it to secrete testosterone, causing the indifferent gonad to create testes. In female embryos, no testosterone is released, and the indifferent gonad produces ovaries. The sex organs take several weeks to develop. The external genital organs are not apparent until about 12 weeks.

At the end of the embryonic period, 8 weeks after conception, the embryo weighs about one seventh of an ounce and is 1 inch long. All the basic organs and body parts have formed in a very rudimentary way. The embryo displays spontaneous reflexive movements, but it is still too small for the movements to be felt by the mother (Hepper, 2015). Serious problems during the embryonic period often cause a miscarriage. Indeed, most miscarriages are the result of chromosomal abnormalities. Organisms with the most severe abnormalities do not survive beyond the first trimester, or 3rd month of pregnancy. It is estimated that up to 45% of all conceptions abort spontaneously, and most occur before the pregnancy is detected (Chou et al., 2020)

Fetal Period (9 Weeks to Birth)

During the **fetal period**, from the 9th week to birth, the organism, now called a **fetus**, grows rapidly, and its organs become more complex and begin to function. The fetus moves spontaneously, the legs kick, and it can suck its thumb (an involuntary reflex) (Einspieler et al., 2021). By the end of the 12th week, the upper limbs have almost reached their final relative lengths, but the lower limbs are slightly shorter than their final lengths relative to the rest of the body (Sadler, 2023).

Limb movements are coordinated by the 14th week, but are too slight to be felt by the mother until about 17 to 20 weeks. The heartbeat gets stronger. Eyelids, eyebrows, fingernails, toenails, and tooth buds form. The first hair to appear is **lanugo**, a fine down-like hair that covers the fetus's body; it is gradually replaced by human hair. The skin is covered with a greasy material called the **vernix caseosa**, which protects the fetal skin from abrasions, chapping, and hardening that can occur with exposure to amniotic fluid (K. L. Moore et al., 2021).

At 21 weeks, rapid eye movements begin, signifying an important time of growth and development for the fetal brain. The brain begins to become more responsive. A startle response has been reported at 22 to 23 weeks, prompted by sudden vibrations and noises (Einspieler et al., 2021). The startle response is a basic reflex controlled by the developing central nervous system and is not a voluntary movement. During weeks 21 to 25, the fetus gains substantial weight, and its body proportions become more like those of a newborn infant. Growth of the fetal body begins to catch up to the head, yet the head remains disproportionately larger than the body at birth.

During the last 3 months of pregnancy, the fetal body grows substantially in weight and length; it typically gains over 5 pounds and grows 7 inches in this period (see Figure 3.3). At about 28 weeks after conception, brain development grows in leaps and bounds. The cerebral cortex develops convolutions and furrows, taking on the brain's characteristic wrinkly appearance (Andescavage et al., 2016). The fetal brain wave pattern shifts to include occasional bursts of activity, similar to the sleep-wake cycles of newborns. By 30 weeks, the pupils of the eyes dilate in response to light. At 35 weeks, the fetus has a firm hand grasp and spontaneously orients itself toward light.

FIGURE 3.3 ■ Prenatal Development

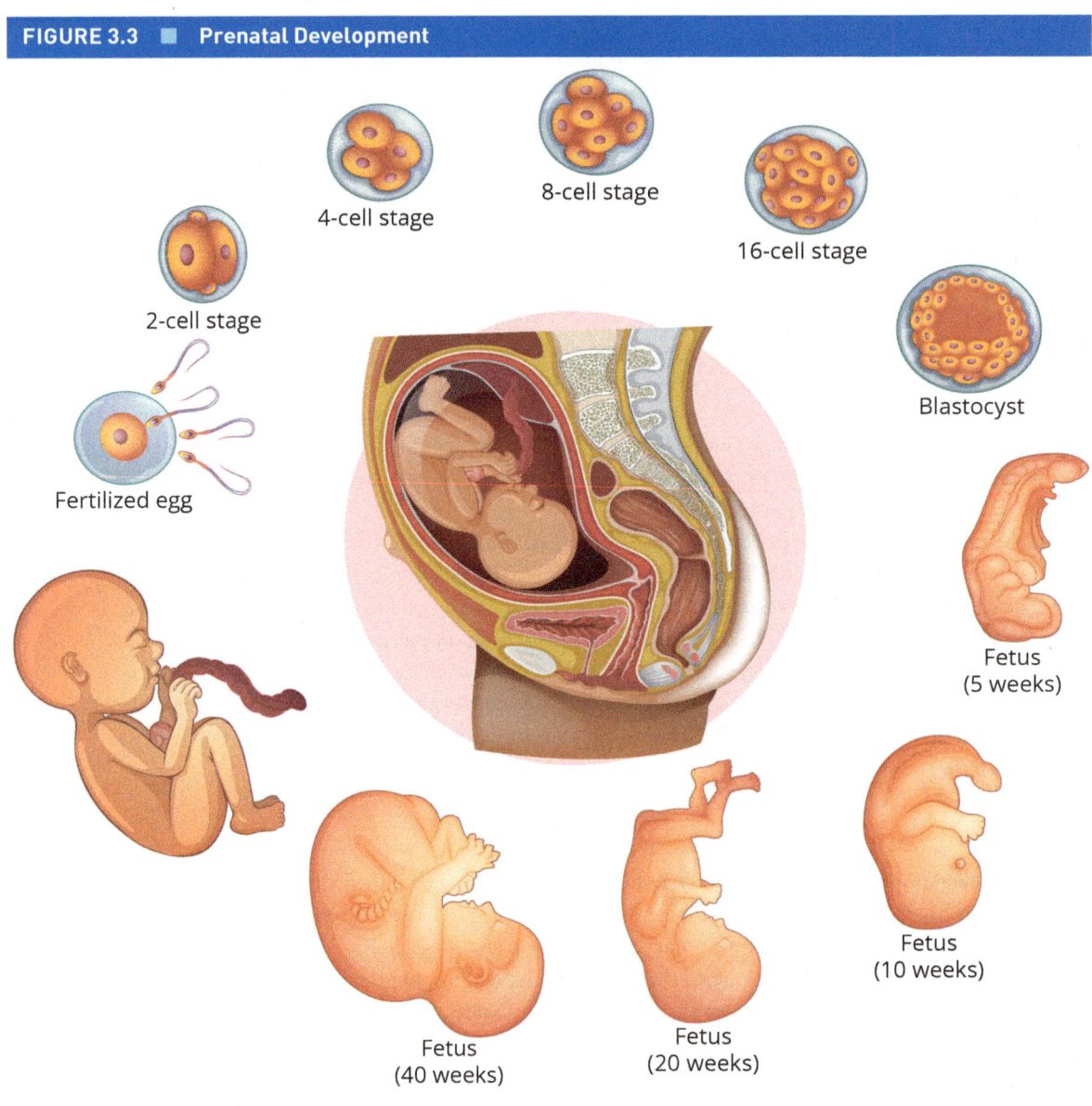

blueringmedia/istock

The expected date of delivery is about 266 days or 38 weeks, from conception (40 weeks from the mother's last menstrual period), but about 1 in every 10 American births is preterm, defined as less than 37 completed weeks of gestation (Carlson, 2024; Martin, 2023). The **age of viability**—the age at which advanced medical care permits a preterm newborn to survive outside the womb—begins at about 22 weeks after conception (K. L. Moore et al., 2021). Although a 22-week fetus born prematurely may survive in intensive care, its immature respiratory system places it at risk; less than 30% of infants born at 22 weeks' gestation survive (Backes et al., 2021). By about 26 weeks, the lungs become capable of breathing air and the premature infant stands a better chance of surviving if given intensive care. About

80% of infants born at 25 weeks survive, and 94% of those born at 27 weeks survive (Myrhaug et al., 2019). As we discuss later in this chapter, premature infants are at heightened risk for short- and long-term impairments and disabilities.

> **THINKING IN CONTEXT 3.1**
>
> 1. "The most critical time in prenatal development is the end because the fetus is most like a baby," explains Rita. To what extent do you agree with Rita? What do we know about the process of prenatal development?
> 2. During what period of prenatal development do most of the body parts form? From your own observations or experience, when do most women learn about their pregnancies? What has developed or is likely developing at this time?

ENVIRONMENTAL INFLUENCES ON PRENATAL DEVELOPMENT

3.2 Examine the effects of teratogens on prenatal development.

Prenatal development unfolds in a predictable way, though the germinal, embryonic, and fetal periods we have discussed. However, environmental factors can interfere with these predictable processes. A **teratogen** is an agent, such as a disease, drug, or other environmental factor, that disrupts prenatal development, that increases the risk of abnormalities and even death (Fraga et al., 2022). Although many substances act as teratogens, it is not always easy to predict the harm caused by them.

Principles of Teratology

The scientific study of the effect of teratogens, known as teratology, examines populations, large groups of women. Conclusions drawn from these studies help us identify relationships among various substances and prenatal development, but we cannot reliably predict the development of specific individuals. Similar exposures to teratogens may not cause the same outcomes in different individuals. Several principles describe how exposure to teratogens can affect prenatal development.

Critical Periods

The effect of exposure to a teratogen depends on the stage of prenatal development when exposure occurs. There are critical periods during prenatal development when the developing organism is more vulnerable to teratogens (Nelson & Gabard-Durnam, 2020). During the germinal stage exposure to teratogens can interfere with cell division and prevent implantation. At this time most women are unaware that they are pregnant. The effects of teratogens at this stage often go unnoticed because the organism simply stops dividing and does not implant to the uterine wall.

During the embryonic period the developing organism is most vulnerable to teratogens (Carlson, 2024). Specific structural abnormalities occur when the embryo is exposed to a teratogen while that part of the body is developing. Each organ of the body has a sensitive period in development during which it is most susceptible to damage from teratogens such as drugs, alcohol, and environmental contaminants (see Figure 3.4). Once a body part is fully formed, it is less likely to be harmed by exposure to teratogens. Some body parts, like the brain, remain sensitive throughout pregnancy.

Dose

The amount of exposure to a teratogen influences its effects on prenatal development. Generally, the larger the dose and the longer the period of exposure, the more damage to prenatal development. Teratogens also differ in their strength. Some teratogens, like alcohol, display a powerful dose–response relationship; heavier and more frequent drinking results in greater damage (Bandoli & Chambers, 2023).

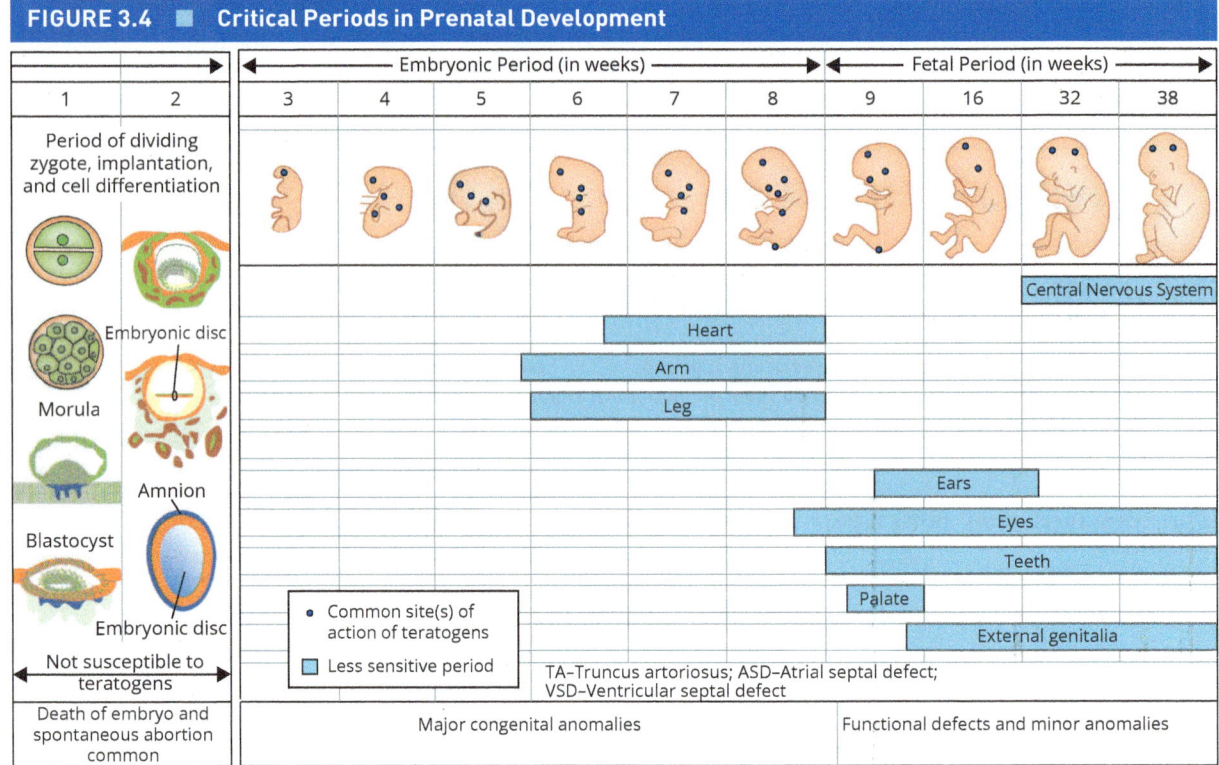

FIGURE 3.4 ■ Critical Periods in Prenatal Development

Individual Differences

Teratogens increase the risk of abnormalities for all organisms, but responses may vary such that some organisms show severe problems, while others have more mild problems, and some may display no problems (Kaminen-Ahola, 2020). Individuals vary in their susceptibility to particular teratogens based on the genetic makeup of both the individual and mother (Gomes et al., 2021). Dizygotic (fraternal) twins may show different effects in response to alcohol exposure in the womb, with one twin showing more adverse effects than the other (Astley Hemingway et al., 2019). The mother's genetic makeup and the prenatal environment also contribute to the likelihood of teratogenic abnormalities.

Complicated Effects

Different teratogens can cause the same congenital (birth) abnormality, and a variety of abnormalities can result from the same teratogen. Also, some teratogenic effects, known as **sleeper effects**, may not be noticeable at birth but appear later in life (Charness et al., 2016). Infants born to women who consumed diethylstilbestrol (DES), a hormone widely prescribed between 1945 and 1970 to prevent miscarriages, were born healthy but as adults were more likely to experience problems with their reproductive systems. Daughters born to mothers who took DES were more likely to develop a rare form of cervical cancer, have miscarriages, and give birth to infants who were premature or low birth weight (Conlon, 2017; Wamakima et al., 2023; Wautier et al., 2020).

Types of Teratogens

As we have discussed, the embryonic stage is the period in which the embryo is most vulnerable. No pregnancy is entirely free of exposure to teratogens. Exposure to prescription, nonprescription, and recreational drugs, and environmental factors, including chemicals, radiation, air pollution, and extremes of heat and humidity is hard to avoid, especially as most women do not become aware of their pregnancies until after the first few weeks of the embryonic stage are past. Still, the vast majority of infants (about 97%) are born each year without congenital abnormalities (Centers for Disease Control and Prevention, 2020; Mai et al., 2019). Next, we examine common teratogens.

Prescription and Nonprescription Drugs

More than 90% of pregnant women take prescription or nonprescription medications (Stanley et al., 2019). Prescription drugs that can act as teratogens include antibiotics, certain hormones, antidepressants, anticonvulsants, and some acne drugs (Tsamantioti & Hashmi, 2024). In several cases, physicians have unwittingly prescribed medication to ease pregnant women's discomfort that caused harm to the fetus. For example, thalidomide, a drug taken by women during the 1950s and 1960s to prevent morning sickness, caused deformities of the child's arms and legs, and, less frequently, damage to the ears, heart, kidneys, and genitals when ingested 4 to 6 weeks after conception (Vargesson, 2022; Vargesson & Stephens, 2021).

Isotretinoin, a form of vitamin A used to treat acne, is a potent teratogen associated with miscarriage as well as severe face, heart, and central nervous system abnormalities and developmental disability (Fallah & Rademaker, 2022; Layton, 2023). The teratogenic effect of isotretinoin is so severe that the U.S. Food and Drug Administration (2010) requires that women prescribed isotretinoin take physician-administered pregnancy tests for 2 months prior to beginning treatment and agree to use two methods of birth control and complete a monthly pregnancy test while taking it.

Nonprescription drugs, such as diet pills and cold medicine, can also cause harm, but research on over-the-counter (OTC) drugs lags far behind research on prescription drugs. We know little about the teratogenic effect of many OTC drugs (Tsamantioti & Hashmi, 2024). Caffeine, found in coffee, tea, cola drinks, and chocolate, is the most common OTC drug consumed during pregnancy, yet its effects on prenatal development are mixed. Some research suggests that low doses of caffeine (200 milligrams or about one cup per day) may be safe (Modzelewska et al., 2019). Indeed, low doses are often prescribed to pregnant women to prevent and treat high blood pressure and preeclampsia (dangerously high blood pressure late in pregnancy that can cause organ damage) (Loussert et al., 2020; Roberge et al., 2017). The risk for negative outcomes, including low birth weight and miscarriage, rise with each 100 milligrams consumed daily (Askari et al., 2023; Jafari et al., 2022; Soltani et al., 2022), leading some researchers to advise that women abstain from caffeine altogether (James, 2021; Qian et al., 2020).

Alcohol

About 10% to 20% of Canadian and U.S. women report consuming alcohol during pregnancy, and about 8% report use late in pregnancy (Gosdin et al., 2022; Umer et al., 2020). Alcohol abuse during pregnancy is the leading cause of developmental disabilities, affecting 1 in 20 school-age children in the United States (Donaldson, 2021; Glass et al., 2023).

Fetal alcohol spectrum disorders refer to the continuum of effects of exposure to alcohol, which vary with the timing and amount of exposure (Popova et al., 2023). Fetal alcohol spectrum disorders are estimated to affect 2% to 5% of children in the United States (Vorgias & Bernstein, 2022). At the extreme end of the spectrum is **fetal alcohol syndrome (FAS)**, a cluster of congenital abnormalities appearing after heavy prenatal exposure to alcohol. FAS is associated with a distinct pattern of facial characteristics (e.g., small head circumference, short nose, small eye opening, and small midface), pre- and postnatal growth deficiencies, reduced brain volume, and deficits in intellectual development, memory, visuospatial skills, motor coordination, and the combined abilities to plan, attend, and problem solve (Boateng et al., 2023; Loock et al., 2020; Wozniak et al., 2019). The effects of prenatal exposure to alcohol persist throughout childhood and adolescence and are associated with cognitive, emotional, and behavioral problems from childhood and adolescence through adulthood (Coles et al., 2022; Grimm et al., 2021; Lees et al., 2020).

Even moderate drinking, defined as 1 drink per day, is harmful because children may be born displaying some but not all FAS problems, *fetal alcohol effects* (Kruithof & Ban, 2021). Consuming 7 to 14 drinks per week during pregnancy is associated with lower birth size, growth deficits through adolescence, and deficits in cognitive development, including attention and memory (Kesmodel et al., 2019; Long & Lebel, 2022). Even less than one drink per day has been associated with poor fetal growth, preterm delivery, and abnormal brain activity in newborns (Mamluk et al., 2017; Sarman, 2018; Shuffrey et al., 2020). Sleeper effects may also occur; infants exposed prenatally to less than one drink per day may display no obvious physical deformities at birth but later, as children, may demonstrate cognitive delays. Scientists have suggested that there is no safe level of drinking (Chu et al., 2022; Popova et al., 2023).

Cigarette Use and E-Cigarette Use

About 7% to 10%, and in some studies as many as 17% of women in the United States report smoking cigarettes during pregnancy (Agrawal et al., 2019; Azagba et al., 2020; Kondracki, 2019). Fetal deaths, premature births, and low birth weight are more common when mothers smoke (Günther et al., 2021; Soneji & Beltrán-Sánchez, 2019).

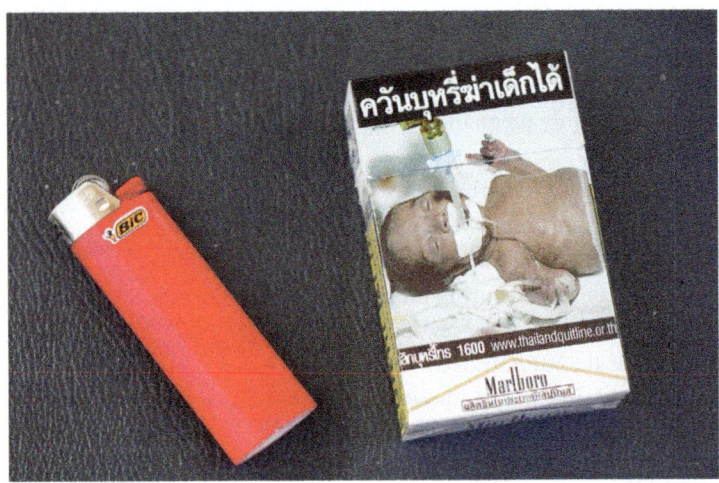

Cigarette packages in many countries include warnings of the dangers smoking poses to prenatal development.

Jan-Otto/istock

Infants exposed to smoke while in the womb are prone to congenital heart abnormalities, respiratory problems, and sudden infant death syndrome and, as children, show more behavior problems, have attention difficulties, and score lower on intelligence and achievement tests (Froggatt, Covey, et al., 2020; Fuemmeler et al., 2023; He et al., 2020). Moreover, maternal smoking during pregnancy increases their offspring's predisposition to illness and disease in childhood, adolescence, and even through middle adulthood (Kaur et al., 2019; Nguyen et al., 2018). There is no safe level of smoking during pregnancy. Even babies born to light smokers (1 to 5 cigarettes per day) show poorer fetal growth, higher rates of low birth weight, and more congenital malformations than do babies born to nonsmokers (Liu et al., 2020; Yang et al., 2022).

About 7% to 15% of women report using e-cigarettes during pregnancy (DeVito et al., 2021; Whittington et al., 2018). E-cigarettes are commonly believed to safer than traditional cigarettes, but this is not true. High temperatures vaporize nicotine as well as components of the e-cigarette device itself, including metals, plastics, rubber, and foam (Wylie et al., 2021). Research examining the long-term effects of prenatal exposure to e-cigarettes is sparse and just emerging, but suggests that e-cigarettes have similar toxic effects on development as traditional cigarettes (Froggatt, Reissland, et al., 2020; Greene & Pisano, 2019; Regan & Pereira, 2021).

The immediate effects of prenatal exposure to e-cigarettes include low birth weight and preterm birth (Regan et al., 2021; Regan & Pereira, 2021). One recent study found that the risk of fetal death was higher in women who vaped a mint or menthol flavor compared to other flavors, suggesting that birth outcomes may vary with e-cigarette characteristics (S. Lin et al., 2023). Exposure to e-cigarette vapor prenatally is associated with increased risk for asthma, cognitive and neurological problems, and poor adjustment to stress in childhood (Aslaner et al., 2022; Froggatt, Reissland, et al., 2020). Quitting cigarette smoking and e-cigarette use before or during pregnancy reduces the risk of adverse pregnancy outcomes (Soneji & Beltrán-Sánchez, 2019).

Marijuana

Roughly 16% of pregnant women report using marijuana, also known as cannabis, during the first trimester of pregnancy, declining to about 5% during the second and third trimester (Hayes et al., 2023; Ko et al., 2020). Prenatal exposure to marijuana is associated with poor fetal growth, low birth weight, preterm birth, and a greater likelihood of requiring intensive neonatal care (Gesterling & Bradford, 2022; Marchand et al., 2022; V. H. Nguyen & Harley, 2022). Neurological correlates of exposure to marijuana include a small head circumference at birth and a thinner cortex, the outer layer of the brain, in late childhood (El Marroun et al., 2016; Gunn et al., 2016; Marchand et al., 2022). Children exposed to marijuana in utero show an increased risk for neurodevelopmental disorders such as ADHD and autism spectrum disorder (Corsi et al., 2020; Roncero et al., 2020). Prenatal exposure to marijuana is associated with impairments in attention, memory, and executive function as well as internalizing problems, such as anxiety and depression, and aggression and behavior problems in childhood that may persist into early adulthood (Grant et al., 2020; Lo et al., 2022; Murnan et al., 2021; Paul et al., 2021). There is no known safe level of marijuana use during pregnancy (Grandy et al., 2022).

Cocaine

Similar to other teratogens, prenatal exposure to cocaine is associated with a range of impairments. Prenatal exposure to cocaine is associated with low birth weight, poor motor skills, difficulty managing arousal and reduced brain volume at birth and in infancy (dos Santos et al., 2018; Grewen et al., 2014). Prenatal cocaine exposure has a small but lasting effect on attention and behavioral control and language skills through early adolescence (Bazinet et al., 2016). In adolescence and emerging adulthood, prenatal exposure to cocaine is associated with poor emotional regulation and behavior problems, which in turn increase the risk of substance abuse (Barbosa-Méndez & Salazar-Juárez, 2020; J.-Y. Kim et al., 2022; Min, Minnes, et al., 2023).

Opioids

Opioids are a class of drugs that include the illegal drugs heroin and synthetic opioids such as fentanyl, as well as pain relievers available legally by prescription, such as oxycodone, morphine, and others. Newborns prenatally exposed to opioids may show addiction and withdrawal symptoms, such as tremors, irritability, abnormal crying, disturbed sleep, and impaired motor control (Boggess & Risher, 2022; Conradt et al., 2019). Prenatal exposure to opioids is associated with low birth weight, smaller head circumference, and altered brain development in newborns (Bailey et al., 2022; Merhar et al., 2020). Children exposed to opioids prenatally tend to show difficulty with attention, managing arousal, learning, and inhibitory control (Levine & Woodward, 2018; Simmons et al., 2023). Throughout childhood into adolescence, children prenatally exposed to opioids perform more poorly than peers on tasks measuring intelligence and executive functioning (such as planning), show more emotional and behavioral problems, and, as adolescents, show reduced brain volume (Azuine et al., 2019; Nygaard et al., 2018; Yeoh et al., 2019).

Environmental Hazards

Prenatal exposure to chemicals, radiation, air pollution, and extremes of heat and humidity can impair development (Gómez-Roig et al., 2021; Yi et al., 2022). Infants prenatally exposed to heavy metals, such as lead and mercury, whether through the mother's ingestion or inhalation, score lower on tests of cognitive ability and intelligence and have higher rates of childhood illness (C. Liu et al., 2022; Shah-Kulkarni et al., 2020).

Exposure to radiation can cause genetic mutations. Many infants born to mothers pregnant during the atomic bomb explosions in Hiroshima and Nagasaki and after the nuclear power accident at Chernobyl displayed many physical deformities, mutations, and intellectual deficits. Prenatal exposure to radiation is associated with problems in physical and cognitive development. Such children are at heightened risk for Down syndrome, reduced head circumference, intellectual disability, poor cognitive and school performance, and cancer (Black et al., 2019; D. S. Chang et al., 2014).

Contextual Influences on Prenatal Substance Use and Perinatal Outcomes

It is well known that substances such as alcohol, marijuana, and opiates negatively affect prenatal development. Given this, the stigma associated with prenatal substance use can prevent some substance-using pregnant women from seeking help (Crawford et al., 2002; Syvertsen et al., 2021). The outcomes of prenatal substance use for women and their infants vary depending on the mix of teratogens to which the fetus is exposed but also with their race and ethnicity, socioeconomic status (SES), and geographic region.

Racial Disparities in Addressing Maternal Substance Use

Should pregnant women be screened for substance use to protect their fetuses and newborns? Many, but not all, pregnant women in the United States are screened for substance use. Women of color and those from low socioeconomic areas are most likely to receive prenatal drug screening (Kravitz et al., 2021). States that conduct prenatal screening often treat maternal substance use as fetal abuse and threaten women who use substances with involuntary treatment or protective custody during pregnancy (Atkins & Durrance, 2020; Seiler, 2016) About half of U.S. states require that substance use by pregnant mothers be reported to child protective services, which may lead to removing the newborn from parental custody or even terminating parental rights altogether (Guttmacher Institute, 2020). These consequences often apply to alcohol use. Over two-thirds of U.S. states have laws related to reporting of alcohol use during pregnancy (Alcohol Policy Information System, 2023).

Policies criminalizing maternal substance use discriminate against women of color and those in low SES brackets because low-income Black and Hispanic women are disproportionately tested and reported to child protective services for substance use (Kravitz et al., 2021). In one California county with universal screening policies, Black and White pregnant women showed similar rates of drug and alcohol use, but Black women were four times more likely than White women to be reported to child protective services after delivery (Roberts & Nuru-Jeter, 2012). Other recent research confirms that Black and Native American mothers are more likely to be reported for alcohol use and marijuana than White mothers (Hoerr et al., 2018; Rebbe et al., 2019a, 2019b).

Criminal sanctions for maternal drug use can discourage women from seeking prenatal and postnatal care and alcohol and substance use treatment, and may undermine the physician-patient relationship (American College of Obstetricians and Gynecologists, 2011; American Medical Association, 2014; McCourt et al., 2022). Such policies can cause women to mistrust medical professionals, which ultimately harms their care if they become reluctant to seek medical care for themselves and their children. Examinations of state policies from 2000–2018 found that punitive prenatal substance use policies did not result in a lower rates of substance exposure at birth and in some cases resulted in increases in substance exposure of up to 18% (Atkins & Durrance, 2020; Meinhofer et al., 2022). Punitive policies may instead deter women from seeking substance use treatment during pregnancy. In contrast, women who live in states that adopt policies that include treatment and support are more likely to seek treatment (Kozhimannil et al., 2019). Perceived stigma may also prevent pregnant women from seeking treatment for alcohol and substance use (Weber et al., 2021). Positive fetal outcomes are supported by substance use treatment that reduces stigma, rewards abstention, invests in family and community supports, and promotes contact with health care and social support services (Barnett et al., 2021; Carroll et al., 2021; Hui et al., 2017)

Teratogen-Context Interactions

Our discussion of teratogens thus far has examined the effects of each teratogen independently, which is somewhat misleading because infants are often exposed to multiple teratogens (J. J. Lee et al., 2023). For example, most infants exposed to opioids or cocaine were also exposed to other substances with teratogenic effects, including tobacco, alcohol, and marijuana, making it difficult to isolate the effect of each drug on prenatal development (Salzwedel et al., 2020). Mothers who use two or more substances, such as opioids and marijuana, are more likely to give birth to premature and low birth weight infants than are those who use one, such as opioids alone (Stein et al., 2020). Teratogenic substances may interact to produce exponentially larger greater effects in combination than apart (Wouldes & Lester, 2023).

In addition, we must be cautious in interpreting findings about illicit drug use and the effects on development because the effects of prenatal exposure to drugs are influenced by parenting and other postnatal (after birth) factors including poverty, inconsistent parenting, and stress (Conradt et al., 2023; S. J. Lee et al., 2020). Parents who abuse substances are more likely to provide poorer quality care, a home environment less conducive to cognitive development, and parent-child interaction that is less sensitive and positive than the environments provided by other parents (Austin et al., 2022; Hatzis et al., 2017). Once contextual factors in the home and neighborhood, such as parenting, the caregiving environment, SES, and exposure to violence and maltreatment are controlled, child and adolescent behavior problems associated with prenatal substance exposure are reduced and often eliminated (Min, Albert, et al., 2023; Viteri et al., 2015)

Disentangling the long-term effects of prenatal exposure to substances, subsequent parenting, and contextual factors is challenging. But it is clear that quality care can lessen the long-term impact of prenatal exposure to substances (Brodie et al., 2019; S. J. Lee et al., 2020; Schuetze et al., 2021).

THINKING IN CONTEXT 3.2

How might contextual factors influence prenatal exposure to teratogens? Apply Bronfenbrenner's bioecological perspective (Chapter 1) to identify contextual factors that might influence prenatal development.

1. Consider the individual: How might a woman's physical, cognitive, or socioemotional development influence the health of her pregnancy and what her embryo and fetus might experience.
2. What interactions in the microsystem (all the people and settings in which they interact) might influence women and their pregnancies?
3. What interactions in the mesosystem (the interrelations among microsystems) might influence women and their pregnancies?
4. To what degree might factors in the exosystem (the outer context in which the microsystem and mesosystem are embedded) affect prenatal development?
5. How might laws, customs, and cultural values (macrosystem) affect women and prenatal outcomes?
6. Considering the biological perspective, brainstorm ways of promoting healthy prenatal development and reducing the influence of teratogens.
7. What specific advice would you provide to a pregnant woman to help her promote a healthy pregnancy?

THE PRENATAL ENVIRONMENT AND PRENATAL CARE

3.3 Consider ways in which parental characteristics and behaviors influence prenatal development

Most discussions about prenatal development emphasize the role of pregnant women. As we discuss further, women's characteristics and behavior, including diet, emotional well-being, and age influence prenatal outcomes. However, men also influence the prenatal environment through genetics and behavior.

Maternal Nutrition

Most women need to consume 2,200 to 2,900 calories per day (and gain about 25 to 30 pounds in total) to sustain a healthy pregnancy (Kaiser et al., 2008). Fetal malnutrition is associated with poor growth before and after birth. Long-term effects include vision impairment, motor and speech disabilities, cognitive difficulties, and, in adulthood, increased risk of heart disease, stroke, and diabetes (Han & Hong, 2019; S. Kim et al., 2017; Tao et al., 2021). Infants who are malnourished can overcome some of the negative effects if they are raised in enriched environments with adequate food and health care. Still, most children who are malnourished before birth remain malnourished; few are raised in enriched environments after birth.

In addition to adequate calories, prenatal development relies on obtaining specific nutrients. For instance, inadequate consumption of folic acid (a B vitamin) very early in pregnancy can result in the formation of neural tube abnormalities stemming from the failure of the neural tube to close.

Spina bifida occurs when the lower part of the neural tube fails to close and spinal nerves begin to grow outside of the vertebrae, often resulting in paralysis (Iskandar & Finnell, 2022). Spina bifida is often accompanied by malformations in brain development and impaired cognitive development (Avagliano et al., 2019). Surgery must be performed before or shortly after birth, but lost capacities cannot be restored (Chmait et al., 2023; Dewan & Wellons, 2019).

Another neural tube abnormality, **anencephaly**, occurs when the top part of the neural tube fails to close and all or part of the brain fails to develop, resulting in death shortly after birth (ten Donkelaar et al., 2023). Neural tube abnormalities can be prevented by consuming .4 to .8mg of folic acid (Kancherla, 2023; U.S. Preventive Services Task Force, 2023). Many foods are fortified with folic acid, but a dietary supplement is safe and ensures that prenatal needs are met. However, many pregnant women consume less than the recommended dose of folic acid (Bibbins-Domingo et al., 2017).

Maternal Illness

Depending on the type and when it occurs, an illness experienced during pregnancy can have grave consequences for the developing fetus. Rubella (German measles) prior to the 11th week of pregnancy can cause a variety of congenital abnormalities, including blindness, deafness, heart abnormalities, and brain damage, but after the first trimester, adverse consequences become less likely (Bouthry et al., 2014; Singh, 2020). Chicken pox can produce congenital abnormalities affecting the arms, legs, eyes, and brain; mumps can increase the risk of miscarriage (Mehta, 2016; Webster et al., 2018). Children born to women infected with mosquito-borne the Zika virus are at risk for *congenital Zika syndrome*, which includes a pattern of abnormalities, such as severe microcephaly characterized by partial skull collapse, damage to the eyes, and body deformities, including restricted range of motion in joints and muscles (D. S. Moore, 2017; Veiga et al., 2021).

Pregnancy increases the risk of experiencing severe illness in response to COVID-19 (Grünebaum et al., 2023). Women infected with COVID-19 are more likely to experience preterm birth, preeclampsia (high blood pressure), low birth weight, and still birth (Villar et al., 2021; Wei et al., 2021). Pregnant women are more likely to be admitted to a hospital and intensive care unit, need oxygen therapy, and to die from complications of COVID-19. Contextual factors are associated with the risk of COVID-19 infection and factors that influence treatment and recovery. Pregnant Black and Hispanic women who live in socially and economically disadvantaged settings with high neighborhood density and less access to health insurance and medical care experience higher risk for COVID-19 infection and negative health outcomes (Emeruwa et al., 2020; Joseph et al., 2020). Vaccination prior to or during pregnancy appears safe and is associated with transmitting COVID-19 antibodies to the fetus (Devera et al., 2024; Rasmussen & Jamieson, 2022).

HIV, the virus that causes *acquired immune deficiency syndrome (AIDS)*, a disease affecting the immune system, can be transmitted prenatally through the placenta, by exposure to body fluids, and breastfeeding (Chilaka & Konje, 2021). Infants and children with HIV are at high risk for a range of illnesses and health conditions, including heart, gastrointestinal, and lung problems; growth stunting; and problems in brain development, which contribute to cognitive and motor impairment; and delays in reaching developmental milestones (K. Harris & Yudin, 2020; McHenry et al., 2018; Wedderburn et al., 2019).

The use of cesarean delivery and prescribing anti-HIV drugs to the mother during the second and third trimesters of pregnancy and to the infant for the first 6 weeks of life have reduced the rate of mother-to-child transmission of HIV to about 1% in the United States and Europe (Blanche, 2020; Selph et al., 2019). Over two thirds of the HIV infected children born from 2002–2013 were to Black or African American mothers (63%) and about 18% to Hispanic or Latina mothers (Taylor et al., 2017). A combination of socioeconomic factors influences these health disparities, such as lack of health insurance, limited health literacy, poverty, and an associated sense of powerlessness, which may prevent women from seeking assistance. HIV medications and treatment are expensive, and an HIV diagnosis is often stigmatizing and may alienate individuals from their communities. Aggressive treatment may further reduce the transmission of HIV to newborns, and research suggests that it may even induce remission (Blanche, 2020; Rainwater-Lovett et al., 2015). However, women of color and those in poverty are less likely to receive HIV treatment.

Maternal Emotional Well-Being

Low birth weight and premature birth are more common when pregnant women experience severe stress, like that associated with living in unsafe environments, experiencing traumatic life events, and experiencing racism, stigma, and discrimination (R. A. Harris et al., 2022; S. R. Liu & Glynn, 2022). Stress hormones cross the placenta, raising the fetus's heart rate and activity level. Long-term exposure to stress hormones in utero is associated with higher levels of stress hormones in newborns and greater release of stress hormones in response to everyday discomfort, such as bathing (McGowan & Matthews, 2018; Nazzari et al., 2019). As a result, newborns exposed to prenatal stress tend to be more irritable and may have difficulties in sleep, digestion, and self-regulation. In childhood, prenatal stress is associated with sleep problems, emotional difficulties, behavior problems, and an increased risk for autism and attention deficit hyperactivity disorder (Clayborne et al., 2021; Lautarescu et al., 2020; van den Heuvel et al., 2021).

Prenatal stress may also have epigenetic effects on development, influencing stress responses throughout the lifespan, especially for members of marginalized groups (Conradt et al., 2020; Mueller et al., 2021). Animal research has suggested that the epigenetic effects of prenatal exposure to stress may be transmitted across generations, potentially affecting multiple cohorts of individuals (Badihian et al., 2019). Prenatal (and postnatal) stress can therefore influence lifelong physical and psychosocial responses to adversity (Lappé & Jeffries Hein, 2021).

Women who experience prenatal stress also tend to experience postnatal stress, making it difficult to disentangle the effects of experiencing stress before and after birth on children (Hartman et al., 2020; Lin et al., 2017). Infants and children exposed to prenatal stress are also exposed to poverty, racism and discrimination, and environmental stressors, which influence their development

Some stress during pregnancy is normal, but exposure to chronic and severe stress during pregnancy poses risks, including low birth weight, premature birth, and a longer postpartum hospital stay.

eggeeggjiew/istock

and reactions to stress. Prenatal and postnatal stress interact to influence children's outcomes. Children who experience prenatal stress show greater emotional problems when they are also exposed to postnatal maternal depression and anxiety as compared with those who are exposed to less maternal postnatal depression (Hartman et al., 2020).

Maternal Age

U.S. women are becoming pregnant at later ages than ever before. Since 1990, the birth rate has increased for women ages 35 to 44, decreased slightly for women ages 24 to 29, and declined more dramatically for women in their early 20s (see Figure 3.5; Osterman et al., 2023). Does maternal age matter? The risk of birth complications increases during the late 30s, especially after age 40. Women who give birth over the age of 40 are at greater risk for complications, including hypertension, gestational diabetes, preterm birth, and miscarriage than younger women (Frick, 2021). Their newborns are at greater risk for low birth weight, respiratory problems, and related conditions requiring intensive neonatal care (Frederiksen et al., 2018; Glick et al., 2021). The risk of chromosomal abnormalities, especially Down syndrome increases sharply with maternal age, especially after age 40 (Akhtar et al., 2022; Xie et al., 2021).

Although risks for complications rise linearly with each year, it is important to realize that the majority of women over age 35 give birth to healthy infants (Marozio et al., 2019). Differences in context and behavior may compensate for some of the risks of advanced maternal age. For example, longer use of oral contraceptives prior to conception is associated with a lower risk of giving birth to a child with Down syndrome (Horányi et al., 2018). Generally, older mothers may have higher SES, have more material resources, and have more education and life experience.

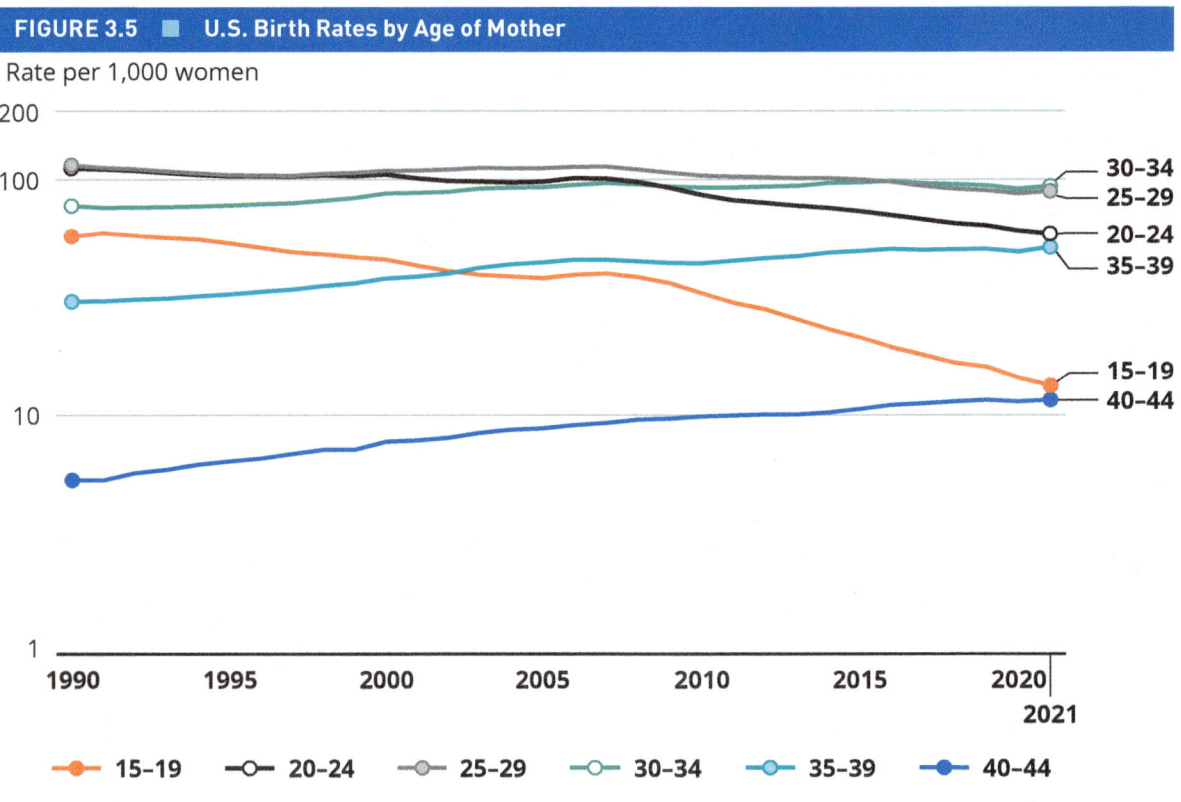

FIGURE 3.5 ■ U.S. Birth Rates by Age of Mother

Source: Osterman, M. J. K., Hamilton, B. E., Martin, J. A., Driscoll, A. K., & Valenzuela, C. P. (2023). Births: Final data for 2021. *National Vital Statistics Reports, 72*(1), 1–53.

Paternal Characteristics and Prenatal Development

It was once thought that biological fathers had no influence on prenatal development—and therefore researchers neglected to study their role. Most obviously, fathers or partners influence the home context. Secondhand smoke from partners is harmful to the developing organism (Braun et al., 2020). Partners' interactions with pregnant mothers can increase maternal stress, with potential negative implications for prenatal development, but they can also be important sources of social support, aiding mothers (Glover & Capron, 2017). We know less about how fathers' health, behavior, and exposure to contextual factors act as biological influences on prenatal development.

Sperm production and quality is influenced by environmental and behavioral factors (Borges et al., 2018). Alcohol abuse, substance abuse, and exposure to toxins such as lead can impair sperm production and quality (Amor et al., 2022; Rodprasert et al., 2023). Smoking is associated with DNA damage and mutations in sperm (Beal et al., 2017; Esakky & Moley, 2016).

Advanced paternal age (over age 40) is associated with damage to sperm and DNA (Gonzalez et al., 2022; Rosiak-Gill et al., 2019). Risks associated with advanced paternal age include congenital abnormalities, chromosomal abnormalities, and developmental disorders such as Down syndrome and autism spectrum disorder (Brandt et al., 2019; Day et al., 2016; Herati et al., 2017).

In addition to DNA, fathers (and mothers) pass on epigenetic markers that can influence their offspring's health throughout life. In one study, men whose fathers smoked when they were conceived had a 50% lower sperm count than the men of nonsmoking fathers (Axelsson et al., 2018). Recall from Chapter 2 that the epigenome determines how DNA is expressed, what genes are turned on and off. The epigenome contains a molecular record or *memory* of a person's life experiences, including health behavior, exposure to toxins, nutritional status, and more (Cirulli, 2021; Perera et al., 2020). These marks can be passed through ova and sperm to offspring and may even be passed to their offspring's children (Curley et al., 2023; Laubach et al., 2024). But it is important to remember that the epigenetic marks we are born with are not set in stone. Some epigenetic marks can be changed after birth through experiences, health care, and behaviors, such as diet and exercise (Galkin et al., 2023; Nellore et al., 2022).

Prenatal Care

Prenatal care, a set of services provided to improve pregnancy outcomes and engage the expectant mother, family members, and friends in health care decisions, is critical for the health of both mother and infant. Prenatal care visits typically include a physical exam, weight check, and diagnostic procedures to assess the fetus's health. These visits also provide women the opportunity to ask questions and for the service provider to provide health care information and advice about nutrition, prenatal care, and preparing for birth. Unfortunately, not all women obtain early prenatal care.

Barriers to Prenatal Care

Nearly one quarter of pregnant women in the United States do not obtain prenatal care until after the first trimester; 6% obtain prenatal care at the end of pregnancy or not at all (Osterman et al., 2023). Inadequate prenatal care is a risk factor for low birth weight and preterm births as well as infant mortality during the first year (Partridge et al., 2012; Xaverius et al., 2016). In addition, use of prenatal care predicts the use of pediatric care, and therefore health and development, throughout childhood (Deaton et al., 2017).

Why do women delay or avoid seeking prenatal care? A common reason is the lack of health insurance (Baer et al., 2019). Government-sponsored health care is available for the poorest mothers, but many low-income mothers do not qualify for care or lack information on how to take advantage of care that may be available. Other common barriers to obtaining prenatal care include lacking transportation, not being able to take time off from work, lacking childcare, and being unaware of one's pregnancy (Heaman et al., 2015; Mazul et al., 2017; Reid et al., 2021). Black and Latina women report nearly twice as many barriers to accessing care as White women (Fryer et al., 2021).

During the COVID-19 pandemic, rates of prenatal care declined because many prenatal care appointments were rescheduled as "virtual" appointments conducted through video conferencing (Erchick et al., 2022). These changes were associated with increased anxiety and depressive symptoms in pregnant women, posing additional risks to their pregnancies (Groulx et al., 2021). Black and marginalized women and those of low SES reported greater stress, anxiety, and depression than White women and those of higher SES (Avalos et al., 2022). Preexisting racial and economic disparities in prenatal care worsened during the pandemic. Birth outcomes also worsened. Compared with the same period the prior year, birth complications and maternal deaths during delivery increased during the COVID-19 pandemic, between March 2020 to April 2021 (Molina et al., 2022).

Race, Ethnicity, and Prenatal Care

There are significant ethnic and socioeconomic disparities in prenatal care. As shown in Figure 3.6, prenatal care is closely linked with maternal education (Blakeney et al., 2019; Stephens et al., 2020). About 86% of women with a college degree obtain first-trimester care, compared with less than two thirds of women with less than a high school diploma (Wen et al., 2021).

Women of color are disproportionately less likely to receive prenatal care during the first trimester and are more likely to receive care beginning in the third trimester or no care (Blakeney et al., 2019; Martin & Osterman, 2023). Generally, Native Hawaiian and Native American women are least likely to obtain prenatal care during the first trimester, followed by Black, Hispanic, Asian American, and White American women (Hamilton et al., 2019; Martin & Osterman, 2023). Ethnic differences are thought to be largely influenced by socioeconomic factors. The ethnic groups least likely to seek early prenatal care are also the most economically disadvantaged members of society and are most likely to live in communities with fewer health resources, including access to physicians and hospitals, sources of health information, and nutrition and other resources.

Prenatal care predicts better birth outcomes, but cultural factors protect some women and infants from the negative consequences of inadequate prenatal care. Known as the *Latina paradox*, Latina mothers, despite low rates of prenatal care, tend to experience low birth weight and

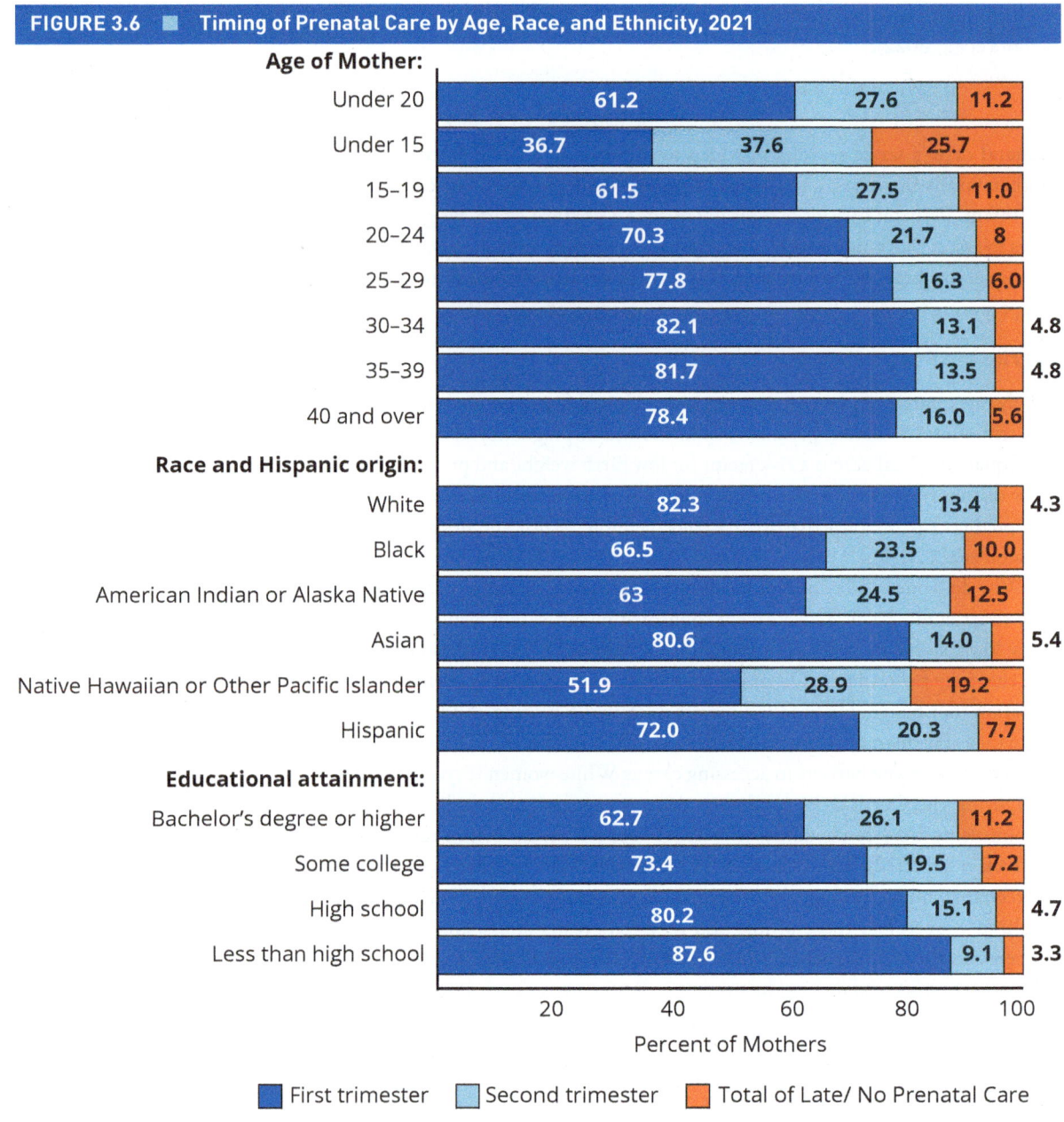

FIGURE 3.6 ■ Timing of Prenatal Care by Age, Race, and Ethnicity, 2021

Source: Osterman et al. (2023).

mortality rates below national averages. These favorable birth outcomes are striking because of the strong and consistent association between SES and birth outcomes. Latinos are among the most socioeconomically disadvantaged ethnic populations in the United States (McGlade et al., 2004; Ruiz et al., 2016).

Several factors may account for the Latina paradox, including strong cultural support for maternity, healthy traditional dietary practices, and the norm of selfless devotion to the maternal role (known as *marianismo*) (Gallegos & Segrin, 2021). Protective cultural factors interact with strong social support networks and informal systems of health care in which women help other women in the community, and warm interpersonal relationships among family members, *familismo*, are highly valued (Gallegos & Segrin, 2021; McGlade et al., 2004).

These cultural factors are thought to underlie the positive birth outcomes seen in Latina women, yet they appear to erode as Latina women acculturate to American society. The birth advantage declines in subsequent American-born generations. Some researchers have called the existence of the Latina paradox into question, because some samples have illustrated that cultural supports cannot easily counter the negative effects of socioeconomic disadvantage (Hoggatt et al., 2012; Sanchez-Vaznaugh et al., 2016). Other research suggests that the Latina paradox is more complicated. One recent study of Puerto Rican women found that women with bicultural acculturation, who identify with both Latina and continental U.S. cultures experience lower stress levels than those with low acculturation (Chasan-Taber et al., 2020). Women's sense of identity may play a role in their perceived stress and perhaps ultimately the health of their pregnancy.

The mixed findings regarding the Latina paradox may also be influenced by complex intersecting social factors, such as geography and politics (Montoya-Williams et al., 2021). Latina women who live on the U.S.-Mexico border are much more likely to have a cesarean birth than those who do not live on the border. This strip of land spans 2,000 miles and four states (Morris et al., 2018). Hot political debates center around this strip, including about immigration, poverty, crime, and whether to construct a physical barrier, a wall, to distinguish each country. The intersecting social disadvantages for Latina women who live on the border may pose multiple threats to their health and the health of their fetuses.

THINKING IN CONTEXT 3.3

1. We have seen that pregnant women and biological fathers influence the prenatal environment. How might contextual factors indirectly influence the fetus, through their effect on women and men? Consider the environments in which adults work and live, outer influences on them (such as the exosystem) and macrosystem factors.
2. Consider barriers to prenatal care. How might intersectional factors, such as age, race, and SES, contribute to the availability and use of prenatal care. Brainstorm two suggestions for increasing women's access to prenatal care.

CHILDBIRTH

3.4 Discuss the process of childbirth and the experience of low birth weight infants.

After about 40 weeks of pregnancy, or 38 weeks after conception, **labor**, the process of birth, begins. During childbirth the fetus emerges from the womb as a neonate, or newborn.

Labor

Labor progresses in three stages. During the first stage of labor, dilation, the cervix dilates or opens to allow the baby's head to pass through (see Figure 3.7). Dilation is the longest stage, typically lasting 8 to 14 hours for a woman having her first child and 3 to 8 hours for subsequent children. It begins when the mother feels regular uterine contractions spaced at 10- to 15-minute intervals. Initial contractions may feel like a backache or menstrual cramps or may be extremely sharp. The **amnion** may rupture, releasing the amniotic fluid that surrounds the fetus (the *water breaking*). The contractions, which gradually become stronger and closer together, cause the cervix to open.

The second stage of labor, delivery, begins when the cervix is fully dilated to 10 cm and the fetus's head is positioned at the opening of the cervix—known as crowning. During this stage, the woman typically feels the urge to push or bear down with each contraction to assist the birth process. Delivery can take from 30 minutes to an hour and a half. It ends when the baby emerges from the mother's body.

In the final stage of labor, the placenta separates from the uterine wall and uterine contractions push it out of the woman's body. This typically happens about 5 to 15 minutes after the baby is born and can take up to a half-hour.

FIGURE 3.7 ■ Stages of Labor

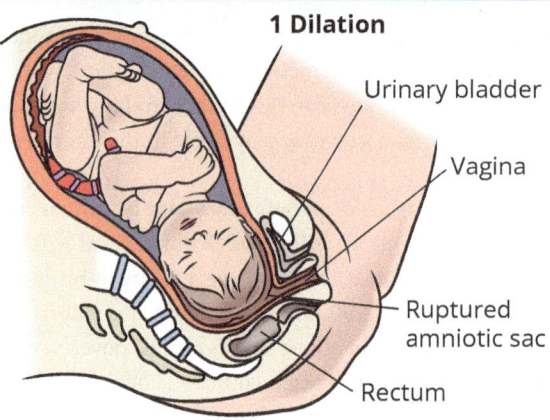
1 Dilation
- Urinary bladder
- Vagina
- Ruptured amniotic sac
- Rectum

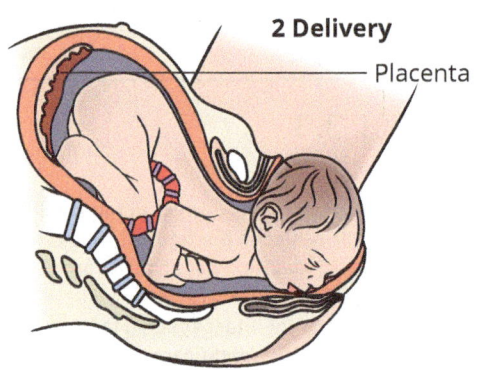
2 Delivery
- Placenta

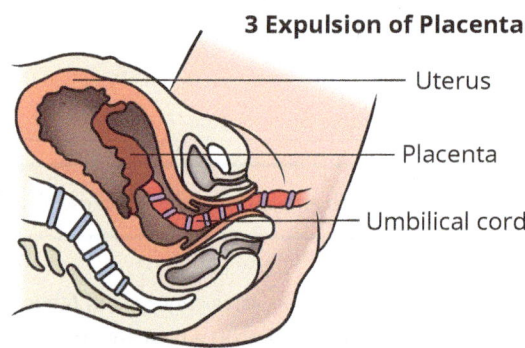
3 Expulsion of Placenta
- Uterus
- Placenta
- Umbilical cord

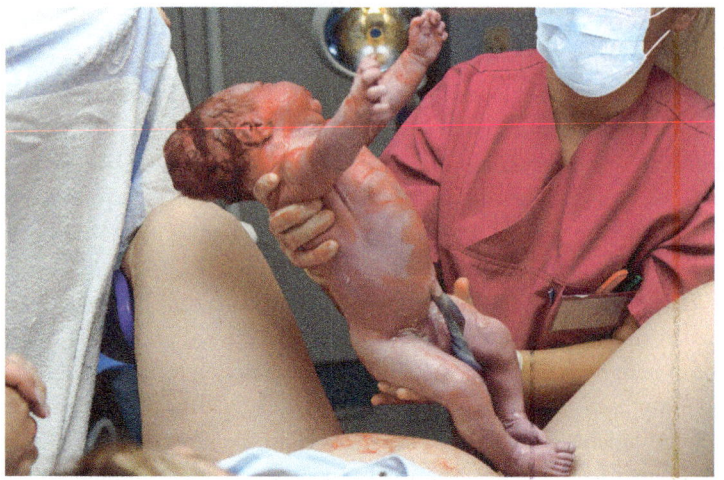

The newborn emerges during the second stage of labor.

delectus/istock

Medication During Delivery

Most women in the United States receive medication during birth, *anesthetics*, painkillers that block body sensations (Butwick et al., 2018; Declercq et al., 2014). Anesthetics are most often dispensed as an *epidural*, injected into a small space between the vertebrae of the lower spine, numbing the lower body (Halliday et al., 2022). Epidurals are effective at reducing pain but can also weaken uterine contractions, lengthen delivery, and may increase the risk of a cesarean section, as discussed next (Gabbe et al., 2016; Herrera-Gómez et al., 2017). An analysis of nearly 15,500 deliveries suggested that newborns exposed to epidural anesthesia did not differ from those exposed to no anesthesia (Wang et al., 2018). The American College of Obstetricians and Gynecologists (2017) has concluded that the proper administration of medication poses few risks to the newborn and recommends pain medication be available to all women.

Cesarean Delivery

In some cases a vaginal birth is not possible because of concerns for the health or safety of the mother or fetus. A fetus in **breech position** is positioned in reverse with its feet or bottom closest to the cervix instead of its head. During a breech birth a fetus may become stuck in the birth canal, potentially cutting off its oxygen supply through the umbilical cord, causing irreversible damage and even death. In such cases the obstetrician may try to turn the baby so that it is head-first. In other cases the fetus is delivered through a **cesarean delivery**, or C-section, a surgical procedure in which the fetus is delivered through an incision in the mother's abdomen.

Cesarean deliveries are also performed when labor progresses too slowly, the head is too large to pass through the pelvis, or the fetus or mother is in danger (Jha et al., 2015; Visscher & Narendran, 2014). About 32% of U.S. births were by cesarean delivery in 2021 (Osterman et al., 2023). Babies delivered by cesarean are exposed to more maternal medication and secrete lower levels of the stress hormones that occur with vaginal birth that are needed to facilitate respiration, enhance circulation of blood to the brain, and help the infant adapt to the world outside of the womb. Interactions between mothers and infants are similar for infants delivered vaginally and by cesarean (Durik et al., 2000).

Natural Childbirth

Natural childbirth is an approach to birth that reduces pain using breathing and relaxation exercises rather than medication. Natural childbirth methods emphasize preparation by pregnant women and their partners about childbirth, helping them reduce their fear, and teaching them pain management techniques. The Lamaze method is a widely known natural childbirth method created by French obstetrician, Ferdinand Lamaze (1956). The Lamaze method emphasizes reducing women's fear and anxiety about labor through education about their bodies, including detailed information about anatomy, pregnancy, and childbirth. When women know what to expect and learn a breathing technique to help them relax, they are better able to manage the pain of childbirth. The Lamaze method relies on the spouse or partner as coach, providing physical and emotional support.

Home Birth

Although common in nonindustrialized nations, home birth is rare, comprising 1.3% of all U.S. births in 2020 (Osterman et al., 2022). The remaining 98% of births occur in hospitals. Most home births are managed by a **midwife**, a healthcare professional, and usually a nurse, specializing in childbirth. Midwives provide health care throughout pregnancy and supervise home births. One review of 50 studies found that the use of midwives, whether as part of a home birthing plan or as part of a plan to birth in a hospital setting, is associated with reduced neonatal mortality, reduced preterm birth, fewer interventions, and more efficient use of medical resources (Renfrew et al., 2014).

Is a home birth safe? A healthy woman, who has received prenatal care and is not carrying twins, is unlikely to encounter problems requiring intervention—and may be a good candidate for a home birth (Wilbur et al., 2015). Although unpredictable events can occur and immediate access to medical facilities can improve outcomes, studies from Europe indicate that home birth is not associated with greater risk of perinatal mortality. Home birth is far more common in many European countries than the United States (20% in the Netherlands, 8% in the United Kingdom) (Brocklehurst et al., 2011; de Jonge et al., 2015). The few U.S. studies examining planned home birth compared with hospital birth have found no difference in neonatal deaths or Apgar scores (see below), and women who have a planned home birth report high satisfaction rates (Jouhki et al., 2017; Zielinski et al., 2015).

Cultural Childbirth Practices

Societies vary in birth customs, including the privacy afforded to giving birth and how newborns are integrated into the community. In the United States, birth is a private event that usually occurs in a hospital, attended by medical personnel and one or two family members. In addition to the expectant mother's partner, a doula can be an important source of support and has become increasingly common in recent decades. A **doula** is a caregiver who aids an expectant mother and her partner throughout the birth process (Kang, 2014). Doulas offer education about pregnancy, delivery, and pain management practices and help the woman create a birth plan. The doula is present during birth, whether at a hospital or other setting, and helps the woman carry out her birth plan. The presence of a doula is associated with less pain medication, fewer cesarean deliveries, and higher satisfaction rates in new mothers (Gabbe et al., 2016; Kozhimannil et al., 2016).

In some cultures, birth is a community event. In a small village in southern Italy, birth usually takes place in a hospital, attended by a midwife (Fogel, 2007; Schreiber, 1977). During labor and immediately after birth immediate and extended family and friends visit and take turns congratulating and kissing the mother and infant, celebrating the mother's contribution to the community.

In South America, the Jahara give birth under a shelter in full view of everyone in the village (Fogel, 2007). On the Indonesian island of Bali, birth occurs in the home with the aid of a midwife and female relatives. Husbands, children, and other family members attend the birth because babies are believed to be reincarnated souls of ancestors. The newborn is immediately integrated into the family and larger community because it viewed as related to many members of the community (Diener, 2000).

The Maya of the Yucatan region of Mexico give birth in the same hammock where they sleep. The father-to-be is present during labor and birth to assist and to witness the suffering that accompanies labor. The pregnant woman's mother is present, as well as sisters, sisters-in-law, mothers-in-law, godmothers, and sometimes neighbors and close friends. The mother and newborn remain inside the house for a week before returning to normal activity after birth to protect them from the influence of evil spirits (Gardiner & Kosmitzki, 2018).

A neighboring ethnic group, the Zinacanteco, place their newborns naked before a fire. The midwife who assisted the mother says prayers asking the gods to look kindly upon the infant. The infant is dressed in a long skirt made of heavy fabric extending beyond the feet; this garment is to be worn throughout the first year. The newborn is then wrapped in several layers of blankets, even covering the face, to protect against losing parts of the soul. These traditional practices are believed to protect the infant from illnesses as well as evil spirits (Brazelton, 1977; Fogel, 2007). Cultures vary in birthing practices.

Newborn Health Screening

After birth, newborns are routinely screened with the **Apgar scale**, which is a quick assessment of the baby's immediate health. As shown in Table 3.1, the Apgar scale consists of five subtests: appearance (color), pulse (heart rate), grimace (reflex irritability), activity (muscle tone), and respiration (breathing). The newborn is rated 0, 1, or 2 on each subscale for a maximum total score of 10. A score of 4 or lower means that the newborn is in serious condition and requires immediate medical attention. The rating is conducted twice, first 1 minute after delivery and again 5 minutes after birth; this timing ensures that hospital staff monitors the newborn over several minutes. A low Apgar score at both time points is associated with an increased risk of neonatal death (Chen et al., 2014). Over 98% of all newborns in the United States achieve a 5-minute score of 7 to 10, indicating good health (Martin et al., 2013).

TABLE 3.1 ■ Apgar Scale

Indicator	Rating (Absence–Presence)		
	0	1	2
Appearance (color)	Blue	Pink body, blue extremities	Pink
Pulse (heart rate)	Absent	Slow (below 100)	Rapid (over 100)
Grimace (reflex irritability)	No response	Grimace	Coughing, crying
Activity (muscle tone)	Limp	Weak and inactive	Active and strong
Respiration (breathing)	Absent	Irregular and slow	Crying, good

Source: Apgar, V. (1953). A proposal for a new method of evaluation in the newborn infant. *Current Research in Anesthesia and Analgesia, 32,* 260–267.

The **Brazelton Neonatal Behavioral Assessment Scale (NBAS)** is a neurobehavioral assessment commonly administered to newborns, especially those who are considered to be at risk (Bartram et al., 2015). It is administered in the first few days after birth to assess the newborn's neurological competence as indicated by the responsiveness to the physical and social environment, perception, and motor skills such as activity level and the ability to bring a hand to the mouth (Nugent, 2013). The NBAS also assesses infants' attention and state changes, including excitability and ability to settle down after being upset. When parents observe and participate in their baby's NBAS screening, they learn about their newborn's perceptual and behavioral capacities and are better able to elicit gazes, quiet fussiness, and tend to be more responsive to their infants (Benzies et al., 2013).

Low Birth Weight and Preterm Infants

About 9% of infants in the United States each year are born with low birth weight, and over 10% are born preterm (Osterman et al., 2023). Infants are classified as **low birthweight** when they weigh less than 2,500 grams (5.5 pounds) at birth; *very low birth weight* refers to a weight less than 1,500 grams (3.5 pounds), and *extremely low birth weight* refers to a weight less than 750 grams (1 lb., 10 oz.). Some low birth weight infants are **preterm** (premature, less than 37 weeks of gestation), or **small for date**, full term but have experienced slow growth and are smaller than expected for their gestational age. Low birth weight infants are at risk for a variety of developmental problems. Indeed, their very survival is far from certain. Low birth weight is the second leading cause of infant mortality (Ahmad et al., 2022).

Characteristics of Low Birth Weight Infants

Many low birth weight infants are diagnosed with respiratory distress syndrome, a condition in which the infant's lungs are not fully developed and cannot provide enough oxygen, leading to erratic breathing and lapses in breathing (Charles et al., 2018). These infants require intensive care and are typically placed in Isolettes that protect them, regulate their body temperature, aid their breathing with the use of respirators, and prevent infection.

Low birth weight infants are at a higher risk for developmental and health problems that correspond closely to their birth weight, with extremely low birth weight infants suffering the greatest problems (Pascal et al., 2018). These problems can include poor growth, cerebral palsy, seizure disorders, neurological difficulties, respiratory problems, and illness (Vollmer & Edmonds, 2019, 2019)

As children and adolescents individuals born low birth weight may show problems with attention, hyperactivity, and cognitive and social problems that may persist into adulthood (Eves et al., 2020; Franz et al., 2018; Jaekel et al., 2018). These problems can make it difficult for low birth weight individuals to interact and respond to stimulation appropriately leading to poor social competence and poor peer relationships, including peer rejection and victimization in childhood and adolescence (Reyes et al., 2021; Ritchie et al., 2018). As adults, low birth weight individuals may be less socially engaged, show poor communication skills, and score high on measures of anxiety (Lærum et al., 2019;

Weider et al., 2023). They may also show accelerated biological aging, posing lifelong risks for health and mortality (van Lieshout et al., 2021)

Parenting a low birth weight infant is stressful because these infants are often easily overwhelmed by stimulation and difficult to soothe (Gardon et al., 2019). Low birth weight infants are often slow to initiate social interactions and look away from adults, resisting adults' attempts to attract their attention (Provasi, 2019). For these reasons adults may find providing sensitive care to low birth weight infants challenging and the infants are at risk to form insecure attachment to their parents (Fuertes et al., 2022; Wolke et al., 2014). Low birth weight infants experience higher rates of child abuse, not only because of their special needs but also because the risk factors for low birth weight, such as prenatal exposure to substances or maternal illness, are also associated with abuse (Cicchetti & Toth, 2015; Puls et al., 2019). Indeed, low SES, a risk factor for low birth weight, may accentuate the childhood cognitive and socioemotional outcomes associated with low birth weight (Hines et al., 2020).

Race, SES, and Low Birth Weight

Socioeconomic disadvantage, race, and low birth weight are complexly interwoven in the United States. In 2021, non-Hispanic Black infants were twice as likely to be born low birth weight (15%) than non-Hispanic White and Hispanic infants (7% and 8%, respectively; Osterman et al., 2023). SES plays a role in these differences, but it is not the whole story, because other factors such as financial and relationship stresses and the experience of racism and discrimination also contribute (Almeida et al., 2018). For example, in a study of over 10,000 Californian women, the most economically disadvantaged Black and White women showed similar low birth weight rates, but increases in income were more strongly associated with improvement in low birth weight rates among White than Black women (Braveman et al., 2015). As SES advantage increased for both White and Black women, the racial disparity in low birth weight outcomes grew. Racial differences in low birth weight are not a function only of income, but also by other factors such as the experience of racism and discrimination (Ncube et al., 2016; Ramraj et al., 2020).

In international comparisons SES has been found to be most strongly linked with low birth weight in the United States, where health care is privatized (Martinson & Reichman, 2016). In a study of five North American cities (Baltimore, Boston, Chicago, Philadelphia, and Toronto, Canada), unemployment and living in a racial or ethnically segregated community were strongly associated with low birth weight in the four U.S. cities, but not in Toronto, where health care is readily available to all (De Maio et al., 2020). Although this study points to the role of health care access in birth outcomes, Black women may have different racial experiences in Canada and the United States. Differences in discrimination, racism, and perceived stress may also play a role in these differing birth outcomes.

Caring for Low Birth Weight Infants

Sensitive caregiving helps low birth weight infants adjust and thrive. One popular and effective intervention known as **kangaroo care** involves skin-to-skin contact between infant and caregiver (Cunningham et al., 2021). The infant is placed upright against the caregiver's chest, under the shirt. As the caregiver goes about daily activities, the infant remains warm and close, hears the voice and heartbeat, smells the body, and feels constant skin-to-skin contact. Babies who receive early and consistent kangaroo care grow more quickly, sleep better, score higher on measures of health, and show more cognitive gains throughout the first year of life (Boundy et al., 2016; Sharma et al., 2019). Kangaroo care is so effective that the majority of hospitals in the United States offer kangaroo care to preterm infants.

Caregiver responses to having a low birth weight infant influence the child's long-term health outcomes, independently of perinatal risk, suggesting that the parenting context is an important influence on infant health (Pierrehumbert et al., 2003; Provasi, 2019). Interventions to promote the development of low birth weight children help caregivers learn coping strategies for interacting with their infants and managing caregiving stress (Boundy et al., 2016; S. M. Chang et al., 2015). When caregivers have knowledge about child development, are involved with their children, and create a stimulating home environment, low birth weight infants tend to have good long-term outcomes and may even catch up to their peers (Jaekel et al., 2015; Lynch & Gibbs, 2017). Sensitive parenting, in which caregivers respond appropriately to the needs and emotions of their children, has a positive impact on the development of low birth weight infants. Low birth weight infants exposed to sensitive parenting may show executive functioning and academic performance similar to normal weight peers, but those exposed to below average levels of sensitive parenting may show lasting deficits (Camerota et al., 2015; Jaekel et al., 2015). Therefore, interventions that focus on parenting skills and support for parents may be effective in promoting healthy development in low birth weight children.

> **THINKING IN CONTEXT 3.4**
>
> 1. Suppose you are planning to give birth. What do you consider in creating a birth plan? Evaluate birth settings and birthing options. What would you choose? Why?
> 2. Recall from Chapter 1 that children play an active role in their own development. How might children born preterm or with low birth weight illustrate this concept? How can contextual factors—the people and places with which preterm and low birth weight infants interact—influence their development, helping them overcome birth disadvantages?

THE NEWBORN

> **3.5** Discuss newborns' ability to sense and learn about the world.

The average newborn is about 20 inches long and weighs about 7.5 pounds. Boys tend to be slightly longer and heavier than girls. Newborns have distinctive features, including a large head (about one quarter of body length) that is often long and misshapen from passing through the birth canal. The newborn's skull bones are not yet fused and will not be until about 18 months of age, allowing the bones to move and the head to mold to the birth canal to facilitate its passage. As a result, the newborn's head may appear misshapen at birth.

A healthy newborn is red-skinned and wrinkly at birth; skin that is bluish in color indicates that the newborn has experienced oxygen deprivation. In such cases, the medical team must quickly provide oxygen and if needed address problems. Some babies emerge covered with *lanugo*, the fuzzy hair that protects the skin in the womb, while others lose their lanugo before birth. The newborn's body is also covered with *vernix caseosa*, a white waxy substance that protects against infection and dries up within the first few days. While many hospital staff wash the vernix caseosa away after birth, research suggests that it is a naturally occurring barrier to infection and should be retained at birth (Jha et al., 2015; Nishijima et al., 2019).

Perceptual Capacities

Until recent decades, it was widely believed that the newborn was perceptually immature—blind and deaf at birth. Developmental researchers now know that the newborn is more perceptually competent than previously imagined. Both taste and smell are well developed at birth. Taste appears to function before birth because research has shown that fetuses swallow sweetened amniotic fluid more quickly than bitter fluid (Ventura & Worobey, 2013). Newborns can discriminate smells and calm in response to familiar smells like the scent of amniotic fluid and their mother's milk (Neshat et al., 2016; Rotstein et al., 2015) The visual capacities of the newborn are more limited and focused primarily on the near environment. Newborn vision is blurry and best at about 18 inches away—the typical distance to a parent's face when holding the infant.

The most impressive newborn capacities for perception and learning are related to hearing. Pregnant women often report that they notice fetal movements in response to loud sounds like a car horn or a door slamming. The fetus responds to auditory stimulation as early as 23 to 25 weeks after conception (Hepper, 2015). By 32 to 34 weeks, the fetus responds to the mother's voice as indicated by a change in heart rate (Hibiya-Motegi et al., 2020; Kisilevsky & Hains, 2011). Before birth, the fetus can discriminate voices and speech sounds and even language features like the rhythm and patterns of poetry (Draganova et al., 2018; Ghio et al., 2021). At birth, newborns show preferences for speech sounds, their mother's voice, their native language, and even stories and music heard prenatally (Moon et al., 1993). Moreover, from birth, newborns are active listeners, paying attention to sounds and naturally taking advantage of opportunities to learn (Vouloumanos et al., 2010).

States of Arousal

Newborns have regular cycles of eating, elimination, and different **states of arousal** or wakefulness. In a typical day, newborns move in and out of six infant states or levels of arousal, as shown in Table 3.2 Most newborns spend about 70% of their time sleeping and wake every 2 to 3 hours. These periods of sleep alternate with shorter periods of wakefulness, which are mainly dedicated to feeding. During the first month, infants often move rapidly from one state to another, falling asleep while feeding. Naps are broken up by periods of drowsiness, alert and unalert activity, and crying.

TABLE 3.2 Newborn States of Arousal

State	Description	Daily Duration in Newborns
Regular sleep	Being fully asleep with little or no body movement. The eyes are closed with no eye movements. The face is relaxed, and breathing is slow and regular.	8–9 hours
Active sleep	Facial grimaces, limb movements, occasional stirring, and eye movement behind closed lids indicate rapid eye movement (REM) sleep. Breathing is irregular.	8–9 hours
Drowsiness	Falling asleep or waking up, eyes open and closed and have a glazed look. Breathing is even but faster than in regular sleep.	Varies
Quiet alertness	Eyes are open and attentive, exploring the world; the body is relatively inactive. Breathing is even.	2–3 hours
Waking activity	Frequent bursts of uncoordinated activity. Breathing is irregular; the face may be relaxed or tense. Fussiness and crying may occur.	1–4 hours

Sources: Prechtl, H. F. R. (1974). The behavioural states of the newborn infant (a review). *Brain Research, 76*(2), 185–212. https://doi.org/10.1016/0006-8993(74)90454-5; Wolff, P. H. (1966). The causes, controls and organization of behavior in the neonate. *Psychological Issues Monograph Series, 5*(1), 1–105.

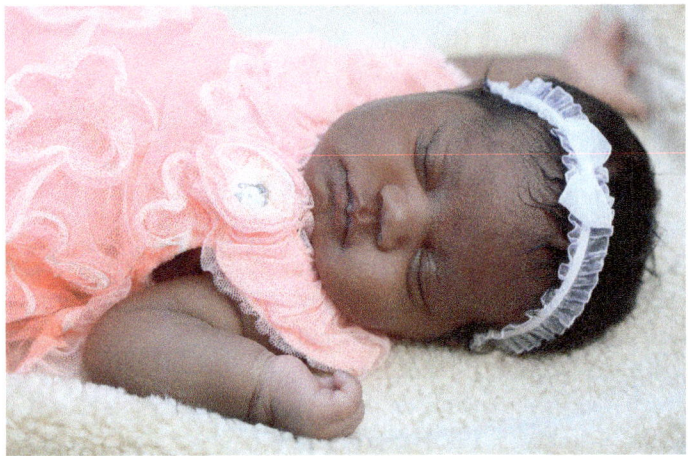

One hypothesis for infants' increased time in sleep is that it provides stimulation and promotes brain development.

Imagesbybarbara/istock

Newborn sleep cycles are brief, lasting from 45 minutes to 2 to 3 hours but are similar to those of adults in that they consist of both **rapid eye movement (REM) sleep** and non-REM sleep (Korotchikova et al., 2016). When a person is in REM sleep, the brain wave activity is remarkably similar to that of the waking state. The eyes move back and forth beneath closed lids; heart rate, blood pressure, and breathing are uneven; and there are slight body movements. REM sleep is associated with dreaming in both children and adults. Neonates spend most of their time, about 18 hours, sleeping each day, half of which is spent in REM sleep, and therefore spend little time in the active alert state in which they get stimulation from the environment (Blumberg et al., 2020; De Beritto, 2020). By ages 3 to 5, children spend about 15% to 20% of their sleep in REM, similar to adults (Grigg-Damberger & Wolfe, 2017; Kobayashi et al., 2004).

Why do newborns spend so much time in REM sleep? REM is a way that the brain stimulates itself, which is important for brain development (Grigg-Damberger & Wolfe, 2017; Wolfe & Ralls, 2019). This view is supported by findings that fetuses and preterm babies, who are even less able to take advantage of external stimulation than are newborns, spend even more time in REM sleep (De Beritto, 2020). In addition, neonates with low REM sleep activity tend to score lower on mental tests at 6 months of age (Arditi-Babchuk et al., 2009). It is clear that sleep serves an important role in fetal and newborn development.

Reflexes

Newborns may seem helpless, but they are innately equipped to respond to the stimulation they encounter in the world. The earliest ways in which infants adapt are through **reflexes**, involuntary and automatic responses to stimuli such as touch, light, and sound. Each reflex has its developmental course (Payne & Isaacs, 2020). Some reflexes disappear early and others persist throughout life (see Table 3.3).

TABLE 3.3 ■ Newborn Reflexes		
Name of Reflex	**Response**	**Developmental Course**
Palmar grasp	Curl fingers around objects that touch the palm	Birth to about 4 months, when it is replaced by voluntary grasp
Rooting	Turn head and tongue toward stimulus when cheek is touched	Disappears over first few weeks of life and is replaced by voluntary head movement
Sucking	Suck on objects placed into the mouth	Birth to about 6 months
Moro	Startle response in reaction to loud noise or sudden change in the position of the head, results in throwing out arms, arching the back, and bringing the arms together as if to grasp something	Birth to about 5 to 7 months
Babinski	Fans and curls the toes in response to stroking the bottom of the foot	Birth to about 8 to 12 months
Stepping	Makes stepping movements as if to walk when held upright with feet touching a flat surface	Birth to about 2 to 3 months
Swimming	Holds breath and moves arms and legs, as if to swim, when placed in water	Birth to about 4 to 6 months

Infants show individual differences in how reflexes are displayed, specifically the intensity of the response. Preterm newborns, for example, show reflexes suggesting a more immature neurological system than full-term newborns (Lomax, 2021). The absence of reflexes may signal neurological deficits.

Early Learning Capacities

Can newborns learn? If we define learning as changing behavior in response to experience, certainly: Animals and even insects learn. Although infants were once believed to be born incapable of sensing and understanding the physical world around them, we now know that they have powerful capacities for learning.

Habituation

Less than 1 day old, cradled next to his mother in the hospital maternity center, Caleb is already displaying the earliest form of learning. He no longer cries each time he hears the loud beep made by the machine that reads his mother's blood pressure. This type of learning is called **habituation**; it occurs when repeated exposure to a stimulus results in the gradual decrease in response (such as in intensity, frequency, or duration) (see Figure 3.8). A fetus may demonstrate habituation as early as 22 to 24 weeks' gestation (Hepper, 2015). Twenty-seven- to 36-week-old fetuses initially respond to vibration and auditory stimuli, such as the sound of a tone. The response declines after repeated exposure, demonstrating

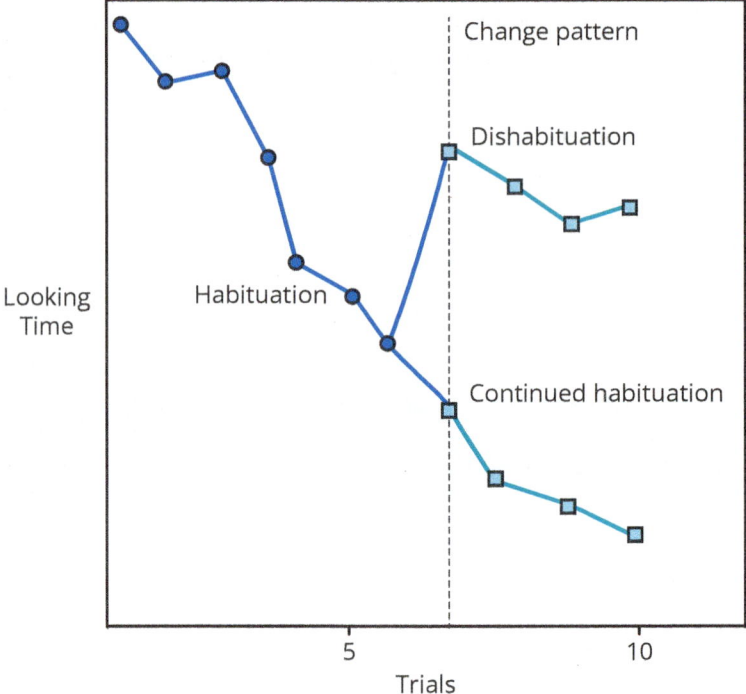

FIGURE 3.8 ■ Habituation

Looking time declines with each trial as the infant habituates to the pattern. Dishabituation, renewed interest, signifies that the infant detects a change in stimulus pattern.

habituation (Muenssinger et al., 2013; Sicard-Cras et al., 2022). Not only can the fetus habituate to stimuli but it also can recall a stimulus for at least 24 hours (van Heteren et al., 2000).

Habituation improves with age, both before and after birth, and is thought to be related to the development of the prefrontal cortex (Nakano et al., 2009). Fetuses with more mature nervous systems habituate more quickly than do those with less well-developed nervous systems, even at the same gestational age (Morokuma et al., 2004). Younger infants and those with low birth weight require more time to habituate than do older and more fully developed infants (Kavšek, 2013; Kavšek & Bornstein, 2010). As the brain matures, infants process information more quickly and learn more about stimuli in fewer exposures. Five- to 12-month-old babies habituate quickly—even after just a few seconds of sustained attention—and in some cases, they can recall the stimulus for weeks, such as recalling faces that they have encountered for brief periods of time (Richards, 1997).

In addition to developmental changes, that are also individual differences in habituation. Some infants habituate quickly and recall what they have learned for a long time. Others require many more exposures to habituate and quickly forget what they have learned. The speed at which infants habituate is associated with cognitive development when they grow older (Sicard-Cras et al., 2022). Fetal habituation predicts measures of information processing ability at 6 months of age (Gaultney & Gingras, 2005). Infants who habituate quickly during the first 6 to 8 months of life tend to show more advanced capacities to learn and use language during the second year of life (Tamis-LeMonda & Bornstein, 1989). Rapid habituation is also associated with higher scores on intelligence tests in childhood (Kavšek, 2004).

Classical Conditioning

In addition to their capacity to learn by habituation, infants are born with a second powerful tool for learning. They can learn through association. Classical conditioning is a form of learning that occurs when an individual associates a neutral stimulus with an unconditioned stimulus that naturally evokes a response. After repeated exposure to the neutral stimulus paired with the unconditioned stimulus the neutral stimulus (now called the conditioned stimulus) evokes the same response as the unconditioned stimulus.

Newborns can demonstrate classical conditioning. For example, 2-hour-old infants were conditioned to suck in response to having their heads stroked when the stroking was paired with the taste of sugar water (Blass et al., 1984). Let's look at this example more closely. Sugar water is an unconditioned stimulus because it naturally evokes the unconditioned response of sucking in infants. Touching or stroking the forehead yielded no response from the 2-hour-old infants; it was a neutral stimulus. When the researcher paired the neutral stimulus (stroking) with the unconditioned stimulus (sugar water), infants soon showed the conditioned response. That is, they associated the stroking with sugar water and thereby responded to the stroke with sucking movements.

Similarly, Lipsitt and Kaye (1964) demonstrated that 2- and 3-day-old infants were able to associate a tone with a nipple and make sucking movements at the sound of the tone. Sleeping neonates can be conditioned to respond to a puff of air to the eye (Tarullo et al., 2016). Even premature infants can demonstrate classical conditioning, although at slower rates than full-term infants (Herbert et al., 2004). Research with chimpanzee fetuses has shown that they display classical conditioning before birth (Kawai, 2010). It is likely that the human fetus can as well.

Newborns tend to require repeated exposures to conditioning stimuli because they process information slowly (Little et al., 1984). As infants grow older, classical conditioning occurs more quickly and to a broader range of stimuli. In a classic study, Watson and Raynor (1920) were able to condition an 11-month-old boy known as Little Albert to show fear in response to a white rat by pairing the rat with a loud noise. Repeated pairings of the white rat with the loud noise made Albert cry; in time, Albert began to cry even when the rat was presented without the noise. This study demonstrated that emotional responses can be classically conditioned. Our capacities to learn through classical conditioning are evident at birth—and persist throughout life.

Operant Conditioning

At birth, babies can learn from experience. Operant conditioning is a type of learning in which behavior is modified by the consequences that follow it. Behaviors increase when they are followed by reinforcement, something that is experienced as pleasurable, and decrease when they are followed by punishment, something unpleasant. In one experiment, researchers played a recording of a newborn's mother's voice when that newborn either increased or decreased its rate of sucking on a pacifier. They then found that the newborns would change their rate of sucking to the level at which they heard the recording, increasing or decreasing the rate of sucking to hear their mothers' voice again (reinforcement) (Moon et al., 1993). Newborns will also change their rate of sucking to see visual designs or hear human voices that they find pleasing (Floccia et al., 1997). Premature infants and even third-trimester fetuses can be operantly conditioned (Thoman & Ingersoll, 1993). A 35-week-old fetus will change its rate of kicking in response to hearing the father talk against the mother's abdomen (Dziewolska & Cautilli, 2006).

As infants develop, they are able to process information more quickly and require fewer pairings of a behavior with a consequence to demonstrate operant conditioning. For example, it takes about 200 trials for 2-day-old infants to learn to turn their heads in response to a nipple full of milk, but 3-month-old infants might require only about 40 trials to learn the same behavior, and 5-month-olds might require fewer than 30 trials (Papousek, 1967). Infants are born ready to learn from experience, and they get better at learning as their brains and bodies develop. In the next chapter we examine brain development and other fundamental biological processes that underlie all learning and behavior.

THINKING IN CONTEXT 3.5

Evolutionary developmental psychologists (see Chapter 1) believe that our behavior and patterns of development are adaptive and serve a purpose for our species (helping infants and children grow into healthy adults). Consider this concept in relation to the newborn's abilities.

1. How might each of the following be adaptive?
   - Newborn states of arousal
   - Newborn reflexes
   - Newborn learning
2. From your perspective, why are we born with these abilities?
3. How can parents and caregivers benefit from learning about newborns' abilities?

APPLY YOUR KNOWLEDGE

Lila and Natalie, best friends since childhood, met for a regular lunch date. Lila excitedly said, "I'm pregnant! We're having a baby!" Natalie expressed her joy for Lila and revealed that she, too, is pregnant. "We've always done everything together," Natalie said, "Why should this be different?" Over the coming months they learned about their developing babies, brainstormed baby names, and planned how to fit an infant into their cramped homes. Although best friends, Lilia and Natalie had very different careers and work settings.

Lila was a chemist who worked in a laboratory, handling various chemicals every day. While she always wore protective gear, including gloves and a lab coat, she sometimes wondered if the chemicals could affect her pregnancy. Her supervisor made sure she avoided working with any known teratogenic substances. However, there were times when Lila needed to use chemicals whose effects were unknown, and she worried about the potential impact on her baby.

Natalie, on the other hand, was a busy elementary school teacher. She spent her days surrounded by children, some of whom came to school sick. Natalie tried her best to maintain good hygiene, washing her hands frequently and using hand sanitizer. Still, she was concerned about contracting infections which could harm her developing baby. Recent outbreaks in the community included measles and rubella. Occasionally, she would also use paint or glue during art projects, and although she tried to choose nontoxic supplies, she couldn't help but worry about the possible effects.

Throughout their pregnancies Lila and Natalie sought prenatal care and their doctors conducted prenatal assessments as needed.

Finally, Lila gave birth to a healthy baby boy, while Natalie had a baby girl who appeared healthy but had a low birth weight. As they compared their experiences and looked forward to raising their children together, they couldn't help but wonder about the role teratogens and environmental influences played in their pregnancies.

1. What are some examples of teratogens and common environmental hazards for prenatal development that pregnant women might encounter in their daily lives? Compare Lila and Natalie's experience with most women's.
2. How can principles of teratology account for the variability in outcomes, such as Lila's healthy baby and Natalie's low birth weight baby?
3. What are the characteristics of low birth weight infants, and what can Natalie expect? How can she best care for her daughter?
4. Like Lila, some pregnant women work in settings that may pose risks to their developing baby. How can they balance the need to work with protecting their babies? What are some strategies that pregnant women can use to minimize exposure to workplace hazards, and what role do employers have in ensuring the safety of their employees and their developing babies? How might this vary across different professions and industries?

CHAPTER SUMMARY

3.1 Describe the three periods of prenatal development.

Fertilization occurs in the fallopian tube. During the germinal period, the zygote begins cell division and travels down the fallopian tube toward the uterus. During the embryonic period from weeks 2 to 8, all the parts of the body begin to form. From 9 weeks until birth, the fetus grows rapidly, and the organs become more complex and begin to function.

3.2 Examine the effects of teratogens on prenatal development.

Teratogens include diseases, drugs, and other agents that influence the prenatal environment to disrupt development. Generally, the effects of exposure to teratogens on prenatal development vary depending on the stage of prenatal development and dose. There are individual differences in effects; different teratogens can cause the same birth defect, a variety of birth defects can result from the same teratogen, and some teratogens show sleeper effects that are not obvious at birth or not visible until many years later. Prescription and nonprescription drugs, maternal illnesses, and smoking and alcohol use can harm the developing fetus. Environmental hazards can also affect prenatal development. Some states require reporting of prenatal substance use, but enforcement and consequences often vary with maternal demographic factors.

3.3 Consider ways in which parental characteristics and behaviors influence prenatal development.

Fetal malnutrition is associated with poor growth before and after birth. Severe stress during pregnancy also poses risks for low birth weight and premature birth, as well as a greater release of stress hormones in newborns. Women who give birth over the age of 40 are at greater risk for hypertension, preterm birth, and miscarriage, and their children are most likely to have Down syndrome. Fathers' age and behavior (such as substance use) may also increase the risk of chromosomal abnormalities and developmental disorders. Biological parents pass on epigenetic markers that can influence their offspring's health throughout life and may even be passed to their offspring's children. Prenatal care is a set of services provided to improve pregnancy outcomes. There are significant racial, ethnic, and socioeconomic disparities in prenatal care that are thought to be largely influenced by socioeconomic factors, because the ethnic groups least likely to obtain early prenatal care are also the most economically disadvantaged members of society and are most likely to live in communities with fewer health resources.

3.4 Discuss the process of childbirth and the experience of low birth weight infants.

Childbirth progresses through three stages. During the first stage, contractions cause the cervix to dilate. During the second stage, the fetus passes through the birth canal. The placenta is passed during the third stage. About one third of U.S. births are by cesarean section, a birth option chosen because of concerns for the health or safety of the mother or fetus. Newborns receive APGAR screening and often additional neonatal assessment. Low birth weight infants, whether preterm or small for date, weigh less than 2,500 grams (5.5 pounds) at birth. The prevalence of low birth weight varies with ethnicity, SES, neighborhood, and access to resources such as prenatal care. Low birth weight infants have more difficulty adapting to their environment and are at higher risk for poor growth and health, cognitive and neurological problems, and challenging relationships with caregivers. When parents are knowledgeable, involved, and create a stimulating home environment, low birth weight infants tend to have good long-term outcomes.

3.5 Discuss newborns' ability to sense and learn about the world.

Newborns can sense the world, but their abilities vary. Newborn vision is poor, but both taste and smell are well developed (Neshat et al., 2016; Rotstein et al., 2015). Hearing emerges in the womb. The fetus can discriminate voices and speech sounds and at birth; newborns show preferences for speech sounds and sounds they have heard prenatally. Newborns have regular cycles of eating and elimination and move in and out of six different states of arousal. Newborns show reflexes, involuntary and automatic responses to stimuli such as touch, light, and sound. Infants show individual differences in how reflexes are displayed, specifically the intensity of the response. The absence of reflexes may signal neurological deficits. Newborns also have powerful capacities for learning through habituation, operant conditioning and classical conditioning.

KEY TERMS

- age of viability
- amnion
- anencephaly
- Apgar scale
- blastocyst
- Brazelton Neonatal Behavioral Assessment Scale (NBAS)
- breech position
- cesarean section
- doula
- embryo
- fetal alcohol spectrum disorders
- fetal alcohol syndrome (FAS)
- fetal period
- fetus
- germinal period
- habituation
- implantation
- labor
- lanugo
- low birthweight
- kangaroo care
- midwife
- natural childbirth
- neonate
- neural tube
- placenta
- prenatal care
- prenatal development
- preterm
- REM sleep
- reflex
- sleeper effects
- small for date
- spina bifida
- states of arousal
- teratogen
- vernix caseosa

Ariel Skelley/Getty Images

4 BRAIN, PERCEPTION, AND MOTOR DEVELOPMENT

LEARNING OBJECTIVES

4.1 Describe the parts of the neuron and processes of brain development.

4.2 Discuss brain development from infancy through adolescence and the role of experience in development.

4.3 Summarize patterns of gross and fine motor development in infancy and childhood.

4.4 Compare biological and contextual influences on motor development.

4.5 Discuss sensory and perceptual development, including the concept of affordances.

Ten-month old Harper's legs wobble with determination as she lets go of the edge of the sofa and stands independently for the very first time. She gurgles with excitement. Within seconds she falls to the floor and scrambles to pull herself up and try again. Less than a year ago, Harper was a newborn barely able to control her flailing arms and legs. Now she can crawl and soon will walk. Learning to crawl, stand, and walk are developmental milestones that integrate our sensory abilities, brain development, and experience. In this chapter, we examine these processes, specifically the interrelations among brain development, motor development, and sensation and perception, during infancy and childhood.

PROCESSES OF BRAIN DEVELOPMENT

4.1 Describe the parts of the neuron and processes of brain development.

The brain is responsible for everything we think, feel, and do. It is the command center of our body. The brain is made up of billions of cells called **neurons**, specialized cells that communicate with other cells to make it possible for people to sense the world, think, move their bodies, and carry out their lives.

The Neuron

Like all other cells in our body, neurons have a cell body and nucleus that contains genes. However, neurons are unique because they are specialized to transmit and receive signals throughout the human body. Neurons have distinct structures that enable them to communicate with other cells (see Figure 4.1). **Dendrites** are the neuron's branching receptors that receive chemical messages (called **neurotransmitters**) from other neurons. These messages are converted into electrical signals and

FIGURE 4.1 ■ Neural Transmission

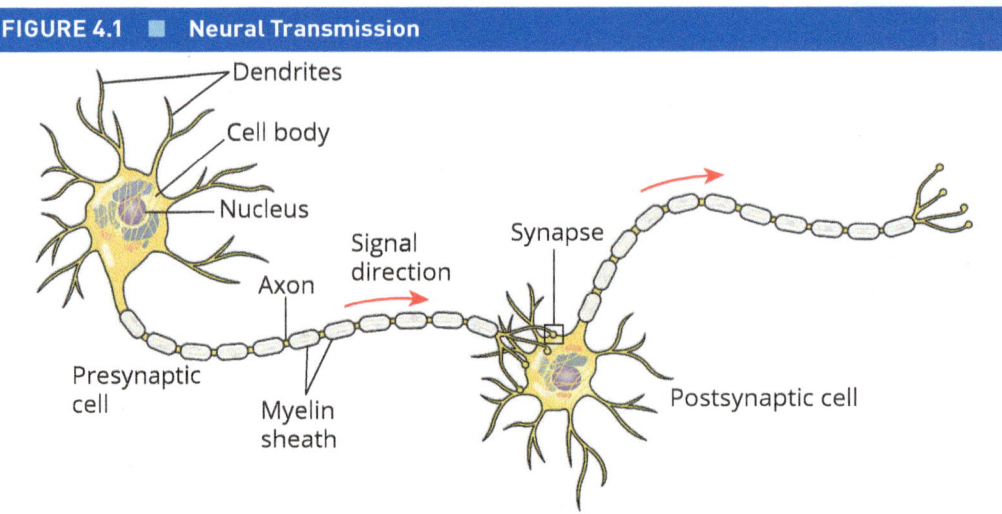

then transmitted along the axon, a long tube-like structure extending from the neuron (Harris, 2022). The axon carries electrical signals to other neurons and to muscles and organs in the body. Neurons, however, do not physically touch. They are separated by a gap called a synapse, which the electrical signal cannot cross. When the electrical signal reaches the end of the axon, the tips (called axon terminals) release neurotransmitters, chemicals that cross the synapse and bind to the dendrites of an adjacent neuron, beginning the process again (Kalat, 2024). This process is how neurons communicate with each other.

Neurons also communicate with sensory and muscle cells. Motor neurons are neurons specialized to transmit messages to muscle cells. When a motor neuron releases a neurotransmitter, the neurotransmitter binds to receptors on the muscle cell, triggering an electrical signal that causes the muscle to contract. Sensory neurons have dendrites that gather information from sensory organs, such as the eyes or ears (Kolb et al., 2023). These dendrites are called sensory receptors, and they are sensitive to specific stimuli such as light or sound. When sensory receptors are stimulated, they transmit electrical signals that trigger the release of neurotransmitters to communicate with other neurons for processing.

Each neuron is a single cell, but each neuron has thousands of synapses, comprising vast networks of interconnected neurons (Holler et al., 2021). Our brains are comprised of about 86 billion neurons that work together, sending and receiving messages to account for all that we experience, feel, think, and do (von Bartheld et al., 2016).

Neurogenesis

Brain development begins well before birth. During the 4th week of prenatal development a structure called the neural tube begins to fuse, forming the foundation for the brain and spinal cord (see Chapter 3). By about 10 weeks the first neurons are created through neurogenesis. Development occurs at an astonishing rate. Thousands of new neurons form each second (Konkel, 2018; Linderkamp & Linderkamp-Skoruppa, 2021).

Neurons are born at the center of the brain and must move to the location in the brain where they will function. This process is called migration. It relies on the work of glial cells, a second type of brain cell that outnumbers neurons (Francis & Cappello, 2021). Glial cells nourish neurons and provide a physical structure to the brain. As shown in Figure 4.2, neurons travel along glial cells to the location of the brain where they will function, often the outer layer of the brain, known as the cortex, and glial cells instruct neurons to form connections with other neurons (Kolb et al., 2023).

FIGURE 4.2 ■ Glial Cells and Neurons

Neurons migrate along the strands of glial cells.

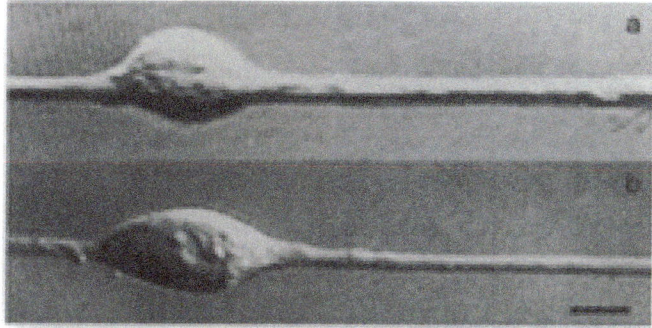
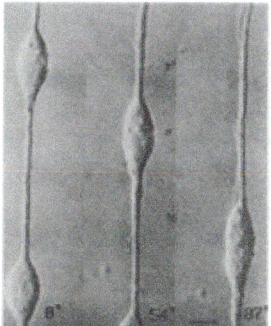
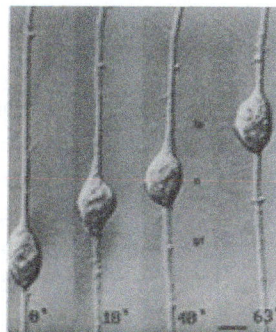

Source: Gasser, U. E., & Hatten, M. E. (1990). Central nervous system neurons migrate on astroglial fibers from heterotypic brain regions in vitro. *Proceedings of the National Academy of Sciences of the United States of America, 87*(12), 4543–4547. https://doi.org/10.1073/pnas.87.12.4543

We are born with more than 100 billion neurons, which is more than we will ever need or have at any other time in our lives. Some neurons die, but neurogenesis continues throughout life and new neurons are formed, although at a much slower pace than during prenatal development (Kolb, 2020; Lucassen et al., 2020).

Synaptogenesis and Pruning

At birth, neural networks are simple with few connections between neurons (Kolb et al., 2023). Early in infancy, the brain undergoes a rapid transformation as the dendrites grow and branch out, increasing synapses with other neurons. This process is called **synaptogenesis**. In response to exposure to stimulation from the outside world, the number of synapses rises dramatically in the first year of life, and the number of dendrites increases 500% by age 2 (Schuldiner & Yaron, 2015; Yu, 2023). Toddlers have more synapses than they will at any other point in life (see Figure 4.3). This explosion in connections in the early years means that the brain makes more connections than it needs, in preparation to receive all kinds of stimulation (Kolb, 2020).

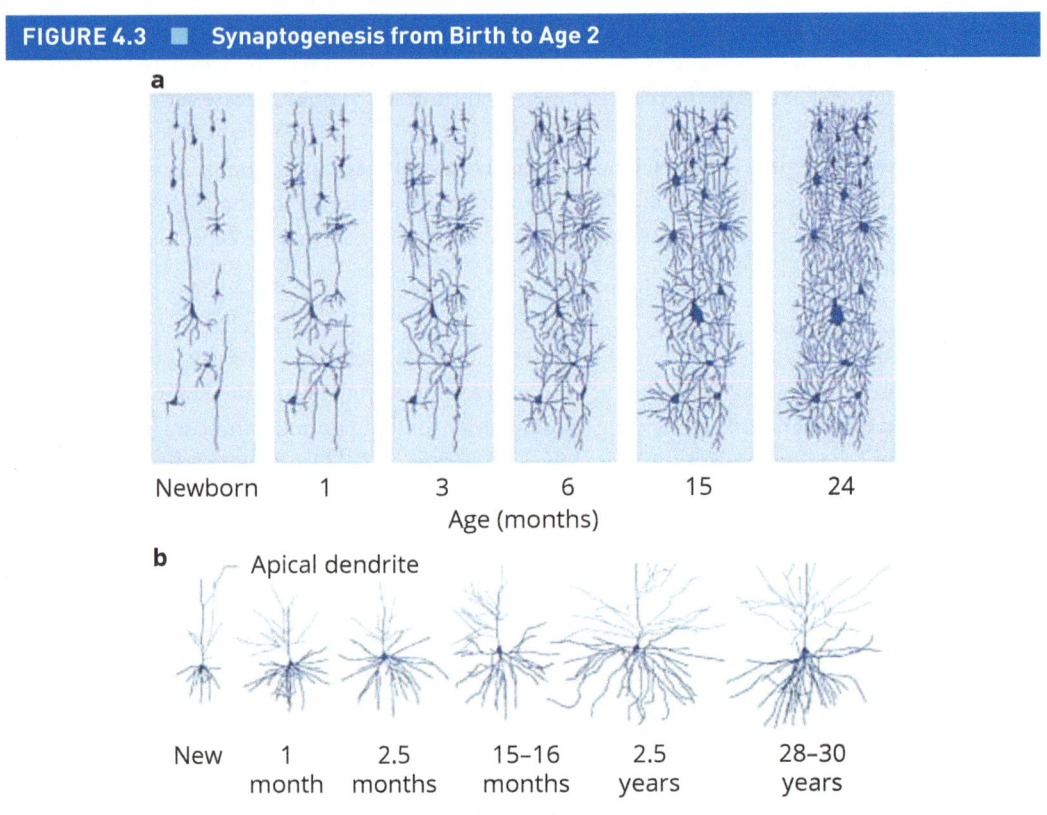

FIGURE 4.3 ■ Synaptogenesis from Birth to Age 2

Source: Adapted from Gilmore, J. H., Knickmeyer, R. C., & Gao, W. (2018). Imaging structural and functional brain development in early childhood. *Nature Reviews Neuroscience, 19*(3), 123–137. https://doi.org/10.1038/nrn.2018.1

Synaptogenesis peaks in different brain regions at different ages (Bosch-Bayard et al., 2022). During the first 5 weeks of life the most active areas of synaptogenesis are in the sensorimotor cortex and subcortical parts of the brain, which are responsible for respiration and other essential survival processes (Nielsen et al., 2023). The visual cortex develops very rapidly between 3 and 4 months and reaches peak density by 12 months of age (Natu et al., 2021; Remer et al., 2017). The prefrontal cortex, the center for higher level thinking and planning, develops more slowly and is not complete until early adulthood (Kolk & Rakic, 2022).

Cortical thickness peaks by 2 years of age, but the surface area continues to develop throughout childhood (Frangou et al., 2022; Gilmore et al., 2018). Any connections that are used become stronger, while those unused eventually shrink, atrophy, and disappear. This process of eliminating unused neural connections, called **synaptic pruning**, improves the efficiency of neural communication by removing *clutter*—excess unused connections. Little-used synapses are pruned in response to experience, an important part of neurological development that leads to quicker and more efficient thought (Bosch-Bayard et al., 2022; Yu, 2023).

Myelination

Growth of our neural networks—connections among our neurons—contributes to advances in thought and behavior. Another important process of brain development is **myelination**, in which the axons of neurons become coated with a fatty substance called myelin that is produced by glial cells (Hughes, 2021). This coating acts as an insulator, allowing electrical impulses to travel faster. Axons coated with myelin transmit neural impulses more quickly than unmyelinated axons. As a result, myelination enables faster communication among neurons, enabling quicker and more efficient neurological function and, ultimately, thought (Lebel & Deoni, 2018).

Myelination begins prenatally but accelerates after birth (Dimond et al., 2020; Gilmore et al., 2018). As myelination progresses infants and children process information more quickly, and their thoughts and behavior become faster, more coordinated, and more complex (Chevalier et al., 2015; de Faria et al., 2021). Myelination proceeds most rapidly from birth to age 4, first in the sensory and motor cortex, and then spreads to other cortical areas through childhood, continuing through adolescence and into early adulthood (Natu et al., 2021)

The Cerebral Cortex

The processes of neural development we have discussed account for the growth of the brain. In addition, neurons specialize to take on different functions. For example, as we discussed, some neurons synapse connect with sensory organs and others with muscles. The 86 billion neurons that form the adult human brain are organized into a variety of structures (see Figure 4.4; Herculano-Houzel, 2020).

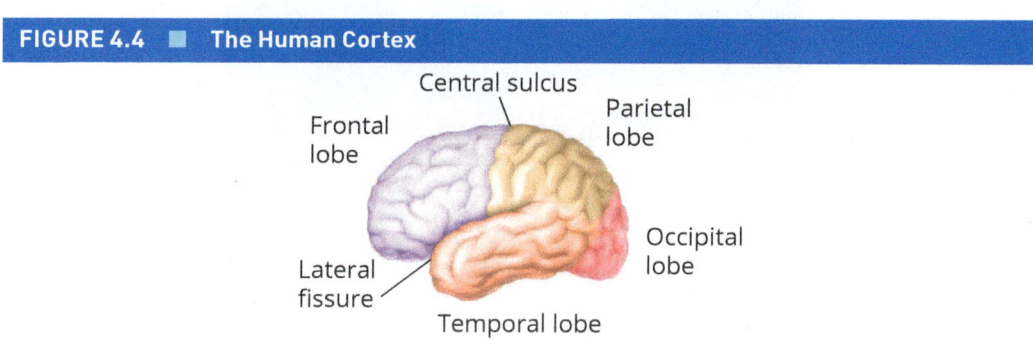

FIGURE 4.4 ■ The Human Cortex

The brain's wrinkled and folded outermost layer is known as the **cortex**. The cortex comprises about 85% of the adult brain's mass. It is comprised of different structures with differing functions, located across four lobes: frontal, temporal, parietal, and occipital.

- The frontal lobes are involved in advanced thought, planning, movement, language, and impulse control.
- The temporal lobe processes auditory information and plays a role in language and memory.
- The parietal lobe integrates sensory input, spatial location, and plays a role in motor control.
- The occipital lobe processes vision.

The four lobes progress on different developmental timetables. The sensory and motor areas tend to develop first (such as the occipital lobe's visual cortex). The frontal lobe, specifically a part called the **prefrontal cortex**, develops throughout infancy, childhood, and adolescence, maturing into early adulthood (Kolk & Rakic, 2022). The prefrontal cortex is the part of the brain responsible for the most advanced cognitive functions known as executive function, higher level thought, including planning, goal setting, controlling impulses, and using cognitive skills and memory to solve problems.

Lateralization

The human brain is divided into two halves, known as hemispheres, which are joined by a thick band of neural fibers known as the **corpus callosum** (see Figure 4.5). The four lobes are present in both hemispheres, but the hemispheres are not identical. Over the course of childhood, the brain undergoes a process called **lateralization** where the right and left hemispheres become specialized to carry out different functions (Kolb, 2020). Each hemisphere of the brain (and the parts of the brain that comprise each hemisphere) is specialized for particular tasks and becomes more specialized with experience (Bisiacchi & Cainelli, 2022). For example, in laboratory studies most adults show more neural activity in the left hemisphere when completing language tasks and in the right when completing spatial tasks.

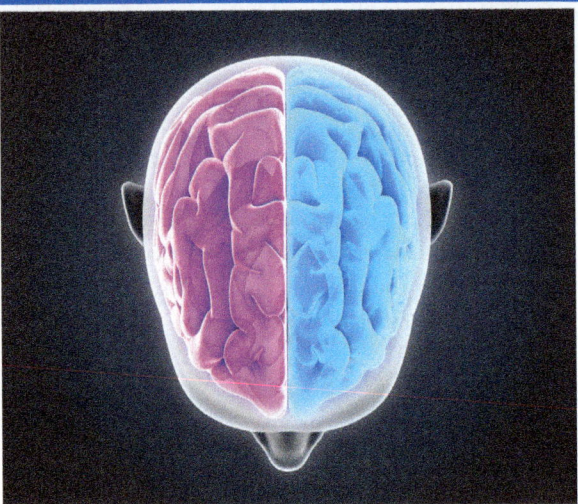

FIGURE 4.5 ■ Hemispheres

Nerthuz/istock

The process of lateralization begins before birth. In the womb, most fetuses face toward the mother's left, which allows the right side of the fetus's body to move more freely (Previc, 1991). This early movement may be one of the first signs of lateralization. Newborns tend to have slightly better hearing from their right ear (Ari-Even Roth et al., 2016). Infants generally display a hand preference, usually favoring the right, which tends to strengthen with use (G. Young, 2016). Over the course of childhood one hemisphere becomes stronger and more adept. This process is known as hemispheric dominance.

As mentioned, most adults show neural activity in their left hemisphere when completing language tasks, suggesting that language is lateralized to the left hemisphere in most adults. Children's language skills are also linked with the development of brain lateralization. Young children who perform better on language tasks use more neural pathways in the left hemisphere and fewer in the right compared to those who are less skilled in language tasks (Walton et al., 2018). Lateralization is an example of how our brains become more specialized with development. However, it is important to remember that complex thinking relies on communication from many parts of the brain on both hemispheres.

THINKING IN CONTEXT 4.1

1. "Neurons are just cells. No big deal," said Kevin. What do you think? Are neurons "just cells?" Consider how they work and what they do.
2. Over the course of our childhoods we become better thinkers, able to think faster and in more sophisticated ways. How do processes of brain development contribute to these advances?

BRAIN DEVELOPMENT

> **4.2** Discuss brain development from infancy through adolescence and the role of experience in development.

Like all parts of the body, the brain forms before birth. Networks of neurons are formed and modified through synaptogenesis and synaptic pruning. At first these networks are simple, but they quickly grow larger and more intricate. Maturation, or biological programming, determines some of this growth, but experience is the true driver of brain development.

Infancy

Exposure to stimulation in the environment—sights, sounds, smells—influences brain development throughout life, especially in infancy. Infants are born ready to learn. Every stimulus they encounter is new. Infants have more neurons than they will ever have at any other time in life, and their neural networks are pruned and shaped through experience. Infancy is said to be a **sensitive period**, an optimal time for brain development when individuals are particularly vulnerable to environmental factors (Cisneros-Franco et al., 2020b). Experience influences brain development in two ways, through experience-expectant growth and experience-dependent growth.

Experience-Expectant Brain Development

At birth we can see light and hear sound. Our brain is wired to process sensory stimuli. In fact, our brain *expects* to encounter sensory stimuli. It is ready, waiting, and *needs* to learn through processing the stimuli we encounter from our senses. The brain depends on experiencing certain basic events and stimuli at key points in time to develop normally (Hodel, 2018; Humphreys & Salo, 2020). This is called **experience-expectant brain development**.

Experience-expectant brain development is demonstrated in sensory deprivation research with animals. When animals are blindfolded and prevented from using their visual system for the first several weeks after birth, they never acquire normal vision. The connections among the neurons that transmit sensory information from the eyes to the visual cortex fail to develop and instead they decay (Hensch, 2022). If only one eye is prevented from seeing, the animal will be able to see well with one eye but will not develop binocular vision, the ability to focus two eyes together on a single object.

The human brain also expects visual experiences in infancy (Röder et al., 2021). Infants born with a congenital cataract in one eye (an opaque clouding that blocks light from reaching the retina) will lose the capacity to process visual stimuli in the affected eye if they do not receive treatment. Even with treatment, subtle differences in facial processing may remain (Maurer, 2017). Sound deprivation has similar effects on the auditory cortex (Mowery et al., 2016).

Brain organization depends on experiencing certain ordinary events early in life, such as opportunities to hear language, see the world, touch objects, and explore the environment (Hensch, 2022; Nelson & Gabard-Durnam, 2020). All infants around the world need these basic experiences during specific times in development to develop normally, and it is difficult to repair errors that are the result of severe deprivation and neglect (Humphreys & Salo, 2020; Malave et al., 2022; Nelson et al., 2019).

Experience-Dependent Brain Development

A second type of development, **experience-dependent brain development**, refers to the growth that occurs in response to learning and experience (Bick & Nelson, 2017; Humphreys & Salo, 2020). Neural networks are shaped through experience's effect on synaptic pruning. Animals raised in stimulating environments with many toys and companions to play with develop brains that are heavier and have more synapses than do those who grow up in standard laboratory conditions (Berardi et al., 2015; Kalat, 2024). Likewise, when animals raised in stimulating environments are moved to unstimulating standard laboratory conditions, their brains lose neural connections. Synapses that are not used are eliminated. This is true for humans, too.

The brain develops in response to experiences that are unique to each individual, such as playing with specific toys or participating in social interactions.
kate_sept2004/istock

Experiences such as learning to stack blocks or crawl on a slippery wood floor are unique to individual infants, and they influence what specific brain areas and functions are developed and reinforced. Experience-dependent development is the result of lifelong experiences that vary by individual based on contextual and cultural circumstances (Cisneros-Franco et al., 2020; Kolb et al., 2014). Enriching experiences, such as interactive play with toy cars and other objects that move; hands-on play with blocks, balls, and cups; and stimulating face-to-face play can all enhance children's development. For example, a longitudinal study that followed more than 350 infants from 5 to 24 months of age found that the quality of mother-infant interactions at 5 months predicted greater brain activity in the prefrontal cortex at 10 and 24 months of age (Bernier et al., 2016). These findings suggest that parenting quality contributes to brain development in infancy, specifically regions associated with executive function, including the ability to plan and engage in goal-directed behavior. In contrast, exposure to deprivation and trauma can have lasting negative effects on brain development (Malave et al., 2022).

Infants who are under-stimulated, such as those who experience maltreatment or who are reared in contexts of deprivation, such as in severely poor and understaffed international orphanages, show deficits in brain volume as well as cognitive and perceptual deficiencies that may persist into adolescence (Chan et al., 2024; Holz et al., 2023; Nelson et al., 2019). Early life adversity, such as child maltreatment, can alter brain development, increase infants' reactivity to stress, and ultimately affect their cognitive and social development (Malave et al., 2022). Subtle differences in stimulation and exposure to stressors, such as those that accompany differences in socioeconomic status (SES), also influence brain development and learning throughout infancy and childhood (Tooley et al., 2021).

Low SES and poverty are consistently associated with negative developmental outcomes through deprivation of resources, such as we have described, as well as through exposure to stress (L. W. Hyde et al., 2020; Tooley et al., 2021). Infants and children reared in poverty tend to have smaller prefrontal cortexes with altered connectivity, especially in the brain networks that support executive function, self-control, and emotion (Chad-Friedman et al., 2021; Luby et al., 2022; Nelson & Gabard-Durnam, 2020). Children reared in poverty often experience stressful events in their homes and neighborhoods that are unpredictable and uncontrollable. Exposure to stress accumulates and influences how children process stimuli in their environment. Cumulative exposure to stress alters neural circuits involved in emotion processing, fear learning, and threat detection, influencing how children's brains respond to unpredictable and uncontrollable events (Engel & Gunnar, 2020). Children show heightened vigilance and reactivity to stress, responses that shape cognitive and socioemotional development. It is not simply household poverty that influences developmental outcomes, neighborhood poverty has similar but independent effects (L. W. Hyde et al., 2022; Luby et al., 2022; Tomlinson et al., 2020). In most cases children experience poverty in the home and neighborhood with exponential effects on their development.

Childhood

During early childhood synaptogenesis continues but at a slower pace than during infancy. The increase in synapses and connections among brain regions helps the brain reach 90% of its adult weight by age 5 and 95% of its adult size by about age 6 (Dubois et al., 2013). Size, however, is deceiving because the brain will undergo substantial development and changes over the coming years. In early childhood, the greatest increases in cortical surface area in the frontal and temporal cortices, which play a role in thinking, memory, language, and planning (Gilmore et al., 2018; Norbom et al., 2021). Brain volume increases throughout middle childhood into early adolescence, especially in the prefrontal cortex (Kolk & Rakic, 2022). Located in the frontal lobe, behind the forehead, the prefrontal cortex is responsible for executive function, the highest level of thinking. Executive function plays a role in attention, working memory, reasoning, planning, and inhibition. Longitudinal research shows increases in prefrontal cortex activity between ages 3 and 7 years, specifically in the lateral prefrontal cortex, which is influential in working memory (Perlman et al., 2016).

Growth and Plasticity

Children's brains tend to grow in spurts with very rapid periods of growth followed by little growth or even reductions in volume due to synaptic pruning (Kolb, 2020; Yu, 2023). Pruning streamlines neural connections and leads to more efficient thought. The natural forming and pruning of synapses enables the human brain to demonstrate **plasticity**, the ability to change its organization and function in response to experience (Di Cristo & Chattopadhyaya, 2020). When young children were given training in music they demonstrated structural brain changes over a period of 15 months that correspond with increases in music and auditory skills (K. L. Hyde et al., 2009).

The brain retains some plasticity throughout life, but plasticity is greatest in early childhood when neurons are forming many synapses, and it declines with pruning (Fandakova & Hartley, 2020). The young child's brain can reorganize itself in response to injury in ways that the adult's brain cannot. Adults who suffered brain injuries as older infants or young children often have fewer cognitive difficulties than adults who were injured later in life. Yet the immature young brain, while offering opportunities for plasticity, is also uniquely sensitive to injury. If a part of the brain is damaged at a critical point in development, functions linked to that region can be irreversibly impaired. However, brain injuries sustained before age 2 and, in some cases, age 3 can result in more global, severe, and long-lasting deficits than those sustained later in childhood (V. A. Anderson et al., 2014; Kolb, 2022), suggesting that a reserve of neurons is needed for the brain to show plasticity. Overall, the degree to which individuals recover from an injury depends on the nature and severity of the injury, their age, their experiences after the injury, and contextual factors supporting recovery, such as interventions (Nelson et al., 2024).

Gray and White Matter

New neural connections form through experience and learning. Synaptogenesis and the accompanying rise in synaptic density are responsible for increases in **gray matter**, which are unmyelinated neurons, and cortical thickness in middle childhood (Di Cristo & Chattopadhyaya, 2020). As in earlier periods of life, unused synapses are pruned, or eliminated. Pruning and the accompanying streamlining of connectivity leads older children to show more focused brain activity on cognitive tasks, as compared with young children who tend to show diffuse patterns of activity throughout multiple parts of the brain (Yu, 2023). As children use fewer regions of the brain they free up processing capacity, leading to improvements in working memory (Abbott & Burkitt, 2023). The processes of synaptogenesis and pruning contribute to advances in information processing as new connections form among neurons and unused *clutter* is eliminated (Mills et al., 2016). Gray matter tends to increase into early adolescence when a new burst of synaptic pruning occurs.

The process of myelination in which neurons become coated with the fatty substance, myelin, continues throughout childhood. Myelinated brain tissue is known as **white matter** because myelin is white. As we have discussed, insulating neurons with myelin increases the speed of neural transmission and contributes to more efficient processing of information. As myelination continues, children's thinking becomes faster, more coordinated, and more complex (de Faria et al., 2021). Myelination occurs throughout the brain but, like synaptogenesis, it is especially prominent in the prefrontal cortex (Cafiero et al., 2019). Myelination continues throughout adolescence and into early adulthood.

Adolescence

It was once believed that brain development ended in childhood, but advances in neuroimaging have revealed that brain structure and function change dramatically during adolescence and into emerging adulthood (Guyer et al., 2023; Morris et al., 2018).

Volume Changes

Puberty is a significant event with cascading effects on development. The increases in sex hormones that accompany puberty, especially testosterone, trigger many changes in the brain. A second burst of synaptogenesis results in a rapid increase of connections among neurons and enhanced plasticity during adolescence (Laube et al., 2020; Vijayakumar, Youssef, Allen, Anderson, Efron, Hazell et al., 2021). The cerebral cortex volume increases by about 1% each year from late childhood through mid-adolescence (Tamnes & Mills, 2020). The rate of growth peaks at about 10.5 years of age in girls and 14.5 in boys (Giedd et al., 2009).

Pruning. Puberty also plays a role in synaptic pruning, which occurs at an accelerated rate during adolescence into emerging adulthood (Juraska, 2024). Synaptic pruning reduces the volume of unmyelinated brain matter and thins and molds the prefrontal cortex. These changes result in markedly more efficient neural connectivity and increase adolescents' capacity for rational thought, planning, and problem solving (Laube et al., 2020).

Similar to brain development in infancy, there are regional differences in the timing and pace of changes in brain volume during adolescence. Specifically, the prefrontal cortex and areas responsible for higher order thinking and regulation are the last to mature. These areas increase in volume and surface area in early adolescence and decrease from late adolescence through the 20s (Guyer et al., 2023; Mills et al., 2016). As unused connections are pruned, functional (used) connections strengthen (Laube et al., 2020). Collectively these changes mark adolescence as a sensitive period for brain development because only in the first years of life are there as many swift and significant changes (Fuhrmann et al., 2015; Gee, 2022).

Gray and white matter. Overall cortical volume declines with pruning, but the brain's two main types of tissue, gray and white matter, show different developmental trajectories, as shown in Figure 4.6. Gray matter reaches its greatest volume in childhood, decreases in adolescence, and stabilizes in early adulthood (Mills & Tamnes, 2024; Tamnes & Mills, 2020). Accelerated synaptic pruning in response to experience reduces the volume of gray matter and thinning and molding the prefrontal cortex during adolescence (Giedd, 2018). White matter occupies about half of the brain; it increases linearly from late childhood through adolescence and continues to develop into early adulthood (Geeraert et al., 2019; Piekarski et al., 2023). Myelination is especially prominent in the prefrontal cortex and the corpus callosum, which increases up to 20% in size during adolescence, speeding communication between the right and left hemispheres (Lebel & Deoni, 2018).

Differences in Timing

During adolescence, different parts of the brain develop at different rates, resulting in temporary imbalances in brain functioning (Tamnes & Mills, 2020). Hormones released with the onset of puberty cause a burst of development in the **limbic system**, a set of brain structures responsible for emotion (see Figure 4.7; Goddings et al., 2019; Vijayakumar, Youssef, Allen, Anderson, Efron, Mundy et al., 2021). Specifically, the amygdala, a limbic structure that plays a role in fear, learning, reward, aggression, and

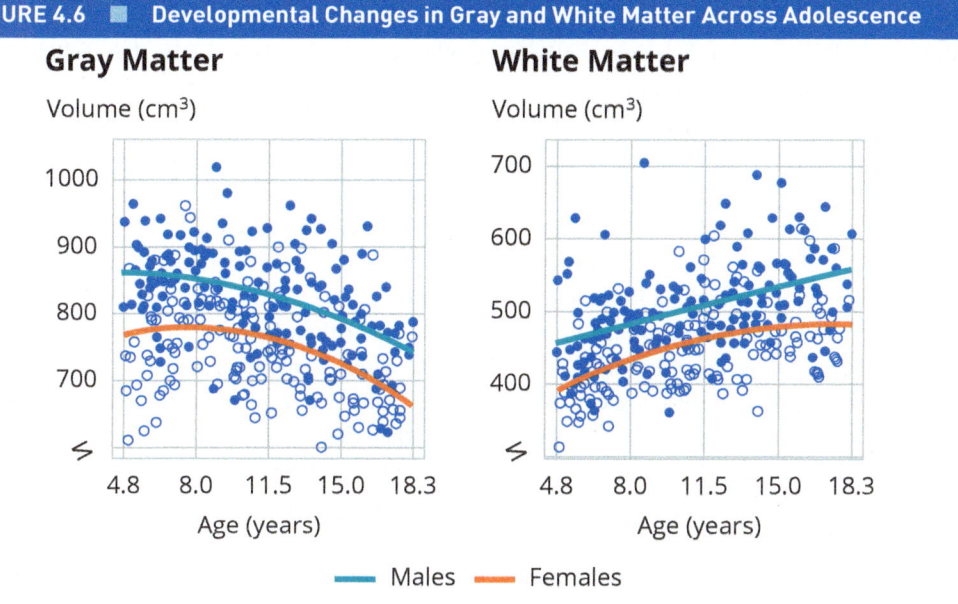

FIGURE 4.6 ■ Developmental Changes in Gray and White Matter Across Adolescence

Source: Brain Development Cooperative Group (2012). Total and regional brain volumes in a population-based normative sample from 4 to 18 years: the NIH MRI Study of Normal Brain Development. *Cerebral Cortex, 22*(1), 1–12. https://doi.org/10.1093/cercor/bhr018

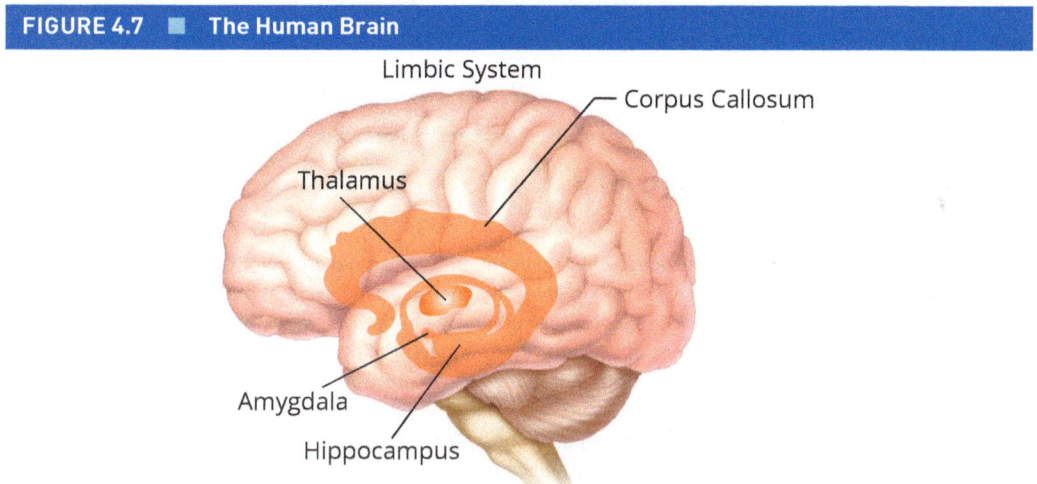

FIGURE 4.7 ■ The Human Brain

sexual behavior, reaches its peak in growth at around 12 to 14 years of age, with greater changes seen in boys (Campbell et al., 2021). The hippocampus, also a part of the limbic system, shows linear growth in adolescence, influencing learning, memory, and aspects of emotional function and stress reactivity.

In contrast, the prefrontal cortex, which is responsible for executive functioning, such as cognitive control, decision making, and planning, undergoes prolonged development that continues into emerging adulthood (Mills & Tamnes, 2024). The different developmental schedules of the limbic system and prefrontal cortex influence adolescents' behavior. When faced with emotionally arousing contexts and stimuli, adolescents tend to show exaggerated activity and connectivity in the amygdala compared to adults and fewer functional connections between the prefrontal cortex and amygdala. In everyday emotionally charged situations, adolescents experience more emotional arousal yet less cortical processing and control than adults. In these situations, adolescents' words and actions may be influenced more by their emotions than their reasoning. The different developmental timetables for these brain structures can account for many *typical* adolescent behaviors (Guyer et al., 2023; Shulman et al., 2016). The volume differences between the prefrontal cortex and parts of the limbic system during adolescence are associated with increased engagement in risk taking behavior (McIlvain et al., 2020).

Reward Sensitivity

Most adults look back on their own adolescence and recall engaging in activities that included an element of risk or were even outright dangerous, such as racing bikes off ramps to soar through the air or driving at fast speeds. Risk taking and adolescence go hand in hand, and the brain plays a large part in such behavior.

At about age 9 or 10, the balance of serotonin and dopamine, neurotransmitters associated with impulsivity, novelty seeking, and rewards, shift in the brain (Goddings et al., 2019; van Duijvenvoorde et al., 2022). Adolescents become much more sensitive to rewards—they notice them and are driven by them. Behavioral control, a function of the prefrontal cortex, is still developing. As a result, adolescents' decisions are biased toward immediate goals rather than long-term consequences (Hansen et al., 2019; van Duijvenvoorde et al., 2016). Risky situations, those that entail an element of danger, become enticing thrills (Spielberg et al., 2014). Adolescents may find themselves drawn to extreme sports, enjoying the high and element of the unknown when they direct their skateboard into the air for a daring turn. These same mechanisms, adolescents' attraction to novelty and enhanced sensitivity to immediate rewards, serve to increase their vulnerability to drugs and alcohol (Hamidullah et al., 2020; Yip et al., 2023).

Developmental shifts in risky behavior are common among adolescents around the world (Duell et al., 2018; Steinberg et al., 2018). Risky activity is thought to decline in late adolescence in part because of increases in adolescents' self-regulatory capacities and the capacities for long-term planning that accompany the maturation of the prefrontal cortex (Dumontheil, 2016; Edelson & Reyna, 2023). The shifting balance between prefrontal and limbic activity and fine-tuning of behavioral control continues into emerging adulthood (Bethlehem et al., 2022; Guyer et al., 2023). Advances in brain development have cascading effects on other areas of development, such as motor development, discussed next.

THINKING IN CONTEXT 4.2

1. How would you explain the process of brain development to a parent? What does a parent need to know? Contrast this with what you believe a teacher needs to know about brain development. How would you tailor your message to your audience, whether parent or teacher?
2. Compare and contrast patterns of brain development in infancy and adolescence. In what ways are they sensitive periods of development? How can we promote healthy development? What are the implications for parenting?
3. How might contextual factors such as parenting, relationships with peers, interactions at school, and neighborhood resources influence brain development? Through what means might SES influence brain development?

MOTOR DEVELOPMENT

4.3 Summarize patterns of gross and fine motor development in infancy and childhood.

Newborns are unable to control their flailing arms and legs. Much of their body movements are the result of reflexes, involuntary motor actions in response to environmental stimuli. Over infancy these simple responses combine and develop into complexly coordinated body movements.

Gross Motor Development

Motor skills evolve in a predictable sequence. **Gross motor development** refers to the ability to control the large movements of the body, such as the arms and legs. Gross motor movements enable us to explore our environment.

Infancy

From birth infants are driven to learn to control their little bodies. Their first gross motor milestone, or achievement, is lifting their heads while lying on their stomachs. Motor development tends to follow a **cephalocaudal pattern of development**, meaning control proceeds from the head down the body. After lifting the head, infants progress through an orderly series of motor milestones: lifting the chest, reaching for objects, rolling over, and sitting up with support (see Figure 4.8). With each milestone infants can see more and do more (Adolph & Hoch, 2019; Long et al., 2022). That is, more of their environment comes into view as infants lift their heads or roll over. Sitting and crawling enable infants to touch and interact with objects and people.

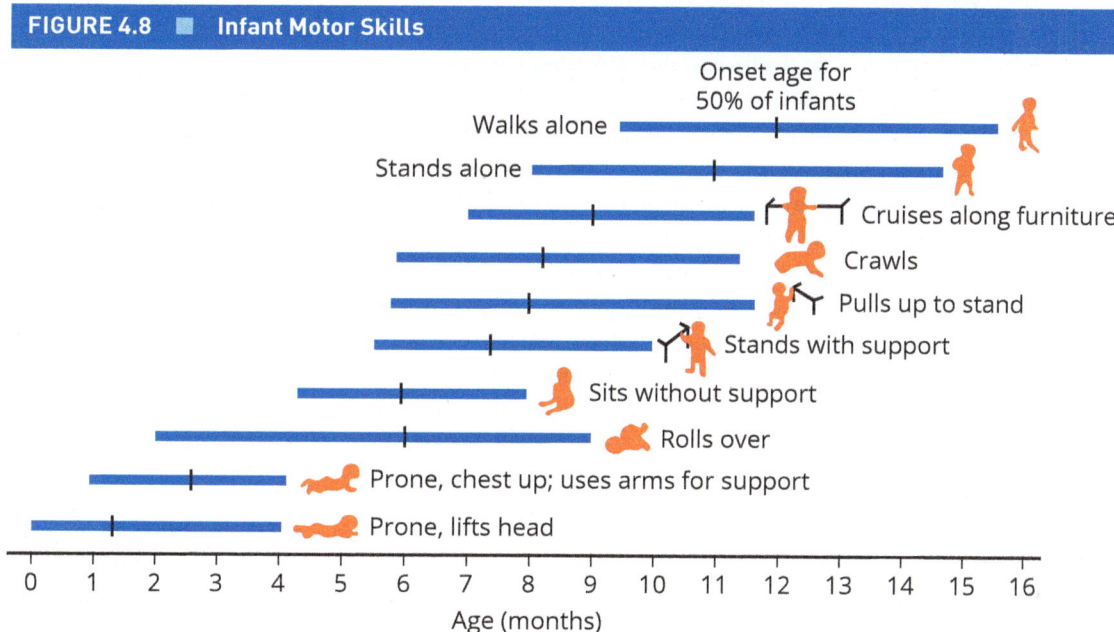

FIGURE 4.8 ■ Infant Motor Skills

Many paths. Although much of motor control proceeds from the head down, there are variations. Some infants sit up before they roll over or walk without ever crawling (Adolph & Robinson, 2015). Similarly, infants reach for toys with their feet weeks before they use their hands, suggesting that early motor development does not necessarily follow a strict cephalocaudal pattern (Galloway & Thelen, 2004).

Posture. The term posture often evokes the image of a person sitting or standing straight, without slouching. Posture is the ability to remain upright and balance. Young infants' eventual ability to raise their heads while on their stomachs is a postural milestone. It requires balance and strength to keep upright, which in this case means using the arms and torso to push up while holding the head upright. Growth, like motor development, is cephalocaudal, meaning infants' heads are disproportionately large relative to their bodies, leading them to be top-heavy. Infants' balance improves with practice.

But postural skill in one position does not translate to other postural skills. Infants who are skilled in pushing themselves up to raise their head and torso cannot immediately balance sitting up independently. Infants topple over many times before they can sit. Sitting requires leg and body strength and the ability to sense one's body position relative to the environment, which is influenced by vision as well as changes in the inner ear that adjusts balance (Kyvelidou & Stergiou, 2018). Sitting marks an important milestone in development: Infants can explore objects with both hands, which opens new opportunities for learning (Kretch et al., 2023; Marcinowski et al., 2019). Sitting, however, does not prepare infants for crawling. Infants who are skilled in sitting topple over when they attempt to crawl. They must adjust their bodies to balance in a new position (D. I. Anderson et al., 2019). Likewise skilled crawlers fall when they attempt to stand. Success in learning this new posture relies on body strength, the use of visual and auditory cues to access one's position in space, and balance.

Crawling. Crawling, moving forward on the hands and knees, usually occurs between 6 and 10 months of age. This milestone changes infants' interactions and experiences. Now infants can move toward desired objects and people, initiating interactions that promote their development (Franchak, 2020). Infants vary in how they crawl (Adolph & Franchak, 2017). Some use their arms to pull and legs to push, some use only their arms or only their legs, and others scoot on their bottoms. Once infants can pull themselves upright while holding on to a chair or table, they begin *cruising*, moving by holding on to furniture to maintain their balance while stepping sideways.

Walking. Most infants walk alone by about 1 year of age, but they take different paths toward walking (Schneider & Iverson, 2023). Some infants move quickly from crawling to walking, others spend more time cruising, and others alternate between crawling, scooting on their bottoms, and cruising before they initiate independent walking. Walking changes their entire visual field. Whereas crawling babies are more likely to look at the floor as they move, walking babies gaze straight ahead at caregivers, walls, and toys (Kretch et al., 2014).

Most beginning walkers, through about 19 months of age, tend to walk in short spurts, a few steps at a time, often ending in the middle of the floor (Hoch et al., 2020). Independent walking influences cognitive, social, and emotional development (Iverson, 2021). Infants who walk attend to and manipulate objects more than those who do not (Veldman et al., 2019). Compared with non-walkers, infants who walk have more sophisticated social interactions with their caregivers, such as directing mothers' attention to particular objects and sharing objects (Yamamoto et al., 2020). Their mothers and caregivers also use more advanced language with these infants (Schneider & Iverson, 2022; West et al., 2023). These behaviors, in turn, are associated with advanced language development relative to non-walkers in both U.S. and Chinese infants (Ghassabian et al., 2016; He et al., 2015; West & Iverson, 2021).

Childhood

Infants' motor abilities, such as skill in walking, prepare them for more elaborate feats in childhood. Children who learn to crawl early tend to show more advanced motor skills in early childhood than their late-crawling peers (Payne & Isaacs, 2025). In this way, there is continuity in motor development. Like infants, children are driven to move and to practice motor skills.

Activity and Coordination. Three-year-old children show the highest level of activity in the lifespan (Gabbard, 2021). Between the ages of 3 and 6 years, children become physically stronger, with increases in bone and muscle strength. As the parts of the brain responsible for sensory and motor skills develop, children gain balance and coordination and can run, stop suddenly and turn, jump, and climb. Complex movements, like those needed to ride a bicycle, are challenging for young children because they require controlling multiple limbs, balancing, and more. But by age 5, most children can throw and catch a ball, climb a ladder, and ride a tricycle. Some 5-year-old children can even skate or ride a bicycle (Gabbard, 2021).

During the school-age years, the gross motor skills developed in early childhood are refined and combined into more sophisticated abilities. Older children can walk heel to toe down the length of a balance beam and turn around and create elaborate jump rope routines that include twisting, turning, and hopping (Payne & Isaacs, 2025). Increases in body size, strength, and coordination contribute to advances in motor skills, which are accompanied by advances in flexibility, balance, and agility. Now children can bend their bodies to do a somersault or carry out a dance routine, balance to jump rope, demonstrate agility to run and change speed and direction rapidly, and have the strength to jump higher and throw a ball farther than ever before.

Context and opportunities for movement. Children's motor abilities unfold with maturation and experience and are also influenced by their context. Preschoolers who regularly engage in moderate to vigorous physical activity tend to show better gross motor coordination (Jones et al., 2020; Silva-Santos et al., 2019).

Children in different contexts have different opportunities to practice motor skills through vigorous physical play and other activities. SES is associated with motor development throughout childhood

(Gosselin et al., 2020; Veldman et al., 2020). SES influences children's development through differences in home and neighborhood environments, such as the availability of supports for indoor play, opportunities for outside play, access to nutrition and health resources, and the availability of caregivers to supervise play (Bellows et al., 2017; Morley et al., 2015). Caregivers' encouragement or discouragement of vigorous active play and outdoor play influences children's opportunities to practice and refine motor skills, and ultimately their gross motor competence (Barnett et al., 2016).

The activities adults favor for children and those activities children practice and master vary with cultural context. Young children of some nations can swim in rough ocean waves that many adults of other nations would not attempt. In one comparison, Brazilian children, raised in a culture that stresses spontaneous, informal, playful, and physically active behavior, tended to outperform British children in comparisons of vigorous activities such as running and jumping (Victora et al., 1990). The British children, on the other hand, immersed in a culture that tended to encourage quiet, independent, and self-contained activities that foster academic achievement, excelled in fine motor tasks compared to the Brazilian children.

Outside play offers opportunities to refine motor skills and develop coordination and strength.

vgajic/istock

Fine Motor Development

Advances in gross motor skills help children move about and develop a sense of mastery of their environment, but it is fine motor skills that permit young children to take responsibility for their own care. **Fine motor development** refers to the ability to control small movements of the fingers such as reaching and grasping. Voluntary reaching plays an important role in cognitive development because it provides new opportunities for interacting with the world. Like other motor skills, reaching and grasping begin as gross activity and are refined with time.

Infancy

Infants' fine motor skills are first displayed as *prereaching*, swinging their arms and extending them toward nearby objects (Ennouri & Bloch, 1996; von Hofsten & Rönnqvist, 1993). By 3 months, infants reach for objects and improve in accuracy, bumping objects and accidentally grasping some (Juett & Kuipers, 2019). Four-month-old infants can successfully reach for and obtain objects. At 5 months, infants can grasp moving objects. By 7 months, the arms can reach independently, and infants are able to reach for an object with one arm rather than both (Spencer et al., 2000). By 10 months, infants can reach for moving objects that change direction (Fagard et al., 2009).

Infants' early reaches and grasps are clumsy. Their hands do not yet move smoothly. Instead their hands tend to move short distances, choppily and in different directions until the object is reached. Grasping requires that infants coordinate their fingers to hold an object. At 4 months most babies use their fingers. At about 7–8 months infants begin to use their thumb and forefinger, known as the pincer grasp, to pick up small objects (Payne & Isaacs, 2025).

As they gain experience with reaching and acquiring objects, infants' attention moves away from focusing on the motor skill (like the ability to coordinate their movement to hit a mobile), to the object itself (the mobile), as well as to the events that occur before and after acquiring the object (how the mobile swings and how grabbing it stops the swinging or how batting at it makes it swing faster). In this way, infants learn about cause and how to solve simple problems.

Childhood

Fine motor skills, such as the ability to button a shirt, pour milk into a glass, assemble puzzles, and draw pictures, involve eye-hand and small muscle coordination improve with age (Bondi et al., 2022). As children get better at these skills, they become more independent and do more for themselves.

Advances in fine motor skills enable children to engage in new hobbies and creative activities.

enigma_images/istock

Many fine motor skills are difficult for young children because they involve both hands and both sides of the brain. Tying a shoelace requires attention, memory of an intricate series of hand movements, and the dexterity to perform them. Although preschoolers struggle with this task, by 5 to 6 years of age, most children can tie their shoes (Payne & Isaacs, 2025). Dexterity is associated with reasoning, and children's ability to use their fingers to aid in counting predicts their mathematical skills (Fischer et al., 2018, 2020; Martzog et al., 2019). Fine motor skills, such as the ability to copy a design, predict the cognitive skills that underlie reading and academic achievement in preschool, kindergarten, and in second grade (Cameron et al., 2012; L. Dinehart & Manfra, 2013; Suggate et al., 2019).

Advances in fine motor control enable older children to develop new interests. School-age children build model cars, braid friendship bracelets, and learn to play musical instruments—all tasks that depend on fine motor control. Such control is particularly important for penmanship. Most 6-year-old children write the alphabet, their names, and numbers in large print, making strokes with their entire arm. With development, children become able to use their wrists and fingers to write. Uppercase letters are usually mastered first; the lowercase alphabet requires smaller movements of the hand that require much practice.

By third grade, most children have the fine motor skills to write in cursive, writing using flowing strokes and connected letters. As computers are increasingly used in classrooms, writing by hand is less commonly used. Several U.S. states have eliminated cursive writing instruction in favor of keyboard instruction. The Common Core in the United States (http://www.corestandards.org) includes print handwriting in the curriculum only in kindergarten and first grade. Still, research suggests that cursive handwriting stimulates neural connections that promote learning (Chemin, 2014; Ose Askvik et al., 2020). Success in cursive writing is associated with academic achievement, especially in reading and writing (L. H. Dinehart, 2015; Semeraro et al., 2019). The ability to write with ease frees cognitive resources that can be redirected toward completing a task. Children also learn new motor skills to help them complete tasks and pursue goals.

THINKING IN CONTEXT 4.3

1. Recall from Chapter 1 that developments in one domain or area, such as motor, have implications for other areas of development. In what ways might motor development illustrate interactions among developmental domains? Give an example.
2. Developmental scientists tend to agree that development is characterized by both continuity and discontinuity (Chapter 1). Give examples from motor development that illustrate the continuous nature of development, with a gradual increase in skills. Identify examples of discontinuous, abrupt, or stage-like changes.

MOTOR DEVELOPMENT AS A DYNAMIC SYSTEM

4.4 Compare biological and contextual influences on motor development.

We have seen that motor skills tend to unfold in a predictable pattern. They are also influenced by experiences, such as opportunities to play. Recall from Chapter 1 that development is influenced by both nature and nurture, and especially the interaction between them. Motor development is the result of complex interactions among biological and contextual factors, as well as the child's goals and behavior.

Biological Influences on Motor Development

Biological factors, such as genetics, play a role in motor development. Identical twins, who share the same genes, are more similar in motor development timing and pace than fraternal twins, who share half of their genes (Smith et al., 2017). But these differences are small. Motor development unfolds with maturation, as individuals grow older. Preterm infants reach motor milestones later than do full-term infants (Boonzaaijer et al., 2021; Gabriel et al., 2009). Cross-cultural research also supports the role of maturation because infants around the world display roughly the same sequence and timing of motor milestones.

Some Native Americans and other cultural groups around the world follow a tradition of tightly swaddling infants to cradleboards. The infants are carried on their mothers' backs during nearly all waking hours for the first 6 to 12 months of their lives. Although this might lead one to expect that swaddled babies will not learn to walk as early as babies whose movements are unrestricted, studies of Hopi Native American infants have shown that swaddling has little impact on when Hopi infants initiate walking (Dennis & Dennis, 1991; Harriman & Lukosius, 1982). Such research suggests that walking is very much the result of a maturational program.

Brain development is crucial in advancing motor skills during infancy and childhood. Synaptic pruning contributes to increased motor speed and reaction time so that 11-year-old children respond twice as quickly as 5-year-old children (Payne & Isaacs, 2025). Growth of the cerebellum (responsible for balance, coordination, and some aspects of emotion and reasoning) and myelination of the cerebellum's connections to the cortex contribute to advances in gross and fine motor skills and speed (Beuriat et al., 2022; Hull, 2020). The cerebellum plays a role in learning sequences of behaviors and refining movement (Li et al., 2019). In addition, brain development improves children's ability to carry out more sophisticated motor activities that require the hands to do different things, such as throwing a ball or playing an instrument (Diamond, 2013). As infants and children gain experience coordinating their motor skills, the connectivity in motor areas of the brain becomes more focused, using fewer neural resources and freeing cognitive space (Nishiyori et al., 2016).

Practice and Motor Development

Much of motor development is driven by maturation, yet contextual factors determine children's opportunities to practice and use their motor skills. In a classic tragic example, about 60 years ago, researchers discovered institutionalized orphans from a developing country who had experienced extreme deprivation. These infants spent their first 2 years of life lying on their backs in their cribs and were never placed in sitting positions or played with; none could walk at 1 to 2 years, and fewer than half could sit up. In addition, most of the 3- to 4-year-old children could not walk well alone (Dennis, 1960). Infants raised in orphanages reach gross motor milestones, including walking, later than home-reared infants (Chaibal et al., 2016). While maturation is necessary for motor development, it is not sufficient. We must also have opportunities to practice our motor skills.

In fact, practice can enhance motor development (Lobo & Galloway, 2012). Newborns' reflexive stepping movements strengthen after practice on a treadmill (Siekerman et al., 2015). When infants practice stepping reflexes each day from 1 to 7 weeks of age, they retain the movements and walk earlier than infants who receive no practice (Vereijken & Thelen, 1997; P. R. Zelazo, 1983). Practice in sitting has a similar effect (N. A. Zelazo et al., 1993). Even 1-month-old infants given postural training showed more advanced control of their heads and necks than other infants (Lee & Galloway, 2012). Similarly, infants who spend supervised playtime on their stomachs each day reach many motor milestones, including rolling over and crawling, earlier than infants who spend little time on their stomachs (Hewitt et al., 2020; Kuo et al., 2008).

In one study, over 2 weeks, young infants received daily play experience with "sticky mittens"— Velcro-covered mitts that enabled them to pick up objects independently, before they could do so on their own (Libertus & Needham, 2010). These infants showed advances in their reaching behavior and greater visual exploration of objects. A comparison group of young infants who passively watched an adult's actions on the objects showed no change. Sticky mittens training in reaching at 3 months of age is associated with object exploration at 15 months of age, consistent with the principle that domains of development, such as motor and cognitive development, interact (Libertus et al., 2016; van den Berg & Gredebäck, 2021). Notably, some researchers suggest that sticky mittens might promote infants' attention to objects and understanding of their own and others' goal directed behavior rather than object exploration (van den Berg et al., 2022; van den Berg & Gredebäck, 2021).

Practice contributes to cross-cultural differences in infant motor development. Different cultures provide infants with different experiences and opportunities for development.

Cultural Styles of Interaction and Motor Development

Babies walk at about a year of age, but cultural and contextual circumstances can speed or delay motor development.

Jeremy van Riemsdyke/Alamy Stock Photo

In many cultures, including several in sub-Saharan Africa and the West Indies, infants attain motor goals like sitting up and walking much earlier than North American infants. Among the Kipsigis of Kenya, parents seat babies in holes dug in the ground and use rolled blankets to keep babies upright in the sitting position (Keller, 2003). The Kipsigis help their babies practice walking at 2 to 3 months of age by holding their hands, putting them on the floor, and moving them slowly forward. Notably, Kipsigis mothers do not encourage their infants to crawl. They view crawling as dangerous because it exposes the child to dirt, insects, and the dangers of fire pits and roaming animals. Crawling is, therefore, virtually nonexistent in Kipsigis infants (Super & Harkness, 2015).

Infants from many sub-Saharan villages, such as the !Kung San, Gusii, and Wolof, are also trained to sit using holes or containers for support and are often held upright and bounced up and down, a social interaction practice that contributes to earlier walking (Lohaus et al., 2011). In some of these cultures, caregivers encourage walking by setting up two parallel bamboo poles that infants can hold on to with both hands, learning balance and stepping skills (Keller, 2003). Similarly, mothers in Jamaica and other parts of the West Indies use a formal handling routine to exercise their babies' muscles, and promote and facilitate early motor behaviors such as standing (Dziewolska & Cautilli, 2006; Hopkins, 1991; Hopkins & Westra, 1989, 1990).

Infants' motor development varies with cultural styles of interaction, such as the West's general cultural emphasis on individualism and Eastern cultures' emphasis on collectivism. In one cross-cultural study comparing infants from German and Cambodian Nso cultures, the Nso infants showed more rapid motor development overall. The Nso practice of proximity, lots of close body contact, and less object play are related to the socialization goals of fostering relationships; they also provide infants with body stimulation that fosters gross motor skills. German mothers displayed a parenting style with less body contact but more face-to-face contact and object play; these socialization practices emphasize psychological autonomy but less gross motor exploration. Nevertheless, the German infants learned how to roll from back to stomach earlier than the Nso infants, likely because Nso infants are rarely placed on their backs and are carried throughout the day (Lohaus et al., 2011).

Although practice can speed development and caregivers in many cultures provide their infants with opportunities for early motor skills, sometimes survival and success require continued dependence on caregivers and delayed motor milestones. For example, crawling may not be encouraged in potentially dangerous environments, such as those with many insects, rodents, or reptiles on the ground. The nomadic Ache of eastern Paraguay discourage their infants from crawling or moving independently. Ache infants walk at 18 to 20 months, compared with the 12-month average of North American infants (Kaplan & Dove, 1987).

Even simple aspects of the childrearing context, such as choice of clothing, can influence motor development. In the 19th century, 40% of American infants skipped crawling, possibly because the long, flowing gowns they wore impeded movement on hands and knees (Trettien, 1990). One study of 13- and 19-month-old infants compared their gait while wearing a disposable diaper, a thicker cloth diaper, and no diaper (Cole et al., 2012). Naked infants demonstrated the most sophisticated walking with fewer missteps and falls. While wearing diapers, infants walked as poorly as they would have done several weeks earlier had they been walking naked. In sum, motor development is largely maturational, but subtle differences across contexts and cultures play a role in its timing.

Dynamic Systems Theory

Motor milestones, such as crawling, may look like sudden advances, seemingly occurring overnight, but they result from infants' daily and even hourly experimentation. Recall from Chapter 1 that many developmental changes may appear stage-like or discontinuous, popping up in their completed form, but these transformations may occur gradually, reflecting continuous changes (Adolph & Hoch, 2019; Thelen, 2000). Long before infants crawl, they lift their heads, use their arms to push up from their tummies, sit while supported, and then sit independently. Lower body strength and improvements in posture enable babies to push up onto all four limbs and, eventually, rock back and forth. From a dynamic systems perspective, crawling emerges gradually as infants' bodies mature, and they experiment with combining many motor skills to move and explore their environment (Adolph et al., 2018).

Every motor behavior, such as crawling or walking, has a long history and is not a stand-alone achievement. According to dynamic systems theory (see Chapter 1), motor development reflects an interaction among developmental domains, maturation, and environment (see Figure 4.9; Adolph & Hoch, 2019; Thelen, 2000). It results from three interrelated influences: (1) physical maturation (infants' central nervous system maturation and physical capacities), (2) the infants' self-directed goals and desire to explore the world, and (3) cultural and environmental supports for exploration.

FIGURE 4.9 ■ Dynamic Systems Theory

The infant's abilities to reach out an arm, stretch, and grasp combine into coordinating reaching movements to obtain desired objects. Motor development proceeds from sitting to crawling, walking, and eventually running. All are the result of infants' blending and coordinating abilities to achieve self-chosen goals, such as obtaining toys, and all are tailored by environmental supports and challenges.

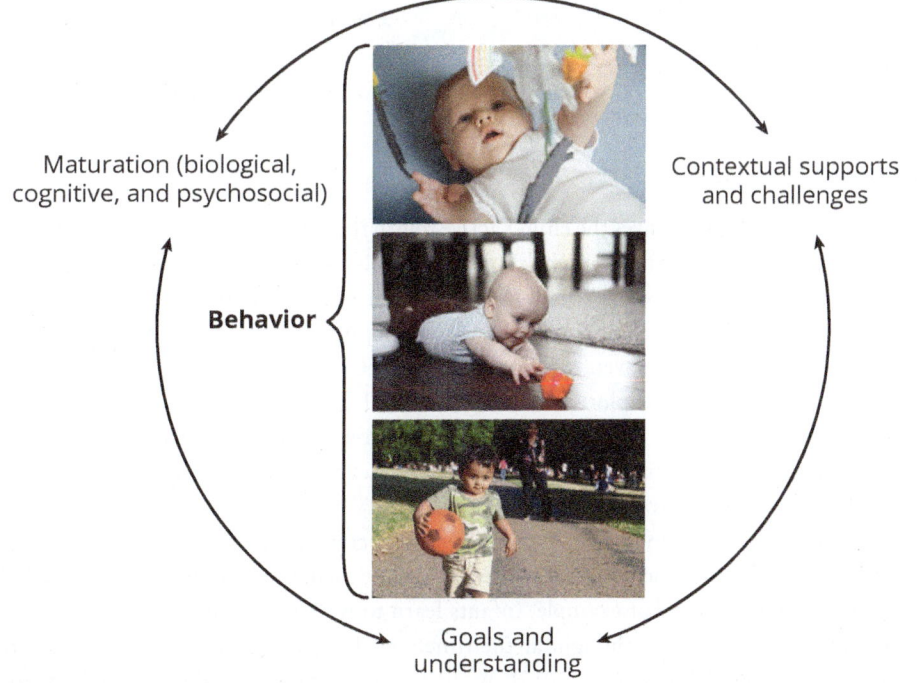

Source: Essentials Collection/istock; harishmarnad/istock

Physical Maturation and Integrated Abilities

Motor skills become more specialized, coordinated, and precise over time. Newborns flail their arms, but months later, they can coordinate reaching to successfully grasp an object with one hand without needlessly flailing the other (D'Souza et al., 2017). These changes occur gradually and entail coordinating many movements, such as sitting upright, holding the head upright, matching motor movements to vision, reaching out an arm, and grasping to obtain a desired object (Corbetta & Snapp-Childs, 2009; Spencer et al., 2000). Infants blend individual motor abilities to permit advances in movement that enable them to explore and control their environments more effectively.

Brain, muscle, and skeletal maturation contribute to motor abilities. Motor development depends on infants' muscle strength. When 40% of infants' weight is supported by a harness, they can stand for longer durations and take more independent steps and steps with one hand than when their weight is unsupported (see Figure 4.10; Kornafel et al., 2023). These findings suggest that the brain maturation needed for walking develops before the necessary muscular and skeletal strength. Practice also matters, as we have seen. Walking skill improves with experience (Hospodar et al., 2021).

FIGURE 4.10 ■ **Unweighting Infants to Discover Their Motor Skills**

Infants can stand for longer durations when their weight is supported, suggesting that the brain maturation needed for walking develops before the necessary muscular strength.

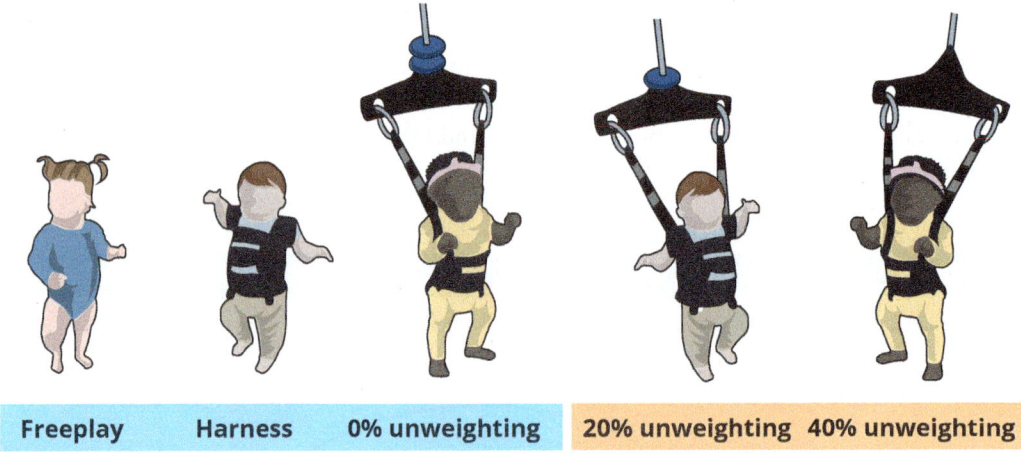

| Freeplay | Harness | 0% unweighting | 20% unweighting | 40% unweighting |

Source: Kornafel, T., Paremski, A. C., & Prosser, L. A. (2023). Unweighting infants reveals hidden motor skills. *Developmental Science, 26,* e13279. https://doi.org/10.1111/desc.13279

Goal-Directed Behavior

Dynamic systems theory emphasizes the child's active role in their development (see Chapter 1). Infants are driven to explore. They use their motor skills to accomplish something, such as picking up a toy or moving to the other side of the room. Infants combine their sensory abilities such as binocular vision and the ability to direct gaze with exploratory hand and foot movements to determine the opportunities a given surface provides for movement. For instance, when 14-month-old infants were tested on a "bridge" of varying widths, they explored the bridge first with quick glances (Kretch & Adolph, 2017). When faced with an impossibly narrow width, infants with walking experience tended to engage in more extensive and time-consuming perceptual and motor exploration, such as touching with hands and feet, to determine whether to cross it.

Infants develop and learn motor skills by revising and combining abilities and skills to fit their goals. They try out behaviors and persist at those that enable them to move closer to the goal, practicing and refining the behavior. For example, infants learn to walk by taking many steps and making many falls, but they persist even though, at the time, crawling is a much faster and more efficient means of transportation (Adolph et al., 2012). Why? Perhaps because upright posture leads to many more interesting sights, objects, and interactions. Upright infants can see and act on more of their environment with two hands free to grasp objects, making walking a very desirable goal (Adolph &

Tamis-LeMonda, 2014). Indeed, walking infants are not deterred by falls, rarely fuss in the process, and continue to practice and eventually master this new skill (Han & Adolph, 2021).

Infants also move simply to move, with no apparent object or destination in sight (Hoch et al., 2019). Infants' goals shift with their abilities and experience. At 12 months most infants have lots of experience crawling. These expert crawlers are more likely to go to a destination, such to obtain an object, than are 12-month-old infants who walk (Hoch et al., 2020). Twelve-month old novice walkers' goals may simply be to gain practice in a new posture, to become expert walkers rather than to obtain an object or reach a destination.

New motor skills provide new possibilities for exploring the environment and new interactions with caregivers that influence opportunities (Franchak, 2020). Because infants can sit independently, caregivers tend to give them more handheld toys and objects, offering new opportunities for cognitive development (Kretch et al., 2022). Infants' goals may shift toward manipulating objects and refining their motor skills to do so. Differences in caregiver interactions and caregiving environments can affect children's goals and their motor skills, including the form they take, the ages of onset, and the overall developmental trend (Adolph & Franchak, 2017).

Social and Cultural Context

According to dynamic systems theory, motor skills do not develop in isolation. They are influenced by the social and cultural contexts in which they occur. Comparisons of mother-infant pairs from six countries revealed large differences in opportunities for infant sitting and infant performance (Karasik et al., 2015). Infants from the United States, Argentina, South Korea, and Italy spent most of their sitting time in places that offered postural support, such as child furniture. In contrast, infants from Kenya and Cameroon spent most of their sitting time in places that offered little postural support, such as the ground or adult furniture, yet these infants tended to show the longest bouts of independent sitting and at the earliest age. Cultural variations in infants' experiences, like these, offer unique opportunities for posture, balance, and locomotion, which generate variation in motor skills both within and between cultures (Karasik & Robinson, 2022).

The home environment plays a critical role in motor development because each child has goals and opportunities that are specific to their particular environment (Adolph & Franchak, 2017). Infants might respond to slippery hardwood floors by crawling on their stomach rather than all fours or by shuffling their feet and hands rather than raising each. Indeed, infants' rate and duration of crawling bouts vary with flooring types. Nine- to 12-month-old infants crawl slower and less efficiently on hardwood floors, compared with carpet and a mat made of woven straw (Choi et al., 2022). Perhaps not surprisingly, simply having space to move about is associated with walking (Hoch et al., 2019). Infants and young children who live in less crowded home environments tend to engage in more spontaneous bouts of walking that contribute to gross motor skills compared to those in more crowded homes (Hospodar et al., 2021; Valadi & Gabbard, 2020).

From a dynamic systems perspective, infants are the drivers of their development. Most infants attain the same motor tasks, such as climbing downstairs, at about the same age, yet differ in how they approach the task. Some might turn around and back down, others descend on their bottoms, and others slide down face first (Berger et al., 2007). By viewing motor development as dynamic systems of action produced by an infant's physical abilities, goal-directed behavior, and environmental supports and opportunities, we can account for the individual differences that we see in motor development.

THINKING IN CONTEXT 4.4

Consider crawling or walking from a bioecological systems perspective (see Chapter 1).

1. What developmental capacities influence infants' motor abilities? Consider their physical, cognitive, and socioemotional development. How might any of these developments influence infants' crawling or walking?

2. What microsystem factors influence infants' motor development? Consider the home and other places where they interact. Consider the people who surround them. How might these influence infants' crawling or walking?
3. How might microsystem factors interact? That is, what is the mesosystem and how might that influence infants' motor development?
4. Consider the larger environment in which infants and their families are embedded, the exosystem. Identify three factors that may affect infants' motor development by affecting the mesosystem and microsystem.
5. How might macrosystem factors—culture and society at large—affect infants' development?

SENSORY AND PERCEPTUAL DEVELOPMENT

4.5 Discuss sensory and perceptual development, including the concept of affordances.

"It's amazing how much she can already sense," Marlan said, awed at the newborn in his arms. "I can't believe she's already looking right at me." "Yes, she's only a few hours old, but she can definitely see you," the nurse said smiling. Newborns are equipped with a full range of senses, ready to experience the world. They can both detect and perceive stimuli, but many of their abilities are immature relative to those of adults. Yet infants' sensory abilities develop rapidly, achieving adult levels within the first year of life (Fen, 2024).

Developmental scientists distinguish between sensation and perception. **Sensation** occurs when our senses detect a stimulus. Our senses, the eyes, ears, tongue, nostrils, and skin, convert visual, auditory, taste, olfactory (smell), and tactile (touch) stimuli into electrical impulses that travel on sensory nerves to the brain where they are processed. **Perception** refers to our brain's sense of the stimulus and our awareness of it. The main challenge of studying infants' sensory abilities is detecting them.

Methods for Studying Infant Perception

How do researchers study infant perception? The simplest method is through *preferential looking tasks* designed to determine whether infants prefer to look at one stimulus or another (Vrabič et al., 2021). In a classic study, alert babies were placed in a chamber and presented with pairs of visual stimuli while an experimenter peeked through a hole in the chamber above them to record what stimuli they looked at most (Fantz, 1961). If the group of infants looks more at one pattern than another it suggests that they can differentiate them. If they look at the pair of stimuli equally it suggests that they cannot tell the difference between them. Research using this method has shown that neonates less than 1 week of age can tell the difference between a face-like pattern, a bull's eye pattern, and a solid disk (Fantz, 1961).

Another method of studying infant perception relies on infants' capacity for habituation, a gradual decline in responding to an unchanging stimulus (see Chapter 3; Kucharský et al., 2024). A researcher examines whether an infant can discriminate between two stimuli, by presenting one until the infant habituates to it. Then a second stimulus is presented. If the infant pays attention to the second stimulus, indicating dishabituation, it suggests that the infant detects that the second stimulus is different from the first. If the infant does not react to the new stimulus, it is assumed that the infant does not perceive the difference between the two stimuli.

Operant conditioning, learning behaviors based on their consequences, is the basis for a third method researchers use to study perception in infants (Schlinger, 2022). Behaviors followed by desirable consequences (reinforcement) tend to increase, and those followed by adverse consequences (punishment) decrease. Research employing this method has shown that newborns will change their rate of sucking on a pacifier, increasing or decreasing the rate of sucking, to hear a tape recording of their mother's voice, a reinforcer (Moon et al., 1993). Other research shows that newborns will change their rate of sucking to see visual designs or hear human voices that they find pleasing (Floccia et al., 1997). Premature infants and even third trimester fetuses can be operantly conditioned (Dziewolska

& Cautilli, 2006; Thoman & Ingersoll, 1993). For example, a 35-week-old fetus will change its rate of kicking in response to hearing the father talk against the mother's abdomen, suggesting that hearing begins in the womb (Dziewolska & Cautilli, 2006).

Vision

It is impossible to know whether the fetus has a sense of vision, but as early as 28 weeks' gestation it responds to bright light directed at the mother's abdomen (Donovan et al., 2020; Reid & Dunn, 2021). At birth, vision is the least developed sense, about 40 times worse than adults, but it improves rapidly (Lewis, 2018). Preferential-looking studies can be used to detect infants' **visual acuity**, their sharpness of vision or ability to see. Infants are presented with stimuli with different frequencies of stripes (Fantz, 1961). Infants who are unable to detect the stripes lose interest in the stimulus and look away from it (see Figure 4.11). Infants reach adult levels of visual acuity between 6 months and 1 year of age.

FIGURE 4.11 ■ Visual Acuity in Infancy

Visual acuity can be tested by presenting infants with stripe patterns of varying widths: 1/8, 1/16, 1/32, and 1/64 inch alongside a gray square of the same brightness, positioned 10 inches away from the infants' eyes. Infants younger than 1 month could discern stripes as fine as 1/8 inch, indicated by preferring to look at the stripes compared to the gray square. Six-month-old infants could detect stripes as narrow as 1/64 inch, suggesting better visual acuity.

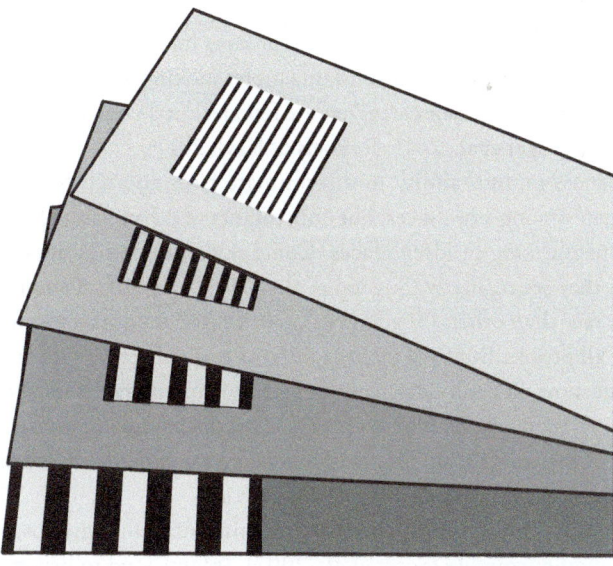

Source: Adapted from Fantz, R. L. (1961). The origin of form perception. *Scientific American, 204,* 66–72.

Newborn Visual Processing

Like acuity, visual tracking, the ability to follow an object's movement with the eyes, is limited at birth but improves quickly. By 2 months of age, infants can follow a slow-moving object smoothly; by 3 to 5 months, their eyes can dart ahead to keep pace with a fast-moving object (Agyei et al., 2016; Fen, 2024). Improvement in vision is due to the increasing maturation of the structures of the eye and the visual cortex, the part of the brain that processes visual stimuli (Weaver et al., 2015).

Newborns prefer particular visual stimuli. Rather than a plain stimulus such as a black or white oval shape, newborns prefer to look at simple patterns, such as a bullseye (Fantz, 1961). How infants explore visual stimuli changes with age (Candy & Aslin, 2020). Until about 1 month of age, infants tend to scan along the outer perimeter of stimuli, a phenomenon known as the **externality effect**. When presented with a face, the infant's gaze will scan along the hairline and not move to the eyes and mouth. Newborns recognize their mothers by their hairline, not by their facial features. By 6 to 7 weeks of age, infants study the eyes and mouth, which hold more information than the hairline, as shown in Figure 4.12 (Hunnius & Geuze, 2004).

FIGURE 4.12 ■ Externality Effect and Face Perception

The externality effect refers to a particular pattern of infant visual processing. When presented with a complex stimulus, such as a face, infants under 2 months of age tend to scan along the outer contours, such as the hairline. Older infants scan the internal features of complex images and faces, thereby processing the entire stimulus.

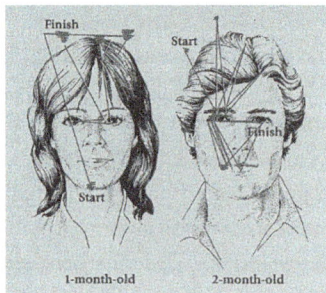

Sources: Adapted from Shaffer, D. R. (2002). *Developmental psychology: Childhood and adolescence* (6th ed., p. 190); Wadsworth/Thomson; Salapatek, P. (1973). Pattern perception in early infancy. In L. B. Cohen & P. Salapatek (Eds.), *Infant perception: From sensation to cognition* (Vol. 1, pp. 133–248). Academic Press.

Face Perception

Newborns prefer to look at faces, and the preference for faces increases with age and experience (A. W. Young, 2021). Between birth and 3 months, infants prefer looking at and can more easily distinguish female faces than male faces when their caregivers are female, but do not show similar preferences when their caregivers are male (Bayet et al., 2015; Rennels & Kayl, 2017).

Experience influences infants' ability to discriminate faces and tell them apart. Ten-month-old infants can discriminate among adult faces, but only infants who have siblings (and therefore exposure to children) discriminate among children's faces (Conte et al., 2022). Infants show similar preferences and abilities for faces they see regularly (Sugden et al., 2014). Most infants more often encounter faces that match their own race than others (Sugden et al., 2014). At 3 months, most infants equally discriminate among faces of all people. But by 9 months, infants easily discriminate among members of their own group or race but show difficulty discriminating faces among members of other groups, typically other races (Markant & Scott, 2018). This tendency is known as the other-race effect, and it increases during the first year of life, suggesting that it is dependent on experience and exposure to same- and other-race faces (Hadders-Algra, 2022; Quinn et al., 2021).

The decline in sensitivity to discriminate faces within unfamiliar groups, such as other races, is an example of **perceptual narrowing** (Scott et al., 2007). Infants tend to become less able to detect or discriminate stimuli not encountered in their environment (Singh, Rajendra et al., 2022). Specifically, babies who have more contact with other-race faces (e.g., through adoption, training, or living in racially diverse communities) show less perceptual narrowing (Bauer et al., 2023; Singh, Phneah et al., 2022).

Some researchers speculate that early perceptual differences in infancy may be associated with the emergence of implicit racial bias in childhood, but more research is needed to understand the social implications of same and other race face discrimination (Quinn et al., 2019; Waxman, 2021). However, just as early experience aids infants' abilities to discriminate faces of other races, childhood contact with members of other races can improve children's ability to distinguish other-race faces (McKone et al., 2019; Pascalis et al., 2020). Noteworthily, the research to date has not sampled diverse populations. It is unclear whether the other-race effect is common to infants in all contexts (Singh, Rajendra et al., 2022).

Color Vision

Like other aspects of vision, color vision improves with age. Newborns can detect some color, but their color vision is poor (Skelton et al., 2022). They can distinguish gray from other colors, such as red, yellow, turquoise, and orange if the stimuli are large and saturated, but they cannot distinguish gray from blue or purple (Lewis, 2018). They also cannot discriminate among colors. That is, although they can see both red and blue, for example, they do not perceive red as different from blue. Early visual experience with color is necessary for normal color perception to develop (Maule et al., 2023). By 4 months, infants process color information similar to adults. They can distinguish many more colors as well as distinctions among closely related colors. Seven-month-old infants detect color categories similar to those of adults; they can group slightly different shades (e.g., various shades of blue) into the same basic color categories as adults do (Clifford et al., 2009).

Depth Perception

Depth perception is the ability to perceive the distance of objects from each other and ourselves. Depth perception permits infants to reach for and successfully grab objects and, later, crawl without bumping into furniture. By observing that newborns prefer to look at three-dimensional objects rather than two-dimensional figures, researchers have found that infants can perceive depth at birth (Slater et al., 1984). However they do not yet have binocular vision; each eye seems to work independently, seeing off to the side but not past the nose (Lewis, 2018). Three- to 4-week-old infants blink their eyes when an object is moved toward their face, as if to hit them, suggesting that they are sensitive to depth cues (Kayed et al., 2008; Náñez & Yonas, 1994). Infants learn about depth by observing and experiencing motion.

A classic series of studies using an apparatus called the *visual cliff* demonstrated that crawling influences how infants perceive depth. The visual cliff, as shown in Figure 4.13, is a Plexiglas-covered table bisected by a plank so that one side is shallow, with a checkerboard pattern right under the glass, and the other side is deep, with the checkerboard pattern a few feet below the glass (E. J. Gibson & Walk, 1960). In this study, crawling babies readily moved from the plank to the shallow side but not to the deep side, even if coaxed by their mothers, suggesting that they perceive the difference in depth (Walk, 1968). The more crawling experience infants have, the more likely they are to refuse to cross the deep side of the visual cliff (Adolph et al., 2021; Bertenthal et al., 1984).

FIGURE 4.13 ■ Visual Cliff

Does this mean that babies cannot distinguish the shallow and deep sides of the visual cliff until they crawl? No, because even 3-month-old infants who are too young to crawl distinguish shallow from deep drops. When placed face down on the glass surface of the deep side of the visual cliff, 3-month-old infants became quieter and showed a decrease in heart rate compared with when they were placed on the shallow side of the cliff (Adolph et al., 2021; Dahl et al., 2013). The young infants can distinguish the difference between shallow and deep drops but do not yet associate fear with deep drops.

As infants gain experience crawling, their depth perception changes. Experienced crawlers rarely fall off the cliff's deep side. They expertly navigate slopes, determining which are safe. In contrast, newly walking infants tumble down the same slopes they easily traverse while crawling (Adolph &

Hoch, 2019). Infants must relearn how to navigate depth from a new position upright. Infants may avoid the deep side of the cliff not out of fear but simply because they perceive that they are unable to navigate the drop successfully; fear might be conditioned through later experiences, but infants are not naturally fearful of heights (Adolph et al., 2014).

Visual Impairment

Visual impairment, either in the form of poor vision or blindness, uniquely affects infants' development. Less than .5% of infants in the United States are identified with a visual impairment within the first year of life (Solebo et al., 2017). The most common cause is cortical visual impairment (CVI), damage to the parts of the brain responsible for vision (Flaxman et al., 2021). CVI occurs more often in preterm infants than in full-term infants. It can also result from trauma and head injuries caused by serious falls or shaken baby syndrome (serious injury caused by forcibly shaking the infant). Infants with CVI are more likely to be diagnosed with multiple disabilities, such as cerebral palsy and developmental disabilities, that influence their adjustment (Chokron & Dutton, 2023; Ozen Tunay et al., 2021).

Vision plays a critical role in cognitive development because infants' earliest exploration of the world is with their eyes. Lack of vision is associated with delayed interest in and manipulation of objects (N. Dale et al., 2017). Infants' visual impairment also affects the people around them. Parents and caregivers of infants with visual impairments experience more parenting stress than other caregivers and greater levels of anxiety and depression (Sakkalou et al., 2018). Caregivers may view infants and children with visual impairments as more challenging to interact with and raise. A child's visual impairment and caregiving needs can affect each member of the family.

In childhood, visual impairment is associated with depression and anxiety (Li et al., 2022). Children may have difficulty participating in class, in physical activities such as gym class, and making friends (Lieberman et al., 2019; Roe, 2019). The absence of light cues for day and night can interfere with sleep for children with visual impairment. As many as 90% have significant sleep problems (Wagner, 2022). Poor sleep can interfere with cognitive development. It can also affect family members, acting as an additional source of stress. Visual impairment resulting from CVI cannot be cured. Treatment focuses on providing children and families with education, support, and assistance in structuring children's homes and learning environments to help them explore and interact with others (N. J. Dale et al., 2019; McDowell, 2023).

Hearing

As noted above, the capacity to hear develops in the womb (Ghio et al., 2021). Newborns are able to hear about as well as adults (Arterberry & Bornstein, 2024). Shortly after birth, neonates can discriminate among sounds, such as tones (Hernandez-Pavon et al., 2008). By 3 days of age, infants will turn their head and eyes in the general direction of a sound, and this ability to localize sound improves over the first 6 months (Litovsky & Ashmead, 1997).

As we discuss in Chapter 9, the process of learning language begins at birth, through listening. Newborns are attentive to voices and can detect their mothers' voices. One-day-old infants prefer to hear speech sounds over similar-sounding nonspeech sounds and the preference for speech sounds persists throughout the first year of life (Issard et al., 2023; May et al., 2018). Newborns can perceive and discriminate nearly all sounds in human languages, but from birth, they prefer to hear their native language (Kisilevsky, 2016). Brain activity in the temporal and left frontal cortex in response to auditory stimuli indicates that newborns can discriminate speech patterns, such as differences in cadence among languages, suggesting an early developing neurological specialization for language (Cabrera & Lau, 2022; Zhang et al., 2022).

Touch

We know much less about the sense of touch in infants, compared with vision and hearing. In early infancy, touch, especially with the mouth, is a critical means of learning about the world (Piaget, 1952). The mouth is the first part of the body to show sensitivity to touch prenatally and remains one of the most sensitive areas to touch after birth.

It was once believed that newborns were too immature to feel pain, but we now know that the capacity to feel pain develops even before birth. In one study, fetuses as early as 24 weeks of age observed with sophisticated ultrasound technology showed facial expressions suggesting distress or pain in response to a needle prick (Reissland et al., 2013). Gentle touches, such as soft strokes or massage, reduces stress responses in both preterm and full-term infants during medical procedures (Dur et al., 2020; Fatollahzade et al., 2020). Similarly, skin-to-skin contact with a caregiver, as in kangaroo care (see Chapter 3), has an analgesic effect, reducing infants' pain response to being stuck with a needle for vaccination (Pandita et al., 2018). Touch has powerful calming effects on us from infancy through adulthood.

Smell and Taste

Smell and taste receptors are functional in the fetus, and preferences are well developed at birth (Bloomfield et al., 2017). Fetuses can process olfactory stimuli (i.e., they can smell), and they prefer familiar odors from the womb for months after birth (Tristão et al., 2021). Newborns recognize their mother's odor and are calmed by it during stressful procedures such as heel-stick tests (Marin et al., 2015; Schaal, 2017). They also display facial expressions suggesting disgust in response to odors of ammonia, fish, and other scents that adults find offensive (Steiner, 1979).

Infants show innate preferences for some tastes (Prescott, 2020; Ross, 2017). Newborns prefer sugar to other substances, and a small dose of sugar can serve as an anesthetic, distracting newborns from pain (Forestell, 2017; Harrison & Bueno, 2023). Both bottle-fed and breastfed newborns prefer human milk—even milk from strangers—to formula (Marlier & Schaal, 2005). The scent of breast milk is calming, slowing premature neonates' heart rate when they are under stress and aiding pain management in infants (Çamur & Erdoğan, 2022; Neshat et al., 2016).

Experience can modify taste preferences, beginning before birth. Fetuses are exposed to flavors in amniotic fluid that influence their preferences after birth (Forestell, 2016; Ustun et al., 2023). In one study, the type of formula fed to infants influenced their taste preferences at 4 to 5 years of age (Mennella & Beauchamp, 2002). Infants fed milk-based formulas and protein-based formulas were more likely to prefer sour flavors at 4 to 5 years of age than infants fed soy-based formulas, who, in turn, were more likely to prefer bitter flavors.

Intermodal Perception

All stimuli we encounter involve more than one type of sensory information. For instance, we see a dog, but we also hear its bark. Not only are infants able to sense in multiple modalities, but they are able to coordinate their senses. **Intermodal perception** is the process of combining information from more than one sensory system (Gerdts, 2021). Sensitivity to intermodal relations among stimuli is critical to perceptual development and learning—and this sensitivity emerges early in life (Lewkowicz et al., 2010). That is, infants expect vision, auditory, and tactile information to occur together (Sai, 2005). Newborns turn their heads and eyes in the direction of a sound source, suggesting that they intuitively recognize that auditory and visual information co-occur and provide information about spatial location (Streri & de Hevia, 2023)

Newborns show a preference for viewing their mother's face at 72, 12, and even just 4 hours after birth (Pascalis et al., 1995). Is this simply inborn? In one study, neonates were able to visually recognize their mother's face only if the face was paired with their mother's voice (they heard her voice while seeing her) at least once after birth (Sai, 2005). Neonates quickly remember the association and then demonstrate a preference for their mothers' face even when it is not paired with her voice. Thus, intermodal perception is evident at birth because neonates can coordinate auditory (voice) and visual (face) stimuli to recognize their mothers. Despite this, intermodal processing is not fully developed at birth. Newborns can visually recognize an object they have previously held but not seen, but they cannot tactually recognize an object they have previously seen but not held, suggesting a role for experience (Lewkowicz & Bremner, 2020; Sann & Streri, 2007).

Intermodal matching, especially touch, plays a role in learning. When 5- to 7-month-old infants listened to abstract patterns of tones while being touched on the knee or elbow, they were more likely to remember the auditory sequences when the accompanying touches matched the auditory pattern of tones (matching audio and tactile stimuli; Lew-Williams et al., 2019). Social touch can influence how infants process and remember stimuli. In another study, 4-month-old infants habituated to a face while their forehead was either stroked with a soft paint brush, stroked by a caregiver, or was not stroked. The infants who were stroked by caregivers looked significantly longer than their peers when shown a new face, suggesting that caregiver touch promoted learning (Della Longa, 2019).

Infant-Context Interactions and Perceptual Development

We have seen that individuals are embedded in and interact dynamically with their contexts. Adopting an ecological perspective, developmental scientists James and Eleanor Gibson explained that perception arises through interactions with the environment (Adolph & Kretch, 2015; E. J. Gibson & Pick, 2000). Children do not patch together small bits of sensory information to build a representation of the world, that is, to understand the physical world. The Gibsons believed that the environment itself provides all the information needed for children to make sense of it (Chong & Proctor, 2020). Individuals perceive the environment directly, without constructing or manipulating sensory information.

Perception arises from action, doing. Infants actively explore their environment first with their eyes, moving their heads and, later, reaching their hands and, eventually, crawling. Perception provides the information infants need to traverse their environment. Through their exploration, infants perceive **affordances**—the nature, opportunities, and limits of objects (Adolph, 2020; E. J. Gibson & Pick, 2000). The features of objects tell infants about their affordances, their possibilities for action, such as whether an object is squeezable, mouthable, catchable, or reachable.

A young child may perceive different affordances (such as how these pots can be used) than an older child.

PeopleImages/istock

Infants' exploration is not random or haphazard. They systematically search to discover the properties of the things around them (Franchak, 2020). From this perspective, perception arises from action, just as it influences action (J. Gibson, 1979). Infants' development, genetics, and motivation influence their ability to explore the environment and discover its affordances. The opportunities objects and environments provide for action, their affordances, vary with children's development. Consider a large pot. A 10-year-old child might consider using it to cook because of their experience of having observed cooking. In contrast, an 18-month-old infant may perceive very different affordances of the pot, such as a drum to bang or a bucket to fill, based on the child's capacities.

We naturally perceive affordances, such as knowing when a surface is safe for walking, by sensing information from the environment and coordinating it with our body sensations, such as our sense of balance (Cole & Adolph, 2023). Physical and cognitive development as well as experience influence the affordances we perceive for interacting in our environment. Vision guides locomotion, influencing infants' ability to balance, avoid collisions, and navigate variations in ground surface, such as carpet, hardwood flooring, or grass (Adolph et al., 2019; Kretch et al., 2014). Infants' locomotive skill improves with experience. But infants' judgments are relative to their specific motor ability and must be relearned with each new posture. Expert crawlers are more skilled at perceiving affordances and can more efficiently navigate a sloped surface, for example, than novice walkers (Adolph, 2020). Newly walking infants must relearn to detect and use perceptual information about body-environment relations to perceive affordances for balance and locomotion (Cole & Adolph, 2023). Perceived affordances influence how we interact with our environments and ultimately our opportunities for learning.

THINKING IN CONTEXT 4.5

1. Discuss infants' both excellent and poor perceptual abilities. How do these abilities influence their interactions with people and objects around them?
2. Evolutionary developmental scientists believe that our developmental path or program is adaptive, serving a purpose for us as a species. How might this be true for our sensory abilities?
3. Consider the objects around you, as you read this chapter. What are they? Considering the concept of affordances, what is the range of activities or opportunities that each object affords? Compare your explanation with what you imagine a young child might say. Do you think a child would perceive similar opportunities for action as you? Explain.

APPLY YOUR KNOWLEDGE

Jorge pushes into a crawling position onto all fours and rocks back and forth. He will soon crawl, about 2 months later than the other babies in the childcare center. Much smaller than his peers, Jorge is new to the childcare center, recently adopted from an overcrowded orphanage in a developing country. At first tiny Jorge barely ate and didn't cry or pay attention to the adults around him. With warm patient care, Jorge soon became comfortable and began to thrive in his new environment.

1. How do motor skills unfold during infancy? Should Jorge's parents worry about his progress? Why or why not?

2. How do environmental factors and children's experiences influence their motor development? Consider Jorge's development.

3. Jorge's parents worry about how his early experiences of deprivation might influence his brain development. Discuss processes of brain development and the role of experience in development. Should Jorge's parents worry? What can they do to help Jorge?

CHAPTER SUMMARY

4.1 Describe the parts of the neuron and processes of brain development.

Brain cells, neurons, are specialized for transmitting and receiving signals. Neurons have distinct structures, such as axons and dendrites, that enable them to communicate with other neurons, sensory and muscle cells. Neurons are born through neurogenesis, which begins prenatally. Brain development occurs through synaptogenesis, synaptic pruning, myelination, and lateralization, which peak in different brain regions at different ages, The brain's wrinkled and folded outermost layer, the cortex, is comprised of 2 hemispheres with four lobes apiece, each with different functions: frontal, temporal, parietal, and occipital.

4.2 Discuss brain development from infancy through adolescence and the role of experience in development.

The environment plays an important role in brain development, especially during infancy, a sensitive period for development. The brain depends on experiencing certain basic events and stimuli at key points in time to develop normally (experience-expectant brain development). It also changes in response to experience (experience-dependent brain development). The quality and type of experiences an individual has in infancy and childhood can positively or negatively impact brain development and future cognitive and social development. Adolescence marks a sensitive period for brain development as puberty triggers a second burst of synaptogenesis and pruning, which molds the prefrontal cortex. The different timing between the early developing limbic system, responsible for emotion, and prefrontal cortex, the seat of reasoning and cognitive control, influences adolescents' behavior. Gray and white matter show different patterns of development.

4.3 Summarize patterns of gross and fine motor development in infancy and childhood.

Gross motor development refers to the ability to control the large movements of the body, such as those of the arms and legs. Fine motor development refers to the ability to control small movements of the fingers, such as reaching and grasping. Infants and children progress through an orderly series of gross and fine motor milestones but there are variations. Motor skills like crawling and walking change infants' interactions and experiences. Infants who walk attend to and manipulate objects more and have more advanced social interactions with their caregivers, which in turn is associated with advanced language development. Motor skills continue to develop and refine over time as children become more skilled in controlling their movements and participating in physical activities. Fine motor skills are also linked to cognitive skills like counting, reading, and writing.

4.4 Compare biological and contextual influences on motor development.

Biological factors such as genetics and maturation, as well as brain development, play a role in motor development. Yet contextual factors, such as opportunities to practice motor skills, are also important. Practice can speed motor development or slow it down. Different cultures provide infants with different experiences and opportunities for practice, contributing to cross-cultural differences in motor development. According to dynamic systems theory motor development reflects an interaction among maturation, the infant's physical capacities, environmental supports, and the infant's desire to explore the world. Infants develop and learn motor skills by revising and combining abilities and skills to fit their goals. Infants' abilities and immediate environments determine whether and how the goal can be achieved. Differences in caregiver interactions and caregiving environments affect children's motor skills, the form they take, the ages of onset, and the overall developmental trend. Children's goals change with abilities and experience. New motor skills provide new possibilities for exploration.

4.5 Discuss sensory and perceptual development, including the concept of affordances.

Infants actively explore their environment using their senses and motor skills to perceive, affordances—the nature, opportunities, and limits of objects. Their emerging skills influence the affordances they perceive, how objects can be used. Vision is the poorest sense at birth but rapidly improves. Visual acuity, pattern perception, visual tracking, and color vision improve over the first few months of life. Neonates are sensitive to depth cues and young infants can distinguish depth, but crawling stimulates the perception of depth and the association of fear with sharp drops. Hearing is the most well-developed sense at birth. Newborns can perceive and discriminate nearly all sounds in human languages, but from birth, they prefer to hear their native language. Touch can soothe and reduce an infant's stress. Smell and taste are well developed at birth, and newborns show early preferences. Intermodal perception is evident at birth because infants can combine information from more than one sensory system.

KEY TERMS

- affordances
- axon
- cephalocaudal pattern of development
- cerebellum
- corpus callosum
- cortex
- dendrites
- experience-dependent brain development
- experience-expectant brain development
- externality effect
- fine motor development
- glial cell
- gray matter
- gross motor development
- intermodal perception
- lateralization
- limbic system
- myelination
- neurogenesis
- neuron
- neurotransmitters
- perception
- perceptual narrowing
- plasticity
- prefrontal cortex
- sensation
- sensitive period
- synapse
- synaptic pruning
- synaptogenesis
- visual acuity
- white matter

ArtMarie/istock

5 PHYSICAL DEVELOPMENT AND HEALTH

> **LEARNING OBJECTIVES**
>
> 5.1 Discuss changes in growth, nutrition, and activity in infancy and childhood.
>
> 5.2 Summarize patterns of physical development in adolescence, including puberty and pubertal timing.
>
> 5.3 Examine health and mortality in infancy and childhood, including injuries, illnesses, childhood obesity, and child abuse.
>
> 5.4 Analyze threats to adolescents' health, such as eating disorders, substance use, and depression and suicide.

"Look Brielle! I can run so fast!" 4-year-old Amir shouted to his babysitter. "Wow! You're getting so big and strong—and fast like a superhero," Brielle replied. "When I first visited you, Amir, you were a tiny baby. You could sit up, but you'd topple over." "No, I wasn't that small," Amir said. "Oh yes you were! I bet that when I close my eyes and blink, you'll be taller and stronger than your big brother. But to grow bigger you'll need to be healthy, right?" "That means, vegetables?" Amir asked. "Yes it does, and healthy exercise, like running around," Brielle said. "I like to run! Want to see me jump?" Amir asked. As Brielle suggested, a task of childhood is to grow taller and stronger. In this chapter we examine growth and influences on health in infancy, childhood, and adolescence.

BODY GROWTH IN INFANCY AND CHILDHOOD

> 5.1 Discuss changes in growth, nutrition, and activity in infancy and childhood.

The most obvious change that infants and children undergo is physical growth. Over the first decade of life, a typical 7.5 pound neonate grows to 10 times its size, about 70 pounds. The first 2 years comprise the period known as infancy and toddlerhood; the term *toddler* refers to toddling, the unsteady gait of babies just learning to walk. Growth during infancy and toddlerhood is so rapid that it is often a surprise to parents. As children enter early childhood, their bodies slim, grow taller, and reshape into proportions similar to adults. How do these developments take place? How do children grow, and what influences their growth?

Patterns of Growth

Throughout childhood, children grow larger and heavier, but growth is uneven. Different parts of the body grow at different rates. Growth generally proceeds in two systematic patterns. First, similar to motor development discussed in Chapter 4, growth is cephalocaudal, meaning it tends to move from the head downward. The head and upper regions of the body develop before the lower areas. For example, recall the fetus's disproportionately large head. During prenatal development, the head grows before the other body parts. Even at birth, the newborn's head is about one fourth the total body length (see Figure 5.1). As the lower parts of the body develop, the head becomes more proportionate to the body. By 3 years of age, children are less top-heavy. Recall that motor development also tends to show this pattern; babies can lift their heads before they push up with their arms, then sit up, and so on.

A second principle that growth and motor development follow is called **proximodistal development** (see Figure 5.2). Growth tends to proceed from the center of the body outward. During prenatal development, the internal organs develop and the torso forms, then arm and leg buds emerge. After birth, the trunk grows ahead of the arms and legs, and the arms and legs tend to grow before the hands and feet. Motor development tends to follow this pattern as infants can swat at objects using their whole arm before reaching with their hands and then grasping with their fingers.

FIGURE 5.1 ■ Body Proportions Throughout Life

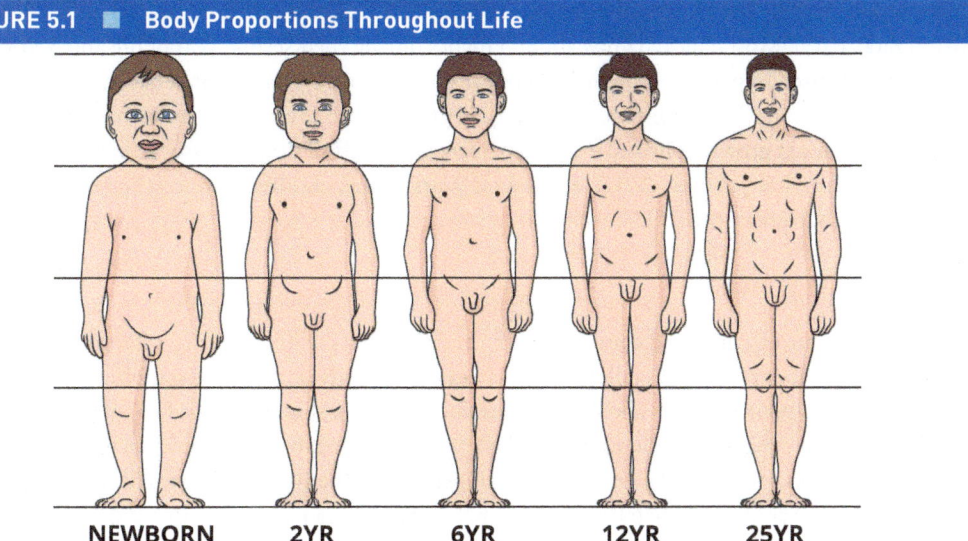

NEWBORN 2YR 6YR 12YR 25YR

Source: Huelke, D. F. (1998). An overview of anatomical considerations of infants and children in the adult world of automobile safety design. *Annual Proceedings / Association for the Advancement of Automotive Medicine, 42,* 93–113.

Growth in Infancy

Even the most casual observer will notice that infants grow substantially larger and heavier over time—but there are many individual differences in growth. How can parents and caregivers tell if a child's development is typical? Researchers have determined that growth follows distinct patterns by compiling information about the height and weight of large samples of children from diverse populations. **Growth norms** are expectations for typical gains and variations in height and weight for children based on their chronological age and ethnic background.

In the first few days after birth, newborns shed excess fluid and typically lose 5% to 10% of their body weight. After this initial loss, infants gain weight quickly. Infants usually double their birth weight at about 4 months, triple it by 12 months, and quadruple it by 30 months (Kliegman & St. Geme, 2025). The average 3-year-old weighs about 31 pounds. Gains in height of 10 to 12 inches can be expected over the first year of life, making the average 1-year-old child about 30 inches tall. This

FIGURE 5.2 ■ Cephalocaudal and Proximodistal Development

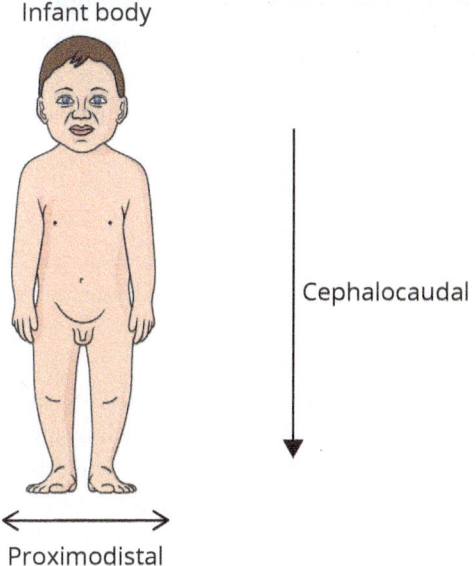

increase is caused by the growth of bone and represents the most significant growth spurt of the lifespan (Ohta, 2019). Most children grow about 5 inches during their second year of life and 3 to 4 inches during their third. To parents, growth may appear slow and steady, but research has shown that it tends to occur in spurts in which an infant or toddler can grow up to one quarter of an inch overnight (Lampl et al., 2001). Infant growth is linked with sleep; increased bouts of sleep are associated with small bursts of growth (Lampl & Johnson, 2011). At about 2 years of age, children have reached one half of their adult height (Kliegman & St. Geme, 2025).

Growth in Childhood

Growth slows during childhood compared with the first 2 years of life. From ages 2 through 6, the average child grows about 2.5 inches taller and gains nearly 5 pounds each year. The typical 6-year-old child weighs about 45 pounds and is about 46 inches tall. Despite a slower growth rate, gradual day-to-day increases in height and weight add up quickly and can seem to sneak up on a child. In middle childhood, children grow 2 to 3 inches and gain 5 to 8 pounds per year, so the average 10-year-old child weighs about 70 pounds and is about 4.5 feet tall. At about age 9, girls begin a period of very rapid growth that continues into adolescence. During this time, girls gain about 10 pounds a year, becoming taller and heavier than same-age boys. It is not until early adolescence, at about age 12, that boys show similar growth.

Body proportions change during childhood as the body "catches up" with the head. The cephalocaudal trend of infancy continues as the trunk, arms, and legs grow rapidly and body proportions become similar to those of adults, slimmer and with longer limbs (Kliegman & St. Geme, 2025). The long bones of the arms and legs grow larger through a process known as **ossification**, the formation of new bone. Ossification results in gains in height and arm-span as the legs and arms grow; bones also become stronger and harder (Lloyd et al., 2019).

There are consistent racial and ethnic differences in growth patterns in many industrialized nations such as Australia, Canada, England, France, and the United States (Natale & Rajagopalan, 2014). Generally, children of African descent tend to be tallest, followed by children of European descent, then Asian, then Latino. Furthermore, 6-year-old African American girls tend to have greater muscle and bone mass than White or Mexican American girls their age (Ellis et al., 1997). However, there are many individual differences.

Sometimes children's growth lags behind their peers. Growth deficiencies can be caused by too little growth hormone circulating in the blood, known as a **growth hormone deficiency**. When such a deficiency is diagnosed, pediatricians can prescribe synthetic growth hormone injections to encourage growth (Hage et al., 2021). Typically children on growth hormone therapy grow about 4 inches or more in the first year of treatment and 3 or more inches in the following 2 years, before the rate of growth declines (Toft, 2018). Growth is contingent on adhering to the treatment schedule and is compromised when injections are late or skipped altogether (van Dommelen et al., 2018). Growth hormones are only prescribed for children with a growth hormone deficiency, not those who are simply shorter than their peers (Boguszewski, 2020). Moreover, growth hormone deficiency is rare, diagnosed in about 1 in 4,000 children (Murray et al., 2016). Most children catch up to their peers' growth without medical intervention.

Nutrition and Growth

Children's bodies require adequate calories and nutrients to grow. The first 2 years of life are a critical window for health and nutrition, a foundation for later development. Early dietary experiences can influence childhood food preferences, and ultimately growth and health.

Breastfeeding

The USDA (Dietary Guidelines Advisory Committee, 2020) and the American Academy of Pediatrics (2012) recommend that infants be breastfed exclusively until about 6 months and, supplement infants' diets with breastmilk through age 1. Most new mothers in the United States (84%) breastfed (Chiang et al., 2021). About one quarter exclusively breastfeed at 6 months and over one third supplement infants' diets with breastmilk at 12 months (Pérez-Escamilla, 2022). Hispanic mothers breastfeed at higher rates than non-Hispanic White mothers, who are more likely to breastfeed than Black mothers (Beauregard et al., 2019; R. Li et al., 2019). Black mothers disproportionately experience barriers to breastfeeding, such as access to breastfeeding resources, lack of social support for breastfeeding, fewer referrals for lactation support, and breastfeeding restrictions at work (Aderibigbe & Lucas, 2023; Jones et al., 2015; K. Robinson et al., 2019). Maternity care facilities in predominantly Black neighborhoods provide less support for breastfeeding, such as the opportunity to room with the newborn or aid in initiating breastfeeding within the first hour of birth, which increases breastfeeding rates, duration, and exclusivity (Pérez-Escamilla et al., 2016; Sipsma et al., 2019). Although Hispanic mothers often experience similar contextual disadvantages as Black mothers, the cultural factors contributing to healthy birth outcomes (discussed in Chapter 3) may also support breastfeeding after birth (Fryer et al., 2018).

Breastfeeding offers benefits for mothers and infants. Mothers who breastfeed have lower rates of diabetes, cardiovascular disease, depression, arthritis, and cancer (Louis-Jacques & Stuebe, 2018; Sattari et al., 2019). Most babies find it easier to digest breast milk than formula (Jiang et al., 2022). In addition, breast milk contains immunizing agents that protect the infant against infections, and breastfed infants tend to experience lower rates of allergies and gastrointestinal symptoms and have fewer visits to physicians (Cabinian et al., 2016; Turfkruyer & Verhasselt, 2015). Breastfeeding for more than 6 months is associated with a reduced risk of childhood obesity and cancer, especially lymphomas (Amitay et al., 2016; Qiao et al., 2020; Victora et al., 2016). The duration of breastfeeding, specifically longer than 6 months, is associated with higher scores in cognitive and language ability from early childhood through adolescence (Isaacs et al., 2010; Lenehan et al., 2020; Whitehouse et al., 2011). However, any differences in cognitive outcomes between breastfed and formula-fed infants are small and are likely influenced by contextual factors associated with breastfeeding, such as socioeconomic status (SES) (Jenkins & Foster, 2014; M.K. & Choi, 2020; Moran-Lev et al., 2021).

Pediatricians recommend breastfeeding, but it is not essential for a healthy infant. Many mothers do not breastfeed, whether by choice or circumstance. Infant formula is a safe and healthy alternative to breast milk because formula production is monitored by the U.S. Food and Drug Administration.

Childhood Food Preferences

Children's appetites vary with their growth. Children's appetite is usually very good during active growth periods, but their appetite declines as their growth slows (Marotz, 2015). This decline is common, but often an undue concern for parents. Children eat when they are hungry and should be provided with frequent opportunities to eat. Generally, children tend to balance their eating, making up for short periods of little food intake with greater consumption later (J. W. Ball et al., 2017).

Children's experiences influence their food preferences. Young children are often sensitive to the sensory quality of foods, including appearance, texture, and shape (Marotz, 2015). Parents model food preferences, and children can acquire food preferences and dislikes through observation (Mahmood et al., 2021). Children often dislike trying new foods. Encouraging children to try a food several times over a few weeks, such as during family dinners, can help them become familiar with the taste and texture, which can increase the likelihood of eating it. Involving children in meal preparation can improve children's interest in and acceptance of new foods.

Children with health conditions and developmental disabilities may have different food needs and experience feeding challenges (Samour & King, 2013). Impaired motor skills may make it difficult or impossible for children to feed themselves. Medications can change children's appetite or their needs for particular nutrients. Children may have difficulty recognizing the body signals for hunger or fullness. Children with autistic spectrum disorders and sensory disorders may restrict their eating to particular textures or colors and require coaxing to eat, especially new foods (Petitpierre et al., 2021). Sensory sensitivity, especially sensitivity to smell and taste, predicts fussy eating in children with neurodevelopmental disorders (Smith et al., 2020).

Malnutrition

Growth is largely maturational, but it is also influenced by health and environmental factors, such as SES (Von Holle et al., 2020). Today's children grow taller and faster than prior generations, and the average adult is taller today than a century ago. Increases in children's growth over the past century are the result of contextual changes such as improved sanitation, nutrition, and access to medical care (Mummert et al., 2018). The largest gains in infant growth have occurred in North America and Europe, followed by South Asia (NCD Risk Factor Collaboration, 2016). Although children of sub-Saharan Africa showed growth gains into the mid-1990s, mass poverty and starvation, poor infrastructure to provide clean water and sanitation, and exposure to the emotional and physical stresses of war and terror have affected growth (Simmons, 2015). It is difficult to assess ethnic differences in growth patterns of children in developing nations because malnutrition and growth stunting are common (de Onis & Branca, 2016).

Marasmus, Kwashiorkor, and Growth Stunting

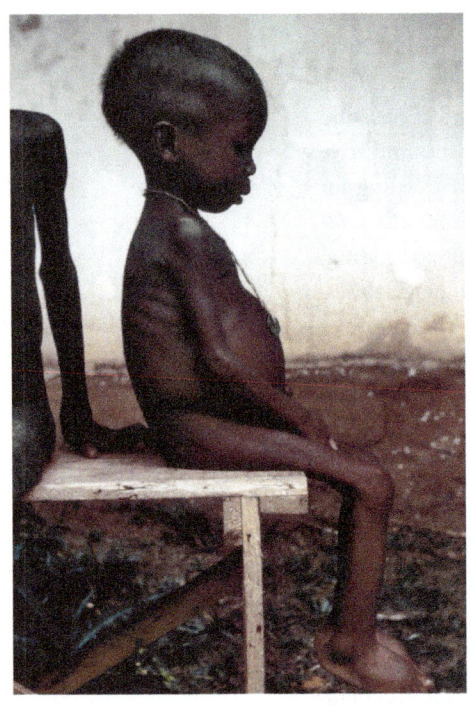

A swollen belly is characteristic of kwashiorkor, an extreme nutritional deficiency.

Dr. Lyle Conrad/CDC

Children who consume a diet that is chronically insufficient in calories, nutrients, and protein can develop **marasmus**, a wasting disease in which the body's fat and muscle are depleted (Kliegman & St. Geme, 2025). Growth stops, the body wastes away, the skin becomes wrinkly and aged looking, the abdomen shrinks, and the body has a hollow appearance. Another disease related to malnutrition is **kwashiorkor**, found in children who experience an insufficient intake of protein, which may occur when a child prematurely abandons breastfeeding, such as after the birth of a younger sibling. It is characterized by lethargy, wrinkled skin, and fluid retention that bloats and swells the stomach, face, legs, and arms. Because the vital organs of the body take all the available nutrients, the other parts of the body deteriorate. Marasmus occurs most often in infants, whereas kwashiorkor tends to occur in older infants and young children (Morley, 2016). Both marasmus and kwashiorkor occur most frequently in developing nations with poor access to resources.

Growth stunting, a reduced or impaired rate of growth, is a worldwide problem, affecting 22% of children globally in 2020 (UNICEF et al., 2021). Undernutrition contributes to growth stunting. Growth stunting affects 43% of children in East African countries, 34% in West Africa, and 35% in South-Central Asia (de Onis & Branca, 2016). Growth stunting is associated with susceptibility to illness, poor overall health, poor cognitive function, and even mortality (Casale et al., 2020; Vaivada et al., 2020). Growth stunting is not common in children from Western nations, such as the United States. Children who enter middle childhood with stunted growth and nutritional deficits often do not catch up, especially if the children remain in the same environments that caused malnourishment (Stein et al., 2010). Instead, stunting continues, resulting in permanent growth deficiencies in adulthood (Soliman et al., 2021; Sonuga-Barke et al., 2022). With improved nutrition and health care, children can show some catchup growth, but worldwide, many children lack access to these basic needs (Scheffler et al., 2021).

Malnutrition and Brain Development

Malnutrition influences development in multiple ways. Malnourished children show cognitive deficits as well as impairments in motivation, curiosity, language, and the ability to effectively interact with the environment throughout childhood and adolescence and even into adulthood (Bosch-Bayard et al., 2022; Galler et al., 2021; Pizzol et al., 2021). Malnourishment damages neurons, as shown in Figure 5.3, resulting in lasting neurological and cognitive deficits.

Malnutrition during the first year of life is associated with depression years later, when those children are 11 to 17 years old (Galler et al., 2010). Among Ghanaian children who survived a severe famine in 1983, those who were youngest at the time of the famine (under age 2) scored lower on cognitive measures throughout childhood and into adulthood than did those who were older (ages 6 to 8) (Ampaabeng & Tan, 2013). Despite these findings, some of the damage caused by malnutrition can be reversed. Motor and mental development can be enhanced if nutrition is reinstated early. Long-term difficulties in attention, learning, and intelligence often remain, even into adulthood (Bosch-Bayard et al., 2022; Galler et al., 2021).

Although malnutrition is common in poor countries, it is also found in some of the world's wealthiest countries. Because of socioeconomic factors, many children in the United States and other

FIGURE 5.3 ■ Effects of Malnourishment on Brain Development

Well-nourished infant

Undernourished infant

Typical brain cells
Extensive branching

Impaired brain cells
Limited branching
Abnormal, shorter branches

Source: de Onis, M., & Branca, F. (2016). Childhood stunting: a global perspective. *Maternal & child nutrition, 12*(Suppl 1), 12–26. https://doi.org/10.1111/mcn.12231

developed countries are deprived of diets that support healthy growth. In 2022, about 17% of U.S. households with children were categorized as *food insecure*. That is, they lacked consistent access to food to support a healthy lifestyle for all adult and child members of the family at some point during the year (Rabbitt et al., 2023). About 9% of children directly experienced food insecurity. As shown in Figure 5.4, rates of food insecurity are higher in Black and Hispanic households (28% and 25% respectively) than White households (12%) and those headed by single parents (21% for homes headed

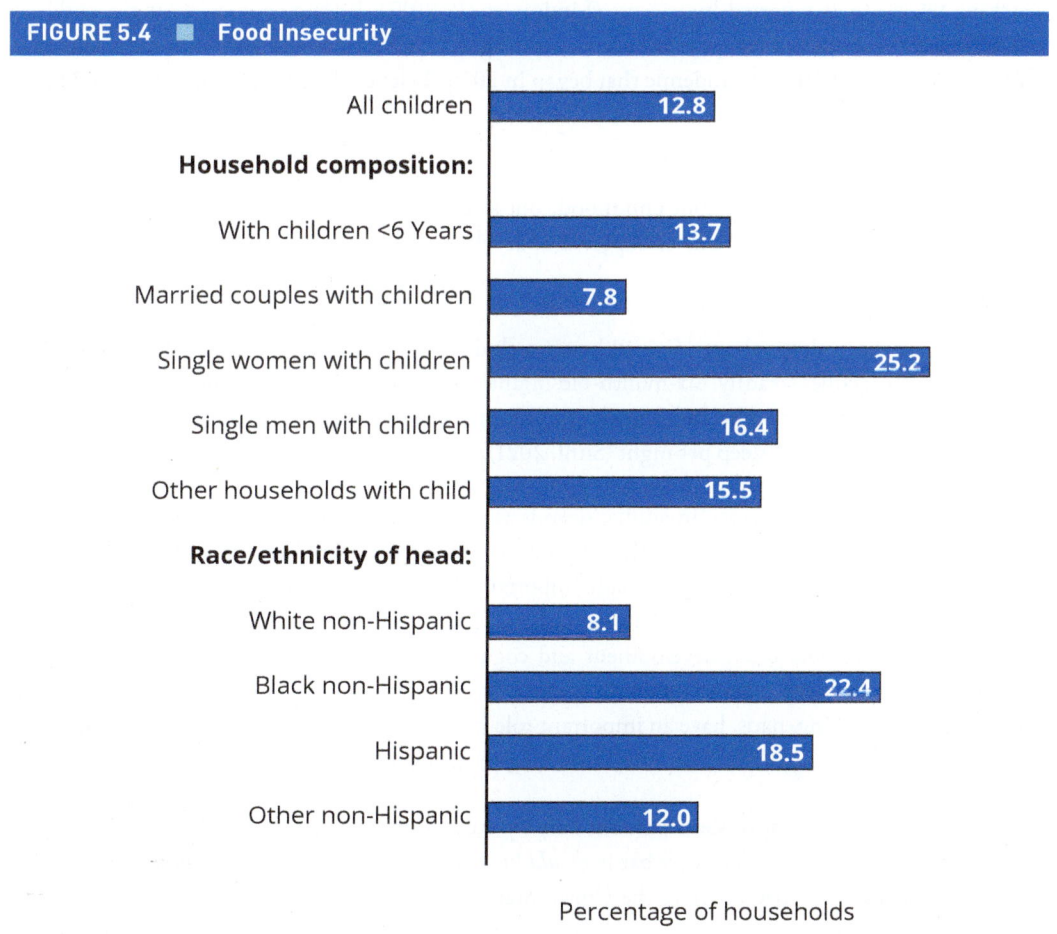

FIGURE 5.4 ■ Food Insecurity

	Percentage of households
All children	12.8
Household composition:	
With children <6 Years	13.7
Married couples with children	7.8
Single women with children	25.2
Single men with children	16.4
Other households with child	15.5
Race/ethnicity of head:	
White non-Hispanic	8.1
Black non-Hispanic	22.4
Hispanic	18.5
Other non-Hispanic	12.0

Source: Coleman-Jensen, A., Rabbitt, M. P., Gregory, C. A., & Singh, A. (2021). *Statistical supplement to household food security in the United States in 2020, AP-091*. Department of Agriculture, Economic Research Service. http://dx.doi.org/10.22004/ag.econ.313486

by single men and 33% for those headed by single women). In the United States and other industrial nations, food insecurity is linked with stunted growth, poor school performance, health and behavior problems, and poor well-being in children (Hines et al., 2021, 2024; Shankar et al., 2017).

Physical Activity

Regular physical activity contributes to health for people of all ages. The Physical Activity Guidelines for Americans advise that all children and adolescents get 60 minutes or more of moderate-to-vigorous physical activity daily (U.S. Department of Health and Human Services, 2018b).

In childhood physical activity is often interwoven into outdoor play carried out with peers on playgrounds, school yards, and recreation centers. Running and chasing games, dancing, biking, jumping rope, and other activities increase children's heart rate and improve cardiovascular health, bone and muscle strength, blood pressure, and immune system health (Drollette & Hillman, 2020; Eather et al., 2020). Children who engage in regular physical activity score higher on attention, memory, and executive function measures, especially planning and cognitive control (Hillman et al., 2019; Sember et al., 2020; Vasilopoulos et al., 2023). In addition, physical activity has been linked to higher levels of self-esteem and lower levels of anxiety, which in turn are associated with higher academic performance in the classroom (Biddle & Vergeer, 2020; Caldas & Reilly, 2018).

Opportunities to play outdoors, especially access to safe playgrounds, are associated with greater levels of physical activity (van Sluijs et al., 2021). Children who live in homes with yards engage in more physical activity than those who live in apartments, and yard size is positively associated with children's level of physical activity (Miller et al., 2020). Children from low-income homes tend to spend less time outdoors, engage in less physically active play, and spend more time in sedentary behaviors, such as watching television as reported by parents (Lindsay et al., 2017). Perhaps not surprisingly, children and adolescents engaged in less physical activity during the quarantines and stay-at-home orders that accompanied the COVID-19 pandemic that began in 2020 (Eyler et al., 2021; Neville et al., 2022).

Sleep

Our sleep needs change throughout childhood, but sleep remains a biological necessity at all ages. Different sleep concerns accompany each period of development.

Infancy

The typical newborn sleeps about 16 to 18 hours each day and wakes every 2 hours to eat (Mäkelä et al., 2018). Sleep declines steadily. Six-month-old infants sleep about 12 hours (Figueiredo et al., 2016). Many continue to wake at night. Infants under 11 months should get 12 to 15 hours of sleep, and toddlers need 11 to 14 hours of sleep per night (Suni, 2021).

REM Sleep and Development. In adults, sleep is associated with memory consolidation, *cementing* memories and learning (Chambers, 2017). Rapid eye movement (REM) sleep, during which their eyes flutter and dreaming occurs, is especially important. Infants spend about 50% of their sleep time in REM sleep, decreasing to about 20% in adulthood. REM sleep is thought to provide infants with stimulation and promote brain development and cognitive growth (Knoop et al., 2021). Similar to findings with adults, sleep is associated with memory formation in infants (G. M. Mason & Spencer, 2022). Daytime sleeping, naps, have an important role in learning and problem solving, beyond nighttime sleep (Horger et al., 2023). Sleep may have long-term effects on cognitive development.

Cultural Variations. Infants' sleep patterns vary by culture, making it difficult to draw conclusions about what is *normal* infant sleep or what it *should* look like (Barry, 2020). For example, newborns in many industrialized countries, such as the United States and the United Kingdom, are often placed to sleep in their own bassinets, whether in their parents' room or in a separate nursery. In these countries, learning to sleep by oneself is viewed as fostering independence and the ability to self-regulate, to develop a sleep schedule (H. L. Ball et al., 1999; McKenna & Volpe, 2007; Schaik et al., 2020).

Co-sleeping, where an infant shares a bed with the mother or with both parents, is common in many countries, including Bangladesh, China, Japan, and Kenya, and is believed to enhance the child's sense of security and attachment to the mother (Morelli et al., 1992; Super & Harkness, 1982; Xiao-na et al., 2010). Infants who sleep with their mothers synchronize their sleep patterns with hers, permitting more awakenings for breastfeeding, yet lengthening the total time that infants sleep (Gettler & McKenna, 2011). In Asia and Latin America, infants are not usually expected to go to bed and sleep alone at a regular time each night. Instead, they are held until they fall asleep and then are placed in the parental bed (Lozoff et al., 1984). Parents' decisions about whether to co-sleep are influenced by their own values and beliefs, which are often shaped by the context in which they live.

Pediatricians in Western nations tend to advise separate sleeping arrangements for parents and infants, citing an increased risk of accidental suffocation and an increased risk of SIDS, especially among mothers who smoke (Mitchell, 2009). Instead, they advise having infants sleep in a crib in the parents' room (Moon & Task Force on Sudden Infant Death Syndrome, 2016b; UK Department of Health, 2005). Despite these warnings, co-sleeping has become more common among Western families for a variety of reasons, such as facilitating breastfeeding, aiding infant and parent sleep, monitoring infants, reducing crying and enhancing bonding, cultural traditions, and environmental reasons (Barry & McKenna, 2022). The American Academy of Pediatrics advises that bedsharing should be abandoned in favor of room sharing, to provide the developmental advantages of co-sleeping and minimize the dangers (Moon et al., 2022)

Childhood

Preschool children should get 10 to 13 hours and school age children 9 to 11 hours of sleep each night (Suni, 2021). Over the course of the evening sleep patterns typically shift so that REM sleep increases. Deep non–REM sleep declines over the sleep period. Sleep problems are more common following traumatic events (Giannakopoulos & Kolaitis, 2021). Common sleep problems children experience include **nightmares** and **sleep terrors**, sometimes called night terrors (Trosman & Ivanenko, 2021). Nightmares are anxiety provoking dreams whereas sleep terrors are more severe. During a sleep terror the child may scream, violently thrash around in bed, and gasp for air. The child may wake or may remain asleep and unaware of the event. Sleep terrors occur during deep sleep and tend to occur earlier in the evening when periods of deep sleep are longest. Sleep terrors are most common in early childhood but may continue into adolescence (Gigliotti et al., 2022). They are often triggered by stress and anxiety. Children who experience nightmares and sleep terrors may dislike going to sleep. They may develop insomnia, insist on leaving the lights on, or cry at bedtime.

Socioeconomic disadvantage and the stress that accompanies household and neighborhood chaos place children at risk for sleep problems and poor sleep (Covington et al., 2021; Giddens et al., 2022; Williamson et al., 2021). Poor sleep may have a cascading effect on development through its influence on brain function, including areas responsible for cognition and emotion. It is associated with problems with attention, working memory, and slower processing speed (Schumacher et al., 2017). Poor sleep is also associated with exaggerated emotional reactivity and poor self-regulation, which can manifest as anxiety, depression, impulsivity, and behavior problems (W. Cheng et al., 2020; Williamson et al., 2020)

THINKING IN CONTEXT 5.1

1. How does growth in infancy and childhood illustrate the influence of biology (nature) and context (nurture)? Give examples. In what ways might biological and environmental factors interact to influence growth in infancy and childhood?
2. What do parents need to know about contextual influences on growth? List five topics that you would include in a lesson for parents who wish to promote their children's physical development.

3. Identify three factors that influence whether women breastfeed. What barriers affect the likelihood of breastfeeding? Consider ways of addressing barriers and aiding women who wish to breastfeed.
4. As director of a childcare center, you'd like to help the infants and children in your center be more physically active. Convincingly explain to parents why physical activity is important. How will you incorporate more physical activity into the center's daily activities and curriculum?

BODY GROWTH AND MATURATION IN ADOLESCENCE

5.2 Summarize patterns of physical development in adolescence, including puberty and pubertal timing.

In contrast to the gradual, steady growth pattern in childhood, adolescents' bodies undergo a dramatic transformation, puberty. **Puberty** is the biological transition to adulthood, in which adolescents mature physically and become capable of reproduction.

Puberty

In late childhood, at about age 8 or 9 in girls and roughly 2 years later in boys, the brain signals the endocrine system to increase the release of sex hormones into the bloodstream (Berenbaum et al., 2015). Levels of testosterone, responsible for male sex characteristics, and estrogen, responsible for female sex characteristics, increase in boys and girls but in different ratios, leading to different patterns of physical development. Although many people view puberty as an event, it is a process that includes many physical changes that occur over about four years but can vary dramatically from 1 to 7 years (Mendle, 2014). Puberty involves the development of reproductive capacity, but that is not the whole story because puberty influences a great variety of body changes, including size, shape, and function.

Growth Spurt

The first outward sign of puberty is the **adolescent growth spurt**, a rapid gain in height and weight that generally begins in girls at about age 10 (as early as age 7 and as late as 14) and in boys at about age 12 (as early as age 9 and as late as 16) (Tinggaard et al., 2012). During this period adolescents grow nearly as fast as infants (Das et al., 2017). The pattern and pace of growth (see Figure 5.5) are similar for most children (Sanders et al., 2017).

Because girls begin their growth spurt about 2 years before boys, 10- to 13-year-old girls tend to be taller, heavier, and stronger than boys their age. By starting their growth spurts 2 years later than girls, boys begin with an extra 2 years of prepubertal growth on which the adolescent growth spurt builds, leading boys to end up taller than girls (Yousefi et al., 2013). On average, the growth spurt lasts about 2 years, but growth in height continues at a more gradual pace for an additional 4 years, ending by about 16 in girls and 18 in boys. Adolescents gain a total of about 10 inches in height. Similar to childhood growth, Black adolescents tend to begin the growth spurt and puberty earlier than same-age non-Black peers (Emmanuel & Bokor, 2017).

Sex differences in body shape emerge during the growth spurt. Boys and girls gain fat and muscle, but in different ratios. Girls gain more fat overall, particularly on their legs and hips, which comes to comprise one fourth of their body weight—nearly twice as much as boys. Boys gain more muscle than girls, especially in their upper bodies, doubling their arm strength between ages 13 and 18 (Payne & Isaacs, 2025). Bone density increases in both boys and girls, and the respiratory and cardiovascular systems mature. Boys become much better at taking in and using oxygen as their hearts and lungs grow larger and function more effectively and the number of red blood cells increases (Sadler, 2017). Consequently, once puberty has begun, boys as a group consistently outperform girls in athletics (Tønnessen et al., 2015).

| FIGURE 5.5 | Sequence of Physical Changes With Puberty |

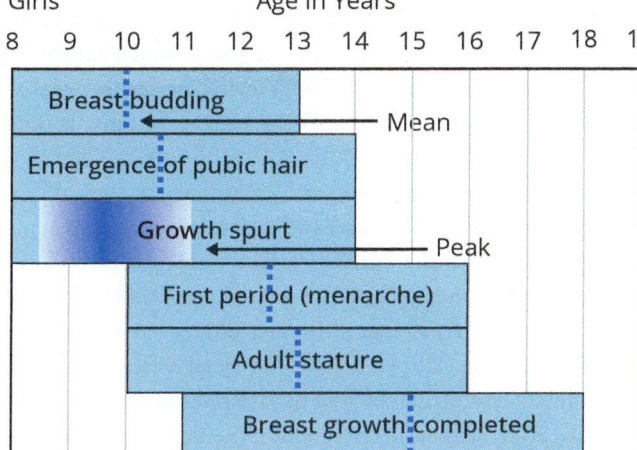

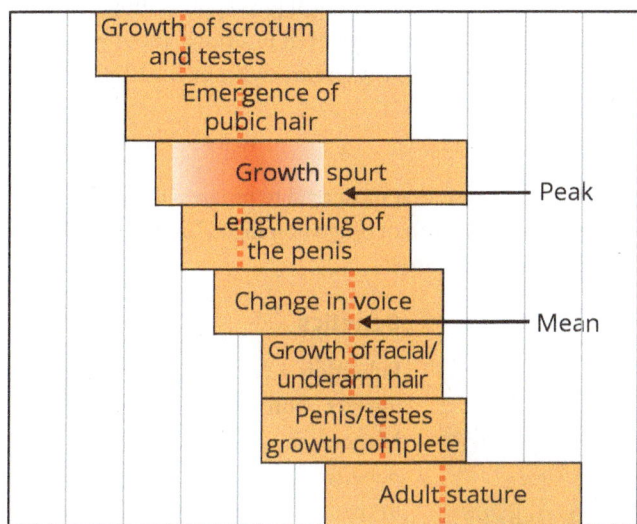

Secondary Sex Characteristics

Most people associate puberty with body changes, such as breast development, deepening of the voice, growth of facial and body hair, and, for many, the emergence of acne. These are examples of **secondary sex characteristics**, body changes that indicate physical maturation but are not directly related to fertility (Hodges-Simeon et al., 2013). In girls, rapid increases in estrogen cause the budding of breasts, which tends to accompany the growth spurt as the first signs of puberty (Emmanuel & Bokor, 2017). Testosterone causes boys' voices to deepen. As their voices change boys may occasionally lose control over their voices and emit unpredictable changes in pitch often experienced as high squeaks, which some refer to as the voice "breaking" (Busch et al., 2019). Girls' voices also deepen, but the change is gradual and not as noticeable as in boys (T. Berger et al., 2019). Oil and sweat glands become more active, resulting in body odor and acne. Hair on the head, arms, and legs becomes darker, and pubic hair begins to grow, first coming in straight and downy and later becoming coarse.

Primary Sex Characteristics

Maturation of the **primary sex characteristics**, the reproductive organs, is less noticeable than secondary sex characteristics but is the function of puberty. In girls, primary sex characteristics include the ovaries, fallopian tubes, uterus, and vagina. In boys, they include the penis, testes, scrotum, seminal vesicles, and prostate gland.

For girls, sexual maturity occurs toward the end of puberty with **menarche**, the first menstruation. **Menstruation** refers to the monthly shedding of the uterine lining, which has thickened in preparation for the possible implantation of a fertilized egg. Although menarche occurs toward the end of puberty, most adolescents and adults view it as a critical marker of puberty because it occurs suddenly and is memorable (Brooks-Gunn & Ruble, 2013).

In North America, the average age of menarche is 12.25. White girls typically experience menarche shortly before turning 13 (roughly 12.7 years of age) and the average Black girl at about 12 (Emmanuel & Bokor, 2017; Martinez, 2020). Generally, Black girls tend to be heavier and enter puberty about a year earlier, reaching pubertal milestones such as the growth spurt and menarche earlier than other girls (Osinubi et al., 2022). Hispanic American girls enter puberty at about the same time as Black girls (Biro et al., 2018; Deardorff et al., 2014). Ethnic and racial differences in the onset of puberty, the accompanying body changes, and menarche lead to variations in girls' day to day experiences and adjustment (Deardorff et al., 2019). However, research on the intersection of ethnicity and race and pubertal timing is scant.

Girls' experiences of menarche are influenced by their knowledge about menstruation as well as their expectations (Brooks-Gunn & Ruble, 2013). Most girls approaching menarche have some knowledge about it and are not afraid because they have been informed about puberty by health education classes and parents (Stidham-Hall et al., 2012; Wigmore-Sykes et al., 2021).

Biological and Contextual Influences on Pubertal Timing

Casual observations of adolescents reveal that most tend to progress through puberty at about the same time, but some begin much earlier or later than others. Biological and contextual factors act together to determine when an adolescent enters puberty.

Young adolescents' physical maturation varies dramatically by individual, as illustrated by these girls, who are all in the same grade.

Bob Daemmrich/Alamy

Genetics

Puberty is a complex trait influenced by many genes that interact with contextual factors (Horvath et al., 2020; Manotas et al., 2022). In support of the role of genetics, pubertal timing for both boys and girls tends to be similar to that of their parents and more similar in identical twins than fraternal twins (Wohlfahrt-Veje et al., 2016; B. Yang et al., 2021). Heredity sets the boundaries of pubertal timing, the earliest and latest age when an individual might begin puberty (Busch, Hagen et al., 2020). But the onset of puberty and whether it is early or late relative to our inherited range is influenced by contextual influences and life experiences more than genes (Saengkaew & Howard, 2022).

Weight and Nutrition

Puberty is triggered by achieving a critical level of body weight, specifically body fat (Tomova, 2016). Girls with a greater body mass index (BMI), especially those who are obese, mature earlier than their peers, and girls who have a low percentage of body fat, whether from athletic training or severe dieting, often experience menarche late relative to other girls (Ferrari et al., 2022; Silventoinen et al., 2022). Accordingly, extreme malnutrition can prevent the accumulation of adequate fat stores needed to support pubertal development, delaying menarche in girls. In many parts of Africa menarche does not occur until about age 14 and as late as age 17, several years later than in Western nations (Garenne, 2020; Tunau et al., 2012). From an evolutionary perspective, the link between body weight and the onset of reproductive maturation may be adaptive because it delays fertility when food and resources are scarce and unlikely to support offspring (Roa & Tena-Sempere, 2014). Similarly, some research suggests that weight affects the onset and tempo of puberty in boys, with higher BMI and obesity associated with earlier puberty but less so as compared with girls and the mechanism is not well understood (Brix et al., 2020; Busch, Højgaard et al., 2020; Bygdell et al., 2021).

Stress

Adolescents' social contexts, especially exposure to stress, influence pubertal timing. Early life stress and the experience of severe stress, such as sexual abuse and maltreatment, can speed the onset of pubertal events, such as public hair development and menarche (Belsky, 2019; Hamlat et al., 2021, 2022).

Chronic stressors, such as poor family relationships, harsh parenting, parents' marital conflict, anxiety, and low SES are associated with early menarche in North American and European girls (Hiatt et al., 2021; Pham et al., 2022; Rickard et al., 2014). The absence of a biological father and the presence of a biological unrelated male, such as a stepfather or a mother's live-in boyfriend, increases the likelihood of early menarche (Gaml-Sørensen et al., 2021; Webster et al., 2014). Household stress, economic adversity, and father absence may hold similar implications for boys' pubertal development, speeding it, but there is much less research on boys' development (Pham et al., 2022; Sun et al., 2017). However, exposure to discrimination is associated with advanced pubertal status in both Black boys and Black girls, supporting the role of stress and adversity in pubertal timing (Argabright et al., 2022).

Lower SES is associated with early pubertal onset in the United States, Canada, and the UK and may account for ethnic differences in pubertal timing (Kelly et al., 2017; Sun et al., 2017). As noted previously, Black and Latina girls tend to reach menarche before White girls, but they are also disproportionately likely to live in low-SES homes and neighborhoods. In many cases ethnic differences in the timing of menarche are reduced or even disappear when SES is considered (Acker et al., 2023; Deardorff et al., 2014). This is consistent with findings that girls who live in similar contextual conditions, especially those of socioeconomic advantage, reach menarche at about the same age, despite having different genetic backgrounds (Obeidallah et al., 2004; L. Tremblay & Larivière, 2020). In contrast, in economically developing countries such as India, Indonesia, Iran, and Pakistan, low SES is associated with delayed puberty because it is also associated with undernutrition and malnutrition (Karim et al., 2021; Nasiri et al., 2020; Öztürk & Güneri, 2020; N. Singh & Singh, 2020).

Secular Trend

Adults commonly lament that children are growing up faster and faster. Biologically speaking, this is true. Contextual influences underlie the **secular trend**, the lowering of the average age of puberty with each generation from prehistoric to the present times (see Figure 5.6; Ohlsson et al., 2019; Papadimitriou, 2016).

Through the 18th century in Europe, puberty occurred as late as age 17 (Tanner, 1990). Globally, the mean age of menarche occurred nearly 2 years earlier in 2002 than 1932 (Leone & Brown, 2020). Worldwide, girls' breast development began on average almost 3 months earlier per decade from 1977 to 2013 (Eckert-Lind et al., 2020). The secular trend parallels increases in the standard of living and average BMI among children in developed countries and is especially influenced by increases in childhood obesity (Ohlsson et al., 2019). The secular trend poses challenges for young people and parents because the biological entry to adolescence is lowering at the same time the societal passage to adulthood is lengthening, making the period of adolescence longer than ever. However, there are some indications that the secular trend has slowed or perhaps even stopped in many nations (Piras et al., 2020; Shi et al., 2023).

Pubertal Timing and Socioemotional Development

While adolescents vary in when they begin and end puberty, based on interacting genetic and contextual factors, for the most part this process falls within the standard age range described previously. Some adolescents, however, mature much earlier or much later than their peers, with implications for their socioemotional development. Early pubertal maturation refers to showing signs of physical

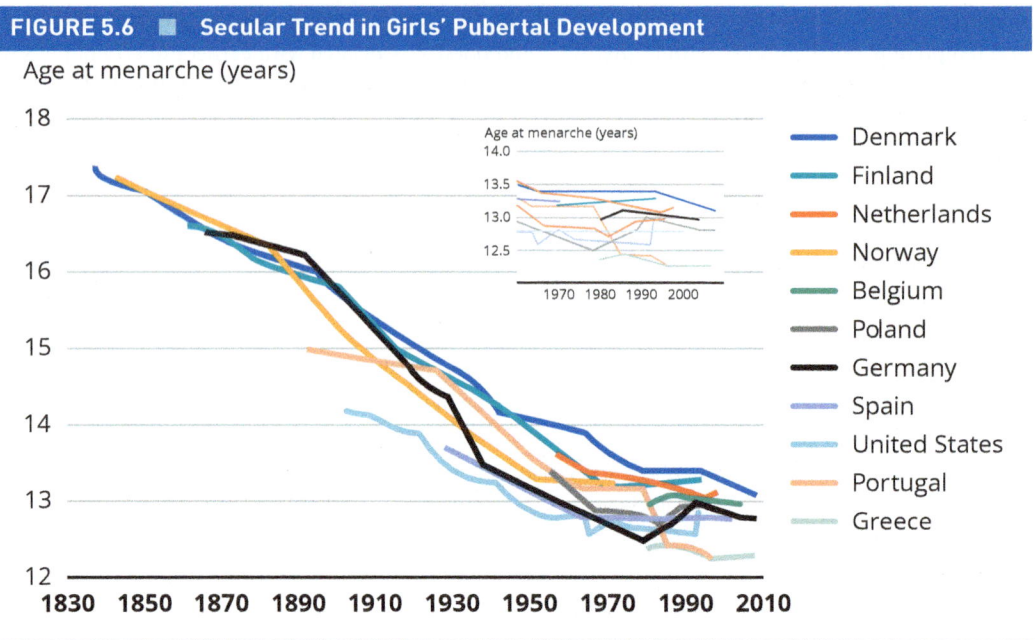

FIGURE 5.6 ■ Secular Trend in Girls' Pubertal Development

Source: Sørensen, K., Mouritsen, A., Aksglaede, L., Hagen, C. P., Mogensen, S. S., & Juul, A. (2012). Recent secular trends in pubertal timing: implications for evaluation and diagnosis of precocious puberty. *Hormone Research in Paediatrics, 77*(3), 137–145. https://doi.org/10.1159/000336325

maturation before age 8 (in girls) or 9 (in boys). Girls who begin puberty after age 13 and boys who begin after age 14 are considered late-maturing adolescents (Pyra & Schwarz, 2019). Early maturation, in particular, poses challenges for both girls' and boys' adaptation.

Adolescents who mature early tend to look older than their years and are more likely to be treated in ways similar to older adolescents, which may be stressful (Rudolph et al., 2014). Around the world, early maturing boys and girls show higher rates of risky activity, including smoking, alcohol and substance use, and aggressive behavior, as well as internalizing problems such as depression, than do same-age peers (Hamlat et al., 2019, 2020; Hoyt et al., 2020).

Early maturing girls experience the greatest risk for adjustment. They tend to feel less positively about their bodies and physical appearance and show higher rates of depression, anxiety, low self-esteem, and problem behavior than girls who mature at average or later ages (Barendse et al., 2022; Bucci & Staff, 2020; Copeland et al., 2019). Some of the problems that early maturing adolescents experience arise because they tend to seek relationships with older peers who are more similar to them in physical maturity than their classmates (Kretsch et al., 2016). Spending time with older peers makes early maturing adolescents, especially girls, more likely to engage in age-inappropriate behaviors, such as early sexual activity and risky sexual activity (Baams et al., 2015; Moore et al., 2014). Early maturing girls tend to date earlier than their peers, are at higher risk of dating violence, and experience more sexual harassment than their peers (F. R. Chen et al., 2017; Skoog & Bayram Özdemir, 2016). Notably, many differences between early maturing adolescents and their peers tend to dissipate over adolescence, as their peers catch up to them in growth, and are indistinguishable after adolescence (Dimler & Natsuaki, 2021).

In contrast to early maturation, the effects of late maturation differ markedly for boys and girls. Late maturation appears to have a protective effect on girls with regard to anxiety and depression (Zimmer-Gembeck et al., 2018). Late maturing boys may experience more social and emotional difficulties. During early adolescence, late maturing boys may be less well liked by their peers and may show body dissatisfaction, anxiety, and depression, but these effects tend to decline with physical maturation (Carter, 2015; Tsai et al., 2023).

Physical Activity

As in childhood, physical activity promotes cardiovascular health, muscle strength, motor control, mental health, and well-being in adolescents (Esteban-Cornejo et al., 2015; McMahon et al., 2017).

Adolescents who regularly engage in physical activity show better cognitive function, including selective attention, processing speed, and general self-efficacy (Reigal et al., 2020). Physical activity is associated with brain development, including myelination and the activation of regions responsible for cognitive processes and self-regulation (Valkenborghs et al., 2019). Advances in self-regulation have a protective effect on mental health and are associated with reduced risk for depression and anxiety in adolescence and emerging adulthood (Belcher et al., 2021; Biddle et al., 2019; Kwan et al., 2020).

By recent estimates, about 18% to 23% of 12- to 17-year-old adolescents meet the recommended 60 minutes of moderate to vigorous physical activity every day (Friel et al., 2020; Merlo, 2020). Declines in physical activity begin in middle childhood, about age 7; typically physical activity is displaced by screen time (Farooq et al., 2018). Longitudinal research with U.S. adolescents has shown that the declines in physical activity during adolescence are consistent across contextual settings, whether rural or urban, and across SES (Metcalf et al., 2015). Socioeconomic disparities in physical activity continue from childhood. Adolescents of low SES are more likely to be sedentary and obese than their more affluent peers; this holds true for adolescents from a variety of developed nations, such as Canada, England, Finland, France, and the United States (Mielke et al., 2017; Vazquez & Cubbin, 2020; Wang & Lim, 2012). Neighborhood SES is associated with opportunities for physical activity, such as the availability of safe parks and outdoor spaces and opportunities for extracurricular activities in the school and community (Gavand et al., 2019; Watts et al., 2016). After school and community sports teams may be more prominent and available in middle income and affluent communities. Similar to findings with children, adolescents physical activity dropped to less than half their usual levels during the COVID-19 pandemic (Nagata et al., 2022; Ng et al., 2020).

Sleep

Puberty causes a shift in adolescents' sleep patterns. The hormone melatonin, which regulates sleep, rises in the bloodstream and increases sleepiness about 2 hours later in adolescents who have begun puberty compared to those who have not (Tarokh et al., 2019). Although adolescents are primed to stay up later than they did as children, sleep is crucial to their development. Adolescents need about 9 hours of sleep each night, yet most high school students in Western countries obtain 7 or fewer hours of sleep on school nights (Galván, 2020; Gariepy et al., 2020). As a result, adolescents tend to report daytime sleepiness, which interferes with their cognitive and emotional functioning.

Similar to other ages, sleep plays an essential role in the neurological processes that influence complex cognitive abilities such as working memory, cognitive flexibility, executive function, and processing speed (Brooks et al., 2022; Fontanellaz-Castiglione et al., 2020). Insufficient sleep impairs adolescents' learning and academic achievement is associated with anxiety, irritability, and depression (Guldner et al., 2023; Shimizu et al., 2020; Vermeulen et al., 2021). Sleep problems are also associated with impulsivity, inaccurate assessment of risks, and heightened engagement in risky behaviors, including cigarette smoking and alcohol and substance use up to 5 years later (Nguyen-Louie et al., 2018; Tashjian & Galván, 2020). Moreover, "catching up" on missed sleep by sleeping longer on the weekends may ineffective in reducing the sleep deficit and may instead increase internalizing and externalizing symptoms, such as anxiety, depression, and antisocial behavior (Fuligni et al., 2018)

Most middle and high schools start earlier than elementary school. Earlier starting times coupled with adolescents' typical shift toward a later bedtime contribute to adolescents' sleep deficits. Delaying school start times increases adolescents' sleep time, improves student school attendance, grades, and disposition (Owens et al., 2017; Winnebeck et al., 2020). Adolescents prefer later start times (Werner et al., 2022). In fall 2022, the state of California began requiring that public school districts start classes no earlier than 8:00 a.m. for middle schools and 8:30 a.m. for high schools (Ziporyn et al., 2022). As of this writing, it is too soon to tell whether these changes benefit adolescents, but they are in line of recommendations by experts that secondary school start times of 8:30 a.m. or later are needed (Blake et al., 2019)

> **THINKING IN CONTEXT 5.2**
>
> 1. How might adolescents' changing bodies affect others around them? Just as our contexts influence us, we influence our contexts. Consider adolescents' families, peers, and teachers. In what ways might pubertal changes affect adolescents' day-to-day interactions and experiences?
> 2. Suppose you could choose whether your child would begin puberty much earlier or much later than their peers. What would you choose? Why?
> 3. Discuss racial and ethnic differences in pubertal timing. What might these differences mean for adolescents' development and overall adjustment?
> 4. Many adolescents get less sleep than they need. Identify barriers to sleep and factors that interfere with obtaining adequate sleep in adolescence. Identify ways of addressing them and improving adolescents' sleep.

THREATS TO INFANTS AND CHILDREN'S HEALTH

> **5.3** Examine health and mortality in infancy and childhood, including injuries, illnesses, childhood obesity, and child abuse.

Infants and children tend to be healthier than ever thanks to advances in medicine, nutrition, sanitation, and knowledge about prenatal development. Today, children's health is threatened most by unintentional injuries, illnesses, and abuse.

Injuries and Mortality

Infant and child mortality, or death, has declined dramatically over the past 100 years. Most of the declines are due to improvements in prenatal care, increasing the number of successful births and healthy newborns. The leading causes of death shift over infancy through adolescence, as discussed next.

Infancy

In infancy, death is most often due to congenital (birth) malformations, complications of low birth weight, sudden infant death syndrome, and unintentional injuries (Ely & Driscoll, 2021). The risk of infant mortality is highest during the first month of life and declines rapidly with age.

Race and SES Differences. Over the past century in the United States, infant mortality has declined for all races and ethnicities. Despite declines, there are large racial disparities in infant mortality rates (see Figure 5.7). Mortality is greatest among infants of non-Hispanic Black women with rates over twice that of infants of non-Hispanic White women and Hispanic women and nearly three times that of non-Hispanic Asian women (Ely & Driscoll, 2021). Infants of Native American/Alaskan Native and Native Hawaiian/Pacific Islander women also show high rates of mortality.

Infant mortality rates vary with SES markers, such as maternal education. Infants whose mothers have less than a high school degree show more than double the rate of mortality than those with mothers with a college degree (G. K. Singh & Yu, 2019). Likewise, the significant income differences linked with education are associated with a higher risk of infant mortality. Poverty rates are at least twice as high among Black, Hispanic, Native Hawaiian/Pacific Islander, and Native American/Alaskan Natives than non-Hispanic Whites (Semega et al., 2020). However, infant mortality rates are highest in Black infants across all income levels (Kothari et al., 2017). Infant mortality is also higher in rural counties than in urban counties in the United States (Ely & Hoyert, 2018).

As with prenatal care, structural factors influence the racial and ethnic differences that characterize infant mortality. Poverty and its interweaving with stress and trauma, poor environmental quality

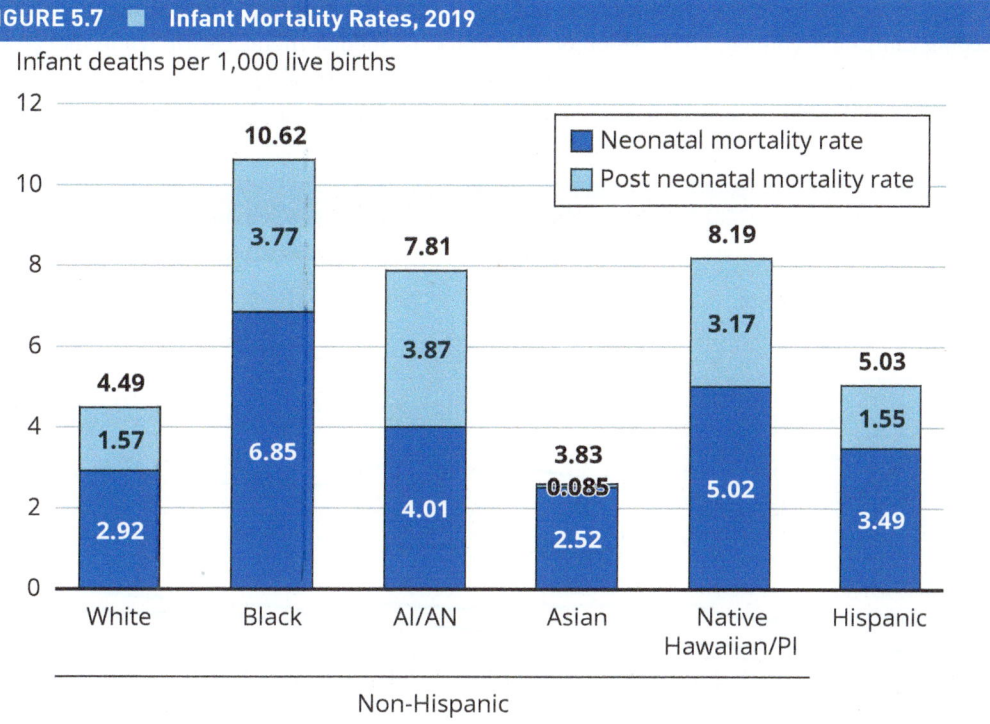

FIGURE 5.7 ■ Infant Mortality Rates, 2019

Source: Ely, D. M., & Driscoll, A. K. (2021). Infant mortality in the United States, 2019: Data from the period linked birth/infant death file. *National Vital Statistics Reports, 70*(14), 1–18. https://doi.org/10.15620/cdc:111053

and exposure to pollution, and discrimination pose risks to maternal and infant health. Risk factors for infant mortality also include little to no prenatal care, lower rates of health insurance, and poor access to health care. In addition to financial constraints, racism, stereotypes, and bias may prevent women of color from regularly accessing health care.

Sudden Infant Death Syndrome. Sudden infant death syndrome (SIDS) is the diagnostic term used to describe the sudden unexpected death of an infant less than 1 year of age that occurs seemingly during sleep and remains unexplained after a thorough investigation, including an autopsy and review of the circumstances of death and the infant's clinical history (Moon & Task Force on Sudden Infant Death Syndrome, 2016b).

Genetic abnormalities, mutations, and prematurity place infants at risk for SIDS (Blackburn et al., 2020; Keywan et al., 2021). Most cases of SIDS occur between the 2nd and 5th month of life (Bajanowski & Vennemann, 2017). Environmental factors associated with SIDS include having infants sleep on their stomach or side, using soft bedding or other inappropriate sleep surfaces (including sofas), bed-sharing, and exposure to carbon monoxide, such as from tobacco smoke (Y. T. Chen et al., 2021; Jullien, 2021).

Native American and Black infants show the highest rates of SIDS in the United States, followed by non-Hispanic Whites (Centers for Disease Control and Prevention [CDC], 2022b). Asian American and Hispanic infants show lower rates of SIDS than White infants. Ethnic differences are likely due to differences in socioeconomic and lifestyle factors associated with SIDS, such as lack of prenatal care, low rates of breast-feeding, maternal smoking, and low maternal age. Cultural practices such as adult-infant bed-sharing, providing infants with soft bedding, and placing the sleeping baby in a separate room from caregivers increase SIDS risk (Erck Lambert et al., 2024; Parks et al., 2017; Tappin et al., 2023).

During the 1990s, SIDS declined dramatically after the American Academy of Pediatrics (1992) recommended that infants be placed for sleep in a nonprone or supine position (i.e., on their backs) as a strategy to reduce the risk of SIDS (see Figure 5.8). Initiated in 1992, the "Back to Sleep" campaign publicized the importance of nonprone sleeping. Between 1992 and 2001, the SIDS rate declined dramatically in the United States and other countries that implemented nonprone/supine sleeping campaigns (Jullien, 2021; Moon & Task Force on Sudden Infant Death Syndrome, 2016a). Recommendations for a safe sleep environment include using a firm sleep surface, avoiding soft bedding and infant overheating, and sharing a room with the infant without sharing a bed (Horne, 2019).

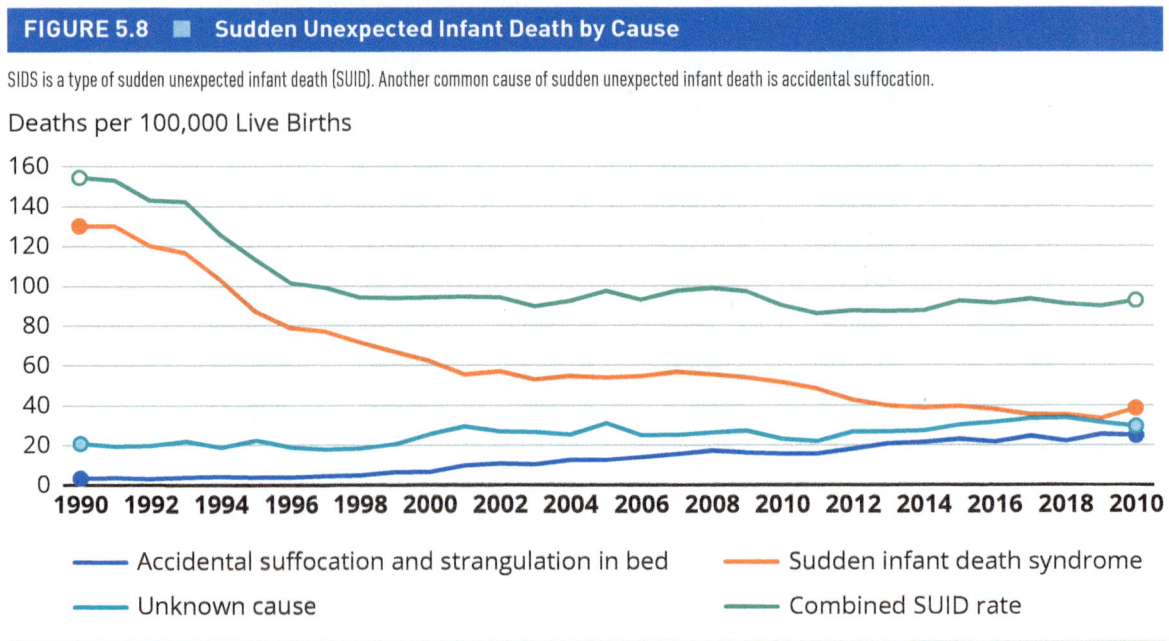

FIGURE 5.8 ■ Sudden Unexpected Infant Death by Cause

SIDS is a type of sudden unexpected infant death (SUID). Another common cause of sudden unexpected infant death is accidental suffocation.

Source: Centers for Disease Control and Prevention (CDC). (2022b). *Trends in sudden unexpected infant death by cause, 1990–2020.* https://www.cdc.gov/sids/data.htm

Childhood

Mortality declines after infancy (but it rises again in adolescence, as we discuss later). In 2021, the leading cause of death in children under age 9 was unintentional injuries. Automobile accidents are the most common cause of fatal injuries (CDC, 2024a). Other leading causes of death are health problems, such as congenital abnormalities, heart disease, and cancer. Alarmingly, homicide was the third and fourth most common cause of death in children under and over 5, respectively (CDC, 2024a). Child maltreatment, discussed later in this chapter, is the most common cause of homicide deaths in children. The most common reason for a visit to the emergency room is a fall. Being hit or struck by objects, cuts, and falling off bikes or skateboards are the other top sources of injuries (CDC, 2022c).

Unintentional injuries are more common in impulsive, overactive, and challenging children, as well as those diagnosed with ADHD (Alexander & Cropper, 2020; Tyrrell & Prasad, 2021). These children are more likely to test limits and protest safety restraints, such as seat belts, wearing a helmet, or holding an adult's hand when crossing the street. Children's risk of injury rises when their parents report feeling little control over their behavior (Acar et al., 2015).

Poor parental and adult supervision are closely associated with childhood injury (Ablewhite et al., 2015; Huynh et al., 2017). Some parents believe that injuries are an inevitable part of child development and may therefore provide less supervision and intervention. Childhood injury is also associated with parental distraction, such as by talking to another parent or phone use (Huynh et al., 2017). Parents who work long hours may find it difficult to keep tabs on their children or feel overwhelmed. In addition, many injuries occur at school, accounting for over 20% of school-age children's visits to the emergency room (Zagel et al., 2019).

Neighborhood disadvantage, characterized by low SES, is associated with higher rates of injuries and bone fractures in children in the United States, Canada, and the United Kingdom (McClure et al., 2015; Rees et al., 2020). Disadvantaged neighborhoods are more likely to have streets, sidewalks, playgrounds, and housing that are poorly designed or maintained, increasing the overall risk of injury (McDonell, 2014).

Contextual factors may increase the risk of injury, but they also offer opportunities for preventing and reducing childhood injuries (Schwebel, 2019). School, community, and media programs can help parents improve supervision and monitoring and teach them about safety risks and how to protect their children. Interventions can also target teachers, school personnel, and schoolchildren, teaching safety skills. At the community level, playgrounds can be designed with safety in mind, including floor surfaces that reduce the risk of injuries after falls. Regular maintenance of playgrounds also supports injury prevention. However, communities often lack the funding to create and maintain safe play spaces, placing residing children at risk.

COVID-19 and Children

Most COVID-19 infections have been documented in adults, but about 7% of COVID-19 infections are in infants and children (Leidman et al., 2021). Typically the incidence of COVID-19 increases with age and presumably, contact with the community. Most infections in children are asymptomatic or include only mild symptoms compared with adults (Ludvigsson, 2020). When children experience symptoms, Black and Hispanic children are 5 to 8 times more likely to be hospitalized than White children (L. Kim et al., 2020). Children are less likely to experience severe infection or death from COVID-19 than adults (Chatziparasidis & Kantar, 2021). All children over 6 months are eligible for COVID-19 vaccinations.

Childhood Asthma

The most common chronic medical condition, affecting about 6% of children age 5 to 11, is **asthma**, a persistent inflammatory disorder of the airways that causes wheezing and coughing (CDC, 2022a; Hoch et al., 2019). When children with asthma are exposed to triggers, such as cold weather, exercise, allergens, emotional stress, and infection, the bronchial tubes contract and fill with mucus, making it difficult for children to breathe.

Asthma has genetic underpinnings that interact with contextual factors, including the home environment and neighborhood (Gruzieva et al., 2021; Willis-Owen et al., 2018). Well insulated homes retain heat efficiently but permit less air circulation, exposing family members to more allergens and toxins from carpeting, secondhand smoke, and furry pets living in the home (Ding et al., 2014; Heinrich, 2011).

Black and Hispanic children are disproportionately likely to develop asthma compared to White children (Zanobetti et al., 2022). These differences are related to racial and ethnic inequities in living situations, including neighborhoods, housing, environmental exposures, and access to health care (Federico et al., 2020; Grant et al., 2022). Low SES neighborhoods influence the risk of developing asthma through high pollution, few parks, poor access to health care, and increased disorder and danger (Chatkin et al., 2022; E. Chen et al., 2019). Children are less likely to play outside in unsafe environments with few green spaces and are more likely to play indoors in enclosed spaces with less circulation (Hartley et al., 2020).

Asthma poses risks to children's development and functioning because children with asthma tend to report more poor health and are more likely to be treated for anxiety and other mental health problems, than are children without asthma (Tomaz Barbosa et al., 2021). Asthma is the most common cause of school absence and is associated with poor academic achievement (Schneider, 2020). In addition, children with asthma are more likely to be bullied than other children, posing additional risks for adjustment (S. P. Joseph et al., 2022).

Childhood Obesity

Children today weigh more than ever before. Obesity has emerged as a serious health problem for children in the United States and western countries in Australia, Europe, South America, and parts of Asia and Africa (Di Cesare et al., 2019; Garrido-Miguel et al., 2019; Spinelli et al., 2019; Xu et al., 2018).

Health care professionals determine whether someone's weight is in the healthy range by examining **body mass index (BMI)**, calculated as weight in kilograms divided by height in meters squared (kg/m^2; World Health Organization, 2009). **Obesity** is defined as having BMI at or above the 95th percentile for height and age, as indicated by the 2000 Centers for Disease Control and Prevention growth charts (Reilly, 2007). About 20% of school-age children are classified as obese (Stierman et al., 2021). Obesity is a growing problem. From 2015 through 2020 children were over four times as likely to be obese than in 1971–1974 as shown in Figure 5.9 (Child Trends, 2018; Stierman et al., 2021).

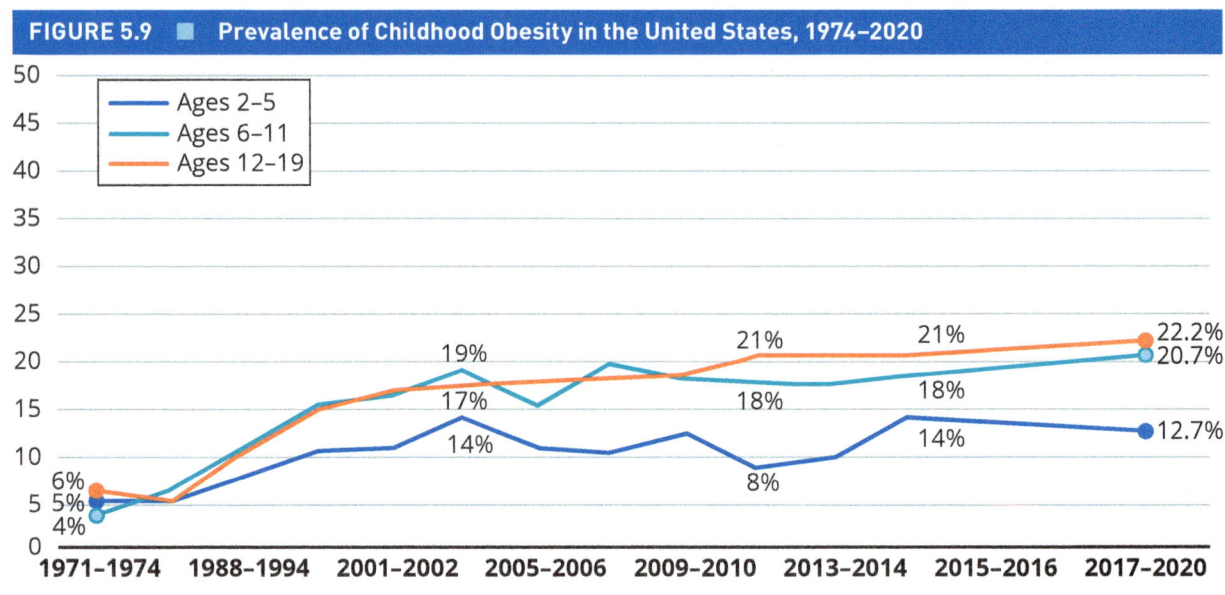

FIGURE 5.9 ■ Prevalence of Childhood Obesity in the United States, 1974–2020

Sources: Adapted from Child Trends. (2018). *Overweight children and youth*; Stierman, B., Afful, J., Carroll, M. D., Chen, T. C., Davy, O., Fink, S., Fryar, C. D., Gu, Q., Hales, C. M., Hughes, J. P., Ostchega, Y., Storandt, R. J., & Akinbami, L. J. (2021). National Health and Nutrition Examination Survey 2017–March 2020 prepandemic data files—development of files and prevalence estimates for selected health outcomes. *National Health Statistics Reports, 2021*(158).

Heredity plays a strong role in obesity, but contextual factors interact with biology to determine whether genetic predispositions to weight gain are fulfilled (Goodarzi, 2018; Loos & Yeo, 2022). Children in low-SES homes are at higher risk for obesity than their peers in high-SES homes (Chung et al., 2016). Low SES communities may increase the likelihood of childhood obesity by offering offer few opportunities for outside play, lack of safe playgrounds with equipment that encourages activity, and the closer proximity of fast-food restaurants to homes and schools (J. Han et al., 2020; Y. Kim et al., 2019).

Physical activity also contributes to body weight, and, as we have discussed, it tends to decline beginning in middle childhood (Farooq et al., 2018). Screen time—time spent in front of a television, computer, or other electronic device with a screen—is a sedentary activity that places children at risk for obesity (Fang et al., 2019). Screen time increases with age and the sedentary nature of screen time and the snacking that tends to accompany it place children at risk for becoming overweight and obese (T. N. Robinson et al., 2017). Perhaps not surprisingly, increases in screen time coupled with reduced outside activity that was commonplace during the lockdowns of the COVID-19 pandemic were associated with weight gain in many children (Jebeile et al., 2022). We discuss children's screen use later in this chapter.

Child and adolescent obesity is associated with short- and long-term health problems, including heart disease, high blood pressure, orthopedic problems, and diabetes (Lee & Kim, 2021; Nowicki et al., 2019; Wühl, 2019). Obese children and adolescents are at risk for peer rejection, depression, low self-esteem, and body dissatisfaction (D. R. Chen & Lu, 2022; E. Robinson et al., 2020). Most youngsters do not outgrow obesity but instead become obese adults (Simmonds 2016).

Programs that effectively reduce obesity in children and adolescents target their screen time and increase their physical activity and time spent outdoors. In addition, successful programs teach children about nutrition and help them reduce their consumption of high-calorie foods and increase their consumption of fruits and vegetables (Kumar & Kelly, 2017; Lobstein et al., 2015).

Child Abuse

Child abuse, also known as *child maltreatment*, is any intentional harm to a minor (an individual under 18 years of age), including actions that harm the child physically, emotionally, sexually, and through neglect (U.S. Department of Health & Human Services, 2024). Each year, there are about 600,000 confirmed cases of abuse or neglect in the United States (U.S. Department of Health & Human Services, 2024). This number is alarming, but it likely underestimates the incidence of child maltreatment because many children experience abuse that is not reported. Neglect (depriving a child of adequate food, clothing, shelter, or medical care) is most common, followed by physical abuse (intentionally injuring a child) and sexual abuse (any sexual activity or inappropriate touching, coerced or persuaded, with a child). Children often experience several forms of abuse at once. It is often difficult for maltreated children to cope and heal because abuse often is not a one-time event; some children experience abuse that persists for years.

Parents are the most common perpetrators of physical abuse and neglect (in over 90% of cases, on average); however unrelated adults known to the child, such as friends of the family, babysitters, and caregivers' partners, are most likely to perpetrate sexual abuse (U.S. Department of Health & Human Services, 2024). Abuse occurs in all types of families and at all socioeconomic levels, but maltreatment is more often discovered in homes characterized by poverty, food and housing insecurity, marital instability, and drug and alcohol abuse (Assink et al., 2019; L. M. Berger et al., 2017; U.S. Department of Health and Human Services, 2018a). Maltreatment is more likely to be discovered in children of disadvantaged families, partly because they are more likely to come into contact with social services, such as when parents seek welfare and other forms of financial assistance or when parental substance use is discovered (H. Kim et al., 2018). Biases regarding low SES may also play a role. For instance, one study of nearly 4,000 children hospitalized for child maltreatment found that low-SES families using public health insurance were more likely to be reported to child protective services than their higher SES counterparts with private health insurance (Rebbe et al., 2022).

Chronic maltreatment influences development of the brain structures that regulate cognition and emotion (Cabrera et al., 2020; W. Yang et al., 2023). School age children who are maltreated tend to score lower on standardized math and reading tests and show poor academic achievement (Ferrara et al., 2023; Ryan et al., 2018). The socioemotional effects of child maltreatment include poor coping skills, low self-esteem, and difficulty managing emotions and social relationships (Cicchetti & Banny, 2014; Lavi et al., 2019). Problems with anxiety, depression, and risky behaviors are common (Cecil et al., 2017; Widom, 2022). Many victims of sexual abuse display symptoms of posttraumatic stress disorder (PTSD), an anxiety disorder that includes flashbacks, nightmares, and feelings of helplessness (Kenny et al., 2020).

Rather than any one factor, it is the accumulation of risk factors that increases the likelihood of child abuse (Vial et al., 2020; M.-Y. Yang & Maguire-Jack, 2018). Children with special needs, such as those with physical and mental disabilities, are at increased risk for maltreatment because they require a great deal of care and present financial and emotional challenges (Font & Berger, 2014; Giardino et al., 2022). Caregivers who abuse children often lack knowledge about child development, have unrealistic expectations for children, and have poor impulse control and coping skills (Wagner et al., 2015). Income loss, involuntary job loss, parental stress, and parental burnout also predict maltreatment (Griffith, 2022; Schenck-Fontaine & Gassman-Pines, 2020).

Maltreatment has negative effects on children. The socioemotional effects are especially daunting and long lasting.

fizkes/istock

Community factors, such as inadequate housing, violence, and poverty, threaten family well-being (Cuartas, 2018; Widom, 2014). Neighborhoods with few community-level support resources, such as parks, childcare centers, preschool programs, recreation centers and churches, are associated with an increased likelihood of child maltreatment (Austin et al., 2020; Molnar et al., 2016). In contrast, neighborhoods with a low turnover of residents, a sense of community, and connections among neighbors support parents and protect against child maltreatment (Molnar et al., 2022; van Dijken et al., 2016).

Effective prevention and early identification of abuse rely on training parents and teachers to recognize the signs of abuse and report suspicions to law enforcement and child protection agencies. All U.S. states and the District of Columbia identify **mandated reporters**. These individuals are legally obligated to report suspected child maltreatment to the appropriate agency, such as child protective services, a law enforcement agency, or a state's child abuse reporting hotline (Child Welfare Information Gateway, 2019). In addition to targeting parents, caregivers, and other adults, effective prevention programs educate children about their bodies and their right not to be touched. When children are exposed to school-based education programs that help them learn how to recognize inappropriate touches, they are more apt to report them to teachers and other adults (Gubbels et al., 2021). Table 5.1 provides a non-exhaustive list of signs of abuse. Not all children who display one or more of the signs on this list have experienced maltreatment, but each sign is significant enough to merit attention.

TABLE 5.1 ■ Signs of Child Abuse and Neglect

The Child:

- Shows sudden changes in behavior or school performance.
- Exhibits extremes in behavior, such as overly compliant or demanding behavior, extreme passivity, withdrawal, or aggression.
- Has not received help for physical or medical problems (e.g., dental care, eyeglasses, immunizations) brought to the parents' attention.
- Has difficulty concentrating or learning problems that appear to be without cause.
- Is very watchful, as if waiting for something bad to happen.
- Frequently lacks adult supervision.
- Has unexplained burns, bruises, broken bones, or black eyes.
- Is absent from school often, especially with fading bruises after returning.
- Comes to school early, stays late, and does not want to go home.
- Is reluctant to be around a particular person or shrinks at the approach of a parent or adult.
- Reports injury by a parent or another adult caregiver.
- Lacks appropriate clothing for the weather.
- Is delayed in physical or emotional development.
- States that there is no one at home to provide care.

The Parent:

- Shows indifference and little concern for the child.
- Denies problems at home or school.
- Blames problems on the child.
- Refers to the child as bad or worthless or berates the child.
- Has demands that are too high for the child to achieve.
- Offers conflicting, unconvincing, or no explanation for the child's injury.
- Uses harsh physical discipline with the child or suggests that caregivers use harsh physical discipline if the child misbehaves.
- Is abusing alcohol or other drugs.

Source: Child Welfare Information Gateway. (2019). *What is child abuse and neglect? Recognizing the signs and symptoms*. Children's Bureau, USDHHS. https://www.childwelfare.gov/resources/what-child-abuse-and-neglect-recognizing-signs-and-symptoms/

THINKING IN CONTEXT 5.3

1. Children live in a variety of contexts, with varying resources and opportunities. Some children face greater risks for poor health than their peers. Discuss health disparities associated with race, ethnicity, and SES. Specifically, discuss two health threats; define them and discuss how contextual factors associated with race, ethnicity, or SES are related to them.
2. Child abuse is a complex problem influenced by the child, caregivers, and the contexts in which they are embedded, such as neighborhood, workplace, community, culture, and so on. Consider child abuse from a bioecological systems perspective (see Chapter 1).
    a. Identify two factors within the child, such as characteristics or behaviors, that might act as risk or protective factors that influence the risk, increasing or decreasing, respectively, the likelihood of abuse.
    b. Consider the microsystem and mesosystem. What are examples of three factors at these levels related to abuse?
    c. Reflect on the children's exosystem. What two factors indirectly affect them?
    d. How does the larger society and culture (macrosystem) matter?

THREATS TO ADOLESCENT HEALTH

5.4 Analyze threats to adolescents' health, such as eating disorders, substance use, and depression and suicide.

Adolescence is generally a healthy period for most young people. Rather than illness, the most significant threats adolescents face to their health stem from their own (and others') behavior, as the mortality statistics suggest. Many adolescents engage in unhealthy weight loss behaviors that can escalate into eating disorders. Other problems that may arise during adolescence and emerging adulthood include substance abuse, depression, and suicide.

Injuries and Mortality

Mortality rises substantially from childhood to adolescence. Recall from Chapter 4 that adolescents' brains are primed to seek rewards, which makes them more likely to engage in risky activities with the potential for injury. Fatal injuries from accidents (from motor vehicles, drowning, pedestrian accidents, and unintentional poisoning, including drug overdoses) are the leading causes of death for adolescents age 10–19 (National Center for Health Statistics, 2022). Suicide is the second leading cause of death for adolescents 10–14 and the third for 15–19. Homicide is the second leading cause of death for older adolescents (and fourth for younger adolescents). Firearms are involved in up to one-half of all adolescent suicides and nearly all adolescent homicides. There are substantial racial differences in mortality in late adolescence, with homicide deaths much more common in Black adolescents and suicide more common in Native American/Alaskan Native and White adolescents.

Contextual factors contribute to ethnic and racial differences in mortality rates during adolescence. Specifically, SES and community factors place Black and American Indian/Alaskan Native youth, who are disproportionately at risk of living in low SES homes and communities, at risk for higher rates of mortality. Economic disadvantage is one of the most robust predictors of violence, especially in urban settings (Bui & Deakin, 2021). Insufficient resources at home and in the neighborhood and exposure to violence and discrimination in the community contribute to Black adolescents' heightened risk of experiencing violence (McCrea et al., 2019). American Indian/Alaskan Native adolescents often live in homes and communities characterized by high levels of poverty. Experiences with discrimination, difficulty acculturating or integrating native customs and beliefs with popular culture, and feeling marginalized contribute to higher rates of suicide among American Indian/Alaskan Native adolescents (Wiglesworth et al., 2022).

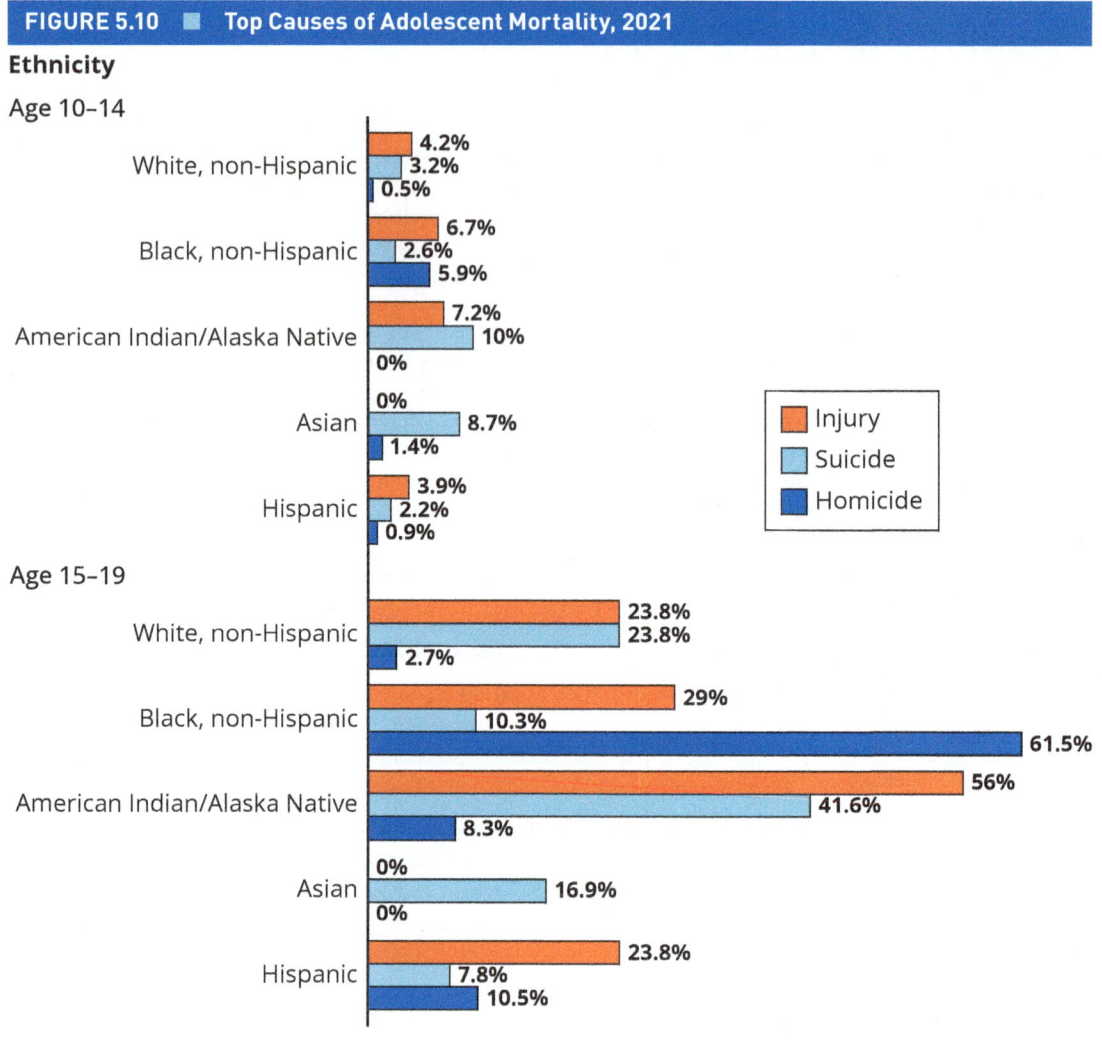

FIGURE 5.10 ■ Top Causes of Adolescent Mortality, 2021

Note. 0 = Insufficient data; rate per 100,000 people

Source: Centers for Disease Control and Prevention. (2024b). *WISQARS leading causes of death visualization tool.* https://www.cdc.gov/injury/wisqars/index.html

Eating Disorders

Adolescents' rapidly changing physique, coupled with media portrayals of "ideal" body shapes, leads many teens to become dissatisfied with their bodies, placing them at risk for eating disorders, such as anorexia nervosa, bulimia nervosa, and binge eating disorder (American Psychiatric Association, 2013). Preoccupation with body shape and weight is common to all eating disorders.

Anorexia Nervosa, Bulimia Nervosa, and Binge Eating Disorder

Individuals with **anorexia nervosa** have a distorted body image, incorrectly viewing themselves as overweight (American Psychiatric Association, 2013). They starve themselves and exercise for hours each day to achieve and maintain a weight substantially lower than expected for height and age (Glashouwer et al., 2019). **Bulimia nervosa** is characterized by recurrent episodes of binge eating, consuming much more food than a similar person would eat in a 2-hour period. Many people use the word *binge* to describe their eating (e.g., "I binged on pizza!"). However, the binge eating that characterizes eating disorders is not simply overeating. Binge eating is uncomfortable. It is associated with a sense of feeling out of control. It typically occurs privately and is accompanied by guilt, shame, and self-disgust afterward. In bulimia nervosa, binge eating is followed by purging, behavior designed to compensate for the binge, such as vomiting, excessive exercise, or use of laxatives (American Psychiatric Association,

2013). Unlike bulimia nervosa, **binge eating disorder** is not accompanied by purges or compensatory behavior (Campbell & Peebles, 2014). Binge eating disorder is diagnosed when binges occur at least once a week for 3 months.

Prevalence of Eating Disorders

Binge eating disorder is the most prevalent eating disorder, occurring in up to 5% of adolescents, followed by bulimia nervosa, which is seen in 1% to 5% (Serra et al., 2020). Anorexia is less common, affecting about 2% of girls age 19 and under (and very few boys), but the starvation accompanying anorexia nervosa makes it the most deadly eating disorder (van Eeden et al., 2021).

Adolescents with eating disorders often have a distorted and negative view of their bodies, coupled with an obsession with weight control and extreme weight-control behaviors.

PeopleImages/istock

Eating disorders occur in all ethnic and socioeconomic groups in Western countries and are increasingly common in Asian and Arab cultures (Alfalahi et al., 2022; Hornberger & Lane, 2021; Melisse et al., 2020; Sahlan et al., 2021). It was once thought that White and Latina girls in the United States, especially those of higher SES, were at higher risk for poor body image and eating disorders than Black girls, who were believed to be protected by cultural and media portrayals valuing voluptuous figures in Black women (Smink et al., 2013). Instead, eating disorders may be undetected in Black girls because of barriers to diagnosis and treatment and a reluctance to seek help (Coffino et al., 2019). Recent research suggests no race or ethnic differences in eating disorders (Z. H. Cheng et al., 2019; Hornberger & Lane, 2021). Race and ethnicity are understudied in this area, with most research articles published over the past 20 years failing to report participant ethnicity (Egbert et al., 2022).

Disordered eating, such as fasting, diet pill use, and purging to control weight, is more common in LGBTQ+ adolescents and those who identify as non-binary than their straight and cisgender peers (Cao et al., 2023; Davidson et al., 2022). Adolescents who identify as transgender show the highest rates of eating disorders, with some studies suggesting that about 16% of transgender youth are diagnosed, and as many as two thirds engage in disordered eating (Hornberger & Lane, 2021; Parker & Harriger, 2020). Discrimination stress contributes to LGBTQ+ adolescents' heightened risk for eating disorders (Geilhufe et al., 2021). Identifying and treating eating disorders in non-binary youth is challenging because most healthcare providers use standard growth charts based on sex, which often do not match non-binary adolescents' body image and goals. Some researchers recommend that health professionals consult growth curves for both the young person's birth-assigned sex and gender identity to establish appropriate treatment goal weight (Nagata et al., 2020).

Influences and Treatment

Stress and traumatic events can trigger disordered eating and increase the risk of developing eating disorders (Touyz et al., 2020). The prevalence of eating disorders rose during the COVID-19 pandemic (Cerniglia & Cimino, 2023). Perceived stress during lockdown was associated with more reported binge eating and dietary restriction (Flaudias et al., 2020). Adolescents with preexisting eating disorder diagnoses showed worse symptoms, greater instability, and greater need for hospitalization during the COVID-19 pandemic (Otto et al., 2021; Spettigue et al., 2021). The need for medical care to treat eating disorders tripled during this period (Feldman et al., 2023).

Treatment for eating disorders addresses patients' weight and shape concerns and psychological conditions such as anxiety and depression through therapy, behavioral training, and perhaps medication (Dalle Grave et al., 2021; Datta et al., 2023; Le Grange et al., 2022). Eating disorders are difficult to treat. In some studies as many as three quarters of adolescents diagnosed with an eating disorder continued to show symptoms 5 years later (Ackard et al., 2011; Herpertz-Dahlmann et al., 2015). Only up to half of individuals fully recover, and anorexia nervosa has the highest mortality rate of all mental disorders (Khalsa et al., 2017).

Alcohol and Substance Use

Generally speaking, in North America, substance use, such as drug, alcohol, and tobacco, tends to increase during adolescence, increasing with each grade in school and peaking in the early 20s (see

Figure 5.11; Schulenberg et al., 2021). Over one third of high school seniors in the United States have tried marijuana, two thirds have tried alcohol, and over thirds report having ever been drunk (Miech et al., 2023). Notably, contrary to popular beliefs about "teenagers these days," regular use of marijuana and alcohol use has declined over the past 20 years (see Figure 5.12).

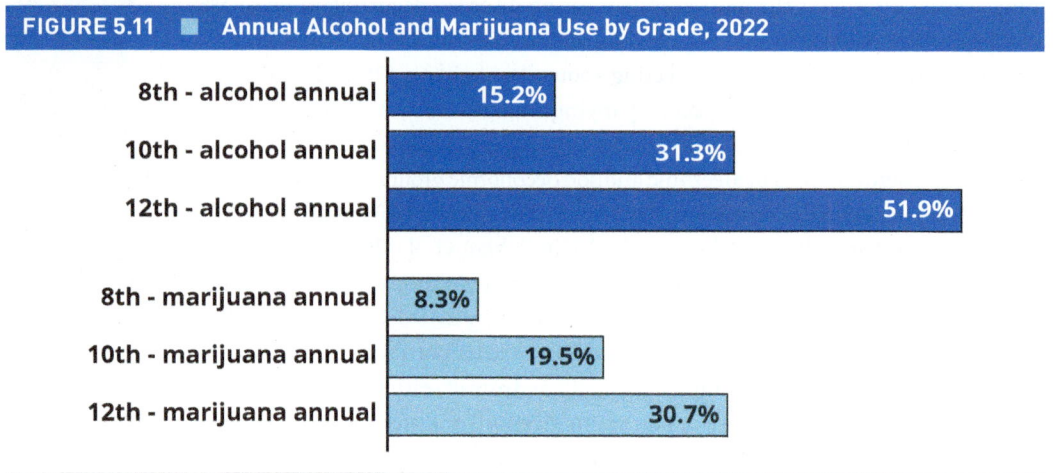

FIGURE 5.11 ■ Annual Alcohol and Marijuana Use by Grade, 2022

Source: Miech, R. A., Johnston, L. D., Patrick, M. E., O'Malley, P. M., Bachman, J. G., & Schulenberg, J. E. (2023). *Monitoring the Future national survey results on drug use, 1975–2022: Secondary school students. Monitoring the Future Monograph Series.* Institute for Social Research, The University of Michigan. http://monitoringthefuture.org/results/publications/monographs

Although most adolescents experiment with alcohol, tobacco, and marijuana, without incident, there are short-term dangers of alcohol and substance use. Adolescents are less sensitive to the cues adults often use to limit their intake, such as motor impairment, sedation, social impairment, and quietness or distress (Spear, 2018). The second most used substance, after alcohol, is marijuana (Hammond et al., 2020). Interestingly, although many states have legalized marijuana, adolescents' use in these states has not increased (Anderson et al., 2019; Hammond et al., 2020).

Alcohol and marijuana use in adolescence, even moderate use, is associated with damage to the brain, including smaller volume and gray matter density in areas responsible for executive control, especially, the frontal cortex (Hamidullah et al., 2020; Müller-Oehring et al., 2018). Substance use is associated with a broad set of neurocognitive deficits in attention, learning, working memory, processing

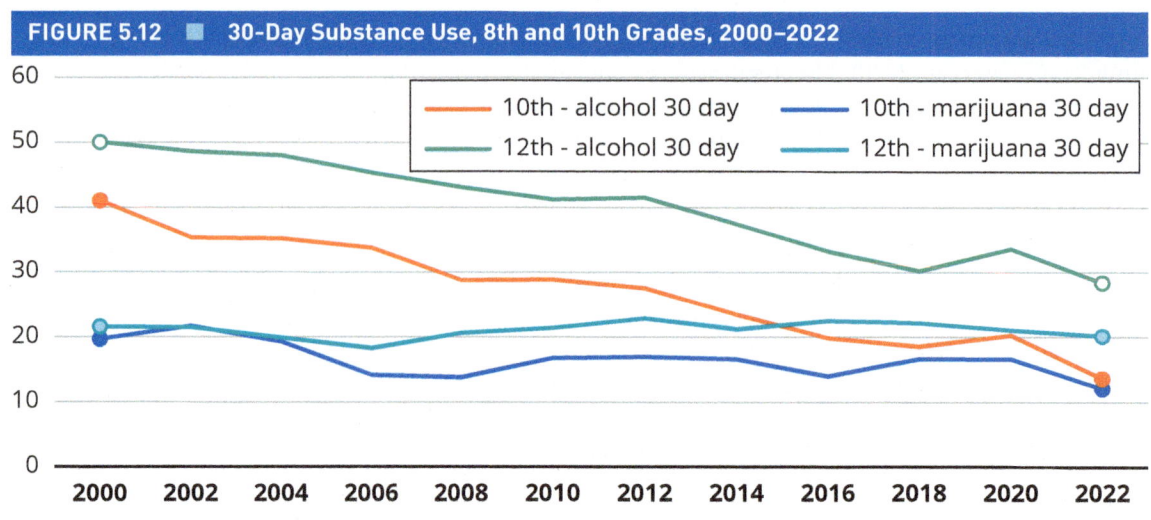

FIGURE 5.12 ■ 30-Day Substance Use, 8th and 10th Grades, 2000–2022

Note. Data shows the percentage for each grade.

Source: Miech et al. (2023).

speed, visuospatial processing, problem solving and executive control (Kroon et al., 2021; Lorenzetti et al., 2020; Lovell et al., 2020). Early onset of marijuana use, before age 18 and especially prior to age 16, is associated with more severe consequences, especially in learning, memory, and executive function (Cyrus et al., 2021; Hammond et al., 2020). Yet there is room for optimism because some research has shown that when alcohol use is discontinued the adolescent brain can grow in volume and show improved executive function (Lisdahl et al., 2013). Given the brain's plasticity, some recovery of neurological function after stopping use is expected, but the degree of recovery is not clear (Hammond et al., 2020; Meruelo et al., 2017).

Alcohol and marijuana use tend to co-occur, making it difficult to disentangle the independent effects of each (Karoly et al., 2020). They are associated with negative consequences that can interfere with adolescents' development, such as academic problems, unwanted sexual encounters, risky sexual activity, externalizing problems, such as aggression and delinquency, and internalizing problems, such as anxiety, depression, and suicide (Coffey & Patton, 2016; Marshall, 2014; Spear, 2018). Finally, marijuana smokers experience many respiratory problems common to tobacco smoking and vaping, such as cough, more frequent chest illnesses, and cancers (Tan & Sin, 2018; Traboulsi et al., 2020)

Most adults with a substance use disorder report using substances before age 18 and developing their disorder by age 20, highlighting the importance of delaying initiation of substance use for as long as possible (Gray & Squeglia, 2018). Warm supportive parenting and monitoring children's whereabouts and friends protect against substance use. Low SES, drug abuse within the family and community, disadvantaged neighborhoods, and early exposure to traumatic life events increase the risk of alcohol and drug abuse in adolescence (Trucco, 2020). Peers play a role in alcohol and substance use, but adolescents tend to overestimate peer use (Yuen et al., 2020). Effective prevention programs help adolescents perceive peer norms accurately and develop coping and life skills to aid in self-regulation and manage challenging social situations (Pedersen et al., 2017; M. Tremblay et al., 2020).

Cigarette and E-Cigarette Use

About 5% of high school seniors report using cigarettes in the past 30 days (compared with one third in 1990) (Miech et al., 2023). Today e-cigarettes (*vaping*) are the most commonly used tobacco product, with about one quarter of 12th graders and one fifth of 10th graders reporting use within the past 30 days (Miech et al., 2023). Many adolescents view e-cigarettes as a safer alternative to conventional cigarettes but that is false (G. Han & Son, 2022). Nicotine and the aerosol created by e-cigarettes include chemicals, heavy metals, and ultrafine particles that reach the lungs and are linked to heightened cardiovascular risk and lung disease (Gawlik et al., 2018; Ghosh et al., 2018; Murthy, 2017). Nicotine stimulates reward pathways in the brain, causing immediate and long-lasting withdrawal symptoms, including irritability, craving, anxiety, and attention deficits. Moreover, e-cigarette users show an increased risk of transitioning to tobacco smoking (Owotomo & Maslowsky, 2021).

Depression and Suicide

About one third of adolescents report sometimes feeling hopeless (U. S. Department of Health and Human Services, 2019). A smaller number, about 13% of 12- to 17-year-old adolescents in the United States. meet the criteria to be diagnosed with depression (American Psychiatric Association, 2013; National Institute of Mental Health, 2019). Depression is characterized by feelings of sadness, hopelessness, and frustration; changes in sleep and eating habits; problems with concentration; loss of interest in activities; and loss of energy and motivation. Depressive symptoms and rates of depression increase in early adolescence and sex differences in prevalence emerge, with girls reporting depression twice as often as boys (Petersen et al., 2018). Depression has long-term consequences for adolescent adjustment, including school dropout, substance abuse, pregnancy, and unemployment and not attending college in emerging adulthood (Clayborne et al., 2019; M. Mason et al., 2019).

Intense and long-lasting depression can lead to thoughts of suicide, death caused by self-directed injuries with the intent to die. Suicide is among the three leading causes of death in adolescents in the United States and many other Western countries, including Australia, Canada, and the United Kingdom (Australian Institute of Health and Welfare, 2016; National Center for Health Statistics.,

2022; Office for National Statistics, 2015; Statistics Canada, 2015). Although depression is more common among girls, suicide is more common in boys (Glenn et al., 2020). For unknown reasons, the U.S. suicide rate for adolescents and emerging adults has increased dramatically over the past 20 years (see Figure 5.13; V. A. Joseph et al., 2022). In the United states, there are marked ethnic and racial differences in adolescent suicide, with Native American or Alaskan Native youth at the highest and Black youth at the lowest risk (V. A. Joseph et al., 2022; Shain, 2019).

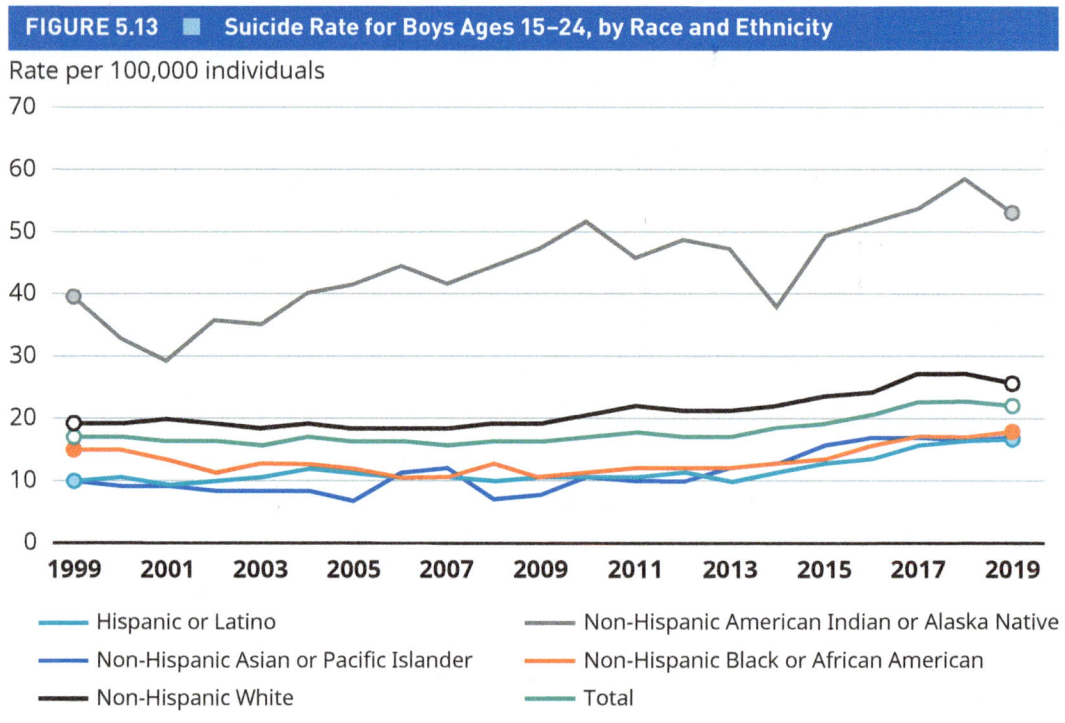

FIGURE 5.13 ■ Suicide Rate for Boys Ages 15–24, by Race and Ethnicity

Sources: Adapted from Ramchand, R., Gordon, J. A., Pearson, J. L. (2021). Trends in suicide rates by race and ethnicity in the United States. *JAMA Network Open, 4*(5), e2111563; Centers for Disease Control and Prevention. (n.d.). *Underlying cause of death 1999–2019*. Accessed December 29, 2020, from https://wonder.cdc.gov/wonder/help/ucd.html; Kochanek, K. D., Xu, J. Q., Arias, E. (2020, December). Mortality in the United States, 2019. NCHS Data Brief, no 395. Accessed April 14, 2021, from h ttps://www.cdc.gov/nchs/data/databriefs/db395-H.pdf

Risk Factors for Depression and Suicide

Genetic factors contribute to the susceptibility to depression in various ways, such as by influencing the brain regions responsible for emotional regulation and stress responses and the production of neurotransmitters that play a role in depression (Lussier et al., 2021). Depression increases the risk of suicide (Carballo et al., 2020). Contextual factors, such as early life stress, neighborhood disadvantage, a poor sense of efficacy in the community, low SES, and the extended experience of stress, contribute to the risk for depression and suicide (Ati et al., 2020; Choi et al., 2021; M. Li et al., 2020; Uddin et al., 2017). Relationships with parents influence adolescents' responses to stressful life events. The long-term effects of stressful life events on depression are buffered by parent-child closeness and worsened by parental depression (Ge et al., 2009; Natsuaki et al., 2014). Family support is a particularly robust protective factor against depression (Lu, 2019; Rueger et al., 2014).

LGBTQ+ youth, especially those who are male or non-binary, experience an exceptionally high risk for suicide, with three times as many attempts as other adolescents (Miranda-Mendizábal et al., 2017; Raifman et al., 2020). In one national study, nearly three quarters of LGBTQ+ youth reported suicide ideation and one quarter reported attempted suicide (Jadva et al., 2021). Adolescents who identify as transgender are at highest risk for suicide, as much as six times more likely to attempt suicide than cisgender peers (Zimlich, 2019). LGBTQ+ adolescents who attempt suicide often list family conflict, peer rejection, bias-based victimization, and poor self-acceptance as influences on their attempts (De Lange et al., 2022; Grossman et al., 2016; Toomey et al., 2018).

COVID-19, Depression, and Suicide

Young people's responses to the COVID-19 pandemic illustrate the importance of contextual factors in mental health. An analysis of over 60 research studies examining adolescents' mental health from before the COVID-19 pandemic through May 2020, after adolescents experienced pandemic quarantines and lock downs, found that up to two thirds of adolescents reported depression symptoms and up to 27% experienced severe depression (compared to typical prevalence level of about 13%) (Panchal et al., 2021). A sample of young adolescents from the United Kingdom showed similar responses, with a 44% increase in self-reported depression from December 2019 through June 2020 (Wright et al., 2021).

Adolescent suicide increased by 25%, during the COVID-19 pandemic, especially in girls (Gracia et al., 2021). In the summer of 2020, emergency room visits for suicide attempts in 12- to 17-year-old girls were 26% higher than the corresponding period in 2019; in 2021, the rate was 51% higher than the corresponding period in 2020, before the pandemic lockdowns (Yard et al., 2021). Suicide-related emergency room visits remained stable for adolescent boys, suggesting that adolescent girls are uniquely vulnerable. The social disruption associated with school closures and lockdowns, especially lack of contact with peers may be particularly challenging for girls.

The COVID-19 pandemic placed multiple stresses on young people, including school closures, disruptions of routines, social isolation, and worries about family illness and economic impacts (Mayne et al., 2021). Risk factors for depression during the pandemic included having a high number of COVID-19 cases in the community and being exposed to a relative doing first-line job responsibilities related to COVID-19 (Panchal et al., 2021). Pandemic-related stresses may be most acutely felt by Black and Latino adolescents and emerging adults from low-income families and communities because of exposure to long-term stressors before the pandemic. Poor access to health services and insurance, barriers to accessing public benefits, chronic poverty, and discrimination may contribute to the pandemic's disproportionate mental health impacts on young people of color (Rothe et al., 2021).

Suicide Prevention

School-based suicide prevention programs teach students and staff to identify the warning signs of suicide, such as those listed in Table 5.2. However, it is important to note that suicide cannot be easily predicted. A recent study of completed suicides by UK adolescents suggested that about one third showed no warning signs, including no known ideation, substance misuse, mental health diagnosis, or recent adverse life events (Rodway et al., 2020). Although many school and community-based programs exist, there is little research examining their effectiveness (Iyengar et al., 2018; Nugent et al., 2019). Treating depression and preventing suicide usually involves therapy, sometimes medication, and increasing support at home, school, and in the peer group (Asarnow & Mehlum, 2019). What can you do to prevent suicide? Encourage and assist others in seeking help when they display risk factors for suicide. When people talk about suicide, it is essential to believe them.

THINKING IN CONTEXT 5.4

1. To what extent do you think adolescents are at heightened risk for body dissatisfaction compared to children and adults? Why? Brainstorm ways of addressing body dissatisfaction. What challenges do you envision in reducing body dissatisfaction and, by extension, potentially reducing the prevalence of eating disorders?
2. Many adults are surprised to learn that adolescent alcohol and substance use has declined over the past two decades. Why do you think these declines have occurred? Consider societal level changes (macrosystem), such as laws, customs, and societal beliefs. How might these have contributed to reductions in alcohol and substance use? What changes might have occurred in high schools, curricula, and at the neighborhood level? How might have adolescents' interactions with family and peers changed?
3. What do you think are the most important points to share with a parent about adolescent suicide? How might you change your message for a high school teacher or coach? Finally, what do adolescents need to know? What are ways of sharing this information with teenagers?

TABLE 5.2 ■ Suicide Warning Signs
Any of the following behaviors can serve as a warning sign of increased suicide risk:
• Change in eating and sleeping habits
• Withdrawal from friends, family, and regular activities
• Acting out behavior or running away
• Drug and alcohol use, especially changes in use
• Unusual neglect of personal appearance
• Marked personality change
• Persistent boredom, difficulty concentrating, or a decline in the quality of schoolwork
• Frequent complaints about physical symptoms, such as stomachaches, headaches, and fatigue
• Loss of interest in pleasurable activities
• Lack of response to praise
• Complaints of being a bad person or feeling rotten inside
• Verbal hints with statements such as the following: "I won't be a problem for you much longer." "Nothing matters." "It's no use." "I won't see you again."
• Putting affairs in order—giving away favorite possessions, cleaning their room, and throwing away important belongings
• Sudden cheerfulness after a period of depression
• Signs of psychosis (hallucinations or bizarre thoughts)
• Most important: Stating "I want to kill myself," or "I'm going to commit suicide."

Source: Adapted from American Academy of Child and Adolescent Psychiatry. (2021). *Suicide in children and teens.* https://www.aacap.org/AACAP/Families_and_Youth/Facts_for_Families/FFF-Guide/Teen-Suicide-010.aspx

APPLY YOUR KNOWLEDGE

"Here I am, right in the center of the back row, the tallest kid in class," 14-year-old Fatima said as she reviewed the class photo from her second grade class. "Now I'm one of the shortest in my grade. And heaviest." she complained to her mother. "Nonsense. I was just like you at your age. You might feel like you stand out now, but the other girls will catch up." "Doubt it," Fatima sighed as she went to her room, "The girls in my class just look at me and gossip. They'll never be like me."

Fatima hopped on to her bed and texted Ralph, "U around?" "Can U hang out?" he asked. Fatima loved hanging out with Ralph and his friends. A high school senior, Ralph knew how to have fun. He and his friends got together almost every day to hang out in the park and vape pot. Sometimes they drank, but beer wasn't as easy to get. Plus, she seemed to fit in with the girls in the group.

Fatima's twin brother, Andre, was a star on the basketball court. Stronger and faster than his peers, Andre was popular with the kids in his class, but his closest friends were not in his class. Like Fatima, Andre preferred spending time with the seniors in his school. The girls were cuter than those in his class and the older boys posed more of a challenge on the basketball court. They were also more fun off the court. The often played what they called "sneaking games" and tried to "get away with stuff." Last week they got away with breaking into the corner store and stealing a case of beer. Andre was scared but soon was exhilarated that they got away with it.

1. Recall from Chapter 1 that some aspects of development are characterized by continuity, gradual linear change, and others by discontinuous stage-like change. Consider Fatima's observation that she was once the tallest child in class and is now the shortest. Which type of change do you think characterizes Fatima's development? Why?

2. Identify influences on growth and health in childhood. How important is early health and physical development for later functioning?

3. How are Fatima and Andre physically different than their peers? How else might they differ physically from their peers? How might physical differences influence socioemotional development, such as their emotions and relationships?

4. What are some of the correlates of early maturation relative to peers? What opportunities does early maturation pose for boys and girls?

5. How might contextual factors influence the physical development in childhood and adolescence? Imagine that Fatima and Andre live in a rural farming community verses a busy urban neighborhood or suburban environment. What opportunities and challenges might these contexts offer for physical development and health in childhood? Adolescence? How might Fatima's and Andre's experiences differ in these two contexts?

6. Adolescents like Fatima and Andre face heightened risk for injuries and health threats. Discuss common threats to adolescents' health. Are Fatima and Andre at equal risk? Why or why not?

CHAPTER SUMMARY

5.1 Discuss changes in growth, nutrition, and activity in infancy and childhood.

Infants experience rapid growth in both the cephalocaudal (head to foot) and proximodistal (center outward) directions during their first year of life. As they begin to grow taller, their body proportions become more like those of adults. Growth is largely maturational, but it can be influenced by health and environmental factors, such as nutrition. Improved sanitation, nutrition, and access to medical care have contributed to an increase in children's growth over the past century in the United States and other industrialized countries. There are also ethnic differences in patterns of growth in many Western countries. Children's appetites vary with their growth, and they develop food preferences based on experience. Malnutrition can lead to marasmus, kwashiorkor, and growth stunting, which is associated with susceptibility to illness, cognitive deficits, poor overall health, and mortality. Physical activity and sleep are associated with cognitive function, brain development, and mental health.

5.2 Summarize patterns of physical development in adolescence, including puberty and pubertal timing.

Puberty is a process of physical maturation that begins at around age 8 or 9 in girls and 10 to12 in boys. The most noticeable signs of pubertal maturation are the growth spurt and secondary sex characteristics. As the primary sex characteristics (the reproductive organs) mature, adolescents become capable of reproduction. Pubertal timing is influenced by genetic and contextual factors including physical health, nutrition, body fat, exposure to stress, SES, and the secular trend. The consequences of early and late maturation differ dramatically for girls and boys. Girls who mature early are at risk for problems with depression, anxiety, and poor body image. Both boys and girls who mature early are more likely to engage in risky and age-inappropriate behaviors such as sexual activity. Late maturation appears to have a protective effect on girls, but findings regarding the effects of late maturation on boys are mixed and less consistent. Physical activity is associated with cognitive, physical, and mental health, but adolescents generally do not meet recommended guidelines for physical activity. Adolescents' sleep tends to shift to a later sleep pattern, which can result in a sleep deficit.

5.3 Examine health and mortality in infancy and childhood, including injuries, illnesses, childhood obesity, and child abuse.

Infant and child mortality have declined dramatically over the past 100 years, with unintentional injuries now the leading cause of death. Asthma, disproportionately found among Black and Latino children due to environmental inequities, can lead to poor health, mental

5.4 **Analyze threats to adolescents' health, such as eating disorders, substance use, and depression and suicide.**

Morality rises substantially in adolescence, with accidents, suicide, and homicide leading causes. Eating disorders include combinations of starvation (anorexia nervosa), binge eating (bulimia nervosa and binge eating disorder), and purging (bulimia nervosa). They are influenced by genetic and contextual factors. Treatment of eating disorders is challenging and often includes medication, therapy, support groups, nutritional education, and sometimes hospitalization to remedy malnutrition. Alcohol and substance use tend to begin in adolescence and are associated with negative short- and long-term effects such as accidents, academic problems, risks for dependence and abuse, and impaired neurological development. Effective prevention and intervention programs provide adolescents with education, teach skills and increase parental awareness. Depression tends to increase over adolescence and is influenced by factors such as early life and long-term stress. LGBTQ+ youth tend to experience high rates of depression and suicide attempts. Family support is a protective factor against depression and suicide.

KEY TERMS

- adolescent growth spurt
- anorexia nervosa
- asthma
- binge eating disorder
- body mass index (BMI)
- bulimia nervosa
- child abuse
- depression
- growth hormone deficiency
- growth norm
- growth stunting
- kwashiorkor
- mandated reporter
- marasmus
- menarche
- menstruation
- nightmare
- obesity
- ossification
- primary sex characteristic
- proximodistal development
- puberty
- secondary sex characteristic
- secular trend
- sleep terror
- suicide
- sudden infant death syndrome (SIDS)

CAREERS IN CHILD DEVELOPMENT: PHYSICAL DEVELOPMENT AND HEALTH

Physical development includes growth and maturation of the body, including the brain, motor skills, and perception abilities. Some careers support child physical development and health prenatally (genetic counselor), at birth (doula and midwife), and throughout childhood and adolescence (pediatric nurses and physicians).

Genetic Counselor

As we saw in Chapter 2, many chromosomal abnormalities are passed through genetic inheritance. Genetic counselors help assess the risk of an individual or couple passing a genetic disorder to their offspring.

Genetic counselors interview individuals and couples to gather information about their family history, educate them about the risks of particular genetic conditions in their offspring, and inform them about the different genetic tests available to them. Genetic counselors also help individuals and couples understand the results of DNA and other laboratory tests and the potential implications for offspring. Genetic counselors typically work in hospital or clinic settings but may work in private practice.

Genetic counselors typically have a master's degree in genetics or genetic counseling from a program certified by the Accreditation Council for Genetic Counseling and pass a national certification exam. Some genetic counselors specialize in cancer, psychiatric, or genomic health. The median annual wage for genetic counselors was $89,990 in 2022 (U.S. Bureau of Labor Statistics, 2024).

Midwife

A midwife is a healthcare professional who supports and cares for women throughout their pregnancy, including delivering babies during childbirth. They collaborate with other healthcare professionals, including obstetricians, nurses, and hospital staff.

There are two main paths to becoming a midwife with different levels of expertise, certification, and autonomy. Some midwives are referred to as direct-entry midwives because, after earning a bachelor's degree, they are trained and certified (through the North American Registry of Midwives) but do not have a nursing degree. The legal status and requirements to become a direct-entry midwife vary by state, but many states do not permit midwives without nursing degrees. Carefully research state requirements before choosing this option.

The second path to becoming a midwife is to earn a nursing degree and complete a master's program in nurse-midwifery and pass an examination administered by the American Midwifery Certification Board to receive the professional designation of certified nurse-midwife. *Certified nurse-midwives* can practice independently in every state. Most people are familiar with the labor and delivery activities of nurse-midwives. Nurse-midwives may focus on all parts of pregnancy and birth, from preconception to postpartum. The nurse-midwife practice includes various services in reproductive health visits, preventative care, and post-menopausal care. They can prescribe medication and admit or discharge patients if needed. The median annual wage for nurse midwives was about $120,880 in 2022 (U.S. Bureau of Labor Statistics, 2024).

Doula

Doulas provide physical, emotional, and educational support to expectant mothers before birth, during labor, and immediately after birth through the first few weeks. Doulas provide education about labor, medication, and comfort during birth. Doulas also support the partner and family, if involved, to aid their participation in the birth process.

The educational requirements to become a doula include a high school degree and completing a doula education program. Some employers prefer college credits or a degree. Doulas work in hospitals, private practices, birth centers, and community organizations. Doulas' earnings vary with work setting, experience, and location. In 2023 doulas in the United States earned, on average, about $70,000 per year (ZipRecruiter, 2023).

Pediatric and Neonatal Nurse

There are many kinds of nurses. Some specialize in working with specific populations, such as infants and children. Becoming a nurse requires earning an associate's degree or bachelor's degree in nursing, obtaining experience, and passing a licensing exam. The associate's degree prepares nurses for entry-level positions. Some employers prefer nurses with bachelor's degrees in nursing. Bachelor's degrees provide more opportunities to advance. Becoming certified as a registered nurse (RN) opens additional opportunities (and higher salaries). Certification as a registered nurse requires 2 years' experience and passing an exam. Opportunities and salary increase with education and experience. In 2021, the median pay for all registered nurses was $81,220, but salaries vary with education, experience, and geographic location (U.S. Bureau of Labor Statistics, 2024).

Pediatric nurses are registered nurses who specialize in caring for patients from infancy through adolescence. Pediatric nurses perform physical examinations, measure vital statistics, educate parents and caregivers, and work alongside other healthcare providers, such as physicians, to promote children's health and well-being. Because their patients are so young, pediatric nurses often develop close connections with them and their families. An understanding of development is critical to the work of pediatric nurses because infants, children, and adolescents have different abilities and needs—and these change with development. Pediatric nurses are found in hospitals, clinics, private practice, schools, and more. Becoming a pediatric nurse involves completing nursing school, gaining experience, and completing a licensure exam. Nurses with at least 5 years' experience and 3,000 hours in pediatrics hours can take the Certified Pediatric Nurse Examination to demonstrate their competence and earn higher salaries.

Neonatal nurses focus on caring for preterm newborns and infants who are preterm, have low birth weight, or are sick and need medical care. They work in neonatal intensive care units (NICUs), specialized units in hospitals that care for newborns needing medical treatment. They feed and care for infants, monitor infants, administer medication and treatments, and work with other health care providers. Neonatal nurses also provide emotional support to parents and educate them about their infants' care. Becoming a neonatal nurse requires a nursing degree, experience, passing a licensure exam, and after earning 2,000 hours in a neonatal setting, earning a passing grade on the Certified Critical Care Registered Nurse Neonatal Exam.

Physician and Pediatrician

Just as there are many types of nurses, there are many medical specialties and types of physicians (or doctors). Becoming a physician requires attending medical school, which entails 4 years of education beyond the bachelor's degree. In addition to passing a licensure examination, physicians complete a 3-year or longer residency program to gain hands-on experience and training within a specialty. Practicing physicians in hospitals, clinics, and private practice can benefit from understanding how people grow and change throughout their lives.

Some specialties related to development include endocrinology (relating to the release and distribution of hormones), psychiatry (relating to mental health), and neurology (relating to the brain and nervous system). Some seek additional specialty certification in their specialty by completing a board examination. Physicians earned a median salary of about $229,000 in 2022 (U.S. Bureau of Labor Statistics, 2024). Salaries vary with the specialty.

Pediatricians are trained physicians specializing in treating infants, children, and adolescents. Not only do they treat illnesses, but they also improve their patients' overall health and well-being. Pediatricians perform routine checkups, provide immunizations and medications, order tests, refer patients to specialists for specific injuries or illnesses, and speak with parents about their child's treatment options. They assess children's growth, determine whether it is in the appropriate range, and devise treatment plans if it is not. Pediatricians work in hospital settings, clinics, and independent practice. Pediatricians complete a 3-year residency in pediatrics, and many complete an exam to become certified by the American Board of Pediatrics. Pediatricians earned a median salary of about $190,000 in 2022 (U.S. Bureau of Labor Statistics, 2024).

Audiologist

Audiologists are health professionals who diagnose and treat hearing and balance disorders for people of all ages. They screen and test children's hearing and diagnose and treat hearing loss, auditory disorders, and balance problems. Many states require that newborns undergo screening for hearing loss. Audiologists help children and parents select hearing aids and other devices to aid hearing and customize them to their needs. Hearing aids are not one size fits all, so customization and helping someone adjust to a hearing aid can take time and multiple visits. They teach children and parents how to use and care for their hearing aids. Audiologists also counsel children and parents on managing hearing impairments and balance problems. Audiologists work in hospitals, schools, physicians' offices, rehabilitation centers, residential healthcare facilities, and private practice.

Becoming an audiologist requires a doctorate in audiology, a 4-year program. About 375 hours of supervised experience and a passing grade on a state licensure exam are needed to practice. The median annual wage for audiologists was $82,680 in 2022 (U.S. Bureau of Labor Statistics, 2024).

Physical Therapist and Physical Therapy Assistant

Physical therapists provide treatment and intervention for individuals suffering from pain, loss of mobility, or other physical disabilities. They are experts in movement, helping people with injuries, disabilities, and health conditions that need treatment and those who want to avoid future problems. Physical therapists work with children with movement difficulties due to conditions such as cerebral palsy, muscular dystrophy, developmental delays, or traumatic brain injury. They evaluate the child's movement and function, develop a personalized treatment plan, and provide treatment such as exercise, stretching, and massage.

Physical therapists assess patients, diagnose their movement difficulties, and develop personalized treatment plans to improve their ability to move, reduce/manage pain, restore function, and prevent disability. Their treatment may involve hands-on therapy, strengthening and stretching exercises, electrical stimulation and other treatments, and patient education. When working with pediatric patients, physical therapists tailor the treatment plan to the child's individual needs and consider their physical development. They collaborate with families to ensure that the child completes their prescribed exercises and offer education and support to help them reach their full potential.

Physical therapy is a doctoral-level health field. To become a physical therapist, earn a Doctor of Physical Therapy degree (DPT), typically a 3-year degree, pass the National Physical Therapy Examination, and then a state licensure exam. The median annual wage for physical therapists was about $97,723 in 2022 (U.S. Bureau of Labor Statistics, 2024).

Another option for those interested in physical therapy is to become a *physical therapy assistant*. Physical therapy assistants support the work of physical therapists in providing treatments and interventions for people suffering pain, loss of mobility, or other physical disabilities. Physical therapy assistants may provide some hands-on work, such as assisting patients with exercises and treatments. Becoming a physical therapy assistant requires completing 2 years of coursework in a physical therapy assistant program and passing an exam to become certified, the standard for practice. The median annual wage for physical therapist assistants was $62,770 in 2022 (U.S. Bureau of Labor Statistics, 2024).

Occupational Therapist and Occupational Therapy Assistant

Occupational therapists specialize in rehabilitating patients of all ages with physical, developmental, or psychological impairments. They work with children who have developmental delays, developmental disorders such as autism spectrum disorder and sensory processing disorder, and other conditions that affect children's movement in everyday settings, such as cerebral palsy, muscular dystrophy, or traumatic brain injury. Unlike physical therapists who focus on treating physical impairment, occupational therapists help people adapt to everyday settings by improving their motor skills, coordination, and balance in daily tasks. These tasks include fine and gross motor skills and motor planning, such as writing, getting dressed, and using utensils.

When working with pediatric patients, occupational therapists identify target areas for developmentally appropriate levels of independence and adaptive skill building. Treatment may include fine motor skills training, play therapy, sensory integration therapy, and gross motor skills training. They work with children and their families to develop treatment plans tailored to the child's individual needs, providing education and support throughout the therapy process.

Like other healthcare professionals, occupational therapists assess patients' problems, determine goals, create interventions to improve patients' ability to perform daily activities and reach their goals, and evaluate outcomes, modifying treatments as needed. They work in various settings, including hospitals, schools, outpatient clinics, and rehabilitation centers, to help patients of all ages lead a fulfilling and independent life. Becoming an occupational therapist requires a master's degree in occupational therapy, passing the National Board for Certification of Occupational Therapy exam, and obtaining state licensure. The median annual wage for occupational therapists was about $93,180 in 2022 (U.S. Bureau of Labor Statistics, 2024).

An option for individuals interested in occupational therapy is to become an *occupational therapy assistant*. Occupational therapy assistants aid occupational therapists by performing support activities, such as guiding patients in stretching and exercising. Becoming an occupational therapy assistant requires the completion of a 2-year occupational therapy assistant program, followed by a certification examination (depending on the state). The median annual wage for occupational therapy assistants was about $64,250 in 2022 (U.S. Bureau of Labor Statistics, 2024).

PART 3
COGNITIVE DEVELOPMENT

Linda Raymond/istock

6 COGNITIVE CHANGE: COGNITIVE-DEVELOPMENTAL AND SOCIOCULTURAL APPROACHES

> ## LEARNING OBJECTIVES
>
> **6.1** Summarize the six substages of sensorimotor reasoning and processes of cognitive development.
>
> **6.2** Discuss the characteristics of preoperational reasoning and young children's abilities.
>
> **6.3** Describe concrete operational reasoning and older children's abilities.
>
> **6.4** Analyze the development of formal operational reasoning and social cognition in adolescence.
>
> **6.5** Examine Vygotsky's sociocultural perspective on cognitive development.

"Look at that, little one!" exclaims Mateo's grandma as she holds up a shiny, colorful ball in front of him. Five-month-old Mateo's eyes widen as he reaches out with both hands, trying to grab the ball. His grandma gently rolls it away, causing Mateo to follow it with his gaze. "He watches everything, like he's trying to figure it all out," she said. In fact, Mateo is trying to figure it out. He is driven to learn. Soon Mateo will show a greater interest in objects, watching them disappear and reappear. His thinking will become more complex as he progresses through toddlerhood and learns language. These are just the first in a lifetime of changes that will transform how Mateo views his world. How do we explain these cognitive changes? Three major perspectives on cognition address this question in different ways. *Cognitive developmental theories* emphasize the structural changes that underlie development, how the content and organization of thinking changes. *Sociocultural theories* point to the role of context and our need to communicate in influencing thought. *Information processing theories* (discussed in Chapter 7) emphasize changes in physical capacities and strategy use as contributors to cognitive change. In this chapter we examine the cognitive developmental and sociocultural approaches to cognitive change throughout life.

PIAGET'S THEORY: SENSORIMOTOR REASONING IN INFANCY

> **6.1** Summarize the six substages of sensorimotor reasoning and processes of cognitive development.

Have you ever looked at an infant's face and wondered, "What's going on in there?" Can infants think? What do they experience? About one 100 years ago, Swiss scholar Jean Piaget (1896–1980) posed this question. He was the first scientist to examine children's thinking systematically, creating the field of cognitive development (Rochat, 2023).

Processes of Cognitive Development

Piaget (1952) was one of the first theorists to view infants and children as active participants in their development. He theorized that infants and children learn by interacting with the world, building their understanding of everyday phenomena, and applying their knowledge to adapt to the world around them. Through these interactions, individuals organize what they learn to construct and refine their cognitive schemas or ways of knowing and interacting with the world. Think of a cognitive schema as a concept, a belief, or something known. We build our concepts or beliefs by engaging with people and things in our environment. We talk to people and touch objects, and our knowledge, our set of cognitive schemas, grows. In childhood and throughout life, we rely on our schemas to make sense of the world. Our schemas are constantly adapting and developing in response to our experiences. Piaget emphasized the importance of two developmental processes that enable us to cognitively adapt to our world: assimilation and accommodation.

Assimilation and Accommodation

Frequently we encounter information that is similar to something we already know. We can apply existing learning strategies to learn that information. **Assimilation** involves integrating a new experience into a preexisting cognitive schema. Suppose that 1-year-old Makayla uses the schema of "grab and shove into the mouth" to learn. She grabs and shoves the rattle into her mouth, learning about the rattle by using her preexisting schema. When Makayla comes across another object, such as mommy's keys, she transfers the schema to it and assimilates the keys by grabbing them and shoving them into her mouth. Makayla develops an understanding of the new objects through assimilation by fitting them into her preexisting schema.

Sometimes we encounter experiences or information that do not fit within an existing schema, so we must adapt and modify the schema in light of the new information. This process is called **accommodation** (see Figure 6.1). Suppose Makayla encounters another object, a beach ball. She tries her schema of grab and shove, but the beach ball won't fit into her mouth; perhaps she cannot even grab it. She must change her schema or create a new one to incorporate the new information—to learn about the beach ball. Makayla may squeeze and mouth the ball instead, accommodating or changing her way of interacting with the new object. Through accommodation, we change our cognitive schemas, our ways of thinking, our knowledge.

FIGURE 6.1 ■ Assimilation and Accommodation

Assimilation   Accommodation

Source: GlobalP/istock; YouraPechkin/istock

As you read these words, perhaps your knowledge about development (a cognitive schema) has changed after reading these new ideas (accommodation). Maybe you were already familiar with these ideas and instead incorporated this information into your existing framework (assimilation). The processes of assimilation and accommodation enable people to adapt to their environment, absorbing the constant flux of information they encounter daily.

Equilibration

People—infants, children, and adults—constantly encounter new information. Some is assimilated into cognitive schemas. Some schemas are accommodated for the new information. Piaget proposed that people are driven to find equilibrium, or a balance between assimilation and accommodation, a process he called **cognitive equilibration**. When assimilation and accommodation are balanced, people neither incorporate new information into their schemas nor change their schemas in light of new information. They do not need to, because their schemas match the outside world and represent it clearly. But a state of cognitive equilibrium is rare and fleeting. More frequently, people experience a mismatch, or cognitive disequilibrium, between their schemas and the world.

Disequilibrium leads to cognitive growth because the mismatch between schemas and reality leads to confusion and discomfort. It motivates children to modify their cognitive schemas so that their view of the world matches reality. Through cognitive equilibration, the coordination of assimilation and accommodation, this modification takes place to restore balance. Equilibration, the drive for cognitive equilibrium, is the basis for cognitive change, propelling individuals through four stages of cognitive development proposed by Piaget. Recall from Chapter 1, these stages represent four progressively more sophisticated forms of reasoning: sensorimotor, preoperational, concrete operational, and formal operational reasoning. Children create and use more sophisticated cognitive schemas with each advancing stage, enabling them to think, reason, and understand their world in more complex ways. The first stage in Piaget's cognitive developmental theory occurs in infancy, sensorimotor reasoning.

Sensorimotor Reasoning

Can infants think? As we noted, Piaget was the first scientist to thoroughly examine this question. He believed infants could think, but their thinking is very different from children's. Sensorimotor reasoning comprises the first stage of Piaget's, from birth to about 2 years old, infants learn about the world through their senses and motor skills. To think about an object, they must act on it by viewing it, listening to it, touching it, smelling it, and tasting it. Piaget (1952) argued that infants are incapable of mental representation—thinking about an object using mental pictures. They cannot remember and think about things and events when they are not present. Instead, to think about an object, an infant must experience it through both the visual and tactile senses. The developmental task of infancy is to develop the ability to think with mental symbols, for infants to think "inside their heads" rather than just using their senses and motor skills. The sensorimotor reasoning period progresses through six substages in which cognition develops from reflexes to intentional action to symbolic representation. At each stage, infants are driven to learn and explore the world.

Substage 1: Reflexes (Birth to 1 Month)

In the first substage, newborns use their reflexes, such as the sucking and palmar grasp reflexes (see Chapter 3), to react to stimuli. During the first month of life, infants strengthen and use these reflexes to learn about their world through assimilation. They apply their reflexive sucking schema to assimilate information and learn about their environment. They also accommodate or modify their sucking schemas to specific objects, sucking differently in response to a bottle versus a pacifier. During the first month of life, newborns strengthen and modify their original reflexive schemas to explore the world around them.

Substage 2: Primary Circular Reactions (1 to 4 Months)

During the second substage, infants begin to make accidental discoveries. Early cognitive growth in the sensorimotor period occurs through engaging in primary circular reactions, which consist of repeating pleasurable or exciting actions involving parts of the body that initially occurred by chance. While flailing his little arms, baby Luke accidentally puts his hand in his mouth. Surprised and delighted by the outcome (his hand in his mouth), baby Luke tries to make it happen again. Therefore, Luke repeats the behavior to experience and explore his body, a primary circular reaction.

Substage 3: Secondary Circular Reactions (4 to 8 Months)

During the third sensorimotor substage, as infants' awareness extends further, they engage in secondary circular reactions, repetitions of actions involving parts of the body that trigger responses in the external environment. Now babies repeat body movements that make interesting events occur in their environment. Baby Aria shakes a rattle to hear its noise and kicks her legs to move a mobile hanging over the crib. Aria demonstrates secondary circular reactions. Aria's attention has expanded to include the environment outside her body, and she is beginning to understand that her actions cause results in the external world. In this way, infants discover new ways of interacting with their environments to continue experiencing sensations and events that they find pleasing.

During the third sensorimotor substage (4 to 8 months), infants' awareness extends to include objects. They repeat actions that have an effect on objects.

keiferpix/istock

Substage 4: Coordination of Secondary Circular Reactions (8 to 12 Months)

Unlike primary and secondary circular reactions, which are discovered by accident, the coordination of secondary circular reactions substage signifies the beginning of intentional behavior. During this substage, infants purposefully coordinate two secondary circular reactions and apply them in new situations to achieve a goal. Piaget described how his son, Laurent, combined the two activities of knocking a barrier out of his way and grasping an object. When Piaget put a pillow in front of a matchbox that Laurent desired, the boy pushed the pillow aside and grabbed the box. In this way, Laurent integrated two secondary circular reactions to achieve a goal. Now planning and goal-directed behavior have emerged.

One of the most significant advances during the coordination of the secondary circular reactions stage is **object permanence**, the understanding that objects continue to exist outside of sensory awareness (e.g., when they are no longer visible). According to Piaget, infants younger than 8 months do not yet have object permanence—out of sight is literally out of mind. An infant loses interest and stops reaching for or looking at a small toy after it is covered by a cloth. Not until 8 to 12 months, during the coordination of secondary circular reactions stage, will an infant search for hidden objects, thus displaying object permanence. This development is an important cognitive advance because it signifies a capacity for mental representation or internal thought. Thinking about an object internally is an essential step toward learning language because language uses symbols: Sounds symbolize and stand for things (e.g., infants must understand that the sound "ball" represents an object, a ball).

Substage 5: Tertiary Circular Reactions (12 to 18 Months)

During the fifth substage, infants begin to experiment with new behaviors to see their results. Piaget described infants as "little scientists" during this period because they move from intentional behavior to systematic exploration. In what Piaget called **tertiary circular reactions**, infants now engage in mini-experiments: active, purposeful, trial-and-error exploration to search for new discoveries (see Figure 6.2). They vary their actions to see how the changes affect the outcomes. Many infants begin to experiment with gravity by dropping objects to the floor while sitting in a highchair. First, an infant throws a ball and watches it bounce. Next, a piece of paper floats slowly down. Then mommy's keys clatter to the floor. And so on. This purposeful exploration is how infants search for discoveries and learn about the world. When presented with a problem, infants in the tertiary circular reactions substage engage in trial-and-error analyses, trying out behaviors until they find the best one to attain their goal.

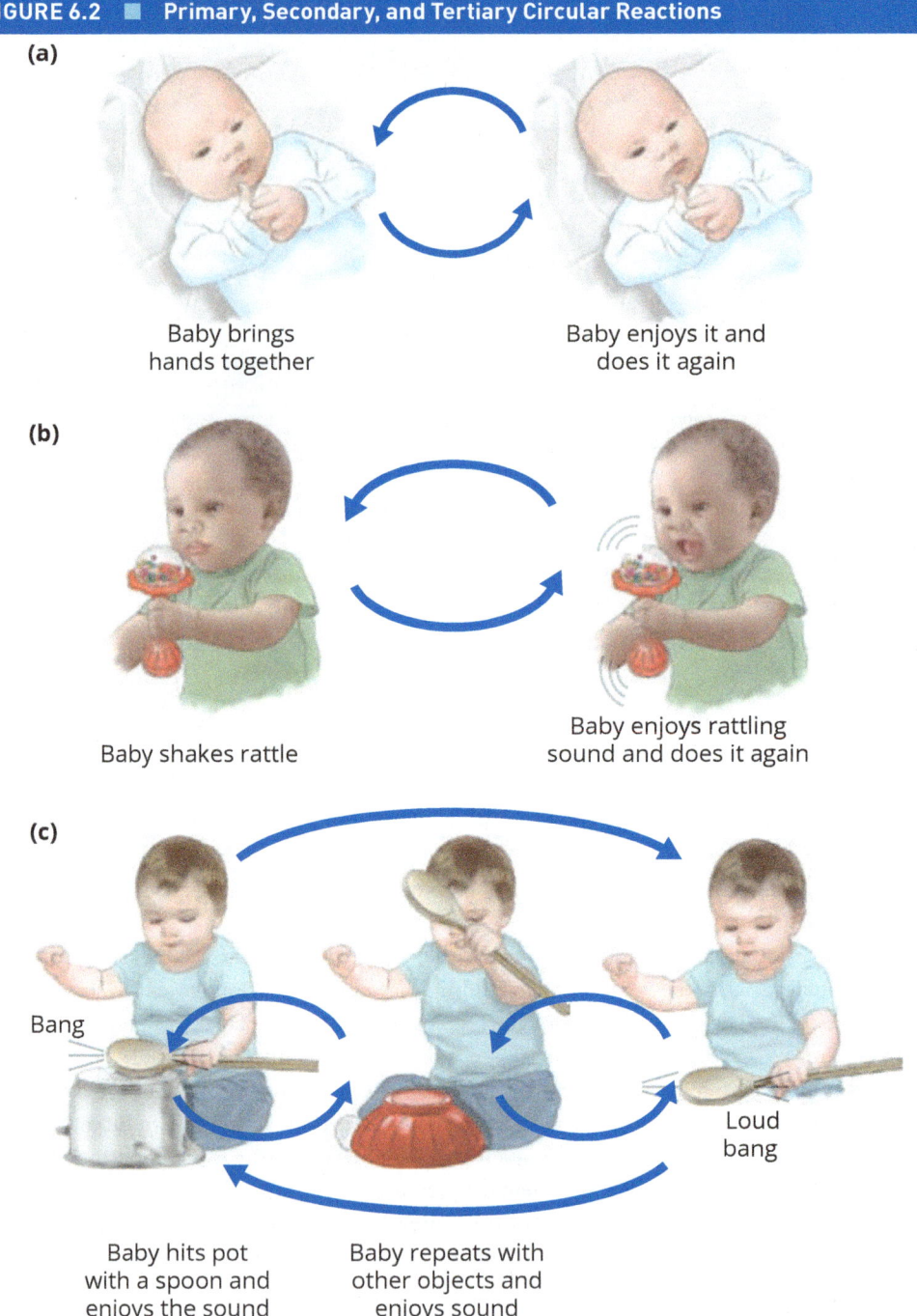

FIGURE 6.2 ■ Primary, Secondary, and Tertiary Circular Reactions

(a) Baby brings hands together / Baby enjoys it and does it again

(b) Baby shakes rattle / Baby enjoys rattling sound and does it again

(c) Baby hits pot with a spoon and enjoys the sound / Baby repeats with other objects and enjoys sound / Loud bang / Bang

Substage 6: Mental Representation (18 to 24 Months)

The sixth sensorimotor substage marks a transition between the sensorimotor and preoperational reasoning stages. Between 18 and 24 months of age, infants develop representational thought, the ability to use symbols such as words and mental pictures to represent objects and actions in memory. In developing this ability, infants are freed from direct experience: They can think about things they no longer see directly in front of them and engage in deferred imitation, imitating actions of an absent model. External physical exploration of the world gives way to internal mental exploration. Children can think through potential solutions and create new solutions without engaging in physical trial and error but simply by considering the possible solutions and their consequences. Table 6.1 summarizes the substages of sensorimotor reasoning.

TABLE 6.1 ■ Substages of Sensorimotor Reasoning		
Substage	**Major Features**	**Example**
Reflexive activity (0–1 month)	Strengthens and adapts reflexes	Newborn shows a different sucking response to a nipple versus a pacifier.
Primary circular reactions (1–4 months)	Repeats motor actions that produce exciting outcomes that are centered toward the body	Infant bats mobile with arm and watches arm move.
Secondary circular reactions (4–8 months)	Repeats motor actions that produce exciting outcomes that are directed toward the environment	Infant bats mobile with arm and watches the mobile move.
Coordination of secondary circular reactions (8–12 months)	Combines secondary circular reactions to achieve goals and solve problems; the beginnings of intentional behavior	Infant uses one hand to lift a bucket covering a ball and the other to grasp the ball. Infant uses both hands to pull a string attached to a ball and eventually reach the ball.
Tertiary circular reactions (12–18 months)	Experiments with different actions to achieve the same goal or observe the outcome and make new discoveries	Toddler hits a pot with a wooden spoon and listens to the sound then hits other objects in the kitchen, such as the refrigerator, stove, or plates, to hear the sound that the spoon makes against the objects.
Mental representation (18–24 months)	Internal mental representation of objects and events; thinking to solve problems rather than relying on trial and error	When confronted with a problem, like a toy that is out of reach on the counter, toddlers consider possible solutions to a problem in their mind, decide on a solution, and implement it.

Evaluating Piaget's Theory: Underestimating Infants

Jean Piaget's theory has historical significance as the first theory of cognitive development (Rochat, 2023). Piaget was the first scientist to examine infants' and children's thinking and ask what develops during childhood and how it occurs. He recognized that motor action and cognition are inextricably linked, a view still accepted by today's developmental scientists (Adolph & Hoch, 2019; Oakes & Rakison, 2020). However, there is criticism of Piaget's sensorimotor reasoning theory, which tends to center around his method for assessing infants' abilities. Newer techniques for studying object permanence have yielded different results.

Measuring the cognitive capabilities of infants and toddlers is very challenging because, unlike older children and adults, infants cannot fill out questionnaires or answer questions. Researchers have had to devise methods of measuring observable behavior that can provide clues to what an infant is thinking. Researchers measure infants' looking behavior by determining what infants look at and for how long. Using such methods, they have found support for some of Piaget's claims and evidence that challenges others. One of the most contested aspects of Piaget's theory concerns his assumption that infants are incapable of mental representation until late in the sensorimotor period (Carey et al., 2015; Crain, 2016). A growing body of research conducted with object permanence and imitation tasks suggests otherwise.

Violation-of-Expectation Tasks

Piaget's method of determining an infant's understanding of object permanence relied on the infant's ability to demonstrate it by uncovering a hidden object. Researchers have posited that many infants may understand that the object is hidden but lack the motor ability to coordinate their hands to demonstrate their understanding physically. Studying infants' looking behavior enables researchers to identify object permanence in younger infants with undeveloped motor skills because it eliminates the need for infants to use motor activity to demonstrate their cognitive competence.

One such research design uses a **violation-of-expectation task**, a task in which a stimulus appears to violate physical laws (Baillargeon et al., 2016; Margoni et al., 2023). Specifically, in a violation-of-expectation task, an infant is shown two events: one that is labeled *expected* because it follows physical laws and a second that is called *unexpected* (or "impossible") because it violates or is incongruous with physical laws (Mireault & Reddy, 2020). If the infant looks longer at the unexpected event, it suggests that they are surprised by it, are aware of physical properties of objects, and can mentally represent them (Stahl & Kibbe, 2022).

In a classic study, developmental researcher Renée Baillargeon (1987) used the violation-of-expectation method to study the mental representation capacities of very young infants. Infants were shown a drawbridge that rotated 180 degrees. Then the infants watched as a box was placed behind the drawbridge to impede its movement. Infants watched as either the drawbridge rotated and stopped after hitting the box (expected event) or did not stop and appeared to move through the box (an "impossible" event). As shown in Figure 6.3, 4-1/2-month-old infants looked longer when the drawbridge appeared to move through the box (the unexpected "impossible" event) than when it stopped after hitting the box, as expected. Baillargeon and colleagues interpreted infants' behavior as suggesting that they maintained a mental representation of the box, even though they could not see it. Therefore, they understood that the drawbridge could not move through the entire box.

FIGURE 6.3 ■ Object Permanence in Young Infants: Baillargeon's Drawbridge Study

(A) Side view of habituation and test displays. Infants were habituated to a 180-degree drawbridge-like motion. (B) In the Experimental Condition, infants completed two types of test trials with a new object, a box. The Impossible Test involved the same full 180-degree rotation from habituation, but now the screen surprisingly passed through the box as it completed its rotation (with the box disappearing as it became obscured). The Possible Test involved a novel shorter rotation of screen up to the point where it would contact the box, where it stopped; this motion was "possible" regarding solidity and object permanence. In the Control Condition, the screen rotations were identical, but no box was presented (such that both motions were equally possible). The results from the test phase are depicted in the right panels of (B). In the Experimental Condition, infants looked longer at the Impossible Test but not the Possible Test. However, in the Control Condition, no preference was observed. They looked equally at the full and partial rotation. These results suggest a violation of infants' expectations regarding object permanence.

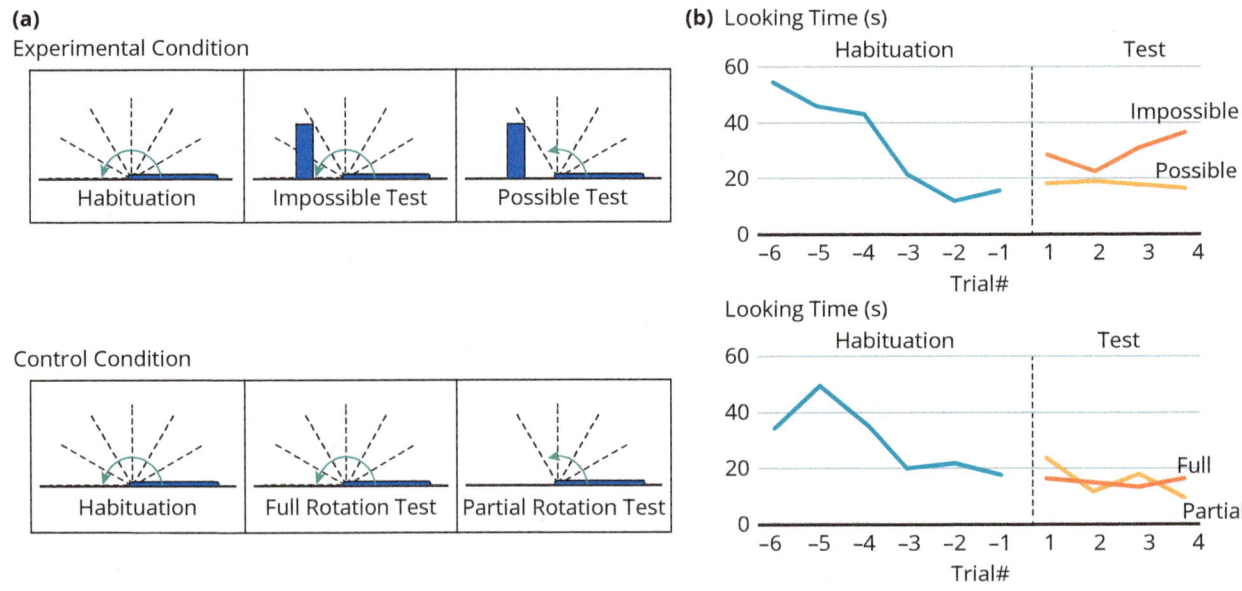

Source: Turk-Browne, N. B., Scholl, B. J., & Chun, M. M. (2008). Babies and brains: Habituation in infant cognition and functional neuroimaging. *Frontiers in Human Neuroscience, 2*, 16. https://doi.org/10.3389/neuro.09.016.2008

Critics argue that these results demonstrate infants' preference for novelty or for greater movement rather than object permanence (Bogartz et al., 2000; Heyes, 2014). Recently researchers have measured infants' pupil size, called pupillometry, as an alternative to looking-time measures of infant attention (Krüger et al., 2019; Zhang & Emberson, 2020) The pupil is a small opening in the eye that dilates, that is, becomes larger, in response to changes in light and also in response to novel or surprising stimuli (Alamia et al., 2019). Two recent studies found that 10-month-old infants' pupillary responses suggested perceptual preferences for stimuli rather than object permanence (Pätzold & Liszkowski, 2020; Sirois & Jackson, 2012). These conclusions are puzzling because Piaget's original tasks demonstrated object permanence at 9 months.

Simple Tasks

Although the violation-of-expectation method is widely used to study infant cognition, its validity is also debated (Rubio-Fernández, 2019). Nevertheless, when considering whether infants display object permanence, studies that use more straightforward tasks have shown support for young infants' competence. Four- and 5-month-old infants will watch a ball roll behind a barrier, gazing at where they expect it to reappear (von Hofsten et al., 2007). When 6-month-old infants are shown an object, and the lights are then turned off, they will reach in the dark for the object (Shinskey, 2012), suggesting that they maintain a mental representation of the object and therefore have object permanence earlier than Piaget believed.

A-Not-B Tasks

Other critics of Piaget's views of infants' capacity for object permanence focus on an error that 8- to 12-month-old infants make, known as the A-not-B error. The A-not-B error involves the following scenario: An infant repeatedly uncovers a toy hidden behind a barrier. He then sees the toy moved from behind one barrier (Place A) to another (Place B), but he continues to look for the toy in Place A, even after watching it be moved to Place B (see Figure 6.4). Piaget theorized that the infant incorrectly, but persistently, searches for the object in Place A because he lacks object permanence.

FIGURE 6.4 ■ A-Not-B Error

The infant continues to look for the ball under Place A, despite having seen the ball moved to Place B.

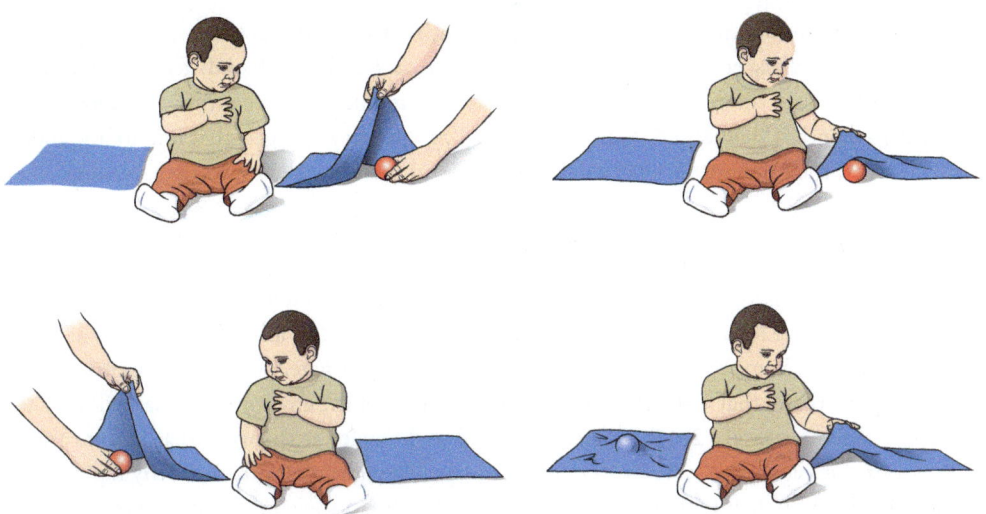

Some researchers point out that infants look at Place B, the correct location, at the same time as they mistakenly reach for Place A, suggesting that they understand the right location of the object (Place B) but cannot keep themselves from reaching for Place A because of neural and motor immaturity (Diamond, 1991). Other researchers propose that infants cannot restrain the impulse to repeat a previously rewarded behavior (Zelazo et al., 1998). Recent research suggests that infant reaching is related to the experimenter's behavior. When the experimenter looks at Place A, the infant reaches for Place A, and when the experimenter looks at Place B, the infant reaches for Place B, suggesting that the A-not-B task measures social behavior rather than cognition (Dunn & Bremner, 2020).

When violation of expectation tasks are used, infants look longer when the impossible event occurs (finding a toy in Place A after watching it move to Place B) than when the expected event occurs (finding the toy in Place B after it was moved there) (Ahmed & Ruffman, 1998). This suggests that infants have an understanding of object permanence, but their limited motor skills prevent them from demonstrating it in A-not-B tasks. One longitudinal study found that infants between 5 and 8 months performed better on an A-not-B looking task than a reaching task (Cuevas & Bell, 2010). However, by 9–10 months, infants performed equally well on both tasks. Age-related changes in performance on

A-not-B and other object permanence tasks may be due to the maturation of brain circuitry controlling motor skills, attentional control, and inhibition (Cuevas & Bell, 2010; Marcovitch et al., 2016).

Deferred Imitation Tasks

Another method of studying infants' capacities for mental representation relies on **deferred imitation**, the ability to repeat an act performed some time ago. Piaget (1962) believed infants under 18 months lacked the mental representation abilities to engage in deferred imitation. However, laboratory research has found that even 6-week-old infants can imitate facial expressions of an unfamiliar adult after a 24-hour delay (Meltzoff & Moore, 1994). Six- and 9-month-old infants also display deferred imitation of unique actions performed with toys, such as taking a puppet's glove off, shaking it to ring a bell inside, and replacing it over a 24-hour delay (Barr et al., 2003).

When infants engage in deferred imitation, they act based on stored representations of actions—memories—a contradiction of Piaget's beliefs about infants' capabilities (Jones & Herbert, 2006). Instead of a stage-like shift in representational capacities, many researchers view deferred imitation, and object permanence itself, as a continuously developing ability (Miller, 2016). Performance on deferred imitation tasks improves throughout the second year of life and infants can remember modeled behaviors for several months and imitate both peers and adults (Hayne et al., 2000; Kolling et al., 2010). They also imitate across contexts, imitating behaviors they learn in childcare settings when at home (Patel et al., 2013). Infants' emotional arousal state also influences their performance on deferred imitation tasks. They are more likely to imitate an action when they are in the same arousal state as when they observed it (e.g., calm) (Seehagen et al., 2021).

The capacity for imitation increases through 30 months of age and also when shorter sequences of behavior are used (Kolling et al., 2010; Kressley-Mba et al., 2005). Individual differences in imitation are stable; children who show lower levels of imitation at 9 months of age continue to score lower on imitation at 14 months (Heimann & Meltzoff, 1996). These findings suggest that infants and toddlers gradually increase their representational capacities in a continuous developmental progression.

Core Knowledge Theory

Despite the criticisms discussed so far, developmental psychologists tend to agree with Piaget's description of infants as active learners. Still, not all agree with his idea that all mental abilities arise from sensorimotor activity. Some researchers believe that infants have innate, or inborn, cognitive abilities, such as perceptual biases that cause them to attend to features of the environment that will help them learn quickly (Bremner et al., 2015). The concept of **core knowledge theory** is that infants are born with several innate knowledge systems, or core domains of thought, that promote early rapid learning and adaptation (Spelke, 2016, 2022). From this perspective, infants encounter such a great amount of sensory information and learn so quickly and that some prewired evolutionary ability to learn rules must be at work. Using the violation-of-expectation method, core knowledge researchers have found that young infants have a basic understanding of the physical properties of objects, such as object permanence, solidity—that objects cannot pass through one another—and gravity (Lin et al., 2022; Margoni et al., 2023).

This view is supported by research that shows that infants have early knowledge of numbers (Cheung & Ansari, 2020; Hyde, 2023; Spelke, 2022). Five-month-old infants can discriminate between small and large numbers of items (Christodoulou et al., 2017). Even newborns are sensitive to large differences in number, distinguishing nine items from three, but they show difficulty distinguishing small numbers from each other (two vs. three items) (Coubart et al., 2014; Di Giorgio et al., 2019). Comparative research has shown that animals display these systems of knowledge early in life and without much experience (Piantadosi & Cantlon, 2017), suggesting that it is possible—and perhaps evolutionarily adaptive—for infants to quickly yet naturally construct an understanding of the world (Bjorklund, 2018).

Critics of core knowledge argue that looking measures only demonstrate discrimination—that young infants can tell the difference between stimuli, but not that they understand the differences between them (Bremner et al., 2015). Others suggest that infants differentiate items based on differences in area instead of number (Mix et al., 2002). It may be that the infant differentiates nine items from three not because of the change in number but simply because nine items take up more space than three. Research has shown that 7-month-old infants can differentiate changes in number and area, are more sensitive to changes in number than area, and prefer to look at changes in number than area (Libertus et al., 2014).

Infants are thought to have an inborn ability to recognize patterns, making them statistical learners who can apply basic inferences to quickly identify patterns in their environment (Denison & Xu, 2019; Köster et al., 2020; Saffran, 2020). When the statistical inferences they make do not match their perception, they show surprise, as indicated by longer looking-time (Sim & Xu, 2019). This surprise may motivate infants to learn and retain information as they naturally try to create and test new hypotheses about the world around them (Stahl & Feigenson, 2019). This process is not conscious. Infants do not know that they are experimenting, but they are driven to learn and explain what they see. In one study, 11-month-old infants did more searching and exploration when presented with a confusing event and stopped when they were given a plausible explanation for the violation (Perez & Feigenson, 2022). When confronted with confusing events, infants spontaneously devise explanations and compare those explanations with what they perceive (Köster et al., 2020).

Overall, Piaget's theory has profoundly influenced how we view the process of cognitive development. But infants and toddlers are more cognitively competent than Piaget imagined, showing signs of representational ability and conceptual thought that he believed were impossible. Developmental scientists agree with Piaget that immature forms of cognition give way to more mature forms, that the individual is active in their development, and that interaction with the environment is critical for cognitive growth.

THINKING IN CONTEXT 6.1

1. Suppose that you are a childcare provider. Design a childcare environment for infants at each sensorimotor stage.
    a. What toys and surroundings might suit an infant in the primary circular reaction substage?
    b. Secondary circular reaction substage?
    c. Coordination of secondary schemas substage?
    d. Tertiary circular reactions substage?
    e. Give an example of assimilation and accommodation in infancy. Using your example, explain the process of equilibration.
2. Do adults experience states of cognitive equilibrium and disequilibrium? Give examples of assimilation and accommodation in an adult's thought. How might this process differ for infants and children?

PREOPERATIONAL REASONING IN EARLY CHILDHOOD

6.2 Discuss the characteristics of preoperational reasoning and young children's abilities.

Four-year-old Dimitri tightly clutched his toy car, "Rocky does not want to ride down that big slide," he said to his big sister. "It will be fun," his 12-year-old Shana said. "Let go of Rocky. His wheels will help him zoom down the slide." "Rocky doesn't want to," said Dimitri. "Hmm. If Rocky really doesn't want to go down the slide, he doesn't have to. Do you want to slide down?" Dimitri nodded his head, "But Rocky's scared." "OK, then hold Rocky and slide down. Show him there's nothing to fear," Shana said. At 4 years old, Dimitri's thinking is much more advanced than it was in infancy. It will continue to grow in leaps and bounds through childhood.

Piaget believed that young children from about ages 2 to 6 demonstrate **preoperational reasoning**, the second stage in his theory of cognitive development. Preoperational reasoning is characterized by a dramatic leap in symbolic thinking that permits young children to use language to communicate their thoughts and desires, interact with others, and play using their thoughts and imaginations to guide their behavior. Symbolic thought enables Dimitri to name his toy "Rocky" and imagine its interests, likes, and dislikes. Despite these developments, preoperational reasoning is limited because children cannot yet perform **cognitive operations**, reversible mental actions. Operations enable children to perform tasks, such as addition and subtraction, mentally rather than physically. Young children's reasoning, therefore, is *preoperational* or before operations.

Characteristics of Preoperational Reasoning

Young children in the preoperational stage show impressive advances in representational thinking, but they are unable to grasp logic and cannot understand complex relationships. Children who show preoperational reasoning tend to make several common errors, including egocentrism, animism, centration, and irreversibility.

Egocentrism

"I like this picture," Ricardo shouts as he holds his mother's smartphone up for her to see. She smiles and explains, "I can't see the picture. All I see is the back of the phone. Turn it around so that I can see the picture." Ricardo flips the phone around, permitting his mother to see the screen. "There it is! Yes, that's a great picture. That was a nice day, remember?" Ricardo did not understand that, although he could see the photo when the smartphone faced him, his mother could not. Ricardo displays **egocentrism**, the inability to take another person's point of view or perspective. Egocentric children view the world from their perspective, assuming that other people share their feelings, knowledge, and even physical view of the world.

The three-mountain task is a classic task used to illustrate preoperational children's egocentrism. The child faces three large mountains at a table (see Figure 6.5). A doll is placed in a chair across the table from the child. The child is asked how the mountains look to the doll. Piaget found that young children in the preoperational stage demonstrated egocentrism because they described the scene from their perspective rather than the doll's. They did not understand that the doll would have a different view of the mountains (Piaget & Inhelder, 1967).

FIGURE 6.5 ■ The Three-Mountains Task

Children who display preoperational reasoning cannot describe the scene depicted in the three mountains task from the point of view of the teddy bear.

Animism

Egocentric thinking can also take the form of **animism**, the belief that inanimate objects are alive. They have feelings, thoughts, and intentions. "It's raining because the sun is sad, and it is crying," 3-year-old Morton explains. Children accept their own explanations for phenomena because they are unable to consider another viewpoint or alternative reason.

Centration

Young children often focus on part of a stimulus, noticing one change and not others, for example. Preoperational children exhibit **centration**, the tendency to focus on one aspect of an object or situation and exclude all others. Children who worry that if they wear a dress, they will become a girl focus entirely on their appearance (the dress) rather than the other characteristics that make them girls or boys.

Centration is illustrated by a classic task that requires the preoperational child to distinguish what something appears to be from what it really is, the **appearance-reality distinction**. In a classic study illustrating this effect, de Vries (1969) presented 3- to 6-year-old children with a cat named Maynard (see Figure 6.6). The children were permitted to pet Maynard. Then, while his head and shoulders were hidden behind a screen (and his back and tail were still visible), a dog mask was placed on Maynard's head. The children were then asked, "What kind of animal is it now?" "Does it bark or meow?" Despite Maynard's body and tail being visible during the transformation, 3-year-old children replied that he was now a dog. Six-year-old children could distinguish Maynard's appearance from reality and explained that he only *looked* like a dog.

FIGURE 6.6 ■ Appearance vs. Reality: Is It a Cat or a Dog?

Young children do not understand that Maynard the cat remained a cat despite wearing a dog mask and looking like a dog.

Source: de Vries, R. (1969). Constancy of generic identity in the years three to six. *Monographs of the Society for Research in Child Development, 34*(3), iii–iv, 1–67. https://doi.org/10.2307/1165683

One reason 3-year-old children fail appearance-reality tasks is that they cannot effectively use dual encoding, the ability to mentally represent an object in more than one way at a time (Doherty & Perner, 2020; Flavell et al., 1986). For example, young children find it challenging to understand that a scale model (like a doll house) can be both an object (something to play with) and a symbol (of an actual house) (MacConnell & Daehler, 2004). They may be distracted by unimportant details. When 3-year-old children are given a 24-hour delay between trials, they forget irrelevant details and are more likely to show symbolic insight to grasp that a scale model can represent an actual room (Sheehan et al., 2020).

Irreversibility

"You ruined it!" cried Johnson after his older sister, Monique, placed a triangular block atop the tower of blocks he had just built. "No, I just put a triangle there to show it was the top and finish it," she explains. "No!" insists Johnson. "OK, I'll take it off," says Monique. "See? Now it's just how you left it." "No. It's ruined," Johnson sighs. Johnson continued to be upset after his sister removed the triangular block, not realizing that she had restored the block structure to its original state by removing the block. Young children's thinking is characterized by **irreversibility**, meaning they do not understand that reversing a process can often undo it and restore the original state.

Preoperational children's irreversible thinking is illustrated by their performance on tasks that measure **conservation**, the understanding that the physical quantity of a substance, such as a number, mass, or volume, remains the same even when its appearance changes (see Figure 6.7). In a typical conservation of liquids task, a child is shown two identical glasses. The same amount of liquid is poured into each glass. After the child agrees that the two glasses contain the same amount of water, the liquid from one glass is poured into a taller, narrower glass and the child is asked whether one glass contains more liquid than the other. Young children in the preoperational stage reply that the taller narrower glass contains more liquid. Why? It has a higher liquid level than the shorter, wider glass. Young children focus on the height of the liquid (an example of centration), ignore the change in width, and do not grasp that the process can be reversed by pouring the liquid back into the shorter, wider glass.

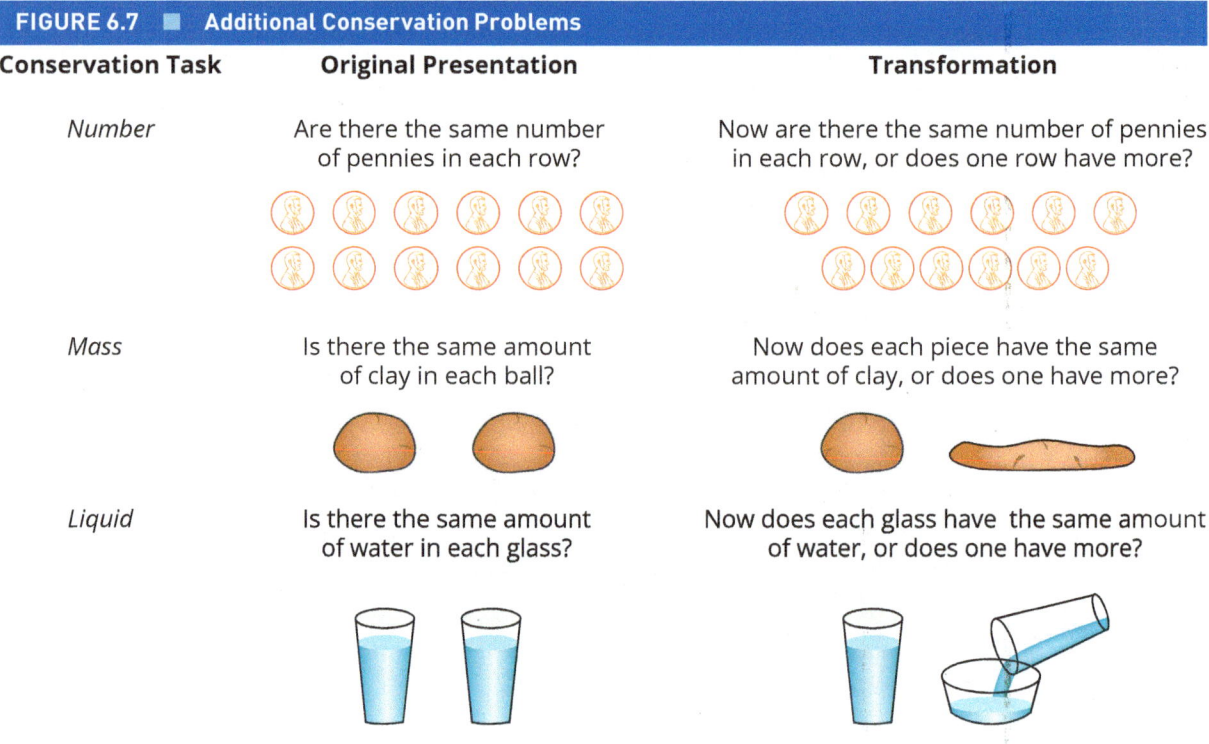

FIGURE 6.7 ■ Additional Conservation Problems

Conservation Task	Original Presentation	Transformation
Number	Are there the same number of pennies in each row?	Now are there the same number of pennies in each row, or does one row have more?
Mass	Is there the same amount of clay in each ball?	Now does each piece have the same amount of clay, or does one have more?
Liquid	Is there the same amount of water in each glass?	Now does each glass have the same amount of water, or does one have more?

Characteristics of preoperational children's reasoning are summarized in Table 6.2.

TABLE 6.2 ■ Characteristics of Preoperational Children's Reasoning

Characteristic	Description
Egocentrism	The inability to take another person's point of view or perspective
Animism	The belief that inanimate objects are alive and have feelings and intentions
Centration	Tendency to focus attention on one part of a stimulus or situation and exclude all others
Irreversibility	Failure to understand that reversing a process can often undo a process and restore the original state

Evaluating Piaget's Theory: Underestimating Young Children

Similar to our discussion of sensorimotor reasoning, research with young children has suggested that Piaget's tests of preoperational thinking underestimated young children. Success in Piaget's tasks appears to depend more on children's language abilities than their actions. To succeed on the three-mountain task discussed earlier, children must not only understand how the mounds look from the other side of the table but must be able to communicate that understanding. Appearance reality tasks require not simply an understanding of dual representation but the ability to express it. If the task is nonverbal, such as requiring reaching for an object rather than talking about it, even 3-year-old children can distinguish appearance from reality (Carlson et al., 2015; Sapp et al., 2000).

Egocentrism and Animism

Simple tasks demonstrate that young children are less egocentric than Piaget posited. When a 3-year-old child is shown a card that depicts a dog on one side and a cat on another, and the card is held up between the researcher, who can see the cat, and the child who can see the dog, the child correctly responds that the researcher can see the cat (Flavell et al., 1981). When the task is relevant to children's everyday lives (i.e., hiding), their performance suggests that they are not as egocentric as Piaget posited (Newcombe & Huttenlocher, 1992). Other research indicates that 3- to 5-year-old children can learn perspective-taking skills through training and retain their perspective-taking abilities 6 months later (Mori & Cigala, 2016).

Likewise, 3-year-old children do not tend to describe inanimate objects with life-like qualities, even when interacting with a robot that can move (Jipson et al., 2016; Okanda et al., 2021). Most 4-year-old children understand that animals grow, and even plants grow, but objects do not (Backschneider et al., 1993). Sometimes young children provide animistic responses. Gjersoe et al. (2015) suggest an emotional component to animistic beliefs. They found that 3-year-olds attribute mental states to toys they are emotionally attached to but not to other favorite toys, even those with which they frequently engage in imaginary play. Finally, children show individual differences in their expressions of animism and reasoning about living things. These differences are linked with aspects of cognitive development such as memory, working memory, and inhibition (Zaitchik et al., 2014).

Reversibility and the Appearance-Reality Distinction

Although young children typically perform poorly on conservation tasks, 4-year-old children can be taught to conserve, suggesting that children's difficulties with reversibility and conservation tasks can be overcome (Gallagher, 2008; Tomasello, 2018). In addition, making the task relevant improves children's performance. Asking children to play a trick on someone (i.e., "Let's pretend that this sponge is a rock and tell Anne that it is a rock when it really is a sponge.") or to choose an object that can be used to clean spilled water (many choose the sponge), illustrates that they can form a dual representation of the sponge as an object that absorbs water and also looks like a rock (Sapp et al., 2000). Three-year-old children can shift between describing an object or situation's real and fake or imagined aspects. In addition, they can describe misleading appearances and functions of objects in response to natural conversational prompts, as compared with the more formal language in the typical prompts used in traditional appearance-reality tasks (e.g., "What is it really and truly?") (Deák, 2006). In sum, preschoolers show an understanding of the appearance-reality distinction, and it develops throughout childhood (Woolley & E Ghossainy, 2013).

Preoperational Reasoning and Education

Early childhood advances in symbolic thinking enable young children to use language, engage in imaginative play, and learn in new ways. Piaget's detailed descriptions of children's abilities have implications for teaching young children and creating supportive childcare and preschool settings (Gray & MacBlain, 2015). Like infants, young children learn by exploring the world. Specifically, they construct their cognitive schemas by interacting with other people, objects, and environments. They integrate new information into their existing schemas (assimilation), and when they encounter material that differs from what they know, children modify their schemas or concepts (accommodation). Discovery learning, in which children are encouraged to explore and *discover* knowledge for themselves rather than be taught rote facts, embodies Piaget's about the active role children play in constructing their understanding of the world.

Education must be age appropriate because, in Piaget's view, cognitive development cannot be rushed. Still, teachers can help young children understand their ideas in more sophisticated ways by asking open-ended questions and encouraging them to express themselves. Children learn by doing. Therefore, helpful interactions focus on the process, such as building a tower rather than the product, the tower's final height. Childcare and preschool settings designed for children's hands, bodies, and minds, with child-sized desks and chairs, seating in small groups rather than rows, and toys that are easily manipulated by tiny hands, meet the needs of children in the preoperational stage of reasoning.

> **THINKING IN CONTEXT 6.2**
>
> 1. Can you remember examples of preoperational reasoning (*mistakes*) in your own thinking when you were a young child? Have you observed a child demonstrating preoperational reasoning? Give examples of animism, centration, irreversibility, or other examples of preoperational reasoning.
> 2. Do all children show preoperational reasoning? Does it appear in some contexts more than others? Or is it universal? Explain your reasoning.
> 3. Can we teach children not to show egocentrism or animism? If we can, should we? Why or why not?
> 4. How would Piaget respond to Questions 2 and 3? Why?

CONCRETE OPERATIONAL REASONING IN MIDDLE CHILDHOOD

> **6.3** Describe concrete operational reasoning and older children's abilities.

With each successive stage in Piaget's theory, children's thinking transforms, new abilities emerge, and reasoning becomes more sophisticated. In middle childhood, a critical ability emerges: logic. When children enter Piaget's third stage, **concrete operational stage of reasoning**, at about age 6 or 7, they become able to use operations, reversible mental actions, to solve problems. Older children can apply operations to think logically. But their logical reasoning is limited to concrete problems that refer to specific or tangible things, such as adding and subtracting apples.

Characteristics of Concrete Operational Reasoning

Older children's newly developed ability to use concrete operations enables them to reason about physical quantities and is evident in their skills in classification and conservation.

Classification

What hobbies did you enjoy as a child? Did you collect and trade coins, rocks, or action figures? School-age children develop interests and hobbies that require advanced thinking skills, such as comparing multiple items across several dimensions. **Classification** is the ability to understand hierarchies, relations among objects, and to simultaneously consider relations between a general category and more specific subcategories, such as cows as a type of farm animal. Several classification skills emerge during the concrete operational stage: transitive inference, seriation, and class inclusion.

Transitive Inference. **Transitive inference** is the ability to infer the relationship between two objects by understanding each object's connection to a third. Present children with three sticks: A, B, and C. Demonstrate that Stick A is longer than Stick B and Stick B is longer than Stick C. Children who reason at the concrete operational stage do not need to physically compare Sticks A and C to know that Stick A is longer than Stick C. They use the information given about the two sticks to infer their relative lengths (Wright & Smailes, 2015). Transitive inference emerges earlier than other concrete operational skills. By about 5 years of age, children can infer that A is longer than C (Goodwin & Johnson-Laird, 2008). Skills in transitive inference contribute to children's growing understanding of mathematics and ability to understand relations among quantities and make inferences based on those relations (F. Schwartz et al., 2020).

Seriation. **Seriation** is the ability to order objects in a series according to a physical dimension, such as height, weight, or color. Ask a child to arrange a handful of sticks in order by length, from shortest to longest. Four- to 5-year-old children can pick out the smallest and largest stick but will arrange the others haphazardly. On the other hand, 6- to 7-year-old children take a more orderly approach. They arrange the sticks by picking out the smallest, the next smallest, and so on (Inhelder & Piaget, 1964).

Class Inclusion. **Class inclusion** involves understanding hierarchical relationships among items. Suppose a child is shown a bunch of flowers, seven daisies, and two roses. She is told that there are nine flowers; seven are called daisies, and two are called roses. The child is then asked, "Are there more daisies or flowers?" Preoperational children will answer that there are more daisies, because they do not understand that daisies are a subclass of flowers. By age 5, children have some knowledge of classification hierarchies and may grasp that daisies are flowers but still not fully understand and apply classification hierarchies to correctly solve the problem (Deneault & Ricard, 2006). By about age 8, children can classify objects, in this case, flowers, and can make quantitative judgments and respond that there are more flowers than daisies (Borst et al., 2013).

In the concrete operational stage, children become capable of classification and can organize these rocks across several dimensions, such as size, color, type, or location.
Ja_Het/istock

Older children often collect items and spend hours sorting their collections along various dimensions. These interests rely on the ability to classify items and arrange them hierarchically. One day Susan sorts her rock collection by geographic location (e.g., the part of the world where it is most common), with subcategories based on hardness and color. She might then reorganize her rocks based on other characteristics, such as age or composition. Susan's interests reflect the logical thinking characteristic of concrete operational reasoning.

Conservation

In a classic conservation problem, a child is shown two identical balls of clay and watches while the experimenter rolls one ball into a long hotdog shape. When asked which piece contains more clay, a child who reasons at the preoperational stage will say that the hotdog shape has more clay because it is longer. Eight-year-old Julio, in contrast, notices that the ball shape is shorter than the hotdog shape but also thicker. He knows that the two forms contain the same amount of clay. At the concrete operational stage of reasoning, Julio now understands that specific characteristics of an object do not change despite superficial changes to the object's appearance. An understanding of reversibility—that an object can be returned to its original state—means Julio realizes that the hotdog-shaped clay can be reformed into its original ball shape.

Most children solve this conservation problem of substances by age 7 or 8. At about age 9 or 10, children also correctly solve conservation of weight tasks (after presenting two equal-sized balls of clay and rolling one into a hotdog shape, "Which is heavier, the hotdog or the ball?"). Conservation of volume tasks (after placing the hotdog- and ball-shaped clay in glasses of liquid: "Which displaces more liquid?") are solved last, at about age 12. The ability to conserve develops slowly, and children show inconsistencies in their ability to solve different types of conservation problems.

Piagetian tasks, such as conservation tasks, offer vivid illustrations of children's abilities. Critics argue that Piaget's explanations for children's reasoning are vague. What causes transformations in reasoning and logic? Information processing theorists believe that children's success on conservation tasks corresponds to the development of processing capacities, such as working memory and the ability to control impulses (see Chapter 7; Borst et al., 2013). In response to the conservation of number tasks, older children show more activity in parts of the temporal and prefrontal cortex and other parts of the brain associated with working memory, inhibitory control, and executive control (Houdé et al., 2011; Poirel et al., 2012). With practice, the cognitive abilities tested in Piagetian tasks become automatic, requiring less attention and fewer processing resources, enabling children to think more complexly

(Case, 1999). Once a child solves a conservation task, the problem becomes routine and requires less attention and mental resources than before, enabling the child to tackle more complicated problems.

Evaluating Piaget's Theory: Context, Culture, and Concrete Operational Reasoning

For Piaget, cognitive development is a universal, step-by-step phenomenon. He believed that all children around the world progress through the same stages. Today's researchers find that the cultural context in which children are immersed plays a critical role in their development (Goodnow et al., 2015). Children worldwide demonstrate concrete operational reasoning, but experience and specific cultural practices play a role in how it is displayed (Manoach et al., 1997).

Schooling and Language

Schooling influences the rate at which principles are understood. Children who have been in school longer tend to do better on transitive inference tasks than same-age children with less schooling (Artman & Cahan, 1993). Formal education is associated with similar patterns of emerging cognitive operations in children from developed and developing countries, including Australia, Britain, Greece, Pakistan, and Zimbabwe (Mpofu & Vijver, 2000; Shayer et al., 1988).

Studies of children from non-Western cultures, especially those without formal schooling, suggest that they achieve conservation and other concrete operational tasks later than those from Western cultures. In Papua New Guinea, conservation of number (typically first to emerge) appears approximately 3 years later than in Western samples, while mastery of more complex tasks (e.g., conservation of area, volume) appears up to 6 years later (Shea, 1985). Scientists debate whether these different patterns of responding represent differences in cognition.

Cultural differences in children's performance on tasks that measure concrete operational reasoning may be influenced by methodology (e.g., how questions are asked and the cultural identity of the experimenter) rather than reflect children's abilities (Gauvain et al., 2015). Generally, children perform better when they are assessed using their native language (Gardiner & Kosmitzki, 2018). For instance, when 10- and 11-year-old Canadian Micmac First Nation children were tested in English on conservation problems (substance, weight, and volume), they performed worse than 10- to 11-year-old white English-speaking children. But when tested in their native language by researchers from their own culture, the children performed similarly to the English-speaking children (Nyiti, 1982).

Familiarity and Contextual Demands

Children are more likely to display logical reasoning when considering substances and materials they are familiar with (Rogoff, 2003). Mexican children who make pottery understand at an early age that clay remains the same when its shape is changed. They demonstrate conservation of substance earlier than other forms of conservation and earlier than children who do not make pottery (Price-Williams et al., 1969). In another striking example, despite having never attended school and scoring low on measures of mathematics achievement, many 6- to 15-year-old children living in the streets of Brazil demonstrate sophisticated logical and computational reasoning. Why? These children sell items such as fruit and candy to earn their living. In addition to pricing their products, collecting money, making change, and giving discounts, the children must adjust prices daily to account for changes in demand, overhead, and the rate of inflation (Saxe, 2005). These children's competence in mathematics was influenced by experience, situational demands, and learning from others. Nevertheless, schooling also matters; children with some schooling were more adept at these tasks than were unschooled children.

Schooling influences the rate at which principles are understood. For example, children who have been in school longer tend to do better on transitive inference tasks than same-age children with less schooling (Artman & Cahan, 1993). Likewise, Zimbabwean children's understanding of conservation is influenced by academic experience, age, and family socioeconomic status (Mpofu & Vijver, 2000).

Culture and context are intertwined. Cultural differences in children's reasoning are influenced by differences in contextual demands. Comparisons of children of five cultures—the indigenous Aranda of Australia, the Inuit of Canada, the Ebrié and the Baoulé of Côte d'Ivoire, and the Kikuya of Kenya—revealed that children's development of spatial and conservation reasoning varied with their group's means of subsistence (e.g., nomadic, hunting-gathering versus sedentary, agricultural farming) (Dasen, 1975, 2022). Conservation reasoning developed more rapidly and earlier in children from strictly agricultural groups (the Kikuyu of Kenya and Baoulé of the Ivory Coast) whose subsistence relies on an understanding of quantity and volume (e.g., seeds, water, and crop growth) than hunting and gathering groups (Aranda and Inuit) (Dasen & Heron, 1981). The opposite trend was observed for spatial reasoning, particularly relevant for nomadic people who rely on spatial skills and coordination to hunt. These different developmental trends reflect cultural differences in the skills that are adaptive and valued within particular societies (Dasen, 1994; Molitor & Hsu, 2019).

Children learn culturally valued skills by interacting with and helping skilled partners.
Javier Mamani/Contributor/Getty

Concrete Operational Reasoning and Education

The constructive nature of thinking—that children actively engage with their surroundings to make sense of the world—is highly relevant to education. The most straightforward implication for parents and teachers is in encouraging curiosity (McDevitt & Ormrod, 2016). School-age children often believe that they should be mastering facts. Instead, adults should support children's reasoning, questioning, and interest in the world. Parents and teachers should encourage and validate children's questions, even if ill-timed. "What a great question, Narvesha! I'll write it on the board so we can discuss it after this activity," Mr. Lopes said. Older children benefit from opportunities to learn from each other through group work and free-play recess.

Like infants and young children, older children learn by exploring the physical world. It's important to provide children with opportunities to explore and experiment with physical objects. Hands-on activities might include grouping objects with similar characteristics, working with clay, and building structures with sticks. Unlike their younger peers, school-age children engage in intellectual exploration and generate simple logical explanations for phenomena. Posing problems and probing children's reasoning and conclusions give children opportunities for this type of learning. Sometimes children misinterpret their observations, confirming misconceptions or drawing the wrong conclusions (Fitzsimmons et al., 2013). Teachers can help children interpret their observations and draw accurate conclusions by creating lessons that combine exploration and guided instruction.

THINKING IN CONTEXT 6.3

1. How does the ability to classify objects and understand hierarchical relationships influence children's understanding of social relationships and complex social structures, like family relationships or peer hierarchies at school?
2. How might contextual and socioeconomic factors relate to children's ability to succeed on tasks measuring concrete operations? Is it possible for a child who reasons at the concrete operational stage to perform poorly on tasks measuring those abilities? Why or why not? If so, under what conditions might a child underperform?

FORMAL OPERATIONAL REASONING IN ADOLESCENCE

> **6.4** Analyze the development of formal operational reasoning and social cognition in adolescence.

Adolescents' thinking is limitless. They daydream about the future, think of alternate endings for stories, and can think about who they are, who they were in the past, and whom they hope to become in the future. The abilities emerge as children develop **formal operational reasoning**, the final stage of Piaget's cognitive-developmental theory, appearing in early adolescence at about age 11 (Inhelder & Piaget, 1958).

Characteristics of Formal Operational Reasoning

Children in the concrete operational stage reason about specific *things*—concepts that exist in reality, including problems concerning how to equitably divide materials, such as a bowl of pudding into five servings. Adolescents in the formal operational stage reason about *ideas*, possibilities that do not exist in reality and that may have no tangible substance, such as whether it is possible to love equitably—to distribute love equally among several targets (Kazi & Galanaki, 2020). Formal operational reasoning entails the ability to think abstractly, logically, and systematically (Inhelder & Piaget, 1958).

Adolescents become capable of reasoning about their own thinking even positing their own existence. Alejandro, for instance, wonders, "I'm thinking about my thinking . . . and I'm thinking about thinking about how I think. Now, how do I know that I am real? Am I just a thought?" The ability to think about possibilities beyond the here and now permits adolescents to plan, generate inferences from available information, and consider ways of solving potential but not yet real problems.

Formal operational thought enables adolescents to engage in **hypothetical-deductive reasoning**, or the ability to consider problems, generate and systematically test hypotheses, and draw conclusions. It is these abilities that underlie the scientific method (see Chapter 1). Piaget constructed tasks to study formal operational reasoning. He tested adolescents' abilities to use scientific reasoning to approach a problem by developing hypotheses and systematically testing them. Consider his famous pendulum task (see Figure 6.8; Inhelder & Piaget, 1958): Adolescents are presented with a pendulum and are asked what determines the speed with which the pendulum swings. They are given materials and told that there are four variables to consider: (1) length of string (short, medium, long), (2) weight (light, medium, heavy), (3) height at which the weight is dropped, and (4) force with which the weight is dropped.

Adolescents who display formal operational reasoning develop hypotheses that they methodically test. They change one variable while holding the others constant (e.g., trying each length of string while keeping the weight, height, and force the same). On the other hand, concrete operational children do not proceed systematically and fail to test each variable independently. Concrete operational children might test a short string with a heavy weight then try a long string and light weight. Solving the pendulum problem requires the scientific reasoning capacities that come with formal operational reasoning.

Evaluating Formal Operational Reasoning

Adolescent thinking is qualitatively different and more rational than children's (Moshman, 2021). Although Piaget believed that cognitive development is a universal process, individuals show varying abilities (Kazi & Galanaki, 2020). Most adolescents and many adults do not display formal operational thinking in Piagetian hypothetical-deductive tasks (Kuhn, 2013). Does this mean that they cannot think abstractly? Likely not.

Opportunities to Apply Formal Operational Reasoning

Piaget (1972) believed that opportunities to use formal operational reasoning influenced its development. Individuals are more likely to show formal operational reasoning when considering material

| FIGURE 6.8 ■ Measuring Formal Operations: The Pendulum Task |

Children and adolescents are presented with a pendulum and are asked what determined the speed with which the pendulum swings. They are given materials and told that there are four variables to consider: (1) length of strong (long, medium, short), (2) weight (light, medium, heavy), (3) height at which the weight is dropped, and (4) force with which the weight is dropped.

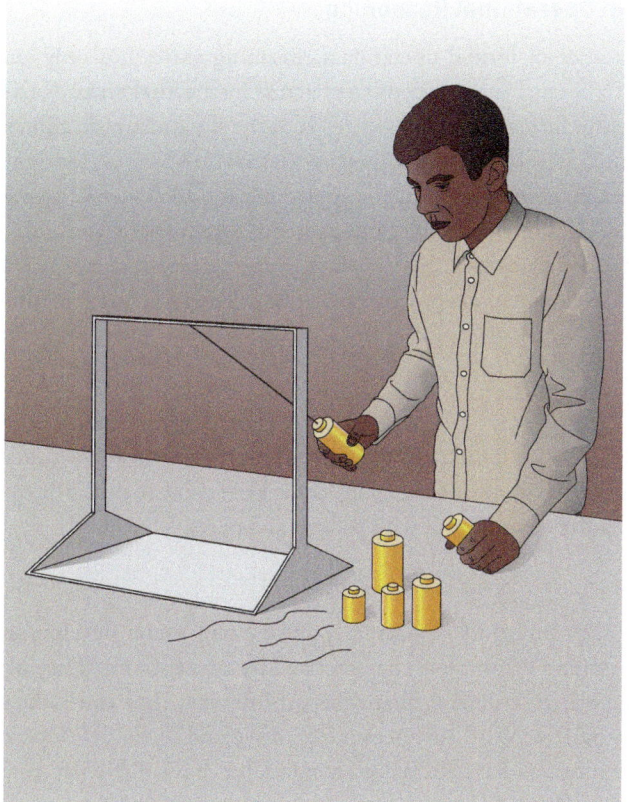

with which they have a great deal of experience. For example, completing college courses is associated with gains in propositional and statistical thought, skills often honed in college and measured in Piagetian tasks (Kuhn, 2012; Lehman & Nisbett, 1990). In one study in the early 1990s, adolescents from 10 to 15 years of age performed better on Piagetian tasks, such as the pendulum task, than adolescents had done over two decades before. The researchers attributed the difference to the fact that (in France, where the studies were done) secondary education was less common in the earlier decades. Therefore adolescents had fewer opportunities to practice the reasoning measured by Piagetian tasks (Flieller, 1999).

Limited Use of Formal Operational Reasoning

Adolescents' application of logic and scientific reasoning improves but is often limited compared with adults. Adolescents tend to choose single-variable solutions to scientific reasoning problems. In one study, sixth-grade students were presented with a detailed pictorial and written information about five variables that were explained to have either a causal or noncausal influence on a hypothetical problem, the likelihood of an avalanche occurring. The sixth graders tended to choose only one variable as the probable cause, varying their choice across trials. A pair of students first chose snow pollution as a cause of an avalanche, referring to the written materials, "Because it shows the snow pollution is high; snow is what causes an avalanche." For a second prediction, the student pair turned to another single variable, slope angle, and, as a third prediction, wind speed. However, the students did not consider how the variables work together (Kuhn et al., 2009).

Although adolescents can demonstrate scientific thinking, many consistently prefer simple one-factor solutions to the complex multiple-variable solutions that tend to characterize complicated real-life problems. They do not yet spontaneously consider the coordinated simultaneous effects of multiple causal influences (Kuhn, 2012). Even adults tend to prefer single-factor solutions to problems, suggesting that, although advanced scientific reasoning becomes possible with formal operations, adolescents and adults may not implement it in daily life (Kuhn, 2020).

Variability in Formal Operational Reasoning

Ultimately, the appearance of formal operational reasoning varies not only across individuals but also within individuals, because it is not consistent across intellectual areas (Kazi & Galanaki, 2020). Instead, the appearance of formal operations varies with the situation, task, context, and the individual's motivation (Birney & Sternberg, 2011; Labouvie-Vief, 2015; Marti & Rodríguez, 2012). Moreover, formal operational reasoning does not suddenly appear in early adolescence. Instead, cognitive change occurs gradually from childhood on, with gains in knowledge, experience, and information processing capacity (Keating, 2012; Moshman, 2021). Finally, most developmental scientists believe that the pinnacle of cognitive development is not in adolescence. Most agree that cognitive growth continues throughout adulthood.

Social Cognition in Adolescence

Adolescents' new abilities for reasoning influence **social cognition**, how they think about other people, relationships, and the social world. Adolescents become better able to take other people's perspectives, which leads to more mature relationships with parents and peers.

Perspective Taking

Perspective-taking ability improves alongside cognitive and social development (Selman, 1980). Recall that young children's thinking is characterized by egocentrism. They often cannot separate their perspective from others, believing that others think what they think, know what they know, and believe what they believe. With advances in cognitive and social development, 6- to 8-year-old children recognize that others have different thoughts but have difficulty comparing others' perspectives with their own. As children approach adolescence (age 8–10), they appreciate that others have different perspectives and taking others' points of view offers a valuable window to interpreting their behavior.

Advances in abstract reasoning between ages 10–12 make **mutual perspective taking** possible. Young adolescents become aware that they can take on other people's points of view and that others attempt to take their own point of view. Now adolescents can consider how their behavior appears to others (take a third person's perspective) and modify their behavior accordingly. By middle adolescence (age 12–15), **societal perspective taking** emerges and adolescents recognize that the social environment, including the larger society, influences people's perspectives and beliefs.

Perspective-taking ability predicts positive peer relations, friendship, and popularity in adolescence (Nilsen & Bacso, 2017). However, like abstract thought, perspective-taking abilities emerge gradually and may not follow an age-based timetable. The ability to use another's perspective in communication and decision making continues to develop in late adolescence (Crone & Fuligni, 2020). Moreover, not all adolescents apply their perspective-taking skills, and many are prone to errors in reasoning and lapses in judgment, as evidenced by the emergence of adolescent egocentrism (Flannery & Smith, 2017).

Adolescent Egocentrism

Adolescents often direct their abstract thinking abilities toward themselves, carefully considering their ideas, beliefs, and experiences. Perspective taking often develops slowly and in a piecemeal fashion. Adolescents often have difficulty separating their own and others' perspectives as they think about themselves. That is, adolescents find it difficult to distinguish their view of what others think of them from reality, what others actually think about them. They show adolescent egocentrism, a perspective-taking error manifested in two phenomena: the imaginary audience and the personal fable (Elkind & Bowen, 1979).

The **imaginary audience** is experienced as self-consciousness. Adolescents tend to feel as if all eyes are on them. This is an error in perspective taking because adolescents misdirect their own preoccupation about themselves to other people and assume that others are focused on them (Elkind & Bowen, 1979). The imaginary audience fuels adolescents' concerns with their appearance and can make the slightest criticism sting painfully because they believe everyone notices and is interested in what happens to them (Alberts et al., 2007).

Adolescents' preoccupation with themselves also leads them to believe they are special, unique, and invulnerable—a belief known as the **personal fable** (Elkind & Bowen, 1979). They believe that their emotions, the highs of happiness and depths of despair that they feel, are different from and more intense than other people's emotions. Others simply do not understand. Beliefs about invulnerability may predispose adolescents to seek risks, to believe that they are immune to the negative consequences of such risky activities as drug use, delinquency, and unsafe sex (Alberts et al., 2007).

One explanation for heightened self-consciousness in adolescence is the imaginary audience, a component of adolescent egocentrism.

skynesher/istock

Both the imaginary audience and the personal fable are thought to increase in early adolescence, peak in middle adolescence, and decline in late adolescence (Elkind & Bowen, 1979). Yet research suggests that adolescent egocentrism may persist into late adolescence and beyond (P. D. Schwartz et al., 2008). One study examined adolescents in 11 countries in Africa, the Americas, Asia, and Europe and found that the sensation-seeking characteristic of the personal fable increased in preadolescence, peaked at around age 19, and declined thereafter (Steinberg et al., 2018). However, when posting to social media, many adolescents painstakingly consider their audience and play to them by sharing content to appear interesting, well-liked, and attractive (Yau & Reich, 2018). Adolescent egocentrism may not completely disappear because, with social media, the imaginary audience may not be entirely imaginary (Terán et al., 2020).

THINKING IN CONTEXT 6.4

How might cognitive development influence adolescents' use of social media?

1. Consider the process of using social media. What abilities are required to effectively participate?
2. How might adolescent egocentrism relate to an adolescent's social media use?
3. How might cognitive development influence an adolescents' understanding and ability to use social media?
4. What should parents know about cognitive development and social media? Should cognitive development inform parent–child conversations about social media use? How?

VYGOTSKY'S SOCIOCULTURAL THEORY

6.5 Examine Vygotsky's sociocultural perspective on cognitive development.

How much of who you are results from your interactions with other people? According to Russian psychologist Lev Vygotsky, we are embedded in a sociocultural context that shapes how we think and whom we become. Like Piaget, Vygotsky believed that we build our understanding of the world around us, but he emphasized social interactions and culture as central to cognitive development (Daniels, 2017; Vasileva & Balyasnikova, 2019).

Cultural Tools

Vygotsky believed that thinking is influenced by our culture. People raised in different cultures think differently because cultures vary in the tools their members share. Cultural tools include not only physical items such as computers, pencils, and paper but also ways of thinking about phenomena, including how to approach math and scientific problems, as well as language itself (Robbins, 2005; Vygotsky, 1978). Spoken language, the ways in which members of a culture communicate about their world, is a cultural tool that shapes thought. The cultural tools we are exposed to influence what we think, the kinds of words we use, how we organize ideas, and *how* we think.

In many cultures, learning occurs through observation, without direct instructional cues from adults (Gaskins & Paradise, 2010; Kärtner et al., 2020). Children raised in agricultural communities where children learn to participate in household tasks at an early age tend to become skilled observational learners, even as infants, which influences how they process stimuli in their world. When 14- to 20-month-old Guatemalan Mayan and middle-class U.S. children were exposed to co-occurring events, such as being given a new toy to explore while other events were happening in the room, U.S. children tended to focus on only one event at a time, the new toy. In contrast, the Mayan children tended to simultaneously monitor multiple events by rapidly shifting their attention from the toy to the environment (Chavajay & Rogoff, 1999). Attending to multiple events, in this case a toy and surrounding environment, maximized the Mayan children's opportunity to learn by observing social interactions that do not involve them. Children's learning opportunities, how they learn, and ultimately how they think, are facilitated by their culture (Kärtner et al., 2020; Legare et al., 2015).

Guided Participation and Scaffolding

Children learn how to use the tools of their culture by interacting with skilled partners who provide guidance. Suppose a child wanted to bake cookies for the first time. Rather than send the child into the kitchen alone, we would probably accompany the child and provide the tools needed to accomplish the task, such as the ingredients, a rolling pin, cookie cutters, and a baking sheet. We would probably show the child how to use each tool, such as how to roll out the dough with the rolling pin. With social interaction and experience, the child adopts and internalizes the tools and knowledge, becoming able to apply them independently. That is, the child learns to bake. Vygotsky argued that in this way, culturally valued ways of thinking and problem solving get passed on to children.

Specifically, children learn through **guided participation** (also known as an *apprenticeship in thinking*), a form of sensitive teaching in which partners are attuned to the needs of children and help them accomplish more than the children could do alone (Rogoff, 2014). As novices, children learn from more skilled, or expert, partners by observing them and asking questions. In this way, children are apprentices, learning how others approach problems. Expert partners provide **scaffolding**, assistance that is tailored to children's needs and enables children to bridge the gap between their current competence level and the task at hand (Mermelshtine, 2017). Consider a child working on a jigsaw puzzle. The child is stumped, unsure of the next step. Suppose a more skilled partner, such as an adult, sibling, or another child who has more experience with puzzles, provides a little bit of assistance, a scaffold. The expert partner might point to a space on the puzzle and encourage the child to find a piece that fits that spot. If the child remains stumped, the partner might point out a piece or rotate it to help the child see the relationship. The partner acts to engage the child and provides support to help the child finish the puzzle, adjusting responses in light of the child's emerging competence.

Scaffolding occurs in formal educational settings, but also informally, any time more skilled persons adjust their interactional style to guide someone to complete tasks that they could not complete alone (Rogoff et al., 2016). Caregivers vary their scaffolding behaviors in response to children's attempts at tasks. They spontaneously use different behaviors depending on the child's attention skills, using more verbal engagement, strategic questions, verbal hints, and verbal prompts when children show difficulty paying attention during a task (Robinson et al., 2009). Two- to 4-year-olds' skills in cognitive control and planning are associated with their caregivers use of scaffolding and verbal guidance (Moriguchi, 2014). Parents and childcare providers often scaffold children's activity, but anyone who is more skilled at a given task, including older siblings and peers, can promote children's cognitive development (Rogoff et al., 2016). Collaboration with more skilled peers improves children's performance on card-sorting tasks, Piagetian tasks, planning, and other academic tasks (Sills et al., 2016). Children's thinking and views of the world are influenced by scaffolding and interactions with members of their culture (Rogoff et al., 2018).

Zone of Proximal Development

As Vygotsky (1962) explained, "What the child can do in cooperation today, he can do alone tomorrow" (p.104). Effective scaffolding works within the **zone of proximal development**, the gap between children's competence level—what they can accomplish independently—and what they can do with assistance of a skilled partner. With time, children internalize the scaffolding lesson and accomplish the task on their own—and their zone of proximal development shifts, as shown in Figure 6.9. Adults tend to naturally provide children with instruction within the zone of proximal development (Rogoff, 2014). When reading a book to a child, adults tend to point to items, label and describe characters' emotional states, explain, ask questions, listen, and respond sensitively, helping the child understand challenging material that is just beyond what the child can understand on their own (Silva et al., 2014).

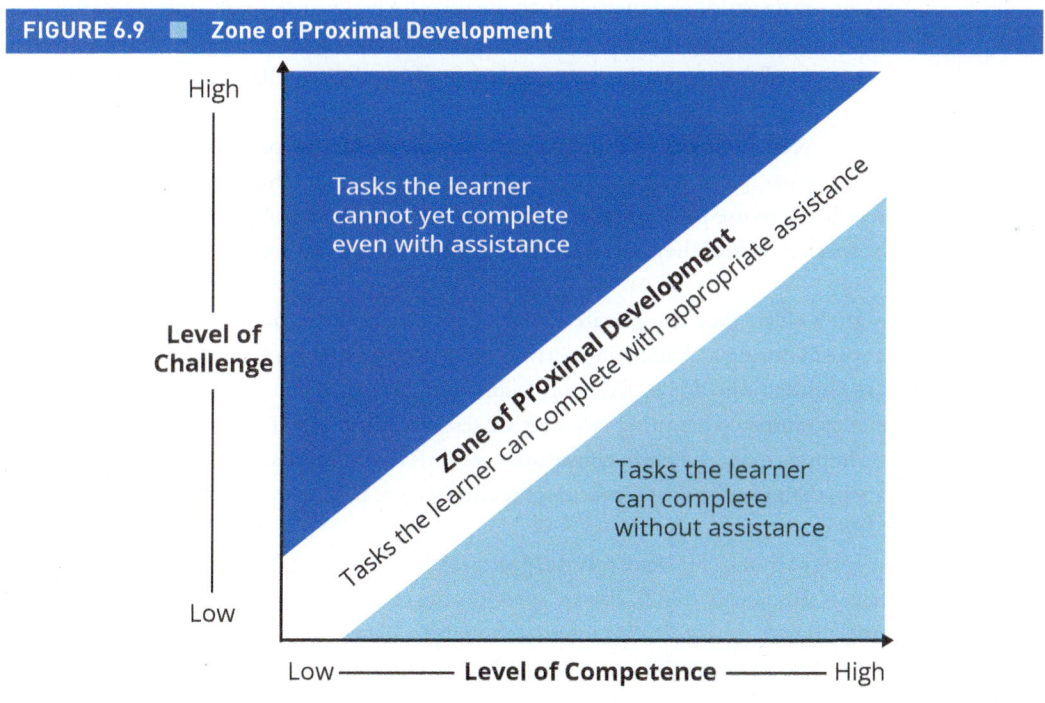

FIGURE 6.9 ■ Zone of Proximal Development

Source: Adapted from Vygotsky, L. (1978). *Mind in society: Development of higher psychological processes* (M. Cole, V. Jolm-Steiner, S. Scribner, & E. Souberman, Eds.). Harvard University Press.

The quality of scaffolding influences children's development. In one study of preschool teachers and children, the degree to which the adult matched children's needs for help in play predicted more autonomous play in children over a 6-month period (Trawick-Smith & Dziurgot, 2011). When parents provided young children specific guidance in considering a conservation of volume problem, such as discussing the size of the containers, asking *how* and *why* questions, and talking about simple math, children were more likely to give correct responses to scientific reasoning problems, including those involving conservation (Vandermaas-Peeler et al., 2016).

Parents and teachers can take advantage of the social nature of learning by assigning children tasks that they can accomplish with some assistance, providing just enough help so that children learn to complete the tasks independently (Taber, 2020). Such learning environments stimulate children to complete more challenging tasks on their own (Wass & Golding, 2014). Through guided play, teachers can develop play environments and settings with materials that encourage exploration and guide children with comments encouraging them to explore, question, or extend their interests (Bodrova & Leong, 2018). Children also scaffold their peers' learning, helping them understand new concepts during play (Ness, 2023).

Private Speech

Parents' guidance acts as a scaffold within the zone of proximal development to help children accomplish challenging tasks. Soon children become able to complete the task independently.

XiXinXing/istock

As Leroy played alone in the corner of the living room, he pretended to drive his toy car up a mountain and said to himself, "It's a high mountain. Got to push it all the way up. Oh no! Out of gas. Now they will have to stay here." Young children like Leroy often talk aloud to themselves, with no intention of communicating with others. This self-talk, called **private speech,** accounts for 20% to 50% of the utterances of children ages 4 to 10 (Berk, 1986). Private speech serves developmental functions. It *is* thinking. Vygotsky theorized that infants and children learn to speak to communicate with members of their culture. In early childhood they begin to use speech known as self-talk, or private speech, to think and guide their own thinking and learning (Vygotsky & Minick, 1987).

Private speech plays a role in self-regulation, the ability to control one's impulses and appropriately direct behavior; this increases during the preschool years (Smolucha & Smolucha, 2022). Children use private speech to plan strategies, solve problems, and regulate themselves so that they can achieve goals. Children are more likely to use private speech while working on challenging tasks and attempting to solve problems, especially when they encounter obstacles or do not have adult supervision (Winsler et al., 2009).

As children grow older, they use private speech more effectively to accomplish tasks. Children who use private speech during a challenging activity are more attentive and involved and show better performance than children who do not (Alarcón-Rubio et al., 2014). When 4- and 5-year-old children completed a complex multistep planning task over six sessions, those who used on-task private speech showed dramatic improvements between consecutive sessions (Benigno et al., 2011). It is worth noting that children vary in their use of private speech; some children use private speech more often than other children (Berk, 1992).

During elementary school, children's private speech tends to become a whisper or a silent moving of the lips (Smolucha & Smolucha, 2022). Private speech is the child's thinking and eventually becomes internalized as *inner speech*, or word-based internal thought, a silent internal dialogue that individuals use every day to regulate and organize behavior (Al-Namlah et al., 2012). Inner speech plays a role in cognitive processing, including short-term memory, planning, and executive function (Alderson-Day & Fernyhough, 2015). Children's use of inner speech varies with the task at hand. They are most likely to use inner speech when completing difficult problems and tasks (Mulvihill et al., 2023; Vissers et al., 2020). As the task becomes more familiar and automatic, the accompanying inner speech declines. Inner speech is common in adults, occurring when we use words to think to ourselves. Adults tend to use more inner speech, and even private speech (talking out loud to ourselves), when completing challenging tasks, supporting its use in self-guidance and self-regulation at all ages (Fernyhough & Borghi, 2023; Racy et al., 2020).

Evaluating Vygotsky's Sociocultural Theory

Vygotsky's zone of proximal development has important implications for education. It supports the use of assisted discovery. Teachers guide and scaffold children's learning rather than relying solely on children's independent or self-guided discovery. Learning is social; therefore, peer engagement and cooperative learning are important for promoting cognitive development. Through instruction, discussion, and play, adults and peers help children grasp new concepts that are seemingly out of reach (Taber, 2020). An educational implication of private speech is that parents and teachers must understand that talking to oneself or inaudible muttering is not misbehavior but, rather, indicates an effort to complete a difficult task or self-regulate behavior.

Although relatively unknown until recent decades, Vygotsky's ideas about the sociocultural nature of cognitive development have influenced prominent systems theories of development, such as Bronfenbrenner's bioecological systems theory (see Chapter 1) (Vasileva & Balyasnikova, 2019). They have been applied in educational settings, supporting the use of assisted discovery, guiding children's learning, and cooperative learning with peers. Effective instruction targets the zone of proximal development; most teachers intuitively seek to help students grasp new concepts that are seemingly just out of reach (Taber, 2020).

Similar to Piaget, Vygotsky's theory has been criticized for a lack of precision. The mechanisms or processes underlying the social transmission of thought are not described (Göncü & Gauvain, 2012). Moreover, constructs such as the zone of proximal development are not easily testable (Wertsch, 1998). Somewhat ahead of his time, Vygotsky described the brain as influencing development and viewed development as a lengthy process (Vasileva & Balyasnikova, 2019). It is understandable that Vygotsky's theory is incomplete, because he died of tuberculosis at the age of 37. We can only speculate about how his ideas might have evolved over a longer lifetime. Nevertheless, Vygotsky provided a new framework for understanding development as a process of transmitting culturally valued tools that influence how we look at the world, think, and approach problems.

THINKING IN CONTEXT 6.5

1. Consider your own cultural context. What are examples of cultural tools? What cultural tools have you adopted?
2. Consider a relatively new cultural tool, the smartphone. What does this tool provide us? Has it shaped our thinking? Do people think in different ways today than they did two decades ago? Are some of those differences related to this *new* cultural tool?
3. Identify an instance in which you used scaffolding to help someone.
4. Can children scaffold other children's learning? What do you think? Why?

APPLY YOUR KNOWLEDGE

Seven-year old Megan sets the large pitcher of lemonade on the table, the most important part of her lemonade stand. Her mother explains, "To make money you need to make sure that you spend less on lemonade and cups than you earn." Showing Megan the price of the lemonade mix and cups and the number of servings each jar of lemonade mix makes, she explains that Megan will make enough money to stay in business if she sells each cup of lemonade for 50 cents. "Don't overfill each cup. See this line?" Megan's mother asks, pointing to a line near the top of the cup. "Pour lemonade up to this line." Nodding, Megan excitedly answers, "OK!"

Megan is pleasantly surprised to see that her lemonade stand is popular with the neighborhood kids and adults. So much so that she runs out of cups. Megan's little brother, Sam, asked "I want to sell lemonade, too. Can I help?" "Sure," Megan replied, "Can you go inside and get more cups?" Sam returned with a stack of cups. "Here they are! Mom says they're all we have left." Megan notices that the new cups are a little bit larger than the first set of cups. As she watches her little brother Sam fill the cup to the top, Megan remembers her mother's warning that if she wants to make enough money to stay in business she shouldn't overfill cups. She tells Sam to pour a little bit less into each cup. "But we're supposed to fill it to the top line," Sam replies. Megan explains, "The new cups are larger so we should fill them with less lemonade." She pours lemonade from an old up into the new, larger cup, "See?" Sam replies, "No. The big cup one has less lemonade."

At the end of the week Megan happily counts her earnings. Her mother reminds her to put aside money to buy more supplies. "How much money do you think we need to buy more lemonade and cups?" she asks. "I don't know," Megan answers. "Well let's see," she responds. "The lemonade powder cost $2 and you needed two jars. How much is that?" "Four!" "How much were the cups? Look at the price sticker" "$1, but we need two, right?" "Yes, so how much are the cups?" "2 dollars." "So how much will our supplies cost?" Megan looks unsure. "How much is the lemonade? How much are the cups? Put those numbers together." "6!" "Exactly. Now, how much money did you make?" "13 dollars." "And how much will you have left after buying supplies? It's how much money you made, take away what you spend on supplies" "7?" "Yes, you earned 7 dollars!"

1. At what Piagetian stage does 7-year-old Megan reason? Explain the evidence for your answer.

2. Consider Megan's younger brother, Sam. What stage does his reasoning suggest? Explain.

3. What role does Megan's mother play in her cognitive advances? Describe her actions from Vygotsky's perspective.

4. What advances in reasoning do 20-year-old Megan and her older sister demonstrate? How do you know? Cite some examples from their conversation.

CHAPTER SUMMARY

6.1 Summarize the six substages of sensorimotor reasoning and processes of cognitive development.

Through interactions with people and objects, individuals organize what they learn to construct and refine their own schemas, or concepts, ideas, and ways of interacting with the world. Assimilation is a cognitive process in which a new experience is integrated into a preexisting schema. Accommodation occurs when we change a schema in light of the new information. Equilibration, the drive for cognitive equilibrium, is the basis for cognitive change, propelling individuals through the four stages of cognitive development proposed by Piaget. During the sensorimotor period, infants move through six substages that transition the infant from strengthening basic reflexes to engaging in primary, secondary, and tertiary circular reactions and demonstrating representational thought. Criticism of the sensorimotor reasoning stage tends to center around the method Piaget used to assess infants' abilities. Research that relies on infants' looking rather than reaching behaviors, such as violation of expectation tasks, suggested that object permanence develops earlier than Piaget believed. Findings with A-not-B tasks and deferred imitation tasks also suggest that young infants' thinking is more advanced than Piaget theorized. Core knowledge theorists argue that infants are born with several innate knowledge systems, or core domains of thought, that enable them to adapt to their world and learn very quickly from birth.

6.2 Discuss the characteristics of preoperational reasoning and young children's abilities.

Young children in the preoperational stage show impressive advances in representational thinking, but they lack the ability to understand logic and complex relationships. Children who show preoperational reasoning tend to make several common errors, including egocentrism, animism, centration, and irreversibility. Egocentrism is the inability to take another person's perspective, while animism is the belief that inanimate objects are alive. Centration is the tendency to focus on one aspect of an object or situation and exclude others, and irreversibility is the inability to understand that reversing a process can restore the original state. Young children cannot solve conservation tasks that test the understanding that the physical quantity of a substance, such as number, mass, or volume, remains the same even when its appearance changes. Research with young children has suggested that Piaget's tests of preoperational thinking underestimated young children. Success on Piaget's tasks appears to depend more on the child's language abilities than actions. Simple tasks demonstrate that young children are less egocentric than Piaget posited, may not consistently display animism, and can be taught to solve conservation tasks. Piaget's descriptions of children's abilities have implications for education, which should be age-appropriate and encourage children to explore, express themselves, and interact with their environment.

6.3 **Describe concrete operational reasoning and older children's abilities.**
At about age 7, children enter the concrete operational state of reasoning, characterized by the development of logical thinking. Children at this stage can use mental operations to solve problems and think logically. They have improved skills in classification and conservation tasks. Classification involves the ability to arrange items hierarchically, such as sorting a rock collection by geographic location of origin. Conservation refers to the understanding that the properties of an object remain unchanged despite its appearance, for example, a child realizing that two differently shaped pieces of clay contain the same amount of material. Children develop conservation skills gradually, with different types of conservation tasks being solved at different ages. Concrete operational reasoning is found in children around the world; however, experience, specific cultural practices, and education play a role in development.

6.4 **Analyze the development of formal operational reasoning and social cognition in adolescence.**
Formal operational reasoning emerges in early adolescence and enables adolescents to think abstractly and to engage in hypothetical-deductive reasoning and use the scientific method. Although Piaget believed that cognitive development is a universal process most adolescents and many adults do not display formal operational thinking in Piagetian hypothetical-deductive tasks. Individuals are more likely to show formal operational reasoning when considering material with which they have a great deal of experience. Adolescents can demonstrate scientific thinking but many consistently prefer simple one-factor solutions over the complex multivariate solutions that characterize everyday problems. The appearance of formal operational reasoning varies across individuals as well as within individuals and varies with situation, task, and context. Adolescents' new abilities for reasoning influence social cognition, and they develop the ability for mutual perspective taking followed by societal perspective taking. Adolescents' perspective taking abilities often manifest in adolescent egocentrism, characterized by the imaginary audience and personal fable, which may influence risk behavior. Both the imaginary audience and the personal fable are thought to peak in middle adolescence and decline in late adolescence.

6.5 **Examine Vygotsky's sociocultural perspective on cognitive development.**
Vygotsky posited that our sociocultural context and social interactions play a central role in shaping how we think and who we become. Vygotsky believed that thinking is influenced by our culture, which includes not just physical items but also ways of thinking about phenomena and language. Our culture shapes how we think and who we become and learning occurs through collaborating with others. Children learn how to use the tools of their culture through guided participation and scaffolding. They learn from more skilled partners who provide guidance and assistance that is tailored to their needs. Children learn from observation and by asking questions, and these expert partners act to engage the child and provide support. Over time, children internalize the instruction, making it part of their skill set, and they thereby master tasks. Effective scaffolding works within the zone of proximal development. Young children use private speech to think and to regulate their behavior and learning. In late childhood private speech is internalized as inner speech and aids children's thinking and problem solving.

KEY TERMS

- accommodation
- animism
- A-not-B error
- appearance–reality distinction
- assimilation
- centration
- class inclusion
- classification
- cognitive equilibration
- cognitive operations
- concrete operational stage of reasoning
- conservation
- core knowledge theory
- deferred imitation
- egocentrism
- formal operational reasoning
- guided participation
- hypothetical–deductive reasoning
- imaginary audience
- irreversibility
- mental representation
- mutual perspective taking
- object permanence
- personal fable
- preoperational reasoning
- primary circular reaction
- private speech
- scaffolding
- secondary circular reaction
- seriation
- social cognition
- societal perspective taking
- tertiary circular reaction
- transitive inference
- violation-of-expectation task
- zone of proximal development

JGI/Jamie Grill/Getty Images

7 INFORMATION PROCESSING THEORY

> **LEARNING OBJECTIVES**
>
> **7.1** Describe information processing theory, including its assumptions, mental stores, and what develops.
>
> **7.2** Examine the development of attention from infancy through adolescence.
>
> **7.3** Discuss the development of working memory and executive function.
>
> **7.4** Summarize changes in memory from infancy through adolescence.
>
> **7.5** Analyze the development of thinking in infants, children, and adolescents.

"Let's play the I Spy game," said Carlo as he drove his children to school. "I spy with my little eye something that is green," he continued. Eight-year-old Ava quickly shouted, "The trees!" while her 5-year-old brother, Max, struggled to find what Carlo was looking at. "Max, you have to keep looking for something that is green," explained Carlo. After a few minutes, Max finally spotted a green sign and shouted, "The sign!" This game can make a car trip pass more quickly. It also tells us about people's cognitive development. Advances in information processing skills, such as attention and working memory, contribute to success in this game.

In contrast with cognitive developmental approach that describes cognitive change as discontinuous or stage-like, information processing theorists argue that thinking changes more gradually, in a continuous fashion. Improvements in information processing make our thinking more complex, faster, and more efficient. In this chapter, we examine the development of the information processing system.

INFORMATION PROCESSING THEORY

> **7.1** Describe information processing theory, including its assumptions, mental stores, and what develops.

Our sociohistorical context influences our development. It also affects scientists' theories. Computers became commercially available in the mid-20th century, enabling users to rapidly and accurately solve challenging problems. Soon scientists began to consider the computer as a metaphor to describe how our minds work. Like a computer, the information processing approach to cognition represents the human mind as designed to manipulate information. A computer's hardware consists of disk drives, RAM, and a processor. The brain and our cognitive structures (such as long-term memory) are our mental hardware. Software are the programs computers run. Our mental software includes the cognitive processes we use to attend to information, store it, and use it to solve problems. Therefore, from an information processing perspective, cognition is a set of interrelated components that enable people to process information by noticing it, taking it in, manipulating it, storing it, and retrieving it (Siegler & Alibali, 2020).

Information Processing Assumptions

Unlike the cognitive-developmental and sociocultural theories we have discussed thus far, information processing theory is not one theory created by one person. Information processing theory is an umbrella term for many theories, each examining a component of cognition, such as attention or memory. Although there are many component theories, information processing theories all share the same three basic assumptions (Wickens & Carswell, 2021).

First, thinking is information processing. Our mind is designed to take in information, manipulate it, store it, retrieve it, and apply it to solve problems. We are built to process information.

Second, cognitive change is a continuous process. With development, we gradually get better at using our cognitive system. However, the system's structure, its components, remains largely the same over the life span (A. Baddeley et al., 2020; Siegler, 2016). This distinguishes information processing theory from Piaget's cognitive-developmental theory; there are no stages.

Third, our cognitive resources are limited (Bjorklund & Myers, 2015; Oberauer et al., 2016). We can only attend to, store, and manipulate so much information at once. Our cognitive system is limited in two basic ways: capacity and speed. Capacity limitations include the amount of information that can be held, how long it can be held, and how it can be processed. With development we get better at holding and manipulating information through our cognitive system despite our system's limitations. The speed with which we manipulate information and think is also limited. With development our thinking becomes faster and more efficient with brain maturation and experience. As we learn strategies to acquire, store, and use knowledge, we expand our processing capacity and process information more quickly.

Mental Stores

According to information processing theory, the mind is composed of three mental stores: sensory memory, working memory, and long-term memory (R. C. Atkinson & Shiffrin, 1968). Throughout our lives, information moves through these three stores, and we use them to manipulate and hold information (see Figure 7.1).

Sensory Memory

Sensory memory is the first step in getting information into the mind. Sensory receptors are found in our eyes, ears, taste buds, and skin. Sensory information enters sensory memory, which holds incoming sensory information in its original form (such as a visual image or sound echo) to determine whether it must be processed or considered (Vandenbroucke et al., 2014). For example, look at this page, then close your eyes. Did you *see* the page for a fraction of a second after you closed your eyes? That image, or icon, represents your sensory memory. Information fades from sensory memory quickly if it is not processed. Visual information decays in about a quarter second, and auditory information lasts about 4 seconds (Radvansky, 2017).

This boy's sensory memory includes the brief image of the flower and its scent.

felixmizioznikov/istock

Working Memory

Every moment a great deal of information rapidly enters our sensory memory. Not surprisingly, much of it is discarded. When we direct our **attention**, or focus our mental resources, on information, it passes from sensory memory to the next part of the information processing system, **working memory** (Oberauer, 2019). Working memory holds and processes information being *worked on* in some way. Working memory consists of at least three components: a short-term store, a processing component, and the **central executive**, a control center that directs mental processes (A. D. Baddeley et al., 2021).

FIGURE 7.1 ■ Information Processing System

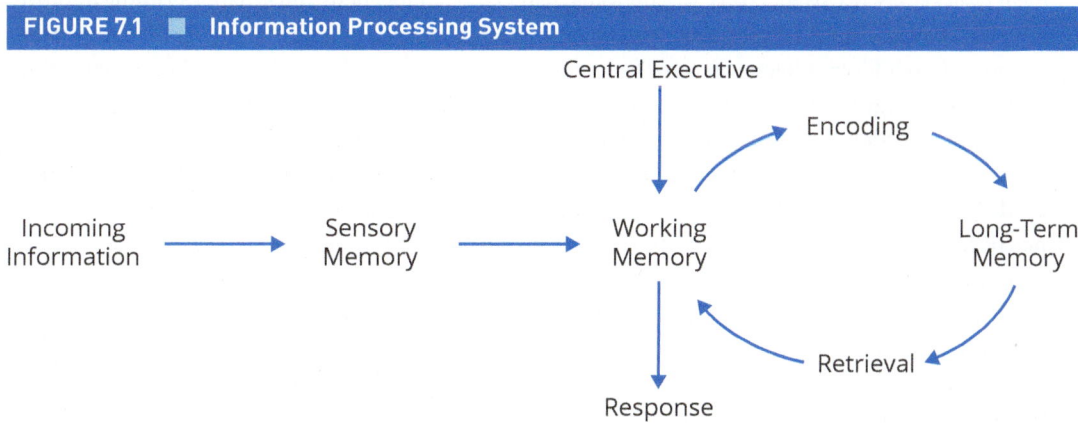

Just as your thoughts constantly change, so do the contents of the short-term store. The short-term store is limited in size and duration. We can hold only so much information in working memory's short-term store (perhaps as many as 9 items, such as words, numbers, or images, and as few as 4 items), and we can hold it for a short period, from seconds to minutes (Radvansky, 2017). This illustrates a core assumption of the information processing system: It has limited capacity (Bjorklund, 2022; Siegler & Alibali, 2020).

The processing component of working memory *works* with or acts on information. Working memory is responsible for manipulating (considering, comprehending), **encoding** (creating a memory), and **retrieval** (recalling) of information. All thoughts—all conscious mental activities—occur within working memory. For example, while reading this paragraph, you might remember other assignments and consider how this material applies to your own experience—activities that tap your working memory.

An essential part of working memory is the central executive, a control mechanism or processor that directs the flow of information and regulates cognitive activities such as attention, action, and problem solving (A. D. Baddeley, 2021; Vandierendonck, 2016). The central executive determines what is important to attend to, combines new information with information already in working memory, and selects and applies strategies for manipulating the information to understand it, make decisions, and solve problems (A. D. Baddeley et al., 2021). Collectively, these cognitive activities are known as **executive function**. The central executive is in charge of mental operations.

Long-Term Memory

As information is manipulated in working memory, it becomes more likely to enter long-term memory, the third mental store. **Long-term memory** is an unlimited store that holds information indefinitely. Information is not manipulated or processed in long-term memory; it is held until it is retrieved to use in working memory (e.g., remembering events and thinking about them).

What Develops

Although information processing theory was initially used to describe adults' thinking, research has shown that infants, children, and adolescents have the same memory stores (A. D. Baddeley et al., 2021; Siegler, 2016). In addition, the structure of the information processing system remains the same throughout the lifespan. We are born with the ability to take in, store, and manipulate information through our sensory, working, and long-term memory. With development, we can process and retain more information and do so more quickly and efficiently to adapt to the world around us.

What develops? **Processing speed**, the speed with which we can complete a mental task, improves. Improvements in processing speed lead to more efficient thinking. Processing speed increases rapidly in early infancy, from 3 months, and continues into adolescence (Saint et al., 2017). Older adolescents can process information to solve problems more rapidly than younger adolescents, who are quicker than children, who are faster than infants.

Gains in processing speed and other information processing capacities are related to brain development (Wickens & Carswell, 2021). Recall from Chapter 4 synaptogenesis and synaptic pruning improve the efficiency of neural connections. Myelination permits quicker physical and cognitive responses. Compared to children, adolescents show faster reaction speed in gym class and are quicker at connecting ideas, making arguments, and drawing conclusions. Children are similarly advanced over infants. From childhood into adolescence, the structure of the prefrontal cortex changes, with decreases in gray matter and increases in white matter, cognition becomes markedly more efficient (Natu et al., 2021; Tamnes & Mills, 2020). Increases in processing speed are also due to expertise, specifically, **automaticity**. With practice, cognitive processes become automatic, requiring little effort and fewer mental resources, such as attention and working memory, and become quicker (Servant et al., 2018). Automaticity is a function of experience. With development, children and adolescents quickly learn from their experiences and naturally apply what they learn to think and solve problems more quickly (Lannoy et al., 2022). When tasks are automatic, they require less thinking—less conscious work. Recall that our cognitive system is limited, therefore freeing up cognitive resources speeds thinking.

In sum, we get better at encoding information, forming memories. We learn strategies for working with our system, effectively deploying attention, paying attention to what is important, memorizing information, and focusing our thoughts. We also become more aware of how our minds work and apply that knowledge in our daily lives. This is called **metacognition**, thinking about our own thinking. We discuss each of these processes in this chapter.

> **THINKING IN CONTEXT 7.1**
>
> 1. Compare the information processing model with Piaget's cognitive developmental perspective. How are the perspectives similar and different? To what extent do you think they are compatible, or work together, to describe how we think?
> 2. Describe the process of thinking and the path that information takes from stimulus, such as something heard or viewed, to forming a memory, and recalling the information for later contemplation. Use terms such as attention, working memory, and long-term memory.

ATTENTION

> 7.2 Examine the development of attention from infancy through adolescence.

Attention refers to our ability to direct our awareness. We must focus our attention to select information to process in working memory, an ability influenced by neurological development, including increases in myelination (G. D. Reynolds & Romano, 2016). Important developments in attention occur over the course of infancy and continue throughout childhood.

Types of Attention

Attention is a finite resource. But we can allocate it in different ways (Gellman, 2020).

Selective attention is the ability to systematically direct one's attention, focusing on relevant information and ignoring distractors. Selective attention enables you to concentrate on reading these words while ignoring distractors such as cars driving by outside your window, your pet dog or cat snoring, and irrelevant thoughts like what's for dinner.

Sustained attention is the ability to remain focused on a stimulus for an extended period. Sustained attention helps you focus on a task, such as reading this chapter, for a long period, perhaps until you finish it.

Divided attention refers to attending to two stimuli at once. Divided attention lets you focus on two tasks, such as reading this chapter while listening to music in the background.

These types of attention, described separately, are interrelated. Selective attention, the ability to tune out distractors, is needed for both sustained and divided attention (Rueda et al., 2023). It is not possible to pay attention over time (sustained) or attend to two stimuli (divided) without the ability to ignore distractors (selective).

Infancy

Newborns can attend to visual stimuli, directing their gaze to orient toward and away from objects, the earliest indicators of attention, but this ability is not fully formed until about 3–4 months of age (Hendry et al., 2019). Attention improves rapidly over infancy with myelination and other advances in brain development (G. D. Reynolds & Romano, 2016).

Researchers apply methods used to study visual perception, such as preferential looking procedures and habituation, to learn about infant attention (see Chapter 4; Hendry et al., 2019; Kucharský et al., 2024). Habituation, reduced responses to a nonchanging stimulus, such as a geometric pattern, tells us that infants get used to and therefore pay less attention to familiar stimuli (Sicard-Cras et al., 2022). Dishabituation, the recovery of responsiveness after a stimulus is changed, shows us when infants detect and direct their attention to the change. Looking time, the amount of time infants spend looking at a stimulus, is often used to measure attention. Recent studies have measured changes in infant heart rate that coincide with phases of attention (Bradshaw et al., 2024). Heart rate rises as infants notice and attend to a stimulus, signifying interest. Heart rate falls, then plateaus with habituation and rises with dishabituation. As infants become more efficient at directing their attention to scan and process visual information, they require less exposure to stimuli to habituate.

The toy keys have captured this infant's attention. How long will it take to habituate to this interesting stimulus?
Catherine Delahaye/Getty Images

With advances in selective attention, infants prefer more complicated and dynamic stimuli—stimuli that change over time—compared with static, unchanging stimuli (Hendry et al., 2019). When 3- to 13-month-old infants were shown displays that included a range of static and moving stimuli, age differences in preferences emerged. At 6.5 months old, infants preferred very complex stimuli, such as video clips, over moderately complex stimuli, such as faces, and little interest in simple stimuli, such as dot patterns (Courage et al., 2006). The onset of walking is associated with gains in selective attention because infants' upright position enables them to see more of their environment, creating new demands and opportunities for attention (Mulder et al., 2022).

Sustained attention emerges at around 2 months of age, but is limited (Krieber-Tomantschger et al., 2022). It increases throughout infancy through early childhood. Whereas a 1-year-old infant attends to a single toy during active play on an average of about 3 seconds, the average time for a 3-year-old child approaches 9 seconds (A. Fisher & Kloos, 2016).

Attention is associated with development in the brain areas responsible for attentional control (Dowe et al., 2020). In response to tasks that challenge attention, infants show widespread activity in the prefrontal cortex (responsible for thinking and planning) at 5.5 months but more specific or localized activity by 7.5 months of age (Ellis et al., 2021; Richards, 2010). Attention at 5 months of age predicts executive function in late infancy through school-age (Blankenship et al., 2019). Attention is vital to memory and learning and predicts language development (Amso & Kirkham, 2021; A. V. Fisher, 2019). Young children's selective attention at age 2.5 years predicts working memory and response inhibition at age 3 (Veer et al., 2017).

Infant attention has been studied within the context of **joint attention** with a caregiver. Joint attention refers to periods when both the caregiver and infant focus on the same object. Joint attention emerges toward the end of the first year of life, improving between 9 and 12 months (Boyer et al., 2020). At 12 months, infants focus for a more extended period when they attend to an object with a caregiver than when they attend to it alone (Wass et al., 2018). Initial studies of joint attention emphasized gaze, infants' ability to identify and follow a stimulus viewed by the caregivers. However, infants and caregivers interact in a range of ways beyond gaze. When caregivers play with infants, they signal their attention and interest in an object through multiple modalities, including talking, handling objects, and looking at objects (see Figure 7.2; Suarez-Rivera et al., 2019). Talking about objects and touching them directs and extends infants' attention to objects (Bánki et al., 2024). The multimodal nature of joint attention is especially useful in understanding it in real life because infants often do not look at their caregivers' faces during object play (Yu & Smith, 2016). Studying joint attention as gaze

FIGURE 7.2 ■ Joint Attention

A. Proportion of all *infant looks at an object with joint attention (JA)* in four categories: with no additional parent behaviors, with parent touch, with parent talk, and with parent touch and talk.

B. Mean proportion of *all infant looks* at an object (with and without JA) that were classified as each category. Infants were most likely to look at an object when jointly attending with a caregiver who touches and talks about it.

(a) Infant looks with joint attention JA

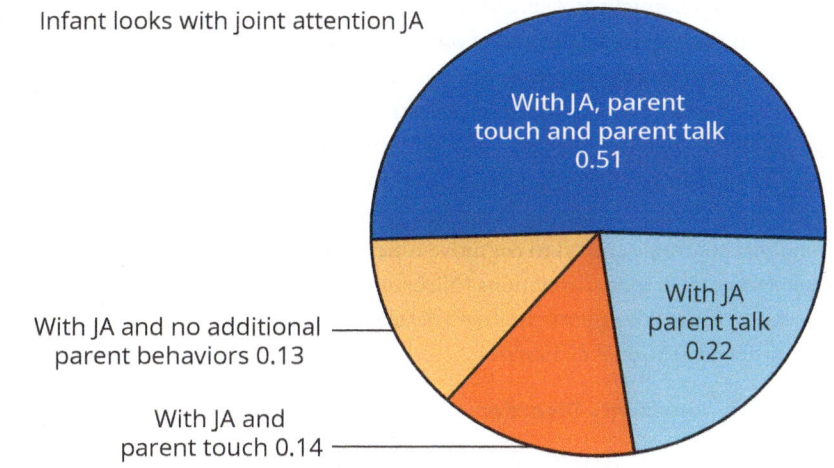

(b) Mean proportion of infant looks that were classified in the five categories

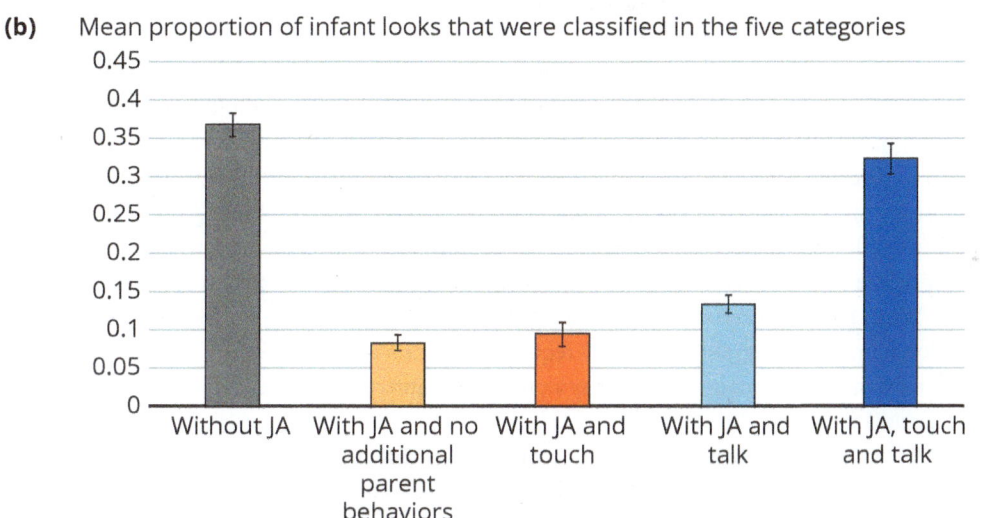

Source: Suarez-Rivera, C., Smith, L. B., & Yu, C. (2019). Multimodal parent behaviors within joint attention support sustained attention in infants. *Developmental Psychology, 55*(1), 96–109. https://doi.org/10.1037/dev0000628

alone can lead to underestimating infants' abilities (Bradley et al., 2023). Perhaps most important, joint attention illustrates the role of social interactions with caregivers and the environment in cognitive development.

Childhood

Dramatic improvements in attention occur early in childhood, particularly sustained attention (Rueda & Conejero, 2020). As children can pay attention for more extended periods, new activities become possible. Preschoolers can listen to an adult read an entire book during story time or attend to a television program for about 30 minutes. But they often struggle with selective attention. It is challenging for them to focus on relevant information and ignore distractions. Their limitations in selective attention can interfere with sustained attention because sustaining attention over time requires the ability to attend selectively.

Developmental Changes

Young children do not search thoroughly when asked to compare detailed pictures and explain what is missing from one. They have trouble focusing on one stimulus and switching their attention to compare it with other stimuli (Hanania & Smith, 2010). For instance, when young children sort cards according to one dimension, such as color, they often have difficulty switching to different sorting criteria, such as by size (Honomichl & Zhe, 2011). Both selective and sustained attention are associated with academic skills at the beginning and end of preschool (Shannon et al., 2021).

Performance on attention tasks improves throughout the elementary school years (Ristic & Enns, 2015). Older children can direct their attention selectively and shift it in response to task demands (Bater & Jordan, 2020). In practice, however, older children only sometimes spontaneously shift their attention without being instructed to do so (Vergauwe et al., 2021). Attentional control improves over childhood, and older children learn how to direct their attention and identify when attention switching is needed. Attentional control is critical to cognitive functioning because it enables us to keep tasks in mind and pursue our goals despite distractions (Niebaum & Munakata, 2020). Advances in working memory and executive function support children's developing skills in attention. Some children, however, experience extreme attentional difficulties.

Attention-Deficit/Hyperactivity Disorder

Attention-deficit/hyperactivity disorder (ADHD) is the most commonly diagnosed neurodevelopmental disorder in children, diagnosed in about 13% of schoolchildren in the United States (Zablotsky et al., 2019; Zgodic et al., 2023). ADHD is characterized by persistent age-inappropriate difficulties with attention and hyperactivity/impulsivity that interfere with performance and behavior in school and daily life (Faraone et al., 2024). Problems with attention and distractibility may appear in different ways, including failing to attend to details, making careless mistakes, not seeming to listen when spoken to directly, not following through on instructions, or difficulty organizing tasks or activities. Impulsivity may include frequent fidgeting, squirming in the seat, and leaving the seat in class; often running or climbing in situations where it is not appropriate; talking excessively, often blurting out an answer before a question is completed; and having trouble waiting a turn (Luo et al., 2019; Nigg et al., 2020). While most children show one or two symptoms of inattention or hyperactivity at some point in their development, a diagnosis of ADHD requires the consistent display of a minimum number of specific symptoms over six months, and the symptoms must interfere with behavior in daily life (American Psychiatric Association, 2013).

ADHD is associated with differences in brain development, specifically, structural abnormalities in parts of the brain responsible for attentional and motor control (Bernanke et al., 2022; Mu et al., 2022). ADHD has genetic roots and is thought to be up to 80% heritable (Sonuga-Barke et al., 2023). However, there are instances in which only one identical twin is diagnosed with ADHD, suggesting a role for epigenetics in determining the degree to which genetic propensities are expressed (Mirkovic et al., 2020; Tistarelli et al., 2020). Environmental influences on ADHD may include premature birth, prenatal exposure to alcohol and drugs, lead exposure, and household chaos (Agnew-Blais et al., 2022; Cabral et al., 2020). Stimulant medication is the most common treatment for ADHD; it increases activity in the parts of the brain that are responsible for attention, self-control, and behavior inhibition (Hawk et al., 2018; Mechler et al., 2022). Behavioral interventions can help children learn strategies to manage impulses and hyperactivity, direct their attention, and monitor their behavior (Antshel, 2020; S. W. Evans et al., 2018). Cognitive and behavioral strategies for managing ADHD are especially important because ADHD is a persistent condition whose symptoms and effects often continue into adulthood (Nigg et al., 2020).

Adolescence

Adolescents are more skilled in attentional tasks, including divided and selective attention, compared to children (Hanania & Smith, 2010; Memmert, 2014). This enables them to better hold information in working memory while processing new information, improving their ability to focus on complex tasks (Theodoraki et al., 2020). At age 13, Julia can tune out distractions in class, pay attention to the teacher, and identify important while taking notes and listening. She can also shift her attention during class discussions to identify new ideas to add to her notes. These advancements in attentional control and information processing help support adolescents' problem-solving skills, including geometry problems, scientific methods, and other challenging problems.

Adolescents frequently test their attentional abilities by multitasking, usually through media activities such as listening to music, texting, or participating in social media while completing another task, like homework (Ettinger & Cohen, 2020). Yet people, including adults, tend to overestimate their ability to multitask (Madore & Wagner, 2019). Cognitive scientists believe the human brain is not designed to perform two or more tasks simultaneously. What appears to be multitasking is actually task-switching, alternating between different tasks (Skaugset et al., 2016)

Media multitasking is associated with poor academic performance (Kokoç, 2021). A review of 56 studies revealed a negative relationship between media multitasking and cognitive control, academic performance, and socioemotional functioning (van der Schuur et al., 2015). Heavy media multitaskers tend to perform worse than light media multitaskers on tasks requiring attention, working memory, long-term memory, and impulse control (Cain et al., 2016). They are also more likely to be distracted and have difficulty attending to one task (Cain et al., 2016; Wiradhany & Koerts, 2021). Causality, however, is difficult to determine. It is unclear whether multitasking leads to poor performance on cognitive tasks or if adolescents with limited attention multitask more (Cain et al., 2016).

There are individual differences in attentional control. In one longitudinal study, media multitasking was linked to poor academic achievement, but it predicted declines in academic achievement over time only for adolescents with poor self-regulation (van der Schuur et al., 2020). Adolescents with better attentional control, even those who multitask, show better academic performance (Kokoç, 2021). Multitasking places demands on two competing brain networks associated with attending to the outside world and focusing on inner thoughts (Lam et al., 2022). The brain must repeatedly switch between them to multitask.

Multitasking places heavy demands on our limited attentional capacities. Although our discussion has focused on attention, working memory and executive function (controlled by the prefrontal cortex, which is still maturing in adolescents) also influence attention (Frick et al., 2022). We discuss these processes next.

Implications for Education and Parenting

One of the most important implications of the findings we have discussed is that attention is a finite resource and is essential for children's learning. Teachers should provide developmentally appropriate tasks and limit the time that students spend on tasks that require sustained attention. For preschoolers, teachers should be aware of their limited selective attention and difficulty ignoring distractions. To maintain attention teachers should structure activities in short time frames, with frequent changes in activities and movement breaks. Teachers can also provide opportunities for sensory play and exploration, because these activities can help develop attentional skills.

For elementary school children, teachers can encourage the development of attentional skills by providing challenging activities, such as puzzles and problem-solving activities. Providing clear instructions and expectations, offering positive feedback and recognition for their efforts, and modeling good attentional skills themselves is also beneficial. Additionally, it is important for teachers to be aware of individual differences in attentional abilities and to provide additional support or accommodations as needed.

For adolescents, teachers may need to teach strategies to manage their attention and multitasking behavior. This includes limiting distractions and prioritizing tasks, encouraging them to focus on one task at a time, and providing opportunities for students to practice switching their attention between different tasks. Teachers can support adolescents' attentional abilities by providing a supportive and engaging learning environment, helping students develop strategies for managing distractions and increasing attentional control, and encouraging them to take breaks and engage in physical activity.

Parents also play an important role in supporting their children's attention and learning. Parents can provide a structured and consistent environment at home, with clear expectations and routines for homework and other tasks. Younger children can develop attention skills through activities such as reading and playing focused games, and parents can work on developing joint attention skills. For older children, parents can set routines, limit distractions, and encourage breaking down tasks into smaller steps. Parents can also limit distractions in the home, such as excessive screen time or loud noises, and create a quiet and comfortable study space for their child. Additionally, parents can model good attention habits themselves, such as focusing on tasks without distraction and limiting their own media multitasking. Finally, parents can work with their child's teacher to identify any attentional challenges and explore strategies for supporting attention and learning at home and at school.

> ### THINKING IN CONTEXT 7.2
>
> 1. Given an example of selective, sustained, and divided attention. How are these forms of attention interrelated?
> 2. What role does brain development play in attention?
> 3. Suppose you were playing with an infant. How would you encourage joint attention? What would you do? What are some of the benefits of joint attention? For emotional or social development?
> 4. Do you multitask? If so, when and under what conditions? Compare your experience with the research findings discussed in this section.

WORKING MEMORY AND EXECUTIVE FUNCTION

> **7.3** Discuss the development of working memory and executive function.

Attention determines what enters working memory and what information we will process. As noted earlier, working memory contains three components: a short-term store where information is held, a processor for manipulating information, and the central executive, which controls working memory processes. The central executive plays a role in attention, determining what information to focus on, directing processing, and influencing memory, deciding what information to retain and how to retain it. In this way working memory and attention interact, influencing each other (Keene et al., 2022). The central executive is responsible for executive control, a set of cognitive processes that include planning, flexible thinking, and cognitive control (Doebel, 2020).

Infancy

Infants' working memory is assessed by observing their reaching and looking behaviors. Delayed response tasks measure the duration of working memory. An object is shown to an infant and is then hidden among several boxes; the infant is allowed to search for the object after a short (e.g., 10-second) delay (Simmering, 2016). Delayed response tasks can be used as soon as infants can reliably reach for items at about 5–6 months of age. Recent research has employed a non-motor visual indicator of working memory: pupil size (Koevoet et al., 2024; Ross-Sheehy & Eschman, 2019). The pupil is the opening in the eye through which light passes. The pupil dilates, or gets larger, in response to cognitive effort, such as when encoding the location of a stimulus as it is moved from Place A to Place B in the A-not-B task (Kaldy & Blaser, 2020).

Working memory capacity, how many items can be held in mind, dramatically increases between 6 months of age, when infants can recall a single item, to 12–14 months, when infants can reliably recall three objects, similar to some adults (Cowan, 2023). Does this mean that infants have similar working memory abilities as adults? Just as attention advances throughout infancy, childhood, and adolescence, so does working memory. Infants may recall objects, but they likely do not process stimuli similarly to adults. In a recent looking-time study, 6-month-old infants demonstrated immediate recall of an object in a hidden place but could not remember the distinct features of the object (Kibbe & Leslie, 2019).

That is, they could recall that an object was hidden, but not *which* object, a ball or a human-like doll head, suggesting that infants' working memory is still developing.

Childhood

In childhood, the storage component of working memory, the short-term store, is commonly assessed by a memory span task in which individuals are asked to recall a series of numbers presented at a rate of about 1 per second. Two- to 3-year-old children could recall about two digits, increasing to about five items at age 7, increasing to about seven by early adulthood (Bjorklund & Myers, 2015). Research employing the more challenging backward memory task, requiring children to repeat a series of numbers backward, suggests that working memory doubles from 5.5 to 11.5 years, from about two digits to four, increasing to about five and one half digits in adulthood (Dobbs & Rule, 1989; M. R. Reynolds et al., 2022). Tests of visual working memory examine children's memory for observed objects. Recall of objects, their locations, and features increases over childhood (Forsberg et al., 2023). Children also get better at updating their working memory, monitoring and recalling changes in stimuli over time (Cheng & Kibbe, 2022). Increases in working memory storage frees cognitive resources and supports advances in selective and sustained attention (Superbia-Guimarães & Cowan, 2023).

The workspace of working memory that manipulates information improves over childhood as the central executive—the director of mental processes—develops. Brain development, specifically pruning in the prefrontal cortex and corpus callosum, supports the development of working memory and executive function (Fiske & Holmboe, 2019; Perone et al., 2018). Between ages 3 and 7, children show increasing prefrontal cortex engagement while completing tasks that measure working memory (Perlman et al., 2016). Neural circuits for visuospatial working memory, auditory working memory, and response inhibition differentiate to enable faster and more efficient processing of these critical cognitive functions (Crone & Steinbeis, 2017; Spencer, 2020). Older children are quicker at matching pictures and recalling spatial information than younger children, and they show more activity in the brain's frontal regions than younger children (Farber & Beteleva, 2011). They can also prioritize information in working memory, devoting more resources to attend to and manipulate information deemed valuable (A. L. Atkinson et al., 2019).

Development of the prefrontal cortex leads to improvements in inhibitory control, or impulse control, the ability to withhold a behavioral response inappropriate in the current context. These advances improve children's capacity for self-regulation, controlling their thoughts and behavior.

Planning

Young children get better at planning, considering the steps needed to complete a particular act, and carrying them out to achieve a goal (Plebanek & Sloutsky, 2019; Rueda, 2013). Preschoolers can create and abide by a plan to complete familiar and not too complex tasks, such as searching for a lost object in a yard. But they need help with more challenging tasks that contain multiple steps, such as planning what to bring for a trip to the park. Young children have difficulty deciding where to begin and how to proceed to complete a task in an orderly way (Ristic & Enns, 2015). When they plan, young children often skip important steps or fail to consider the order of steps (Martin-Ordas, 2018). They also need help carrying out their plans as they quickly lose focus.

School-age children's growing executive functions help them devise and carry out plans more effectively than young children. They can control their attention and deploy it selectively, focusing on the relevant information and ignoring other information, compared with younger children, who are easily distracted and fidget (Cowan, 2023). Starting around age 6 or 7, children begin to spontaneously monitor the cognitive demands of tasks and guide their behavior (Niebaum & Munakata, 2020). They can plan tasks with multiple steps, considering the sequence of steps before they begin (Tecwyn et al., 2014).

Inhibitory Control

Growing executive function abilities enable children to become more skilled at controlling and deploying their cognitive resources to pursue goals (Doebel, 2020). They get better at inhibiting impulses to engage in task-irrelevant actions and can keep focused on a task.

Children's skills in inhibitory control, or impulse control, influence their behavior at home, school, and with peers. Inhibitory control contributes to emotional regulation, children's understanding, expression, and control of emotions, which contributes to social development (Li et al., 2020). Preschool children who score high on measures of executive function and inhibitory control show greater social competence, including more adaptive responses to peer conflict, than other children (Caporaso et al., 2019). For instance, a study that followed 8- to 12-year-old children over a year found that children with poor impulse control were more likely to experience peer rejection (Lecce et al., 2020). Children who are skilled in emotional regulation tend to be better able to resist their impulses and adjust to school (Savina, 2020).

Advances in working memory and executive function are associated with language, reading, writing, and mathematics skills (Allen et al., 2019; Spiegel et al., 2021). The demands of formal schooling, such as learning in a classroom with peers, directing attention to a teacher's lesson, follow directions, and completing independent work, rely on working memory and executive function skills. Academic success is influenced by working memory and executive function, yet the school context also promotes these cognitive abilities (Peng & Kievit, 2020). Children in first grade show greater increases in working memory over the school year than their same-age peers in kindergarten (Davidson et al., 2023). Working memory shows greater improvements during the school year than during the summer months (Finch, 2019). In one study of Australian schoolchildren, the amount of schooling was a better predictor of working memory than chronological age (Roberts et al., 2015). In addition, high-quality warm and positive relationships with teachers are associated with higher scores on working memory tasks during elementary school (de Wilde et al., 2016; Koşkulu-Sancar et al., 2023).

Adolescence

With brain development, working memory improves in early adolescence, reaching adult-like levels in late adolescence by about age 19 and continues to improve into the 20s (Laureys et al., 2022; Malagoli & Usai, 2018). Developments in working memory are primarily driven by changes in the central executive and permit individuals to deploy their attention and memory to solve problems effectively.

Inhibitory control shows gradual but substantial gains in adolescence through emerging adulthood (Laureys et al., 2022; Theodoraki et al., 2020). Increases in inhibitory control enable adolescents to adapt their responses to the situation. They can inhibit well-learned responses when inappropriate to the situation, speeding cognitive processing (Gyurkovics et al., 2020). Immature inhibitory processes can contribute to outbursts when it seems as if adolescents speak before considering their feelings or the potential consequences of their actions. The neurological changes that underlie response inhibition continue to develop into the 20s, and still maturing immature capacities are thought to contribute to the risk-taking behavior common in adolescence (Crone et al., 2018; Kray et al., 2021).

Exposure to Poverty and Executive Function

Working memory and executive function improve with age and experience and are also influenced by contextual factors. Severe stress is associated with impaired working memory and inhibitory control in childhood and adolescence (Johnson et al., 2021; Mirabolfathi et al., 2020). Poverty is a stressor that poses significant risks to the development of executive function (Tooley et al., 2021).

Exposure to long-term poverty is associated with a reduced surface area and volume in the prefrontal cortex and parts of the brain associated with executive function, learning, cognitive control, and emotional processing (Gur et al., 2019; Noble & Giebler, 2020; Rakesh & Whittle, 2021). Socioeconomic status (SES) differences are apparent in brain development and emerge early (Yaple & Yu, 2020). In one study, differences in brain volume linked to SES were apparent in 5-week-old infants (Betancourt et al., 2016). SES is more closely related to brain structure and cognition in children from low SES homes than high SES homes (Hair et al., 2015; Noble et al., 2015). That is, the detrimental effect of low SES contexts is a greater influence on children's development than the positive effect of high SES contexts. Chronic poverty is especially damaging because the neurological and cognitive deficits accumulate over childhood, with lifelong implications (Dickerson & Popli, 2016).

One of the ways poverty affects development is through household chaos, a combination of household instability and disorder (K. Andrews et al., 2021; Marsh et al., 2020). Children reared in economic uncertainty are more likely to experience disruptions in home settings and relationships through household moves and adults moving in and out of the home (Pascoe et al., 2016). Impoverished environments often include household crowding, lack of structure, and excessive ambient noise in the home or neighborhood (G. W. Evans & Kim, 2013). Infants and children reared in environments of household chaos may be overwhelmed by stimulation combined with less developmentally appropriate support, with negative effects on cognitive development. The effects of a chaotic home environment begin early. A chaotic environment has been shown to negatively affect visual processing speed for complex stimuli in 5.5-month-old infants (Tomalski et al., 2017). SES has early and prolonged effects on children's brain development, increasing over time with lifelong implications for cognitive and language development (Tooley et al., 2021).

SES is associated with executive function and performance on tasks that require attention switching, working memory, and response inhibition (Last et al., 2018; Theodoraki et al., 2020). A cross-sectional study of adolescents and emerging adults aged 9 to 25 showed an inverse association between SES and executive function across all ethnicities (Last et al., 2018). Adolescents from high-income families show greater activation of the prefrontal cortex during working memory tasks than those from low-income families, and prefrontal activity better predicted math achievement in high-income adolescents (Finn et al., 2017). Adolescents in low SES homes and neighborhoods may experience greater challenges in developing the cognitive control capacities needed for sound decision making (Lawson et al., 2018). However, contextual factors can also buffer the adverse effects of low SES. For example, low SES adolescents who perceive greater academic support at school perform better on executive function tasks, specifically inhibition, than their peers (Piccolo et al., 2018).

Implications for Education and Parenting

Parents and teachers who aim to enhance children's working memory and executive function should engage them in discussions, and encourage them to think critically, observe, and ask questions. For preschoolers, teachers can incorporate games and activities that challenge working memory. Simon Says, memory matching games, and repeating sequences of numbers or words can help improve students' working memory. Hands-on, interactive learning experiences, including sorting objects, playing memory games, and completing puzzles can help improve working memory. Pretend play and activities that require children to think about and plan out the steps to complete a task can help develop their executive function skills. A structured and supportive learning environment with clear expectations and routines can also help regulate young children's behavior and emotions.

For school-aged children, teachers can teach memory skills, like grouping information to recall, using mnemonic devices, and providing opportunities for repetition and practice. Classroom activities that require children to switch between tasks, attend to multiple sources of information, and make decisions based on available information can also help improve executive function skills. Taking breaks, engaging in physical activity, and providing a structured learning environment with clear expectations and routines can also support self-regulation. Encouraging children to reflect on their learning and problem solve can also help enhance their executive function skills.

Teachers can help older children and adolescents develop self-regulation skills, such as goal-setting, prioritizing tasks, and managing distractions, to help them better control their working memory and attention. Active participation, such as asking questions and discussing what they are learning, can help engage working memory and improve learning outcomes. A structured environment with clear routines and expectations can also help manage attention and prioritize tasks. Teachers can also help manage stress and emotional regulation by teaching coping strategies and creating a supportive classroom environment.

Parents can support their children in similar ways at home, with a structured environment that supports self-regulation. For young children, activities that involve attention and memory, such as

Puzzles can improve children's working memory and executive function.

fizkes/istock

following directions, completing puzzles, and playing memory games, can help improve working memory. Encouraging play, exploration, reading books, and telling stories together can build attention, memory, and language skills.

For older children and adolescents, parents can encourage problem solving and decision making by having them make choices and solve problems independently. Playing strategy games, using educational technology, and engaging in creative activities can also support working memory and executive function skills. Regardless of age, parents and teachers can enhance children's working memory and executive function by providing a supportive and stimulating environment, participating in activities that promote these skills, and being positive and encouraging.

> ### THINKING IN CONTEXT 7.3
>
> 1. How are attention, working memory, and executive function interrelated? Give an example of how they influence our ability to solve problems.
> 2. What is inhibitory control, and what does it mean for children's daily activities? Give examples of how increasing inhibitory control affects children's and adolescents' behavior.
> 3. Identify contextual factors that might influence the development of cognitive abilities, like working memory and executive function. To what degree do children vary in their exposure to positive and negative contextual factors? Explain. What might be some of the long-term effects?

LONG-TERM MEMORY

> **7.4** Summarize changes in memory from infancy through adolescence.

Our attention and working memory are limited, as we have discussed. In contrast, long-term memory is thought to have no bounds. A memory is formed when information is encoded into long-term memory. However, long-term memory relies on attention and working memory (Amso & Kirkham, 2021; Forsberg et al., 2022). We must attend to information and process it to encode it in long-term memory. Information that is not attended to, processed, or encoded will not be retained.

We remember many different kinds of stimuli. We recall dates, names, and places. We also recall specific experiences, mental representations of previous moments in the past. There are several types of memory (Tulving, 2002). **Semantic memory** refers to the recall of information, facts, and experiences. Our memories are influenced by our experiences. **Episodic memory** is the recall of information associated with a particular time, place, or person that is not personally relevant (Courage & Howe, 2022). Recalling a specific word learned in class or that appeared on a list of words in an experiment are examples of episodic memory. When episodic memories have personal relevance and are tied to particular experiences and a sense of self, they are called **autobiographical memories**.

When does memory begin? When can we recall our experiences?

Infancy

The earliest form of episodic memory, observed in neonates, is **recognition memory**, the ability to recognize a previously encountered stimulus. Habituation studies measuring looking time and brain activity demonstrate that newborns can recall visual and auditory stimuli (Muenssinger et al., 2013; Streri et al., 2013). With age, infants require fewer trials or presentations to recall a stimulus and retain it for progressively longer periods of time (Cuevas & Sheya, 2019; Howe, 2015). Infants can also remember motor activities. In one classic study, 2- to 3-month-old infants were taught to kick their foot, tied to a mobile with a ribbon, to make the mobile move. One week later, when the infants were reattached to the mobile, they kicked vigorously, indicating their memory of the first occasion. The infants would kick even 4 weeks later if the experimenter gave the mobile a shake to remind them of its movement (Rovee-Collier & Bhatt, 1993). Researchers believe that recognition memory is a form of episodic memory, a memory for having viewed a stimulus, but is not a memory of a personal experience.

Young infants were taught to kick their foot to make an attached mobile move. When tested 1 week later, the infants remembered and kicked their legs vigorously to make the mobile move.

Deferred Imitation

Researchers use deferred imitation tasks to study infants' long-term memory. Infants observe an experimenter engage in a novel behavior with an unfamiliar object. After a delay, the infants are given the object. If they display the novel behavior more often than infants who have not viewed the object, it suggests they have formed a memory of the object and action. Deferred imitation of simple experimenter-modeled actions involving brief delays appears at around 6 months (Barr et al., 2005). With age infants can remember more complicated sets of actions, with fewer exposures and for longer periods (Cuevas & Sheya, 2019). Nine-month-old infants shown a two-step sequence of actions (e.g., hanging a plate from a bar and striking it with a mallet) can imitate the action after a 1-month delay, if they viewed the event at least three times, but not if it was viewed less than three times. Long-term memory appears to increase rapidly because 13-, 16-, and 20-month-old infants can imitate a more complicated three-step sequence of actions over a longer delay, with older infants showing higher levels of deferred imitation than younger infants (see Figure 7.3; Bauer et al., 2000). Memory holds complex implications for other types of development. As indicated by performance on deferred imitation tasks, infants' memory at 9 months, predicts language development at 16 months of age (Sundqvist et al., 2016).

Infants' memory is influenced by contextual factors (Cuevas & Sheya, 2019). They are most likely to remember events that take place in familiar contexts and in which they are actively engaged (Cuevas & Davinson, 2022). Infants' emotional state also influences their performance in memory tasks. Nine-month-old infants showed better recall in a deferred imitation task when their state at encoding, when the memory was made, matched their state at retrieval (calm or animated) (Seehagen et al., 2021). Generally, infants create memories more quickly and retain them for more extended periods with age. As we develop, we amass a great deal of information in long-term memory, organize it in increasingly sophisticated ways, and encode and retrieve it more efficiently and with less effort.

Childhood Amnesia

Although infants show impressive abilities to recognize and remember objects viewed and sequences modeled, they are not yet capable of autobiographical memory (Riggins & Bauer, 2022). Recalling objects and behaviors observed is different from remembering events personally experienced. A study examining about 11,000 reports of early memories of events and personal experiences found that nearly none occurred before age 2 (Akhtar et al., 2018). Initially called infant amnesia, and more commonly **childhood amnesia**, adults cannot recall events from infancy.

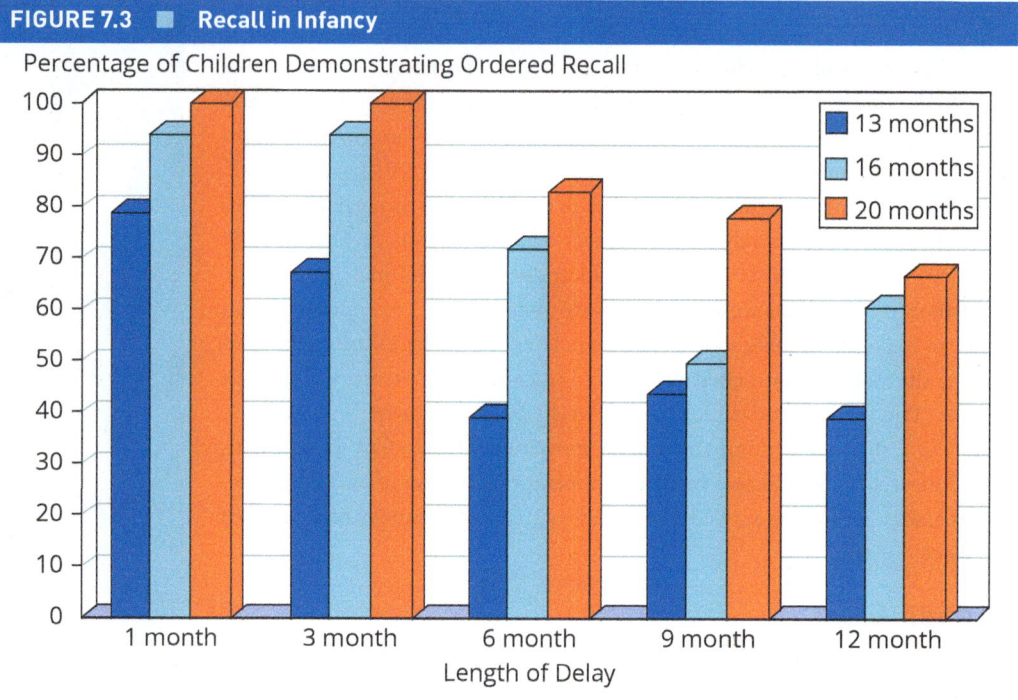

FIGURE 7.3 ■ Recall in Infancy

Source: Bauer, P. J. (2002). Long-term recall memory: Behavioral and neuro-developmental changes in the first 2 years of life. *Current Directions in Psychological Science, 11*(4), 137–141. https://doi.org/10.1111/1467-8721.00186

Why are memories from infancy unavailable? Some researchers believe infant amnesia is a retrieval problem (Howe, 2015). The information is stored, but over time we lose the ability to retrieve it because the context in which these memories were formed is too different from the context in which they are being retrieved (Madsen & Kim, 2016). A second explanation focuses on storage processes, suggesting that infants cannot store memories, so the information is unavailable to recall (Howe, 2019, 2022). The hippocampus, a part of the brain that plays a role in memory, is not mature enough to process and store memories until childhood (Ramsaran et al., 2019; Riggins et al., 2020). Other researchers point to the role of language in thought. Recall from Chapter 6 that Vygotsky believed that thought has its origins in language; children's thinking changes, becoming more sophisticated, as they acquire language. Our earliest memories tend to coincide with our emerging language abilities. In addition, autobiographical memory relies on a sense of self as having experienced the event (Riggins & Bauer, 2022). According to this view, infants cannot yet sense themselves as individuals having experienced an event; therefore, it is not encoded (Ross et al., 2020). As we discuss in Chapter 11, the sense of self begins to emerge during the second year of life.

Interestingly, the rate of forgetting shifts over childhood. As children grow older, so does the age of their earliest memory (Courage & Howe, 2022). When 4- to 13-year-old children were interviewed about their earliest memory and interviewed a second time 2 years later, the average earliest age of memory increased from 32 months to about 40 months (Peterson et al., 2011). These results, paired with findings from deferred imitation studies, suggest that infants may form memories, but their memories are more fragile than children's. Children's more durable memories are partially the result of using strategies to remember (Schwartz, 2018).

Childhood

Developments in attention and working memory enable children to manipulate information, think about and use it in increasingly sophisticated ways. These processes also influence children's ability to form lasting memories, to encode and retrieve it from long-term memory.

Autobiographical Memory

Young children report fewer memories of events than do older children and adults, but their autobiographical memory improves steadily from age 3 to 6, with advances in language and executive function

(Nieto et al., 2018; Schwartz, 2018). By age 3, children can retrieve and report specific memories over delays of 18 months or longer, especially memories that have personal significance or are highly stressful (Bauer & Larkina, 2014; Nuttall et al., 2014). Unique or new events, such as a trip to the circus, are better recalled than common events (Fivush et al., 1983). Frequent events tend to blur together. Young children are better at remembering things they did than things they simply watched.

How caregivers talk with children about a shared experience can influence how well they remember it (Fivush, 2019; Haden & Fivush, 1996). Caregivers with an elaborative conversational style discuss new aspects of an experience, provide more information to guide a child through a mutually rewarding conversation, and affirm the child's responses. They may ask questions, expand children's responses, and help the child tell their stories. Three-year-olds whose caregivers use an elaborative style engage in longer conversations about events, remember more details and tend to remember the events better at ages 5 and 6 (Fivush, 2011; Fivush & Zaman, 2014). Caregivers use of an elaborative style of reminiscing is associated with children's ability to provide greater detailed personal memory, both concurrently and longitudinally (Wu & Jobson, 2019).

Autobiographical memory becomes more durable over childhood. It becomes more complete, coherent, and complex (Bauer et al., 2019; Habermas et al., 2010). Children's memory nearly doubles, and they can better organize their reports by time and include more information about the place (Bauer & Larkina, 2017; Morris et al., 2010). Older children tend to include causal connections, such as *because*, that help explain the course of events (Bauer, 2015).

Memory Strategies

Age differences in episodic memory are especially pronounced in open recall tasks, such as, "Tell me about your birthday party." Age differences in recall tend to disappear when the recall is supported by prompts and cues questions, and cues, such as, "Who was at your birthday party? What did you eat?" (Bauer & Larkina, 2016). Generally, preschool children can accurately recognize stimuli they have encountered before (recognition memory) (Myers & Perlmutter, 2014). They are less able to recall a stimulus without cues or seeing it again. Why do young children perform so poorly in recall tasks? Young children are not very effective at using **memory strategies**, cognitive activities (*tricks*) that make them more likely to remember (Schwartz, 2018). Strategy use increases with advances in executive function, working memory, and attention (Coughlin et al., 2018). Common memory strategies include rehearsal, organization, and elaboration.

Rehearsal refers to systematically repeating information to retain it in working memory. A child may say a phone number over and over so that they do not forget it before writing it down. Children do not spontaneously and reliably apply rehearsal until after the first grade (Miller et al., 2015; Morey et al., 2018).

Shortly after rehearsal appears, children start to use **organization**, grouping or chunking items by theme or type, such as animals, flowers, and furniture, to aid recall. When memorizing a list of words, a child might organize them into meaningful groups or chunks—foods, animals, objects, and so forth. Growth in working memory is partially attributed to an increase in the number of chunks children can retain with age (Cowan et al., 2010). Ten-year-old children, but not 7-year-old children, spontaneously used organization as a memory strategy, and adults use this strategy more frequently than children (Horn et al., 2021).

A third strategy, **elaboration**, entails creating an imagined scene or story to link the material to be remembered. To remember to buy bread, milk, and butter, a child might imagine a slice of buttered bread balancing on a glass of milk. It is not until the later school years that children use elaboration without prompting and apply it to various tasks (Schneider & Ornstein, 2015). As metacognition and metamemory skills, and the executive function that underlies these abilities, improve, children get better at choosing, using, and combining memory strategies, and their recall improves dramatically (Stone et al., 2016). For example, fifth-grade students who use more sophisticated memory strategies are more successful in delayed recall tasks in which they are asked to read a passage and then recall it after a delay (Jonsson et al., 2014).

Although preschool-age children can be taught strategies, they generally do not transfer their learning and do not apply it to new tasks (Titz & Karbach, 2014). Young children's limited working memory and difficulty inhibiting irrelevant stimuli prevent them from applying strategies to new tasks (Savina, 2020). They cannot apply the strategy because they cannot simultaneously retain both the material to be learned and the strategy to be used. Instead, new information competes with the information the child is attempting to recall (Hamilton et al., 2022). The development of executive function, working memory, and attention enables older children to effectively use memory strategies (Stone et al., 2016).

Knowledge and Experience

Over time children acquire increasing amounts of information that they naturally organize in meaningful ways. As children learn more about a topic, their knowledge structures become more elaborate and organized, while the information becomes more familiar and meaningful. It is easier to recall new information about topics we are already familiar with, and existing knowledge about a topic makes it easier to learn more about it (Ericsson & Moxley, 2013). Familiarity with a task or type of information can explain why young children can sometimes perform as well as adults. In one study, parents read a novel rhyming verse and a word list as their 4-year-old children's bedtime story for 10 consecutive days. When asked to recall the verse, the 4-year-old children outperformed their parents and a set of young adults who also listened to it (Király et al., 2017). The children and adults did not differ in the ability to recall the gist of the verse. Unlike adults, young children are immersed in a culture of verse and rely on oral transmission of information, since they cannot read, which is likely at the root of their skill relative to adults.

During middle childhood, children develop vast knowledge bases and organize information into elaborate hierarchical networks that enable them to apply strategies in more complex ways and remember more material than ever before—and more easily than ever before. Fourth grade students who are experts at soccer show better recall of a list of soccer-related items than do students who are soccer novices, though the children do not differ on recall of non-soccer-related items (Schneider & Bjorklund, 1992). The soccer experts tend to organize the lists of soccer items into groups or categories; their knowledge helps them organize the soccer-related information with little effort, using fewer resources on organization and permitting the use of more working memory for problem solving and reasoning. Novices, in contrast, lack a knowledge base to aid their attempts at organization. Children's experiences, then, influence their memory, thinking, and reasoning.

The strategies that children use to tackle cognitive tasks vary with culture. In fact, daily tasks themselves vary with our cultural context. Children in Western cultures receive lots of experience with tasks requiring them to recall bits of information, leading them to develop considerable expertise in memory strategies such as rehearsal, organization, and elaboration. In contrast, research shows that people in non-Western cultures with no formal schooling often do not use or benefit from instruction in memory strategies such as rehearsal (Rogoff & Chavajay, 1995). Instead, they refine memory skills that are adaptive to their way of life. They may rely on spatial cues for memory, such as when recalling items within a three-dimensional miniature scene. Australian Aboriginal and Guatemalan Mayan children perform better at these tasks than children from Western cultures (Rogoff & Waddell, 1982). Moreover, how children recall experiences is influenced by cultural values, such as emphasizing the individual (individualism) or the community (collectivism), different emphases on emotion, and differences in language (Wang, 2021). Cultural and contextual demands influence the cognitive strategies we learn and prefer and how we use our information processing system to gather, manipulate, and store knowledge.

Memory Suggestibility

We have seen that children's memory skills improve with age. When can their memories be trusted as accurate? Children as young as 3 years have been called on to relate their memories of events they have experienced or witnessed, including abuse, maltreatment, and domestic violence (Pantell & Committee on Psychosocial Aspects of Child and Family Health, 2017). Are children's memories vulnerable to suggestion? Can we trust their memories?

Although retrieval cues can help young children recall events and experiences, preschool-age children may be more vulnerable to suggestion than school-age children or adults (Brown & Lamb, 2015;

La Rooy et al., 2011). This is especially true after repeated questioning (La Rooy et al., 2011). In one study, preschoolers were questioned every week about events that had either happened or not happened to them; by the 11th week, nearly two thirds of the children falsely reported having experienced an event (Ceci et al., 1994). In another study, children were asked if they could remember several events, including a fictitious instance of getting their finger caught in a mousetrap; almost none initially recalled these events. After repeated suggestive questioning, more than half of 3- and 4-year-olds and two fifths of 5- and 6-year-olds said they recalled these events—often vividly (Poole & White, 1991, 1993). Children often discuss events they have experienced with parents, who help them establish narratives, scaffolding them to relay their experiences to others. Parents who exert greater control and help in structuring their child's recall may inadvertently increase the likelihood of false reports (Principe & London, 2022).

However, young children also can resist repeated suggestions. In one study, 4- and 7-year-old children either played games with an adult confederate (e.g., dressing up in costumes, playing tickle, being photographed) or merely watched the games (Ceci & Bruck, 1998). Eleven days later, each child was interviewed about the earlier events by an adult who included misleading questions that were often followed up with suggestions relevant to child abuse. Even the 4-year-olds resisted the false suggestions about child abuse. But children also vary. Some children can resist social pressure and suggestive questioning better than others (Uhl et al., 2016). Children with intellectual impairments show greater suggestibility than their non-impaired peers (Klemfuss & Olaguez, 2018). Perhaps not surprisingly, a meta-analysis of 37 studies suggested that language development, specifically the ability to express and articulate ideas and experiences, is associated with reduced suggestibility in children age 2 through 17 (Perez et al., 2022).

Although children are more vulnerable, it is important to note that adults' memories are also influenced by suggestion. Indeed, recent research suggests that in some situations, adults are *more* likely than children to make quick associations between suggestive details about unexperienced events and prior experiences, making them more vulnerable to suggestion (Otgaar et al., 2018). Like children, adults exposed to misleading information or inconsistent with their experiences are more likely to perform poorly during memory interviews—and repeated questioning has a similar effect on performance (Wysman et al., 2014).

Adolescence

Like other cognitive abilities, long-term memory develops in adolescence. Adolescents become better able to determine what is essential to attend to, combine new information with information already in working memory, and select and apply strategies for manipulating the information to understand it, make decisions, and solve problems (Andersson, 2008; A. Baddeley, 2016). Adolescents are more likely than children to use memory strategies such as organizing new material into patterns and connecting new material with what is already known (Camos et al., 2018). Generally, we know less about memory in adolescence than in infancy and childhood.

Experience contributes to cognitive gains. Adolescents know more than children, permitting them more opportunities to associate new material with old, enhancing encoding and long-term memory (Keating, 2012). These advances in knowledge and strategy use result in more sophisticated, efficient, and quick thinking and learning. Adolescents can retain more information at once, better integrate prior experiences and knowledge with new information, and combine information in more complex ways (Cowan et al., 2010; Gaillard et al., 2011). Specifically, brain development influences adolescents' growing capacities for executive function, permitting greater cognitive control and regulation of attention, thinking, and problem-solving (Carlson et al., 2013; Crone et al., 2018).

Implications for Education and Parenting

Both parents and teachers can support children's memory development in a variety of ways. For young children, focus on play-based activities, such as matching games, sorting games, and memory games. Activities that can help preschoolers include rhymes and songs, storytelling, role-playing, games, picture books, hands-on activities, and flashcard activities. Parents and teachers can adopt an elaborative conversational style when discussing shared experiences or information with students. This involves asking questions, expanding on students' responses, and helping students tell their stories.

School-age children can be taught memory strategies like rehearsal, organization, and elaboration, and can be encouraged to use these strategies when learning new information (Cottini, 2023). Teachers can design lessons and activities that allow students to practice their memory skills, such as recalling information, organizing it, and applying memory strategies. They can also promote hands-on learning experiences, such as field trips, hands-on experiments, and interactive lessons, that help children build their memory skills by allowing them to experience new things and create connections between new information and what they already know. Technology, such as educational apps and games, can help children practice and improve their memory skills.

Adolescents can learn more advanced memory strategies like mnemonics to help them remember information more effectively. Encouraging active learning, such as through discussions, debates, and other interactive activities, can help students process and integrate new information. Parents and teachers can foster critical thinking skills by encouraging adolescents to analyze, evaluate, and make connections between different pieces of information. In addition, parents and teachers can encourage the use of technology, such as flashcards, memory games, and other memory-enhancing tools, to practice and improve memory skills. Self-reflection can help adolescents reflect on their learning experiences and think about what strategies have been effective for them in the past. This can help them become more effective memory learners.

At all ages, parents and teachers can create a supportive learning environment that supports children's cognitive development, helping them connect new information with what students already know, making it easier for them to learn and recall information.

THINKING IN CONTEXT 7.4

Design a game to help children develop memory skills.

1. What kind of game would you design? Video game, board game, or other?
2. What age would you target?
3. How would your game work?
4. What skills would it develop?

THINKING

7.5   Analyze the development of thinking in infants, children, and adolescents.

Do you remember your earliest thoughts? What did you believe as a preschooler? Elementary school student? The ability to think and manipulate ideas is so ingrained in adults that they often have trouble remembering a time when thinking was not second nature to them. What do infants and children think? How does thinking develop?

Infancy

Nineteenth-century psychologist William James (1890) famously described infants' world as "one great blooming, buzzing confusion." Today we know that infants are not actually confused by their surroundings. We have seen that infants are born able to perceive, attend to, and interact with their environment. They naturally group the stimuli they encounter—objects, people, and events—by similarities, forming categories. **Categorization** is a mental process that enables people of all ages to organize, store, and retrieve information in memory (Owen & Barnes, 2021; Quinn, 2016). Categorization is an adaptive process that helps us respond efficiently to new stimuli from a common class without treating each stimulus as entirely novel. Various techniques are used to study categorization in infancy, including habituation tasks and sequential touching tasks.

Habituation Tasks

Developmental researchers use basic learning capacities like habituation to study how infants categorize objects, similar to how they study perception and attention (Rigney & Wang, 2015). For example, infants are habituated to stimuli belonging to one category (e.g., fruit: apples and oranges). Then they are presented with a new stimulus of the same category (e.g., a pear or a lemon) and a stimulus of a different category (e.g., a cat or a horse). If the infant dishabituates or shows renewed interest by looking longer at the new stimulus (e.g., cat), it suggests that the infant perceives it as belonging to a different category from that of the previously encountered stimuli (L. B. Cohen & Cashon, 2006). Using this method, researchers have learned that 3-month-old infants categorize pictures of dogs and cats differently based on perceived differences in facial features (Quinn et al., 1993).

Infants' earliest categories are based on the perceived similarity of objects (Lafontaine et al., 2020; Rakison & Butterworth, 1998). By 4 months, infants can form categories based on perceptual properties, grouping objects similar in appearance, including shape, size, and color (Quinn, 2016; Rekow et al., 2020). As early as 7 months of age, infants use conceptual categories based on perceived function and behavior, and patterns in their brain waves correspond to their identification of novel and familiar categories (Mandler, 2004; Quinn et al., 2010). Seven- to 12-month-old infants use many categories to organize objects, such as food, furniture, birds, animals, vehicles, kitchen utensils, and more, based on both perceptual similarity and perceived function and behavior, such as motion (Bornstein & Arterberry, 2010; Oakes, 2010; Sučević et al., 2021).

Sequential Touching Tasks

In addition to habituation, researchers use sequential touching tasks to study the conceptual categories that older infants create (Perry, 2015). In these tasks, infants are presented with a collection of objects from two categories (e.g., four animals and four vehicles), and their patterns of touching are recorded. If the infants recognize a categorical distinction among the objects, they touch those from within a category in succession more than would be expected by chance. Using this method, researchers have shown that 12- to 30-month-old toddlers organize objects at a global level and then at more specific levels. They categorize at more inclusive levels (e.g., broader categories, such as animals or vehicles) before less inclusive levels (e.g., types of animals or types of vehicles) and before even less inclusive levels (e.g., specific animals or vehicles) (Bornstein & Arterberry, 2010).

Infants' and toddlers' everyday experiences and exploration contribute to their growing capacity to recognize commonalities among objects, group them in meaningful ways, and use these concepts to think and solve problems (Spriet et al., 2022). Recognizing categories is a way of organizing information that allows for more efficient thinking, including storing and retrieving information in memory (Owen & Barnes, 2021). Therefore, advances in categorization are critical to cognitive development. The cognitive abilities that underlie categorization also influence language development, because words represent categories, ways of organizing ideas and things.

Childhood

Thinking becomes more complex over the childhood years. Children become increasingly aware of the process of thinking and their thoughts. This awareness of the mind is known as **theory of mind**, which refers to children's awareness of their own and other people's mental processes. Theory of mind is part of the broader concept of metacognition, knowledge of how the mind works, and the ability to control the mind (Lockl & Schneider, 2007).

Theory of Mind

Between the ages of 2 and 5, young children's theory of mind grows and changes (Bower, 1993; Flavell et al., 1995; Wellman, 2017). By age 3, children understand the difference between thinking about a cookie and having a cookie. They know that having a cookie means that one can touch, eat, or share it, while thinking about a cookie does not permit such actions (Astington, 1993). Young children also understand that other people have thoughts and desires. For example, they know that a child who wants a cookie will be happy after receiving one and sad after not having one (Moses et al., 2000). Similarly, they understand that a child who believes they are having hot oatmeal for breakfast will be surprised after receiving cold spaghetti (Wellman & Banerjee, 1991). Theory of mind is commonly assessed by examining children's abilities to understand that people can hold different beliefs about an object or event.

False belief tasks. Young children typically do not understand that people can hold different beliefs and that some beliefs may be incorrect. This lack of understanding is evident in false belief tasks. In a classic false-belief task, young children are presented with a box of Band-Aids and are surprised to find that it contains pencils rather than Band-Aids. What will other children think when they receive the Band-Aids box? Children who have not yet developed a theory of mind will believe that other children will share their knowledge and expect the Band-Aid box to hold pencils (Flavell, 1993). The children do not yet understand that the other children hold different, false beliefs. In addition, young children tend to claim that they knew all along that the Band-Aid box contained pencils (Birch, 2005). They confuse their present knowledge with their memories for prior knowledge and have difficulty remembering ever having believed something that contradicts their current view (Bernstein et al., 2007).

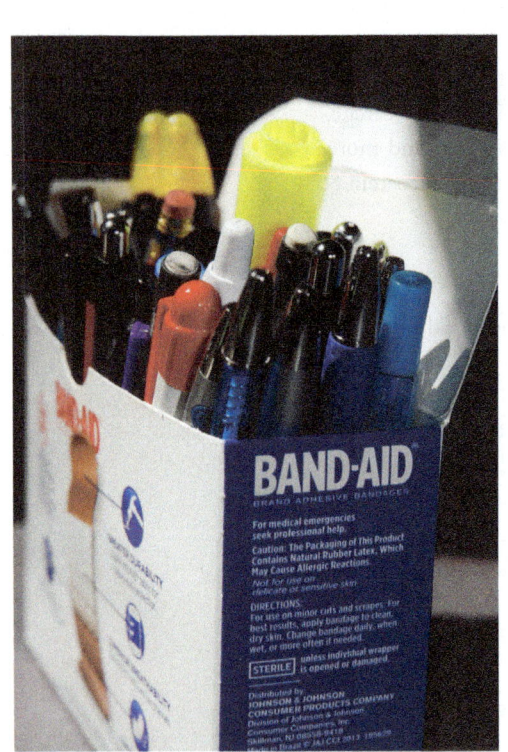

After closing this box filled with pens and markers, the child who understands false belief knows that other people will assume that there are Band-Aids in this box.

Theory of mind, as evidenced by false-belief tasks, emerges at about 3 years of age and shifts reliably between 3 and 4 years of age (Grosse Wiesmann et al., 2017). By age 3, children can understand that two people can believe different things, and by 4 can understand that people who are presented with different versions of the same event develop different beliefs (Eisbach, 2004; Rakoczy et al., 2007). By age 4 or 5, children become aware that they and other people can hold false beliefs (Moses et al., 2000).

Cognitive skills and false-belief understanding. Advanced cognition is needed for children to learn abstract concepts such as belief. Performance on false-belief tasks, such as the Band-Aid/pencil box task, is associated with measures of executive function, the abilities that enable complex cognitive functions such as planning, decision making, and goal setting (Doenyas et al., 2018; Sabbagh et al., 2006). As executive functioning improves, children become better able to reflect on and learn from experience, which promotes the development of theory of mind (Benson et al., 2013). One longitudinal study following children ages 2 to 4 found that gains in executive functioning predicted children's performance on false-belief tasks (Hughes & Ensor, 2007). Children's performance on false-belief tasks is closely related to language development, competence in sustaining conversations, and reading comprehension (Hughes & Devine, 2015; Lecce & Devine, 2022). Preschoolers with higher scores on theory of mind measures are more likely than their peers to share resources and play cooperatively with friends. Theory of mind continues to develop throughout childhood, influencing social skills such as third- and fourth-grade children's ability to identify faux pas or transgressions of social norms (Osterhaus & Koerber, 2021).

Context, Culture, and Theory of Mind

Children in many countries, including Canada, China, India, Thailand, Norway, and the United States, show the onset and development of theory of mind between the ages of 3 and 5 (Callaghan et al., 2005; Wellman et al., 2011). Conversations about people's thoughts predict children's understanding of false beliefs (Rakoczy, 2022; Slaughter et al., 2007). Cultural differences in caregiver-child interactions influence patterns of theory of mind development.

Cultural variations. North American and Chinese children develop theory of mind in early childhood, but along different paths (Wellman, 2017). Chinese culture emphasizes collectivism and interdependence among community members. Chinese parents' conversations with children focus on shared knowledge that community members must learn. U.S. parents emphasize cultural values of individuality and independence. They comment more on children's thinking, including differences in people's thoughts. U.S. children, and other children from individualistic cultures, develop an understanding of individual beliefs before shared knowledge. Chinese children tend to show the reverse pattern: an early understanding of the knowledge aspect of theory of mind and later understanding of beliefs (Wellman, 2017). Children from Iran and Turkey follow a pattern of theory of mind development similar to those from China, learning about shared knowledge before individual beliefs (Shahaeian et al., 2011).

Research with Samoan and Vanuatu children of the South Pacific confirms the relevance of culture on theory of mind. Compared to Western samples, Samoan and Vamuatu children showed delayed development in theory of mind and a prolonged transition to succeeding in theory of mind tasks (Dixson et al., 2018; Mayer & Träuble, 2015). This finding is consistent with the Pacific Island cultural doctrine of opacity of mind, which deemphasizes internal mental states as explanations for behavior (Slaughter & Perez-Zapata, 2014). In these cultures, children are not exposed to discussions about the mind and get little experience considering other people's thoughts. Therefore, the slow progression of Samoan and Vanuatu children on theory of mind tasks can be attributed to the lack of cultural emphasis on internal mental states. A study of Pacific families living in New Zealand found that mothers with a stronger Pacific cultural identity referred to beliefs less often when talking to their children than mothers whose Pacific identities were weaker (Slaughter & Perez-Zapata, 2014; Taumoepeau, 2015). Interestingly, Vanuatuan children who lived in towns showed more advanced performance than those who lived in rural settings, suggesting that the social contexts within a given cultural setting also influence how children come to understand the nature of people's thoughts (Dixson et al., 2018).

Similarly, a study of 8-year-old children from Peru used a culturally appropriate version of the Band-Aid box task in which a sugar bowl contained tiny potatoes (Vinden, 1996). The children initially believed the bowl contained sugar. However, after learning that it contained potatoes, they answered typical false-belief questions incorrectly, predicting that others would respond that the bowl contained potatoes. Even at age 8, well after Western children succeeded in similar tasks, the Peruvian children responded incorrectly, unable to explain why others might initially believe that the bowl contained sugar and be surprised to learn otherwise. Similar to the Samoan and Vanuatuan children, children in this isolated farming village were exposed to discussions that deemphasized internal mental states as causes for behavior. With little discussion of false beliefs or deceiving others, the children tended to develop theory of mind later than Western children (Vinden, 1996).

Conversations about thoughts and beliefs. Everyday conversations aid children in developing a theory of mind because such conversations tend to center around and provide examples of mental states and their relationship with behavior. When parents and other adults speak with children about mental states, emotions, and behaviors, as well as discuss causes and consequences, children develop a more sophisticated understanding of other people's perspectives (Devine & Hughes, 2019; Sodian et al., 2020). Children with secure attachments to their caregivers tend to have more advanced theory of mind skills, likely because sensitive caregivers engage children in conversation and help them regulate their emotions (Szpak & Białecka-Pikul, 2020). In addition, siblings provide young children with opportunities for social interaction, pretend play, and practice with deception. Children with siblings perform better on false-belief tests than only children (McAlister & Peterson, 2013).

Children can be trained in perspective-taking. Conversation about deceptive objects (e.g., a pen that looked like a flower) improves performance on false-belief tasks (Lohmann & Tomasello, 2003). When children are presented with a series of deceptive objects and are shown the appearance and real states of the objects, along with an explanation, 3-year-olds show improvements in false-belief tasks (Lohmann & Tomasello, 2003). Discussion emphasizing the existence of a variety of possible perspectives about an object can improve performance in false-belief tasks—dialogue can facilitate the development of theory of mind (Bernard & Deleau, 2007). When North American and European children engage in discussion about the thoughts, beliefs, and desires of characters in stories, especially stories in which characters play tricks to surprise or deceive one another, their performance in subsequent false-belief tasks improves (Ruffman, 2023; Slaughter & Perez-Zapata, 2014).

Metacognition

Theory of mind is a precursor to the development of metacognition, which refers to our ability to think about our thinking (Lecce et al., 2015). Young children understand that the mind is where thinking takes place. Between ages 3 and 5, children come to understand that thoughts cannot be observed and that people can hold different beliefs, including false beliefs (Pillow, 2008). They begin to understand that someone can think of one thing while doing something else, that a person whose eyes and ears are covered can think, and that thinking is different from talking, touching, and knowing (Flavell et al., 1995). However, young children tend to see the mind as a static container for information and do not understand that the mind is always active, even when we are not (Flavell, 1999). They assume that the absence of visible indicators of thinking indicates the absence of thought.

It is not until middle childhood that children begin to grasp the dynamic nature of the mind and its constant activity (Chandler & Carpendale, 1998). Metacognition improves with the development of the prefrontal cortex, enabling older children to monitor their thinking and allocate their effort accordingly spontaneously (Niebaum & Munakata, 2020). Like theory of mind, metacognition is supported by conversations with caregivers about mental states and thinking (Geurten & Léonard, 2023).

Metacognition includes several components, most notably **metamemory**, which involves understanding our memory and using strategies to enhance it. Young children typically show limited knowledge of memory functions, contributing to their poor performance on memory tasks (Pillow, 2008). For example, while 6- and 7-year-olds understand the role of deliberate practice in memory and practice without being prompted, 4-year-olds show no knowledge of deliberate practice (Brinums et al., 2018).

Metamemory improves steadily throughout elementary school and contributes to memory advances (Cottini et al., 2018; Schneider & Ornstein, 2015). By 8 or 9, children can accurately evaluate their knowledge and apply it to learn more effectively. Older children perform better on cognitive tasks because they can evaluate the task and determine how to approach it, considering their knowledge, attention span, and motivation (Forsberg et al., 2021). They also can choose and monitor the use of memory strategies that will enable them to store and retrieve needed information successfully (Schneider & Pressley, 2013). These abilities improve with neural maturation and experience and allow children to become mindful of their thinking and better able to consider the requirements of a task; determine how to tackle it; and monitor, evaluate, and adjust their activity to complete the task (Ardila, 2013).

Adolescence

Advances in attention, working memory, and executive function, coupled with a growing knowledge base and faster processing, mean that adolescents can think faster, more efficiently, and more complexly than ever before. Improvements in metacognition enable adolescents to be mindful of their reasoning, with implications for decision making.

Metacognition

Adolescents not only have better thinking skills than children, but they are also more aware of their ideas and thought processes and can reflect on thinking itself, metacognition (Schneider et al., 2022). Metacognitive ability develops dramatically between ages 11 and 17 with the development of the hippocampus, implicated in memory, and prefrontal cortex, responsible for executive function (Ghetti & Fandakova, 2020; Weil et al., 2013). As metacognition develops, adolescents become more planful about their cognitive system, enabling them to better take in, manipulate, and store information (Ardila, 2013; van der Stel & Veenman, 2013). They can monitor their thinking and learning and deploy strategies that enhance information representation, storage, and retrieval. Eleventh grader Travis explains, "Studying for a biology exam is really different from studying for a history exam. In biology, I visualize the material, but when I study for history, I make up stories to help me remember it all." Travis illustrates the metacognitive skills that emerge in adolescence because he can evaluate his understanding and adjust his strategies to the content in ways that help him learn best. Improvements in metacognition predicts mathematics achievement (Muncer et al., 2021). Adolescents' abilities to apply metacognition in real-world settings continue to develop into late adolescence and early adulthood.

Metacognition enables adolescents to reason about problems in new ways. By considering their cognitive strategies and experimenting and reflecting on their experiences, adolescents begin to appreciate logical reasoning, which they increasingly apply to everyday situations (Ardila, 2013; van der Stel & Veenman, 2013). As adolescents become able to reason about reasoning, they show improvements in manipulating abstract ideas and engaging in the hypothetical-deductive thinking characteristic of scientific reasoning (Kuhn, 2013). They are also better able to evaluate others' thinking and advice. They can evaluate their ideas and others' ideas and are less likely than children to take others' advice when they deem it misleading—they can judge and compare with knowledge (Moses-Payne et al., 2021).

Decision Making

Adolescents approach thinking and decision making in more complex ways than children, but their thinking is still developing. In some ways and under some conditions, their thinking is like adults. In other ways, not. Under laboratory conditions, adolescents can demonstrate logical decision making that aligns with their goals and is comparable to adults (Icenogle & Cauffman, 2021; Reyna & Rivers, 2008). Comparisons of adolescents' and adults' decisions on hypothetical dilemmas—such as whether to engage in substance use, have surgery, have sex, or drink and drive—show that adolescents and adults often generate similar consequences to each decision option, spontaneously mention similar risks and benefits of each option, and rate the harmfulness of risks in similar ways (Edelson & Reyna, 2021; Kwak et al., 2015). However, the hypothetical decisions that comprise laboratory studies are very different from the everyday decisions they face.

Decisions adolescents make in everyday life have personal relevance, require quick thinking, are emotional, and often are made in the presence and influence of others. Recall from Chapter 4 the mismatch between the development of the limbic system, responsible for emotion, and the prefrontal cortex. Adolescents often feel strong emotions and impulses that they find challenging to regulate due to the still-immature condition of their prefrontal cortex (A. O. Cohen & Casey, 2017; McIlvain et al., 2020). Therefore, laboratory studies of decision making are less helpful in understanding how young people compare with adults when they must make choices that are important or occur in stressful situations in which they must rely on experience, knowledge, and intuition (Steinberg, 2013). When faced with unfamiliar, emotionally charged situations, spur-of-the-moment decisions, pressures to conform, poor self-control, and risk and benefit estimates that favor good short-term and bad long-term outcomes, adolescents tend to reason more poorly than adults (Breiner et al., 2018; Icenogle & Cauffman, 2021).

Furthermore, adolescents are more sensitive to rewards than adults. Adolescents tend to place more importance on the potential benefits of decisions (e.g., social status, pleasure) than on the potential costs or risks (e.g., physical harm, short- and long-term health issues) (Javadi et al., 2014; Shulman & Cauffman, 2013). In the presence of rewards and peers perceived as rewarding, adolescents show heightened activity in the brain systems that support reward processing and reduced activity in the areas responsible for inhibitory control, compared with adults (J. L. Andrews et al., 2021; Smith et al., 2015). Activity in the brain's reward center predicts alcohol use in 16- to 18-year-old adolescents (Swartz et al., 2020). Social rewards, such as a sense of belonging and avoiding peer rejection, are powerful influences on adolescent decision making (Tomova et al., 2021). Risky activity is thought to decline in late adolescence through emerging adulthood as the prefrontal cortex matures and self-regulatory capacities and long-term planning abilities improve (Icenogle et al., 2019).

Adult guidance can aid adolescents in learning how to make good decisions. Such guidance may involve discussing how to consider options, including the pros and cons of each and the likelihood of each, and how to weigh information to come to a decision. In addition, experience in making decisions, and learning from successes and failures, coupled with developments in cognition, self-control, and emotional regulation, leads to adolescent decision making that is more reflective, confident, and successful.

Moreover, not all risk taking is harmful. Adolescents' heightened tendency for risk taking is often viewed as a risk to their health, but some adolescents engage in positive risk taking (Duell & Steinberg, 2021). A positive risk is socially acceptable, holds the potential for both desirable and undesirable outcomes, and is uncertain. Examples of positive risks include trying out for a sports team, running for student government, engaging in challenging physical activities (such as skateboarding), enrolling in a difficult course, or initiating a new friendship. Each of these activities is accompanied by risk for success or failure, social risk (acceptance or rejection), and uncertainty. Positive risks may be constructive for development.

Implications for Education and Parenting

Parents and teachers play an important role in advancing children's and adolescents' thinking skills. For young children, parents and teachers can provide opportunities for social interaction, pretend play, and conversations about mental states and emotions. They can support the development of children's thinking and perspective-taking development by engaging in everyday conversations involving mental states, emotions, and behaviors (Léonard et al., 2023). Additionally, discussing the causes and consequences of events, including the thoughts, beliefs, and desires of characters in stories, can help children understand the perspectives of others. Parents and teachers can also foster metacognition in children by encouraging them to reflect on their thought processes and knowledge and evaluate their and others' ideas (Zhao et al., 2022).

Although adolescents have better thinking skills and are more aware of their thought processes than children, their decisions can be influenced by emotions and the presence of others. Parents and teachers can foster metacognition by helping adolescents reflect on their thinking and learning processes. This can be done by encouraging adolescents to reflect on their own thinking processes and evaluate their understanding of a topic through self-assessment, goal setting, and monitoring their own progress.

Parents and teachers should provide opportunities for adolescents to engage in decision-making activities that require reflection and logical reasoning while also acknowledging their challenges in making real-life decisions. Classroom opportunities for abstract reasoning and hypothetical-deductive thinking can help adolescents develop advanced logic. Encouraging students to analyze and evaluate information, arguments, and evidence through debates, discussions, and written assignments can also help improve their thinking skills.

Finally, parents and teachers should emphasize the importance of self-control and regulation in thinking and decision making. Support for self-regulation included assistance with planning, prioritization, and limit setting, critical tools of thinking with lifelong benefits.

THINKING IN CONTEXT 7.5

1. How does children's context influence the development of theory of mind? What are some cultural differences in theory of mind, and what kinds of interactions promote the development of theory of mind? To what extent do you think U.S. children experience cultural and contextual differences in interactions that might shape the development of theory of mind?
2. Consider a parent's perspective on thinking. How might advances in children and adolescents' thinking abilities influence their interactions with parents? What challenges and rewards might these pose for parents?
3. Despite their rapid advances in information processing and reasoning skills, in everyday life adolescents often make poor decisions. What are some of the reasons for this? To what degree should adolescents be protected by the consequences of poor decisions? How?

APPLY YOUR KNOWLEDGE

Twelve-year-old Mia and her 7-year-old brother Leo eagerly anticipated their town's annual bike race. Mia was no stranger to the event, having participated in it for the past 3 years. However, this was Leo's first time, and he had less experience riding a bike than his sister.

With several years of experience biking around the neighborhood, Mia could easily recall how to navigate the neighborhood streets and could follow the race route without effort. On the other hand, Leo was still getting the hang of balancing and steering his bike through the uneven and windy streets, making it difficult to stay aware of his surroundings.

On race day, the siblings arrived early. Mia took the time to check her bike's tire pressure and secure her helmet while Leo looked around and tried to remember the course. As the race began, Mia sped along with ease. Her familiarity with the course enabled her to make split-second decisions about when to speed up or slow down. She anticipated and avoided obstacles, such as pedestrians and parked cars, and maintained a steady pace ahead of most other racers.

Leo faced more challenges. Despite his determination, he struggled to keep up with the other bikers, forgetting parts of the route information and veering off course. Focused on pedaling, steering, and remembering the route, Leo almost collided with parked cars and other bikers. Leo's pace was slower, and he found it hard to catch up with his sister and the other racers.

As the race drew to a close, Mia triumphantly crossed the finish line among the first racers, greeted by cheers from the spectators. Leo finished several minutes later, out of breath but proud of his accomplishment.

1. How did the siblings' prior experience impact their performance in the race? Explain these differences from an information processing perspective.

2. Define attention, working memory, and executive function. How did differences in these information processing factors account each child's performance?

3. Leo wants to improve his performance. Referring to cognitive factors, give him advice on how to improve.

CHAPTER SUMMARY

7.1 Describe information processing theory, including its assumptions, mental stores, and what develops.

Information processing theory is a collection of theories that examine how humans process information. It assumes that thinking is a form of information processing, that cognitive change is a continuous process, and that our cognitive resources are limited. The mind is composed of three mental stores: sensory memory, working memory, and long-term memory. Sensory memory holds incoming sensory information for a fraction of a second. Working memory holds and processes information that is being actively *worked on*. It consists of a short-term store, a processing component, and the central executive, a control center that directs mental processes. The processing component of working memory is responsible for manipulating, encoding, and retrieving information. The central executive directs the flow of information and regulates cognitive activities such as attention, action, and problem solving. Development includes increases in processing speed and automaticity.

7.2 Examine the development of attention from infancy through adolescence.

Attention refers to our ability to direct our awareness and focus on relevant information. Types of attention include selective attention (ignoring distractors), sustained attention (remaining focused for an extended period), and divided attention (attending to two stimuli at once). Over the course of infancy, infants' preferences shift to complex and dynamic stimuli over simple stimuli. Joint attention emerges toward the end of the first year of life and highlights the role of social interaction in cognitive development. In childhood, gains in sustained attention occur before selective attention. Attention is linked to academic skills and improves over childhood. About 10% of children are diagnosed with attention-deficit/hyperactivity disorder (ADHD), characterized by persistent difficulties with attention and hyperactivity/impulsivity. Adolescents are more skilled in attentional tasks, such as divided and selective attention, than children. Multitasking, typically through media activities, is common among adolescents, but cognitive scientists believe the brain is not designed to perform multiple tasks at the same time. Multitasking is associated with poor academic performance, but there are individual differences in attentional control. Multitasking places heavy demands on attentional capacities, which are influenced by working memory and executive function, which are controlled by the still-developing prefrontal cortex.

7.3 Discuss the development of working memory and executive function.

Working memory capacity increases dramatically from 6 months of age to 12–14 months, when infants can recall three objects, similar to some adults. The greatest improvements in memory occur in early childhood, and by 8 years old, children recall about half as many items as adults. Brain development, specifically in the prefrontal cortex and corpus callosum, leads to advances in working memory and executive function, allowing for quicker matching of pictures, better recall of spatial information, and better prioritization of information in working memory. Advances in executive function, especially inhibitory control, continue through adolescence. These advances in working memory and inhibitory control are associated with improved language, reading, writing, and mathematics skills and continue to improve into adulthood. Contextual factors influence the development of executive function, and exposure to poverty is especially harmful.

7.4 Summarize changes in memory from infancy through adolescence.

Infants have impressive recognition memory abilities and can remember objects and simple sequences modeled after a delay, but they do not yet have autobiographical memory. Infants' memory is influenced by contextual factors, emotional state, and personal engagement. Infants' memories become more durable with age. Infant amnesia is the phenomenon where adults cannot recall events from infancy. It is believed that the brain development, language, and a sense of self are crucial to autobiographical memory and contribute to infant amnesia. Children's memory skills improve as they get older, with advances in language, executive function, and attention. Autobiographical memory improves steadily from ages 3 to 6, and caregivers can influence memory by using an elaborative conversational style. Memory strategies, such as rehearsal, organization, and elaboration, are used more effectively as executive function, working memory, and attention improve. Children's knowledge and experience also influence their memory and cognitive abilities. Children's memories can be vulnerable to suggestion, especially preschool-age children, but some children can resist suggestive questioning better than others. Adolescents become can better determine what is essential to attend to, combine new information with information already in working memory, and select and apply strategies for manipulating the information to understand it, make decisions, and solve problems.

7.5 Analyze the development of thinking in infants, children, and adolescents

Young infants categorize objects by their perceived similarity, an early form of thinking. By 4 months, they form categories based on perceptual properties and by 7 months based on perceived function and behavior. Theory of mind, an awareness of the mind, develops between ages 2 and 5, as measured by false belief tasks. Conversations about mental states aid children in developing a theory of mind, and cultural differences in caregiver-child interactions influence patterns of theory of mind development. Theory of mind is a precursor to the development of metacognition, which refers to our ability to think about our thinking. Metamemory is an aspect of metacognition, which improves steadily throughout elementary school and contributes to memory advances. Adolescents have better metacognitive and reasoning abilities. However, when it comes to decision making, adolescents tend to prioritize potential rewards over potential risks, and their ability to reason and control their emotions may be compromised in emotionally charged situations.

KEY TERMS

- attention
- attention-deficit/hyperactivity disorder
- autobiographical memory
- categorization
- central executive
- divided attention
- elaboration
- episodic memory
- executive function
- joint attention
- long-term memory
- memory strategy
- metacognition
- metamemory
- organization
- processing speed,
- recognition memory
- rehearsal
- selective attention
- Semantic memory
- sensory memory
- sustained attention
- theory of mind
- working memory

Jose Luis Pelaez Inc/Getty Images

8 INTELLIGENCE

> **LEARNING OBJECTIVES**
>
> **8.1** Explain five theories of intelligence.
>
> **8.2** Discuss ways of measuring intelligence in childhood and adolescence.
>
> **8.3** Analyze contextual influences on intelligence.
>
> **8.4** Summarize four neurodevelopmental conditions, including the role of contextual factors in disability.

Eight-year-old Willa sits at the kitchen table doing her homework as her father cooks dinner. Willa throws her pencil down. "I hate math. I'm just not good at it." Her father responds, "Well, first you should practice. That's how you'll get better at math. Just like you practice piano and get better every day." "That's not the same," Willa says. "I'm really good at piano. My teacher says I'm better than anyone at school . . . even the high school students." "Sure, but practice helps," he answers. Willa replies, "I'm really good at piano. But that doesn't mean I'm smart. I can't even do math and the smartest people are all good at math."

What do you think? Is Willa right? Are children either smart—or not? Do you have to excel at math to be smart? Does Willa's piano playing count as smartness? What exactly does it mean to be smart? In this chapter, we examine the development of intelligence, what Willa referred to as smartness. We first consider the question of how to define intelligence.

APPROACHES TO UNDERSTANDING INTELLIGENCE

> **8.1** Explain five theories of intelligence.

What does it mean to be intelligent? At its simplest, **intelligence** refers to an individual's ability to adapt to their environment and circumstances (Sternberg, 2021). Some theories describe intelligence as a single ability. Others view intelligence as multifaceted. Some theories emphasize cognitive abilities such as attention, working memory, and processing speed. Others include creativity, interpersonal skills, and even athletic abilities. What all theories of intelligence hold in common is that there are individual differences in people's intellectual abilities, ways in which people vary, that are stable or consistent over time (Deary et al., 2021).

Psychometric Approach

A popular description of intelligence comes from the psychometric approach, which emphasizes measuring individual differences in traits or characteristics. From this perspective, intelligence is composed of a set of psychological traits or characteristics that can be measured and vary among people, accounting for differences in performance or ability (Coyle, 2021; Furr, 2021). Psychometricians typically administer a battery of tests to a large number of people and analyze patterns in performance across the different tests to identify common factors or underlying abilities that may be responsible for the observed patterns in performance.

In an early influential theory, Charles Spearman (1904) explained intelligence as a single general ability he called *g*. This factor was thought to be responsible for individuals' performance on all mental tests. Most children's performance, however, varies across tasks, suggesting that *g* may oversimplify intelligence. Thurstone and Thurstone (1941) proposed that intelligence is instead comprised of several distinct abilities, called primary mental abilities, such as verbal comprehension, numerical skill, spatial reasoning, and memory. People vary in their pattern of strengths and weaknesses across the skills. Some show exceptional word comprehension skills and can comprehend difficult texts. Others are skilled in spatial reasoning and can quickly identify, sort, and place objects.

More recent theories describe intelligence as consisting of both general and specific components. John Carroll (1996, 2005) explained intelligence as a hierarchy with three tiers. At the top is *g*, broad ability, which is broken down into a second tier that includes abilities such as memory and learning, visual perception, audio perception, and processing speed. Each of these abilities can be broken down into component skills, representing a third tier. For example, memory and learning consist of skills in memory span and associative memory; visual perception includes visualization, spatial perception, and the ability to recognize an item when only a tiny part of it is shown. A hierarchical approach accounts for the complexity of intelligence: It is a broad ability composed of specific skills.

Information Processing and Intelligence

If you believe that intelligent people are quicker, more efficient thinkers, then you probably agree with the information-processing approach to intelligence. The information-processing abilities we discussed in Chapter 7, such as attention, working memory, and processing speed, underlie performance in all cognitive tasks, including intelligence tests, and are therefore important indicators of intellectual ability that are evident at birth and persist for a lifetime (Kovacs & Conway, 2019; Rey-Mermet et al., 2019). At all ages, people who process information rapidly and efficiently learn and adapt to their environment quickly, markers of intelligence (Troche et al., 2018).

Habituation tasks are often used to measure information-processing abilities in infants because they indicate how quickly an infant learns: Infants who learn quickly look away from an unchanging stimulus (or habituate) rapidly. Infants who are fast habituators, who quickly get used to unchanging stimuli, score higher on measures of intelligence in infancy, childhood, adolescence, and even emerging adulthood than slow habituating peers (Fagan, 2011; Kavšek, 2013). Infant reaction time and preferences for novelty over familiarity are indicators of attention, working memory, and processing speed and predict intelligence and cognitive abilities through late adolescence (Bornstein, 2020; Rose et al., 2012).

Children's processing speed predicts intelligence scores in childhood and adolescence (Redick et al., 2012; Schubert & Frischkorn, 2020). Likewise, working memory is associated with measures of intelligence in childhood and adolescence into emerging adulthood (Giofrè et al., 2013; Schneider & Niklas, 2017). The highest level of cognitive control, executive function, the ability to direct information through the cognitive system to guide thoughts and actions, is also associated with intelligence (Chen et al., 2019). From an information-processing perspective, intelligence is rooted in cognitive processing skills; intelligent children think quickly, complexly, and efficiently.

Neurological Development and Intelligence

All our thoughts and behavior, including intelligence, are the result of brain activity. Neuroscientists study brain structure and function as determinants of intelligence (Haier, 2023). Brain volume and cortical thickness are positively associated with children's and adolescents' intelligence, indicating that differences in brain structure can be associated with individual differences in intelligence (Pietschnig et al., 2015; Schmitt et al., 2019). Intelligence is positively associated with increased gray matter throughout the brain and in the areas of the brain responsible for processing sensory experiences (occipital and temporal cortices) and abstract thought (frontal cortex) (Basten et al., 2015; Hilger et al., 2020). Myelinated white matter has also been linked to intelligence, primarily through its influence on processing speed and working memory (Bathelt et al., 2019; Privado et al., 2014).

In addition to these structural differences, brain activity changes predictably during different cognitive tasks. For instance, there is greater activity in the frontal and parietal brain regions (areas responsible for working memory and executive function) during cognitive tasks, including those commonly used in intelligence tests (Basten et al., 2015; Margolis et al., 2013). In addition, there are individual differences in the structure and connectivity of brain regions activated during cognitive tasks that correspond to performance on measures of intelligence. Children who score higher on measures of verbal intelligence show a different pattern of connectivity among brain regions than low scoring children, suggesting that they process and integrate information across different brain regions more efficiently (Khundrakpam et al., 2017). Intelligence therefore may emerge from patterns of connectivity and efficiency (Cohen & D'Esposito, 2021). Individuals with higher intelligence may exert less neural effort, showing smaller changes in brain activation while performing a given cognitive task than other people (Neubauer & Fink, 2009; Takeuchi et al., 2018).

While we have gained valuable insights into the relationship between brain functioning and intelligence, much remains unknown. Correlations between brain structure, neural activity, and intelligence tell us that these variables are related, but they do not explain why. It is still unclear whether the observed differences in brain structure and activity are causes or consequences of individual differences in intelligence. Alternatively, perhaps they are influenced by other factors. Determining how smart brains differ and in what patterns and regions of activity is only a first step in understanding how intelligence evolves from the brain. A complete explanation of intelligence requires accounting for intelligent, adaptive behavior.

Triarchic Theory of Intelligence

Most developmental scientists would agree that intelligence enables us to adapt to our rapidly changing environments. Rather than a single ability, psychologist Robert Sternberg (1985, 2018) views intelligence as a set of mental abilities that permits individuals to adapt to any context and to select and modify the sociocultural contexts in which they live and behave. Sternberg's **triarchic theory of intelligence** poses three interacting forms of intelligence: analytical, creative, and practical (see Figure 8.1; Sternberg, 2011, 2020). Individuals may have strengths in any or all of them.

Analytical intelligence refers to information processing capacities, such as how efficiently people acquire knowledge, process information, engage in metacognition, and generate and apply strategies to solve problems. *Creative intelligence* taps insight and the ability to deal with novelty. People with creative intelligence respond to new tasks quickly and efficiently. They learn easily, compare information with what is already known, develop new ways of organizing information, and display original thinking. *Applied intelligence* influences how people deal with their surroundings: how well they evaluate their environment, select and modify it, and adapt it to fit their needs and external demands.

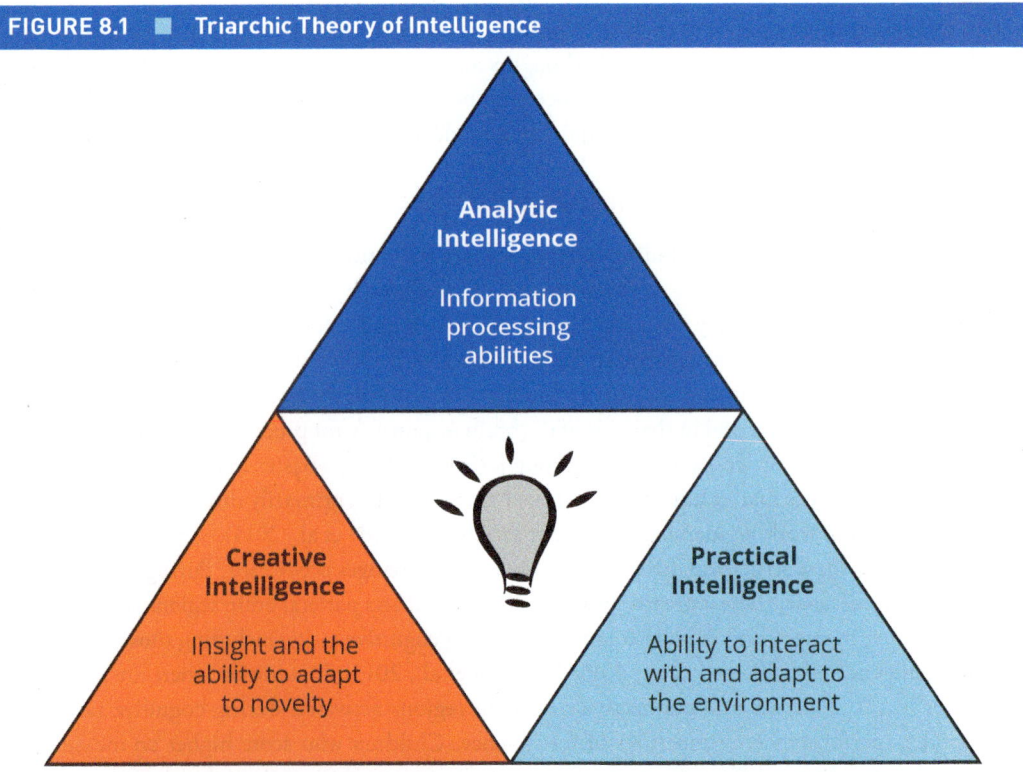

FIGURE 8.1 ■ Triarchic Theory of Intelligence

Source: Adapted from Sternberg, R. J. (2011). The theory of successful intelligence. In R. J. Sternberg & S. B. Kaufman (Eds.), *The Cambridge handbook of intelligence* (pp. 504–527). Cambridge University Press.

Intelligent people apply their analytical, creative, and applied abilities to suit the setting and problems at hand (Sternberg, 2018). Some situations require careful analysis, others the ability to think creatively, and yet others the ability to solve problems quickly in everyday settings. Many situations tap more than one form of intelligence.

Intelligence tests typically measure analytical ability, which is thought to be associated with school success. However, these tests do not measure creative and practical intelligence, which are better predictors of success outside of school. Some people are successful in everyday settings but less so in school and therefore may obtain low scores on traditional intelligence tests despite being successful in their careers and personal lives. In this way, intelligence tests can underestimate the intellectual strengths of some children (Sternberg, 2020).

Cultures vary in terms of which specific skills are thought to constitute intelligence, but the three mental abilities that underlie intelligent behavior—analytic, creative, and applied intelligence—are recognized across cultures. Still, the relative importance ascribed to each may differ (Sternberg & Grigorenko, 2008). In Western cultures, someone who invests a great deal of effort into learning, enjoys it, and enthusiastically seeks opportunities for lifelong learning is considered intelligent. In contrast, other cultures emphasize applied intelligence. The Chinese Taoist tradition emphasizes the importance of humility, freedom from conventional standards of judgment, and awareness of the self and the outside world (Yang & Sternberg, 1997). In many African cultures, conceptions of intelligence revolve around the skills that maintain harmonious interpersonal relations (Ruzgis & Grigorenko, 1994). Chewa adults in Zambia emphasize social responsibilities, cooperativeness, obedience, and respectfulness as important to intelligence. Likewise, Kenyan parents emphasize responsible participation in family and social life (Serpell, 1974; Serpell & Jere-Folotiya, 2008; Super & Harkness, 1982).

Views of intelligence even vary within a given context (Sternberg, 2021). When parents were asked about the characteristics of an intelligent child in the first grade of elementary school, White American parents emphasized cognitive capacities. Parents who were immigrants from Cambodia, Mexico, the Philippines, and Vietnam, on the other hand, pointed to motivation, self-management, and social skills (Okagaki & Sternberg, 1993), suggesting that characteristics valued as intelligent vary across cultures and that children within the same context may be immersed in different cultures (Sternberg, 2021). Once again, we see the interaction of context and culture as influences on development.

Multiple Intelligences

A skilled dancer, a champion athlete, an award-winning musician, and an excellent communicator all have talents that are not measured by traditional intelligence tests. According to Howard Gardner (Gardner, 2017; Gardner et al., 2018) intelligence is the ability to solve problems or create culturally valued products. Specifically, Gardner's **multiple intelligence theory** proposes at least eight independent kinds of intelligence, shown in Figure 8.2. Multiple intelligence theory expands the use of the term *intelligence* to refer to skills not usually considered intelligence by experts and has led to a great deal of debate among intelligence theorists and researchers (Kaufman, Kaufman et al., 2013).

According to multiple intelligence theory, each person has a unique pattern of intellectual strengths and weaknesses. A person may be gifted in dance (bodily-kinesthetic intelligence), communication (verbal-linguistic intelligence), or music (musical intelligence), yet score low on intelligence tests. Each form of intelligence is thought to be biologically based, and each develops on a different timetable (Gardner, 2017). Assessing multiple intelligences requires observing the products of each form of intelligence (e.g., how well a child can learn a tune, navigate an unfamiliar area, or learn dance steps), which at best is a lengthy proposition and at worst is nearly impossible (Barnett et al., 2006). Through extended observations, an examiner can identify patterns of strengths and weaknesses in individuals and help them understand and achieve their potential (Gardner et al., 2018).

The theory of multiple intelligences is an optimistic perspective that allows everyone to be intelligent in their own way, viewing intelligence as broader than book learning and academic skills. Educators who adopt this view may create enriching educational experiences that target the many forms of intelligence and help students develop a range of physical, creative, and academic talents (Cavas & Cavas, 2020). Multiple intelligences theory has been criticized for not being grounded in research (Waterhouse, 2006). However, some neuroscientists have noted that each type of

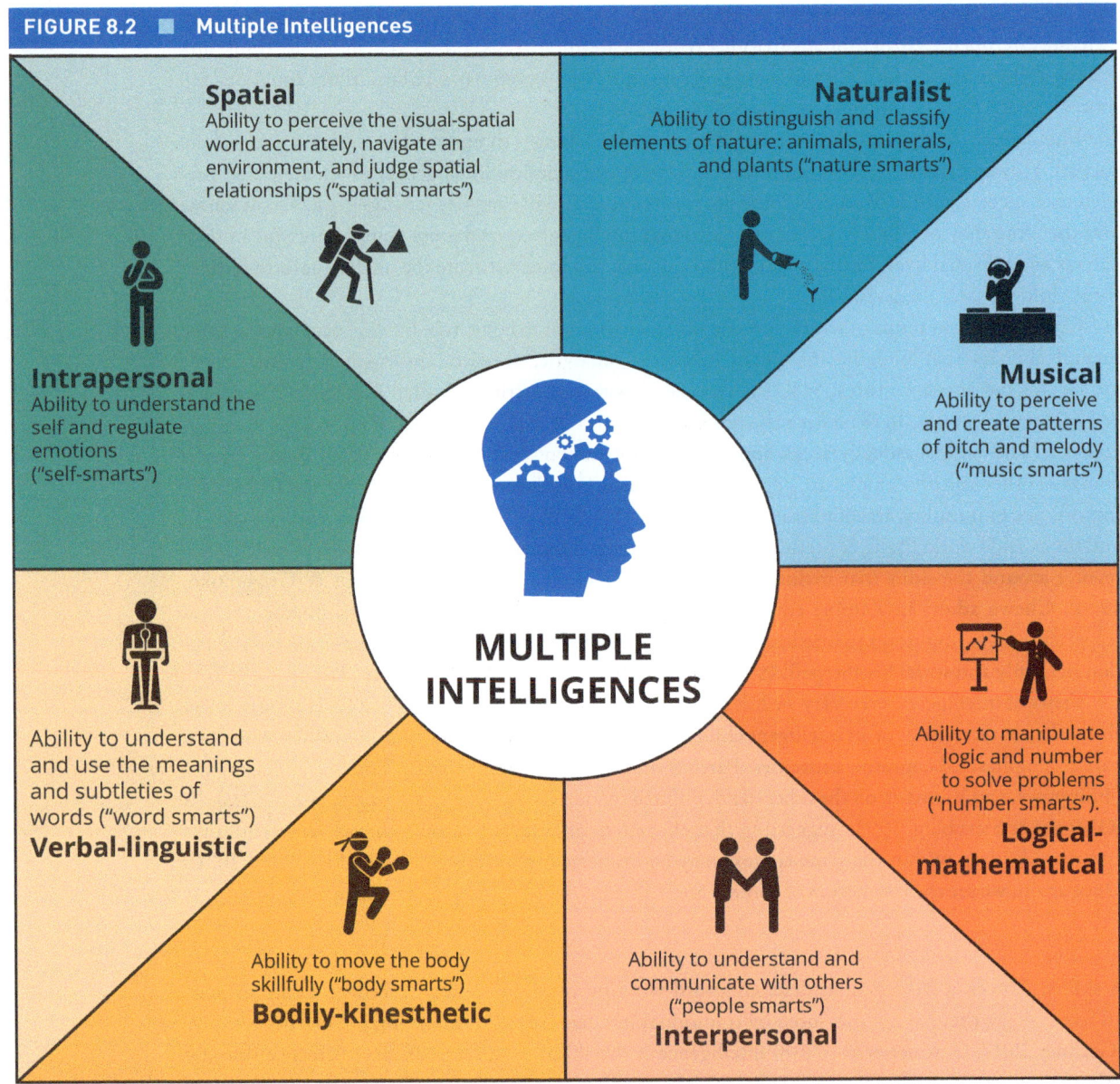

FIGURE 8.2 Multiple Intelligences

Source: Adapted from Gardner, H. (2017). Taking a multiple intelligences (MI) perspective. *Behavioral and Brain Sciences, 40*, e203. https://doi.org/10.1017/S0140525X16001631

intelligence corresponds to specific neurological processes, suggesting a biological basis for multiple intelligences (Shearer, 2020; Shearer & Karanian, 2017). A critical contribution of multiple intelligence theory is the recognition that traditional intelligence tests measure a specific set of mental abilities and ignore others.

Emotional Intelligence

We have seen that intelligence refers to the ability to adapt. Both triarchic and multiple intelligence theories emphasize intellectual and social abilities that help us navigate our world. Emotional intelligence, on the other hand, emphasizes our ability to adapt to interpersonal and intrapersonal contexts, that is, our interactions with people and ourselves. **Emotional intelligence** includes the ability to perceive, understand, manage, and respond appropriately to other people's emotions as well as our own (Caruso et al., 2019; Salovey & Mayer, 1989). It is a crucial component of *people skills* that enable us to form and sustain successful relationships, including friendships (Goleman, 1996; Goleman & Boyatzis, 2017). For example, 9-year-old Stacey acted quickly when she heard the boys teasing her friend. "Don't listen to them. Those boys don't know anything. Let's play together and forget about them."

In support of the adaptive advantage posed by emotional intelligence, research has shown that individuals who score high in measures of emotional intelligence tend to show less physically reactive responses to stress and release lower levels of stress hormones, during stressful situations (De la Barrera et al., 2021; Lea et al., 2019). This suggests that emotional intelligence can provide an adaptive advantage in the face of stress. It may not be surprising, then, that emotional intelligence is associated with well-being and mental health in children, adolescents, and adults (Pauletto et al., 2021; Villanueva et al., 2022). Emotional intelligence is linked with prosocial behavior and high-quality satisfying friendships and social relationships (Frederickson et al., 2012; Mavroveli et al., 2007). It is also associated with academic achievement in children, adolescents, and college students (MacCann et al., 2019; Sanchez-Ruiz et al., 2013).

Emotional intelligence, the ability to understand, manage, and respond appropriately to others' and our own emotions, enables us to form and sustain successful relationships.

Flashpop/Getty Images

There are individual differences in emotional intelligence, but it is malleable. Interventions that offer practice in perceiving, interpreting, understanding, and managing emotions have shown that emotional intelligence skills can be taught (Dacre Pool & Qualter, 2012; Schutte et al., 2013). Several dozen studies have shown that training can improve emotional intelligence skills in children and adolescents, at least modestly (Kotsou et al., 2019; Mattingly & Kraiger, 2019; Petrides et al., 2016).

> ## THINKING IN CONTEXT 8.1
>
> 1. Which theory or theories best explain intelligence, our ability to adapt to our environment? Explain how your chosen theory can help a child adapt to challenging environments.
> 2. Compare the role of context across the various theories of intelligence. How well do multiple intelligence theory, the triarchic theory, and emotional intelligence account for contextual or environmental influences on intelligence?
> 3. As a teacher, you are considering applying intelligence theories in your classroom. Which theory do you choose? How might you apply it in class (such as in activities or discussions)?

MEASURING INTELLIGENCE

> 8.2 Discuss ways of measuring intelligence in childhood and adolescence.

We have seen that most theories of intelligence describe it as a complex trait composed of many abilities. Intelligence tests measure the skills that comprise intelligence. Such tests can be administered in group settings to large numbers of children simultaneously or to children individually.

Group Administered Tests

Group testing examines large numbers of people at once. The Army Alpha test was the first group-administered test created for adults (Yoakum & Yerkes, 1920). This pencil-and-paper test was developed during World War I to place Army recruits in positions appropriate to their intellectual abilities (Wasserman, 2018). Descendants of this early group-administered test are given routinely in school settings as a quick way of analyzing the intellectual abilities of groups of children, including their strengths and weaknesses, which aids professionals in planning educational curricula. These multiple-choice tests also identify children who need further assessment with individually administered tests.

The Cognitive Abilities Test (CogAT) is a widely used group-administered test of reasoning skills for K–12 students (Lohman, 2011). It is administered by paper and pencil and takes about an hour to complete. The CogAT assesses three types of reasoning: verbal, quantitative, and nonverbal. Verbal reasoning items include reading comprehension, analogies, grouping words based on shared characteristics, and sentence completion. Quantitative items examine children's abilities to reason about numbers and patterns. Tasks include identifying the missing number in a sequence of numbers that follows a pattern, number analogies, comparing quantities, and using mathematical concepts to solve problems. The Nonverbal Battery includes items that do not rely on language skills, which tend to correspond to schooling and experience with reading and academic skills (Lohman & Gambrell, 2012). Nonverbal items assess different aspects of nonverbal reasoning, such as identifying patterns of geometric shapes, mentally rotating figures, and classifying figures. The CogAt gives a quick and effective assessment of students' skills and aids in identifying students who may require additional testing and educational resources (Warne, 2015).

Individually Administered Tests

Is a child's behavior and development typical for their age? Is a toddler in need of early intervention? Does a child's score on a group-administered test like the CogAT suggest that they need further evaluation? Is the score particularly high or low? Does it match teacher or parent observations? Children in each of these scenarios can benefit from an individualized assessment. Individual intelligence tests measure cognitive skills. Children also show unique patterns of strengths and weaknesses in abilities. Some people show exceptional skills in word comprehension and can comprehend difficult texts. Others are skilled in mathematical reasoning and can compute long strings of numbers quickly and easily. These tests have shown that individual differences in intelligence scores correspond to differences in children's reasoning and problem-solving abilities (Sackett et al., 2017). Intelligence tests have been devised for children of all ages. They vary in the specific tasks, but all measure abilities thought to underlie infants' and children's ability to adapt to their world.

Bayley Scales of Infant Development

At 3 months of age, Baby Lourdes can lift and support her upper body with her arms when on her stomach. She grabs and shakes toys with her hands and enjoys playing with others. Lourdes' pediatrician tells her parents that her development is right on track for babies her age and that she shows typical levels of infant intelligence. Standardized tests permit the pediatrician to determine Lourdes' development relative to other infants her age.

The most often used standardized measure of infant intelligence is the Bayley Scales of Infant Development III (BSID-III), commonly called Bayley-III (see Figure 8.3). This test is appropriate for infants from 1 month through 42 months of age (Bayley, 1969, 2005). The Bayley-III consists of five scales: three consisting of infant responses and two of parent responses. The *Motor Scale* measures gross and fine motor skills, such as grasping objects, drinking from a cup, sitting, and climbing stairs. The *Cognitive Scale* includes items such as attending to a stimulus or searching for a hidden toy. The *Language Scale* examines comprehension and production of language, such as following directions and naming objects. The *Social-Emotional Scale* is derived from parental reports regarding behavior such as the infant's responsiveness and play activity. Finally, the *Adaptive Behavior Scale* is based on parental reports of the infant's ability to

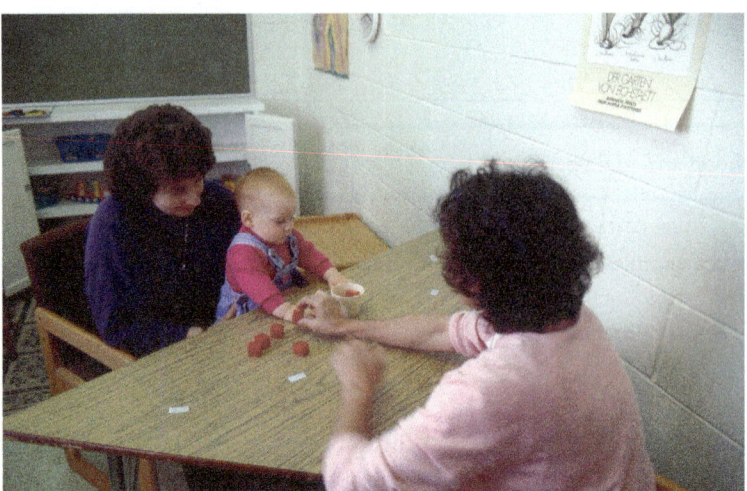

Infant assessment tests, such as the BSID-III, examine cognitive, language, social-emotional, and motor abilities, such as infants' skill in manipulating objects.

Cliff Moore/Science Source

FIGURE 8.3 ■ Block Design Task

Source: Monica Wierzbicki/Body Scientific Intl.

adapt in everyday situations, including the infant's ability to communicate, regulate their emotions, and display certain behaviors.

The Bayley-III provides a comprehensive profile of an infant's current functioning, but infants' performance often varies considerably from one testing session to another (Bornstein et al., 1997). Scores vary with infants' states of arousal and motivation. This suggests that pediatricians and parents must exert great care in interpreting scores—particularly poor scores—because an infant's performance may be influenced by factors other than developmental functioning. Infants who perform poorly on the Bayley-III should be re-examined.

Although Bayley-III scores tell us about an infant's current abilities, they do not predict performance on tests of intelligence and executive function in childhood (Gould et al., 2019; Luttikhuizen dos Santos et al., 2013; Månsson et al., 2019). Even Nancy Bayley (1949), who invented the Bayley Scales, noted in a longitudinal study that infant performance was not related to intelligence scores at age 18. Why is infant intelligence relatively unrelated to later intelligence? Consider what infant tests measure: perception and motor skills, responsiveness, and language skills. The ability to grasp an object, crawl up stairs, or search for a hidden toy—items that appear on the Bayley-III—are not measured by childhood intelligence tests. Instead, intelligence tests administered in childhood examine more complex and abstract abilities such as verbal reasoning, verbal comprehension, and problem solving.

If the Bayley-III does not predict later intelligence, why administer it? Infants whose performance is poor relative to age norms may suffer from serious developmental problems that can be addressed through intervention (Del Rosario et al., 2021). The abilities measured by the Bayley-III are critical indicators of neurological health. They are useful for charting developmental paths, diagnosing neurological disorders, and detecting intellectual disabilities in infants and toddlers. Thus, the Bayley-III is primarily used as a screening tool to identify infants who can benefit from medical and developmental intervention.

Stanford-Binet Test

French psychologist Alfred Binet and his student, Theodore Simon, created the first intelligence test in 1905. The test was commissioned by the French Ministry of Education and aimed to identify children who required additional support to succeed in school (Wasserman, 2018). The resulting Binet-Simon test assessed children's ability to reason verbally and numerically, solve problems, and think logically. A descendant of this test, the Stanford Binet Test, is still used today.

Mental Age. Binet believed that the cognitive abilities that comprise intelligence mature with age, leading older children to score higher on intelligence tests than younger children. Binet and Simon assessed children of all ages, recording the level of performance and the items that children typically answer correctly at each age. Most 7-year-olds could pass some items but few 6-year-olds could do the same. Similarly, items for older children, 12 years of age, could not be correctly answered by younger children. Binet defined a child's **mental age** as the child's performance relative to same-age children. Most children's mental age corresponds to their chronological age (age in years) (K. C. Peterson et al., 2020). Children whose mental age is greater than their chronological age have a high level of intelligence. In contrast, children whose mental age is less than their chronological age have a low level of intelligence.

Intelligence Quotient. In 1917, American psychologist Lewis Terman at Stanford University adapted the Binet-Simon test for use with English-speaking children, creating the Stanford-Binet Intelligence Scale, which is still in use today. The test yields an **intelligence quotient (IQ)** score, defined as mental age (MA) divided by chronological age (CA), multiplied by 100 (IQ = MA/CA × 100). An IQ score of 100 indicates average intelligence, specifically that a child can correctly answer the same items as same-age peers (Wasserman, 2018).

Stanford-Binet 5. Today's Stanford-Binet Intelligence Scales (Fifth Edition), called *Stanford-Binet 5*, measures intelligence as five intellectual abilities that are assessed with verbal and nonverbal tasks: knowledge, quantitative reasoning, visual-spatial processing, working memory, and fluid reasoning (which measures the speed of processing). The Stanford-Binet 5 no longer uses the concept of mental age. Instead, IQ scores reflect how individuals' performance is compared with test norms, standards of performance based on average scores. Norms were created by assessing a large representative sample of people (2 years of age through adults) from many socioeconomic and racial backgrounds (K. C. Peterson et al., 2020). The resulting IQ scores reflect how well or poorly individuals perform compared to same-age peers. The Stanford-Binet 5 remains one of the most popular IQ tests today.

Weschler Tests

The Weschler tests are a set of widely used measures of intelligence constructed by psychologist David Wechsler (1944), who viewed intelligence as "the global capacity of a person to act purposefully, to think rationally, and to deal effectively with his environment." The children's test, the Wechsler Intelligence Scale for Children (WISC-V), is appropriate for children aged 6 through 16. In addition to the WISC, there are Wechsler tests for preschoolers (the Wechsler Preschool and Primary Scale of Intelligence, or WPPSI) and adults (the Wechsler Adult Intelligence Scale, or WAIS) (Beaujean & Woodhouse, 2020). Each contains similar subtests that measure verbal and nonverbal abilities.

The WISC-V is composed of 10 subtests that comprise an overall measure of IQ as well as five indexes: verbal comprehension, visual-spatial, fluid reasoning, working memory, and processing speed (Wechsler, 2014). The WISC tests verbal abilities that tap vocabulary and knowledge and factual information that is influenced by culture. It also tests nonverbal abilities, such as tasks that require the child to arrange materials, such as blocks and pictures, that are thought to be less influenced by culture. The nonverbal subtests require little language proficiency, which enables children with speech disorders and those who do not speak English to be fairly assessed. Supplemental subtests are included to aid examiners in further assessing a child's capacities in a given area. Table 8.1 presents the subtests and sample items that comprise the WISC-V. By carefully examining a child's pattern of subtest scores, a professional can determine whether a child has specific learning needs, whether gifted or challenged (Flanagan & Alfonso, 2017). As with the Stanford-Binet, a score of 100 is defined as average performance for a person's age. A person's full-scale IQ is a combination of verbal and performance scores.

The WISC-V is standardized on samples of children who are geographically and ethnically representative of the total population of the United States, creating norms that permit comparisons among children who are similar in age and ethnic background (Beaujean & Woodhouse, 2020; Sattler, 2014). In Canada, an adapted WISC, standardized with children representative of the Canadian population, is available in English and French (Wechsler, 2014). The WISC has been adapted and used in many

TABLE 8.1 ■ Sample Items Measuring the Five Wechsler Intelligence Scale for Children Indices	
WISC-V Index	**Sample Item**
Verbal Comprehension Index (VCI)	Vocabulary: What does amphibian mean?
Visual Spatial Index (VSI)	Block design: In this timed task, children are shown a design composed of red-and-white blocks, are given a set of blocks, and are asked to put together the blocks to recreate the design.
Fluid Reasoning Index (FRI)	Matrix reasoning: Children are shown an array of pictures with one missing. They must select the picture that completes the array.
Working Memory Index (WMI)	Digit span: Children are read lists of numbers and asked to repeat them as heard or in reverse order.
Processing Speed Index (PSI)	Coding: In this timed task, children are shown a code that converts numbers into symbols and are asked to transcribe lists of numbers into code.

other countries, including Austria, France, Germany, Greece, Japan, Lithuania, the Netherlands, Slovenia, Sweden, Switzerland, Taiwan, and the United Kingdom, with few differences (Fons Van de Vijver et al., 2019; Georgas et al., 2003). During the COVID-19 pandemic, procedures for remote administration of the WISC online were developed and tested in U.S. children, with comparable overall estimates of IQ (Wright, 2020).

Stability and Change in Intelligence in Childhood and Adolescence

We have seen that measures of intelligence in infancy are not good predictors of IQ in childhood or adolescence. What about childhood measures of intelligence? IQ shows increasing stability starting at about age 4 (Sameroff et al., 1993). The long-term stability of intelligence increases with age. The correlation between IQ measured at age 5 and again in young adulthood is about 0.50, and it is about 0.80 by 10 years of age (Bjorklund & Myers, 2015). Research on groups of children indicates that mean intelligence scores remain relatively stable from childhood to adulthood. However, when we consider individuals, we see that there are also large individual differences in stability (Sackett et al., 2017; Watkins et al., 2022).

When elementary school students were evaluated twice over a period of approximately 3 years, on average each children's scores stayed largely the same (differing by one point or less). But about one quarter of the children's scores differed by 10 or more points up to, for one child, 29 points (Watkins & Smith, 2013). There are not many studies examining long-term stability in children's IQ scores, but the results of this study suggest that intelligence is stable for most children but shows substantial change and variation among others. Similar to other domains of development, intellectual development is characterized by both stability and change and is influenced by dynamic interactions among the individual and context.

In sum, intelligence tests are helpful tools for describing distinct patterns of abilities among children. IQ scores are strong predictors of academic achievement (Sternberg, 2020). Nevertheless, it is important to remember that IQ scores are one indicator of cognitive ability, but not the only indicator. Developmental scientists tend to view IQ tests as rough gauges rather than precise indicators of intelligence, because intelligence is a broad ability with many facets (Kranzler & Floyd, 2020; Sternberg, 2021).

THINKING IN CONTEXT 8.2

1. Suppose you were asked to create an intelligence test. What skills or abilities would you measure? What would a child with high scores show? Low scores? What theory does your test best fit?
2. To what extent do you think intelligence tests like the WISC or CogAT match the content taught in school? What kinds of experiences might help children improve their verbal skills? Quantitative? Nonverbal? Are some abilities more easily modified than others? In your view, do schools offer opportunities for children to modify the abilities assessed by intelligence tests?

CONTEXTUAL INFLUENCES ON INTELLIGENCE

> **8.3** Analyze contextual influences on intelligence.

Like all facets of development, intelligence is influenced by dynamic interactions among biology and context. Heredity is thought to play a role in intelligence, but there is no single gene responsible for IQ (Franić et al., 2015). Like many other characteristics, intelligence is polygenetic, influenced by complex combinations of genes (von Stumm & Plomin, 2021). In addition, genes are not independent influences on intelligence but instead act in conjunction with children's contexts (Harden, 2021).

Sociohistorical Context and IQ

Our sociohistorical context, *when* we live, influences our development. For example, average scores on intelligence tests have increased with each generation since the 1930s (Lynn, 2013). This is known as the Flynn effect and was first documented by James Robert Flynn (1987, 1998), who found that intelligence scores increased by about nine points for verbal measures and 15 points for nonverbal measures with each generation over 60 years. Recent research on children and adolescents born between 1957 and 1999 showed a three-point increase in IQ measures every decade (Giangrande et al., 2022).

The Flynn effect is thought to result from multiple contextual factors, including improvements in education and nutrition, increasing environmental stimulation and education, and technological advancements (Flynn & Weiss, 2007). Each generation is exposed to more information and ideas than the previous one, and this exposure likely influences their thinking (te Nijenhuis, 2013). More substantial generational increases occur in developing regions, such as rural Kenya (T. C. Daley et al., 2003), compared with developed regions where changes in IQ have slowed (Pietschnig & Voracek, 2015). The rise in average IQ scores over the past century reflects the changing cognitive demands of society (Flynn, 2020). As society becomes more complex, so too do average IQ scores. When a society reduces its demands, the average IQ can be expected to fall.

Some researchers argue that the Flynn effect may not entirely reflect generational changes in IQ but may instead result from changes in measures used to evaluate intelligence (O'Keefe & Rodgers, 2020). Intelligence measures such as the WISC are routinely revised. One study suggested that when changes in measures are controlled, the Flynn effect is reduced or even disappears (Platt et al., 2019).

Kenyan children show an especially pronounced Flynn effect, influenced by contextual changes in education, health, and nutrition.

Andrew Aitchison/Contributor/Getty Images

Socioeconomic Status and IQ

As another example of the role of contextual influences on intelligence, the heritability of IQ tends to vary with children's environment (Sauce & Matzel, 2018). Children from low socioeconomic status (SES) backgrounds who are adopted into higher SES homes typically score 12 points or higher on IQ tests than their biological siblings raised by birth parents or adopted into lower SES homes (Duyme et al., 1999).

While genes play a large role in determining the IQ scores of children from high SES homes, they play a smaller role for those from low SES homes (Nisbett et al., 2013; Scarr, 1992). Why? SES refers to the economic and social status of a person or group, including education, income, and occupation, which influence people's access to resources, opportunities, and often, basic necessities (Antonoplis, 2023). Children reared in high SES homes tend to have greater access to resources in the home and community, such as quality schools, safe neighborhoods, green spaces to play, and access to health care. Their parents tend to have more education, work in more prestigious and higher-earning jobs, and can provide more economic and educational resources, such as books, toys, and activities. Children in high SES homes also tend to encounter more child-directed speech than those in low SES homes (Jiang et al., 2024). Because of this contextual support, children from higher SES homes are more likely to achieve their genetic potential for IQ, making genetics a larger factor in the differences seen between individuals (Gottschling et al., 2019).

On the other hand, children from lower SES environments experience contextual stressors that interfere with their development and can prevent them from realizing their genetic potential for intelligence. Many children from impoverished homes live in communities that lack consistent access to basic necessities, such as clean drinking water, health care, and safe schools. They are more likely to be exposed to toxins in the home and community, such as lead paint, air pollution, and industrial contaminants and wastes (Alvarez et al., 2022; Weisner et al., 2023). SES contributes to differences in nutrition, living conditions, school resources, intellectual stimulation, and exposure to contextual stressors and threats, such as discrimination. Any of or all these factors can influence cognitive and psychosocial factors related to IQ, such as motivation, self-concept, and academic achievement (Kriegbaum et al., 2018; Plomin & Deary, 2015). As a result, IQ scores for children from lower SES homes are more influenced by the context and opportunities that children have experienced rather than genetic endowment (Flynn & Sternberg, 2019; Sauce & Matzel, 2018). In sum, socioeconomic status is a strong predictor of children's intelligence scores (Korous et al., 2022; von Stumm, 2017).

Group Differences and the Majority Culture

A consistent and controversial finding in the intelligence literature is that Black children as a group tend to score 10 to 15 points lower on standardized IQ tests than non-Hispanic White children (Rindermann & Thompson, 2013). Hispanic children tend to score between non-Hispanic Black and non-Hispanic White children, while Asian American children tend to score similarly or slightly higher than non-Hispanic White children (Neisser et al., 1996; Nisbett et al., 2013). Before examining the reasons for these findings, it is crucial to note that focusing solely on group differences overlooks important facts. First, individuals of all races and ethnicities show a wide range of functioning. Second, there is overlap in the IQ scores of children from all racial and ethnic backgrounds. For instance, over 20% of Black children score higher on IQ tests than any other children, whether Black or non-Hispanic White (Rindermann & Thompson, 2013). Therefore, many researchers argue that group comparisons are not meaningful, because there are more differences among individuals within each group than between the groups (C. E. Daley & Onwuegbuzie, 2011). Contextual differences associated with race and ethnicity, including SES, are more important influences on intelligence scores than race itself (Henry et al., 2020).

According to some experts, IQ tests tap the thinking style and language of the majority culture rather than intelligence itself (Heath, 1989; Helms, 1992). School provides children with exposure to information and ways of thinking that are valued by the majority culture and measured by IQ tests. As a result, IQ scores tend to show small increases with each year of schooling, improve during the school year, and decrease over the summer break (Flynn & Sternberg, 2019; Huttenlocher et al., 1998).

This seasonal drop in IQ scores is more significant for children from low SES backgrounds (Nisbett et al., 2013).

In turn, IQ scores are a robust predictor of childhood academic achievement. Children with higher IQs tend to earn above-average grades in school and are more likely to remain in school (Kriegbaum et al., 2018; Mackintosh, 2011). Schooling provides children with exposure to information and ways of thinking that are valued by the majority culture and reflected in IQ tests. Therefore, a correlation between IQ and school achievement may emerge because the test items require the very kinds of learned abilities and ways of thinking that are also the currency of schooling (Richardson & Norgate, 2015). Additionally, children of the same age who have more years of schooling tend to have higher IQ scores than those who are less educated, and correlations between IQ and school achievement tend to increase with age, suggesting that schooling influences IQ as well (Cliffordson & Gustafsson, 2008; Sternberg, 2020; Sternberg, et al., 2001).

Language differences also may explain some group differences in intelligence. For example, Latino and Native American children tend to perform better on nonverbal tasks than ones that require the use of language (Neisser et al., 1996). But even nonverbal sorting tasks can be influenced by culture. When presented with a series of cards depicting objects (such as bird and dog) and activities or actions (such as run and fly) and told to sort the cards into meaningful groupings, children from Western cultures tend to sort the cards by object, putting bird and dog in the same category of *animal*. Children of the Kpelle tribe in Nigeria instead sorted the cards by action, placing bird with fly, because birds fly (Sternberg, 1985). Learning experiences and opportunities also influence children's scores on nonverbal tasks. Performance on spatial reasoning tasks is associated with experience with spatially oriented video games (Subrahmanyam & Greenfield, 1996).

Stereotypes and IQ

Context can influence IQ both directly, by providing resources, and indirectly, through shared beliefs about the nature of intelligence and about the characteristics of individuals deemed intelligent. Children are immersed in contexts that send subtle and overt messages about the nature of intelligence and stereotypes about group differences in intelligence. Negative stereotypes can affect the performance of children on intelligence tests. Children may underperform due to fear or anxiety that they will confirm negative stereotypes about their group. This phenomenon is known as **stereotype threat** (Seo & Lee, 2021; Spencer et al., 2016; Steele & Aronson, 1995).

Research has shown that Black and Hispanic American children perform less well on verbal tasks when they are aware of negative racial and ethnic stereotypes and are told that the task is a "test" examining academic ability compared to their non-Hispanic White peers. However, when they are told that the task is "not a test," they perform better (McKown & Strambler, 2009; McKown & Weinstein, 2003; Wasserberg, 2014). Conversely, children who reject negative stereotypes and do not believe that they apply to them tend to show higher engagement and achievement (Nasir et al., 2017).

Although stereotype threat is most often examined as an influence on academic performance in children of color, it may also apply to other intersectional categories, such as SES and gender (Jaxon et al., 2019). For example, children from low SES homes who are aware of negative stereotypes about SES and ability tend to perform more poorly on standardized tests, such as IQ, and in academics (Durante & Fiske, 2017). Girls who believe negative stereotypes about girls' ability to do math tend to show more poor mathematics achievement than girls who reject gender stereotypes (Herts et al., 2020).

Reducing Cultural Bias in IQ Tests

Given the well-documented impact of context on intelligence, how can we minimize cultural bias in IQ tests? This is a challenging issue because some items on IQ tests may be more familiar to children from certain backgrounds than others. For example, questions about snow may be biased against children who live in climates that are warm year-round, and some children may be more familiar with word problems about cows than about subways.

One way to reduce cultural bias in IQ tests is to include questions that are culture-fair, that are familiar to people from all SES and ethnic backgrounds. An item might ask how a bird and a fish are different, assuming that all children have experience with these two common animals. Still, it is difficult to eliminate bias completely because children from varying backgrounds naturally have diverse experiences. Moreover, verbal tasks may place some children at a disadvantage.

IQ tests that rely heavily on verbal tasks are more likely to show differences in performance across ethnic, racial, and socioeconomic groups. As the Weschler IQ tests have been revised to reduce verbal subtests that are thought to be influenced by culture, group differences in children's performance have declined. Newer versions of the WISC rely less on spoken language and tend to show smaller differences between White and Black children (Weiss et al., 2016).

Learning experiences and opportunities also influence children's scores on nonverbal tasks. For example, performance on spatial reasoning tasks is associated with playing spatially oriented video games (Quiroga et al., 2019). Similarly, familiarity with test materials can affect performance. In one study, Zambian and English children were asked to reproduce patterns using different media (wire, pencil and paper, or clay). Both groups performed equally well with clay but the Zambian children excelled in the wire medium, with which they were accustomed, while the English children performed best with pencil and paper (Serpell & Simatende, 2016). Differences in familiarity with test materials can produce marked differences in test results. To truly understand individuals' intelligence, we must use measures that are responsive to contextual differences and variations in socialization and enculturation that influence responses—and corresponding IQ scores.

THINKING IN CONTEXT 8.3

1. Consider intelligence from the perspective of Bronfenbrenner's bioecological systems theory (see Chapter 1). List factors at each bioecological level—microsystem, mesosystem, exosystem, and macrosystem—that might influence children's intelligence scores.
2. Considering this perspective, what factors might influence group differences in intelligence? Identify factors at each level and explain how variations in these bioecological factors might account for group differences in intelligence.

NEURODEVELOPMENTAL CONDITIONS

> **8.4** Summarize four neurodevelopmental conditions, including the role of contextual factors in disability.

An important theme of development is that it is characterized by individual differences. Although development generally follows a predictable pattern, the specific path, pace, and outcomes may vary among individuals. Some children are born with or develop impairments that affect their physical, cognitive, or socioemotional functioning. These impairments are often referred to as **developmental disabilities**, which include a range of conditions resulting from impairments in physical functioning, learning, language, and behavior (see Figure 8.4; Zablotsky & Black, 2020).

Over the past half-century, the nature of childhood disability has dramatically shifted. Advances in medicine and improvements in public health, such as prenatal diagnostic tests, increased knowledge about teratogens and prenatal development, and greater access to medical care, have led to a decline in the prevalence of physical disabilities in children, including cerebral palsy, limb and other birth abnormalities, and sensory impairments (Houtrow et al., 2014; Young, 2021). However, there has been an increase in the incidence of neurodevelopmental conditions, leading to an overall increase in childhood disability in recent decades (Graham et al., 2017; Houtrow et al., 2014; Zablotsky et al., 2019). Common neurodevelopmental conditions include autistic spectrum disorder, attention-deficit/hyperactivity disorder, and intellectual disability.

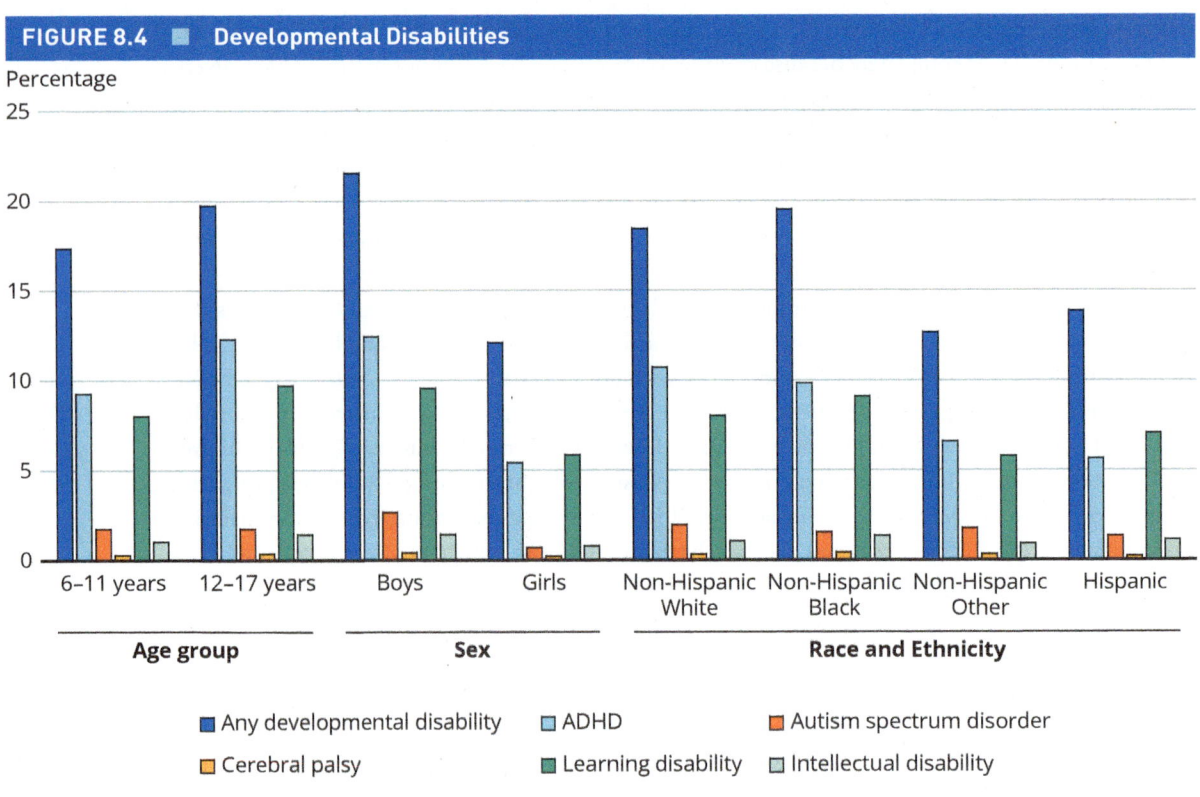

FIGURE 8.4 ■ Developmental Disabilities

Source: Adapted from Zablotsky, B., Black, L. I., Maenner, M. J., Schieve, L. A., Danielson, M. L., Bitsko, R. H., Blumberg, S. J., Kogan, M. D., & Boyle, C. A. (2019). Prevalence and trends of developmental disabilities among children in the United States: 2009–2017. *Pediatrics* 144(4), e20190811. https://doi.org/10.1542/peds.2019-0811

As we begin our discussion, it is important to acknowledge that developmental scientists have begun to adopt the term **neurodiversity** to describe differences in brain functioning rather than the term "disability" (Dwyer, 2022). This shift reflects a growing understanding that there is a wide range of individual differences in cognitive and behavioral functioning that should not be stigmatized (Pellicano & den Houting, 2022). The term *disability* can be problematic because it implies that a child is not meeting a normative standard of development and can focus on deficits and limitations. In contrast, the concept of neurodiversity emphasizes that there is natural variation in human brain function and that different neurological profiles have unique perspectives and abilities and should be valued.

Autism Spectrum Disorders

Autism spectrum disorders (ASD) are a group of neurodevelopmental disorders that vary in severity and are characterized by deficits in social communication and repetitive behaviors (Lord et al., 2020, 2022). About 2.3% of children in the United States are diagnosed with ASD, and boys are about four times as likely to be diagnosed than girls (Hirota & King, 2023; Masi et al., 2017). The degree of social and communication impairments can range from minor difficulties with social comprehension and perspective-taking to an inability to use nonverbal or spoken language. A common characteristic of ASD is repetitive behaviors, such as rocking, hand-flapping, twirling, and repeating sounds, words, or phrases (Hodges et al., 2020). Some children with ASD experience sensory dysfunction, perceiving visual, auditory, and tactile stimulation as intense and even painful (Morimoto et al., 2021).

ASD is associated with atypical brain development characterized by altered neural connectivity and sensitivity (McPartland et al., 2021; Zhang & Roeyers, 2019). Some areas of the brain show exaggerated pruning, while others exhibit heightened connectivity (Rafiee et al., 2022). The sensorimotor areas of the brain tend to show heightened connectivity, which may account for the sensory difficulties and motor features associated with ASD (Hull et al., 2017; Morimoto et al., 2021). However, the areas of the brain responsible for inhibitory control and self-regulation tend to show less connectivity, suggesting that children with ASD may experience difficulty controlling their impulses (Voorhies et al., 2018).

In addition, individuals with ASD show fewer neural connections within and reduced interconnectivity among areas involved in detecting facial expressions, social behavior, emotion, social communication, and perspective-taking (Cheng et al., 2015; Sato & Uono, 2019). Collectively these neurological differences mean that children with ASD may experience difficulty with theory of mind (Kana et al., 2015). That is, they may find it challenging to consider mental states, which are essential to communication.

While children are typically diagnosed with ASD between the ages of 3 and 4, some ASD symptoms can be observed in infancy (van 't Hof et al., 2021). Infants with ASD may show delays in motor milestones and social development, such as following another person's gaze, smiling at others, and vocalizing in response to others (Franchini et al., 2023; Tanner & Dounavi, 2021). In one study, researchers found that infants who were later diagnosed with ASD began showing less attention to other people's eyes by 2 months of age (Jones & Klin, 2013). Likewise, brain scans show that infants' brains differentiate people's faces from objects, but infants with ASD show similar brain activity in response to both faces and objects, suggesting that they view faces and objects similarly (McCleery et al., 2009). Early recognition that faces are special stimuli that are linked with social stimulation is important for developing communication skills, emotional attachments, and theory of mind.

Children with ASD show a wide range of intellectual functioning, and about 1 in 3 children with autism also have an intellectual disability (Shenouda et al., 2023). Children with ASD often experience difficulties with working memory, requiring more time to process information (Habib et al., 2019; Wang et al., 2017). They may benefit from instruction that emphasizes modeling, hands-on activities, and concrete examples and teaches skills for generalizing learning from one setting or problem to another (Kent et al., 2020; Lord et al., 2020).

Specific Learning Disorder

Once referred to as a learning disability, **specific learning disorders (SLD)** are diagnosed when children demonstrate a measurable discrepancy between aptitude and achievement in a particular academic area given their age, intelligence, and amount of schooling (American Psychiatric Association, 2013). Despite normal intelligence and sensory function, children with SLDs struggle with academic achievement. An estimated 1 in 5 children in the United States has a specific learning disorder (Horowitz et al., 2017). SLDs can manifest in several ways, reflecting different patterns of brain function, and influencing reading, writing skills, mathematics, and other cognitive skills (Grigorenko et al., 2020).

The most commonly diagnosed SLD is **developmental dyslexia**, a disorder that affects reading. Children with dyslexia have reading achievements below that predicted by age or IQ. Children with dyslexia demonstrate difficulty in matching letters to sounds and with word recognition and spelling despite adequate instruction, intelligence, and intact sensory abilities (R. L. Peterson & Pennington, 2012; Snowling et al., 2020). Dyslexia is estimated to affect 20% of the school population, and boys and girls are equally affected (S. E. Shaywitz et al., 2021).

Dyslexia is influenced by genetics (Gialluisi et al., 2021). Children with dyslexia have a neurological difficulty in processing speech sounds. During speech tasks, they use different brain regions than other children, and they often have difficulty recognizing that words consist of small units of sound strung together and represented visually by letters (Richlan, 2019; B. A. Shaywitz & Shaywitz, 2020). Abnormalities in the brain areas responsible for reading can be seen in 11-year-olds with dyslexia but not in young children who have not been exposed to reading, suggesting that the brain abnormalities associated with dyslexia occur after reading commences (Clark et al., 2014). Other research suggests a role for visual attention and difficulty integrating visual attention, executive function, and reading-related brain networks (Taran et al., 2022). Successful interventions include training in phonics and supporting emerging skills by linking letters, sounds, and words through writing and reading from developmentally appropriate texts (Snowling, 2013).

Developmental dyscalculia is a disorder that affects mathematics ability. Dyscalculia is thought to affect about 5% of students and is less well understood than developmental dyslexia (Kaufmann,

Mazzocco et al., 2013; Rapin et al., 2016). Children with developmental dyscalculia find it challenging to learn mathematical concepts such as counting, addition, and subtraction and often have a poor understanding of these concepts (Kucian & von Aster, 2015). In early elementary school, they may use relatively ineffective strategies for solving math problems, such as using their fingers to add large sums. Research suggests that it is influenced by brain connectivity and suboptimal recruitment of regions needed for mathematical cognition difficulty with working memory and executive function, specifically visuospatial short-term memory and inhibitory function (Castaldi et al., 2020; McCaskey et al., 2020). Children with dyscalculia are usually given intensive practice to help them understand numbers, including the use of an abacus (a counting tool consisting of a frame with beads) to help visualize numbers—but there is much to learn about this disorder (Bryant et al., 2016; Fuchs et al., 2017; Lu et al., 2020)

Developmental dysgraphia is a disorder that affects writing abilities. It is closely related to dyslexia and may manifest as difficulties with spelling, poor handwriting, and trouble conveying thoughts on paper, leading children to show writing performance below that expected based on their grades (Döhla & Heim, 2016; Döhla et al., 2018). Developmental writing disorders occur in about 7%–15% of school-aged children and are more common in boys (Horowitz et al., 2017). Like dyslexia, children with dysgraphia experience difficulties with working memory and executive function, especially response inhibition, and fMRI scans suggest different patterns of brain connectivity (Richards et al., 2015). An estimated third to half of children with dysgraphia also have dyslexia (Chung et al., 2020)

Writing relies on motor and sensory skills in addition to cognition. Children with dysgraphia may hold their pencil in a tight, awkward grip, show poor body posture while writing, and produce illegible handwriting. Children with dysgraphia may avoid writing tasks, say words aloud or tire quickly while writing, omit words in sentences, and have difficulty organizing and conveying ideas on paper. Teachers may identify children with dysgraphia when they notice a large discrepancy between their understanding demonstrated by speech and written work.

Teachers and parents can help children with dysgraphia by focusing on the sensory and motor aspects (Berninger & Wolf, 2009). Paper with raised lines can provide a sensory guide to help children learn to write within the lines. Providing children with dysgraphia with a range of pens and pencils to sample for comfort can also be helpful, as can training children in handwriting, but permitting them to use print or cursive letters, whichever is most comfortable. Children with dysgraphia often benefit from using a keyboard, which is often easier than manipulating a pen, but a keyboard should not completely replace handwriting. Like other SLDs, managing dysgraphia often requires learning and practicing skills.

Sensory Processing Disorder

"No!! It's too loud!" Ryan cries and retreats to the corner, rocking. The other children, unperturbed by the sound, watch Ryan and then go back to playing. It is estimated that, perhaps like Ryan, between 5% and 16% of children experience **sensory processing disorder (SPD)**, an extreme difficulty processing and responding to sensory stimuli that interferes with daily functioning (Ahn et al., 2004; Ben-Sasson et al., 2009; Galiana-Simal et al., 2020). Children with SPD may overreact or underreact to sensory stimuli, making it difficult to respond appropriately to everyday sights, sounds, smells, and tactile stimuli.

SPD is caused by the atypical processing of sensory stimuli in the brain. Children with SPD show abnormalities in the parts of the brain involved in multimodal sensory integration, especially the parietal and occipital regions (Chang et al., 2016). Brain scans also tend to show structural differences in the connections among sensory pathways and the parts of the brain responsible for higher-order thinking, the frontal cortex, suggesting that children with SPD may experience difficulty making sense of sensory stimuli, integrating sensory and social stimuli, and inhibit inappropriate responses to stimuli (Owen et al., 2013).

SPD may take several forms (Goodman-Scott & Lambert, 2015; Miller et al., 2009; Mulligan et al., 2021). Some children with SPD experience sensory over-responsivity; they have a shallow sensory threshold, and their sensory system overreacts to stimuli, causing children to be easily overwhelmed. Other children with SPD experience sensory under-responsivity, a high sensory threshold, meaning they often do not notice or process sensory input. For example, a child with sensory under-responsivity may not hear the teacher and miss social signals because they do not notice visual cues like facial expressions. A third group of children with SPD crave and seek intense stimulation. These children may appear impulsive and unpredictable because they are often constantly in motion, running, jumping, tapping, humming, and fighting to receive sensations from their environment.

Atypical sensory processing and SPD often co-occur with other developmental disorders, such as ASD and attention deficit hyperactivity disorder (ADHD) (Crasta et al., 2020; Little et al., 2018). Researchers debate whether SPD is a distinct disorder or a feature of some developmental disorders (Galiana-Simal et al., 2020). There is a lack of research or agreement about the nature of SPD. It is included as a diagnosis in some diagnostic manuals but not in the *Diagnostic and Statistical Manual of Mental Disorders* (*DSM*) or the *International Statistical Classification of Diseases* (Goodman-Scott & Lambert, 2015). The American Academy of Pediatrics recommends that SPD should not be diagnosed, given the lack of a clear definition (Zimmer & Desch, 2012).

SPD poses social and cognitive risks for children. Children with SPD often have difficulty playing with other children and experience more internalizing problems, such as anxiety and depression (Boterberg & Warreyn, 2016). They experience higher risks for frequent conflict with peers because of their difficulty processing and generating adaptive responses to sensory input (Cosbey et al., 2012). Children with SPD find it harder to make and sustain friendships. They tend to be less aware of other children's social cues and spend more time in solitary play and play that is less mature than their peers. Moreover, parents of children with SPD report higher levels of parental stress than parents of children without sensory deficits (Gourley et al., 2013).

Treatment for SPD involves exposing children to sensory stimuli in a controlled environment. Sensory integration therapy is a specialized treatment to meet a child's specific sensory challenges (Galiana-Simal et al., 2020). Through therapy and play, children are exposed to sensory stimuli and aided in developing coping and problem-solving skills to help them organize sensory input and promote self-regulation and appropriate responses (Critz et al., 2015).

Intellectual Disability

Intellectual disability (ID) is a condition in which an individual has low intellectual functioning, typically defined by an IQ score below 70 (American Psychiatric Association, 2013; Schalock et al., 2021). Individuals with ID display a wide range of functioning. Some individuals have severe disabilities and require constant care. Others with mild delays may as adults live independently, hold jobs, and raise families. About 75% or more of ID cases are mild (Patel et al., 2020). As adults, most people with mild ID can be employed and maintain independence in daily activities. Difficulty in adaptation, modifying behavior in light of situational demands, is essential to a diagnosis of intellectual disability.

The *DSM* identifies three types of adaptive functioning: conceptual, social, and practical. Individuals diagnosed with ID must show deficiencies in at least one type of adaptive functioning:

- Conceptual skills: These are cognitive skills related to thinking, learning, and remembering. They include understanding and using language, reading, writing, counting, telling time, and solving math problems.

- Social skills: These are interpersonal skills, including the ability to follow rules, understand others, make and keep friends, and solve social problems. They include making eye contact, turn taking, and managing conflict.

- Practical skills: These are activities of daily living, including personal care, practicing, safety, having school and work skills, using money, and participating in recreational activities. They include getting dressed, grooming, using the telephone, showing up on time, paying for items at a store, and engaging in hobbies or clubs.

In defining ID, the American Association on Intellectual and Developmental Disabilities emphasizes the degree of support people require in conceptual, social, and practical skills rather than IQ or impairment in adaptive functioning (Schalock et al., 2021). Support may include formal assistance provided by health care providers, mental health professionals, teachers, and professional caregivers or human service agencies. It may also include informal support from family, friends, and community members.

ID has both genetic and contextual influences. Although many cases of intellectual disability have no identifiable cause, genetic and chromosomal disorders, including Down syndrome, some sex-linked disorders, phenylketonuria, and mutation, may be responsible for approximately one fourth to one half of identified intellectual disability cases (Ilyas et al., 2020; Vissers et al., 2016). Contextual influences on intellectual disability include neglect, childbirth trauma, and factors associated with poverty, such as lack of access to health care and poor nutrition (Burack et al., 2021; Patel et al., 2020). Biological and contextual factors tend to interact. Prenatal exposure to teratogens, such as maternal use of alcohol or drugs, malnutrition, or poor prenatal care, influences biological development, which in turn influences the child's ability to adapt to stimuli, and may place the child at risk for experiences that may increase the likelihood of intellectual disability.

A supportive and engaging environment with toys, books, and warm and intellectually stimulating interactions with caregivers during infancy and early childhood, coupled with help and guidance through the school years, can enhance the outcomes of children with intellectual disabilities (Burack et al., 2021; Gorter et al., 2014; Guralnick, 2017). Interventions targeted to the needs of children with mild or moderate disability can help them become independent and, as adults, live autonomously in the community. Support and training in communication skills are important because adults with ID tend to report communication difficulties in work and community settings (Smith et al., 2020). Children with profound disabilities require greater levels of assistance and more consistent care. As adults, people with profound intellectual disabilities often reside in institutional settings that can meet their many needs. However, centers that provide care during the day as well as in-home assistance services, are important alternatives to institutional care, because they are less costly and allow individuals with profound intellectual disabilities to remain with their families in their homes and communities.

Children with intellectual and learning disabilities in mainstreamed classrooms learn alongside their nondisabled peers.

zoranm/Getty Images

Context and Disability: Race and SES

Contextual influences such as access to health resources play a role in the prevalence and treatment of childhood disability. Children in low SES homes are more likely to be diagnosed with neurodevelopmental disabilities than children of high SES (Durkin et al., 2017; Zablotsky et al., 2019, 2020). Disability rates are higher among children in rural communities, which tend to offer fewer health and social services than urban communities (Zablotsky et al., 2019; Zablotsky & Black, 2020).

There are also racial and ethnic differences in diagnoses of developmental disorders that may implicate contextual influences. Non-Hispanic White children are more likely to be diagnosed with ADHD and ASD than non-Hispanic Black and Hispanic children, with Hispanic children being the least likely to be diagnosed. On the other hand, learning disabilities show a different pattern. Non-Hispanic Black children are more likely to be diagnosed with learning disabilities than non-Hispanic White and Hispanic children, with Hispanic children again having the lowest rates of diagnosis (Bax et al., 2019; Zablotsky et al., 2019). Black, Hispanic, and Asian children tend to be diagnosed later than White children, which is concerning, because early diagnosis and intervention can significantly impact developmental outcomes (Barnard-Brak et al., 2021). In general, Black children are less likely to be diagnosed with disabilities than other children. They are also less likely to receive services, highlighting systemic issues that must addressed (Gallegos et al., 2021).

While research has shown racial and socioeconomic disparities in diagnosing developmental disorders, it is important to note that these findings are complex and may not tell the whole story. These differences in diagnoses rates may reflect actual differences in the incidence of these disorders or, perhaps more likely, may instead reflect the impacts of SES, bias, and other societal influences. Black children may experience similar rates of developmental disabilities as White children but may be less likely to be diagnosed (Bax et al., 2019; Morgan et al., 2017). SES and race are intertwined, and families in low SES homes and communities may lack access to professionals who can evaluate and diagnose their children.

Schools in disadvantaged neighborhoods are more likely to be overcrowded, with fewer resources to identify children with special needs. In addition, race and ethnicity may influence how teachers and school staff interpret children's behavior in the classroom, potentially leading to the under-identification of developmental disabilities in Black children. Racial biases about intelligence or academic ability may also play a role in under-identifying Black children for developmental disability screening, and teachers and staff may be unaware of their biases (Slobodin & Masalha, 2020). For example, disruptive behavior in White children may be more likely to be attributed to attentional difficulties, while such behavior in Black children is assumed to be related to learning disabilities or oppositional behavior disorders (Bax et al., 2019; Fadus et al., 2020; Fish, 2019). In this way, White children may be channeled toward assessment for attention problems and be diagnosed with ADHD and Black children to be evaluated for learning disabilities and behavioral problems—both with potentially life-long consequences. Children who are not identified or diagnosed with developmental disabilities or who are mislabeled as problematic or oppositional may miss out on early interventions and support, which can have long-term impacts on their educational and social outcomes.

Giftedness

Giftedness is an aspect of atypical neurodevelopment often overlooked in discussions of developmental differences. The first definition of giftedness came from the psychometric tradition, typically defining giftedness as high intelligence, as indicated by an IQ score of 130 or greater. However, more recent theories, such as the triarchic theory of intelligence and multiple intelligence theory, have expanded the definition of intelligence to include exceptional talents and creativity in various domains, including art, music, creative writing, dance, and sports (Baccassino & Pinnelli, 2023; Mcclain & Pfeiffer, 2012). This broader definition recognizes that giftedness may manifest in many different ways and that gifted individuals may have diverse learning profiles and needs.

Gifted children share several characteristics. First, they have exceptional ability or talent in a particular domain, such as music, math, or another area, that is substantially above average, and they show outstanding performance (Sternberg & Ambrose, 2021). Second, gifted children are passionate about their area of talent. They are highly motivated to create exceptional works and are often deeply engaged in their area of interest. Third, exceptional performance requires creativity. Gifted persons are creative, and gifted individuals are known for their creativity in identifying problems, generating ideas, and applying their knowledge to understand and solve problems and produce original work (Kaufman et al., 2012; Renzulli, 2020). Gifted children require challenging and supportive environments, both at home and in school, with access to stimulating peers and opportunities for further development and exploration of their talents (Baccassino & Pinnelli, 2023). Without encouragement, support, and stimulation, talent may deteriorate, underscoring the importance of nurturing giftedness through appropriate and targeted educational and social interventions.

Despite recent broad definitions of giftedness, most U.S. states still emphasize high IQ or academic performance in identifying children for gifted education (Worrell et al., 2019). Usually, a teacher or parent referral is the first step in identifying a child for gifted services, followed by further assessment, which usually involves an IQ test. Unfortunately, Black children are underrepresented in gifted programs. While they make up about 15% of the U.S. student population, only 9% of students enrolled in gifted programs each year are Black. Compare this to White students, who comprise roughly 50% of students and make up about 60% of those identified as gifted (Pearman & McGee, 2022). The underidentification of giftedness in Black children is due to a complex interplay of factors, including SES differences in homes and communities that affect children's development and learning, such as access to educational resources and the availability of gifted education programs (Ford et al., 2021; Worrell & Dixson, 2022). In addition, biases and misattributions of behavior can also contribute to the mislabeling of developmental disorders in Black children. Finally, recall our discussion of IQ tests and group differences observed in IQ tests.

There are two general approaches to educating gifted children: enrichment and acceleration (Chandra Handa, 2019). The enrichment approach covers the same curriculum as a typical class for children of the student's age but in greater depth, breadth, or difficulty. Students may share the classroom with their average-ability peers and receive enriched content after school, on Saturday, during the summer, or through more challenging assignments (Kim, 2016). In contrast, an accelerated program covers the curriculum at a more advanced pace in conjunction with student mastery. A student might skip grade levels in particular subjects, such as mathematics, or may skip a grade entirely. Both types of education occur in K–12 schools, but school funding plays a role in determining students' opportunities for gifted education.

THINKING IN CONTEXT 8.4

1. Suppose you were a second-grade teacher. What behaviors would you look for to signal a child who may require assessment? Would you look for the same behaviors in boys and girls? Why or why not? What would you look for in older students, such as fifth graders? Describe any similarities and differences.
2. How do contextual factors influence the likelihood of neurodevelopmental conditions, including giftedness? Identify factors in the home, both physical and social, school, and community.

APPLY YOUR KNOWLEDGE

Jayla frowns slightly as she reads the test question: "Which one is not like the others: 'river,' 'mountain,' 'lake,' or 'pool'?" Unsure of the word "pool," she guesses, "Maybe 'mountain,' because it's not water?" Jayla encounters other unfamiliar words in the test, "saucer" and "yacht." She also finds some scenarios confusing, such as questions about skiing and gardening. "This test is really long," she says to herself.

The following afternoon in art class, Jayla shines brightly as she expertly molds clay into an intricate sculpture. At her after-school pottery class, her instructor, Mr. Singh, compliments her, saying, "Incredible detail, Jayla! Your sense of form is outstanding. Let's refine the texture a bit, and you'll create masterpieces."

Later in the week, the school counselor, Ms. Thompson, holds a meeting with the school principal and Jayla's teachers, including Mr. Singh. Ms Thompson begins the discussion, stating, "I wanted to check in with you all about Jayla's performance at school. The scores on her recent intelligence test suggests a significant gap between her verbal and spatial abilities. I'd like to learn more about your experiences with Jayla."

As the teachers take turns sharing their insights, Mr. Singh remarks, "Jayla has an exceptional talent for visual arts." Her science teacher notes, "Jayla keeps up with the class well." Her language arts teacher, however, says cautiously, "Jayla is diligent yet struggles with vocabulary and complex reading tasks."

Reflecting on the feedback, Ms. Thompson concludes, "Jayla's scores suggest lower verbal abilities compared to her spatial skills. Yet her academic performance is solid. Let's keep an eye on her performance in language arts and in tasks that require reading comprehension. I will keep an eye on her, particularly in literacy-heavy subjects." She decides to share these insights with Jayla's parents, saying, "It's important we provide her with the support she might need."

1. Identify reasons why Jayla might be unfamiliar with some words and terms used in the intelligence test. How might tests be modified to be fair to children of all backgrounds? What do you recommend?

2. Why might Jayla have scored higher on the performance scale than the verbal scale? Discuss developmental reasons that might underlie her performance. Are there other possible reasons?

3. How might Jayla's performance be explained using multiple intelligence theory? The triarchic theory of intelligence?

CHAPTER SUMMARY

8.1 Explain five theories of intelligence.

The psychometric approach measures individual differences in traits to explain intelligence. Early theories proposed a single general ability, but more recent theories describe intelligence as a set of specific abilities such as information processing skills. Information processing skills underlie performance in cognitive tasks and are important indicators of intellectual ability evident from birth. The neurological theory points to brain structure and activity and neural efficiency as influences on intelligence. The triarchic theory views intelligence as a set of mental abilities that permits individuals to adapt to any context and consists of analytical, creative, and practical intelligence. Gardner's multiple intelligence theory proposes at least eight independent kinds of intelligence, including bodily-kinesthetic, musical, and interpersonal intelligence. Emotional intelligence emphasizes our ability to adapt to interpersonal and intrapersonal contexts, including our interactions with people and ourselves, and includes the ability to perceive, understand, manage, and respond appropriately to emotions.

8.2 Discuss ways of measuring intelligence in childhood and adolescence.

Group testing allows for the examination of large groups of people and has been used since World War I to assess intellectual abilities and place recruits in appropriate positions. The Cognitive Abilities Test (CogAT) is a commonly used group-administered test for K–12 students that assesses verbal, quantitative, and nonverbal reasoning skills. While group testing is useful for identifying children who may need additional assessment, individually administered tests are important for measuring unique patterns of strengths and weaknesses in cognitive abilities. The Bayley Scales of Infant Development III is a widely used standardized measure of infant intelligence, providing information about neurological health and developmental problems that may require intervention. The Stanford-Binet Intelligence Scale and the Weschler Intelligence tests are commonly used measures of childhood intelligence. Intelligence tests are strong predictors of academic achievement. Long-term intelligence scores shows both stability and change, depending on the individual and context.

8.3 Analyze contextual influences on intelligence.

The development of intelligence is influenced by the sociohistorical context in which people live. The Flynn effect, where intelligence scores increase with each generation, has been attributed to factors such as improvements in education, nutrition, environmental stimulation, and technology. Persistent group differences are found in IQ scores, but contextual factors are thought to account for group differences. SES is a strong predictor of intelligence scores. SES contributes to IQ through differences in nutrition, living conditions, school resources, intellectual stimulation, and life circumstances. Children's awareness of negative stereotypes may lead to stereotype threat and may influence their performance on intelligence tests. IQ tests that rely heavily on verbal tasks are more likely to show ethnic, racial, and SES differences. One way to reduce cultural bias in IQ tests is to include questions that are culture-fair and rely less on verbal measures.

8.4 **Summarize four neurodevelopmental conditions, including the role of contextual factors in disability.**

Developmental scientists have begun to adopt the term *neurodiversity* to describe differences in brain functioning. Autism spectrum disorder (ASD) is a group of neurodevelopmental disorders characterized by deficits in social communication and repetitive behaviors. Specific learning disorders (SLDs) are diagnosed when children demonstrate a measurable discrepancy between aptitude and achievement in a particular academic area given their age, intelligence, and amount of schooling. Dyslexia, a disorder that affects reading, and dyscalculia, a disorder that affects mathematics ability, are the most commonly diagnosed SLDs. Dysgraphia is a disorder that affects writing abilities and is closely related to dyslexia. Intellectual disability (ID) refers to a condition in which an individual has low intellectual functioning and displays deficiencies in at least one type of adaptive functioning. Children in low SES homes are more likely to be diagnosed with neurodevelopmental disabilities than children of high SES, and there are racial and ethnic differences in diagnoses of developmental disorders that may implicate contextual influences. Most U.S. states still emphasize high IQ or academic performance in identifying children for gifted education, and Black children are underrepresented in gifted programs.

KEY TERMS

autism spectrum disorder
developmental disabilities
developmental dyscalculia
developmental dysgraphia
developmental dyslexia
emotional intelligence
intellectual disability
intelligence

intelligence quotient
mental age
multiple intelligence theory
neurodiversity
sensory processing disorder (SPD)
specific learning disorder (SLD)
stereotype threat
triarchic theory of intelligence

Charles Gullung/Getty Images

9 LANGUAGE DEVELOPMENT

> **LEARNING OBJECTIVES**
>
> **9.1** Identify five components of language.
>
> **9.2** Examine patterns of language development during infancy and toddlerhood.
>
> **9.3** Summarize patterns of language development in childhood and adolescence.
>
> **9.4** Contrast nativist, learning, interactionist, and contextual contributors to language development.

Eleven-month-old Luca is wide-eyed as his father rolls a ball to him and says, "Ball!" "Ba!" says Luca. Unlike the random cooing and babbling sounds he made a few months ago, Luca is beginning to show that he understands words. He also tries to say them. By 26 months of age, Luca can express his desires with simple phrases like, "Want milk!" and "Cookie, please." Soon after, his expressions will become more elaborate, and by 3 years of age Luca will hold conversations with his preschool playmates about toys, play, and pretend characters and activities. Luca's growing ability to use words to represent objects, experiences, thoughts, and feelings enables him to think and to communicate with others in increasingly flexible and adaptive ways, transforming his social world and influencing his socioemotional development. In this chapter we examine the dramatic changes in language that occur during infancy and childhood.

FOUNDATIONS OF LANGUAGE

> **9.1** Identify five components of language.

What is language? At its simplest, language is a system of associations between sounds and meaning. Learning language requires learning how to combine a limited number of sounds (or gestures in the case of sign language) according to rules specific to that language.

Language and Development

Language is a powerful social tool that facilitates communication. It allows us to share our ideas and desires with others and learn about other people's thoughts and desires. Infants are naturally inquisitive. They are driven to explore their world, building their understanding. Infants can point, reach, grasp, and hand toys to caregivers, but their communication is limited to nonverbal means. Although they can communicate with gestures and facial expressions, the emergence of language makes new forms of complex and efficient communication and learning possible.

Through language, infants can ask for information, express their curiosity, and seek out new experiences. Caregivers respond differently to infants with language than those who do not have language. They use more words, listen more, and use more sophisticated speech patterns with infants who can talk (Dailey & Bergelson, 2022). These interactions stimulate cognitive and social development as infants learn to use language to explore their world and build relationships with others.

Communication begins well before infants can speak.
miodrag ignjatovic/Getty Images

As young children develop language skills, they become more proficient in communicating with others. They can make friends, share their thoughts and feelings, and display a sense of empathy for others (Brazzelli et al., 2022). Language enables children to comfort others and provide emotional support, building stronger relationships and enhancing social development (Mulvey & Jenkins, 2021).

Components of Language

Infants learn that sounds can signify people, places, and things. Soon they know how to combine sounds to communicate ideas about people, places, and things. As children learn language, they can distinguish its component sounds, combine sounds to form words, combine words to create sentences, and use language to communicate with others. To master language, children must learn to use the five essential components that underlie all languages: phonology, morphology, semantics, syntax, and pragmatics.

Phonology

Phonology refers to the basic units of sounds (known as **phenomes**) used in a given language and the rules for combining them to create meaning (Singleton & Shulman, 2020; Zsiga, 2024). All spoken languages use a finite number of phonemes, with approximately 200 sounds used in all known languages and around 45 sounds used in the English language (Owens, 2020). Each language has its own unique set of phonemes and rules for combining them, known as its phonology.

Infants must learn how to detect, discriminate, and later produce the unique speech sounds used in their language, such as the differences among *b, d,* and *p* sounds. As children continue to develop, they refine their phonological skills and learn to use the different sounds and combinations of sounds to form words and sentences. Nonnative languages often sound strange to us because they often use different speech sounds and combinations that are unfamiliar to us. It is challenging to learn a new language as an adult because we must learn to detect and discriminate new speech sounds and combine them in new ways.

Morphology

As infants attend to and discriminate sounds, learning phonology, they also learn that sounds have meaning. A **morpheme** is the smallest unit of language that has meaning (Ramat, 2021). Some words consist of a single morpheme, such as cat or dog. Others consist of multiple morphemes combined to create more complex meanings. For example, the word *cooked* consists of two morphemes, *cook* and *-ed*. The morpheme *cook* has its own meaning, while the morpheme *-ed* is added to signify that the cooking occurred in the past. This is an example of how morphemes can be combined to change their meaning. The rules for combining morphemes into words are known as **morphology** (Mithun, 2019). It is the structure of words and how they are formed. As children's understanding of morphology advances, they can communicate more effectively and in more sophisticated ways, such as by changing the tense to communicate events in the past.

Syntax

Learning a language involves more than just acquiring a vocabulary. It also involves learning the rules for combining words to form meaningful sentences. **Syntax** refers to the rules that govern how words can be combed to form grammatically correct sentences (Owens, 2020; Singleton & Shulman, 2020). Syntax enables individuals to communicate effectively with others by creating clear and understandable sentences.

For example, consider the following sentences:

A. Dozer bit Freddy.

B. Freddy bit Dozer.

C. Dozer Freddy bit.

A child who understands the basic syntax rules would understand that Sentences A and B have different meanings. They would also recognize that Sentence C is nonsensical because the order of the words does not make grammatical sense.

As children develop their language skills they become more proficient in their understanding of syntax and can use more sophisticated sentence structures to express their ideas and thoughts, conveying different meanings and making their communication more precise and effective. Our understanding of **grammar**, or the combination of morphology and syntax, develops throughout childhood and adolescence.

Semantics

Semantics refers to the meaning or content of words and sentences (Singleton & Shulman, 2020). It involves understanding the relationship between words and their referents in the world around us. Infants' first words and their expanding vocabularies illustrate their growing understanding of semantics. As infants begin to learn language, they associate sounds with specific objects and events in their environment. For example, they may learn to associate the sound *baba* with their bottle or the sound *doggie* with a dog.

As they continue developing their language skills, children expand their vocabularies and learn more advanced concepts and relationships between words. For example, a child may learn the word *happy* and begin to understand that it is associated with positive emotions. They may then use this word to describe their own feelings or to understand the emotions of others. As their understanding of the meaning of words and sentences grows, children become more skilled at using language to express themselves and communicate effectively.

Pragmatics

The final component of language is **pragmatics**—understanding how to use language to communicate effectively (Birner, 2021). It includes understanding the intention that a whispered word or gesture may convey, combining spoken language with body language, detecting the social appropriateness of spoken words, and ensuring that listeners have enough information to understand a message. Five-year-old Destiny knows that she must speak differently, using different words and structures, when talking to her 2-year-old sister than to her older brother. She learns to tailor and edit her speech in light of her audience. Eleven-year-old Marques asks to share a cookie with his friend ("Yo! Gimme a cookie!") using very different language and intonation than he does when asking his grandmother for a cookie ("May I please have a cookie?"). While we begin to show some competence in pragmatics in infancy, our grasp of pragmatics develops well into adolescence and is refined during adulthood (Gerstenberg, 2020; Zufferey, 2020).

Learning to speak a language involves developing each of these parts of speech. Infants begin this process by learning to discriminate, understand, and form sounds for words. They gradually learn the meanings of words and sentences and how to put words together meaningfully. Children also learn how to tailor their speech for the audience and acquire the cultural nuances reflected in their language. Children accomplish this in just a few years—an astonishing feat.

THINKING IN CONTEXT 9.1

1. Describe a complex activity, such as how to ride a bike, cook a particular dish, or play a challenging video game.
2. Imagine that you had to explain this activity to a child. Would your approach or language change? If so, how?
3. What if your audience were teenagers? How would your explanation differ?
4. How would your explanation change if your audience were experts?

LANGUAGE DEVELOPMENT IN INFANCY AND TODDLERHOOD

> **9.2** Examine patterns of language development during infancy and toddlerhood.

"You just love to hear Mommy talk, don't you?" Velma asked as newborn Jayson stared up at her. Is Jayson attending to his mother? Is he interested in his mother's speech? As described in Chapter 4, hearing emerges well before birth, and evidence suggests that newborns can recall sounds heard in the womb (Henriques et al., 2022). Jayson recognizes his mother's voice and naturally tunes in, which will help him learn language, a critical task for infancy and toddlerhood. Language development has important implications for the child's cognitive, social, and emotional development. Gaining the ability to use words to represent objects, experiences, thoughts, and feelings permits children to think and communicate with others in increasingly flexible and adaptive ways.

Early Preferences for Speech Sounds

Newborn infants are primed to learn language. Recall from Chapter 4 that neonates naturally attend to speech and prefer to hear human speech sounds, especially their native language, as well as stories and sounds they heard prenatally (Henriques et al., 2022; Movalled et al., 2023). Infants naturally notice the complex patterns of sounds around them and organize sounds into meaningful units (Saffran, 2020). They recognize frequently heard words, such as their names. By 4.5 months of age, infants recognize their names and will turn their heads to hear their own names but not others, even when the other names have a similar sound pattern (e.g., Annie and Johnny) (Mandel et al., 1995). Four- to 6-month-old infants tend to pay particular attention to vowel sounds, and, toward the end of the first year, consonants (Chládková & Paillereau, 2020).

Although infants can perceive and discriminate sounds that comprise all human languages at birth, their developing capacities and preferences are influenced by context (Gervain, 2022; Hoff et al., 2022). The Japanese language does not discriminate between the consonant sounds of *r* in rip and *l* in lip. Japanese adults learning English find it very difficult to discriminate between the English pronunciations of these *r* and *l* sounds, yet until about 6 to 8 months of age, Japanese and U.S. infants are equally able to distinguish these sounds. By 10 to 12 months, however, discrimination of *r* and *l* improves for U.S. infants and declines for Japanese infants. This likely occurs because U.S. infants hear these sounds often, whereas Japanese infants do not (Kuhl et al., 2006). As they are exposed to their native language, they become more attuned to the sounds (and distinctions between sounds) that are meaningful in their own language and less able to distinguish speech sounds that are not used in that language (Nallet & Gervain, 2021; Reh et al., 2021).

Despite infants' growing preferences for speech sounds they hear often, infants' speech discrimination abilities remain malleable (Kuhl, 2016). In one study, 9-month-old English-learning American infants engaged in 12 interactive sessions with an adult speaker of Mandarin Chinese over the course of 4 to 5 weeks (Kuhl et al., 2003). After the sessions, the infants were tested on a Mandarin phonetic contrast that does not occur in English. The infants discriminated the contrast as well as same-aged Mandarin-learning infants and retained the contrast for several days. The relevance of context is also illustrated by the infants' loss of the ability to discriminate the Mandarin contrast several days after training, presumably without ongoing exposure to the Mandarin language (Fitneva & Matsui, 2015).

Social input, such as the quality of caregiver-infant interactions, plays a critical role in the timing of infants' narrowing of speech sound discrimination. Specifically, infants who experience high-quality interactions with their caregivers, characterized by frequent speech and contingent social feedback, show a narrowing earlier, as early as 6 months of age (Elsabbagh et al., 2013; Kuhl, 2021). We discuss caregiver-infant interactions later in this chapter.

Speech discrimination is associated with language development. Native-language discrimination ability between 6 and 7 months predicts the rate of language growth between 11 and 30 months

(Kuhl, 2015; Uhler et al., 2022). In addition, speech discrimination at 11 months is associated with spoken grammar at 6 years of age as well as the risk of developing speech-language disorders (Zhao et al., 2021).

Prelinguistic Communication

At birth, crying is the infant's only means of communication. Infants soon learn to make many more sounds, like gurgles, grunts, and squeals. Between 2 and 3 months of age, infants begin **cooing**, making deliberate vowel sounds like *ahhhh*, *ohhhh*, and *eeeee*. Infants' first coos sound like one long vowel. These vocal sounds are a form of vocal play; they are likely to be heard when babies are awake, alert, and contented. At the cooing stage, infants already use pauses consistent with spoken conversation's turn-taking pattern. With age, the quality of coos changes to include different vowel-like sounds and combinations of vowel-like sounds (Owens, 2020). **Babbling**, repeating strings of consonants and vowels, such as "ba-ba-ba" and "ma-ma-ma," begins to appear at about 6 months of age.

At first, babbling is universal. All babies do it, and the sounds they make are similar no matter what language their parents speak or in what part of the world they are raised. But infants soon become sensitive to the ambient language around them, and it influences their vocalizations (Quam & Roberts, 2023). In one study, French adults listened to the babbling of a French 8-month-old and a second 8-month-old from either an Arabic-speaking or a Cantonese-speaking family. Nearly three quarters of the time, the adults correctly indicated which baby in the pair was French (Boysson-Bardies et al., 1984). By the end of the first year, infants' babbling sounds more like real speech, because they begin to vary the pitch of their speech in ways that reflect the inflections of their native languages (Andruski et al., 2013).

In spoken English, declarative sentences are characterized by a pitch that falls toward the end of the sentence, whereas in questions, the pitch rises at the end of the sentence. Older babies' babbling mirrors these patterns when they are raised by English-speaking parents, while babies reared with Japanese or French as their native languages show intonation patterns similar to those of the respective languages (Levitt et al., 1992). Longitudinal observations of infants raised in Catalan-speaking environments likewise show that their babbling shifts to mirror intonations in native speech (Esteve-Gilbert et al., 2013).

Language acquisition is a socially interactive process: Babies learn by hearing others speak and noticing the reactions that their vocalizations evoke in caregivers (Kuhl, 2016; Quam & Roberts, 2023). Social interaction elicits vocalizations, and infants modify their babbling in response to caregiver interactions (Zhang et al., 2024). As caregivers respond to infants' babbling, infants restructure their babbling, changing the phonological pattern of sounds in response to their caregivers' infant-directed speech (Lopez et al., 2020). By 10 months, babble sounds match what infants see and hear (Laing & Bergelson, 2020). Babbling repertoires reflect infants' developing morphology and are a foundation for word learning (Ramsdell et al., 2012).

Putting Words Together

Language development follows a predictable pattern, from prelinguistic communication to learning words to stringing words together to communicate with others.

First Words

Eleven-month-old Jervan's mother hands him his bottle. "Here's your bottle." "Ba!" Jarvan says with delight. Jervan now understands many words and is beginning to try to utter them. Throughout language development, babies' **receptive language** (what they can understand) exceeds their **productive language** (what they can produce themselves) (Tamis-Lemonda & Bornstein, 2015). That is, infants understand more words than they can use. Research suggests that infants may understand some commonly spoken words as early as 6 to 9 months of age, long before they can speak (Bergelson & Swingley, 2012; Dehaene-Lambertz & Spelke, 2015). Infants' vocalizations at 6 months predict their receptive language at 12 months (Werwach et al., 2021).

At about 1 year of age, infants, on average, speak their first word. At first, infants use one-word expressions, called **holophrases**, to express complete thoughts. A first word might be a complete word or a syllable. Usually, the word has more than one meaning, depending on the context in which it is used. "Da" might mean "I want that," "There's Daddy!" or "What's that?" Caregivers usually hear and understand first words before other adults do. The first words infants use are those they hear often or are meaningful for them, such as their name, the word no, or the word for their caregiver. Infants reared in English-speaking homes tend to use nouns first, because they are concrete and easily understood (Waxman et al., 2013). The word *dog* refers to a specific thing—an animal—and is easier to understand than a verb, such as *goes*. In contrast, infants reared in homes in which Japanese, Korean, or Mandarin Chinese is spoken tend to learn verbs very early in their development in response to the greater emphasis on verbs in their native languages (Waxman et al., 2013).

Regardless of what language a child speaks, early words tend to be used in the following ways (MacWhinney, 2015; Owens, 2020):

- Request or state the existence or location of an object or person by naming it (car, dog, outside).
- Request or describe the recurrence of an event or receipt of an object (again, more).
- Describe actions (eat, fall, ride).
- Ask questions (What? That?).
- Attribute a property to an object (hot, big).
- Mark social situations, events, and actions (no, bye).

Learning Words

"I can't believe how quickly Matthew picks up new words. It's time for us to be more careful about what we say around him," warned Elana. Her husband agreed, "He's only two years old and has quite a vocabulary. Who would think that he'd learn so many words so quickly?" By 13 months of age, children begin to quickly learn the meaning of new words and understand that words correspond to particular things or events (Woodward et al., 1994). Most infants of Matthew's age expand their vocabularies rapidly, often to the surprise of their parents. Infants learn new words through **fast mapping**, a process of quickly acquiring and retaining a word after hearing it applied a few times (Kan & Kohnert, 2008; Marinellie & Kneile, 2012).

Infants learn to map names with objects before their first birthday and before they produce language (Clerkin & Smith, 2022). Word learning is linked with social development. At about 7–8 months, infants begin pointing to objects, directing their attention and their caregiver's attention, and initiating social interaction, which leads to learning new words (Moore et al., 2019). Infants learn more about objects and are more likely to link words with objects in the presence of eye gaze cues when both the infant and speaker attend to the object when the infant hears the new word (Çetinçelik et al., 2021).

Older infants get better at using social information to learn words, and they accumulate a larger vocabulary, which aids in word learning (Bergelson, 2020). Two-year-olds can learn a word even after a single brief exposure under ambiguous conditions or after overhearing a speaker use the word when talking to someone else (Remon et al., 2020; Spiegel & Halberda, 2011). Between 24 and 30 months, infants can learn new words even when their attention is distracted by other objects or events (Moore et al., 1999). Children's knowledge and interests influence their vocabulary development. They are more likely to learn words that are related to those they know and label objects, actions, and events that they find interesting (Mani & Ackermann, 2018).

Interestingly, not all children engage in fast mapping to the same extent. Children's individual differences in traits, such as shyness and approachability, are associated with the effective use of fast mapping. In novel situations, children who are shy do not attend to objects as much as other children, whereas children who score high in measures of approachability spend more time focusing on objects (Axelsson et al., 2022; M. Hilton et al., 2019). Children must focus their attention on objects to learn their names.

Fast mapping improves with age and accounts for the **vocabulary spurt**—a rapid vocabulary learning period between 16 and 24 months of age (Owens, 2020). During this period, infants apply their word-learning strategies to learn multiple words of varying difficulty seemingly at once. Within weeks, infants increase their vocabulary from 50 words to over 400 (Bates et al., 1988). As shown in Figure 9.1, infants vary in the speed of word acquisition, with some showing a rapid increase in vocabulary before others (Samuelson & McMurray, 2017). In addition, although fast mapping helps infants learn many new words, their own speech lags behind what they can understand because young children have difficulty retrieving words from memory (Owens, 2020). The speed with which infants learn new words during the vocabulary spurt predicts their vocabulary size as preschoolers (Rowe, 2012). Infants who rapidly expand their knowledge of words during the vocabulary spurt tend to have larger vocabularies in preschool than their peers, who acquire new words at a slower pace.

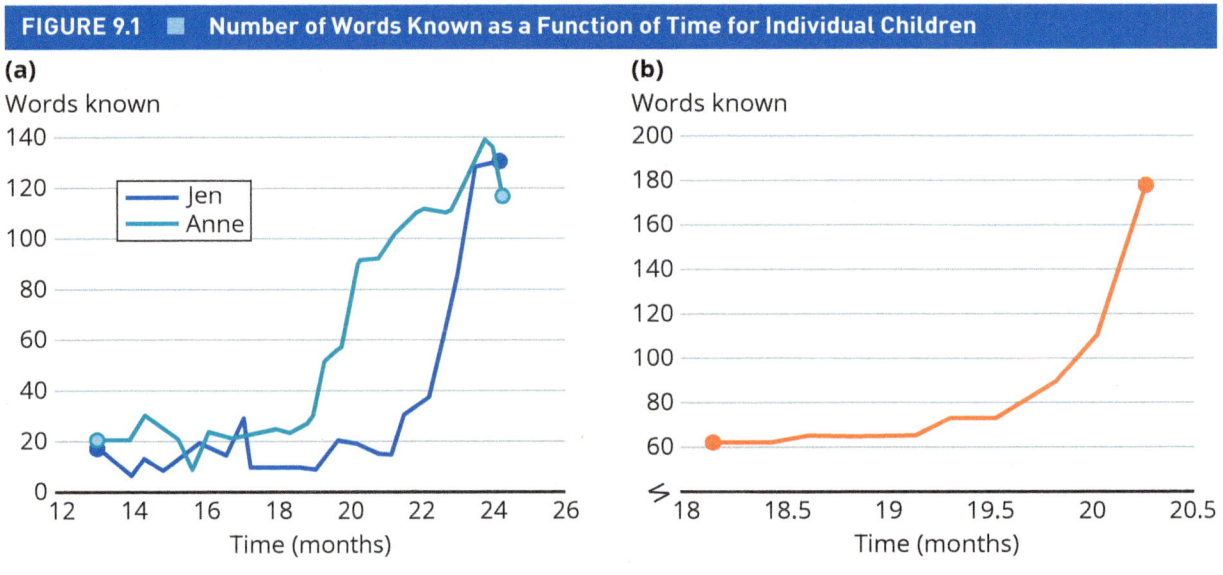

FIGURE 9.1 ■ Number of Words Known as a Function of Time for Individual Children

Source: Samuelson, L. K., & McMurray, B. (2017). What does it take to learn a word? *Wiley Interdisciplinary Reviews: Cognitive Science, 8*(1–2), e1421. https://doi.org/10.1002/wcs.1421

As children learn words, we see two interesting kinds of mistakes that tell us about how words are acquired. **Underextension** refers to applying a word more narrowly than it is usually applied, so the word's use is restricted to a single object. The word *cup* might refer to Daddy's cup but not to the general class of cups. Later, the opposite tendency appears. **Overextension** refers to applying a word too broadly. Cow might refer to cows, sheep, horses, and all farm animals. Overextension suggests that the child has learned that a word can signify a whole class of objects. As children develop a larger vocabulary and get feedback on their speech, they demonstrate fewer errors of overextension and underextension (Brooks & Kempe, 2014; Ferreira Pinto & Xu, 2021).

Two-Word Utterances

At about 21 months of age, or usually about 8 to 12 months after they say their first word, most children compose their first simple two-word sentences, such as "Kitty come" or "Mommy milk." These utterances are known as **telegraphic speech** and use a few precise words to express a thought. Like other milestones in language development, telegraphic speech is universal among toddlers. Children around the world use two-word phrases to express themselves. It is worth noting that telegraphic speech does not completely replace holophrases. Children continue to produce holophrases in addition to telegraphic speech and continue to produce utterances of varying lengths as they acquire more advanced speech (Xu et al., 2023).

Language development follows a predictable path. Children between 20 and 30 months of age begin to follow the rules for forming sentences in a given language. Soon they become more comfortable with using plurals, past tense, articles (e.g., *a* and *the*), prepositions (e.g., *in* and *on*), and conjunctions (e.g., *and* and *but*). By 2.5 years of age, children demonstrate an awareness of the communicative purpose of speech and the importance of being understood (Owens, 2020). In one experiment, 2.5-year-old children asked an adult to hand them a toy. Children were more likely to repeat and clarify their request when the adult's verbal response indicated misunderstanding ("Did you say to put the toy on the shelf?") than when the adult appeared to understand the request (Shwe & Markman, 1997).

Infant Gesture

Infants can communicate through simple gestures, such as pointing and nodding, before they can speak (Vallotton et al., 2017). Using gestures and joint attention, directing an adult's attention to an object, predicts later vocabulary development (Cameron-Faulkner, 2020; Cameron-Faulkner et al., 2021; Rowe et al., 2022). Infants' pointing also predicts their language development (Kirk et al., 2022).

Although signing may not accelerate language development, it offers opportunities for parent-infant interaction and play.

SDI Productions/istock

Infants' early use of gestures has led scientists to explore using symbolic gestures, or "baby signing," as a means of communication (Goodwyn & Acredolo, 1998). Baby signing programs, including videos, classes, books, and cue cards, became popular among parents, claiming they could accelerate language development and improve parent-child relationships (Nelson et al., 2012). However, a review of research studies on baby signing programs found methodological weaknesses, such as a lack of control groups or no random assignment, that hindered drawing conclusions (Johnston, 2005). In a longitudinal study, 8-month-old infants were randomly assigned to one of three groups: baby sign training, verbal training, or non-intervention. At 20 months of age, language development was similar for all infants, regardless of their group, indicating that baby signing did not accelerate language development (Kirk et al., 2013).

While baby-signing programs may lack scientific support for accelerating language development, they may promote frequent parent-infant interaction, which can contribute to cognitive, language, and social development (Mueller & Sepulveda, 2014; Zammit & Atkinson, 2017). However, a recent study observed infants at 4, 7, and 11 months of age and found that vocalizations outnumbered gestures at all ages, suggesting that gestures are less common than thought (Burkhardt-Reed et al., 2021). Rich infant-caregiver interactions are essential for early development, and if baby signing is helpful in parents' estimation and does not rush or pressure infants, there is no reason to discourage its use.

Language Development in Bilingual Infants

We have seen that, from birth, infants attend to speech sounds. Through exposure to speech, they rapidly tune into the language they hear, learning the sounds that comprise their language. How, then, is language learning influenced by exposure to two languages? Brain scans suggest that 12-month-old bilingual infants' responses to language are similar to those of monolingual infants, suggesting that they are on the same timetable for language learning (Ferjan Ramírez et al., 2017). Notably, bilingual infants retain the ability to discriminate phonetic speech sounds of other languages long after monolingual peers have narrowed their perception to native language sounds (Sebastian-Galles & Santolin, 2020).

Language development is promoted through exposure to speech during frequent, high-quality social interactions. The proportion of each language bilingual infants hear can vary day to day, depending on who is caring for them and the proportion of infant-directed versus other-directed speech they hear (Orena et al., 2020). In bilingual babies, the amount of infant-directed speech heard in one-to-one interactions influences the growth of that language but is unrelated to the growth of the second language (De Houwer et al., 2018). For example, hearing lots of high-quality Spanish in interactions with a caregiver predicts the growth of Spanish but not English. Whether in one language or two, language growth is related to the quality and quantity of infant-directed speech they hear (Gámez et al., 2023; Kalashnikova & Carreiras, 2022).

Typically infants exposed to two languages from birth babble and produce their first words at the same age as those exposed to one language. Bilingual infants' vocabulary develops similarly to monolingual infants (Höhle et al., 2020; Ramirez & Kuhl, 2016). Although bilingual infants show a smaller vocabulary than monolingual infants in a single language, combined across both languages, bilingual children's vocabulary tends to be equal to or greater than monolingual children's (Byers-Heinlein et al., 2024).

Trilingual infants—those exposed to three languages—show a similar pattern whereby growth in each language is related to input quantity and quality (Côté et al., 2022). Some research suggests bilingual infants learn new words better than their monolingual peers (Singh et al., 2018). Their exposure to the sounds of multiple languages contributes to their ability to flexibly learn new sounds. In sum, language development is influenced by interactions with expert speakers. This is true whether learning one, two, three, or more languages.

Language Development in Deaf Infants

About 2 out of 1,000 U.S. infants are born with profound hearing loss, which can put them at risk for impaired language development (Centers for Disease Control, 2019). Infants are sensitive to language from birth, so early intervention is crucial for deaf infants to achieve positive language outcomes. Universal neonatal hearing screening and early intervention to promote access to visual and/or spoken language are now standard policies in almost all industrialized countries (Lederberg et al., 2013; National Center for Hearing Assessment and Management, 2019). Research has shown that language outcomes improve dramatically when hearing loss is identified at birth and intervention is implemented by 6 months of age (Cole & Flexer, 2016).

Infants with hearing loss usually wear hearing aids, and those with profound hearing loss may eventually receive cochlear implants, which convert auditory information into electrical signals that are transmitted to the brain. While the U.S. Food and Drug recommends cochlear implantation after 12 months of age, research suggests that earlier implantation, before 9 months and even as early as 6 months of age, is safe and can lead to better language outcomes (C. Chen et al., 2023; Deep et al., 2021; Karltorp et al., 2020). However, early implantation may not be covered by health insurance, limiting access to early intervention for families with lower incomes (X. Liu et al., 2021).

Hearing loss in infancy can limit infants' sensory input and disrupt social interactions with caregivers, which can affect cognitive skills such as memory, attention, learning, and information processing—all essential for speech and language development (Kronenberger & Pisoni, 2018; Morgan et al., 2021). Early auditory deprivation may affect brain development and reduce the neurological ability to detect and respond to speech signals, making it difficult for children to learn language (Wang et al., 2018). Sensory deprivation at birth can have dramatic effects on the organization of the brain, which can interfere with its normal development (see Chapter 4).

Interventions to promote language development in infants with hearing loss focus on empowering parents, improving the parent-child relationship, and increasing parents' knowledge about their infants' abilities and communication skills, such as by encouraging child-directed speech (Wright et al., 2021). These interventions are successful in promoting school readiness (Meinzen-Derr et al., 2020). Infants' outcomes are influenced by contextual factors such as the availability and use of family support from professionals, access to sign language instruction and the ability of family members to learn sign language, and access to professional services and technology (Lederberg et al., 2013). Children with hearing loss may be especially sensitive to variations in environmental quality, such as the quality and quantity of caregiver interactions (Levine et al., 2016). Engaging and responsive infant-directed speech, gestures, and touching can help infants interact with and develop a warm and supportive bond with caregivers who can support their development (Yoshinaga-Itano et al., 2020).

> **THINKING IN CONTEXT 9.2**
>
> 1. Recall from Chapter 1 that domains of development interact. How might other types of development, such as cognitive, motor, and perceptual skills, influence language development in infancy? How might infants' emerging language skills influence development in other domains?
> 2. Infants are primed to learn language and play an active role in their language development. Explain and provide examples considering dual-language learners, deaf infants, or infant gesture.

LANGUAGE DEVELOPMENT IN CHILDHOOD AND ADOLESCENCE

9.3 Summarize patterns of language development in childhood and adolescence.

Language is refined throughout childhood and continues to change in subtle ways into adolescence. Early childhood is a particularly important time for language learning.

Early Childhood

Toddlers tend to use telegraphic speech, but their language development continues quickly. Young children learn to use multiple elements of speech, such as plurals, adjectives, and the past tense. Children's vocabulary and grammar become dramatically more complex during early childhood, enabling them to communicate and think in new ways.

Vocabulary

By the age of 3, the average child has a vocabulary of 900 to 1,000 words. Vocabulary acquisition continues at a rapid pace. Children tend to learn words that they often hear, especially those that label things and events that interest them or that they encounter in meaningful contexts (Ackermann et al., 2020; Mani & Ackermann, 2018). By age 6, most children have a vocabulary of about 14,000 words, meaning they learn a new word every 1 to 2 hours every day (Owens, 2020). Most 5-year-olds can quickly understand and apply most words that they hear, especially when used in context or explained with examples. Preschoolers acquire words by making inferences given the context—and inferential learning is associated with better retention than learning through direct instruction (Zosh et al., 2013).

Children continue to use fast mapping as a strategy to quickly learn the meaning of a new word after hearing it once or twice in a specific context (Kucker et al., 2015). As they gain experience, they get better at fast mapping new words. In addition to fast mapping, children also apply other strategies to learning words. **Logical extension**, for instance, is a strategy children use to extend a word to other objects in the same category (Owens, 2020). When learning that a dog with spots is called a Dalmatian, a child may refer to a Dalmatian bunny (a white bunny with black spots) or a Dalmatian horse. Children learn to make words their own and apply them to all the situations they want to discuss (Behrend et al., 2001).

At about age 3, children demonstrate the **mutual exclusivity assumption** in learning new words: They assume that objects have only one label or name and a new word is assumed to be a label for an unfamiliar object rather than a synonym or second label for a familiar object (Lewis et al., 2020). When young children were shown one familiar object and one unfamiliar object and were asked to identify the object referred to by a nonsense syllable, the children reached for the unfamiliar object, indicating that they expect new words to label new objects; they do not expect synonyms (Markman & Wachtel, 1988). Similarly, young children use the mutual exclusivity assumption to learn the names of different parts of objects, such as the brim of a hat, the cab of a truck, or a bird's beak (M. B. Hansen & Markman, 2009). Four- and 5-year-old children get better at selectively applying the mutual exclusivity principle, understanding that a given object can have multiple labels (Kalashnikova et al., 2016;

Lewis et al., 2020). In the absence of social cues indicating otherwise, preschoolers use a familiar object as a cue leading them to match a novel object with a novel word (Yildiz, 2020).

Preschoolers can learn words from watching educational videos, but they tend to learn more during video chats with adults and even more during in-person interactions (Samudra et al., 2022; Tsuji et al., 2021). Children learn best with parents, teachers, siblings, and peers in in-person interactive contexts. Effective learning contexts include turn taking, joint attention, and scaffolding experiences that provide hints about the meaning of new words (Anderson et al., 2021; Donnelly & Kidd, 2021; MacWhinney, 2015). Vocabulary instruction during storybook time and class discussion helps preschoolers learn new words (Madsen et al., 2022). Children exposed to high-quality learning environments at age 3, characterized by responsive adults, extended talk, and scaffolding of children's conversations, show higher verbal ability at age 5 (J. E. Hansen & Broekhuizen, 2021). Young children's language development has far reaching effects. Expressive vocabulary during the first 3 years of life is associated with language ability in high school at age 15 (Dale et al., 2023).

Syntax and Pragmatics

Young children quickly learn to combine words into sentences in increasingly sophisticated ways that follow the rules of syntax or grammar (de Villiers & de Villiers, 2014). Three-year-old children tend to use plurals (cats), possessives (cat's), and past tense (walked) (Park et al., 2012). They also tend to understand pronouns such as *I, you*, and *we*.

Like telegraphic speech, young children's sentences are short, leaving out words like *a* and *the*. However, their speech is more sophisticated than telegraphic speech because they include some pronouns, adjectives, and prepositions. Four- and 5-year-olds use four- to five-word sentences and can express declarative, interrogative, and imperative sentences (Turnbull & Justice, 2016). Context influences the acquisition of syntax. Four-year-old children will use more complex sentences with multiple clauses, such as "I'm resting because I'm tired," if their parents use such sentences (Huttenlocher et al., 2002). Children often use run-on sentences, in which ideas and sentences are strung together. Parental conversations and support for language learning are associated with faster and more correct language use (MacWhinney, 2015). Teachers' use of advanced syntax during instructional activities and interactions predicts preschoolers' and kindergarteners' vocabulary (Farrow et al., 2020)

"See? I goed on the slide!" called out Leona. **Overregularization errors** such as Leona's are very common in young children. They occur because young children are still learning exceptions to grammatical rules and are applying grammatical rules too stringently (Owens, 2020). For example, one rule is to add *s* to a word to create a plural noun. But there are many exceptions to this rule. Overregularization is expressed when children refer to *foots, gooses, tooths*, and *mouses*, illustrating that the child understands and applies the rules. Adult speakers find this usage awkward, but it is actually a sign of the child's increasing grammatical sophistication. And despite all the common errors young children make, one study of 3-year-olds showed that nearly three quarters of their utterances were grammatically correct. The most common error was in making tenses (e.g., *eat/eated, fall/falled*) (Eisenberg et al., 2012). By the end of the preschool years, most children use syntax appropriately and confidently.

In addition to improvements in vocabulary and syntax, children demonstrate a greater understanding of the pragmatics of language, how to use language to communicate effectively (Owens, 2020). Young children engage the people around them in conversation. They get better at conversational turn taking, alternating between listening and speaking. Parents often marvel at the sophistication of their "baby's" thoughts. Young children carry on conversations about objects, their surroundings, and their feelings. The content of their conversations is limited by their cognitive skills, especially egocentrism. Young children find it difficult to take another's perspective. As children's ability to think ahead and consider the future improves, they can increasingly talk about things that have not yet happened, such as a trip or party. Preschoolers recognize the need to adjust their speech to their conversational partner, such as by speaking more simply to a toddler sibling than a peer or an adult.

Bilingual Language Learning

We have seen that infants who are exposed to two languages tend to build distinct language systems from birth (MacWhinney, 2015). The pace of learning two languages is influenced by various factors, such as the degree to which the two languages differ, how often the child hears each language, and how clearly the speakers enunciate speech sounds (Pace et al., 2021; Werker, 2012).

Young children who are bilingual typically have words in both languages for the same thing, which goes against the mutual exclusivity assumption that characterizes monolingual vocabulary learning (Nicoladis & Laurent, 2020). For instance, a bilingual child might say "all done" in English and "*pau*" in Hawaiian. In contrast, monolingual children learn synonyms for words much later (Littschwager & Markman, 1994). This difference suggests that bilingual children know that the words are part of two separate language systems and that a label is appropriate to a specific language. Children whose parents value bilingualism and retaining a first language are more likely to receive support for two languages at home (Mak et al., 2023).

Bilingual young children also learn two sets of rules for combining words and do not mix grammatical rules for the two languages. For example, bilingual children learning French and German do not incorrectly use German words with French syntax or vice versa (Meisel, 1989). Moreover, they tend to select the appropriate language to use and adjust their communication with their partner, which suggests that they are aware that they know two languages and that others may not (Gampe et al., 2019).

Bilingual children's language development typically follows the path of each language, including the pattern of vocabulary and grammatical development and is influenced by the quantity and quality of the input in each language (Hoff, 2020; Parra et al., 2011). Similar to findings with infants, when each language is measured separately, bilingual young children tend to lag behind their monolingual peers in vocabulary and grammar in each language, but their combined vocabularies for both languages tend to be similar in size to the vocabulary of monolingual children (see Figure 9.2; Hindman & Wasik, 2015; Hoff et al., 2012). Recent research has extended this finding to older children, 6–13 years old, where the gap between monolingual and bilingual Norwegian children was reduced or disappeared when vocabulary in both languages was measured (Monsrud et al., 2022). Still other research suggests that the total vocabulary growth in bilingual children may be even greater than that of monolinguals (Bialystok, 2020; Hoff et al., 2014). Children who learn more than one language tend to be oriented toward and detect novelty—new sounds, words, and syntax—which challenges and likely promotes the development of attention and working memory processes—and contributes to advances in language development (Kuzyk et al., 2020; Singh, 2021).

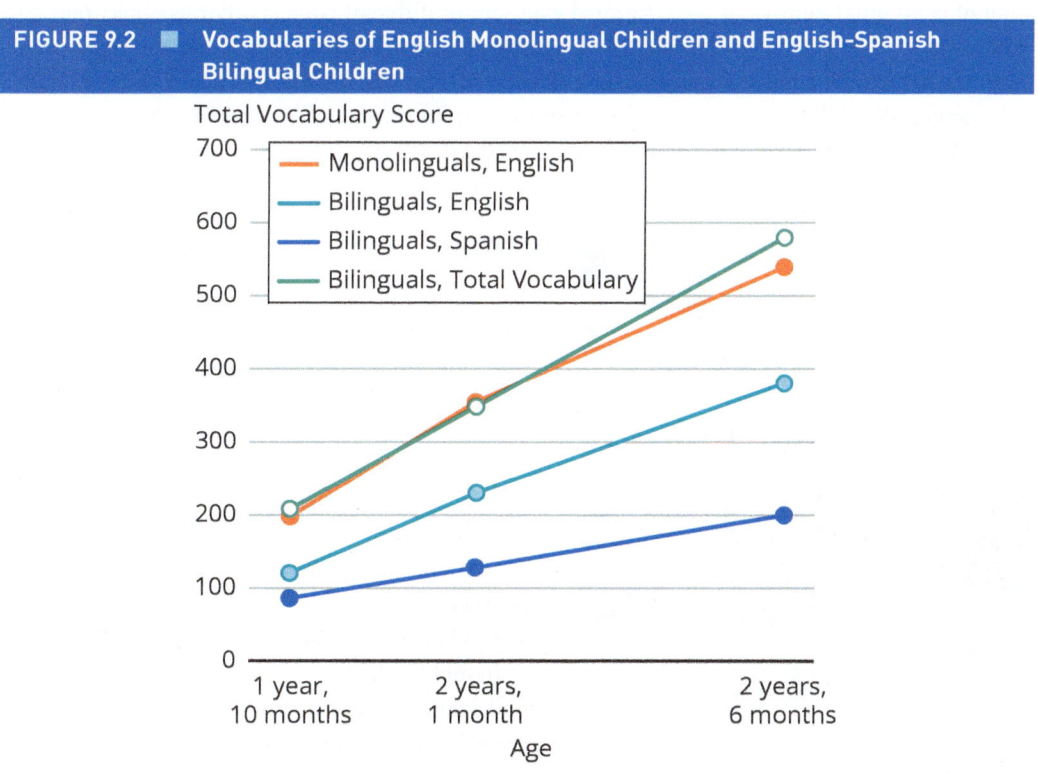

FIGURE 9.2 ■ Vocabularies of English Monolingual Children and English-Spanish Bilingual Children

Source: Adapted from Hoff, E., Core, C., Place, S., Rumiche, R., Señor, M., & Parra, M. (2012). Dual language exposure and early bilingual development. *Journal of Child Language, 39*(1), 1–27. https://doi.org/10.1017/S0305000910000759

School-Age Children and Adolescents

School-age children expand their vocabulary and develop a more sophisticated understanding of grammar, rules that permit combining words to express ideas and feelings. Children's knowledge of pragmatics, how language is used in everyday contexts, grows and becomes more sophisticated during middle childhood. Advances in cognition, especially working memory, executive function, and attention, play a role in children's language development (Chow et al., 2021; Hill & Wagovich, 2020).

Vocabulary

School-age children's increases in vocabulary are not as noticeable to parents as the changes that occurred in infancy and early childhood. Nevertheless, 6-year-old children's vocabularies expand by four times by the end of the elementary school years and six times by the end of formal schooling (Clark, 2017). When they encounter ambiguous words that might refer to multiple objects, children, like adults, seek additional information, and in laboratory settings, choose additional training (Zettersten & Saffran, 2021). Most words that children encounter relate to already known words; children learn these words more quickly than ambiguous words and, when compared with adults, retain them as well (Floyd & Goldberg, 2021).

Children learn that many words can describe a given action, but the words often differ slightly in meaning (e.g., walk, stride, hike, march, tread, strut, and meander) (Hoff, 2016). They become more selective in using words, choosing the right word to meet their needs. As their vocabularies grow, children learn that some words can have more than one meaning, such as run ("The jogger runs down the street," "The clock runs fast," etc.). They begin to appreciate that some words have psychological meanings as well as physical ones (e.g., a person can be smooth, and a surface can be smooth). This understanding that words can be used in more than one way leads 8- to 10-year-old children to understand similes and metaphors (e.g., a person can be described as "cold as ice" or "sharp as a tack") (Katz, 2017).

Everyday experiences shape our vocabulary, how we think, and how we speak. Words are often acquired incidentally from speaking with others and reading rather than through explicit vocabulary instruction. Reading is a primary source of vocabulary expansion in school-age children (Sparapani et al., 2018; Wasik et al., 2016). Some complex words, such as scientific terms, require the acquisition of conceptual knowledge over repeated exposure in different contexts. For example, one study examined 4- to 10-year-old children's knowledge of two scientific terms, eclipse and comet, before and after the natural occurrence of a solar eclipse. Two weeks after the solar eclipse and without additional instruction, the children showed improvement in their knowledge of eclipses but not comets; older and younger children did not differ in their knowledge (Best et al., 2006). Similar to infancy and early childhood, older children learn words through exposure.

Language skills open the door to new opportunities, such as reading, which in turn is associated with advances in cognitive and language development.

FatCamera/istock

Grammar

Older children become increasingly aware of and knowledgeable about the nature and qualities of language, known as **metalinguistic awareness** (Melogno et al., 2022; Simard & Gutiérrez, 2018). Language arts classes in elementary school teach children about the parts of language and the syntax of sentences, aiding children as they further develop their ability to think about their use of language. By 8 years of age, children can analyze the grammatical acceptability of their utterances and spontaneously self-correct many of their errors (Hanley et al., 2016).

In middle childhood, school children better understand grammatical structures. They begin to use the passive voice ("The dog is being fed"), the auxiliary *have* ("I have already fed the dog"), and conditional sentences ("If I had been home earlier, I would have fed the dog")

(Clark, 2017). Despite these advances, school-age children often have difficulty understanding spoken sentences, of which the meaning depends on subtle shifts in intonation (Turnbull & Justice, 2016). An example can be found in the sentence, "John gave a lollipop to David, and he gave one to Bob." With the emphasis placed on *and*, the sentence can be taken to mean that John gave a lollipop to both David and Bob; whereas if the emphasis is on *he*, the sentence can be assumed to mean that John gave a lollipop to David, and David gave a lollipop to Bob.

Experience with language and exposure to varied constructions influence grammatical development. Most English-speaking children find passive-voice sentences (e.g., "The boy was struck by the car") difficult to understand and therefore, master passive-voice sentences later than other structures (Armon-Lotem et al., 2016). In contrast, the Inuit children of Arctic Canada hear and speak the Inuktitut language, which emphasizes full passives; they produce passive voice sentences in their language sooner than children from other cultures (Allen & Crago, 1996). The culture and language systems in which children are immersed influence their use of language and, ultimately, how they communicate. Throughout middle childhood, sentence structure and use of grammar become more sophisticated, children become better at communicating their ideas, and their understanding of pragmatics improves. Metalinguistic awareness and improvements in grammar influence reading comprehension and academic achievement (Hung & Loh, 2021; Prentza, 2021).

Pragmatics

Recall that pragmatics refers to the practical application of language to communicate (Owens, 2020). With age and improvements in perspective-taking skills, specifically theory of mind, that come with cognitive development, children are more likely to change their speech in response to listeners' needs (M.-R. Liu & Chen, 2020). When faced with an adult who will not give them a desired object, 9-year-old children are more polite in restating their request than 5-year-old children (Ninio, 2014). Children speak to adults differently than to other children, and they speak differently on the playground than in class or at home. In addition, older children begin to understand that there is often a distinction between what people say and what they mean.

One example of pragmatics that develops in middle childhood is the use of *irony*, choosing a word or expression that conveys the opposite of its literal meaning (Pexman, 2022). Many contextual, linguistic, and developmental factors influence the processing and comprehension of irony, such as cognitive flexibility, theory of mind, the ability to interpret intonation and facial expressions, and the capacity to evaluate how well a statement matches the situation (Pexman, 2022; Zajączkowska & Abbot-Smith, 2020). Children at the ages of 5 to 6 become capable of recognizing irony when they can understand that a speaker might believe something different from what has been said. Yet most children at this age tend to interpret irony as sincere, relying on the person's statement and disregarding other cues in the story, such as intonation and gestures. Cognitive development permits children to detect the discrepancy between what the speaker says and what they believe.

Children's ability to understand ironic remarks continues to develop through middle childhood, and by age 8, children can recognize and use simple forms of irony (Glenwright & Pexman, 2010). Even in adolescence, the understanding of irony is still developing; children as old as 13 do not reliably distinguish irony, intended to joke or mock, from deception, intended to conceal information (Filippova & Astington, 2008).

Bilingual Language Learning

About one in three U.S. children under the age of 17 speak a language other than English at home (Child Trends, 2019). We have seen that bilingual children tend to have a combined vocabulary similar to monolingual children, but often a smaller vocabulary for each language. About one in five bilingual children struggle with speaking English at school (Federal Interagency Forum on Child and Family Statistics, 2017).

When it comes to teaching English to children who speak a different language at home, the most common approach in the United States is through English **immersion**, which places second-language-speaking children in English-speaking classes, requiring them to learn English and course content simultaneously (Bucknam & Hood, 2021). Research is mixed on whether immersion is associated with a loss in children's native language use (Baus et al., 2013; Neveu et al., 2022). Reductions in native language use associated with immersion may be associated with slower development of executive function (Kubota et al., 2020).

An alternative approach is **dual-language learning** (or dual-language immersion), where English-speaking and non-English-speaking students learn together in both languages, and both languages are valued equally. Advocates of dual-language learning argue that bringing a child's native language into the classroom sends children the message that their cultural heritage is respected and strengthens their cultural identity and self-esteem (Ramírez, 2020). Children exposed to dual-language immersion tend to retain their native language while learning the new language, and native language skills may contribute to developing skills in the new language (Castro et al., 2011; Mancilla-Martinez et al., 2020). Dual-language learning approaches, which encourage students to retain their native language while learning English, are more effective than immersion approaches at promoting successful learning of English as well as overall academic achievement (Relji et al., 2015). Children's skills in their native language transfer to influence literacy and skills in the new language (Macswan et al., 2017).

Learning a second language during childhood may affect proficiency in the first or native language, with the second language potentially becoming dominant, and used more often (Hoff, 2016). Nonetheless, children's competence in both languages tends to steadily improve, often with the second language increasing more rapidly (Oppenheim et al., 2020). The quality and quantity of exposure to each language matter. In 7- to 9-year-old bilingual children whose native language was Chinese, exposure to Chinese at home and during extracurricular activities predicted higher receptive and expressive vocabulary in their native language 2 years later regardless of their proficiency in their second language, English (S. H. Chen et al., 2021). Similarly, an older sibling's use of a first language is associated with the development of that language (Taylor & Kan, 2021). This is also true for learning a second language. Interactions with older siblings who speak a second language predict vocabulary and fluency in a second language in school-age children (Sorenson Duncan & Paradis, 2020).

Peers also matter. In one study, Chinese children who were under the age of 9 when they immigrated to New York City reported preferring English to Mandarin 1 year later and were more proficient in English 3 years later than children who were older than age 9 at the time of immigration (Jia & Aaronson, 2003). Why the difference? The younger children in this study tended to become friends with children who spoke English and spent more time interacting with peers who spoke English than the older children, who spent more time with Chinese-speaking peers. Children's interactions with peers and others in the community influence their bilingual language acquisition and use, and the language that is used most becomes dominant.

The ability to speak more than one language is thought to have cognitive advantages. Individuals who master two or more languages tend to score higher on measures of memory, selective attention, analytical reasoning, mathematics, and cognitive flexibility (Bialystok, 2020; Hartanto et al., 2018). Bilingual children tend to score higher on measures of executive function, particularly the ability to control attention and ignore misleading information (Barac et al., 2014; Bialystok, 2015). However, meta analyses suggest that the relationships between bilingualism and executive function are complex, often small, vary by the study, and are influenced by contextual factors, such as exposure to code-switching (Gunnerud et al., 2020; Lowe et al., 2021).

Code-switching, or alternation between languages, is common, and bilingual children often hear parents and caregivers switching between a first and second language. But code-switching taxes working memory and executive function because it requires individuals to retain and manipulate multiple forms of words. Recall from Chapter 7 that working memory and executive function are limited cognitive resources. For that reason code-switching carries processing costs in terms of production and comprehension (van Hell, 2022). Recent research suggests that the frequency of exposure to code-switching can affect language ability differently depending on children's verbal working memory. For children with high verbal working memory, greater exposure to code-switching is associated with higher levels of language ability, whereas for children with lower verbal working memory, greater exposure to code-switching is associated with lower levels of language ability (Kaushanskaya & Crespo, 2019).

Nonetheless the ability to communicate with others in all the contexts in which children live is undoubtedly beneficial for their development. When children can speak, read, and write in two or more languages, they can participate in the contexts and cultures in which they are immersed.

> **THINKING IN CONTEXT 9.3**
>
> 1. Children's advances in language enable them to have more complicated relationships with parents and peers. Discuss the social implications of gains in childhood in vocabulary, grammar, and pragmatics.
> 2. Suppose you were the parent of a preschooler who does not speak English. How might you help your child learn a second language? What challenges might you expect?
> 3. What are some benefits of a child learning a second language? Consider cognitive development. Can you identify other developmental benefits, such as for social development?

EXPLANATIONS FOR LANGUAGE DEVELOPMENT

> 9.4 Contrast nativist, learning, interactionist, and contextual contributors to language development.

Over the first 2 years of life, children transform from wailing newborns who communicate their needs through cries to toddlers who can use words to articulate their needs, desires, and thoughts. Developmental scientists have offered several explanations for infants' rapid acquisition of language (see Table 9.1). Some explanations emphasize the role of the environment in accounting for language, whereas others emphasize biological factors.

TABLE 9.1 ■ Theories of Language Development

Theory	Description
Learning theory	Language is learned through reinforcement, punishment, and imitation. The quantity and quality of the parents' verbal interactions with the child and responses to the child's communication attempts influence the child's rate of language development. Learning theory cannot account for young children's unique utterances and errors.
Nativist theory	Despite wide variations in circumstances, living situations, and contexts, children around the world achieve language milestones at about the same time, suggesting an innate ability. An inborn language acquisition device (LAD) equipped with universal grammar permits children to quickly and efficiently analyze everyday speech and determine its rules. Researchers have not identified the LAD or universal grammar Chomsky thought underlies all languages. Language does not emerge in a finished form. Instead, children learn to string words together over time based on their experiences and trial and error.
Interactionist theory	Children have an inborn sensitivity to language and discriminate a wide variety of speech sounds, including those that adults can no longer distinguish. Exposure to language influences children's sensitivity to speech sounds, and the ability to detect sounds not used in their native language declines throughout the first year of life. Language acquisition occurs in a social context. Children learn language by interacting with more mature, expert speakers who can speak at their developmental level.

Learning Theory

Baby Howie gurgles, "Babababa!" His parents encourage him excitedly, "Say bottle; ba-ba!" Howie squeals, "Babababa!" "Yes! You want your ba-ba!" Parents play an important role in language development. They provide specific instruction and communicate excitement about their infants' developing competence, encouraging infants to practice new language skills.

Learning theorist B. F. Skinner (1957) proposed that language, like all other behaviors, is learned through operant conditioning: reinforcement and punishment. From birth, infants make sounds at random. Caregivers respond to infants' early utterances with interest and attention, imitating and reinforcing their verbal behavior (Petursdottir & Mellor, 2017). Infants repeat the sounds, and caregivers reward sounds that resemble adult speech with attention, smiles, and affection. Infants imitate sounds that adults make and repeat sounds that are reinforced. From this perspective, imitation and reinforcement shape children's language development. The quantity and quality of the parents' verbal interactions with the child and responses to the child's communication attempts to influence the child's rate of language development (Nikolaus & Fourtassi, 2023).

Critics of learning theory point out that it cannot account for all language development because it cannot explain the unique utterances and errors that young children make (Berwick et al., 2013). Children's word combinations are complex and varied—they cannot be acquired solely by imitation and reinforcement. Toddlers often put words together in ways they likely never heard (e.g., "Mommy milk"). Young children make grammatical errors, such as "*feets*" instead of "feet" or "winned" instead of "won," which cannot be the result of imitation. Certainly, young children not only repeat things they hear (sometimes to parents' chagrin!), but they also construct unique phrases and combinations of words. Despite these criticisms, reinforcement from parents and caregivers is powerful encouragement for children. However, language development cannot be completely explained by learning theory alone. Despite wide variations in circumstances, living situations, and contexts, infants worldwide achieve language milestones at about the same ages, suggesting a biological component to language development.

Nativist Theory

The nativist perspective posits that language development is an innate process. Linguist Noam Chomsky (1959, 2017) argued that language acquisition involves behavior that is too complicated to be learned solely through conditioning. He observed that all young children learn the essentials of grammar, the rules of language, at an early age and that there are many similarities across the world's languages. This suggests that the human mind has an innate capacity to learn language.

Chomsky proposed that infants are born with a **language acquisition device (LAD)**, an innate system of language learning that enables them to quickly and efficiently analyze everyday speech and determine its rules, regardless of their native language, whether Chinese, English, German, or Urdu (Yang et al., 2017). The LAD contains a storehouse of rules, universal grammar, which applies to all human languages. As infants hear spoken language, they naturally notice its linguistic properties and acquire it. From a nativist perspective, language is a biologically driven learning mechanism triggered by exposure to language (Friederici, 2017).

The nativist perspective can account for children's unique utterances and grammatical mistakes because children are biologically primed to learn language and do not rely solely on learning (Bouchard, 2021). Moreover, languages share many properties, such as ways of indicating tense, forming questions, and distinguishing between singular and plural nouns, suggesting universal processes similar to Chomsky's universal grammar (Samuels, 2019).

Critics of Chomsky's nativist perspective point out that it does not explain the process of language development and how it occurs (Ibbotson & Tomasello, 2016). Furthermore, although there are similarities across languages, there are also individual differences in language learning and in languages beyond what Chomsky proposed (Dąbrowska, 2015). Language acquisition is a process in which children string words together over time based on their experiences and trial and error (Tomasello, 2012). It does not occur as quickly or effortlessly as Chomsky described (Miller, 2016).

Interactionist Theory

Scientists have long debated whether language development is influenced by nature or nurture. Nativist theory represents the *nature* side of this debate, that language is inborn and simply unfolds with development. In contrast, learning theory describes language as shaped by the environment. Today most developmental scientists advocate for an interactionist perspective, theorizing that biological and environmental factors interact dynamically to influence development.

Biological Influences

Genetics plays a role in language development. Researchers have identified multiple genes that work together in combination and in an epigenetic fashion with environmental factors to affect language development (Dediu & Christiansen, 2016; Fisher, 2017; Verhoef et al., 2021).

Evolutionary developmental theorists explain language as having evolved through natural selection. From this perspective, language gave some of our early human ancestors an advantage in survival and reproduction over those who did not have language (Berwick & Chomsky, 2016; Hauck, 2020). Specifically, language evolved as an adaptation that fulfilled early humans' need to communicate information beyond what could be conveyed by simple calls and hoots (Benítez-Burraco & Progovac, 2020; Bretas et al., 2020). It is believed that the growth of human communities led to more complex social dynamics, which may have driven the evolution of larger and more sophisticated human brains that became capable of language (Hauser et al., 2014; Tamariz & Kirby, 2016). The same areas of the brain are used to process virtually all languages, suggesting biological commonalities or universalities (Malik-Moraleda et al., 2022).

Language in adults is largely governed by the left hemisphere. Two areas in the brain's left hemisphere are vital for language and distinguish humans from other primates: Broca's and Wernicke's (Friederici, 2017; Jäncke et al., 2021). **Broca's area** controls the ability to use language for expression. Damage to this area inhibits the ability to speak fluently, leading to language production errors. Wernicke's area is responsible for language comprehension. Damage to **Wernicke's area** impairs the ability to understand the speech of others and sometimes affects the ability to speak coherently. Broca's and Wernicke's areas work together because interacting with others requires listening, comprehending what others say, and producing language to share our thoughts (Ono et al., 2022).

The brain is wired for language at birth. Three-month-olds, newborns, and even premature newborns activate the same brain networks as adults in response to language (Nallet & Gervain, 2021). Speech sounds produce more activity in the left hemisphere of newborns' brains, while nonspeech sounds elicit more activity in the right hemisphere, similar to adults (Vannasing et al., 2016). In response to hearing language, 3-month-old infants show functional neural activity that is similar but less refined, focused, and organized than that of adults (Dehaene-Lambertz, 2017). Activity in the language areas of the cortex increases from infancy through adulthood (Paquette et al., 2015).

Myelination is associated with language development in infancy. Myelin density at 7 months of age predicted language production at 24 and 30 months old as well as the rate of language growth (Corrigan et al., 2022). Myelinated brain matter, white matter, in infancy is associated with children's language abilities in kindergarten (Zuk et al., 2021). In addition, white matter at age 2 is associated with the quality of parent-infant interaction during infancy, suggesting that the brain changes in response to experience and environmental factors (Huber et al., 2023).

Environmental Influences

Interactionist theory describes biological and environmental factors as reciprocal influences on each other and development. Recall that infants are born able to perceive and discriminate sounds that comprise all human languages at birth. Over the first year of life, infants become less sensitive to sounds not used in their native language (Levine et al., 2016). These declines are due to infants' environment, specifically, exposure to the native language and little to no exposure to other languages.

The quality of language input from parents and the number of words children hear is related to their vocabulary size at age 2 (Hoff & Naigles, 2002). Infants not only need to hear spoken language, but they also need others to interact and talk with them. Children whose mothers address a great deal of speech to them develop vocabulary more rapidly. They are faster at processing words they know and producing speech than children whose mothers speak to them less often (Weisleder & Fernald, 2013). The number of words and different grammatical structures used in maternal speech and grammatical complexity predict the size of children's vocabulary and understanding of grammar (Hadley et al., 2011; Huttenlocher et al., 2010).

Although parents do not reliably reinforce correct grammar, they tend to communicate in ways that tell young children when they have made errors and show how to correct them (Saxton, 1997). Adults often respond to children's utterances with expansions, which are enriched versions of the children's statements. If a child says, "Bottle fall," the parent might respond, "Yes, the bottle fell off the table." Adults also tend to recast children's sentences into new grammatical forms. "Kitty go" might be recast into "Where is the kitty going?" When children use grammatically correct statements, parents maintain and extend the conversation (Bohannon & Stanowicz, 1988). When adults recast and expand young children's speech, the children tend to acquire grammatical rules more quickly and score higher on tests of expressive language ability than when parents rely less on these conversational techniques (Abraham et al., 2013; Taumoepeau, 2016). We discuss caregiver-directed speech further in the next section.

In sum, an interactionist approach to language development emphasizes the dynamic and reciprocal influence of biology and environment, or context. Infants are equipped with biological propensities and processing capacities that permit them to perceive and analyze speech and learn to speak. Infants are motivated to communicate with others, and language is a tool for communication. Interactions with others provide important learning experiences, which help infants expand their language capacities to communicate with others (Fitneva & Matsui, 2015). From this perspective, contextual influences, like those we discuss next, play a vital role in language development.

Contextual Influences on Language Development

Language development occurs in a social context. Babies learn language by interacting with more mature, expert speakers who can speak at their developmental level. Caregivers who are responsive to infants, who act on infants' smiles, gestures, and vocalizations, foster language development (and other forms of development, such as cognitive and emotional development).

Exposure to Infant-Directed Speech

Most adults naturally speak to young infants in a sing-song way that attracts their attention. **Infant-directed speech** uses repetition, short words and sentences, high and varied pitch, and long pauses (Broesch, 2021). Both monolingual and bilingual infants prefer listening to infant-directed speech than to typical adult speech, and they prefer adults who use infant-directed speech (Byers-Heinlein et al., 2021). EEG recordings show that babies—even newborns—demonstrate more neural activity in response to infant-directed speech than adult speech, suggesting that they can better attend to it and distinguish the sounds (Háden et al., 2020; Nencheva & Lew-Williams, 2022). Infant-directed speech exaggerates sounds, helping infants hear and distinguish sounds and enabling them to map sounds to meanings (Estes & Hurley, 2013; Genovese et al., 2020). Infants are more likely to learn words presented by infant-directed speech than those presented through adult-directed speech (Cox & Haebig, 2022).

Most of the research in this area has examined mothers, but fathers also show infant-directed speech (Ferjan Ramírez, 2022). Adults naturally talk to infants, and infant-directed speech has been documented in many languages and cultures in Africa, Asia, Australia, Europe, and North America (C. B. Hilton et al., 2022; Many Babies Consortium, 2020). Patterns of infant-directed speech are so similar across cultures that adults can discriminate it from adult-directed speech even if they do not speak the language. When adults in the Turkana region of northwestern Kenya listened to speech produced in English by North American mothers, they could discriminate between infant-directed and adult-directed speech, suggesting that infant-directed speech is recognizable to adults of many cultures (Bryant et al., 2012).

Through infant-directed speech, adults attract infants' attention by using shorter words and sentences, higher and more varied pitch, repetition, and a slower rate. Infants prefer listening to infant-directed speech, and infant-directed speech appears cross-culturally.

damircudic/istock

Cultural Differences in Infant-Directed Speech. Infant-directed speech has been documented cross-culturally, but there are exceptions.

For example, in Samoa, caregivers do not address infants directly until they begin to crawl. Parents tend to interpret their vocalizations as indicators of physiological state rather than as attempts to communicate. Because of the status hierarchy in Samoa, child-directed speech is uncommon in adults because it would reflect someone of higher status (i.e., an adult) adjusting their speech to someone of lower status (Ochs & Schieffein, 1984). Instead, older children are tasked with responding to infants' vocalizations, and it is largely older children who talk with infants (Lieven & Stoll, 2010).

Similarly, the Kaluli of Papua New Guinea do not engage in infant-directed speech. They believe that infants cannot understand language (Ochs & Schieffein, 1984). Infants are carried facing outward rather than toward the mother. Kaluli infants learn language by hearing adults speak to each other, modeling language use rather than speaking to infants. Only when children themselves begin to talk do parents start talking to them, and then they focus on teaching them what to say (Rowe & Weisleder, 2020).

Culture even shapes the types of words that infants learn. In Asian cultures such as Japan, China, and Korea that stress interpersonal harmony, children tend to acquire verbs and social words much more quickly than do North American toddlers (Gopnik & Choi, 1995; Tardif et al., 2008). Observations of U.S. and Japanese mother-infant interactions reveal different emphases in play, with U.S. mothers responding to infant object play more than social play, and Japanese mothers responding more to social play (Tamis-LeMonda et al., 1992). North American infants' first words tend to include more referential language or naming words such as *ball, dog, cup*, and the like. In contrast, Japanese infants tend to use more expressive language or words that are used mainly in social interaction, such as *please* and *want* (Fernald & Morikawa, 1993). Dutch-, English-, French-, Hebrew-, Italian-, and Spanish-speaking infants tend to prefer using more nouns than verbs (Bassano, 2000; Bornstein et al., 2004; Tardif et al., 1997). Cultures vary in common practices and contexts of infant-directed communication, yet all infants learn language on roughly similar timeframes, supporting the decisive role of maturation.

Changes in Infant-Directed Speech. Caregivers naturally adjust their infant-directed speech to the child's needs. As babies' babbling begins to sound more like language, parents tune in and treat the vocalizations in a new way. They respond by associating word-like vocalizations with objects and events, encouraging vocabulary growth. As infants' comprehension increases, parents adjust their language to match, using more complicated words and sentences (Englund & Behne, 2006; Genovese et al., 2020). Even as they learn speech, infants continue to display preferences for some features of infant-directed speech. A study of 12- and 16-month-old infants indicated that they preferred the high pitch and pitch variability of infant-directed speech but not the shorter utterances or simplified syntax (Segal & Newman, 2015).

Parental responsiveness to infants' vocalizations predicts the size of infants' vocabularies, the diversity of infants' communications, and the timing of language milestones (Alvarenga et al., 2022; Tamis-LeMonda et al., 2014). Infants of highly responsive mothers achieved language milestones such as first words, vocabulary spurt, and telegraphic speech 4 to 6 months earlier than infants of low-responsive mothers (Tamis-LeMonda et al., 2001). Parental responsiveness and consistency of responsiveness at 12, 24, and 26 months predicted children's language scores at 7 years (Levickis et al., 2023). Parental responsiveness is also associated with the language skills of adopted children, supporting the contextual influence of parents in language development (Stams et al., 2002).

Socioeconomic Status and Language Development

Language development unfolds within the home context. Neighborhood and household socioeconomic status (SES) influences the home environment and children's development. As early as age 3, children from low SES backgrounds know fewer words and score more poorly on standardized language measures and tests than their higher SES counterparts (see Figure 9.3; Golinkoff et al., 2019; Levine et al., 2020). The link between household SES and influence is indirect, associated with the home language and literacy environment, including caregiver-child discussion and the availability of reading and educational materials (Luo et al., 2021).

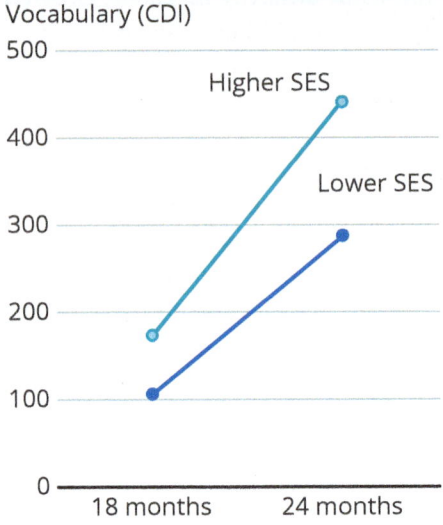

FIGURE 9.3 ■ Mean Number of Spoken Words Reported on the MacArthur/Bates CDI by Age and SES (HI)

Source: Fernald, A., Marchman, V. A., & Weisleder A. (2013). SES differences in language processing skill and vocabulary are evident at 18 months. *Developmental Science, 16*(2), 234–248. https://doi.org/10.1111/desc.12019

SES and Child Directed Speech. As noted previously, most of the research into parents' influence on children's language development focuses on mothers. Mothers with higher incomes, higher education levels, and more prestigious careers tend to direct a greater amount of language and more diverse and complex language to their young children than mothers of low SES (Hart & Risley, 1995; Rowe, 2018). Naturalistic research with children 3 to 30 months of age showed that children in higher maternal education homes heard more child-directed speech than those in lower-maternal education homes (Bergelson et al., 2019).

How powerful is SES in language outcomes? In a classic study, Hart and Risley (1995) assessed a small sample of 42 children and their mothers monthly over 2.5 years, up to about age 3. The researchers measured differences in language exposure and extrapolated their estimates to conclude that by age 4, children of high SES families encounter an average of 30 million more words in their interactions with their mothers than children from the lowest SES families, a difference referred to as the "30 million word gap." In this study, SES differences in maternal language predicted vocabulary and literacy skills many years later, contributing to lifelong gaps in competency.

Recent research has called into question the 30-million-word gap, which was based only on language spoken directly to the child and not overhead language (Sperry et al., 2019). Observations of young children from middle-class, working-class, and poor communities revealed that when overheard speech is included, that is, the total number of words children hear are taken into account, the gap in language exposure disappeared (Sperry et al., 2019). A recent meta-analysis of 19 studies found large differences in child-directed speech correlated to SES, but no differences by SES when considering all speech (Dailey & Bergelson, 2022).

Critics argue that child-directed speech differs greatly from overhead speech and that the quality of child-directed speech is a much better predictor of language development than simply the quantity of heard speech (Golinkoff et al., 2019). While laboratory research shows that children can learn from overheard speech, it is back and forth conversations between caregivers and children that fuel language development. What caregivers communicate and how they communicate is more important than the specific number of words communicated (Masek et al., 2021). In addition, although the quality of maternal child-directed speech is related to SES, there is considerable variation within each SES group (Rowe, 2018; Schwab & Lew-Williams, 2016). Conclusions that there are never SES differences in language environments can harm disadvantaged children as it could imply that no intervention is needed.

Race and Socioeconomic Intersections and Language Development. Discussions of SES and development are incomplete without considering the effects of other intersectional factors, such as race and ethnicity. SES and race are intertwined in many studies, such that the families from low SES contexts also happen to be families of color, making it difficult to determine if a set of findings are related to SES differences, racial and ethnic differences, or a combination of both. Conclusions about the quality of mother-infant interactions in low SES contexts may lead researchers to erroneously conclude, for example, that African American mothers talk less with their young children simply because the low SES mothers also tended to be African American. Early studies that confounded SES and race concluded that African American mothers speak less to their children, ask fewer questions, and elicit lower-quality speech than other mothers (Anderson-Yockel & Haynes, 1994; Brooks-Gunn & Markman, 2005). Yet in these early studies, it was impossible to determine whether maternal language was related to SES, race, or both.

One recent study of maternal language input disentangled maternal education and race by examining four groups of mothers: African American and non-African American mothers with a high school education or less and African American and non-African American mothers with education beyond high school (Vernon-Feagans et al., 2020). In this study, maternal education, not race, accounted for differences in maternal language input. Maternal education influences children's language input and the resources available to support children's development and education (Hindman et al., 2014; Vernon-Feagans et al., 2020).

Differences in education can place families at risk for low SES and negatively affect the quality of child-directed speech. However, scarcity of resources and heightened stress can also influence caregiver-child interactions. In contexts of social and economic vulnerability and high stress, maternal sensitivity is diminished, while children simultaneously require more responsiveness to adapt (Alvarenga et al., 2022). A recent study found that caregivers who were prompted to reflect on financial scarcity spoke less to their 3-year-olds in a subsequent play session than a control group (Ellwood-Lowe et al., 2022). This study also found that middle to high SES caregivers had fewer back and forth exchanges with their young children at the end of the month when they were more likely aware of financial hardship than at the beginning of the month. Structural constraints specific to low SES circumstances may affect how much parents speak to their children (Ellwood-Lowe et al., 2022).

Overall, caregiver responsiveness and the quality of caregiver speech input predict children's language development from infancy through late childhood (Owens, 2020; Schwab & Lew-Williams, 2016). Early interventions to promote language development tend to focus on the caregiver-child dyad. Interventions to help caregivers promote children's language development emphasize child-directed speech during play and activities such as shared book reading (Dowdall et al., 2020; Hindman et al., 2016). Programs for preschoolers and older children focus on improving vocabulary, developing storytelling skills, practicing active listening, and improving children's confidence in speaking (Hulme et al., 2020).

THINKING IN CONTEXT 9.4

1. Consider language development from Bronfenbrenner's bioecological systems theory. Identify four microsystem and mesosystem factors that might influence children's language learning. Provide at least two examples of exosystem factors that might influence children's language development. How might the macrosystem influence language?
2. Consider the various perspectives on language development. From the nativist perspective, what can parents do to promote language development in their infants? What advice would learning theorists provide? Provide advice to parents about language development from the interactionist perspective.

APPLY YOUR KNOWLEDGE

At 8 months old, Maya often babbles in her high chair while her mother, Priya, prepares dinner in their small but cozy kitchen. Priya frequently turns to smile and respond to Maya's sounds. "Oh you want your keys?" Priya asks as Maya gurgles excitedly, reaching out for the play set of keys. Priya continues to talk with Maya as she cooks.

Nine-year-old Anil, Maya's older brother, walks into the kitchen after finishing his homework. "Mom! Maya can't talk yet. I bet she doesn't even understand what you're saying," he says with a smirk. Priya smiles and responds, "Maya understands more than you realize, Anil. You were much the same way as a baby. We had many conversations before you said a single word." "So you're teaching Maya to speak?" Anil asks. "No. Maya is teaching herself, learning by watching and listening," Priya explains.

"I wish I could teach myself. Then, I wouldn't have to go to school," Anil said. "What's wrong with school? I though you liked school," Priya replied.

"It's just . . . it's hard, Mom," Anil confessed. "There are a lot of kids in class, and the teacher can't help everyone. I feel like she never talks to me. And sometimes it's so noisy that it's hard to focus." "I know, Anil, you have to try," Priyam advises. She worries about Anil's education. The school is overcrowded and it seems that teachers quickly come and go. The school is located at a busy intersection, yet the neighborhood feels like a ghost town. Many neighborhood businesses closed during the COVID-19 pandemic and have not reopened, leaving vacant storefronts.

Priya nodded, understanding the gravity of the situation. "I know it's tough, but remember, learning can happen anywhere—not just in school. We'll keep doing our reading every night, and maybe we can find some new ways to help you learn, just like how Maya is learning now."

1. Discuss how Priya's interaction with Maya supports her early language development. Why is it important for caregivers to respond to infants' babbles and gestures?

2. Priya and Anil have contrasting views of influences on language development. What theories of language development correspond to their views?

3. Compare and contrast the informal learning environment provided by Priya for Maya with the formal educational setting Anil experiences. How might these environments influence their learning and development? Recommend strategies parents can use to support language development in both early and later childhood and across contexts.

4. The neighborhood's changes due to the COVID-19 pandemic have affected the local school and community. What are some of the broader implications of such social and economic changes on children's development? How might these changes influence their language development?

SUMMARY

9.1 Identify five components of language.

Language is a system of associations between sounds and meaning that facilitates communication and learning. Children must learn to use the five basic components of language: phonology, morphology, syntax, semantics, and pragmatics. Phonology refers to the basic units of sounds used in a given language and the rules for combining them, while morphology refers to the rules for combining morphemes into words. Syntax refers to the rules for combining words to form grammatically correct sentences, while semantics refers to the meaning or content of words and sentences. Pragmatics involves understanding how to use language to communicate effectively, including tailoring speech for different audiences and detecting the social appropriateness of spoken words.

9.2 **Examine patterns of language development during infancy and toddlerhood.**
Newborns have the ability to hear all sounds in the human voice spectrum, but their ability to perceive nonnative speech sounds declines within their first year of life. As infants progress from cooing to babbling and their first words, exposure to their native language allows them to become more attuned to the meaningful sounds and distinctions in their language, while losing the ability to distinguish nonnative speech sounds. Infants learn new words through a process called fast mapping, but their own speech development lags behind their understanding, leading to underextension and overextension errors. As children reach 20 to 30 months of age, they begin to follow the rules for forming sentences in their language. Language development is a socially interactive process, and infants can communicate through gestures before they can speak. In fact, their use of gestures can predict later vocabulary development. Bilingual infants learn at the same rate as monolingual infants, and the quantity and quality of speech they hear in each language influences their development in that language. Language development is greatly influenced by interactions with expert speakers, whether the child is learning one, two, three, or more languages.

9.3 **Summarize patterns of language development in childhood and adolescence.**
Young children build vocabulary, learning words by making inferences and applying strategies such as fast mapping, logical extension, and the mutual exclusivity assumption. They learn to combine words into sentences in increasingly sophisticated ways that follow the complex rules of syntax or grammar, but often make overregularization errors. Effective learning contexts for vocabulary and language development include turn taking, joint attention, and scaffolding experiences. School-age children continue to develop their language skills, expanding their vocabulary and understanding of grammar and pragmatics. Children also become more aware of how language is used in different contexts, and their ability to understand irony improves. English immersion and dual-language learning are two approaches used to teach children a second language. The quality and quantity of exposure to each language matter, and interactions with peers and others in the community influence bilingual language acquisition and use. Speaking more than one language may have cognitive advantages, but code-switching can tax working memory and executive function. Nonetheless, being able to communicate in multiple languages allows children to participate in the different contexts and cultures in which they live.

9.4 **Contrast nativist, learning, interactionist, and contextual contributors to language development.**
Learning theory poses that language is learned through modeling, imitation, and reinforcement. Nativist theorists pose that the human brain has an innate capacity to learn language, called a language acquisition device. An interactionist perspective proposed that both biological and environmental factors interact to influence language. Language may have evolved to aid early humans' needs to communicate. We have innate perceptual biases for discriminating and listening to language, and the brain is wired for language at birth. At the same time, language acquisition occurs in a social context in which adults use infant-directed speech to catch the infant's attention and facilitate language development by responding in ways that foster language learning, such as by using expansions and recasts. Contextual influences include exposure to infant-directed speech, which varies with culture and development, and home SES.

KEY TERMS

babbling
Broca's area
code-switching
cooing

dual-language learning
fast mapping
grammar
holophrase

immersion
infant-directed speech
language acquisition device (LAD)
logical extension
metalinguistic awareness
morpheme
morphology
mutual exclusivity assumption
overextension
overregularization errors
phenomes

phonology
pragmatics
productive language
receptive language
semantics
syntax
telegraphic speech
underextension
vocabulary spurt
Wernicke's area

CAREERS IN CHILD DEVELOPMENT: COGNITIVE DEVELOPMENT

Understanding what children know and how they think can be beneficial for anyone who has contact with children. However, certain careers place a particular emphasis on this knowledge.

Early Childhood Educator

Early childhood educators work as preschool teachers as well as in educational programs and interventions designed to promote school readiness, such as Head Start. Preschool teachers prepare young children for kindergarten by introducing them to the classroom environment and helping them acclimate to it. Preschool teachers create educational and social programs to promote young children's cognitive and socioemotional development. They employ different educational techniques, such as storytelling, educational play, and media, to teach children, help them develop their creativity, and help them improve their social competencies and self-esteem. They provide children opportunities to interact with each other and help them resolve conflicts. They record children's process, identify needs, and communicate with parents.

Early childhood educators also work in educational programs and interventions outside of preschool, such as Head Start. Head Start is a free, federally funded program designed to help 3- to 5-year-old children from impoverished homes prepare (or get a "head start") for school entry. Like preschool teachers, Head Start teachers develop and administer the curriculum, such as teaching letters and numbers, record children's process, report developmental concerns, and meeting with parents. They also support the mission of Head Start, promoting the health and well-being of underserved children and their families. Head Start helps children and their parents access health and family services, such as medical and dental care, get healthy meals and snacks, and support for parents.

About three quarters of Head Start teachers hold bachelor's degrees, but the qualifications to become a preschool teacher vary by state and school. While some private schools might require an associate's degree, public schools generally require a bachelor's degree in early childhood education or a related field and completing a licensure exam. The median wage for preschool teachers was about $37,000 in 2023, but salaries vary by state and school (U.S. Bureau of Labor Statistics, 2024).

Elementary Education

Elementary school teachers instruct children in grades K through 5 or 6, depending on the school. Some elementary schools include children through Grade 8. Although not visible to children and parents, much of elementary school teachers' work is conducted outside class. They develop educational goals and construct plans for each day of class, including selecting reading and other materials, developing activities, creating lectures, choosing discussion topics and preparing questions, grading student work, recording and assessing student progress, communicating with parents, and submitting reports to administrators. Most people are familiar with elementary school teachers' classroom activities, such as instructing, working to maintain student attention, managing behavior problems, and creating intellectual and emotional connections with students.

Becoming a teacher requires earning a bachelor's degree in education, which includes an internship experience in an elementary school classroom. Some colleges offer intensive 1-year programs for aspiring teachers with bachelor's degrees in other fields. Teachers must pass a state licensing or certification exam. Elementary school teachers earned a median salary of about $63,700 in 2023 (U.S. Bureau of Labor Statistics, 2024).

Secondary Education: Middle School Teacher and High School Teacher

Middle school teachers typically work with students in Grades 6 through 8, but sometimes as early as fourth grade and as late as ninth grade. Secondary school teachers typically work with students in Grades 9 through 12. Many activities of elementary school, middle school, and high school teachers are similar. All develop educational goals and construct plans for each day of class, teach, record, and assess student progress, communicate with parents, and submit reports to administrators. High school, and often middle school, teachers typically specialize in one, or sometimes two, subjects such as English or math. They usually teach several sections of students over the day, whereas elementary school teachers usually teach the same group of students all day.

Middle schools are often smaller than high schools. Middle school teachers often have smaller classes than high school teachers (but larger than elementary school classrooms). In middle school, changing classes often involve entire classes of students moving from teacher to teacher so that a group of students remains together in all classes. Frequently middle school teachers work together to create a cohesive experience for students. High school students move from class to class individually. Teachers may not share the same students and may work more independently. Middle and high school teachers are often tasked with maintaining order during breaks, such as when students change classes, during lunch periods, and study halls. They also are frequently involved in after-school activities, such as clubs.

Becoming a middle or high school teacher requires earning a bachelor's degree in education, often specializing in a specific subject (e.g., history, biology, or math), and completing an internship experience in the classroom. Teachers must pass a state licensing or certification exam. The median annual salary for middle school and high school teachers was about $64,000 in 2023 (U.S. Bureau of Labor Statistics, 2024).

Special Education

Special education teachers conduct the same activities as elementary school teachers but specialize in working with students with special education needs, including developmental and learning disabilities. They may assist general education teachers in identifying and assessing children with special needs. Special education teachers work with a team, including the parent, general teacher, counselor or school psychologist, and administrator, to create an individualized education program (IEP) for each student with special needs. The IEP is a detailed plan and set of supports that is the cornerstone of a special needs child's education. Special education teachers adjust class lessons to fit the child's needs, as outlined in the IEP. They monitor students' progress, record their observations and evaluations, update parents on students' progress, and meet with the IEP team to evaluate and adjust learning goals as needed.

Becoming a special education teacher requires a bachelor's degree in special education, including supervised teaching and passing a certification exam. Some states require a master's degree. In 2023, special education teachers earned a median salary of about $66,000 (U.S. Bureau of Labor Statistics, 2024).

ESL Teacher

An English as a Second Language (ESL) teacher educates students whose first language is not English. They work with nonnative speakers of all ages. ESL teachers instruct students on reading, writing, and conversing in English to improve their communication skills so that they can succeed at school, work, and in the community. They prepare lesson plans, adapt their lessons to accommodate student differences in age, ability, and progress, and prepare progress reports. ESL teachers' instructional style must be flexible to adjust to students of different ages and backgrounds. They must be knowledgeable about different cultures as they encounter students from many backgrounds. ESL teachers often act as formal and informal mentors, advisors, and liaisons to students and families who are new to a community or require assistance with communication.

Schools employ ESL teachers, but many work with adult learners in community centers, high schools, and colleges. Becoming an ESL teacher requires a bachelor's degree, a teaching internship, completion of a state licensure exam, and completion of an add-on certification to teach ESL, which requires an additional exam. The median salary for ESL teachers was about $61,000 in 2023 (U.S. Bureau of Labor Statistics, 2024).

Neuropsychological Technician

A neuropsychological technician is a healthcare professional who, under the supervision of a neuropsychologist, administers and scores standardized neuropsychological tests to children, adolescents, and adults as part of a larger psychological evaluation completed by a licensed psychologist. Neuropsychological technicians prepare test materials, administer and interpret neuropsychological tests, prepare reports on test results, and support neuropsychologists by maintaining patient records, scheduling appointments, and completing other administrative work.

Neuropsychological technicians work in hospitals, clinics, schools, research facilities, and private practice, often alongside a neuropsychologist or psychiatrist. They may work as part of a team with other healthcare professionals, such as occupational therapists, speech-language pathologists, and social workers. Typically, neuropsychological technicians hold a bachelor's degree in psychology or a related field, although some employers may prefer candidates with a master's degree in psychology or neuropsychology. In 2023, neuropsychological technicians earned a median salary of about $48,000 (Salary.com, n.d.).

Speech-Language Pathologist

Speech-language pathologists work with children and adults who have problems with speech and communication. Their patients may be unable to speak at all or have problems such as stuttering, unusually high-pitched voice, difficulty making specific sounds, or difficulty swallowing. Speech-language pathologists assess and diagnose speech difficulties, create and carry out treatment plans, and monitor patient progress, modifying the treatment plan as needed. They also counsel individuals and families on how to cope with communication and swallowing disorders. Many speech-language pathologists work in schools, evaluating children for speech and language disorders and working with teachers, school personnel, and parents to carry out individual and group programs and provide counseling and support. Speech-language pathologists also work in hospitals, private practice, and those who work with adults may be found in nursing and residential care.

Becoming a speech-language pathologist requires a master's degree from a speech-language pathology program accredited by the Council on Academic Accreditation in Audiology and Speech-Language Pathology. To practice, graduates must also be licensed through their state licensing board, which typically requires supervised experience and an exam. In some states, speech-language pathologists in schools may need a teaching certification. The median annual wage for speech-language pathologists was about $89,000 in 2023 (U.S. Bureau of Labor Statistics, 2024).

Developmental Psychologist

Psychologists study human behavior, including physical, cognitive, and socioemotional functioning, and apply their findings to improve people's lives. Developmental psychologists study people of all ages to learn about how their behavior changes over their lifetime. The topics and findings discussed throughout this book are the result of research in developmental psychology.

Developmental psychologists often conduct research in university, social service, and government settings on various topics, such as studying memory, executive function, behavioral problems such as aggression, emotional regulation, and attachment. Some of this research is basic, intended to further knowledge and theory. Others, sometimes called applied developmental psychologists, conduct applied research designed to address children and families' needs in everyday settings.

Developmental psychologists design and empirically evaluate programs provided by hospitals, social service agencies, mental health clinics, and schools. For example, a developmental psychologist might evaluate the impact of a behaviorally oriented program administered in a hospital or clinic setting, such as the effect of prenatal care and education on adolescent mothers and the effects on infant health outcomes. Others serve as consultants who provide teachers with information about behavioral management and instructional techniques appropriate for troubled adolescents.

Applied developmental psychologists also work in direct service, providing assessment, consultation, and treatment to individuals and families. They conduct developmental assessments of children and adolescents who have suffered injuries or who are suspected of having developmental delays. Frequently, applied developmental psychologists in hospital and service settings work with a multidisciplinary team of physicians, social workers, physical therapists, and other professionals to determine the best course of treatment or intervention for patients. Applied developmental psychologists are also found in social services agencies and court settings, where they evaluate families who wish to provide foster parenting, determine parental fitness for regaining child custody after the loss of parental rights, or participate as part of a multidisciplinary team to assist children who have suffered abuse during the subsequent investigation and court process.

How do you become a psychologist? The specific method varies by psychology subfield, but all psychologists attend graduate school and earn doctoral degrees. Earning a doctoral degree typically takes 4 to 5 years of study, including 2 to 3 years of coursework and one or two comprehensive exams that test students' knowledge of the field and ability to think critically about it. After completing coursework and exams, students begin the final requirement: a dissertation, an independent research project that makes discoveries and a unique contribution to the field.

Applied developmental psychologists who plan to assess and treat individuals must seek state licensure. Typically, licensure eligibility requires at least 4,000 hours of supervised field experience, with at least 2,000 hours postdoctoral, passing a written national examination and a written examination covering ethical and legal issues within a particular state and an oral examination in some states.

PART 4

SOCIOEMOTIONAL DEVELOPMENT

Nitat Termmee/Getty Images

10 EMOTIONAL DEVELOPMENT

> **LEARNING OBJECTIVES**
>
> **10.1** Describe how emotions are experienced and expressed in infancy, childhood, and adolescence.
>
> **10.2** Discuss the development of emotional regulation from infancy through adolescence.
>
> **10.3** Analyze the role of temperament and goodness of fit in children's development.
>
> **10.4** Examine the development of attachment, its stability, and associated outcomes.

Just weeks old, baby Rosalind would wriggle and squirm, spreading her arms and kicking her legs vigorously whenever she felt hungry, uncomfortable, or in need of a diaper change. Her parents were quick to respond to her cries, soothing her with gentle touches and soft coos. Rosalind began to prefer interacting with attentive adults who cared for her. Soon baby Rosalind began to smile and gurgle when held. In turn, Rosalind's parents played with her and were delighted to see her animated, excited responses. As a toddler, her emerging language skills enabled Rosalind to express her needs in words. She learned that words are powerful tools that can convey emotions ("I love you, Mommy"). With time, Rosalind began to use words to help her manage strong emotions and difficult situations. When the neighbor's loud dog barked, Rosalind distracted herself by singing. Rosalind expressed her ideas and feelings to everyone around her, leading to new and more complex relationships with her parents and siblings. Rosalind also learned that it is sometimes best to hold in emotions that might hurt other people's feelings—instead of telling Grandma that she had really wanted a video game for her birthday, she thanked her for the puzzle toy she gave her.

EMOTIONAL EXPERIENCE

> **10.1** Describe how emotions are experienced and expressed in infancy, childhood, and adolescence.

Emotions are so integral to our daily experience that we often do not notice their existence until they become intense, such as a toddler's tantrum when picked up, a child's cry of frustration when told to put away a toy, and an adolescent's anger when told they cannot attend a party. However, emotions can also be subtle, such as a giggle in response to a joke, a feeling of pride after being told "good job," and a sense of contentment when drawing or painting a picture. Even very young infants feel emotions, as discussed next.

Infants' Emotional Experience

Are we born with the ability to feel emotions? Researchers rely on infants' behavior and facial expressions as clues to their emotional state since infants cannot describe their experiences and feelings. Newborns show facial expressions that are associated with interest, distress, disgust, and happiness or contentment (Izard et al., 2010). The earliest and most reliable emotion newborns display is distress, often expressed through crying, wailing, and flailing their arms and bodies to signal their need for attention from caregivers. Infants' facial expressions are remarkably similar to those of adults, but we do not know whether internal emotional states accompany their facial expressions (Sullivan & Lewis, 2003). We cannot ask infants what they feel, so it is unclear whether newborns experience the emotions their faces show.

Primary Emotions

Primary emotions, also known as basic emotions, including happiness, sadness, interest, surprise, fear, anger, and disgust, are experienced by people worldwide. Primary emotions emerge in infants at about the same ages in all cultures studied, indicating that they are inborn (Izard et al., 2010). Infants start to display anger, sadness, joy, surprise, and fear between 2 and 7 months of age.

Research with adults suggests that emotions result from interactions among richly connected subcortical brain structures, such as the brainstem and limbic system, as well as parts of the cerebral cortex (Celeghin et al., 2017; Palomero-Gallagher & Amunts, 2022). These brain structures develop prenatally and exist in animals, implying that emotions serve a biological purpose, are crucial to survival, and are likely experienced by infants (Rolls, 2017; Turner, 2014).

Emotions develop in predictable ways (see Table 10.1). Although basic emotions are believed to be inborn, their expressions and the conditions that elicit them change in the first few months of life. Newborns smile, and smiling is one of the most important emotional expressions in infancy. Newborn smiles are reflexive, involuntary, and linked with shifts in arousal state (e.g., going from being asleep to drowsy wakefulness), and they occur frequently during periods of rapid eye movement (REM) sleep (Challamel et al., 2020; Kawakami et al., 2008). By about 3 weeks, infants smile while awake and alert and in response to familiar sounds, voices, and tastes (Sroufe & Waters, 1976).

TABLE 10.1 ■ Milestones in Emotional Development

Approximate Age	Milestone
Birth	Basic emotions Discriminates mother
2–3 months	Social smile Distinguishes happiness, anger, surprise, and sadness
6–8 months	Fear, stranger anxiety, and separation protest occur
7–12 months	Social referencing
18–24 months	Self-conscious emotions appear. Develops vocabulary for talking about emotions

As infants' vision improves during the second month of life, they smile more in response to visual stimuli, such as bright objects catching their attention (Sroufe, 1997). The **social smile**, which occurs in response to familiar people, emerges between 6 and 10 weeks of age and is a crucial milestone in infant development because it shows social engagement (Messinger & Fogel, 2007). The social smile plays a significant role in initiating and maintaining social interactions between infants and adults, particularly by enhancing caregiver-child bonding. Parents are enthralled when their baby shows delight in seeing them, and the parents' happy response encourages their baby to smile even more (Beebe et al., 2016).

As infants grow, laughs begin to accompany their smiles, and they laugh more often and at more things. They may show clear expressions of joy, and intense happiness, as early as 2.5 months of age while playing with a parent and at 3 to 4 months of age in response to stimuli that they find highly arousing (Messinger et al., 2019). By 6 months of age, an infant may laugh at unusual sounds or sights, such as when mommy puts a bowl on her head or makes a funny face. Laughing at unusual events illustrates infants' increasing cognitive competence because they know what to expect and are surprised when something unexpected occurs. By a year of age, infants can smile deliberately to engage an adult. Infants' emotions tend to elicit more frequent verbal responses from parents than negative emotions (Fields-Olivieri et al., 2020).

Negative emotions also change over time. Distress is evident at birth when newborns experience the discomfort of hunger, a heel prick at a doctor's appointment, or a change in temperature. Anger appears at about 6 months of age (Dollar & Calkins, 2019). Initially, anger is elicited by physical restrictions, such as being restrained in a highchair or while being dressed. Being unable to obtain a desired toy can also evoke frustration and anger. Between 8 and 20 months of age, infants gradually become more reactive, and anger is more easily aroused, involving varied elicitors and responses (Braungart-Rieker et al., 2010). Infants' increasing ability to understand and predict other people's actions can lead them to show anger at anticipated events, such as becoming upset when mommy puts on her jacket to leave home or when grandma takes out the towels in preparation for bath time.

During the second year of life, temper tantrums become common when toddlers' attempts at autonomy are thwarted, and they experience frustration or stress. The intensity of anger escalates with the child's stress level (Potegal et al., 2007). Some toddlers show extreme tantrums, lie on the floor, scream, and jerk their arms and legs. Other children's tantrums are more subtle. They may whine, mope, and stick out their lower lip. Like adults, infants' emotional expressions are unique to them, and they display emotional responses to stimuli tied to their own experiences (Camras, 2019).

Self-Conscious Emotions

Emotional development is an orderly process in which complex emotions build on the foundation of simple emotions. The development of **self-conscious emotions**, or secondary emotions, including empathy, pride, embarrassment, shame, and guilt, depends on cognitive development and an awareness of self (Tracy & Weidman, 2021). Self-conscious emotions do not begin to emerge until about 15 to 18 months of age, and they primarily develop during the second and third years of life (M. Lewis, 2019).

For toddlers to experience self-conscious emotions, they must have a sense of self, observe themselves and others, be aware of standards and rules, and compare their behavior to those standards (M. Lewis, 2016; M. Lewis & Minar, 2022). Feelings of pride arise from accomplishing a personally meaningful goal, while guilt derives from realizing that one has violated a standard of conduct. Caregiver interactions, especially evaluations of infant behavior, influence the initial forms of many self-conscious emotions (Goodvin et al., 2015). Self-conscious emotions shape social behavior, social interactions, and relationships throughout life, underscoring their importance in emotional development (Tracy & Weidman, 2021).

What cognitive and social capacities are needed to display embarrassment?
manonallard/istock

Recognizing Others' Emotions

Early in life, infants can discriminate facial expressions that indicate emotion. In one study, 2-day-old infants habituated to a face showing either happiness or disgust successfully discriminated between the two, suggesting an early sensitivity to facial expressions (Addabbo et al., 2018). Newborns have been shown to discriminate happy faces from fearful ones (Farroni et al., 2007; Ruba & Repacholi, 2020). From an evolutionary perspective, infants may be innately prepared to attend to facial displays of emotion because such displays are biologically significant, and the ability to recognize them is crucial for human survival (Bjorklund & Hart, 2022).

Between 2 and 4 months of age, infants can detect emotional expressions such as happiness, anger, surprise, and sadness (Bornstein et al., 2013). The ability to compare and distinguish between emotional expressions develops gradually. Five-month-old infants can distinguish sadness from disgust, happiness from surprise, and sadness from anger, but they are unable to discriminate anger from disgust (White et al., 2019). Six-and-one-half-month-old infants can identify and match happy, angry, and sad emotions portrayed on faces, and also body movements indicating emotion (Hock et al., 2017).

In addition to recognizing the emotional expressions of others, infants respond to them. Between 6 and 10 months of age, infants begin to use **social referencing**, looking to caregivers' or other adults' emotional expressions to find clues for how to interpret and respond to ambiguous events (Ehli et al., 2020; Walle et al., 2017). Social referencing influences infants' emotional reactions and, ultimately, behavior. When toddlers grab the sofa to pull themselves up to stand, turn, and then tumble over as they take a step, they often look to their caregivers to determine how to interpret their fall. If caregivers respond with fearful facial expressions, infants are likely also to be fearful, but if caregivers instead smile, infants will probably remain calm and return to their attempts at walking. The use of social referencing is one way infants demonstrate their understanding that others experience emotions and thoughts.

Like adults, older infants tend to show a negativity bias, avoiding harm by attending to and following cues indicating negative attitudes toward an object more closely than neutral or happy attitudes (Liberman, 2022; Norris, 2021). In the case of fearful messages, infants' behavior may be more influenced by the emotional message conveyed by adults' speech than the facial expressions themselves (Biro et al., 2014; Ruba & Repacholi, 2020).

Infants' use of social referencing changes with development. Ten-month-old infants show selective social referencing. They monitor the caregiver's attention and do not engage in social referencing when the adult is not attending or engaged (Stenberg, 2017). At 12 months, infants use referential cues such as the caregiver's body posture, gaze, and voice direction to determine what objects the caregivers' emotional responses refer to (Brooks & Meltzoff, 2008). They can correctly interpret body expressions of adults' emotion (Vuong & Geangu, 2023). Twelve-month-old infants are more likely to use a caregiver's cues as guides in ambivalent situations when the caregiver responds promptly to the infants' behavior (Stenberg, 2017). Social referencing reflects infants' growing understanding of the emotional states of others, allowing them to observe, interpret, and use emotional information from others to learn about the world and form their own interpretations and responses to events (Wu et al., 2021).

Stranger Wariness

Many infants around the world display **stranger wariness** (also known as *stranger anxiety*), a fear of unfamiliar people. In many, but not all, cultures, stranger wariness emerges at about 6 months and increases throughout the first year of life, beginning to decrease after about 15 months of age (Bornstein et al., 2013; Sroufe, 1977). Locomotion, infant success in crawling or walking, tends to precede the emergence of stranger wariness, suggesting interconnections among motor and emotional development (Brand et al., 2020). From an evolutionary perspective, stranger wariness may have emerged to protect infants as they became able to initiate new interactions with unknown and potentially unsafe adults (Hahn-Holbrook et al., 2010).

Whether infants show stranger wariness depends on their overall disposition, past experience, and the situation in which they meet a stranger (Salvadori et al., 2022; R. A. Thompson & Limber, 1991). The pattern of stranger wariness varies among infants. Some show rapid increases and others show slow increases in stranger wariness; once wariness has been established, some infants show steady decline and others show more rapid changes. Twin studies suggest that these patterns are influenced by genetics because the patterns of change are more similar among monozygotic twins (identical twins who share 100% of their genes) than dizygotic twins (fraternal twins who share 50% of their genes) (Brooker et al., 2013).

Among North American infants, stranger wariness is generally expected by parents and caregivers. However, infants of the Efe people of Zaire, Africa, show little stranger wariness. This is likely related to the Efe collective caregiving system, in which Efe babies are passed from one adult to another, relatives and nonrelatives alike (Tronick et al., 1992), and the infants form relationships with the many people who care for them (Meehan & Hawks, 2013). In contrast, babies reared in Israeli kibbutzim (cooperative agricultural settlements that tend to be isolated and subjected to terrorist attacks), tend to demonstrate widespread wariness of strangers. By the end of the first year, when infants look to others for cues about how to respond emotionally, kibbutz babies display far greater anxiety than babies reared in Israeli cities (Saarni et al., 1998). In this way, stranger wariness may be adaptive, modifying infants' drive to explore in light of contextual circumstances (Easterbrooks et al., 2012).

Stranger wariness illustrates the dynamic interactions between the individual and context (LoBue & Adolph, 2019). Infant's emotionality and temperamental style, tendencies toward social interaction, and, of course, past experiences with strangers are important. Parental expectations and anxiety also matter. Infants whose mothers report greater stress reactivity, who experience more anxiety and negative affect in response to stress, show higher rates of stranger wariness (Brooker et al., 2013; Waters et al., 2014). Characteristics of the stranger (e.g., their height), the familiarity of the setting, and how quickly the stranger approaches influence how the infant appraises the situation (LoBue et al., 2019).

Infants are more open when the stranger is sensitive to the infant's signals and approaches at the infant's pace (Mangelsdorf, 1992). Not all infants show stranger wariness. Instead, whether how and how long infants demonstrate stranger wariness is the result of the dynamic interplay among individual characteristics, experiences, and context (LoBue & Adolph, 2019).

Children's Emotional Experience

Over the first few months of life, infants display the full range of basic emotions. As their cognitive and social capabilities develop, they can experience complex social emotions, such as embarrassment. The social world plays a role in emotional development. Adults interact with infants, provide opportunities to observe and practice emotional expressions, and assist in regulating emotions. Much of emotional development is the result of the interplay of infants' emerging capacities and the contexts in which they are raised. Through this process, infants become capable of new and more complicated emotions and relationships with others and develop a greater sense of self-understanding, social awareness, and self-management. These processes collectively are referred to as **emotional competence** (Salisch et al., 2022).

Advances in cognition, language, and a growing sense of self enable children to recognize, understand, and talk about their emotions in increasingly advanced ways (Bell et al., 2019; Shablack & Lindquist, 2019). As children develop emotional competence they are better able to appraise others' emotions and influences on emotions, infer causes and consequences of others' emotions, and regulate their emotional reactions (Camras & Halberstadt, 2017; Goodvin et al., 2015)

Understanding Others' Emotions

As he watches his mother leave, preschooler Donald begins to cry. His classmate Amber tells the teacher, "Donald is sad. He misses his mommy," and she brings Donald a toy. "Don't be sad," she says. By 3 to 4 years of age, children recognize and name emotions based on their expressive cues. By age 4, children begin to understand that external factors (such as losing a toy) can affect emotion and can predict a peer's emotion and behavior (such as feeling sad and crying or feeling angry and hitting things) (Goodvin et al., 2015).

The emergence of theory of mind has profound implications for emotional development (Weimer et al., 2021). As children begin to take other people's perspectives, they can apply their understanding of emotions to understand and help others, such as recognizing that a sibling is sad and offering a hug. Children can begin to appreciate the role of internal factors, such as desires, on emotion and behavior (Wellman, 2017). By age 5, most children understand that desire can motivate emotion, and many understand that people's emotional reactions to an event can vary based on their desires.

Elementary school children are more likely to refer to internal causes, such as thoughts or desires, as motivations for emotions rather than external causes, such as breaking a toy (Flavell et al., 2001). At about age 6 to 7, children incorporate their growing understanding of beliefs into their attributions for emotion; they begin to appreciate that a person's belief will determine their emotional reaction to a situation (Lagattuta et al., 2015; Pons et al., 2004). In one study, 4-, 5-, and 7-year-old children listened to scenarios depicting a child alone or accompanied by another person (mother, father, friend) who encounters a scary creature. With age, children were more likely to realize that different people will experience different intensities of fear in the same situation and that people's beliefs and fears could change with the use of strategies (such as reminding oneself that the creature is not real) (Sayfan & Lagattuta, 2009). Older children's concept of emotion expands to include a temporal element, for example, that emotional intensity tends to gradually dissipate over time; that emotions can be triggered by thinking about past events; and that personal background, experiences, and personality influence emotional reactions (Goodvin et al., 2015; Lagattuta et al., 2015).

Although a basic grasp of emotion emerges early, it is not until late childhood that children can appreciate that people can have mixed or conflicting emotions; they can feel both happy and sad or fearful (De Rosnay et al., 2014; Pons et al., 2004). In one study, 4- to 11-year-old children listened to a story about a child who got a new kitten to replace one that ran away. Most 5-year-old children believed that the child would feel happy about the new kitten and rejected the idea that the child might feel both happy about the new kitten and sad about the lost kitten. Yet most 7- to 8-year-olds and nearly all 10- to 11-year-olds thought the child would feel mixed emotions (Donaldson & Westerman, 1986). Other research supports the finding that by age 8, most children can recognize that a person can have mixed emotions and that when presented with emotional stimuli, such as a movie with a bittersweet ending, children themselves can report experiencing both happy and sad emotions (Larsen et al., 2007).

Social Interaction and Emotional Understanding

Interactions with others are essential in advancing children's understanding of emotions. When parents talk about emotions and explain their own and their child's emotions, preschoolers can better evaluate and label others' emotions and show better adjustment (Ogren & Johnson, 2020; S. F. Thompson et al., 2020). Children's interactions with siblings offer important opportunities to practice identifying emotions, decoding the causes of emotions, anticipating the emotional responses of others, and using their emotional understanding to influence their relationships and affect the behavior of others (Kramer, 2014).

Young children also often enact emotions in pretend sociodramatic play, providing experience and practice in understanding emotions and their influence on social interactions (Goodvin et al., 2015). Pretend play with siblings and peers gives children practice in acting out feelings, considering others' perspectives, implementing self-control, regulating aggression, and improving the children's understanding of emotion (Hoffmann & Russ, 2012; Laurent et al., 2018). One study showed that preschoolers' sociodramatic play predicted their expressiveness, knowledge, and emotion regulation 1 year later (Lindsey & Colwell, 2013). Parent-child interactions remain an important influence on emotional development throughout elementary school (Castro et al., 2015).

Classrooms also offer many opportunities for children of all ages to learn about emotions through play, modeling, and direct instruction (K. M. Lewis et al., 2021; Valiente et al., 2020). Book reading is associated with emotional development in young and older children (Batini et al., 2020). Adults who accompany book reading with discussion about the characters, their emotions, and their motivations can help advance preschoolers' emotional understanding (Schapira & Aram, 2020). Preschool teachers also engage in emotion coaching, helping young children understand the emotions they feel and see in others (Curby et al., 2022; Yelinek & Grady, 2019). Likewise, elementary school teachers who model emotional strategies and help students identify and practice positive interactions with others promote positive development (K. M. Lewis et al., 2021).

Masks and Emotion Recognition

The use of masks during the COVID-19 pandemic raised concerns about their impact on children's ability to recognize emotions in others. Several recent studies have explored this issue with varying results. One recent study found that children and adults had difficulty inferring emotions when masks covered their faces, but young children (ages 3–5) were particularly poor at identifying emotions (Gori et al., 2021). School-aged children (7–12 years old) also showed worse emotion recognition of masked faces, with more pronounced effects for happy, sad, and fearful faces than angry and neutral faces (Chester et al., 2023). In this study, children whose families reported greater social disruption in response to the pandemic have more difficulty identifying emotions of masked faces. This could be because these children spent more time at home with unmasked family members and therefore become less proficient at reading masked faces than their peers. Stress may also play a role in impairing children's ability to read others' emotions. However, another study involving preschoolers found that they were able to recognize emotions in pictures of masked adults about as well as those with unmasked adults, suggesting resilience (Schneider et al., 2022). Three- to 5-year-old children can identify emotions on masked faces when the emotion is explicitly stated or implicitly inferred, similar to real-world scenarios where emotional expressions accompany social interaction (Giordano et al., 2024). These overall mixed findings point to the role of individual differences and circumstances in shaping development.

Adolescents' Emotional Experience

Similar to other periods of development, in adolescence emotional development is intertwined with cognitive development. In early adolescence, around age 12, young people can understand simultaneous conflicting emotions (Coe-Odess et al., 2019). As their abstract reasoning skills improve, they gain insight into their own emotions and can understand that the same event can trigger different emotional responses. Adolescents begin to compare emotions across situations, predict emotional reactions in themselves and others, and experience emotions in response to memories of past events and anticipation of future events (Phillips & Power, 2018).

A popular, though inaccurate, view of adolescence is the moody teenager slamming the door to their room: Is adolescence a time of extreme emotional volatility? The popular belief that adolescence is a tumultuous time for both teenagers and parents can be traced back to the work of psychologist G. Stanley Hall (1904), who is often regarded as the "father of adolescence." Hall believed that puberty, the biological transition to reproductive maturity, triggered an inevitable and extreme upheaval known as storm and stress, which he believed was universal among adolescents.

Research over the last century has shown that Hall's beliefs about the nature of adolescence and adolescent moodiness are not entirely accurate. While every adolescent experiences puberty and biological changes undoubtedly influence behavior, it is only during the early stages of puberty that hormones rapidly increase and fluctuate enough to cause erratic and powerful shifts in adolescents' emotions and behavior (Reiter & Lee, 2001). Pubertal hormones are only weakly and inconsistently related to adolescent mood (Balzer et al., 2015; Duke et al., 2014). As discussed in Chapter 4, adolescents' experiences of puberty vary depending on factors such as the age of onset, the duration and intensity of changes, their temperament and emotional-regulation skills, and environmental supports (Hollenstein & Lougheed, 2013). Therefore, developmental scientists agree that while some adolescents may experience emotional volatility, it is not driven by hormones, or an inevitable or universal feature of adolescence (Arnett, 1999; Larson & Ham, 1993).

A research method known as event sampling has helped us learn about adolescents' emotional experience. In studies that employ the *event sampling method* participants carry pagers and report their experiences and feelings at random points throughout the day (Larson & Csikszentmihalyi, 2014; Richards & Larson, 1993). Studies using this method have shown that adolescents often experience more intense emotions that vary with their context, and they experience more shifts in context than many adults throughout the day (home, school, peers, after-school activities) (Bailen et al., 2019; Larson et al., 2014). Shifts in mood may be related to encountering surprises, unexpected events and experiences (Gregorová et al., 2024). Therefore, differences in adolescents' and adults' emotional experiences may be related to their varying shifts in context.

Generally, the frequency of positive emotions tends to decline and negative emotions tend to increase over adolescence (Larson, Moneta, et al., 2002). Specifically, older adolescents experience less frequent and less intense positive emotions and more frequent negative emotions than children and younger adolescents (Frost et al., 2015; Larson et al., 2014; Reitsema et al., 2021). Adolescents also experience more negative emotions than adults and more extremes of emotion, with a broader range of highs and lows (Coe-Odess et al., 2019; Larson, Wilson, et al., 2002). However, adolescents' negative moods are also less stable and quicker to dissipate than adults.

Brain development plays a critical role in adolescents' emotional experience. Recall from Chapter 4 that the limbic system, including the amygdala, implicated in aggression, develops rapidly in early adolescence. Adolescents tend to experience greater amygdala activity in response to triggers than adults, suggesting greater emotional reactivity and potentially negative emotions (C. Tamnes & Mills, 2020). The prefrontal cortex, the seat of reasoning and cognitive control, determines how emotions are interpreted, controlled, and acted on. The prefrontal cortex develops later and on a longer path throughout adolescence into early adulthood. Adolescents are likely to feel strong emotions before they can control them (Herd et al., 2020). With brain maturation, adolescents become better able to regulate their emotions.

> **THINKING IN CONTEXT 10.1**
>
> 1. Identify examples of how infants' experience and expression of self-conscious emotions are influenced by their interactions with others and their physical and cultural context. How might infants' self-conscious emotions impact their social interactions and relationships?
> 2. How might social referencing and stranger wariness reflect adaptive responses to a context? Why does stranger wariness vary among children and cultures?
> 3. Give examples of how children's cognitive development influences and is influenced by advances in emotional development.
> 4. Consider your emotional experience during adolescence. Do you recall experiencing strong emotions or rapid shifts in mood? If so, what do you think may have contributed these shifts? What aspects of your context may have influenced your emotional experience as an adolescent, whether it was intense and unstable or more mellow and stable?

EMOTIONAL REGULATION

> **10.2** Discuss the development of emotional regulation from infancy through adolescence.

Infants and children can identify emotions, but can they control their emotions? **Emotion regulation** is the ability to control emotions. It involves managing intense feelings and determining when and how to release them. Emotion regulation becomes important as children become aware of social standards and rules, such as how anger can be displayed.

Infancy

How do infants regulate emotions? Young infants rely on caregivers to help them manage strong emotions by holding them, rocking them, and limiting their access to over arousing stimuli (Gee & Cohodes, 2021).

Managing Emotions

During the first 2 to 3 months of life infants manage negative emotions by sucking vigorously on their hands or objects. At about 3 months of age infants start to use voluntary motor behaviors, such as turning their bodies away from distressing stimuli (Baker, 2018). Smiling is also thought to serve a purpose in regulating emotions, because it allows infants to control aspects of a situation without losing touch with it. When infants get excited and smile, they often look away briefly. This involuntary behavior may be a way of breaking themselves away from the stimulus and allowing them to regroup, preventing overstimulation. Smiling is associated with a decline in heart rate, suggesting that it is a relaxation response to decrease infants' level of arousal.

At 6 months, infants are more likely to use gaze aversion and fussing as primary emotion regulatory strategies, while at 12 months of age, they are more likely to use self-soothing (e.g., thumb sucking, rocking themselves) and distraction (chewing on objects, playing with toys) (Crowell, 2021). Responsive caregiving that acts in line with children's responses, helping them orient or move toward or away from overwhelming stimuli can help infants and toddlers regulate their emotions (Stifter & Augustine, 2019). With advances in cognition and motor control the infant can explore the environment by walking, initiate social interactions, and remember past experiences (Baker, 2018). By 18 months of age, toddlers actively attempt to change distressing situations, such as by moving away from upsetting stimuli, and they begin to use distraction, such as by playing with toys or talking (Crockenberg & Leerkes, 2004; Feldman et al., 2011). The caregiving environment plays a large role in infants' and toddlers' emerging abilities to engage in self-regulation. Warm and supportive interactions with parents and other caregivers can help infants understand their emotions and learn how to manage them.

Caregiver Sensitivity

Caregivers play a critical role in helping infants manage and regulate their emotions. They use various soothing behaviors, such as soft vocalizations and minimizing exposure to overwhelming stimuli, to help very young infants regulate their emotions (Spinelli & Mesman, 2018). Sensitive caregivers are attuned to infants' emotional reactions and try to satisfy their needs, elicit positive responses and minimize negative ones, and maintain an optimal level of arousal (stimulating but not overwhelming) (Baker, 2018). When mothers respond promptly to their 2-month-old infants' cries, these infants cried for shorter durations, were better able to manage their emotions, and stopped crying more quickly than other infants at 4 months of age (Jahromi & Stifter, 2007). Responsive parenting that is attuned to infants' needs helps infants develop skills in emotion regulation, especially in managing negative emotions like anxiety, as well as their physiological correlates, such as accelerated heart rate (Feldman et al., 2011; Samdan et al., 2020). Caregiver sensitivity predicts self-regulation during stressful situations in infancy through middle childhood (Morawska et al., 2019; Rattaz et al., 2022).

Responsive parenting helps infants learn to manage their emotions and self-regulate.
kate_sept2004/istock

The form that caregiver sensitivity and adaptive responsiveness take can vary with culture and socialization goals (Bornstein & Esposito, 2020). Caregivers from Western individualist societies socialize their infants to Western values, such as independence. In a Western context, pausing to encourage infants to self-soothe fosters autonomy, a cultural value. In non-Western contexts that value collectivism, responding immediately to infant cries encourages interdependence, connections with others, and community. Appropriate responses to infants vary with cultural context—and no cultural context is better or worse in promoting emotional development (Raval & Walker, 2019).

Therefore, cultures often have particular beliefs about how much responsiveness is appropriate when babies cry and fuss, as well as expectations about infants' abilities to regulate their own emotions (Halberstadt & Lozada, 2011). The !Kung hunter-gatherers of Botswana, Africa, respond to babies' cries nearly immediately (within 10 seconds), whereas Western mothers tend to wait a considerably longer period before responding to infants' cries (e.g., 10 minutes) (Barr et al., 1991). Fijian mothers tend to be more responsive than U.S. mothers to negative facial expressions in their infants (Broesch et al., 2016). Gusii mothers focus on protection and nurturance to protect infants from harm and disease. Like !Kung mothers, Gusii mothers respond immediately to their babies' cries, but responsivity tends to be nonverbal and subtle, so much so that researchers once believed that they were not responsive (Mesman et al., 2018). Infants from non-Western cultures are thought to cry very little because they are carried often. In one study, infants born to parents who were recent immigrants from Africa cried less than U.S. infants, illustrating the role of culture in influencing infant cries (Bleah & Ellett, 2010).

Overall, parents and caregivers use a variety of strategies to help infants learn to manage emotions, including direct intervention, modeling, selective reinforcement, control of the environment, verbal instruction, and touch (Stifter & Augustine, 2019; Waters et al., 2017). These strategies change as the infants grow older. Touching becomes a less common regulatory strategy with age, whereas vocalizing and distracting techniques increase (Meléndez, 2005). When mothers guide infants to regulate their emotions, they tend to engage in distraction and mother-oriented strategies, such as seeking help, during frustrating events (J. C. Thomas et al., 2017). Parents who model emotion regulation strategies, such as using distraction, are more likely to have toddlers who use those strategies to soothe themselves in stressful situations (Schoppmann et al., 2019).

Dynamic Caregiver-Infant Interactions

Infants' interactions with their caregivers are dynamic and undergo continuous transformations as infants develop. Infants' growing motor and language skills, such as crawling, creeping, walking, and talking, introduce new challenges and opportunities for their interactions with parents and caregivers as well as their socioemotional growth (Adolph & Franchak, 2017). As crawling begins, parents and caregivers respond with happiness and pride, positive emotions that encourage infants' exploration. As infants gain motor competence, they wander further from their parents (Thurman & Corbetta, 2017). Crawling increases a toddler's capability to attain goals—a capability that, while often satisfying to the toddler, may involve hazards.

As infants become more mobile, emotional outbursts become more common. Parents report that advances in locomotion are accompanied by toddlers' increased frustration as they attempt to move in ways that often exceed their abilities or are not permitted by parents (Clearfield, 2011; Pemberton Roben et al., 2012). When mothers recognize the dangers posed to toddlers by objects such as houseplants, vases, and electrical appliances, they sharply increase their expressions of anger and fear, which leads to anger and fear in their toddlers. At this stage, parents actively monitor toddlers' whereabouts, protect them from dangerous situations, and expect them to comply—a dynamic that is often a struggle, amounting to a test of wills. At the same time, these struggles help the child begin to develop a grasp of mental states in others that are different from their own.

Although all caregivers can influence infants' emotional development, research has tended to focus on infants' interactions with mothers (Islamiah et al., 2023). Mothers and infants systematically influence and coregulate each other's emotions and behaviors (Buhler-Wassmann & Hibel, 2021; Rattaz et al., 2022). Mothers regulate infant emotional states by interpreting their emotional signals, providing appropriate arousal, modeling emotional responses, and reciprocating and reinforcing infant reactions. Infants influence their mother's emotions through their responsiveness to her initiations and stimulation, and by responding to her emotions (Bornstein et al., 2012; Hajal & Paley, 2020). The limited research examining fathers shows similar associations. Sensitive parenting by fathers, including relationship quality, positive and supportive responses to infants' expression of emotions, and modeling of emotional regulation strategies is associated with infants' emotional regulation skills (Islamiah et al., 2023). By experiencing a range of emotional interactions—times when their emotions mirror those of their caregivers and times when their emotions are different from those of their caregivers—infants learn how to transform negative emotions into neutral or positive emotions and regulate their emotional states (Guo et al., 2015).

Childhood

Throughout childhood, children make great strides in regulating their emotions and become better able to manage how they experience and express emotions. These developments in emotion regulation are influenced by cognitive abilities, especially executive function, and language development (Bell et al., 2019; Stifter & Augustine, 2019).

Strategies

Emotion regulation strategies develop over time and influence children's emotional experience (Eisenberg et al., 2015). By age 4, children can explain simple strategies for reducing emotional arousal, such as limiting sensory input (covering their eyes), self-talk ("It's not scary"), self-soothing (thumb sucking), or changing their goals ("I want to play blocks," after having been excluded by children who are playing a different game) (R. A. Thompson & Goodvin, 2007). At 6 to 7 years old, children continue to rely on behavioral strategies like fleeing from distressing situations and by about age 8 begin to report using cognitive strategies like distraction (Pons et al., 2004; Zimmer-Gembeck & Skinner, 2016). School-age children learn how to redirect their attention, reconceptualize situations ("It's not so bad"), and increasingly use cognitive strategies to regulate their emotions (Crowell, 2021; Riediger & Bellingtier, 2022). Overall, children become more reflective and strategic in managing their emotions as they age. Self-regulation helps children manage difficult circumstances, but the specific mechanisms they use vary with context (Eisenberg et al., 2015). For example, a child who assertively responds to a bully by protesting loudly when a teacher is nearby but quietly tolerates it when adults are absent may be showing two forms of competent emotion regulation, adaptive to each specific context (R. A. Thompson, 2011). As children grow, they become more aware of the contexts in which it is appropriate to express certain emotions (Quiñones-Camacho & Davis, 2020). Learning to cope with and change intense emotions is adaptive.

Emotional Display Rules

By middle childhood, children understand that emotions can be intentionally hidden, as well as appreciate the concept of emotional display rules (D. C. Jones et al., 1998; Misailidi, 2006). These rules involve masking socially undesirable true feelings in favor of more socially appropriate emotional expression that preserves relationships, avoids hurting others' feelings, and protects self-esteem (Goodvin et al., 2015). For instance, young children may express their displeasure with a gift by rejecting it outright, saying "I don't want this!", because they are not yet aware of the social implications of their behavior. As children enter middle childhood, they begin to understand the concept of emotional display rules and learn to manage their emotional behavior accordingly. Unlike younger children, they will likely express gratitude for an undesirable gift, even if their true feelings differ, by providing fake smiles and keeping their feelings private (Goodvin et al., 2015; Kromm et al., 2015).

As in infancy, the development of emotional understanding and display rules concerning emotion emerges from parent-child interactions (Malatesta & Haviland, 1982). Parents react to and shape their children's emotional expressions, which can vary depending on cultural beliefs about emotion (Friedlmeier et al., 2011).

Cultural Socialization

Parents remain important resources for emotional management in childhood. Mothers' emotional awareness and management skills influence children's emotional regulation skills (Crespo et al., 2017). Responsive parenting, such as framing experiences for children, explaining expectations and strategies for emotional management, and modeling emotion regulation, can foster children's emotion regulation skills (Sala et al., 2014; Sosa-Hernandez et al., 2020; Stifter & Augustine, 2019). Conversely, dismissive or hostile reactions to children's emotions prevent them from learning to manage and not be overwhelmed by their emotions (Speyer et al., 2022; Zeman et al., 2013).

In Western parent-child dyads, the encouragement of emotional expression and provision of instrumental support (scaffolding) is viewed as supportive and thought to be associated with children's emotion knowledge and social competence. In contrast, punitive, harsh responses that minimize children's emotions are labeled as nonsupportive and are associated with poor emotional competence in children. U.S. parents tend to endorse supportive socialization responses more than those that are unsupportive (Cassano et al., 2007). Still parents offer more support in helping children manage some emotions than others. For example, parents of school-age children in the United States tend to be more understanding and provide more emotional and instrumental support in response to children's sadness than anger, similar to parents in India who also are more responsive to sadness than anger (Shipman & Zeman, 2001; Zeman & Garber, 1996).

In the South Asian country of Nepal, naturalistic observation of Tamang (Indigenous inhabitants) and Brahman (Hindu upper caste) families illustrate cultural differences in emotional socialization of intense emotions, such as anger. One study showed that Tamang mothers discouraged children's anger by scolding and teasing, perhaps reflecting the Tamang culture's Buddhist values of minimizing emotion, as well as their low social status relative to Brahmans (Cole et al., 2006). Brahman parents, on the other hand, responded to children's anger with reasoning, not encouragement or punishment. Tamang and Brahman parents also differed in responses to shame. Tamang parents responded to children's shame with a combination of ignoring, reasoning, and nurturing. Brahman parents ignored shame, perhaps because shame is inconsistent with the Brahman high social caste. Among school-age children, Brahman children showed a greater awareness of the need to conceal anger as compared with Tamang or U.S. children (Cole et al., 2006). These findings suggest that emotional socialization varies even within collectivist societies, perhaps reflecting the myriad contexts that can coexist within a society (Friedlmeier et al., 2011).

As children develop their emotion regulation skills, they begin to feel more in control of their emotional experience (McClelland et al., 2015; Saarni & Carolyn, 2000). Emotional regulation plays a key role in children's ability to adapt to their environment, including the unique demands of the school setting (Harrington et al., 2020). Children who can direct their attention and distract themselves when distressed or frustrated tend to be well-behaved students and are often liked by their peers (Frenzel et al., 2023; McClelland & Cameron, 2011). Furthermore, these skills in emotion regulation are associated with social competence and overall adjustment (J. Deneault & Ricard, 2013).

Adolescence

Emotion regulation skills, such as recognizing, monitoring, evaluating, and modifying emotional reactions, continue to develop throughout adolescence and into emerging adulthood (Fombouchet et al., 2023; Sanchis-Sanchis et al., 2020). These skills are influenced by cognitive and brain development as well as interaction with others in the social environment (Fombouchet et al., 2023). The ability to regulate emotions is crucial for forming and maintaining interpersonal relationships and influences mental health (Daniel et al., 2020; Phillips & Power, 2018).

Adolescents use a wider variety of emotion regulation strategies than children, including more proactive strategies such as seeking emotional support and reflecting on their experiences and feelings, and fewer passive regulation strategies such as avoidance and denial (Coe-Odess et al., 2019; Silvers, 2022). Throughout adolescence, the range of coping strategies increases, and adolescents switch between strategies more flexibly, enabling them to adapt to a multitude of situations.

A key emotional regulation strategy is cognitive reappraisal, which involves reconsidering a situation from a different perspective. The capacity for cognitive reappraisal increases rapidly from childhood through mid-adolescence (Silvers, 2020; Theurel & Gentaz, 2018). However, not all adolescents consistently use this strategy in their everyday lives, and its use does not show consistent age-related increases (De France & Hollenstein, 2022; Fombouchet et al., 2023; Silvers & Guassi Moreira, 2019). Despite this, cognitive reprisal is associated with effectively managing distressing emotions and overall psychological well-being, and it can buffer adolescents' responses to stressors, such as those that accompanied the COVID-19 pandemic (Chervonsky & Hunt, 2019; Kuhlman et al., 2021).

Concealment, which involves minimizing how and which emotions are expressed to achieve social goals, is a common emotion regulation strategy used by adolescents. While masking an emotion can sometimes be adaptive, such as when experiencing peer victimization, it is not always beneficial (Herd & Kim-Spoon, 2021). With development, adolescents learn when and how to mask their emotions while also gaining the social and self-awareness to know when to do so. Distancing, or stepping back from an emotional situation, also becomes common during adolescence (Nook et al., 2020).

Contextual factors can pose risks for emotional regulation. Household chaos and the stress associated with low socioeconomic status (SES) homes and neighborhoods can influence families' emotional climate and interactions, which in turn can influence adolescents' emotional regulation skills (Herd et al., 2020). Responsive caregiving by parents, characterized by supervision, acceptance, and support, remains an important influence on emotional regulation in adolescence. Parenting practices that invalidate adolescents' emotions or exert psychological control are linked to adolescent emotion regulation difficulties (Silvers, 2022). Poor peer interactions, such as bullying, are associated with impaired emotion regulation processes measured behaviorally and in the brain (Herd & Kim-Spoon, 2021). Adolescents' experiences can influence emotional regulation and are also influenced by their emotional regulation skills.

Overall, emotion regulation increases with age (Sanchis-Sanchis et al., 2020). Adolescents can modulate intense emotions, learn to self soothe and attend to emotions, separate momentary emotional experiences from their overall sense of self, maintain interpersonal relationships that prompt strong emotions, and use cognitive skills to understand the nature and source of emotions (Phillips & Power, 2018; Silvers, 2022). These developments have significant and enduring consequences for emotional experience, socioemotional development and mental health in adolescence and adulthood (Azpiazu Izaguirre et al., 2021; Daniel et al., 2020).

> **THINKING IN CONTEXT 10.2**
>
> 1. How do other domains of development, such as cognition, language, and motor skills, support emotional regulation in infants, children, and adolescents? Give examples for each stage.
> 2. How does the influence of parents and caregivers on children's emotional regulation change over time, from infancy to adolescence? Explain.
> 3. What strategies could be used to teach children and adolescents cognitive reappraisal for emotional regulation? How might developmental factors, such as age and cognitive ability, influence your lesson and the effectiveness of these strategies?

TEMPERAMENT

> **10.3** Analyze the role of temperament and goodness of fit in children's development.

Some babies are easygoing. They sleep through the night, happily eat new foods, and smile often, adapting to the rhythm of each day. People, even babies, tend to react to the world in predictable ways. **Temperament**, the characteristic way in which an individual approaches and reacts to people and situations, is thought to be one of the basic building blocks of emotion and personality (Strelau, 2020). Temperament has strong biological determinants; behavior genetics research has shown genetic bases for temperament (Saudino & Micalizzi, 2015; Zwir et al., 2020). Yet the expression of temperament reflects reciprocal interactions among genetic predispositions, maturation, and experience (C. Liu et al., 2023; Rothbart & Posner, 2022). Every infant behaves in a characteristic, predictable style that is influenced by their inborn tendencies toward arousal and stimulation as well as by experiences with adults and contexts (Gartstein et al., 2024; Planalp & Goldsmith, 2020). In other words, every infant displays a particular temperament style.

Styles of Temperament

Begun in 1956, the New York Longitudinal Study is a pioneering study of temperament that followed 133 infants into adulthood. Early in life, the infants in the study demonstrated differences in nine characteristics that are thought to capture the essence of temperament (Buss & Plomin, 1984; Chess & Thomas, 1991; Goldsmith et al., 1987):

1. *Activity level.* Some babies wriggle, kick their legs, wave their arms, and move around a great deal, whereas other babies tend to be more still and stay in one place.
2. *Regularity.* Some infants are predictable in their patterns of eating, sleeping, and defecating; other babies are not predictable.
3. *Approach-withdrawal.* Some babies tend to approach new situations, people, and objects, whereas others withdraw from novelty.
4. *Adaptability.* Some babies get used to new experiences and situations quickly; others do not.
5. *Intensity of reaction.* Some babies have very extreme reactions, giggling exuberantly and crying with piercing wails. Other babies show more subdued reactions, such as simple smiles and soft, whimpering cries.
6. *Threshold of responsiveness.* Some babies notice many types of stimuli—sights, sounds, and touch sensations—and react to them. Other infants notice few types of stimuli and seem oblivious to changes.

7. *Quality of mood.* Some babies tend toward near-constant happiness, while others tend toward irritability.

8. *Distractibility.* Some babies can be easily distracted from objects or situations, while others cannot.

9. *Attention span.* Some babies play with one toy for a long time without becoming bored, whereas others get bored easily.

Some aspects of infant temperament, particularly activity level, irritability, attention, and approach-withdrawal (sometimes called sociability), show stability for months and years at a time and in some cases even into adulthood (Lemery-Chalfant et al., 2013; Papageorgiou et al., 2014; Sieber & Zmyj, 2022). Infants' growing ability to regulate their attention and emotions holds implications for some components of temperament, such as rhythmicity, distractibility, and intensity of reaction.

The expression of these nine characteristics that comprise temperament can be grouped into three temperament profiles (A. Thomas & Chess, 1977; A. Thomas et al., 1970):

1. **Easy temperament:** Easy babies are often in a positive mood, even-tempered, open, adaptable, regular, and predictable in biological functioning. They establish regular feeding and sleeping schedules easily. About 40% of the longitudinal sample were categorized as having an easy temperament.

2. **Difficult temperament:** Difficult babies are active, irritable, and irregular in biological rhythms. They are slow to adapt to changes in routine or new situations, show intense and frequent unpleasant moods, react vigorously to change, and have trouble adjusting to new routines. About 10% of the sample fell into this category.

3. **Slow-to-warm-up temperament:** Just as it sounds, slow-to-warm-up babies tend to be inactive, moody, and slow to adapt to new situations and people. They react to new situations with mild irritability but adjust more quickly than do infants with difficult temperaments. Roughly 15% of the infants in the sample showed these characteristics.

Although it may seem as if all babies could be easily classified, about one third of the infants in the New York Longitudinal Study did not fit squarely into any of the three categories but displayed a mix of characteristics, such as eating and sleeping regularly but being slow to warm up to new situations (A. Thomas et al., 1970; A. Thomas & Chess, 1977). Individuals vary and sometimes show patterns of behavior and development that differ from research findings and models. Further research is needed to understand these differences.

Another influential model of temperament, by Mary Rothbart, includes three dimensions (Rothbart, 2011; Rothbart & Bates, 2007):

1. Extraversion/surgency—the tendency toward positive emotions. Infants who are high in extraversion/surgency approach experiences with confidence, energy, and positivity, as indicated by smiles, laughter, and approach-oriented behaviors.

2. Negative affectivity—the tendency toward negative emotions, such as sadness, fear, distress, and irritability.

3. Effortful control—the ability to focus attention, shift attention, and inhibit responses to manage arousal. Infants who are high in effortful control are able to regulate their arousal and soothe themselves.

From this perspective, temperament reflects individual differences in biological reactivity and control (Rothbart & Posner, 2022). It includes how easily we react to or become emotionally aroused by stimuli, as well as how well we are able to control our emotional arousal (Rothbart, 2011). Some infants and children are better able to distract themselves, focus their attention, and inhibit impulses than others. The ability to self-regulate and manage emotions and impulses is associated with positive long-term adjustment, including school readiness, academic achievement, social competence, and resistance to stress (Chen & Schmidt, 2015; Potmesilova & Potmesil, 2021). Generally speaking, a difficult temperament poses risks to adjustment (MacNeill & Pérez-Edgar, 2020). Preterm infants are predisposed to experience difficult temperaments as they tend to show greater arousal, difficulty focusing their attention, and trouble regulating their arousal than full-term infants (Cassiano et al., 2020; Reyes et al., 2019).

Infant temperament tends to be stable over the first year of life but less so than childhood temperament, which can show stability over years, even into adulthood (Bornstein et al., 2019; Strelau, 2020). In infancy, temperament is especially open to environmental influences, such as interactions with others (Bornstein et al., 2015; Gartstein et al., 2016). Young infants' temperament can change with experience, neural development, and sensitive caregiving (e.g., helping babies regulate their negative emotions) (Goodvin et al., 2015; Jonas et al., 2015). As infants gain experience and learn how to regulate their states and emotions, those who are cranky and difficult may become less so. By the second year of life, styles of responding to situations and people are better established, and temperament becomes more stable. Temperament at age 3 remains stable, predicting temperament at age 6 and personality traits at age 26 (Dyson et al., 2015).

Context and Goodness of Fit

Like all aspects of development, temperament is influenced by reciprocal reactions among individuals and their contexts. An important influence on socioemotional development is the **goodness of fit** between the child's temperament and the environment around them, especially the parents' temperaments and child-rearing methods (Chess & Thomas, 1991; Dong et al., 2022).

Infant Temperament

The specific behaviors that comprise adaptive parenting vary with the infants' temperament (MacNeill & Pérez-Edgar, 2020). Infants are at particular risk for poor outcomes when their temperaments show poor goodness of fit to the settings in which they live. If an infant who is fussy, difficult, and slow to adapt to new situations is raised by a patient and sensitive caregiver who provides time for them to adapt to new routines, the infant may become less cranky and more flexible over time. The infant may adapt their temperament style to match their context so that later in childhood they may no longer be classified as difficult and no longer display behavioral problems. If, on the other hand, a child with a difficult temperament is reared by a parent who is insensitive, coercive, and difficult in temperament, the child may not learn how to regulate their emotions and may have behavioral problems and adjustment difficulties that influence caregiving and worsen with age, even into adolescence and beyond (Gölcük & Berument, 2021). When children are placed in low-quality caregiving environments, those with difficult temperaments respond more negatively and show more behavior problems than do those with easy temperaments (Poehlmann et al., 2011).

Infant temperament both is influenced by and influences their bond with caregivers (Le Bas et al., 2020). Infants' temperament weeks after birth is associated with maternal bonding and the emerging mother-infant relationship (Takács et al., 2020). Goodness of fit at 4 and 8 months of age predicts a close bond with caregivers at 15 months (Seifer et al., 2014; Takács et al., 2020). An infant's temperament tends to be stable over time because certain temperamental qualities evoke certain reactions from others, promoting goodness of fit. Babies with an *easy* temperament usually get the most positive reactions from others, whereas babies classified as *difficult* receive mixed reactions (Chess & Thomas, 1991). An easy baby tends to smile often, eliciting smiles and positive interactions from others, including parents, which in turn reinforce the baby's easy temperamental qualities (Planalp et al., 2017; Wittig & Rodriguez, 2019). Conversely, a difficult baby may evoke more frustration and negativity from caregivers as they try unsuccessfully to soothe the baby's fussing. Mothers who view their 6-month-old infants as difficult may be less emotionally available to them (Kim & Teti, 2014). Babies' emotionality and negative emotions predict their mothers' perception of parenting stress and poor parenting behaviors, which in turn can influence their interactions (Oddi et al., 2013; Paulussen-Hoogeboom et al., 2007). Mothers of difficult infants may question their own parenting competence (Takács et al., 2019).

Caregiver Temperament and Expectations

Goodness of fit is also related to caregivers' temperament and their expectations about their infants and their ability to parent (Grady & Karraker, 2017). In one study, mothers who, *prior to giving birth*, considered themselves less well equipped to care for their infants were found to be more likely to have infants who showed negative aspects of temperament, such as fussiness, irritability, and difficulty being soothed (Verhage et al., 2013). This suggests that perceptions of parenting may shape views of infant temperament—and thereby shape temperament itself. In other research, 3 months after giving birth, new mothers' feelings of competence were positively associated with infant temperament. Mothers' beliefs about their ability to nurture are shaped by the interaction between their infants' traits and their own parenting self-efficacy, as well as their opportunities for developing successful caregiving routines (Verhage et al., 2013). This contextual dynamic has been found to hold true across cultures. Both British and Pakistani mothers in the UK reported fewer problems with their infants' temperaments at 6 months of age when the mothers had a greater sense of parenting efficacy and displayed more warm and less hostile parenting styles (Prady et al., 2014).

Socioemotional development is a dynamic process in which infants' behavior and temperament styles influence the family processes that shape their development. Sensitive and patient caregiving is not always easy with a challenging child, and adults' own temperamental styles influence their caregiving. A poor fit between the caregiver's and infant's temperaments can make an infant fussier and crankier. When a difficult infant is paired with a parent with a similar temperament—one who is impatient, irritable, and forceful—behavioral problems in childhood and adolescence are likely (Rubin et al., 1998; Strelau, 2020).

Experience and Goodness of Fit

Experience can influence children's biological functioning in ways that influence temperament. Exposure to extreme adversity, especially early in life, can exacerbate young children's reactivity to stress, heightening biological reactions to stress such as the release of stress hormones. As a result, such children can become more temperamentally wary and irritable (Ashman & Dawson, 2002; Wiik & Gunnar, 2009).

Infants from disenfranchised groups may be especially vulnerable to environmental stress. One study presented Black and White infants with tasks designed to evoke stress (such as the *still face task* in which the caregiver temporarily presents the infant with a still face that is nonresponsive to the infants' behavior). At 4 months of age the infants showed similar levels of the stress hormone cortisol, but at 12 months Black infants showed higher levels of cortisol than White infants (Dismukes et al., 2018). Racial differences in SES, experiences of discrimination, and urban life stressors may contribute to differences in infants' stress reactivity with potentially lifelong implications. Notably, supportive relationships can buffer stress reactivity. For example, children who are temperamentally reactive are able to respond to stress adaptively in the presence of a sensitive caregiver (Engel & Gunnar, 2020). However, caregivers' ability to provide sensitive care can vary with environmental stressors. Adverse experiences and contexts can impair parenting.

Children's environments change over time in ways that can also influence goodness of fit. As children mature, parents, teachers, and other adults increasingly expect more competent, self-controlled behavior; the school setting requires compliance, initiative, and cooperation; and children increasingly participate with adults in circumstances (like church or concerts) in which they must understand and enact socially appropriate behavior. A particular temperamental profile may fit well with environmental demands and opportunities at one age (e.g., low persistence or attention span in infancy) but may be a poor fit later (e.g., the same characteristics in the school years). In this way, the goodness of fit is developmentally and contextually dynamic, and influences the stability of temperamental attributes over time as well as later personality (Dong et al., 2022; Goodvin et al., 2015).

Cultural Differences in Temperament

Researchers have observed consistent cultural differences in temperament that are rooted in cultural norms for how individuals are perceived. Japanese mothers view their infants as interdependent beings who must learn the importance of relationships and connections with others (Rothbaum et al., 2000). North American mothers, on the other hand, view their task as shaping babies into autonomous beings (Kojima, 1986). Whereas Japanese mothers tend to interact with their babies in soothing ways, discouraging strong emotions, North American mothers are active and stimulating (Rothbaum et al., 2000). Differences in temperament result, such that Japanese infants tend to be more passive, less irritable and vocal, and more easily soothed when upset than North American infants (Kojima, 1986; M. Lewis et al., 1993; Rothbaum et al., 2000). Culture influences the behaviors that parents view as desirable and the means that parents use to socialize their infants (Chen & Schmidt, 2015; Davidov, 2021; Kagan, 2013). Culture, therefore, plays a role in how emotional development—in this case, temperament—unfolds.

In some cultures, infants cry very little, perhaps because they are in constant contact with their mothers, supporting responsive caregiving.

John S Lander/Contributor/Getty Images

Asian cultures often prioritize low arousal and emotionality and socialize infants in line with these values. Chinese American, Japanese American, and Hmong children tend to display lower levels of irritability and less physical activity, but also lower levels of positive emotions, and they engage in more self-quieting and self-control than do European American children (Friedlmeier et al., 2015; Senzaki et al., 2021; Slobodskaya et al., 2013; Super & Harkness, 2010). Similarly, a comparison of toddlers from Chile, Poland, South Korea, and the United States showed that the South Korean toddlers scored highest on measures of control, combined with low levels of activity (Krassner et al., 2017). Outward control, however, may be accompanied by internal stress. In one study, 4-month-old Japanese infants receiving an inoculation showed a pronounced cortisol response, suggesting that they were experiencing great stress, but they cried little. A comparison group of U.S. infants showed a great distress and took longer to calm down, but showed a lower cortisol response. Although the Japanese babies appeared quiet and calm, they were *more* physiologically stressed than the U.S. infants. Cultural views of the nature of arousal and emotional regulation influence parenting behaviors and ultimately infants' responses to stressors (Davidov, 2021; Friedlmeier et al., 2015).

What constitutes an adaptive match between infant temperament and context—goodness of fit—varies with culture and potentially with the many contexts within a culture (Dong et al., 2022). Sometimes these relationships are surprising. Consider the Maasai, an African semi-nomadic ethnic group. In times of drought, when the environment becomes extremely hostile, herds of cattle and goats die, and infant mortality rises substantially. Under these challenging conditions, infants with difficult temperaments tend to survive at higher rates than do those with easy temperaments. Infants who cry and are demanding are attended to, are fed more, and are in better physical condition than easy babies, who tend to cry less and therefore are assumed to be content (Gardiner & Kosmitzki, 2018). Thus, the Maasai infants with difficult temperaments demonstrate higher rates of survival because their temperaments better fit the demands of the hostile context in which they are raised. Temperament, therefore, must be considered in context.

THINKING IN CONTEXT 10.3

1. In your view, are extreme changes in temperament possible, such as moving from an easy temperament to difficult, or the reverse? Why? If so, how might these changes occur?
2. Give examples of contextual factors in the home, childcare or school settings, and community that might influence goodness of fit, and thereby infants' temperament and adjustment.

ATTACHMENT

> **10.4** Examine the development of attachment, its stability, and associated outcomes.

Monroe gurgles and cries out while lying in his crib. As his mother enters the room, he squeals excitedly. Monroe's mother smiles as she reaches into the crib, and Monroe giggles with delight as she picks him up. Monroe and his mother have formed an important emotional bond called attachment.

What Is Attachment?

Attachment refers to a lasting emotional tie between two people who strive to maintain closeness to the other and act to ensure the relationship continues (Fraley & Shaver, 2021). Attachment relationships serve as an important backdrop for emotional and social development. Our earliest attachments are with our primary caregivers, most often our mothers. It was once thought that feeding determined patterns of attachment. Freud, for example, emphasized the role of feeding and successful weaning on infants' personalities and well-being. Behaviorist theorists explain attachment as the result of infants associating their mothers with food, a powerful reinforcer that satisfies a biological need. Certainly, feeding is important for infants' health and well-being and offers opportunities for the close contact needed to develop attachment bonds, but feeding itself does not determine attachment.

In one famous study, baby rhesus monkeys were reared with two inanimate surrogate *mothers*: one made of wire mesh and another covered with terrycloth (see Figure 10.1). The baby monkeys clung to the terrycloth mother despite being fed only by the wire mother, suggesting that attachment bonds are not based on feeding but rather on contact comfort (Harlow & Zimmerman, 1959). So how does an attachment form, and what is its purpose?

Bowlby's Ethological Theory of Attachment

John Bowlby, a British psychiatrist, posed that early family experiences influence emotional disturbances not through feeding practices, conditioning, or psychoanalytic drives, but via inborn tendencies to form close relationships. Specifically, Bowlby (1969, 1988) developed an ethological theory of attachment that characterizes it as an adaptive behavior that evolved because it contributed to the survival of the human species. Inspired by ethology (the study of animal behavior), particularly by Lorenz's work on the imprinting of geese (see Chapter 1) and by observations of interactions of monkeys, Bowlby posited that humans are biologically driven to form attachment bonds with other humans. An attachment bond between caregivers and infants ensures that the two will remain in close proximity, thereby aiding the survival of the infant and, ultimately, the species. From this perspective, caregiving responses are inherited and are triggered by the presence of infants and young children.

Infants' Signals and Adults' Responses

From birth, babies develop a repertoire of behavior signals to which adults naturally attend and respond, such as smiling, cooing, and clinging. Crying is a particularly effective signal because it conveys negative emotion that adults can judge reliably, and it motivates adults to relieve the infants' distress. Adults are innately drawn to infants, find infants' signals irresistible, and respond in kind. One study found that nearly 700 mothers in 11 countries (Argentina, Belgium, Brazil, Cameroon, France, Kenya, Israel, Italy, Japan, South Korea, and the United States) tended to respond to their infants' cries and distress by picking up, holding, and talking to their infants (Bornstein et al., 2017). Infants' behaviors, immature appearance, and even smell draw adults' responses (Kringelbach et al., 2016). Infants, in turn, are attracted to caregivers who respond consistently and appropriately to their signals. During the first months of life, infants rely on caregivers to regulate their states and emotions—to soothe them when they are distressed and help them establish and maintain an alert state (R. A. Thompson, 2013). Attachment behaviors provide comfort and security to infants because they bring babies close to adults who can protect them.

FIGURE 10.1 ■ Harlow's Study: Contact Comfort and the Attachment Bond

This infant monkey preferred to cling to the cloth-covered mother even if fed by the wire mother. Harlow concluded that attachment is based on contact comfort rather than feeding.

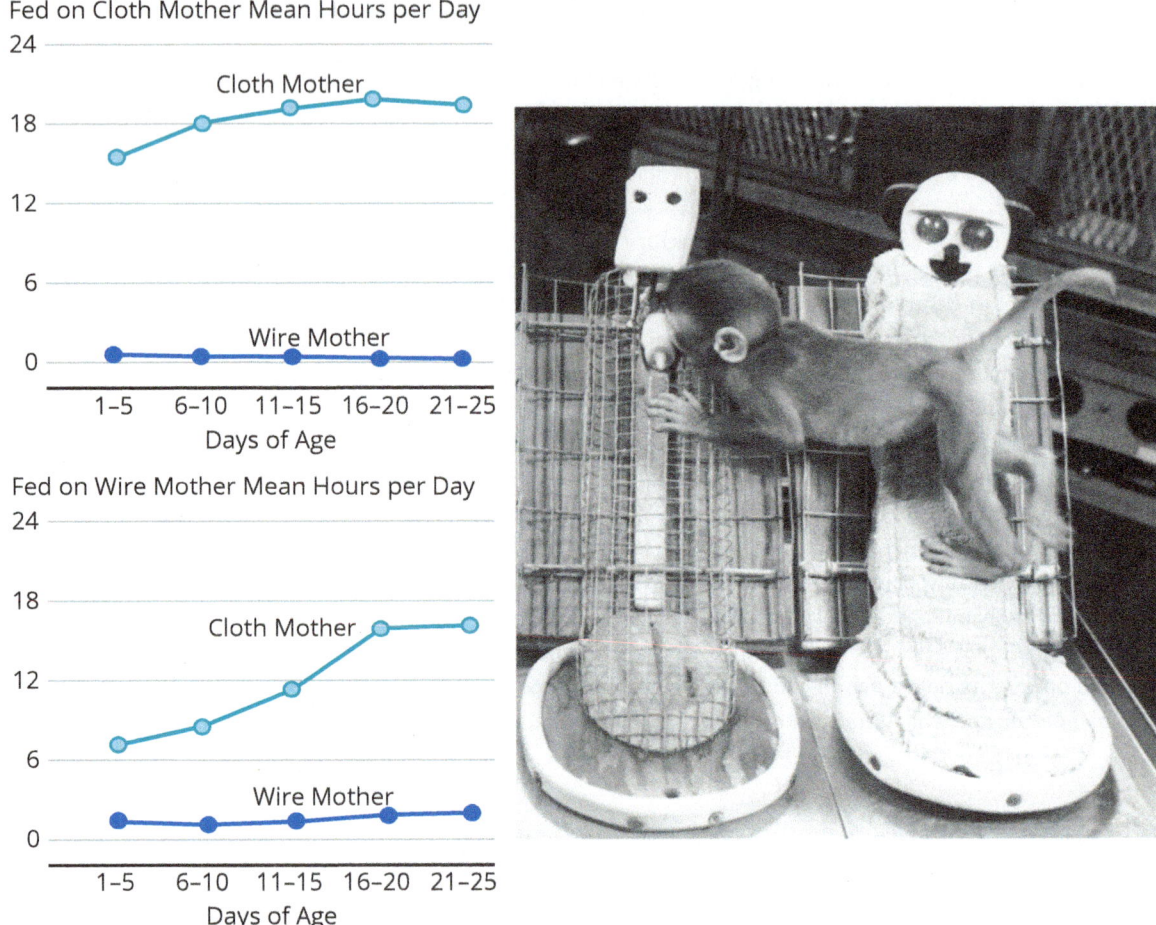

Source: Harlow, H. F. (1958). The nature of love. *American Psychologist, 13*(12), 673–685. https://doi.org/10.1037/h0047884; Photo Researchers Inc/Science Source.

The hormone oxytocin plays a role in attachment, suggesting a biological component to caregiver-infant attachment. Research with mothers and infants shows that both experience a rise in oxytocin during interactions characterized by sensitive caregiving and with secure attachment (Kohlhoff et al., 2017, 2022). Fathers show similar increases in oxytocin when they interact with their children (Gettler et al., 2021; Morris et al., 2021). In addition, fMRI results show greater brain activity when mothers see their infant's face, compared to other infant faces, and greater activity in areas associated with rewards in response to seeing happy, but not sad, infant faces (Strathearn et al., 2008). In response to their infants' cries, Chinese, Italian, and U.S. mothers show brain activity in regions associated with auditory processing, emotion, and intention, suggesting automatic responses to infant expressions of distress (Bornstein et al., 2017).

Phases of Attachment

Bowlby proposed that attachment formation progresses through several developmental phases during infancy, from innate behaviors that bring the caregiver into contact with the infant to a mutual attachment relationship. Infants' behavior becomes increasingly organized, adaptable, and intentional with each phase.

Phase 1: Pre-Attachment—Indiscriminate Social Responsiveness (birth to 2 months): Infants instinctively elicit caregiving responses from caregivers by crying, smiling, and making eye contact with adults. Infants respond to any caregiver who reacts to their signals, whether parent, grandparent, childcare provider, or sibling.

Phase 2: Attachment in the Makings—Discriminating Sociability (2 through 6–7 months): When caregivers are sensitive and consistent in responding to babies' signals, babies learn to associate their caregivers with the relief of distress, forming the basis for an initial bond. Babies begin to discriminate among adults and prefer familiar people. They direct their responses toward a particular adult or adults who can best soothe them.

Phase 3: Clear-Cut Attachments—Discriminating Sociability (7 to 24 months): Infants develop attachments to specific caregivers who attend to, accurately interpret, and consistently respond to their signals. Infants can gain proximity to caregivers through their own motor efforts, such as crawling. As attachments form, infants may experience **separation anxiety** (sometimes called *separation protest*), a reaction to separations from an attachment figure that is characterized by distress, crying, and clinging (Lamb & Lewis, 2015). Separation anxiety tends to increase between 8 and 15 months of age then declines. This pattern appears across cultures as varied as those of the United States, Israeli kibbutzim, and !Kung hunter-gatherer groups in Africa (Kagan et al., 1994). Separation anxiety declines as infants develop reciprocal relationships with caregivers and can understand and predict parents' patterns of separation and return, reducing their confusion and distress.

Phase 4: Reciprocal Relationships—Multiple Attachments (24 to 30 months and onward): With advances in cognitive and language development, children can engage with their primary caregiver as partners, taking turns and initiating interactions within the attachment relationship. They begin to understand others' emotions and goals and apply this understanding through strategies such as social referencing. They also begin to develop attachment relationships with other responsive adults.

Ainsworth's Strange Situation and Attachment Classifications

Virtually all infants form an attachment to their parents, but Canadian psychologist Mary Salter Ainsworth (1940) proposed that infants differ in **security of attachment**—the extent to which they feel that parents can reliably meet their needs. Like Bowlby, Ainsworth believed that infants must develop a dependence on parents, viewing them as a metaphorical secure base, to feel comfortable exploring the world (Salter, 1940). To examine attachment, Mary Ainsworth developed the **Strange Situation**, a structured observational procedure that reveals the security of attachment when the infant is placed under stress. As shown in Table 10.2, the Strange Situation is a structured observation task consisting of eight 3-minute-long episodes performed in a specific sequence. In each segment, the infant is with the parent (typically the mother), with a stranger, with both parent and stranger, or alone. Researchers observe infants' exploration of the room, their reaction when the mother leaves the room, and, especially, their responses during reunions, when the mother returns.

TABLE 10.2 ■ The Strange Situation

Event	Attachment Behavior Observed
Experimenter introduces mother and infant to playroom and leaves.	
Infant plays with toys and parent is seated.	Mother as secure base
Stranger enters, talks with caregiver, and approaches infant.	Reaction to unfamiliar adult
Mother leaves room; stranger responds to baby if upset.	Reaction to separation from mother
Mother returns and greets infant.	Reaction to reunion
Mother leaves room.	Reaction to separation from mother
Stranger enters room and offers comfort to infant.	Reaction to stranger and ability to be soothed by stranger
Mother returns and greets infant. Tries to interest the infant in toys.	Reaction to reunion

On the basis of responses to the Strange Situation, infants are classified into one of several attachment types (Ainsworth et al., 1978).

- **Secure Attachment** The securely attached infant uses the parent as a secure base, exploring the environment and playing with toys in the presence of the parent, but regularly checking in (e.g., by looking at the parent or bringing toys). The infant shows mild distress when the parent leaves. On the parent's return, the infant greets the parent enthusiastically, seeks comfort, and then returns to individual play. About two thirds of North American infants who complete the Strange Situation are classified as securely attached (Lamb & Lewis, 2015).

- **Insecure-Avoidant Attachment** Infants who display an insecure-avoidant attachment show little interest in the mother and busily explore the room during the Strange Situation. The infant is not distressed when the mother leaves and may react to the stranger in similar ways as to the mother. The infant ignores or avoids the mother on return or shows subtle signs of avoidance, such as failing to greet her or turning away from her. About 15% of samples of North American infants' responses to the Strange Situation reflect this style of attachment (Lamb & Lewis, 2015).

- **Insecure-Resistant Attachment** Infants with an insecure-resistant attachment show a mixed pattern of responses to the mother. The infant remains preoccupied with the mother throughout the procedure, seeking proximity and contact, clinging even before the separation. When the mother leaves, the infant is distressed and cannot be comforted. During reunions, the infant's behavior suggests resistance, anger, and distress. The infant might seek proximity to the mother and cling to her while simultaneously pushing her away, hitting, or kicking. About 10% of North American infants tested in the Strange Situation fall into this category (Lamb & Lewis, 2015).

- **Insecure-Disorganized Attachment** A fourth category was added later to account for the small set of infants (10% or below) who show inconsistent, contradictory behavior in the Strange Situation. The infant with insecure-disorganized attachment shows a conflict between approaching and fleeing the caregiver, suggesting fear (Main & Solomon, 1986). Infants showing insecure-disorganized attachment experience the greatest insecurity, appearing disoriented and confused, and may show extreme fear of the caregiver.

These attachment classifications have been studied over five decades. A recent meta-analysis of 285 studies examining over 20,000 parent-child dyads in 20 countries conducted between 1987 and 2020 found similar proportions of attachment types, with over 50% of infants globally showing secure attachment, regardless of parent-child race or gender (Madigan et al., 2023).

Secure Base and Internal Working Models

Attachment is crucial for infants' development. When infants are securely attached to their caregivers, they feel confident to explore using their attachment figure as a **secure base**, or foundation, to return to when frightened. Attachment therefore has a cascading effect on other aspects of development. Infants who use their caregivers as a secure base develop motor skills as they explore their environment. Exploration challenges their cognitive abilities, and they get experience interacting with others, advancing their socioemotional development.

Attachment also influences infants' emerging sense of self because it becomes internalized and represented as an **internal working model**, a mental model of the caregiving relationship and infants' expectations for care. Internal working models include infants' expectations about whether they are worthy of love, of whether their attachment figures will be available during times of distress, and how they will be treated. The internal working model influences the development of self-concept, or sense of self, in infancy and guides later relationships throughout life (Bretherton & Munholland, 2016; R. A. Thompson et al., 2022).

Secure parent-child attachments are associated with positive socioemotional development in infancy that extends through childhood and adolescence. Insecure attachment is associated with poor responses to interpersonal stress, including elevated cortisol levels and other markers of physiological reactivity (Groh & Narayan, 2019). Insecure attachment in infancy, especially disorganized attachment, is associated with long-term negative outcomes, including less positive and more negative affect, poor emotional regulation, poor social competence, and higher rates of antisocial behavior, depression, and anxiety from childhood into adulthood (Cooke et al., 2019; Groh et al., 2017; Zajac et al., 2020).

Influences on Attachment

The most important determinant of infant attachment is the caregiver's ability to consistently and sensitively respond to the child's signals (Ainsworth et al., 1978; Behrens et al., 2011).

Sensitive Caregiving

Infants become securely attached to caregivers who are sensitive and offer high-quality responses to their signals, who accept their role as caregiver, who are accessible and cooperative with infants, who are not distracted by their own thoughts and needs, and who feel a sense of efficacy (Woodhouse et al., 2020). Mothers of securely attached infants provide stimulation and warmth and consistently synchronize or match their interactions with their infants' needs (Beebe et al., 2010; Gerlach et al., 2022). Secure mother-infant dyads show more positive interactions and fewer negative interactions compared with insecure dyads (Guo et al., 2015; Hoehl et al., 2021). The goodness of fit between the infant and the parent's temperament influences attachment, supporting the role of reciprocal interactions in attachment (Seifer et al., 2014).

Infants' experience of perinatal stress, adversity in the weeks after birth, may increase their risk for insecure attachment (Thiel et al., 2021). Preterm infants who are born very early often require prolonged hospitalization and separation from their mothers, potentially disrupting caregiver-infant physical contact and interaction. Preterm infants and their parents tend to experience heightened stress, which is associated with reduced caregiver sensitivity and a greater risk for insecure attachment (Fuertes et al., 2024; Gonçalves et al., 2020). However, a recent meta-analysis of hundreds of studies conducted globally suggested that preterm status, medical conditions, and neurodevelopmental disabilities were not associated with an increased risk for insecure attachment (Madigan et al., 2023). Adversity may pose risks for insecure attachment, but attachment outcomes ultimately depend on caregiver responsiveness, which can promote resilience in the face of adversity (Gerlach et al., 2022).

Insecure attachment is associated with caregiving that is rigid, unresponsive, inconsistent, and demanding (Venta & Abate, 2021). The insecure-avoidant attachment pattern is associated with parental unavailability or rejection. Insecure-resistant attachment is associated with inconsistent and unresponsive parenting, sometimes offering overstimulating and intrusive care and other times care that is not attentive to the infant's signals. Disorganized attachment is more common among infants who have been abused or raised in particularly poor caregiving environments, but disorganized attachment itself is not an indicator of abuse (Granqvist et al., 2017). In many cases, insecure attachment responses may represent adaptive infant responses to poor caregiving environments (Weinfield et al., 2008). Toddlers who show an avoidant attachment tend to rely on self-regulated coping rather than turning to others (Zimmer-Gembeck et al., 2017). Not relying on an unsupportive parent may represent a good strategy for infants.

Caregiver Depression

When caregivers experience challenges, they often have difficulty providing responsive, nurturing care (Dozier & Bernard, 2023). Depression can interfere with caregivers' ability to recognize their infants' needs and provide sensitive care. Both mothers and fathers can become depressed, which can disrupt attachment, but most of the research to date has examined mothers (Ertekin Pinar & Ozbek, 2022). The hormonal and social changes that accompany pregnancy and new motherhood place women at risk for postpartum depression, depression that occurs in the months after childbirth. However, depression can occur at any time in life.

Mothers who are depressed tend to view their infants differently than nondepressed mothers and independent observers (Newland et al., 2016). They are more likely to identify negative emotions (i.e., sadness) than positive emotions (i.e., happiness) in infant faces and tend to disengage faster from infant emotional expressions (Vismara et al., 2021; Webb & Ayers, 2015). Challenging behaviors, such as fussiness and crying, and difficult temperaments tend to elicit more negative responses from depressed mothers (Newland et al., 2016).

Mothers who are depressed tend to be less responsive to their babies, show less affection, use more negative forms of touch, and show more negative emotions and behaviors such as withdrawal, intrusiveness, hostility, coerciveness, and insensitivity (Jennings et al., 2008; Śliwerski et al., 2020). Given the poor parent-child interaction styles that accompany maternal depression, it may not be surprising that infants of depressed mothers show a variety of negative outcomes, including insecure attachment, overall distress, withdrawn behavior, poor social engagement, and difficulty regulating emotions (Barnes & Theule, 2019; Granat et al., 2017). They tend to show greater physiological arousal in response to stressors, difficulty reading and understanding others' emotions and are at risk for later problems in development (Y. Liu et al., 2017; Prenoveau et al., 2017; Suurland et al., 2017). The ongoing reciprocal interactions between mothers and infants account for the long-term negative effects of maternal depression.

Yet low sensitivity is not always associated with poor outcomes. Infants can develop secure attachments to less sensitive caregivers as long as their basic needs are met and they maintain a calm regulated state (Cassidy et al., 2005). One study of 4.5-month-old infants from predominantly Black, White, and Hispanic low SES homes found that caregiver provision of a secure base (meeting basic needs and fostering a sense of calm) predicted attachment even in the presence of caregiver insensitivity (Woodhouse et al., 2020). Infants' brains may predispose them to form attachments, regardless of the quality of care (Opendak & Sullivan, 2019). In addition, infants develop attachments to other members of the family system, such as fathers (Cabrera et al., 2014; Dagan & Sagi-Schwartz, 2018; Lickenbrock & Braungart-Rieker, 2015).

Attachment occurs within a larger family system. Attachments with one caregiver influence and are influenced by those with other caregivers, and the multiple attachment relationships among family members influence the family's interactions as a whole (Brown et al., 2022). Caregivers benefit from secure attachment to their infants. Attachment reduces mothers' depressive symptoms, improves their physiological regulation of stress and physical health, and can aid resilience to trauma and other stressors in addition to improving mother-child interactions (Norholt, 2020).

Father-Infant Attachment

Fathers and infants develop attachment bonds. Similar to mothers, oxytocin rises when fathers first hold their newborn and when they touch their infants (Gettler et al., 2021; Morris et al., 2021). Fathers interact with their newborns much like mothers do. They provide similar levels of care by cradling the newborn and performing tasks like diaper changing, bathing, and feeding (Combs-Orme & Renkert, 2009). This is true of fathers globally, in Western and non-Western contexts, such as the Kadazan of Malaysia and Aka and Bofi of Central Africa (B. S. Hewlett & MacFarlan, 2010; Hossain et al., 2007; Madigan et al., 2023).

Men and women often have different interaction and communication patterns with infants, with women engaging in more care and soothing behaviors and men more stimulating play (Morawska, 2020). Fathers tend to engage in more unpredictable rough-and-tumble play that is often met with positive reactions and arousal from infants and children (Amodia-Bidakowska et al., 2020). Stimulating and responsive father-infant interactions are associated with secure attachment (Bakermans-Kranenburg & van IJzendoorn, 2023; Olsavsky et al., 2020).

Differences in mothers' and fathers' interaction styles appear in many cultures, including France, India, Italy, and Switzerland, as well as among African American, European American, and Hispanic American families in the United States (Best et al., 1994; Hossain et al., 1997; Roopnarine et al., 1992). Interaction styles differ more in some cultures than in others. For example, German, Israeli kibbutzim, and Swedish, fathers, as well as fathers in the Aka ethnic group of Africa's western Congo basin, are not more playful than mothers (Frodi et al., 1983; B. Hewlett, 2008; B. S. Hewlett et al., 1998;

Sagi et al., 1985). Furthermore, overall and across cultures, infants demonstrate similar attachments to both mothers and fathers (Lamb & Lewis, 2015; Madigan et al., 2023).

Like mothers, father-child interaction is associated with social competence, independence, and cognitive development (Brown & Aytuglu, 2020; Cabrera et al., 2018). Fathers provide opportunities to practice arousal management by providing high-intensity stimulation and excitement, like tickling, chasing, and laughing. Fathers who are sensitive, supportive, and appropriately challenging during play promote father-infant attachment relationships (Lickenbrock & Braungart-Rieker, 2015; Olsavsky et al., 2020). The positive social, emotional, and cognitive effects of father-child interaction continue from infancy into childhood and adolescence (Cabrera et al., 2018; A.-A. Deneault et al., 2021). In addition, an infant's secure attachment relationship with one caregiver can compensate for the negative effects of an insecure attachment to another caregiver (Boldt et al., 2014; Dagan & Sagi-Schwartz, 2018). Finally, throughout this discussion we have used the terms father and mother, however, caregiver gender identity, sexual orientation, or biological or adoptive status have no bearing on infant attachment relationships (Feugé et al., 2020; Madigan et al., 2023; McConnachie et al., 2020).

Fathers tend to have different interaction styles than mothers. Father-infant interaction tends to be play-oriented. This is true of fathers in Western contexts as well as those in non-Western contexts, such as the Kadazan of Malaysia and Aka and Bofi of Central Africa.

kate_sept2004/istock

Stability of Attachment

Attachment patterns tend to be stable over infancy and early childhood, especially when securely attached infants receive continuous responsive care (McIntosh et al., 2024; Opie et al., 2021). Yet attachment can change. The loss of a parent, parental divorce, a parent's psychiatric disorder, and physical abuse, as well as changes in family stressors, adaptive processes, and living conditions, can transform a secure attachment into an insecure attachment pattern later in childhood or adolescence (Feeney & Monin, 2016; Lyons-Ruth & Jacobvitz, 2016).

Attachment is complex and influenced by contextual factors outside the parent-infant relationship. Conflict among parents is associated with lower levels of attachment security (E. S. Tan et al., 2018). Contextual factors such as low SES, family and community stressors, and the availability of supports influence attachment stability through their effect on parents' emotional and physical resources and the quality of parent-infant interactions (Booth-LaForce et al., 2014; R. A. Thompson, 2016; Van Ryzin et al., 2011). Caregivers who experience intimate violence or reside in communities that threaten physical and emotional safety may provide less sensitive caregiving (Coe et al., 2021; O'Sullivan & Monk, 2020).

Challenging life circumstances and contexts associated with insecure attachment, such as caregiver physical and mental health problems, low SES, and environmental stress, may persist throughout the life span and contribute to the long-term continuity of poor outcomes (Granqvist et al., 2017; Zelekha & Yaakobi, 2020). Longitudinal research suggests that insecure attachment may be passed from generation to generation. Caregivers who have experienced insensitive parenting may be less sensitive to their infants' needs, thereby transmitting their own insecure attachment to their children (Raby et al., 2015; Risi et al., 2021).

Cultural Variations in Attachment Classifications

Infants of all cultures become attached to their caregivers. Infants in many countries, including Germany, Holland, Japan, and the United States, approach the Strange Situation in similar ways

(O'Shaughnessy, 2023; Sagi et al., 1991). Secure and insecure attachment patterns occur in a wide variety of cultures in Africa, Asia, Europe, the Middle East, and North America (Cassibba et al., 2013; Jin et al., 2012; Madigan et al., 2023).

Nevertheless, there are subtle differences in attachment across cultures. The behaviors that characterize sensitive caregiving vary with culturally specific socialization goals, values, and beliefs of the parents, family, and community (Keller, 2019; Mesman et al., 2016). For example, German mothers' behavior is influenced by the shared cultural belief that infants should become independent at an early age and should learn that they cannot rely on the mother's comfort at all times. German infants are more likely than U.S. infants to show an insecure-avoidant pattern of attachment. To observers raised in the United States, German mothers may seem unresponsive to their children's crying, yet they are demonstrating sensitive childrearing within their context (Grossmann et al., 1985).

Generally, insecure-avoidant attachments are more common in Western European countries, and insecure-resistant attachments are more prevalent in Japan and Israel (see Figure 10.2; Van Ijzendoorn & Kroonenberg, 1988). Because Western cultures emphasize individuality and independence, Western parents might interpret insecure-resistant behavior as clingy. Instead, parents from collectivist cultures that emphasize the importance of relationships may view insecure-resistant attachment as successful bonding (Gardiner & Kosmitzki, 2018; Keller, 2018). However, it is critical to note that the Strange Situation itself is a Western measure, developed in the United States. Cultural differences in infants' behavior in the Strange Situation may not reflect differences in attachment. That is, the behaviors that reflect sensitive caregiving and those that illustrate secure attachment may vary with culture because they are adaptations to different circumstances (O'Shaughnessy, 2023; Rothbaum et al., 2000).

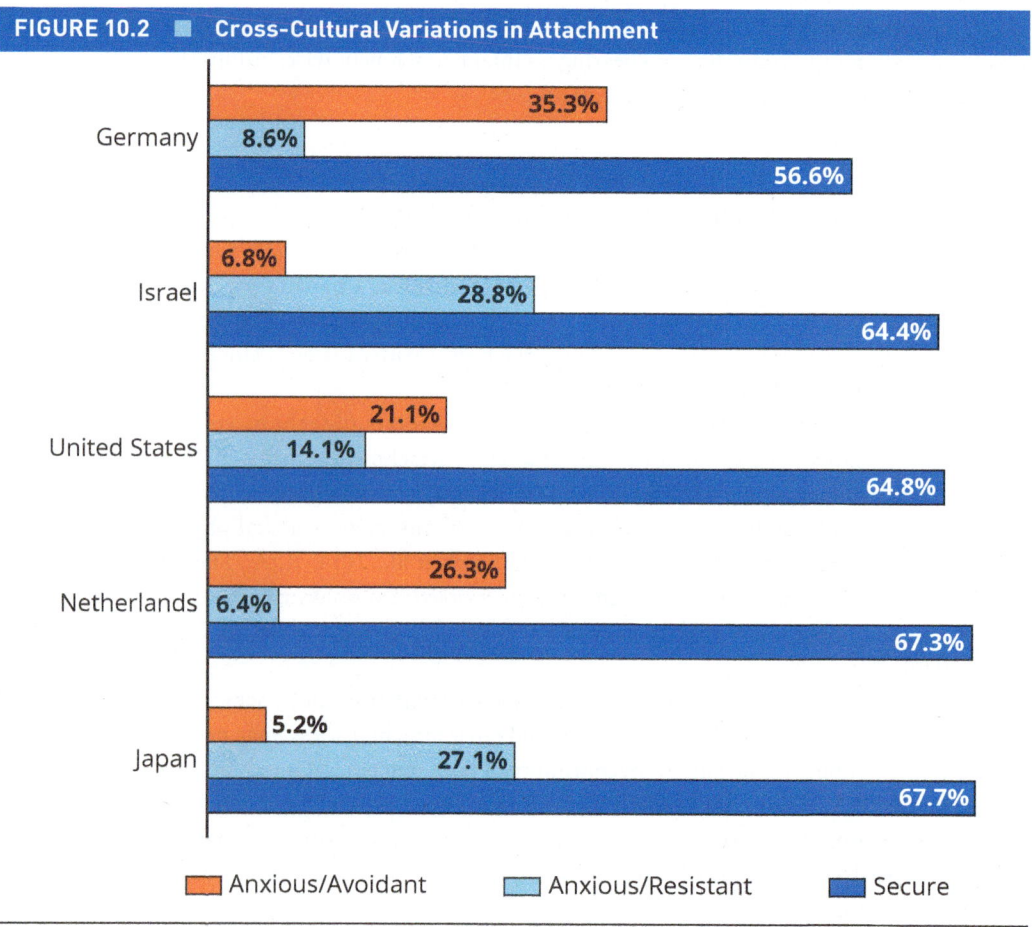

FIGURE 10.2 ■ Cross-Cultural Variations in Attachment

Germany: Anxious/Avoidant 35.3%, Anxious/Resistant 8.6%, Secure 56.6%
Israel: Anxious/Avoidant 6.8%, Anxious/Resistant 28.8%, Secure 64.4%
United States: Anxious/Avoidant 21.1%, Anxious/Resistant 14.1%, Secure 64.8%
Netherlands: Anxious/Avoidant 26.3%, Anxious/Resistant 6.4%, Secure 67.3%
Japan: Anxious/Avoidant 5.2%, Anxious/Resistant 27.1%, Secure 67.7%

Source: Adapted from Van Ijzendoorn M. H., & Kroonenberg, P. M. (1988). Cross-cultural patterns of attachment: A meta-analysis of the strange situation. *Child Development, 59*(1), 147–156. https://doi.org/10.2307/1130396

For example, insecure-resistant behavior as measured by the Strange Situation in Japanese samples of infants can be attributed to cultural childrearing practices that foster mother-infant closeness and leave infants unprepared for the separation episodes (Takahashi, 1990). The Strange Situation may be so stressful for them that they resist comforting. Similarly, infants who are raised in small, close-knit Israeli kibbutz communities do not encounter strangers in their day-to-day lives, so the introduction of a stranger in the Strange Situation procedure can be overly challenging for them. At the same time, kibbutz-reared infants spend much of their time with their peers and caregivers and see their parents infrequently and therefore may prefer to be comforted by people other than their parents (Sagi et al., 1985).

Dogon infants from Mali, West Africa, show rates of secure attachment that are similar to those of Western infants, but the avoidant attachment style is not observed (McMahan True et al., 2001). Dogon infant care practices diminish the likelihood of avoidant attachment because the infant is in constant proximity to the mother. Infant distress is promptly answered with feeding, and infants feed on demand, which reduces the risk of avoidant attachment.

Although most research on attachment has focused on the mother-infant bond, we know that infants form multiple attachments (Dagan & Sagi-Schwartz, 2018; R. A. Thompson et al., 2022). Consider the Efe foragers of the Democratic Republic of Congo, in which infants are cared for by many people, as adults' availability varies with their hunting and gathering duties (Morelli, 2015). Efe infants experience frequent changes in residence and camp, exposure to many adults, and frequent interactions with multiple caregivers. It is estimated that the Efe infant will typically come into contact with 9 to 14, and sometimes as many as 20, people within a 2-hour period. Efe infants are reared in an intensely social community and develop many trusting relationships—many attachments to many people (Morelli, 2015). The Western emphasis on mother-infant attachment may fail to acknowledge the many other attachment bonds that Efe infants form. All infants must develop attachments with some caregivers—but which caregivers, whether mothers, fathers, or other responsive adults, matter less than the bonds themselves.

Attachment in Childhood and Adolescence

Attachments and internal working models established in infancy influence children and adolescents' relationships and socioemotional development. Just as in infancy, children with a secure attachment tend to be confident, emotionally expressive, and capable of displaying positive and negative emotions. When upset, they can be comforted by parents who are sensitive to their needs. Children with an insecure-avoidant attachment tend to avoid relying on their parents for support and they show little distress in stressful situations. Children who show an insecure-resistant attachment tend to be ambivalent toward their parents, directing anger to their parents at the same time as they approach them for comfort. Children with a disorganized attachment tend to lack a consistent strategy for relating to their parents. They may appear scared and act unpredictably in stressful situations.

Preschool and school-age children who are securely attached as infants tend to be more curious, empathetic, self-confident, and socially competent, and they have more positive interactions and close friendships with peers than those who are insecurely attached (Boldt et al., 2014; Groh et al., 2017; Veríssimo et al., 2014). The advantages of secure attachment continue into adolescence. Adolescents who were securely attached in infancy and early childhood are more socially competent; tend to be better at making and keeping friends and functioning in a social group; and demonstrate better emotional regulation, self-esteem, and academic performance (Hong et al., 2023; Keizer et al., 2019; Rogers et al., 2022).

Children and adolescents with an insecure attachment pattern may develop negative views of themselves and the social world, feeling unworthy of love and seeing others as untrustworthy and negative. They tend to have more difficulty regulating their emotions and experience more negative emotions depression and behavior problems than securely attached children and adolescents (Cooke et al., 2018; de Vries et al., 2016). Those with insecure-resistant and insecure-avoidant attachments tend to view their attachment figures as unavailable, leading to a heightened risk for depression, negative self-image, low self-esteem, and a reduced sense of self-control (Khan et al., 2020; R. Tan et al., 2023). In contrast, the insecure-resistant pattern is associated with anxiety, because parents may alternate between rejecting and overprotective behaviors, limiting exploration. In addition, insecure-avoidant and disorganized attachment are linked to an increased risk of aggression, delinquency, substance use, and other risk behaviors (Buist, 2018). Over time, experience with attachment figures influences children's and adolescents' internal working models of self, which are used to engage in new relationships (Bowlby, 1973; Bretherton & Munholland, 2016). Attachment tends to be stable throughout adolescence, but as adolescents become more independent their attachment relationships change in form, function, and security (J. D. Jones et al., 2018). Adolescents and parents renegotiate their relationship and their positions and roles in the family, often resulting in increased conflict and insecurity. Generally, the quality of adolescent-parent attachment tends to temporarily decrease from early to middle adolescence, followed by a gradual increase until late adolescence (Buist, 2018). Even securely attached adolescents tend to increase emotional distance from parents, preferring peers to parents for attachment functions such as proximity seeking and separation protest and even a secure base (Buist, 2018). These changes in parent-adolescent relationships help adolescents become self-reliant and autonomous.

THINKING IN CONTEXT 10.4

1. In what ways does attachment illustrate the developmental principle that individuals play an active role in their development (see Chapter 1)? Explain.
2. Infants reared in impoverished orphanages may receive little attention and experience few meaningful interactions with caregivers. What might these experiences mean for the development of attachment? What outcomes and behaviors might you expect from children reared under such conditions? In your view, what can be done to help such children?
3. Attachment is only important in infancy. Agree or disagree? Explain your reasoning.

APPLY YOUR KNOWLEDGE

Eighteen-month-old Stefana toddles across the floor to her mother, gripping her mother's leg as she cries. "Ah, come here, hija," her mother, Perda, says as she scoops Stefana into her arms and soothes her, "Are you tired? Let's take a nap." As she puts Stefana in her crib Perda reminds herself that Stefana has come a long way.

From Day 1 Stefana was a challenge, as Perda's mother puts it. She cried through the day and night on most days. It was hard to determine what caused her to cry. Was the room too loud or too cold? Did she just wake up on the "wrong side of the crib"? Stefana was unpredictable, to say the least, sometimes liking specific foods—and other times spitting them out. Sometimes she napped and often she didn't. "Challenging or not, I'm here for my little girl," Perda thought.

At 18 months, Stefana is still unpredictable, but she is more easily soothed. Now when she hears a loud noise, like a truck backfiring outside, she no longer wails. Instead she looks to her mother and soon goes back to playing.

The childcare center teacher has noted that Stefana now adjusts much more easily to her mother leaving. When Perda goes to work, Stefana cries at first but sucks her thumb and begins to play shortly thereafter. She beams and runs to Perda when she returns every afternoon.

1. How would you describe Stefana's temperament? How do Stefana and Perda's temperament styles interact?
2. How would you describe Stefana's attachment style?
3. What long-term outcomes do you expect for Stefana?
4. Suppose Stefana lived in a different context, with a caregiver who shares her temperament or perhaps as an orphan in an orphanage that is understaffed and underfunded. Or perhaps with a loving mother but in an unsafe, unpredictable war zone. How might these contexts contribute to Stefana's emotional development?

CHAPTER SUMMARY

10.1 Describe how emotions are experienced and expressed in infancy, childhood, and adolescence.

Infants communicate their emotions through facial expressions and behavior, with basic emotions believed to be inborn and emerging at similar ages across cultures. Infants use social referencing to determine how to interpret and respond to ambiguous events, influenced by individual characteristics, experiences, and context. The development of self-conscious emotions, such as empathy, pride, embarrassment, shame, and guilt, depends on cognitive development and self-awareness. Culture shapes emotional expression and influences children's interactions with parents. As children develop emotional competence, they can recognize and understand others' emotions, infer causes and consequences, and appreciate the role of internal factors in emotions. Social interactions with parents, siblings, peers, and teachers offer important opportunities to practice identifying emotions, decoding their causes, anticipating emotional responses, and using emotional understanding to influence relationships and behavior. Adolescents understand emotions in more complex ways. While some adolescents may experience emotional volatility, it is not inevitable or universal. Brain development plays a role in adolescents' emotional experience. Adolescents are likely to feel strong emotions before they can control them, but with brain maturation, they become better able to regulate their emotions.

10.2 Discuss the development of emotional regulation from infancy through adolescence.

Infants rely on caregivers to help them manage their emotions. Caregivers who are attuned to infants' emotional reactions and respond promptly to their cries help infants develop skills in emotion regulation, particularly in managing negative emotions like anxiety. Caregiver sensitivity varies with cultural context. Parents use a variety of strategies to help infants learn to manage emotions, such as direct intervention, modeling, selective reinforcement, control of the environment, verbal instruction, and touch. Infants' interactions with their caregivers are dynamic and undergo continuous transformations as infants develop. Children's emotional development is influenced by cognitive abilities, executive function, and language development. Strategies for regulating emotions change with age and context, with children becoming more reflective and strategic in managing their emotions as they grow older. In adolescence, emotion regulation skills continue to develop, with adolescents using a wider variety of strategies, including cognitive reappraisal and concealment. Responsive caregiving by parents and positive interactions with peers remain important influences on emotional regulation. The development of emotion regulation has significant and enduring consequences for emotional experience, socioemotional development, and mental health in adolescence and adulthood.

10.3 Analyze the role of temperament and goodness of fit in children's development.

Temperament, the characteristic way in which an individual approaches and reacts to people and situations, has a biological basis. Children are classified into three temperament styles: easy, slow-to-warm-up, and difficult. Three dimensions also characterize temperament: extraversion/surgency, negative affectivity, and effort control. Temperament is influenced by the interaction of genetic predispositions, maturation, and experience. Temperament tends to be stable, but there are developmental and individual differences. Temperament is shaped by interactions between individuals and their environments. An important influence on socioemotional development is the goodness of fit between the child's temperament and the environment around them, especially the parent's temperament and child-rearing methods. Adaptive parenting behaviors differ based on the infant's temperament, with infants at risk of poor outcomes when their temperament mismatches their surroundings. Infant temperament tends to remain stable over time, with certain qualities evoking specific reactions from others that reinforce those temperamental traits. Cultural differences also play a role, with parents from different cultures socializing infants to prioritize different behaviors.

10.4 Examine the development of attachment, its stability, and associated outcomes.

Attachment refers to emotional bonds between people. Our earliest attachments are with our caregivers. Infants vary in the security of attachment. Using the Strange Situation, infants are categorized as securely attached or insecurely attached (insecure-avoidant, insecure-resistant, or insecure-disorganized). Attachment is influenced by the caregiver's ability to respond sensitively to the child's signals. Children develop multiple attachments and attachment patterns tend to be stable into childhood. The attachment bond developed during infancy is internally represented as working model of self. Secure attachments in infancy are associated with social competence and socioemotional health, continuing into childhood and adolescence. Attachment patterns are seen in a wide variety of cultures around the world, but the behaviors that make up sensitive caregiving vary with the socialization goals, values, and beliefs of the family and community, which may vary by culture.

KEY TERMS

attachment
emotion regulation
emotional competence
goodness of fit
insecure–avoidant attachment
insecure–disorganized attachment
insecure–resistant attachment
internal working model
primary emotions
secure attachment

secure base
security of attachment
self-conscious emotion
separation anxiety
social referencing
social smile
Strange Situation
stranger wariness
temperament

harpazo_hope/Getty Images

11 SELF, IDENTITY, AND PERSONALITY

> **LEARNING OBJECTIVES**
>
> **11.1** Discuss the development of self-concept from infancy through adolescence.
>
> **11.2** Describe patterns of change in self-esteem over childhood and adolescence.
>
> **11.3** Summarize processes of identity development, including its influences and outcomes.
>
> **11.4** Analyze the process of ethnic-racial identity development, including its influences, and its role in adjustment.
>
> **11.5** Examine achievement motivation and its influences.

"Hello baby," Nelson greeted his new nephew. "What's going on in there? Are you aware that you are a separate individual, a unique 'you'?" he asked. Nelson's sister, Jen, teased, "Don't pressure my baby. He's just a day old, it's hard to say for sure. But I'm sure he'll show us in time." Jen is right. We do not know what newborns feel and whether they are aware of their own existence, but it is clear that the sense of self becomes evident over infancy and grows and changes with development. In this chapter, we examine the development of self from infancy through adolescence.

SELF-CONCEPT

> **11.1** Discuss the development of self-concept from infancy through adolescence.

What are five words that describe you? A child might answer, "I'm a boy. I like dogs. Blue is my favorite color." How would you respond to the question? The words or phrases you use to describe yourself are examples of **self-concept**. Self-concept refers to our knowledge and beliefs about ourselves, including our traits and characteristics. It is how we see and describe ourselves and our traits. Our self-concept changes, becoming more complex, over childhood and adolescence.

Infancy

What do babies know about themselves? Do they have a sense of self? When do they know they are separate from the people and things surrounding them? Self-concept begins with self-awareness. Are infants aware of themselves? This is a difficult question to answer because infants cannot tell us what they perceive, think, or feel. Researchers look at infants' behavior to deduce what infants know.

Self-Awareness

Four-month-old Camille delights in realizing that she can make the mobile above her crib move by kicking her feet. This understanding that she can influence objects suggests that she has a sense of herself as distinct from her environment (Rochat, 1998). Before infants can understand their own actions, they must begin to see themselves as physically separate from the world around them.

Some developmental scientists believe that infants are born able to distinguish themselves from the surrounding environment (Meltzoff, 1990; Rochat, 2019). For instance, newborns show distress when hearing a recording of another infant's cries but not when hearing their own, indicating that they can distinguish between others and themselves, suggesting a primitive notion of self (Dondi et al., 1999). Similarly, newborns can imitate specific facial expressions made by adults, which also suggests a basic awareness of self and others (Meltzoff, 2007; Rochat, 2018).

However, other scientists argue that self-awareness does not emerge until around 3 months of age (Neisser, 1993). Infants' sense of body awareness develops through interactions and physical contact with their mothers (Montirosso & McGlone, 2020). Early tactile experiences, particularly gentle affective touch from caregivers, aid in developing body awareness and self-other differentiation (Della

Longa et al., 2020). Some researchers believe that early self-awareness is indicated by infants' recognition of the consequences of their body movements (Langfur, 2013). As infants interact with people and objects, they learn that their behaviors have effects, which leads them to experiment to see how their behaviors influence the world around them. This awareness helps them differentiate themselves from their environments and develop a sense of self (Bigelow, 2020). A recent study examined infants' awareness of themselves in relation to others. Sixteen month old infants saw their parent wearing a sticker on either their forehead or cheek. When given a sticker, half of the infants placed it on themselves (rather than an object), specifically on the location on their own face matching their parents' placement, suggesting an awareness of themselves in relation to their parents (Kampis et al., 2022).

Self-Recognition

One way of studying self-awareness in infants is to examine their reactions to viewing themselves in a mirror. When do they show **self-recognition**, the ability to recognize or identify the self? In the mirror self-recognition test, also known as the rouge or mark test, a mark is applied to an infant's face without their knowledge, and they are placed in front of a mirror (Bard et al., 2006). If the infant recognizes themselves in the mirror, they will notice the mark and touch their face.

Mirror recognition develops gradually and systematically (Brandl, 2018). Three-month-old infants attend and react positively to their mirror image. By 8 to 9 months, they react to the tandem movement of the mirror image with themselves and play with the image, treating it as if it is another baby (Bullock & Lutkenhaus, 1990). Some 15- to 17-month-old infants show signs of self-recognition, but it is not until 18 to 24 months that most infants demonstrate self-recognition by touching their nose when they notice the rouge mark in the mirror (Cicchetti et al., 1997). Success in this task depends on cognitive development, particularly the ability to hold a mental representation, an image in their mind. Infants must be able to retain a memory of their own image to display self-recognition in the mirror task (Cuevas & Davinson, 2022).

This toddler recognizes herself in the mirror, as shown by her touching the rouge mark on her face.

Thierry Berrod, Mona Lisa Production/Science Source

There are cultural differences in mirror recognition. Infants from Western cultures tend to demonstrate mirror recognition earlier than those from non-Western cultures such as Cameroon, Vanuatu, and Zambia (Cebioğlu & Broesch, 2021; Ross et al., 2017). One possible explanation is that Western parents' emphasis on autonomy and independence through object-focused and face-to-face interactions, may contribute to earlier mirror recognition in their infants (Keller et al., 2005). However, research has not supported this as cultural differences in parenting behaviors were unrelated to infants' mirror recognition performance (Kärtner et al., 2011; Ross et al., 2017). In some cultures, children may have low motivation to remove a mark from their face in the mirror recognition task due to cultural norms or compliance with authority figures (Courage et al., 2004; Rochat et al., 2012). Interestingly, experience with mirrors does not appear to be a significant factor in performance on the test, as toddlers from rural populations with little familiarity with mirrors have performed similarly to their urban counterparts after becoming familiarized with the mirror (Kärtner et al., 2012). Culture-specific norms of expressive behavior and motivation for tactile exploration.

Mirror recognition is not the only indicator of a sense of self—and may not be the earliest indicator. Infants' brains respond to seeing images of their own faces before they can succeed in the mirror task (Stapel et al., 2017). Eighteen-month-old infants viewed photographs of their own face, the face of an unfamiliar infant, the face of their caregiver, and the face of an unfamiliar caregiver, while their brain activity was registered via electroencephalography (EEG). The infants showed more brain activity in response to their own faces, suggesting self-recognition, yet only one half of these infants succeeded in the mirror task. A recent study suggests that infants show more brain activity in response to seeing their own face than another infant's face or their mother's face, suggesting an early awareness of self (Rigato et al., 2024) In addition, the mirror recognition task recruits areas in the brain associated with self-reflection in adults. Toddlers who exhibit mirror self-reflection show increased functional connectivity in these areas compared to those toddlers who do not yet show mirror self-recognition, suggesting that mirror self-recognition may be a good indicator of a sense of self in infancy (Bulgarelli et al., 2019).

Toddlers' emerging self-awareness has important implications for socioemotional development. They begin to experience complex self-conscious emotions, such as embarrassment, shame, guilt, jealousy, and pride (Lewis & Carmody, 2008). An understanding of self is needed before children can be aware of being the focus of attention and feel embarrassment, identify with others' concerns and feel shame, or desire what someone else has and feel jealousy toward them (Botto & Rochat, 2018). In a study of 15- to 24-month-old infants, only those who recognized themselves in the mirror looked embarrassed when an adult gave them overwhelming praise. They smiled, looked away, and covered their faces with their hands. The infants who did not recognize themselves in the mirror did not show embarrassment (Lewis, 2011). A developing sense of self and the self-conscious emotions accompanying it leads toddlers to have more sophisticated social interactions with caregivers and others, all of which contribute to the development of self-concept. Self-recognition predicts emotional knowledge such that children who showed early self-recognition showed greater emotional knowledge at 4.5 years (Lewis & Minar, 2022).

Emerging Self-Concept

In toddlerhood, between 18 and 30 months of age, children's sense of self-awareness expands beyond self-recognition to include a **categorical self**, a self-description based on broad categories such as sex, age, and physical characteristics (Stipek et al., 1990). Toddlers describe themselves as *big, strong, girl/boy*, and *baby/big kid*. Children use their categorical selves as a guide to behavior. Once toddlers label themselves by gender, they spend more time playing with toys stereotyped for their own gender. Applying the categorical self as a guide to behavior illustrates toddlers' advancing capacities for self-control.

At about the same time, as toddlers display the categorical self, they begin to show another indicator of their growing self-understanding. As toddlers become proficient with language and their vocabulary expands, they begin to use many personal pronouns and adjectives, such as *I, me*, and *mine*, suggesting a sense of self in relation to others (Bates, 1990; Rochat, 2019). Claims of possession (*My toy!*) emerge by about 21 months and illustrate children's clear representation of *I* versus other, a milestone in self-definition and the beginnings of self-concept (Levine, 1983; Rochat, 2010).

Childhood

Three- and 4-year-old children tend to understand and describe themselves concretely, using observable descriptors including appearance, general abilities, favorite activities, possessions, and simple psychological traits (Harter, 2012a). Ryder explains, "I'm four years old. I have black hair. I'm happy, my doggie is white, and I have a television in my room. I can run really fast. Watch me!" Ryder's self-description, his self-concept, is typical of children his age. Soon children begin to include emotions and attitudes in their self-descriptions, such as "I'm sad when my friends can't play," suggesting an emerging awareness of their internal characteristics (Thompson & Virmani, 2010).

In middle childhood, self-concept shifts from concrete descriptions of behavior to trait-like psychological constructs (e.g., popular, smart, good looking). Consider this school-age child's self-description: "I'm pretty popular.... That's because I'm nice to people and helpful and can keep secrets. Mostly I am nice to my friends, although if I get in a bad mood, I sometimes say something that can be a little mean" (Harter, 2012b). Like most older children, this child's self-concept describes abilities and personality traits rather than specific behaviors.

Compared to younger children who tend to describe themselves in all-or-none terms, older children include both positive and negative traits in their self-descriptions. Children learn more about themselves through interactions with parents, teachers, and peers (Pesu et al., 2016). Older children come to understand that their traits can vary with the context, and that a person can be nice or mean, depending on the situation. The all-or-none trait descriptions in early childhood transform into complex integrations of psychological traits in middle to late childhood. By about 9 years of age, children describe and evaluate themselves across a range of domains, including a physical self-concept (referring to physical attributes and attractiveness), academic self-concept (school performance), athletic self-concept (physical skills), social self-concept (social relationships with peers and others), and beliefs about behavioral conduct (whether they can behave appropriately) (Harter, 2012a, 2012b). Children's self-concept is associated with their behavior. Children's academic self-concept, such as beliefs about math and reading abilities, predicts their academic achievement into adolescence (Cvencek et al., 2018; Susperreguy et al., 2018). For many children domain specific self-concept tends to be stable from childhood throughout adolescence and into emerging adulthood (Putnick et al., 2020).

Children's conceptions of themselves are influenced by their interactions with parents and the cultural context in which they are raised. In one study, preschool through second-grade U.S. and Chinese children were asked to recount autobiographical events and describe themselves in response to open-ended questions (Wang, 2004). The U.S. children often provided detailed accounts of their experiences. They focused on their own roles, preferences, and feelings and described their personal attributes and inner traits positively. In contrast, Chinese children provided relatively skeletal accounts of past experiences and focused on social interactions and daily routines. They often described themselves in neutral or modest tones, referring to social roles and context-specific personal characteristics. These differences are consistent with cultural values of independence in the United States and collectivism in China. In another study, U.S. preschool children reported feeling more sadness and shame in response to failure and more pride in response to success than did Japanese preschool children (Lewis et al., 2010). The Japanese preschool children displayed few negative emotions in response to failure but showed self-conscious embarrassment in response to success. Culture influences how children come to define and understand themselves and even the emotions with which they self-identify (Thompson & Virmani, 2010).

Adolescence

A more complex, differentiated, and organized self-concept emerges in adolescence (Harter, 2012a). Adolescents use multiple abstract and varied labels to describe themselves in various domains, such as academics, social skills, physical abilities, appearance, and emotional regulation skills (Esnaola et al., 2020). As young people recognize that their feelings, attitudes, and behaviors may change with the situation, they begin to use qualifiers in their self-descriptions (e.g., "I'm sort of shy") (Balakrishnan, 2020). Adolescents' awareness of the situational variability in their psychological and behavioral qualities is evident in statements such as, "I'm assertive in class, speaking out and debating my classmates, but I'm quieter with my friends. I don't want to stir up trouble." Many young adolescents find these inconsistencies confusing and wonder who they really are, contributing to their challenge of forming a balanced and consistent sense of self.

As adolescents become able to consider the future, imagine their future lives, and wonder how they might change over time, they identify an *ideal self*, who they aspire to be. Adjustment is influenced by the match between the adolescents' personal characteristics, their *real self*, and their aspirational *ideal self*. A discrepancy between the ideal self and the real self is associated with symptoms of depression, low self-esteem, and poor school grades (Ferguson et al., 2010; Stevens et al., 2014). Adolescents who show poor stability or consistency in their self-descriptions tend to experience higher rates of depressive and anxiety symptoms throughout adolescence (Van Dijk et al., 2014).

Experiences in the home, school, and community influence adolescents' self-concept. Warm, accepting, and firm parenting provides support and give-and-take to promote the development of adolescent self-concept (S. M. Lee et al., 2006; Van Dijk et al., 2014). At school, particularly among high school students, perceived teacher support and communal values predict positive academic and behavioral self-concept (Dasgupta et al., 2022; Dudovitz et al., 2017). Peer acceptance and support are also associated with a positive self-concept in adolescence (Fernández-Zabala et al., 2020). Adolescents' evaluations of their self-concepts are the basis for self-esteem, as discussed next.

THINKING IN CONTEXT 11.1

1. In what ways might infants' developing sense of self be influenced by their emotional development, temperament, and attachment to caregivers? How might these interact to influence infants' self-awareness?

2. What role does cognitive development play in self-concept? Give examples.
3. How might contextual factors, such as those that accompany being raised in an inner city, suburban neighborhood, rural environment, or nomadic society, influence infants', children's, and adolescents' developing sense of self? Would you expect the same pattern of development across all contexts? Why or why not? Would infants, children, and adolescents develop similarly in each context? Why or why not?

SELF-ESTEEM

11.2 Describe patterns of change in self-esteem over childhood and adolescence.

Self-concept refers to our descriptions of ourselves, while **self-esteem** is our self-evaluation ("How well do I like myself?"). Self-esteem involves feelings of self-worth, self-acceptance, and self-respect, qualities that rely on cognitive development and a sense of self that emerge in childhood and develop throughout life (Orth & Robins, 2019).

Early Childhood

Young children tend to evaluate themselves positively. They tend to have a high sense of self-esteem that does not always match their abilities. Three-year-old Dorian exclaims, "I'm the smartest! I know all my ABCs! Listen! A, B, C, F, G, L, M, V!" Like Dorian, many young children are excited but also unrealistically positive about their abilities (Harter, 2012a; Hennefield & Markson, 2022; Zell et al., 2019). They may underestimate the difficulty of tasks and believe that they will always be successful. Even after failing a task several times, they often continue to believe that the next try will bring success.

Young children's overly optimistic perspective on their skills can be attributed to their cognitive development, secure attachment with caregivers, and the overwhelmingly positive feedback they usually receive when they attempt a task (Goodvin et al., 2008; Verschueren, 2020). These unrealistically positive expectations serve a developmental purpose: They contribute to young children's growing sense of initiative and aid them in learning new skills.

Young children maintain their positive views about themselves because they do not yet engage in **social comparison**. They do not compare other children's performance with their own. With advances in cognition and social experience, children begin to learn their relative strengths and weaknesses, and their self-evaluations become more realistic (Gerber, 2020; Rochat, 2013). Between ages 4 and 7, children's self-evaluations become linked with their performance. In one study, children's self-evaluations declined when they failed tasks assigned by an adult as well as those they perceived as important (Cimpian et al., 2017). Self-esteem is promoted by sensitive caregiving that supports children's attempts at difficult tasks, emphasizes the value of effort, provides realistic feedback, helps children take pride in success, and provides unconditional support (Brummelman & Sedikides, 2020).

Middle Childhood

Self-esteem tends to increase throughout elementary school and is associated with academic achievement (Orth et al., 2018; Y. Wang et al., 2021). As children get better at taking other people's perspectives, they receive feedback about their abilities from parents, teachers, and peers, and they begin to evaluate their abilities more objectively. Whereas preschoolers tend to have unrealistically positive self-evaluations, school-age children's self-esteem becomes more realistic (Boseovski, 2010). Children evaluate their characteristics, abilities, and performance compared to peers, which influences their overall sense of competence (Gerber, 2020; Harter, 2012b). Self-esteem is influenced by children's ability to balance feedback from themselves and others. Children whose self-evaluations depend heavily on approval from others are at risk for poor self-esteem (Moore & Smith, 2018).

In elementary school, self-esteem becomes more complex, tied to specific domains, such as academic, social, and athletic ability (Orth et al., 2020). School-aged children's self-evaluations are more closely linked to their abilities, beliefs, and behavior (Davis-Kean et al., 2009). Their self-esteem is tied closely to abilities that they view as important. For example, a 10-year-old might say, "Even though I'm not doing well in those subjects, I still like myself as a person because Math and Science just aren't that important to me. How I look and how popular I am are more important" (Harter, 2012b). Poor academic grades will not likely affect this child's self-esteem. Children's self-esteem also shapes their interests. They tend to report feeling most interested in activities in which they perform well and areas that they view as their strengths (Denissen et al., 2007).

Positive parent-child interactions and a secure attachment to parents predict a positive sense of self-esteem throughout childhood (Krauss et al., 2020; Magro et al., 2019; X. Wang et al., 2023). Self-esteem is nurtured by warm caregivers who feel competent in their role as parents, express positive emotions, acceptance, and the sense that the child matters (Álvarez & Szücs, 2023). Children internalize the view of themselves as worthy individuals, and this internalized view is at the core of self-esteem (Verschueren, 2020). However, when parents overvalue their children's attributes, overpraise their performance, and over-encourage them to stand out from others, children may develop a sense of narcissism, viewing themselves as superior to others (Brummelman, 2018). In sum, as in early childhood, school-age children's self-esteem is best fostered within the context of warm and accepting parent-child interactions, parental encouragement for realistic and meaningful goals, and praise that is connected to children's performance (Brummelman & Sedikides, 2020; Coulombe & Yates, 2022).

Adolescence

As adolescents' self-conceptions become more differentiated, so do their self-evaluations. Adolescents evaluate themselves, in global terms, as self-esteem. They also evaluate themselves in specific areas, such as academics, athletic ability, and social competence (Esnaola et al., 2020; Orth et al., 2020). Adolescents develop a positive sense of self-esteem when they evaluate themselves favorably in areas they view as important. For instance, sports accomplishments are more closely associated with physical self-esteem in adolescent athletes, who tend to highly value physical athleticism, but athleticism is less closely related to self-esteem in nonathletes (Wagnsson et al., 2014). Similarly, adolescents with high academic self-esteem tend to spend more time and effort on schoolwork, view academics as more important, and continue to demonstrate high academic achievement (Preckel et al., 2013).

Shifts in Self-Esteem

The advances in perspective-taking abilities and self-reflection that lead early adolescents to be more aware of others can also lead them to be more self-conscious and self-critical. Self-esteem tends to decline in early adolescence, at about 11 years of age, reaching its lowest point at about 13 years before rising (Orth, 2017). Instability or fluctuations in self-image tend to increase and peak in early adolescence between ages 12 and 14 (Thomaes et al., 2011). This pattern of decline is true across gender and ethnicity, although girls tend to show lower self-esteem (Onetti et al., 2019; von Soest et al., 2016).

Declines in global self-esteem are influenced by the multiple transitions that young adolescents undergo, such as body changes and the emotions accompanying those changes, as well as adolescents' self-comparisons to their peers (Schaffhuser et al., 2017). Girls reach puberty earlier than boys; girls' pubertal transitions tend to accompany school transitions, which are associated with temporary declines in self-esteem. Most adolescents view themselves more positively as they progress from early adolescence through the high school years, and for most adolescents, these shifts in self-esteem are small (Bachman et al., 2011; von Soest et al., 2016).

Racial and Ethnic Differences

Black adolescents tend to have higher self-esteem than peers of other races and ethnicities (see Figure 11.1; Bachman et al., 2011; Erol & Orth, 2011; Louie & Wheaton, 2019). From early to late adolescence, the relative position of White and Hispanic adolescents shifts, with Hispanic adolescents showing dramatic increases in self-esteem relative to White adolescents. Asian American adolescents tend to score particularly low on measures of self-esteem compared to their peers (Bachman et al., 2011).

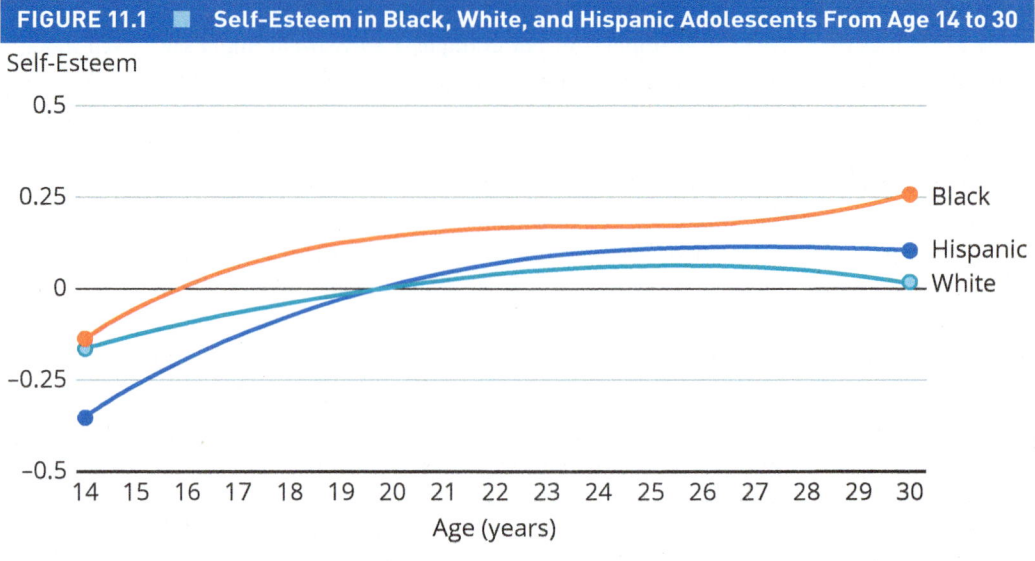

FIGURE 11.1 ■ Self-Esteem in Black, White, and Hispanic Adolescents From Age 14 to 30

Source: Adapted from Erol, R. Y., & Orth, U. (2011). Self-esteem development from age 14 to 30 years: A longitudinal study. *Journal of Personality and Social Psychology, 101*(3), 607–619. https://doi.org/10.1037/a0024299

Despite often experiencing racism and discrimination, Black adolescents' self-esteem may be protected by their immersion in close-knit Black communities, which offer young people support, guidance, and connections to adults who provide positive feedback. Black Americans tend to receive more social support from their religious communities than White Americans (Louie et al., 2022). These connections are a source of support that influences Black adolescents' self-conceptions and feelings of worth. Self-esteem rises with the number of close connections Black adolescents have to family, school, religion, peer, and neighborhood networks (Rose et al., 2019). Self-esteem, in turn, buffers some of the adverse effects of experiencing discrimination on Black adolescents' mental health (Smith & Nicholson, 2022).

Hispanic adolescents are often immersed in similar communities that emphasize relationships and family ties that buffer the effect of negative experiences and discrimination on adolescents' self-evaluations (Ortiz, 2020). Culture also plays a role in influencing Asian American adolescents' typically low self-evaluations (Chen & Graham, 2018). Asian cultures tend to emphasize interdependence and collectivism, valuing the community over the individual (Markus & Kitayama, 2010). Promoting self-esteem can run contrary to these values (Heine & Hamamura, 2007).

Self-Esteem and Adjustment

Adolescents' sense of self-worth has implications for their behavior and well-being (Katsantonis et al., 2023). Those with high self-esteem tend to be more confident, more willing to reject advice they deem poor, more likely to speak up, and more sure of themselves (Baumeister & Vohs, 2018; Cvencek & Greenwald, 2020). Adolescents with high self-esteem have more self-compassion—they are kind to themselves. They are more likely to perceive experiences and failures as opportunities for self-awareness rather than self-judge (Barry et al., 2015). High self-esteem is associated with academic achievement, positive relationships with parents and peers, and mental health (Orth & Robins, 2022). Low self-esteem, on the other hand, is associated with risky behavior, including alcohol and substance use, and a higher risk for school drop out (Lawrence & Adebowale, 2023; C. G. Lee et al., 2018; Pederson et al., 2022). Persistently low self-esteem is associated with adjustment difficulties, such as depression, that can persist throughout the lifespan (Fiorilli et al., 2019; Orth, 2017).

Contextual Influences on Self-Esteem

Family and peers are meaningful contexts for the development of self-esteem (Harris & Orth, 2020). Positive parent-adolescent relationships characterized by warmth, firmness, and parents' emotional availability, are associated with higher estimates of self-worth and better adjustment in adolescents from Australia, China, Germany, Italy, the Netherlands, and the United States (Babore et al., 2017; Harris et al., 2015; Keizer et al., 2019; Miconi et al., 2017). In contrast, neglectful parenting, parent-adolescent conflict, and parental feedback that is critical, inconsistent, and not contingent on behavior predict the development of poor self-esteem (Huey et al., 2020; Pinquart & Gerke, 2019).

Peer acceptance can buffer the negative effects of a distant relationship with parents (Birkeland et al., 2014). Adolescents who feel supported and well-liked by peers tend to show high self-esteem in adolescence, emerging adulthood, and young adulthood through age 35 (Gruenenfelder-Steiger et al., 2016; Sánchez-Queija et al., 2017; Vanhalst et al., 2013). Longitudinal data collected over 5 years suggested that self-esteem predicted social support quality increasingly over time from ages 13 to 18 (Marshall et al., 2014). The direction of influence between peer relationships and self-esteem is difficult to interpret and complicated; it is likely a two-way relationship in which self-esteem influences and is influenced by social support (Harris & Orth, 2020).

Adolescents benefit from friendships with peers of different ethnicities. Cross-ethnic friendships are associated with self-esteem, well-being, and less victimization. Why are friendships with diverse peers so beneficial?

Giuseppe Lombardo/Getty Images

THINKING IN CONTEXT 11.2

1. Consider self-esteem from an evolutionary developmental perspective.
   a. How might young children's overly optimistic self-evaluations be adaptive to their development?
   b. How might developing more realistic self-evaluations be adaptive for older children?
   c. Might changes in self-esteem over adolescence be adaptive? Why or why not?
2. What advice would you give a parent who wishes to promote their child's self-esteem? How might this advice vary with the age of the child?

IDENTITY

11.3 Summarize processes of identity development, including its influences and outcomes.

Who are you? What makes you, you? These questions pertain to your identity, your sense of self. As adolescents come to understand their characteristics, they begin to construct an **identity**, a sense of self that is coherent and consistent over time (Erikson, 1950). According to psychologist Erik Erikson, the developmental task of adolescence is to establish a sense of identity by considering their past and hopes for the future and determining values, beliefs, and goals regarding vocation, politics, religion, and sexuality. Successfully resolving this process leads to **identity achievement**, constructing a coherent sense of self after exploring various possibilities. Erikson emphasized adolescence as the prime time for identity development, but today much of the work of identity development occurs in early adulthood, specifically emerging adulthood (age 18–25) (Arnett & Mitra, 2020).

Psychosocial Moratorium

A key assumption of identity theory is individuals must actively explore identity alternatives before committing to a particular identity (W. Meeus, 2023). Having the time and space to do the hard work of figuring oneself out is crucial for a successful identity search. Adolescents are best positioned to construct an identity when they experience what Erikson (1950) referred to as a **psychosocial moratorium**, a time-out period that provides more freedom and autonomy than childhood but is without the full autonomy and responsibilities of adulthood.

This period allows adolescents the opportunity to explore possibilities of who they might become. Adolescents might try different career aspirations, contemplate becoming an actor one week and a lawyer the next, or explore personalities and desires. Some adolescents examine their religion more closely and consider their beliefs, perhaps learning about other religions. As adolescents explore possible identities, they make choices and become increasingly confident about their choices over time. Those who successfully engage in this process emerge with a sense of identity—an understanding of who they are and where they are going. The unsuccessful resolution of the identity search is confusion, withdrawing from the world, and isolating oneself from loved ones, parents, and peers.

Identity development is a dynamic process in which individuals shift between certainty and uncertainty as they explore identity alternatives and examine their commitment to a particular identity structure (Galliher et al., 2017). Adolescents navigate these shifts in certainty daily, moment-to-moment, with changes in circumstances and moods (Branje et al., 2021). Uncertainty is often uncomfortable, motivating young people to seek resolution and reduce the discomfort. Longitudinal research following individuals from early to late adolescence suggests that adolescents' uncertainty in identity precedes commitment making at the within-person level from early to late adolescence for interpersonal identity (Becht et al., 2017). For the past half century, Erikson's ideas about identity have influenced thinking in this area.

Identity Status

How do we study identity? Researchers study identity with large samples of people using interview and survey measures. The most common approach is to classify individuals' progress in identity development into four categories known as **identity status**, the degree to which individuals have explored possible selves, and whether they have committed to specific beliefs and goals (Marcia, 1966). The identity status model conceptualizes Erikson's ideas about identity development as combinations of exploration and commitment making.

Identity statuses reflect how individuals view and respond to the world (Hall, 2018). Figure 11.2 summarizes four identity statuses, or categories, describing a person's identity development. The least mature status is **identity diffusion** (not having explored or committed to a sense of self), characterized by pervasive uncertainty with little motive for resolution. Individuals who are in the **identity foreclosed** status have prematurely chosen an identity without having engaged in exploration; they tend to be inflexible and view the world in black and white, right and wrong, terms. The moratorium status, reflecting Erikson's previously discussed psychosocial moratorium, involves an active exploration of ideas and a sense of openness to possibilities coupled with some uncertainty. As uncertainty is experienced as discomfort, young people are highly motivated to seek resolution and reduce the discomfort. The fourth category, identity achievement status, requires that individuals construct a sense of self through reflection, critical examination, and exploring or trying out new ideas and belief systems and that they have formed a commitment to a particular set of ideas, values, and beliefs. Identity diffusion and foreclosure become less common in late adolescence when moratorium and identity achievement are more prevalent.

Individuals' identity status refers to their identity situation at a given point in life (Kroger & Marcia, 2011). Young people typically shift among identity statuses over adolescence, but the specific pattern of identity development varies among adolescents (W. H. J. Meeus, 2011). Some remain in one identity status, such as identity moratorium, for most of adolescence, while others experience multiple transitions. The most common shifts in identity status are from the least mature statuses, identity diffusion and identity foreclosure, to the most mature statuses, moratorium and achievement, in middle and late adolescence (Branje, 2022; de Moor et al., 2022). The overall proportion

FIGURE 11.2 ■ Identity Status

	Commitment	
	Present	**Absent**
Exploration — Present	**Identity Achievement** Commitment to an identity after exploring multiple possibilities. Associated with an active problem-solving style, high self-esteem, feelings of control, high moral reasoning, and positive views of work and school.	**Moratorium** Active exploration of identity alternatives without having committed to an identity. Associated with openness to experience, an active problem-solving style, anxiety and discomfort, and experimentation, including alcohol or substance use.
Exploration — Absent	**Identity Foreclosure** Commitment to an identity without having explored multiple possibilities. Associated with avoiding reflection or exploration of identity alternatives, rigidity, and a lack of openness to new information and ideas, especially if they contract their position.	**Identity Diffusion** Has neither committed to an identity nor explored alternatives Associated with avoidance, tending not to solve personal problems in favor of letting issues decide themselves, academic difficulties, apathy, alcohol, and substance use.

Sources: Marcia, J. E. (1966). Development and validation of ego-identity status. *Journal of Personality and Social Psychology, 3*(5), 551–558; Meeus, W. H. J. (2011). The study of adolescent identity formation 2000–2010: A review of longitudinal research. *Journal of Research on Adolescence, 21*(1), 75–94. https://doi.org/10.1111/j.1532-7795.2010.00716.x

of young people in the moratorium status tends to increase during adolescence, peaking at about age 19 and declining over emerging adulthood as young people gradually commit to identities (Kroger et al., 2010).

Domains of Identity

Identity is not an all-or-nothing concept. People form a sense of identity across many different domains or areas, and the relative salience of each domain can vary over the course of development (Branje et al., 2021; McAdams & Zapata-Gietl, 2015). The pace and pattern of development differ across identity domains, and adolescents with a strong sense of identity in one domain do not necessarily have a strong sense of identity in other domains (Goossens, 2001; Klimstra et al., 2016). For instance, having chosen a career, an adolescent may demonstrate identity achievement with regard to vocation yet remain diffused about political ideology, never having considered political affiliations.

As young people develop a sense of identity, they increasingly perceive themselves as adults.

istock/FatCamera

Some identity domains may remain unexplored. For example, persistent and increasing levels of identity diffusion have been commonly found in the political and religious domains, continuing through middle adulthood (Fadjukoff et al., 2016). Researchers often group different identity domains under two broad umbrella domains: interpersonal (i.e., friendships and dating) and ideological (i.e., occupation, religion, and politics) (Schwartz, 2001; Schwartz et al., 2015). Frequently there is little convergence or overlap in identity processes in ideological and relational domains (Luyckx et al., 2014). In one study of late adolescents, the interpersonal domains (relationships with friends, family, and dates) were most prominent, but occupational identity was the only ideological realm explored (McLean et al., 2016). Similarly, other research with emerging adults suggests that the relational domain correlates more closely with global identity than occupational and ideological (Vosylis et al., 2018). We look to our relationships and contexts to make sense of ourselves.

Influences on Identity Development

Identity is constructed through relationships and interactions with parents and peers (Branje, 2022). Relationships with parents are renegotiated as adolescents claim more and more autonomy, gaining space to develop their own sense of identity (W. H. J. Meeus & de Wied, 2007). When parents provide a sense of security and autonomy, adolescents tend to be more comfortable exploring their world, using their parents as a secure base to return to (Schwartz et al., 2013, 2015). Adolescents who feel connected to their parents, supported and accepted by them, but who also feel that they are free and encouraged to develop and voice their views are more likely to engage in the exploration necessary to advance to the moratorium and achieved statuses (Branje, 2022; Schwartz et al., 2015; Trost et al., 2020). Conversely, adolescents who are not encouraged or permitted to explore are more likely to show the foreclosed status. For example, a 14-year-old in a family of doctors who has not considered any careers and comes to a decision, after much prodding by their parents and grandparents, that they want to be a doctor may be in the identity foreclosed status.

The degree of freedom and support that adolescents are afforded for exploration varies with contextual factors related to family and community, such as socioeconomic status (SES) (Vosylis et al., 2021). Adolescents from high SES homes may have fewer responsibilities to work outside the home, may reside in communities with more extracurricular opportunities, and may be more likely to attend postsecondary education than their peers from low SES homes—all factors that support the exploration needed for identity achievement (Kroger, 2015; Spencer et al., 2015). Adolescents who lack support and encouragement to explore alternatives will likely experience identity diffusion, because they lack opportunities to seek out and make commitments to possible selves (Hall & Brassard, 2008; Reis & Youniss, 2004). Contexts of trauma and uncertainty can disrupt identity development. For instance, adolescents who are refugees show higher levels of identity diffusion and detachment than first- and second-generation immigrants (Zettl et al., 2022). Neighborhood adversity poses a risk to identity development as concerns about safety and poor access to resources may inhibit adolescents' exploration (W. Meeus, 2023).

Peers also influence identity development as adolescents use them as a mirror to view their emerging identities and as an audience to which they relay their self-narratives (Branje, 2022; McAdams & Zapata-Gietl, 2015). Adolescents who feel supported and respected by peers are more likely to explore identity alternatives (Ragelienė, 2016). As with parents, conflict with peers harms identity development as adolescents often feel less free to explore identity alternatives and lack a supportive peer group to offer input on identity alternatives, which holds negative implications for identity development, such as identity foreclosure or diffusion (Branje et al., 2021; Hall & Brassard, 2008). In emerging adulthood, romantic relationships are an important context for identity development as the attachment to partners provides security for exploration, similar to infants' secure base (Pittman et al., 2011). Romantic partners influence each other reciprocally, illustrating the many interactions between individuals and the people in their immediate contexts (Wängqvist et al., 2016).

Outcomes Associated With Identity Development

Identity achievement is associated with positive outcomes, such as high self-esteem, a mature sense of self, feelings of control, high moral reasoning, and positive views of work and school (Jespersen et al., 2013; Spencer et al., 2015). On the other hand, adolescents in the moratorium status often feel puzzled and overwhelmed by the many choices before them (Lillevoll et al., 2013). The process of sorting through and determining commitments in the educational and relationship domains can be stressful, is associated with negative mood and, at its extreme, can be paralyzing and curtail their exploration of identity (Branje et al., 2021; Crocetti et al., 2009; Klimstra et al., 2016). Individuals in the identity foreclosure status tend to take a rigid and inflexible stance. Closed to new experiences, they avoid reflecting on their identity choice, and reject information that may contradict their position.

Finally, while it is developmentally appropriate for early adolescents to have neither explored nor committed to a sense of identity, by late adolescence identity diffusion is uncommon and has been considered indicative of maladjustment (Kroger et al., 2010). Identity-diffused adolescents keep life on hold. They do not seek—and may even avoid—the meaning-making experiences needed to form a sense of identity (Carlsson et al., 2016). Adolescents in the identity-diffused status tend to use a cognitive style that is characterized by avoidance. Academic difficulties, general apathy, organization and time management problems, alcohol and substance abuse, and delinquent and antisocial behavior are associated with identity diffusion and often precede it (Bogaerts et al., 2021; Crocetti, 2017; Mercer et al., 2017). However, identity is not a one-time event. It is an ongoing construction that continues over the lifespan, not just in adolescence and emerging adulthood.

THINKING IN CONTEXT 11.3

1. How do physical and cognitive development influence adolescents' sense of self and identity? Consider the interplay between identity development and factors such as puberty, brain development, and decision-making skills. Conversely, how might adolescents' emerging sense of identity influence their decision-making and development?
2. In what ways do interactions with parents, peers, school, community, and broader societal forces shape the construction of identity? Give examples.
3. How might the experience of trauma influence identity development?

ETHNIC-RACIAL IDENTITY

11.4 Analyze the process of ethnic-racial identity development, including its influences, and its role in adjustment.

Constructing an identity involves integrating self-conceptions, self-evaluations, and experiences into a coherent and consistent sense of self. Race and ethnicity influence this process. Whereas children's self-concepts and descriptions of race tend to focus on observable characteristics, adolescents' increasing cognitive abilities enable more sophisticated self-conceptions that include abstract beliefs and experiences regarding race and ethnicity. **Ethnic-racial identity** refers to a sense of membership to an ethnic or racial group including the attitudes, values, and culture associated with that group (whether Latino, Asian American, African American, European American, etc.) within a specific sociohistorical context (Phinney & Ong, 2007; Rivas-Drake et al., 2014; Umaña-Taylor, 2016b). Early experiences influence children's understanding of race, their self-conceptions, and ultimately their ethnic-racial identity.

Infancy

Infants' developing cognitive abilities do not support the ability to think about or understand race. But just as their perceptual abilities enable them to categorize objects by appearance, they also categorize people by appearance (Waxman, 2021). Between 3 and 6 months infants prefer to look at familiar social and racial stimuli, including a preference for ethnic-racial groups to which they have been most exposed (C. D. Williams et al., 2020). Usually these ethnic-racial preferences mirror the infant's own ethnicity or race.

Similar to the perceptual narrowing that accompanies language development whereby they become less able to distinguish sounds that they do not encounter, infants become less able to recognize faces from unfamiliar ethnic-racial groups, compared to faces from familiar ethnic-racial groups (Quinn et al., 2018). This tendency to recognize same-race faces better than other-race faces appears in Asian American, Black, White, and Latino infants (Timeo et al., 2017). This pattern is not due to an intrinsic racial bias, but instead to contextual factors, like regular exposure to people of a particular race or ethnicity (Quintana, 1998). In support of this, infants exposed to racially diverse social networks and from racially diverse neighborhoods, who encounter people of other races, show less preference for their own race over other race faces compared with infants from less diverse, more homogenous neighborhoods (Arnold et al., 2023; H. G. Hwang et al., 2021).

Childhood

Young children's cognitive abilities enable them to form simple understandings of ethnicity and race. They tend to associate observable characteristics, such as skin, hair, and eye color, with race (C. D. Williams et al., 2020). Similar to their inability to grasp conservation (e.g., that physical quantities such as liquid remain unchanged despite changes in appearance; see Chapter 6), young children may view race as a temporary and changeable characteristic (Quintana, 1998; Roberts & Gelman, 2017).

Young children's understanding of ethnicity and race is shaped through their interactions with adults and members of their contexts (Waxman, 2021). They are exposed to messages about skin color, its associated characteristics, and its acceptability, which can influence their racial preferences. For example, 3- and 4-year-old White children have been shown to have a pro-White bias in their preferences for dolls, peers, and toys (Perszyk et al., 2019; Sturdivant & Alanis, 2021; A. Williams & Steele, 2019). Young children of color may also demonstrate a preference for lighter skin or internalize racial biases (Jordan & Hernandez-Reif, 2009; Kaufman & Wiese, 2012). Although research is only beginning to examine how information about race and racial preferences influence young children's sense of self, it is likely that young children internalize race-related messages into their early self-understanding.

Parents tend to delay conversations about race and may unwittingly communicate racial biases to children, underestimating children's understanding and ability to process such information (Pirchio et al., 2018; Sullivan et al., 2021). In a recent study, about one quarter of parents reported talking to their young child (age 5 or under) about race in the previous week, increasing to two thirds of parents with children under age 12 (Sullivan et al., 2022). As shown in Figure 11.3, discussions of race increased with age and at all ages parents of color were more likely than White parents to talk with their children about race. Parents and teachers can counter discriminatory messages by adopting an anti-bias framework that helps young children learn about race through storybook reading and discussion (Beneke et al., 2019; Curenton et al., 2022).

By middle childhood many children begin to use ethnic and racial group terms as self-descriptors (Spencer & Markstrom-Adams, 1990; Umaña-Taylor et al., 2014). Older children's understanding of race reflects their cognitive development, specifically the more logical, systematic thinking of concrete operational reasoning (Quintana, 1998). Bias declines dramatically in late childhood, about age 9 (Aboud & Steele, 2017; A. Williams & Steele, 2019).

Older children continue to build their understanding of race, by considering labels and developing more complex understandings and preferences (C. D. Williams et al., 2020). They have greater exposure to the role of race in social life through interactions with peers, at school, and in the community.

FIGURE 11.3 ■ **Proportion of Parent-Child Conversations About Race, by Age and Race**

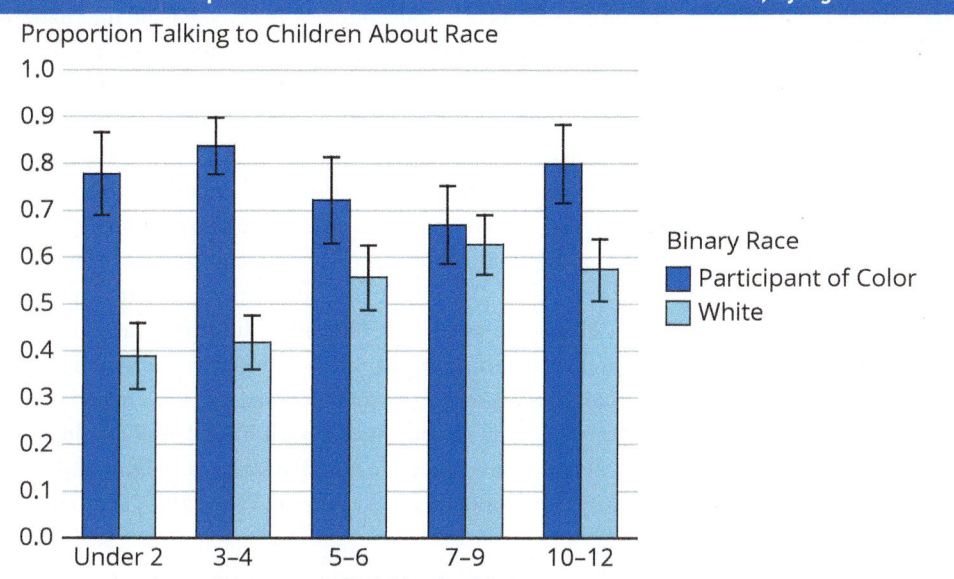

Source: Sullivan, J., Wilton, L., & Apfelbaum, E. P. (2022). How age and race affect the frequency, timing, and content of conversations about race with children. *Child Development, 93*(3), 633–652. https://doi.org/10.1111/cdev.13787

Race may become more relevant and visible to them as older children participate in new contexts, such as new schools and neighborhood playgrounds.

Older children may witness or be subjected to negative race-relevant experiences such as stereotyping based on their ethnic or racial group membership, discrimination, bullying, and racism by peers, adults, and even teachers. However, they have more advanced cognitive and social skills that they can use to draw meaning from their experiences and cope. As they enter adolescence, their understanding of ethnicity and race broadens, and they start to develop a sense of identity.

Ethnic-Racial Identity in Adolescence

The task of identity formation is central to adolescence and encompasses exploring and considering possibilities in many domains, including racial and ethnic heritage. Many adolescents of color construct identities while immersed in contexts rife with racism and prejudice that are displayed as discrimination. Young people's sense of ethnic-racial identity influences how they experience, interpret, and respond to discrimination (Yip, 2018). Many individuals develop a sense of identity that includes both ethnicity and race (e.g., Black and Latino) (Woolverton & Marks, 2023). Other adolescents, however, do not consider their ethnic-racial identity.

Like other components of a sense of self, ethnic-racial identity develops and changes over time as individuals explore, gain experience, and make choices in various contexts. Adolescents examine their ethnic-racial identity by learning about the cultural practices associated with their ethnicity or race by reading, attending cultural events, and talking to members of their culture (Romero et al., 2014). In addition to exploration, the process of ethnic-racial identity development involves internalizing values from one's ethnic and racial group (D. L. Hughes et al., 2017). As adolescents develop a sense of belonging to their cultural community, they may become committed to an ethnic-racial identity.

Similar to Marcia's identity status model discussed previously, ethnic-racial identity can be described by three statuses (Phinney, 1989; Phinney & Ong, 2007). The *unexamined status* includes adolescents who have not explored the meaning of their ethnicity or race and show no clear personal understanding of or commitment to their race and ethnicity. The *exploration status* represents a moratorium in which the individual engages in an active search for information about the meaning of ethnic and racial group membership for them, without having committed. The *achievement status* refers to having explored ethnicity or race, considering its meaning, and having accepted and internalized ethnicity or race as part of one's sense of self identity. Ethnic-racial identity achievement results in commitment to and affirmation of one's ethnic or racial group as well as participation in identity-relevant contexts. That is, adolescents who demonstrate ethnic-racial identity achievement are engaged in their ethnic and racial community and participate in their culture.

During adolescence, young people move from an unexplored and uncommitted ethnic-racial identity to a secure sense of ethnic-racial identity through a period of exploration and meaning making (Phinney & Chavira, 1992). Early and middle adolescents tend to have a less clear and committed sense of ethnic-racial identity and engage in more exploration compared to older adolescents and emerging adults (D. L. Hughes et al., 2017). However, the ethnic-racial identity statuses are not stages and regression to lower statuses is part of the normative identity development process in response to experience as adolescents seek to make meaning from their experiences (Syed et al., 2007). Exploration and commitment tend to continue into adulthood, and development can persist throughout adulthood. The development of ethnic-racial identity is cyclical and dynamic, shaped by people's interactions within their contexts (D. L. Hughes et al., 2017; Phinney & Ong, 2007).

Adolescents with a strong sense of ethnic-racial identity tend to have better emotional and social adjustment and well-being compared to those who have a weak or no identification with their ethnicity. Ethnic-racial identity is associated with positive outcomes, such as school achievement in adolescents from diverse backgrounds, including of African American, Chinese, European, Latino, and Mexican households (Douglass & Umaña-Taylor, 2017; Kyere & Huguley, 2020; Shen et al., 2022; M. T. Wang et al., 2020). A strong sense of ethnic-racial identity is also linked to better socioemotional functioning, including self-esteem and optimism, and fewer emotional and behavior problems than is seen in those who do not or only weakly identify with ethnicity (Monroe et al., 2023; Umaña-Taylor & Rivas-Drake, 2021; Wantchekon & Umaña-Taylor, 2021).

Influences on Ethnic-Racial Identity

The exploration and commitment process that is key to identity achievement also underlies establishment of a sense of ethnic-racial identity (Yip, 2014). Like other aspects of identity, ethnic-racial identity is influenced by family, peer, school, neighborhood, and societal contexts (Pasco et al., 2021; Sladek et al., 2022).

Parents

The family is a particularly important context for ethnic-racial identity formation, as close and warm family relationships are associated with more well-developed ethnic identities. Parents promote ethnic and cultural socialization and pride by teaching children about the history, culture, and heritage associated with their ethnicity (Umaña-Taylor & Hill, 2020). Parents who provide positive ethnic socialization messages promote a sense of group identity (Douglass & Umaña-Taylor, 2016).

Ethnic socialization. Research suggests that there are group differences in ethnic socialization practices. Parents' ethnic socialization practices pass down cultural heritage, traditions, and customs to children and often emphasize the experience of ethnic minority status. Parents of color tend to engage in higher levels of ethnic socialization than White parents (Harding et al., 2017; Sullivan et al., 2022). Black and Latino youth and their parents tend to report a greater emphasis on preparing their adolescents to manage bias than parents of youth from other ethnic groups (Aral et al., 2022; Else-Quest & Morse, 2015). In contrast, a recent meta-analysis suggested that White parents are more likely to emphasize equality and fairness for all, that everyone is the same and has equal opportunities to succeed (Simon, 2021). The messages parents of color send to take pride in one's culture and prepare for bias are influenced by their own as well as their children's experiences with discrimination (Holloway & Varner, 2021). For example, parents tend to engage in more ethnic-racial socialization after their children report experiencing discrimination

(Y. Wang et al., 2023). These socialization practices may buffer the effects of discrimination and racism on their adolescents' adjustment.

Cultural socialization, to the extent that it teaches youth about the traditions and history of their ethnic group, is likely to foster ethnic-racial identity exploration and commitment (S. C. Nelson et al., 2018; Sanchez et al., 2017; Umaña-Taylor & Hill, 2020). Among Mexican-origin preadolescents, parental cultural socialization in fifth grade predicted the development of ethnic pride, affirming one's identity, in seventh grade (Hernández et al., 2014). Similarly, Umaña-Taylor et al. (2009) studied a predominantly Mexican-origin high school sample and found that high familial ethnic socialization during middle adolescence predicted increased exploration and ethnic-racial identity resolution 2 years later. Parental ethnic socialization also predicts ethnic-racial identity exploration and commitment in emerging adulthood (S. C. Nelson et al., 2018).

Adolescents are more likely to construct a favorable ethnic identity when they learn about their culture's values, language, and history, celebrate cultural traditions, and regularly interact with parents and peers within their culture.

istock/kali9

Adolescents' perception of their ethnic socialization, including their view of the extent to which they adopt the customs and values of their culture, is linked with ethnic-racial identity (D. Hughes et al., 2009; M. T. Wang et al., 2020). Adolescents' reports of their experiences of racial socialization have been found to predict their level of exploration and commitment to their ethnic-racial identity and whether they have an achieved ethnic-racial identity status (Seaton et al., 2012).

Perceived pressure. Sometimes, however, strong ethnic socialization messages from the family and ethnic community are perceived as pressure and stressful. Adolescents may experience discontinuity between the two worlds of home and ethnic community and school and society in general (Yoon et al., 2017). Parents who are immigrants may emphasize cultural socialization and devalue acculturation. Some may work long hours, with little time or energy to aid their children's adjustment. Parents who grew up as members of a racial or ethnic majority in their home country or in a country that is ethnically homogeneous, may be unaware of or lack the knowledge to help their children cope with the challenges of navigating two different cultures. Language barriers can prevent meaningful communication between parents and teachers and school administrators (Boutakidis et al., 2011).

Alternatively, parents might restrict adolescents from participating in the larger culture out of fear that assimilation will undermine cultural values. One study of Vietnamese American adolescents living in an ethnic enclave in southern California provides an example. Most of the adolescents felt that their parents encouraged them to embrace their heritage, make friends, and engage in activities within the Vietnamese community rather than become involved with the larger community of school and neighborhood (Vo-Jutabha et al., 2009). As one boy explained, "My parents expect me to speak Vietnamese consistently. Every now and then they just say that I forgot it and that I don't know how to speak it anymore. . . . Of course, I understand it and my parents expect me to be in a Viet Club or something. But I mean c'mon, really c'mon" (Vo-Jutabha et al., 2009, pp. 683–684). Another girl added, "I think living in the Asian community kinda stops me from branching out. I live in this area and all of my friends are mostly Asian and I want to have other friends" (Vo-Jutabha et al., 2009, p. 680). Adolescents who perceive excessive parental pressure and restrictions might respond with rebellion and rejection of ethnic heritage.

Peers

Similar to other aspects of identity, peers play a role in the development of an ethnic-racial identity (Y. Wang & Lin, 2023). Adolescents may first be drawn to peers and make friendships based on superficial similarities, like appearance and perceived group membership in a race or ethnicity. Over time more sophisticated processes, such as intimacy and identity, become important for sustaining the friendship. Indeed, a longitudinal study of sixth- and seventh-grade students found that having more diverse friends at the beginning of the academic year predicted increases in ethnic-racial identity exploration 1 year later (Rivas-Drake et al., 2017). In addition, over time, adolescents' ethnic-racial identity become more like their peers. Exposure to an ethnically diverse friendship network may prompt greater engagement in activities that help adolescents learn about their own ethnic-racial background.

Other research supports the role of peers in ethnic-racial identity. Among African American adolescents, high levels of peer acceptance by and popularity among African American peers is associated with a strong sense of ethnic-racial identity (Rivas-Drake et al., 2014; Rock et al., 2011). Similarly, college student friendship dyads tend to show similar levels of ethnic-racial identity exploration and commitment (Syed & Juan, 2012). Peers may support ethnic-racial identity development by communicating experiences and beliefs about ethnicity and race. For example, recent research with diverse emerging adults suggested that the messages that peers communicate about prejudice and discrimination predicted ethnic-racial identity commitment (S. C. Nelson et al., 2018). On days when adolescents report more interactions supportive of their ethnic-racial identity, they engage in more prosocial behaviors and report more positive feelings about their race-ethnicity (Y. Wang, 2021). Peers provide a sense of community that can bolster young people's sense of commitment to an ethnic-racial identity and offer a buffer against stress from prejudice and discrimination (Jugert et al., 2020; Rivas-Drake et al., 2017).

Teachers and Schools

Teachers and school personnel can sometimes unintentionally convey stereotypical, discriminatory, or racist messages to students. Adolescents of color may perceive discrimination in the classroom, such as feeling that their teachers call on them less, grade them more harshly, or discipline them more severely than other students. Discrimination at school has negative consequences for students' grades, academic self-concept, school engagement, and overall adjustment (Hood et al., 2017; McWhirter et al., 2018). For example, Navajo ninth- and 10th-grade adolescents who perceived discrimination showed lower psychosocial adjustment and higher substance use than their peers over a 1-year period (Galliher et al., 2011). Ethnic and racial minority adolescents often receive confusing messages to embrace their heritage while routinely experiencing discrimination, making the path to exploring and achieving ethnic-racial identity challenging and painful (McLean et al., 2015).

To address ethnic-racial socialization, many schools are incorporating related programming and messages that educate students about the meaning of being a part of a particular ethnic-racial group, promote awareness of different cultures, examine mainstream U.S. norms, and explore the role of race in students' lives (Saleem & Byrd, 2021). Positive ethnic-racial socialization messages at school have been consistently associated with greater exploration and resolution in middle school and high school as well as positive attitudes toward people of different races and ethnicities (Byrd & Legette, 2022; Rivas-Drake et al., 2020). Research has shown that Black and Latino students in these programs experience positive outcomes such as stronger feelings of belonging and connection to their ethnic group, improved academic outcomes (including increased school engagement, academic competence, and academic self-concept), and better psychosocial outcomes such as increased happiness and reduced stress (Saleem & Byrd, 2021; Thomas et al., 2022).

Discrimination and Ethnic-Racial Identity

As they become more skilled at considering other people's perspectives, adolescents of color may become more aware of and sensitive to negative stereotypes about their race or ethnicity. Negative messages, unequal treatment, and discrimination pose challenges to developing a positive sense of ethnic-racial identity (McLean et al., 2015). Adolescents from various racial and ethnic groups, both native born and immigrant, report experiences of discrimination on average 1–2 times a week (D. Hughes et al., 2016; Umaña-Taylor, 2016a). These experiences are associated with low self-esteem, depression, low social competence, behavior problems, and distress (Mrick & Mrtorell, 2011; Rivas-Drake et al., 2014).

Discrimination and ethnic-racial identity are interwoven and influence each other. Adolescents who feel a strong sense of belonging to a race or ethnicity, view the race or ethnicity as important to their overall self, or are in the process of exploring their ethnic-racial identity are more likely to report experiences with discrimination (Brittian et al., 2015; Del Toro et al., 2021; Gonzales-Backen et al., 2018). For instance, Latino adolescents with a higher sense of ethnic-racial identity belonging reported more discrimination a year later (Meca et al., 2020).

The experience of discrimination can also prompt adolescents to seek information about, and increase identification with, their ethnic and racial group, and reject negative discriminatory stereotypes (Mims & Williams, 2020; Yip, 2018). Adolescents who reported higher levels of perceived discrimination also reported higher levels of ethnic-racial identity exploration 1 year later (Del Toro et al., 2021; Meca et al., 2020). Difficult experiences with racism and discrimination can prompt adolescents to reflect on their interactions with people and places, and the larger sociohistorical context, which in turn can shape the formation and development of their ethnic-racial identity. A strong sense of ethnic-racial identity can sensitize adolescents to racism and discrimination, but it can also provide protection, reducing the negative impact of racial discrimination on well-being (Umaña-Taylor & Rivas-Drake, 2021; Yip et al., 2022).

THINKING IN CONTEXT 11.4

1. What kinds of race-related experiences and knowledge do children have? Identify ways that children learn about race and examples of the kinds of messages they encounter.
2. Is ethnicity or race an important part of your sense of self? Why or why not? Have you experienced shifts in your experience of ethnicity or race from childhood to adulthood? What factors might influence whether an adolescent is aware and feels a sense of ethnic-racial identity?
3. Discuss the complex effects of ethnic-racial identity, specifically how it can sensitize adolescents to discrimination yet also help them cope. In what ways might ethnic-racial identity act a protective factor for youths of color, promoting resilience despite hardships?

ACHIEVEMENT MOTIVATION

11.5 Examine achievement motivation and its influences.

Whether playing a sport, practicing an instrument, or participating in class, some children are more driven to succeed than others. **Achievement motivation** is the willingness to persist in challenging tasks and meet high standards of accomplishment (Wigfield, Eccles, et al., 2015). Achievement motivation is closely tied to children's beliefs about their abilities. Its roots lie in infants' earliest experiences and interactions with the world.

Mastery Motivation

Two-year-old Ariana concentrates as she grasps the large wooden puzzle piece and places it on the puzzle board. Despite several unsuccessful attempts, Ariana persists and rotates the piece again until it finally falls into place. Ariana beams with pride, her face lighting up with satisfaction. The ability to reason about the puzzle piece and manipulate it with her tiny fingers is the result of Ariana's growing cognitive and motor skills, as well as socioemotional development. Infants' drive to explore and influence their environment by stacking objects, opening and closing cabinets, and completing puzzles reflects their growing sense of mastery motivation and their desire to explore, understand, and "master" their environment (Barrett & Morgan, 2018).

All infants seek to learn about and control objects around them, but there are individual differences in mastery motivation and its display (Kenward et al., 2009). Some activities and goals appeal more to one infant than another, and some infants are more motivated to complete tasks than others. When toddlers' attempts are met with indifference or negativity by caregivers, they lose interest in exploring. Mastery motivation is fostered by engaging and nurturing caregiving environments in which infants have opportunities, support, and encouragement to exert control over objects and interactions (Lucca et al., 2019; W. Wang et al., 2023). Caregiving that is harsh, controlling, and critical when children do not succeed can generate shame and inhibit children's desire to persist and try after failing (Dweck & Master, 2009; Liao et al., 2021).

Infants' and young children's sense of mastery motivation influences their emerging self-concept and how they understand and manage success and failure. **Mastery motivation** predicts self-regulation and school readiness and influences children's views of their abilities and motivation to achieve (Fung et al., 2019; MacPhee et al., 2018).

Achievement Motivation

Children's early experiences with success and failure influence their beliefs about their abilities, how they approach tasks, and their motivation to persist in difficult tasks. Several types of beliefs influence achievement motivation.

Achievement Attributions

Children's beliefs about the causes of their performance, whether success or failure, are known as **achievement attributions**. Some children attribute their performance to internal factors, such as skills, ability, and effort, while others attribute it to external factors, such as luck or circumstances (Wigfield et al., 2021). A child who excels on an exam may attribute it to their ability or effort (internal attribution) or an easy exam (external attribution). In contrast, a failing grade might be attributed to poor effort or poor ability (internal attribution) or the difficulty of the exam (external attribution). Both internal and external attributions can be adaptive, depending on the situation and factors involved.

Achievement motivation is fostered by internal attributions that explain success as the result of effort or ability and failure as the result of effort. External attributions that account for failure due to circumstances can also be adaptive. However, it is important to note that this is not the whole story regarding achievement motivation and attributions.

Mindset

The usefulness of internal attributions depends on children's views of their abilities. Along with attributing success or failure to internal or external causes, children also vary in their **mindset** or the degree to which they believe their abilities and characteristics can be modified (Dweck & Yeager, 2019; Yeager & Dweck, 2020). Children with a *growth mindset* view their skills and characteristics as changeable and believe they can grow and improve, while those with a *fixed mindset* believe their skills and characteristics cannot be changed (Bernecker & Job, 2019; Kapasi & Pei, 2022).

A growth mindset fosters achievement motivation because children believe that effort can lead to improvement in their abilities. On the other hand, children who hold a fixed mindset will be less motivated to try because they cannot change their abilities. Children's beliefs about the malleability of their abilities influence their motivation and achievement.

Goals

Children's goals influence their motivation and success in completing tasks. Children who set **learning goals** tend to focus on the process of learning and developing their abilities (Wigfield et al., 2019). This goal orientation is often accompanied by a growth mindset and openness to change. When reviewing an exam, children with a learning goal orientation will examine feedback and seek information about incorrect answers to improve their understanding. Their focus is on growth and improvement.

In contrast, children who believe their abilities are fixed tend to focus on **performance goals**, which are concerned with demonstrating their ability and receiving positive feedback (Wigfield et al., 2019). These goals prioritize validating their abilities and, in some cases, outperforming other children. When reviewing exams, children with performance goals tend to be more concerned with whether they got the item right rather than reviewing and learning from incorrect answers.

Learning goals support achievement motivation because they prioritize the process of developing abilities and using feedback to improve. Children who focus on performance goals may lose motivation when they are unsuccessful because they are not interested in learning or do not believe they can improve.

Mastery Orientation and Helpless Orientation

Children's attributions, mindset, and goals collectively determine their achievement motivation and influence how they approach difficult tasks. Those who attribute their performance to internal factors, have a growth mindset, and focus on learning exhibit a **mastery orientation**. They believe that success results from hard work and that failures can be controlled through factors such as effort (Haimovitz & Dweck, 2017). These children focus on the process of completing a task rather than just the outcome, and when faced with obstacles, they adopt a growth mindset and try to change or adapt their behavior (Muenks et al., 2018; J. Song et al., 2020). They believe they can improve and are more likely to bounce back from failure and take steps to improve their performance.

Other children respond to success and failure in maladaptive ways. Children with an external attribution style, a fixed mindset, and a focus on performance goals may exhibit a **helpless orientation**. They attribute their failures to their ability and believe that they cannot succeed while attributing their successes to external factors such as luck or an easy test. Children with a helpless orientation are overwhelmed by challenges, are self-critical, feel incompetent, and avoid difficult tasks (Dweck, 2017). They also tend to have a fixed mindset, believing their skills and characteristics cannot be changed. Poor performance confirms these children's negative views of their ability and sense of helplessness.

Achievement motivation is a powerful predictor of academic success beyond intelligence, cognitive abilities, and prior performance (Bostwick et al., 2020; Steinmayr et al., 2019). A mastery orientation has been shown to predict subsequent classroom engagement, seeking help from teachers, and higher grades in children and adolescents (Duchesne et al., 2019; N. Y. Hwang et al., 2019; Yeager & Dweck, 2020). Importantly, achievement motivation can be improved, mindset can be changed, and a mastery orientation can be fostered through sensitive interactions with others: parents, teachers, and peers (See Table 11.1; Canning & Limeri, 2023; Kapasi & Pei, 2022).

TABLE 11.1 ■ Mastery Orientation and Helpless Orientation		
	Mastery Orientation	**Helpless Orientation**
Mindset	Growth	Fixed
Goal Orientation	Learning goals	Performance goals
Attribution for success	Ability	Luck Easy exam / circumstance
Attribution for Failure	Lack of effort Difficult exam/circumstance	Ability

Source: Adapted from Bernecker, K., & Job, V. (2019). Mindset theory. In K. Sassenberg & M. L. W. Vliek (Eds.), *Social psychology in action: Evidence-based interventions from theory to practice* (pp. 179–191). Springer International. https://doi.org/10.1007/978-3-030-13788-5_12

Contextual Influences on Achievement Motivation

Children's beliefs about their abilities and attributions for their performance are influenced by their contexts and interactions with parents, teachers, and peers.

Parents

Parents influence children's achievement motivation through their beliefs and attitudes about ability, success, and failure (Haimovitz & Dweck, 2016). Children who are raised by parents with a growth mindset tend to be more persistent and motivated to succeed (Y. Song et al., 2022). When parents believe that ability cannot be changed, they may limit opportunities for children to improve, ignore positive changes, and interfere when children try a difficult task, inhibiting their desire to succeed and fostering helplessness (Orkin et al., 2017).

Warm and supportive parenting can boost children's self-esteem and help them recognize their abilities. Parents who promote their children's autonomy, encourage exploration, and allow them to solve their own problems foster a mastery orientation (Raftery et al., 2012). In contrast, excessive control and harsh criticism can inhibit children's motivation. Children and adolescents who feel emotionally supported by their parents are more likely to pursue mastery goals, experience less test anxiety, and achieve higher academic success (Hayek et al., 2022; J. Song et al., 2015).

Positive parental interactions have far-reaching effects on child development.
Maskot/Getty Images

The type of feedback adults provide plays a large role in children's beliefs about their abilities. *Person praise*, which focuses on the qualities of the individual (e.g., "You're so smart! You did it!"), is often used by well-intentioned adults to make children feel good. However, this type of praise can lead children to reinforce beliefs in a fixed mindset (e.g. "I'm good at this task because I'm smart" or "I failed because I'm not smart") (Haimovitz & Dweck, 2017). In the face of failure or criticism, person praise can result in a heightened sense of helplessness, because it implies that ability is fixed and cannot be changed (Dweck & Yeager, 2019). *Process praise*, in contrast, emphasizes the role of effort, a changeable ability, in success ("Great job! You studied hard, and your performance shows it!"). This type of praise fosters a growth mindset (Brummelman & Sedikides, 2020). Effective praise should imply that success results from controllable, malleable forces, minimize the role of external control, promote autonomy, and provide specific, accurate information about the quality of performance to build a resilient sense of competence (Corpus & Good, 2020).

Parents also influence children through the home environment they provide. SES influences children's motivation through the availability of opportunities and resources and through parents' behavior. Children need opportunities to explore and try new things, as well as parents who are able to recognize and take advantage of these opportunities (Archer et al., 2012; Simpkins et al., 2013). Research has shown that children and adolescents who grow up in high SES families show a greater mastery orientation and higher levels of achievement motivation, better academic performance, and greater involvement in organized after-school activities than their middle or low SES counterparts (Manganelli et al., 2021; Wigfield, Eccles, et al., 2015; Wigfield et al., 2021).

A growth mindset is thought to be beneficial for achievement motivation, but a recent study found that it only positively predicted achievement among students from more advantaged families and not among those from less advantaged families (King & Trinidad, 2021). Parents' educational attainment supports their children's academic success through their beliefs and expectations and cognitive stimulation provided in and outside of the home (Davis-Kean et al., 2021).

Teachers

Teachers who form close, warm relationships with students promote higher levels of academic motivation and engagement (Heatly & Votruba-Drzal, 2019; Silinskas & Kikas, 2022). Children who perceive their teachers as supportive, providing a positive learning environment, and encouraging autonomy tend to work harder in class and show higher achievement than students who lack this belief (Affuso et al., 2023; Wigfield, Muenks, et al., 2015). When students view their teachers as unsupportive, they are more likely to attribute their performance to external factors, such as luck or the teacher, and to withdraw from class participation. As students' achievement declines, teachers may further doubt their abilities, creating a vicious cycle between helpless attributions and poor achievement (Filippello et al., 2020; Skinner et al., 2020). Teachers who relate failure back to their students' effort are supportive of their students and stress learning goals over performance goals are more likely to have mastery-oriented students (Brummelman & Sedikides, 2020; Yeager & Dweck, 2020).

Peers

The peer group influences achievement motivation through children and adolescents' beliefs about their friends' behavior and attitudes as well as their perception of implicit norms of the group (Wigfield et al., 2021). Older children and adolescents tend to affiliate with students who share their academic competence, grades, and orientation toward school, and they become more similar to friends over time through their interactions (Fujiyama et al., 2021; Gremmen et al., 2017; Rambaran et al., 2017). Having best friends who value academics is positively associated with high achievement motivation, while adolescents who view their friends as resistant to classroom norms are likely to have poor achievement motivation (R. M. Nelson & DeBacker, 2008).

Perceived acceptance by peers is also positively associated with achievement motivation. Children and adolescents who feel valued and respected by their peers and who have high quality friendships are likely to have high achievement motivation (R. M. Nelson & DeBacker, 2008; Wentzel et al., 2021). Those who perceive greater emotional support from their peers also report stronger mastery goals (J. Song et al., 2015). Peer relationships influence children's beliefs about their ability, interest, and motivation to achieve.

THINKING IN CONTEXT 11.5

1. How does the type of praise (process vs person) affect a child's view of their abilities and motivation to succeed? What might be some of the long-term implications of praise?
2. How should parents and teachers who are interested in promoting a growth mindset hand a child's failure? What are some ways of turning failures into growth opportunities?
3. How do peers influence children's mindset and achievement? Give examples of positive and negative ways peers might affect a child's or adolescents' achievement.

APPLY YOUR KNOWLEDGE

At 7 years of age, Kenya described herself as an athlete, a good teammate, and smart. She had dreams of becoming a soccer player, believing that she was fast, strong, and coordinated. But try as she might, she couldn't score a goal. By age 9, Kenya spent a lot of time on the sidelines, watching her teammates and hoping the coach would send her onto the field. She started to dislike going to practice because she couldn't keep up during team runs. "I'm just not good at this. There's no point. I'm not going to improve." At age 12, Kenya didn't make the team. At first, she was crushed and felt terrible about herself.

Kenya focused on her schoolwork and soon discovered that she was much better at math than her classmates. Kenya's teacher encouraged her to take a math placement test, and Kenya's high score led her to be placed in an advanced algebra class. She continued to excel and decided that she wanted a career in science or math, but she wasn't sure which.

At 17, Kenya entered college with a mix of excitement and trepidation. She was a year younger than most students, having skipped a year of high school. Kenya was nervous about orientation and meeting other first-year students. One activity required students to define themselves and their career goals and write their responses on a small sticky note to be posted on the wall. "I want to major in premed, go to medical school, and be a surgeon at a prestigious hospital, just like my mother," Kenya wrote. However, she was also considering her passion for math and science.

Later, after meeting her advisor to register for classes, Kenya wondered why she should have to take classes in subjects unrelated to medicine, like art, history, and English. Her advisor explained that general education courses will broaden her horizons and help her explore new topics and better understand herself. Kenya didn't think those classes were necessary.

Kenya excitedly enrolled in a math course, but she failed her first exam. She was confused, "I don't get it. I skipped senior year. I'm supposed to be smart! I guess I'm not."

1. Describe Kenya's self-concept, including examples of her ideal and real self. How did her self-concept change over time?

2. Describe Kenya's mindset. How is it related to her performance in sports and academics? In your view, how effective is Kenya's mindset in supporting her motivation and performance? What, if anything, could she do differently?

3. What identity status does Kenya demonstrate, and what factors contribute to this status? Provide examples to support your choice and discuss how Kenya's experiences and interactions may have influenced her identity development.

4. How might Kenya's experiences and interactions with others have influenced her developing sense of self and identity? What role might Kenya's interactions with her parents, peers, and coaches have played in her beliefs about her abilities and potential?

5. What advice would you give Kenya to help her navigate college and develop a helpful mindset and cultivate positive sense of self and identity? What resources or support might help her?

CHAPTER SUMMARY

11.1 Discuss the development of self-concept from infancy through adolescence.

Self-awareness emerges in early infancy. In toddlerhood the sense of self-awareness expands beyond self-recognition to include a categorical self, such as sex, age, and physical characteristics, which guides behavior. Children first understand themselves in concrete and unrealistically positive terms, but with age self-concept becomes correlated with skills, accomplishments, and external indicators of competence. As children move from early childhood to middle childhood, self-concept includes trait-like psychological constructs. Older children include both positive and negative traits to describe themselves and differentiate among multiple types of self-concept. Cognitive advances enable adolescents to use more labels to describe themselves and the labels they choose become more abstract, complex, situational, and often contradictory. They begin to identify an ideal verses actual self whose match influences well-being. At all ages, self-concept is influenced by interactions with parents and experiences in the home, school, and community.

11.2 Describe patterns of change in self-esteem over childhood and adolescence.

Self-esteem refers to an individual's self-evaluation, including feelings of self-worth, self-acceptance, and self-respect. Young children's self-esteem is very positive. They often overestimate their abilities and underestimate the difficulty of tasks. School-age children's sense of self-esteem is influenced by social comparison and becomes more realistic, connected to their abilities, and more comprehensive. Adolescents evaluate themselves with respect to multiple dimensions and relationships. They develop a positive sense of self-esteem when they evaluate themselves favorably in the areas that they view as important. Overall, global self-esteem tends to decline in early adolescence reaching its lowest point at about 13. Despite disadvantages and discrimination, Black adolescents tend to have high self-esteem compared to other-ethnic peers, influenced by cultural values and supports. High self-esteem is associated with positive adjustment, academic achievement, and mental health whereas low self-esteem is associated with risky behaviors and adjustment difficulties. Family and peers are significant contexts for the development of self-esteem.

11.3 Summarize processes of identity development, including its influences and outcomes.

Identity refers to an individual's sense of self. It is constructed by integrating self-conceptions and self-evaluations to construct a sense of self that is coherent and consistent over time. Identity achievement represents the successful resolution of this process, the culmination of a successful psychosocial moratorium. Researchers classify individuals' progress in identity development into four identity status categories: moratorium, identity diffusion, identity foreclosure, and identity achievement status. Adolescents shift among identity statuses, with the least mature status being identity diffusion and the most mature status being identity achievement. We establish an identity in multiple domains, often at different times. Identity is influenced by interactions with parents and peers. Identity achievement is associated with positive adjustment and identity diffusion is associated with negative outcomes. Although the task of forming an identity is first encountered during adolescence, it is a lifespan task.

11.4 Analyze the process of ethnic-racial identity development, including its influences, and its role in adjustment.

Infants do not understand race, but they categorize people and object by appearance. Children's understanding of race parallels their cognitive development. In middle childhood, children begin to use race and ethnicity as descriptors. Ethnic-racial identity refers to a sense of membership to an ethnic or racial group including the attitudes, values, and culture associated with that group within a specific sociohistorical context. Adolescents explore their ethnic-racial identity by learning about the cultural practices associated with their race. Similar to that of identity, ethnic-racial identity is characterized into three statuses: unexamined, exploration, and achievement. Individuals move through the ethnic-racial identity generally, from unexamined, to exploration, to achieved in response to new experiences and opportunities for making meaning of their ethnicity or race. Adolescents with strong sense of ethnic identity tend to show better adjustment and coping skills as well as fewer emotional and behavior problems than their peers. A strong sense of ethnic-racial identity can reduce the magnitude of the effects of racial discrimination.

11.5 Examine achievement motivation and its influences.

Achievement motivation refers to the drive to persist in challenging tasks and meet high standards of accomplishment. It stems from infants' early experiences and their sense of mastery motivation, which is their desire to explore and learn about their environment. This sense of mastery motivation affects their self-concept and approach to success and failure. Key factors that contribute to achievement motivation include attributional style, mindset, and goals. Children who attribute their performance to internal factors, have a growth mindset, and focus on learning exhibit a mastery orientation, believing that success results from effort and that they can improve. Children who exhibit a helpless orientation have an external attribution style, a fixed mindset, and focus on performance goals, attributing their failures to ability and their successes to external factors and tend to avoid hard tasks. Parents, teachers, and peers all play a role in shaping a child's achievement motivation through their provision of support and beliefs about achievement.

KEY TERMS

achievement attributions	learning goals
achievement motivation	mastery motivation
categorical self	mastery orientation
ethnic-racial identity	mindset
helpless orientation	performance goals
identity	psychosocial moratorium
identity achievement	self-concept
identity diffusion	self-esteem
identity foreclosed	self-recognition
identity status	social comparison

mladenbalinovac/Getty Images

12 MORAL DEVELOPMENT

Part 4 • Socioemotional Development

> **LEARNING OBJECTIVES**
>
> **12.1** Summarize the development of moral reasoning and its influences in childhood and adolescence.
>
> **12.2** Analyze the progression of prosocial behavior and its contextual influences.
>
> **12.3** Examine common forms of aggressive and antisocial behavior in childhood and adolescence.
>
> **12.4** Describe the development of religiosity and spirituality in childhood and adolescence.

"Am I a good boy?" 10-year-old Vidal asked his father. "You're a boy who does good things," Ramon replied. "Will I always be good?" Vidal asked. "If you do good things. Think about other people. How do they feel? What is fair to everyone? Help others. Show that you care. That's what it means to be good. I know you can do that," Ramon said. "Pop, that sounds hard," Romeo replied. "Sometimes it will come easily, and other times it will take work. But I know you can do it. You have a good heart, son." The exchange between Vidal and Romeo calls attention to the role of morality in development. How do children come to understand *right* and *wrong*? In this chapter, we examine how people reason about fairness and learn to engage in moral behavior, including helping others and controlling aggression.

MORAL REASONING

> **12.1** Summarize the development of moral reasoning and its influences in childhood and adolescence.

Children are constantly faced with moral questions and dilemmas in their everyday lives, such as whether it is acceptable to take a cookie from the cookie jar without asking, to break a rule, or to steal, even if it would help another person. These experiences are opportunities for children to learn about right and wrong and develop a sense of morality. **Moral reasoning**, the process of making judgments about right and wrong, is influenced by children's cognitive abilities and develops in a predictable pattern (Killen & Dahl, 2021; Vozzola & Senland, 2022). As children grow, they actively construct their understanding of justice and fairness through social experiences with adults and peers (Dahl, 2018, 2019; Killen & Smetana, 2015).

Piaget began studying morality by asking children about their understanding of the rules of marbles. Fewer children play marbles today. If you were to study children's understanding of rules today, what game would you choose?

Yamtono_Sardi/istock

Reasoning About Rules: Piaget's Theory

Cognitive-developmental theorist Jean Piaget (1932), whose theory we discussed in Chapter 6, studied how children understand rules. He observed children playing marbles, a common schoolyard game in Piaget's time, and asked them questions about how to play the game. What are the rules? Where do the rules come from? Have the rules for playing marbles always been the same? Can they be changed? Piaget found that preschool-age children did not understand rules clearly, and their play was not guided by them. The youngest children engaged in solitary play without consideration for rules, tossing and rolling the marbles about as they pleased. Through his observations, Piaget concluded that moral thinking develops in stages similar to those in his theory of cognition.

Children enter the first stage of Piaget's theory of morality, **heteronomous morality** (also known as the morality of constraint), by age 6. In this stage, children first become aware of rules and view them as unalterable and absolute. The children interviewed by Piaget believed that people have always played marbles in the same way and that the rules cannot be changed. At this stage, moral behavior is consistent with the rules set by authority figures. Young children see rules, including those created in play, as absolute and view behavior as either right or wrong. They also believe violating rules merits punishment, regardless of intent (DeVries & Zan, 2003; Nobes & Pawson, 2003). For example, young children may believe that there is only one way to play softball, such as how their coach advocates, and they may view this as the *right way* to play. Preschoolers will hold to this rule, explaining that it is simply the right way to play. It is not until middle childhood that children develop more flexible views of fairness.

As children enter elementary school and spend more time with their peers, their understanding of rules becomes more flexible. In middle childhood, at about age 7, children enter the second stage of Piaget's scheme, **autonomous morality** (also known as the morality of cooperation). Now children begin to see rules as products of group agreement and tools to improve cooperation. For instance, older children are likely to recognize a rule that the youngest children must be the first to bat at the piñata at a children's party is a way to help the youngest children, who are less likely to be successful. They might agree that the rule promotes fairness or might argue to abandon the rule because it gives younger children an unfair advantage. At this stage, children view a need for shared agreement on rules and consequences for violations (Chiari & de Morais, 2024). Piaget's theory of moral reasoning inspired Lawrence Kohlberg, who created perhaps the most well-known theory of moral reasoning.

Reasoning About Justice: Kohlberg's Theory

Psychologist Lawrence Kohlberg (1969, 1976) adopted a cognitive developmental perspective of moral development and proposed that children construct their understanding of fairness through their interactions with others. Kohlberg investigated moral development by posing hypothetical dilemmas about justice, fairness, and rights that place obedience to authority and law in conflict with helping someone. Is stealing ever permissible—even to help someone? Individuals' responses to this question change with development. Kohlberg believed that moral reasoning progresses through a universal order of six stages, grouped into three levels representing qualitative changes or shifts in conceptions of justice.

Beginning in early childhood and persisting until about age 9, children demonstrate what Kohlberg called **preconventional reasoning**. At this level, children's behavior is governed by self-interest. In Stage 1, children's moral judgments are first motivated by the desire to avoid punishment ("Don't steal because you don't want to go to jail"). In Stage 2, children become motivated by rewards for complying. Children who demonstrate preconventional reasoning account for *good* or moral behavior as a response to external forces rather than an expression of altruistic motivations. They have not yet internalized societal norms, and their behavior is motivated by desires rather than internalized principles.

At about age 9, children transition to the second level of Kohlberg's scheme, **conventional moral reasoning**. Children can now take others' perspectives and are motivated by reciprocity, seeking to be accepted and avoid disapproval. Rules maintain relationships. In Stage 3, children uphold rules to please others, gain affection, and be considered good people—honest, caring, and nice. The Golden Rule motivates their behavior: "Do unto others as you would have them do unto you." At Stage 4, which emerges in adolescence, perspective taking expands beyond individuals to include society's rules. Adolescents accept rules as tools to maintain social order and believe everyone has a duty to uphold the rules. They view rules as universal and as such must be enforced for everyone.

Not until adolescence, according to Kohlberg, do people become capable of demonstrating advanced moral thinking, **postconventional moral reasoning**. This level involves autonomous decision making based on moral principles that value respect for individual rights above all else. Postconventional moral thinkers at Stage 5 recognize that their self-chosen principles of fairness and justice may sometimes conflict with the law, and they view laws and rules as flexible and part of the social contract meant to further human interests. They believe that laws and rules should be followed because they bring good to people but that they can be changed if they are inconsistent with the needs and rights of the majority. If laws are unjust and harm more people than they protect, they can be broken.

The final, most advanced, and most rare stage of reasoning, Stage 6, is based on abstract ethical principles that are universal, valid for all people regardless of law, such as equality and respect for human dignity. Although improvement in cognitive development make postconventional reasoning possible, the highest forms of postconventional reasoning are rare. Table 12.1 compares Piaget's and Kohlberg's models of reasoning.

TABLE 12.1 ■ Moral Development: Piaget and Kohlberg's Theories					
	Piaget's Stages		**Kohlberg's Levels***		
	Stage 1: Morality of Constraint	Stage 2: Morality of Cooperation	Level 1: Preconventional Moral Reasoning	Level 2: Conventional Moral Reasoning	Level 3: Postconventional Moral Reasoning
Cognitive-developmental stage	Preoperational Reasoning	Concrete Operational Reasoning	Preoperational Reasoning	Concrete Operational Reasoning	Formal Operational Reasoning
Perspective	Individualistic. Children cannot take the perspective of others; they assume that everyone sees the world as they do.	Multiple. Children can take the perspective of others; they see that more than one point of view is possible and that others do not necessarily view issues as they do.	Individualistic. Children cannot take the perspective of others; they focus on their own needs.	Community. Children take the perspective of the community at large; there is an emphasis on societal rules and welfare.	Rational and moral. Adolescents and adults take the perspective of all persons, a universal perspective. They rationally consider social contracts and attachments. Sometimes what is right contradicts the law. People and human dignity come first.
View of justice	Absolute. Children see acts as either right or wrong, with no shades of gray. The wrongness of an act is defined by punishment.	Relative. Children see that there is often more than one point of view. Acts are seen as right or wrong regardless of punishment.	Absolute. Acts are either right or wrong, defined by punishment and rewards.	Absolute. Right or wrong acts are defined by social approval.	Universal. Abstract principles of justice apply to all individuals, situations and societies.
Understanding of rules	Rules are unalterable and sacred.	Rules are created by people and can be changed if it suits people's needs.	Rules are unalterable and imposed by authority figures.	Rules are unalterable and act to uphold the community.	Rules are meant to benefit individuals, communities, and societies. They can be changed or broken if they are not just or conflict with moral principles.
Reason for compliance with rules	Rules are obeyed out of a sense of obligation to conform to authority and to avoid punishment.	Rules that are just are obeyed for their own sake rather than under threat of punishment.	Rules are followed to gain rewards and avoid punishment.	Rules are followed out of a sense of duty to please others and gain social approval, which is more important than other rewards.	Individuals follow universal principles of justice, such as respecting human dignity. Rules that reflect these principles are followed.

Note: *Each level comprises two stages.

Sources: Adapted from Hoffman, M. L. (1970). Conscience, personality, and socialization technique. *Human Development, 13*, 90–126. https://doi.org/10.1159/000270884; Kohlberg, L. (1981). *Essays on moral development.* Harper & Row; Piaget, J. (1932). *The moral judgment of the child.* Harcourt Brace.

Developmental Changes in Moral Reasoning

Kohlberg's (1969) theory was based on longitudinal research with a group of boys, ages 10, 13, and 16, who were periodically interviewed over three decades. Kohlberg discovered that the boys' reasoning progressed through sequential stages and in a predictable order. Kohlberg measured moral reasoning by presenting individuals with hypothetical dilemmas that examine how people make decisions when fairness and people's rights are pitted against obedience to authority and law. Participants' explanations of how they arrived at their decisions reveal developmental shifts in moral reasoning that correspond to cognitive development. The Heinz dilemma is the most well-known example of hypothetical conflicts that Kohlberg (1969) used to study moral development.

> Near death, a woman with cancer learns of a drug that may save her. The woman's husband, Heinz, approaches the druggist who created the drug, but the druggist refuses to sell the drug for anything less than $2,000. After borrowing from everyone he knows, Heinz has only scraped together $1,000. Heinz asks the druggist to let him have the drug for $1,000 and he will pay him the rest later. The druggist says that it is his right to make money from the drug he developed and refuses to sell it to Heinz. Desperate for the drug, Heinz breaks into the druggist's store and steals the drug. Should Heinz have done that? Why or why not?

At the preconventional level, decisions are influenced by self-interest, the desire to gain rewards and avoid punishments. Children might respond that Heinz should not steal the drug because he will go to prison, or that he should steal the drug to avoid his wife's anger or to receive her affection. Conventional moral reasoning is socially driven. School-age children might argue that Heinz should steal the drug because good people help their wives or because it is his duty as a husband. Alternatively, they might say that Heinz should not steal the drug because good people do not steal or because following rules maintains social order; what would happen if everyone stole? At the postconventional level of reasoning, adolescents might explain that stealing is against the law, but laws are intended to help people and, in this case, stealing the drug is intended to help Heinz's wife. Moreover, the value of a life is exponentially greater than that of the drug, suggesting that Heinz should steal the drug.

Kohlberg's theory of moral reasoning has led to over five decades of research. Many studies have confirmed that individuals proceed through the first four stages of moral reasoning in a slow, gradual, and predictable fashion (Boom et al., 2007; Chiari & de Morais, 2024; Dawson, 2002). Research has shown that preconventional reasoning decreases by early adolescence. Conventional reasoning, specifically Stage 3, increases through middle adolescence, and Stage 4 reasoning increases from middle to late adolescence and becomes typical of most individuals by early adulthood. Research suggests, however, that few people's reasoning moves beyond conventional moral reasoning (Stage 4). Postconventional reasoning at Stage 5 is rare, even in adults (Kohlberg et al., 1983). Research generally has not supported the existence of Stage 6, the hypothesized most advanced type of moral reasoning; however, Stage 6 represents an end goal state to which human development strives (Kohlberg & Ryncarz, 1990).

Influences on Moral Reasoning

Moral development is influenced by social interaction, specifically how parents and caregivers discuss moral issues, such as those involving telling the truth, harming others, and respecting property rights (Mammen & Paulus, 2023; Vozzola & Senland, 2022). Reasoning develops when individuals have opportunities to engage in discussions characterized by mutual perspective taking and opportunities to consider different points of view. Caregivers who engage children and adolescents in discussions about personal experiences, local issues, and media events, while presenting alternative points of view and asking questions, can promote moral reasoning. When children and adolescents encounter reasoning that is slightly more complex than their own, they may be prompted to reconsider their own thinking and advance their reasoning. Caregivers who are warm and engage their children in discussion, listen with sensitivity, and use humor can promote the development of moral reasoning (Carlo et al., 2011; Pinquart & Fischer, 2022).

Interactions with peers in and out of school can also promote moral reasoning when adolescents share different perspectives and engage each other with in-depth discussions (F. C. Power et al., 1989).

Adolescents who report having more close friendships in which they engage in deep conversations tend to show more sophisticated moral reasoning than do teens who have little social contact (Schonert-Reichl, 1999). They also report feeling positive emotions when they make unselfish moral decisions (Malti et al., 2013). Moral reasoning is inherently social. Consequently, some have argued that the social basis of morality means that men and women should reason in very different ways.

Gender and Moral Reasoning

A common criticism of Kohlberg's theory of moral reasoning is that his initial research was conducted with samples of only boys. Early research that studied both men and women suggested gender differences in moral reasoning, with men typically showing Stage 4 reasoning, characterized by concerns about law and order, and women showing Stage 3 reasoning, characterized by concerns about maintaining relationships (Poppen, 1974). Researchers (Gilligan, 1982) argued that Kohlberg's theory neglected a distinctively feminine mode of moral reasoning, known as a **care orientation**, which is characterized by empathy, a desire to maintain relationships, and a responsibility to not cause harm. Gilligan argued that this care orientation was predominantly used by women, while the **justice orientation**, based on the abstract principles of fairness and individualism captured by Kohlberg, was predominantly used by men (Gilligan & Attanucci, 1988).

Although researchers acknowledge that more than one mode of moral reasoning exists, subsequent research has shown that moral orientations are not linked with gender (Knox et al., 2004; Kohlberg et al., 1983); boys, girls, men, and women display similar reasoning that combines concerns of justice (e.g., being fair) with those of care (e.g., being supportive and helpful), and any sex differences are small (Jaffee & Hyde, 2000; Weisz & Black, 2002). The most mature forms of moral reasoning incorporate both justice and care concerns.

Culture and Moral Reasoning

Cross-cultural studies of Kohlberg's theory show that the sequence of moral development he identified appears in all cultures (Boom et al., 2007) but that people in non-Western cultures rarely score above the conventional level, specifically Stage 3 (Gibbs et al., 2007). Morality and appropriate responses to ethical dilemmas are culturally defined and vary based on cultural perspectives (Goldschmidt et al., 2022). Western cultures tend to place a higher emphasis on individual rights and justice-based reasoning, while non-Western cultures tend to value collectivism and care-based reasoning, focusing on human interdependence. In one recent study, Han Chinese, Euro-Canadians, and Chinese-Canadians 7 to 17 years of age reasoned about scenarios in which protagonists told either lies to protect or truths to harm. Cultural variations in moral evaluations emerged such that the Han Chinese children emphasized collective cultural values, Euro-Canadians emphasized individuality, and Chinese-Canadians displayed variations of perspectives in their judgments (Lo et al., 2020).

In collectivist cultures, moral dilemmas are defined in terms of responsibility to the entire community rather than just the individual (Miller, 2018). This emphasis on the needs of others is characteristic of Stage 3 in Kohlberg's justice-oriented scheme. However, moral values are relative to the cultural context, and different cultures may place different weights on care and justice orientations. Stage 3 reasoning is an advanced form of reasoning in collectivist cultures because it embodies principles most valued in these cultures, concepts such as interdependence and relationships. Individuals in all cultures can reason using both care and justice orientations, even though their cultural context may emphasize one over the other.

Moral Reasoning and Behavior

With increases in moral reasoning, adolescents are more likely to act in ways that align with their beliefs (Smetana et al., 2014). Adolescents who demonstrate higher levels of moral reasoning are more likely to share with and help others and are less likely to engage in antisocial behavior such as cheating, aggression, or delinquency (Brugman, 2010; Comunian & Gielen, 2000). Nevertheless, the relationship between moral reasoning and behavior is not always clear-cut. While some studies have found a relationship between low levels of moral reasoning and delinquency, other studies have found no such relationship (Leenders & Brugman, 2005; Tarry & Emler, 2007). Interventions for youth who engage in delinquent behavior tend to successfully advance moral reasoning yet tend to have no effect on recidivism or repeated delinquent behavior (Heynen et al., 2024). It seems that the degree to which moral reasoning is associated with behavior varies with adolescents' beliefs about the behavior. Adolescents' moral reasoning may only predict their behavior in situations they deem as moral choices, but not in the many situations they view as personal choices or social conventions (Berkowitz & Begun, 1995; Brugman, 2010).

Children's Conceptions of Moral, Social, and Personal Issues

Moral reasoning refers to how we think about moral issues, those concerning fairness, justice, or right and wrong. Every day we make decisions about many issues that do not concern morality. When can children differentiate moral rules from suggestions and customs?

Young Children

Social experiences, such as sibling disputes over toys, help young children develop conceptions about fairness (Dahl, 2018; Killen & Smetana, 2015). They judge intent to harm, a moral violation, harshly. In one study, 3- and 4.5-year-old children viewed an interchange in which one puppet struggled to achieve a goal, was helped by a second puppet, and was violently hindered by a third puppet. When asked to distribute biscuits, the 4.5-year-olds but not 3-year-olds were more likely to give more biscuits to the helper than the hinderer puppet. Most explained the unequal distribution by referring to the helper's prosocial behavior or the hinderer's antisocial behavior (Kenward & Dahl, 2011). Three-year-olds can succeed in generating intent-based judgments, however, in response to simplified tasks (Margoni & Surian, 2020).

As early as 3 years of age, children can differentiate between *moral issues*, imperatives that concern people's rights and welfare, and *social conventions* or social customs (Smetana & Yoo, 2023; Smetana et al., 2018). They judge stealing an apple, a moral violation, more harshly than violating a social convention, such as eating with one's fingers (Smetana et al., 2014). Moral rules are seen as less violable, less contingent on authority, and less alterable than social conventions (Smetana, 2013; Turiel & Nucci, 2017).

In addition to moral and conventional issues, between ages 3 and 5, children identify *personal issues*, matters of personal choice that do not violate rights, across home and school settings (Turiel & Nucci, 2017). Individuals, including preschoolers, believe that they have control over matters of personal choice, unlike moral issues whose violations are inherently wrong.

Older Children

School-age children's thinking about moral issues becomes more nuanced. They distinguish among moral issues, such as unfair distributions, physical harm, and psychological harm (Smetana & Ball, 2019; Yoo & Smetana, 2022). Elementary school children judge bullying as wrong independent of rules and more wrong than other moral issues, such as lapses in truth-telling—and both were judged more wrong than etiquette transgressions (Thornberg et al., 2016). With advances in cognitive development, children can take multiple perspectives and become better able to consider the situation and weigh a variety of variables in making decisions. Five- to 11-year-old children become increasingly tolerant of necessary harm; that is, violating moral rules to prevent injury to others (Jambon & Smetana, 2014).

School-age children also discriminate among social conventions that have a purpose from those with no obvious purpose. Social conventions that serve a purpose, such as preventing injuries (e.g., not running indoors), are evaluated as more important and more similar to moral issues than social conventions with no obvious purpose (e.g., avoiding a section of the school yard despite no apparent danger) (Smetana & Yoo, 2023; Yoo & Smetana, 2022). School-age children also consider intent and context. Canadian 8- to 10-year-old children understood that a flag serves as a powerful symbol of a country and its values—and that burning it purposefully is worse than accidentally burning it. The 10-year-old children also understood that flag burning is an example of freedom of expression and can be used to express disapproval of a country or its activities. They agreed that if a person were in a country that is unjust, burning its flag would be acceptable (Helwig & Prencipe, 1999).

How adults discuss moral issues, such as truth telling, harm, and property rights, influences how children come to understand these issues. When adults, especially parents, discuss moral issues in ways that are sensitive to the child's developmental needs, children develop more sophisticated conceptions of morality and advance in their moral reasoning (Padilla-Walker & Memmott-Elison, 2020). As we have seen, there are cultural differences in how people think about moral and conventional issues—and these conceptualizations are communicated, internalized, and transformed by children as they construct their own concepts about morality.

Culture

Cross-cultural research suggests that children from diverse cultures in Africa, Asia, Europe, North and South America, and Southeast Asia differentiate moral, social conventional, and personal issues (Killen et al., 2002; Turiel, 1998; Yau & Smetana, 2003). However, cultural differences in socialization contribute to children's conceptions. Although 3 to 7-year-old children from China and the United States considered personal issues as permissible and up to the child rather than the adults, their consideration of moral transgressions varied (Yau & Smetana, 2003; Zhao & Kushnir, 2019). The Chinese children tended to focus on the consequences of the acts for others' welfare and fairness, as compared with the emphasis on avoiding punishment common in Western samples of preschoolers (Yau & Smetana, 2003). These differences are consistent with cultural preferences for collectivism and individualism.

Whereas Western parents tend to emphasize individuality and independence, Chinese parents tend to emphasize children's obligations to the family and community (Chao, 1995; Yau & Smetana, 2003). One study of 4-year-old Chinese children and their mothers showed that the mothers consistently drew children's attention to transgressions, emphasizing the consequences for others. The children learned quickly and were able to spontaneously discuss their mothers' examples and strategies, as well as reenact them in their own interactions, and their explanations reflected their own understanding of rules and expectations in their own terms rather than reflecting simple memorization (X. Wang et al., 2008).

In sum, children and adolescents develop and hone their understanding of justice and fairness through social interaction at home, at school, and with peers. Children and adolescents regularly encounter moral and conventional issues, such as lying to a friend, not completing homework, violating a household rule, and problems of fairness and sharing. These everyday experiences—opportunities to take perspective—advance moral reasoning.

THINKING IN CONTEXT 12.1

1. Besides cognitive development, what other factors may influence children's decisions about right and wrong? Could physical maturation or socioemotional development potentially influence moral reasoning?
2. How might moral development impact socioemotional development, including children's emotional experiences, self-understanding, and relationships with others?
3. To what extent do contextual factors, such as socioeconomic status, race, ethnicity, and culture, influence the development of moral reasoning? How might these factors shape children's understanding of what is moral and just?
4. Can moral reasoning be taught? Why or why not? If so, how?
5. How might cultural values and context shape children's understanding of moral, conventional, and personal choices? How might the home and neighborhood environment influence children's views and beliefs about what is right and wrong?

PROSOCIAL BEHAVIOR

> **12.2** Analyze the progression of prosocial behavior and its contextual influences.

Eighteen-month-old Lionel placed the block on his baby brother's lap, while he was seated in an infant chair, and exclaimed, "Dat!" "You want your brother to have the block, Lionel? Good job sharing your block, Lionel!" said his babysitter. Infants and toddlers, like Lionel, engage in sharing (Paulus, 2014; Svetlova et al., 2010). Sharing and helping are examples of **prosocial behavior**, voluntary behavior intended to benefit another person (Eisenberg et al., 2015). **Empathy**, the capacity to understand someone's feelings, often motivates prosocial behavior (Stern & Cassidy, 2018).

Helping

When does helping emerge? A series of research studies using the violation-of-expectation method (see Chapter 6) suggested that simple conceptions of prosocial behavior may emerge in infants as young as 3 months old, such as their preference for looking at characters that help rather than hinder others (Van de Vondervoort & Hamlin, 2016). In one scenario, a character is shown pushing a ball up a hill. A second character may either help or hinder the effort by pushing the ball back down the hill. Four- to 6-month-old babies prefer the helper over the hinderer and prefer viewing helpers get rewarded and hinderers punished suggesting a sensitivity to intent (Hamlin, 2013, 2014). Infants tend to frown more and display more and display more physiological arousal in response to viewing hinderers (Tan & Hamlin, 2024). Infants may have a basic sense of empathy well before they can demonstrate it through prosocial behavior (Stout et al., 2021). Top of Form

Even toddlers as young as 16 months can exhibit simple forms of prosocial behavior in the form of **instrumental assistance**, such as helping adults, even unfamiliar experimenters, by bringing them a needed object (Thompson & Newton, 2013). However, between ages 1 and 3, children are more likely to help caregivers than strangers (Reschke et al., 2023). At 16 months infants are more likely to help an unfamiliar experimenter if an unknown adult modeled the behavior suggesting that modeling is a way that infants learn prosocial behavior (Schuhmacher et al., 2019).

At 3.5 years of age, children show more complex forms of prosocial behavior. Compared to 18-month-old children, 3.5-year-olds are more likely to help an adult by bringing a needed object, to do so autonomously without the adult's specific request, and to select an object appropriate to the adult's need (Svetlova et al., 2010). Generally, instrumental helping increases between 18 months and 26 months (Song et al., 2022).

Between 18 and 24 months of age, toddlers show increasingly prosocial responses to others' emotional and physical distress and even show nervous system activation indicating their own distress (Hepach et al., 2012; Hoffman, 2007). Toddlers also show positive emotions, in response to seeing others being helped (Hepach et al., 2023). Sympathy for others motivates early prosocial behavior in toddlers (Grueneisen & Warneken, 2022). But their responses are limited by their poor perspective-taking ability. Toddlers tend to offer the aid that they themselves would prefer, such as bringing their own mother to help a distressed peer (Hepach et al., 2012). Although they can respond prosocially to distressed others, spontaneous prosocial behavior not prompted by adults is rare in toddlerhood (Eisenberg et al., 2015).

Young children often engage in prosocial behavior for egocentric motives, such as the desire for praise and to avoid punishment and disapproval. Situational factors also influence young children's judgments about whether to help (Dahl & Paulus, 2019). They are more likely to help when there is little cost to themselves but are less likely to help as the cost of helping someone else increases.

As theory of mind develops, children begin to become aware of others' perspectives and their prosocial behavior becomes more advanced in motivation and form (Imuta et al., 2016; Vonk et al., 2020). Older children's prosocial behavior becomes motivated by empathy and concern for others as well as internalized societal values for good behavior (Eisenberg et al., 2013). Like adults, young children's judgments about whether to help are influenced by considerations such as people's welfare and needs as well as the situation (Dahl & Paulus, 2019). At age 5 children feel more positive emotions in response to actively helping someone than just watching (Hepach et al., 2023). In addition, positive emotions following helping are greater when an audience is watching, suggesting a strategic motivation to improve their reputation by helping (Hepach et al., 2023). Older children also engage in prosocial behavior strategically to achieve goals such as to improve their reputation, to be chosen as social partners, or to elicit reciprocal assistance (Grueneisen & Warneken, 2022).

Sharing

In addition to helping, children display prosocial behavior by sharing, which tends to increase throughout toddlerhood into early childhood (Song et al., 2022). Children's views of when and how to share change with development (Damon, 1977, 1988). Sharing involves judgments concerning **distributive justice**—how to divide goods fairly (Damon, 1977, 1988). How should a candy bar be divided among three siblings? Does age matter? Height? Hunger? How much the child likes chocolate? Children's reasoning about distributive justice undergoes predictable changes as they grow older.

Developmental Changes

Three-year-old children conceptualize fair sharing as strict equality, where each child should get the same amount of candy, no matter what (Damon, 1977; Enright et al., 1984). Using nonverbal measures, researchers have shown that 3-year-old children identify and react negatively to unfair distributions of stickers, especially if they receive fewer than another child (LoBue et al., 2011). Despite endorsing norms of sharing, behavioral studies show that 3-, 4-, and 6-year-old children tend to favor themselves but they become more likely to share with age (Qiu et al., 2017; C. E. Smith et al., 2013). Sharing behavior is also influenced by context. After working together actively to obtain rewards in a collaboration task, most 3-year-old children share equally with a peer (Warneken et al., 2011).

Between 3 and 5 years of age, young children show selectivity in sharing. Young children share more with children and adults who show prosocial behaviors such as sharing and helping others, and they view helping as less acceptable if the recipient is trying to steal (Dahl & Brownell, 2019; Kuhlmeier et al., 2014). Four- and 5-year-olds report an obligation to share, but often allocate rewards based on observable characteristics, such as age, size, or other obvious physical characteristics (e.g., "The oldest should get more candy"). Often these decisions are based on personal desires and characteristics that adults would deem irrelevant, such as, "Girls should get more because they're girls!" When told that they must make an unequal distribution, 5-year-olds tend to share more with others whom they expect will reciprocate and more with friends than with peers they dislike (Paulus & Moore, 2014). They are also more likely to share with friends and persons known to them than strangers.

Young children show prosocial behaviors, such as sharing.
FatCamera/Getty Images

As with moral reasoning, children progress from self-serving reasons for sharing, expressed in early childhood (e.g., "I get more candy because I want it" or "I share candy so that Mikey will play with me") to more mature conceptions of distributive justice, including considerations of need, in middle childhood (Damon, 1977). At around 7 years of age, children start taking merit and effort into account and believe that extra candy should go to the child who has excelled or worked especially hard (Kienbaum & Mairhofer, 2022). By 8 years of age children tend to prefer fair allocations, forgoing opportunities to allocate more to themselves (Qiu et al., 2017). They also can act on the basis of benevolence, believing that others at a disadvantage should get special consideration (C. E. Smith & Warneken, 2016). For example, extra candy should go to the child who does not get picked to play on a sports team or a child who is excluded from an activity. Between ages 8 and 10, children begin to coordinate and balance competing claims, such as those of need, effort, and merit (Kienbaum & Mairhofer, 2022; C. E. Smith & Warneken, 2016).

Notably, young children's perspectives on sharing shifts from an emphasis on equality to equity, and they begin to consider others' wealth and distribute more resources to poor others than rich others (Paulus et al., 2018). Children who have more contact with children of lower wealth are more likely to allocate resources based on wealth, allocating more to a low wealth peer than high wealth peer (Elenbaas, 2019).

Prosocial Behavior in Adolescence

Adolescents' prosocial reasoning and behavior tend to improve from early through late adolescence, alongside improvements in moral reasoning, perspective taking, and emotional control (Crone & Achterberg, 2022; Eisenberg et al., 2005; te Brinke et al., 2023; Van der Graaff et al., 2018). Like children, adolescents show selectivity in helping behaviors. Generally adolescents show higher mean levels of prosocial behavior toward friends than toward either parents or strangers (Güroglu et al., 2014; Padilla-Walker & Christensen, 2011). Prosocial behavior toward family tends to remain stable or decrease over time, while prosocial behavior toward friends increases over time (Padilla-Walker et al., 2015).

Cognitive, emotional, and social development influence the display of prosocial behavior in adolescence. Abstract reasoning enables adolescents to engage in perspective taking and advances in emotional understanding contribute to empathic concern, the ability to understand and feel concern for another's emotional experience (Eisenberg et al., 2015). Individual differences in perspective taking among adolescents predicts adolescents' giving behavior in economic games, which adolescents must decide how much of a given quantity, such as coins, tokens, or candy, to give to others (Güroglu et al., 2014; te Brinke et al., 2023).

Perspective taking and empathic concern facilitate positive peer relationships and prosocial behavior. As adolescents become more peer-oriented, with increasing interactions with peers, developing more intimate relationships with peers, and becoming more interested in romantic relationships, their behaviors tend to become more other-oriented, with opportunities for prosocial behavior (Wentzel, 2014). Engaging in prosocial behavior may foster adolescents' tendency to show perspective taking and empathic concern, as well as improve relations with peers (Van der Graaff et al., 2018).

Prosocial Behavior and Adjustment

Prosocial behavior is associated with many positive outcomes. In childhood, prosocial behavior is associated with positive peer relationships, mental health, and social competence (Malti & Dys, 2018). Prosocial children tend to show low levels of aggressive and problem behaviors (Zondervan-Zwijnenburg et al., 2022). They tend to be successful in school and score high on measures of vocabulary, reading, and language—perhaps because prosocial children are friendly and interact with teachers and peers (Eisenberg et al., 2015; Miller & Hastings, 2020). Childhood prosocial behavior is associated with having friends and positive relationships with peers in early adolescence (Ma et al., 2020).

These positive outcomes continue and increase in adolescence. Prosocial behavior is associated with self-esteem, social competence and approval, academic achievement, and high-quality relationships (El Mallah, 2020; Padilla-Walker, Carlo, et al., 2018; Xiao et al., 2019). Moreover, longitudinal research suggests that prosocial behavior is negatively associated with internalizing and externalizing problems such as anxiety, depression, aggression, risky behaviors, substance use, delinquency, and association with deviant peers (Memmott-Elison & Toseeb, 2022; Memmott-Elison et al., 2020; Padilla-Walker et al., 2020; Padilla-Walker, Memmott-Elison, et al., 2018).

Influences on Prosocial Behavior

Prosocial behavior is influenced by many interacting factors, including biology and genes, family contexts, the larger social context, and the development of reasoning skills.

Biological Influences

Genetic factors are believed to contribute to individual differences in prosocial behavior (Waldman et al., 2011). Studies on twins have shown that identical twins show more similar reports of prosocial behavior than do their fraternal twin peers (Knafo-Noam et al., 2015). Several genes have been implicated in prosocial tendencies, including one that influences the hormone oxytocin, which is associated with attachment and other socioemotional behaviors (Carter, 2014).

A child's inborn temperament influences how the child regulates emotion, which affects their ability to feel empathy for others in distress and, in turn, whether empathetic feelings result in personal distress or prosocial behavior (Eisenberg et al., 2015). Children who struggle to regulate their emotions may react to others in distress with heightened physiological arousal, such as increased heart rate and brain activity in regions associated with negative emotions, suggesting a feeling of being overwhelmed that can interfere with prosocial responding (Miller, 2018). Other research suggests that shyness may inhibit young children's learning opportunities to practice prosocial behaviors, which can hinder their ability to respond empathically and prosocially (MacGowan & Schmidt, 2021).

Brain development also plays a role in emotional control and prosocial behavior in children and adolescents (Do et al., 2019; Walsh et al., 2023). A recent 3-year fMRI study of adolescents and emerging adults found that higher prosociality was associated with more advanced brain development, as indicated by greater cortical thinning of brain regions related to social cognition and behavior control (Ferschmann et al., 2019). Prosocial behavior increases as self-regulation improves over adolescence (Andrews et al., 2021).

Family Influences

Prosocial behaviors, such as sharing, comforting, and helping emerge through everyday interactions with caregivers from birth (Dahl & Brownell, 2019). Rich interactions with parents engage the emotions, cognitions, and behaviors critical to prosocial responding (Brownell, 2016; Reschke et al., 2023; Wong et al., 2021). The secure attachment that accompanies warm, sensitive parenting aids in the development of emotional regulation, a predictor of empathy and prosocial responding throughout childhood (Beier et al., 2019; Elhusseini et al., 2023; Spinrad & Gal, 2018). Parents of prosocial children draw attention to models of prosocial behavior in peers and in media, such as in storybooks, movies, and television programs. Parents may also describe feelings and model sympathetic concern and the use of language to discuss feelings. Young children whose parents do these things are more likely to use words to describe their thoughts and emotions and attempt to understand others' emotional states (Taylor et al., 2013).

Parents also actively encourage prosocial behavior through modeling and including children, even toddlers, in caregiving and household caregiving activities (Kärtner et al., 2021; Schuhmacher et al., 2019). Parents can scaffold and support toddlers' participation in caregiving and helping through compliments, encouragement, guidance, and praise (Dahl & Brownell, 2019). Scaffolding increases helping even in 6- to 9-month-old infants (Dahl et al., 2022). Parents' encouragement of children's participation in household cleanup routines predicts children's willingness to help another adult in a new context (Hammond & Carpendale, 2015). Children's prosocial behavior emerges out of prosocial activity shared with adults, and parental encouragement promotes its development (see Figure 12.1; Brownell, 2016; Carpendale & Wallbridge, 2023).

The relationship between parents and children is bidirectional, with children playing a role in their development by influencing their parents (Miller & Hastings, 2020). For instance, a study found that maternal sensitivity influenced children's prosocial behavior from preschool through sixth grade and that prosocial behavior, in turn, predicted mothers' subsequent sensitivity, suggesting that mothers and children influence each other (Newton et al., 2014). Children who exhibit kindness, compassion, and helpfulness tend to elicit responsive and warm parenting from their mothers, further reinforcing their prosocial behavior.

Parent-child interactions that involve support and developmentally appropriate limits or rules are associated with higher rates of prosocial behavior in 1st-, 5th-, 10th-, and 12th-grade students (Carlo et al., 2018; Yavuz et al., 2022). Warmth is especially influential in supporting prosocial behavior in adolescents (Carlo et al., 2011; Padilla-Walker et al., 2015; Putnick et al., 2018).

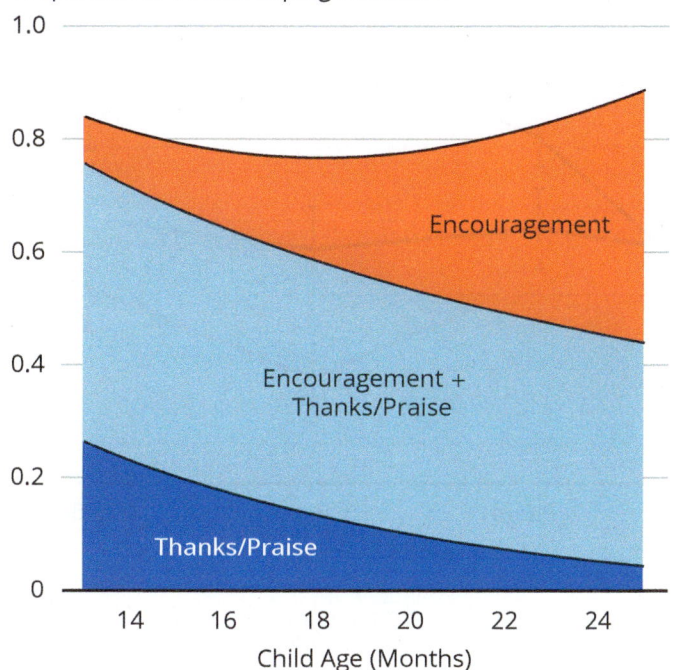

FIGURE 12.1 ■ Proportion of Situations in Which Caregivers Give Praise and Encouragement to Toddlers

Source: Dahl, A., & Brownell, C. A. (2019). The social origins of human prosociality. *Current Directions in Psychological Science, 28*(3), 274–279. https://doi.org/10.1177/0963721419830386

Siblings offer opportunities to learn and practice helping and other prosocial behavior (Hughes et al., 2018). Older siblings who display positive emotional responsiveness promote preschoolers' emotional and social competence. Children with siblings tend to develop a theory of mind earlier than those without siblings (Kramer, 2014). The perspective-taking and cognitive skills that comprise theory of mind promote emotional understanding and prosocial behavior. Affectionate sibling relationships also predict prosocial behavior in adolescence (Harper et al., 2016)

Peer Influences

Prosocial behavior is associated with positive peer relationships—and these relationships influence prosocial behavior. Similar to relationships with parents, close high-quality friendships predict prosocial behavior (Silke et al., 2018). Peers can influence prosocial behavior through modeling and communicating values and norms (Busching & Krahé, 2020). Adolescents whose peers model prosocial behaviors, promote prosocial values and norms, or discourage deviant or aggressive behavior also show higher levels of a variety of prosocial behaviors (Farrell et al., 2017). Furthermore, prosocial behavior is associated with peer acceptance, with longitudinal research suggesting that prosocial behavior can help rejected adolescents become more accepted by peers (Chávez et al., 2022).

Peers also influence adolescent behavior through their reactions. In one study, 12- to 16-year-old adolescents made decisions about the allocation of coins between themselves and a group of anonymous peers who provided either prosocial feedback (liking the decision to give more coins to others), antisocial feedback (liking the decision to keep more coins to oneself), or no feedback (van Hoorn et al., 2016). As shown in Figure 12.2 prosocial behavior increased after prosocial feedback, decreased after antisocial feedback, and, when no feedback was provided, prosocial behavior remained stable and did not change over multiple consecutive decisions. Peers influence adolescents' prosocial behavior in both positive and negative ways.

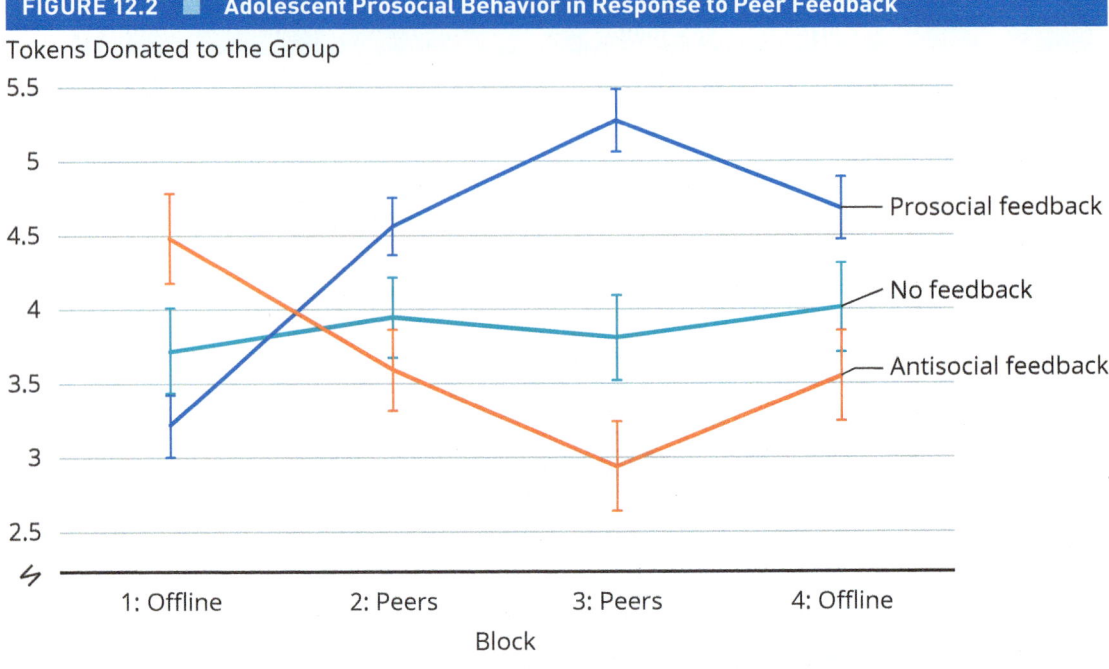

FIGURE 12.2 ■ Adolescent Prosocial Behavior in Response to Peer Feedback

Source: van Hoorn, J., van Dijk, E., Meuwese, R., Rieffe, C., & Crone, E. A. (2016). Peer influence on prosocial behavior in adolescence. *Journal of Research on Adolescence, 26*(1), 90–100. https://doi.org/10.1111/jora.12173

Cultural Context

Collectivist cultures, in which people live with extended families, work is shared, and the maintenance of positive relationships with others is emphasized, tend to promote prosocial values and behavior more so than do cultures that emphasize the individual, as is common in most Western cultures (Eisenberg et al., 2015). One study of mother-child dyads in Japan and the United States found that the Japanese mothers of 4-year-old children tended to emphasize mutuality in their interactions, stressing the relationship (e.g., "This puzzle is difficult for us. Let's see if we can solve it."). In contrast, the U.S. mothers tended to emphasize individuality (e.g., "This puzzle is hard for you, isn't it? Let's see you try again.") (Dennis et al., 2002). These different styles influence how children display empathy, whether as sharing another's emotion or simply understanding another's emotion.

Culture subtly influences children's ideas about sharing and fairness. Young children from Brazil, China, Fiji, Peru, Tibet, and the United States move from emphasizing self-interest to increasing fairness (Robbins et al., 2016; Rochat et al., 2009). Recently 4- to 11-year-old children in 13 diverse countries ranging from collectivist (China, Cuba, Taiwan) to individualist (Canada, the United States) were asked to distribute rewards among hypothetical recipients. Children of all cultures shifted from equality-based to equity-based distribution. However, the age and degree to which children favored equity varied with countries' levels of individualism and collectivism. Children from more individualistic cultures favored equitable distributions at an earlier age than children from more collectivist cultures overall (Huppert et al., 2019). When presented with a hypothetical equality-based context in which recipients differed in regard to wealth and merit, children from the most individualistic cultures endorsed equitable distributions to a greater degree than children from more collectivist cultures. But in an empathy-based context, when recipients differed in injury-status, children from the most collectivist cultures exhibited greater preferences to distribute resources equitably compared to children from more individualistic cultures.

In another study Filipino and American fifth graders were presented with hypothetical scenarios that required them to distribute resources. All the children preferred equal division of the resources regardless of merit or need, but the Filipino and American children offered different explanations of their choices that were related to their culture (Carson & Banuazizi, 2008). U.S. children emphasized that the characters in the scenario performed equally and therefore deserved equal amounts of the resources, reflecting U.S. culture's emphasis on individuality and merit. Filipino children, on the other hand, tended to be more concerned with the interpersonal and emotional consequences of an unequal distribution, in line with their culture's emphasis on the collective and the importance of interpersonal relationships (Carson & Banuazizi, 2008). With age children of all cultures increasingly prefer equitable distributions, but cultural values influence how they understand and account for their choices (Noh, 2020).

> **THINKING IN CONTEXT 12.2**
>
> 1. Prosocial development is linked with perspective-taking ability. What other types of development influence children and adolescent's capacities for prosocial behavior? Discuss.
> 2. What can parents and teachers do to encourage children's prosocial tendencies? What about those of adolescents?
> 3. Many studies of prosocial behavior examine sharing and instrumental assistance. Can you identify another way of studying prosocial behavior in older children or adolescents? What other behaviors might indicate prosociality?

AGGRESSION AND ANTISOCIAL BEHAVIOR

> 12.3 Examine common forms of aggressive and antisocial behavior in childhood and adolescence.

Whereas prosocial behavior is intended to help others, antisocial behavior is intended to hurt others or break rules. **Aggression** is a form of antisocial behavior designed to harm others. All children engage in some aggressive behavior, just as all children engage in some prosocial behavior. Aggression takes different forms as children grow older.

Aggression

Despite their increasing capacities for empathy and prosocial behavior, young children often display aggressive behavior, behavior that can harm or violate the rights of others. Most infants and children engage in some physically aggressive behaviors, such as hitting, biting, or kicking, at least some of the time (Tremblay et al., 2004). The most common form of aggression seen in infancy and early childhood is **instrumental aggression**, which is used to achieve a goal, such as obtaining a toy (Hay et al., 2011). For instance, a child who grabs a crayon out of another child's hand is often motivated to obtain the crayon, not to hurt the other child. In addition to toys, preschool children often battle over space ("I was sitting there!").

Instrumental aggression is often displayed by sociable and confident children, usually during play, and increases from toddlerhood into early childhood as children begin to play with other children and act in their own interests (Hay, 2016). However, there are individual differences in aggression that are apparent by 6 months of age and persist through early childhood. Excessive rage, irritation, and using physical force in infancy and early childhood predict problematic levels of aggressiveness in later childhood (Dugré & Potvin, 2022; Perhamus & Ostrov, 2020).

By ages 4 to 5, physical aggression begins to decline and verbal aggression becomes more frequent as most children develop the self-control to resist aggressive impulses and the language skills to express their needs (Eisner & Malti, 2015). Verbal aggression is a form of **relational aggression**, intended to harm others' social relationships (Ostrov & Godleski, 2010). In preschool and elementary school, relational aggression often takes the form of name calling and excluding peers from play (Pellegrini & Roseth, 2006).

Physical aggression continues to decline throughout elementary school and high school (Eisner & Malti, 2015). A small minority of children show high levels of aggression that increase over childhood, placing them at risk for long-term problems with aggression and antisocial behavior (Hay, 2016; Kjeldsen et al., 2014). These children may be more likely to have experienced coercive parenting and family dysfunction, and have mothers with a history of antisocial behavior, which can inhibit the development of emotional regulation and self-management skills (F. Wang et al., 2013). Effective emotion regulation is critical to controlling aggressive impulses, and children who struggle to develop these skills are likely to continue displaying aggressive behavior (Ersan, 2020; Gower et al., 2014). Aggression is associated with poor relationships and rejection from peers and school performance in childhood and adolescence (Vuoksimaa et al., 2021; Yue & Zhang, 2023). Children who show high levels of aggression often direct it toward their peers, often in the form of bullying.

Bullying

Bullying, also known as *peer victimization*, occurs when a child or adolescent repeatedly attempts to harm another through physical, verbal, or social means, such as by hitting, kicking, name-calling, teasing, shunning, or humiliating them (Olweus, 2013). Bullying is a widespread problem affecting children and adolescents in many countries, with estimated rates ranging from 15% to 25% of children in Australia, Austria, England, Finland, Germany, Norway, and the United States (Eyuboglu et al., 2021; Lebrun-Harris et al., 2020; Zych et al., 2017). Physical bullying is most prevalent in childhood, while verbal and relational forms increase across childhood and persist through adolescence (Finkelhor et al., 2009). In a recent survey of parents of about 50,000 children found that 22% of children age 6–11 and 21% of adolescents age 12–17 experienced bullying victimization in the past year (Lebrun-Harris et al., 2020). In adolescence, peer victimization tends to peak early, typically during middle school and tends to decrease by the end of high school (Hymel & Swearer, 2015).

In addition to traditional bullying, cyberbullying has emerged as a significant concern. Cyberbullying is bullying carried out online via social media, email, or text messaging. An estimated 5% to 15% of U.S. adolescents experience cyberbullying (Nagata et al., 2022; Zycha et al., 2015). International estimates range from 19% to 45% of adolescents in 42 countries (Craig et al., 2020). Cyberbullying often co-occurs with traditional bullying, leading some experts to suggest that bullying may begin and migrate online (Carvalho et al., 2021; Johansson & Englund, 2021). Indeed, a study examining 11- to 16-year-old adolescents over an 18-month period, traditional, offline, bullying victimization predicted later cyberbullying victimization (Camacho et al., 2023).

Children Who Bully

Boys and girls who engage in bullying tend to be impulsive and aggressive. Boys tend to show physical aggression and target both boys and girls. Girls who bully tend to target other girls, using verbal and relational aggression to threaten relationships by methods such as ridiculing, embarrassing, and spreading rumors (Murray-Close et al., 2016).

Bullying, particularly in the form of relational aggression, is often motivated by the desire to attain and maintain high social status and a powerful dominant position in the peer group (Hensums, Brummelman, et al., 2023; van der Ploeg et al., 2020). Children and adolescents who are socially skilled at relational aggression are frequently perceived by peers as popular, cool, and powerful (Juvonen & Graham, 2014; Wiertsema et al., 2023). In fact, bullying can be useful in maintaining prestige and high social status among peers. As evidence of this, many bullies report having no difficulty making friends and receiving similar levels of support from their classmates as other children (Menesini & Salmivalli, 2017). Bullies may become more popular over time, but their aggression also poses risks for rejection (Hensums, Brummelman, et al., 2023; Wiertsema et al., 2023).

Children and adolescents who engage in online and offline bullying often experience maladaptive and rejecting parenting, including inconsistent and poor parental involvement and support, as well as inadequate supervision (Bullo & Schulz, 2022; Nocentini et al., 2019). Parents of bullies are more likely to prefer coercive control and physical discipline, and may be permissive toward aggressive behavior, even encouraging children to retaliate for perceived provocation (Gómez-Ortiz et al., 2016; Hinduja & Patchin, 2022; Rajendran et al., 2016). Children and adolescents who bully tend to experience higher rates of depression than peers who are uninvolved in bullying, but less than victims of bullying (Serafini et al., 2023; Ye et al., 2023).

Children who show physical forms of bullying, such as hair pulling, are often reared in homes with poor supervision, coercive control, and physical discipline.
SolStock/ Getty Images

Children who are Bullied

Children who are bullied are often perceived as different from their peers, as more quiet, inhibited, and cautious than other children (Juvonen & Graham, 2014). Children with neurodevelopmental conditions, such as ADHD, experience higher rates of victimization (Abregú-Crespo et al., 2024; Cuba Bustinza et al., 2022). Likewise, children with physical differences, such as being overweight, are more likely to be bullied (Cheng et al., 2022). Victims of bullying often report experiencing intrusive, overprotective, and critical parenting, which can increase their vulnerability to bullying (Menesini & Salmivalli, 2017). Common social and emotional characteristics of victims of bullying, such as nonassertiveness, passivity, having few friends, and experiencing anxiety, depression, and poor emotional control, are often present in children prior to peer victimization and are then amplified by victimization (Cooley et al., 2021; Husky et al., 2020; Kaufman et al., 2022).

In response to bullying, many children may choose to avoid contact, such as by not going to school and refusing to go to certain places (Waasdorp & Bradshaw, 2011). A sample of adolescents from Australia showed that nearly half of bullied adolescents did *not* seek help (Matuschka et al., 2022). Those with poorer prosocial skills, lower perceived social support, and higher Internet use were less likely to seek help for bullying victimization. Children may respond in ways that reinforce the behavior of the bullies, such as becoming defensive, crying, or further withdrawing. Older children who experience frequent victimization may respond with rage and a greater desire to retaliate, making them more likely to engage in **reactive aggression**, an aggressive response to an insult, confrontation, or frustration (Arseneault, 2018). Intense feelings of hostility may even motivate victims to engage in bullying behavior, turning into perpetrators themselves (Walters & Espelage, 2022).

Many, but not all, victims of bullying are passive and withdrawn. Children who are aggressive may respond with hostility and poor self-control, potentially escalating the situation and inviting aggressive exchanges with others (Arseneault, 2018; Swearer & Hymel, 2015; van Dijk et al., 2017). Some children are **bully-victims**, meaning they share characteristics of both bullies and victims (Hymel & Swearer, 2015; O'Connor, 2021). There is often an overlap between bullies and victims, and the perpetration of bullying can lead to future victimization, and vice versa (Walters, 2021). In one study, experiencing offline bullying was associated with perpetrating cyberbullying, and later offline bullying in adolescents, over an 18-month period (Camacho et al., 2023).

Bully-victims often display high levels of anxiety and depression, as well as low rates of social acceptance and self-esteem common to other victims, but they also show more aggression, impulsivity, and poor self-control than do other victims (Drubina et al., 2023; van Dijk et al., 2017). These children may have difficulty managing their emotions, increasing their risk for reactive aggression and acting out behaviors that invite aggressive exchanges with others. They tend to have problems in peer relationships and are often disliked by their classmates (Arseneault, 2018). Children who are bully-victims are more likely than other victimized children to experience anxiety and depression in late adolescence and in early adulthood—and even into middle adulthood (Evans-Lacko et al., 2017; McDougall & Vaillancourt, 2015).

Experiencing repeated victimization, online or offline, is associated with negative emotional, academic, and behavioral correlates that may persist into adulthood (Moore et al., 2017). Victims of cyberbullying tend to view it as more harsh and uncontrollable than traditional forms of bullying because unlike offline bullying, which occurs in a specific place, such as school, cyberbullying is asynchronous and can occur at any time, without the victim's presence. As a result, victims may feel powerless and unable to escape, leading to heightened feelings of distress (Eyuboglu et al., 2021; Nesi et al., 2018). Adjustment problems associated with bullying include anxiety, depression, suicidal ideation, poor health, and heightened alcohol and substance use (Halliday et al., 2021; Hysing et al., 2019; Kretschmer et al., 2017; Moore et al., 2017). Peer victimization is associated with poor academic performance, which can have life-long consequences as academic achievement influences educational and career opportunities (Hysing et al., 2019; Laith & Vaillancourt, 2022).

Bullying Intervention

Reducing peer victimization is challenging because it occurs within a system of peers, teachers, and contexts, both in and out of school. Successful school-based interventions to combat bullying address multiple perspectives, including victims, bullies, and other members of the school community (Gaffney et al., 2021; Hensums, de Mooij, et al., 2023; Hutson et al., 2018; Nese et al., 2014). Interventions for cyberbullying are most often implemented in schools, as part of an overall antibullying strategy, and address the interacting roles of victims and bullies (Kumar & Goldstein, 2020; Polanin et al., 2022). Interventions can help victims change their negative self-perceptions, acquire the skills needed to maintain relationships with peers, and teach them to respond to bullying in ways that do not reinforce their attackers (Olweus & Limber, 2010). Learning to identify, understand, and manage one's own and other people's emotions, as well as direct anger in safe and appropriate ways, is helpful for all adolescents (Hutson et al., 2018).

Teachers can influence the classroom climate by becoming aware of bullying, being willing to intervene, and fostering an atmosphere of warm and respectful communication (Burger et al., 2022; Cornell et al., 2015). It is especially important to address bystanders—students who witness episodes of bullying but do not act. Bystanders reinforce bullies' behaviors and increase bullying (Kärnä et al., 2010; Salmivalli, 2014). School and class norms can influence whether bystanders intervene, especially if parents reinforce norms (Grassetti et al., 2018; Pozzoli et al., 2012). Parents tend to advise children to intervene and tell an adult in response to physical bullying and to help the victim in response to emotional attacks (Grassetti et al., 2020). Classmates can be encouraged to support one another when bullying events occur: Rather than being bystanders or egging the bully on, they can tell a teacher, refuse to watch, and even, if safe, encourage bullies to stop.

Stopping bullying requires awareness and change within the school (Jenkins et al., 2021). Schools must review and modify practices with an eye toward identifying how class environment and procedures may maintain or increase bullying (Fink et al., 2018; Nese et al., 2014). In recognition of the pervasiveness and seriousness of bullying, specific bully-related policies are included in public school laws in most states. Addressing the problem of bullying requires that children, teachers, and parents voice concerns about bullying; that schools develop policies against bullying; that teachers supervise and monitor children during lunch and recess times; and that parents learn how to identify and change victims' and bullies' behaviors.

Addressing bullying is tricky with adolescents. Interventions to combat bullying in younger groups tend to focus on the more observable forms of bullying common in childhood. The relational bullying more common in adolescence is much less visible and often goes unnoticed by adults. Existing interventions for bullying may not address the reasons for peer victimization in adolescence. For example, antibullying interventions for children tend to emphasize social and emotional skills. However, adolescents often victimize others through relational aggression, not because they lack social and emotional regulation skills, but because relational aggression enhances their social status (such as making the teen seem "cool") (Yeager et al., 2018). It is difficult to design effective interventions to target behaviors that adolescents find useful, making addressing adolescent bullying a difficult problem.

Delinquency

During adolescence young people experiment with new ideas, activities, and limits. For many adolescents, experimentation takes the form of delinquent activity (juvenile offending, or **delinquency**). At least one-half of adolescents are involved in some violation of a law each year, usually without coming into contact with the police (Gurley, 2011).

Most delinquent acts are limited to adolescence and do not continue into adulthood (Moffitt, 2017; Pulkkinen et al., 2020). But a small number of adolescents begin engaging in antisocial behavior in childhood. Usually these children show multiple problem behaviors, may have their first contact with the criminal justice system by age 12 or earlier, and engage in more serious offenses in adolescence, indicating that they are at risk of becoming repeat offenders who continue criminal activity in adulthood (Baglivio et al., 2014; Eme, 2020).

Adolescent delinquent activity typically occurs in the presence of peers. Antisocial activity generally begins in early adolescence, is sustained by affiliation with similar peers, continues into middle adolescence and then declines in late adolescence. Research with adolescents from nine countries has shown that opportunities for and peer support of aggression predict delinquency (Lansford et al., 2020). Brain development plays a large role in risky activity, such as delinquent behavior. Recall from Chapter 4, that adolescents experience heightened sensitivity to rewards, exaggerated emotional responses, and executive function, controlled by a still-developing prefrontal cortex (Andrews et al., 2021; Tamnes & Mills, 2020). With advances in brain development, and the corresponding shifts in cognition, and emotional regulation, antisocial activity declines (Carroll et al., 2023).

Some delinquent activity is common in adolescence, but not all teenagers engage in delinquent or antisocial acts. Delinquent activity is more common among adolescents with a greater drive for sensation seeking and poor impulse control, who experience poor parental monitoring, who spend more unstructured time with peers (especially antisocial peers), and who are more susceptible to peer influence (Hoeben et al., 2016; Huijsmans et al., 2021; Vaughan et al., 2022). Parenting that is inconsistent, controlling, and accompanied by harsh punishment can magnify impulsive, defiant, and aggressive tendencies in adolescents (Kapetanovic et al., 2019; Liu et al., 2021).

Addressing adolescent delinquency requires looking beyond the individual to consider contextual factors that contribute to delinquency. Communities with pervasive poverty often have limited educational, recreational, and employment activities, are subject to over-policing, offer access to drugs and firearms, present opportunities to witness and be victimized by violence, and allow exposure to gangs who offer protection and companionship, all of which contribute to the onset of antisocial behavior (Booth & Shaw, 2023; McCrea et al., 2019; Winters, 2020).

Protecting children and adolescents involves fostering resilience through support systems, such as relationships with parents, other adults, and prosocial peers. Parenting programs that help parents develop supportive parent-child relationships, communication skills, and appropriate discipline and monitoring practices can prevent delinquent activity in children and adolescents (Beelmann et al., 2023). In schools, support from teachers and high-quality instruction can increase adolescents' school engagement, which serves as a protective factor (Lamari-Fisher & Bond, 2021).

After school activities, particularly those involving athletic activity and sports, are effective in preventing delinquent activity by keeping adolescents occupied and promoting connections with peers and the school (Jugl et al., 2021). Furthermore, advances in social and emotional competencies are positively associated with social and academic adjustment and are also linked with fewer behavioral problems and emotional distress (Domitrovich et al., 2017; Osher et al., 2016; Weissberg, 2019). It is essential to recognize that adolescent delinquency is a complex problem whose causes extend well beyond the individual adolescent.

> **THINKING IN CONTEXT 12.3**
>
> 1. How does bullying differ from childhood into adolescence? From your observations, what forms might it take at each age? Why do these changes occur? Which do you think is easier to prevent or intervene in?
> 2. How does the nature of aggression change over childhood and into adolescence? What developmental factors contribute to these changes?
> 3. What are the roles of physical, cognitive, and socioemotional development in delinquent activity during adolescence? Give examples of each. What are the roles of peers and parents in influencing delinquent behavior?

RELIGION AND SPIRITUALITY

> 12.4 Describe the development of religiosity and spirituality in childhood and adolescence.

When people consider their values and beliefs concerning moral and prosocial behavior, they often associate them with religion. **Religiosity** refers to the practice of a religion, including adopting its values and beliefs and participating in its customs, rituals, and community. **Spirituality** refers to the perception and experience of transcendent beings, such as a god or gods, and the search for meaning and purpose in life in ways that benefit others and society (King et al., 2021). Religiosity and spirituality are separate but overlapping concepts (Paul Victor & Treschuk, 2020). Spirituality may occur within or outside the context of religion. On the other hand, an individual might attend church and participate in religious instruction but may not reflect on its meaning or feel spiritually engaged. In adulthood the sense of religiosity may expand to include a spiritual search for meaning and purpose, encompassing both religiosity and spirituality. Nevertheless, some people may be spiritual but not religious, pursuing a sense of meaning in life without participating in organized religion. What does religion mean to children?

Religiosity in Childhood

Most people have their first experiences with religion as children. Children learn about religion through formal education, such as by attending Sunday school or parochial schools. Parents play an important role in religious socialization and encourage their children to adopt their religious beliefs (L. Power & McKinney, 2013). Most children are similar to their parents regarding religiosity and preferences (Stearns & McKinney, 2019).

Children's understanding of religion is related to their cognitive and moral development. Younger children tend to adhere to religious rituals inflexibly, emphasizing the importance of specific actions without appreciating the symbolic meaning beyond them. Older children have a more nuanced understanding of rules and interpret rituals in more sophisticated ways, appreciating their symbolism. They tend to place more emphasis on the intention behind the ritual than on its accuracy of performance, similar to adults (Moulin-Stozek & James, 2022).

Religiosity in Adolescence

Adolescents' views of religion are complicated. In the United States, most (85%) of adolescents aged 13 to 17 report believing in God or a universal spirit (Pew Research Center, 2020). Similarly, a large scale survey of adolescents and emerging adults aged 12 to 25 across 8 countries and 5 continents revealed that over three quarters report identifying with some religious affiliation and two thirds report following God or a higher power as an important life goal (Benson et al., 2012). About 40% of U.S. teenagers say they attend religious services at least once or twice a month, but religious practice, including attendance at religious services, declines throughout adolescence (Hardie et al., 2016; Pew Research Center, 2020).

Adolescents' understanding of religion is influenced by their cognitive development. Their advances in abstract thinking enable them to consider metaphysical concepts, such as the existence of God, and engage in metacognition to evaluate their understanding and beliefs (Labouvie-Vief, 2006). Adolescents can integrate and weigh information from multiple sources with their emotions and experiences to construct personal religious beliefs. As a result, their religious beliefs tend to become less rigid and more flexible. For many adolescents, religiosity becomes less about rituals and specific practices, such as attending religious services, and more about spirituality, searching for answers to life's meaning and establishing beliefs (Lopez et al., 2011). They may view God as a creator and promoter of goodness and fairness, but many may perceive God as peripheral to daily life unless problems arise (Barry et al., 2018).

During adolescence, many young people examine their feelings about religion as a part of their identity exploration. Their search for a sense of self is often intertwined with their concerns about life's greater meaning and purpose. Religion can provide a framework to explore these existential questions (Ream & Savin-Williams, 2006). Figuring out how religion fits into their lives is a critical part of identity development (Erikson, 1959). As young people move toward identity resolution, religiosity tends to increase (Duriez et al., 2008). However, recall from Chapter 11, identity achievement is rare in adolescence (Branje, 2022).

Adolescents often develop strong religious beliefs and interests, such as these boys who are learning about the Koran.

Godong/Getty Images

Religious Socialization

Parents play an important role in the religious socialization of children and adolescents. Most U.S. children and adolescents tend to share similar religious beliefs, attend religious services at a similar frequency and are oriented toward the same general religious traditions as their parents (Pew Research Center, 2020). Parents and grandparents serve as models, engaging in religious practices such as including religious discussions, praying at family meals, reading sacred texts as a family, and other family rituals (Barry et al., 2018; Dollahite & Thatcher, 2008; Layton et al., 2011). Church attendance provides children with unique opportunities to socialize regularly with family, friends, and neighbors (Jones et al., 2022), creating a community of support. Parents may also encourage their children to participate in particular activities, such as religious youth groups, to promote their religious development.

However, religious development is not solely the result of passive socialization. Children and adolescents actively converse with their parents about religion, sharing their views and asking questions, indicating that learning about religion is an active process in which they construct meaning (Boyatzis & Janicki, 2003). Religious socialization is a bidirectional relational process in which parents and children give and take. A positive religious socialization process involves parental religious teaching, reasonable expectations, warmth, and consistent modeling, along with autonomy granting and respect for children's views, which can foster positive relationships and support religious development in children and adolescents (Barrow et al., 2021).

The quality of parent-child relationships influences the effectiveness of parental religious socialization (Goeke-Morey & Cummings, 2017). A warm relationship creates a positive context for discussions about religion (Goodman & Dyer, 2020). Adolescents who have close relationships with parents are more likely than other adolescents to attend weekly worship services with their families (Day et al., 2009). Adolescents with secure attachments to their parents or who rate their relationship with their parents positively tend to show similar levels of religiosity as their parents (Ream & Savin-Williams, 2006). Insecurely attached adolescents might disaffiliate with religion to break from religious family members with whom they have dysfunctional relationships. Still, others might seek religion-based attachments that were lacking in their family systems, developing strong attachments to religious figures, for example (Granqvist, 2002; King et al., 2009).

Religious beliefs and practices are also modeled and socialized through peer relationships. Adolescents tend to affiliate with peers who share similar interests and values, including religious beliefs, especially among highly religious adolescents (French et al., 2012; C. Smith & Snell, 2009). Religious groups provide contexts for friendship formation through various activities and social gatherings. Some adolescents look to friendships as valuable spiritual guides (Birkinshaw 2015). Participation in religious activities with a peer is associated with increased attendance (Tratner et al., 2020). Through shared activities, adolescents tend to socialize with one another, becoming more similar in values, attitudes, and behaviors, including religious beliefs and practices.

Religiosity and Adjustment

Religious involvement is associated with numerous positive psychosocial and behavioral outcomes in children and adolescents, including high self-esteem, prosocial behavior, well-being, and academic achievement (Barry et al., 2018; Hardy & King, 2019). More significantly, religiosity is negatively associated with and may protect against adjustment and behavioral problems, such as depression, substance use, delinquency, and sexual risk taking (Aggarwal et al., 2023; Hardy et al., 2022; Koletić et al., 2023; Peviani et al., 2019). For example, in a longitudinal sample of African American adolescents followed from age 12 to 18, religiosity served a protective role against the effect of stressful life events, such as neighborhood disorganization, violence, and discrimination, on depression over time (Lee & Neblett, 2019). Religiosity shows a similar protective effect against negative peer experiences, such as peer victimization, and internalizing symptoms and the effect of parental substance use on adolescent substance use (Helms et al., 2015; Schnitker et al., 2021).

Factors that promote religiosity, such as supportive parent and peer relationships, are also known to protect adolescents against risk. Highly religious parents are more likely to engage in effective parenting practices, such as communication, warmth, and monitoring, than their less religious peers (Snider et al., 2004). Part of the buffering effect of religiosity on adjustment and risky behavior occurs through religiosity's positive influence on parenting and the parent-child relationship (Goeke-Morey & Cummings, 2017). In a longitudinal study of African American adolescents and their parents, parental religiosity predicted positive parenting and adolescent religiosity, which in turn were negatively associated with affiliating with sexually permissive peers and risky sexual activity in girls (Landor et al., 2011). In boys, although parental religiosity predicted authoritative parenting and adolescent religiosity, authoritative parenting was not associated with risky sexual activity, suggesting gender differences in sexual socialization regardless of parent religiosity.

The religious community provides a network of social support and opportunities for high-quality social relationships that may serve a protective role on adolescents. Social support from a religious community is negatively associated with risky behaviors, including alcohol and substance use (Peviani et al., 2019; Schnitker et al., 2021). Religiosity and participation in religious communities may promote healthy behaviors in adolescents by fostering emotion regulation (Vishkin et al., 2014). Achieving the goals and standards articulated by religious communities, such as regular attendance at religious services and participation in prosocial community groups, encourages adolescents to monitor and regulate their behavior, promoting self-control (Hardy et al., 2020). Indeed, research with early adolescents suggests that religiosity is inversely associated with substance use and other risk behaviors through its influence on executive function and self-regulation mechanisms, including the ability to resist impulses and delay gratification (Holmes et al., 2019; Kim-Spoon et al., 2015).

THINKING IN CONTEXT 12.4

1. Children and adolescent's understanding of religion reflects their cognitive development. Consider preoperational, concrete operational, and formal operational reasoning (see Chapter 6). How might a child at each stage think about religion?
2. How does religiosity change during adolescence, and what factors contribute to these changes?
3. What is the relationship between religiosity and adjustment in children and adolescents? How does religiosity protect against behavioral and emotional problems? How might religiosity contribute to resilience (see Chapter 10)?

APPLY YOUR KNOWLEDGE

"I want that!" Julissa exclaimed as she kicked a ball out of Daryl's hands. "Hey!" he yelled as the ball hurtled toward his friend, knocking him down. "Are you ok? Don't cry," Daryl told his friend as Julissa chased the ball. Daryl handed his friend a toy truck. "You can play with this," he instructed.

Later that day during snack time the teacher told Daryl to distribute the crackers. He gave each child exactly 3 crackers because that's what the teacher does. It's the rule. Julissa protested, claiming that girls should get more than boys. "Why?" Daryl asked. "Because girls are better," Julissa answered. When Daryl counted three crackers for Julissa, she announced, "You're not invited to my birthday party!"

After school Daryl told his mother about Julissa's proclamation. "She wasn't very nice, was she?" Daryl's mother asked, "How did that make you feel?" "Bad," he answered. After a hug Daryl's mother encouraged him to go play outside with his best friend who lived next door.

1. Compare Julissa's and Daryl's prosocial and aggressive behavior. What is typical for young children?
2. How does children's understanding of rules and sharing change over time?
3. What role do parents play in influencing children's prosocial and aggressive behavior?
4. What advice would you provide Daryl's parents? Julissa's parents?

CHAPTER SUMMARY

12.1 Summarize the development of moral reasoning and its influences in childhood and adolescence.

Psychologists Jean Piaget and Lawrence Kohlberg both proposed that children's moral reasoning develops in stages. Piaget suggested that children progress from the morality of constraint in early childhood to the morality of cooperation in middle childhood, while Kohlberg's theory posits that moral reasoning progresses through three levels representing qualitative changes in conceptions of justice: preconventional reasoning, conventional reasoning, and postconventional reasoning. Reasoning advances with issue-focused discussions in which multiple perspectives are presented. Children between ages 3 and 5 can differentiate between moral issues (imperatives concerning people's rights and welfare), social conventions or customs, and personal issues (matters of personal choice that do not violate rights). School-age children's thinking about moral issues becomes more nuanced as they become better able to consider multiple perspectives and variables in decision making. The relationship between moral reasoning and behavior is not always clear-cut, and cultural values influence conceptions of justice, social conventions, and moral reasoning,

12.2 Analyze the progression of prosocial behavior and its contextual influences.

Prosocial behavior, which includes helping and sharing, emerges in infancy. Young infants display a preference for characters that help others over those that hinder them, and by 16 months, toddlers can exhibit instrumental assistance. As children grow older, their prosocial behavior becomes more complex. Children progress from self-serving reasons for sharing in early childhood to more mature conceptions of distributive justice, including considerations of need, in middle childhood. Adolescents show improvement in prosocial reasoning and behavior as they develop cognitive, emotional, and social abilities. Prosocial behavior is associated with many positive outcomes, including positive peer relationships, mental health, social competence, and academic achievement. It is negatively associated with internalizing and externalizing problems.

12.3 Examine common forms of aggressive and antisocial behavior in childhood and adolescence.

Aggression is a form of antisocial behavior that can harm or violate the rights of others. While most children engage in some aggressive behavior, the type and frequency of aggression vary as children grow older. Physical aggression declines in childhood while verbal and relational aggression, such as name-calling and exclusion, becomes more frequent into adolescence. Bullying occurs when a child or adolescent repeatedly attempts to harm another through physical, verbal, or social means. Bullying can lead to negative emotional, academic, and behavioral correlates that may persist into adulthood. Children who engage in bullying often experience maladaptive and rejecting parenting, while victims of bullying often have intrusive, overprotective, and critical parenting. Successful interventions to combat bullying address multiple perspectives, including victims, bullies, and other members of the school. Many adolescents engage in delinquent activity but most stop before adulthood. The risk factors for delinquent activity include developmental factors, poor parental monitoring, affiliation with antisocial peers, and contextual factors such as poverty and exposure to violence. Protective factors include supportive relationships with parents, adults, and prosocial peers, high-quality instruction, and involvement in after-school activities.

12.4 Describe the development of religiosity and spirituality in childhood and adolescence.

Religiosity refers to the practice of a religion, while spirituality refers to the search for meaning and purpose in life. Children and adolescents learn about religion through formal education and parental socialization. Adolescents' views of religion become more flexible and focused on spirituality, searching for answers to life's meaning and establishing beliefs. Parental religious socialization involves both passive and active processes, and the quality of parent-child relationships influences the effectiveness of religious socialization. Peer relationships also contribute to religious beliefs and practices. Religiosity is associated with numerous positive psychosocial and behavioral outcomes in children and adolescents. It is also negatively associated with and may serve a protective role against adjustment and behavioral problems. Supportive parent and peer relationships and social support from the religious community contribute to religiosity's protective effects. The religious community also provides a network of social support and opportunities for high-quality social relationships. Religiosity and participation in religious communities may promote healthy behaviors in adolescents by fostering emotion regulation and self-control.

KEY TERMS

- aggression
- autonomous morality
- bullying
- bully-victim
- care orientation
- conventional moral reasoning
- delinquency
- distributive justice
- empathy
- heteronomous morality
- instrumental aggression
- instrumental assistance
- justice orientation
- moral reasoning
- postconventional moral reasoning
- preconventional reasoning
- prosocial behavior
- reactive aggression
- relational aggression
- religiosity
- spirituality

Digital Vision/Getty Images

13 GENDER

> **LEARNING OBJECTIVES**
>
> **13.1** Summarize sex differences and gender stereotypes in physical, cognitive, and socioemotional development.
>
> **13.2** Compare and contrast biological, cognitive, and contextual explanations for gender typing.
>
> **13.3** Examine gender identity in childhood and adolescence.
>
> **13.4** Describe the development of transgender identity in children and adolescents.
>
> **13.5** Discuss sexual activity in adolescence.

In recent years, gender reveal parties have become popular among expectant couples who bat a piñata, pop a balloon, or cut a cake to reveal pink or blue ribbons, confetti, or icing revealing the gender of their unborn child. Pink: It's a girl! Blue: It's a boy! What does gender mean for our development? We often make generalizations about the behaviors and traits we expect to see in girls and boys, women and men. In this chapter, we examine common beliefs about gender, influences on gender, and developmental changes in how sex and gender are experienced across the life span.

SEX DIFFERENCES AND GENDER STEREOTYPES

> **13.1** Summarize sex differences and gender stereotypes in physical, cognitive, and socioemotional development.

Many people use the terms sex and gender interchangeably, but to developmental scientists, sex and gender have distinct meanings. **Sex** is biological and determined by genes—specifically, by the presence of a Y chromosome in the 23rd pair of chromosomes—and is usually indicated by the appearance of infants' genitals. **Gender**, on the other hand, is socially constructed and refers to the characteristics of men and women, how they think, feel, and behave, and the roles they adopt in a particular society, known as gender roles (Mencarini, 2023). **Gender identity** refers to a person's awareness and self-categorization of their gender (Shelton, 2023).

Gender Stereotypes

Throughout history, most societies have expected males and females to participate in different gender roles based on family and community needs. Women's traditional roles as child bearers and caregivers led to the expectation that they should be nurturing, kind, gentle, and sensitive to others. At the same time, men were expected to provide for and protect the family, requiring traits such as dominance, independence, strength, and power (Best & Puzio, 2019). These gender roles have often fueled **gender stereotypes**, generalized and often exaggerated beliefs about the activities, attitudes, skills, and characteristics considered appropriate for individuals based on their categorization as male or female in a given culture. Gender stereotypes include cultural expectations for the attitudes and feelings men and women should have, what roles they should occupy, and what they should not do.

Gender stereotypes appear in many cultures, with adults in 30 countries generally agreeing on the traits characteristic of men and women (Guimond et al., 2013; Kosakowska-Berezecka et al., 2024; Lockenhoff et al., 2014). In recent decades, the roles and activities of women in Western countries have shifted, often in ways contrary to gender stereotypes. For example, girls' participation in organized sports has increased dramatically, accounting for 43% of high school athletes today, compared with 7% in 1971–1972 (National Coalition for Women and Girls in Education, 2022). Women earned about 60% of bachelor's degrees in 2023, compared with 43% in 1970 (National Center for

Education Statistics, 2024). They also represent 47% of the U.S. workforce, up from 38% in 1970s (U.S. Department of Labor, 2023).

Despite these changes, women who are married to men tend to hold disproportionate caregiving and household responsibilities. Even in dual-earner families, women tend to remain the primary caregivers to children, creating a "second-shift" responsibility for women (Dominguez-Folgueras, 2022). Women are more likely than men to leave the workforce after having children (U.S. Bureau of Labor Statistics, 2022). During the COVID-19 pandemic, women were more likely than men to leave jobs due to the closing of schools and unavailability of child care, reduced work hours and unemployment, and the need to care for family members (Flor et al., 2022; Yavorsky et al., 2021).

Gender differences in activities inform our societal expectations about women and men, influencing the stereotypes we hold about gender roles (Bhatia & Bhatia, 2021). Thus, gender stereotypes in the United States have remained largely unchanged over the past three decades, with women rated by adults as more communal than men and men as more instrumental than women during both the early 1980s and the early 2010s (Haines et al., 2016). A recent examination of U.S. public opinion polls conducted from 1946 to 2018 suggests that traditional gender stereotypes about personal characteristics remain common despite women being increasingly viewed as occupationally competent (Eagly et al., 2020). Similarly, an analysis of over 80 studies conducted in 29 countries over 30 years (1984–2014) found that young adolescents endorse stereotypical gender roles, such as toughness, physical strength, and competitiveness for boys, and attractiveness, physical weakness, vulnerability, and compliance for girls (Kågesten et al., 2016).

Gender stereotypes are pervasive. But are they true? Our examination of the role of gender in development begins with a basic question: How do boys and girls differ?

Sex Differences

Boys and girls, men and women, may look different and are often treated differently, but a great body of research suggests that average sex differences in cognitive abilities and social behaviors are small and trivial at all ages in life (Hyde & DeLamater, 2020; Riva, 2023). Boys' and girls' abilities and behaviors overlap, and there is a great deal of variability or differences within each sex, more so than between the sexes overall (Brown et al., 2020). This means there are many more differences and a greater variety of differences among boys and girls than between boys and girls. Therefore, generalizations about sex differences should be understood as referring to the average, but not necessarily to any individual. To date, the research on sex differences has examined chromosomal sex, categorizing children as male or female based on chromosomes and gender assigned at birth. Therefore, the following sections examine differences between boys and girls in physical, cognitive, and socioemotional abilities. However, as discussed later in this chapter, some children do not identify with their gender assigned at birth (Diamond, 2020).

Physical Abilities

Throughout childhood, girls and boys are comparable in weight and height and show similar growth rates. Girls tend to display better fine motor skills and balance than boys in early childhood and perform similarly or better on most gross motor skills except for the upper body coordination needed to throw a ball (Matarma et al., 2020; Peyre et al., 2019). On the other hand, boys tend to be more physically active than girls, even before birth, and this difference increases during childhood. Boys typically engage in more physical, active play, including rough-and-tumble interactions that involve playful aggression and overall body contact (Scott & Panksepp, 2003; P. K. Smith & StGeorge, 2023). As we have seen in Chapter 5, puberty, the process of reproductive maturation, causes most boys to become bigger, stronger, and faster than most girls. Boys continue to show more physical activity than girls in adolescence and adulthood (Du et al., 2019; Rosselli et al., 2020).

Boys show higher rates of physical aggression than girls, including play fighting.

Photo and Co/Getty Images

Cognitive Abilities

There is no evidence to support the idea of sex differences in intelligence, executive functioning, or working memory, but research has identified subtle sex differences in several specific cognitive tasks (Grissom & Reyes, 2018; Reynolds et al., 2022). Differences in verbal ability are small but emerge in infancy, with girls beginning to talk earlier and having a more extensive vocabulary than boys up to age 5 (Petersen, 2018; Peyre et al., 2019). Infant girls tend to be held and talked to more often than boys; recall from Chapter 9 that infant-directed speech promotes language development. Their early verbal skills enable girls to interact with caregivers in more advanced ways, further supporting their language development. Girls tend to perform better than boys on reading comprehension and verbal fluency tasks, albeit by a small margin, throughout adolescence in all industrialized countries (Wallentin, 2020). Yet these subtle gender differences tend to fade as children grow older. Adult women tend to perform better on verbal memory tasks involving words, sentences, and prose, but most tests of verbal abilities themselves show few to no differences (Asperholm et al., 2019; Barel & Tzischinsky, 2018).

Boys tend to perform better on a specific type of spatial reasoning task known as *mental rotation*, the ability to recognize a stimulus that has been rotated in space (see Figure 13.1; Hines, 2015; Lauer et al., 2019). As infants, boys are slightly more likely than girls to recognize stimuli that have been rotated (Enge et al., 2023). Males' advantage in spatial rotation ability persists and increases from childhood into adulthood (Newcombe, 2020; van Tetering et al., 2019). Elementary school children tend to agree with gender stereotypes that girls are less proficient in mental rotation tasks than boys—and girls performed worse when spatial tasks were described as math problems versus art problems, suggesting that gender stereotypes may play a role in girls' performance on spatial tasks (Neuburger et al., 2015). Note that sex differences appear only on spatial tasks measuring mental rotation (Barel & Tzischinsky, 2018; Newcombe, 2020). Other spatial tasks show few to no differences.

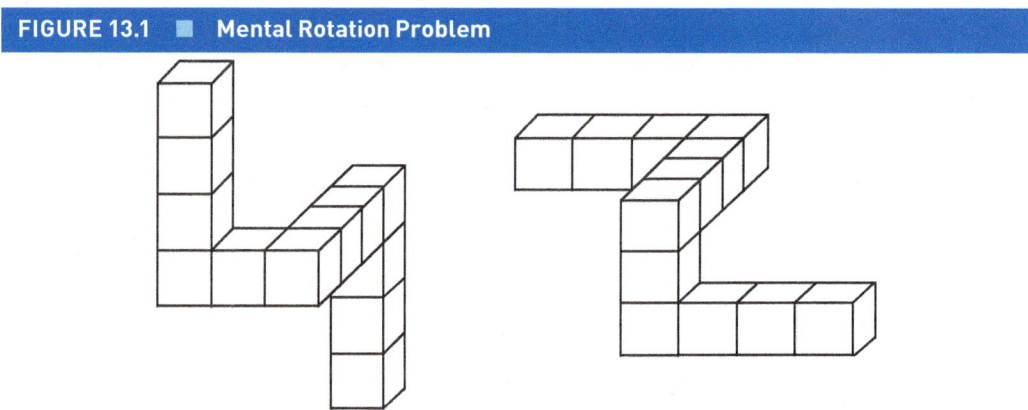

FIGURE 13.1 ■ Mental Rotation Problem

Sex differences in math abilities are mixed. Early studies suggested small differences such as girls performing better on computational math tests and boys performing better at mathematical reasoning tasks (Byrnes & Takahira, 1993; Leahey & Guo, 2001). More recent analyses have found no sex differences in children's understanding of math concepts and school performance in math (Geary et al., 2023; Girelli, 2023; Hines, 2015). However, in high school, boys tend to earn slightly higher scores on the mathematics portion of the Scholastic Aptitude Test (SAT) (U.S. Department of Education, 2023). Sex differences in math SAT scores were once substantial, but the gap has markedly declined in recent decades and is now negligible (Hutchison et al., 2019).

General differences in math scores are largely social in origin. In one recent study, parents rated math as a difficult subject, and males (fathers and sons) were more likely than females (mothers and daughters) to report liking math (Hildebrand et al., 2023). There are sex differences in attitudes about math, with girls showing higher levels of math anxiety and less confidence in their math ability than boys (Herts & Levine, 2020). In addition, parents and teachers often believe that boys are better at math than girls, even when they earn comparable test scores. Consequently, girls' advances in mathematics performance reflect increasing emphases by educational institutions, government, and industry to encourage girls to enter careers in the sciences, suggesting that socialization influences how boys and girls approach math (Dasgupta & Stout, 2014; Master, 2021).

Similarities and Differences in Socioemotional Abilities

From an early age, girls are better able to manage and express their emotions than boys (Weinberg et al., 1999). While girls tend to express happiness and sadness more often than boys, boys express more anger (Chaplin & Aldao, 2013). Girls also express complex emotions such as shame and guilt, which require further cognitive and social development, more frequently than boys (Else-Quest et al., 2012). In infancy, childhood, and adolescence, girls are more accurate at identifying facial expressions, such as happy or sad, than boys (Thompson & Voyer, 2014).

The most marked social difference between boys and girls is in aggression. Physical aggression peaks in early childhood between ages 2 and 4, and boys tend to exhibit more physical aggression than girls from childhood into adolescence and adulthood (Eliot, 2021; Tevlin, 2021). Sex differences in inhibitory control emerge by 3 months, and boys show less inhibitory control and more impulsivity than girls throughout childhood, adolescence, and adulthood (Cross et al., 2011; Gaillard et al., 2021). Differences in activity and the ability to restrain impulses contribute to sex differences in physical aggression.

However, sex differences in aggression are not so simple. Preschool-aged children begin to use verbal and relational aggression, harm within relationships, including name calling and excluding peers from play. Boys and girls transition away from physical aggression at different rates (Padgett & Tremblay, 2020). In middle childhood, girls tend to show more relational aggression, which expands to include withdrawing from friendships, spreading rumors, and humiliating peers (Ostrov & Godleski, 2010; Swit et al., 2024). This difference in relational aggression widens in adolescence and disappears in early adulthood. Nonetheless, relational and physical aggression often overlap in older children (Else-Quest & Hyde, 2018; Slawinski et al., 2019).

In summary, despite gender stereotypes, actual sex differences are varied and essentially nonexistent. While some physical differences between boys and girls exist, cognitive and socioemotional differences are small and overlap significantly. Sex differences are greatest for aggression, with boys and girls exhibiting different forms throughout development. Overall, boys and girls are more alike than different.

THINKING IN CONTEXT 13.1

1. Why do you think adults commonly believe that boys and girls are radically different from each other?
2. Imagine that you were asked to create a 20-second video for social media on the topic of sex differences in children. What is your message? What information is most important to include? Why?

GENDER TYPING

13.2 Compare and contrast biological, cognitive, and contextual explanations for gender typing.

Three-year-old Camila calls out, "I want the pink dress, just like a princess." Demarco pushes his truck and proclaims, "This monster truck is going to drive over the battlefield." Ask any adult and they will likely tell you that boys and girls are very different. Yet we have seen that boys and girls show reliable differences in only a few domains of development. But boys and girls do, on average, adopt different gender roles, a process called **gender typing** (Patterson & Vannoy, 2023). How do we explain the acquisition of gender roles? There are many influences on gender typing and even more proposed explanations. Some of these explanations emphasize biological factors. Others focus on cognitive influences, and still others turn to contextual influences. A sufficient explanation of gender development integrates aspects of each.

Biological Explanations

Biological explanations of gender typing point to the role of evolution and look to differences in biological structures, especially the brain, and hormones as contributors to sex differences in psychological and behavioral functioning (Pasterski & Bibonas, 2022).

Evolution

From an evolutionary perspective, males' and females' behavior adapted over millennia to the challenges they faced. As providers and protectors, males developed aggressive and competitive traits, which were advantageous in securing, providing for, and protecting a mate, thereby passing along their genetic inheritance (Geary, 2021; Wong & Buda, 2020). Females became more nurturing because it was adaptive to care for the young to ensure their genes survived and were passed along to the next generation. Most mammalian species demonstrate a preference for same-sex playmates, with males being more active and aggressive and females more nurturing, suggesting that such gender differences in behavior may be adaptive across species, including our own (Beatty, 1992; de Waal, 1993). Gendered behavior, therefore, appears to promote the survival of the individual and the species.

Genes

Biological differences begin at conception with the union of sex chromosomes (see Chapter 2), either XX (female) or XY (male). Genetic information on the Y chromosome leads to the formation of testes and the subsequent production of higher testosterone levels in males (Reale et al., 2023). In animals, testosterone produced prenatally influences neural survival and connectivity, leading to subtle sex differences in brain structure and function (Nugent & McCarthy, 2011; Ostatnikova et al., 2020).

Hormones

Hormones also contribute to sex differences in interests and behaviors. Early exposure to relatively high levels of testosterone promotes male-typical behavior development. When females are prenatally exposed to high levels of male sex hormones (e.g., in the case of congenital adrenal hyperplasia, a genetic disorder that causes excess androgen production beginning prenatally), they show more active aggressive play and fewer caregiving activities in early childhood, compared with peers exposed to normative levels of testosterone (Kung et al., 2024; Spencer et al., 2021). Hormonally influenced differences in behavioral styles influence children's play; children choose to play with children who have similar styles, resulting in a preference for same-sex playmates (Berenbaum, 2018). In this way, biological factors influence the behaviors associated with gender roles.

Cognitive Explanations

Other explanations for gender role development rely on understanding children's thinking. Cognitive development, individuals' capacity for thought and reasoning, influences how children and adolescents understand gender.

Cognitive Developmental Theory

According to the cognitive-developmental theory of gender (Kohlberg, 1966), children and adolescents construct their understanding of gender in the same way they construct their understanding of the world: by interacting with people and things and thinking about their experiences. By 3 to 4 months of age, infants can distinguish between female and male faces (Quinn et al., 2002). Between

18 and 24 months of age, most children develop the ability to label gender groups and to use gender labels in their speech (C. L. Martin & Ruble, 2010).

Gender Identity. **Gender identity**, awareness of whether one is a boy or a girl, typically emerges at about age 2 (Patterson & Vannoy, 2023). Once children label themselves as male or female, they classify the world around them, as well as their own behaviors, according to those labels (e.g., like me, not like me) (Kohlberg, 1966). In this way, children construct their own understandings of what it means to be a boy or a girl and thereby begin to acquire gender roles. By 2 to 2.5 years of age, once children have established a gender identity, they show more interest in stereotypically associated with their own gender (e.g., dolls for girls, cars for boys) and a preference for playing with children of their own sex (Silva & Alves, 2020; Zosuls et al., 2009).

Gender Stability. **Gender stability**, the understanding that gender generally does not change, emerges at around age 3. Still, children's grasp of gender tends to emphasize appearance, and they therefore tend to believe that wearing a dress, for example, can change a child from boy to girl. Between ages 3 and 5, after acquiring gender stability, children show an increase in stereotype knowledge, evaluate their own gender more positively, and tend to show more rigidly sex-typed beliefs and behaviors (Halim et al., 2013; Jhuremalani et al., 2022; King et al., 2021). For instance, girls may insist on wearing dresses, while boys may refuse to wear anything with a hint of femininity. In contrast, children with positive attitudes toward other genders tend to have more flexible views on gender appropriateness and exhibit less gender-stereotyped behavior (Halim et al., 2017).

Gender Constancy. Only as children come to understand Piagetian conservation tasks (see Chapter 6) do they come to realize that a boy will always be a boy, even if he changes his appearance, such as by growing long hair or wearing a skirt; and a girl will remain a girl no matter what she wears or which activities she chooses. **Gender constancy** refers to the child's understanding that gender does not change and that they will always be the same regardless of appearance, activities, or attitudes (Kohlberg, 1966).

Initially, gender constancy may further gender typing, as children become more aware of and pay more attention to gender norms (Arthur et al., 2009). Children's endorsement of gender stereotypes peaks in middle childhood. Their knowledge of stereotypes expands to include beliefs about personality, interests, and achievement (Jhuremalani et al., 2022; Miller et al., 2024). Elementary school children describe reading, spelling, art, and music as appropriate subjects for girls and mathematics and athletics as for boys (Kurtz-Costes et al., 2014; Passolunghi et al., 2014). As a result, girls tend to report negative feelings about math and perceive math as a "male subject" (Cvencek et al., 2011). By age 6, girls are less likely than boys to believe that members of their gender are *really, really smart*. Also at age 6, girls begin to avoid activities said to be for children who are really, really smart; lump more boys into the really, really smart category; and steer themselves away from games intended for the really, really smart (Bian et al., 2017). Gender stereotypes are powerful and influence children's preferences and views of their own abilities.

A full understanding of gender constancy includes the awareness that a person's sex is a biological characteristic, which typically occurs by about 7 years of age (Halim, 2016; Silva & Alves, 2020). Children with a more mature grasp of gender constancy may be less afraid to engage in cross-gender-typed activities because they understand that their gender will remain the same despite their interests or behavior (Halim et al., 2017). As children grow older, they tend to develop more flexible and less stereotyped views of gender because they recognize that gender is independent of appearance and behavior. Gender stereotypical preferences for movies and television programs decline from middle childhood to early adolescence (Kanka et al., 2019).

Gender Schema Theory

Psychologist Sandra Bem (1983) proposed that once children begin to label themselves as boys and girls, they begin to form a **gender schema**. A gender schema is a mental structure that organizes gender-related information and represents children's understanding of what it means to be male or female, similar to Piaget's concept of schemes (Canevello, 2020; Weisgram, 2016). As children's gender schema forms, it is used to organize the information they encounter. Children notice and even search for differences between boys and girls, such as preferred clothes, toys, and activities (Cook et al., 2022). Children also notice that their culture classifies men and women as different and encompassing gendered roles. Children then use their gender schemas as guides for their behavior and attitudes and gender typing occurs (Leung, 2020; Weisgram, 2016). In this way, gender development is influenced by self-socialization.

When presented with gender-neutral toys, children first try to identify whether they are for boys or girls before deciding whether to play with them (Miller et al., 2006). When told that an attractive toy is for the other sex, children will avoid playing with it and expect same-sex peers to avoid it as well. A review of 75 research studies found that boys and girls preferred gender-typical over gender-atypical toys and preferred toys consistent with their gender over other-gender-consistent toys (Davis & Hines, 2020). Young children play with peers who engage in similar amounts of gender-typed activities, such as playing dress-up or with tools, and, over time, they engage in increasingly similar levels of gender-typed activities, contributing to sex segregation in children's play groups (C. L. Martin et al., 2013).

Gender schemas are such an important organizing principle that they can influence children's memory. Preschoolers tend to notice and recall information that is consistent with their gender schemas, and they may misremember gender-inconsistent events in gender-consistent ways (Cook et al., 2022; Leung, 2020). For instance, in a classic study, children who viewed others behaving in ways contrary to gender-stereotypes, such as boys baking cookies or girls playing with toy trucks, tended to misrecall the event, distorting it in ways that are gender consistent or forgetting entirely (Signorella & Liben, 1984). Not until around age 8 do children notice and recall information that contradicts their gender schemas and even then, elementary school children have been shown to misremember gender-inconsistent story information (Frawley, 2008). Children's knowledge and beliefs about gender and gender roles influence their own gender roles and behavior. The world they are immersed in also holds implications for gender role development.

Contextual Explanations

A contextual approach to gender development explains gender typing as the result of children's interactions with the sociocultural context in which they are raised. Children construct their gender identities through these interactions. Children learn gender-typical behavior by observing parents, especially their same-sex parent, peers, other adults, and even characters in stories and television programs (Bandura & Bussey, 2004). They use models as guides for their behavior and receive feedback from others. Children use observations and experiences to build their understanding of gender and gender schemas and construct their gender identity, which influences their interactions with others and their gender socialization (Bem, 1983; Kohlberg, 1966; Silva & Alves, 2020).

Parents

Gender socialization begins early in life, initially with parents. From birth, boys and girls have different social experiences (Morawska, 2020).

Gendered Interactions. Parents perceive sons and daughters differently, have different expectations for them, and interact differently with them from birth. Their infant-directed speech to boys is more likely to focus on promoting gross motor skills, such as bouncing games, and to girls fine motor skills, such as patting hands (Dinkel & Snyder, 2020). These differences in speech are related to parents' gendered perceptions of their children's motor abilities. Mothers of 11-month-old infant boys had more accurate perceptions of their child's crawling ability, while mothers of girls underestimated their child's crawling ability even when there was no actual gender difference in crawling ability (Mondschein et al., 2000).

Moreover, parents tend to talk more to their daughters than sons from birth through early childhood (K. Johnson et al., 2014; Morawska, 2020). This difference in infant-directed speech likely contributes to girls' advanced language skills relative to boys. Parents also talk differently to girls than boys. They tend to refer more to emotions and use a greater range of emotion words, especially those stereotypically associated with girls, such as sadness, when speaking to their daughters (Mascaro et al., 2017). Parents use more warm, encouraging and empathetic speech with girls and are more accepting of displays of emotion from girls than boys (Lambie & Lindberg, 2016). In contrast, parents are more likely to discuss anger with boys, expect and accept displays of anger from them, and boys expect less punishment for displays of anger than girls (Dollar & Calkins, 2019). Throughout childhood parents model aggression more with sons, displaying more anger and physical control, such as spanking, toward sons than daughters (Endendijk et al., 2017).

Gendered Toys and Play. A visit to the toy aisle at a store with baby dolls on one side and cars on the other reveals much about gender socialization. From birth, boys tend to receive toys that focus on action and competition, such as cars, trains, and sports equipment; while girls are more likely to receive toys that focus on cooperation, nurturance, and physical attractiveness, such as baby dolls, Easy-Bake Ovens, and play makeup (MacPhee & Prendergast, 2019; Morawska, 2020). Throughout childhood, parents tend to stereotype certain toys as boys' toys or girls' toys, provide their children with gendered toys, reinforce play with same-gender toys, and discourage play with cross-gender toys, regardless of children's actual toy preferences (Brown et al., 2020; Etaugh & Liss, 1992). Young children pick up on these messages and develop interests and preferences for gendered toys (Weisgram, 2022). In one study, 3- and 5-year-old children identified "girl toys" and "boy toys" and predicted that their parents would approve of their playing with gender-appropriate toys and disapprove of choices to play with cross-gender toys (Freeman, 2007).

Girls are more often encouraged to engage in gender-atypical play, such as with trucks, than boys.

Emma Kim/Getty Images

Boys tend to be more strongly encouraged to engage in gendered play than girls (Brown et al., 2020). Parents, especially fathers, tend to show more discomfort with sex-atypical play in boys (e.g., playing with dolls) than girls (e.g., playing with trucks) (Sullivan et al., 2018); and fathers' gender talk is especially influential in children's gender attitudes (de Vries et al., 2022). Boys but not girls tend to increase the time spent playing with sex-typical toys (i.e., boy toys) over childhood (Todd et al., 2018).

Autonomy Support. Parents tend to encourage boys' independent play, demands for attention, and even attempts to take toys from other children. In contrast, parents tend to direct girls' play, assist, refer to emotions, and encourage them to participate in household tasks (Hines, 2015).

As children enter adolescence parents continue to foster autonomy in boys, allowing them more independence than girls. Parents tend to monitor and restrict adolescent girls' behavior more than boys, because girls are often viewed as more vulnerable (McHale et al., 2003). However, an examination of 126 studies suggests a cohort or generational shift in parents' behavior toward children and adolescents (Endendijk et al., 2016). Specifically, studies published during the 1970s and 1980s reported that parents directed more autonomy-supportive strategies toward boys than toward girls, but from 1990 onward, parents directed somewhat more autonomy-supportive strategies toward girls than toward boys. Yet adolescents whose parents express traditional attitudes toward gender roles are more likely to hold traditional attitudes themselves (Tenenbaum & Leaper, 2003).

Peers

The peer group also serves as a powerful influence on gender typing in young children. As children begin to label people based on gender (at about age 2), they begin to show a preference for same-gender peers over other-gender peers (Powlishta et al., 1993). This preference increases over childhood. As early as age 3, peers reinforce gender-typed behavior with praise, imitation, or participation (Rose et al., 2022). Young children tend to show more disapproval of boys who engage in cross-gender behavior than girls. Preschoolers often act as gender-enforcers, excluding boys and girls who engage in cross-gender activities. Children who spend more time with gender-enforcing peers tend to play more with same-sex peers and show more gender-stereotyped attitudes than other children (Xiao et al., 2019).

Girls and boys show different play styles that contribute to gendered preferences in playmates. Boys use more commands, threats, and force; girls use more gentle tactics, such as persuasion, acceptance, and verbal requests, which are effective with other girls but ignored by boys (Leaper, 2022). Girls, therefore, may find interacting with boys unpleasant, because boys pay little attention to their attempts at interaction and are generally nonresponsive. Differences in play styles influence boys' and girls' choices of play partners and contribute to sex segregation (Coyle & Fulcher, 2022; Weisgram, 2022). Peer and parental attitudes tend to be similar and reinforce each other, because both are part of a larger sociocultural system of socialization agents (Bandura & Bussey, 2004). By the time children reach middle childhood and adolescence, gender atypical behavior is associated with exclusion and peer victimization (Roberts et al., 2013; Zosuls et al., 2016).

Media

Children's television, books, and G-rated movies tend to depict the world as gender stereotyped, and these media depictions can promote gender-typed behavior in children (Aubrey & Roberts, 2020; Ward & Grower, 2020). Typical children's media displays more male than female characters, with male characters in action roles such as officers or soldiers in the military and female characters as more likely to have domestic roles, be in romantic relationships, be described as meek, or be in need of help (which is usually provided by male characters) (Casey et al., 2021; Filipović, 2018; Tsao, 2020; Walsh & Leaper, 2019). Coloring books display similar patterns, with more male than female characters, and male characters are depicted as older, stronger, more powerful, and more active than female characters (e.g., as superheroes vs. princesses) (Fitzpatrick & McPherson, 2010). Children's media is rife with princess characters that send powerful messages about gender norms and roles (Golden & Jacoby, 2018). One study of 4- and 5-year-old children found that nearly all had viewed media featuring Disney princess heroines, and two thirds of girls played with Disney princess toys at least once a week compared with only 4% of the boys. Engagement with Disney princess toys and media was associated with more female gender-stereotypical behavior in girls 1 year later, even after controlling for initial levels of gender-stereotypical behavior (Coyne et al., 2016). In support of television's influence on gender typing, a study of several Canadian towns that gained access to television for the first time showed a marked increase in children's gender-stereotyped attitudes 2 years after television was introduced (Kimball, 1986).

Adolescents are also exposed to gender stereotypes in media (Aubrey & Roberts, 2020). Those who watch more mainstream media programs tend to endorse more gender stereotypes (Koletić, 2017; Peter & Valkenburg, 2009; Ward & Grower, 2020). Do media preferences influence gender stereotyping or do gendered interests influence media preference? It is likely that media preferences and gendered interests influence each other.

Reducing Gender Stereotyping

Children are immersed in a gendered world, and they quickly learn and internalize messages about gender as they interact with the people and things around them. Parents who wish to reduce gender stereotyping in their children must begin by examining their own views and gender-related behavior. Parents can model gender neutral attitudes and beliefs by engaging in nontraditional activities, such as men cooking dinner and women taking out the garbage. Parents can encourage mixed gender play dates that include a broad range of activities.

Teachers can organize classrooms to be less gender salient, such as by encouraging all children to take turns playing in the kitchen, block area, and sandbox (Farago et al., 2022). Some preschools are committed to creating gender-neutral classroom environments in which teachers typically refrain from using gendered language and actively work to counteract gender stereotypes. Children in these settings typically show more gender-neutral behaviors and attitudes. One study examined preschool children in Sweden, a country with relatively egalitarian gender attitudes (Shutts et al.,

2017). Some of the children attended a typical preschool and others attended a gender-neutral preschool with policies and practices aimed at actively creating a gender-neutral environment. Although all Swedish schools are required by law to aim for gender equality in classrooms, the gender-neutral preschool included additional practices to reduce the salience of gender. For example, teachers avoided using gendered language (including the use of a gender-neutral pronoun and not *boy* or *girl*), modifying stories and songs to counteract rather than reinforce traditional gender roles and family structures, and avoiding some behaviors traditionally directed at one gender (e.g., commenting on the attractiveness of girls' clothes). Children exposed to the gender-neutral preschool setting showed less in-gender favoritism ("Girls are better than boys!") and less stereotyping. They were less likely to limit their play to same-sex peers.

In addition to encouraging children to befriend boys and girls and play with a wide range of toys, including nontraditional toys, parents and teachers can help children recognize gender stereotyping and sexism in the world around them (Bigler & Pahlke, 2019). Parents and teachers can point out and correct stereotypes. Opportunities arise daily. When 4-year-old Aaron insisted, "Only boys can be doctors!" his father replied, "Is that true? Remember Dr. Lopes? She's a woman—and a doctor. And remember the nurse who gave you a shot, Aaron?" "He's a man," Aaron replied. "Yes—and he's a nurse. Men can be nurses, and women can be doctors." Exposure to such counter-stereotypical models can help reduce gender stereotyping in children (Olsson & Martiny, 2018). Even small doses of education can reduce gender stereotyping. For example, British elementary school children exposed to a weekly 30-minute classroom lesson over a 4-month period learned to identify and challenge gender stereotypes and explore similarities between and among boys and girls (Spinner et al., 2021). Children encounter messages about gender daily. Each of these instances is an opportunity to reduce stereotyping and encourage children to be more flexible and tolerant. Table 13.1 summarizes theoretical explanations for gender typing.

TABLE 13.1 ■ Theories of Gender Typing	
Theoretical Explanation	
Biological	Describes gender role development in evolutionary and biological terms. Males adapted to become more aggressive and competitive and females more nurturing because it ensured that their genes were passed to the next generation. Gender differences may also be explained by subtle differences in brain structure as well as differences in hormones.
Cognitive	The emergence of gender identity leads children to classify the world around them according to gender labels, and they begin to show more interest in gender-appropriate toys. Children show an increase in stereotype knowledge, evaluate their own gender more positively, and demonstrate rigidity of gender-related beliefs. Gender constancy furthers gender typing as children attend more to norms of their sex. According to gender schema theory, once children can label their sex, their gender schema forms and becomes an organizing principle. Children notice differences between males and females in preferred clothes, toys, and activities, as well as how their culture classifies males and females as different and encompassing different roles. Children then use their gender schemas as guides for their behavior and attitudes, and gender typing occurs.
Contextual	Contextual explanations rely on social learning and the influence of the sociocultural context in which children are raised. Males and females have different social experiences from birth. Gender typing occurs through socialization, through a child's interpretation of the world around them, and modeling and reinforcement from parents, peers, and teachers.

THINKING IN CONTEXT 13.2

1. Recall from Chapter 1 that development is influenced by nature and nurture. What roles do nature and nurture play in gender development? In your view, does either have greater influence?
2. In your experience, do parents treat boys and girls differently? Do teachers? To what extent do adults influence children's gender typing?
3. How does gender typing illustrate the interaction of different types of development, such as cognitive, socioemotional, and physical development?

GENDER IDENTITY IN CHILDHOOD AND ADOLESCENCE

13.3 Examine gender identity in childhood and adolescence.

Once young children categorize themselves as either boys or girls, they start to see the world through the lens of gender and develop extensive knowledge of gender stereotypes and gendered behavior (Cook et al., 2022). Elementary school children's cognitive abilities allow them to think about gender in more complex ways. They begin to organize their knowledge about gender as a collective, enabling them to compare themselves with the gender collective. This emerging ability for social comparison leads them to develop conceptions of the typical or ideal person of their gender and compare their own qualities to these standards to estimate their similarity to their gender collective (Leung, 2020).

Most research examining gender socialization and gender identity examines how boys and girls adopt the gender identities that correspond to their chromosomal sex and their sex assigned at birth (Cook et al., 2022; Perry et al., 2019). However, evidence suggests that children who do not identify with their sex assigned at birth experience similar changes in gender identity (Olson & Gülgöz, 2018). We discuss these children later in this chapter.

Dimensions of Gender Identity

In middle childhood, children's gender identity expands as they begin to compare themselves with others. Several dimensions of gender identity rise in importance: Felt same-gender typicality and felt other-gender typicality, gender contentedness, and felt pressure to conform to gender roles.

Felt Gender Typicality

Felt same-gender typicality and **felt other-gender typicality** are beliefs children hold about their similarity to members of their gender and the other gender, including the group's characteristics, skills, and interests (Perry et al., 2019). While it was once believed that gender identity was unidimensional, with individuals holding traits typical of the male or female gender, most experts now believe that male-typical and female-typical characteristics are independent. Individuals may identify as **androgynous**, identifying with characteristics of both genders (Bem, 1974). In support of this, children's felt same-gender typicality and felt other-gender typicality are not highly correlated; many children believe they hold characteristics typical of both genders (C. L. Martin et al., 2017).

Children who feel high levels of same-gender typicality perceive themselves as sharing the characteristics and traits that are typically associated with their gender. They tend to have high self-esteem, high social competence, and secure relationships and are viewed positively by their peers as likable, prosocial, and rarely victimized (Corby et al., 2007; Perry et al., 2019). Less is known about the consequences of felt other-gender typicality, but it appears that effects depend on the child's level of felt same-gender typicality. When accompanied by perceived same-gender typicality, feeling other-gender typicality is associated with positive adjustment (Pauletti et al., 2017). However, if children do not feel same-gender typical, feeling other-gender typical may expose them to risks, such as emotional distress, low self-esteem, peer victimization, and poor adjustment, especially when parents are less accepting of atypicality (Xiao et al., 2022, 2023; Zosuls et al., 2016).

Gender Contentedness

Gender contentedness refers to children's satisfaction with the gender they were assigned at birth (e.g., being born a girl or boy) and involves their evaluation of their gender, including comparing the benefits and drawbacks of being male or female (e.g., rating whether they sometimes wish they were the other gender) (Egan & Perry, 2001). High levels of gender contentedness are associated with positive outcomes, such as high self-esteem, social competence, secure attachments to others, better relationships with peers, and few internalizing problems (e.g., depression, social withdrawal, sadness, anxiety) (Menon, 2011; Pauletti et al., 2017).

Girls are more likely than boys to express dissatisfaction with their gender, but the negative consequences of such discontent tend to be less severe for girls. This is because having cross-gender interests is more likely to enhance a girl's popularity, whereas boys with such interests are more likely to be victimized (Braun & Davidson, 2017). Low gender contentedness is more distressing when children perceive pressure to conform to gender stereotypes (Perry et al., 2019). Children who are gender nonconforming and those who identify as transgender tend to display poor gender contentedness.

Felt Pressure to Conform to Gender Roles

Felt pressure to conform to gender roles refers to pressure children feel to avoid other-gender behavior. It includes anticipating negative consequences such as ridicule, criticism, and shaming from parents, peers, and even oneself for engaging in behavior characteristic of the other gender (Jackson et al., 2021; Nielson et al., 2020). Children who feel this pressure tend to view the world through a gendered lens, perceive the genders as polar opposites, classify behavior as either appropriate or inappropriate for their gender, and adopt same-gender-stereotyped attributes while avoiding those associated with the other gender.

Children who feel high levels of pressure to conform to gender roles may experience adjustment problems (Carver et al., 2003; Pauletti et al., 2014; Perry et al., 2019; Yunger et al., 2004). In girls, such pressure is associated with problems such as poor self-esteem, depression, poor attachments to parents and friends, and poor peer relationships. Boys tend to feel even higher pressure to conform, especially those who feel more similar to their own gender (and less similar to the other gender), and as this pressure rises, they may show higher levels of aggression, low prosocial behavior, and biases against girls (Nielson et al., 2020). Peer groups tend to show similar beliefs about the pressure to conform to gender roles, and their beliefs become more similar over time (Kornienko et al., 2016). Children's beliefs about the pressure to conform to gender roles are shaped through their daily interactions with peers, including discussion and modeling (Schroeder & Liben, 2020). Generally, felt pressure for gender differentiation tends to decline over the school years.

Adolescents tend to feel less pressure to conform to gender roles than children.
Vladimir Vladimirov/Getty Images

Gender Typing and Sexual Orientation

What is the relationship between gender typing and sexuality? Is there a link between holding male-typical or female-typical characteristics and sexual orientation? While the media may portray gay men as overtly feminine and lesbian women as masculine, the relationship between gender nonconformity and sexual orientation is complex. Some studies suggest that gender nonconformity and sexual orientation are related, and others suggest that they are independent (Marino et al., 2023; Martin-Storey, 2016). However, most of the research on the link between childhood gender nonconformity and sexual orientation is based on retrospective reports in which adults recall their childhood behavior (Li et al., 2017). Retrospective reports may be biased because our memories of past events are subtly influenced by our subsequent attitudes, behaviors, and experiences (Gottschalk, 2003). Prospective research, on the other hand, follows participants over time, enabling researchers to study behaviors as they unfold.

Prospective studies of 4,500 and 6,000 children found that parent reports of gender-typicality at ages 2.5 through 5 predicted adolescents' sexual orientation at ages 15 and 21 (Li et al., 2017; Xu et al., 2021). Another study of over 10,000 middle and high school students surveyed again 7 and 14 years later, in emerging adulthood and early adulthood, respectively, found average group differences in gender-nonconforming behavior as well as substantial individual variability (Kahn & Halpern, 2019). While, on average gay and lesbian participants reported more gender-nonconforming behavior than their heterosexual counterparts, many gender-nonconforming young people identified as heterosexual, indicating that gender-typed behaviors vary among all sexual orientations. In other words, sexual orientation cannot be inferred from gender-typed behavior. Both gay and heterosexual men may adopt male-stereotyped traits, stereotyped female traits, or both male- and female-stereotyped traits (androgyny). This is also true for lesbian women and bisexual men and women.

Gender Identity in Adolescence

One of adolescence's most important developmental tasks is identity development, forming a comprehensive sense of self. As part of this process, adolescents form a multidimensional sense of self by exploring different identity possibilities and making commitments in each area. Gender identity is a particularly salient aspect of self for many adolescents.

Gender Identity

During late childhood through early adolescence, children continue to refine their views of their felt same and other-gender typicality, gender contentedness, and felt pressure for gender conformity (Perry et al., 2019; Patterson & Vannoy, 2023). Through personal reflection and input from others, adolescents judge and commit to each facet of gender identity. Individuals vary in how they proceed in considering the various facets of gender identity and when each is achieved (Steensma et al., 2013). Once established, these dimensions of gender identity are relatively stable but may change over adolescence, emerging adulthood, and adulthood, just like other aspects of identity (Branje et al., 2021).

Most of the research on gender identity in adolescence has focused on felt gender typicality. Generally, the degree to which adolescents view themselves as typical of their gender predicts adolescent adjustment, including measures of mental health and popularity with peers, especially in boys (Egan & Perry, 2001; Jewell & Brown, 2014). Associations between felt gender typicality and adjustment are influenced by interactions with parents and peers, especially feelings of acceptance and rejection (Kleiser Polk & Mayeux, 2023; Loso et al., 2023; Zosuls et al., 2016). For example, one longitudinal study found that low felt gender typicality in seventh grade was associated with peer victimization, which in turn predicted increased social anxiety and somatic problems (feeling physically ill) in eighth grade (D. S. Smith & Juvonen, 2017). Generally, adolescents who feel gender atypical perceive pressure from parents and peers to act in gender-typical ways and tend to show more internalizing problems, such as anxiety, and are more likely to experience peer victimization than other adolescents (T. Hu et al., 2024; Narita et al., 2024).

Gender Intensification

With the onset of puberty, physical development takes center stage. As their bodies mature and they look more like adults, adolescents are often treated differently by others and become acutely aware of their appearance and their gender. Although gender flexibility tends to increase in late childhood (Banse et al., 2010), rigidity tends to rebound in early adolescence. Despite more flexible and abstract thinking, adolescents often express stereotyped views about gender roles. For example, one meta-analysis of 30 years of research conducted in 29 countries found that young adolescent boys and girls tended to endorse gender-stereotyped norms, such as toughness and competition as representative of masculinity and weakness and attractiveness as representative of femininity (Kågesten et al., 2016). Boys were more likely to endorse stereotypical gender norms, and girls tended to express more flexible views of gender.

Gender typing and gender-stereotyped behavior tend to rise in early adolescence; a phenomenon called **gender intensification** (Klaczynski et al., 2020; Nielson et al., 2024; Priess & Lindberg, 2018). Boys may feel greater pressure from parents, peers, and themselves, to become more masculine and less feminine (Jackson et al., 2021). To a lesser extent, girls may experience the reverse, greater pressure to become more feminine and less masculine. Indeed, longitudinal surveys of adolescents conducted at the beginning and end of their first year of middle school found an increase in masculinity scripts for boys but not girls (Rogers et al., 2017).

Like young children, adolescents tend to negatively evaluate peers who violate expectations for gendered behavior, such as by engaging in behaviors or expressing interests stereotyped for the other sex (Toomey et al., 2014). Boys who are perceived as less masculine and girls as less feminine than peers may feel less accepted, be less popular, and experience higher rates of victimization (Kleiser Polk & Mayeux, 2023).

However, not all adolescents experience gender intensification, leading researchers to debate its existence (Korlat et al., 2021; Priess & Lindberg, 2018). Longitudinal research with African American youth found that young girls and boys show knowledge of gender stereotypes, but from ages 9 to 15, they show declines in traditional gender attitudes that level off through age 18 (Lam et al., 2017). In the United States and other Western cultures, boys are now free to be more expressive, and girls are encouraged to be more independent than they were in the past (Sravanti & Sagar Kommu, 2020). In late adolescence, even individuals who displayed gender intensification earlier tend to become more flexible in their thinking and adoption of gender roles.

THINKING IN CONTEXT 13.3

1. How do cognitive and social factors interact to shape the development of gender identity in childhood and adolescence? How do children's and adolescents' perceptions of gender influence their behavior and adjustment?
2. Does gender intensification occur in adolescence? Discuss your own observations. How do these compare with the research findings?
3. Compare the influence of parents and peers on gender identity. Which do you think is more influential? Why?

TRANSGENDER IDENTITY

13.4 Describe the development of transgender identity in children and adolescents.

Our previous discussion has focused on gender and gender identity development in children with a **cisgender** identity, individuals whose gender identity matches the sex they were assigned at birth (typically determined by their chromosomal sex and external genitalia). Most of the research on gender socialization and gender identity has centered around cisgender development, examining how boys and girls adopt gender identities that align with their sex assigned at birth (Perry et al., 2019).

However, more recent research has challenged the idea that gender is limited to two distinct categories, male and female, commonly called the gender binary (Diamond, 2020). Instead, some developmental scientists view gender as a more fluid and multifaceted construct. A growing body of research examines individuals with a **transgender identity** who do not identify with the sex assigned to them at birth (deMayo et al., 2022). A transgender woman identifies as female but was assigned a male sex at birth, while a transgender man identifies as male but was assigned a female sex at birth. Despite this growing body of research, most studies on gender development to date have still focused on cisgender individuals (deMayo et al., 2022). This means that our understanding of transgender individuals and their development is relatively limited.

About .5% to 1% of adolescents and adults identify themselves as transgender, although the true figure may be higher (Crissman et al., 2017; Gates, 2011; Safer & Tangpricha, 2019; Zucker, 2017). Studies of high school students in 10 and 14 states found that 1.8% and 1.7% identified as transgender, respectively (Johns et al., 2019; Miller-Jacobs et al., 2023). A review of multiple population-based studies found that 1.2% to 2.7% of children and adolescents surveyed identified as transgender (Zhang et al., 2020). Although the prevalence of transgender identity is still not well documented, most people adopt a cisgender identity, one that is congruent with their chromosomal sex.

Childhood

Transgender children's gender development is quite similar to that of cisgender children (Olson & Gülgöz, 2018). Like gender-conforming children, transgender children show preferences for peers, toys, clothing, and activities typically associated with their expressed gender; choose stereotypically gendered outfits; and report that they are more similar to children of their expressed gender than to children of the other gender (Fast & Olson, 2018; Gülgöz et al., 2022; Rubin et al., 2020). We have seen that parents, peers, and teachers tend to discourage gender nonconformity in children, especially boys (Halpern & Perry-Jenkins, 2016; Spivey et al., 2018). Transgender children resist such pressure, insist on their gender identity, and explain that they were born in their expressed identity (Gülgöz et al., 2019).

Are transgender children's preferences genuine? Research suggests yes. In one study, 5- to 12-year-old transgender children, their cisgender siblings, and unrelated cisgender children completed self-report and implicit (without awareness) measures of gender identity and preferences (Olson et al., 2015). The transgender children's self-reports and implicit, less controllable, measures of preferences were consistent with their expressed gender and were indistinguishable from those of cisgender children who shared their gender identity. In middle to late childhood, transgender children tend to show more flexible views of gender stereotypes than cisgender children. For example, one study suggested that 6- to 8-year-old transgender children and their siblings were less likely to endorse gender stereotypes than unrelated children and viewed gender nonconformity as more acceptable in peers (Olson & Enright, 2018).

While in the past, parents may have ignored children's wishes or outright prohibited them from adopting a transgender identity, some parents today adopt a different approach, permitting their children to socially transition to the gender identity they identify with. A **social gender transition** entails matching children's everyday experiences with their gender identities, such as by changing the pronoun used to describe them, perhaps their name, and their appearance, including hair and clothing. In this way, children live according to their gender identity rather than their sex assigned at birth. This type of social transitioning is reversible and nonmedical.

Whether or not parents should support children's desire to live presenting as their gender identity is hotly debated by parents, schools, and the U.S. legal system (Block, 2023; Turban et al., 2021). Little research has compared children who have and have not socially transitioned (R. Hall et al., 2024). Some studies have found that older children who have *not* socially transitioned reported increased rates of anxiety and depression (Ryan et al., 2010; Simons et al., 2013). Others have found no differences (R. Hall et al., 2024). Yet other studies of socially transitioned transgender children suggest feelings of validation and levels of depression and anxiety no different from gender-consistent children (Horton, 2023; Olson et al., 2016).

It is also important to recognize that not all gender nonconforming children who do not adopt behavior consistent with their sex assigned at birth develop a transgender identity (Deardorff et al., 2019; Ristori & Steensma, 2016). Many ultimately develop a gender identity that aligns with their sex assigned at birth. It is difficult to predict whether a gender-nonconforming child will develop a transgender identity. However, it is estimated that nearly 50% of transgender youth identify as such before age 12; many report knowing before age 8, and some as early as preschool (Deardorff et al., 2019; Fast & Olson, 2018; Olson, 2016). In one study, 94% of children with a transgender identity who socially transitioned retained a transgender identity 5 years later (Olson et al., 2022).

Adolescence

The heightened attention to gender that accompanies the onset of puberty can be distressing for adolescents with a transgender identity, posing risks for adjustment as their bodies change in ways that do not align with their expressed gender (Pulice-Farrow et al., 2020). Recall that the physical changes of puberty may be accompanied by gender intensification, increased social pressure to conform to gender standards. Transgender adolescents who feel pressure to conform to their sex assigned at birth may be particularly prone to adjustment difficulties.

Adjustment

As compared with their cisgender peers, adolescents with a transgender identity, regardless of race and ethnicity, experience elevated stress and higher rates of mental health problems, including self-harm, depression, anxiety, and suicidal ideation (thinking about suicide) (Becerra-Culqui et al., 2018; Price-Feeney et al., 2020; Thoma et al., 2019; Vance et al., 2021). Transgender adolescents commonly experience harassment, discrimination, and higher levels of peer victimization and are more likely to report feeling unsafe at school than their cisgender peers (Hatchel et al., 2019; Pampati et al., 2020). Notably, by age 9 many transgender children are more susceptible to mental health problems than their cisgender peers (D. H. Russell et al., 2022).

A social transition to an adolescent's self-identified sex can promote resilience in transgender adolescents. Social transitioning and parental support of social transitions are associated with better mental health outcomes, including lower rates of anxiety and depression (Durwood et al., 2017, 2021). Using one's chosen name and style of dress can be self-affirming, with mental health benefits (Ehrensaft et al., 2018; S. T. Russell et al., 2018). A sense of acceptance and the ability to live as one's expressed gender may buffer stresses that tend to accompany gender nonconformity. Adolescents' acceptance and adjustment to a transgender identity varies with individual and contextual factors, such as whether the adolescent has transitioned and the degree of available support.

Gender Affirming Support

Gender identity, like other facets of identity, is influenced by interactions with others. The reactions and support children and adolescents receive in response to their emerging gender identity influences their adjustment. Close, supportive relationships with family and peers are associated with positive adjustment (Johns et al., 2018; Pariseau et al., 2019).

Family. Family dynamics, how caregivers respond to, adjust to, and learn from their children, and how caregivers interact with one another influences adjustment (Bhattacharya et al., 2020). Parental connectedness and support of transgender adolescents' social transitions, and especially using the adolescent's preferred pronouns and name, are associated with positive mental health (Hale et al., 2021; K. C. Johnson et al., 2020; Olsavsky et al., 2023; Tankersley et al., 2021).

Peers. Although much of the research examines the damaging effects of peer victimization, peer relationships can also promote health and adjustment. When transgender adolescents feel supported by peers they report a positive sense of self and fewer mental health problems (Hatchel et al., 2019; Kia et al., 2021). Social support has a protective effect on transgender adolescents, buffering the negative effects of victimization on anxiety and depression (Durwood et al., 2021). In addition, some transgender adolescents seek support through online peer interactions and communities, which can also buffer the negative effects of victimization (Allen et al., 2019; Selkie et al., 2020).

School. Students who identify as transgender seek a sense of safety and belonging at school (Mackie et al., 2021; Tankersley et al., 2021). Relationships with supportive teachers are associated with less absenteeism, better academic performance, and positive coping with peer difficulties (Poteat et al., 2021; Seelman et al., 2015). Transgender students who attend schools with clear policies against bullying, LGBT-inclusive curricula, and the presence of a Gay-Straight Alliance (GSA) or other gender-inclusive student group tend to report feeling more connected to adults at school and school itself, as well as report feeling safer and are more engaged (Hazel et al., 2019; Marx & Kettrey, 2016).

Schools with gender-affirming policies can aid transgender adolescents' adjustment, but many students do not attend schools with such policies. For example, a national survey of over 23,000 U.S. secondary students found that only about 20% of LGBTQ students reported being taught positive representations about LGBTQ people, history, or events in their school (Kosciw et al., 2018). In addition, only about half of U.S. secondary students report the availability of a GSA in their schools (Kosciw et al., 2018). The school context offers important opportunities to support transgender students and to reduce the incidence of peer victimization, but many adolescents attend schools with few resources.

Gender-Affirming Health Care

In contrast to a social gender transition, in which adolescents adopt the presentation and expression associated with one's gender identity, a **medical gender transition** is a medical process that involves physical changes to the body. This can involve both developmental changes, body changes that are induced by hormone therapy, and permanent changes to the body through breast augmentation or reduction and gender reassignment surgery. Older children who identify as transgender, in consultation with their parents and pediatrician, may take medication to delay the onset of puberty and reproductive maturation. This involves using **puberty suppressors**, prescribed by endocrinologists (physicians who specialize in the endocrine system and hormones) to inhibit sex hormones and prevent the onset of pubertal changes. Bottom of Form

Puberty suppression prevents the development of cisgender sex characteristics, is reversible, and can provide transgender adolescents and their families with valuable time to explore and understand their gender identity, make mature, informed decisions, and develop coping skills (Panagiotakopoulos et al., 2020; Ramos et al., 2021). Research has shown that early intervention with hormone-suppressing medication, early in puberty and prior to age 15, was associated with reduced risk of depression, self-harm, suicidal ideation and the need for psychoactive medication (Green et al., 2022; Sorbara et al., 2020). Similarly, prior to receiving puberty suppression treatment Dutch adolescents showed more internalizing and poor peer relations compared with peers, but after treatment experienced fewer emotional and behavioral problems and showed similar or better psychological functioning compared with cisgender peers (Miesen et al., 2020)

Research has suggested that puberty suppression is a safe and effective option associated with positive mental health outcomes in transgender adolescents (Bonifacio et al., 2019; Chen et al., 2023; Olsavsky et al., 2023). However, further research is needed to inform professional practices (Rew et al., 2021; Rosenthal, 2021). Gender affirming care also includes social and psychological intervention in which psychologists, social workers, and other health providers support transgender adolescents and help their families support their social transition.

Sunny Bryant, a transgender child from Texas, has testified before the Texas House of Representatives and the Texas Senate advocating for transgender youth.

Francois Picard/Contributor/Getty Images

However, many transgender adolescents lack access to medical and social interventions. Gender affirming medical care, often limited outside of large cities and banned in some states, is expensive, posing large barriers for adolescents and their parents who seek support and treatment (Puckett et al., 2018; Safer & Chan, 2019). Transgender adolescents report less use of health care, fewer physician visits and health checkups and report their health is poorer than their cisgender peers, suggesting that they may have fewer opportunities to interact with health care professionals who can offer assistance (Rider et al., 2018). Transgender adolescents who live in states that ban gender affirming care experience higher rates of depression (Miller-Jacobs et al., 2023).

Adolescents and their parents report many obstacles to gender-affirming care, such as the availability of medical care sensitive to transgender adolescents' needs, a general lack of education about treatment options, experience of bias, fear of rejection, and, especially, economic barriers (Kearns et al., 2021; Kidd et al., 2023). Puberty suppression medication, for instance, is often not covered by medical insurance and can be prohibitively expensive (Rew et al., 2021; Stevens et al., 2015). Adolescents from low socioeconomic homes and communities with limited access to healthcare resources are particularly vulnerable to these barriers and are less likely to obtain gender affirming care (Safer & Chan, 2019).

> **THINKING IN CONTEXT 13.4**
>
> 1. How do family, peer, and school environments influence the development of transgender identity in children and adolescents? Discuss specific ways these contexts can either support or hinder transgender youth.
> 2. How might the experiences of transgender youth differ based on their intersecting identities, such as race, ethnicity, and socioeconomic status? Provide examples to illustrate these differences.
> 3. Why might the onset of puberty be particularly challenging for transgender adolescents? Discuss the role of gender intensification and social pressures during this developmental stage.
> 4. What are some of the potential risks and benefits of early access to gender-affirming medical care, such as puberty suppression? Identify barriers to accessing gender-affirming healthcare. How might these barriers vary by geographic location, socioeconomic status, and other factors?

SEXUAL ACTIVITY IN ADOLESCENCE

13.5 Discuss sexual activity in adolescence.

Prevalence of Sexual Activity

Many adults are surprised to learn that the percentage of high school students who have ever had sexual intercourse is at an all-time low, down from 54% in 1991 to 38% in 2021 (Federal Interagency Forum on Child and Family Statistics, 2023). The percentage of students who have ever had intercourse dropped even lower, to 30%, in 2021; however, the reduction is likely related to the social distancing and lockdowns that accompanied the COVID-19 pandemic. At the time of this writing, it is unclear whether adolescent sexual activity will rebound to the prepandemic, 2019, level.

An important trend over the past three decades is that fewer adolescents initiate sexual activity in the early years of high school. As shown in Figure 13.2, between 1991 and 2021, sexual activity declined for all students, but most dramatically for ninth-grade students (Federal Interagency Forum on Child and Family Statistics., 2021). Of those who have had intercourse, 73% reported opposite-sex partners only in 2019 (76% in 2021) (Centers for Disease Control and Prevention, 2023). About one quarter of high school students (27%) reported having had intercourse within the previous 3 months in 2019 (and about 21% in 2021).

As shown in Figure 13.2, the proportion of adolescents who have ever engaged in sexual intercourse declined from 2005 to 2021. This trend is especially visible among Black adolescents and, to a lesser extent, among Hispanic adolescents, but not among White adolescents (see Figure 13.3; Centers for Disease Control and Prevention, 2020; Ethier et al., 2018). Racial and ethnic differences in adolescent sexual activity are intertwined with the socioeconomic and contextual factors that are correlated with race and ethnicity.

Early sexual activity and greater sexual experience are more common in adolescents reared in stressful contexts, such as low socioeconomic status homes and neighborhoods where community ties are weak (Minnis et al., 2022; Orihuela et al., 2020). In addition, racial differences in rates of pubertal maturation influence sexual activity. African American girls experience puberty earlier than other girls, and early maturation is a risk factor for early sexual activity (Osinubi et al., 2022; Vasilenko, 2022). Given that adolescents of color continue to face contextual risks for early sexual initiation, it is unclear why they have experienced greater declines in sexual initiation and activity than White adolescents.

Understanding and becoming comfortable with one's sexuality is a developmental task for adolescents. In late adolescence, sexual activity is associated with positive self-esteem and well-being and is not associated with psychological problems such as anxiety, depression, or problem behavior (Harries et al., 2018; Nogueira Avelar e Silva et al., 2018). Although initiating sexual activity in the later high

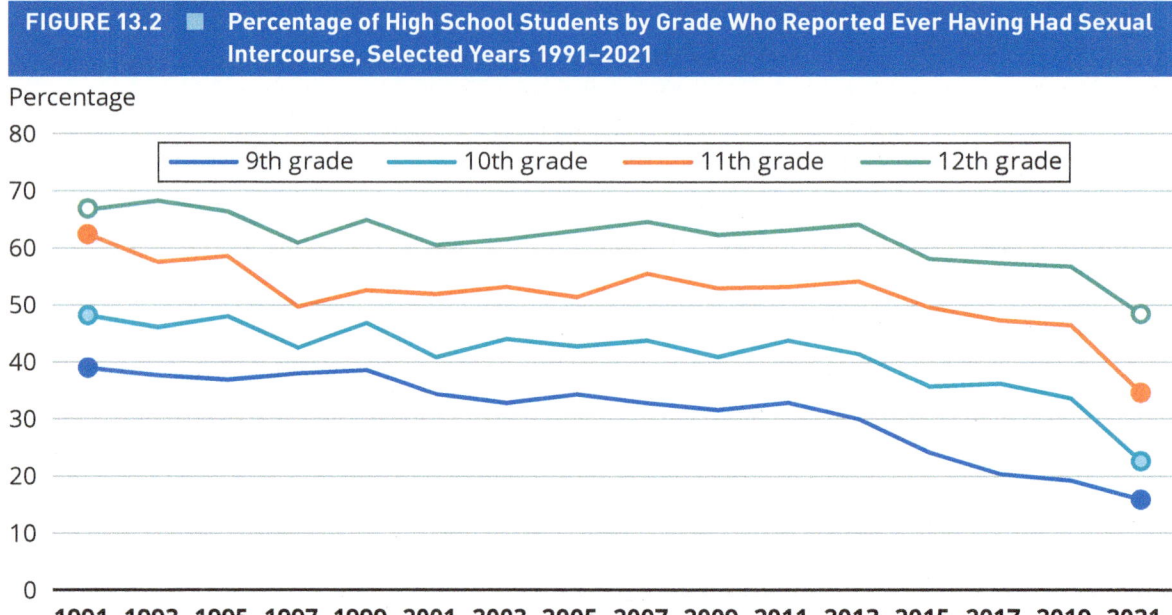

FIGURE 13.2 ■ Percentage of High School Students by Grade Who Reported Ever Having Had Sexual Intercourse, Selected Years 1991–2021

Note. Students were asked, "Have you ever had sexual intercourse?" Data are collected biannually.

Source: Federal Interagency Forum on Child and Family Statistics. (2023). *Sexual activity.* America's Children: Key National Indicators of Well-Being, 2023. https://www.childstats.gov/americaschildren/beh4.asp

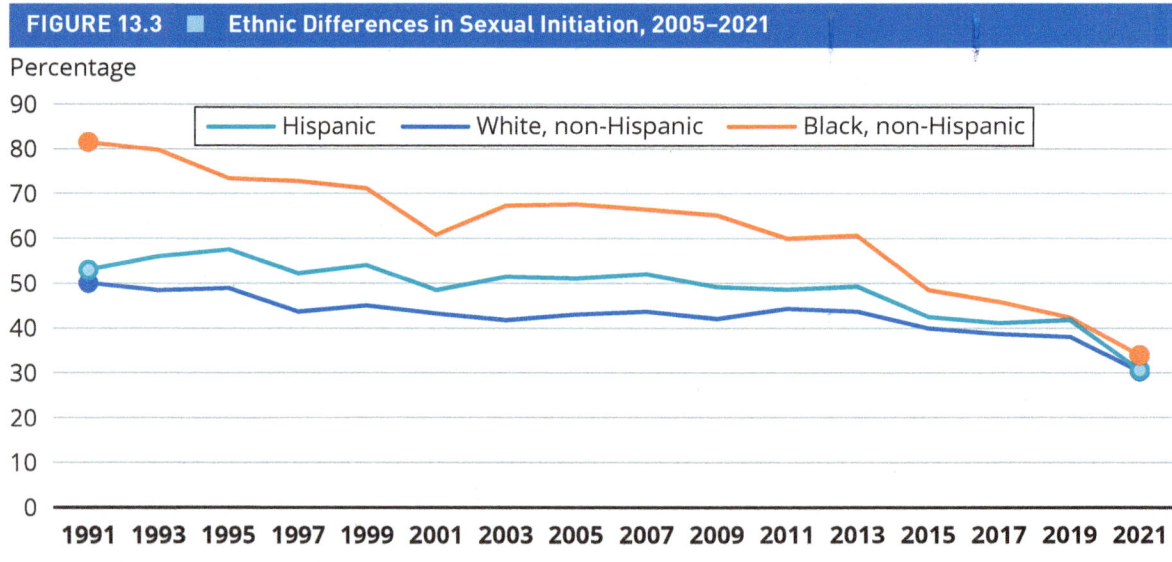

FIGURE 13.3 ■ Ethnic Differences in Sexual Initiation, 2005–2021

Source: Centers for Disease Control and Prevention. (2023). Youth risk behavior surveillance—United States, 2021. *Morbidity and Mortality Weekly Report, 72*(1). https://www.cdc.gov/mmwr/volumes/72/su/pdfs/su7201-H.pdf

school years is not associated with poor adjustment, early sexual initiation, prior to age 16, poses risks to development. Early sexual activity is associated with attitudes that are more accepting of risk taking and engaging in more risky behaviors, such as taking sexual risks, alcohol and substance use, poor academic achievement, and delinquency, as well as having a larger number of adolescent pregnancies and sex partners relative to peers (Vasilenko, 2022; Warner, 2018).

Lesbian, Gay, and Bisexual Adolescents

Sexual orientation refers to an enduring pattern of emotional, romantic, and sexual attraction to opposite-sex partners (heterosexual), same-sex partners (gay or lesbian), or partners of both sexes (bisexual) (Ervin et al., 2023). It is important to note that being cisgender or transgender signifies one's gender identity, which is separate from one's sexual orientation, whether they are gay, lesbian, or bisexual (Baams & Kaufman, 2023). Research on the intersection of transgender identity and sexual orientation is rare. Consequently many researchers study transgender adolescents alongside LGB adolescents. Wherever possible, the following discussion distinguishes LGB and transgender adolescents.

The process of determining sexual orientation often entails exploring and considering alternatives. Many preadolescents and young adolescents engage in sex play with members of the same sex, yet ultimately develop a heterosexual orientation. Researchers today view sexual orientation as a dynamic spectrum, ranging from exclusive opposite-sex attraction and relations to exclusive same-sex attraction and relations, with multiple sexual orientations in between (Hopkins & Richardson, 2021; Savin-Williams, 2021). For example, one longitudinal study followed nearly 14,000 youth from ages 12 to 33 and found three general patterns of sexual attraction: heterosexual (88%), mostly heterosexual (10%), and LGB (2%) (Calzo et al., 2017).

Many people experience attractions that fluctuate and vary over time (Kaestle, 2019). A 3-year study of high school students found one third of girls and 10% of boys reported fluidity in sexual attractions (Stewart et al., 2019). Reporting of same-sex attraction and behavior among adolescents and emerging adults is not stable. Longitudinal data with over 10,000 7th- to 12th-grade students over a 6-year period revealed some migration over time in both directions—from opposite-sex attraction and behavior to same-sex attraction and behavior and vice versa (Saewyc, 2011). Stability in same-sex attractions develops over time, from late adolescence through emerging and early adulthood (Y. Hu et al., 2016; Srivastava et al., 2022). After a period of questioning and exploration, adolescents may commit to a sexual orientation and integrate their sexuality into their overall sense of identity. Adoption of a sexual orientation is not a linear process.

Also, sexual attraction does not always match behavior; many people experience attractions that they do not act on and engage in behaviors that may not match with sexual orientation (Li & Davis, 2020). In addition, a small minority of people report a stable asexual orientation, feeling no sexual attraction whatsoever (Brunning & McKeever, 2021; Su & Zheng, 2023).

The onset of sexual activity can precede, co-occur, or follow self-identification as gay or lesbian; however, most often first sex typically occurs after, not before, the individual recognizes that they are gay or lesbian (W. J. Hall et al., 2021). Although it was once thought that same-sex sexual experiences served to test or confirm a lesbian or gay identity, it instead appears that young people often embrace a lesbian or gay identity prior to experiencing same-sex behavior (Baams & Kaufman, 2023). Adolescents of all sexual orientations tend to engage in similar levels of sexual activity. In the annual Youth Risk Behavior Survey conducted by the Centers for Disease Control and Prevention (2020), 33% of the adolescents who identified as lesbian, gay, or bisexual reported ever having sex (compared with 29% of those who identify as heterosexual) and 22% reported being sexually active within the past 3 months (compared with 21% of heterosexual youth).

We have seen that sexual activity is a normative experience for late adolescents and associated with well-being (Vasilenko, 2022). Research examining LGB youth has tended to emphasize the risks they experience with much less attention to the developmental correlates of sexual activity. Constructing an identity as a young person who is lesbian, gay, bisexual, or transgender can be complicated by the prejudice and discrimination that many LGBT youth experience in their schools and communities. LGBT adolescents experience more harassment and victimization by peers and report a more hostile peer environment than their heterosexual peers (Fish et al., 2023). Perceived discrimination and victimization by peers contribute to LGBT adolescents' increased risk for poor mental health and behavioral problems, such as depression, self-harm, suicide, running away, poor academic performance, substance use, and risky sexual practices (Barnett et al., 2019; Fish, 2020; White et al., 2018).

Support from parents and peers can buffer the negative effects of stigmatization and victimization for LGBT individuals and is associated with high self-esteem and positive adjustment (McConnell et al., 2016; Skoog & Kapetanovic, 2021; Watson et al., 2019). Within the school setting, supports such as knowledgeable teachers and counselors, vigilance against bullying, and the presence of GSA student groups aid LGBT students' adjustment and promote resilience (Gower et al., 2018; Lessard et al., 2020).

Parents, Peers, and Adolescent Sexual Activity

Adolescents who report close relationships with parents tend to initiate sex at a later age and report lower rates of sexual activity overall than their peers with poor relationships with their parents (McDade et al., 2020; Reis et al., 2023). Warm parenting, regularly shared family activities (e.g., outings, game nights, or shared dinners), and parental monitoring of adolescents' activities are associated with lower rates of sexual activity and fewer sexual partners (Hurst et al., 2022; Kaestle et al., 2021).

When parents and children communicate about sexuality—specifically, when they have open conversations characterized by warmth, support, and humor—adolescents tend to show a later onset of sexual activity and engage in less sexual risk taking than their peers (Hurst et al., 2022; Verbeek et al., 2020). However, while communication about risky sexual activity is associated with engaging in safer sex, it does *not* prevent sexual activity itself. Why? Sexual exploration and experimentation is a normative developmental task for adolescents and sexual intercourse is common in late adolescence.

Adolescents who believe that their peers, especially their best friends, are sexually active have more positive attitudes about and are more approving of sexual activity, are more likely to initiate sexual activity, engage in sex more frequently, and accumulate a greater number of sexual partners than those with peers who are less sexually active (Friedman et al., 2019; Hiatt et al., 2017).

Contraceptive Use

Adolescents often encounter information about contraceptives in health and sexual education classes at school (Maziarz et al., 2020). Most sexually active high school students report using contraceptives within the past year, most commonly condoms (Lindberg et al., 2021). However, many adolescents use condoms only sporadically and inconsistently (Pazol et al., 2015). Only about one half of high school students report using a condom during their last intercourse (Centers for Disease Control and Prevention, 2020). Common reasons given for not using condoms include not planning to have sex, the belief that pregnancy is unlikely, and difficulty communicating and negotiating the use of condoms (A. Z. Johnson et al., 2015). Adolescents' knowledge and access to condoms are the best predictors of their consistent use (Jaramillo et al., 2017). Yet in one recent survey of nearly 800 high school superintendents, only 7% of schools offered condoms to high school students (Demissie et al., 2019).

Adolescent Pregnancy

The birth rate for 15- to 19-year-old girls in the United States has dropped dramatically from 117 per 1,000 girls in 1990 to 16.7 per 1,000 girls in 2019 (J. A. Martin et al., 2021; Osterman et al., 2022). The decline in adolescent birth rates over the past 30 years can be attributed to an increase in contraceptive use, including hormonal birth control methods such as the contraceptive pill and IUD (Lindberg et al., 2021). Despite overall declines over the past three decades, the United States continues to have one of the highest teen birth rates in the developed world (Sedgh et al., 2015). In addition, ethnic and socioeconomic disparities place vulnerable teens at heightened risk for adolescent pregnancy and birth. Hispanic, African American, and American Indian/Alaska Native adolescents, as well as those from low socioeconomic status homes and communities—both rural and urban—have the highest adolescent birth rates in the United States (Burrus, 2018).

Girls who experience menarche early, relative to peers, tend to engage in sexual behavior earlier than their same-age peers and experience higher risks of pregnancy (De Genna et al., 2011). Similarly, poor academic achievement, delinquency, substance use, depression, and affiliation with deviant peers are risk factors for early sexual activity and adolescent pregnancy (Carlson et al., 2014; Fortenberry, 2013). Low socioeconomic status homes and neighborhoods are associated with a higher risk of adolescent pregnancy, influenced by lack of access to health services, after school activities, and weak community ties.

Outcomes of Adolescent Pregnancy

Adolescent mothers are less likely than their peers to achieve many of the typical markers of adulthood on a conventional schedule, such as completing high school, entering a stable marriage, and becoming financially and residentially independent (Johansen et al., 2020). Lack of resources such as child care, housing, and financial support are associated with poor educational outcomes; adolescent mothers with child care and financial resources tend to show higher educational attainment (Hans, 2024). Although adolescent pregnancy is associated with negative outcomes, the risk factors for adolescent pregnancy are also those that place youth at risk for negative adult outcomes in general, such as extreme poverty, family instability, and few educational and community supports (SmithBattle & Flick, 2023). It is therefore difficult to determine the degree to which outcomes are caused by adolescent pregnancy itself or the contextual conditions that are associated with it. Adolescent fathers are similar to adolescent mothers in that they are more likely than their peers to have poor academic performance, higher school dropout rates, finite financial resources, and lowered income potential (Shpiegel et al., 2022).

Infants born to adolescent mothers are at risk for preterm birth and low birth weight (Ranjbar et al., 2023). Children of adolescent mothers tend to be at risk for negative developmental outcomes such as conduct and emotional problems, cognitive and developmental delays, poor academic achievement, risky behavior and adolescent pregnancy (Cederbaum et al., 2020; Cresswell et al., 2022; Liu et al., 2018). These outcomes are influenced by the characteristics of adolescents who are likely to become mothers, as well as the consequences of having a child at a young age (e.g., low level of maternal education, low socioeconomic status, frequent caretaker and residence changes, poor parenting) (Gorry, 2023; SmithBattle et al., 2024). Children of adolescent mothers can demonstrate resilience and adjustment despite these risks. Positive adjustment is predicted by secure attachment, low maternal depressive symptoms, and positive parenting on the part of the mother, characterized by warmth, discussion, and stimulation (Hua, 2023; Powers et al., 2021).

Supports for Adolescent Parents

Adolescent parents are more likely to be successful when they have a range of economic, educational, and social supports. Effective supports for adolescent parents include access to health care and affordable childcare, encouragement to stay in school, and training in vocational skills, parenting skills, and coping skills (Hua, 2023). Interventions that emphasize promoting high-quality parent-infant interactions are associated with positive cognitive development in infants (Baudry et al., 2017). Social support predicts increased parenting self-efficacy and parental satisfaction (Angley et al., 2015; Flaherty & Sadler, 2022). Relationships with adults who are close and supportive and provide guidance predict completing high school. Adolescent parents who share caregiving with their parents or other adults obtain support and learn parenting skills, becoming increasingly competent at parenting over time (Zambrano et al., 2023). Adolescent parents also benefit from relationships with adults who are sensitive not only to their needs as parents but also to their own developmental needs for autonomy and support.

Sexuality Education

Many schools provide comprehensive sexuality education, educational programs designed to promote healthy adolescent development and provide medically accurate information including information about safe sex while emphasizing age-appropriate physical, mental, emotional and social dimensions of human sexuality (Miedema et al., 2020). They promote adolescents' overall health, including sexual and reproductive health, consent and sexual rights, positive views of sexuality, the prevention of violence, support of diversity, and the promotion of healthy relationships (Bordogna et al., 2023; Schneider & Hirsch, 2020).

Public opinion polls in the United States suggest strong support for comprehensive approaches to sex education that include information about abstinence and education about sexuality, condoms and contraception, and provide access to condoms and contraception for sexually active adolescents (Kantor & Levitz, 2017; Santelli et al., 2017). Likewise, health professionals have overwhelmingly supported comprehensive sexuality education (American College of Obstetricians and Gynecologists.,

2016; American Public Health Association., 2014; Breuner et al., 2016). Systematic reviews consistently find that comprehensive sexuality education programs tend to show efficacy in delaying initiation of intercourse in addition to promoting other protective behaviors, such as condom use (Breuner et al., 2016; Goldfarb & Lieberman, 2021).

> **THINKING IN CONTEXT 13.5**
>
> 1. Identify factors at each of Bronfenbrenner's bioecological levels that might influence sexual activity in adolescence.
> 2. Identify factors at each level: microsystem, mesosystem, exosystem, and macrosystem.
> 3. How might interventions apply this information to reduce sexual activity and increase safe-sex practices among adolescents?

APPLY YOUR KNOWLEDGE

Four-year-old Tony loved his preschool classroom. He liked painting on the big easel, building with the big blocks, and playing in the pretend house and kitchen. One day he pretended to bake a cake with his friend Ashley. They busily stirred imaginary batter in bowls then poured it into a pan and slid it into the pretend over.

Ryan barged in and shouted, "Hey! What are you doing? That's girl stuff!"

"No, it's not. It's cooking," said Tony.

"Only girls cook in a kitchen and only girls wear aprons. Boys and girls do different things. Boys are better," Ryan said.

Tony looked down at the apron he was wearing and frowned. "But I'm not a girl," he said. That afternoon Tony said to his older sister, "I don't want to be a girl anymore."

"Why would you think you're a girl?" she asked.

"I make a cake at school. And I wore an apron. Ryan says only girls do that. I don't want to be a girl. I'm not gonna wear an apron. No more cooking."

"Ryan's wrong. You can cook all you want and wear an apron, too. It won't change who you are. It won't make you a girl."

1. Why does Tony think he will become a girl? Discuss Tony's and Ryan's understandings of gender and how you expect it to develop over time, referring to cognitive developmental concepts, such as gender identity, gender stability, and gender constancy.
2. Ryan believes that boys and girls are fundamentally different and that boys are superior. What evidence is there to support his view? Discuss sex differences in childhood.
3. In your view, what are the most important influences on gender typing? Weigh biological, cognitive, and contextual explanations. Considering these, how would you explain gender development to a friend?
4. How might the preschool environment and classroom norms influence Tony's and Ryan's understandings of gender roles and expectations? How can teachers help children develop more inclusive views of gender?
5. How do societal and cultural factors, such as media representations of gender and gender stereotypes in popular culture, shape children's understanding of gender? What can parents and educators do to help children develop critical thinking skills and resist gender stereotypes and biases?

CHAPTER SUMMARY

13.1 Summarize sex differences and gender stereotypes in physical, cognitive, and socioemotional development.

Sex is biological, determined by genes, and usually indicated by the appearance of infants' genitals. Gender is determined by socialization and the roles that the individual adopts. Gender stereotypes are beliefs about the activities, attitudes, skills, and characteristics labeled as appropriate for males or females in a given culture. Until puberty boys and girls are physically similar. While girls tend to display better fine motor skills and balance than boys in early childhood, boys tend to be more active. Sex differences in cognitive abilities are small or negligible. Girls tend to have better verbal abilities, while boys tend to perform better on mental rotation tasks. In terms of socioemotional development, from an early age, girls are better able to manage and express their emotions than boys. Physical aggression is more common in boys and relational aggression more common in girls, but there is overlap. Overall, boys and girls are more alike than different.

13.2 Compare and contrast biological, cognitive, and contextual explanations for gender typing.

Biological explanations for gender typing rely on evolution, genetics, and hormones. Evolutionary theory suggests that gendered behavior promotes survival of the individual and the species. Hormones, especially testosterone, influence behavior. According to cognitive developmental theory, children construct their understanding of gender by interacting with people and things and thinking about their experiences. Gender identity, awareness of whether one is a boy or a girl, typically emerges at about age 2, followed by gender stability and gender constancy. Gender schema theory proposes that once children begin to label themselves as boys and girls, they form a gender schema that organizes gender-related information and represents their understanding of what it means to be male or female. Gender schemas are used to guide behavior and attitudes. Gender development is shaped by socialization and interactions with various agents in the sociocultural context. Parents' gender-based expectations and behaviors influence children's gender socialization. Gendered toys and play also contribute to gender typing, especially if parents reinforce play with same-gender toys and discourage play with cross-gender toys. Children show a preference for same-gender peers, who tend to influence gender typing through praise and imitation. Media depictions of gender also promote gender-typed behavior in children. To reduce gender stereotyping, adults can model gender-neutral attitudes and beliefs, encourage mixed-gender interactions, and organize environments and classrooms to reduce gender salience and stereotypes.

13.3 Examine gender identity in childhood and adolescence.

In middle childhood, children's gender identity expands, and several dimensions of gender identity rise in importance: felt same-gender typicality, felt other-gender typicality, gender contentedness, and felt pressure to conform to gender roles. Felt same-gender typicality and felt other-gender typicality refer to children's beliefs about their similarity to members of their gender and the other gender and are associated with positive adjustment when felt at high levels. Gender contentedness involves children's satisfaction with the gender they were assigned at birth and is also associated with positive outcomes. Felt pressure to conform to gender roles refers to the extent to which children feel pressure to avoid other-gender behavior, and high levels of this pressure may lead to adjustment problems. With the onset of puberty, adolescents become more acutely aware of their appearance and gender. Many perceive greater social pressure to adhere to gender-stereotyped roles and behaviors, a phenomenon referred to as gender intensification. However, research findings on gender intensification are mixed and adolescents tend to become more flexible in their thinking and adoption of gender roles by late adolescence.

13.4 Describe the development of transgender identity in children and adolescents.
Transgender children do not identify with the sex assigned to them at birth, but nonetheless show gender development that is similar to that of cisgender children, with both groups showing preferences for activities and peers typically associated with their expressed gender. Research suggests that transgender children's preferences are genuine, and they tend to show more flexible views of gender stereotypes than cisgender children. Social gender transitioning is reversible and nonmedical, involving matching children's everyday experiences with their gender identity. Studies suggest that socially transitioned transgender children have mental health outcomes no different from gender-consistent children. The onset of puberty can be distressing for transgender adolescents. Adolescents with a transgender identity experience elevated stress and higher rates of mental health and social problems. Support from family, peers, and schools that affirm transgender identity can promote positive adjustment and resilience. Gender-affirming medical care, including puberty suppression, is associated with positive mental health outcomes for transgender adolescents, but many face barriers in accessing care.

13.5 Discuss sexual activity in adolescence.
Fewer high school students have had sexual intercourse than ever before. Early sexual activity is associated with engaging in more risky behaviors. Close relationships with parents tend to delay the initiation of sexual activity but communication about risky sexual activity does not prevent sexual activity itself. Sexual exploration and experimentation are normative developmental tasks for adolescents, and sexual intercourse is common in late adolescence. The use of contraceptives among sexually active high school students is inconsistent, and access to contraceptives and knowledge about their use are the best predictors of consistent use. Adolescent pregnancy rates have declined, but racial and ethnic disparities exist. Adolescent pregnancy is associated with poor outcomes for parents and children. Effective supports for adolescent parents can promote positive outcomes. Comprehensive sexuality education programs that provide medically accurate information, including information about safe sex, are strongly supported and effective in delaying initiation of intercourse and promoting protective behaviors.

KEY TERMS

- Androgynous
- Cisgender
- Felt other-gender typicality
- Felt same-gender typicality
- Gender
- Gender constancy
- Gender identity
- Gender intensification
- Gender schema
- Gender stability
- Gender stereotypes
- Gender typing
- Medical gender transition
- Puberty suppressors
- Sex
- Sexual orientation
- Social gender transition
- Transgender identity

CAREERS IN CHILD DEVELOPMENT: SOCIOEMOTIONAL DEVELOPMENT

There are many ways to work with children, help them manage problems, and optimize their development, at all levels of education.

Social Worker
Social workers work with individuals and families of all ages, providing counseling and identifying and helping them access needed resources. Social workers are advisers who advocate for others during transitions, crises, and challenging circumstances. They help families navigate often confusing federal and state programs to obtain needed assistance, such as access to the WIC program, which promotes the health of low-income women, infants, and children by providing nutritious food, housing

assistance, medical treatment, and other aid. Social workers may educate and counsel on topics such as parenting and coping skills, in both individual and group counseling sessions. A bachelor's degree may offer preparation for entry-level positions in social work; a master's degree in social work (MSW) provides many more opportunities, including independent practice as a clinical social worker.

Clinical social workers obtain master's degrees, additional supervised experience, and pass a certification exam to become licensed clinical social workers (LCSW). Clinical social workers provide psychological treatment, including diagnosing and treating psychological, emotional, and behavioral disorders and working with doctors and other medical professionals. They are employed in various settings, including hospitals, schools, community mental health centers, social service agencies, and private practice. The median salary for clinical social workers was about $58,000 in 2023 (U.S. Bureau of Labor Statistics, 2024).

Substance Abuse Counselor

Substance abuse counselors provide support to individuals experiencing drug and alcohol problems. They teach adults how to modify their behavior to progress toward recovery. They evaluate patients, develop treatment and recovery plans, facilitate individual and group therapy sessions, teach coping skills, monitor patients' progress, and revise treatment plans as needed. Substance abuse counselors collaborate with psychiatrists, doctors, nurses, social workers, and corrections departments. They are found in hospitals, individual and family services, mental health and substance abuse facilities, and state and local governments.

Substance abuse counseling requires a master's degree in substance abuse counseling, followed by 3,000 hours of supervised experience and completion of a licensure exam. However, states vary in their requirements to practice. Certified substance abuse counselors may be employed at the bachelor's level in many states. Frequently bachelor's level certification involves completing several courses in drug and alcohol abuse counseling, 300 to 600 hours of supervised training, and a certification exam (usually from the Association for Addiction Professionals, but some states maintain their own accreditation requirements). Substance abuse counselors' median salary was $54,000 in 2023 (U.S. Bureau of Labor Statistics, 2024).

Child Life Specialist

A child's hospitalization poses many challenges for parents and families. Children are often afraid and may not understand why they are away from home and why they are ill. Parents worry about their children and balancing their responsibilities to the hospitalized child, other children, and work. Enter the child life specialist.

Child life specialists work in medical settings to help children and families navigate the process of illness, injury, disability, and hospitalization. They help children and families better understand a process, procedure, or other element of a medical experience. Child life specialists apply age-appropriate strategies to minimize children's trauma and improve their understanding of medical diagnoses and treatment plans. They educate children and families and support parents in the physically and emotionally demanding process of caring for hospitalized or disabled children. Child life specialists help children reduce their anxiety and promote positive development. They may implement group programs, therapies, and activities with children, such as play activities, to encourage free expression and promote social and emotional development and feelings of competence.

Child life specialists collaborate with healthcare teams to coordinate and manage care. These teams may include social workers, chaplains, nurses, and doctors. They primarily work in hospitals but can also work in medical clinics, hospices, dental offices, schools, camps, and even patients' homes.

Becoming a child life specialist requires a bachelor's degree in child life studies or a related field like social work or psychology. Becoming a child life specialist requires certification. In addition to a bachelor's degree, certification requires a 600-hour internship experience and a passing Child Life Professional Certification Examination score. In 2023, the average salary of child life specialists was about $60,000 (Salary.com, n.d.b).

Applied Behavior Analyst

Many children engage in challenging behavior that parents and teachers must curb, such as aggressive behavior, disruptive classroom behavior, and impulsivity. Applied behavior analysts identify problematic behaviors and devise treatment plans to modify those behaviors. Applied behavior analyses apply psychological principles to modify people's behavior. They work with people of all ages. Applied behavior analysts who work with children are sometimes called *child behavior specialists*.

Applied behavior analysts work to improve individuals' social, communication, academic, and adaptive skills. They assess children's behavior, work with children and parents to set goals, devise and implement treatments, and monitor change. Applied behavior analysts teach parents, teachers, and support professionals how to implement behavioral interventions, such as operant conditioning and reinforcement, at home, school, and in other settings. They observe children, monitor their progress, and write reports. They communicate with teachers, families, and staff about the children's progress and needs.

Behavior analysts often work in special education settings to help children with special needs self-regulate their behavior. They often join healthcare provider teams and consult with doctors, therapists, and psychologists. They work in hospitals, private clinics, schools, patients' homes, and private practice.

Training to become an applied behavior analyst consists of completing a master's degree, including behavioral analysis coursework, completing 800–1,500 hours of supervised experience (depending on placement), and passing the Board Certified Behavior Analyst Exam. In some states, applied behavior analysts are licensed as professional counselors. The median salary for a board-certified applied behavior analyst was about $72,000 in 2023 (Salary.com, n.d.a).

Bachelor's degree holders may become *assistant behavior analysts* and support the work of applied behavior analysts under their supervision. Assistant applied behavior analysts are required by most states to seek certification and become licensed as board-certified assistant behavior analysts. A bachelor's degree with coursework in principles of learning and behavior analysis and ethics, 500–1,000 hours of supervised experience, and a passing score on the Board Certified Assistant Behavior Analyst Certification Examination are basic requirements for becoming a board-certified assistant behavior analyst. The median salary for a board-certified assistant applied behavior analyst was about $50,000 in 2023 (Salary.com, n.d.a).

Clinical Psychologist and Counseling Psychologist

Many careers enable professionals to provide counseling and mental health assistance. A psychologist is perhaps the most well-known of these careers. Psychologists who provide counseling are most often trained in clinical or counseling psychology. Both clinical psychologists and counseling psychologists provide individual assessment and therapy and create and evaluate therapeutic programs for individuals and groups. Despite these similarities, clinical and counseling psychology are distinct fields with different emphases. Traditionally, clinical psychology focuses on assessing and treating mental disorders to alleviate distress and behavior problems. Counseling psychology also treats distress but focuses on improving well-being over the lifespan, focusing on normative functioning rather than disorder. In practice, however, clinical and counseling psychology engage in similar counseling and therapeutic activities.

Clinical and counseling psychologists work in various settings including private practices, hospitals and medical centers, community mental health centers, schools, university or college counseling centers, criminal justice settings, and specialty clinics. Some psychologists specialize in a particular topic, such as health psychology; age, such as geropsychology; or topic, such as eating disorders or parenting problems. In addition to direct service delivery, clinical and counseling psychologists engage in intervention, program development, and evaluation. Some become administrators who manage other mental health workers or an entire agency or organization.

Use of the title psychologist requires state licensure. Clinical and counseling psychologists earn doctoral degrees, which include supervised experience and the completion of a dissertation, typically requiring conducting original research. After obtaining a doctoral degree, clinical and counseling psychologists complete an additional year of supervised experience then a national licensure exam. Many states require an additional state licensure exam. The median salary for clinical and counseling psychologists was about $96,000 in 2023 (U.S. Bureau of Labor Statistics, 2024).

Intervention Research

There are many prevention and intervention programs designed to promote positive development in childhood and adolescence. These programs are conducted in a variety of settings, such as schools, after-school programs, community centers, and nonprofit centers. Individuals work in these programs in various roles, as workers, counselors, and social workers who implement the programs or as planners and researchers who create, assess, evaluate, and revise them.

Researchers may fulfill several roles in intervention research. Some researchers study social problems to provide information to other professionals who create interventions. They might study ways of preventing adolescent pregnancy or how to increase the prevalence of girls and underrepresented minorities in science, technology, engineering, and mathematics at all levels of education. Other researchers assess the effectiveness of programs. A researcher at a social service agency might examine the effectiveness of new drug-control interventions like mandatory minimum sanctions, residential and group home treatments for youthful offenders identified as drug users, and school-based prevention programs. The results of this research are used to improve programs.

Individuals in intervention research are employed at nonprofit agencies, universities, think tanks (research centers), and government. They conduct research to gather information about social problems and policies, assess and improve programs for children, youth, and families, and write reports and other documents to inform policymakers and the public. Researchers at educational nonprofit organizations such as the Educational Testing Service might study ways of accommodating standardized test-takers with disabilities.

Assistant-level research positions are often available to bachelor's degree holders. Additional education and credentialling requirements depend on the position. Direct service work implementing interventions might require licensure or certification as a counselor. Research skills honed in a master's program in quantitative research, psychology, human development, or another related field can enable individuals to work on research teams. Doctoral degrees (such as in psychology) offer the most opportunities to lead research teams and create programs.

PART 5
CONTEXTS OF DEVELOPMENT

Michael Heffernan/ Getty Images

14 FAMILIES

> ### LEARNING OBJECTIVES
>
> **14.1** Describe the family system.
>
> **14.2** Examine parenting, including parenting styles, discipline, conflict, and monitoring.
>
> **14.3** Compare the various forms families take.
>
> **14.4** Analyze the challenges faced by families with incarcerated, deployed, or migrant members, as well as the impact of the COVID-19 pandemic on families.

"It's mine! Willie took my game again! Mom!" Gabby yelled. "It was mine first. I let you use it, remember?" Willie replied. "I don't care whose toy it is. In this family we talk, not shout, and we share, right kids?" Mom said. "You may not realize it, but when you yell at each other, it affects me, too. We are a family, and what you do affects me, and what I do affects you. Do you understand?" "Fine," they replied simultaneously. Sibling arguments are common, but this mother's response emphasizes an important principle regarding families: Every member influences every other member. In this chapter, we examine how families influence child and adolescent development.

THE FAMILY AS A SYSTEM

> **14.1** Describe the family system.

Children and adolescents play an active role in their development by interacting with the people and environments around them. They influence family members and are influenced by them. Parents socialize children and adjust their parenting in response to their children's behavior. Siblings also influence each other, and their interactions shape their relationships with their parents as well as their parents' relationship with each other. These reciprocal interactions among family members constitute a system, a set of interconnected parts that work together as a network (see Chapter 1).

Family systems theory examines the interactive and bidirectional nature of relationships within families. The family system is part of the mesosystem in Bronfenbrenner's (2005) bioecological systems theory, but Bronfenbrenner's mesosystem is broader and includes individuals' interactions outside of the family. From a family systems perspective, each family member affects and is affected by others in the family unit. As family members interact with each other over time, their interactions begin to form stable patterns of behavior that result in a balanced state of equilibrium (Bowen, 1978; Updegraff & Perez-Brena, 2023). However, changes in any individual or relationship can lead to shifts in the others. Developmental milestones, such as a child starting school or an adolescent entering puberty, can affect the entire family and disrupt their equilibrium. Changes in family circumstances, such as a divorce, move, birth of a new child, or change in socioeconomic status (SES), can require the family to adapt and establish a new equilibrium.

Central to family systems theory is the developmental concept of *reciprocal interaction*, in which children and parents influence each other dynamically over time (Baltes et al., 1998; Lerner et al., 2015). Each family member's development is influenced by and also influences their interactions with other family members. For example, parents' relationship and marital quality influence their children (Chiang & Bai, 2022). Therefore, we must consider not only children's development but also parents' development to understand family dynamics.

Changing Child

Children's development influences their parents. Many new parents report feeling unprepared for their infants' constant needs, accompanied by added housework, financial demands, loss of sleep, and less leisure time (Galatzer-Levy et al., 2011; Lévesque et al., 2020). These pressures can lead to a reduced sense of well-being and self-esteem and even depression (Grolleman et al., 2023; van Scheppingen et al., 2018). The demands of new parenthood are also accompanied by rewards, such as experiencing a greater sense of meaning and satisfaction in life (Brajša-Žganec et al., 2023; Brandel et al., 2018).

As children reach developmental milestones such as crawling, walking, and talking, parents experience both excitement and new stresses as they learn to keep their children safe. Parents begin to realize that their children are their own little people with unique personalities and needs. Children become increasingly aware of the world around them, and parents must navigate their children's growing curiosity and desire for independence. Children's entry to school brings new responsibilities for parents as they become more involved in their children's education and extracurricular activities. Just as parents become proficient at meeting children's developmental demands at a given age, children advance, posing new challenges and requiring a transformation of skills.

As adolescents enter puberty, their bodies take on adult proportions and functions, leading them to be increasingly treated like adults. Adolescents often find these changes stressful, which can also be true for parents. As pubertal changes peak, conflict with parents tends to rise, and parent-child relationships become more volatile, with many ups and downs (Marceau et al., 2015; Peltz et al., 2024).

With cognitive maturation, adolescents become able to reason more effectively than ever. They are more likely to expect parents to provide reasons for rules and can counter parental arguments, often with sound rationales. Parents are often surprised by their adolescents' new abilities to argue, especially if they were used to explaining rules by stating, "Because I said so," and may find this change stressful.

Socioemotional tasks such as identity development lead adolescents to explore and consider many options in areas such as sexuality, friendship and romantic relationships, career, and others. Frequently adolescents explore and consider options that parents may find distasteful, potentially causing conflict. As adolescents' attention turns to peers, they seek distance from parents and seek to become independent; important tasks for adolescents may be difficult for parents as they are undergoing their own changes as they enter and progress through middle adulthood.

Changing Parent

Human development is a lifelong process, and parents age as their children do, resulting in unique developmental needs. In 2021, the mean age for first birth was 27.3, up from 21.4 in 1970 and 25 in 2000 (Mathews & Hamilton, 2002; Osterman et al., 2023). Most adults in their 30s advance in their careers and often juggle conflicting demands at home and work (Mehta et al., 2020).

Most parents are around age 40 when their first child enters adolescence, marking their transition to middle adulthood. As the stresses and rewards of parenting change over childhood into adolescence, the effects of parenthood on adults' mental and physical health also shift (R. W. Simon & Caputo, 2019). Although caring for infants and young children is physically demanding and associated with a greater sense of parenting role overload, parents of adolescents report poorer life satisfaction, self-esteem, self-efficacy, and more depressive symptoms than parents of infants and young children (Nomaguchi & Milkie, 2023; Pollmann-Schult, 2014).

Advances in cognition and socioemotional development empower adolescents to reason and engage in more sophisticated conversations, negotiations, and arguments than ever before. It may not be surprising that parents tend to report that adolescence is the most stressful stage of parenting (Nomaguchi & Milkie, 2020). Parental dissatisfaction tends to reach its lowest point in early adolescence when conflict increases most rapidly (Luthar & Ciciolla, 2016; Meier et al., 2018).

For many middle-aged parents, part of the challenge of raising adolescents is the sharp contrast between the developmental trajectories and tasks of adolescence and those of middle adulthood. Adolescents' physical maturation can make parents aware of the passing of time, their age, and their limited lifespan. As adolescents begin their identity search, parents may reevaluate their sense of self, priorities, and goals, revising their sense of identity (Soenens et al., 2019; Steinberg, 2001). Turning points in life, such as a child's entry to adolescence, as well as normative age-related changes can prompt growth and change in adults' identity (Kuther & Burnell, 2019; Moen & Wethington, 1999).

Siblings

About 80% of children in the United States have at least one sibling (U.S. Census Bureau, 2023). By middle childhood, children spend more time with siblings than with parents (Dunn, 2002). Siblings are an important influence on each other's development.

Childhood

Siblings who usually offer each other social support and assistance can sometimes come into conflict.

StockPlanets/ istock

Interactions with siblings offer young children opportunities to understand other people's thoughts and practice taking their perspectives, advancing theory of mind (see Chapter 7; Devine & Hughes, 2018). Through interactions with siblings, children learn relationship skills such as sharing and conflict resolution (Howe et al., 2022; Xiao et al., 2022). They learn that relationships continue even through arguments and anger. Siblings offer each other social support and help each other manage academic, family, and peer issues and the anxiety and depressive symptoms that can accompany them (Fry et al., 2021; Howe et al., 2022). Close, supportive relationships with siblings are associated with better adjustment to difficult and traumatic experiences, such as parental divorce, bullying, and even child maltreatment (L. Kramer et al., 2018; van Dijk et al., 2022).

Sibling relationships are also often characterized by patterns of ambivalence and conflict (J. Kramer & Arnold, 2020). Sibling rivalry tends to rise in middle childhood as children increasingly engage in social comparison. Parents, teachers, peers, other family members—and children themselves—naturally compare siblings' characteristics, interests, and accomplishments (McHale et al., 2012). Children who feel that a sibling receives more affection, approval, or resources from parents may feel resentful, which may harm the sibling relationship.

Conflict, even fighting and violence, are common among siblings. In one study, nearly three quarters of families reported physical violence between siblings, and over 40% of children had been kicked, bitten, or punched by a sibling within the past year (Feinberg et al., 2012). Parents increasingly report mediating sibling conflicts into middle childhood, peaking at about age 8, when parents reduce their mediation efforts and increasingly permit siblings to interact independently (Beyens et al., 2019). Some sibling conflict is inevitable and can help children develop important relationship skills, such as conflict resolution, communication, and emotion regulation (Howe et al., 2022; L. Kramer et al., 2018).

Frequent and intense sibling conflict is associated with poor adjustment, depression, peer aggression, and antisocial behaviors (Buist & Vermande, 2014; Coyle et al., 2017). Children who experience chronic victimization by siblings are at higher risk for peer victimization (Tucker et al., 2019). Sibling victimization tends to increase with family adversities, such as loss, illness, and other transitions, especially in boys, and declines as families adjust and overcome adversity (Toseeb et al., 2020; Tucker et al., 2019). In contrast, research on children in foster care suggests that warm sibling relationships are a source of support and are associated with resilience to adversity (Wojciak et al., 2018).

Adolescence

Adolescents with close and warm relationships with parents tend to also have positive sibling relationships characterized by less conflict than those with less warm parental relationships (C. Liu & Rahman, 2022; Ruff et al., 2018). The process of autonomy seeking that increases distance between parents and adolescents also influences the sibling relationship.

In most families, siblings have a natural hierarchy influenced by age. Older siblings generally are physically, socially, and cognitively advantaged over their younger siblings, considered more capable than their siblings, and are often involved in the caretaking of siblings. Therefore older siblings tend to have greater power than younger siblings (Tucker et al., 2010). The largest power discrepancies between siblings appear to be present during childhood and early adolescence and decrease in magnitude as siblings move through adolescence.

Older siblings serve as sources of advice and role models for both positive and negative behaviors (Waid et al., 2020). Siblings engage in similar levels of risk behaviors, such as delinquency and externalizing problems, alcohol and other substance use and sexual attitudes and behaviors during adolescence (Defoe et al., 2023; Huijsmans et al., 2019). Siblings shape adolescents' views about what behaviors are popular or desirable through modeling, self-disclosure, and even coaching and encouragement (Whiteman et al., 2017). Siblings also exert a positive influence on each other. Sibling support is associated with academic engagement and school achievement (M. T. Wang et al., 2019).

Over adolescence, the family network shifts to a more peripheral position (including siblings), and peers become more central (Updegraff & Perez-Brena, 2023). As adolescents seek greater autonomy from the family and spend more time with peers, they spend less time with siblings and the emotional intensity of the relationship (positive and negative) declines as does the involvement (McHale et al., 2012). Although adolescents tend to spend less time with siblings, younger siblings' drive for equality often results in increased conflict, especially during early adolescence (Lindell & Campione-Barr, 2017). Generally, sibling relationships become more egalitarian with age and development, as younger siblings become more equally matched in these capacities with their older siblings (Campione-Barr, 2017).

Ultimately the quality of the sibling relationships influences adolescents' well-being (Jensen et al., 2023; Solmeyer et al., 2014). Sibling conflict is a risk factor for problem behaviors. Adolescents who engage their siblings in excessive arguments or deliberately attempt to bother or harm a sibling may apply this interpersonal approach in other relationships, making it more likely that they will be involved with similarly aggressive peers (Gallagher et al., 2018). In contrast, sibling relationships offer opportunities to learn about intimacy. High-quality sibling relationships are associated with romantic competence in late adolescence (Doughty et al., 2015).

Only Children

As shown in Figure 14.1, family size has shrunk over the past four decades. In 2021, about 20% of children lived in one-child households, as or only children (U.S. Census Bureau, 2023). Only children are commonly stereotyped as spoiled and overly dependent on their parents. Fortunately, research fails to support these biases. Instead, only children tend to show positive adjustment, have high self-esteem, and be high achievers (M. Li et al., 2021; Sheng et al., 2022). Only children tend to receive greater attention from parents and develop closer relationships with them than children with siblings who must share their parents' attention (Y. Liu & Jiang, 2021). We have seen that siblings offer opportunities to learn interpersonal and conflict-resolution skills. In both early and middle childhood, only children are more likely than their peers to show poor interpersonal skills and difficulty with self-control (Downey et al., 2015). Yet other research suggests that only children are more prosocial, less lonely, tend to have similar numbers of high-quality friendships, and generally show similar rates of adjustment as their peers with siblings (Gerhardt, 2016; Y. Li et al., 2024; Lin et al., 2021). Overall, it appears that only children are similar to those with siblings.

Much of what we know about only children comes from studying children in China. Until 2015, under Chinese policy, married couples were permitted to give birth to only one child. Known as the one-child policy, it was implemented in 1979 to curb population growth by restricting the number of children married couples could have. The policy was most strictly implemented in urban areas, and couples in rural areas could request permission for two children if the first child was a girl and the couple waited 4 to 5 years between births (Yang, 2007).

At the core of the one-child policy was a set of incentives and penalties for infractions (McLoughlin, 2005). In exchange for limiting parents' childbearing, the Chinese government provided greater opportunities and resources for only children at the national, community, and household levels. The one-child policy was intended to give Chinese school-age only children advantages over those with siblings,

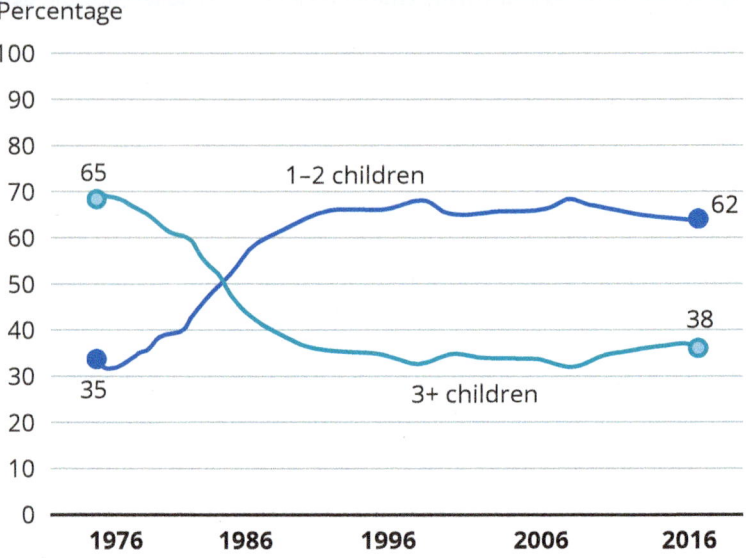

FIGURE 14.1 ■ Percentage of Mothers Who Have Given Birth to 1 to 2 and 3 or More Children, United States

Source: Bialik, K. (2018). *Middle children have become rarer, but a growing share of Americans now say three or more kids are 'ideal.'* Pew Research Center.

specifically, more attention and resources. Research suggests that Chinese only children scored higher than those with siblings on measures of IQ but did not differ on psychosocial measures such as dependence, helping behaviors, independence, aggression, friendliness, curiosity, self-confidence, peer relationships, social competence, and academic achievement (Chen et al., 1994; Guo et al., 2005; D. Wang et al., 2000).

Given Chinese culture's tradition of valuing boys, the one-child policy was implicated in high rates of female infanticide and sex-selective abortions, leading to a significant gender imbalance (Mosher, 2006). A rapidly aging population, coupled with a much smaller workforce due to slowed population growth, prompted a change to the one-child policy (Dai et al., 2022). In 2015, China ended the policy, permitting couples to apply to have two children, which was soon extended to three children (Scharping, 2019). Fewer couples than expected have had second and third children, suggesting that the one-child policy may have changed perceived norms on family size (Holliday, 2014). A recent survey of Chinese adults revealed that about 60% intended to have a second child and only about 13% a third (Jing et al., 2022). The one-child policy in China has provided a unique opportunity to study the effects of being an only child. However these findings are influenced by the unique sociocultural and historical context.

THINKING IN CONTEXT 14.1

1. Describe your family system. How has your development influenced your parents and family members? How might have your parents' and families' development influenced your interactions? Give examples.
2. What are some of the advantages and disadvantages of having siblings? What are the advantages and disadvantages of being an only child? Compare this with your experience.

PARENTING

14.2 Examine parenting, including parenting styles, discipline, conflict, and monitoring.

Relationships between parents and children begin at birth and continue throughout life. How parents and caregivers interact with and discipline their children has a lasting impact on their relationship and the child's overall adjustment.

Parenting Styles

Parenting is a complex process that involves the interplay between parent and child characteristics. Just as children's temperaments and interactional styles vary, parents also display different patterns of behaviors that shape their interactions and relationships with their children. **Parenting style** is the emotional climate of the parent-child relationship, characterized by the degree of warmth, support, and boundaries that parents provide. The parenting style parents adopt influences their efficacy, their relationship with their children, and their children's development. Parenting styles are displayed as enduring sets of parenting behaviors that occur across situations forming childrearing climates, combining warmth and acceptance with varying degrees of limits and rule setting. In a classic series of studies, Diana Baumrind (1971, 2013) examined 103 preschoolers and their families through interviews, home observations, and other measures. She identified several parenting styles and their effects on children (see Figure 14.2).

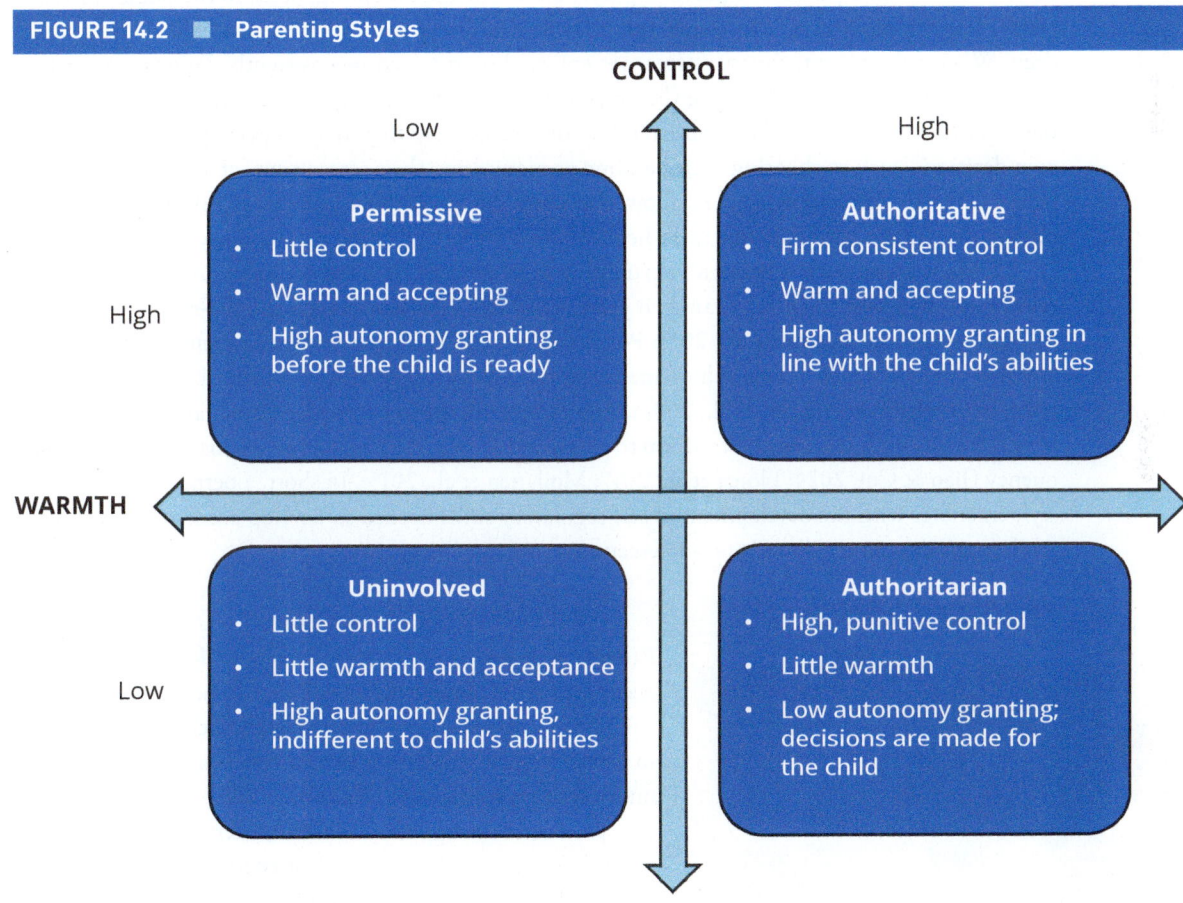

FIGURE 14.2 ■ Parenting Styles

Authoritarian Parenting Style

Baumrind classified the **authoritarian parenting style** as emphasizing behavioral control and obedience over warmth. Authoritarian parents require children to conform to parental rules without question. Rule breaking tends to be accompanied by forceful punishment, such as yelling, threatening, or spanking. Parents with an authoritarian style are less supportive and warm, perhaps even appearing cold and detached. Authoritarian parenting is also characterized by psychological control, not permitting children to think for themselves, explore, or make their own decisions.

Children raised by authoritarian parents tend to be withdrawn, mistrustful, anxious, and angry (Rose et al., 2018). They tend to have difficulty in peer interactions, show aggression and can react with hostility to frustrating peer interactions (Gagnon et al., 2013; D. Li et al., 2024; Marcone et al., 2020). Children reared with harsh, controlling parenting show more behavioral problems and display less prosocial behavior than other children from early childhood through adolescence (Baumrind et al., 2010; Pinquart, 2017; Wong et al., 2021). Furthermore, since parents and children mutually influence each other, harsher parenting tends to lead to more behavior problems in children, which, in turn, tends to increase negative interactions with parents.

In adolescence, authoritarian parenting's emphasis on psychological control and punishment (e.g., "my way or the highway") inhibits healthy adjustment (Milevsky, 2016). Psychological control impedes the development of autonomy and is linked with low self-esteem, depression, low academic competence, and antisocial behavior in adolescence through early adulthood in young people from Africa, the Americas, Asia, Europe, and the Middle East (Bornstein & Putnick, 2018; Chad-Friedman et al., 2023; Zhai et al., 2024). Moreover, adolescents' perceptions of negative or controlling parenting behavior, not parents' own views, predict behavior problems (Dimler et al., 2017).

Permissive Parenting Style

Parents who adopt a **permissive parenting style** are warm and accepting, often to the point of indulgence. They emphasize self-expression and place few rules and behavioral expectations on their children. When rules are set, they are often not enforced or enforced inconsistently. Permissive parents often allow their children to monitor their own behavior, granting autonomy at a young age and without regard for developmental appropriateness. For instance, children may be permitted to make their own decisions, such as choosing their bedtime or monitoring their screen time, at an early age, often before they can. Adolescents may be allowed to come and go without a curfew. Children and adolescents often lack the self-regulation skills necessary to appropriately limit their activity.

Children raised with a permissive parenting style tend to be more socioemotionally immature, rebellious, impulsive, and bossy than their peers. They also show less self-control, self-regulatory capacity, and persistence (Hoeve et al., 2011; Piotrowski et al., 2013). A permissive parenting style places children at risk for poor school achievement and more behavior problems, which can pose long-term risks for development (Jewell et al., 2008). Adolescents reared in permissive homes are more likely to have difficulty with self-control, conform to peers, and show more behavior problems, including delinquency (Jiao & Cui, 2024; Llorca et al., 2017; Moilanen et al., 2015). In short, a permissive parenting style interferes with the development of self-regulatory skills needed to develop academic and behavioral competence in childhood and adolescence.

Uninvolved Parenting Style

Parents with an **uninvolved parenting style** prioritize their needs over those of their children. Parents who are under stress, emotionally detached, or depressed often lack time or energy to devote to their children, which can place them at risk for an uninvolved parenting style (Baumrind, 2012). Uninvolved parents provide little support or warmth, exert minimal control, and fail to recognize their children's need for affection and direction. Children reared in neglectful homes show less knowledge about emotions than children raised with other parenting styles (Sullivan et al., 2010). Uninvolved parenting can negatively affect children's cognitive, emotional, social, and even physical development. Children reared with an uninvolved style tend to engage in less physical activity and report more poor health than those reared by other styles (Watson et al., 2023). At its extreme, uninvolved parenting can take the form of rejection and neglect, forms of child maltreatment that are associated with emotional and behavioral problems (Zhang & Wang, 2023).

Uninvolved parenting can make children feel invisible. Extreme forms of uninvolved parenting constitute neglect.

MoMo Productions/ Getty Images

Authoritative Parenting Style

The most positive developmental outcomes are associated with what Baumrind called the **authoritative parenting style**. Authoritative parents are both warm and sensitive to children's needs while also being firm in their expectations that children conform to appropriate standards of behavior. They exert reasonable control while engaging their children in discussions about standards and granting them developmentally appropriate levels of autonomy, permitting decision making appropriate to the children's abilities (Baumrind, 2013). When rules are violated, authoritative parents explain what went wrong and impose limited, developmentally appropriate punishments closely tied to the misdeed. Authoritative parents value and foster their children's individuality. They encourage their children to have their own interests, opinions, and decisions while still controlling their children's behavior. Authoritative parents' use of open discussion, joint decision making, and firm but fair limit-setting helps children and adolescents feel valued, respected, and encouraged to think for themselves (Hart et al., 2019).

Children raised by authoritative parents tend to display confidence, self-esteem, and curiosity and score higher on measures of social skills, prosocial behavior, executive function, and academic achievement (Ali et al., 2023; Helm et al., 2020; Lavrič & Naterer, 2020; Wong et al., 2021). The positive effects of authoritative parenting continue into adolescence. In adolescents of diverse ethnic and socioeconomic groups, and in countries around the world, authoritative parenting fosters autonomy, self-reliance, self-esteem, academic competence, and a positive view of the value of work (Bornstein & Putnick, 2018). Parental support and acceptance are associated with reduced levels of depression, psychological disorders, and behavior problems in adolescence (Pinquart, 2017). Even in households where parents have different parenting styles, authoritative parenting in at least one parent predicts positive adjustment and buffers the negative outcomes associated with other styles in adolescence (Hoeve et al., 2011; McKinney & Renk, 2011). Authoritative parents' use of open discussion, joint decision making, and firm but fair limit setting helps adolescents feel valued, respected, and encouraged to think for themselves. In addition, a 3-year study of 9th- and 11th-grade students found that both maternal and paternal authoritative styles are associated with greater sibling support 3 years later compared with authoritarian styles (Milevsky, 2022).

As children grow older parents must adjust their parenting techniques to match their children's increased ability to reason and desire for independence. Authoritative parents tend to use less direct management and instead begin to share power—for example, by guiding and monitoring children's behavior from a distance, communicating expectations, and allowing children to be in charge of moment-to-moment decision making (Hawes & Tully, 2020; Lamb & Lewis, 2015). Parents increasingly use reasoning with older children by pointing out the consequences of their behavior, explaining how they affect others, and appealing to the child's self-concept and sense of values (Hawes & Tully, 2020). This approach helps children understand the reasons behind rules, take responsibility for their actions, and become more independent while fostering close relationships with parents.

Discipline

Discipline encompasses the methods parents use to teach and socialize their children toward acceptable behavior. Learning theory can account for the effect of parents' discipline strategies on children's behavior. Specifically, the consequences of a child's behavior, whether reinforced or punished, influence their future behavior. For reinforcement to be effective, it must be viewed as rewarding to the child and can be either tangible, such as money or candy, or intangible, such as attention or a smile. Consistency is essential for changing a child's behavior. Effective reinforcement is administered consistently when the desired behavior occurs. Over time, the reinforcement becomes internalized by the child and the behavior itself becomes reinforcing and associated with pleasurable feelings and, eventually, a positive sense of accomplishment.

Physical Punishment

Physical punishment, also known as corporal punishment or spanking, is prohibited in 60 countries (Grogan-Kaylor et al., 2018, 2021). However, it remains legal but controversial in many parts of the world, with many parents reporting that spanking is acceptable, appropriate, and sometimes necessary (Chiocca, 2017; Dorn, 2023). Most adults in the United States report being spanked as children without harm, and 80% of parents report spanking their young children (Gershoff et al., 2018). Why is spanking a contentious issue if it occurs in many cultures?

Spanking has been shown to have negative effects on children. Research suggests that physical punishment tends to increase children's compliance only temporarily, if at all (Heilmann et al., 2021). Punishment often directs children's attention to themselves and their feelings rather than how their behavior affects others, increasing children's emphasis on themselves rather than empathetic and prosocial motives (McCord, 1996). It can also promote the very behavior that parents aim to stop, because punishment models the use of aggression to resolve conflict and other problems, teaching children that might makes right (Sege & Siegel, 2018). Longitudinal studies have linked physical punishment to behavior problems, internalizing problems, such as anxiety and depression, and low self-esteem in childhood and adolescence, as well as mental health problems that can last into adulthood (Heilmann et al., 2021; Mendez et al., 2016; Ward et al., 2021).

Physical punishment can damage parent-child interactions and relationships (Laible et al., 2020; Sege & Siegel, 2018). When a parent loses self-control and yells, screams, or hits a child, the child may feel helpless, become fearful of the parent, avoid them, and become passive. In one recent study, corporal punishment at age 3 was linked to a decline in the quality of parent-child interaction by age 5, suggesting that physical punishment may erode the parent-child relationship (Laible et al., 2020). Moreover, a recent study following children from age 3 to 5 found that spanking had nearly identical effects as adverse childhood experiences on externalizing behavior, leading the scientists to conclude that physical punishment is a source of early life stress, similar to child maltreatment (Ma et al., 2021). Given this similarity, experts have concluded that parents should avoid physical punishment (Gershoff et al., 2018).

What can parents do about their children's undesirable behavior? There are alternatives to physical punishment that can effectively reduce undesirable behavior in children. Nonphysical punishment, such as time out from reinforcement, also called *time out*, can be effective, in small doses and within specific contexts. Time out involves removing a child from the situation and its rewarding stimuli, including social contact, for a short period (Dadds & Tully, 2019). Implemented correctly, time out effectively reduces inappropriate behavior (Lawrence et al., 2021; Morawska & Sanders, 2011).

To be effective, punishment should occur immediately after the dangerous or undesirable behavior, be administered calmly and consistently, be clearly connected to the behavior, and be explained to the child (Lieneman & McNeil, 2023). The purpose of punishment is to deter the child from engaging in dangerous or unwanted behavior, to make them comply but not to make them feel guilty. Effective punishment is administered calmly, privately, within the context of a warm parent-child relationship, and it is accompanied by an explanation so that the child understands the reason for the punishment (Baumrind, 2013).

It is worth noting that even experts debate the effects of mild "nonabusive" spanking. Some argue that it may be effective as a "backup method" when young children fail to cooperate with milder tactics, such as time out (Larzelere et al., 2019). Despite estimates that the majority of parents spank their children, recent evidence with a sample of over 16,000 parents suggests that the use of spanking has declined dramatically over the past 25 years (see Figure 14.3; Mehus & Patrick, 2021). These findings are encouraging, but pediatricians and developmental scientists agree that parents can benefit from education about alternative discipline strategies.

Inductive Discipline

Inductive discipline, methods that use reasoning, are effective alternatives to spanking in changing a child's behavior (AAP Committee on Psychosocial Aspects of Child and Family Health, 1998; Lawrence et al., 2021). Examples of inductive methods include helping children find and use words to express their feelings. Another inductive method is to give children choices (e.g., peas or carrots), permitting them to feel some control over the situation and be empowered. Parents who use inductive techniques model effective conflict resolution and help children to become aware of the consequences of their actions; the use of inductive discipline is part of the authoritative parent's repertoire (Lawrence

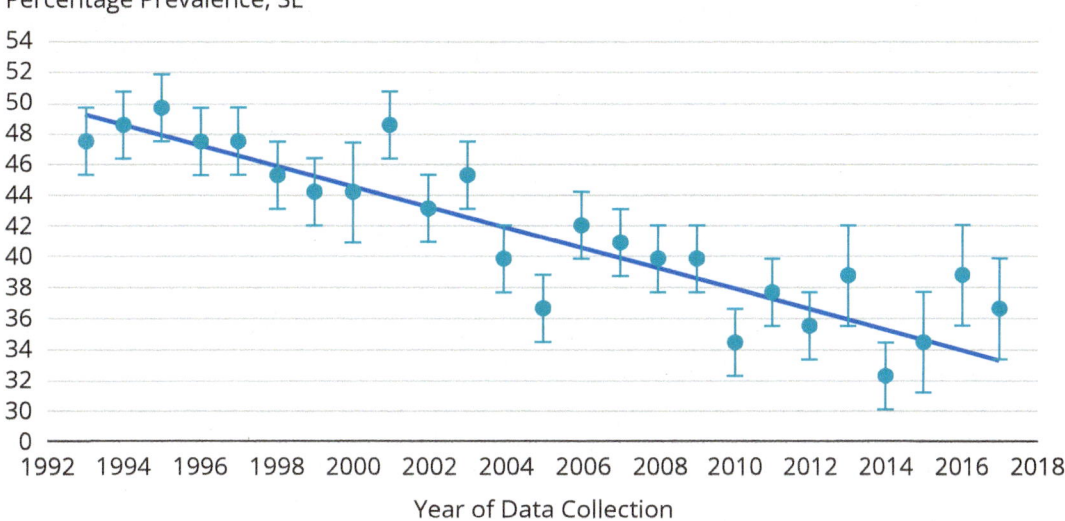

FIGURE 14.3 ■ Trend in Prevalence of Spanking Within the Past Year Among 35-Year-Old Parents From 1993 to 2017

Source: Mehus, C. J., & Patrick, M. E. (2021). Prevalence of spanking in US national samples of 35-year-old parents from 1993 to 2017. *JAMA pediatrics*, *175*(1), 92–94. https://doi.org/10.1001/jamapediatrics.2020.2197

et al., 2021). Inductive methods are very effective in helping children internalize rules and standards and adopt positive social skills (Choe et al., 2013; Tompkins & Villaruel, 2021). One study of 54 African American kindergarten-aged children from an inner city found that those whose mothers used inductive reasoning were more likely to see that hurting other people is not just a question of breaking the rules, but is wrong, as compared with children whose mothers reported taking away privileges (Jagers et al., 1996).

Developmental professionals agree that discipline that relies on a warm parent-child relationship, clear expectations, communication, and limit-setting is most effective in modifying children's behavior.

Culture, Context, and Parenting

The strategies parents use to control children's behavior vary depending on factors such as the parent's and child's personalities, the child's age, the parent-child relationship, the parent's knowledge about child development, and cultural customs and expectations (Vally & El Hichami, 2020). There is no single way to parent. Instead, there are many cultural variations in parenting, and the effectiveness of disciplinary techniques may differ by cultural context (Cauce, 2008).

Cross Cultural Comparisons

Parents' beliefs about how to promote children's positive adjustment vary across cultures, and what is considered adaptive in one culture may be viewed as maladaptive in another (Olson et al., 2019). For example, European American mothers tend to stress the importance of building self-esteem in their preschoolers, whereas Taiwanese mothers tend to describe self-esteem as undesirable because it may evoke maladaptive behaviors such as stubbornness, rudeness, or poor self-control (Miller & Fung, 2012; Miller et al., 2002). North American parents permit and encourage children to express emotions, including anger, while Japanese parents encourage children to refrain from displaying strong emotions (Zahn-Waxler et al., 1996). Cultures that value independence, assertiveness, and expressiveness, such as the United States and Canada, tend to view shy, inhibited behavior as a sign of social incompetence (Rubin et al., 2009). In contrast, cultures that emphasize social harmony, such as China, Indonesia, and Korea, tend to view inhibited behavior and emotional restraint positively, seek to promote inhibited behavior, and associate such behavior with positive adjustment in children (Chen, 2018; E. H.

Lee et al., 2013). Cultural differences in beliefs about children's desirable characteristics can motivate cultural differences in parenting behavior (Bornstein et al., 2018).

Chinese parents tend to describe their parenting as relatively controlling and do not emphasize individuality and choice (Chao, 2001). They are directive and view exerting control as a way of teaching children self-control and encouraging high achievement (Huntsinger et al., 1998). Yet most Chinese parents couple the emphasis on control with warmth (Xu et al., 2005). Authoritative parenting is associated with emotion regulation, cognitive and social competence, and fewer behavioral problems in young children from collectivist cultures, such as Indonesia and China, and individualist cultures, such as Australia and the United States (Haslam et al., 2020).

Although it is commonly believed that the effects of physical punishment are determined by cultural differences in its acceptability, a recent analysis found that harsh parenting was associated with negative outcomes in children from the Arabian Peninsula, East and South-East Asia, Latin America, North Africa, North America, and Western Europe (Pinquart, 2021). In addition, authoritarian parenting and power assertive discipline are associated with difficulties in emotion regulation, poor social competence, anxiety, poor behavior, and poor academic achievement in children and adolescents of diverse cultures and countries, including Australia, China, the European Union, 25 countries in Africa, and the United States (Cuartas, 2021, 2022; Ward et al., 2021).

North American Children

Is strict control always harmful to North American children? Research has identified a disciplinary style common in African American families that combines strict parental control with affection (Tamis-LeMonda et al., 2009). This approach emphasizes the importance of obedience and strict control in helping children develop self-control. African American parents who use controlling strategies coupled with warmth tend to raise children who are more cognitively mature and socially competent than their peers raised using other approaches. This difference is particularly apparent in children reared in low-income homes and communities, where vigilant, strict parenting enhances children's safety (Silveira et al., 2021; Weis & Toolis, 2010).

While physical discipline is associated with behavioral problems in European American children, it appears to protect some African American children from conduct problems during adolescence (Lansford et al., 2004). The warmth and affection provided by strict but warm African American parents buffer some of the negative consequences of strictness (McLoyd & Smith, 2002; Stacks et al., 2009). How children perceive parental discipline and intention is crucial in determining its effect. Children tend to evaluate parental behavior in light of their culture and the emotional tone of the relationship. African American children and children in low-income homes reared by strict but warm parents often see this discipline style as a sign of concern for their well-being (Y.-E. Lee et al., 2016).

However, the effects of culture and neighborhood context on parenting behaviors in African American families in the United States are challenging to disentangle, as African American families are disproportionately represented in disadvantaged neighborhoods (McLoyd et al., 2019). Does strict discipline embody cultural beliefs about parenting, or is it a response to raising children in a disadvantaged environment? Parental perceptions of danger and their own distress influence how they parent (Cuellar et al., 2013; Murry et al., 2008). Therefore, parenting behaviors, including discipline, must be considered within a cultural and environmental context, because there is no one-size-fits-all approach to parenting,

Parent–Adolescent Relationships

Adolescence marks a change in parent-child relationships. As they advance cognitively and develop a more complicated sense of self, adolescents strive for autonomy, the ability to make and carry out their own decisions, and they begin to rely less on parents. They also can demonstrate better self-understanding and more rational decision making and problem solving, creating a foundation for parents to treat adolescents less like children and grant them more decision-making responsibility. The parenting challenge of adolescence is to offer increasing opportunities for adolescents to develop and practice autonomy while providing protection from danger and the consequences of poor decisions (Kobak et al., 2017). Parents may doubt their own importance to their adolescent children, but a large body of research shows that parents play a critical role in adolescent development alongside that of peers.

Conflict

Conflict between parents and adolescents tends to increase in early adolescence as adolescents seek autonomy and recognize that their parents are fallible and capable of mistakes (Meeus, 2016). Adolescents report having three or four conflicts or disagreements with parents over a typical day (Adams & Laursen, 2007). Most of these conflicts are mundane and center around household responsibilities, privileges, relationships, curfews, cleaning of the adolescent's bedroom, choices of media, or music volume (Huey et al., 2017). Conflict tends to peak in middle adolescence and decline from middle to late adolescence and emerging adulthood as young people become more independent (Branje, 2018; Smetana & Rote, 2019).

There is continuity in parenting and relationships from childhood to adolescence and parent-adolescent interactions are reciprocal, with parents and adolescents influencing each other over time. For instance, daily diaries by adolescents reveal that anger both predicts conflict with parents and is also a consequence of conflict (LoBraico et al., 2020). As parents engage in more negative interactions, adolescents focus more on angry interpersonal interactions and less on happy interactions (Lucas-Thompson et al., 2020).

Age-related shifts in conflict are supported by research with diverse samples, with some small differences (Smetana & Rote, 2019). Some research suggests that conflicts develop earlier and are more frequent among European Americans as compared with adolescents of other ethnicities and races (Smetana, 2011). Contextual factors may contribute to these differences, such as in cultural values, including individualism, collectivism, family solidarity, and respect for elders, as well as neighborhood and community influences, including resources, SES, and privilege.

A common source of conflict for adolescents from immigrant families concerns acculturation, specifically mismatches between adolescents and parents (Fuligni & Tsai, 2015). Research with families of Latino and Asian heritage suggests that parent-adolescent gaps in acculturation, when it reflects clashes in values, may lead to conflicts over everyday issues. In one study of Arab American adolescents, the larger the acculturation gap between parents and adolescents (as perceived by adolescents), the greater the conflict (Goforth et al., 2015).

Frequent arguments charged with negative emotions are harmful to adolescents. Parent-adolescent conflict is associated with internalizing problems, such as depression; externalizing problems, such as aggression and delinquency; and academic and social problems, including social withdrawal and poor peer relationships, in Black, Latino, Asian, and White adolescents (Hofer et al., 2013; Moreno et al., 2017; Skinner & McHale, 2016; Weymouth et al., 2016).

Although severe conflict is harmful, within the context of warm parental relationships, some conflict is conducive to adolescent development, helping adolescents learn to regulate emotions and resolve conflicts (Branje, 2018; Silva et al., 2020). Adolescent-parent conflict can be distressing to adolescents, but some degree of conflict is associated with better adjustment than either no conflict or very frequent conflict (Smetana & Rote, 2019). Disagreements have a purpose: transforming adolescent parent relationships from hierarchical in early adolescence to more symmetrical in late adolescence (Meeus, 2016). Despite the increase in conflicts, most adolescents and parents continue to have warm, close, and communicative relationships characterized by love and respect (Hart et al., 2019).

Parents' task in raising adolescents is to balance autonomy granting with guidance. Authoritative parenting best accomplishes this feat because it is characterized by warmth, support, and limits. Authoritative parents' use of open discussion, joint decision making, and firm but fair limit setting helps adolescents feel valued, respected, and encouraged to think for themselves (Romm & Metzger, 2021). Generally, emotional support by parents tends to increase and psychological control continues to decline during emerging adulthood (Desjardins & Leadbeater, 2017; Smetana & Rote, 2019)

Monitoring

Effective parenting involves balancing granting adolescents' autonomy with protecting them. One way to achieve this balance is through **parental monitoring**, which refers to parents being aware of their child's whereabouts and companions. Parental monitoring coupled with autonomy support is associated with positive adjustment and well-being, including academic achievement and fewer risk behaviors, such as early sexual initiation, substance use, and delinquent activity in youth across ethnicity and SES (Lopez-Tamayo et al., 2016; Merrin et al., 2019; Rodríguez-Meirinhos et al., 2020). Adolescents communicate more openly, and monitoring strategies are most effective within the context of warm family relationships (Kapetanovic & Skoog, 2021).

Adolescents living in poor, high-risk communities may benefit from more active and restrictive forms of parental monitoring, such as daily discussions about activities and behavioral limit setting, which may protect them from community dangers (Bendezú et al., 2018; Burton & Jarrett, 2000). However, when parents monitor too closely and restrict autonomy, such as monitoring in ways that adolescents perceive as intrusive or controlling, adolescents are likely to conceal their activities from their parents, lie, and continue to do so over time (Baudat et al., 2020; Rote & Smetana, 2016). Some mild concealment, white lies, and partial truths may serve a developmental purpose, helping adolescents establish autonomy (Lionetti et al., 2019). While adolescents are entitled to their own thoughts and increasing privacy, secrecy is associated with behavior problems including substance use and delinquency (Baudat et al., 2022; Marceau et al., 2020). One cross-cultural study of nearly 1,100 young adolescents from 12 cultural groups in nine countries including China, Colombia, Italy, Jordan, Kenya, Philippines, Sweden, Thailand, and the United States found that adolescent secrecy is associated with externalizing problems in all cultures (Kapetanovic et al., 2020). Generally speaking, adolescents with positive relationships with parents conceal less and those with negative relationships conceal more (Dykstra et al., 2020; Rote et al., 2020).

Effective parental monitoring is accompanied by warmth and is balanced with respect for adolescents' autonomy and privacy. But the specific practices that comprise effective parental monitoring change as adolescents grow older. Parents and adolescents tend to have different views of parental monitoring, with adolescents reporting greater parental requests for information and exerting more control (De Los Reyes et al., 2019; Ingoglia et al., 2021). Adolescents' and parents' perceptions of parental monitoring remain mismatched through late adolescence, with parents, but not adolescents, reporting declines in parental requests for information from adolescents (Lionetti et al., 2019). From middle to late adolescence, parental knowledge and control naturally decline as adolescents establish a private sphere, spend more time out of the home, and disclose less (Masche, 2010; M.-T. Wang et al., 2011).

THINKING IN CONTEXT 14.2

1. What challenges do parents face in modifying their parenting styles as infants grow into children and children into adolescents?
2. Parents and children influence each other dynamically. Provide examples of this process, how children influence their parents and are also influenced by their parents. How do parent-child interactions change over childhood into adolescence?
3. Parent-adolescent relationships are commonly viewed as, at best, strained and, at worst, hostile. Compare these popular views of parent-adolescent relationships to the research on parenting.

FAMILY CONSTELLATIONS

14.3 Compare the various forms families take.

We are all embedded in families, by birth, adoption, or choice, that influence our development. In earlier generations, it was assumed that most families conformed to a traditional model composed of a husband, wife, and one or more children born to them. Since the turn of the 21st century, however, we have increasingly recognized that families may take many forms, as we now explore.

Same-Sex Parented Families

About 15% of same-sex couples raise minor children (23% of lesbian and 7% of gay couples), compared with 39% of different-sex couples (U.S. Census Bureau, 2022). Most children raised by LGBT parents are the biological children of these parents (Taylor, 2020), though LGBT parents are more likely to adopt children than heterosexual parents (Figure 14.4). Just as same-sex couples have only recently won the right to marry (in 2015), it was only in 2017 that joint adoption by same-sex couples became legal in all U.S. states (Movement Advancement Project, 2018). Before this ruling, most U.S. states permitted adoption by LGBT single adults, but few permitted same-sex couples to jointly adopt (J. A. Raley et al., 2013).

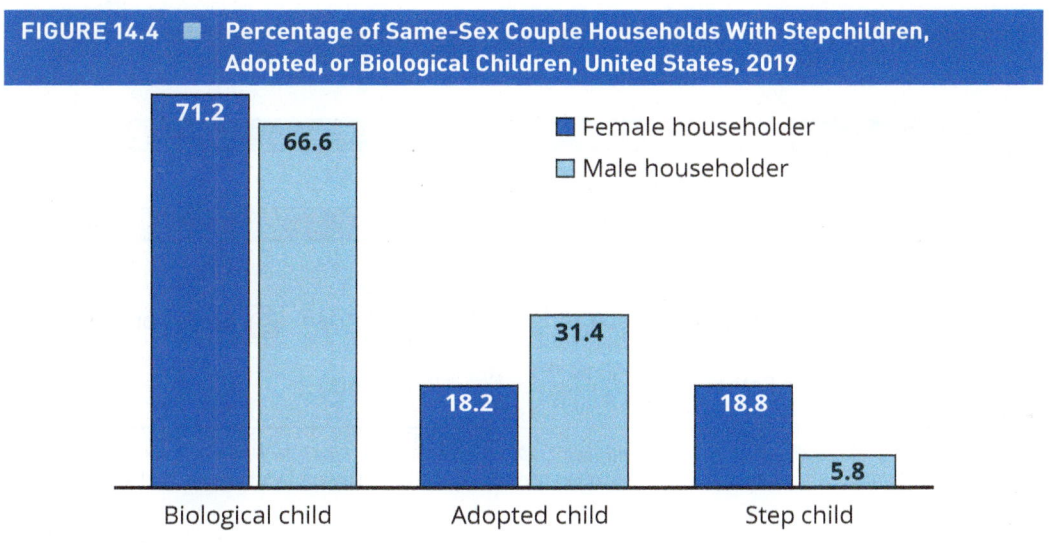

FIGURE 14.4 ■ Percentage of Same-Sex Couple Households With Stepchildren, Adopted, or Biological Children, United States, 2019

Source: Taylor, D. (2020). *Fifteen percent of same-sex couples have children in their household.* America Counts: Stories Behind the Numbers. U.S. Census Bureau. https://www.census.gov/library/stories/2020/09/fifteen-percent-of-same-sex-couples-have-children-in-their-household.html

More than three decades of research conducted in the United States, the United Kingdom, Belgium, and the Netherlands has failed to reveal important differences in the adjustment or development of children and adolescents reared by same-sex couples compared with those reared by other couples (Farr et al., 2019; Fedewa et al., 2014; Patterson, 2017). Specifically, children and adolescents raised by lesbian mothers or gay fathers do not differ from other children on measures of social competence and emotional development, including empathy and emotional regulation (H. Bos & Gartrell, 2020; Farr, 2017; Imrie & Golombok, 2020; K. A. Simon & Farr, 2022). Instead, some studies have suggested that children raised by gay and lesbian parents show higher academic achievement and show fewer social and behavioral problems and lower levels of aggression than other children (Kabátek & Perales, 2021; Mazrekaj et al., 2020; Suárez et al., 2023).

Moreover, children raised by lesbian mothers and gay fathers show similar patterns of gender identity and gender role development as children raised by heterosexual parents—they are not more likely to identify as gay or lesbian in adulthood (H. M. W. Bos et al., 2018; Farr et al., 2019; Schumm & Crawford, 2019). Researchers have concluded that a family's social and economic resources, the strength of the relationships among members of the family, and the presence of stigma are far more important variables than parental gender or sexual orientation in affecting children's development and well-being (Farr, 2017; Imrie & Golombok, 2020).

One-Parent Families

About 20% of U.S. children under age 18 live with one parent, most commonly with their mother (Westrick-Payne & Wiborg, 2021). Figure 14.5 shows children's living arrangements, by race and ethnicity. Black children are disproportionally likely to live in a one-parent home with their mother (42%) compared with Hispanic (21%), White (11%), and Asian children (7%).

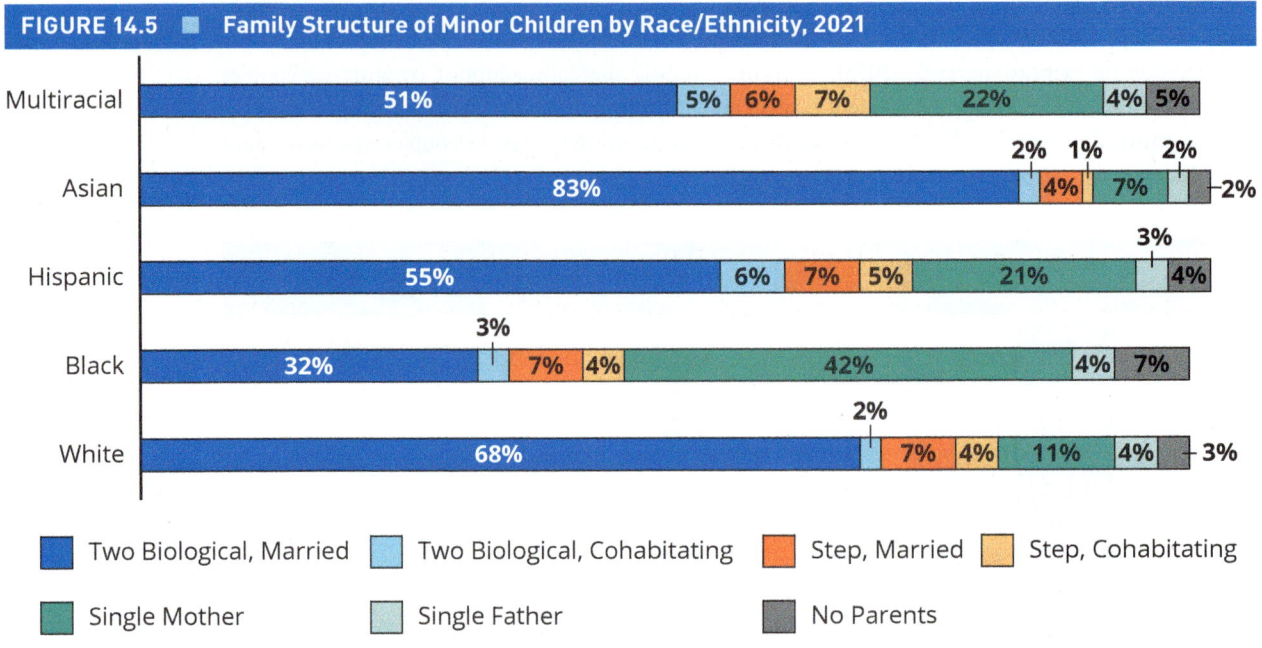

FIGURE 14.5 ■ Family Structure of Minor Children by Race/Ethnicity, 2021

Source: Westrick-Payne, K. K., & Wiborg, C. E. (2021). *Children's family structure, 2021. Family Profiles, FP-21-26.* National Center for Family & Marriage Research. https://www.bgsu.edu/ncfmr/resources/data/family-profiles/payne-wiborg-children-family-structure-2021-fp-21-26.html

There are various paths to creating a one-parent family, such as divorce, death, or having never married. The correlates of being raised in a one-parent home therefore vary. Some children in one-parent homes show more physical, mental health, and behavioral problems, and others show similar emotional and behavioral adjustment as those reared in two-parent homes (Kroese et al., 2020; Lut et al., 2021; Waldfogel et al., 2010; Zadeh, 2020). These diverse findings are likely related to the parenting stress that may accompany single parenthood, particularly in low socioeconomic contexts (Peverill et al., 2021; Reiss et al., 2019). Children in one-parent mother homes, regardless of ethnicity, are disproportionately likely to live in poverty (Cancian & Meyer, 2018; Wimer et al., 2021). Poverty rates are also high for one-parent father families. Children in low SES and poor homes are more likely to experience hunger, have poor access to health care, attend schools with fewer resources, experience residential instability, and live in unsafe neighborhoods with few social connections. Poverty poses risks to all children, but children in one-parent families may have fewer connections with adults who can help them adjust.

It is important to recognize that differences in adjustment between children raised by one or two parents are small; most children raised in one-parent homes are well adjusted (Lamb, 2012; Zadeh, 2020). In addition, there are more differences among children in one-parent homes than between children in one-parent homes and two-parent homes. Many of the differences associated with family structure are reduced or disappear when researchers take SES into account, suggesting that differences in child well-being across family types are strongly influenced by family income, access to resources, and the stresses that accompany economic difficulties (Ryan et al., 2015).

Around 25% of children under age 18 live with a single parent, most commonly with their mother. Children raised in one-parent households are generally well-adjusted.

Andrew Holbrooke/ Contributor/ Getty Images

Increasingly women become single parents by choice. Children reared by single-by-choice parents tend to live in higher socioeconomic homes than other children reared by single parents—and they tend to experience positive adjustment and few problems (Golombok, 2017; Imrie & Golombok, 2020). Parenting stress and success are influenced by access to economic and social resources (Jones et al., 2021). Conclusions about one-parent families are also complicated because frequently a parent's cohabiting partner also occupies the home, with social, caregiving, and financial implications.

Cohabiting Families

There are many kinds of families, and not all are formed through marriage. An estimated 40% of children will spend some time in a cohabiting-parent family before they reach age 12 (Manning, 2015). Unmarried cohabiting couples tend to have shorter, less stable relationships than married couples (Smock & Schwartz, 2020). Children living in cohabiting households are much more likely to be exposed to family instability, including parental separation, conflict in the home, and transitions in family life than children of married parents, which can influence their adjustment (Cavanagh & Fomby, 2019). However, cohabiting couples with high-quality relationships tend to coparent effectively (Broderick et al., 2019).

Children of unmarried cohabiting parents who have close caring relationships with them and whose union is stable develop as well as their counterparts whose parents' marriages are stable (Rose-Greenland & Smock, 2013). But there is little research on children's outcomes. A recent study of children in the UK found that children in cohabiting families showed more behavior problems than those in married families, but the differences were minor (Jarvis et al., 2023).

On average, children raised in cohabiting-parent families have economic situations that are better than those of many children in one-parent families (e.g., higher parental education and family earnings) but more economically stressful than those reared in married two-parent families (e.g., greater poverty and food insecurity) (Kennedy & Fitch, 2012; Manning, 2015). The effect of cohabitation on children likely varies with family SES and with contextual norms.

Divorced and Divorcing Families

Since 1960, divorce rates have tripled in many industrialized nations. In the United States, the divorce rate has declined over the past three decades from its peak of 5.3 per 1,000 people in 1981 to 2.4 in 2022, but this rate is high compared to other countries (National Center for Health Statistics, 2015, 2024).

For many decades, it was assumed that divorce caused significant and irreparable harm to children. Instead, most researchers today take a neutral stance, viewing divorce as a common transition that many children experience. Divorce is associated with internalizing and externalizing problems, but the effects are often small and transient, vary by particular outcome, and do not apply to all children uniformly (Amato & Anthony, 2014; Tullius et al., 2022; Weaver & Schofield, 2015). Variations in child, parent, and family characteristics and contexts influence children's adjustment to parental divorce, but the first year following the divorce tends to be the most challenging for children. Most children show improved social and emotional adjustment within 2 years after the divorce, suggesting that most children of divorce are resilient (Baert & Van der Straeten, 2021; Lamb, 2012). What initially appear to be effects of divorce are instead a complex combination of parent, child, and contextual factors that precede and follow the divorce in conjunction with the divorce itself (Amato & Anthony, 2014; Zemp & Bodenmann, 2018).

Divorce triggers a reconfiguration of family roles, and parenting responsibilities shift disproportionately onto the resident parent. After divorce, children most often live with their mothers and experience a drop in income that influences their access to resources and opportunities (Van Winkle & Leopold, 2021). One-parent-headed households often move to more affordable housing, causing additional changes in children's school, community, and circle of friends, reducing children's access to social support and opportunities to play with friends. Custodial parents might also increase the hours they work, leading to less contact with their children. These changes contribute to inconsistencies in family routines, activities, and parental monitoring before, during, and after the divorce. High-quality family relationships, including positive interactions with the noncustodial parent and low levels of parent-parent conflict, can buffer children against these stressors (Bastaits & Mortelmans, 2016; Cao et al., 2022; Weaver & Schofield, 2015).

Divorce tends to be preceded by a period of uncertainty and tension, often characterized by increases in conflict between parents that may continue for several years after the divorce (R. K. Raley & Sweeney, 2020). In fact, harmful family processes, such as parental conflict, poor parent-child interactions, and ineffective parenting strategies, may precede parental divorce by as much as 8 to 12 years (Drapeau et al., 2009; Potter, 2010). These processes take a toll on children's emotional and psychological health. Chronic exposure to parental conflict is associated with increased physiological arousal, an elevated stress response, and poorer adjustment (Davidson et al., 2014; Davies & Martin, 2014; Van Eldik et al., 2020). In turn, children's difficulties adapting, such as behavior problems, can increase parental conflict (Drapeau et al., 2009). Longitudinal research following children of married parents has found that children whose parents later divorce show many of the problems typical of children of divorce, such as anxiety, depression, delinquency, and poor academics, long before the divorce takes place (Cao et al., 2022; R. K. Raley & Sweeney, 2020). But not all parents display high levels of conflict. When researchers take into account the quality of parenting and children's exposure to conflict, the link between parental divorce and children's adjustment lessens, suggesting that parenting strategies and relationships are more important influences on children's adjustment than divorce (Cao et al., 2022; Sanders & Kirby, 2014).

Blended Families

Between 10% and 15% of U.S. children live in blended families, composed of a biological parent and a nonrelated adult, most commonly a mother and stepfather (Pew Research Center, 2015; Westrick-Payne & Wiborg, 2021). Blended families, also known as stepfamilies or reconstituted families, can involve multiple transitions, including divorce, remarriage, and moves to new homes, neighborhoods, and schools. Both parents and adolescents living in stepfamilies tend to show lower physical health and higher symptoms of distress than those in first-marriage families (Gath, 2022). It can be difficult for blended families to integrate and balance the many relationships among custodial, noncustodial, and stepparents, as well as grandparents and extended family members (Nixon et al., 2016). As stepfamilies become more complex, with increasing numbers of biologically and nonbiologically related individuals, challenges to children's adjustment also increase (S. L. Brown et al., 2015). Navigating relationships with new stepsiblings can be stressful for children (R. K. Raley & Sweeney, 2020).

Children's age influences their adaptation to a blended family. School-age children and adolescents tend to display more difficulties in adjusting to remarriage than younger children (Ganong, Coleman,

& Russell, 2015). Although adjusting to being part of a blended family can entail transitions that may be stressful, most children reared in stepfamilies do not differ from those raised in one-parent families in terms of cognitive, academic, and social outcomes and many are similar to children in first-marriage families (Ganong & Coleman, 2017). Indeed, entering a stepfamily is associated with improved adjustment, especially when stepparents and parents agree on childrearing rules and roles, communicate clearly, and parent with warmth (Ganong, Sanner, et al., 2022). Most blended families experience an increase in income that can also contribute to children's well-being (Ryan et al., 2015).

Overall, blended families adapt more easily, and children show better adjustment when parents work to maintain close bonds with their children and participate in family activities to improve cohesion (Ganong, Coleman, et al., 2022). Stepparents can form closer relationships with children by focusing on building warm friendships and adopting their new roles slowly rather than rushing or forcing relationships (Doodson & Morley, 2006; Zemp & Bodenmann, 2018). Children in stepfamilies fare best when coparents work collaboratively, manage conflicts, keep children out of parental issues, and prioritize children's well-being (Ganong, Sanner, et al., 2022).

Adoptive Families

Over 66,000 children were adopted in the United States in 2019. Adoptions fell during the COVID-19 pandemic to about 58,000 in 2020 and 54,000 in 2021 (Office of the Administration for Children & Families & U.S. Department of Health & Human Services, n.d.). Individuals and other-sex and same-sex couples have similar motives for adopting children as those who raise biological children (Jennings et al., 2014; Malm & Welti, 2010). They include reasons such as valuing family ties, continuing a family line, feeling that parenting is a life task, and the desire for a nurturing relationship with a child (Costa & Tasker, 2018; Goldberg et al., 2012).

Adoption and Child Outcomes

Overall, adoptive children tend to spend more time with their parents and have more educational resources than other children (Zill, 2015). Adoptive children tend to be raised by parents with higher levels of education and income than other children (Drozd et al., 2018). This is partly due to self-selection and partly because of the screening that adoptive parents must undergo before they can adopt. In kindergarten, adopted children do not differ from nonadopted children in reading and math scores (Tan et al., 2017). Yet many adopted children show less engagement in class and tend to have more academic difficulties than other children. Longitudinal research suggests that adoption is associated with lower academic attainment achievement across childhood, adolescence, and emerging adulthood compared with nonadopted comparison groups (A. Brown et al., 2017; Wiley, 2017).

Adopted children may show more behavior problems and adjustment difficulties than their nonadoptive peers, in some cases persisting into adulthood (A. Brown et al., 2017; Palacios & Brodzinsky, 2010). However, findings are mixed. For many children, emotional difficulties are transitional. Some research suggests no differences between adopted and nonadopted children in internalizing problems, such as anxiety and depression (A. Brown et al., 2019; Wiley, 2017). This is supported by longitudinal research that followed adoptees into middle adulthood and showed few differences in psychological distress; differences were accounted for by differences in childhood family circumstances (Sehmi et al., 2020).

Children's experiences prior to adoption, especially any neglect and maltreatment, and their developmental status at the time of adoption influence their short- and long-term adjustment (Balenzano et al., 2018; Blake et al., 2022; Hornfeck et al., 2019). Adopted children tend to experience greater stress prenatally, early in life, before adoption, and during the adoption process, which can influence their long-term adjustment after adoption (Pace et al., 2022; Wiley, 2017). The quality of the relationship between adoptive parents and children influences children's outcomes and the long-term effects of preadoption adversity (Farr & Grotevant, 2019). When children develop close bonds with adoptive parents, they tend to experience reductions in internalizing and externalizing problems and show better emotional understanding and regulation, social competence, and self-esteem (Paine et al., 2021; Schoemaker et al., 2020). These positive effects are also observed in children who have experienced emotional neglect, and those effects hold regardless of the age of adoption (Barone et al., 2017; Brodzinsky et al., 2022).

Transracial Adoption

About one third of adoptions involve a child or adolescent adopted by parents of a different race, with Black children most commonly being adopted by White families (Kalisher et al., 2020). While transracial adoption provides children with loving and stable homes, it also presents them with unique challenges related to belonging to families who do not share their racial and cultural backgrounds. Transracial adoptees may feel different from their family members and friends and may experience an increased risk of social and emotional harm such as bullying, racial and ethnic microaggression, and adoption stigma, as well as academic delays (Branco & Brott, 2018). In particular, racial and adoption microaggressions can negatively affect their sense of identity and well-being (White et al., 2022).

Transracial adoptive children, particularly adolescents, may have limited resources to learn about their heritage and may struggle with ethnic and racial socialization and identity development (Wiley, 2017). Ethnic and racial socialization helps adolescents of color manage discrimination and bias. However, children raised by parents of a different race or ethnicity may encounter few racial models (Castner & Foli, 2022). Adolescents who were adopted by parents of a different race may have difficulty identifying ethnic-racial identity alternatives, and the process of identity exploration may be slower for them than for nonadopted adolescents of color. Despite this, most transracially adopted individuals eventually develop a firm sense of identity, including ethnic-racial identity (Hrapczynski & Leslie, 2019b). Racial and ethnic socialization and a positive sense of ethnic-racial identity are associated with healthy adoptee outcomes, including a positive sense of self, high self-esteem, and well-being (Montgomery & Jordan, 2018).

Parents can support their adoptive children's ethnic and racial socialization and identity development by exposing them to their racial and ethnic heritage and providing opportunities for them to learn and interact with people who identify with their race and ethnicity (Hrapczynski & Leslie, 2019b). Ethnic-racial identity is supported when parents encourage adolescents' exploration. Research with Mexican American children adopted by White parents suggests that ethnic-racial identity was associated with living in diverse neighborhoods, parents' awareness of the children's culture, and encouragement for children to learn about and participate in their culture (Montgomery & Jordan, 2018). In addition, children and adolescents experience less discrimination distress when parents acknowledge and validate children's experiences, discuss discrimination and racism, and prepare them for bias (Castner & Foli, 2022; Hrapczynski & Leslie, 2019a).

Overall, close relationships with adoptive parents who engage them in cultural activities are positively associated with academic performance (Montgomery et al., 2020). Transracially adopted children show the most positive self-esteem and sense of well-being and the least distress when they integrate their racial and cultural heritage with their adoptive culture rather than denying either their adoptive or racial heritage (Mohanty, 2015).

Grandparent-Headed Families

About 3% of children are raised by their grandparents (U. S. Census Bureau, 2024). Children raised in grandparent-headed households are disproportionally likely to be Black, Native American, and Hispanic (Dolbin-MacNab & O'Connell, 2021; Joshi & Lebrun-Harris, 2022). Grandparents often obtain custody of their grandchildren in response to parental absence or incapacitation from physical and mental illness, substance abuse, incarceration, or death (Hayslip et al., 2017).

Children reared by their grandparents often have experienced threats to their development, such as witnessing or being victimized by violence, having a parent incarcerated or in jail, or living with someone with a mental illness or substance use problem (G. C. Smith et al., 2024). These experiences are traumatic to both grandparent and child, posing risks for adjustment to both. Children living in grandparent-headed households tend to show more physical health conditions, such as asthma, and overall poor health, as well as higher rates of developmental conditions including ADHD, learning disabilities, and speech and language disorders than their peers (Rapoport et al., 2020; Xu et al., 2022).

Emotional and behavioral problems, including anxiety, depression, anger issues, and disruptive behavior, are common as well as overall poor well-being (Y. Wang et al., 2024).

Contextual factors increase the likelihood of and pose challenges to custodial grandparenting. Nearly half (45%) of grandparent-headed households live in poverty (Carlson, 2021). Grandparent-headed households tend to experience higher rates of food insufficiency, less education, and higher rate of unemployment and are more likely to rely on public insurance than other households (Joshi & Lebrun-Harris, 2022).

Grandparent caregiving is not part of typical adult development and can be particularly stressful for adults (Hayslip & Blumenthal, 2016). Grandparent caregivers may grapple with their own losses, including grief and anger toward the parent, heightened stress, and financial difficulties. They tend to suffer more mental and physical health problems than their peers who do not care for grandchildren, especially when their grandchildren experience emotional and behavioral problems (Doley et al., 2015; Whitley & Fuller-Thomson, 2018). Despite these challenges, custodial grandparents show similar interactions with children, emotional support, and coping skills as custodial parents (Joshi & Lebrun-Harris, 2022; Rapoport et al., 2020). Grandparents who feel that they have a social support network to turn to for emotional and physical assistance tend to show better adjustment, fewer problems, and a greater sense of well-being and life satisfaction (Hayslip et al., 2017; Mendoza et al., 2020)

THINKING IN CONTEXT 14.3

1. Considering the many forms families take, identify common factors that contribute to children and adolescent well-being and other positive outcomes across all types of families.
2. How do the experiences of adopted children differ from those of nonadopted children? What are some of the unique issues faced by children in transracial adoptive families, and how can parents support their children's ethnic and racial identity development? What strategies can help children cope with the potential social and emotional risks associated with transracial adoption?
3. What are some of the issues faced by children growing up in one-parent families, and how do they vary across different socioeconomic contexts?
4. How do cohabiting families differ from married families, and what are the implications of these differences for children's well-being and development? What are some factors that contribute to the stability of cohabiting relationships, and how do they affect children's experiences?

CHALLENGES FOR FAMILIES

14.4 Analyze the challenges faced by families with incarcerated, deployed, or migrant members, as well as the impact of the COVID-19 pandemic on families.

Many children face circumstances within their families that can impede healthy development. While all children and families experience some transitions, such as relocating to new neighborhoods and schools, some deal with more serious ones. This section examines several family circumstances that pose challenges for children's and adolescents' development, including parental incarceration, deployment, migrant status, and the COVID-19 pandemic.

Parental Incarceration

By age 14, about 1 in 14 U.S. children experiences a resident parent leaving for jail or prison (Poehlmann-Tynan & Turney, 2020). Children with parents who are incarcerated tend to show more psychological and behavioral problems, such as anxiety, symptoms of trauma, health vulnerabilities, antisocial behavior, and delinquency (Kjellstrand et al., 2020; Luk et al., 2023; Poehlmann-Tynan & Turney, 2020; Wildeman et al., 2018).

Children of color and low-income children are disproportionately likely to experience parental incarceration, and their adjustment to parental incarceration is associated with the contextual factors that are intertwined with race and SES (Bruns & Lee, 2019). Children with incarcerated parents often experience multiple co-occurring adversities before and after incarceration, including family instability, parental substance use, parenting stress, poverty, residential instability, and homelessness (Arditti & Johnson, 2020; Muentner et al., 2023; Wildeman et al., 2018). The circumstances surrounding the incarceration—such as witnessing criminal activity, arrest, or judicial proceedings—may be traumatic, posing further risks to children's well-being (Metcalfe et al., 2023). Children with incarcerated parents may experience stigma, and shame may impede their social interactions, relationships, and learning at school, with peers and in the community (Turney & Goodsell, 2018).

Within the home context, incarceration increases economic hardship and strains family processes, with implications for parenting. Parental incarceration is stressful for caregivers, posing mental health risks that may negatively impact parenting (Bradshaw et al., 2021). Resident parents may find children more trying, be more easily irritated or angry, and report more difficulty coping with children, which influences children's health and behavior, potentially creating a negative cycle between parents and children (Jackson et al., 2022). Children with incarcerated parents are more likely to experience harsh punishment and less supervision than their peers (Arditti & Johnson, 2020). They are also more likely to enter the child welfare system (de Haan et al., 2019; Morrison & Drake, 2023). Close nurturing relationships between youth and their caregivers can help children and families adapt to the emotional and social challenges of parental incarceration and promote children's well-being (Luk et al., 2023; P. S. Smith, 2019). Policies and interventions that support children's relationships with parents, including visits that allow one-on-one physical contact while the parent is in prison or jail, parenting support and instruction, and re-entry assistance to aid transitions and support family reunions after the parent's release (Mihalec-Adkins & Shlafer, 2022; Pritzl et al., 2022).

Parental Deployment

Over one third of the 1.6 million active duty military members had children in 2019 (Department of Defense, 2020). A parent's transition to active duty, or deployment, places great demands on the family because it includes parental separation and the risk of injury or death of the service member (Wright et al., 2013). The at-home spouse experiences additional responsibilities and stress as they adjust to single parenting. Children with deployed parents experience unique stressors, such as indirect exposure to and awareness of conflict and violence, and exposure to a family member who may return from combat with physical or psychological injuries (Park, 2011).

Children with a deployed parent tend to experience more emotional and behavioral difficulties than their civilian peers, which tend to increase with deployment length (Cramm et al., 2019; Foran et al., 2017; Mulholland et al., 2020). Since deployment is associated with imminent danger of parental injury or even death, these symptoms likely are due to greater worries (Cunitz et al., 2019). Although anxiety symptoms are common, behavioral problems are more varied and inconsistent (Williamson et al., 2018). Military families tend to experience economic stability and the support of a community of other military families, which aid them in coping with adversity.

Children and families are often surprised that the parent's *return* from active duty and reintegration into the family and community is stressful for children, spouses, and marriages (DeVoe et al., 2020). Children's adjustment is influenced by the length of parental deployment and parental distress—both the at-home spouse and returned parent (Aikins & Aikins, 2024; Williamson et al., 2018). Children are also affected by the reunited couple's interactions and relationships (O'Neal & Mancini, 2021). The returning parent's adjustment influences their spouse and children. For example, physical injuries are associated with poor mental health in children and parents (Brickell et al., 2024; Hisle-Gorman & Susi, 2021).

Studies of service members have documented anger, aggression, and post-traumatic stress disorder (PTSD) symptoms as frequently reported problems for combat veterans returning from war

(Mathewson-Chapman & Chapman, 2020; Russell & Russell, 2019). PTSD symptoms affect parenting behaviors, child discipline and supervision, and involvement and interest in the child's activities, resulting in impaired parent-child interactions (Banneyer et al., 2017; Giff et al., 2019). PTSD symptoms in parents are associated with anxiety, depression, and behavioral problems in children (Cramm et al., 2019; Foran et al., 2017). Successful interventions address the family's stress and aid parent and child adjustment with education about stress, emotion regulation skills, problem solving, skills, and family communication (Creech et al., 2014).

Migrant Families

The Latino population in the United States has experienced significant growth, increasing by 23% over the past decade, which outpaces the nation's overall growth of 7% (Krogstad et al., 2023; Passel et al., 2022). Latinos comprised approximately one fifth of the U.S. population in 2021. While undocumented migration has received much attention in recent years, only about 13% of Latino people in the United States are undocumented (Lonas, 2021). Despite this, a recent study found that nearly a third of U.S.-born Latinos and about half of immigrant Latinos worry that they or someone close to them could be deported, with about 80% of immigrants who are not U.S. citizens and lack a green card reporting this concern (Moslimani, 2022).

Families with undocumented members face a range of complex problems, including severe financial stress, fear of deportation, inadequate access to higher education, and heightened uncertainty about the future (Chavez-Dueñas & Adames, 2022; Talleyrand & Vojtech, 2018). Undocumented families are more likely to live in poverty, but their undocumented status can preclude them from obtaining economic support, such as food stamps. Adults cannot work legally and frequently find work in the underground labor market for low wages and often under exploitative working conditions.

Children and adolescents in homes with undocumented family members often live in fear of the detention and removal of those family members and, perhaps not surprisingly, tend to show higher levels of anxiety and depressive symptoms than other children and adolescents (Kam et al., 2018; Rayburn et al., 2021). The removal of an undocumented parent can have profound consequences for the family. The loss of a parent's income can be economically devastating. Emotional burdens for children and adolescents include coping with distressed relatives while managing their own distress. Older children and adolescents may take on adult roles in the family, such as responsibility for siblings, in the wake of one or more parents' detention and removal. They may be encouraged to stay at home and remain out of school during removal proceedings, potentially influencing their academic achievement and peer relationships. Many develop a fear of authority figures. Feelings of fear, isolation, anger, and hopelessness can interfere with healthy development.

When adolescents are undocumented themselves, the cognitive and socioemotional changes of adolescence often bring a heightened awareness of their undocumented status. Recall from Chapter 11 that ethnic-racial identity, the extent to which adolescents identify with and affirm their ethnic heritage, is a protective factor associated with positive mental health and academic outcomes (Rivas-Drake et al., 2014). For many adolescents, ethnic identity is a valuable resource for coping with acculturation-related stress. However, ethnic-racial identity may not protect Latino youth who experience unauthorized legal status and may view their ethnic group as unwanted and rejected by society. Undocumented youth risk developing a negative ethnic-racial identity due to the stress, stigma, and politicization associated with their unauthorized status (Rodriguez, 2017; Suárez-Orozco, 2017).

In addition, adolescents with undocumented status face practical issues in balancing normative social experiences, such as driving, working, and planning for college, with the barriers posed by undocumented status. Barriers to accessing driver's licenses, college, and employment block their economic and educational progress, preventing adolescents with undocumented status from improving their economic situation (Abrego & Gonzales, 2010; Talleyrand & Vojtech, 2018). As they grow older, undocumented adolescents' family and financial responsibilities may increase. Still, lacking permission to work legally, they may be pressed to work in similar low-wage and exploitative working conditions as their parents, contributing to a cycle of poverty (Diaz-Strong & Gonzales, 2023). Ultimately, adolescents with undocumented status face hurdles that can impact their psychological and economic well-being throughout adulthood.

COVID-19 and Families

The COVID-19 pandemic has significantly affected families' lives, including elevated stress, anxiety, and depression in parents and children (Eales et al., 2021; Gayatri & Irawaty, 2022).

Family System

The COVID-19 pandemic presented unique stressors for families because many children attended school online while parents worked remotely.
zoranm/istock

Parents have been faced with a unique combination of stressors during the pandemic, including unemployment, economic instability, changes to work roles, and the burden of meeting children's social and educational needs with the closure of schools. The threat to their health and that of loved ones, and the reductions in social support that accompanied lockdowns added to parents' distress.

Parenting tasks shifted during the pandemic, with home confinement, new demands on shared home space, and restrictions on routine activities, such as playgrounds. Monitoring children's at-home learning posed additional stress, because on days when children were working on school tasks and especially when parents were heavily involved in learning parents reported more negative parent-child interactions, lower parental and child positive affect, and higher child negative affect, which were linked with poor well-being for both parents and children (Schmidt et al., 2021).

The accumulation of stressors during the pandemic was associated with heightened risk for anxiety, depression, substance use, and conflicts with partners and children (Prime et al., 2020; Whaley & Pfefferbaum, 2023). Marital conflict between stressed partners also affected the entire family system and was associated with lower quality parenting (W. K. Lee & Joo, 2024; Roos et al., 2021). Many families experienced declines in family cohesion, increased conflict, and harsh discipline, which predicted children's internalizing and externalizing problems (Fosco et al., 2022). Coparenting quality declined for many couples, which also contributed to increases in children's internalizing and externalizing problems and parental depression (Feinberg et al., 2022).

Parents' emotional health influences their children's behavior. Parents who experienced more COVID-19 pandemic-related stressors reported that their children showed more anxiety and withdrawal, fear, acting out, and pandemic-related concerns (Aviles et al., 2024; Singletary et al., 2022). Caregiver depression predicted low-quality parenting and disrupted parent-child relationships (Roos et al., 2021). Although parents' distress during the lockdown predicted increases in harsh parenting, declines in responsive parenting and parent-child relationship quality, these negative effects were buffered by partner support and cooperative coparenting (McRae et al., 2021). Parents' relationships with their partners influence their relationships with their children, serving as protective when their relationships are positive and risk factors when their relationship is poor.

Racial Disparities

The COVID-19 pandemic has disproportionately affected Black families in the United States, worsening preexisting vulnerabilities (Whaley & Pfefferbaum, 2023). Black children and adults have shown higher infection, hospitalization, and mortality rates than other races and ethnicities (Mackey et al., 2021). For example, Black Americans represent 13% of the U.S. population but account for 33% of COVID-19 hospitalizations and 34% of COVID-19 deaths (Anaele et al., 2021). Black children, along with Latino children, have experienced greater illness severity, and 65% of the children who have died from COVID-19 were Black (Fernandes et al., 2021).

These disparities can be understood within the context of individual, institutional, and structural racism in the United States. The experience of discrimination and microaggressions are stressors that negatively affect children's and adults' physical and mental health, increasing their vulnerability to illness (Benner et al., 2018). Black youth and their families are more likely to suffer from preexisting conditions, such as asthma, which increase the severity of COVID-19 symptoms. Black Americans are more likely to live in overcrowded and underserviced housing areas, experience food insecurity, and have poor access to healthcare, all markers of structural racism that increase their susceptibility to infection, hospitalization, and mortality (Abrams et al., 2022). Black Americans were also more likely to work in essential industries, such as food service, public transit, and health care, that continued to work during the pandemic, increasing their exposure to COVID-19 (The Lancet, 2020). Childcare was often unavailable, leaving children without adult supervision. Economic stressors, including unemployment, food insecurity, difficulty paying bills, and housing instability, are related to family conflict and changes in family interactions that affect the family system (M.-T. Wang et al., 2021).

Black children are more likely to attend schools in low SES or poor neighborhoods with limited resources, including limited access to technology (Bogan et al., 2022). Remote learning during the pandemic has exposed inequities in access to the Internet, with Black children being more likely to lack adequate technology and Internet access for virtual learning. Poor low-resource schools were also less likely to provide adequate remote education. Black youth faced increased stress due to disconnection from school and reduced contact with peers, relatives, and adult role models who could provide necessary support.

High COVID-19 death rates meant that Black families were also overrepresented among those experiencing bereavement due to the high COVID-19 mortality rate. The disruption of traditional grief, funeral, and burial practices due to social distancing measures and travel restrictions further exacerbated the burden of death and loss in the Black community. Black children were disproportionately impacted by acute, chronic, and traumatic stressors due to the pandemic and racial trauma, leading to heightened exposure to sociocultural stressors that affect their overall psychological functioning and emotional well-being. These experiences highlight the need to develop and fund support and interventions to promote their resilience and recovery.

THINKING IN CONTEXT 14.4

1. How can nurturing relationships between children and their caregivers serve as a protective factor for children who experience risks to their development, such as parental incarceration, deployment, or undocumented status? What specific caregiving behaviors and practices are most beneficial for children in these situations?
2. How do ethnicity, race, and SES intersect to influence children's experiences and outcomes related to incarceration, deployment, migrant status, and pandemic experiences? How can understanding these intersections help us better support children and families from marginalized communities facing these challenges?
3. In what ways do parents' mental health and responses to challenging family circumstances, such as those discussed in this section, impact children's and adolescents' health development? What are some ways of supporting parents' mental health and well-being to promote positive outcomes for their children?
4. What are the potential long-term psychological and emotional effects of the COVID-19 pandemic on children, particularly those from marginalized communities? How can families, educators, and mental health professionals work together to support the recovery and resilience of these children?

APPLY YOUR KNOWLEDGE

Samantha and Tom are parents to two children: 12-year-old Emma and 7-year-old Ethan. The parents have contrasting styles of interacting with their children, which has become a persistent source of conflict in their marriage, and often a source of stress for the children. One evening, Emma excitedly declares, "I'm going to stay up to watch the season finale of my favorite show!" Samantha responds with a smile, "Sure, honey." Tom disagrees, shaking his head. "Absolutely not. It's a school night. Go to your room and study." Samantha rolls her eyes, countering, "Relax, Tom. They won't fall behind in school if they stay up and watch a show." Tom insists, "The rules are the rules. No screens after 8 pm."

A little bit later Samantha visits Emma's room with earbuds in hand. "Shh. Don't tell your father. Use these and your father won't hear you watch your show." "Thanks Mom!"

Samantha and Tom's parenting clashes often leave their children puzzled about what is expected of them. Emma starts avoiding her father and, following her mother's suggestion, disregards his rules, spending time with her friends and on her tablet instead. When Tom discovers her disobedience, Emma is usually confined to her room without her tablet, which her mother frequently sneaks to her.

Emma's activities attract so much attention from their father that Ethan increasingly feels overlooked and resentful. He begins picking fights with his sister more often. Frustrated, he exclaims, "Everyone worries about Emma. What about me?"

Ultimately, Samantha and Tom decide to divorce, which brings new challenges to the family's adjustment. Emma and Ethan continue to live in their family home with their mother, but they struggle to adapt. Samantha must work longer hours to support the family, and the children aren't used to having their mother away so often. Emma starts to have sleep troubles and begins to cut classes at school. Ethan worries that something will happen to his father and he'll disappear from their lives. His anxious feelings make it hard for him to concentrate in class.

After a long day at work, Samantha is exhausted and looking forward to some quiet time alone. "Mom, you're starting to sound more like Dad," Emma cries when her mother forbids her from staying up late. Frustrated, Samantha replies, "Just go to your room."

As Samantha and Tom navigate their new co-parenting arrangement, they continue to argue during pick-ups and drop-offs. Ethan asks Emma, "When will everything feel normal again? When will mom be like she used to?" Emma replied, "They said getting divorced would make it better. I'm still waiting for them to keep their promise."

1. Describe Samantha and Tom's parenting styles. How do they contrast? How do these different approaches to parenting and discipline affect the children and family as a whole?
2. Apply the family systems model to this family. Describe the interactions among family members over time, including how divorce affects the family system.
3. Discuss the effects of the parents' conflict on Emma and Ethan and how their behavior and emotional well-being are affected by the tension between their parents.
4. Analyze the process and effects of the divorce on the family, and suggest factors that influence children's adjustment to divorce.
5. Discuss how parent-child relationships change as children become adolescents, and how these may affect Emma's behavior and relationship with her parents.

CHAPTER SUMMARY

14.1 Describe the family system.

Family systems theory views the family as a set of interconnected and interdependent parts that work together as a network. Family systems theory examines the bidirectional and reciprocal interactions among family members. Children and adolescents play an active role in their development and their interactions with their families, and these interactions shape their relationships with their parents and siblings. As children develop, parents must adapt their parenting, and the family system must frequently adjust to maintain equilibrium. Changes in any individual or relationship can lead to shifts in the others. Changes in family circumstances can also require the family to adapt and establish a new equilibrium. Close, supportive sibling relationships are associated with better adjustment. Some conflict can help children develop relationship skills, but frequent and intense sibling conflict is associated with poor adjustment. During adolescence, as young people seek greater autonomy from their families, they spend less time with their siblings, and the emotional intensity of their relationships declines. Positive sibling relationships are associated with romantic competence in late adolescence. Only children tend to have positive adjustment and high achievement but are more likely to have interpersonal difficulties than children with siblings.

14.2 Examine parenting, including parenting styles, discipline, conflict, and monitoring.
Parenting styles are enduring sets of parenting behaviors. Authoritarian parents emphasize control and obedience over warmth. Parents who are permissive are warm and accepting but have few rules and expectations for children. Uninvolved parents provide little support or warmth and little control. Authoritative parents are warm and sensitive to children's needs but also are firm. Children and adolescents of authoritative parents show the most positive outcomes. Parenting behaviors must be considered within their cultural context. Discipline refers to the methods parents use to teach and socialize their children toward acceptable behavior. Physical punishment has been shown to have negative effects on children. Effective alternatives to spanking include time out and inductive discipline. Punishment should be used sparingly and administered calmly, consistently, and with clear connections to the behavior. Conflict between parents and adolescents tends to increase during early adolescence, but warm and communicative relationships are still common. Parental monitoring is associated with positive adjustment and well-being in adolescents but should be balanced with respect for autonomy and privacy.

14.3 Compare the various forms families take.
Families come in many forms. There are no significant differences in the adjustment or development of children raised by same-sex couples compared to those raised by opposite sex couples. Children in one-parent families are at higher risk for adjustment problems and living in poverty. Cohabiting couples tend to have shorter and less stable relationships than married couples, but when their relationship is close and stable children show similar adjustment as their counterparts from married parent homes. Divorce is associated with adjustment problems for children, but the effects are often small and vary by outcome. Blended families involve multiple transitions and challenges for children, but many children are similar to those raised in first-marriage households. Among adopted children, positive relationships with adoptive parents are associated with reductions in internalizing and externalizing problems, better emotional understanding and regulation. Transracial adoptees may struggle with ethnic and racial socialization and identity development. Adoptive parents can support their children's ethnic and racial socialization and identity development by exposing them to their racial and ethnic heritage, validating children's experiences, and discussing discrimination and racism.

14.4 Analyze the challenges faced by families with incarcerated, deployed, or migrant members, as well as the impact of the COVID-19 pandemic on families.
Children with incarcerated parents are at higher risk of experiencing psychological and behavioral problems. Parental incarceration can also pose economic hardship and strains family processes, potentially leading to negative parent-child interactions. Interventions focus on supporting the family and re-entry. Deployment of a parent in the military poses challenges including parental separation and the risk of injury or death of the service member. Children with deployed parents experience emotional and behavioral difficulties. The deployed parent's adjustment after their return can also influence children's well-being. Parenting and relationship support aids families of deployed parents. Undocumented families face severe

financial stress, fear of deportation, and inadequate access to higher education, as well as high rates of anxiety and depressive symptoms. Undocumented status can prevent children and adolescents from normative experiences, negatively affect their ethnic-racial identity, and pose barriers to education and employment that can impact their psychological and economic well-being throughout adulthood. The COVID-19 pandemic resulted in health problems and elevated stress, anxiety, and depression in parents and children. It has disproportionately affected Black families in the United States in terms of health, education, and economics.

KEY TERMS

Authoritarian parenting style
Authoritative parenting style
Discipline
Family systems theory
Inductive discipline

Parental monitoring
Parenting style
Permissive parenting style
Uninvolved parenting style

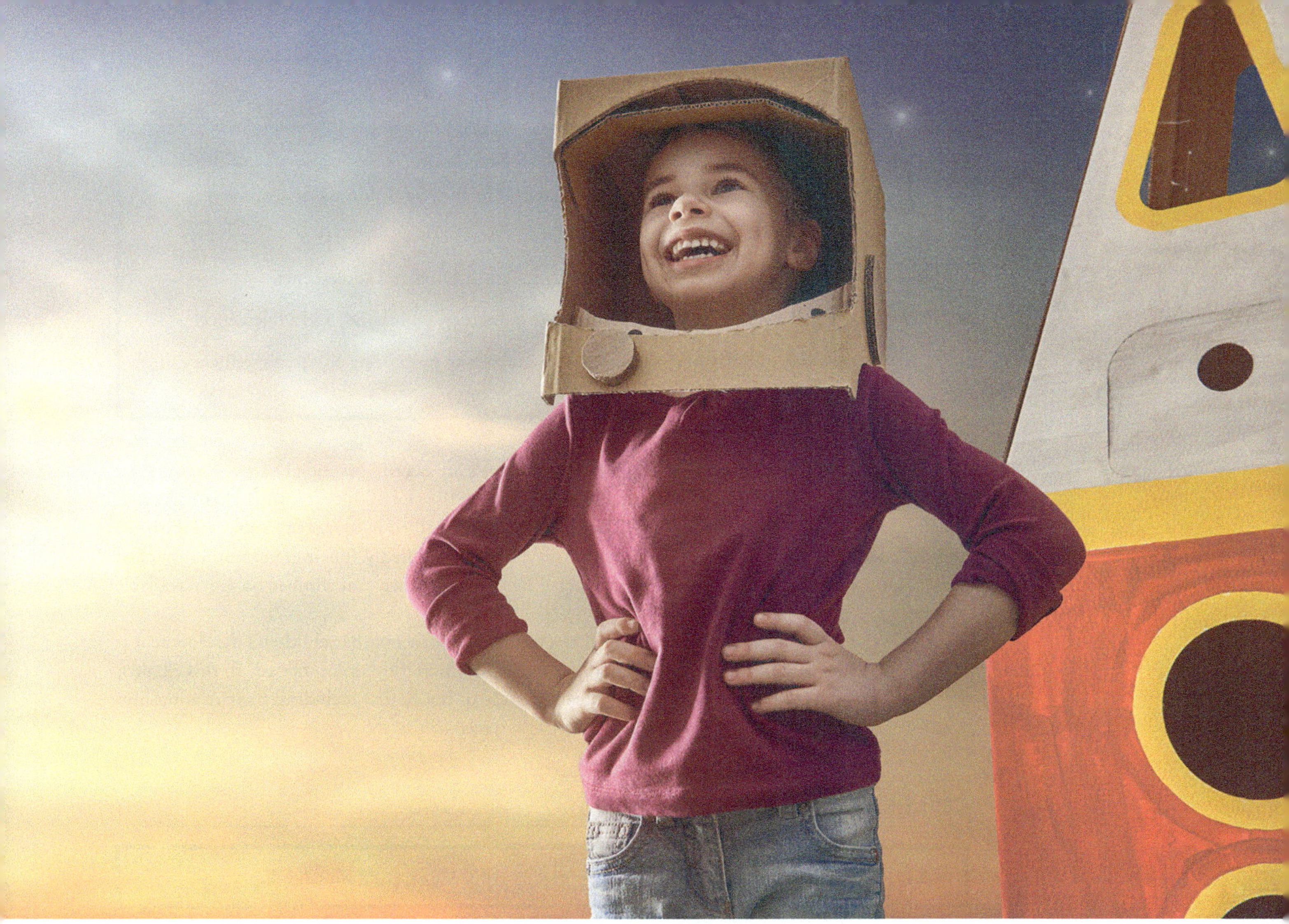

Choreograph/istock

15 CONTEXTS OF DEVELOPMENT

> ## LEARNING OBJECTIVES
>
> **15.1** Discuss the range of forms play takes and its influence on children's development.
>
> **15.2** Examine peer relationships in childhood and adolescence.
>
> **15.3** Analyze the school context and its influence on children and adolescents.
>
> **15.4** Summarize the effects of screen media use in infancy, childhood, and adolescence.
>
> **15.5** Discuss the interplay of risk and protective factors in promoting children's resilience to adversity.

"Let's be pirates!" declared 5-year-old Ramon. "Okay. Here's my sword," his friend Leo said, raising the plastic wiffleball bat. Ramon and Leo ran to the playhouse at the end of the yard, where Leo's sister sat playing. "There's the boat. Let's get her!" Ramon cried. Leo explained to his sister, "You're on the boat, and we're pirates coming to get you." "I'll run!" she exclaimed excitedly. Their grandmother watched from the porch as the children created stories, acted them out together, and climbed on every available surface.

Throughout this book we have examined the fundamental theme that children's development is influenced by their interactions with the many contexts in which they are immersed. In this chapter, we examine children's interactions with contexts outside of the home, including their relationships with peers, experiences in school, and interactions with screen media.

CHILDREN'S PLAY

> **15.1** Discuss the range of forms play takes and its influence on children's development.

Play offers essential learning opportunities for children and contributes to physical, cognitive, and socioemotional development. Running, jumping, and balancing games help children learn to control their bodies, coordinate their senses, and practice new motor skills. Through play, children learn to perspective take and understand other children's viewpoints, manage challenging situations, regulate emotions, practice creativity, express their thoughts and desires, and solve problems (Russ, 2022). Child-directed play, in which children play freely without adult direction is especially important for cognitive and social development.

Play and Cognitive Development

Children learn through play. According to cognitive-developmental theorist Jean Piaget (1962), children actively explore and construct their understanding of the world through play. Early play is simple, such as a toddler bouncing a ball and chasing it across the room. They begin to play with peers in early childhood. Their growing cognitive and emotional capacities, such as their advances in theory of mind and emotional regulation, enable them to join peer groups, manage conflict, and select and keep playmates (Schlesinger et al., 2020). Playing with other children may push them to learn to take the perspective of others and develop less egocentric ways of thinking (Piaget, 1962). Moreover, successfully playing with peers requires that young children learn to manage their emotions and carefully control their behavior to match their peers' and the setting (Coplan & Arbeau, 2009).

Young children's emerging cognitive abilities make certain types of play possible. In make believe or **representational play**, children pretend that one object is something else. Understanding that an object, such as a block, can also symbolize something else, such as a make believe telephone, is a cognitive feat that prepares children for learning symbols such as letters and numbers (Berk & Winsler, 1995; Vygotsky, 1976). Following the rules of pretend play, such as pretending that a block is a telephone, gives children practice controlling their impulses and regulating their behavior. Preschoolers can observe the rules in simple games, such as Simon Says, matching games, and games with spinners and dice, opening new opportunities for playing with other children and further development (Rubin et al., 2015).

Social Development and Early Friendships

Advances in social development in early childhood enable children to include others in their play. Social play evolves over a series of steps that occur over the ages of 2 to 5 (Parten, 1932). Toddlers' play is characterized by *nonsocial activity*, including inactivity, watching another child play, and solitary play. *Parallel play* then emerges, where children play alongside each other but do not interact. Play later progresses to include social interaction in *associative play*, in which children play alongside each other and exchange toys and talk about each other's activities. Finally, *cooperative play* represents the most advanced form of play because children play together and work toward a common goal, such as building a bridge or engaging in make believe play (Fehr et al., 2020). These forms of play emerge in order but are not a strict developmental sequence because later behaviors do not necessarily replace earlier ones (Yaoying & Xu, 2010). Solitary play declines with age, but it can still occupy up to a third of kindergarteners' playtime (Dyer & Moneta, 2006).

Children engage in solitary play for a variety of reasons. Some activities, such as coloring, are best completed alone. Sometimes young children play alone to have time for self-reflection (J. C. Katz & Buchholz, 1999). Solitary play can provide opportunities for children to regulate themselves or control their environment (Luckey & Fabes, 2005). As children progress through preschool social play becomes more common, children have more playmates, longer play episodes, and more varied contacts, promoting social development (Jaggy et al., 2023; Russ, 2022).

The earliest friendships emerge through children's play, and most young children can name a friend (Quinn & Hennessy, 2010). Young children generally understand friends as companions who live nearby, share toys, and have similar expectations for play. Friends are a source of amusement and excitement. Friends share, imitate each other, and initiate social interactions with each other (van Hoogdalem et al., 2013). As children enter preschool, they spend more time interacting with peers, especially same-sex peers. While proximity and play dimensions are emphasized in young children's friendships, research suggests that preschool friendships can also be characterized by emotional qualities such as support and closeness, and high-quality friendships are more likely to endure over the school year (Carter, 2023; Y. Wang et al., 2019). Through peer interactions, young children gain social competence, communication, and emotional regulation skills that permit them to have more complicated—and rewarding—relationships in later childhood and adolescence (Schlesinger et al., 2020).

Sociodramatic Play

Children act out themes and stories in their play. Simple forms of dramatic play begin in toddlerhood, when a 2-year-old feeds or punishes a stuffed animal (Frahsek et al., 2010). With advances in reasoning and opportunities to interact with other children, the most advanced type of play, **sociodramatic play**, emerges. In sociodramatic play, children interact with other children, take on roles, and act out stories (Lillard, 2015; Vasc & Lillard, 2020). They imitate people and experiences they have had or observed. Representational play is part of sociodramatic play as children make believe that they are adults, animals, or superheroes and incorporate pretend objects into their play. Sociodramatic play is social, involving two or more children, and it is interactive, requiring children to talk with each other as they act out their stories. It emerges in early childhood and becomes more frequent and complex from ages 3 to 6, often with intricate storylines (Rubin et al., 2015).

By pretending to be mothers, astronauts, cartoon characters, and other persons, children learn how to explain their ideas and emotions and develop a sense of self-concept as they differentiate themselves from the roles they play (Coplan & Arbeau, 2009). Pretending to be sad, angry, or afraid in pretend scenarios helps children develop emotional control (T. R. Goldstein & Lerner, 2018). Both boys and girls engage in sociodramatic play, though girls engage in more such play than boys. Sociodramatic play offers important opportunities for development because children learn through social interactions.

Children model higher-level thinking and interaction skills, scaffold less skilled peers, and help them reach their potential (Vygotsky, 1978). Sociodramatic play helps children explore social rules and conventions, promotes language skills, and is associated with social competence (Gioia & Tobin, 2010; Newton & Jenvey, 2011).

Rough-and-Tumble Play

Rough-and-tumble play, which includes running, climbing, chasing, jumping, and play fighting, is seen around the world.
yellowsarah/istock

Some sociodramatic play is accompanied by **rough-and-tumble play**, characterized by vigorous physical activity: running, climbing, chasing, jumping, and play fighting (StGeorge & Fletcher, 2020). Children's rough-and-tumble play is seen around the world and can be distinguished from aggression by the presence of a play face, smiling, and laughing (Coome, 2021). Rough-and-tumble play serves developmental purposes. It is carefully orchestrated and requires self-control, emotional regulation, and social skills. Children learn to assert themselves, interact with other children, and engage in physical play without hurting other children (P. K. Smith & StGeorge, 2023). Rough-and-tumble play exercises children's gross motor skills and helps them develop muscle strength and control. Rough-and-tumble play is common in animals and appears to elicit a positive affect that buffers the effects of stress, suggesting that it promotes resilience (Burgdorf et al., 2017; Pellis et al., 2023).

Both boys and girls engage in rough-and-tumble play, but boys do so at much higher rates. This is also true of most mammalian species (Marley et al., 2022). In one observation of preschool children, about 80% of the rough-and-tumble play instances occurred in boys (Tannock, 2011). It is estimated that 5% of preschool children's play is rough-and-tumble play, peaking at 10% in late childhood from about age 8 to 10, and falling to about 4% in adolescence (Coome, 2021).

Rough-and-tumble play often accompanies sociodramatic play (Fehr et al., 2020). Many children engage in superhero play, for instance, pretending to be media characters with extraordinary abilities, including strength, the ability to fly or to transform themselves into other beings. Children act out scenarios, running, jumping, and chasing. They take turns pretending to be "bad guys" and "good guys" (Frost et al., 2012). Similar to other forms of sociodramatic play, superhero play promotes children's emotional and social development. Children pretend to be powerful characters and pretend to experience different emotions, advancing their understanding of and ability to regulate their emotions as well as learning how to manage aggression (Vasc & Lillard, 2020; Veiga et al., 2022). Superhero play promotes friendships between children because it involves sharing common interests and cooperating with each other.

Imaginary Companions

"You stay here, and I'll get the cookies," Katie told her friend Madison. "Does Madison want cookies, too?" asked Mommy. "Of course!" replied Katie as she placed two cookies at a place setting in front of an empty chair. **Imaginary companions** or friends are common in early childhood, as early as ages 2 to 3, and occur in about 40% of young children (McAnally et al., 2020). According to parents' reports, there is no clear triggering event that marks the emergence of most imaginary companions (Taylor et al., 2009). Children who experience adversity, such as those in foster care, are no more or less likely to report imaginary friends (Aguiar et al., 2017). Children appear to come up with them on their own. Imaginary companions often represent extensions of real people known to the child, especially those the child admires or characters from stories, television, or movies. Imaginary companions are usually human, although they may take the form of animals, aliens, and monsters (Armah & Landers-Potts,

2021). The sense of what an invisible friend looks like is stable and can be retained for years. Imaginary companions may be a marker for creativity as children who create imaginary companions are more likely to report vivid imagery and elaborate storylines in daydreams, dreams, and pretend games (Trionfi & Reese, 2009).

Relationships with imaginary friends appear to resemble those with real friends and provide similar benefits, especially companionship (Gleason & Kalpidou, 2014). Children create realistic relationships with their imaginary companions, including pretend conflicts, feeling angry with them, and finding them unavailable to play (Taylor, 1999). Their similarity with real friends has sometimes caused concern in parents who fear that children create imaginary companions because they are lonely and have no playmates. On the contrary, research suggests that children with pretend friends are particularly sociable by nature and do not differ from other children regarding the number of playmates or peer acceptance (Gleason & Kalpidou, 2014). By interacting with imaginary companions children may practice social interactions, social roles, and emotions (Gleason, 2017). In fact, children with imaginary companions are better at communicating with peers and show more advanced theory of mind and understanding of emotion than their peers (Giménez-Dasí et al., 2016; Roby & Kidd, 2008). One study of 5-year-olds found that those with imaginary friends could better understand and talk about mental characteristics than those with only actual friends (P. E. Davis et al., 2014). Perhaps imaginary companions and the mental gymnastics that create and sustain them indicate psychosocial health rather than deficits.

Culture and Play

Although children worldwide play, peer activities take different forms in different cultures. In collectivist societies, children tend to play games that emphasize cooperation. For example, children in Ghana play a game called *Ampe*. They form a circle, clap, chant, and jump. A leader and a challenger at the center jump simultaneously and thrust one foot forward. If they choose the same foot, the leader stays; if not, the challenger becomes the new leader. Every child has a turn as leader and challenger, and all children actively create the rhythm and cheer each other on, encouraging unity and cooperation (Owusu & Obuo Addo, 2023). In contrast, children from Western cultures that emphasize individual rights are inclined to play competitive games such as follow the leader, hide and seek, and duck, duck, goose! However, it is important to note that both cooperative and competitive play can be found in all cultures. Like other aspects of development, play is shaped by the context in which it occurs.

Children's play varies with contextual circumstances, such as the amount of household work common for children in a given culture, the availability of toys, and parental encouragement of play (Gaskins, 2014). Children of the Nyansongo community of Kenya are expected to help with household and agricultural work as well as child and animal care (Edwards, 2000). Parents tend to discourage outside play to minimize aggression with neighbors, and they do not stimulate children's play by joining or making suggestions. Children tended to combine play with work and play with kin. When boys were herding cattle and goats, for instance, they played tag and created hurdles out of sticks. The children engaged in little roleplay, likely because they had real babies to look after and adult work to do.

In contrast, young children in Juxtlahuaca, Mexico, have much more unstructured time (Edwards, 2000). Adults generally do not stimulate play, but they also do not discourage it. Children's work entails running errands for adults, but they spend much of their time in the courtyard playing simple games such as tag and ball. Girls tend to engage in role-play, pretending to tend house, sew, and make tortillas. Boys tended to spin tops, and play with toy cars on roads they created with mud.

As expectations for work decline and support for play increases, more sophisticated forms of play become common. In Taira, Okinawa, where parents tend to be heavily involved in physical work, young children are seldom given chores and are permitted to wander and play in the courtyards (Edwards, 2000). The children attend a community nursery in the morning where they are taught turn taking and other cooperative skills that are useful in play. Older children supervise younger ones as they play in large groups. Children play rule-based games, such as marbles. They draw in the sand, construct houses of bamboo sticks, and dig. Taira children also engage in a great deal of sociodramatic play including house, animal care, and robber and ghost themes. Again we see that children's play varies with contextual opportunities to play and adult support for play.

> ### THINKING IN CONTEXT 15.1
>
> 1. "Play is a luxury. Children don't need it," Mara says. What do you think? Discuss some of the developmental functions of play. Do different types of play serve different functions?
> 2. How do cognitive and social development impact the types of play that children engage in, and how does play, in turn, promote further development?
> 3. What are the roles of rough-and-tumble and sociodramatic play in children's development?
> 4. Should children be encouraged to have imaginary companions?

PEER RELATIONSHIPS

> **15.2** Examine peer relationships in childhood and adolescence.

Much of children's and adolescents' development occurs within the peer context. Most preschoolers can name a friend, but friendship becomes more complex over elementary, middle, and high school.

Friendship

Our caregivers organize our earliest social interactions, often a byproduct of their social get-togethers. We learn how to be a friend by observing adults and other siblings. Our attachments and relationships with caregivers teach us about interactive synchrony, give-and-take. In childhood, play partners transform into true friendships, characterized by reciprocity and give-and-take. Through interactions with peers, young children develop social competence, communication, and emotional regulation skills, a foundation for more sophisticated and rewarding relationships in later childhood and adolescence (Schlesinger et al., 2020).

Who are children's and adolescents' friends?

For young children, friends are companions who live nearby and share toys and similar expectations for play (Afshordi & Liberman, 2021). Throughout childhood and adolescence, friendships are rooted in similarity. School-age children choose friends who share interests, play preferences, personality characteristics, cognitive ability, and intelligence, likely because these characteristics influence the capacity to take other people's perspectives and reciprocate (Boutwell et al., 2017; Ilmarinen et al., 2017). In adolescence, close friends and best friends tend to be similar in orientation toward risky activity, such as willingness to try drugs and engage in delinquency and dangerous behaviors such as unprotected sex (Osgood et al., 2022; Richmond et al., 2019; Trinh et al., 2019). Through interaction, friends tend to become even more similar to each other (Chang, 2022). In childhood and adolescence, friends tend to share demographics, such as age, ethnicity, and socioeconomic status (SES), as well as similar peer status (Bravo et al., 2022; Laursen, 2017; Markiewicz & Doyle, 2016).

Contextual characteristics, such as the ethnic diversity of a neighborhood or school, influence children's choices of friends within and outside of their own ethnic group. In schools and neighborhoods that are ethnically, racially, and socioeconomically diverse, children and adolescents are more likely to report having at least one close friend of another race (Bohman & Miklikowska, 2021; Lessard et al., 2019). Cross-ethnic friendships are less common than same-ethnic friendships but are associated with unique benefits. Adolescents of color who have cross-ethnic friends perceive less discrimination, are less likely to exclude others, feel less vulnerable to peer victimization, and show higher rates of self-esteem and well-being over time than those without cross-ethnic friends (Bagci et al., 2014; Elenbaas et al.,

2020; Graham et al., 2014; Kawabata & Crick, 2011). In addition, members of cross-ethnic friendships show lower levels of and greater declines in racial prejudice over time than their peers without cross-ethnic friendships (Titzmann et al., 2015).

Friendship Qualities

In middle childhood, friendship is a reciprocal relationship in which children are responsive to each other's needs and trust each other (Maunder & Monks, 2019). School-age children differentiate among best friends, good friends, and casual friends, depending on how much time they spend together and how much they share with one another (Rubin et al., 2015). Older children, especially girls, tend to have fewer but closer friends; by age 10, most children report having a best friend (Erdley & Day, 2016). Shared values and loyalty become important components of friendship by 9 to 10 years of age (Bagwell & Bukowski, 2018; Rubin et al., 2015). Violations of trust, such as divulging secrets, breaking promises, and not helping a friend in need, can break up a friendship. Similarly, adolescent friendships are characterized by intimacy, self-disclosure, trust, and reciprocity, especially for girls (Kitts & Leal, 2021; Krammer et al., 2023). Boys tend to emphasize the recreational qualities of friendship more than girls (Rudolph & Dodson, 2022). Adolescents expect their friends to be there for them, stand up for them, and not share their secrets or harm them.

Communicating with others and forming mutually self-disclosing supportive relationships help adolescents develop perspective taking, empathy, self-concept, and a sense of identity (French & Cheung, 2018). Longitudinal research suggests bidirectional interactions such that adolescents with high-quality friendships tend to engage in more self-disclosure, and self-disclosure in turn predicts high-quality friendships (Costello et al., 2024). Supportive and empathetic friends encourage prosocial behavior, promote psychological health, reduce the risk of delinquency, and help adolescents manage stress, such as the challenges of school transitions (Hiatt et al., 2015; Wentzel, 2014).

Friendship continues to have positive benefits, and the nature of friendship continues to change from adolescence into emerging adulthood and early adulthood (Miething et al., 2017). Close, supportive friendships are associated with positive adjustment and well-being, including self-esteem, prosocial behavior, and less peer victimization (Bagwell, 2020; Luijten et al., 2023; Maunder & Monks, 2019). Poor friendship quality, on the other hand, is associated with poor adjustment and internalizing problems such as depression and anxiety (Schwartz-Mette et al., 2020; Troop-Gordon et al., 2019).

Friendship Stability

High-quality friendships, characterized by sharing, mutual perspective taking, and intimacy, tend to endure (Asher & Weeks, 2018; Hiatt et al., 2015; Poulin & Chan, 2010). Nevertheless, because friendship is based largely on similarities and proximity, friendships may come and go as children and adolescents develop new interests or when they change contexts, such as when they change extracurricular activities, neighborhoods, schools, or even begin a new school year (Laursen, 2017; Meter & Card, 2016). Friendships that take place in multiple contexts, such as school, neighborhood, and extracurricular contexts, are more likely to endure than those that occur in only one context (Meter & Card, 2016). About one third to one half of friendships in early adolescence are unstable year-to-year, with young people regularly losing friends and making new friendships (Poulin & Chan, 2010). After early adolescence, friendships become more stable, with young people retaining most of their friendships over a school year.

Friendship dissolution or loss is common, with the majority of adolescents reporting that they have "broken up" with a friend (Flannery & Smith, 2021). Friendship dissolution is associated with emotional and behavioral problems, such as depression, anger, anxiety, and acting-out behaviors. These problems may precede friendship loss and contribute to children's and adolescents' poor adjustment afterward (Dryburgh et al., 2022; Lessard & Juvonen, 2018).

However, many friendships are downgraded rather than lost. For example, a best friendship may dissolve but the former best friends may remain good friends with a lesser degree of intimacy (Bowker & Weingarten, 2022). Adolescents may find the rejection and loss of intimacy painful, but the friendship endures. Downgraded friendships appear to be stressful only if the adolescent does not have a current best friendship (Bowker et al., 2024). Many children replace "lost" friendships with "new" friendships (Wojslawowicz Bowker et al., 2006). One recent study found that having new friendships and a larger friendship network at school was more predictive of perceived social adjustment than having maintained friendships over time; the loss of friendships only predicted poor adjustment when it was the loss of much of a peer group (S. Ferguson et al., 2022). For many children and adolescents, the importance of stable friendships may have less to do with the relationship's length and more to do with simply having a buddy by one's side who can provide companionship, recreation, validation, caring, help, and guidance.

Peer Acceptance, Popularity, and Rejection

Beginning in middle childhood, peer evaluations become vital sources of self-validation, self-esteem, and confidence (LaFontana & Cillessen, 2010). **Peer acceptance**, the degree to which peers view a child as a worthy social partner becomes important in middle childhood.

Children who are exceptionally well-liked by their peers are said to be **popular**. Popular children tend to have a variety of positive characteristics, including helpfulness, trustworthiness, assertiveness, and friendliness and are perceived as fun and prosocial (Laursen et al., 2020; Lease et al., 2020). They are skilled in self-control, emotional regulation, and social information processing (van den Berg et al., 2017). That is, popular children are good at reading social situations, problem solving, self-disclosure, and conflict resolution (Blandon et al., 2010). Theory of mind predicts popularity throughout childhood (Slaughter et al., 2015). Positive social competencies and prosocial behaviors are cyclical; children who excel at social interaction continue to do so, their peers tend to reciprocate, and positive effects on peer relationships increase (Laible et al., 2014; M. Wang et al., 2019).

Some popular children do not show the prosocial and empathetic characteristics typical of popularity. Some popular children are disliked (McDonald & Asher, 2018; Romera et al., 2019). These children and adolescents have high peer status yet show antisocial and aggressive behavior toward pursuing goals (Lansu, 2023). Often labeled by peers and teachers as tough, these children are socially skilled yet show antisocial and aggressive behavior (Seo et al., 2023; Shi & Xie, 2012). Aggressive popular children show social competencies similar to prosocial popular children, yet also share many characteristics of children who are rejected by their peers (Kornbluh & Neal, 2016; Marks, 2017).

Children who experience **peer rejection** tend to be disliked and shunned. Children with poor communication, emotional control, and social information-processing skills risk peer rejection (Bierman et al., 2014; Hladik & Hrbackova, 2021; van der Wilt et al., 2019). Boys and girls with behavior problems experience a heightened risk for peer rejection—and peer rejection, in turn, is associated with increases in behavior problems throughout elementary school and rule-breaking in adolescence (Prabaharan & Spadafora, 2020; Quarmley et al., 2022). Rejected children's behavior tends to be characterized by either withdrawal or aggression.

Withdrawn-rejected children tend to isolate themselves from peers, rarely initiate contact with peers, and speak less frequently than their peers (Duffy et al., 2020; Rubin & Chronis-Tuscano, 2021). They tend to spend most of their time playing alone and on the periphery of the social scene, often because of shyness or social anxiety. When socially withdrawn children experience peer rejection, they tend to become more withdrawn and even more disliked by their peers (Coplan et al., 2013). Despite this, socially withdrawn children are just as likely to have a best friend as other children (Rubin et al., 2006).

Not all rejected children are withdrawn. **Aggressive-rejected children** are confrontational, hostile, impulsive, and hyperactive (Duffy et al., 2020; Hall et al., 2022). They enter peer groups in destructive ways that disrupt the group's interaction or activity and direct attention to themselves. Aggressive-rejected children tend to have difficulty taking other children's perspectives and tend to react aggressively to slights by peers, quickly assuming hostile intentions (Fite et al., 2013; Laible et al., 2014). Children whose parents show little warmth and use coercive discipline are likely to have poor social skills, show aggressive behavior, threaten other children, and are more likely to be rejected by other children (Lansford, 2014).

Both aggressive-rejected and withdrawn-rejected children misinterpret other children's behaviors and motives, have trouble understanding and regulating their emotions, are poor listeners, and are less socially competent than other children (Ladd & Kochenderfer-Ladd, 2016). Peer rejection further hinders social development by depriving children of opportunities to learn and practice interacting with peers, resolving conflict, and regulating emotions (Prabaharan & Spadafora, 2020). Peer rejection is associated with short- and long-term problems, such as loneliness, anxiety, depression, low self-esteem, low academic achievement, and, in adolescence, delinquency and school dropout (Cooley & Fite, 2016; LoParo et al., 2023; Schwartz et al., 2015). Table 15.1 summarizes characteristics associated with popular children and those who are rejected.

TABLE 15.1 ■ Characteristics of Popular and Rejected Children and Adolescents

	Characteristic	Outcomes
Popular Children and Adolescents	Helpful, trustworthy, assertive Cognitively skilled and achievement oriented Socially skilled, able to self-disclose and provide emotional support Good social problem-solving skills and conflict-resolution skills Prosocial orientation Assume others have good intentions A minority is also antisocial and aggressive. They interact with others in a hostile way, using physical or relational aggression, and are likely to bully other children.	Positive characteristics are strengthened through experience and peer approval. Positive peer evaluations are sources of self-validation, self-esteem, confidence, and attention from peers, and they influence adjustment. Without intervention, the minority of popular children who are aggressive are likely to continue patterns of physical or relational aggression in response to peer approval and acceptance.
Aggressive-rejected Children and Adolescents	Confrontational, hostile toward other children Impulsive and hyperactive Difficulty with emotional regulation Difficulty taking others' perspectives Assume that their peers are out to get them Poor social skills Misinterpret other children's behaviors and motives	Similar outcomes for both types of rejected children Negative characteristics are strengthened. Few opportunities to learn and practice social skills, conflict resolution, and emotional regulation Anxiety, depression, and low self-esteem Behavior problems
Withdrawn-rejected Children and Adolescents	Passive, timid, and socially awkward Socially withdrawn, isolate themselves from others Anxious Poor social skills Fear being disliked by peers Misinterpret other children's behaviors and motives	Poor academic achievement Increased physical and relational aggression over time Withdrawal and loneliness

Cliques and Crowds

Adolescents' close friendships expand from one-on-one relationships to include small tightly knit groups of friends known as **cliques**. Like most close friends, members of cliques tend to share similarities such as demographics and attitudes (Lansford et al., 2009). Cliques are a context for adolescents' social interactions. The behavior, norms, and values that clique members share derive from interactions among the group members. A norm of spending time exercising together and snacking afterward, as well as valuing health and avoiding smoking, alcohol, and drugs, may emerge in a clique whose members are athletes. Belonging to a peer group gives adolescents a sense of inclusion, worth, support, and companionship (W. E. Ellis & Zarbatany, 2017).

Dating typically begins through the intermingling of mixed-sex peer groups.
wundervisuals/istock

In early adolescence, cliques tend to be sex segregated, composed of either boys or girls. Girls' groups tend to be smaller than boys' groups but both are similarly tight-knit (Gest et al., 2007). By mid-adolescence, cliques become mixed and often form the basis for dating (Connolly et al., 2004). By late adolescence, especially after high school graduation, mixed-sex cliques tend to split up as adolescents enter college and the workforce (Connolly & Craig, 1999).

In contrast with cliques, which are an expansion of intimate friendships, **crowds** are larger and looser groups based on shared characteristics, interests, and reputation. Rather than voluntarily joining, adolescents are sorted into crowds by their peers. Members of a crowd may or may not interact with one another; however, because of similarities in appearance, activities, and perceived attitudes, their peers consider them members of the same group (Pivnick et al., 2020). Crowds differentiate young people based on behaviors such as sexual activity, academic achievement, psychiatric symptoms, and health risks such as alcohol and substance use (Jordan et al., 2019; Stalgaitis et al., 2019, 2020).

Adolescent crowds have been found in nearly all U.S. secondary schools large enough to have multiple social groups (Cross, 2018). Common categories of peer groups found in Western nations include Populars/Elites (high in social status), Athletes/Jocks (athletically oriented), Academics/Brains (academically oriented), and Partiers (highly social; care little about academics). Other types of crowds include Nonconformists (unconventional in dress and music), Deviants (defiant; engage in delinquent activity), and Normals (not clearly distinct on any particular trait) (Delsing et al., 2007; Sussman et al., 2007; Verkooijen et al., 2007). Populars and jocks are generally rated by adolescents as higher in social status than brains and partiers (Helms et al., 2014).

In middle adolescence, as their cognitive and classification capacities increase, adolescents begin to classify their peers in more complex ways, and hybrid crowds emerge, such as *popular-jocks* and *partier-jocks*. As with cliques, crowds decline in late adolescence, especially after young people leave high school. Recent research suggests that crowds may continue into emerging adulthood as college students self-identify into crowds along four dimensions: social, scholastic, athletic, and counterculture (Hopmeyer & Medovoy, 2017).

Peer Conformity

Most young adolescents feel some pressure to conform to peer norms. Such pressure peaks at about age 14 and declines through age 18 and after (see Figure 15.1; Steinberg & Monahan, 2007). Adolescents experience the greatest pressure to conform to day-to-day activities and personal choices such as appearance (clothing, hairstyle, makeup) and music. Peer influence occurs within the context of friendship—and we have seen that adolescents tend to select peers who are similar to themselves (Erdley & Day, 2016; Gremmen et al., 2017). Through peer influence, friends become more similar, which supports the friendship and fosters group harmony (Laursen & Veenstra, 2023). It can be difficult to determine when adolescent behavior, especially risk behavior, results from conforming to peer influence or is simply a shared activity with friends (Daspe et al., 2019; McCoy et al., 2019). Despite this, there are clear developmental trends in risky activity among adolescents and their peers over time suggesting that young adolescents are more susceptible to peer influence than older adolescents, especially for antisocial behaviors such as delinquent activity, peaking at about age 14 (Sumter et al., 2018).

It is not simply peer behavior that influences adolescent behavior, but it is adolescents' perceptions of peer behavior, and beliefs about peers' activity, that predict engaging in risky activities such as smoking, substance use, and even sexting, sending sexually explicit text messages (Maheux et al.,

FIGURE 15.1 ■ Age Differences in Resistance to Peer Influence

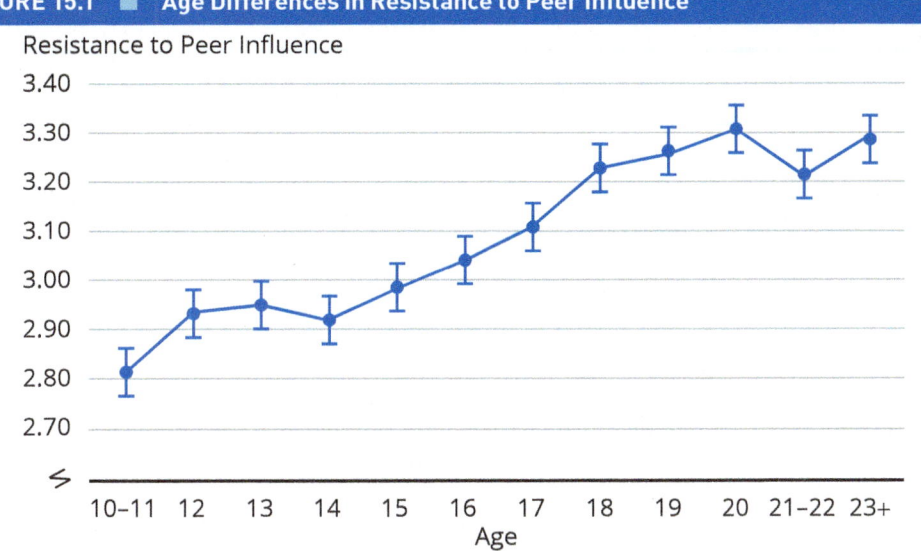

Source: Steinberg, L., & Monahan, K. C. (2007). Age differences in resistance to peer influence (Fig. 1, p. 1536). *Developmental Psychology, 43*(6), 1531–1543. https://doi.org/10.1037/0012-1649.43.6.1531

2020; Watts et al., 2024). In addition, adolescents naturally engage in more risk in the presence of peers, even without encouragement (Laursen & Faur, 2022; Van Hoorn et al., 2017). Young people vary in how they perceive and respond to peer influence based on factors such as age, personal characteristics, peer status, and context, such as the presence of norms (Field et al., 2024; Pei et al., 2020). Adolescents are especially vulnerable to the negative effects of peer pressure during transitions such as entering a new school and undergoing puberty and when they are uncertain of their status in the peer group (Brechwald & Prinstein, 2011; W. E. Ellis & Zarbatany, 2017). Adolescents are more likely to conform to best friends' behavior when they share a high-quality and satisfying relationship (Hiatt et al., 2017).

Peer influence is not always negative. Adolescents also report pressure from their friends to engage in prosocial and positive behaviors such as getting good grades, performing well athletically, getting along with parents, and avoiding smoking (Farrell et al., 2017; Hofmann & Müller, 2018; Wentzel, 2014). In laboratory experiments, adolescents were likely to show prosocial behavior after believing that anonymous peers approved of their prosocial actions, such as sharing coins with others (van Hoorn et al., 2016). Knowing when and how much to conform to others is a skill children and adolescents must learn to adapt to their social world, and a skill that remains useful in adulthood (Laursen & Veenstra, 2023). Ultimately, susceptibility to peer influence tends to decline with advances in psychosocial maturity that support independent decision making.

THINKING IN CONTEXT 15.2

1. Identify two common misconceptions about peer relationships in childhood and adolescence. Why do many people hold mistaken beliefs about these issues?
2. What are the characteristics of popular children and those whom their peers reject? Under what conditions might these characteristics overlap? How might this affect children's and adolescents' peer relationships?
3. How does peer conformity influence adolescent behavior? What factors contribute to susceptibility to peer pressure, and what are the short- and long-term effects of conforming to peer norms?

SCHOOL

> **15.3** Analyze the school context and its influence on children and adolescents.

All children enter first grade at about age 6. Many children attend kindergarten prior to entering elementary school, but only 19 states require children to complete kindergarten (Kelley et al., 2020). Early education is important for children's cognitive, social, and emotional development and is a foundation for later learning.

Educational Approaches

There are many perspectives on education that can be grouped into two general approaches that differ in instructional emphasis. Some preschool and elementary school classrooms emphasize **direct instruction**. Sometimes called academically centered or teacher-centered instruction, these programs provide structured learning environments in which teachers select instructional strategies and convey information to children (S. D. Powell, 2019). Learning activities typically include drills, quizzes, presentations, and recitations of definitions, facts, and lists. Children's learning is assessed through quizzes and exams that often involve selecting responses, such as multiple-choice or fill-in-the-blank items. Direct instruction supports children's learning, but critics argue it encourages passive learning by over-emphasizing teacher talk and learning and comprehending facts rather than higher-level thinking (Burden & Byrd, 2019; Mason & Otero, 2021). Today facts are readily available via the Internet. Children must develop skills in evaluating and applying information (Borich, 2017).

A second approach, often referred to as student-centered, is the **constructivist classroom**, influenced by Piaget and Vygotsky's perspectives on cognitive development. Constructivist instruction involves students in their learning (S. D. Powell, 2019). Children are viewed as active constructors of their own understanding through interactions with their worlds—through observing, interacting with objects and people, and engaging in a variety of activities that allow them to manipulate materials and interact with teachers and peers (Kostelnik et al., 2015). Children learn by doing, through play, and learn to problem solve, get along with others, communicate, and self-regulate.

Rather than convey and drill information, in a constructivist classroom, teachers engage children in problem-solving activities in which they investigate a problem, examine relevant information, and devise conclusions. Teachers ask questions to encourage student exploration and nurture reflection and thought about the process rather than emphasize a single correct answer. Constructivist approaches also encourage peer interaction. Cooperative learning, role-playing, simulations, and debates permit students to interact, share their ideas, and learn from one another (Burden & Byrd, 2019).

Montessori schools, first created in the early 1900s by the Italian physician and educator Maria Montessori (1870–1952), exemplify the constructivist approach because children are viewed as having a hand in their own development and are given freedom in choosing their activities (Lillard, 2021). Teachers act as facilitators, providing a range of activities and materials, demonstrating ways of exploring them, and providing help when the child asks. The Montessori approach fosters independence, self-regulation, and cognitive and problem-solving skills (Ackerman, 2019).

Rather than advocate for direct instruction or constructivist approaches, many educators call for **developmentally appropriate practice**, tailoring instruction to the child's age, recognizing individual differences, and the need for hands-on, active teaching methods (Kostelnik et al., 2015; Thompson & Stanković-Ramirez, 2021). Teachers provide educational support in the form of learning goals, instruction, and feedback, but they also emphasize emotional support and help children learn to manage their own behavior (S. Anderson & Phillips, 2017). Teachers are supported with explicit instruction in the strategies needed to support young children's literacy, language, math, social, and self-regulatory development (Markowitz et al., 2018). Developmentally appropriate practice is responsive, child-centered, and associated with higher reading and math scores during first grade (Lerkkanen et al., 2016).

Early Childhood Education Interventions

About 53% of 3- and 4-year-old children enroll in preschool (Griffiths, 2023). Children who attend preschool show advantages in literacy and math, compared to children who do not attend preschool (Johnson et al., 2023). They show higher rates of college graduation and higher wages compared to their peers (Bustamante et al., 2022). However, young children's developmental needs extend beyond education, and children from low SES homes are less likely to attend preschool. One of the most successful early childhood education and intervention programs in the United States, **Project Head Start**, was created by the federal government to provide economically disadvantaged children with nutritional, health, and educational services during their early childhood years, prior to kindergarten (Ramey & Ramey, 1998). Parents of Head Start children also receive assistance, such as education about child development, vocational services, and programs addressing their emotional and social needs (Zigler & Styfco, 2004).

Over the past four decades, a great deal of research has been conducted on the effectiveness of Head Start. The most common finding is that Head Start improves cognitive and academic performance, with gains in literacy and achievement scores in elementary school (Carr et al., 2023; Welsh et al., 2020). Yet some research has suggested that the cognitive effects of Head Start may fade over time such that, by late childhood, Head Start participants perform similarly to the control group of low SES children who have not participated in Head Start (U.S. Department of Health and Human Services & Administration for Children and Families, 2010).

Early intervention may not compensate for the pervasive and long-lasting effects of poverty-stricken neighborhoods and inadequate public schools (Schnur & Belanger, 2000; Welshman, 2010). At the same time, there are long-term advantages of attending Head Start. Compared with children who do not participate in Head Start, those who do so have greater parental involvement in school, show higher math achievement scores in middle school, are less likely to be held back a grade or have problems with chronic absenteeism in middle school, and are more likely to graduate from high school and college (Bailey et al., 2021; Joo, 2010; Phillips et al., 2016). Head Start is associated with other long-lasting social and physical effects, such as social adjustment and health-related outcomes, including immunizations, and lower rates of adolescent pregnancy and delinquency (Duncan & Magnuson, 2013; Huston, 2008; Welsh et al., 2020). Despite these findings, only one third of children in poverty are enrolled in Head Start (Guevara, 2022).

Additional evidence for the effectiveness of early childhood education interventions comes from the Carolina Abecedarian Project and the Perry Preschool Project, carried out during the 1960s and 1970s (Berčnik & Rožman Krivec, 2020). Both programs enrolled children from families with incomes below the poverty line and emphasized providing stimulating preschool experiences to promote motor, language, and social skills as well as cognitive skills, including literacy and math. Special emphasis was placed on rich, responsive adult-child verbal communication as well as nutrition and health services from birth to school age. Children in these programs achieved higher reading and math scores in elementary school than their non-enrolled peers (Campbell & Ramey, 1994). As adolescents and emerging adults, they showed higher rates of high school graduation and college enrollment, as well as lower rates of substance abuse and pregnancy (Campbell et al., 2002; Muennig et al., 2011; Pages et al., 2022). At ages 30 and 40, early intervention participants showed higher levels of education and income (Campbell et al., 2012; Schweinhart et al., 2005). Researchers continue to study and apply the Abecedarian approach today in playgroups, preschools, and other settings (Page et al., 2019; Sparling & Meunier, 2019).

The success of early education intervention programs has influenced a movement in the United States toward comprehensive prekindergarten (PreK) programs. Young children who participate in high-quality PreK programs enter school with greater readiness to learn and score higher on reading and math tests than their peers (Ricciardi et al., 2021; Sierens et al., 2020). Although all young children appear to benefit from PreK programs, children from low-income homes benefit the most (Slicker & Hustedt, 2019). During 2022–2023, 44 states provided preschool programs (Friedman-Krauss et al., 2022). However, only 46% of 4-year-olds and 17% of 3-year-olds attended state-funding or public preschools (Friedman-Krauss et al., 2024). Preschool attendance declined during the COVID pandemic, but the rate of decline was disproportionately large for low-income children (Figure 15.2).

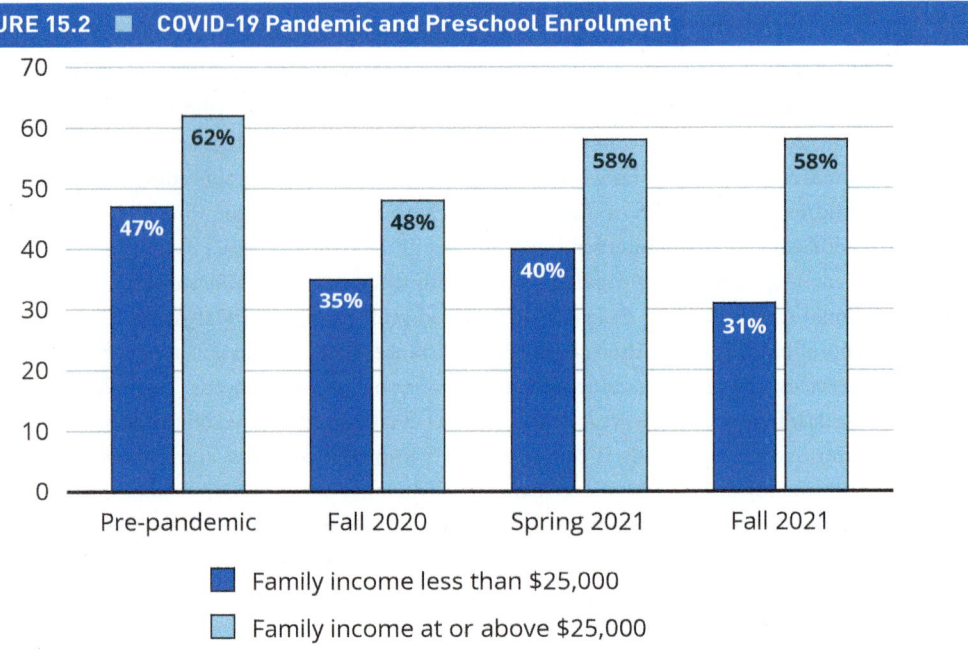

FIGURE 15.2 ■ COVID-19 Pandemic and Preschool Enrollment

■ Family income less than $25,000
■ Family income at or above $25,000

Source: Friedman-Krauss, A. H., Barnett, A. H., Hodges, K. S., Garver, K. A., Jost, T. M., Weisenfeld, G., & Duer, J. (2024). *The state of preschool 2023: State preschool yearbook.* National Institute for Early Education Research. https://nieer.org/yearbook/2023

Children's Access to Digital Technology

All school-age children in the United States have access to computers or tablets at school, and broadband Internet is available to all schools (National Science Foundation, 2018). Not all schools provide access to current technology, however, and the quality of Internet access varies across school systems. Schools in rural areas and low SES communities are less likely to have access to current technology or may have fewer opportunities to access computers and tablets given fewer resources.

Computers and tablets offer children new learning opportunities. Effective educational applications engage children and foster active learning through discovery. For example, children may learn social studies, math, and science by playing and reflecting on computer simulations, games, and interactive cartoons (Chauhan, 2017; Guan et al., 2024). Perhaps not surprisingly, children tend to prefer learning by tablet games compared to traditional classroom instruction (Dunn et al., 2018). Digital learning environments are especially effective in fostering learning outside of the classroom at home (Chauhan, 2017; Daoud et al., 2021). Computer and tablet-based games and interventions improve attention, working memory, and other cognitive skills (Arabiat et al., 2023).

Unfortunately, children's home access to technology varies with geography and SES (V. S. Katz et al., 2018). Rural families and those living in poverty are more likely than others to report access to high-speed Internet as a major problem (Anderson, 2018). While more than 90% of families with school-age children living in low SES homes report having Internet access, many report that their connectivity is constrained by interrupted or slow service, outdated devices, or having to share devices (Rideout & Katz, 2016). In 2021, nearly a third of children in low SES homes did not have access to broadband Internet (Frausel & Burroughs, 2023, pp. 2019–2021). Inequity in home access to technology is often referred to as the *homework gap* because of the challenges that students face when trying to do their homework. Inequities increase as teachers incorporate more technology-based learning into assignments and the effects magnify with each grade (Moore et al., 2018). Children with poor access to technology at home typically report using their smartphone and cellular data plan, a poor substitute for computers and high-speed Internet. School and community initiatives that provide children with tablets or inexpensive computers for home use hold promise for improving children's access to technology and closing the homework gap (Wenger, 2018).

The large socioeconomic differences in children's access to technology and Internet became apparent during the COVID-19 pandemic, which closed schools in many states and forced schoolchildren to quickly transition to remote learning from home (Masonbrink & Hurley, 2020). As shown in Figure 15.3, children's access to a computer and Internet resources during the COVID-19 pandemic varied dramatically with education and ethnicity, with children most educationally at risk also facing barriers to access (Friedman et al., 2021). Students with better access to high-speed Internet-enabled devices showed higher levels of engagement in remote learning after controlling for family SES and education (Domina et al., 2021).

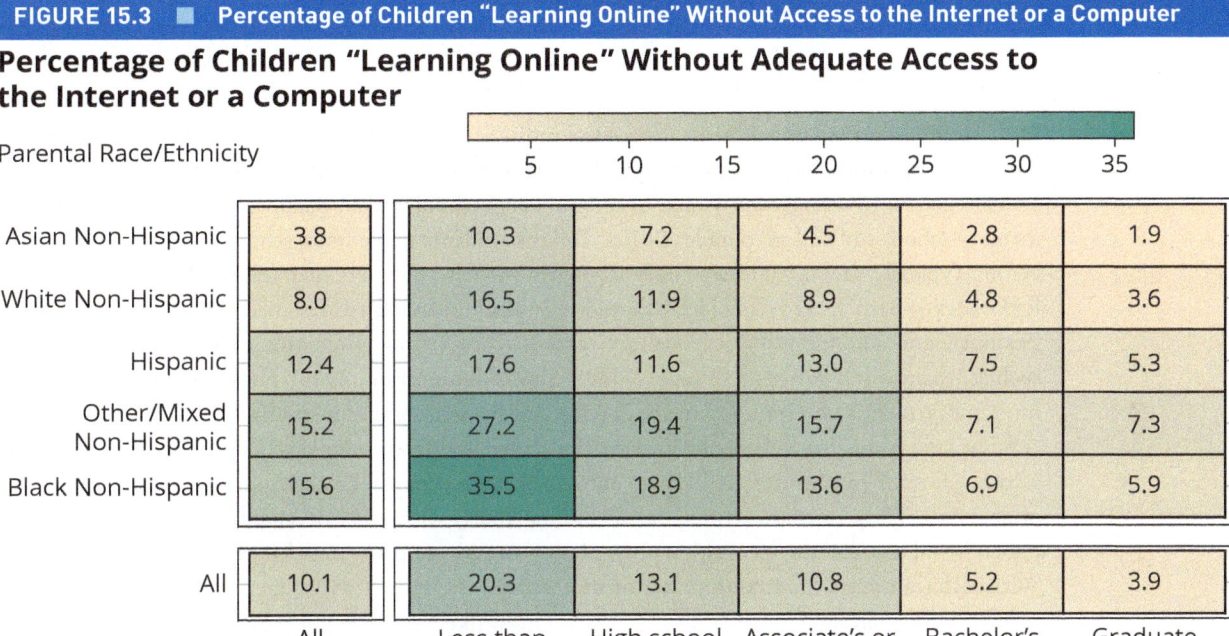

FIGURE 15.3 ■ Percentage of Children "Learning Online" Without Access to the Internet or a Computer

Percentage of Children "Learning Online" Without Adequate Access to the Internet or a Computer

Parental Race/Ethnicity	All	Less than High school	High school	Associate's or Some College	Bachelor's	Graduate
Asian Non-Hispanic	3.8	10.3	7.2	4.5	2.8	1.9
White Non-Hispanic	8.0	16.5	11.9	8.9	4.8	3.6
Hispanic	12.4	17.6	11.6	13.0	7.5	5.3
Other/Mixed Non-Hispanic	15.2	27.2	19.4	15.7	7.1	7.3
Black Non-Hispanic	15.6	35.5	18.9	13.6	6.9	5.9
All	10.1	20.3	13.1	10.8	5.2	3.9

Parental Education

Source: Friedman, J., York, H., Mokdad, A. H., & Gakidou, E. (2021). U.S. children "learning online" during COVID-19 without the Internet or a computer: Visualizing the gradient by race/ethnicity and parental educational attainment. *Socius, 7,* 2378023121992607. https://doi.org/10.1177/2378023121992607

Educating Children With Special Needs

School systems must meet the needs of a diverse population of children, many with special educational needs. Children with intellectual and learning disabilities require assistance to overcome obstacles to learning. The U.S. Individuals with Disabilities Education Improvement Act mandates that children with disabilities receive services to determine their educational needs, devise an individualized education plan (IEP), and provide educational opportunities similar to those experienced by children without disabilities (Forbringer, 2020).

An IEP is a plan tailored to each student's specific abilities and educational needs. It is a written plan created by a team of individuals, including a school psychologist or school counselor, the child's teacher, parents, and sometimes other professionals, such as vision or hearing specialists, depending on the child's disability. The IEP is specialized, goal-directed, and guided by student performance (Heward, 2018). At least once yearly, the school staff, professionals, and parents convene to assess the child's progress and revise the IEP accordingly.

In the United States and Canada, legislation mandates that children with disabilities be placed in the *least restrictive* environment or classrooms as similar as possible to classrooms for children without learning disabilities. Whenever possible, children are to be educated in the general classroom, with their peers, for all or part of the day and provided with a teacher or paraprofessional specially trained to meet their needs (Mastropieri & Scruggs, 2017). This is known as *inclusion*. Children's responses to inclusion vary with the severity of their disabilities and the quality and quantity of support provided in the classroom (Lewis et al., 2017). Most experts agree that inclusion works best when children receive instruction in a resource room that meets their specialized needs for part of the school day and the regular classroom for the rest of the school day (Heward, 2018). When children are placed in regular classrooms with peers of all abilities, they have multiple opportunities to learn from peers and may be better prepared to learn and work alongside people of all abilities (Salend, 2015). Interaction with peers and cooperative learning assignments that require children to work together to achieve academic goals help students with learning disabilities learn social skills and form friendships with peers.

School Transitions

Most children in the United States experience multiple school transitions during their education. In previous generations, students typically only experienced one school transition: from elementary or primary school (kindergarten–Grade 8) to secondary school, which includes the years between elementary school and college (Grades 9–12). Today's students make more school transitions than ever before. Typically, they attend elementary school through Grade 5 or 6, then transition to middle school for Grades 6–8, then high school for Grades 9–12. Middle schools are designed to give students greater flexibility and autonomy than elementary schools while encouraging strong connections to adults, such as teachers and parents (National Middle School Association, 2003). High school students have more opportunities for autonomy and to develop skills in self-regulation, motivation, and organization.

The transitions from elementary to middle school and from middle school to high school entail a complete shift in contexts, including changes in environments, teachers, standards, support, and, often, peers. These transitions often occur simultaneously with other developmental changes, such as puberty, and can disrupt friendships when peers transition to different schools (Felmlee et al., 2018). With each transition, the school environment, teachers, and standards change, sometimes in ways that conflict with adolescents' needs. Adolescents are most likely to experience difficulties when there is a poor match between their developmental needs and what the school environment affords in its organization and characteristics (Eccles & Roeser, 2011).

The adjustment difficulties associated with school transitions can be stressful for many adolescents and often result in declines in academic achievement (Booth & Gerard, 2014; Felmlee et al., 2018). Student engagement and motivation may also decrease, while feelings of loneliness, anxiety, depression, and behavior problems may increase (Coelho et al., 2017; Duchesne et al., 2019; Meyer & Schlesier, 2022). For most students, these adjustment difficulties are temporary, and their achievement recovers within 1 to 2 years as they adapt to their new schools (Crosnoe et al., 2015). However, students who perceive the school transition as more stressful than their peers tend to show greater and long-term drops in motivation and academic achievement and feel less connected to school (S. E. Goldstein et al., 2015). Students with lower academic ability, lower self-esteem, and who are unprepared for middle or high school are particularly vulnerable to poor school and peer transitions and depressive symptoms (Coelho et al., 2017).

Connections With Teachers

Students face increasingly stringent academic standards as they transition from elementary school to middle school and then to high school. Middle school classrooms offer fewer opportunities for student autonomy and decision making, involve more frequent, formal evaluations, and feature increased teacher emphasis on classroom management compared to elementary school classrooms (Eccles & Roeser, 2015). Over the first year of middle school, students tend to perceive a decline in emotional support from teachers and reduced educational clarity (Lazarides et al., 2021). This sense of disconnection can persist and increase into high school, with students feeling less connected to and valued by their teachers (Shubert et al., 2020).

Research suggests that many teachers' views align with their students, and middle and junior high school teachers may hold different beliefs about students than elementary school teachers, such as trusting them less, even when they teach students of the same chronological age (Midgley et al., 1995). Teacher self-efficacy declines with each grade level in secondary school, which is concerning because confident teachers set high expectations for students, subsequently predicting student success (Eccles & Roeser, 2015). The decline is more pronounced for teachers in low SES schools and communities, likely influenced by poor access to resources and increased stress (Cooper et al., 2010). This mismatch of adolescents' changing developmental needs and school resources contributes to declines in academic performance, motivation, and overall functioning, including increases in anxiety and depressive symptoms (Benner et al., 2017; Booth & Gerard, 2014; Coelho et al., 2017).

Racial and Ethnic Differences

Changes in school demographics, particularly changes in the ethnic composition of schools, can pose challenges to adolescents' adjustment (Douglass et al., 2014). Black and Latino students may be more vulnerable to the negative effects of school transitions than non-Hispanic White students (Burchinal et al., 2006; Espinoza & Juvonen, 2011). In one study, high achieving Black boys and Latina girls showed the greatest losses in academic achievement, whereas White girls tend to show the greatest stability in academic status between middle school and high school (Sutton et al., 2018). Research with adolescents from 17 diverse urban schools in the southeast United States found that nearly half of Black and Latino students reported perceiving ethnic-racial discrimination by teachers and peers in the year following the transition to middle school (Marraccini et al., 2022). Risks to academic achievement tend to accumulate over time, with disadvantaged students facing disproportionate risks, as they may be less prepared to meet the heightened demands of high school.

Students of all races and ethnicities, including African American, Latino, Asian, and White adolescents, fare best in diverse schools with ethnic groups of relatively equal size (Nishina et al., 2019). Students in diverse schools perceive their teachers as more fair, report feeling safer, less victimized, and less lonely, and report more positive attitudes toward students of other ethnicities (Juvonen et al., 2018). When students feel that their ethnic group is well represented in their high school, they are more likely to feel a sense of belonging, supporting their connections with school and academic achievement (Benner & Graham, 2009; Graham et al., 2022).

Contextual Influences on Academic Achievement

Children's and adolescents' adjustment to school transitions and academic success are influenced by their relationships with parents, peers, teachers, and schools.

Parents

Authoritative parenting, characterized by consistent warmth and firm limits, supports academic motivation and performance in children and adolescents regardless of race, ethnicity, and SES (Dotterer et al., 2014; Pinquart, 2017). Parents promote academic achievement by setting high, but realistic expectations and being active and involved in their child's education, including getting to know their children's teachers, monitoring their academic progress, and ensuring that their child is taking appropriately rigorous classes (Benner et al., 2021; Boonk et al., 2018). Parent-school involvement is particularly beneficial for disadvantaged students and those with poor prior achievement because it communicates the importance of education and models academic engagement and problem solving (Benner et al., 2016; Suizzo et al., 2023).

Peers

Children and adolescents tend to choose friends who share interests and similarities, including academic achievement, and through their interactions they become more similar (Gremmen et al., 2019; Véronneau et al., 2010). Positive peer support can protect children and adolescents at risk for poor school outcomes. For example, in a study of African American adolescents, peer support predicted emotional engagement in school, which was related to their academic achievement (Golden et al., 2018). Positive interpersonal relationships with peers during the transition to secondary school predicted higher well-being and academic achievement (Kiuru et al., 2020). Adolescents report trying harder at school when they believe their friends value academics (Rambaran et al., 2017).

Teachers

Children look to teachers for guidance in understanding themselves.
Kali9/Getty Images

Teachers foster students' achievement by creating an environment that supports students' needs including high expectations, emotional support, and autonomy (Alley, 2019; Eccles & Roeser, 2011; Madjar & Cohen-Malayev, 2016). Children and adolescents who report high levels of teacher support and feel connected to their schools tend to be more engaged and confident and show better emotional health, including lower rates of depressive and anxiety symptoms, as well as earn higher grades (Benner et al., 2021; Burns, 2020; Engels et al., 2021; Kidger et al., 2012; Zee et al., 2021). The student-teacher relationship is reciprocal: Students who feel that they have a close relationship with their teacher tend to have teachers who report a similarly close relationship (Prewett et al., 2019).

Schools

Effective schools foster personalized learning and strong positive connections between adults and students, enabling teachers to meet students' individual needs and develop students' sense of belonging (Burden & Byrd, 2019; Yager et al., 2013). Students who feel a sense of belonging to the school as a whole and experience meaningful, positive connections with adults and students are more likely to persist and be motivated academically (M.-T. Wang & Hofkens, 2020). Finally, effective schools develop connections with the community they are immersed in, between the school, parents, and the larger community. These schools have high parental involvement and are attuned to parents' and students' socioeconomic, cultural, and language needs (Rutledge et al., 2015).

THINKING IN CONTEXT 15.3

1. What are the benefits and drawbacks of the direct instruction approach versus the constructivist approach in early childhood education? To what extent are these approaches used in elementary and secondary school? To what degree should teachers strike a balance between the two? What would that look like?
2. How do the frequency and nature of school transitions affect adolescents' academic achievement and emotional well-being? How well does the environment match adolescents' developmental needs? What contextual factors might determine goodness of fit? How can we enhance the fit between adolescents' needs and school opportunities and resources?
3. In your view, how might the COVID-19 pandemic affect children's education? What do you expect? How might children vary? Why? What are the implications of inequities in access to digital technology and the Internet for children's learning, especially during the COVID-19 pandemic? How can school and community initiatives improve access to technology and help close the homework gap?

MEDIA

15.4 Summarize the effects of screen media use in infancy, childhood, and adolescence.

Children and adolescents use screen media daily through televisions, smartphones, tablets, and computers. Media is another context for development.

Screen Media Use in Infancy

On average, infants and toddlers spend approximately an hour daily engaged with screen media, mainly videos and television (Rideout & Robb, 2020). Although most parents believe that age-appropriate videos can positively impact development, longitudinal studies offer no evidence of long-term benefits of media use in infancy (American Academy of Pediatrics Council on Communications and Media, 2016; Ribner & McHarg, 2021). Instead, more frequent exposure to media and mobile devices is associated with poorer language and self-regulation in infants (Lawrence & Choe, 2021; McHarg et al., 2020).

Infants learn more readily from interactions with people than from videos watched on screens (Barr, 2010; Guellai et al., 2022). When caregivers watch videos with infants and talk to them about the content, they spend more time looking at the screen, learn more from the media, and show greater language knowledge as toddlers (Linebarger & Vaala, 2010; Tu et al., 2024). But it is not clear that caregiver co-viewing of media is better than parent-infant interaction by itself (Courage, 2017). Infant screen media use is not harmful, but it likely will not enhance learning. Delaying infants' introduction to screen media, limiting use, and interacting with infants during media use during infancy is associated with better cognitive performance in infancy and in preschoolers (Guellai et al., 2022; Stockdale et al., 2022; Supanitayanon et al., 2020).

Infants and toddlers learn more from interacting with their parents and other caregivers than they do from watching infant-directed educational content.

LucaLorenzelli/istock

Screen Media Use in Childhood and Adolescence

Young children between ages 2 and 4 use screen media for about 2.5 hours daily (Rideout & Robb, 2020). Unlike infants, young children can benefit from educational media. Limited screen time, watching educational programs, and co-viewing screen media with caregivers may promote young children's language skills (Madigan et al., 2020). Preschoolers who frequently watch the educational show, *Sesame Street*, score higher on many school readiness skills, such as knowing letters and numbers as well as writing their name, earn higher scores on standardized measures of vocabulary, view school and people of other ethnicities more positively, and adapt better to school (Kirkorian et al., 2008). In contrast, noneducational programs and those created for general audiences, particularly those that contain violence, are associated with attention problems, motivation problems, and aggressive behavior in early childhood and later (Barr et al., 2010).

Children between ages 5 and 8 use screen media for about 3 hours daily. More than two thirds of school-age children have their own mobile devices and use media independently, without their parents. Most children watch online videos that they select themselves. Nearly half of parents say getting their children to stop using media can be difficult. Limited use of computers, smartphones, and tablets is not harmful to children (Przybylski & Weinstein, 2019). Heavy screen use, however, is associated with impairments in attention, executive functioning, academic performance, mental health, and behavior problems (Eirich et al., 2022; Jusienė et al., 2020; Santos et al., 2022). Heavy screen use is associated with less sleep time and poor sleep, and it displaces time that would be spent in physical play, which contributes to the growth of motor skills and overall physical health, including weight (Liu et al., 2022; Oswald et al., 2020; Schwarzfischer et al., 2020).

Screen use increases over childhood, with children aged 8–12 spending about 5.5 hours and adolescents aged 13 to 18 spending about 8.5 hours on screen media daily in 2021 (Rideout et al., 2022). Over three quarters of adolescents report watching videos, over two thirds use social media, and over half watch television daily.

Children's use of media use is influenced by their context. Low SES households are more likely to experience household chaos, which is associated with increased use of screen media (Emond et al., 2018; Larsen & Jordan, 2020). On average, children and adolescents from low-SES homes spend nearly 2 hours more per day with screen media than their peers from higher-income homes (Rideout & Robb, 2020; Rideout et al., 2022). Black and Hispanic children and adolescents tend to use screen media more often, up to 2 hours more per day than their White peers. Although screen media use increased by 17% from 2019 to 2021, ethnic, racial, and SES disparities in media use remained consistent (Rideout & Robb, 2021). During the COVID-19 pandemic, the majority of children and adolescents (aged 8 to 18 years) reported that media use was important for having fun (91%), maintaining a positive mood (84%), and staying connected with friends and family (83%). Screen media poses both risks and benefits for children and adolescents.

Media Violence

Much of the attention on the effects of media on children and adolescents has focused on the effects of exposure to violence in media. Violence is prevalent in television and movies and has increased over the decades (Martins & Riddle, 2022; Riddle & Martins, 2022). Likewise, an analysis of a cross-section of television shows rated for children, adolescents, and adults found that violence was pervasive, occurring in 70% of episodes overall and for 2.3 seconds per minute of each episode (Gabrielli et al., 2016). How does exposure to media violence influence children and adolescents?

Television

Regular exposure to television violence in childhood has been associated with aggressive behavior in adolescence and adulthood (C. A. Anderson et al., 2003; Eisner & Malti, 2015; Huesmann, 2007). A classic longitudinal study examined school-age children annually and found increasing rates of aggression in children who watched more television violence, especially when they identified with the aggressor and perceived the violence as realistic (Huesmann et al., 1984; Huesmann & Eron, 1986). Fifteen years later, the children who habitually watched more television violence were more aggressive as young adults (Huesmann et al., 2003). In another study, preschoolers' viewing of violent television was associated with emotional distress, poor classroom engagement, poor academic achievement and motivation at age 12 (Pagani et al., 2023).

However, it is important to note that findings regarding television violence are based on correlational studies, and such studies do not establish causality (see Chapter 1). Any effects of exposure to television violence are gradual and likely cumulative over time (Krahé, 2012). Children exposed to violence regularly are more likely to be desensitized to its effects and view aggression as more acceptable than children who watch less violent television (Calvert, 2015).

In adolescence, television violence may affect attitudes toward violence, desensitizing adolescents to the effects of violence and increasing aggressive thoughts and expectations for hostile and aggressive behavior from others (Calvert, 2015; Wiedeman et al., 2015). Viewing media violence is associated with aggressive behavior in adolescence, but individuals vary in their susceptibility (Khurana et al., 2019). Adolescents have more advanced cognitive abilities than children, including more sophisticated moral reasoning and the ability to reason and reflect on what they see, which may affect their responses to televised violence.

Other factors, such as experiences at home, with peers, at school, and in the community, also influence violence. Family factors, such as harsh parenting, maltreatment, and exposure to domestic violence, are particularly important predictors of aggressive behavior in childhood and adolescence (Labella & Masten, 2018). Peer rejection has also been associated with higher levels of anger and frustration, more lenient moral judgments of antisocial media content, and a greater preference for antisocial media clips (Plaisier & Konijn, 2013). Additionally, personality factors such as a predisposition toward aggression can influence adolescents' media preferences (Rydell, 2016). Adolescents select media that match their interests. Therefore, more aggressive adolescents tend to prefer more violent media than adolescents who are less aggressive (Breuer et al., 2015). The effects of exposure to television violence on behavior may vary with adolescents' predispositions and the interactions they experience in their immediate contexts (C. J. Ferguson, 2013a).

Video Games

Unlike television, where users are observers, users actively participate in video games. They are immersed in often realistic worlds in which they might shoot and kill zombies, "bad guys," and sometimes innocent people and "good guys." A 2011 U.S. Supreme Court case, *Brown v. Entertainment Merchants Association*, considered whether a California law to limit adolescents' access to violent video games was constitutional. After evaluating research summarized by psychologists, physicians, and other researchers and health professionals, the Court concluded that the evidence on video game violence was not persuasive and could not justify the state's strict guidelines for regulating adolescents' access to violent video games (C. J. Ferguson, 2013b). In the decade since this ruling, research has shown mixed results.

Research suggests short- and long-term harmful effects, such as increased aggressive thoughts and feelings, physiologic arousal, aggressive behavior, desensitization to violence, and decreased prosocial behavior and empathy (Bushman & Anderson, 2023; Greitemeyer, 2022). A recent 10-year study following adolescents into emerging adulthood found several paths of violent video game use. Heavy (4%) and moderate (23%) users in early adolescence showed declines in video game use over adolescence, followed by a small rebound in emerging adulthood. The majority of adolescents (73%) were low users in early adolescence and increased their use into emerging adulthood, but at all times engaged in less violent video game play than their peers. Notably, although all the adolescents showed similar levels of aggressive behavior in early adolescence, the moderate users were the most aggressive in emerging adulthood (Coyne & Stockdale, 2021). This is consistent with a meta-analysis of 21 studies that found a small but consistent effect of video games on aggression, although the relationship declines when prior aggression is controlled (Burkhardt & Lenhard, 2021).

Other longitudinal studies of children and adolescents found no association between exposure to shooter games in which players hunt and shoot animated people and increases in aggressive behavior, behavior problems, or delinquency (Lobel et al., 2017; S. Smith et al., 2018). Large reviews of research suggest that any relationships between video games and aggressive behavior and reduced prosocial behavior are negligible or nonexistent once family factors and other variables are considered (DeCamp & Ferguson, 2017; C. J. Ferguson, 2015). For example, a study of Spanish high school students found that personality factors and association with deviant peers predicted aggressive behavior over a 1-year period; yet playing violent video games was not associated with aggressive behavior after controlling for personality and peers (López-Fernández et al., 2021).

Many interactions in the family, peer, school, and neighborhood context contribute to adolescent violence, as discussed in Chapter 12. Individual differences, such as personality factors and interests, also play a role. More aggressive adolescents are likely to seek out media with aggressive or violent content that matches their interests (Saleem et al., 2012; Wiedeman et al., 2015). While adolescents can be negatively influenced by violent media, research has shown that children and adolescents who are generally more aggressive tend to be more strongly influenced by exposure to violent media (Coyne, Warburton, et al., 2023; Wiedeman et al., 2015). One longitudinal study found that physical aggression in 14- to 17-year-olds predicted the later use of violent video games, suggesting that adolescents select video games that match their interests, in this case, aggressive (Breuer et al., 2015). Adolescents who feel excluded may also experience heightened preferences for violent games; the combination of exclusion and violent game playing can influence aggressive inclinations (Plaisier & Konijn, 2013). However, as with the research on television violence, these studies are correlational.

Social Media and Adolescent Development

About 85% of adolescents report using social media, and the frequency of social media use has skyrocketed over the past decade, along with the proliferation of smartphones (M. Anderson & Jiang, 2018b; Rideout et al., 2022).

Adolescents' Views of Social Media

Adolescents report using social media to share their thoughts and emotions with friends, offer support, and feel like they have people who will support them through tough times (Atske et al., 2022; Uhls et al., 2017). Most adolescents report feeling better connected to their friends through social media activity and know more about friends' lives and feelings (M. Anderson & Jiang, 2018a; Lenhart, 2015). In one study of over 3,000 early adolescents, social media use was positively linked with reports of friendship quality and bonding (Antheunis et al., 2016). Adolescents tend to associate their social media use with positive rather than negative emotions, such as feeling included rather than excluded or confident rather than insecure (M. Anderson & Jiang, 2018a). These positive effects of social media use may have been magnified during the COVID-19 pandemic as social media permitted adolescents to remain in contact, often constant contact, with peers as well as practice autonomy, independence, and social exploration—self-presentation (Hamilton et al., 2022).

However, social interactions on social media can also be stressful. About one third of boys and nearly half of girls say that they get overwhelmed by social media "because of all the drama" (Atske et al., 2022). About one quarter of boys and over one third of girls say that social media can make them feel left out by their friends or pressured to post content that will get lots of comments or likes. In fact, 40% of adolescents say they at least sometimes decide not to post something on social media because they worry people might use it to embarrass them (Atske et al., 2022). Despite this, adolescents view the impact of social media on their lives as mostly positive (32%) or neutral (59%). Adolescents are more likely to say that social media has a negative effect on same-age peers (32%) than themselves (9%). This difference raises questions about adolescents' reasoning about social media use.

Effects of Social Media

Most of the research examining the effects of social media has focused on its potentially negative impact on adolescents, with mixed conclusions (Schønning et al., 2020). Some studies have suggested a link between heavy social media and low self-esteem, anxiety, and depression (Bányai et al., 2017; Twenge et al., 2020), but others found no consistent relationship (Heffer et al., 2019; Houghton et al., 2018). Similarly, recent meta-analyses and large-scale studies with thousands of adolescents have reported only small and inconsistent effects between social media use and psychological well-being and mental health (Odgers & Jensen, 2020; Orben, 2020; Valkenburg et al., 2022). However, individual differences in these relationships might be masked, as social media use may be differentially associated with outcomes depending on individual differences and contextual factors (Sarmiento et al., 2020; Vannucci & McCauley Ohannessian, 2019). It is also worth noting that even tiny effects can be experienced as significant by the affected individuals (Odgers et al., 2020). A negative effect may not be common but nevertheless it is important to the person affected by it.

Social Media and Development

Although adults often express concerns about the dangers of social media, it can serve developmental functions for adolescents (Parent, 2023). Adolescents use social media to develop and maintain friendships (Uhls et al., 2017). Online interactions can give adolescents a sense of belonging and offer new opportunities for practicing social skills, sharing, and intimacy. Through posting, liking, and commenting, adolescents learn how about the norms of online social behavior (Moreno & Uhls, 2019). Adolescents report more opportunities for self-disclosure on social media than in real life, because they can carefully compose and edit messages without the potential discomfort accompanying real-time interpersonal interaction (Best et al., 2014; Popat & Tarrant, 2023). While real-life interactions are essential for social development, initial online forays can make adolescents feel closer to friends, which can support in-person interactions.

Social media also offers opportunities for identity development. Through social media, adolescents can explore and choose how to present themselves, posting certain photographs and texts that reflect their emerging identities, gaining feedback from their peers, and engaging in social comparison with peers (Wood et al., 2016). Adolescents can experiment by revealing and expressing different characteristics representing different aspects of themselves, who they hope to be, and their multiple intersecting identities (Michikyan & Suárez-Orozco, 2016). Most adolescents agree that people get to show different sides of themselves on social media that they cannot show offline, and most adolescents (and adults) carefully plan how they will present themselves (Lenhart, 2015; Nesi et al., 2018).

In addition, social media may have a special role in the development of adolescents who are marginalized or who are questioning their identity. Social media gives access to diverse peers in other geographic locations, allowing adolescents to find like-minded peers and those with similar experiences and interests. Adolescents in isolated communities or who feel different from peers can connect with similar peers, making social connections and friendships that may be unavailable offline (Nesi et al., 2018). For example, adolescents attempting to understand their gender and sexual identities may learn about themselves and "try on" an identity through online interactions with other questioning peers (Michikyan & Suárez-Orozco, 2016; Tovar et al., 2023). Through social media interactions with similar peers and in a safe space, adolescents without offline friends can feel less lonely and more confident (Coyne, Weinstein, et al., 2023). Most adolescents report that social media positively contributes to their lives (Uhls et al., 2017).

Social media is part of the fabric of daily life for adolescents. It has transformed adolescents' social lives in ways that affect their cognitive, social, and emotional development. Although much of the research has examined the potentially harmful effects of social media on adolescents, social media is simply another context in which adolescents interact with both positive and negative influences.

THINKING IN CONTEXT 15.4

1. Your friend is the parent of a 6-month-old infant. Provide advice regarding the infant's use of screen media.
2. As a parent, will you permit your child to watch violent videos or play violent video games? Why or why not? Explain how you would address the various types of media. Discuss your personal policy and explain the rationale.
3. How does social media affect adolescent development? What are the positive and negative effects of use, and how do these effects influence development?

RISK AND RESILIENCE

15.5 Discuss the interplay of risk and protective factors in promoting children's resilience to adversity.

Children live and interact with a complex web of interconnected contexts that influence their development. While some of these contexts and interactions promote children's well-being, others threaten it. Experience with early life stress, foster care, and exposure to violence are contextual circumstances that pose risks to development. Children's responses and their resulting developmental outcomes depend on their personal characteristics and their interactions with the people and settings that surround them.

Exposure to Early Life Stress

Very young infants may not have explicit memories of specific experiences and events, but early exposure to trauma may affect their development in ways that can last a lifetime. Maladaptive contexts not only present risks for physical harm, but the experience of trauma also can invisibly and over the long-term elevate risks to children's emotional development and mental health (Juruena et al., 2020; Mueller & Tronick, 2019).

Early childhood trauma can have a biological impact on emotional development. The experience of early social adversity in infancy may cause epigenetic changes to the genes responsible for regulating the endocrine system, which controls hormone production and release throughout life (Agorastos et al., 2019; Nicolaides et al., 2024). Infancy and early childhood may be a particularly plastic time in development with greater potential for epigenetic changes that may sensitize individuals' stress responses throughout their lifetime (Laurent et al., 2016; Mariani Wigley et al., 2021). These changes can affect brain development and function (Herzberg & Gunnar, 2020). Early life stress is associated with higher levels of internalizing and externalizing problems in school children (de Maat et al., 2022)

However, not all infants and young children exhibit heightened reactivity in response to early-life stress (Hegde & Mitra, 2020). Some infants exposed to trauma show lower levels of stress hormones and reduced reactivity to stress (al'Absi et al., 2021; Turecki & Meaney, 2016). The developmental outcomes of early life stress are influenced by the timing and intensity of the adversity. Exposure to particularly intense and chronic stress early in development may initially result in hyperactive stress responses, which can eventually lead to blunted responses (Laurent et al., 2016). Blunted responses may reflect adaptations to chronically stressful situations. Conversely, exposure to unpredictable stressors may lead to heightened stress reactivity as individuals adapt to volatile and unexpected situations (Blair, 2010). While both heightened and blunted stress responses may be adaptive attempts to optimize survival in nonoptimal caregiving environments, these adaptations may also carry behavioral costs, such as increased distress when confronted with stress and long-term anxiety and depressive symptoms, which negatively affect developmental trajectories (Laurent et al., 2016).

While early life stress poses risks to emotional development, the quality of the caregiving environment also influences the developing stress response system and can offer opportunities for plasticity (Hegde & Mitra, 2020). Caregivers can regulate and buffer infants' hormonal and behavioral responses to threats (Howell et al., 2017). Sensitive, consistent, and predictable caregiving promotes a sense of safety in infants, which can shape infants' physiological reactions to current and future stress (Gee & Cohodes, 2021). That is, sensitive caregiving can reduce the negative epigenetic effects of early life stress (Janusek et al., 2019; Mariani Wigley et al., 2022; Provenzi et al., 2020). Warm parenting within a predictable stimulating environment with supportive adults and family can help infants develop the self-regulation skills to adapt to adverse contexts. Unfortunately, trauma can disrupt the caregiving system, making adaptation difficult.

Foster Care

Foster care is a child welfare arrangement where a child is temporarily placed outside the home because the parents cannot provide care or safety. Although intended as a temporary placement, many children and adolescents remain in the foster care system for months and years.

Children and adolescents in foster care face various risks for adjustment prior to entering care, including maltreatment, abandonment, family breakdown, parental substance abuse or prenatal exposure to substances (Leloux-Opmeer et al., 2016; Marcellus & Badry, 2023). Many have preexisting problems, including physical and mental health, emotional, cognitive, and behavioral problems and problems at school (Engler et al., 2022; Farruggia et al., 2018). The nature of foster care, including its instability, can worsen these processes. Children and adolescents in foster care experience multiple transitions in and out of care, including returning to their parents' home when the parents are deemed able to care for them and moving from foster home to foster home.

Children and adolescents in foster care often enter the system with many pressing problems that can challenge the adults who care for them (Konijn et al., 2019). Parenting stress, in turn, is associated with increases in behavior problems (West et al., 2023). Foster children's adjustment relies on warm and supportive relationships, especially a close relationship with a specific caregiver, family member, or adult. Relationships can provide a sense of stability, security, and belonging. Children and adolescents in foster care also benefit from stable housing placements that enable them to develop these relationships. Effective interventions for children in foster care help them develop skills in coping, communication, help seeking, and emotional regulation (Blakeslee et al., 2023). Peer and adult mentorship can support their social development and offer encouragement to succeed in school (Nuñez et al., 2022; Taussig et al., 2020).

Interventions that target foster parents also help the children they foster. Effective interventions promote sensitive parenting, developmentally appropriate discipline, parenting knowledge and attitudes, and they reduce parenting stress, enabling adults to effectively raise a child they foster, which is associated with positive child outcomes (Schoemaker et al., 2020).

Many adolescents in foster care for a long period "age out" of the system, transitioning to independence once they reach adulthood. About 18,000 adolescents face this transition annually (Administration for Children and Families, 2019). The transition is often difficult because adolescents in foster care often have not experienced the same guidance, support, and encouragement as their non–foster care peers. Emancipated youth experience high rates of homelessness because they lack the social ties that many young adults rely on, such as living at home and receiving financial support from their parents (Bender et al., 2015). They also display high rates of psychological, behavioral, and social problems (Farruggia et al., 2018).

A successful transition from foster care requires that youth have access to various services and opportunities, including education, employment, and reliable transportation to school and work (Rome & Raskin, 2019). Access to basic resources such as food, mental health, and housing is critical. Assistance with education, including identifying, applying to, and funding schools, is also important. Employment assistance includes job placement, résumé building, and interviewing skills. Foster care alumni agree that life skills, such as cooking, budgeting, and life management, are important to learn before transitioning out of foster care (Armstrong-Heimsoth et al., 2021). A connection and positive relationships with at least one person supports youth who are transitioning from foster care (Stubbs et al., 2023). A mentor or other adult from a foster care organization can monitor progress and provide guidance. Young people are more likely to be aware of and utilize services when mentors provide monitoring, communication, and encouragement. Early initiation of services, easily accessible information, and individualized programs can help young people successfully transition from foster care to independent adult functioning (Häggman-Laitila et al., 2019).

Neighborhood and Community Violence

Violence is a pervasive problem for many communities. Children may be exposed to violence in many settings, such as at the playground, on the way to school, in the neighborhood, and outside their homes. The chronic and unpredictable nature of community violence presents a constant threat to children's and parents' sense of safety (Ceballo et al., 2022). These experiences can leave children feeling as if danger is ever-present and inescapable. Chronic exposure to community violence may lead children to believe that the world is a dangerous and unpredictable place and parents cannot offer protection (Farver et al., 2005). As children become more independent and spend more time with peers and away from home, their exposure to violence tends to increase (Gollub et al., 2019). However, school-age children's emerging skills in emotional regulation leave them ill-equipped to process these traumatic experiences and manage their emotions (Estrada et al., 2023; Saraiya et al., 2013).

Children who live in communities of chronic violence may show symptoms of post-traumatic stress disorder (PTSD) and anxiety, including fear of being alone, worries for their safety and the safety of loved ones, and difficulty sleeping (Birkeland et al., 2022; Wright et al., 2016). They also risk experiencing academic problems, behavior problems, and increased risk taking during adolescence, including carrying a gun (Baiden et al., 2024; DiClemente & Richards, 2022; Schneider, 2020). Additionally, exposure to community violence is associated with aggressive and disruptive behavior in children and higher rates of bullying other children (J. P. Davis et al., 2020). Prolonged exposure to high levels of violence can also increase the risk of desensitization in children, making them less sensitive to the impact of violence (Gaylord-Harden et al., 2016).

Parents play a crucial role in how children process their experiences, especially in the face of community violence. Parents' ability to regulate their own experience of trauma and manage their own stress and emotions influences children's adjustment (Halevi et al., 2016). However, parents exposed to community violence may feel alienated from their community and unsafe, which can lead to distress, frustration, and a sense of helplessness. These factors can compromise parenting and contribute to harsh, controlling parenting (Guo et al., 2018; Sim et al., 2018). When dealing with their grief, fear, and anxiety, parents may be less available for physical and emotional caregiving, which in turn predicts poor child adjustment (Farver et al., 2005). Parents exposed to community violence also experience heightened risk for depression (Chen & Lee, 2021; Dempsey et al., 2016). Parents face many challenges, but those who can instill a sense of warmth and security are best able to support their children's needs and promote well-being (Saraiya et al., 2013).

Interventions to help children exposed to violence in their communities tend to emphasize teaching cognitive strategies for coping, such as connecting thoughts with feelings and identifying constructive strategies for processing traumatic memories (Ali-Saleh Darawshy et al., 2020). Such programs also teach social problem-solving skills and stress management, including relaxation techniques. Effective interventions to combat the effects of community violence support parents and provide children with safe spaces, such as after-school community centers, that allow children to interact with each other and caring adults in a safe context that permits them to develop skills in coping, conflict resolution, and emotional regulation (Yule et al., 2019).

War and Terror

War and terrorism can have a profound impact on the lives of children, disrupting their home, school, and community environments. The sudden chaos of war can interfere with children's daily routines and place safe concerns at the forefront of their minds. Traumatic experiences such as hearing bomb blasts, witnessing deaths, fleeing home and community in search of safety, and sudden losses of loved ones can unravel the contextual and social fabric of children's and families' lives (Bürgin et al., 2022; Werner, 2012).

Acts of war and terror affect children, families, and communities with dire consequences for development.

SOPA Images/LightRocket/Getty Images

Refugee children who are displaced from their homes and countries are particularly vulnerable, experiencing heightened risk for PTSD symptoms, sleep difficulties, depression, and behavior problems (Hazer & Gredebäck, 2023; Murray, 2019). Children exposed to war may also display heightened vigilance to threats, prolonged fear of being alone, safety concerns, preoccupations with danger, and aggression (Huesmann et al., 2016; Michalek et al., 2022). A recent study of Syrian refugee children exposed to war found that over 80% experienced high levels of PTSD, depression, and behavior problems (McEwen et al., 2022). About two thirds of the children still displayed symptoms related to these issues even 1 year later.

Intervening to assist children in war zones is difficult due to the danger and difficulty of accessing families. However, relationships with parents can protect children from the negative effects of exposure to war (Al-Yagon et al., 2022). Interventions to assist refugee children promote children's attachment to parents and caregivers by ensuring that children stay physically and emotionally close to their parents (Bürgin et al., 2022). Parents who can instill a sense of warmth and security can best support their children's needs and promote healthy adjustment (Saraiya et al., 2013). Parents are an important source of support, but they also experience trauma. A recent meta-analysis showed, perhaps not surprisingly, that parenting behaviors varied with parents' exposure to danger (Eltanamly et al., 2021). Parents with more exposure to war showed less warmth and more harshness toward their children, which influenced children's adjustment, such as PTSD symptoms, depression and anxiety, social problems, and externalizing behavior. Parents who lived under threat, but not war, tended to show more warmth and overprotection. Interventions that support refugee parents aim to lower their stress, improve their well-being, and increase parenting knowledge and skills so that they can support their children (Miller et al., 2020).

Teachers and school-based interventions can help children adjust to the trauma (Asarnow, 2011). However, refugee children lose their daily school routine and must adapt to a new environment, peers, school, and often language (Murray, 2019). Restoring educational routines can provide structure and support children in regulating their emotions, behavior, and relationships. When schools are closed, locally trained paraprofessionals can help families establish educational resources until children can return to their usual schools.

Government policies regarding resettlement, adults' access to employment, family access to mental and physical health care, and access to education influence refugee children's adjustment (Arakelyan & Ager, 2021). No intervention can erase the effects of exposure to the trauma of war and terror, but interventions can help bolster the factors that promote resilience to adversity.

Resilience

Many children exposed to extraordinary circumstances and difficult environments, such as early life adversity, community violence, war, and poverty, show positive adjustment despite their experiences. These children demonstrate **resilience**, the ability to respond or perform positively in the face of adversity or disadvantage (Cutuli et al., 2021; Masten et al., 2023). Resilience is determined by a complex interplay of risk factors and protective factors (Rutter, 2023).

Risk factors are conditions that threaten healthy development and functioning (Luthar et al., 2015; Masten et al., 2016). They are associated with a higher likelihood of negative outcomes, such as psychological, behavioral, and health problems, including anxiety, depression, frequent illnesses and hospitalizations, poor academic achievement, and delinquent activity (Masten et al., 2021). Each of these poor outcomes poses cascading risks to future development and adjustment. Risk factors are cumulative and their effects interact, making adjustment more challenging as children and families face more threats (Mesman et al., 2021).

Fortunately, protective factors can buffer some of the poor outcomes that accompany adverse circumstances and contexts. **Protective factors** are associated with positive adjustment and may arise from within the child, from the family or extended family, and from the community (Traub & Boynton-Jarrett, 2017; Twum-Antwi et al., 2020). Warm relationships with caregivers and other adults, active engagement at school and the community, participation in routines, and church attendance are protective factors that promote adjustment and can reduce the negative outcomes associated with adversity (Masten et al., 2021; K. M. Powell et al., 2020).

Resilient children can manage their trauma and anxiety and show high self-esteem, low levels of depression, and few behavioral problems (Cutuli et al., 2021; Nabors, 2022). They tend to have personal characteristics that protect them from adversity and help them learn from experience, such as an easy temperament, a sense of competence, self-control, good information processing and problem-solving skills, friendliness, and empathy (Collado-Soler et al., 2023; Twum-Antwi et al., 2020). Children who engage in more prosocial behavior tend to show greater resilience to war's damaging effects than children who are less prosocial (Guido et al., 2021). A fundamental characteristic of resilience is the ability to regulate one's emotions and behavior (Mesman et al., 2021). Resilient individuals also have a proactive orientation, take initiative, believe in their own effectiveness, and have a positive sense of self (Brodie et al., 2019; Pérez-González et al., 2017).

Avenues for fostering resilience include promoting children's strengths and bolstering children's executive function skills, self-appraisals, and sense of efficacy (B. J. Ellis et al., 2017; Masten et al., 2023; Twum-Antwi et al., 2020). Resilience is accompanied by strong and supportive relationships with caregivers or adults who provide warm guidance and firm support (Arditti & Johnson, 2020; Labella & Masten, 2018). Effective supports for children who are at risk target parents' mental health and self-care skills, aid parents in establishing routines, promote parenting skills, and help parents understand the impact of trauma on children (Humphreys et al., 2022; Nabors, 2022). Table 15.2 illustrates characteristics that promote resilience in children. Resilient children illustrate an important finding: Exposure to adversity in childhood does not necessarily lead to maladjustment; many children thrive despite challenging experiences.

TABLE 15.2 Characteristics of Resilient Children		
Individual Competencies	**Family Competencies and Characteristics**	**School and Community Characteristics**
Coping skills	Close relationships with parents and caregivers	Access to local churches
Easy temperament	Organized home	After-school programs
Emotional regulation abilities	Parental involvement in children's education	Availability of emergency services
Good cognitive abilities	Positive family climate	Mentoring programs and opportunities to form relationships with adults
Intelligence	Postsecondary education of parents	Health care availability
Positive outlook	Provision of support	Instruction in conflict management
Positive self-concept	Religiosity and engagement with the church	Opportunity to develop and practice leadership skills
Religiosity	Socioeconomic advantage	Peer programs, such as big brother/big sister programs
Self-efficacy (feeling of control over one's destiny)	Warm but assertive parenting	Programs to assist developing self-management skills
Talents valued by others		Public safety
		Support networks outside of the family, such as supportive adults and peers
		Ties to prosocial organizations
		Well-funded schools with highly qualified teachers
		Youth programs

Sources: Adapted from Cutuli, J. J., Herbers, J. E., Masten, A. S., & Reed, M. G. J. (2021). Resilience in development. In C. R. Snyder, S. J. Lopez, L. M. Edwards, & S. C. Marques (Eds.), *The Oxford handbook of positive psychology* (pp. 74–88). Oxford; Masten, A. S., Lucke, C. M., Nelson, K. M., & Stallworthy, I. C. (2021). Resilience in development and psychopathology: Multisystem perspectives. *Annual Review of Clinical Psychology, 17,* 521–549. https://doi.org/10.1146/annurev-clinpsy-081219-120307; Powell, K. M., Rahm-Knigge, R. L., & Conner, B. T. (2020). Resilience protective factors checklist (RPFC): Buffering childhood adversity and promoting positive outcomes. *Psychological Reports, 124*(4), 1437–1461. https://doi.org/10.1177/0033294120950288

THINKING IN CONTEXT 15.5

Apply Bronfenbrenner's bioecological systems theory to consider children's resilience to social problems. Choose any of the social issues we have discussed in this section (such as early life adversity). Identify risk and protective factors that may influence a child's adjustment. Specifically:

1. Consider the child's personality, skills, and development. What factors might promote resilient responses? What might hinder resilience?
2. Consider the microsystem. How might the people and places in which children interact influence their response to adversity?
3. How might the microsystem factors identified interact (mesosystem)?
4. What exosystem influences play a role in increasing or decreasing children's resilience?
5. How might macrosystem factors affect the bioecological system? How might these outside factors influence resilience?

APPLY YOUR KNOWLEDGE

Nine-year-old Lavette walks home from school alone, quietly singing to herself as she passes the empty playground around the corner from her home. "Mom says don't go in there alone," she reminds herself. "Sure, I might fall off the slide or something, but Mom's not worried about that. It's those high school kids. She says it's dangerous. I know, I see the fights." Lavette continues, stepping around the glass from a shattered car window. "Another one," she mutters. "Mom says to be careful and look around before going into our building," Lavette reminds herself as she pulls her keys out of her pocket. Finally, she enters the quiet apartment and settles down with her tablet to watch some videos. Lavette's phone rings. "Hi, Mom. Yes, I'm home, no problems."

Soon Lavette gets a text from her best friend. "Say hi?" Lavette grabs her tablet and soon her friend Paula is smiling back. They chat all afternoon about kids at school, music, and their shared interest in dancing. The friends have danced in a club for years, but it was recently placed on hold because of a shooting outside the community center. The director quit, saying that it's unsafe, and they haven't found another.

"Die!!" screamed 11-year-old Anton. "Anton! Be quiet!" Lavette shouted. "There he goes again, yelling at his video game. The first time I heard him yell about shooting someone, I thought it was real and I was scared. Now I know he's just playing his creepy killing video game," she tells Paula. "Ugh. It's too realistic," Paula replies. "We see enough of that on our way to school."

1. How does Lavette and Paula's friendship compare to friendships typically seen in children of their age group?

2. What challenges does community violence pose for children's development? How do Lavette, Paula, and Anton demonstrate resilience? What strategies and behaviors have they developed to support their well-being?

3. Discuss the research regarding violent video game use and development. Is Anton's reaction unusual? Should his mother be concerned?

4. How has technology supported Lavette and Paula's friendship. In what ways might their friendship be different if such technology were not available?

5. Identify risk and protective factors that Lavette, Paula, and Anton experience. Consider individual and contextual factors in their lives. How might these collectively influence their capacity for resilience?

6. If a counselor at the community center wanted to foster resilience in the local children, what characteristics would they seek to foster in the children, and what environmental changes could be made to support these characteristics? What specific suggestions might the counselor make for Lavette, Paula, and Anton?

CHAPTER SUMMARY

15.1 Discuss the range of forms play takes and its influence on children's development.

Play contributes to physical, cognitive, and socioemotional development. Types of play include nonsocial activity, parallel play, associative play, and cooperative play. Sociodramatic play, where children interact with other children, take on roles, and act out stories, helps children explore social rules and conventions, promotes language skills, and is associated with social competence. Rough-and-tumble play, characterized by vigorous physical activity, helps children assert themselves, interact with other children, and engage in physical play without hurting others. Imaginary companions are common in early childhood and provide similar benefits to real friends, including companionship, social interactions, social roles, and emotional regulation. Culture also shapes children's play. Children in collectivist societies tend to play games that emphasize cooperation, while children in Western cultures that emphasize individual rights tend to play competitive games. Children's play also varies with contextual circumstances, such as the amount of household work that is common for children in a given culture, the availability of toys, and parental encouragement of play.

15.2 Examine peer relationships in childhood and adolescence.

In childhood and adolescence, friends tend to be chosen based on similarity. Friendship qualities such as trust, loyalty, and shared values become important with age. High-quality friendships endure, but friendships may come and go. Friendship instability and loss are associated with emotional and behavioral problems. Close, supportive friendships are associated with positive adjustment and well-being. Popular children are well-liked by their peers and have a variety of positive characteristics. Some popular children instead exhibit antisocial and aggressive behavior. Children who experience peer rejection tend to be disliked and shunned. Adolescents form close friendships that expand to include cliques, small groups of tight-knit friends who share similarities such as demographics and attitudes. Cliques provide adolescents with a sense of inclusion, worth, support, and companionship. In contrast to cliques, crowds are larger and looser groups based on shared characteristics, interests, and reputation. Peer influence occurs within the context of friendship and includes both risky and prosocial behavior. Susceptibility to peer influence tends to decline with advances in psychosocial maturity that support independent decision making.

15.3 Analyze the school context and its influence on children and adolescents.

Education can be approached in two ways: teacher-centered direct instruction or student-centered constructivist instruction. Early childhood education and intervention programs have been successful in improving cognitive performance and long-lasting social and physical outcomes for economically disadvantaged children, but poverty and inadequate public schools can have long-lasting effects. Technology is an important tool, but access remains a challenge for low SES and rural communities. Children with special needs are entitled to an IEP, and legislation mandates they be educated in the least restrictive environment possible. School transitions can be challenging due to changes in environments, teachers, standards, support, and peers. Negative effects occur when there is a poor match between adolescents' developmental needs and what the school environment affords in its organization and characteristics.

15.4 Summarize the effects of screen media use in infancy, childhood, and adolescence.

Frequent exposure to screen media in infants is associated with poorer language and self-regulation skills. However, young children can benefit from educational media if they watch limited screen time and educational programs, co-viewing with caregivers. Screen use increases over childhood into adolescence and at higher rates for children of color and those in low SES homes. Exposure to violence on television has been associated with aggressive behavior in children and aggressive thoughts but not behavior in adolescents. Large comprehensive reviews of research suggest that relationships between video games and aggressive behavior and reduced prosocial behavior are negligible once family factors and other variables are considered. Social media has both positive and negative effects on adolescents. Most adolescents feel better connected to their friends through social media activity, but it can also be stressful. There are inconsistent findings on the relationship between social media use and psychological well-being. Social media serves developmental functions for adolescents by helping them develop and maintain friendships and offering opportunities for identity development.

15.5 Discuss the interplay of risk and protective factors in promoting children's resilience to adversity.

Resilience is the ability to respond positively to adversity or disadvantage and is determined by the interplay of risk and protective factors. Risk factors threaten healthy development and functioning and are associated with negative outcomes, while protective factors promote positive adjustment. Early life stress can have long-term effects on children's stress response system. Children in foster care often enter with preexisting problems that may become worse with multiple transitions and placement instability. Exposure to community violence and war are associated with PTSD and adjustment difficulties. Sensitive, consistent, and warm parenting supports children's emotional development and adjustment to adversity. Interventions that promote children's coping, help seeking, and emotional regulation skills help them adjust. Interventions that teaching parenting skills, address caregivers' distress, and reduce parenting stress also support children.

KEY TERMS

- Aggressive-rejected children
- Clique
- Constructivist classroom
- Crowd
- Developmentally appropriate practice
- Direct instruction
- Foster care
- Imaginary companions
- Montessori school
- Peer acceptance
- Peer rejection
- Popular
- Project Head Start
- Protective factor
- Representational play
- Resilience
- Risk factors
- Rough-and-tumble play
- Sociodramatic play
- Withdrawn-rejected children

CAREERS IN CHILD DEVELOPMENT: CONTEXTS OF DEVELOPMENT

Lifespan development occurs in all the contexts in which we live, such as home, school, and work. There are career opportunities within each of these contexts.

Preschool and Child Care Center Director

Visitors to childcare centers are most familiar with the childcare worker or teacher who cares for infants and toddlers. Who hires and supervises the childcare workers? Who creates and administers programs? Who oversees the operations of the center? Childcare directors or administrators may not have daily contact with each infant, but their work affects infants and parents daily.

Childcare directors are responsible for operating and leading the work of a childcare center. They create or play a lead role in constructing the center's mission statement which outlines the philosophy that guides the center's work. Childcare directors lead teachers in creating instructional resources to use in class and develop policies such as scheduling outside time, naps, and other activities. They are also responsible for running the business, including advertising, maintaining financial records, and directing human resources. Directors may market the center, take parents on tours of the facility, write budgets, and prepare annual reports. Human resource activities include hiring, overseeing, and evaluating employees and mediating disputes.

The requirements for becoming a childcare director vary by state and center. Some require a bachelor's degree (or higher) in early childhood education. Others require a high school diploma. Some states and centers may require experience as a childcare staff member before becoming a director. Most require directors of childcare centers to have certification, such as the National Administration Credential (NAC), which requires completion of a 45-hour course. The 2023 median salary for childcare directors was about $51,000 (U.S. Bureau of Labor Statistics, 2024).

Recreation Worker

Recreation workers organize activities to help people to stay active, improve fitness, and have fun. They develop, plan, organize, and direct recreational activities for people of all ages (e.g., aerobics, arts and crafts, performing arts, camping, or recreational sports). Some recreation workers are camp counselors who lead and supervise children and adolescents in outdoor activities such as swimming, boating, horseback riding, camping, hiking, sports, music, drama, and art. Other recreation workers might work in youth programs or church activities. In residential camps recreation workers may assume a therapeutic role in helping adolescents build social and problem-solving skills.

Recreation workers are employed in educational settings, park and recreational centers, community activity centers, health clubs and fitness centers, country clubs, medical and rehabilitation centers, and nursing homes. A position as an entry-level recreation worker generally does not require a bachelor's degree, but a college diploma creates opportunities for advancement to supervisory positions. The mean annual wage for recreation workers was about $34,000 in 2023 (U.S. Bureau of Labor Statistics, 2024).

School Counselor

School counselors, sometimes called guidance counselors, help students understand and cope with social, behavioral, and personal problems. School counselors use counseling skills to identify and prevent problems and aid students in learning skills to enhance their personal, social, and academic growth. They work with parents, teachers, principals, medical professionals, and social workers to address the issues that may be inhibiting a student's learning and school performance. School counselors may provide special services such as substance abuse prevention programs, conflict management, parenting education training, and supervising peer counseling programs. They work with individuals, small groups, or entire classes.

Whereas school psychologists work with students with special needs, school counselors are available to all students, often leaving their doors open for students to visit as they choose. They may identify students who are distressed and may need further assistance from a school psychologist. School counselors may also play a role in helping students prepare to apply to college or make plans for after graduation.

Becoming a school counselor requires a master's degree, supervised experience, and obtaining school counseling certification. Some states require public school counselors to have both counseling and teaching certificates. The median salary for school counselors was about $62,000 in 2023 (U.S. Bureau of Labor Statistics, 2024).

School Psychologist

School psychologists work with schoolchildren to improve their educational experience, mental health, and behavior. School psychologists engage in various activities, such as consultation, assessment, intervention and prevention, educational or training services, research, and program development. Educational services may take the form of teaching educators classroom management techniques, learning strategies, and ways to identify at-risk children. School psychologists help teachers and schools by teaching educators how to identify children who may have learning disorders or are at risk of mental health problems, providing skills training for parents and teachers to cope with disruptive behavior, and developing school initiatives to promote student social development and create a safe environment, such as bullying and substance use prevention.

School psychologists spend much of their time assessing children. They use instruments and diagnostic tools to evaluate the nature of a student's academic or behavioral problem and identify the most appropriate intervention. School psychologists evaluate students' academic skills and learning aptitudes, personality and emotional development, social skills, learning environment and school climate, eligibility for special education, and effectiveness of intervention strategies. They then teach and train children, teachers, parents, and others who interact with the child. School psychologists also provide counseling for children, parents, and families, such as family therapy, substance abuse counseling, and grief counseling. They counsel individuals and groups of children in skills training, such as social skills, coping strategies, and problem solving.

Becoming a school psychologist requires education beyond the master's degree. School psychologists obtain either a specialist-level degree or a doctoral degree. The specialist-level degree comprises 60 credits, whereas the doctoral degree entails 90 credits. Both specialist and doctoral levels require year-long 1,200-hour supervised internships. School psychologists must seek state licensure, typically an exam. In 2023, school psychologists earned a median salary of about $85,000 (U.S. Bureau of Labor Statistics, 2024).

Marriage and Family Therapists

Marriage and family therapists are counselors that adopt a family system perspective, the recognition that all family members interact and influence each other as a dynamic system, similar to the bioecological perspective we have discussed throughout this book. When conducting therapy, marriage and family therapists consider the set of relationships in which a person is embedded. They treat many problems, such as depression, marital problems, anxiety, parent-child relationship difficulties, and substance abuse. Marriage and family therapists emphasize short-term therapy designed to change specific behaviors and communication patterns and promote people's strengths.

Marriage and family therapists are found in mental health centers, hospitals, community centers, and private practice. Becoming a marriage and family therapist requires earning a master's degree in marital and family therapy, which includes an internship. They must also complete 2 years (3,000 hours) of supervised clinical experience and pass a licensure exam to practice independently. In 2023, marriage and family therapists earned a median salary of about $59,000 (U.S. Bureau of Labor Statistics, 2024).

User Design and Usability

Products are designed for specific purposes, often for specific populations, such as children or older adults. Products designed for young children might have bright colors, large buttons, and a stimulating sensory component such as a beeping noise or flashing lights. A variety of professionals work to create products that are accessible, functional, and attractive. Positions in user design carry many titles, such as usability specialist, user experience strategist, and user interface designer. What all these *user-oriented* titles have in common is an emphasis on understanding how people use and interact with a product and improving their experience.

User experience designers work with all kinds of products, such as toys, computer hardware and software, electronic equipment, and cars. Some work on teams to create product prototypes and test and modify them based on input from potential users. Human development knowledge can help create websites, apps, and video games with users' development in mind. For example, an understanding of how attention, perception, and cognition changes with age can help user experience designers create software that is easily understood, meaningful, and engaging for children of different ages. This might include creating software layouts and backgrounds that are sensitive to children's developmental or sensory needs, by including larger text and icons and contrasting colors that are easily distinguished. They might record and analyze users' behaviors when they try to accomplish a task using a software product. They interview users about their experience with the product: Was it easy to use? What confused them about the interface? The resulting knowledge is used to improve the design.

Preparation for user experience careers emphasizes experience over a specific major or degree. Web design, graphic design, computer programming, and an understanding of human development and behavior are helpful. Some colleges offer bachelor's and master's degrees in user design, as well as one or two semester programs and certifications in user design. The median salary in this field is $68,000 at lower experience levels, ranging to $120,000 with years of expertise (Salary.com, 2022).

Toy and Media Research

Some toys captivate young children yet fail to interest older children. How do companies create toys that meet children's specific interests of a given age? It requires knowledge of development to make toys fun and educational. Some companies employ people to conduct toy development research. These researchers might speak with children about their interests and assess children's reactions to prototypes of toys or current toys in the market. They might conduct focus groups with parents and children to determine their views about specific products and to get feedback on toy designs. The resulting knowledge is used to improve the product. They may also determine how to market particular toys based on their observations of children.

These same techniques may be applied to create children's media. Understanding development helps media creators design television and other media to fit children's attention spans and interests. Focus groups and observations can help media creators design effective media. Positions in toy and media research might hold the job title of *market research analyst*, which earned a median salary of about $75,000 in 2023 (U.S. Bureau of Labor Statistics, 2024). The level of education required for a market research or product development position varies with the employer. Entry-level positions usually require a bachelor's degree. The average market research assistant salary at all experience levels was $65,000 in 2023 (Salary.com, 2024). These positions might include other titles, so reviewing the organizational structure of specific companies is a useful way of learning about opportunities in these areas.

GLOSSARY

accommodation: In Piaget's theory, the process by which schemas are modified or new schemas created in light of experience.

Achievement attributions: Children's beliefs about the causes of their performance, whether success or failure.

Achievement motivation: The willingness to persist at challenging tasks and meet high standards of accomplishment.

adolescent growth spurt: The first outward sign of puberty, refers to a rapid gain in height and weight that generally begins in girls at about age 10 and in boys about age 12.

adoption: A legal process in which a person assumes the parenting rights and responsibilities of a child.

affordances: Refers to the actional properties of objects—their nature, opportunities, and limits.

age of viability: The age at which the fetus may survive if born prematurely; begins about 22 weeks after conception.

Aggression: A form of antisocial behavior intended to harm others through physical, verbal, or relational actions.

Aggressive-rejected children: Children who are confrontational and hostile toward peers and are shunned by peers.

amniocentesis: A prenatal diagnostic procedure in which a small sample of the amniotic fluid is extracted from the mother's uterus and subject to genetic analysis.

amnion: A membrane that surrounds the fetus and contains amniotic fluid.

Androgynous: Identifying with characteristics of both genders.

anencephaly: A neural tube defect that results in the failure of all or part of the brain to develop, resulting in death prior or shortly after birth.

animism: The belief that inanimate objects are alive and have feelings and intentions; a characteristic of preoperational reasoning.

anorexia nervosa: An eating disorder characterized by compulsive starvation and extreme weight loss and accompanied by a distorted body image.

A-not-B error: An object permanence error in which an infant uncovers an object several times in one place (Place A), and continues to search for the object in Place A even after seeing the object moved to a new location, Place B.

Apgar scale: A quick assessment that evaluates a baby's immediate health at birth, including appearance, pulse, grimace, activity, and respiration.

appearance–reality distinction: The ability to recognize that an object can appear to be something different from what it actually is; marks children's ability to represent an object in multiple ways.

applied developmental science: A field that studies lifespan interactions between individuals and the contexts in which they live, and applies research findings to real-world settings to create interventions and influence social policy.

artificial insemination: A means of conception in which sperm are injected into the vagina by a means other than sexual intercourse.

assimilation: In Piaget's theory, the process by which new experiences are interpreted and integrated into preexisting schemas.

assisted reproductive technology (ART): alternative methods of conception that rely on medical technology

asthma: a persistent inflammatory disorder of the airways that causes wheezing and coughing

attachment: A lasting emotional tie between two individuals.

attention: The ability to direct one's awareness.

attention-deficit/hyperactivity disorder: A condition characterized by persistent difficulties with attention and/or impulsivity; people with ADHD often face challenges fulfilling expectations for performance and behavior in school and daily life.

Authoritarian parenting style: An approach to childrearing that emphasizes high behavioral control and low levels of warmth and autonomy granting.

Authoritative parenting style: An approach to childrearing in which parents are warm and sensitive to children's needs, grant appropriate autonomy, and exert firm control.

autism spectrum disorder: Refers to a family of disorders that range in severity and are marked by social and communication challenges, often accompanied by restrictive and repetitive behaviors.

autobiographical memories: The recollection of a personally meaningful event that took place at a specific time and place in one's past.

Autonomous morality: Piaget's second stage of morality in which children have a more flexible view of rules as they begin to value fairness and equality and account for factors like act, intent, and situation.

autonomy: The ability to make and carry out decisions independently.

Axon: part of the neuron; long tube-like structure that extends from the neuron and carries electrical signals to other neurons.

babbling: An infant's repetition of syllables such as "ba-ba-ba-ba" and "ma-ma-ma," which begins at about 6 months of age.

behavior genetics: The field of study that examines how genes and environment combine to influence the diversity of human traits, abilities, and behaviors.

behaviorism: A theoretical approach that studies how observable behavior is controlled by the physical and social environment through conditioning.

binge eating disorder: An eating disorder characterized by binges, consuming an abnormally large amount of food (thousands of calories) in a single sitting coupled with a feeling of being out of control.

bioecological systems theory: Created by Urie Bronfenbrenner, this theory poses that individuals are embedded in a series of interacting contexts, systems, which reciprocally influence the individual

blastocyst: A thin-walled, fluid-filled sphere containing an inner mass of cells from which the embryo will develop; is implanted into the uterine wall during the germinal period.

body mass index (BMI): A measure of body fat based on weight in kilograms divided by height in meters squared (kg/m2).

Brazelton Neonatal Behavioral Assessment Scale (NBAS): The most common neurobehavioral assessment administered to newborns that is administered a few days after birth to assess neurological functioning, including the strength of 20 inborn reflexes, responsiveness to the physical and social environment, and changes in state.

breech position: A feet-first birth position that poses risks to the neonate's health; often results in a cesarean section.

Broca's area: The region in the brain that controls the ability to use language for expression; damage to the area inhibits fluent speech.

bulimia nervosa: An eating disorder characterized by recurrent episodes of binge eating and subsequent purging usually by induced vomiting and the use of laxatives.

Bullying: An ongoing interaction in which a child repeatedly attempts to inflict physical, verbal, or social harm on another child; also known as *peer victimization*.

Bully-victim: An individual who attacks or inflicts harm on others and who is also attacked or harmed by others; the child is both bully and victim.

canalization: The tendency for a trait that is biologically programmed to be restricted to only a few outcomes.

Care orientation: Gilligan's feminine mode of moral reasoning, characterized by a desire to maintain relationships and a responsibility to avoid hurting others.

case study: An in-depth examination of a single individual (or small group of individuals).

Categorical self: A self-description based on broad categories such as sex, age, and physical characteristics that children use to guide their behavior.

categorization: An adaptive mental process in which objects are grouped into conceptual categories, allowing for organized storage of information in memory, efficient retrieval of that information, and the capacity to respond with familiarity to new stimuli from a common class.

central executive: In information processing, the part of our mental system that directs the flow of information and regulates cognitive activities such as attention, action, and problem solving.

centration: The tendency to focus on one part of a stimulus, situation, or idea and exclude all others; a characteristic of preoperational reasoning.

Cephalocaudal pattern of development: The principle that growth proceeds from the head downward; the head and upper regions of the body develop before the lower regions.

cerebellum: Subcortical (below the cortex) part of the brain responsible for body movements, balance, and coordination.

cesarean section: A surgical procedure that removes the fetus from the uterus through the abdomen; also known as a C-section.

child abuse: Any intentional harm to a minor (under the age of 18), including repeated actions that harm the child physically, emotionally, sexually, or through neglect; also known as child maltreatment.

child assent: A child's agreement to participate in a study or procedure.

chorionic villus sampling (CVS): Prenatal diagnostic test that is conducted on cells sampled from the chorion to detects chromosomal abnormalities.

chromosome: rod-like molecules that contain DNA

chronosystem: In bioecological systems theory, temporal context, referring to how people and contexts change over time.

Cisgender: An individual who identifies with his or her sex assigned at birth.

class inclusion: Involves understanding hierarchical relationships among items.

classical conditioning: A form of learning in which an environmental stimulus becomes associated with stimuli that elicit reflex responses

classification: Involves organizing items into groups based on similar characteristics.

Clique: A tightly knit peer group of about three to eight close friends who share similarities such as demographics and attitudes.

Code-switching: Alternating between languages.

Cognitive equilibration: Balance between assimilation and accommodation.

Cognitive operations: Reversible mental actions.

cognitive schemas: A mental representation, such as concepts, ideas, and ways of interacting with the world.

cognitive-developmental theory: A perspective posited by Piaget that views individuals as active explorers of their world, learning by interacting with the world around them, and describes cognitive development as progressing through stages.

Cohort: A generation of people born at the same time, influenced by the same historical and cultural conditions.

Computerized tomography (CT scan): Compilation of multiple x-ray images thatcreates a 3-D picture of a person's brain, providing images of brain structures, bone, brain vasculature, and tissue

concrete operational stage of reasoning: Piaget's third stage of reasoning, from about 6 to 11, in which thought becomes logical and is applied to direct tangible experiences but not to abstract problems.

conservation: The principle that a physical quantity, such as number, mass, or volume, remains the same even when its appearance changes; understood in concrete operational reasoning in Piaget's theory.

Constructivist classroom: Educational approach that that involves children in their own learning. Encourages children to actively build their own understanding of the world through observing, interacting with objects and people, and engaging in a variety of activities; also called child-centered.

context: conditions in which a person develops, including aspects of the physical and social environment such as family, neighborhood, culture, and historical time period.

continuous change: An aspect of development that unfolds slowly and gradually over time.

Conventional moral reasoning: The second level of Kohlberg's theory in which moral decisions are based on conforming to social rules.

cooing: An infant's repetition of sounds, such as "ahhhh," "ohhh," and "eeee," that begins between 2 and 3 months of age.

core knowledge theory: A framework explaining that infants are born with several innate knowledge systems or core domains of thought that enable early rapid learning and adaptation.

corpus callosum: A thick band of nerve fibers that connects the left and right hemispheres of the brain, allowing communication.

correlational research: A research design that measures relationships among participants' measured characteristics, behaviors, and development.

cortex: The outermost part of the brain containing the greatest numbers of neurons and accounting for thought and consciousness.

cross-sectional research: A developmental research design that compares people of different ages at a single point in time to infer age differences.

Crowd: A large category of adolescents grouped based on perceived shared characteristics, interests, and reputation, but not necessarily friends.

culture: A set of customs, knowledge, attitudes, and values shared by a group of people and learned through interactions with group members.

Debriefing: Informing participants about the purpose and results of their research after the study is completed; carrying out the ethical principle of honesty in research.

deferred imitation: Imitating the behavior of an absent model; illustrates infants' capacity for mental representation.

Delinquency: Juvenile offending; illegal behavior by minors.

Dendrites: part of the neuron; branching neural receptors that receive chemical messages from neurotransmitters

deoxyribonucleic acid (DNA): The chemical structure, shaped like a twisted ladder, that contains all of the body's genes.

dependent variable: The behavior under study in an experiment; it is expected to be affected by changes in the independent variable.

depression: An emotional disorder characterized by feelings of sadness, hopelessness; changes in sleep, eating habits, and concentration; loss of interest in activities; and loss of energy and motivation.

development: The processes by which individuals grow and change, as well as the ways in which they stay the same over time.

Developmental disabilities: range of conditions resulting from impairments in physical functioning, learning, language, and behavior

developmental domains: types of development, including physical development, cognitive development, and socioemotional development.

developmental dyscalculia: A specific learning disorder that affects mathematics ability.

developmental dysgraphia: A specific learning disorder that affects writing abilities.

developmental dyslexia: The most commonly diagnosed specific learning disorder characterized by unusual difficulty in matching letters to sounds and difficulty with word recognition and spelling despite adequate instruction and intelligence and intact sensory abilities.

Developmentally appropriate practice: An educational approach that tailors instruction to the age of the child, recognizing individual differences and the need for hands-on active teaching methods.

developmental science: The study of human development at all points in life, from conception to death.

Diffusion tensor imaging (DTI): uses an MRI machine to track how water molecules move in and around the fibers connecting different parts of the brain, measure the brain's white matter, and determine changes that occur with development.

Direct instruction: An approach to education that emphasizes structured learning environments in which teachers select instructional strategies and convey information to children; also known as academically centered instruction

Discipline: The methods a parent uses to teach and socialize children.

Discontinuous Change: An aspect of development that is characterized by abrupt or stage-like change.

Distributive justice: Judgements on how to divide goods fairly.

divided attention: attending to two stimuli at once

dizygotic (DZ) twin: Occurs when two ova are released and each is fertilized by a different sperm, and the resulting offspring share 50% of the genetic material; also known as a *fraternal twin*.

dominant–recessive inheritance: A form of genetic inheritance in which the phenotype reflects only the dominant allele of a heterozygous pair.

doula: A caregiver who provides support to an expectant parent and the birthing partner throughout the birth process.

Down syndrome: A condition in which a third, extra chromosome appears at the 21st site; also known as *trisomy 21*. Down syndrome is associated with distinctive physical characteristics accompanied by developmental disability.

dual-language learning: an approach to language learning in which children are taught and develop skills in two languages

dynamic systems theory: A developmental framework that emphasizes interactions between biological maturation, environmental circumstances and constraints, and individuals' drive to engage the world; previously mastered skills are combined to provide more complex and effective ways of exploring and controlling the environment.

egocentrism: Piaget's term for children's inability to take another person's point of view or perspective and to assume that others share the same feelings, knowledge, and physical view of the world.

elaboration: A memory strategy in which one imagines a scene or story to link the material to be remembered.

Electroencephalography (EEG): method of measuring electrical activity patterns produced by the brain via electrodes placed on the scalp

embryo: Prenatal organism between about 2 and 8 weeks after conception; a period of major structural development.

emotion regulation: The ability to adjust and control one's emotional state to influence how and when emotions are expressed.

emotional competence: skill in understanding emotions including self-understanding, social awareness, and self-management.

Emotional intelligence: includes the ability to perceive, understand, manage, and respond appropriately to others' emotions as well as our own

Empathy: The capacity to understand another person's emotions and concerns.

epigenetics: A perspective that development results from dynamic interactions between genetics and the environment such that the expression of genetic inheritance is influenced by environmental forces.

episodic memory: Memory for everyday experiences.

Ethnic-racial identity: A sense of membership to a racial or ethnic group and viewing the attitudes and practices associated with that group as an enduring part of the self.

ethology: Emphasizes the evolutionary basis of behavior and its adaptive value in ensuring survival of a species.

evolutionary developmental theory: A perspective that applies principles of evolution and scientific knowledge about the interactive influence of genetic and environmental mechanisms to understand the adaptive value of developmental changes that are experienced with age.

executive function: The set of cognitive operations that support planning, decision making, and goal-setting abilities, such as the ability to control attention, coordinate information in working memory, and inhibit impulses.

exosystem: In bioecological systems theory, social settings in which an individual does not participate but has an indirect influence on development.

experience-dependent brain development: Brain growth and development in response to experiences.

experience-expectant brain development: Brain growth and development that are dependent on basic environmental experiences, such as visual and auditory stimulation, in order to develop normally.

experiment: A research procedure that uses control to determine causal relationships among variables.

externality effect: Refers to a particular pattern of infant visual processing.

Family systems theory: A theory that emphasizes the interactions among family members, viewing the family as a system of interconnected and interdependent parts, such that each family member affects the entire system.

fast mapping: A process by which children learn new words after only a brief encounter, connecting it with their own mental categories.

Felt other-gender typicality: The degree to which one feels similar to members of a different gender (and dissimilar to members of the same gender), including characteristics, skills, and interests.

Felt same-gender typicality: The degree to which one feels similar to members of their gender including characteristics, skills, and interests.

fetal alcohol spectrum disorders: The continuum of physical, mental, and behavioral outcomes caused by prenatal exposure to alcohol.

fetal alcohol syndrome (FAS): The most severe form of fetal alcohol spectrum disorder accompanying heavy prenatal exposure to alcohol, including a distinct pattern of facial characteristics, growth deficiencies, and deficits in intellectual development.

fetal MRI: Applies MRI technology to image the fetus's body and diagnose malformations.

fetal period: Occurs during the ninth week of prenatal development to birth, in which the fetus grows rapidly, and its organs become more complex and begin to function.

fetoscopy: A technique that uses a small camera, inserted through a small incision on the mother's abdomen or cervix and placed into the amniotic sac to examine and perform procedures on the fetus during pregnancy.

fetus: The prenatal organism from about the ninth week of pregnancy to delivery; a period of rapid growth and maturation of body structures.

fine motor development: The ability to control small movements of the fingers such as reaching and grasping.

formal operational reasoning: Piaget's fourth stage of cognitive development, characterized by abstract, logical, and systematic thinking.

Foster care: A child welfare arrangement where a child is temporarily placed outside the home because the family cannot provide care or safety.

fragile X syndrome: An example of a dominant–recessive disorder carried on the X chromosome characterized by intellectual disability, cardiac defects, and behavioral mannerisms common in individuals with autistic spectrum disorders; occurs in both males and females but is more severe in males.

Functional magnetic resonance imaging (fMRI): measures brain activity with a powerful magnet that uses radio waves and to measure blood oxygen level, an indicator of brain activity

gamete: A reproductive cell; sperm in males and ovum in females.

Gender: Identification with and adoption of socially constructed norms, roles, and characteristics for males and females, known as the gender binary, and may also include nonbinary identities. Often determined by socialization.

Gender constancy: The understanding that gender does not change and that they will always be the same regardless of appearance, activities, or attitudes. Reflects an awareness that sex is a biological characteristic. Occurs in middle childhood.

Gender identity: Awareness and labeling oneself by gender.

Gender intensification: The view that young adolescents become sensitive to gender stereotypes and are increasingly likely to adhere to gender stereotypes.

Gender schema: A mental structure that organizes gender-related information and represents children's understanding of what it means to be male or female (or a nonbinary gender), similar to Piaget's concept of schemas.

Gender stability: The understanding that gender generally does not change, but emphasizes appearance (e.g., clothes, hair, and behavior). Occurs in early childhood.

Gender stereotypes: Refers to broad generalized judgments of the activities, attitudes, skills, and characteristics deemed appropriate for men and women in a given culture.

Gender typing: The process in which young children acquire the characteristics and attitudes that are considered appropriate for their gender in their society.

gene: The basic unit of heredity; a small segments of DNA that provide instructions for the cell to manufacture proteins.

genetic counseling: A medical specialty that helps prospective parents determine the probability that their children will inherit genetic defects and chromosomal abnormalities.

gene–environment correlation: The idea that many of an individual's traits are supported by their genes and environment; there are three types of correlations: passive, reactive, and active.

gene–environment interactions: Refer to the dynamic interplay between genes and our environment in determining characteristics, behavior, physical, cognitive, and social development as well as health.

genomic imprinting: The instance when the expression of a gene is determined by whether it is inherited from the mother or father.

genotype: An individual's collection of genes that contain instructions for all physical and psychological characteristics, including hair, eye color, personality, health, and behavior.

germinal period: Also referred to as the period of the zygote; refers to the first 2 weeks after conception.

glial cell: A type of brain cell that nourishes neurons and provides structure to the brain.

goodness of fit: The compatibility between a child's temperament and their environment, especially the parent's temperament and childrearing methods; the greater the degree of match, the more favorable the child's adjustment.

grammar: The rules of language.

gray matter: Unmyelinated neurons.

gross motor development: The ability to control large movements of the body, such as walking and jumping.

growth hormone deficiency: too little growth hormone circulating in the blood causing growth deficiency

growth norm: The expectation for typical gains and variations in height and weight for children based on their chronological age and ethnic background.

growth stunting: A reduced growth rate.

guided participation: Also known as apprenticeship in thinking; the process by which children learn from others who guide them, providing a scaffold to help them accomplish more than the child could do alone.

habituation: The gradual decline in the intensity, frequency, or duration of a response when repeatedly exposed to a stimulus; indicates learning.

Helpless orientation: An orientation characterized by a fixed mind-set and the attribution of poor performance to internal factors.

hemophilia: An X-linked chromosomal disorder involving abnormal blood clotting.

Heteronomous morality: Piaget's first stage of morality when children become aware of rules and view them as absolute and unalterable.

holophrase: A one-word expression used to convey a complete thought.

hypothesis: A proposed explanation for a phenomenon that can be tested.

hypothetical-deductive reasoning: The ability to consider propositions and probabilities, generate and systematically test hypotheses, and draw conclusions.

Identity: A coherent organized sense of self that includes values, attitudes, and goals to which one is committed.

Identity achievement: The identity state in which, after undergoing a period of exploration, a person commits to self-chosen values and goals.

Identity diffusion: The identity state in which an individual has not undergone exploration or committed to self-chosen values and goals.

Identity foreclosure (identity foreclosed): The identity state in which an individual has not undergone exploration but has committed to values and goals chosen by an authority figure.

Identity status: The degree to which individuals have explored possible selves and whether they have committed to specific beliefs and goals, assessed by administering interview and survey measures, and categorized into four identity statuses.

imaginary audience: A manifestation of adolescent egocentrism in which they assume that they are the focus of others' attention.

Imaginary companions: Pretend friends; common in early childhood.

Immersion: in the U.S., second-language-speaking children are placed in English-speaking classes in which they learn language and course content simultaneously

implantation: The process by which the blastocyst becomes attached to the uterine wall, completed by about 10 days after fertilization.

incomplete dominance: A genetic inheritance pattern in which both genes are expressed in the phenotype.

independent variable: The factor proposed to change the behavior under study in an experiment; it is systematically manipulated during an experiment.

Inductive discipline: Strategy to control children's behavior that relies on reasoning and discussion.

infant-directed speech: Uses shorter words and sentences, higher and more varied pitch, repetitions, a slower rate, and longer pauses; also known as motherese.

information processing theory: A perspective that uses a computer analogy to describe how the mind receives information and manipulates, stores, recalls, and uses it to solve problems.

informed consent: A participant's informed (knowledge of the scope of the research and potential harm and benefits of participating), rational, and voluntary agreement to participate in a study.

insecure-avoidant attachment: An attachment pattern in which an infant shows little distress when separated from a caregiver and avoids connecting with the caregiver during reunions, such as during the Strange Situation.

insecure-disorganized attachment: An attachment pattern in which an infant shows inconsistent, contradictory behavior with the caregiver (such as in the Strange Situation), suggesting a conflict between approaching and fleeing the caregiver.

insecure-resistant attachment: An attachment pattern in which an infant shows anxiety and uncertainty, including great distress at separation from the caregiver (such as during the Strange Situation) and simultaneously seeks and avoids contact upon the caregiver's return.

Instrumental aggression: Behavior that hurts someone else to achieve a goal such as gaining a possession.

Instrumental assistance: Tangible help.

Intellectual disability: a condition in which an individual has low intellectual functioning, typically defined by an IQ score below 70

intelligence: An individual's ability to adapt to their environment and circumstances.

Intelligence quotient: a score resulting from an intelligence test. In the Stanford-Binet Intelligence scale, IQ is defined as mental age (MA) divided by chronological age (CA), multiplied by 100 (IQ = MA/CA × 100).

intermodal perception: The process of combining information from more than one sensory system such as visual and auditory senses.

internal working model: A set of expectations about one's worthiness of love and the availability of attachment figures during times of distress.

Intersectionality: the dynamic interrelations of social categories, such as gender, race and ethnicity, sexual orientation, socioeconomic status, immigration status, age, and disabilities, and the interwoven systems of power and privilege that accompany social category membership

in vitro fertilization: Fertilization, the creation of zygotes, through mixing sperm with ova that have been surgically removed from the woman's body.

irreversibility: A characteristic of preoperational reasoning in which a child does not understand that an action can be reversed and a thing restored to its original state.

Jacob's syndrome: A sex chromosome abnormality experienced by men in which they produce high levels of testosterone; also known as XYY syndrome.

Joint attention: joint attention refers to periods when two people focus on the same object.

Justice orientation: A male mode of moral reasoning proposed by Gilligan that emphasizes the abstract principles of fairness and individualism.

justice: The ethical principle that requires that risks and benefits of research participation must be spread equitably across individuals and groups.

Kangaroo care: An intervention for low birth weight babies in which the infant is placed vertically against the parent's chest, under the shirt, providing skin-to-skin contact.

Klinefelter syndrome: Sex chromosome abnormality in which a male has an extra X chromosome (XXY).

kwashiorkor: A malnutrition disease in children caused by deprivation of protein and calories and characterized by lethargy, bloating and swelling of the stomach.

labor: Typically occurs at about 40 weeks of pregnancy, or 38 weeks after conception; also known as *childbirth*.

language acquisition device (LAD): In Chomsky's theory, an innate facilitator of language that allows infants to quickly and efficiently analyze everyday speech and determine its rules, regardless of their native language.

lanugo: A fine, down-like hair that covers the fetus's body.

lateralization: The process by which the two hemispheres of the brain become specialized to carry out different functions.

Learning goals: Goals that emphasize the process of learning and developing abilities.

limbic system: A collection of brain structures responsible for emotion.

logical extension: A strategy children use to increase their vocabulary in which they extend a new word to other objects in the same category.

longitudinal research: A developmental study in which one group of participants is studied repeatedly to infer age changes.

long-term memory: The component of the information processing system that is an unlimited store that holds information indefinitely, until it is retrieved to manipulate working memory.

low birthweight: Classifies infants who weigh less than 2,500 grams (5.5 pounds) at birth.

macrosystem: In bioecological systems theory, the sociohistorical context—cultural values, laws, and cultural values—in which the microsystem, mesosystem, and exosystem are embedded, posing indirect influences on individuals.

mandated reporter: A professional who is legally obligated to report suspected child maltreatment to law enforcement.

marasmus: A wasting disease in which the body's fat and muscle are depleted; growth stops and the body wastes away, taking on a hollow appearance.

Mastery motivation: Infants' drive to explore, understand, and master their environment

Mastery orientation: Achievement orientation characterized by attributing success to internal factors and a growth mindset to believe that poor performance can be improved.

Medical gender transition: A process supervised by medical professions in which transgender individuals undergo body changes to match their gender identity. Medical transition can involve body changes that are induced by hormone therapy, surgery, and cosmetic procedures to regions including the face, chest, genitals, and other body parts.

meiosis: The process by which a gamete is formed, containing one half of the cell's chromosomes, producing ova and sperm with 23 single, unpaired chromosomes.

memory strategy: Deliberate cognitive activities that make an individual more likely to remember information.

menarche: The first menstrual period.

menstruation: The monthly shedding of the uterine lining, which has thickened in preparation for the implantation of a fertilized egg.

mental age: a child's performance relative to same-age children.

mental representation: An internal depiction of an object; thinking of an object using mental pictures.

mesosystem: In bioecological systems theory, the relations and interactions among microsystems.

metacognition: The ability to think about thinking; knowledge of how the mind works.

metalinguistic awareness: awareness and knowledge about the nature and qualities of language

metamemory: An aspect of metacognition that refers to the understanding of memory and how to use strategies to enhance memory.

microsystem: In bioecological systems theory, the innermost level of context, which includes an individual's immediate physical and social environment.

midwife: A health care professional, usually a nurse, who specializes in childbirth; midwives provide health care throughout pregnancy and supervise home births.

Mindset: The degree to which individuals believe that their abilities and characteristics are modifiable.

mitosis: The process of cell duplication in which DNA is replicated and the resulting cell is genetically identical to the original.

monozygotic (MZ) twin: Occurs when the zygote splits apart early in development, and the resulting offspring share 100% of their genetic material; also known as an *identical twin*.

Montessori school: A child-centered educational approach, first created during the early 1900s by the Italian physician and educator Maria Montessori (1870–1952), in which children are viewed as active constructors of their own development and are given freedom in choosing their activities.

Moral reasoning: The process of making judgments about right and wrong; influenced by children's cognitive abilities and develops in a predictable pattern.

morpheme: is the smallest unit of language that has meaning

Morphology : the rules for combining morphemes into words

multiple intelligence theory: Gardner's proposition that human intelligence is composed of a varied set of abilities.

mutation: A sudden permanent change in the structure of genes.

mutual exclusivity assumption: When learning new words, young children assume that objects have only one label or name.

mutual perspective taking: Adolescents' understanding that they take other people's point of view at the same time as others attempt to take their own point of view.

myelination: The process in which neurons are coated in a fatty substance, myelin, which contributes to faster neural communication.

natural childbirth: An approach to birth that reduces pain through the use of breathing and relaxation exercises.

naturalistic observation: A research method in which a researcher views and records an individual's behavior in natural, real-world settings.

Nature-Nurture Debate: A debate within the field of human development regarding whether development is caused by nature (genetics or heredity) or nurture (the physical and social environment).

Neonate: newborn

neural tube: Forms during the third week after conception and will develop into the central nervous system (brain and spinal cord).

Neurodiversity: a term that describes differences and natural variations in brain functioning and performance

neurogenesis: The production of new neurons.

neuron: A nerve cell that stores and transmits information; billions of neurons comprise the brain.

Neurotransmitters: chemical messenger that carries messages among neurons

niche-picking: An active gene–environment correlation in which individuals seek out experiences and environments that complement their genetic tendencies.

nightmare: An anxiety-provoking dream.

noninvasive prenatal testing (NIPT): A prenatal diagnostic that samples cell-free fetal DNA from the mother's blood for chromosomal abnormalities.

Nonshared environment: Environmental factors that are unique to individuals and may contribute to differences among individuals, such as siblings.

obesity: In children, defined as having a body mass index at or above the 95th percentile for height and age.

object permanence: The understanding that objects continue to exist outside of sight.

observational learning: Learning that occurs by watching and imitating models, as posited by social learning theory.

Ontogenetic development: developmental changes within the individual, including interacting biological, cognitive, and socioemotional traits

open-ended interview: A research method in which a researcher asks a participant questions using a flexible, conversational style and may vary the order of questions, probe, and ask follow-up questions based on the participant's responses.

operant conditioning: A form of learning in which behavior increases or decreases based on environmental consequences.

organization: Memory strategy in which items to remember are categorized or grouped by theme or type.

ossification: The process of cartilage being converted into bone.

overextension: A vocabulary error in which the infant applies a word too broadly to a wider class of objects than appropriate.

overregularization errors: Grammatical mistakes that children make because they apply grammatical rules too stringently to words that are exceptions.

Parental monitoring: Parents' awareness of their children's activities, whereabouts, and companions.

Parenting style: Sets of childrearing behaviors a parent uses across situations to form a childrearing climate.

Peer acceptance: Likeability or the degree to which a child is viewed as a worthy social partner by peers.

Peer rejection: An ongoing interaction in which a child is deliberately excluded by peers.

perception: The mental processing of sensory information, which is then interpreted as sight, sound, smell, taste, or touch.

perceptual narrowing: A decline in sensitivity to discriminate faces within unfamiliar groups.

Performance goals: Goals that emphasize the process of learning and developing abilities.

Permissive parenting style: A childrearing approach characterized by high levels of warmth and low levels of control or discipline.

personal fable: A manifestation of adolescent egocentrism in which adolescents believe their thoughts, feelings, and experiences are more special and unique than anyone else's, as well as the sense that they are invulnerable.

Phenomes: basic units of sounds used in a given language

phenotype: The observable physical or behavioral characteristics of a person's eye color, hair color, or height.

phenylketonuria (PKU): A recessive disorder that prevents the body from producing an enzyme that breaks down phenylalanine (an amino acid) from proteins that, without treatment, leads to buildup that damages the central nervous system.

Phonology: the basic units of sounds used in a given language and the rules for combining them

placenta: The principal organ of exchange between the mother and the developing organism, enabling the exchange of nutrients, oxygen, and wastes via the umbilical cord.

plasticity: A characteristic of development that refers to malleability or openness to change in response to experience.

polygenic inheritance: Occurs when a trait is a function of the interaction of many genes, such as with height, intelligence, and temperament.

Popular: Individuals who receive many positive ratings from peers indicating that they are accepted and valued by peers.

Positron emission tomography (PET): technique to examine brain activity by injecting a small dose of radioactive material into the participant's blood stream

Postconventional moral reasoning: Kohlberg's third level of moral reasoning emphasizing autonomous decision making based on principles such as valuing human dignity.

pragmatics: The practical application of language for everyday communication.

Preconventional reasoning: Kohlberg's first level of reasoning in which young children's behavior is governed by punishment and gaining rewards.

prefrontal cortex: Located in the front of the brain and responsible for higher thought, such as planning, goal setting, controlling impulses, and using cognitive skills and memory to solve problems.

prenatal care: A set of services provided to improve pregnancy outcomes and engage the expectant parent, family members, and friends in pregnancy-related health care decisions.

Prenatal development: The development process from conception until birth.

preoperational reasoning: Piaget's second stage of cognitive development, between about ages 2 and 6, characterized by advances in symbolic thought, but thought is not yet logical.

preterm: A birth that occurs 35 or fewer weeks after conception.

primary circular reaction: Infants' repeating an action that produced an interesting outcome involving their body; a sensorimotor substage in Piaget's theory.

primary emotions: Emotions that are universal in humans, appear early in life, and are thought to have a long evolutionary history, includes happiness, interest, surprise, fear, anger, sadness, and disgust.

primary sex characteristic: The reproductive organs; in females, this includes the ovaries, fallopian tubes, uterus, and vagina, and in males, this includes the penis, testes, scrotum, seminal vesicles, and prostate gland.

private speech: Self-directed speech that children use to guide their behavior; from Vygotsky's theory

Processing speed: the speed with which we can complete a mental task,

productive language: Language individuals can produce or generate on their own.

Project Head Start: Early childhood intervention program that provides low-income children with nutritional, health, and educational services, as well as helps parents become involved in their children's development.

Prosocial behavior: Actions that are oriented toward others for the pure sake of helping, without a reward.

Protective factor: Variable that is thought to reduce the poor outcomes associated with adverse circumstances.

proximodistal development: The principle that growth and development proceed from the center of the body outward.

psychoanalytic theory: A perspective introduced by Freud that development and behavior is influenced by inner drives, memories, and conflicts of which an individual is unaware and cannot control.

Psychosocial moratorium: In Erikson's theory, a period in which the individual is free to explore identity possibilities before committing to an identity.

puberty: The biological transition to reproductive maturity.

Puberty suppressors: Medication that inhibits sex hormones and prevents the onset of pubertal changes.

punishment: In operant conditioning, the process in which a behavior is followed by an aversive or unpleasant outcome that decreases the likelihood of a response.

Questionnaire: A survey or set of questions used to collect data.

random assignment: A method of assigning participants that ensures each participant has an equal chance of being assigned to the experimental group or control group.

range of reaction: The concept that a genetic trait may be expressed in a wide range of phenotypes dependent on environmental opportunities and constraints.

Reactive aggression: An aggressive response to an insult, confrontation, or frustration.

receptive language: Language that one can understand.

reciprocal determinism: A perspective positing that individuals and their environment interact and influence each other.

recognition memory: The ability to identify a previously encountered stimulus.

reflex: Involuntary and automatic responses to stimuli such as touch, light, and sound.

rehearsal: A mnemonic strategy that involves systematically repeating information to retain it in working memory.

reinforcement: In operant conditioning, the process by which a behavior is followed by a desirable outcome increases the likelihood of a response.

Relational aggression: Nonphysical acts aimed at harming a person's connections with others, such as by exclusion and rumor spreading.

Religiosity: Involves a relationship with a religion, a set of doctrinal beliefs and behaviors shared by a community, and religious practice, participation in its prescribed rituals and practices; sometimes overlaps with spirituality.

REM sleep: Rapid eye movement sleep, in which an individual's brain wave activity is similar to that of the waking state while asleep.

Representational play: Make-believe play where children pretend that one object is something else.

Resilience: The ability to adapt to serious adversity.

Risk factors: Individual or contextual challenges that tax an individual's coping capacities and can evoke psychological stress.

Rough-and-tumble play: A form of play characterized by vigorous physical activity such as running, climbing, chasing, jumping, and play fighting.

scaffolding: Temporary support that permits a child to bridge the gap between their current competence level and the task at hand.

scientific method: The process of forming and answering questions using systematic observations and gathering information.

secondary circular reaction: Infants' repeating an action that triggers an interesting outcome in the environment; a sensorimotor substage in Piaget's theory.

secondary sex characteristic: Physical traits appear during puberty but are not directly related to fertility, such as breast development and the growth of body hair.

secular trend: Changes in an aspect of development from one generation to the next

secure attachment: The attachment pattern in which an infant uses the caregiver as a secure base from which to explore, seeks contact during reunions, and is easily comforted by the caregiver.

secure base: The use of a caregiver as a foundation from which to explore and return to for emotional support.

security of attachment: The extent to which an individual feels that an attachment object, such as a caregiver, can reliably meet their needs; measured by the Strange Situation.

selective attention: The ability to focus on relevant stimuli and ignore others.

Self-concept: The set of attributes, abilities, and characteristics that a person describes themselves with.

self-conscious emotion: Emotion that requires cognitive development and an awareness of self, such as empathy, embarrassment, shame, and guilt.

Self-esteem: The emotional evaluation of one's own worth.

Self-recognition: The ability to identify the self, typically measured as mirror recognition.

Semantic memory: refers to recall of information, facts, and experiences.

Semantics: the meaning or content of words and sentences

sensation: The physical response of sensory receptors when a stimulus is detected (e.g., activity of the sensory receptors in the eye in response to light); awareness of stimuli in the senses.

sensitive period: A period during which experience has a particularly powerful role in shaping developmental outcomes.

sensory memory: The first step in the information processing system in which stimuli are stored for a brief moment in its original form to enable it to be processed.

sensory processing disorder (SPD): an extreme difficulty processing and responding to sensory stimuli that interferes with daily functioning

separation anxiety: Also known as separation protest; occurs when infants respond to the departure of an attachment figure with distress and crying.

sequential research: A developmental design in which multiple groups of participants of different ages are followed over time, combining cross-sectional and longitudinal research.

seriation: A type of classification that involves ordering objects in a series according to a physical dimension such as height, weight, or color.

Sex: Determined by the presence of a Y chromosome in the 23rd pair of chromosomes and usually indicated by the genitals; usually assigned at birth.

Sexual orientation: An enduring pattern of emotional, romantic, and sexual attraction to opposite-sex partners (heterosexual), same-sex partners (gay or lesbian), or partners of both sexes (bisexual).

sickle cell anemia: a recessive disorder in which red blood cells become crescent, or sickle, shaped.

sleeper effects: Teratogenic outcomes or effects that are not visible until many years later.

sleep terror: An episode of screaming, flailing, and fear while asleep.

small for date: Describes an infant who is full term but who has significantly lower weight than expected for the gestational age.

social cognition: reasoning about other people, relationships, and the social world.

Social cognitive theory: Albert Bandura's theory conceptualizing children's development as the result of interactions among their physical and social environment, their cognition and personal characteristics, and behavior.

Social comparison: The tendency to compare and judge one's abilities, achievements, and behaviors in relation to others.

Social gender transition: A process by which transgender individuals adopt social changes to match their gender identity, such as by changing pronouns and appearance.

Social policy: local, state, or federal governments' plans and actions to support or improve the welfare of its people

social referencing: Seeking information from caregivers about how to interpret unfamiliar or ambiguous events by observing their emotional expressions and reactions.

social smile: A smile that emerges in response to seeing familiar people; occurs in an infant between 6 and 10 weeks after birth.

societal perspective taking: The recognition that the social environment, including the larger society, influences people's perspectives and beliefs.

sociocultural theory: Vygotsky's theory that individuals acquire culturally relevant ways of thinking through social interactions with members of their culture.

Sociodramatic play: An advanced type of play where children interact with other children, take on roles, and act out stories.

Sociohistorical context: the time period in which we live and its unique historical circumstances

specific learning disorder (SLD): Diagnosed in children who demonstrate a measurable discrepancy between aptitude and achievement in a particular academic area given their age, intelligence, and amount of schooling.

spina bifida: A neural tube that results in spinal nerves growing outside of the vertebrae, often resulting in paralysis and developmental disability.

Spirituality: The perception and experience of transcendent beings, like God, and the search for meaning and purpose in life in ways that benefit others and society.

States of arousal: Level of wakefulness and engagement with the environment, ranging from sleep to waking activity and quiet alertness.

Stereotype threat: phenomenon when individuals' awareness of negative stereotypes influences their performance on intelligence and other tests.

Strange Situation: A structured laboratory procedure that measures the security of attachment by observing infants' reactions to being separated from the caregiver in an unfamiliar environment.

stranger wariness: Also known as stranger anxiety; an infant's expression of fear of unfamiliar people.

structured interview: A research method in which each participant is asked the same set of questions in the same way.

structured observation: An observational measure in which an individual's behavior is viewed and recorded in a controlled environment; a situation created by the experimenter.

sudden infant death syndrome (SIDS): The sudden unexpected death of an infant less than 1 year of age that occurs seemingly during sleep and remains unexplained after a thorough investigation.

Suicide: Death caused by self-directed injuries with the intent to die.

surrogacy: An alternative form of reproduction known in which a woman (the surrogate) is impregnated and carries a fetus to term and agrees to turn the baby over to a woman, man, or couple who will raise it.

sustained attention: The ability to remain focused on a stimulus for an extended period of time.

synapse: The intersection or gap between the axon of one neuron and the dendrites of other neurons; the gap that neurotransmitters must cross.

synaptic pruning: The process by which synapses, neural connections that are seldom used, disappear.

synaptogenesis: The process in which neurons form synapses and increase connections between neurons.

Syntax: the rules for combining words to form sentences, including which combinations are correct, or grammatical, and which are not

telegraphic speech: Two-word utterances produced by toddlers that communicate only the essential words.

temperament: Characteristic differences among individuals in emotional reactivity, self-regulation, and activity that influence reactions to the environment and are stable and appear early in life.

teratogen: An environmental factor that causes damage to prenatal development.

tertiary circular reaction: In Piaget's theory, repeating an action to explore and experiment in order to see the results and learn about the world.

theory: An organized set of observations to describe, explain, and predict a phenomenon.

theory of mind: Children's awareness of their own and other people's mental processes and realization that other people do not share their thoughts.

Transgender identity: An identity or sense of self that does not align with the sex assigned at birth.

transitive inference: A classification skill in which a child can infer the relationship between two objects by understanding each object's relationship to a third object.

triarchic theory of intelligence: Sternberg's theory positing three independent forms of intelligence: analytical, creative, and applied.

Triple X syndrome: Chromosomal disorder in which an individual is born with three X chromosomes. Often unnoticed

Turner syndrome: Sex chromosome abnormality in which a female is born with only one X chromosome; girls with Turner syndrome show abnormal growth patterns, abnormalities in primary and secondary sex characteristics, and other disorders.

ultrasound: Prenatal diagnostic procedure in which high-frequency sound waves are directed at the mother's abdomen to provide clear images of the womb projected onto a video monitor.

underextension: A vocabulary error in which the infant applies a word too narrowly to a single object rather than the more appropriate, wider class of objects.

Uninvolved parenting style: A childrearing style characterized by low levels of warmth and acceptance coupled with little control or discipline.

vernix caseosa: Greasy material that protects the fetal skin from abrasions, chapping, and hardening that can occur from exposure to amniotic fluid.

violation-of-expectation task: A task in which a stimulus appears to violate physical laws.

visual acuity: Sharpness of vision.

Vocabulary spurt: a period of rapid vocabulary learning that occurs from about 16 to 24 months of age.

Wernicke's area: The region of the brain that is responsible for language comprehension; damage to this area impairs the ability to understand others' speech and sometimes the ability to speak coherently.

white matter: Myelinated brain tissue.

Withdrawn-rejected children: Children who are withdrawn and passive and are shunned by peers.

working memory: The component of the information processing system that holds and processes information that is being manipulated, encoded, or retrieved and is responsible for maintaining and processing information used in cognitive tasks.

zone of proximal development: Vygotsky's term for the tasks that children cannot do alone but can exercise with the aid of more skilled partners.

zygote: A fertilized ovum.

REFERENCES

AAP Committee on Psychosocial Aspects of Child and Family Health. (1998). Guidance for effective discipline. *Pediatrics*, *101*, 723–728. https://doi.org/10.1542/peds.101.4.723

Abacan, M. A., Alsubaie, L., Barlow-Stewart, K., Caanen, B., Cordier, C., Courtney, E., Davoine, E., Edwards, J., Elackatt, N. J., Gardiner, K., Guan, Y., Huang, L. H., Malmgren, C. I., Kejriwal, S., Kim, H. J., Lambert, D., Lantigua-Cruz, P. A., Lee, J. M. H., Lodahl, M., & &#hellip;1; Wicklund, C. (2019). The global state of the genetic counseling profession. *European Journal of Human Genetics*, *27*(2), 183–197. https://doi.org/10.1038/s41431-018-0252-x

Abbott, R., & Burkitt, E. (2023). Learning and memory. In *Child development and the brain* (2nd ed., pp. 175–198). Policy Press.

Ablewhite, J., Peel, I., McDaid, L., Hawkins, A., Goodenough, T., Deave, T., Stewart, J., Kendrick, D., Peden, M., Oyegbite, K., Ozanne-Smith, J., Hyder, A., Branche, C., Rahman, A., Joffe, A., Lalani, A., Sethi, D., Towner, E., Vincenten, J., & &#hellip;1; Kessel, A. (2015). Parental perceptions of barriers and facilitators to preventing child unintentional injuries within the home: A qualitative study. *BMC Public Health*, *15*(1), 280. https://doi.org/10.1186/s12889-015-1547-2

Aboud, F. E., & Steele, J. R. (2017). Theoretical perspectives on the development of implicit and explicit prejudice. In A. Rutland, D. Nesdale, & C. S. Brown (Eds.), *The Wiley handbook of group processes in children and adolescents* (pp. 165–183). John Wiley & Sons. https://doi.org/10.1002/9781118773123.ch8

Abraham, L. M., Crais, E., & Vernon-Feagans, L. (2013). Early maternal language use during book sharing in families from low-income environments. *American Journal of Speech-Language Pathology*, *22*(1), 71–83. https://doi.org/10.1044/1058-0360(2012/11-0153

Abramowicz, J. S. (2019). Ultrasound in reproductive medicine: Is it safe? In L. A. Stadtmauer & I. Tur-Kaspa (Eds.), *Ultrasound imaging in reproductive medicine* (pp. 3–17). Springer International. https://doi.org/10.1007/978-3-030-16699-1_1

Abrams, E. M., Greenhawt, M., Shaker, M., Pinto, A. D., Sinha, I., & Singer, A. (2022). The COVID-19 pandemic: Adverse effects on the social determinants of health in children and families. *Annals of Allergy, Asthma & Immunology*, *128*(1), 19–25. https://doi.org/10.1016/j.anai.2021.10.022

Abrego, L. J., & Gonzales, R. G. (2010). Blocked paths, uncertain futures: The postsecondary education and labor market prospects of undocumented Latino youth. *Journal of Education for Students Placed at Risk*, *15*(1–2), 144–157. https://doi.org/10.1080/10824661003635168

Abregú-Crespo, R., Garriz-Luis, A., Ayora, M., Martín-Martínez, N., Cavone, V., Á, Carrasco, M., Fraguas, D., Martín-Babarro, J., Arango, C., & Díaz-Caneja, C. M. (2024). School bullying in children and adolescents with neurodevelopmental and psychiatric conditions: A systematic review and meta-analysis. *Lancet Child & Adolescent Health*, *8*(2), 122–134. https://doi.org/10.1016/S2352-4642(23)00289-4

Acar, E., Dursun, O. B., S, Esin, İ., Öğütlü, H., Özcan, H., & Mutlu, M. (2015). Unintentional injuries in preschool age children: Is there a correlation with parenting style and parental attention deficit and hyperactivity symptoms. *Medicine*, *94*(32), e1378. https://doi.org/10.1097/MD.0000000000001378

Ackard, D. M., Fulkerson, J. A., & Neumark-Sztainer, D. (2011). Stability of eating disorder diagnostic classifications in adolescents: Five-year longitudinal findings from a population-based study. *Eating Disorders*, *19*(4), 308–322. https://doi.org/10.1080/10640266.2011.584804

Acker, J., Mujahid, M., Aghaee, S., Gomez, S., Shariff-Marco, S., Chu, B., Deardorff, J., & Kubo, A. (2023). Neighborhood racial and economic privilege and timing of pubertal onset in girls. *Journal of Adolescent Health*, *72*(3), 419–427. https://doi.org/10.1016/j.jadohealth.2022.10.013

Ackerman, D. J. (2019). The Montessori preschool landscape in the United States: History, programmatic inputs, availability, and effects. *ETS Research Report Series*, 1–20. https://doi.org/10.1002/ets2.12252 *2019*(1)

Ackermann, L., Hepach, R., & Mani, N. (2020). Children learn words easier when they are interested in the category to which the word belongs. *Developmental Science*, *23*(3), e12915. https://doi.org/10.1111/desc.12915

Adams, R. E., & Laursen, B. (2007). The correlates of conflict: Disagreement is not necessarily detrimental. *Journal of Family Psychology*, *21*(3), 445–458. https://doi.org/10.1037/0893-3200.21.3.445

Addabbo, M., Longhi, E., Marchis, I. C., Tagliabue, P., & Turati, C. (2018). Dynamic facial expressions of emotions are discriminated at birth. *PLoS ONE*, *13*(3), e0193868. https://doi.org/10.1371/journal.pone.0193868

Aderibigbe, O., & Lucas, R. (2023). Exclusive breastfeeding in African American women: A concept analysis. *Journal of Advanced Nursing*, *79*(5), 1699–1713. https://doi.org/10.1111/jan.15301

Administration for Children and Families. (2019). *AFCARS Report #26*. https://www.acf.hhs.gov/cb/resource/afcars-report-26

Adolph, K. E. (2020). An ecological approach to learning in (not and) development. *Human Development*. https://doi.org/10.1159/000503823 *63*(3–4

Adolph, K. E. (2020). An ecological approach to learning in (not and) development. *Human Development*, *63*(3–4), 180–201. https://doi.org/10.1159/000503823

Adolph, K. E., Cole, W. G., Komati, M., Garciaguirre, J. S., Badaly, D., Lingeman, J. M., Chan, G. L. Y., & Sotsky, R. B. (2012). How do you learn to walk? Thousands of steps and dozens of falls per day. *Psychological Science*, *23*(11), 1387–1394. https://doi.org/10.1177/0956797612446346

Adolph, K. E., & Franchak, J. M. (2017). The development of motor behavior. *Wiley Interdisciplinary Reviews: Cognitive Science*, *8*(1–2), e1430. https://doi.org/10.1002/wcs.1430

Adolph, K. E., & Hoch, J. E. (2019). Motor development: Embodied, embedded, enculturated, and enabling. *Annual Review of Psychology*, *70*(1), 141–164. https://doi.org/10.1146/annurev-psych-010418-102836

Adolph, K. E., Hoch, J. E., & Cole, W. G. (2018). Development (of walking): 15 suggestions. *Trends in Cognitive Sciences*, *22*(8), 699–711. https://doi.org/10.1016/j.tics.2018.05.010

Adolph, K. E., Hoch, J. E., & Ossmy, O. (2019). James Gibson's Ecological Approach to Locomotion and Manipulation. In *Perception as Information Detection* (pp. 222–236). Routledge. https://doi.org/10.4324/9780429316128

Adolph, K. E., Kaplan, B. E., & Kretch, K. S. (2021). Infants on the edge: Beyond the visual cliff. In *Developmental psychology: Revisiting the classic studies* (pp. 36–55). Sage Publications Ltd.

Adolph, K. E., & Kretch, K. S. (2015). Gibson's theory of perceptual learning. In H. Keller (Ed.), *International encyclopedia of social and behavioral sciences*. Elsevier.

Adolph, K. E., Kretch, K. S., & LoBue, V. (2014). Fear of Heights in Infants? *Current Directions in Psychological Science*, 23(1), 60–66. https://doi.org/10.1177/0963721413498895

Adolph, K. E., & Robinson, S. R. (2015). Motor development. In L. S. Liben & Ulrich. Müller (Eds.), *Handbook of child psychology and developmental science* (pp. 1–45). John Wiley & Sons. https://doi.org/10.1002/9781118963418.childpsy204

Adolph, K. E., & Tamis-LeMonda, C. S. (2014). The costs and benefits of development: The transition from crawling to walking. *Child Development Perspectives*, 8(4), 187–192. https://doi.org/10.1111/cdep.12085

Aertsen, M., Diogo, M. C., Dymarkowski, S., Deprest, J., & Prayer, D. (2020). Fetal MRI for dummies: What the fetal medicine specialist should know about acquisitions and sequences. *Prenatal Diagnosis*, 40(1), 6–17. https://doi.org/10.1002/pd.5579

Affuso, G., Zannone, A., Esposito, C., Pannone, M., Miranda, M. C., De Angelis, G., Aquilar, S., Dragone, M., & Bacchini, D. (2023). The effects of teacher support, parental monitoring, motivation and self-efficacy on academic performance over time. *European Journal of Psychology of Education*, 38(1), 1–23. https://doi.org/10.1007/s10212-021-00594-6

Afshordi, N., & Liberman, Z. (2021). Keeping friends in mind: Development of friendship concepts in early childhood. *Social Development*, 30(2), 331–342. https://doi.org/10.1111/sode.12493

Aggarwal, S., Wright, J., Morgan, A., Patton, G., & Reavley, N. (2023). Religiosity and spirituality in the prevention and management of depression and anxiety in young people: A systematic review and meta-analysis. *BMC Psychiatry*, 23(1), 729. https://doi.org/10.1186/s12888-023-05091-2

Agnew-Blais, J. C., Wertz, J., Arseneault, L., Belsky, D. W., Danese, A., Pingault, J.-B., Polanczyk, G. V., Sugden, K., Williams, B., & Moffitt, T. E. (2022). Mother's and children's ADHD genetic risk, household chaos and children's ADHD symptoms: A gene-environment correlation study. *Journal of Child Psychology and Psychiatry*, 63(10), 1153–1163. https://doi.org/10.1111/jcpp.13659

Agorastos, A., Pervanidou, P., Chrousos, G. P., & Baker, D. G. (2019). Developmental trajectories of early life stress and trauma: A narrative review on neurobiological aspects beyond stress system dysregulation. *Frontiers in Psychiatry*, 10, 118. https://doi.org/10.3389/fpsyt.2019.00118

Agrawal, A., Rogers, C. E., Lessov-Schlaggar, C. N., Carter, E. B., Lenze, S. N., & Grucza, R. A. (2019). Alcohol, cigarette, and cannabis use between 2002 and 2016 in pregnant women from a nationally representative sample. *JAMA Pediatrics*, 173(1), 95–96. https://doi.org/10.1001/jamapediatrics.2018.3096

Aguiar, N. R., Mottweilier, C. M., Taylor, M., & Fisher, P. A. (2017). The imaginary companions created by children who have lived in foster care. *Imagination, Cognition and Personality*, 36(4), 340–355. https://doi.org/10.1177/0276236617700590

Agyei, S. B., van der Weel, F. R. R., & van der Meer, A. L. H. (2016). Development of visual motion perception for prospective control: Brain and behavioral studies in infants. *Frontiers in Psychology*, 7, 100. https://doi.org/10.3389/fpsyg.2016.00100

Ahmad, F. B., Cisewski, J. A., & Anderson, R. N. (2022). Provisional mortality data—United States, 2021. *Morbidity and Mortality Weekly Report*, 71(17), 597–600.

Ahmad, M. A., Weiler, Y., Joyeux, L., Eixarch, E., Vercauteren, T., Ourselin, S., Deprest, J., & Vander Poorten, E. (2023). 3D vs. 2D simulated fetoscopy for spina bifida repair: A quantitative motion analysis. *Scientific Reports*, 13(1), Article 1. https://doi.org/10.1038/s41598-023-47531-9

Ahmed, A., & Ruffman, T. (1998). Why do infants make A not B errors in a search task, yet show memory for location of hidden objects in a non-search task? *Developmental Psychology*, 34, 441–453. https://doi.org/10.1037/0012-1649.34.3.441

Ahn, R. R., Miller, L. J., Milberger, S., & McIntosh, D. N. (2004). Prevalence of parents' perceptions of sensory processing disorders among kindergarten children. *American Journal of Occupational Therapy*, 58(3), 287–293. https://doi.org/10.5014/ajot.58.3.287

Aikins, J. W., & Aikins, D. (2024). Maternal processes contributing to child internalizing and externalizing symptoms: Comparing military, two-parent, and single-parent families. *Journal of Child and Family Studies*, 33, ages 1590–1601. https://doi.org/10.1007/s10826-024-02798-y

Ainsworth, M. D. S., Blehar, M. C., Waters, E., & Wall, S. (1978). *Patterns of attachment*. Erlbaum.

Akhtar, F., & Bokhari, S. R. A. (2024). *Down syndrome*. StatPearls. http://www.ncbi.nlm.nih.gov/books/NBK526016/

Akhtar, F., Rizwan, S., & Bokhari, A. (2022). *Down syndrome*. StatPearls. https://www.ncbi.nlm.nih.gov/books/NBK526016/

Akhtar, S., Justice, L. V., Morrison, C. M., & Conway, M. A. (2018). Fictional first memories. *Psychological Science*, 29(10), 1612–1619. https://doi.org/10.1177/0956797618778831

Akolekar, R., Beta, J., Picciarelli, G., Ogilvie, C., & D'Antonio, F. (2015). Procedure-related risk of miscarriage following amniocentesis and chorionic villus sampling: A systematic review and meta-analysis. *Ultrasound in Obstetrics & Gynecology*, 45(1), 16–26. https://doi.org/10.1002/uog.14636

Al-Namlah, A. S., Meins, E., & Fernyhough, C. (2012). Self-regulatory private speech relates to children's recall and organization of autobiographical memories. *Early Childhood Research Quarterly*, 27(3), 441–446. https://doi.org/10.1016/j.ecresq.2012.02.005

Al-Yagon, M., Garbi, L., & Rich, Y. (2022). Children's resilience to ongoing border attacks: The role of father, mother, and child resources. *Child Psychiatry & Human Development*, 54, 1015–1026. https://doi.org/10.1007/S10578-021-01303-6

al'Absi, M., Ginty, A. T., & Lovallo, W. R. (2021). Neurobiological mechanisms of early life adversity, blunted stress reactivity and risk for addiction. *Neuropharmacology*, 188, 108519. https://doi.org/10.1016/j.neuropharm.2021.108519

Alamia, A., VanRullen, R., Pasqualotto, E., Mouraux, A., & Zenon, A. (2019). Pupil-linked arousal responds to unconscious surprisal. *Journal of Neuroscience*, 39(27), 5369–5376. https://doi.org/10.1523/JNEUROSCI.3010-18.2019

Alarcón-Rubio, D., Sánchez-Medina, J. A., & Prieto-García, J. R. (2014). Executive function and verbal self-regulation in childhood: Developmental linkages between partially internalized private speech and cognitive flexibility. *Early*

Childhood Research Quarterly, 29(2), 95–105. https://doi.org/10.1016/j.ecresq.2013.11.002

Alberry, M. S., Aziz, E., Ahmed, S. R., & Abdel-fattah, S. (2021). Non invasive prenatal testing (NIPT) for common aneuploidies and beyond. *European Journal of Obstetrics and Gynecology and Reproductive Biology, 25*(8). https://doi.org/10.1016/j.ejogrb.2021.01.008

Alberts, A., Elkind, D., & Ginsberg, S. (2007). The personal fable and risk-taking in early adolescence. *Journal of Youth and Adolescence, 36*(1), 71–76. https://doi.org/10.1007/s10964-006-9144-4

Alcohol Policy Information System. (2023). *Alcohol and pregnancy reporting requirements*. https://alcoholpolicy.niaaa.nih.gov/apis-policy-topics/reporting-requirements/23

Alderson-Day, B., & Fernyhough, C. (2015). Inner speech: Development, cognitive functions, phenomenology, and neurobiology. *Psychological Bulletin, 141*(5), 931–965. https://doi.org/10.1037/bul0000021

Alegría, M., O'Malley, I. S., Smith, R., Useche Rosania, A., Boyd, A., Cuervo-Torello, F., Williams, D. R., & Acevedo-Garcia, D. (2023). Addressing health inequities for children in immigrant families: Psychologists as leaders and links across systems. *American Psychologist, 78*(2), 173–185. https://doi.org/10.1037/amp0001016

Alexander, K., & Cropper, R. (2020). Injury, Accident, and Injury Prevention. In K. Sweeny, M. L. Robbins, & L. M. Cohen (Eds.), *The Wiley encyclopedia of health psychology* (pp. 61–66). John Wiley & Sons. https://doi.org/10.1002/9781119057840.CH189

Alfalahi, M., Mahadevan, S., Balushi, R. al., Chan, M. F., Saadon, M. A., Al-Adawi, S., & Qoronfleh, M. W. (2022). Prevalence of eating disorders and disordered eating in Western Asia: A systematic review and meta-analysis. *Eating Disorders, 30*(5). https://doi.org/10.1080/10640266.2021.1969495

Ali, N., Ullah, A., Khan, A. M., Khan, Y., Ali, S., Khan, A., Bakhtawar, Khan., A, Din., U, M., Ullah, R., Khan, U. N., Aziz, T., & Ahmad, M. (2023). Academic performance of children in relation to gender, parenting styles, and socioeconomic status: What attributes are important. *PLoS ONE, 18*(11), e0286823. https://doi.org/10.1371/journal.pone.0286823

Ali-Saleh Darawshy, N., Gewirtz, A., & Marsalis, S. (2020). Psychological intervention and prevention programs for child and adolescent exposure to community violence: A systematic review. *Clinical Child and Family Psychology Review, 23*(3), 365–378. https://doi.org/10.1007/s10567-020-00315-3

Alisic, E., Krishna, R. N., Robbins, M. L., & Mehl, M. R. (2016). A comparison of parent and child narratives of children's recovery from trauma. *Journal of Language and Social Psychology, 35*(2), 224–235. https://doi.org/10.1177/0261927X15599557

Allen, K., Higgins, S., & Adams, J. (2019). The relationship between visuospatial working memory and mathematical performance in school-aged children: A systematic review. *Educational Psychology Review, 31*(3), 509–531. https://doi.org/10.1007/s10648-019-09470-8

Allen, L. R., Watson, L. B., & VanMattson, S. B. (2019). young adults' reflections on adolescent sources of extra-familial support. *Journal of LGBT Youth, 17*(1), 1–23. https://doi.org/10.1080/19361653.2019.1591323

Allen, S. E. M., & Crago, M. B. (1996). Early passive acquisition in Inuktitut. *Journal of Child Language, 23*(1), 129–156. https://doi.org/10.1017/S0305000900010126

Alley, K. M. (2019). Fostering middle school students' autonomy to support motivation and engagement. *Middle School Journal, 50*(3), 5–14. https://doi.org/10.1080/00940771.2019.1603801

Almeida, J., Bécares, L., Erbetta, K., Bettegowda, V. R., & Ahluwalia, I. B. (2018). Racial/ethnic inequities in low birth weight and preterm birth: The role of multiple forms of stress. *Maternal and Child Health Journal, 22*(8), 1154–1163. https://doi.org/10.1007/s10995-018-2500-7

Alvarenga, P., Á, Cerezo, M., & Kuchirko, Y. (2022). Impact of maternal verbal responsiveness on infant language development. In P. Alvarenga, M. Á. Cerezo, & Y. Kuchirko (Eds.), *The maternal sensitivity program: A model for promoting infant development in challenging contexts* (pp. 21–30). Springer International. https://doi.org/10.1007/978-3-030-84212-3_2

Alvarez, C. H., Calasanti, A., Evans, C. R., & Ard, K. (2022). Intersectional inequalities in industrial air toxics exposure in the United States. *Health & Place, 77*, 102886. https://doi.org/10.1016/j.healthplace.2022.102886

Álvarez, C., & Szücs, D. (2023). Maternal cognitions and cognitive, behavior and emotional development in middle childhood. *Current Research in Behavioral Sciences, 4*, 100098. https://doi.org/10.1016/j.crbeha.2023.100098

Amato, P. R., & Anthony, C. J. (2014). Estimating the effects of parental divorce and death with fixed effects models. *Journal of Marriage and Family, 76*(2), 370–386. https://doi.org/10.1111/jomf.12100

American, Psychiatric Association. (2013). *Diagnostic and statistical manual of mental disorders DSM-5*. Author.

American Academy of Child and Adolescent Psychiatry. (2021). *Suicide in children and teens*. https://www.aacap.org/AACAP/Families_and_Youth/Facts_for_Families/FFF-Guide/Teen-Suicide-010.aspx

American Academy of Pediatrics. (1992, June). AAP Task Force on Infant Positioning and SIDS: Positioning and SIDS. *Pediatrics, 89*(6), 1120–1126. https://doi.org/10.1542/peds.89.6.1120

American Academy of Pediatrics. (2012). Breastfeeding and the use of human milk. *Pediatrics, 129*(3), e827–e841. https://doi.org/10.1542/peds.2011-3552

American Academy of Pediatrics Council on Communications and Media. (2016). Media and Young Minds. *Pediatrics, 138*(5), e20162591. https://doi.org/10.1542/peds.2016-2591

American College of Obstetricians and Gynecologists. (2011). *Substance abuse reporting and pregnancy: The role of the obstetrician–gynecologist*. American College of Obstetricians and Gynecologists.

American College of Obstetricians and Gynecologists. (2016). *ACOG committee opinion. Comprehensive Sexuality Education*. https://www.acog.org/Clinical-Guidance-and-Publications/Committee-Opinions/Committee-on-Adolescent-Health-Care/Comprehensive-Sexuality-Education

American College of Obstetricians and Gynecologists. (2017). Obstetric analgesia and anesthesia: Practice bulletin No. 177. *Obstetrics & Gynecology, 129*(4), e73–e89. https://doi.org/10.1097/AOG.0000000000002018

American College of Obstetricians and Gynecologists. (2024). *Current ACOG guidance: NIPT summary of recommendations*. https://www.acog.org/advocacy/policy-priorities/non-invasive-prenatal-testing/current-acog-guidance

American Medical Association. (2014). *Pregnant women's rights*. http://www.ama-assn.org/ama/pub/physician-resources/legal-topics/litigation-center/case-summaries-topic/pregnant-womens-rights.page

American Psychiatric Association. (2013). *Diagnostic and statistical manual of mental disorders DSM-5.*

American Psychological Association. (2010). *Ethical principles of psychologists and code of conduct*.

American Public Health Association. (2014). *Sexuality education as part of a comprehensive health education program in K to 12 schools*. https://www.apha.org/policies-and-advocacy/public-health-policy-statements/policy-database/2015/01/23/09/37/sexuality-education-as-part-of-a-comprehensive-health-education-program-in-k-to-12-schools

Amir, D., & McAuliffe, K. (2020). Cross-cultural, developmental psychology: Integrating approaches and key insights. *Evolution and Human Behavior*, 41(5), 430–444. https://doi.org/10.1016/j.evolhumbehav.2020.06.006

Amitay, E. L., Dubnov Raz, G., & Keinan-Boker, L. (2016). Breastfeeding, other early life exposures and childhood leukemia and lymphoma. *Nutrition and Cancer*, 68(6), 968–977. https://doi.org/10.1080/01635581.2016.1190020

Amodia-Bidakowska, A., Laverty, C., & Ramchandani, P. G. (2020). Father-child play: A systematic review of its frequency, characteristics and potential impact on children's development. *Developmental Review*, 57, 100924. https://doi.org/10.1016/j.dr.2020.100924

Amor, H., Hammadeh, M. E., Mohd, I., & Jankowski, P. M. (2022). Impact of heavy alcohol consumption and cigarette smoking on sperm DNA integrity. *Andrologia*, 54(7), e14434.

Ampaabeng, S. K., & Tan, C. M. (2013). The long-term cognitive consequences of early childhood malnutrition: The case of famine in Ghana. *Journal of Health Economics*, 32(6), 1013–1027. https://doi.org/10.1016/j.jhealeco.2013.08.001

Amso, D., & Kirkham, N. (2021). A multiple-memory systems framework for examining attention and memory interactions in infancy. *Child Development Perspectives*, 15(2). https://doi.org/10.1111/cdep.12410

Anaele, B. I., Doran, C., & McIntire, R. (2021). Visualizing COVID-19 mortality rates and African-American populations in the USA and Pennsylvania. *Journal of Racial and Ethnic Health Disparities*, 8(6), 1356–1363. https://doi.org/10.1007/s40615-020-00897-2

Anderson, C. A., Berkowitz, L., Donnerstein, E., Huesmann, L. R., Johnson, J. D., Linz, D., Malamuth, N. M., & Wartella, E. (2003). The influence of media violence on youth. *Psychological Science in the Public Interest*, 4(3), 81–110. https://doi.org/10.1111/j.1529-1006.2003.pspi_1433.x

Anderson, D. I., He, M., Gutierrez, P., Uchiyama, I., & Campos, J. J. (2019). Do balance demands induce shifts in visual proprioception in crawling infants? *Frontiers in Psychology*, 10(JUN). https://doi.org/10.3389/fpsyg.2019.01388

Anderson, D. M., Hansen, B., Rees, D. I., & Sabia, J. J. (2019). Association of marijuana laws with teen marijuana use. *JAMA Pediatrics*, 173(9). https://doi.org/10.1001/jamapediatrics.2019.1720

Anderson, M. (2018). *About a quarter of rural Americans say access to high-speed internet is a major problem*. Pew Research Center. https://www.pewresearch.org/fact-tank/2018/09/10/about-a-quarter-of-rural-americans-say-access-to-high-speed-internet-is-a-major-problem/

Anderson, M., & Jiang, J. (2018a). *Teens and their experiences on social media*. Pew Research Center. https://www.pewinternet.org/2018/11/28/teens-and-their-experiences-on-social-media/

Anderson, M., & Jiang, J. (2018b). *Teens, social media & technology 2018*. Pew Research Center. www.pewinternet.org/2018/05/31/teens-social-media-technology-2018/

Anderson, N. J., Graham, S. A., Prime, H., Jenkins, J. M., & Madigan, S. (2021). Linking quality and quantity of parental linguistic input to child language skills: A meta-analysis. *Child Development*, 92(2), 484–501. https://doi.org/10.1111/cdev.13508

Anderson, S., & Phillips, D. (2017). Is pre-k classroom quality associated with kindergarten and middle-school academic skills? *Developmental Psychology*, 53(6), 1063–1078. https://doi.org/10.1037/dev0000312

Anderson, V. A., Spencer-Smith, M. M., Coleman, L., Anderson, P. J., Greenham, M., Jacobs, R., Lee, K. J., & Leventer, R. J. (2014). Predicting neurocognitive and behavioural outcome after early brain insult. *Developmental Medicine and Child Neurology*, 56(4), 329–336. https://doi.org/10.1111/dmcn.12387

Anderson-Yockel, J., & Haynes, W. O. (1994). Joint book-reading strategies in working-class African American and white mother-toddler dyads. *Journal of Speech, Language, and Hearing Research*, 37(3), 583–593. https://doi.org/10.1044/jshr.3703.583

Andersson, U. (2008). Working memory as a predictor of written arithmetical skills in children: The importance of central executive functions. *British Journal of Educational Psychology*, 78(2), 181–203.

Andescavage, N. N., Plessis, du., A, McCarter., R, Serag., A, Evangelou., I, Vezina., G, Robertson., R, & Limperopoulos, C. (2016). Complex trajectories of brain development in the healthy human fetus. *Cerebral Cortex*, 27(11), 5274–5283. https://doi.org/10.1093/cercor/bhw306

Andrews, J. L., Ahmed, S. P., & Blakemore, S. J. (2021). Navigating the social environment in adolescence: The role of social brain development. *Biological Psychiatry*, 89(2), 109–118. https://doi.org/10.1016/j.biopsych.2020.09.012

Andrews, J. L., Ahmed, S. P., & Blakemore, S. J. (2021). Navigating the social environment in adolescence: The role of social brain development. *Biological Psychiatry*, 89(2), 109–108. https://doi.org/10.1016/j.biopsych.2020.09.012

Andrews, K., Atkinson, L., Harris, M., & Gonzalez, A. (2021). Examining the effects of household chaos on child executive functions: A meta-analysis. *Psychological Bulletin*, 147, 16–32. https://doi.org/10.1037/bul0000311

Andruski, J. E., Casielles, E., & Nathan, G. (2013). Is bilingual babbling language-specific? Some evidence from a case study of Spanish–English dual acquisition. *Bilingualism: Language and Cognition*, 17(3), 660–672. https://doi.org/10.1017/S1366728913000655

Angley, M., Divney, A., Magriples, U., & Kershaw, T. (2015). Social support, family functioning and parenting competence in adolescent parents. *Maternal and Child Health Journal*, 19(1), 67–73. https://doi.org/10.1007/s10995-014-1496-x

Antheunis, M. L., Schouten, A. P., & Krahmer, E. (2016). The role of social networking sites in early adolescents' social lives. *Journal of Early Adolescence*, 36(3), 348–371. https://doi.org/10.1177/0272431614564060

Antonarakis, S. E., Skotko, B. G., Rafii, M. S., Strydom, A., Pape, S. E., Bianchi, D. W., Sherman, S. L., & Reeves, R. H. (2020). Down syndrome. *Nature Reviews Disease Primers*, 6(1), 1–20. https://doi.org/10.1038/s41572-019-0143-7

Antonoplis, S. (2023). Studying Socioeconomic Status: Conceptual Problems and an Alternative Path Forward. *Perspectives on Psychological Science*, 18(2), 275–292. https://doi.org/10.1177/17456916221093615

Antshel, K. M. (2020). Attention-deficit/hyperactivity disorder in childhood. In S. Hupp & J. D. Jewell (Eds.), *The encyclopedia of child and adolescent development* (pp. 1–11). Wiley. https://doi.org/10.1002/9781119171492.wecad504

Apgar, V. (1953). A proposal for a new method of evaluation in the newborn infant. *Current Research in Anesthesia and Analgesia*, *32*, 260–267.

Arabiat, D., Al Jabery, M., Robinson, S., Whitehead, L., & Mörelius, E. (2023). Interactive technology use and child development: A systematic review. *Child: Care, Health and Development*, *49*(4), 679–715. https://doi.org/10.1111/cch.13082

Arakelyan, S., & Ager, A. (2021). Annual research review: A multilevel bioecological analysis of factors influencing the mental health and psychosocial well-being of refugee children. *Journal of Child Psychology and Psychiatry*, *62*(5), 484–509. https://doi.org/10.1111/JCPP.13355

Aral, T., Juang, L. P., Schwarzenthal, M., & Rivas-Drake, D. (2022). The role of the family for racism and xenophobia in childhood and adolescence:. *Review of General Psychology*, *26*(3), 327–341. https://doi.org/10.1177/10892680211056320

Archer, L., DeWitt, J., Osborne, J., Dillon, J., Willis, B., & Wong, B. (2012). Science aspirations, capital, and family habitus: How families shape children's engagement and identification with science. *American Educational Research Journal*, *49*(5), 881–908. https://doi.org/10.3102/0002831211433290

Ardila, A. (2013). Development of metacognitive and emotional executive functions in children. *Applied Neuropsychology. Child*, *2*(2), 82–87. https://doi.org/10.1080/21622965.2013.748388

Arditi-Babchuk, H., Feldman, R., & Eidelman, A. I. (2009). Rapid eye movement (REM) in premature neonates and developmental outcome at 6 months. *Infant Behavior & Development*, *32*(1), 27–32. https://doi.org/10.1016/j.infbeh.2008.09.001

Arditti, J. A., & Johnson, E. I. (2020). A family resilience agenda for understanding and responding to parental incarceration. *American Psychologist*, *77*(1), 56–70. https://doi.org/10.1037/amp0000687

Argabright, S. T., Moore, T. M., Visoki, E., DiDomenico, G. E., Taylor, J. H., & Barzilay, R. (2022). Association between racial/ethnic discrimination and pubertal development in early adolescence. *Psychoneuroendocrinology*, *140*, 105727. https://doi.org/10.1016/j.psyneuen.2022.105727

Ari-Even Roth, D., Hildesheimer, M., Roziner, I., & Henkin, Y. (2016). Evidence for a right-ear advantage in newborn hearing screening results. *Trends in Hearing*, *20*. https://doi.org/10.1177/2331216516681168

Armah, A., & Landers-Potts, M. (2021). A review of imaginary companions and their implications for development. *Imagination, Cognition and Personality*, *41*(1), 31–53. https://doi.org/10.1177/0276236621999324

Armon-Lotem, S., Haman, E., Jensen de López, K., Smoczynska, M., Yatsushiro, K., Szczerbinski, M., van Hout, A., Dabašinskienė, I., Gavarró, A., Hobbs, E., Kamandulytė-Merfeldienė, L., Katsos, N., Kunnari, S., Nitsiou, C., Sundahl Olsen, L., Parramon, X., Sauerland, U., Torn-Leesik, R., & van der Lely, H. (2016). A large-scale cross-linguistic investigation of the acquisition of passive. *Language Acquisition*, *23*(1), 27–56. https://doi.org/10.1080/10489223.2015.1047095

Armstrong-Carter, E., Wertz, J., & Domingue, B. W. (2021). Genetics and child development: Recent advances and their implications for developmental research. *Child Development Perspectives*, *15*(1), 57–64. https://doi.org/10.1111/cdep.12400

Armstrong-Heimsoth, A., Hahn-Floyd, M., Williamson, H. J., Kurka, J. M., Yoo, W., & Rodríguez De Jesús, S. A. (2021). Former foster system youth: Perspectives on transitional supports and programs. *Journal of Behavioral Health Services & Research*, *48*(2), 287–305. https://doi.org/10.1007/s11414-020-09693-6

Arnett, J. J. (1999). Adolescent storm and stress, reconsidered. *American Psychologist*, *54*(5), 317–326.

Arnett, J. J., & Mitra, D. (2020). Are the features of emerging adulthood developmentally distinctive? A comparison of ages 18–60 in the United States. *Emerging Adulthood*, *8*(5), 412–419. https://doi.org/10.1177/2167696818810073

Arnold, S. H., Burke, N., Leshin, R. A., & Rhodes, M. (2023). Infants' visual attention to own-race and other-race faces is moderated by experience with people of different races in their daily lives. *Journal of Experimental Psychology: General*. https://doi.org/10.1037/xge0001492 Advance online publication

Arseneault, L. (2018). Annual research review: The persistent and pervasive impact of being bullied in childhood and adolescence: Implications for policy and practice. *Journal of Child Psychology and Psychiatry*, *59*(4), 405–421. https://doi.org/10.1111/jcpp.12841

Arterberry, M. E., & Bornstein, M. H. (2024). *Development in infancy*. Routledge.

Arthur, A. E., Bigler, R. S., & Ruble, D. N. (2009). An experimental test of the effects of gender constancy on sex typing. *Journal of Experimental Child Psychology*, *104*(4), 427–446. https://doi.org/10.1016/j.jecp.2009.08.002

Artman, L., & Cahan, S. (1993). Schooling and the development of transitive inference. *Developmental Psychology*, *29*(4), 753–759. https://doi.org/10.1037/0012-1649.29.4.753

Asarnow, J. R. (2011). Promoting stress resistance in war-exposed children. *Journal of the American Academy of Child & Adolescent Psychiatry*, *50*(4), 320–322. https://doi.org/10.1016/j.jaac.2011.01.010

Asarnow, J. R., & Mehlum, L. (2019). Practitioner review: Treatment for suicidal and self-harming adolescents – advances in suicide prevention care. *Journal of Child Psychology and Psychiatry, and Allied Disciplines*, *60*(10), 1046–1054. https://doi.org/10.1111/jcpp.13130

Asch, A., & Marmor, R. (2020). *Assisted reproduction—The Hastings Center*. Hastings Center Bioethics Briefings.

Asher, S. R., & Weeks, M. S. (2018). Friendships in childhood. In A. L. Vangelisti & D. Perlman (Eds.), *The Cambridge handbook of personal relationships* (pp. 119–134). Cambridge University Press. https://doi.org/10.1017/9781316417867.011

Ashman, S. B., & Dawson, G. (2002). Maternal depression, infant psychobiological development, and risk for depression. In S. H. Goodman & I. H. Gotlib (Eds.), *Children of depressed parents: Mechanisms of risk and implications for treatment* (pp. 37–58). American Psychological Association. https://doi.org/10.1037/10449-002

Ask, H., Cheesman, R., Jami, E. S., Levey, D. F., Purves, K. L., & Weber, H. (2021). Genetic contributions to anxiety disorders: Where we are and where we are heading. *Psychological Medicine*, *51*(13), 2231–2246. https://doi.org/10.1017/S0033291720005486

Askari, M., Bazshahi, E., Payande, N., Mobaderi, T., Fahimfar, N., & Azadbakht, L. (2023). Relationship between caffeine intake and small for gestational age and preterm birth: A dose-response meta-analysis. *Critical Reviews in Food Science and Nutrition*, 1–11. https://doi.org/10.1080/10408398.2023.2177606

Aslaner, D. M., Alghothani, O., Saldaña, T. A., Ezell, K. G., Yallourakis, M. D., MacKenzie, D. M., Miller, R. A., Wold, L. E., & Gorr, M. W. (2022). E-cigarette vapor exposure in utero causes long-term pulmonary effects in offspring. *American Journal of Physiology-Lung Cellular and Molecular Physiology*, *323*, L676–L682. https://journals.physiology.org/doi/full/10.1152/ajplung.00233.2022

Asperholm, M., Högman, N., Rafi, J., & Herlitz, A. (2019). What did you do yesterday? A meta-analysis of sex differences in episodic memory. *Psychological Bulletin*, *145*(8), 785–821. https://doi.org/10.1037/bul0000197

Assink, M., van der Put, C. E., Meeuwsen, M. W. C. M., de Jong, N. M., Oort, F. J., Stams, G. J. J. M., & Hoeve, M. (2019). Risk factors for child sexual abuse victimization: A meta-analytic review. *Psychological Bulletin*, *145*(5), 459–489. https://doi.org/10.1037/bul0000188

Astington, J. W. (1993). *The child's discovery of the mind*. Harvard University Press.

Astley Hemingway, S. J., Bledsoe, J. M., Davies, J. K., Brooks, A., Jirikowic, T., Olson, E. M., & Thorne, J. C. (2019). Twin study confirms virtually identical prenatal alcohol exposures can lead to markedly different fetal alcohol spectrum disorder outcomes-fetal genetics influences fetal vulnerability. *Advances in Pediatric Research*, *5*(23). https://doi.org/10.24105/apr.2019.5.23

Ati, N. A. L., Paraswati, M. D., & Windarwati, H. D. (2020). What are the risk factors and protective factors of suicidal behavior in adolescents? A systematic review. *Journal of Child and Adolescent Psychiatric Nursing*, *34*(4), 7–18. https://doi.org/10.1111/jcap.12295

Atkins, D. N., & Durrance, C. P. (2020). State policies that treat prenatal substance use as child abuse or neglect fail to achieve their intended goals. *Health Affairs (Project Hope)*, *39*(5), 756–763. https://doi.org/10.1377/hlthaff.2019.00785

Atkinson, A. L., Waterman, A. H., & Allen, R. J. (2019). Can children prioritize more valuable information in working memory? An exploration into the effects of motivation and memory load. *Developmental Psychology*, *55*(5), 967–980. https://doi.org/10.1037/dev0000692

Atkinson, R. C., & Shiffrin, R. M. (1968). Human memory: A proposed system and its control processes. *Psychology of Learning and Motivation*, *2*, 89–195. https://doi.org/10.1016/S0079-7421(08)60422-3

Atske, S., Vogels, E. A., Perrin, A., & Raine, L. (2022). *Connection, creativity and drama: Teen life on social media in 2022*. Pew Research Center: Internet, Science & Tech. https://www.pewresearch.org/internet/2022/11/16/connection-creativity-and-drama-teen-life-on-social-media-in-2022/

Aubrey, J. S., & Roberts, L. (2020). Effects of media use on development of gender role beliefs. In J. Bulck (Ed.), *The international encyclopedia of media psychology* (pp. 1–12). John Wiley & Sons. https://doi.org/10.1002/9781119011071.iemp0081

Austin, A. E., Gest, C., Atkeson, A., Berkoff, M. C., Puls, H. T., & Shanahan, M. E. (2022). Prenatal substance exposure and child maltreatment: A systematic review. *Child Maltreatment*, *27*(2), 290–315. https://doi.org/10.1177/1077559521990116

Austin, A. E., Lesak, A. M., & Shanahan, M. E. (2020). Risk and protective factors for child maltreatment: A review. *Current Epidemiology Reports*, *7*(4), 334–342. https://doi.org/10.1007/s40471-020-00252-3

Australian Institute of Health and Welfare. (2016). *Leading causes of death*. http://www.aihw.gov.au/deaths/leading-causes-of-death/

Avagliano, L., Massa, V., George, T. M., Qureshy, S., Bulfamante, G. P., & Finnell, R. H. (2019). Overview on neural tube defects: From development to physical characteristics. *Birth Defects Research*, *111*(19), 1455–1467. https://doi.org/10.1002/bdr2.1380

Avalos, L. A., Nance, N., Zhu, Y., Croen, L. A., Young-Wolff, K. C., Zerbo, O., Hedderson, M. M., Ferrara, A., Ames, J. L., & Badon, S. E. (2022). Contributions of COVID-19 pandemic-related stressors to racial and ethnic disparities in mental health during pregnancy. *Frontiers in Psychiatry*, *13*, 837659. https://doi.org/10.3389/fpsyt.2022.837659

Aviles, A. I., Betar, S. K., Cline, S. M., Tian, Z., Jacobvitz, D. B., & Nicholson, J. S. (2024). Parenting young children during COVID-19: Parenting stress trajectories, parental mental health, and child problem behaviors. *Journal of Family Psychology*, *38*(2), 296–308. https://doi.org/10.1037/fam0001181

Axelsson, E., Othman, N. N., & Kansal, N. (2022). Temperament and children's accuracy and attention during word learning. *Infant Behavior and Development*, *69*, 101771. https://doi.org/10.1016/j.infbeh.2022.101771

Axelsson, J., Sabra, S., Rylander, L., Rignell-Hydbom, A., Lindh, C. H., & Giwercman, A. (2018). Association between paternal smoking at the time of pregnancy and the semen quality in sons. *PLoS ONE*, *13*(11), e0207221. https://doi.org/10.1371/journal.pone.0207221

Azagba, S., Manzione, L., Shan, L., & King, J. (2020). Trends in smoking during pregnancy by socioeconomic characteristics in the United States, 2010–2017. *BMC Pregnancy and Childbirth*, *20*(1), 52. https://doi.org/10.1186/s12884-020-2748-y

Azmitia, M., Peraza, P. D. G., Thomas, V., Ajayi, A. A., & Syed, M. (2023). The promises and challenges of using an intersectional framework to study identity development during adolescence and early adulthood. In *APA handbook of adolescent and young adult development* (pp. 391–405). American Psychological Association. https://doi.org/10.1037/0000298-024

Azpiazu Izaguirre, L., Fernández, A. R., & Palacios, E. G. (2021). Adolescent life satisfaction explained by social support, emotion regulation, and resilience. *Frontiers in Psychology*, *12*, 694183. https://www.frontiersin.org/articles/10.3389/fpsyg.2021.694183

Azuine, R. E., Ji, Y., Chang, H. Y., Kim, Y., Ji, H., Dibari, J., Hong, X., Wang, G., Singh, G. K., Pearson, C., Zuckerman, B., Surkan, P. J., & Wang, X. (2019). Prenatal risk factors and perinatal and postnatal outcomes associated with maternal opioid exposure in an urban, low-income, multiethnic US population. *JAMA Network Open*, *2*(6), e196405. https://doi.org/10.1001/jamanetworkopen.2019.6405

Baams, L., Dubas, J. S., Overbeek, G., & van Aken, M. A. G. (2015). Transitions in body and behavior: A meta-analytic study on the relationship between pubertal development and adolescent sexual behavior. *Journal of Adolescent Health*, *56*(6), 586–598. https://doi.org/10.1016/j.jadohealth.2014.11.019

Baams, L., & Kaufman, T. M. L. (2023). Sexual orientation and gender identity/expression in adolescent research: Two decades in review. *Journal of Sex Research*, *60*(7), 1004–1019. https://doi.org/10.1080/00224499.2023.2219245

Babore, A., Carlucci, L., Cataldi, F., Phares, V., & Trumello, C. (2017). Aggressive behaviour in adolescence: Links with self-esteem and parental emotional availability. *Social Development*, *26*(4), 740–752. https://doi.org/10.1111/sode.12236

Baccassino, F., & Pinnelli, S. (2023). *Giftedness and gifted education: A systematic literature review*. Frontiers in Education. https://www.frontiersin.org/articles/10.3389/feduc.2022.1073007

Bachman, J. G., O'Malley, P. M., Freedman-Doan, P., Trzesniewski, K. H., & Donnellan, M. B. (2011). Adolescent self-esteem: Differences by race/ethnicity, gender, and age. *Self and Identity*, *10*(4), 445–473. https://doi.org/10.1080/15298861003794538

Backes, C. H., Rivera, B. K., Pavlek, L., Beer, L. J., Ball, M. K., Zettler, E. T., Smith, C. V., Bridge, J. A., Bell, E. F., & Frey, H. A. (2021). Proactive neonatal treatment at 22 weeks of gestation: A systematic review and meta-analysis. *American Journal of Obstetrics and Gynecology, 224*(2), 158–174. https://doi.org/10.1016/j.ajog.2020.07.051

Backschneider, A. G., Shatz, M., & Gelman, S. A. (1993). Preschoolers' ability to distinguish living kinds as a function of regrowth. *Child Development, 64*, 1242–1257. https://doi.org/10.1111/j.1467-8624.1993.tb04198.x

Baddeley, A. (2016). Working memory. In R. J. Sternberg, S. T. Fiske, & D. J. Foss (Eds.), *Scientists making a difference: One hundred eminent behavioral and brain scientists talk about their most important contributions* (pp. 119–122). Cambridge University Press.

Baddeley, A., Eysenck, M. W., & Anderson, M. C. (2020). *Memory*. Routledge.

Badihian, N., Daniali, S. S., & Kelishadi, R. (2019). Transcriptional and epigenetic changes of brain derived neurotrophic factor following prenatal stress: A systematic review of animal studies. *Neuroscience and Biobehavioral Reviews*. https://doi.org/10.1016/j.neubiorev.2019.12.018

Baer, R. J., Altman, M. R., Oltman, S. P., Ryckman, K. K., Chambers, C. D., Rand, L., & Jelliffe-Pawlowski, L. L. (2019). Maternal factors influencing late entry into prenatal care: A stratified analysis by race or ethnicity and insurance status. *Journal of Maternal-Fetal & Neonatal Medicine, 32*, 1–7. https://doi.org/10.1080/14767058.2018.1463366

Baert, S., & Van der Straeten, G. (2021). Secondary school success in times of parental divorce. *Family Relations, 70*(2), 575–586. https://doi.org/10.1111/fare.12476

Bagci, S. C., Rutland, A., Kumashiro, M., Smith, P. K., & Blumberg, H. (2014). Are minority status children's cross-ethnic friendships beneficial in a multiethnic context? *British Journal of Developmental Psychology, 32*(1), 107–115. https://doi.org/10.1111/bjdp.12028

Baglivio, M. T., Jackowski, K., Greenwald, M. A., & Howell, J. C. (2014). Serious, violent, and chronic juvenile offenders. *Criminology & Public Policy, 13*(1), 83–116. https://doi.org/10.1111/1745-9133.12064

Bagni, C., & Zukin, R. S. (2019). A synaptic perspective of fragile X syndrome and autism spectrum disorders. *Neuron, 101*(6), 1070–1088. https://doi.org/10.1016/j.neuron.2019.02.041

Bagwell, C. L. (2020). Friendship in childhood. In S. Hupp & J. D. Jewell (Eds.), *The encyclopedia of child and adolescent development* (pp. 1–14). Wiley. https://doi.org/10.1002/9781119171492.wecad278

Bagwell, C. L., & Bukowski, W. M. (2018). Friendship in childhood and adolescence: Features, effects, and processes. In W. M. Bukowski, B. Laursen, & K. H. Rubin (Eds.), *Handbook of peer interactions, relationships, and groups* (pp. 371–390). Guilford Press. https://psycnet.apa.org/record/2018-00748-019

Baião, R., Fearon, P., Belsky, J., Teixeira, P., Soares, I., & Mesquita, A. (2020). Does 5-HTTLPR moderate the effect of the quality of environmental context on maternal sensitivity? Testing the differential susceptibility hypothesis. *Psychiatric Genetics, 30*(2), 49–56. https://doi.org/10.1097/YPG.0000000000000247

Baiden, P., Park, Y., LaBrenz, C. A., & Childress, S. (2024). Exposure to neighborhood violence and gun carrying among adolescents in the United States: Findings from a population-based study. *Journal of Interpersonal Violence*, 08862605241231616. https://doi.org/10.1177/08862605241231616

Bailen, N. H., Green, L. M., & Thompson, R. J. (2019). Understanding emotion in adolescents: A review of emotional frequency, intensity, instability, and clarity:. *Emotion Review, 11*(1), 63–73. https://doi.org/10.1177/1754073918768878

Bailey, B. A., Shah, D. S., Boynewicz, K. L., Justice, N. A., & Wood, D. L. (2022). Impact of in utero opioid exposure on newborn outcomes: Beyond neonatal opioid withdrawal syndrome. *Journal of Maternal-Fetal & Neonatal Medicine, 35*(25), 9383–9390. https://doi.org/10.1080/14767058.2022.2035713

Bailey, M. J., Sun, S., & Timpe, B. (2021). Prep school for poor kids: The long-run impacts of Head Start on human capital and economic self-sufficiency. *American Economic Review, 111*(12), 3963–4001. https://doi.org/10.1257/aer.20181801

Baillargeon, R. (1987). Object permanence in 3 1/2- and 4 1/2-month-old-infants. *Developmental Psychology, 23*(5), 655–664. https://doi.org/10.1037//0012-1649.23.5.655

Baillargeon, R., Scott, R. M., & Bian, L. (2016). Psychological reasoning in infancy. *Annual Review of Psychology, 67*(1), 159–186. https://doi.org/10.1146/annurev-psych-010213-115033

Bajanowski, T., & Vennemann, M. (2017). Sudden infant death syndrome (SIDS). In M. M. Houck (Ed.), *Forensic pathology* (pp. 259–266). Elsevier.

Baker, J. M., Klabunde, M., Jo, B., Green, T., & Reiss, A. L. (2020). On the relationship between mathematics and visuospatial processing in Turner syndrome. *Journal of Psychiatric Research, 121*, 135–142. https://doi.org/10.1016/J.JPSYCHIRES.2019.11.004

Baker, S. (2018). The effects of parenting on emotion and self-regulation. In M. R. Sanders & A. Morawska (Eds.), *Handbook of parenting and child development across the lifespan* (pp. 217–240). Springer International. https://doi.org/10.1007/978-3-319-94598-9_10

Bakermans-Kranenburg, M. J., & van IJzendoorn, M. H. (2015). The hidden efficacy of interventions: Gene x environment experiments from a differential susceptibility perspective. *Annual Review of Psychology, 66*(1), 381–409. https://doi.org/10.1146/annurev-psych-010814-015407

Bakermans-Kranenburg, M. J., & van IJzendoorn, M. H. (2023). Sensitive responsiveness in expectant and new fathers. *Current Opinion in Psychology, 50*, 101580. https://doi.org/10.1016/j.copsyc.2023.101580

Balakrishnan, A. (2020). Self-concept, Expressions of the. In B. J. Carducci, C. S. Nave, A. D. Fabio, D. H. Saklofske, & C. Stough (Eds.), *The Wiley encyclopedia of personality and individual differences* (pp. 369–373). Wiley. https://doi.org/10.1002/9781119547174.ch240

Balenzano, C., Coppola, G., Cassibba, R., & Moro, G. (2018). Pre-adoption adversities and adoptees' outcomes: The protective role of post-adoption variables in an Italian experience of domestic open adoption. *Children and Youth Services Review, 85*, 307–318. https://doi.org/10.1016/j.childyouth.2018.01.012

Ball, H. L., Hooker, E., & Kelly, P. J. (1999). Where will the baby sleep? Attitudes and practices of new and experienced parents regarding co-sleeping with their new-born infants. *American Anthropologist, 101*, 1–9. http://dx.doi.org/10.1525/aa.1999.101.1.143

Ball, J. W., Bindler, R. C., Cowen, Kay., & Shaw, M. Rose. (2017). *Principles of pediatric nursing: Caring for children*. Pearson College Division. https://www.pearson.com/us/higher-education/program/Ball-Principles-of-Pediatric-Nursing-Caring-for-Children-7th-Edition/PGM311969.html

Baltes, P. B. (1987). Theoretical propositions of life-span developmental psychology: On the dynamics between growth and decline. *Developmental Psychology, 23*, 611–626.

Baltes, P. B., Lindenberger, U., & Staudinger, U. M. (1998). Life-span theory in developmental psychology. In R. M. Lerner (Ed.), *Handbook of child psychology: Theoretical models of human development* (Vol. 1, pp. 1029–1143). Wiley.

Balzer, B. W. R., Duke, S.-A., Hawke, C. I., & Steinbeck, K. S. (2015). The effects of estradiol on mood and behavior in human female adolescents: A systematic review. *European Journal of Pediatrics, 174*(3), 289–298. https://doi.org/10.1007/s00431-014-2475-3

Bandoli, G., & Chambers, C. D. (2023). Protective and risk factors. In O. A. Abdul-Rahman & C. L. M. Petrenko (Eds.), *Fetal alcohol spectrum disorders: A multidisciplinary approach* (pp. 17–31). Springer International. https://doi.org/10.1007/978-3-031-32386-7_2

Bandura, A. (2010). Vicarious learning. In D. Matsumoto (Ed.), *Cambridge dictionary of psychology* (p. 344). Cambridge University Press.

Bandura, A. (2011). But what about that gigantic elephant in the room? In R. Arkin (Ed.), *Most underappreciated: 50 prominent social psychologists describe their most unloved work*. Arkin (pp. 51–59). Oxford University Press.

Bandura, A. (2012). Social cognitive theory. In P. A. M. Van Lange, A. W. Kruglanski & E. T. Higgins (Eds.), *Handbook of theories of social psychology* (Vol. 1, pp. 349–373). SAGE.

Bandura, A. (2018). Toward a psychology of human agency: Pathways and reflections. *Perspectives on Psychological Science, 13*(2), 130–136. https://doi.org/10.1177/1745691617699280

Bandura, A., & Bussey, K. (2004). On broadening the cognitive, motivational, and sociostructural scope of theorizing about gender development and functioning: Comment on Martin, Ruble, and Szkrybalo (2002). *Psychological Bulletin, 130*(5), 691–701.

Banneyer, K. N., Koenig, S. A., Wang, L. A., & Stark, K. D. (2017). A review of the effects of parental PTSD: A focus on military children. *Couple and Family Psychology: Research and Practice, 6*(4), 274–286. https://doi.org/10.1037/cfp0000093

Banse, R., Gawronski, B., Rebetez, C., Gutt, H., & Bruce Morton, J. (2010). The development of spontaneous gender stereotyping in childhood: Relations to stereotype knowledge and stereotype flexibility. *Developmental Science, 13*(2), 298–306. https://doi.org/10.1111/j.1467-7687.2009.00880.x

Bányai, F., Zsila, Á., Király, O., Maraz, A., Elekes, Z., Griffiths, M. D., Andreassen, C. S., & Demetrovics, Z. (2017). Problematic social media use: Results from a large-scale nationally representative adolescent sample. *PLoS ONE, 12*(1), e0169839. https://doi.org/10.1371/journal.pone.0169839

Barac, R., Bialystok, E., Castro, D. C., & Sanchez, M. (2014). The cognitive development of young dual language learners: A critical review. *Early Childhood Research Quarterly, 29*(4), 699–714. https://doi.org/10.1016/j.ecresq.2014.02.003

Barbosa-Méndez, S., & Salazar-Juárez, A. (2020). Prenatal and postnatal cocaine exposure enhances the induction and expression of locomotor sensitization to cocaine in rats. *Reproductive Toxicology, 93*, 235–249. https://doi.org/10.1016/j.reprotox.2020.03.001

Barbot, B., Hein, S., Trentacosta, C., Beckmann, J. F., Bick, J., Crocetti, E., Liu, Y., Rao, S. F., Liew, J., Overbeek, G., Ponguta, L. A., Scheithauer, H., Super, C., Arnett, J., Bukowski, W., Cook, T. D., Côté, J., Eccles, J. S., Eid, M., & &#hillip1; van IJzendoorn, M. H. (2020). Manifesto for new directions in developmental science. *New Directions for Child and Adolescent Development*, 135–149. https://doi.org/10.1002/cad.20359 *2020*(172)

Bard, K. A., Todd, B. K., Bernier, C., Love, J., & Leavens, D. A. (2006). Self-awareness in human and chimpanzee infants: What is measured and what is meant by the mark and mirror test? *Infancy, 9*(2), 191–219. https://doi.org/10.1207/s15327078in0902_6

Barel, E., & Tzischinsky, O. (2018). Age and sex differences in verbal and visuospatial abilities. *Advances in Cognitive Psychology, 2*(14), 51–61. https://doi.org/10.5709/ACP-0238-X

Barendse, M. E. A., Byrne, M. L., Flournoy, J. C., McNeilly, E. A., Guazzelli Williamson, V., Barrett, A.-M. Y., Chavez, S. J., Shirtcliff, E. A., Allen, N. B., & Pfeifer, J. H. (2022). Multimethod assessment of pubertal timing and associations with internalizing psychopathology in early adolescent girls. *Journal of Psychopathology and Clinical Science, 131*(1), 14–25. https://doi.org/10.1037/abn0000721

Bargh, J. A. (2013). Our unconscious mind. *Scientific American, 310*(1), 30–37. https://doi.org/10.1038/scientificamerican0114-30

Barnard-Brak, L., Morales-Alemán, M. M., Tomeny, K., & McWilliam, R. A. (2021). Rural and racial/ethnic differences in children receiving early intervention services. *Family & Community Health, 44*(1), 52. https://doi.org/10.1097/FCH.0000000000000285

Barnes, J., & Theule, J. (2019). Maternal depression and infant attachment security: A meta-analysis. *Infant Mental Health Journal, 40*(6), 817–834. https://doi.org/10.1002/imhj.21812

Barnett, A. P., Molock, S. D., Nieves-Lugo, K., & Zea, M. C. (2019). Anti-LGBT victimization, fear of violence at school, and suicide risk among adolescents. *Psychology of Sexual Orientation and Gender Diversity, 6*(1), 88–95. https://doi.org/10.1037/sgd0000309

Barnett, E. R., Knight, E., Herman, R. J., Amarakaran, K., & Jankowski, M. K. (2021). Difficult binds: A systematic review of facilitators and barriers to treatment among mothers with substance use disorders. *Journal of Substance Abuse Treatment, 126*, 108341. https://doi.org/10.1016/j.jsat.2021.108341

Barnett, L. M., Lai, S. K., Veldman, S. L. C., Hardy, L. L., Cliff, D. P., Morgan, P. J., Zask, A., Lubans, D. R., Shultz, S. P., Ridgers, N. D., Rush, E., Brown, H. L., & Okely, A. D. (2016). Correlates of gross motor competence in children and adolescents: A systematic review and meta-analysis. *Sports Medicine, 46*(11), 1663–1688. https://doi.org/10.1007/s40279-016-0495-z

Barnett, S. M., Ceci, S. J., & Williams, W. M. (2006). Is the ability to make a bacon sandwich a mark of intelligence? And other issues: Some reflections on Gardner's theory of multiple intelligences. In J. A. Schaler (Ed.), *Howard Gardner under fire: The rebel psychologist faces his critics* (pp. 95–114). Open Court.

Barone, L., Lionetti, F., & Green, J. (2017). A matter of attachment? How adoptive parents foster post-institutionalized children's social and emotional adjustment. *Attachment & Human Development, 19*(4), 323–339. https://doi.org/10.1080/14616734.2017.1306714

Barr, R. (2010). Transfer of learning between 2D and 3D sources during infancy: Informing theory and practice. *Developmental Review, 30*(2), 128–154. https://doi.org/10.1016/j.dr.2010.03.001

Barr, R. G., Konner, M., Bakeman, R., & Adamson, L. (1991). Crying in !Kung San infants: A test of the cultural specificity hypothesis. *Developmental Medicine & Child Neurology, 33*(7), 601–610. https://doi.org/10.1111/j.1469-8749.1991.tb14930.x

Barr, R., Lauricella, A., Zack, E., & Calvert, S. L. (2010). Infant and early childhood exposure to adult-directed and child-directed television programming. *Merrill-Palmer Quarterly, 56*(1), 21–48. https://psycnet.apa.org/doi/10.1353/mpq.0.0038

Barr, R., Marrott, H., & Rovee-Collier, C. (2003). The role of sensory preconditioning in memory retrieval by preverbal infants. *Learning & Behavior*, *31*(2), 111–123.

Barr, R., Rovee-Collier, C., & Campanella, J. (2005). Retrieval protracts deferred imitation by 6-month-olds. *Infancy*, *7*(3), 263–283. https://doi.org/10.1207/s15327078in0703_3

Barrett, K. C., & Morgan, G. A. (2018). Mastery motivation: Retrospect, present, and future directions. *Advances in Motivation Science*, *5*, 1–39. https://doi.org/10.1016/BS.ADMS.2018.01.002

Barrow, B. H., Dollahite, D. C., & Marks, L. D. (2021). How parents balance desire for religious continuity with honoring children's religious agency. *Psychology of Religion and Spirituality*, *13*, 222–234. https://doi.org/10.1037/rel0000307

Barry, C. M., Nelson, L. J., & Abo-Zena, M. M. (2018). Religiousness in adolescence and emerging adulthood. In *Encyclopedia of Adolescence* (pp. 3101–3126). Springer International. https://doi.org/10.1007/978-3-319-33228-4_265

Barry, C. T., Loflin, D. C., & Doucette, H. (2015). Adolescent self-compassion: Associations with narcissism, self-esteem, aggression, and internalizing symptoms in at-risk males. *Personality and Individual Differences*, *77*, 118–123. https://doi.org/10.1016/J.PAID.2014.12.036

Barry, C.-J. S., Walker, V. M., Cheesman, R., Davey Smith, G., Morris, T. T., & Davies, N. M. (2023). How to estimate heritability: A guide for genetic epidemiologists. *International Journal of Epidemiology*, *52*(2), 624–632. https://doi.org/10.1093/ije/dyac224

Barry, E. S. (2020). What is "normal" infant sleep? Why we still do not know. *Psychological Reports*, *124*(2), 651–692. https://doi.org/10.1177/0033294120909447

Barry, E. S., & McKenna, J. J. (2022). Reasons mothers bedshare: A review of its effects on infant behavior and development. *Infant Behavior and Development*, *66*, 101684. https://doi.org/10.1016/j.infbeh.2021.101684

Bartram, S. C., Barlow, J., & Wolke, D. (2015). The Neonatal Behavioral Assessment Scale (NBAS) and Newborn Behavioral Observations system (NBO) for supporting caregivers and improving outcomes in caregivers and their infants. In S. C. Bartram (Ed.), *Cochrane database of systematic reviews*. John Wiley & Sons. https://doi.org/10.1002/14651858.CD011754

Bassano, D. (2000). Early development of nouns and verbs in French: Exploring the interface between lexicon and grammar. *Journal of Child Language*, *27*(3), 521–559. https://doi.org/10.1017/S0305000900004396

Bastaits, K., & Mortelmans, D. (2016). Parenting as mediator between post-divorce family structure and children's well-being. *Journal of Child and Family Studies*, *25*(7), 2178–2188. https://doi.org/10.1007/s10826-016-0395-8

Basten, U., Hilger, K., & Fiebach, C. J. (2015). Where smart brains are different: A quantitative meta-analysis of functional and structural brain imaging studies on intelligence. *Intelligence*, *51*, 10–27. https://doi.org/10.1016/j.intell.2015.04.009

Bater, L. R., & Jordan, S. S. (2020). Selective attention. In Virgil. Zeigler-Hill & K. Shackelford. Todd (Eds.), *Encyclopedia of personality and individual differences* (pp. 4624–4628). Springer. https://doi.org/10.1007/978-3-319-24612-3_1904

Bates, E. (1990). Language about me and you: Pronominal reference and the emerging concept of self. In D. Cicchetti & M. Beeghly (Eds.), *The self in transition: Infancy to childhood* (pp. 165–182). University of Chicago Press.

Bates, E., Bretherton, I., & Snyder, L. (1988). *From first words to grammar*. Cambridge University Press.

Bateson, P. (2015). Human evolution and development: An ethological perspective. In W. F. Overton & P. C. M. Molenaar (Eds.), *Handbook of child psychology and developmental science: Theory and method* (Vol. 1, pp. 208–243). Wiley.

Bathelt, J., Scerif, G., Nobre, A. C., & Astle, D. E. (2019). Whole-brain white matter organization, intelligence, and educational attainment. *Trends in Neuroscience and Education*, *15*, 38–47. https://doi.org/10.1016/j.tine.2019.02.004

Batini, F., Luperini, V., Cei, E., Izzo, D., & Toti, G. (2020). The association between reading and emotional development: A systematic review. *Journal of Education and Training Studies*, *9*(1), 12–50. https://doi.org/10.11114/jets.v9i1.5053

Baudat, S., Mantzouranis, G., Van Petegem, S., & Zimmermann, G. (2022). How do adolescents manage information in the relationship with their parents? A latent class analysis of disclosure, keeping secrets, and lying. *Journal of Youth and Adolescence*, *51*(6), 1134–1152. https://doi.org/10.1007/s10964-022-01599-0

Baudat, S., Van Petegem, S., Antonietti, J. P., & Zimmermann, G. (2020). Parental solicitation and adolescents' information management: The moderating role of autonomy-supportive parenting. *Journal of Child and Family Studies*, *29*(2), 426–441. https://doi.org/10.1007/s10826-019-01687-z

Baudry, C., Tarabulsy, G. M., Atkinson, L., Pearson, J., & St-Pierre, A. (2017). Intervention with adolescent mother-child dyads and cognitive development in early childhood: A meta-analysis. *Prevention Science*, *18*(1), 116–130. https://doi.org/10.1007/s11121-016-0731-7

Bauer, P. J. (2002). Long-term recall memory: Behavioral and neuro-developmental changes in the first 2 years of life. *Current Directions in Psychological Science*, *11*(4), 137–141. https://doi.org/10.1111/1467-8721.00186

Bauer, P. J. (2015). A complementary processes account of the development of childhood amnesia and a personal past. *Psychological Review*, *122*(2), 204–231. https://doi.org/10.1037/A0038939

Bauer, P. J., & Larkina, M. (2014). The onset of childhood amnesia in childhood: A prospective investigation of the course and determinants of forgetting of early-life events. *Memory*, *22*(8), 907–924. https://doi.org/10.1080/09658211.2013.854806

Bauer, P. J., & Larkina, M. (2016). Predicting remembering and forgetting of autobiographical memories in children and adults: A 4-year prospective study. *Memory*, *24*(10), 1345–1368. https://doi.org/10.1080/09658211.2015.1110595

Bauer, P. J., & Larkina, M. (2017). Predictors of age-related and individual variability in autobiographical memory in childhood. *Memory*, *27*(1), 63–78. https://doi.org/10.1080/09658211.2017.1381267

Bauer, P. J., Larkina, M., Güler, E., & Burch, M. (2019). Long-term autobiographical memory across middle childhood: Patterns, predictors, and implications for conceptualizations of childhood amnesia. *Memory*, *27*(9), 1175–1193. https://doi.org/10.1080/09658211.2019.1615511

Bauer, P. J., Wenner, J. A., Dropik, P. L., & Wewerka, S. S. (2000). Parameters of remembering and forgetting in the transition from infancy to early childhood. *Monographs of the Society for Research in Child Development*, *65*(4), i–1–vi.204.

Bauer, T., Hall, C., Bursalıoğlu, A., & Guy, M. W. (2023). Community diversity and the other-race effect in infancy. *Frontiers in Psychology*, *1*(4). https://www.frontiersin.org/journals/psychology/articles/10.3389/fpsyg.2023.1214075

Baumeister, R. F., & Vohs, K. D. (2018). Revisiting our reappraisal of the (surprisingly few) benefits of high self-esteem. *Perspectives on Psychological Science*, 13(2), 137–140. https://doi.org/10.1177/1745691617701185

Baumrind, D. (1971). Current patterns of parental authority. *Developmental Psychology*, 4(Monograph 1), 1–103. https://psycnet.apa.org/doi/10.1037/h0030372

Baumrind, D. (2012). Differentiating between confrontive and coercive kinds of parental power-assertive disciplinary practices. *Human Development*, 55(2), 35–51. https://doi.org/10.1159/000337962

Baumrind, D. (2013). Authoritative parenting revisited: History and current status. In R. E. Larzelere, A. S. Morris, & A. W. Harrist (Eds.), *Authoritative parenting: Synthesizing nurturance and discipline for optimal child development* (pp. 11–34). APA http://psycnet.apa.org/buy/2012-15622-002

Baumrind, D., Larzelere, R. E., & Owens, E. B. (2010). Effects of preschool parents' power assertive patterns and practices on adolescent development. *Parenting: Science & Practice*, 10(3), 157–201. https://doi.org/10.1080/15295190903290790

Baus, C., Costa, A., & Carreiras, M. (2013). On the effects of second language immersion on first language production. *Acta Psychologica*, 142(3), 402–409. https://doi.org/10.1016/j.actpsy.2013.01.010

Bax, A. C., Bard, D. E., Cuffe, S. P., McKeown, R. E., & Wolraich, M. L. (2019). The association between race/ethnicity and socioeconomic factors and the diagnosis and treatment of children with attention-deficit hyperactivity disorder. *Journal of Developmental & Behavioral Pediatrics*, 40(2), 81–91. https://doi.org/10.1097/DBP.0000000000000626

Bayet, L., Quinn, P. C., Tanaka, J. W., Lee, K., Gentaz, É., & Pascalis, O. (2015). Face gender influences the looking preference for smiling expressions in 3.5-month-old human infants. *PLoS ONE*, 10(6), e0129812. https://doi.org/10.1371/journal.pone.0129812

Bayley, N. (1949). Consistency and variability in the growth of intelligence from birth to eighteen years. *Pedagogical Seminary and Journal of Genetic Psychology*, 75(2), 165–196. https://doi.org/10.1080/08856559.1949.10533516

Bayley, N. (1969). *Manual for the Bayley scales of infant development*. Psychological Corporation.

Bayley, N. (2005). *Bayley scales of infant and toddler development*. Psychological Corporation.

Bazinet, A. D., Squeglia, L., Riley, E., & Tapert, S. F. (2016). Effects of drug exposure on development. In K. J. Sher (Ed.), *The Oxford handbook of substance use and substance use disorders* (Vol. 2, pp. 215–254). Oxford University Press. https://doi.org/10.1093/oxfordhb/9780199381708.013.21

Beal, M. A., Yauk, C. L., & Marchetti, F. (2017). From sperm to offspring: Assessing the heritable genetic consequences of paternal smoking and potential public health impacts. *Mutation Research/Reviews in Mutation Research*, 773, 26–50. https://doi.org/10.1016/j.mrrev.2017.04.001

Beatty, W. W. (1992). Gonadal hormones and sex differences in nonreproductive behaviors. In A. A. Gerall, H. Moltz, & I. L. Ward (Eds.), *Handbook of behavioral neurobiology: Vol. 11. Sexual differentiation* (pp. 85–128). Plenum.

Beaujean, A. A., & Woodhouse, N. (2020). Wechsler Intelligence Scale for Children (WISC). In B. J. Carducci, C. S. Nave, J. S. Mio, & R. E. Riggio (Eds.), *The Wiley encyclopedia of personality and individual differences* (pp. 465–471). Wiley. https://doi.org/10.1002/9781118970843.ch147

Beauregard, J. L., Hamner, H. C., Chen, J., Avila-Rodriguez, W., Elam-Evans, L. D., & Perrine, C. G. (2019). Racial disparities in breastfeeding initiation and duration among U.S. infants born in 2015. *MMWR*, 68(34), 745–748. https://doi.org/10.15585/mmwr.mm6834a3

Becerra-Culqui, T. A., Liu, Y., Nash, R., Cromwell, L., Flanders, W. D., Getahun, D., Giammattei, S. V., Hunkeler, E. M., Lash, T. L., Millman, A., Quinn, V. P., Robinson, B., Roblin, D., Sandberg, D. E., Silverberg, M. J., Tangpricha, V., & Goodman, M. (2018). Mental health of transgender and gender nonconforming youth compared with their peers. *Pediatrics*, 141(5), e20173845. https://doi.org/10.1542/peds.2017-3845

Becht, A. I., Nelemans, S. A., Branje, S. J. T., Vollebergh, W. A. M., Koot, H. M., & Meeus, W. H. J. (2017). Identity uncertainty and commitment making across adolescence: Five-year within-person associations using daily identity reports. *Developmental Psychology*, 53(11), 2103–2112. https://doi.org/10.1037/dev0000374

Beebe, B., Jaffe, J., Markese, S., Buck, K., Chen, H., Cohen, P., Bahrick, L., Andrews, H., & Feldstein, S. (2010). The origins of 12-month attachment: A microanalysis of 4-month mother-infant interaction. *Attachment & Human Development*, 12(1–2), 3–141. https://doi.org/10.1080/14616730903338985

Beebe, B., Messinger, D., Bahrick, L. E., Margolis, A., Buck, K. A., & Chen, H. (2016). A systems view of mother-infant face-to-face communication. *Developmental Psychology*, 52(4), 556–571. https://doi.org/10.1037/a0040085

Beelmann, A., Arnold, L. S., & Hercher, J. (2023). Parent training programs for preventing and treating antisocial behavior in children and adolescents: A comprehensive meta-analysis of international studies. *Aggression and Violent Behavior*, 68, 101798. https://doi.org/10.1016/j.avb.2022.101798

Behrend, D. A., Scofield, J., & Kleinknecht, E. E. (2001). Beyond fast mapping: Young children's extensions of novel words and novel facts. *Developmental Psychology*, 37(5), 698–705. https://doi.org/10.1037/0012-1649.37.5.698

Behrens, K. Y., Parker, A. C., & Haltigan, J. D. (2011). Maternal sensitivity assessed during the Strange Situation Procedure predicts child's attachment quality and reunion behaviors. *Infant Behavior & Development*, 34(2), 378–381. https://doi.org/10.1016/j.infbeh.2011.02.007

Beier, J. S., Gross, J. T., Brett, B. E., Stern, J. A., Martin, D. R., & Cassidy, J. (2019). Helping, sharing, and comforting in young children: Links to individual differences in attachment. *Child Development*, 90(2), e273–e289. https://doi.org/10.1111/cdev.13100

Beitsch, R. (2017). *As surrogacy surges, new parents seek legal protections*. Pew Charitable Trusts.

Belcher, B. R., Zink, J., Azad, A., Campbell, C. E., Chakravartti, S. P., & Herting, M. M. (2021). The roles of physical activity, exercise, and fitness in promoting resilience during adolescence: Effects on mental well-being and brain development. *Biological Psychiatry: Cognitive Neuroscience and Neuroimaging*, 6(2), 225–237. https://doi.org/10.1016/j.bpsc.2020.08.005

Bell, M. A., Wolfe, C. D., Diaz, A., & Liu, R. (2019). Cognition and emotion in development. In V. LoBue, K. Pérez-Edgar, & K. A. Buss (Eds.), *Handbook of emotional development* (pp. 375–403). Springer. https://doi.org/10.1007/978-3-030-17332-6_15

Bellows, L. L., Davies, P. L., Courtney, J. B., Gavin, W. J., Johnson, S. L., & Boles, R. E. (2017). Motor skill development in low-income, at-risk preschoolers: A community-based longitudinal intervention study. *Journal of Science and Medicine in Sport*,

20(11), 997–1002. https://doi.org/10.1016/J.JSAMS.2017.04.003

Belsky, J. (2019). Early-life adversity accelerates child and adolescent development. *Current Directions in Psychological Science*, *28*(3). https://doi.org/10.1177/0963721419837670

Bem, S. L. (1974). The measurement of psychological androgyny. *Journal of Consulting and Clinical Psychology*, *42*(2), 155–162.

Bem, S. L. (1983). Gender schema theory and its implications for child development: Raising gender-aschematic children in a gender-schematic society. *Signs*, *8*, 598–616.

Ben-Sasson, A., Carter, A. S., & Briggs-Gowan, M. J. (2009). Sensory over-responsivity in elementary school: Prevalence and social-emotional correlates. *Journal of Abnormal Child Psychology*, *37*(5), 705–716. https://doi.org/10.1007/s10802-008-9295-8

Bender, K., Yang, J., Ferguson, K., & Thompson, S. (2015). Experiences and needs of homeless youth with a history of foster care. *Children and Youth Services Review*, *55*, 222–231. https://doi.org/10.1016/j.childyouth.2015.06.007

Bendezú, J. J., Pinderhughes, E. E., Hurley, S. M., McMahon, R. J., & Racz, S. J. (2018). Longitudinal relations among parental monitoring strategies, knowledge, and adolescent delinquency in a racially diverse at-risk sample. *Journal of Clinical Child and Adolescent Psychology*, *47*(sup1), S21–S34. https://doi.org/10.1080/15374416.2016.1141358

Beneke, M. R., Park, C. C., & Taitingfong, J. (2019). An inclusive, anti-bias framework for teaching and learning about race with young children. *Young Exceptional Children*, *22*(2), 74–86. https://doi.org/10.1177/1096250618811842

Benigno, J. P., Byrd, D. L., McNamara, J. P., Berg, W. K., & Farrar, M. J. (2011). Talking through transitions: Microgenetic changes in preschoolers' private speech and executive functioning. *Child Language Teaching and Therapy*, *27*(3), 269–285. https://doi.org/10.1177/0265659010394385

Benítez-Burraco, A., & Progovac, L. (2020). A four-stage model for language evolution under the effects of human self-domestication. *Language & Communication*, *73*, 1–17. https://doi.org/10.1016/j.langcom.2020.03.002

Benner, A. D., Boyle, A. E., & Bakhtiari, F. (2017). Understanding students' transition to high school: Demographic variation and the role of supportive relationships. *Journal of Youth and Adolescence*, *46*(10), 2129–2142. https://doi.org/10.1007/s10964-017-0716-2

Benner, A. D., Boyle, A. E., & Sadler, S. (2016). Parental involvement and adolescents' educational success: The roles of prior achievement and socioeconomic status. *Journal of Youth and Adolescence*, *45*(6), 1053–1064. https://doi.org/10.1007/s10964-016-0431-4

Benner, A. D., Fernandez, C. C., Hou, Y., & Gonzalez, C. S. (2021). Parent and teacher educational expectations and adolescents' academic performance: Mechanisms of influence. *Journal of Community Psychology*, *49*(7), 2679–2703. https://doi.org/10.1002/jcop.22644

Benner, A. D., & Graham, S. (2009). The transition to high school as a developmental process among multiethnic urban youth. *Child Development*, *80*(2), 356–376. https://doi.org/10.1111/j.1467-8624.2009.01265.x

Benner, A. D., Wang, Y., Shen, Y., Boyle, A. E., Polk, R., & Cheng, Y.-P. (2018). Racial/ethnic discrimination and well-being during adolescence: A meta-analytic review. *American Psychologist*, *73*, 855–883. https://doi.org/10.1037/amp0000204

Benson, J. E., Sabbagh, M. A., Carlson, S. M., & Zelazo, P. D. (2013). Individual differences in executive functioning predict preschoolers' improvement from theory-of-mind training. *Developmental Psychology*, *49*(9), 1615–1627. https://doi.org/10.1037/a0031056

Benson, P. L., Scales, P. C., Syvertsen, A. K., & Roehlkepartain, E. C. (2012). Is youth spiritual development a universal developmental process? An international exploration. *Journal of Positive Psychology*, *7*(6), 453–470. https://doi.org/10.1080/17439760.2012.732102

Benzies, K. M., Magill-Evans, J. E., Hayden, K., Ballantyne, M., Raju, T., Higgins, R., Stark, A., Leveno, K., Anderson, P., Doyle, L., Bhutta, A., Cleves, M., Casey, P., Cradock, M., Anand, K., Moster, D., Terje, R., Markestad, T., Petrini, J., & &#hillip1; Dahl, L. (2013). Key components of early intervention programs for preterm infants and their parents: A systematic review and meta-analysis. *BMC Pregnancy and Childbirth*, *13*(Suppl 1), S10. https://doi.org/10.1186/1471-2393-13-S1-S10

Berardi, N., Sale, A., & Maffei, L. (2015). Brain structural and functional development: Genetics and experience. *Developmental Medicine & Child Neurology*, *57*(s2), 4–9. https://doi.org/10.1111/dmcn.12691

Berčnik, S., & Rožman Krivec, L. (2020). Compensatory programs in preschool education. In M. Sardoč (Ed.), *Handbook of equality of opportunity* (pp. 1–25). Springer International. https://doi.org/10.1007/978-3-319-52269-2_74-1

Berenbaum, S. A. (2018). Beyond pink and blue: The complexity of early androgen effects on gender development. *Child Development Perspectives*, *12*(1), 58–64. https://doi.org/10.1111/cdep.12261

Berenbaum, S. A., Beltz, A. M., & Corley, R. (2015). The importance of puberty for adolescent development: Conceptualization and measurement. *Advances in Child Development and Behavior*, *48*, 53–92. https://doi.org/10.1016/bs.acdb.2014.11.002

Bergelson, E. (2020). The comprehension boost in early word learning: Older infants are better learners. *Child Development Perspectives*, *14*(3), 142–149. https://doi.org/10.1111/cdep.12373

Bergelson, E., Casillas, M., Soderstrom, M., Seidl, A., Warlaumont, A. S., & Amatuni, A. (2019). What do North American babies hear? A large-scale cross-corpus analysis. *Developmental Science*, *22*(1), e12724. https://doi.org/10.1111/DESC.12724

Bergelson, E., & Swingley, D. (2012). At 6–9 months, human infants know the meanings of many common nouns. *Proceedings of the National Academy of Sciences of the United States of America*, *109*(9), 3253–3258. https://doi.org/10.1073/pnas.1113380109

Berger, L. M., Font, S. A., Slack, K. S., & Waldfogel, J. (2017). Income and child maltreatment in unmarried families: Evidence from the earned income tax credit. *Review of Economics of the Household*, *15*(4), 1345–1372. https://doi.org/10.1007/s11150-016-9346-9

Berger, S. E., Theuring, C., & Adolph, K. E. (2007). How and when infants learn to climb stairs. *Infant Behavior and Development*, *30*(1), 36–49. https://doi.org/10.1016/j.infbeh.2006.11.002

Berger, T., Peschel, T., Vogel, M., Pietzner, D., Poulain, T., Jurkutat, A., Meuret, S., Engel, C., Kiess, W., & Fuchs, M. (2019). Speaking voice in children and adolescents: Normative data and associations with BMI, Tanner stage, and singing activity. *Journal of Voice*, *33*(4), 580.e21–580.e30. https://doi.org/10.1016/j.jvoice.2018.01.006

Berk, L. E. (1986). Development of private speech among preschool children. *Early Child Development and Care*, *24*, 113–136. https://doi.org/10.1080/0300443860240107

Berk, L. E. (1992). The extracurriculum. In P. W. Jackson (Ed.), *Handbook of research on curriculum* (pp. 1003–1043). Macmillan.

Berk, L. E., & Winsler, A. (1995). *Scaffolding children's learning: Vygotsky and early childhood education (NAEYC. In Research into Practice Series*. National Association for the Education of Young Children. Vol. 7)

Berkowitz, M. W., & Begun, A. L. (1995). Assessing how adolescents think about the morality of substance use. *Drugs & Society*, 8(3-4), 111–124. https://doi.org/10.1300/J023v08n03_09

Bernanke, J., Luna, A., Chang, L., Bruno, E., Dworkin, J., & Posner, J. (2022). Structural brain measures among children with and without ADHD in the Adolescent Brain and Cognitive Development Study cohort: A cross-sectional US population-based study. *Lancet Psychiatry*, 9(3), 222–231. https://doi.org/10.1016/S2215-0366(21)00505-8

Bernard, S., & Deleau, Michel. (2007). Conversational perspective-taking and false belief attribution: A longitudinal study. *British Journal of Developmental Psychology*, 25(3), 443–460. https://doi.org/10.1348/026151006X171451

Bernecker, K., & Job, V. (2019). Mindset theory. In K. Sassenberg & M. L. W. Vliek (Eds.), *Social psychology in action: Evidence-based interventions from theory to practice* (pp. 179–191). Springer International. https://doi.org/10.1007/978-3-030-13788-5_12

Bernier, A., Calkins, S. D., & Bell, M. A. (2016). Longitudinal associations between the quality of mother-infant interactions and brain development across infancy. *Child Development*, 87(4), 1159–1174. https://doi.org/10.1111/cdev.12518

Berninger, V. W., & Wolf, B. J. (2009). *Teaching students with dyslexia and dysgraphia: Lessons from teaching and science*. Paul H. Brookes. https://psycnet.apa.org/record/2009-08969-000

Bernstein, D. M., Atance, C., Meltzoff, A. N., & Loftus, G. R. (2007). Hindsight bias and developing theories of mind. *Child Development*, 78(4), 1374–1394. https://doi.org/10.1111/j.1467-8624.2007.01071.x

Bertenthal, B. I., Campos, J. J., & Barrett, K. (1984). Self-produced locomotion: An organizer of emotional, cognitive, and social development in infancy. In R. Emde & R. Harmon (Eds.), *Continuities and discontinuities in development* (pp. 174–210). Plenum.

Berwick, R. C., & Chomsky, N. (2016). *Why only us: Language and evolution*. MIT Press.

Berwick, R. C., Chomsky, N., & Piattelli-Palmarini, M. (2013). Poverty of the stimulus stands: Why recent challenges fail. In M. Piattelli-Palmarini & R. C. Berwick (Eds.), *Rich languages from poor inputs* (pp. 18–42). Oxford University Press. https://doi.org/10.1093/acprof:oso/9780199590339.003.0002

Best, D. L., House, A. S., Barnard, A. E., & Spicker, B. S. (1994). Parent-child interactions in France, Germany, and Italy: The effects of gender and culture. *Journal of Cross-Cultural Psychology*, 25(2), 181–193. https://doi.org/10.1177/0022022194252002

Best, D. L., & Puzio, A. R. (2019). Gender and culture. In D. Matsumoto & H. C. Hwang (Eds.), *The handbook of culture and psychology* (pp. 235–291). https://doi.org/10.1093/oso/9780190679743.003.0009

Best, P., Manktelow, R., & Taylor, B. (2014). Online communication, social media and adolescent wellbeing: A systematic narrative review. *Children and Youth Services Review*, 41, 27–36. https://doi.org/10.1016/j.childyouth.2014.03.001

Best, R. M., Dockrell, J. E., & Braisby, N. R. (2006). Real-world word learning: Exploring children's developing semantic representations of a science term. *British Journal of Developmental Psychology*, 24(2), 265–282. https://doi.org/10.1348/026151005X36128

Betancourt, L. M., Avants, B., Farah, M. J., Brodsky, N. L., Wu, J., Ashtari, M., & Hurt, H. (2016). Effect of socioeconomic status (SES) disparity on neural development in female African-American infants at age 1 month. *Developmental Science*, 19(6), 947–956. https://doi.org/10.1111/desc.12344

Bethlehem, R. a. I., Seidlitz, J., White, S. R., Vogel, J. W., Anderson, K. M., Adamson, C., Adler, S., Alexopoulos, G. S., Anagnostou, E., Areces-Gonzalez, A., Astle, D. E., Auyeung, B., Ayub, M., Bae, J., Ball, G., Baron-Cohen, S., Beare, R., Bedford, S. A., Benegal, V., & &#hillip1; Alexander-Bloch, A. F. (2022). Brain charts for the human lifespan. *Nature*, 604, 525–533. https://doi.org/10.1038/s41586-022-04554-y

Beuriat, P. A., Cristofori, I., Gordon, B., & Grafman, J. (2022). The shifting role of the cerebellum in executive, emotional and social processing across the lifespan. *Behavioral and Brain Functions*, 18(1), 1–11. https://doi.org/10.1186/S12993-022-00193-5/FIGURES/4

Beyens, I., Valkenburg, P. M., & Piotrowski, J. T. (2019). Developmental trajectories of parental mediation across early and middle childhood. *Human Communication Research*, 45(2), 226–250. https://doi.org/10.1093/hcr/hqy016

Bhatia, N., & Bhatia, S. (2021). Changes in gender stereotypes over time: A computational analysis. *Psychology of Women Quarterly*, 45, 106–125. https://doi.org/10.1177/0361684320977178

Bhattacharya, N., Budge, S. L., Pantalone, D. W., & Katz-Wise, S. L. (2020). Conceptualizing relationships among transgender and gender diverse youth and their caregivers. *Journal of Family Psychology*, 35(5), 595–605. https://doi.org/10.1037/fam0000815

Bialik, K. (2018). *Middle children have become rarer, but a growing share of Americans now say three or more kids are 'ideal.'*. Pew Research Center. https://www.pewresearch.org/short-reads/2018/08/09/middle-children-have-become-rarer-but-a-growing-share-of-americans-now-say-three-or-more-kids-are-ideal/

Bialystok, E. (2015). Bilingualism and the development of executive function: The role of attention. *Child Development Perspectives*, 9(2), 117–121. https://doi.org/10.1111/cdep.12116

Bialystok, E. (2020). Bilingual effects on cognition in children. In *Oxford research encyclopedia of education*. Oxford University Press. https://doi.org/10.1093/acrefore/9780190264093.013.962

Bian, L., Leslie, S.-J., & Cimpian, A. (2017). Gender stereotypes about intellectual ability emerge early and influence children's interests. *Science*, 355(6323), 389–391. https://doi.org/10.1126/science.aah6524

Bianchi, E., & Wright, G. J. (2016). Sperm meets egg: The genetics of mammalian fertilization. *Annual Review of Genetics*, 50(1), 93–111. https://doi.org/10.1146/annurev-genet-121415-121834

Bibbins-Domingo, K., Grossman, D. C., Curry, S. J., Davidson, K. W., Epling, J. W., Garcia, F. A. R., Kemper, A. R., Krist, A. H., Kurth, A. E., Landefeld, C. S., Mangione, C. M., Phillips, W. R., Phipps, M. G., Pignone, M. P., Silverstein, M., & Tseng, C. W. (2017). Folic acid supplementation for the prevention of neural tube defects US preventive services task force recommendation statement. *JAMA*, 317(2), 183–189. https://doi.org/10.1001/jama.2016.19438

Bick, J., & Nelson, C. A. (2017). Early experience and brain development. *Wiley Interdisciplinary Reviews: Cognitive Science*, 8(1-2), e1387. https://doi.org/10.1002/wcs.1387

Biddle, S. J. H., Ciaccioni, S., Thomas, G., & Vergeer, I. (2019). Physical activity and mental health in children and adolescents: An updated review of reviews and an analysis of causality. *Psychology of Sport and Exercise*, 42, 146–155. https://doi.org/10.1016/j.psychsport.2018.08.011

Biddle, S. J. H., & Vergeer, I. (2020). Mental health benefits of physical activity for young people. In T. Brusseau, S. Fairclough, & D. Lubans (Eds.), *The Routledge handbook of youth physical activity* (pp. 121–147). Routledge. https://doi.org/10.4324/9781003026426-8

Bierman, K. L., Kalvin, C. B., & Heinrichs, B. S. (2014). Early childhood precursors and adolescent sequelae of grade school peer rejection and victimization. *Journal of Clinical Child and Adolescent Psychology*, 44(3), 367–379. https://doi.org/10.1080/15374416.2013.873983

Bigelow, A. E. (2020). Self-knowledge. In J. B. Benson (Ed.), *Encyclopedia of infant and early childhood development* (pp. 95–106). Elsevier. https://doi.org/10.1016/B978-0-12-809324-5.05882-X

Bigler, R. S., & Pahlke, E. (2019). "I disagree! Sexism is silly to me!" Teaching children to recognize and confront gender biases. In R. K. Mallett & M. J. Monteith (Eds.), *Confronting prejudice and discrimination*. Elsevier. https://doi.org/10.1016/B978-0-12-814715-3.00012-6

Birch, S. A. J. (2005). When knowledge is a curse: Biases in mental state attribution. *Current Directions in Psychological Science*, 14, 25–29. https://doi.org/10.1111/j.0963-7214.2005.00328.x

Bird, R. J., & Hurren, B. J. (2016). Anatomical and clinical aspects of Klinefelter's syndrome. *Clinical Anatomy*, 29(5), 606–619. https://doi.org/10.1002/ca.22695

Birkeland, M. S., Breivik, K., & Wold, B. (2014). Peer acceptance protects global self-esteem from negative effects of low closeness to parents during adolescence and early adulthood. *Journal of Youth and Adolescence*, 43(1), 70–80. https://doi.org/10.1007/s10964-013-9929-1

Birkeland, M. S., Skar, A.-M. S., & Jensen, T. K. (2022). Understanding the relationships between trauma type and individual posttraumatic stress symptoms: A cross-sectional study of a clinical sample of children and adolescents. *Journal of Child Psychology and Psychiatry*, 63(12), 1496–1504. https://doi.org/10.1111/jcpp.13602

Birkinshaw, S. (2015). Spiritual friends: An investigation of children's spirituality in the context of British urban secondary education. *British Journal of Religious Education*, 37(1), 83–102. https://doi.org/10.1080/01416200.2014.902806

Birner, B. J. (2021). *Pragmatics: A slim guide*. Oxford University Press.

Birney, D. P., & Sternberg, R. J. (2011). The development of cognitive abilities. In M. H. Bornstein & M. E. Lamb (Eds.), *Developmental science: An advanced textbook* (pp. 353–388). Psychology Press.

Birney, D. P., & Sternberg, R. J. (2011). The development of cognitive abilities. In M. H. Bornstein & M. E. Lamb (Eds.), *Developmental science: An advanced textbook* (6th ed., pp. 353–388). Psychology Press.

Biro, F. M., Pajak, A., Wolff, M. S., Pinney, S. M., Windham, G. C., Galvez, M. P., Greenspan, L. C., Kushi, L. H., & Teitelbaum, S. L. (2018). Age of menarche in a longitudinal US cohort. *Journal of Pediatric and Adolescent Gynecology*, 31(4), 339–345. https://doi.org/10.1016/j.jpag.2018.05.002

Biro, S., Alink, L. R. A., van IJzendoorn, M. H., & Bakermans-Kranenburg, M. J. (2014). Infants' monitoring of social interactions: The effect of emotional cues. *Emotion*, 14(2), 263–271. https://doi.org/10.1037/a0035589

Bisiacchi, P., & Cainelli, E. (2022). Structural and functional brain asymmetries in the early phases of life: A scoping review. *Brain Structure and Function*, 227(2), 479–496. https://doi.org/10.1007/s00429-021-02256-1

Bjorklund, D. F. (2018). Behavioral epigenetics: The last nail in the coffin of genetic determinism. *Human Development*, 61(1), 54–59. https://doi.org/10.1159/000481747

Bjorklund, D. F. (2018). A metatheory for cognitive development (or "Piaget is Dead" revisited). *Child Development*. https://doi.org/10.1111/cdev.13019

Bjorklund, D. F. (2020). *How children invented humanity: The role of development in human evolution*. Oxford University Press.

Bjorklund, D. F., & Hart, S. L. (2022). Infancy through the lens of evolutionary developmental science. In L. Hart. Sybil & F. Bjorklund. David (Eds.), *Evolutionary perspectives on infancy* (pp. 3–15). Springer. https://doi.org/10.1007/978-3-030-76000-7_1

Bjorklund, D. F., & Hart, S. L. (2022). Infancy through the lens of evolutionary developmental science. In S. L. Hart & D. F. Bjorklund (Eds.), *Evolutionary Perspectives on Infancy* (pp. 3–15). Springer. https://doi.org/10.1007/978-3-030-76000-7_1

Bjorklund, D. F., & Myers, A. (2015). The development of cognitive abilities. In M. H. Bornstein & M. E. Lamb (Eds.), *Developmental science: An advanced textbook* (pp. 391–441). Psychology Press.

Black, S. E., Bütikofer, A., Devereux, P. J., & Salvanes, K. G. (2019). This is only a test? Long-run and intergenerational impacts of prenatal exposure to radioactive fallout. *Review of Economics and Statistics*, 101(3), 531–546. https://doi.org/10.1162/rest_a_00815

Blackburn, J., Chapur, V. F., Stephens, J. A., Zhao, J., Shepler, A., Pierson, C. R., & Otero, J. J. (2020). Revisiting the neuropathology of sudden infant death syndrome (SIDS). *Frontiers in Neurology*, 11, 594550. https://doi.org/10.3389/fneur.2020.594550

Blair, C. (2010). Stress and the development of self-regulation in context. *Child Development Perspectives*, 4(3), 181–188. https://doi.org/10.1111/j.1750-8606.2010.00145.x

Blake, A. J., Ruderman, M., Waterman, J. M., & Langley, A. K. (2022). Long-term effects of pre-adoptive risk on emotional and behavioral functioning in children adopted from foster care. *Child Abuse and Neglect*, 13(0). https://doi.org/10.1016/j.chiabu.2021.105031

Blake, A. J., Ruderman, M., Waterman, J. M., & Langley, A. K. (2022). Long-term effects of pre-adoptive risk on emotional and behavioral functioning in children adopted from foster care. *Child Abuse and Neglect*, 130(Pt 2), 105031. https://doi.org/10.1016/j.chiabu.2021.105031

Blake, M. J., Latham, M. D., Blake, L. M., & Allen, N. B. (2019). Adolescent-sleep-intervention research: Current state and future directions. *Current Directions in Psychological Science*, 28(5), 475–482. https://doi.org/10.1177/0963721419850169

Blakeney, E. L., Herting, J. R., Bekemeier, B., & Zierler, B. K. (2019). Social determinants of health and disparities in prenatal care utilization during the Great Recession period 2005-2010. *BMC Pregnancy and Childbirth*, 19(1), 1–20. https://doi.org/10.1186/s12884-019-2486-1

Blakeslee, J. E., Kothari, B. H., & Miller, R. A. (2023). Intervention development to improve foster youth mental health by targeting coping self-efficacy and help-seeking. *Children and Youth Services Review*, 144, 106753. https://doi.org/10.1016/j.childyouth.2022.106753

Blanche, S. (2020). Mini review: Prevention of mother–child transmission of HIV: 25 years of continuous progress toward the eradication of pediatric AIDS? *Virulence*, 11(1), 14–22. https://doi.org/10.1080/21505594.2019.1697136

Blandon, A. Y., Calkins, S. D., Grimm, K. J., Keane, S. P., & O'Brien, M. (2010). Testing a developmental cascade model of emotional and social competence and early peer acceptance. *Development and Psychopathology*, 22(4), 737–748. https://doi.org/10.1017/S0954579410000428

Blankenship, T. L., Slough, M. A., Calkins, S. D., Deater-Deckard, K., Kim-Spoon, J., & Bell, M. A. (2019). Attention and executive functioning in infancy: Links to childhood executive function and reading achievement. *Developmental Science*, 22(6), e12824. https://doi.org/10.1111/desc.12824

Blasi, C. H. (2020). Evolutionary Developmental Psychology. In T. K. Shackelford (Ed.), *The SAGE handbook of evolutionary psychology* (pp. 51–72). SAGE. https://doi.org/10.4135/9781529739435.N3

Blass, E. M., Ganchrow, J. R., & Steiner, J. E. (1984). Classical conditioning in newborn humans 2–48 hours of age. *Infant Behavior and Development*, 7, 223–235.

Blau, N. (2016). Genetics of phenylketonuria: Then and now. *Human Mutation*, 37(6), 508–515. https://doi.org/10.1002/humu.22980

Bleah, D. A., & Ellett, M. L. (2010). Infant crying among recent African immigrants. *Health Care for Women International*, 31(7), 652–663. https://doi.org/10.1080/07399331003628446

Block, J. (2023). Raft of US state laws restrict access to treatments for gender dysphoria. *BMJ*, 380, 533. https://doi.org/10.1136/bmj.p533

Bloomfield, F. H., Alexander, T., Muelbert, M., & Beker, F. (2017). Smell and taste in the preterm infant. *Early Human Development*, 114, 31–34. https://doi.org/10.1016/j.earlhumdev.2017.09.012

Blumberg, M. S., Dooley, J. C., & Sokoloff, G. (2020). The developing brain revealed during sleep. *Current Opinion in Physiology*, 15, 14–22. https://doi.org/10.1016/j.cophys.2019.11.002

Boateng, T., Beauchamp, K., Torres, F., Ruffaner-Hanson, C. D., Pinner, J. F. L., Vakamudi, K., Cerros, C., Hill, D. E., & Stephen, J. M. (2023). Brain structural differences in children with fetal alcohol spectrum disorder and its subtypes. *Frontiers in Neuroscience*, 1(7). https://www.frontiersin.org/journals/neuroscience/articles/10.3389/fnins.2023.1152038

Bodrova, E., & Leong, D. J. (2018). Tools of the mind: A Vygotskian early childhood curriculum. In M. Fleer & B. van Oers (Eds.), *International handbook of early childhood education* (pp. 1095–1111). Springer. https://doi.org/10.1007/978-94-024-0927-7_56

Bogaerts, A., Claes, L., Buelens, T., Verschueren, M., Palmeroni, N., Bastiaens, T., & Luyckx, K. (2021). Identity synthesis and confusion in early to late adolescents: Age trends, gender differences, and associations with depressive symptoms. *Journal of Adolescence*, 87, 106–116. https://doi.org/10.1016/j.adolescence.2021.01.006

Bogan, E., Adams-Bass, V. N., Francis, L. A., Gaylord-Harden, N. K., Seaton, E. K., Scott, J. C., & Williams, J. L. (2022). "Wearing a mask won't protect us from our history": The impact of COVID-19 on Black children and families. *Social Policy Report*, 35(2), 1–33. https://doi.org/10.1002/sop2.23

Bogartz, R. S., Shinskey, J. L., & Schilling, T. H. (2000). Object permanence in five-and-a-half-month-old infants? *Infancy*, 1(4), 403–428. https://doi.org/10.1207/S15327078IN0104_3

Boggess, T., & Risher, W. C. (2022). Clinical and basic research investigations into the long-term effects of prenatal opioid exposure on brain development. *Journal of Neuroscience Research*, 100(1), 396–409. https://doi.org/10.1002/jnr.24642

Boguszewski, M. C. S. (2020). Growth hormone deficiency and replacement in children. *Reviews in Endocrine and Metabolic Disorders*, 22(1), 101–108. https://doi.org/10.1007/S11154-020-09604-2

Bohannon, J. N., & Stanowicz, L. (1988). The issue of negative evidence: Adult responses to children's language errors. *Developmental Psychology*, 24(5), 684–689. https://doi.org/10.1037/0012-1649.24.5.684

Bohman, A., & Miklikowska, M. (2021). Does classroom diversity improve intergroup relations? Short- and long-term effects of classroom diversity for cross-ethnic friendships and anti-immigrant attitudes in adolescence. *Group Processes & Intergroup Relations*, 24(8), 1372–1390. https://doi.org/10.1177/1368430220941592

Boldt, L. J., Kochanska, G., Yoon, J. E., & Koenig Nordling, J. (2014). Children's attachment to both parents from toddler age to middle childhood: Links to adaptive and maladaptive outcomes. *Attachment & Human Development*, 16(3), 211–229. https://doi.org/10.1080/14616734.2014.889181

Bondi, D., Robazza, C., Lange-Küttner, C., & Pietrangelo, T. (2022). Fine motor skills and motor control networking in developmental age. *American Journal of Human Biology*, 34(8), e23758. https://doi.org/10.1002/AJHB.23758

Bonifacio, J. H., Maser, C., Stadelman, K., & Palmert, M. (2019). Management of gender dysphoria in adolescents in primary care. *Canadian Medical Association Journal*, 191(3), E69–E75. https://doi.org/10.1503/cmaj.180672

Bonomi, M., Rochira, V., Pasquali, D., Balercia, G., Jannini, E. A., & Ferlin, A. (2017). on behalf of the Klinefelter ItaliaN Group (KING). Klinefelter syndrome (KS): Genetics, clinical phenotype and hypogonadism. *Journal of Endocrinological Investigation*, 40(2), 123–134. https://doi.org/10.1007/s40618-016-0541-6

Boom, J. J., Wouters, H., & Keller, M. (2007). A cross-cultural validation of stage development: A Rasch re-analysis of longitudinal socio-moral reasoning data. *Cognitive Development*, 22(2), 213–229. https://doi.org/10.1016/j.cogdev.2006.10.005

Boonk, L., Gijselaers, H. J. M., Ritzen, H., & Brand-Gruwel, S. (2018). A review of the relationship between parental involvement indicators and academic achievement. *Educational Research Review*, 24, 10–30. https://doi.org/10.1016/j.edurev.2018.02.001

Boonzaaijer, M., Suir, I., Mollema, J., Nuysink, J., Volman, M., & Jongmans, M. (2021). Factors associated with gross motor development from birth to independent walking: A systematic review of longitudinal research. *Child: Care, Health and Development*, 47(4), 525–561. https://doi.org/10.1111/CCH.12830

Booth, J. M., & Shaw, D. S. (2023). Examining parental monitoring, neighborhood peer anti-social behavior, and neighborhood social cohesion and control as a pathway to adolescent substance use. *Journal of Child and Family Studies*, 32(2), 626–639. https://doi.org/10.1007/s10826-022-02514-8

Booth, M. Z., & Gerard, J. M. (2014). Adolescents' stage-environment fit in middle and high school: The relationship between students' perceptions of their schools and themselves. *Youth & Society*, 46(6), 735–755. https://doi.org/10.1177/0044118X12451276

Booth-LaForce, C., Groh, A. M., Burchinal, M. R., Roisman, G. I., Owen, M. T., & Cox, M. J. (2014). Caregiving and contextual sources of continuity and change in attachment security from infancy to late adolescence. *Monographs of the Society for Research in Child Development*, 79(3), 67–84. https://doi.org/10.1111/mono.12114

Bordogna, A. L., Coyle, A. C., Nallamothu, R., Manko, A. L., & Yen, R. W. (2023). Comprehensive sexuality education to reduce pregnancy and STIs in adolescents in the

United States: A systematic review and meta-analysis. *American Journal of Sexuality Education, 18*(1), 39–83. https://doi.org/10.1080/15546128.2022.2080140

Borges, E., Braga, D. P. de A. F., Provenza, R. R., Figueira, R. de C. S., Iaconelli, A., & Setti, A. S. (2018). Paternal lifestyle factors in relation to semen quality and in vitro reproductive outcomes. *Andrologia, 50*(9), e13090. https://doi.org/10.1111/and.13090

Borich, G. D. (2017). *Effective teaching methods: Research-based practice.* Pearson.

Bornstein, M. H. (2020). Intelligence in infancy. In R. J. Sternberg (Ed.), *The Cambridge handbook of intelligence* (pp. 124–154). Cambridge University Press. https://doi.org/10.1017/9781108770422.008

Bornstein, M. H., & Arterberry, M. E. (2010). The development of object categorization in young children: Hierarchical inclusiveness, age, perceptual attribute, and group versus individual analyses. *Developmental Psychology, 46*(2), 350–365. https://doi.org/10.1037/a0018411

Bornstein, M. H., Arterberry, M. E., & Lamb, M. E. (2013). *Development in infancy: A contemporary introduction.* Psychology Press.

Bornstein, M. H., Cote, L. R., Maital, S., Painter, K., Park, S.-Y., Pascual, L., Pêcheux, M.-G., Ruel, J., Venuti, P., & Vyt, A. (2004). Cross-linguistic analysis of vocabulary in young children: Spanish, Dutch, French. Hebrew, Italian, Korean, and American English. *Child Development, 75*(4), 1115–1139. https://doi.org/10.1111/j.1467-8624.2004.00729.x

Bornstein, M. H., & Esposito, G. (2020). Cross-Cultural Perspectives on Parent–Infant Interactions. In C. S. Tamis-LeMonda & J. J. Lockman (Eds.), *The Cambridge Handbook of Infant Development: Brain, Behavior, and Cultural Context* (pp. 805–832). Cambridge University Press. https://doi.org/10.1017/9781108351959.029

Bornstein, M. H., Hahn, C.-S., Putnick, D. L., & Pearson, R. (2019). Stability of child temperament: Multiple moderation by child and mother characteristics. *British Journal of Developmental Psychology, 37*(1), 51–67. https://doi.org/10.1111/bjdp.12253

Bornstein, M. H., & Putnick, D. L. (2018). Parent—adolescent relationships in global perspective. In J. E. Lansford & P. Banati (Eds.), *Handbook of adolescent development research and its impact on global policy.* Oxford.

Bornstein, M. H., Putnick, D. L., & Esposito, G. (2017). Continuity and stability in development. *Child Development Perspectives, 11*(2), 113–119. https://doi.org/10.1111/cdep.12221

Bornstein, M. H., Putnick, D. L., Gartstein, M. A., Hahn, C.-S., Auestad, N., & O'Connor, D. L. (2015). Infant temperament: Stability by age, gender, birth order, term status, and socioeconomic status. *Child Development, 86*(3), 844–863. https://doi.org/10.1111/cdev.12367

Bornstein, M. H., Putnick, D. L., Rigo, P., Esposito, G., Swain, J. E., Suwalsky, J. T. D., Su, X., Du, X., Zhang, K., Cote, L. R., De Pisapia, N., & Venuti, P. (2017). Neurobiology of culturally common maternal responses to infant cry. *Proceedings of the National Academy of Sciences of the United States of America, 114*(45), E9465–E9473. https://doi.org/10.1073/pnas.1712022114

Bornstein, M. H., Putnick, D. L., & Suwalsky, J. T. D. (2018). Parenting cognitions → parenting practices → child adjustment? The standard model. *Development and Psychopathology, 30*(2), 399–416. https://doi.org/10.1017/S0954579417000931

Bornstein, M. H., Slater, A., Brown, E., Roberts, E., & Barrett, J. (1997). Stability of mental development from infancy to later childhood: Three "waves" of research. In G. Bremner, A. Slater, & G. Butterworth (Eds.), *Infant development: Recent advances* (pp. 191–215). Psychology Press.

Bornstein, M. H., Suwalsky, J. T. D., & Breakstone, D. A. (2012). Emotional relationships between mothers and infants: Knowns, unknowns, and unknown unknowns. *Development and Psychopathology, 24*(1), 113–123. https://doi.org/10.1017/S0954579411000708

Borst, G., Poirel, N., Pineau, A., Cassotti, M., & Houdé, O. (2013). Inhibitory control efficiency in a Piaget-like class-inclusion task in school-age children and adults: A developmental negative priming study. *Developmental Psychology, 49*(7), 1366–1374. https://doi.org/10.1037/a0029622

Bos, H., & Gartrell, N. (2020). Lesbian-mother families formed through donor insemination. In A. E. Goldberg & K. R. Allen (Eds.), *LGBTQ-parent families: Innovations in research and implications for practice* (pp. 25–44). Springer International. https://doi.org/10.1007/978-3-030-35610-1_2

Bos, H. M. W., Kuyper, L., & Gartrell, N. K. (2018). A population-based comparison of female and male same-sex parent and different-sex parent households. *Family Process, 57*(1), 148–164. https://doi.org/10.1111/famp.12278

Bosch-Bayard, J., Biscay, R. J., Fernandez, T., Otero, G. A., Ricardo-Garcell, J., Aubert-Vazquez, E., Evans, A. C., & Harmony, T. (2022). EEG effective connectivity during the first year of life mirrors brain synaptogenesis, myelination, and early right hemisphere predominance. *NeuroImage, 252*, 119035. https://doi.org/10.1016/j.neuroimage.2022.119035

Bosch-Bayard, J., Razzaq, F. A., Lopez-Naranjo, C., Wang, Y., Li, M., Galan-Garcia, L., Calzada-Reyes, A., Virues-Alba, T., Rabinowitz, A. G., Suarez-Murias, C., Guo, Y., Sanchez-Castillo, M., Rogers, K., Gallagher, A., Prichep, L., Anderson, S. G., Michel, C. M., Evans, A. C., Bringas-Vega, M. L., & &#hillip1; Valdes-Sosa, P. A. (2022). Early protein energy malnutrition impacts life-long developmental trajectories of the sources of EEG rhythmic activity. *NeuroImage, 254*, 119144. https://doi.org/10.1016/j.neuroimage.2022.119144

Boseovski, J. J. (2010). Evidence for "rose-colored glasses": An examination of the positivity bias in young children's personality judgments. *Child Development Perspectives, 4*(3), 212–218. https://doi.org/10.1111/j.1750-8606.2010.00149.x

Bostwick, K. C. P., Collie, R. J., Martin, A. J., & Durksen, T. L. (2020). Teacher, classroom, and student growth orientation in mathematics: A multilevel examination of growth goals, growth mindset, engagement, and achievement. *Teaching and Teacher Education, 94*, 103100. https://doi.org/10.1016/j.tate.2020.103100

Boterberg, S., & Warreyn, P. (2016). Making sense of it all: The impact of sensory processing sensitivity on daily functioning of children. *Personality and Individual Differences, 92*, 80–86. https://doi.org/10.1016/j.paid.2015.12.022

Botto, S. V., & Rochat, P. (2018). Sensitivity to the evaluation of others emerges by 24 months. *Developmental Psychology, 54*(9), 1723–1734. https://doi.org/10.1037/DEV0000548

Bouchard, D. (2021). Three conceptions of nativism and the faculty of language. *Language Sciences, 85*, 101384. https://doi.org/10.1016/j.langsci.2021.101384

Boundy, E. O., Dastjerdi, R., Spiegelman, D., Fawzi, W. W., Missmer, S. A., Lieberman, E., Kajeepeta, S., Wall, S., Chan, G. J., Lawn, J., E, Cousens., S, Zupan., J, Bryce., J, Black., R, E., Victora., C, G, Charpak., N, Ruiz., J, G. ... C, F. (2016). Kangaroo mother care and neonatal outcomes: A meta-analysis. *Pediatrics, 365*(9462), 891–900. https://doi.org/10.1542/peds.2015-2238

Boutakidis, I. P., Chao, R. K., & Rodríguez, J. L. (2011). The role of adolescents' native language fluency on quality of communication and respect for parents in Chinese and Korean immigrant families. *Asian American Journal of Psychology*, *2*(2), 128–139. https://doi.org/10.1037/a0023606

Bouthry, E., Picone, O., Hamdi, G., Grangeot-Keros, L., Ayoubi, J.-M., & Vauloup-Fellous, C. (2014). Rubella and pregnancy: Diagnosis, management and outcomes. *Prenatal Diagnosis*, *34*(13), 1246–1253. https://doi.org/10.1002/pd.4467

Boutwell, B. B., Meldrum, R. C., & Petkovsek, M. A. (2017). General intelligence in friendship selection: A study of preadolescent best friend dyads. *Intelligence*, *64*, 30–35. https://doi.org/10.1016/j.intell.2017.07.002

Bowen, M. (1978). *Family therapy in clinical practice*. Jason Aronson.

Bower, B. (1993). A child's theory of mind. *Science News*, *144*, 40–42.

Bowker, J. C., & Weingarten, J. (2022). Chapter nine—Temporal approaches to the study of friendship: Understanding the developmental significance of friendship change during childhood and adolescence. In J. J. Lockman (Ed.), *Advances in Child Development and Behavior* (Vol. 63, pp. 249–272). JAI. https://doi.org/10.1016/bs.acdb.2022.04.005

Bowker, J. C., Weingarten, J. P., Etkin, R. G., & Dirks, M. A. (2024). When best friendships end: Young adolescents' responses to hypothetical best friendship dissolution and associations with real-life friendship outcomes. *Frontiers in Developmental Psychology*, *2*, 1369085. https://www.frontiersin.org/articles/10.3389/fdpys.2024.1369085

Bowlby, J. (1969). *Attachment and loss* (Vol. 1). Basic Books.

Bowlby, J. (1969). Attachment and loss. In *Attachment* (Vol. 1). Basic Books.

Bowlby, J. (1973). *Attachment and loss* (Vol. 2). Basic Books.

Bowlby, J. (1988). *A secure base: Clinical applications of attachment theory*. Routledge.

Boyatzis, C. J., & Janicki, D. L. (2003). Parent-child communication about religion: Survey and diary data on unilateral transmission and bi-directional reciprocity styles. *Review of Religious Research*, *44*(3), 252–270. https://doi.org/10.2307/3512386

Boysson-Bardies, B. D., Sagart, L., Durand, C., Eimas, P. D., Siqueland, E. R., Jusczyk, P., Vigorito, J., Kuhl, P. K., & Oller, D. K. (1984). Discernible differences in the babbling of infants according to target language. *Journal of Child Language*, *11*(1), 1–15. https://doi.org/10.1017/S0305000900005559

Bradshaw, D., Creaven, A.-M., & Muldoon, O. T. (2021). Parental incarceration affects children's emotional and behavioral outcomes: A longitudinal cohort study of children aged 9 to 13 years. *International Journal of Behavioral Development*, *45*, 310–316. https://doi.org/10.1177/0165025421995918

Brain Development Cooperative Group. (2012). Total and regional brain volumes in a population-based normative sample from 4 to 18 years: the NIH MRI Study of Normal Brain Development. *Cerebral Cortex*, *22*(1), 1–12. https://doi.org/10.1093/cercor/bhr018

Brajša-Žganec, A., Džida, M., Brkljačić, T., Lipovčan, Kaliterna., L, & Lučić, L. (2023). The well-being of parents in the year after childbirth. *Journal of Family Issues*, *44*(9), 2446–2468. https://doi.org/10.1177/0192513X221096799

Bralten, J., Klemann, C., Mota, N., Witte, W. D., Arango, C., Fabbri, C., Kas, M., Wee, N. van der., Penninx, B., Serretti, A., Franke, B., & Poelmans, G. (2019). Genetic underpinnings of sociability in the UK Biobank. *bioRxiv*, 781195. https://doi.org/10.1101/781195

Branco, S. F., & Brott, P. E. (2018). The elementary school counselor's voice in counseling transracially adopted students. *Professional School Counseling*, *21*(1), 1096-2409-21.1. https://doi.org/10.5330/1096-2409-21.1.26

Brand, R. J., Escobar, K., & Patrick, A. M. (2020). Coincidence or cascade? The temporal relation between locomotor behaviors and the emergence of stranger anxiety. *Infant Behavior and Development*, *58*, 101423. https://doi.org/10.1016/j.infbeh.2020.101423

Brandel, M., Melchiorri, E., & Ruini, C. (2018). The dynamics of eudaimonic well-being in the transition to parenthood: Differences between fathers and mothers. *Journal of Family Issues*, *39*, 2572–2589. https://doi.org/10.1177/0192513X18758344

Brandes, N., Weissbrod, O., & Linial, M. (2022). Open problems in human trait genetics. *Genome Biology*, *23*(1), 1–32. https://doi.org/10.1186/S13059-022-02697-9

Brandl, J. L. (2018). The puzzle of mirror self-recognition. *Phenomenology and the Cognitive Sciences*, *17*(2), 1–26. https://doi.org/10.1007/s11097-016-9486-7

Brandt, J. S., Cruz Ithier, M. A., Rosen, T., & Ashkinadze, E. (2019). Advanced paternal age, infertility, and reproductive risks: A review of the literature. *Prenatal Diagnosis*, *39*(2), 81–87. https://doi.org/10.1002/pd.5402

Branje, S. (2018). Development of parent-adolescent relationships: Conflict interactions as a mechanism of change. *Child Development Perspectives*, *12*(3), 171–176. https://doi.org/10.1111/cdep.12278

Branje, S. (2022). Adolescent identity development in context. *Current Opinion in Psychology*, *45*, 101286. https://doi.org/10.1016/j.copsyc.2021.11.006

Branje, S., de Moor, E. L., Spitzer, J., & Becht, A. I. (2021). Dynamics of identity development in adolescence: A decade in review. *Journal of Research on Adolescence*, *31*(4), 908–927. https://doi.org/10.1111/jora.12678

Braun, M., Klingelhöfer, D., Oremek, G. M., Quarcoo, D., & Groneberg, D. A. (2020). Influence of second-hand smoke and prenatal tobacco smoke exposure on biomarkers, genetics and physiological processes in children—An overview in research insights of the last few years. *International Journal of Environmental Research and Public Health*, *17*(9), 3212. https://doi.org/10.3390/ijerph17093212

Braun, S. S., & Davidson, A. J. (2017). Gender (non)conformity in middle childhood: A mixed methods approach to understanding gender-typed behavior, friendship, and peer preference. *Sex Roles*, *77*(1), 16–29. https://doi.org/10.1007/s11199-016-0693-z

Braungart-Rieker, J. M., Hill-Soderlund, A. L., & Karrass, J. (2010). Fear and anger reactivity trajectories from 4 to 16 months: The roles of temperament, regulation, and maternal sensitivity. *Developmental Psychology*, *46*(4), 791–804. https://doi.org/10.1037/a0019673

Braveman, P. A., Heck, K., Egerter, S., Marchi, K. S., Dominguez, T. P., Cubbin, C., Fingar, K., Pearson, J. A., & Curtis, M. (2015). The role of socioeconomic factors in Black-White disparities in preterm birth. *American Journal of Public Health*, *105*(4), 694–702. https://doi.org/10.2105/AJPH.2014.302008

Bravo, A., Ortega-Ruiz, R., Veenstra, R., Engels, M. C., & Romera, E. M. (2022). Friendship selection and influence processes for popularity in early and mid-adolescents. *Journal of Adolescence*, *94*(1), 45–56. https://doi.org/10.1002/jad.12004

Brazelton, T. B. (1977). Implications of infant development among the Mayan Indians of Mexico. In P. H. Liederman, S. R. Tulikn, & A. Rosenfeld (Eds.), *Culture and infancy* (pp. 336–352). Academic Press.

Brazzelli, E., Pepe, A., & Grazzani, I. (2022). Prosocial behavior in toddlerhood: The contribution of emotion knowledge, theory of mind, and language ability. *Frontiers in Psychology, 13*, 897812. https://doi.org/10.3389/fpsyg.2022.897812

Brechwald, W. A., & Prinstein, M. J. (2011). Beyond homophily: A decade of advances in understanding peer influence processes. *Journal of Research on Adolescence, 21*(1), 166-179. https://doi.org/10.1111/j.1532-7795.2010.00721.x

Breiner, K., Li, A., Cohen, A. O., Steinberg, L., Bonnie, R. J., Scott, E. S., Taylor-Thompson, K., Rudolph, M. D., Chein, J., Richeson, J. A., Dellarco, D. V., Fair, D. A., Casey, B. J., & Galván, A. (2018). Combined effects of peer presence, social cues, and rewards on cognitive control in adolescents. *Developmental Psychobiology, 60*(3), 292-302. https://doi.org/10.1002/dev.21599

Bremner, J. G., Slater, A. M., & Johnson, S. P. (2015). Perception of object persistence: The origins of object permanence in infancy. *Child Development Perspectives, 9*(1), 7-13. https://doi.org/10.1111/cdep.12098

Bretas, R. V., Yamazaki, Y., & Iriki, A. (2020). Phase transitions of brain evolution that produced human language and beyond. *Neuroscience Research, 161*, 1-7. https://doi.org/10.1016/j.neures.2019.11.010

Bretherton, I., & Munholland, K. (2016). The internal working model construct in light of contemporary neuroimaging research. In J. Cassidy & P. R. Shaver (Eds.), *Handbook of Attachment: Theory, Research, and Clinical Applications* (pp. 63-88).

Breton, C. V., Landon, R., Kahn, L. G., Enlow, M. B., Peterson, A. K., Bastain, T., Braun, J., Comstock, S. S., Duarte, C. S., Hipwell, A., Ji, H., LaSalle, J. M., Miller, R. L., Musci, R., Posner, J., Schmidt, R., Suglia, S. F., Tung, I., Weisenberger, D., & &#hillip1; Fry, R. (2021). Exploring the evidence for epigenetic regulation of environmental influences on child health across generations. *Communications Biology, 4*(1), 1-15. https://doi.org/10.1038/s42003-021-02316-6

Breuer, J., Vogelgesang, J., Quandt, T., & Festl, R. (2015). Violent video games and physical aggression: Evidence for a selection effect among adolescents. *Psychology of Popular Media Culture, 4*(4), 305-328. https://doi.org/10.1037/ppm0000035

Breuner, C. C., & Mattson, G. (2016). & Committee on Psychosocial Aspects of Child and Family Health. Sexuality education for children and adolescents. *Pediatrics, 138*(2), e20161348.

Brickell, T. A., Wright, M. M., Sullivan, J. K., Varbedian, N. V., Gillow, K. C., Baschenis, S. M., French, L. M., & Lange, R. T. (2024). Health outcomes in children living in military families caring for a service member or veteran with traumatic brain injury. *Journal of Child and Family Studies, 33*(3), 908-923. https://doi.org/10.1007/s10826-023-02683-0

Briley, D. A., Livengood, J., Derringer, J., Tucker-Drob, E. M., Fraley, R. C., & Roberts, B. W. (2019). Interpreting behavior genetic models: Seven developmental processes to understand. *Behavior Genetics, 49*(2), 196-210. https://doi.org/10.1007/s10519-018-9939-6

Brinke, te., W. L., van de Groep, S., van der Cruijsen, R., & Crone, E. A. (2023). Variability and change in adolescents' prosocial behavior across multiple time scales. *Journal of Research on Adolescence, 33*(2), 575-590. https://doi.org/10.1111/jora.12827

Brinums, M., Imuta, K., & Suddendorf, T. (2018). Practicing for the future: Deliberate practice in early childhood. *Child Development, 89*(6), 2051-2058. https://doi.org/10.1111/cdev.12938

Brittian, A. S., Kim, S. Y., Armenta, B. E., Lee, R. M., Umaña-Taylor, A. J., Schwartz, S. J., Villalta, I. K., Zamboanga, B. L., Weisskirch, R. S., Juang, L. P., Castillo, L. G., & Hudson, M. L. (2015). Do dimensions of ethnic identity mediate the association between perceived ethnic group discrimination and depressive symptoms? *Cultural Diversity and Ethnic Minority Psychology, 21*(1), 41-53. https://doi.org/10.1037/a0037531

Brix, N., Ernst, A., Lauridsen, L. L. B., Parner, E. T., Arah, O. A., Olsen, J., Henriksen, T. B., & Ramlau-Hansen, C. H. (2020). Childhood overweight and obesity and timing of puberty in boys and girls: Cohort and sibling-matched analyses. *International Journal of Epidemiology, 49*(3), 834-844. https://doi.org/10.1093/ije/dyaa056

Brocklehurst, P., Hardy, P., Hollowell, J., Linsell, L., Macfarlane, A., McCourt, C., Marlow, N., Miller, A., Newburn, M., Petrou, S., Puddicombe, D., Redshaw, M., Rowe, R., Sandall, J., Silverton, L., & Stewart, M. (2011). Perinatal and maternal outcomes by planned place of birth for healthy women with low risk pregnancies: The Birthplace in England national prospective cohort study. *BMJ, 343*, d7400. https://www.bmj.com/content/343/bmj.d7400

Broderick, A. V., Brelsford, G. M., & Wadsworth, M. E. (2019). Interparental relationships among low income, ethnically diverse, two-parent cohabiting families. *Journal of Child and Family Studies, 28*(8), 2259-2271. https://doi.org/10.1007/s10826-019-01442-4

Brodie, N., Keim, J. L., Silberholz, E. A., Spector, N. D., & Pattishall, A. E. (2019). Promoting resilience in vulnerable populations. *Current Opinion in Pediatrics, 31*(1), 157-165. https://doi.org/10.1097/MOP.0000000000000722

Brodzinsky, D., Gunnar, M., & Palacios, J. (2022). Adoption and trauma: Risks, recovery, and the lived experience of adoption. *Child Abuse and Neglect, 13*(0). https://doi.org/10.1016/j.chiabu.2021.105309

Brodzinsky, D., Gunnar, M., & Palacios, J. (2022). Adoption and trauma: Risks, recovery, and the lived experience of adoption. *Child Abuse and Neglect, 130*, 105309. https://doi.org/10.1016/j.chiabu.2021.105309

Broesch, T. (2021). Motherese. In T. K Shackelford & V. A. Weekes-Shackelford (Eds.), *Encyclopedia of evolutionary psychological science* (pp. 5263-5264). Springer. https://doi.org/10.1007/978-3-319-19650-3_3326

Broesch, T., Rochat, P., Olah, K., Broesch, J., & Henrich, J. (2016). Similarities and differences in maternal responsiveness in three societies: Evidence from Fiji, Kenya, and the United States. *Child Development, 87*(3), 700-711. https://doi.org/10.1111/cdev.12501

Bronfenbrenner, U. (2005). The bioecological theory of human development. In U. Bronfenbrenner (Ed.), *Making human beings human: Bioecological perspectives on human development* (pp. 3-15). SAGE.

Bronfenbrenner, U., & Morris, P. A. (2006). The bioecological model of human development. In R. M. Lerner & W. Damon (Eds.), *Handbook of child psychology: Theoretical models of human development* (Vol. 1, pp. 793-828). Wiley.

Brooker, R. (2022). *Concepts of genetics*. McGraw-Hill.

Brooker, R. J., Buss, K. A., Lemery-Chalfant, K., Aksan, N., Davidson, R. J., & Goldsmith, H. H. (2013). The development of stranger fear in infancy and toddlerhood: Normative development, individual differences, antecedents, and outcomes. *Developmental Science, 16*(6), 864-878. https://doi.org/10.1111/desc.12058

Brooks, P. J., & Kempe, V (Eds.). (2014). *Encyclopedia of language development*. SAGE.

Brooks, R., & Meltzoff, A. N. (2008). Infant gaze following and pointing predict accelerated vocabulary growth through two years of age: A longitudinal, growth curve modeling study. *Journal of Child Language*, *35*(1), 207–220. https://doi.org/10.1017/s0305000900700829x

Brooks, S. J., Katz, E. S., & Stamoulis, C. (2022). Shorter duration and lower quality sleep have widespread detrimental effects on developing functional brain networks in early adolescence. *Cerebral Cortex Communications*, *3*(1), tgab062. https://doi.org/10.1093/texcom/tgab062

Brooks-Gunn, J., & Markman, L. B. (2005). The contribution of parenting to ethnic and racial gaps in school readiness. *Future of Children*, *15*(1), 139–168. https://doi.org/10.1353/foc.2005.0001

Brooks-Gunn, J., & Ruble, D. N. (2013). Developmental processes in the experience of menarche. In A. Baum, J. E. Singer, & J. L. Singer (Eds.), *Issues in child health and adolescent health: Handbook of psychology and health* (pp. 117–148). Psychology Press.

Brown, A., Waters, C. S., & Shelton, K. H. (2017). A systematic review of the school performance and behavioural and emotional adjustments of children adopted from care. *Adoption & Fostering*, *41*(4), 346–368. https://doi.org/10.1177/0308575917731064

Brown, A., Waters, C. S., & Shelton, K. H. (2019). The educational aspirations and psychological well-being of adopted young people in the UK. *Adoption & Fostering*, *43*(1), 46–59. https://doi.org/10.1177/0308575919826900

Brown, C., Fine, A., & Cauffman, E. (2023). Youth and the justice system. In *APA handbook of adolescent and young adult development* (pp. 665–676). American Psychological Association. https://doi.org/10.1037/0000298-040

Brown, C. S., Biefeld, S. D., & Tam, M. J. (2020). *Gender in childhood*. Cambridge University Press. https://doi.org/10.1017/9781108874281

Brown, D. A., & Lamb, M. E. (2015). Can children be useful witnesses? It depends how they are questioned.. *Child Development Perspectives*, *9*(4), 250–255. https://doi.org/10.1111/cdep.12142

Brown, G. L., & Aytuglu, H. A. (2020). Father-Child Attachment Relationships. In H. E. Fitzgerald, K. von Klitzing, N. J. Cabrera, J. Scarano de Mendonça, & T. Skjøthaug (Eds.), *Handbook of Fathers and Child Development: Prenatal to Preschool* (pp. 273–290). Springer International. https://doi.org/10.1007/978-3-030-51027-5_18

Brown, G. L., Mangelsdorf, S. C., Neff, C., Shigeto, A., Aytuglu, A., & Thomas, C. R. (2022). Infant attachment configurations with mothers and fathers: Implications for triadic interaction quality and children's parental preferences. *Early Childhood Research Quarterly*, *58*, 155–164. https://doi.org/10.1016/j.ecresq.2021.09.004

Brown, H. R., Harvey, E. A., Griffith, S. F., Arnold, D. H., & Halgin, R. P. (2017). Assent and dissent: Ethical considerations in research with toddlers. *Ethics & Behavior*, *27*(8), 651–664. https://doi.org/10.1080/10508422.2016.1277356

Brown, S. L., Manning, W. D., & Stykes, J. B. (2015). Family structure and child well-being: Integrating family complexity. *Journal of Marriage and the Family*, *77*(1), 177–190. https://doi.org/10.1111/jomf.12145

Brownell, C. A. (2016). Prosocial behavior in infancy: The role of socialization. *Child Development Perspectives*, *10*(4), 222–227. https://doi.org/10.1111/cdep.12189

Brugman, D. (2010). Moral reasoning competence and the moral judgment-action discrepancy in young adolescents. In W. Koops, D. Brugman, & T. J. Ferguson (Eds.), *The development and structure of conscience* (pp. 119–133). Psychology Press.

Brummelman, E. (2018). The emergence of narcissism and self-esteem: A social-cognitive approach. *European Journal of Developmental Psychology*, *15*(6), 756–767. https://doi.org/10.1080/17405629.2017.1419953

Brummelman, E., & Sedikides, C. (2020). Raising children with high self-esteem (but not narcissism). *Child Development Perspectives*, *14*(2), 83–89. https://doi.org/10.1111/cdep.12362

Brunning, L., & McKeever, N. (2021). Asexuality. *Journal of Applied Philosophy*, *38*(3), 497–517. https://doi.org/10.1111/japp.12472

Bruns, A., & Lee, H. (2019). Racial/ethnic disparities. In J. M. Eddy & J. Poehlmann-Tynan (Eds.), *Handbook on children with incarcerated parents: Research, policy, and practice* (pp. 37–52). Springer International. https://doi.org/10.1007/978-3-030-16707-3_4

Bryant, B. R., Bryant, D. P., Porterfield, J., Dennis, M. S., Falcomata, T., Valentine, C., Brewer, C., & Bell, K. (2016). The effects of a tier 3 intervention on the mathematics performance of second grade students with severe mathematics difficulties. *Journal of Learning Disabilities*, *49*(2), 176–188. https://doi.org/10.1177/0022219414538516

Bryant, G. A., Liénard, P., & Barrett, H. C. (2012). Recognizing infant-directed speech across distant cultures: Evidence from Africa. *Journal of Evolutionary Psychology*, *10*(2), 47–59. https://doi.org/10.1556/jep.10.2012.2.1

Bubac, C. M., Miller, J. M., & Coltman, D. W. (2020). The genetic basis of animal behavioural diversity in natural populations. *Molecular Ecology*, *29*(11), 1957–1971. https://doi.org/10.1111/mec.15461

Bucci, R., & Staff, J. (2020). Pubertal timing and adolescent delinquency. *Criminology*, *58*(3), 537–567. https://doi.org/10.1111/1745-9125.12245

Bucknam (Afang, Sun., 孙阿芳, & Hood, S. J. (2021). Student language use in a one-way Mandarin immersion classroom. *RELC Journal*, *52*(3), 425–439. https://doi.org/10.1177/0033688219888060

Bühler, J. L., & Nikitin, J. (2020). Sociohistorical context and adult social development: New directions for 21st century research. *American Psychologist*, *75*(4), 457–469. https://doi.org/10.1037/AMP0000611

Buhler-Wassmann, A. C., & Hibel, L. C. (2021). Studying caregiver-infant co-regulation in dynamic, diverse cultural contexts: A call to action. *Infant Behavior and Development*, *64*, 101586. https://doi.org/10.1016/j.infbeh.2021.101586

Bui, L., & Deakin, J. (2021). What we talk about when we talk about vulnerability and youth crime: A narrative review. *Aggression and Violent Behavior*, *58*, 101605. https://doi.org/10.1016/j.avb.2021.101605

Buist, K. L. (2018). Attachment during adolescence. In R. J. R. Levesque (Ed.), *Encyclopedia of Adolescence* (pp. 1–6). Springer International. https://doi.org/10.1007/978-3-319-32132-5_4-2

Buist, K. L., & Vermande, M. (2014). Sibling relationship patterns and their associations with child competence and problem behavior. *Journal of Family Psychology*, *28*(4), 529–537. https://doi.org/10.1037/a0036990

Bulgarelli, C., Blasi, A., de Klerk, C. C. J. M., Richards, J. E., Hamilton, A., & Southgate, V. (2019). Fronto-temporoparietal connectivity and self-awareness in 18-month-olds: A resting state fNIRS study. *Developmental Cognitive Neuroscience*, *38*, 100676. https://doi.org/10.1016/j.dcn.2019.100676

Bull, M. J. (2020). Down syndrome. *New England Journal of Medicine, 382*(24), 2344–2352. https://doi.org/10.1056/NEJMra1706537

Bullo, A., & Schulz, P. J. (2022). Parent-child communication, social norms, and the development of cyber aggression in early adolescence. *Journal of Youth and Adolescence, 51*(9), 1774–1786. https://doi.org/10.1007/s10964-022-01625-1

Bullock, M., & Lutkenhaus, P. (1990). Who am I? Self-understanding in toddlers. *Merrill-Palmer Quarterly, 36*, 217–238.

Burack, J. A., Evans, D. W., Russo, N., Napoleon, J. S., Goldman, K. J., & Iarocci, G. (2021). Developmental perspectives on the study of persons with intellectual disability. *Annual Review of Clinical Psychology, 17*, 339–363. https://doi.org/10.1146/annurev-clinpsy-081219-090532

Burchinal, M., Roberts, J. E., Zeisel, S. A., Hennon, E. A., & Hooper, S. (2006). Social risk and protective child, parenting, and child care factors in early elementary school years. *Parenting: Science & Practice, 6*(1), 79–113. https://psycnet.apa.org/doi/10.1207/s15327922par0601_4

Burden, P. R., & Byrd, D. M. (2019). *Methods for effective teaching: Meeting the needs of all students*. Pearson. https://www.pearson.com/us/higher-education/product/Burden-Methods-for-Effective-Teaching-Meeting-the-Needs-of-All-Students-8th-Edition/9780134695747.html

Burgdorf, J., Kroes, R. A., & Moskal, J. R. (2017). Rough-and-tumble play induces resilience to stress in rats. *NeuroReport, 28*(17), 1122–1126. https://doi.org/10.1097/WNR.0000000000000864

Burger, C., Strohmeier, D., & Kollerová, L. (2022). Teachers can make a difference in bullying: Effects of teacher interventions on students' adoption of bully, victim, bully-victim or defender roles across time. *Journal of Youth and Adolescence, 51*(12), 2312–2327. https://doi.org/10.1007/s10964-022-01674-6

Bürgin, D., Anagnostopoulos, D., Anagnostopoulos, D., Doyle, M., Eliez, S., Fegert, J., Fuentes, J., Hebebrand, J., Hillegers, M., Karwautz, A., Kiss, E., Kotsis, K., Pejovic-Milovancevic, M., Räberg Christensen, A. M., Raynaud, J.-P., Crommen, S., Ç, Çetin, F., Boricevic, V. M., Kehoe, L., & &#hillip1; Fegert, J. M. (2022). Impact of war and forced displacement on children's mental health—Multilevel, needs-oriented, and trauma-informed approaches. *European Child & Adolescent Psychiatry, 1*, 1–9. https://doi.org/10.1007/S00787-022-01974-Z

Burkhardt, J., & Lenhard, W. (2021). A meta-analysis on the longitudinal, age-dependent effects of violent video games on aggression. *Media Psychology, 25*(3), 499–512. https://doi.org/10.1080/15213269.2021.1980729

Burkhardt-Reed, M. M., Long, H. L., Bowman, D. D., Bene, E. R., & Oller, D. K. (2021). The origin of language and relative roles of voice and gesture in early communication development. *Infant Behavior and Development, 65*, 101648. https://doi.org/10.1016/j.infbeh.2021.101648

Burns, E. C. (2020). Factors that support high school completion: A longitudinal examination of quality teacher-student relationships and intentions to graduate. *Journal of Adolescence, 84*, 180–189. https://doi.org/10.1016/j.adolescence.2020.09.005

Burrus, B. B. (2018). Decline in adolescent pregnancy in the United States: A success not shared by all. *American Journal of Public Health, 108*(S1), S5–S6. https://doi.org/10.2105/ajph.2017.304273

Burton, L. M., & Jarrett, R. L. (2000). the mix, yet on the margins: The place of families in urban neighborhood and child development research. *Journal of Marriage and Family, 62*(4), 1114–1135. https://doi.org/10.1111/j.1741-3737.2000.01114.x

Busch, A. S., Hagen, C. P., & Juul, A. (2020). Heritability of pubertal timing: Detailed evaluation of specific milestones in healthy boys and girls. *European Journal of Endocrinology, 183*(1), 13–20. https://doi.org/10.1530/EJE-20-0023

Busch, A. S., Højgaard, B., Hagen, C. P., & Teilmann, G. (2020). Obesity is associated with earlier pubertal onset in boys. *Journal of Clinical Endocrinology & Metabolism, 105*(4), e1667–e1672. https://doi.org/10.1210/clinem/dgz222

Busch, A. S., Hollis, B., Day, F. R., Sørensen, K., Aksglaede, L., Perry, J. R. B., Ong, K. K., Juul, A., & Hagen, C. P. (2019). Voice break in boys-temporal relations with other pubertal milestones and likely causal effects of BMI. *Human Reproduction, 34*(8), 1514–1522. https://doi.org/10.1093/humrep/dez118

Busching, R., & Krahé, B. (2020). With a little help from their peers: The impact of classmates on adolescents' development of prosocial behavior. *Journal of Youth and Adolescence, 49*(9), 1849–1863. https://doi.org/10.1007/s10964-020-01260-8

Bushman, B. J., & Anderson, C. A. (2023). Solving the puzzle of null violent media effects. *Psychology of Popular Media, 12*(1), 1–9. https://doi.org/10.1037/ppm0000361

Busnelli, A., Dallagiovanna, C., Reschini, M., Paffoni, A., Fedele, L., & Somigliana, E. (2019). Risk factors for monozygotic twinning after in vitro fertilization: A systematic review and meta-analysis. *Fertility and Sterility, 111*(2), 302–317. https://doi.org/10.1016/j.fertnstert.2018.10.025

Buss, A. H., & Plomin, R. (1984). *Temperament: Early developing personality traits*. Erlbaum.

Bustamante, A. S., Dearing, E., Zachrisson, H. D., & Vandell, D. L. (2022). Adult outcomes of sustained high-quality early child care and education: Do they vary by family income? *Child Development, 93*(2), 502–523. https://doi.org/10.1111/cdev.13696

Butler, G., Srirangalingam, U., Faithfull, J., Sangster, P., Senniappan, S., & Mitchell, R. (2023). Klinefelter syndrome: Going beyond the diagnosis. *Archives of Disease in Childhood, 108*(3), 166–171. https://doi.org/10.1136/archdischild-2020-320831

Butler, M. G., Miller, J. L., & Forster, J. L. (2019). Prader-Willi syndrome—clinical genetics, diagnosis and treatment approaches: An update. *Current Pediatric Reviews, 15*(4). https://doi.org/10.2174/1573396315666190716120925

Butts, S. F. (2021). Health disparities of African Americans in reproductive medicine. *Fertility and Sterility, 116*(2). https://doi.org/10.1016/j.fertnstert.2021.06.041

Butwick, A. J., Bentley, J., Wong, C. A., Snowden, J. M., Sun, E., & Guo, N. (2018). United States state-level variation in the use of neuraxial analgesia during labor for pregnant women. *JAMA Network Open, 1*(8), e186567. https://doi.org/10.1001/jamanetworkopen.2018.6567

Byers-Heinlein, K., Gonzalez-Barrero, A. M., Schott, E., & Killam, H. (2024). Sometimes larger, sometimes smaller: Measuring vocabulary in monolingual and bilingual infants and toddlers. *First Language, 44*(1), 74–95. https://doi.org/10.1177/01427237231204167

Byers-Heinlein, K., Tsui, A. S. M., Bergmann, C., Black, A. K., Brown, A., Carbajal, M. J., Durrant, S., Fennell, C. T., Fiévet, A. C., Frank, M. C., Gampe, A., Gervain, J., Gonzalez-Gomez, N., Hamlin, J. K., Havron, N., Hernik, M., Kerr, S., Killam, H., Klassen, K., & &#hillip1; Wermelinger, S. (2021). A multilab study of bilingual infants: Exploring the preference for infant-directed speech. *Advances in Methods and Practices in Psychological Science, 4*(1). https://doi.org/10.1177/2515245920974622

Bygdell, M., Kindblom, J. M., Jansson, J.-O., & Ohlsson, C. (2021). Revisiting the critical weight hypothesis for regulation of pubertal timing in boys. *American Journal of Clinical Nutrition*, *113*(1), 123–128. https://doi.org/10.1093/ajcn/nqaa304

Byrd, A. L., & Manuck, S. B. (2014). MAOA, childhood maltreatment, and antisocial behavior: Meta-analysis of a gene-environment interaction. *Biological Psychiatry*, *75*(1), 9–17. https://doi.org/10.1016/j.biopsych.2013.05.004

Byrd, A. L., Manuck, S. B., Hawes, S. W., Vebares, T. J., Nimgaonkar, V., Chowdari, K. V., Hipwell, A. E., Keenan, K., & Stepp, S. D. (2018). The interaction between monoamine oxidase A (MAOA) and childhood maltreatment as a predictor of personality pathology in females: Emotional reactivity as a potential mediating mechanism. *Development and Psychopathology*. https://doi.org/10.1017/S0954579417001900

Byrd, C. M., & Legette, K. B. (2022). School ethnic-racial socialization and adolescent ethnic-racial identity. *Cultural Diversity and Ethnic Minority Psychology*, *28*(2), 205–216. https://doi.org/10.1037/cdp0000449

Byrnes, J. P., & Takahira, S. (1993). Explaining gender differences on SAT-math items. *Developmental Psychology*, *29*(5), 805–810. https://doi.org/10.1037/0012-1649.29.5.805

Cabinian, A., Sinsimer, D., Tang, M., Zumba, O., Mehta, H., Toma, A., Sant'Angelo, D., Laouar, Y., Laouar, A., Nguyen, T., Vieira-Silva, S., Liston, A., Raes, J., Ouellette, A., Selsted, M., Cunliffe, R., Rose, F., Keyte, J., Abberley, L., & &#hillip1; Richardson, B. (2016). Transfer of maternal immune cells by breastfeeding: Maternal cytotoxic T lymphocytes present in breast milk localize in the Peyer's patches of the nursed infant. *PLoS ONE*, *11*(6), e0156762. https://doi.org/10.1371/journal.pone.0156762

Cabral, M. D. I., Liu, S., & Soares, N. (2020). Attention-deficit/hyperactivity disorder: Diagnostic criteria, epidemiology, risk factors and evaluation in youth. *Translational Pediatrics*, *9*(S1), S104–S113. https://doi.org/10.21037/tp.2019.09.08

Cabrera, C., Torres, H., & Harcourt, S. (2020). The neurological and neuropsychological effects of child maltreatment. *Aggression and Violent Behavior*, *54*, 101408. https://doi.org/10.1016/j.avb.2020.101408

Cabrera, L., & Lau, B. K. (2022). The development of auditory temporal processing during the first year of life. *Hearing, Balance and Communication*, *20*(3), 155–165. https://doi.org/10.1080/21695717.2022.2029092

Cabrera, N. J., Fitzgerald, H. E., Bradley, R. H., & Roggman, L. (2014). The ecology of father-child relationships: An expanded model. *Journal of Family Theory & Review*, *6*(4), 336–354. https://doi.org/10.1111/jftr.12054

Cabrera, N. J., Volling, B. L., & Barr, R. (2018). Fathers are parents, too! Widening the lens on parenting for children's development. *Child Development Perspectives*, *12*(3), 152–157. https://doi.org/10.1111/cdep.12275

Caceres, V., Murray, T., Myers, C., & Parbhoo, K. (2022). Prenatal genetic testing and screening: A focused review. *Seminars in Pediatric Neurology*, *42*, 100976. https://doi.org/10.1016/j.spen.2022.100976

Cafiero, R., Brauer, J., Anwander, A., & Friederici, A. D. (2019). The concurrence of cortical surface area expansion and white matter myelination in human brain development. *Cerebral Cortex*, *29*(2), 827–837. https://doi.org/10.1093/cercor/bhy277

Cain, M. S., Leonard, J. A., Gabrieli, J. D. E., & Finn, A. S. (2016). Media multitasking in adolescence. *Psychonomic Bulletin & Review*, *23*(6), 1932–1941. https://doi.org/10.3758/s13423-016-1036-3

Caldas, S. J., & Reilly, M. S. (2018). The influence of race–ethnicity and physical activity levels on elementary school achievement. *Journal of Educational Research*, *111*(4), 473–486. https://doi.org/10.1080/00220671.2017.1297925

Callaghan, T., Rochat, P., Lillard, A., Claux, M. L., Odden, H., Itakura, S., Tapanya, S., & Singh, Saraswati. (2005). Synchrony in the onset of mental-state reasoning. *Psychological Science*, *16*(5), 378–384. https://doi.org/10.1111/j.0956-7976.2005.01544.x

Calvert, S. L. (2015). Children and digital media. In R. M. Lerner (Ed.), *Handbook of child psychology and developmental science* (pp. 1–41). John Wiley & Sons. https://doi.org/10.1002/9781118963418.childpsy410

Calzo, J. P., Masyn, K. E., Austin, S. B., Jun, H.-J., & Corliss, H. L. (2017). Developmental latent patterns of identification as mostly heterosexual versus lesbian, gay, or bisexual. *Journal of Research on Adolescence*, *27*(1), 246–253. https://doi.org/10.1111/jora.12266

Camacho, A., Runions, K., Ortega-Ruiz, R., & Romera, E. M. (2023). Bullying and cyberbullying perpetration and victimization: Prospective within-person associations. *Journal of Youth and Adolescence*, *52*(2), 406–418. https://doi.org/10.1007/s10964-022-01704-3

Cameron, C. E., Brock, L. L., Murrah, W. M., Bell, L. H., Worzalla, S. L., Grissmer, D., & Morrison, F. J. (2012). Fine motor skills and executive function both contribute to kindergarten achievement. *Child Development*, *83*(4), 1229–1244. https://doi.org/10.1111/j.1467-8624.2012.01768.x

Cameron-Faulkner, T. (2020). The emergence of gesture during prelinguistic interaction. In C. F. Rowland, A. L. Theakston, B. Ambridge, & Twomey. K. E (Eds.), *Current perspectives on child language acquisition: How children use their environment to learn* (pp. 173–187). American Speech-Language-Hearing Association. https://doi.org/10.1075/tilar.27.08cam

Cameron-Faulkner, T., Malik, N., Steele, C., Coretta, S., Serratrice, L., & Lieven, E. (2021). A cross-cultural analysis of early prelinguistic gesture development and its relationship to language development. *Child Development*, *92*(1), 273–290. https://doi.org/10.1111/CDEV.13406

Camerota, M., Willoughby, M. T., Cox, M., Greenberg, M., Family, & Life, Project Investigators. (2015). Executive function in low birth weight preschoolers: The moderating effect of parenting. *Journal of Abnormal Child Psychology*, *43*(8), 1551–1562. https://doi.org/10.1007/s10802-015-0032-9

Camos, V., Barrouillet, P., & Barrouillet, P. (2018). *Working memory in development*. Routledge. https://doi.org/10.4324/9781315660851

Camp, K. M., Parisi, M. A., Acosta, P. B., Berry, G. T., Bilder, D. A., Blau, N., Bodamer, O. A., Brosco, J. P., Brown, C. S., Burlina, A. B., Burton, B. K., Chang, C. S., Coates, P. M., Cunningham, A. C., Dobrowolski, S. F., Ferguson, J. H., Franklin, T. D., Frazier, D. M., Grange, D. K., & &#hillip1; Young, J. M. (2014). Phenylketonuria Scientific Review Conference: State of the science and future research needs. *Molecular Genetics and Metabolism* (Vol. 112, pp. 87–122). https://doi.org/10.1016/j.ymgme.2014.02.013 2

Campbell, C. E., Mezher, A. F., Eckel, S. P., Tyszka, J. M., Pauli, W. M., Nagel, B. J., & Herting, M. M. (2021). Restructuring of amygdala subregion apportion across adolescence. *Developmental Cognitive Neuroscience*, *100883*. https://doi.org/10.1016/j.dcn.2020.100883

Campbell, F. A., Pungello, E. P., Burchinal, M., Kainz, K., Pan, Y., Wasik, B. H., Barbarin, O. A., Sparling, J. J., & Ramey, C. T. (2012). Adult outcomes as a function of an early childhood educational program: An Abecedarian Project follow-up. *Developmental Psychology*, *48*(4), 1033–1043. https://doi.org/10.1037/a0026644

Campbell, F. A., & Ramey, C. T. (1994). Effects of early intervention on intellectual and academic achievement: A follow-up study of children from low-income families. *Child Development*, *65*(2), 684–698. https://doi.org/10.1111/j.1467-8624.1994.tb00777.x

Campbell, F. A., Ramey, C. T., Pungello, E., Sparling, J., & Miller-Johnson, S. (2002). Early childhood education: Young adult outcomes from the Abecedarian Project. *Applied Developmental Science*, *6*(1), 42–57. https://psycnet.apa.org/doi/10.1207/S1532480XADS0601_05

Campbell, K., & Peebles, R. (2014). Eating disorders in children and adolescents: State of the art review. *Pediatrics*, *134*(3), 582–592. https://doi.org/10.1542/peds.2014-0194

Campione-Barr, N. (2017). The changing nature of power, control, and influence in sibling relationships. *New Directions for Child and Adolescent Development*, 7–14. https://doi.org/10.1002/cad.20202 2017(156)

Camras, L. A. (2019). Facial expressions across the life span. In V. LoBue, K. Pérez-Edgar, & K. A. Buss (Eds.), *Handbook of emotional development* (pp. 83–103). Springer International. https://doi.org/10.1007/978-3-030-17332-6_5

Camras, L. A., & Halberstadt, A. G. (2017). Emotional development through the lens of affective social competence. *Current Opinion in Psychology*, *17*, 113–117. https://doi.org/10.1016/J.COPSYC.2017.07.003

Çamur, Z., & Erdoğan, Ç. (2022). The effects of breastfeeding and breast milk taste or smell on mitigating painful procedures in newborns: Systematic review and meta-analysis of randomized controlled trials. *Breastfeeding Medicine*, *17*, 793–804. https://doi.org/10.1089/bfm.2022.0134

Cancian, M., & Meyer, D. R. (2018). Reforming policy for single-parent families to reduce child poverty. *Russell Sage Foundation Journal of the Social Sciences*, *4*(2), 91–112. https://doi.org/10.7758/rsf.2018.4.2.05

Candy, T. R., & Aslin, R. N. (2020). Visual sensory development. In J. B. Benson (Ed.), *Encyclopedia of infant and early childhood development* (2nd ed., pp. 435–445). Elsevier. https://doi.org/10.1016/B978-0-12-809324-5.21842-7

Canevello, A. (2020). Gender schema theory. In V. Zeigler-Hill & T. K. Shackelford (Eds.), *Encyclopedia of personality and individual differences* (pp. 1741–1743). Springer International. https://doi.org/10.1007/978-3-319-24612-3_978

Canning, E. A., & Limeri, L. B. (2023). Theoretical and methodological directions in mindset intervention research. *Social and Personality Psychology Compass*, *17*(6), e12758. https://doi.org/10.1111/spc3.12758

Cao, H., Fine, M. A., & Zhou, N. (2022). The Divorce Process and Child Adaptation Trajectory Typology (DPCATT) model: The shaping role of predivorce and postdivorce interparental conflict. *Clinical Child and Family Psychology Review*, *25*(3), 500–528. https://doi.org/10.1007/s10567-022-00379-3

Cao, Z., Cini, E., Pellegrin, D., & Fragkos, K. C. (2023). The association between sexual orientation and eating disorders-related eating behaviours in adolescents: A systematic review and meta-analysis. *European Journal of Eating Disorders Review*, *31*(1), 46–64. https://doi.org/10.1002/erv.2952

Caporaso, J. S., Boseovski, J. J., & Marcovitch, S. (2019). The individual contributions of three executive function components to preschool social competence. *Infant and Child Development*, *28*(4), e2132. https://doi.org/10.1002/icd.2132

Carballo, J. J., Llorente, C., Kehrmann, L., Flamarique, I., Zuddas, A., Purper-Ouakil, D., Hoekstra, P. J., Coghill, D., Schulze, U. M. E., Dittmann, R. W., Buitelaar, J. K., Castro-Fornieles, J., Lievesley, K., Santosh, P., Arango, C., Sutcliffe, A., Curran, S., Selema, L., Flanagan, R., & &#hillip1; Aitchison, K. (2020). Psychosocial risk factors for suicidality in children and adolescents. *European Child and Adolescent Psychiatry*, *29*(6). https://doi.org/10.1007/s00787-018-01270-9

Carey, A. L., Rentscher, K. E., & Mehl, M. R. (2020). Naturalistic observation of social interactions. In *The Wiley encyclopedia of health psychology* (pp. 373–383). John Wiley & Sons. https://doi.org/10.1002/9781119057840.ch87

Carey, S., Zaitchik, D., & Bascandziev, I. (2015). Theories of development: In dialog with Jean Piaget. *Developmental Review*, *38*, 36–54. https://doi.org/10.1016/J.DR.2015.07.003

Carlberg, C., & Molnar, F. (2019). *Human epigenetics: How science works*. Springer.

Carlo, G., Mestre, M. V., Samper, P., Tur, A., & Armenta, B. E. (2011). The longitudinal relations among dimensions of parenting styles, sympathy, prosocial moral reasoning, and prosocial behaviors. *International Journal of Behavioral Development*, *35*(2), 116–124. https://doi.org/10.1177/0165025410375921

Carlo, G., White, R. M. B., Streit, C., Knight, G. P., & Zeiders, K. H. (2018). Longitudinal relations among parenting styles, prosocial behaviors, and academic outcomes in U.S. Mexican adolescents. *Child Development*, *89*(2), 577–592. https://doi.org/10.1111/cdev.12761

Carlson, B. M. (2024). *Human embryology and developmental biology* (7th ed.). Elsevier. https://www.us.elsevierhealth.com/human-embryology-and-developmental-biology-9780323881685.html

Carlson, D. L., McNulty, T. L., Bellair, P. E., & Watts, S. (2014). Neighborhoods and racial/ethnic disparities in adolescent sexual risk behavior. *Journal of Youth and Adolescence*, *43*(9), 1536–1549. https://doi.org/10.1007/s10964-013-0052-0

Carlson, L. (2021). *Grandchildren living in grandparent-headed households, 2019* (Family Profiles, FP-21-07). National Center for Family & Marriage Research. https://www.bgsu.edu/ncfmr/resources/data/family-profiles/carlson-grandchildren-grandparent-headed-households-2019-fp-21-07.html

Carlson, S. M., Claxton, L. J., & Moses, L. J. (2015). The relation between executive function and theory of mind is more than skin deep. *Journal of Cognition and Development*, *16*(1), 186–197. https://doi.org/10.1080/15248372.2013.824883

Carlson, S. M., Zelazo, P. D., & Faja, S. (2013). Executive function. In P. D. Zelazo (Ed.), *The Oxford handbook of developmental psychology* (Vol. 1, pp. 706–743). Oxford University Press. https://doi.org/10.1093/oxfordhb/9780199958450.013.0025

Carlsson, J., Wängqvist, M., & Frisén, A. (2016). Life on hold: Staying in identity diffusion in the late twenties. *Journal of Adolescence*, *47*, 220–229. https://doi.org/10.1016/j.adolescence.2015.10.023

Caron, C. (2020, April 18). Surrogacy is complicated. Just ask New York. *New York Times*. https://www.nytimes.com/2020/04/18/parenting/pregnancy/surrogacy-laws-new-york.html

Carone, N., Baiocco, R., Lingiardi, V., & Barone, L. (2020). Gay and heterosexual single father families created by surrogacy: Father-child relationships, parenting quality, and children's psychological adjustment. *Sexuality Research and Social Policy*, *17*, 711–728. https://doi.org/10.1007/s13178-019-00428-7

Carone, N., Lingiardi, V., Chirumbolo, A., & Baiocco, R. (2018). Italian gay father families formed by surrogacy: Parenting, stigmatization, and children's psychological adjustment. *Developmental Psychology*, *54*(10), 1904–1916. https://doi.org/10.1037/dev0000571

Carpendale, J. I. M., & Wallbridge, B. (2023). From action to ethics: A process-relational approach to prosocial development. *Frontiers in Psychology*, *1*(4). https://www.frontiersin.org/journals/psychology/articles/10.3389/fpsyg.2023.1059646

Carr, R. C., Vernon-Feagans, L., & Burchinal, M. R. (2023). Head Start in low-wealth, rural communities: Evidence from the Family Life Project. *Early Education and Development*, *34*(7), 1590–1611. https://doi.org/10.1080/10409289.2022.2109392

Carroll, J. B. (1996). A three-stratum theory of intelligence: Spearman's contribution. In I. Dennis & P. Tapsfield (Eds.), *Human abilities* (pp. 1–17). Lawrence Erlbaum.

Carroll, J. B. (2005). The three-stratum theory of cognitive abilities. In D. P. Flanagan & P. L. Harrison (Eds.), *Contemporary intellectual assessment: Theories, tests, and issues* (2nd ed., pp. 69–76). Guilford Press.

Carroll, J. J., El-Sabawi, T., & Ostrach, B. (2021). The harms of punishing substance use during pregnancy. *International Journal of Drug Policy*, *98*, 103433. https://doi.org/10.1016/j.drugpo.2021.103433

Carroll, S. L., Mikhail, M. E., & Burt, S. A. (2023). The development of youth antisocial behavior across time and context: A systematic review and integration of person-centered and variable-centered research. *Clinical Psychology Review*, *101*, 102253. https://doi.org/10.1016/j.cpr.2023.102253

Carson, A. S., & Banuazizi, A. (2008). "That's not fair": Similarities and differences in distributive justice reasoning between American and Filipino children. *Journal of Cross-Cultural Psychology*, *39*(4), 493–514. https://doi.org/10.1177/0022022108318134

Carson, S. A., & Kallen, A. N. (2021). Diagnosis and management of infertility: A review. *JAMA*, *326*(1), 65–76. https://doi.org/10.1001/jama.2021.4788

Carter, C. (2023). Navigating young children's friendship selection: Implications for practice. *International Journal of Early Years Education*, *31*(2), 519–534. https://doi.org/10.1080/09669760.2021.1892600

Carter, C. S. (2014). Oxytocin pathways and the evolution of human behavior. *Annual Review of Psychology*, *65*(1), 17–39. https://doi.org/10.1146/annurev-psych-010213-115110

Carter, R. (2015). Anxiety symptoms in African American youth. *Journal of Early Adolescence*, *35*(3), 281–307. https://doi.org/10.1177/0272431614530809

Caruso, D. R., Mayer, J. D., Bryan, V., Phillips, K. G., & Salovey, P. (2019). Measuring emotional and personal intelligence. In M. W. Gallagher & S. J. Lopez (Eds.), *Positive psychological assessment: A handbook of models and measure* (pp. 233–245). American Psychological Association.

Carvalho, M., Branquinho, C., & de Matos, M. G. (2021). Cyberbullying and bullying: Impact on psychological symptoms and well-being. *Child Indicators Research*, *14*(1), 435–452. https://doi.org/10.1007/s12187-020-09756-2

Carver, K., Joyner, K., & Udry, J. R. (2003). *National estimates of adolescent romantic relationships*. Lawrence Erlbaum Associates.

Casale, D., Desmond, C., & Richter, L. M. (2020). Catch-up growth in height and cognitive function: Why definitions matter. *Economics & Human Biology*, *37*, 100853. https://doi.org/10.1016/J.EHB.2020.100853

Case, R. (1999). Cognitive development. In M. Bennett (Ed.), *Developmental psychology: Achievements and prospects* (pp. 36–54). Taylor and Francis.

Casey, K., Novick, K., & Lourenco, S. F. (2021). Sixty years of gender representation in children's books: Conditions associated with overrepresentation of male versus female protagonists. *PLoS ONE*, *16*(12), e0260566. https://doi.org/10.1371/journal.pone.0260566

Caspi, A., McClay, J., Moffitt, T. E., Mill, J., Martin, J., Craig, I. W., Taylor, A., & Poulton, R. (2002). Role of genotype in the cycle of violence in maltreated children. *Science*, *297*(5582), 851–854. https://doi.org/10.1126/science.1072290

Cassano, M., Perry-Parrish, C., & Zeman, J. (2007). Influence of gender on parental socialization of children's sadness regulation. *Social Development*, *16*(2), 210–231. https://doi.org/10.1111/j.1467-9507.2007.00381.x

Cassiano, R. G. M., Provenzi, L., Linhares, M. B. M., Gaspardo, C. M., & Montirosso, R. (2020). Does preterm birth affect child temperament? A meta-analytic study. *Infant Behavior and Development*, *58*, 101417. https://doi.org/10.1016/j.infbeh.2019.101417

Cassibba, R., Sette, G., Bakermans-Kranenburg, M. J., & van IJzendoorn, M. H. (2013). Attachment the Italian way: In search of specific patterns of infant and adult attachments in Italian typical and atypical samples. *European Psychologist*, *18*(1), 47–58. https://doi.org/10.1027/1016-9040/a000128

Cassidy, J., Woodhouse, S. S., Cooper, G., Hoffman, K., Powell, B., & Rodenberg, M. (2005). Examination of the precursors of infant attachment security: Implications for early intervention and intervention research. In L. J. Berlin, Y. Ziv, L. Amaya-Jackson, & M. T. Greenberg (Eds.), *Enhancing Early Attachments: Theory, Research, Intervention, and Policy* (pp. 34–60). Guilford Press. https://psycnet.apa.org/record/2005-08750-002

Castaldi, E., Piazza, M., & Iuculano, T. (2020). Learning disabilities: Developmental dyscalculia. In A. Gallagher, C. Bulteau, D. Cohen, & J. L. Michaud (Eds.), *Handbook of clinical neurology* (Vol. 174, pp. 61–75). Elsevier B.V. https://doi.org/10.1016/B978-0-444-64148-9.00005-3

Castner, J., & Foli, K. J. (2022). Racial identity and transcultural adoption. *Online Journal of Issues in Nursing*, *27*(1), 5. https://www.doi.org/10.3912/OJIN.Vol27No01Man05

Castro, D. C., Páez, M. M., Dickinson, D. K., & Frede, E. (2011). Promoting language and literacy in young dual language learners: Research, practice, and policy. *Child Development Perspectives*, *5*(1), 15–21. https://doi.org/10.1111/j.1750-8606.2010.00142.x

Castro, V. L., Halberstadt, A. G., Lozada, F. T., & Craig, A. B. (2015). Parents' emotion-related beliefs, behaviors, and skills predict children's recognition of emotion. *Infant and Child Development*, *24*(1), 1–22. https://doi.org/10.1002/icd.1868

Cattelan, S., Devigili, A., Santacà, M., & Gasparini, C. (2023). Female reproductive fluid attracts more and better sperm: Implications for within-ejaculate cryptic female choice. *Biology Letters*, *19*(6), 20230063. https://doi.org/10.1098/rsbl.2023.0063

Cauce, A. M. (2008). Parenting, culture, and context: Reflections on excavating culture. *Applied Developmental Science*, *12*(4), 227–229. https://doi.org/10.1080/10888690802388177

Cavagnari, B. M., Guerrero-Vaca, D. J., Carpio-Arias, T. V., Duran-Aguero, S., Vinueza-Veloz, A. F., Robalino-Valdivieso, M. P., Morejón-Terán, Y. A., & Vinueza-Veloz, M. F. (2023). The double burden of malnutrition and gross motor development in infants: A cross-sectional study. *Clinical Nutrition*, *42*(7), 1181–1188. https://doi.org/10.1016/j.clnu.2023.05.001

Cavanagh, S. E., & Fomby, P. (2019). Family instability in the lives of American children. *Annual Review of Sociology*, *45*(1), 493–513. https://doi.org/10.1146/annurev-soc-073018-022633

Cavas, B., & Cavas, P. (2020). Multiple intelligences theory—Howard Gardner. In B. Akpan & T. J. Kenned. (Eds.), *Science education in theory and practice* (pp. 405–418). Springer. https://doi.org/10.1007/978-3-030-43620-9_27

Ceballo, R., Alers-Rojas, F., Mora, A. S., & Cranford, J. A. (2022). Exposure to community violence: Toward a more expansive definition and approach to research. *Child Development Perspectives, 16*(2), 96–102. https://doi.org/10.1111/cdep.12448

Cebioğlu, S., & Broesch, T. (2021). Explaining cross-cultural variation in mirror self-recognition: New insights into the ontogeny of objective self-awareness. *Developmental Psychology, 57*, 625–638. https://doi.org/10.1037/dev0001171

Ceci, S. J., & Bruck, M. (1998). The ontogeny and durability of true and false memories: A fuzzy trace account. *Journal of Experimental Child Psychology, 71*, 165–169. https://doi.org/10.1006/jecp.1998.2468

Ceci, S. J., Huffman, M. L., Smith, E., & Loftus, E. F. (1994). Repeatedly thinking about a non-event: Source misattributions among preschoolers. *Consciousness and Cognition, 3*, 388–407. https://doi.org/10.1006/ccog.1994.1022

Cecil, C. A. M., Viding, E., Fearon, P., Glaser, D., & McCrory, E. J. (2017). Disentangling the mental health impact of childhood abuse and neglect. *Child Abuse & Neglect, 63*, 106–119. https://doi.org/10.1016/j.chiabu.2016.11.024

Cederbaum, J. A., Jeong, C. H., Yuan, C., & Lee, J. O. (2020). Sex and substance use behaviors among children of teen mothers: A systematic review. *Journal of Adolescence, 79*, 208–220. https://doi.org/10.1016/j.adolescence.2020.01.008

Celeghin, A., Diano, M., Bagnis, A., Viola, M., & Tamietto, M. (2017). Basic emotions in human neuroscience: Neuroimaging and beyond. *Frontiers in Psychology, 8*, 1432. https://doi.org/10.3389/fpsyg.2017.01432

Centers for Disease Control. (2019). *Data and statistics about hearing loss in children*. Hearing Loss in Children https://www.cdc.gov/ncbddd/hearingloss/data.html

Centers for Disease Control. (2024). *ART success rates*. https://www.cdc.gov/art/artdata/index.html

Centers for Disease Control and Prevention. (2020). *Youth risk behavior survey: Data summary and trends report 2009–2019*.

Centers for Disease Control and Prevention. (2020). *Data & statistics on birth defects*. https://www.cdc.gov/ncbddd/birthdefects/data.html

Centers for Disease Control and Prevention. (2023). Youth risk behavior surveillance—United States, 2021. *Morbidity and Mortality Weekly Report, 72*(1). https://www.cdc.gov/mmwr/volumes/72/su/pdfs/su7201-H.pdf

Centers for Disease Control and Prevention (CDC). (2022a). *Most recent national asthma data; national current asthma1 prevalence. (2020)* https://www.cdc.gov/asthma/most_recent_national_asthma_data.htm

Centers for Disease Control and Prevention (CDC). (2022b). *Trends in sudden unexpected infant death by cause, 1990–2020*. https://www.cdc.gov/sids/data.htm

Centers for Disease Control and Prevention (CDC). (2022c). *WISQARS nonfatal injury reports, 2000–2020*. https://wisqars.cdc.gov/nonfatal-reports

Centers for Disease Control and Prevention (CDC). (2024a). *Underlying cause of death, 2018–2021, single race results form*. http://wonder.cdc.gov/ucd-icd10-expanded.html

Centers for Disease Control and Prevention (CDC). (2024b). *WISQARS leading causes of death visualization tool*. https://www.cdc.gov/injury/wisqars/index.html

Centers for Disease Control and Prevention (CDC). Cerniglia, L., & Cimino, S. (n.d.). Underlying cause of death 1999–2019. Eating disorders and internalizing/externalizing symptoms in adolescents before and during the COVID-19 pandemic. *Journal of the American Nutrition Association, 42*(5), 445–451. https://doi.org/10.1080/07315724.2022.2063206 December 29, 2020, from 2023 https://wonder.cdc.gov/wonder/help/ucd.html

Çetinçelik, M., Rowland, C. F., & Snijders, T. M. (2021). Do the eyes have it? A systematic review on the role of eye gaze in infant language development. *Frontiers in Psychology, 11*, 3627. https://doi.org/10.3389/FPSYG.2020.589096

Chad-Friedman, E., Botdorf, M., Riggins, T., & Dougherty, L. R. (2021). Early childhood cumulative risk is associated with decreased global brain measures, cortical thickness, and cognitive functioning in school-age children. *Developmental Psychobiology, 63*(2), 192–205. https://doi.org/10.1002/dev.21956

Chad-Friedman, E., Jordan, L. S., Chad-Friedman, S., Lemay, E., Olino, T., Klein, D. N., & Dougherty, L. R. (2023). Parent and child depressive symptoms and authoritarian parenting: Reciprocal relations from early childhood through adolescence. *Clinical Psychological Science, 12*(3), 403–420. 21677026231170871. https://doi.org/10.1177/21677026231170871

Chaibal, S., Bennett, S., Rattanathanthong, K., & Siritaratiwat, W. (2016). Early developmental milestones and age of independent walking in orphans compared with typical home-raised infants. *Early Human Development, 101*, 23–26. https://doi.org/10.1016/j.earlhumdev.2016.06.008

Chakravorty, S., & Williams, T. N. (2015). Sickle cell disease: A neglected chronic disease of increasing global health importance. *Archives of Disease in Childhood, 100*(1), 48–53. https://doi.org/10.1136/archdischild-2013-303773

Challamel, M.-J., Hartley, S., Debilly, G., Lahlou, S., & Franco, P. (2020). A video polysomnographic study of spontaneous smiling during sleep in newborns. *Journal of Sleep Research, 30*(3), e13129. https://doi.org/10.1111/jsr.13129

Chambers, A. M. (2017). The role of sleep in cognitive processing: Focusing on memory consolidation. *Wiley Interdisciplinary Reviews: Cognitive Science, 8*(3), e1433. https://doi.org/10.1002/wcs.1433

Chan, S. Y., Ngoh, Z. M., Ong, Z. Y., Teh, A. L., Kee, M. Z. L., Zhou, J. H., Fortier, M. V., Yap, F., MacIsaac, J. L., Kobor, M. S., Silveira, P. P., Meaney, M. J., & Tan, A. P. (2024). The influence of early-life adversity on the coupling of structural and functional brain connectivity across childhood. *Nature Mental Health, 2*(1), Article 1. https://doi.org/10.1038/s44220-023-00162-5

Chan, W., Kwok, Y., Choy, K., Leung, T., & Wang, C. (2013). Single fetal cells for non-invasive prenatal genetic diagnosis: Old myths new prospective. *Medical Journal of Obstetrics and Gynecology, 1*(1), 1004.

Chandler, M. J., & Carpendale, J. I. (1998). Inching toward a mature theory of mind. In M. Ferrari & R. J. Sternberg (Eds.), *Self-awareness: Its nature and development* (pp. 148–190).

Chandra Handa, M. (2019). Leading differentiated learning for the gifted. *Roeper Review, 41*(2), 102–118. https://doi.org/10.1080/02783193.2019.1585213

Chang, C.-Y. (2022). Selection or influence? The position-based method to analyzing behavioral similarity in adolescent social networks. *International Journal of Adolescence and Youth, 27*(1), 149–165. https://doi.org/10.1080/02673843.2022.2043915

Chang, D. S., Lasley, F. D., Das, I. J., Mendonca, M. S., & Dynlacht, J. R. (2014). Radiation effects in the embryo and fetus. In *Basic radiotherapy physics and biology* (pp.

313–316). Springer International. https://doi.org/10.1007/978-3-319-06841-1_32

Chang, S. M., Grantham-McGregor, S. M., Powell, C. A., Vera-Hernández, M., Lopez-Boo, F., Baker-Henningham, H., Walker, S. P., Hackman, DA., Farah, MJ., Meaney, MJ., Hertzman, C., Boyce, T., Grantham-McGregor, S., Cheung, YB., Cueto, S., Glewwe, P., Richter, L., Strupp, B., Walker, SP., & &#hillip1; Aboud, F. (2015). Integrating a parenting intervention with routine primary health care: A cluster randomized trial. *Pediatrics, 136*(2), 272–280. https://doi.org/10.1542/peds.2015-0119

Chang, Y.-S., Gratiot, M., Owen, J. P., Brandes-Aitken, A., Desai, S. S., Hill, S. S., Arnett, A. B., Harris, J., Marco, E. J., & Mukherjee, P. (2016). White matter microstructure is associated with auditory and tactile processing in children with and without sensory processing disorder. *Frontiers in Neuroanatomy, 9*, 169. https://doi.org/10.3389/fnana.2015.00169

Chao, R. K. (1995). Chinese and European American cultural models of the self reflected in mothers' childrearing beliefs. *Ethos, 23*(3), 328–354. http://dx.doi.org/10.1525/eth.1995.23.3.02a00030

Chao, R. K. (2001). Extending research on the consequences of parenting style for Chinese Americans and European Americans. *Child Development, 72*, 1832–1843. https://doi.org/10.1111/1467-8624.00381

Chaplin, T. M., & Aldao, A. (2013). Gender differences in emotion expression in children: A meta-analytic review. *Psychological Bulletin, 139*(4), 735–765. https://doi.org/10.1037/a0030737

Charles, E., Hunt, K. A., Harris, C., Hickey, A., & Greenough, A. (2018). Small for gestational age and extremely low birth weight infant outcomes. *Journal of Perinatal Medicine, 47*(2), 247–251. https://doi.org/10.1515/jpm-2018-0295

Charness, M. E., Riley, E. P., & Sowell, E. R. (2016). Drinking during pregnancy and the developing brain: Is any amount safe? *Trends in Cognitive Sciences, 20*(2), 80–82. https://doi.org/10.1016/j.tics.2015.09.011

Chasan-Taber, L., Kini, N., Harvey, M. W., Pekow, P., & Dole, N. (2020). The association between acculturation and prenatal psychosocial stress among Latinas. *Journal of Immigrant and Minority Health, 22*(3), 534–544. https://doi.org/10.1007/s10903-019-00909-2

Chatkin, J., Correa, L., & Santos, U. (2022). External environmental pollution as a risk factor for asthma. *Clinical Reviews in Allergy and Immunology, 62*(1), 72–89. https://doi.org/10.1007/s12016-020-08830-5

Chatziparasidis, G., & Kantar, A. (2021). COVID-19 in children with asthma. *Lung, 199*(1), 7–12. https://doi.org/10.1007/S00408-021-00419-9

Chauhan, S. (2017). A meta-analysis of the impact of technology on learning effectiveness of elementary students. *Computers & Education, 105*, 14–30. https://doi.org/10.1016/j.compedu.2016.11.005

Chavajay, P., & Rogoff, B. (1999). Cultural variation in management of attention by children and their caregivers. *Developmental Psychology, 35*(4), 1079–1090.

Chávez, D. V., Salmivalli, C., Garandeau, C. F., Berger, C., & Kanacri, B. P. L. (2022). Bidirectional associations of prosocial behavior with peer acceptance and rejection in adolescence. *Journal of Youth and Adolescence, 51*(12), 2355–2367. https://doi.org/10.1007/s10964-022-01675-5

Chavez-Dueñas, N. Y., & Adames, H. Y. (2022). Parenting while undocumented: An intersectional socialization approach. *Current Opinion in Psychology, 47*, 101441. https://doi.org/10.1016/j.copsyc.2022.101441

Chemin, A. (2014). *Handwriting vs typing: Is the pen still mightier than the keyboard*. The Guardian. https://www.theguardian.com/science/2014/dec/16/cognitive-benefits-handwriting-decline-typing

Chen, D., Berona, J., Chan, Y-M., Ehrensaft, D., Garofalo, R., Hidalgo, M. A., Rosenthal, S. M., Tishelman, A. C., & Olson-Kenned., J. (2023). Psychosocial functioning in transgender youth after 2 years of hormones. *New England Journal of Medicine, 388*(3), 240–250. https://doi.org/10.1056/NEJMoa2206297

Chen, D. R., & Lu, H. H. (2022). Social alienation of adolescents with obesity in classrooms: A multilevel approach. *Journal of Adolescence, 94*(1), 81–91. https://doi.org/10.1002/JAD.12001

Chen, E., Hayen, R., Le, Van., Austin, M. K., Shalowitz, M. U., Story, R. E., & Miller, G. E. (2019). Neighborhood social conditions, family relationships, and childhood asthma. *Pediatrics, 144*(2). https://doi.org/10.1542/PEDS.2018-3300/76892

Chen, F. R., Rothman, E. F., & Jaffee, S. R. (2017). Early puberty, friendship group characteristics, and dating abuse in US girls. *Pediatrics, 139*(6), e20162847. https://doi.org/10.1542/peds.2016-2847

Chen, L.-W., Wu, Y., Neelakantan, N., Chong, M. F.-F., Pan, A., van Dam, R. M., Wardlaw, T., Lawn, J., Cousens, S., Zupan, J., Mcmillen, I., Maslova, E., Bhattacharya, S., Lin, S., Michels, K., Eteng, M., Eyong, E., Akpanyung, E., Agiang, M., & &#hillip1; Rehm, J. (2014). Maternal caffeine intake during pregnancy is associated with risk of low birth weight: A systematic review and dose-response meta-analysis. *BMC Medicine, 12*(1), 174. https://doi.org/10.1186/s12916-014-0174-6

Chen, S. H., Zhou, Q., & Uchikoshi, Y. (2021). Heritage language socialization in Chinese American immigrant families: Prospective links to children's heritage language proficiency. *International Journal of Bilingual Education and Bilingualism, 24*(8), 1193–1209. https://doi.org/10.1080/13670050.2018.1547680

Chen, W. Y., & Lee, Y. (2021). Mother's exposure to domestic and community violence and its association with child's behavioral outcomes. *Journal of Community Psychology, 49*(7), 2623–2638. https://doi.org/10.1002/jcop.22508

Chen, X. (2018). Culture, temperament, and social and psychological adjustment. *Developmental Review, 50*, 42–53. https://doi.org/10.1016/j.dr.2018.03.004

Chen, X., & Graham, S. (2018). Doing better but feeling worse: An attributional account of achievement—Self-esteem disparities in Asian American students. *Social Psychology of Education, 21*(4). https://doi.org/10.1007/s11218-018-9447-9

Chen, X., Rubin, K. H., & Li, B. (1994). Only children and sibling children in urban China: A re-examination. *International Journal of Behavioral Development, 17*(3), 413–421. https://doi.org/10.1177/016502549401700302

Chen, X., & Schmidt, L. A. (2015). Temperament and Personality. In R. Lerner (Ed.), *Handbook of Child Psychology and Developmental Science* (pp. 1–49). John Wiley & Sons. https://doi.org/10.1002/9781118963418.childpsy305

Chen, Y., Spagna, A., Wu, T., Kim, T. H., Wu, Q., Chen, C., Wu, Y., & Fan, J. (2019). Testing a cognitive control model of human intelligence. *Scientific Reports, 9*, 2898. https://doi.org/10.1038/s41598-019-39685-2

Chen, Y. T., Liu, C. L., Chen, C. J., Chen, M. H., Chen, C. Y., Tsao, P. N., Chou, H. C., & Chen, P. C. (2021). Association between short-term exposure to air pollution and sudden infant death syndrome. *Chemosphere, 27*(1). https://doi.org/10.1016/j.chemosphere.2020.129515

Cheng, C., & Kibbe, M. M. (2022). Development of updating in working memory in 4–7-year-old children. *Developmental Psychology, 58*(5), 902–912. https://doi.org/10.1037/dev0001337

Cheng, S., Kaminga, A. C., Liu, Q., Wu, F., Wang, Z., Wang, X., & Liu, X. (2022). Association between weight status and bullying experiences among children and adolescents in schools: An updated meta-analysis. *Child Abuse & Neglect*, *134*, 105833. https://doi.org/10.1016/j.chiabu.2022.105833

Cheng, W., Rolls, E., Gong, W., Du, J., Zhang, J., Zhang, X. Y., Li, F., & Feng, J. (2020). Sleep duration, brain structure, and psychiatric and cognitive problems in children. *Molecular Psychiatry*, *26*(8), 3992–4003. https://doi.org/10.1038/s41380-020-0663-2

Cheng, W., Rolls, E. T., Gu, H., Zhang, J., & Feng, J. (2015). Autism: Reduced connectivity between cortical areas involved in face expression, theory of mind, and the sense of self. *Brain*, *138*(5), 1382–1393. https://doi.org/10.1093/brain/awv051

Cheng, Z. H., Perko, V. L., Fuller-Marashi, L., Gau, J. M., & Stice, E. (2019). Ethnic differences in eating disorder prevalence, risk factors, and predictive effects of risk factors among young women. *Eating Behaviors*, *32*, 23–30. https://doi.org/10.1016/j.eatbeh.2018.11.004

Chervonsky, E., & Hunt, C. (2019). Emotion regulation, mental health, and social wellbeing in a young adolescent sample: A concurrent and longitudinal investigation. *Emotion*, *19*, 270–282. https://doi.org/10.1037/emo0000432

Chess, S., & Thomas, A. (1991). Temperament and the concept of goodness of fit. In J. Strelau & A. Angleitner (Eds.), *Explorations in Temperament: International Perspectives on Theory and Measurement* (pp. 15–28). Plenum. https://doi.org/10.1007/978-1-4899-0643-4_2

Chester, M., Plate, R. C., Powell, T., Rodriguez, Y., Wagner, N. J., & Waller, R. (2023). The COVID-19 pandemic, mask-wearing, and emotion recognition during late-childhood. *Social Development*, *32*(1), 315–328. https://doi.org/10.1111/sode.12631

Cheung, P., & Ansari, D. (2020). Early understanding of number. In S. Hupp & J. D. Jewell (Eds.), *The encyclopedia of child and adolescent development* (pp. 1–12). Wiley. https://doi.org/10.1002/9781119171492.wecad133

Chevalier, N., Kurth, S., Doucette, M. R., Wiseheart, M., Deoni, S. C. L. S., Dean, D. C. D., O'Muircheartaigh, J., Blackwell, K. A., Munakata, Y., LeBourgeois, M. K., Kail, R., Fry, A., Hale, S., Fry, A., Hale, S., Salthouse, T., McAuley, T., White, D., Nettelbeck, T., & &#hillip1; Greenstein, D. (2015). Myelination is associated with processing speed in early childhood: Preliminary insights. *PLoS ONE*, *10*(10), e0139897. https://doi.org/10.1371/journal.pone.0139897

Chhangur, R. R., Weeland, J., Overbeek, G., Matthys, W., Orobio de Castro, B., van der Giessen, D., & Belsky, J. (2017). Genetic moderation of intervention efficacy: Dopaminergic genes, the incredible years, and externalizing behavior in children. *Child Development*, *88*(3), 796–811. https://doi.org/10.1111/cdev.12612

Chiang, K. V., Li, R., Anstey, E. H., & Perrine, C. G. (2021). Racial and ethnic disparities in breastfeeding initiation — United States, 2019. *Morbidity and Mortality Weekly Report*, *70*(21), 769–774. http://dx.doi.org/10.15585/mmwr.mm7021a1

Chiang, S.-C., & Bai, S. (2022). Reciprocal influences among marital relationship, Parent–adolescent relationship, and youth depressive symptoms. *Journal of Marriage and Family*, *84*(4), 962–981. https://doi.org/10.1111/jomf.12836

Chiari, C., & de Morais, M. L. (2024). Moral judgment competence: The main theoretical contributions of Piaget, Kohlberg, and Lind. In P. U. R. Bataglia, C. P. Alves, & E. M. P. P. R. Parente (Eds.), *Studies on Moral Competence: Proposals and Dilemmas for Discussion* (pp. 67–76). Springer Nature Switzerland. https://doi.org/10.1007/978-3-031-52139-3_5

Chilaka, V. N., & Konje, J. C. (2021). HIV in pregnancy – An update. *European Journal of Obstetrics & Gynecology and Reproductive Biology*, *256*, 484–491. https://doi.org/10.1016/j.ejogrb.2020.11.034

Child Trends. (2018). *Overweight children and youth*. https://www.childtrends.org/indicators/overweight-children-and-youth

Child Trends. (2019). *Dual language learners*. https://www.childtrends.org/indicators/dual-language-learners

Child Welfare Information Gateway. (2019). *What is child abuse and neglect? Recognizing the signs and symptoms*. https://www.childwelfare.gov/resources/what-child-abuse-and-neglect-recognizing-signs-and-symptoms/

Chiocca, E. M. (2017). American parents' attitudes and beliefs about corporal punishment: An integrative literature review. *Journal of Pediatric Health Care*, *31*(3), 372–383. https://doi.org/10.1016/j.pedhc.2017.01.002

Chládková, K., & Paillereau, N. (2020). The what and when of universal perception: A review of early speech sound acquisition. *Language Learning*, *70*(4), 1136–1182. https://doi.org/10.1111/LANG.12422

Chmait, R. H., Monson, M. A., & Chon, A. H. (2023). Advances in fetal surgical repair of open spina bifida. *Obstetrics & Gynecology*, *141*(3), 505. https://doi.org/10.1097/AOG.0000000000005074

Choe, D. E., Olson, S. L., & Sameroff, A. J. (2013). The interplay of externalizing problems and physical and inductive discipline during childhood. *Developmental Psychology*, *49*(11), 2029–2039. https://doi.org/10.1037/a0032054

Choi, J. K., Teshome, T., & Smith, J. (2021). Neighborhood disadvantage, childhood adversity, bullying victimization, and adolescent depression: A multiple mediational analysis. *Journal of Affective Disorders*, *279*, 554–562. https://doi.org/10.1016/j.jad.2020.10.041

Choi, J., Ogawa, T., Takesue, S., Muraki, S., Inoue, Y., Abe, H., & Yamanoi, E. (2022). Different flooring surfaces affect infants' crawling performance. *Applied Ergonomics*, *98*, 103553. https://doi.org/10.1016/j.apergo.2021.103553

Chokron, S., & Dutton, G. N. (2023). From vision to cognition: Potential contributions of cerebral visual impairment to neurodevelopmental disorders. *Journal of Neural Transmission*, *130*(3), 409–424. https://doi.org/10.1007/s00702-022-02572-8

Chomsky, N. (1959). Review of B. F. Skinner's verbal behavior. *Language*, *35*, 26–58.

Chomsky, N. (2017). Language architecture and its import for evolution. *Neuroscience & Biobehavioral Reviews*, *81*, 295–300. https://doi.org/10.1016/J.NEUBIOREV.2017.01.053

Chong, I., & Proctor, R. W. (2020). On the evolution of a radical concept: Affordances according to Gibson and their subsequent use and development. *Perspectives on Psychological Science*, *15*(1). https://doi.org/10.1177/1745691619868207

Chou, B., Bienstock, J. L., & Satin, A. J. (2020). *The Johns Hopkins manual of gynecology and obstetrics*. Wolters Kluwer.

Chow, J. C., Ekholm, E., & Bae, C. L. (2021). Relative contribution of verbal working memory and attention to child language. *Assessment for Effective Intervention*, *47*(1), 3–13. https://doi.org/10.1177/1534508420946361

Christ, S. E., Clocksin, H. E., Burton, B. K., Grant, M. L., Waisbren, S., Paulin, M. C., Bilder, D. A., White, D. A., & Saville, C. (2020). Executive function in phenylketonuria (PKU): Insights from the behavior rating inventory of executive function (BRIEF) and a large sample of individuals with PKU.

Neuropsychology, 34, 456–466. https://doi.org/10.1037/neu0000625

Christodoulou, J., Lac, A., & Moore, D. S. (2017). Babies and math: A meta-analysis of infants' simple arithmetic competence. *Developmental Psychology, 53*(8), 1405–1417. https://doi.org/10.1037/dev0000330

Chu, J. T. W., McCormack, J., Marsh, S., Wells, A., Wilson, H., & Bullen, C. (2022). Impact of prenatal alcohol exposure on neurodevelopmental outcomes: A systematic review. *Health Psychology and Behavioral Medicine, 10*(1), 973–1002. https://doi.org/10.1080/21642850.2022.2129653

Chung, A., Backholer, K., Wong, E., Palermo, C., Keating, C., & Peeters, A. (2016). Trends in child and adolescent obesity prevalence in economically advanced countries according to socioeconomic position: A systematic review. *Obesity Reviews, 17*(3), 276–295. https://doi.org/10.1111/obr.12360

Chung, P. J., Patel, D. R., & Nizami, I. (2020). Disorder of written expression and dysgraphia: Definition, diagnosis, and management. *Translational Pediatrics, 9*(Suppl 1), S46–S54. https://doi.org/10.21037/tp.2019.11.01

Cicchetti, D., & Banny, A. (2014). A developmental psychopathology perspective on child maltreatment. In M. Lewis & K. D. Rudolph (Eds.), *Handbook of developmental psychopathology* (pp. 723–741). Springer. https://doi.org/10.1007/978-1-4614-9608-3

Cicchetti, D., Rogosch, F. A., Toth, S. L., & Spagnola, M. (1997). Affect, cognition, and the emergence of self-knowledge in the toddler offspring of depressed mothers. *Journal of Experimental Child Psychology, 67*(3), 338–362.

Cicchetti, D., & Toth, S. L. (2015). Child maltreatment. In M. E. Lamb (Ed.), *Handbook of child psychology and developmental science* (Vol. 3, pp. 1–51). John Wiley & Sons. https://doi.org/10.1002/9781118963418.childpsy313

Cimpian, A., Hammond, M. D., Mazza, G., & Corry, G. (2017). Young children's self-concepts include representations of abstract traits and the global self. *Child Development, 88*(6), 1786–1798. https://doi.org/10.1111/cdev.12925

Cirulli, F. (2021). Embedding early experiences into brain function: Perspectives from behavioral epigenetics. In L. Provenzi & R. Montirosso (Eds.), *Developmental human behavioral epigenetics* (Vol. 23, pp. 157–165). Academic Press. https://doi.org/10.1016/B978-0-12-819262-7.00009-X

Cisneros-Franco, J. M., Voss, P., Thomas, M. E., & de Villers-Sidani, E. (2020). Chapter 8—Critical periods of brain development. In A. Gallagher, C. Bulteau, D. Cohen, & J. L. Michaud (Eds.), *Handbook of clinical neurology* (Vol. 173, pp. 75–88). Elsevier. https://doi.org/10.1016/B978-0-444-64150-2.00009-5

Clark, E. V. (2017). *Language in children: A brief introduction.* Routledge. https://www.routledge.com/Language-in-Children/Clark/p/book/9781138906075

Clark, K. A., Helland, T., Specht, K., Narr, K. L., Manis, F. R., Toga, A. W., & Hugdahl, K. (2014). Neuroanatomical precursors of dyslexia identified from pre-reading through to age 11. *Brain : A Journal of Neurology, 137,* 3136–3141. https://doi.org/10.1093/brain/awu229

Clayborne, Z. M., Nilsen, W., Torvik, F. A., Gustavson, K., Bekkhus, M., Gilman, S. E., Khandaker, G. M., Fell, D. B., & Colman, I. (2021). Prenatal maternal stress, child internalizing and externalizing symptoms, and the moderating role of parenting: Findings from the Norwegian mother, father, and child cohort study. *Psychological Medicine, 53*(6), 2437–2447. https://doi.org/10.1017/S0033291721004311

Clayborne, Z. M., Varin, M., & Colman, I. (2019). Systematic review and meta-analysis: Adolescent depression and long-term psychosocial outcomes. *Journal of the American Academy of Child & Adolescent Psychiatry, 58*(1), 72–79. https://doi.org/10.1016/j.jaac.2018.07.896

Clearfield, M. W. (2011). Learning to walk changes infants' social interactions. *Infant Behavior & Development, 34*(1), 15–25. https://doi.org/10.1016/j.infbeh.2010.04.008

Clerkin, E. M., & Smith, L. B. (2022). Real-world statistics at two timescales and a mechanism for infant learning of object names. *Proceedings of the National Academy of Sciences, 119*(18), e2123239119. https://doi.org/10.1073/pnas.2123239119

Clifford, A., Franklin, A., Davies, I. R. L., & Holmes, A. (2009). Electrophysiological markers of categorical perception of color in 7-month old infants. *Brain & Cognition, 71*(2), 165–172. https://doi.org/10.1016/j.bandc.2009.05.002

Cliffordson, C., & Gustafsson, J.-E. (2008). Effects of age and schooling on intellectual performance: Estimates obtained from analysis of continuous variation in age and length of schooling. *Intelligence, 36*(2), 143–152. https://doi.org/10.1016/j.intell.2007.03.006

Coe, J. L., Huffhines, L., Gonzalez, D., Seifer, R., & Parade, S. H. (2021). Cascades of risk linking intimate partner violence and adverse childhood experiences to less sensitive caregiving during infancy. *Child Maltreatment, 26*(4), 409–419. https://doi.org/10.1177/10775595211000431

Coe-Odess, S. J., Narr, R. K., & Allen, J. P. (2019). Emergent emotions in adolescence. In V. LoBue, K. Pérez-Edgar, & K. A. Buss (Eds.), *Handbook of emotional development* (pp. 595–625). Springer. https://doi.org/10.1007/978-3-030-17332-6_23

Coelho, V. A., Marchante, M., & Jimerson, S. R. (2017). Promoting a positive middle school transition: A randomized-controlled treatment study examining self-concept and self-esteem. *Journal of Youth and Adolescence, 46*(3), 558–569. https://doi.org/10.1007/s10964-016-0510-6

Coffey, C., & Patton, G. C. (2016). Cannabis use in adolescence and young adulthood. *Canadian Journal of Psychiatry, 61*(6), 318–327. https://doi.org/10.1177/0706743716645289

Coffino, J. A., Udo, T., & Grilo, C. M. (2019). Rates of help-seeking in US adults with lifetime DSM-5 eating disorders: Prevalence across diagnoses and differences by sex and ethnicity/race. *Mayo Clinic Proceedings, 94*(8), 1415–1426. https://doi.org/10.1016/j.mayocp.2019.02.030

Cohen, A. O., & Casey, B. J. (2017). The neurobiology of adolescent self-control. In T. Egner (Ed.), *The Wiley handbook of cognitive control* (pp. 455–475). John Wiley & Sons. https://doi.org/10.1002/9781118920497.ch26

Cohen, J. R., & D'Esposito, M. (2021). An integrated, dynamic functional connectome underlies intelligence. In A. K. Barbey, R. J. Haier, & S. Karama (Eds.), *The Cambridge handbook of intelligence and cognitive neuroscience* (pp. 261–281). Cambridge University Press. https://doi.org/10.1017/9781108635462.017

Cohen, L. B., & Cashon, C. H. (2006). Infant cognition. In D. Kuhn, R. S. Siegler, W. Damon, & R. M. Lerner (Eds.), *Handbook of child psychology* (Vol. 2, pp. 214–251). John Wiley & Sons.

Cole, E. Bingham., & Flexer, C. Ann. (2016). *Children with hearing loss: Developing listening and talking, birth to six.* Plural.

Cole, P. M., Tamang, B. L., & Shrestha, S. (2006). Cultural variations in the socialization of young children's anger and shame. *Child Development, 77*(5), 1237–1251. https://doi.org/10.1111/j.1467-8624.2006.00931.x

Cole, W. G., & Adolph, K. E. (2023). Learning to move in a changing body in a changing world. *Integrative and Comparative*

Biology, 63(3), 653–663. https://doi.org/10.1093/icb/icad083

Cole, W. G., Lingeman, J. M., & Adolph, K. E. (2012). Go naked: Diapers affect infant walking. *Developmental Science, 15*(6), 783–790. https://doi.org/10.1111/j.1467-7687.2012.01169.x

Coleman-Jensen, A., Rabbitt, M. P., Gregory, C. A., & Singh, A. (2021). *Statistical supplement to household food security in the United States in 2020, AP-091.* Department of Agriculture, Economic Research Service. http://dx.doi.org/10.22004/ag.econ.313486

Coles, C. D., Grant, T. M., Kable, J. A., Stoner, S. A., Perez, A., & Disorders, the C. I. on F. A. S. (2022). Prenatal alcohol exposure and mental health at midlife: A preliminary report on two longitudinal cohorts. *Alcoholism: Clinical and Experimental Research, 46*(2), 232–242. https://doi.org/10.1111/acer.14761

Collado-Soler, R., Trigueros, R., Aguilar-Parra, J. M., & Navarro, N. (2023). Emotional intelligence and resilience outcomes in adolescent period, is knowledge really strength? *Psychology Research and Behavior Management, 16,* 1365–1378. https://doi.org/10.2147/prbm.S383296

Combs-Orme, T., & Renkert, L. E. (2009). Fathers and their infants: Caregiving and affection in the modern family. *Journal of Human Behavior in the Social Environment, 19*(4), 394–418. https://doi.org/10.1080/10911350902790753

Comunian, A. L., & Gielen, U. P. (2000). Sociomoral reflection and prosocial and antisocial behavior: Two Italian studies. *Psychological Reports, 87*(1), 161–176. https://doi.org/10.2466/pr0.2000.87.1.161

Conlon, J. L. (2017). Diethylstilbestrol. *Journal of the American Academy of Physician Assistants, 30*(2), 49–52. https://doi.org/10.1097/01.jaa.0000511800.91372.34

Connolly, J., & Craig, W. (1999). Conceptions of cross-sex friendships and romantic relationships in early adolescence. *Journal of Youth & Adolescence, 28*(4), 481–509. https://psycnet.apa.org/doi/10.1023/A:1021669024820

Connolly, J., Craig, W., Goldberg, A., & Pepler, D. (2004). Mixed-gender groups, dating, and romantic relationships in early adolescence. *Journal of Research on Adolescence, 14,* 185–207. https://psycnet.apa.org/doi/10.1111/j.1532-7795.2004.01402003.x

Conradt, E., Camerota, M., Maylott, S., & Lester, B. M. (2023). Annual research review: Prenatal opioid exposure – a two-generation approach to conceptualizing neurodevelopmental outcomes. *Journal of Child Psychology and Psychiatry, 64*(4), 566–578. https://doi.org/10.1111/jcpp.13761

Conradt, E., Carter, S. E., & Crowell, S. E. (2020). Biological embedding of chronic stress across two generations within marginalized communities. *Child Development Perspectives, 14*(4), 208–214. https://doi.org/10.1111/CDEP.12382

Conradt, E., Flannery, T., Aschner, J. L., Annett, R. D., Croen, L. A., Duarte, C. S., Friedman, A. M., Guille, C., Hedderson, M. M., Hofheimer, J. A., Jones, M. R., Ladd-Acosta, C., McGrath, M., Moreland, A., Neiderhiser, J. M., Nguyen, R. H. N., Posner, J., Ross, J. L., Savitz, D. A., & &#hillip1; Lester, B. M. (2019). Prenatal opioid exposure: Neurodevelopmental consequences and future research priorities. *Pediatrics, 144*(3). https://doi.org/10.1542/peds.2019-0128

Conte, S., Baccolo, E., Bulf, H., Proietti, V., & Macchi Cassia, V. (2022). Infants' visual exploration strategies for adult and child faces. *Infancy, 27*(3). https://doi.org/10.1111/infa.12458

Conte, S., & Richards, J. (2021). Attention in early development. In O. Braddick (Ed.), *Oxford research encyclopedia of psychology.* Oxford University Press. https://doi.org/10.1093/acrefore/9780190236557.013.52

Cook, R. E., Martin, C. L., Nielson, M. G., & Xiao, S. X. (2022). Contemporary cognitive approaches to gender development: New schemas, new directions, and new conceptualizations of gender. In D. P. VanderLaan & W. I. Wong (Eds.), *Gender and sexuality development: Contemporary theory and research* (pp. 125–157). Springer International. https://doi.org/10.1007/978-3-030-84273-4_5

Cooke, J. E., Kochendorfer, L. B., Stuart-Parrigon, K. L., Koehn, A. J., & Kerns, K. A. (2018, September 20). Parent-child attachment and children's experience and regulation of emotion: A meta-analytic review. *Emotion.* https://doi.org/10.1037/emo0000504

Cooke, J. E., Kochendorfer, L. B., Stuart-Parrigon, K. L., Koehn, A. J., & Kerns, K. A. (2019). Parent-child attachment and children's experience and regulation of emotion: A meta-analytic review. *Emotion, 19*(6), 1103–1126. https://doi.org/10.1037/emo0000504

Cooley, J. L., Blossom, J. B., Tampke, E. C., & Fite, P. J. (2021). Emotion regulation attenuates the prospective links from peer victimization to internalizing symptoms during middle childhood. *Journal of Clinical Child and Adolescent Psychology, 51*(4), 495–504. https://doi.org/10.1080/15374416.2020.1731819

Cooley, J. L., & Fite, P. J. (2016). Peer victimization and forms of aggression during middle childhood: The role of emotion regulation. *Journal of Abnormal Child Psychology, 44*(3), 535–546. https://doi.org/10.1007/s10802-015-0051-6

Coome, L. A. (2021). Boys' rough-and-tumble play. In T. K. Shackelford & V. A. Weekes-Shackelford (Eds.), *Encyclopedia of evolutionary psychological science* (pp. 714–717). Springer International. https://doi.org/10.1007/978-3-319-19650-3_667

Cooper, A. R. (2022). Intravaginal embryo culture: A successful alternative to standard IVF that may improve access to care. *Current Opinion in Obstetrics and Gynecology, 34*(4), 179–183.

Cooper, S. M., Burnett, M., Golden, A., Butler-Barnes, S., & Inniss-Thompson, M. (2022). School discrimination, discipline inequities, and adjustment among black adolescent girls and boys: An intersectionality-informed approach. *Journal of Research on Adolescence, 32*(1), 170–190. https://doi.org/10.1111/jora.12716

Cooper, S. M., Kurtz-Costes, B., & Rowley, S. J. (2010). The schooling of African American children. In J. L. Meece & J. S. Eccles (Eds.), *Handbook of research on schools, schooling and human development* (pp. 275–292). Routledge.

Copeland, W. E., Worthman, C., Shanahan, L., Costello, E. J., & Angold, A. (2019). Early pubertal timing and testosterone associated with higher levels of adolescent depression in girls. *Journal of the American Academy of Child and Adolescent Psychiatry, 58*(12), 1197–1206. https://doi.org/10.1016/j.jaac.2019.02.007

Coplan, R. J., & Arbeau, K. A. (2009). Peer interactions and play in early childhood. In K. H. Rubin, W. M. Bukowski, & B. Laursen (Eds.), *Handbook of peer interactions, relationships, and groups* (pp. 143–161). Guilford Press.

Coplan, R. J., Rose-Krasnor, L., Weeks, M., Kingsbury, A., Kingsbury, M., & Bullock, A. (2013). Alone is a crowd: Social motivations, social withdrawal, and socioemotional functioning in later childhood. *Developmental Psychology, 49*(5), 861–875. https://doi.org/10.1037/a0028861

Corbetta, D., & Snapp-Childs, W. (2009). Seeing and touching: The role of sensory-motor experience on the development of infant reaching. *Infant Behavior &*

Development, 32(1), 44–58. https://doi.org/10.1016/j.infbeh.2008.10.004

Corby, B. C., Hodges, E. V. E., & Perry, D. G. (2007). Gender identity and adjustment in Black, Hispanic, and White preadolescents. *Developmental Psychology, 43*(1), 261–266. https://doi.org/10.1037/0012-1649.43.1.261

Cornell, D., Shukla, K., & Konold, T. (2015). Peer victimization and authoritative school climate: A multilevel approach. *Journal of Educational Psychology, 107*(4), 1186–1201. https://doi.org/10.1037/edu0000038

Corpus, J. H., & Good, K. (2020). The effects of praise on children's intrinsic motivation revisited. In *Psychological Perspectives on Praise* (pp. 39–47). Routledge.

Corrigall, K. A., & Schellenberg, E. G. (2015). Predicting who takes music lessons: Parent and child characteristics. *Frontiers in Psychology, 6*, 282. https://doi.org/10.3389/fpsyg.2015.00282

Corrigan, N. M., Yarnykh, V. L., Huber, E., Zhao, T. C., & Kuhl, P. K. (2022). Brain myelination at 7 months of age predicts later language development. *NeuroImage, 263*, 119641. https://doi.org/10.1016/j.neuroimage.2022.119641

Corsi, D. J., Donelle, J., Sucha, E., Hawken, S., Hsu, H., El-Chaâr, D., Bisnaire, L., Fell, D., Wen, S. W., & Walker, M. (2020). Maternal cannabis use in pregnancy and child neurodevelopmental outcomes. *Nature Medicine, 26*(10), 1536–1540. https://doi.org/10.1038/s41591-020-1002-5

Cosbey, J., Johnston, S. S., Dunn, M. L., & Bauman, M. (2012). Playground behaviors of children with and without sensory processing disorders. *OTJR: Occupational Therapy Journal of Research, 32*(2), 39–47. https://doi.org/10.3928/15394492-20110930-01

Costa, P. A., & Tasker, F. (2018). "We wanted a forever family": Altruistic, individualistic, and motivated reasoning motivations for adoption among LGBTQ individuals. *Journal of Family Issues, 39*(18), 4156–4178. https://doi.org/10.1177/0192513X18810948

Costello, M. A., Pettit, C., Hellwig, A. F., Hunt, G. L., Bailey, N. A., & Allen, J. P. (2024). Adolescent social learning within supportive friendships: Self-disclosure and relationship quality from adolescence to adulthood. *Journal of Research on Adolescence*, 1–13. https://doi.org/10.1111/jora.12947

Côté, S. L., Gonzalez-Barrero, A. M., & Byers-Heinlein, K. (2022). Multilingual toddlers' vocabulary development in two languages: Comparing bilinguals and trilinguals. *Journal of Child Language, 49*(1), 114–130. https://doi.org/10.1017/S030500092000077X

Cottini, M., Basso, D., & Palladino, P. (2018). The role of declarative and procedural metamemory in event-based prospective memory in school-aged children. *Journal of Experimental Child Psychology, 166*, 17–33. https://doi.org/10.1016/j.jecp.2017.08.002

Coubart, A., Izard, V., Spelke, E. S., Marie, J., & Streri, A. (2014). Dissociation between small and large numerosities in newborn infants. *Developmental Science, 17*(1), 11–22. https://doi.org/10.1111/desc.12108

Coughlin, C., Leckey, S., & Ghetti, S. (2018). Development of episodic memory: Processes and implications. In Ghetti. Simona (Ed.), *Stevens' handbook of experimental psychology and cognitive neuroscience* (pp. 1–25). John Wiley & Sons. https://doi.org/10.1002/9781119170174.epcn404

Coulombe, B. R., & Yates, T. M. (2022). Maternal caregiving, prosocial behavior, and self-esteem in middle childhood. *Social Development, 31*(3), 639–655. https://doi.org/10.1111/sode.12576

Courage, M. L. (2017). Screen media and the youngest viewers: Implications for attention and learning. In F. C. Blumberg & P. J. Brooks (Eds.), *Cognitive development in digital contexts* (pp. 3–28). Elsevier. https://doi.org/10.1016/B978-0-12-809481-5.00001-8

Courage, M. L., Edison, S. C., & Howe, M. L. (2004). Variability in the early development of visual self-recognition. *Infant Behavior & Development, 27*(4), 509–532. https://doi.org/10.1016/j.infbeh.2004.06.001

Courage, M. L., & Howe, M. L. (2022). Autobiographical memory: Early onset and developmental course. In M. L. Courage & N. Cowan (Eds.), *The development of memory in infancy and childhood* (3rd ed., pp. 238–261). Psychology Press.

Courage, M. L., Reynolds, G. D., & Richards, J. E. (2006). Infants' attention to patterned stimuli: Developmental change from 3 to 12 months of age. *Child Development, 77*(3), 680–695. https://doi.org/10.1111/j.1467-8624.2006.00897.x

Covington, L. B., Patterson, F., Hale, L. E., Teti, D. M., Cordova, A., Mayberry, S., & Hauenstein, E. J. (2021). The contributory role of the family context in early childhood sleep health: A systematic review. *Sleep Health, 7*(2), 254–265. https://doi.org/10.1016/j.sleh.2020.11.010

Cowan, N. (2023). Working memory and child development with its windfalls and pitfalls. In R. Logie, N. Cowan, S. Gathercole, R. Engle, & Z. Wen (Eds.), *Memory in science for society: There is nothing as practical as a good theory*. Oxford University Press. https://doi.org/10.1093/oso/9780192849069.003.0009

Cowan, N., Hismjatullina, A., AuBuchon, A. M., Saults, J. S., Horton, N., Leadbitter, K., & Towse, J. (2010). With development, list recall includes more chunks, not just larger ones. *Developmental Psychology, 46*(5), 1119–1131. https://doi.org/10.1037/a0020618

Cox, C. M., Thoma, M. E., Tchangalova, N., Mburu, G., Bornstein, M. J., Johnson, C. L., & Kiarie, J. (2022). Infertility prevalence and the methods of estimation from 1990 to 2021: A systematic review and meta-analysis. *Human Reproduction Open*, hoac051. https://doi.org/10.1093/hropen/hoac051

Cox, C. R., & Haebig, E. (2022). Child-oriented word associations improve models of early word learning. *Behavior Research Methods, 55*, 16–37. https://doi.org/10.3758/S13428-022-01790-Y

Coyle, E. F., & Fulcher, M. (2022). Social influences on gender development: Theory and context. In D. P. VanderLaan & W. I. Wong (Eds.), *Gender and sexuality development: Contemporary theory and research* (pp. 101–124). Springer International. https://doi.org/10.1007/978-3-030-84273-4_4

Coyle, S., Demaray, M. K., Malecki, C. K., Tennant, J. E., & Klossing, J. (2017). The associations among sibling and peer-bullying, social support and internalizing behaviors. *Child & Youth Care Forum, 46*(6), 895–922. https://doi.org/10.1007/s10566-017-9412-3

Coyle, T. R. (2021). Defining and measuring intelligence: The psychometrics and neuroscience of g. In A. K. Barbey, S. Karama, & R. J. Haier (Eds.), *The Cambridge handbook of intelligence and cognitive neuroscience* (pp. 3–25). Cambridge University Press. https://doi.org/10.1017/9781108635462.003

Coyne, S. M., Linder, J. R., Rasmussen, E. E., Nelson, D. A., & Birkbeck, V. (2016). Pretty as a princess: Longitudinal effects of engagement with Disney princesses on gender stereotypes, body esteem, and prosocial behavior in children. *Child Development, 87*(6), 1909–1925. https://doi.org/10.1111/cdev.12569

Coyne, S. M., & Stockdale, L. (2021). Growing up with Grand Theft Auto: A 10-year study of longitudinal growth of violent video game play in adolescents.

Cyberpsychology, Behavior, and Social Networking, 24(1), 11-16. https://doi.org/10.1089/cyber.2020.0049

Coyne, S. M., Warburton, W., Swit, C., Stockdale, L., & Dyer, W. J. (2023). Who is most at risk for developing physical aggression after playing violent video games? An individual differences perspective from early adolescence to emerging adulthood. *Journal of Youth and Adolescence, 52*(4), 719-733. https://doi.org/10.1007/s10964-023-01739-0

Coyne, S. M., Weinstein, E., Sheppard, J. A., James, S., Gale, M., Van Alfen, M., Ririe, N., Monson, C., Ashby, S., Weston, A., & Banks, K. (2023). Analysis of social media use, mental health, and gender identity among US youths. *JAMA Network Open, 6*(7), e2324389. https://doi.org/10.1001/jamanetworkopen.2023.24389

Craig, W., Boniel-Nissim, M., King, N., Walsh, S. D., Boer, M., Donnelly, P. D., Harel-Fisch, Y., Malinowska-Cieślik, M., Gaspar de Matos, M., Cosma, A., Van den Eijnden, R., Vieno, A., Elgar, F. J., Molcho, M., Bjereld, Y., & Pickett, W. (2020). Social media use and cyber-bullying: A cross-national analysis of young people in 42 countries. *Journal of Adolescent Health,* S100-S108. https://doi.org/10.1016/j.jadohealth.2020.03.006 66(6, Supplement

Crain, W. C. (2016). *Theories of development: Concepts and applications.* Routledge.

Cramm, H., Mccoll, M. A., Aiken, A. B., & Williams, A. (2019). The mental health of military-connected children: A scoping review. *Journal of Child and Family Studies, 28,* 1725-1735. https://doi.org/10.1007/s10826-019-01402-y

Crane, T. (2016). The unity of unconsciousness. *Proceedings of the Aristotelian Society, 117*(1), 1-21. https://doi.org/10.1093/arisoc/aox001

Crasta, J. E., Salzinger, E., Lin, M. H., Gavin, W. J., & Davies, P. L. (2020). Sensory processing and attention profiles among children with sensory processing disorders and autism spectrum disorders. *Frontiers in Integrative Neuroscience, 14,* 22. https://doi.org/10.3389/fnint.2020.00022

Crawford, A. D., Mcglothen-Bell, K., Recto, P., Mcgrath, J. M., Scott, L., Brownell, E. A., & Cleveland, L. M. (2002). Stigmatization of pregnant individuals with opioid use disorder. *Women's Health Reports, 3*(1), 172-179. https://doi.org/10.1089/WHR.2021.0112

Creech, S. K., Hadley, W., & Borsari, B. (2014). The impact of military deployment and reintegration on children and parenting: A systematic review. *Professional Psychology: Research and Practice, 45*(6), 452-463. https://doi.org/10.1037/a0035055

Crenshaw, K. (1989). *Demarginalizing the intersection of race and sex: A black feminist critique of antidiscrimination doctrine, feminist theory and antiracist politics.* University of Chicago Legal Forum. 1989(8) https://chicagounbound.uchicago.edu/uclf/vol1989/iss1/8

Crespo, L. M., Trentacosta, C. J., Aikins, D., & Wargo-Aikins, J. (2017). Maternal emotion regulation and children's behavior problems: The mediating role of child emotion regulation. *Journal of Child and Family Studies, 26*(10), 2797-2809. https://doi.org/10.1007/s10826-017-0791-8

Cresswell, L., Faltyn, M., Lawrence, C., Tsai, Z., Owais, S., Savoy, C., Lipman, E., & Van Lieshout, R. J. (2022). Cognitive and mental health of young mothers' offspring: A meta-analysis. *Pediatrics, 150*(5), e2022057561. https://doi.org/10.1542/peds.2022-057561

Crissman, H. P., Berger, M. B., Graham, L. F., & Dalton, V. K. (2017). Transgender demographics: A household probability sample of US adults, 2014. *American Journal of Public Health, 107*(2), 213-215. https://doi.org/10.2105/AJPH.2016.303571

Critz, C., Blake, K., & Nogueira, E. (2015). Sensory processing challenges in children. *Journal for Nurse Practitioners, 11*(7), 710-716. https://doi.org/10.1016/j.nurpra.2015.04.016

Crocetti, E. (2017). Identity formation in adolescence: The dynamic of forming and consolidating identity commitments. *Child Development Perspectives, 11*(2), 145-150. https://doi.org/10.1111/cdep.12226

Crocetti, E., Klimstra, T., Keijsers, L., Hale lii, W. W., & Meeus, W. H. J. (2009). Anxiety trajectories and identity development in adolescence: A five-wave longitudinal study. *Journal of Youth & Adolescence, 38*(6), 839-849. https://doi.org/10.1007/s10964-008-9302-y

Crockenberg, S. C., & Leerkes, E. M. (2004). Infant and maternal behaviors regulate infant reactivity to novelty at 6 months. *Developmental Psychology, 40*(6), 1123-1132. https://doi.org/10.1037/0012-1649.40.6.1123

Crone, E. A., & Achterberg, M. (2022). Prosocial development in adolescence. *Current Opinion in Psychology, 44,* 220-225. https://doi.org/10.1016/j.copsyc.2021.09.020

Crone, E. A., & Fuligni, A. J. (2020). Self and others in adolescence. *Annual Review of Psychology, 71*(1), 447-469. https://doi.org/10.1146/annurev-psych-010419-050937

Crone, E. A., Peters, S., & Steinbeis, N. (2018). Executive function: Development in adolescence. In S. A. Wiebe & J. Karbach (Eds.), *Executive function: Development across the life span* (pp. 58-72). Routledge.

Crone, E. A., & Steinbeis, N. (2017). Neural perspectives on cognitive control development during childhood and adolescence. *Trends in Cognitive Sciences, 21*(3), 205-215. https://doi.org/10.1016/J.TICS.2017.01.003

Crosnoe, R., Benner, A. D., Crosnoe, R., & Benner, A. D. (2015). Children at school. In R. M. Lerner (Ed.), *Handbook of child psychology and developmental science* (pp. 1-37). John Wiley & Sons. https://doi.org/10.1002/9781118963418.childpsy407

Cross, C. P., Copping, L. T., & Campbell, A. (2011). Sex differences in impulsivity: A meta-analysis. *Psychological Bulletin, 137*(1), 97-130. https://doi.org/10.1037/a0021591

Cross, J. R. (2018). Crowds. In R. J. R. Levesque (Ed.), *Encyclopedia of adolescence* (pp. 573-580). Springer. https://doi.org/10.1007/978-1-4419-1695-2_44

Crowell, J. A. (2021). Development of emotion regulation in typically developing children. *Child and Adolescent Psychiatric Clinics, 30*(3), 467-474. https://doi.org/10.1016/j.chc.2021.04.001

Cuartas, J. (2018). Neighborhood crime undermines parenting: Violence in the vicinity of households as a predictor of aggressive discipline. *Child Abuse & Neglect, 76,* 388-399. https://doi.org/10.1016/J.CHIABU.2017.12.006

Cuartas, J. (2021). Corporal punishment and early childhood development in 49 low- and middle-income countries. *Child Abuse & Neglect, 120,* 105205. https://doi.org/10.1016/j.chiabu.2021.105205

Cuartas, J. (2022). Corporal punishment and child development in low- and middle-income countries: Progress, challenges, and directions. *Child Psychiatry & Human Development, 54,* 1607-1623. https://doi.org/10.1007/s10578-022-01362-3

Cuba Bustinza, C., Adams, R. E., Claussen, A. H., Vitucci, D., Danielson, M. L., Holbrook, J. R., Charania, S. N., Yamamoto, K., Nidey, N., & Froehlich, T. E. (2022). Factors associated with bullying victimization and bullying perpetration in children and adolescents with ADHD: 2016 to 2017 National Survey of Children's Health. *Journal of Attention Disorders, 26*(12), 1535-1548. https://doi.org/10.1177/10870547221085502

Cuellar, J., Jones, D. J., & Sterrett, E. (2013). Examining parenting in the neighborhood context: A review. *Journal of Child* and Family Studies, 24(1), 195–219. https://doi.org/10.1007/s10826-013-9826-y

Cuevas, K., & Bell, M. A. (2010). Developmental progression of looking and reaching performance on the A-not-B task. Developmental Psychology, 46(5), 1363–1371. https://doi.org/10.1037/a0020185

Cuevas, K., & Davinson, K. (2022). The development of infant memory. In L. Courage. Mary & Nelson. Cowan (Eds.), The development of memory in infancy and childhood (pp. 31–59). Psychology Press. https://doi.org/10.4324/9781003016533-2

Cuevas, K., & Davinson, K. (2022). The development of infant memory. In M. L. Courage & N. Cowan (Eds.), The development of memory in infancy and childhood (pp. 31–59). Psychology Press. https://doi.org/10.4324/9781003016533-2

Cuevas, K., & Sheya, A. (2019). Ontogenesis of learning and memory: Biopsychosocial and dynamical systems perspectives. Developmental Psychobiology, 61(3), 402–415. https://doi.org/10.1002/dev.21817

Cunitz, K., Dölitzsch, C., Kösters, M., Willmund, G. D., Zimmermann, P., Bühler, A. H., Fegert, J. M., Ziegenhain, U., & Kölch, M. (2019). Parental military deployment as risk factor for children's mental health: A meta-analytical review. Child and Adolescent Psychiatry and Mental Health, 13(1), 1–10. https://doi.org/10.1186/s13034-019-0287-y

Cunningham, C., Patton, D., Moore, Z., O'Connor, T., Bux, D., & Nugent, L. (2021). Neonatal kangaroo care—What we know and how we can improve its practice: An evidence review. Journal of Neonatal Nursing, 28(6), 383–387. https://doi.org/10.1016/j.jnn.2021.10.004

Curby, T. W., Zinsser, K. M., Gordon, R. A., Ponce, E., Syed, G., & Peng, F. (2022). Emotion-focused teaching practices and preschool children's social and learning behaviors. Emotion, 22, 1869–1885. https://doi.org/10.1037/emo0000988

Curenton, S. M., Harris, K., Rochester, S. E., Sims, J., & Ibekwe-Okafor, N. (2022). Promoting racial literacy in early childhood: Storybooks and conversations with young black children. Child Development Perspectives, 16(1), 3–9. https://doi.org/10.1111/cdep.12440

Curley, J. P., Mashoodh, R., & Champagne, F. A. (2023). Transgenerational epigenetics. In T. O. Tollefsbol (Ed.), Handbook of epigenetics (3rd ed., pp. 465–478). Academic Press. https://doi.org/10.1016/B978-0-323-91909-8.00023-2

Cutuli, J. J., Herbers, J. E., Masten, A. S., & Reed, M. G. J. (2021). Resilience in development. In C. R. Snyder, S. J. Lopez, L. M. Edwards, & S. C. Marques (Eds.), The Oxford handbook of positive psychology (pp. 74–88).

Cvencek, D., Fryberg, S. A., Covarrubias, R., & Meltzoff, A. N. (2018). Self-concepts, self-esteem, and academic achievement of minority and majority North American elementary school children. Child Development, 89(4), 1099–1109. https://doi.org/10.1111/cdev.12802

Cvencek, D., & Greenwald, A. G. (2020). Self-esteem, Expressions of. In The Wiley encyclopedia of personality and individual differences (pp. 399–404). Wiley. https://doi.org/10.1002/9781119547174.ch245

Cvencek, D., Meltzoff, A. N., & Greenwald, A. G. (2011). Math-gender stereotypes in elementary school children. Child Development, 82(3), 766–779. https://doi.org/10.1111/j.1467-8624.2010.01529.x

Cyrus, E., Coudray, M. S., Kiplagat, S., Mariano, Y., Noel, I., Galea, J. T., Hadley, D., Dévieux, J. G., & Wagner, E. (2021). A review investigating the relationship between cannabis use and adolescent cognitive functioning. Current Opinion in Psychology, 38, 38–48. https://doi.org/10.1016/j.copsyc.2020.07.006

D., Kochanek, K., Q., Xu, J., & Arias, E. (2020, December). Mortality in the United States, 2019. NCHS Data Brief, (no 395). April 14, 2021, from https://www.cdc.gov/nchs/data/databriefs/db395-H.pdf

Dąbrowska, E. (2015). What exactly is universal grammar, and has anyone seen it? Frontiers in Psychology, 6, 852. https://doi.org/10.3389/fpsyg.2015.00852

Dacre Pool, L., & Qualter, P. (2012). Improving emotional intelligence and emotional self-efficacy through a teaching intervention for university students. Learning and Individual Differences, 22(3), 306–312. https://doi.org/10.1016/j.lindif.2012.01.010

Dadds, M. R., & Tully, L. A. (2019). What is it to discipline a child: What should it be? A reanalysis of time-out from the perspective of child mental health, attachment, and trauma. American Psychologist, 74(7), 794–808. https://doi.org/10.1037/amp0000449

Dagan, O., & Sagi-Schwartz, A. (2018). Early attachment network with mother and father: An unsettled issue. Child Development Perspectives, 12(2), 115–121. https://doi.org/10.1111/cdep.12272

Dagli, A. I., Mathews, J., & Williams, C. A. (2021). Angelman Syndrome. In M. P. Adam, J. Feldman, G. M. Mirzaa, R. A. Pagon, S. E. Wallace, L. J. Bean, K. W. Gripp, & A. Amemiya (Eds.), GeneReviews®. University of Washington. http://www.ncbi.nlm.nih.gov/books/NBK1144/

Dahl, A. (2018). New beginnings: An interactionist and constructivist approach to early moral development. Human Development, 61(4–5), 232–247. https://doi.org/10.1159/000492801

Dahl, A. (2019). The science of early moral development: On defining, constructing, and studying morality from birth. Advances in Child Development and Behavior, 56, 1–35. https://doi.org/10.1016/bs.acdb.2018.11.001

Dahl, A., & Brownell, C. A. (2019). The social origins of human prosociality. Current Directions in Psychological Science, 28(3), 274–279. https://doi.org/10.1177/0963721419830386

Dahl, A., Campos, J. J., Anderson, D. I., Uchiyama, I., Witherington, D. C., Ueno, M., & Barbu-Roth, M. (2013). The epigenesis of wariness of heights. Psychological Science, 24, 1361–1367. https://doi.org/10.1177/0956797613476047

Dahl, A., Goeltz, M. T., & Brownell, C. A. (2022). Scaffolding the emergence of infant helping: A longitudinal experiment. Child Development, 93(3), 751–759. https://doi.org/10.1111/cdev.13710

Dahl, A., & Paulus, M. (2019). From interest to obligation: The gradual development of human altruism. Child Development Perspectives, 13(1), 10–14. https://doi.org/10.1111/cdep.12298

Dai, K., Shen, S., & Cheng, C. (2022). Evaluation and analysis of the projected population of China. Scientific Reports, 12(1), 3644. https://doi.org/10.1038/s41598-022-07646-x

Dailey, S., & Bergelson, E. (2022). Language input to infants of different socioeconomic statuses: A quantitative meta-analysis. Developmental Science, 25(3), e13192. https://doi.org/10.1111/desc.13192

Dale, N. J., Sakkalou, E., O'Reilly, M. A., Springall, C., Sakki, H., Glew, S., Pissaridou, E., De Haan, M., & Salt, A. T. (2019). Home-based early intervention in infants and young children with visual impairment using the Developmental Journal: Longitudinal cohort study. Developmental Medicine & Child Neurology, 61(6), 697–709. https://doi.org/10.1111/dmcn.14081

Dale, N., Sakkalou, E., O'Reilly, M., Springall, C., De Haan, M., & Salt, A. (2017). Functional vision and cognition in infants with congenital disorders of the peripheral visual system. *Developmental Medicine & Child Neurology, 59*(7), 725–731. https://doi.org/10.1111/dmcn.13429

Dale, P. S., Paul, A., Rosholm, M., & Bleses, D. (2023). Prediction from early childhood vocabulary to academic achievement at the end of compulsory schooling in Denmark. *International Journal of Behavioral Development, 47*(2), 123–134. https://doi.org/10.1177/01650254221116878

Daley, C. E., & Onwuegbuzie, A. J. (2011). Race and intelligence. In R. J. Sternberg & S. B. Kaufman (Eds.), *The Cambridge handbook of intelligence* (pp. 293–308). Cambridge University Press.

Daley, T. C., Whaley, S. E., Sigman, M. D., Espinosa, M. P., & Neumann, C. (2003). IQ on the rise: The Flynn effect in rural Kenyan children. *Psychological Science, 14*(3), 215–219. https://doi.org/10.1111/1467-9280.02434

Dallagiovanna, C., Vanni, V. S., Somigliana, E., Busnelli, A., Papaleo, E., Villanacci, R., Candiani, M., & Reschini, M. (2021). Risk factors for monozygotic twins in IVF-ICSI cycles: A case-control study. *Reproductive Sciences, 28*(5), 1421–1427. https://doi.org/10.1007/s43032-020-00406-0

Dalle Grave, R., Sartirana, M., Sermattei, S., & Calugi, S. (2021). Treatment of eating disorders in adults versus adolescents: Similarities and differences. *Clinical Therapeutics, 43*(1), 70–84. https://doi.org/10.1016/j.clinthera.2020.10.015

Damon, W. (1977). *The social world of the child*. Jossey-Bass.

Damon, W. (1988). *The moral child*. Free Press.

Daniel, S. K., Abdel-Baki, R., & Hall, G. B. (2020). The Protective Effect of Emotion Regulation on Child and Adolescent Wellbeing. *Journal of Child & Family Studies, 29*(7), 2010–2027. https://doi.org/10.1007/s10826-020-01731-3

Daniels, H. (2017). *Introduction to Vygotsky* (3rd ed.). Taylor and Francis. https://doi.org/10.4324/9781315647654

Daniels, H. (2017). Introduction to the third edition. In H. Daniels (Ed.), *Introduction to Vygotsky* (pp. 1–34). Taylor and Francis. https://doi.org/10.4324/9781315647654

Daoud, R., Starkey, L., Eppel, E., Vo, T. D., & Sylvester, A. (2021). The educational value of internet use in the home for school children: A systematic review of literature. *Journal of Research on Technology in Education, 53*, 353–374. https://doi.org/10.1080/15391523.2020.1783402

Das, J. K., Salam, R. A., Thornburg, K. L., Prentice, A. M., Campisi, S., Lassi, Z. S., Koletzko, B., & Bhutta, Z. A. (2017). Nutrition in adolescents: Physiology, metabolism, and nutritional needs. *Annals of the New York Academy of Sciences*, 21–33. https://doi.org/10.1111/nyas.13330 *1393*(1)

Dasen, P. R. (1975). Concrete operational development in three cultures. *Journal of Cross-Cultural Psychology, 6*(2), 156–172. https://doi.org/10.1177/002202217562002

Dasen, P. R. (1994). Culture and cognitive development from a Piagetian perspective. In W. J. Lonner & R. Malpass (Eds.), *Psychology and culture* (pp. 145–149). Allyn & Bacon.

Dasen, P. R. (2022). Culture and cognitive development. *Journal of Cross-Cultural Psychology, 53*(7/8), 789–816.

Dasen, P. R., & Heron, A. (1981). Crosscultural tests of Piaget's theory. In H. C. Triandis & A. Heron (Eds.), *Handbook of cross-cultural psychology: Developmental psychology* (Vol. 4, pp. 295–341). Allyn & Bacon.

Dasgupta, N., & Stout, J. G. (2014). Girls and women in science, technology, engineering, and mathematics. *Policy Insights from the Behavioral and Brain Sciences, 1*(1), 21–29. https://doi.org/10.1177/2372732214549471

Dasgupta, N., Thiem, K. C., Coyne, A. E., Laws, H., Barbieri, M., & Wells, R. S. (2022). The impact of communal learning contexts on adolescent self-concept and achievement: Similarities and differences across race and gender. *Journal of Personality and Social Psychology, 123*, 537–558. https://doi.org/10.1037/pspi0000377

Dash, G. F., Karalunas, S. L., Kenyon, E. A., Carter, E. K., Mooney, M. A., Nigg, J. T., & Feldstein Ewing, S. W. (2023). Gene-by-environment interaction effects of social adversity on externalizing behavior in ABCD youth. *Behavior Genetics, 53*(3), 219–231. https://doi.org/10.1007/s10519-023-10136-z

Daspe, M., Arbel, R., Ramos, M. C., Shapiro, L. A. S., & Margolin, G. (2019). Deviant peers and adolescent risky behaviors: The protective effect of nonverbal display of parental warmth. *Journal of Research on Adolescence, 29*(4), 863–878. https://doi.org/10.1111/jora.12418

Datta, N., Matheson, B. E., Citron, K., Van Wye, E. M., & Lock, J. D. (2023). Evidence based update on psychosocial treatments for eating disorders in children and adolescents. *Journal of Clinical Child & Adolescent Psychology, 52*(2), 159–170. https://doi.org/10.1080/15374416.2022.2109650

Davidov, M. (2021). Cultural moderation of the effects of parenting: Answered and unanswered questions. *Child Development Perspectives, 15*(3), 189–195. https://doi.org/10.1111/cdep.12422

Davidson, C., Shing, Y. L., McKay, C., Rafetseder, E., & Wijeakumar, S. (2023). The first year in formal schooling improves working memory and academic abilities. *Developmental Cognitive Neuroscience, 60*, 101205. https://doi.org/10.1016/j.dcn.2023.101205

Davidson, K. W., Barry, M. J., Mangione, C. M., Cabana, M., Chelmow, D., Coker, T. R., Davis, E. M., Donahue, K. E., Jaén, C. R., Kubik, M., Li, L., Ogedegbe, G., Pbert, L., Ruiz, J. M., Silverstein, M., Stevermer, J., & Wong, J. B. (2022). Screening for eating disorders in adolescents and adults: US preventive services task force recommendation statement. *JAMA, 327*(11), 1061–1067. https://doi.org/10.1001/jama.2022.1806

Davidson, R. D., O'Hara, K. L., & Beck, C. J. A. (2014). Psychological and biological processes in children associated with high conflict parental divorce. *Juvenile and Family Court Journal, 65*(1), 29–44. https://doi.org/10.1111/jfcj.12015

Davies, P., & Martin, M. (2014). Children's coping and adjustment in high-conflict homes: The reformulation of emotional security theory. *Child Development Perspectives, 8*(4), 242–249. https://doi.org/10.1111/cdep.12094

Davis, J. P., Ingram, K. M., Merrin, G. J., & Espelage, D. L. (2020). Exposure to parental and community violence and the relationship to bullying perpetration and victimization among early adolescents: A parallel process growth mixture latent transition analysis. *Scandinavian Journal of Psychology, 61*(1), 77–89. https://doi.org/10.1111/sjop.12493

Davis, J. T. M., & Hines, M. (2020). How large are gender differences in toy preferences? A systematic review and meta-analysis of toy preference research. *Archives of Sexual Behavior, 49*(2), 373–394. https://doi.org/10.1007/s10508-019-01624-7

Davis, P. E., Meins, E., & Fernyhough, C. (2014). Children with imaginary companions focus on mental characteristics when describing their real-life friends. *Infant and Child Development, 23*(6), 622–633. https://doi.org/10.1002/icd.1869

Davis, S. M., Soares, K., Howell, S., Cree-Green, M., Buyers, E., Johnson, J., & Tartaglia, N. R. (2020). Diminished ovarian reserve in girls and adolescents with trisomy X syndrome. *Reproductive Sciences,*

27, 1985–1991. https://doi.org/10.1007/s43032-020-00216-4

Davis-Kean, P. E., Jager, J., & Andrew Collins, W. (2009). The self in action: An emerging link between self-beliefs and behaviors in middle childhood. *Child Development Perspectives*, *3*(3), 184–188. https://doi.org/10.1111/j.1750-8606.2009.00104.x

Davis-Kean, P. E., Tighe, L. A., & Waters, N. E. (2021). The role of parent educational attainment in parenting and children's development. *Current Directions in Psychological Science*, *30*(2), 186–192. https://doi.org/10.1177/0963721421993116

Dawson, T. L. (2002). New tools, new insights: Kohlberg's moral judgement stages revisited. *International Journal of Behavioral Development*, *26*(2), 154–166. https://doi.org/10.1080/01650250042000645

Day, J., Savani, S., Krempley, B. D., Nguyen, M., & Kitlinska, J. B. (2016). Influence of paternal preconception exposures on their offspring: Through epigenetics to phenotype. *American Journal of Stem Cells*, *5*(1), 11–18.

Day, R. D., Jones-Sanpei, H., Smith Price, J. L., Orthner, D. K., Hair, E. C., Moore, K. A., & Kaye, K. (2009). Family processes and adolescent religiosity and religious practice: View from the NLSY97. *Marriage and Family Review*, *45*(2–3), 289–309. https://doi.org/10.1080/01494920902735109

De Beritto, T. V. (2020). Newborn sleep: Patterns, interventions, and outcomes. *Pediatric Annals*, *49*(2), e82–e87. https://doi.org/10.3928/19382359-20200122-01

De France, K., & Hollenstein, T. (2022). The development of cognitive reappraisal for regulating emotions: Infancy to adolescence. In D. Dukes, A. C. Samson, & E. A. Walle (Eds.), *The Oxford handbook of emotional development* (p. 0). Oxford University Press. https://doi.org/10.1093/oxfordhb/9780198855903.013.5

De Genna, N., Larkby, C., & Cornelius, M. (2011). Pubertal timing and early sexual intercourse in the offspring of teenage mothers. *Journal of Youth & Adolescence*, *40*(10), 1315–1328. https://doi.org/10.1007/s10964-010-9609-3

De Houwer, A., Miller, D., Bayram, F., Rothman, J., & Serratrice, L. (2018). The role of language input environments for language outcomes and language acquisition in young bilingual children. In D. Miller, F. Bayram, J. Rothman, & L. Serratrice (Eds.), *Bilingual cognition and language: The state of the science across its subfields* (pp. 127–154).

De la, Barrera., U, Villanueva., L, Montoya-Castilla., I, & Prado-Gascó, V. (2021). How much emotional attention is appropriate? The influence of emotional intelligence and subjective well-being on adolescents' stress. *Current Psychology*, *42*, 5131–5143. https://doi.org/10.1007/s12144-021-01763-y

De Lange, J., Baams, L., Van Bergen, D. D., Bos, H. M. W., & Bosker, R. J. (2022). Minority stress and suicidal ideation and suicide attempts among LGBT adolescents and young adults: A meta-analysis. *LGBT Health*, *9*(4). https://doi.org/10.1089/lgbt.2021.0106

De Los, Reyes., A, Ohannessian., M, C., & Racz, S. J. (2019). Discrepancies between adolescent and parent reports about family relationships. *Child Development Perspectives*, *13*(1), 53–58. https://doi.org/10.1111/cdep.12306

De Maio, F., Ansell, D., & Shah, R. C. (2020). Racial/ethnic minority segregation and low birth weight in five North American cities. *Ethnicity & Health*, *25*, 915–924. https://doi.org/10.1080/13557858.2018.1492706

De Paepe, M. (2022). Multiple gestation: The biology of twinning. In C. J. Lockwood, J. Copel, J. Louis, L. Dugoff, R. M. Silver, R. Resnik, & T. Moore (Eds.), *Creasy and Resnik's maternal-fetal medicine—e-book principles and practice*. Elsevier.

De Rosnay, M., Fink, E., Begeer, S., Slaughter, V., Peterson, C., Astington, J. W., Jenkins, J. M., Banerjee, R., Henderson, L., Brinton, B., Fujiki, M., Deleau, M., Rosnay, M., Hughes, C. H., Dorval, B., Eckerman, C. O., Ervin-Tripp, S., Frith, U., Lalonde, C. E., & … Liu, D. (2014). Talking theory of mind talk: Young school-aged children's everyday conversation and understanding of mind and emotion. *Journal of Child Language*, *41*(5), 1179–1193. https://doi.org/10.1017/S0305000913000433

Deák, G. O. (2006). Do children really confuse appearance and reality? *Trends in Cognitive Sciences*, *10*(12), 546–550. https://doi.org/10.1016/j.tics.2006.09.012

Deardorff, J., Abrams, B., Ekwaru, J. P., & Rehkopf, D. H. (2014). Socioeconomic status and age at menarche: An examination of multiple indicators in an ethnically diverse cohort. *Annals of Epidemiology*, *24*(10), 727–733. https://doi.org/10.1016/j.annepidem.2014.07.002

Deardorff, J., Hoyt, L. T., Carter, R., & Shirtcliff, E. A. (2019). Next steps in puberty research: Broadening the lens toward understudied populations. *Journal of Research on Adolescence*, *29*(1), 133–154. https://doi.org/10.1111/jora.12402

Deary, I. J., Cox, S. R., & Hill, W. D. (2021). Genetic variation, brain, and intelligence differences. *Molecular Psychiatry*, *27*, 335–353. https://doi.org/10.1038/s41380-021-01027-y

Deater-Deckard, K. (2001). Nonshared environmental processes in social emotional development: An observational study of identical twin differences in the preschool period. *Developmental Science*, *4*(2), 1–7.

Deater-Deckard, K., & O'Connor, T. (2000). Parent-child mutuality in early childhood: Two behavioral genetic studies. *Developmental Psychology*, *36*(5), 561–571.

Deaton, A. E., Sheiner, E., Wainstock, T., Landau, D., & Walfisch, A. (2017). 613: Does lack of prenatal care predict later lack of child care? *American Journal of Obstetrics and Gynecology*, *216*(1), S359–S360. https://doi.org/10.1016/j.ajog.2016.11.347

DeCamp, W., & Ferguson, C. J. (2017). The impact of degree of exposure to violent video games, family background, and other factors on youth violence. *Journal of Youth and Adolescence*, *46*(2), 388–400. https://doi.org/10.1007/s10964-016-0561-8

Declercq, E. R., Sakala, C., Corry, M. P., Applebaum, S., & Herrlich, A. (2014). Major survey findings of Listening to MothersSM III: Pregnancy and birth. *Journal of Perinatal Education*, *23*(1), 9–16. https://doi.org/10.1891/1058-1243.23.1.9

Dediu, D., & Christiansen, M. H. (2016). Language evolution: Constraints and opportunities from modern genetics. *Topics in Cognitive Science*, *8*(2), 361–370. https://doi.org/10.1111/tops.12195

Deep, N. L., Purcell, P. L., Gordon, K. A., Papsin, B. C., Roland, J. T., Jr., & Waltzman, S. B. (2021). Cochlear implantation in infants: Evidence of safety. *Trends in Hearing*, *25*, 23312165211014696. https://doi.org/10.1177/23312165211014695

de Faria, O., Pivonkova, H., Varga, B., Timmler, S., Evans, K. A., & Káradóttir, R. T. (2021). Periods of synchronized myelin changes shape brain function and plasticity. *Nature Neuroscience*, *24*(11), 1508–1521. https://doi.org/10.1038/S41593-021-00917-2

Defoe, I. N., Treffers, S., & Stams, G. J. (2023). Research review: Siblings matter. A multi-level meta-analysis on the association between cannabis use among adolescent siblings. *Journal of Child Psychology and Psychiatry*, *64*(11), 1532–1544. https://doi.org/10.1111/jcpp.13836

de Haan, B., Mienko, J. A., & Eddy, J. M. (2019). The interface of child welfare and parental criminal justice involvement: Policy and practice implications for the children of incarcerated parents. In J. M. Eddy & J. Poehlmann-Tynan (Eds.), *Handbook on children with incarcerated parents: Research, policy, and practice* (pp. 279–294). Springer International. https://doi.org/10.1007/978-3-030-16707-3_19

Dehaene-Lambertz, G. (2017). The human infant brain: A neural architecture able to learn language. *Psychonomic Bulletin & Review, 24*(1), 48–55. https://doi.org/10.3758/s13423-016-1156-9

Dehaene-Lambertz, G., & Spelke, E. S. (2015). The infancy of the human brain. *Neuron, 88*(1), 93–109. https://doi.org/10.1016/j.neuron.2015.09.026

de Jonge, A., Geerts, C., van der Goes, B., Mol, B., Buitendijk, S., & Nijhuis, J. (2015). Perinatal mortality and morbidity up to 28 days after birth among 743 070 low-risk planned home and hospital births: A cohort study based on three merged national perinatal databases. *BJOG: An International Journal of Obstetrics & Gynaecology, 122*(5), 720–728. https://doi.org/10.1111/1471-0528.13084

Del Rosario, C., Slevin, M., Molloy, E. J., Quigley, J., & Nixon, E. (2021). How to use the Bayley scales of infant and toddler development. *Archives of Disease in Childhood: Education and Practice Edition, 106*, 108–112. https://doi.org/10.1136/archdischild-2020-319063

Del Toro, J., Hughes, D., & Way, N. (2021). Inter-relations between ethnic-racial discrimination and ethnic-racial identity among early adolescents. *Child Development, 92*(1), e106–e125. https://doi.org/10.1111/cdev.13424

DelGiudice, M. (2018). Middle childhood: An evolutionary-developmental synthesis. In N. Halfon, C. B. Forrest, R. M. Lerner, & E. M. Faustman (Eds.), *Handbook of life course health development* (pp. 95–107). Springer. https://doi.org/10.1007/978-3-319-47143-3_5

Della Longa, L. (2019). Tune to touch: Affective touch enhances learning of face identity in 4-month-old infants. *Developmental Cognitive Neuroscience, 35*, 42–46. https://doi.org/10.1016/j.dcn.2017.11.002

Della Longa, L., Filippetti, M. L., Dragovic, D., & Farroni, T. (2020). Synchrony of caresses: Does affective touch help infants to detect body-related visual–tactile synchrony? *Frontiers in Psychology, 10*, 2944. https://www.frontiersin.org/articles/10.3389/fpsyg.2019.02944

Delsing, M. J. M. H., Bogt, ter., M, T. F., Engels, R. C. M. E., & Meeus, W. H. J. (2007). Adolescents' peer crowd identification in the Netherlands: Structure and associations with problem behaviors. *Journal of Research on Adolescence, 17*(2), 467–480. https://doi.org/10.1111/j.1532-7795.2007.00530.x

de Maat, D. A., Schuurmans, I. K., Jongerling, J., Metcalf, S. A., Lucassen, N., Franken, I. H. A., Prinzie, P., & Jansen, P. W. (2022). Early life stress and behavior problems in early childhood: Investigating the contributions of child temperament and executive functions to resilience. *Child Development, 93*(1), e1–e16. https://doi.org/10.1111/cdev.13663

deMayo, B. E., Jordan, A. E., & Olson, K. R. (2022). Gender development in gender diverse children. *Annual Review of Developmental Psychology, 4*, 207–229. https://doi.org/10.1146/annurev-devpsych-121020-034014

Demissie, Z., Clayton, H. B., & Dunville, R. L. (2019). Association between receipt of school-based HIV education and contraceptive use among sexually active high school students—United States, 2011–2013. *Sex Education, 19*(2), 237–246. https://doi.org/10.1080/14681811.2018.1501358

de Moor, E. L., Sijtsema, J. J., Weller, J. A., & Klimstra, T. A. (2022). Longitudinal links between identity and substance use in adolescence. *Self and Identity, 21*, 113–136. https://doi.org/10.1080/15298868.2020.1818615

Dempsey, J., McQuillin, S., Butler, A. M., & Axelrad, M. E. (2016). Maternal depression and parent management training outcomes. *Journal of Clinical Psychology in Medical Settings, 23*(3), 240–246. https://doi.org/10.1007/s10880-016-9461-z

Deneault, A.-A., Bakermans-Kranenburg, M. J., Groh, A. M., Fearon, P. R. M., & Madigan, S. (2021). Child-father attachment in early childhood and behavior problems: A meta-analysis. *New Directions for Child and Adolescent Development, 43*–66. https://doi.org/10.1002/CAD.20434

Deneault, J., & Ricard, M. (2006). The assessment of children's understanding of inclusion relations: Transitivity, asymmetry, and quantification. *Journal of Cognition and Development, 7*(4), 551–570. https://doi.org/10.1207/s15327647jcd0704_6

Deneault, J., & Ricard, M. (2013). Are emotion and mind understanding differently linked to young children's social adjustment? Relationships between behavioral consequences of emotions, false belief, and SCBE. *The Journal of Genetic Psychology, 174*(1), 88–116. https://doi.org/10.1080/00221325.2011.642028

Denison, S., & Xu, F. (2019). Infant statisticians: The origins of reasoning under uncertainty. *Perspectives on Psychological Science, 14*(4), 499–509. https://doi.org/10.1177/1745691619847201

Denissen, J. J. A., Zarrett, N. R., & Eccles, J. S. (2007). I like to do it, I'm able, and I know I am: Longitudinal couplings between domain-specific achievement, self-concept, and interest. *Child Development, 78*(2), 430–447.

Dennis, T. A., Cole, P. M., Zahn-Waxler, C., & Mizuta, I. (2002). Self in context: Autonomy and relatedness in Japanese and U.S. mother-preschooler dyads. *Child Development, 73*(6), 1803–1817. https://doi.org/10.1111/1467-8624.00507

Dennis, W. (1960). Causes of retardation among institutional children: Iran. *Journal of Genetic Psychology, 96*, 47–59.

Dennis, W., & Dennis, M. G. (1991). The effect of cradling practices upon the onset of walking in Hopi children. *Journal of Genetic Psychology, 152*(4), 563–572.

de Onis, M., & Branca, F. (2016). Childhood stunting: A global perspective. *Maternal & Child Nutrition, 12*(Suppl 1), 12–26. https://doi.org/10.1111/mcn.12231

Department of Defense. (2020). *2019 Demographics profile: Active duty families.* https://download.militaryonesource.mil/12038/MOS/Infographic/2019-demographics-active-duty-families.pdf

Desjardins, T., & Leadbeater, B. J. (2017). Changes in parental emotional support and psychological control in early adulthood. *Emerging Adulthood, 5*(3), 177–190. https://doi.org/10.1177/2167696816666974

Devera, J. L., Gonzalez, Y., & Sabharwal, V. (2024). A narrative review of COVID-19 vaccination in pregnancy and breastfeeding. *Journal of Perinatology, 44*(1), Article 1. https://doi.org/10.1038/s41372-023-01734-0

de Villiers, J. G., & de Villiers, P. A. (2014). The role of language in theory of mind development. *Topics in Language Disorders, 34*(4), 313–328. https://doi.org/10.1097/TLD.0000000000000037

Devine, R. T., & Hughes, C. (2019). Let's talk: Parents' mental talk (not mind-mindedness or mindreading capacity) predicts children's false belief understanding. *Child Development, 90*(4), 1236–1253. https://doi.org/10.1111/cdev.12990

Devine, R. T., & Hughes, C. H. (2018). Let's talk: Parents' mental talk (not mind-mindedness or mindreading capacity) predicts children's false belief understanding. *Child Development, 90*(4), 1236–1253. https://doi.org/10.1111/cdev.12990

DeVito, E. E., Fagle, T., Allen, A. M., Pang, R. D., Petersen, N., Smith, P. H., & Weinberger, A. H. (2021). Electronic nicotine delivery systems (ENDS) use and pregnancy I: ENDS use behavior during pregnancy. *Current Addiction Reports*, 8(3), 347–365. https://doi.org/10.1007/S40429-021-00380-w

Devlin, B., Daniels, M., & Roeder, K. (1997). The heritability of IQ. *Nature*, 388(6641), Article 6641. https://doi.org/10.1038/41319

DeVoe, E. R., Ross, A. M., Spencer, R., Drew, A., Acker, M., Paris, R., & Jacoby, V. (2020). Coparenting across the deployment cycle: Observations from military families with young children. *Journal of Family Issues*, 41(9), 1447–1469. https://doi.org/10.1177/0192513X19894366

de Vries, E. E., van der Pol, L. D., Toshkov, D. D., Groeneveld, M. G., & Mesman, J. (2022). Fathers, faith, and family gender messages: Are religiosity and gender talk related to children's gender attitudes and preferences? *Early Childhood Research Quarterly*, 59, 21–31. https://doi.org/10.1016/j.ecresq.2021.10.002

de Vries, R. (1969). Constancy of generic identity in the years three to six. *Monographs of the Society for Research in Child Development*, 34(3), iii–1–iv.67. https://doi.org/10.2307/1165683

DeVries, R., & Zan, B. (2003). When children make rules. *Educational Leadership*, 61(1), 64–67.

de Vries, S. L. A., Hoeve, M., Stams, G. J. J. M., & Asscher, J. J. (2016). Adolescent-parent attachment and externalizing behavior: The mediating role of individual and social factors. *Journal of Abnormal Child Psychology*, 44(2), 283–294. https://doi.org/10.1007/s10802-015-9999-5

de Waal, F. B. M. (1993). Sex differences in chimpanzee (and human) behavior: A matter of social values? In M. Hechter, L. Nadel, & R. E. Michod (Eds.), *The origin of values* (pp. 285–303). Aldine de Gruyter.

Dewan, M. C., & Wellons, J. C. (2019). Fetal surgery for spina bifida. *Journal of Neurosurgery: Pediatrics*, 24(2), 105–114. https://doi.org/10.3171/2019.4.PEDS18383

de Wilde, A., Koot, H. M., & van Lier, P. A. C. (2016). Developmental links between children's working memory and their social relations with teachers and peers in the early school years. *Journal of Abnormal Child Psychology*, 44(1), 19–30. https://doi.org/10.1007/s10802-015-0053-4

Di Cesare, M., Sorić, M., Bovet, P., Miranda, J. J., Bhutta, Z., Stevens, G. A., Laxmaiah, A., Kengne, A. P., & Bentham, J. (2019). The epidemiological burden of obesity in childhood: A worldwide epidemic requiring urgent action. *BMC Medicine*, 17(1), 1–20. https://doi.org/10.1186/s12916-019-1449-8

Di Cristo, G., & Chattopadhyaya, B. (2020). Development of neuronal circuits: From synaptogenesis to synapse plasticity. In C. Bulteau. Anne Gallagher, D. Cohen, & J. L. Michaud (Eds.), *Handbook of clinical neurology* (Vol. 173, pp. 43–53). Elsevier B.V. https://doi.org/10.1016/B978-0-444-64150-2.00005-8

Di Giorgio, E., Lunghi, M., Rugani, R., Regolin, L., Dalla Barba, B., Vallortigara, G., & Simion, F. (2019). A mental number line in human newborns. *Developmental Science*, 22(6), e12801. https://doi.org/10.1111/desc.12801

Diamond, A. (1991). Neuropsychological insights into the meaning of object concept development. In S. Carey & R. Gelman (Eds.), *The epigenesis of mind: Essays on biology and cognition* (pp. 67–110). Psychological Assessment Resources.

Diamond, A. (2013). Executive functions. *Annual Review of Psychology*, 64, 135–168. https://doi.org/10.1146/annurev-psych-113011-143750

Diamond, L. M. (2020). Gender fluidity and nonbinary gender identities among children and adolescents. *Child Development Perspectives*, 14(2), 110–115. https://doi.org/10.1111/cdep.12366

Diaz-Strong, D. X., & Gonzales, R. G. (2023). The divergent adolescent and adult transitions of Latin American undocumented minors. *Child Development Perspectives*, 17(1), 3–9. https://doi.org/10.1111/cdep.12478

Dickerson, A., & Popli, G. K. (2016). Persistent poverty and children's cognitive development: Evidence from the UK Millennium Cohort Study. *Journal of the Royal Statistical Society Series A: Statistics in Society*, 179(2), 535–558. https://doi.org/10.1111/rssa.12128

DiClemente, C. M., & Richards, M. H. (2022). Community violence in early adolescence: Assessing coping strategies for reducing delinquency and aggression. *Journal of Clinical Child & Adolescent Psychology*, 51(2), 155–169. https://doi.org/10.1080/15374416.2019.1650365

Dieke, A. C., Zhang, Y., Kissin, D. M., Barfield, W. D., & Boulet, S. L. (2017). Disparities in assisted reproductive technology utilization by race and ethnicity, United States, 2014: A commentary. *Journal of Women's Health*, 26(6), 605–608. https://doi.org/10.1089/jwh.2017.6467

Diener, M. (2000). Gift from the Gods: A Balinese guide to early child rearing. In J. DeLoache & A. Gotleib (Eds.), *A world of babies: Imagined childcare guiles for seven societies*. Cambridge University Press.

Dietary Guidelines Advisory Committee. (2020). *Scientific report of the 2020 Dietary Guidelines Advisory Committee: Advisory Report to the Secretary of Agriculture and the Secretary of Health and Human Services*. U.S. Department of Agriculture, Agricultural Research Service.

Dimler, L. M., & Natsuaki, M. N. (2021). Trajectories of violent and nonviolent behaviors from adolescence to early adulthood: Does early puberty matter, and, if so, how long? *Journal of Adolescent Health*, 68, 523–531. https://doi.org/10.1016/j.jadohealth.2020.06.034

Dimler, L. M., Natsuaki, M. N., Hastings, P. D., Zahn-Waxler, C., & Klimes-Dougan, B. (2017). Parenting effects are in the eye of the beholder: Parent-adolescent differences in perceptions affects adolescent problem behaviors. *Journal of Youth and Adolescence*, 46(5), 1076–1088. https://doi.org/10.1007/s10964-016-0612-1

Dimond, D., Rohr, C. S., Smith, R. E., Dhollander, T., Cho, I., Lebel, C., Dewey, D., Connelly, A., & Bray, S. (2020). Early childhood development of white matter fiber density and morphology. *NeuroImage*, 210, 116552. https://doi.org/10.1016/j.neuroimage.2020.116552

Dinehart, L. H. (2015). Handwriting in early childhood education: Current research and future implications. *Journal of Early Childhood Literacy*, 15(1), 97–118. https://doi.org/10.1177/1468798414522825

Dinehart, L., & Manfra, L. (2013). Associations between low-income children's fine motor skills in preschool and academic performance in second grade. *Early Education & Development*, 24(2), 138–161. https://doi.org/10.1080/10409289.2011.636729

Ding, G., Ji, R., & Bao, Y. (2014). Risk and protective factors for the development of childhood asthma. *Paediatric Respiratory Reviews*, 16(2), 133–139. https://doi.org/10.1016/j.prrv.2014.07.004

Dinkel, D., & Snyder, K. (2020). Exploring gender differences in infant motor development related to parent's promotion of play. *Infant Behavior and Development*, 59, 101440. https://doi.org/10.1016/j.infbeh.2020.101440

Dismukes, A., Shirtcliff, E., Jones, C. W., Zeanah, C., Theall, K., & Drury, S. (2018). The development of the cortisol response to dyadic stressors in Black and White infants. *Development and Psychopathology*,

30(5). https://doi.org/10.1017/S0954579418001232

Dixson, H. G. W., Komugabe-Dixson, A. F., Dixson, B. J., & Low, J. (2018). Scaling theory of mind in a small-scale society: A case study from Vanuatu. *Child Development*, *89*(6), 2157–2175. https://doi.org/10.1111/cdev.12919

Do, K. T., McCormick, E. M., & Telzer, E. H. (2019). The neural development of prosocial behavior from childhood to adolescence. *Social Cognitive and Affective Neuroscience*, *14*(2), 129–139. https://doi.org/10.1093/scan/nsy117

Dobbs, A. R., & Rule, B. G. (1989). Adult age differences in working memory. *Psychology and Aging*, *4*, 500–503. https://doi.org/10.1037/0882-7974.4.4.500

Doebel, S. (2020). Rethinking executive function and its development. *Perspectives on Psychological Science*, *15*(4), 942–956. https://doi.org/10.1177/1745691620904771

Doenyas, C., Yavuz, H. M., & Selcuk, B. (2018). Not just a sum of its parts: How tasks of the theory of mind scale relate to executive function across time. *Journal of Experimental Child Psychology*, *166*, 485–501. https://doi.org/10.1016/j.jecp.2017.09.014

Doherty, M. J., & Perner, J. (2020). Mental files: Developmental integration of dual naming and theory of mind. *Developmental Review*, *56*, 100909. https://doi.org/10.1016/j.dr.2020.100909

Döhla, D., & Heim, S. (2016). Developmental dyslexia and dysgraphia: What can we learn from the one about the other? *Frontiers in Psychology*, *6*, 2045. https://doi.org/10.3389/fpsyg.2015.02045

Döhla, D., Willmes, K., & Heim, S. (2018). Cognitive profiles of developmental dysgraphia. *Frontiers in Psychology*, *9*, 2006. https://doi.org/10.3389/fpsyg.2018.02006

d'Oiron, R. (2019). Carriers of hemophilia A and hemophilia B. In R. A. Kadir, P. D. James, & C. A. Lee (Eds.), *Inherited bleeding disorders in women* (2nd ed., pp. 65–82). John Wiley & Sons. https://doi.org/10.1002/9781119426080.ch5

Dolbin-MacNab, M. L., & O'Connell, L. M. (2021). Grandfamilies and the opioid epidemic: A systemic perspective and future priorities. *Clinical Child and Family Psychology Review*, *24*(2), 207–223. https://doi.org/10.1007/s10567-021-00343-7

Doley, R., Bell, R., Watt, B., & Simpson, H. (2015). Grandparents raising grandchildren: Investigating factors associated with distress among custodial grandparent. *Journal of Family Studies*, *21*(2), 1–19. https://doi.org/10.1080/13229400.2015.1015215

Dollahite, D. C., & Thatcher, J. Y. (2008). Talking about religion. *Journal of Adolescent Research*, *23*(5), 611–641. https://doi.org/10.1177/0743558408322141

Dollar, J. M., & Calkins, S. D. (2019). The development of anger. In V. LoBue, K. Pérez-Edgar<, & K. A. Buss (Eds.), *Handbook of emotional development* (pp. 199–225). Springer International. https://doi.org/10.1007/978-3-030-17332-6_9

Domina, T., Renzulli, L., Murray, B., Garza, A. N., & Perez, L. (2021). Remote or removed: Predicting successful engagement with online learning during COVID-19. *Socius*. https://doi.org/10.1177/23780231209882007

Dominguez-Folgueras, M. (2022). It's about gender: A critical review of the literature on the domestic division of work. *Journal of Family Theory & Review*, *14*(1), 79–96. https://doi.org/10.1111/jftr.12447

Domitrovich, C. E., Durlak, J. A., Staley, K. C., & Weissberg, R. P. (2017). Social-emotional competence: An essential factor for promoting positive adjustment and reducing risk in school children. *Child Development*, *88*(2), 408–416. https://doi.org/10.1111/cdev.12739

Donaldson, S. K., & Westerman, M. A. (1986). Development of children's understanding of ambivalence and causal theories of emotions. *Developmental Psychology*, *22*(5), 655–662. https://doi.org/10.1037/0012-1649.22.5.655

Donaldson, T. (2021). Diagnostic history: Prenatal exposure to alcohol and other teratogens. In N. N. Brown (Ed.), *Evaluating fetal alcohol spectrum disorders in the forensic context* (pp. 1–17). Springer. https://doi.org/10.1007/978-3-030-73628-6_1

Dondi, M., Simion, F., & Caltran, G. (1999). Can newborns discriminate between their own cry and the cry of another newborn infant? *Developmental Psychology*, *35*, 418–426. https://doi.org/10.1037//0012-1649.35.2.418

Dong, S., Dubas, J. S., & Deković, M. (2022). Revisiting goodness of fit in the cultural context: Moving forward from post hoc explanations. *Child Development Perspectives*, *16*(2), 82–89. https://doi.org/10.1111/CDEP.12446

Donkelaar, ten., J, H., Copp, A. J., Bekker, M., Renier, W. O., Hori, A., & Shiota, K. (2023). Neurulation and Neural Tube Defects. In H. J. ten. Donkelaar, M. Lammens, & A. Hori (Eds.), *Clinical neuroembryology: Development and developmental disorders of the human central nervous system* (pp. 249–312). Springer International. https://doi.org/10.1007/978-3-031-26098-8_4

Donnelly, S., & Kidd, E. (2021). The longitudinal relationship between conversational turn-taking and vocabulary growth in early language development. *Child Development*, *92*(2), 609–625. https://doi.org/10.1111/CDEV.13511

Donovan, T., Dunn, K., Penman, A., Young, R. J., & Reid, V. M. (2020). Fetal eye movements in response to a visual stimulus. *Brain and Behavior*, *10*(8), e01676. https://doi.org/10.1002/brb3.1676

Doodson, L., & Morley, D. (2006). Understanding the roles of non-residential stepmothers. *Journal of Divorce & Remarriage*, *45*(3/4), 109–130. https://doi.org/10.1300/J087v45n03_06

Dorn, A. van. (2023). The strange endurance of corporal punishment. *Lancet Child & Adolescent Health*, *7*(3), 154–155. https://doi.org/10.1016/S2352-4642(23)00019-6

dos Santos, J. F., de Melo Bastos, Cavalcante., C, Barbosa., T, F., Gitaí, D. L. G., Duzzioni, M., Tilelli, C. Q., Shetty, A. K., & de Castro, O. W. (2018). Maternal, fetal and neonatal consequences associated with the use of crack cocaine during the gestational period: A systematic review and meta-analysis. *Archives of Gynecology and Obstetrics*, *298*(3), 487–503. https://doi.org/10.1007/s00404-018-4833-2

Dotterer, A. M., Lowe, K., & McHale, S. M. (2014). Academic growth trajectories and family relationships among African American youth. *Journal of Research on Adolescence*, *24*(4), 734–747. https://doi.org/10.1111/jora.12080

Doughty, S. E., McHale, S. M., & Feinberg, M. E. (2015). Sibling experiences as predictors of romantic relationship qualities in adolescence. *Journal of Family Issues*, *36*(5), 589–608. https://doi.org/10.1177/0192513X13495397

Douglass, S., & Umaña-Taylor, A. J. (2016). Time-varying effects of family ethnic socialization on ethnic-racial identity development among Latino adolescents. *Developmental Psychology*, *52*(11), 1904–1912. https://doi.org/10.1037/dev0000141

Douglass, S., & Umaña-Taylor, A. J. (2017). Examining discrimination, ethnic-racial identity status, and youth public regard among Black, Latino, and White adolescents. *Journal of Research on Adolescence*, *27*(1), 155–172. https://doi.org/10.1111/jora.12262

Douglass, S., Yip, T., & Shelton, J. N. (2014). Intragroup contact and anxiety among ethnic minority adolescents: Considering ethnic identity and school diversity transitions. *Journal of Youth and Adolescence*, *43*(10), 1628–1641. https://doi.org/10.1007/s10964-014-0144-5

Dowdall, N., J, Melendez-Torres, G., Murray, L., Gardner, F., Hartford, L., & Cooper, P. J. (2020). Shared picture book reading interventions for child language development: A systematic review and meta-analysis. *Child Development*, *91*(2), e383–e399. https://doi.org/10.1111/cdev.13225

Dowe, K. N., Planalp, E. M., Dean, D. C., Alexander, A. L., Davidson, R. J., & Goldsmith, H. H. (2020). Early microstructure of white matter associated with infant attention. *Developmental Cognitive Neuroscience*, *45*, 100815. https://doi.org/10.1016/j.dcn.2020.100815

Downey, D. B., Condron, D. J., & Yucel, D. (2015). Number of siblings and social skills revisited among American fifth graders. *Journal of Family Issues*, *36*(2), 273–296. https://doi.org/10.1177/0192513X13507569

Dozier, M., & Bernard, K. (2023). Intervening early: Socioemotional interventions targeting the parent-infant relationship. *Annual Review of Developmental Psychology*, *5*(5), 115–135. https://doi.org/10.1146/annurev-devpsych-120621-043254

Draganova, R., Schollbach, A., Schleger, F., Braendle, J., Brucker, S., Abele, H., Kagan, K. O., Wallwiener, D., Fritsche, A., Eswaran, H., & Preissl, H. (2018). Fetal auditory evoked responses to onset of amplitude modulated sounds. A fetal magnetoencephalography (fMEG) study. *Hearing Research*, *363*, 70–77. https://doi.org/10.1016/j.heares.2018.03.005

Drapeau, S., Gagne, M.-H., Saint-Jacques, M.-C., Lepine, R., & Ivers, Hans. (2009). Post-separation conflict trajectories: A longitudinal study. *Marriage & Family Review*, *45*(4), 353–373. https://psycnet.apa.org/doi/10.1080/01494920902821529

Drollette, E. S., & Hillman, C. H. (2020). Cognitive and academic benefits of physical activity for school-age children. In T. Brusseau, S. Fairclough, & D. Lubans (Eds.), *The Routledge handbook of youth physical activity* (pp. 148–169). Routledge. https://doi.org/10.4324/9781003026426-9

Drozd, F., Bergsund, H. B., Hammerstrøm, K. T., Hansen, M. B., & Jacobsen, H. (2018). A systematic review of courses, training, and interventions for adoptive parents. *Journal of Child and Family Studies*, *27*(2), 339–354. https://doi.org/10.1007/s10826-017-0901-7

Drubina, B., Kökönyei, G., Várnai, D., & Reinhardt, M. (2023). Online and school bullying roles: Are bully-victims more vulnerable in nonsuicidal self-injury and in psychological symptoms than bullies and victims? *BMC Psychiatry*, *23*(1), 945. https://doi.org/10.1186/s12888-023-05341-3

Dryburgh, N. S. J., Ponath, E., Bukowski, W. M., & Dirks, M. A. (2022). Associations between interpersonal behavior and friendship quality in childhood and adolescence: A meta-analysis. *Child Development*, *93*(3), e332–e347. https://doi.org/10.1111/cdev.13728

D'Souza, H., Cowie, D., Karmiloff-Smith, A., & Bremner, A. J. (2017). Specialization of the motor system in infancy: From broad tuning to selectively specialized purposeful actions. *Developmental Science*, *20*(4), e12409. https://doi.org/10.1111/desc.12409

Du, Y., Liu, B., Sun, Y., Snetselaar, L. G., Wallace, R. B., & Bao, W. (2019). Trends in adherence to the Physical Activity Guidelines for Americans for aerobic activity and time spent on sedentary behavior among US adults, 2007 to 2016. *JAMA Network Open*, *2*(7), e197597. https://doi.org/10.1001/jamanetworkopen.2019.7597

Dubois, J., Dehaene-Lambertz, G., Kulikova, S., Poupon, C., Hüppi, P. S., & Hertz-Pannier, L. (2013). The early development of brain white matter: A review of imaging studies in fetuses, newborns and infants. *Neuroscience*, *276*, 48–71. https://doi.org/10.1016/j.neuroscience.2013.12.044

Duchesne, S., Larose, S., & Feng, B. (2019). Achievement goals and engagement with academic work in early high school: Does seeking help from teachers matter? *Journal of Early Adolescence*, *39*(2), 222–252. https://doi.org/10.1177/0272431617737626

Dudovitz, R. N., Chung, P. J., & Wong, M. D. (2017). Teachers and coaches in adolescent social networks are associated with healthier self-concept and decreased substance use. *Journal of School Health*, *87*(1), 12–20. https://doi.org/10.1111/josh.12462

Duell, N., & Steinberg, L. (2021). Adolescents take positive risks, too. *Developmental Review*, *62*, 100984. https://doi.org/10.1016/j.dr.2021.100984

Duell, N., Steinberg, L., Icenogle, G., Chein, J., Chaudhary, N., Di Giunta, L., Dodge, K. A., Fanti, K. A., Lansford, J. E., Oburu, P., Pastorelli, C., Skinner, A. T., Sorbring, E., Tapanya, S., Uribe Tirado, L. M., Alampay, L. P., Al-Hassan, S. M., Takash, H. M. S., Bacchini, D., & Chang, L. (2018). Age patterns in risk taking across the world. *Journal of Youth and Adolescence*, *47*(5), 1052–1072. https://doi.org/10.1007/s10964-017-0752-y

Duffy, A. L., Gardner, A. A., & J, Zimmer-Gembeck, M. (2020). Peer rejection and dislike. In S. Hupp & J. D. Jewell (Eds.), *The encyclopedia of child and adolescent development* (pp. 1–13). Wiley. https://doi.org/10.1002/9781119171492.wecad191

Dugré, J. R., & Potvin, S. (2022). Developmental multi-trajectory of irritability, anxiety, and hyperactivity as psychological markers of heterogeneity in childhood aggression. *Psychological Medicine*, *52*(2), 241–250. https://doi.org/10.1017/S0033291720001877

Duke, S. A., Balzer, B. W. R., & Steinbeck, K. S. (2014). Testosterone and its effects on human male adolescent mood and behavior: A systematic review. *The Journal of Adolescent Health: Official Publication of the Society for Adolescent Medicine*, *55*(3), 315–322. https://doi.org/10.1016/j.jadohealth.2014.05.007

Dumontheil, I. (2016). Adolescent brain development. *Current Opinion in Behavioral Sciences*, *10*, 39–44. https://doi.org/10.1016/j.cobeha.2016.04.012

Duncan, G. J., & Magnuson, K. (2013). Investing in preschool programs. *Journal of Economic Perspectives*, *27*(2), 109–132. https://doi.org/10.1257/jep.27.2.109

Dunn, J. (2002). Sibling relationships. In P. K. Smith & C. H. Hart (Eds.), *Blackwell handbook of childhood social development* (pp. 223–237). Blackwell.

Dunn, J., Gray, C., Moffett, P., & Mitchell, D. (2018). 'It's more funner than doing work': Children's perspectives on using tablet computers in the early years of school. *Early Child Development and Care*, *188*(6), 819–831. https://doi.org/10.1080/03004430.2016.1238824

Dunn, K., & Bremner, J. G. (2020). Investigating the social environment of the A-not-B search task. *Developmental Science*, *23*(3), e12921. https://doi.org/10.1111/desc.12921

Dur, Ş., Çağlar, S., Yıldız, N. U., Doğan, P., Güney, Varal., & İ. (2020). The effect of Yakson and gentle human touch methods on pain and physiological parameters in preterm infants during heel lancing. *Intensive and Critical Care Nursing*, *61*, 102886. https://doi.org/10.1016/j.iccn.2020.102886

Durante, F., & Fiske, S. T. (2017). How social-class stereotypes maintain inequality. *Current Opinion in Psychology*, *18*, 43–48. https://doi.org/10.1016/j.copsyc.2017.07.033

Duriez, B., Smits, I., & Goossens, L. (2008). The relation between identity styles and religiosity in adolescence: Evidence from a longitudinal perspective. *Personality and Individual Differences*, 44(4), 1022–1031. https://doi.org/10.1016/j.paid.2007.10.028

Durik, A., Hyde, J., & Clark, R. (2000). Sequelae of cesarean and vaginal deliveries: Psychosocial outcomes for mothers and infants. *Developmental Psychology*, 36, 251–260.

Durkin, M. S., Maenner, M. J., Baio, J., Christensen, D., Daniels, J., Fitzgerald, R., Imm, P., Lee, L. C., Schieve, L. A., Van Naarden Braun, K., Wingate, M. S., & Yeargin-Allsopp, M. (2017). Autism spectrum disorder among US children (2002–2010): Socioeconomic, racial, and ethnic disparities. *American Journal of Public Health*, 107(11), 1818–1826. https://doi.org/10.2105/AJPH.2017.304032

Durwood, L., Eisner, L., Fladeboe, K., Ji, C., Barney, S., McLaughlin, K. A., & Olson, K. R. (2021). Social support and internalizing psychopathology in transgender youth. *Journal of Youth and Adolescence*, 50(5), 841–854. https://doi.org/10.1007/S10964-020-01391-Y

Durwood, L., McLaughlin, K. A., & Olson, K. R. (2017). Mental health and self-worth in socially transitioned transgender youth. *Journal of the American Academy of Child and Adolescent Psychiatry*, 56(2), 116–123.e2. https://doi.org/10.1016/j.jaac.2016.10.016

Dussias, P. E., & Miller, K. (2022). Eye-tracking methods in child SLA research. In *Research methods for understanding child second language development*. Routledge.

Duyme, M., Dumaret, A. C., & Tomkiewicz, S. (1999). How can we boost IQs of "dull children"?: A late adoption study. *Proceedings of the National Academy of Sciences of the United States of America*, 96(15), 8790–8794. https://doi.org/10.1073/PNAS.96.15.8790

Dweck, C. S. (2017). The journey to children's mindsets-and beyond. *Child Development Perspectives*, 11(2), 139–144. https://doi.org/10.1111/cdep.12225

Dweck, C. S., & Master, A. (2009). Self-theories and motivation. In K. R. Wentzel & D. B. Miele (Eds.), *Handbook of motivation at school* (pp. 123–140). Routledge.

Dweck, C. S., & Yeager, D. S. (2019). Mindsets: A view from two eras. *Perspectives on Psychological Science*, 14(3), 481–496. https://doi.org/10.1177/1745691618804166

Dwyer, P. (2022). The neurodiversity approach(es): What are they and what do they mean for researchers? *Human Development*, 66(2), 73–92. https://doi.org/10.1159/000523723

Dyer, S., & Moneta, G. B. (2006). Frequency of parallel, associative, and co-operative play in British children of different socioeconomic status. *Social Behavior & Personality: An International Journal*, 34(5), 587–592. http://dx.doi.org/10.2224/sbp.2006.34.5.587

Dykstra, V. W., Willoughby, T., & Evans, A. D. (2020). A longitudinal examination of the relation between lie-telling, secrecy, parent-child relationship quality, and depressive symptoms in late-childhood and adolescence. *Journal of Youth and Adolescence*, 49(2), 438–448. https://doi.org/10.1007/s10964-019-01183-z

Dyson, M. W., Olino, T. M., Durbin, C. E., Goldsmith, H. H., Bufferd, S. J., Miller, A. R., & Klein, D. N. (2015). The structural and rank-order stability of temperament in young children based on a laboratory-observational measure. *Psychological Assessment*, 27(4), 1388–1401. https://doi.org/10.1037/pas0000104

Dziewolska, H., & Cautilli, J. (2006). The effects of a motor training package on minimally assisted standing behavior in a three-month-old infant. *The Behavior Analyst Today*, 7(1), 111–120.

Dziewolska, H., & Cautilli, J. (2006). The effects of a motor training package on minimally assisted standing behavior in a three-month-old infant. *The Behavior Analyst Today*, 7(1), 111–120. http://dx.doi.org/10.1037/h0100149

E, Lauer., J., Yhang, E., & Lourenco, S. F. (2019). The development of gender differences in spatial reasoning: A meta-analytic review. *Psychological Bulletin*, 145(6), 537–565. https://doi.org/10.1037/bul0000191

Eagly, A. H., Nater, C., Miller, D. I., Kaufmann, M., & Sczesny, S. (2020). Gender stereotypes have changed: A cross-temporal meta-analysis of U.S. public opinion polls from 1946 to 2018. *American Psychologist*, 75(3), 301–315. https://doi.org/10.1037/amp0000494

Eales, L., Ferguson, G. M., Gillespie, S., Smoyer, S., & Carlson, S. M. (2021). Family resilience and psychological distress in the COVID-19 pandemic: A mixed methods study. *Developmental Psychology*, 57, 1563–1581. https://doi.org/10.1037/dev0001221

Easterbrooks, M. A., Bartlett, J. D., Beeghly, M., & Thompson, R. A. (2012). Social and emotional development in infancy. In I. B. Weiner, R. M. Lerner, M. A. Easterbrooks, & J. Mistry (Eds.), *Handbook of Psychology, Developmental Psychology* (p. 752). John Wiley & Sons.

Eather, N., Ridley, K., & Leahy, A. (2020). Physiological health benefits of physical activity for young people. In T. Brusseau, S. Fairclough, & D. Lubans (Eds.), *The Routledge handbook of youth physical activity*. Routledge.

Ebeh, D. N., & Jahanfar, S. (2021). Association between maternal race and the use of assisted reproductive technology in the USA. *SN Comprehensive Clinical Medicine*, 3(5). https://doi.org/10.1007/s42399-021-00853-z

Eccles, J. S., & Roeser, R. W. (2011). Schools as developmental contexts during adolescence. *Journal of Research on Adolescence*, 21(1), 225–241. https://doi.org/10.1111/j.1532-7795.2010.00725.x

Eccles, J. S., & Roeser, R. W. (2015). School and community influences on human development. In M. H. Bornstein & M. E. Lamb (Eds.), *Developmental science: An advanced textbook* (pp. 645–727). Psychology Press.

Eckert-Lind, C., Busch, A. S., Petersen, J. H., Biro, F. M., Butler, G., Bräuner, E. V., & Juul, A. (2020). Worldwide secular trends in age at pubertal onset assessed by breast development among girls: A systematic review and meta-analysis. *JAMA Pediatrics*, 174(4), e195881–e195881. https://doi.org/10.1001/jamapediatrics.2019.5881

Edelson, S. M., & Reyna, V. F. (2021). How fuzzy-trace theory predicts development of risky decision making, with novel extensions to culture and reward sensitivity. *Developmental Review*, 62, 100986. https://doi.org/10.1016/j.dr.2021.100986

Edelson, S. M., & Reyna, V. F. (2023). Decision making in adolescence and early adulthood. In *APA handbook of adolescent and young adult development* (pp. 107–122). American Psychological Association. https://doi.org/10.1037/0000298-007

Edwards, C. P. (2000). Children's play in cross-cultural perspective: A new look at the six cultures study. *Cross-Cultural Research*, 34(4), 318–338. https://psycnet.apa.org/doi/10.1177/106939710003400402

Egan, S. K., & Perry, D. G. (2001). Gender identity: A multidimensional analysis with implications for psychosocial adjustment. *Developmental Psychology*, 37(4), 451–463. https://doi.org/10.1037/0012-1649.37.4.451

Egbert, A. H., Hunt, R. A., Williams, K. L., Burke, N. L., & Mathis, K. J. (2022). Reporting racial and ethnic diversity in eating disorder research over the past 20 years. *International Journal of Eating Disorders*,

55(4), 455–462. https://doi.org/10.1002/EAT.23666

Eggen, P. (2020). Information processing and human memory. In G. Noblit (Ed.), *Oxford research encyclopedia of education*. Oxford University Press. https://doi.org/10.1093/acrefore/9780190264093.013.86

Ehli, S., Wolf, J., Newen, A., Schneider, S., & Voigt, B. (2020). Determining the function of social referencing: The role of familiarity and situational threat. *Frontiers in Psychology*, *11*, 538228. https://doi.org/10.3389/fpsyg.2020.538228

Ehrensaft, D., Giammattei, S. V., Storck, K., Tishelman, A. C., & Keo-Meier, C. (2018). Prepubertal social gender transitions: What we know; what we can learn—A view from a gender affirmative lens. *International Journal of Transgenderism*, *19*(2), 251–268. https://doi.org/10.1080/15532739.2017.1414649

Einspieler, C., Prayer, D., & Marschik, P. B. (2021). Fetal movements: The origin of human behaviour. *Developmental Medicine & Child Neurology*, *63*(10), 1142–1148. https://doi.org/10.1111/dmcn.14918

Eirich, R., McArthur, B. A., Anhorn, C., McGuinness, C., Christakis, D. A., & Madigan, S. (2022). Association of screen time with internalizing and externalizing behavior problems in children 12 years or younger: A systematic review and meta-analysis. *JAMA Psychiatry*, *79*(5), 393–405. https://doi.org/10.1001/jamapsychiatry.2022.0155

Eisbach, A. O. (2004). Children's developing awareness of diversity in people's trains of thoughts. *Child Development*, *75*(6), 1694–1707. https://doi.org/10.1111/j.1467-8624.2004.00810.x

Eisenberg, N., Cumberland, A., Guthrie, I. K., Murphy, B. C., & Shepard, S. A. (2005). Age changes in prosocial responding and moral reasoning in adolescence and early adulthood. *Journal of Research on Adolescence*, *15*(3), 235–260. https://doi.org/10.1111/j.1532-7795.2005.00095.x

Eisenberg, N., Spinrad, T. L., & Knafo-Noam, A. (2015). Prosocial development. In *Handbook of child psychology and developmental science* (pp. 1–47). John Wiley & Sons. https://doi.org/10.1002/9781118963418.childpsy315

Eisenberg, N., Spinrad, T. L., & Knafo-Noam, A. (2015). Prosocial development. In *Handbook of Child Psychology and Developmental Science* (pp. 1–47). John Wiley & Sons. https://doi.org/10.1002/9781118963418.childpsy315

Eisenberg, N., Spinrad, T. L., & Morris, A. S. (2013). Prosocial development. In P. D. Zelazo (Ed.), *The Oxford handbook of developmental psychology* (Vol. 2, pp. 300–324). Oxford University Press. https://doi.org/10.1093/oxfordhb/9780199958474.013.0013

Eisenberg, S. L., Guo, L.-Y., & Germezia, M. (2012). How grammatical are 3-year-olds? *Language, Speech, and Hearing Services in Schools*, *43*(1), 36–52. https://doi.org/10.1044/0161-1461(2011/10-0093

Eisner, M. P., & Malti, T. (2015). Aggressive and violent behavior. In R. M. Lerner (Ed.), *Handbook of child psychology and developmental science* (pp. 1–48). John Wiley & Sons. https://doi.org/10.1002/9781118963418.childpsy319

Eisner, M. P., & Malti, T. (2015). Aggressive and violent behavior. In M. E. Lamb (Ed.), *Handbook of child psychology and developmental science* (pp. 1–48). John Wiley & Sons. https://doi.org/10.1002/9781118963418.childpsy319

El Mallah, S. (2020). Conceptualization and measurement of adolescent prosocial behavior: Looking back and moving forward. *Journal of Research on Adolescence*, *30*, 15–38. https://doi.org/10.1111/JORA.12476

El Marroun, H., Tiemeier, H., Franken, I. H. A., Jaddoe, V. W. V., van der Lugt, A., Verhulst, F. C., Lahey, B. B., & White, T. (2016). Prenatal cannabis and tobacco exposure in relation to brain morphology: A prospective neuroimaging study in young children. *Biological Psychiatry*, *79*(12), 971–979. https://doi.org/10.1016/J.BIOPSYCH.2015.08.024

Elder, G. H., Shanahan, M. J., & Jennings, J. A. (2015). Human development in time and place. In M. H. Bornstein & T. Leventhal (Eds.), *Handbook of child psychology: Ecological settings and processes* (Vol. 4, pp. 6–54). Wiley.

Elenbaas, L. (2019). Interwealth contact and young children's concern for equity. *Child Development*, *90*(1), 108–116. https://doi.org/10.1111/cdev.13157

Elenbaas, L., Rizzo, M. T., & Killen, M. (2020). A developmental-science perspective on social inequality. *Current Directions in Psychological Science*, *29*(6), 610–616. https://doi.org/10.1177/0963721420964147

Elhusseini, S., Rawn, K., El-Sheikh, M., & Keller, P. S. (2023). Attachment and prosocial behavior in middle childhood: The role of emotion regulation. *Journal of Experimental Child Psychology*, *225*, 105534. https://doi.org/10.1016/j.jecp.2022.105534

Eliot, L. (2021). Brain development and physical aggression: How a small gender difference grows into a violence problem. *Current Anthropology*, *62*(S23), S66–S78. https://doi.org/10.1086/711705

Elkind, D., & Bowen, R. (1979). Imaginary audience behavior in children and adolescents. *Developmental Psychology*, *15*(1), 38–44. https://doi.org/10.1037/0012-1649.15.1.38

Ellis, B. J., Bianchi, J., Griskevicius, V., & Frankenhuis, W. E. (2017). Beyond risk and protective factors: An adaptation-based approach to resilience. *Perspectives on Psychological Science*, *12*(4), 561–587. https://doi.org/10.1177/1745691617693054

Ellis, C. T., Skalaban, L. J., Yates, T. S., & Turk-Browne, N. B. (2021). Attention recruits frontal cortex in human infants. *Proceedings of the National Academy of Sciences of the United States of America*, *118*(12), e2021474118. https://doi.org/10.1073/pnas.2021474118

Ellis, K. J., Abrams, S. A., & Wong, W. W. (1997). Body composition of a young, multi-ethnic female population. *American Journal of Clinical Nutrition*, *65*, 724–731.

Ellis, W. E., & Zarbatany, L. (2017). Understanding processes of peer clique influence in late childhood and early adolescence. *Child Development Perspectives*, *11*(4), 227–232. https://doi.org/10.1111/cdep.12248

Ellwood-Lowe, M. E., Foushee, R., & Srinivasan, M. (2022). What causes the word gap? Financial concerns may systematically suppress child-directed speech. *Developmental Science*, *25*(1), e13151. https://doi.org/10.1111/desc.13151

Elsabbagh, M., Hohenberger, A., Campos, R., Van Herwegen, J., Serres, J., de Schonen, S., Aschersleben, G., & Karmiloff-Smith, A. (2013). Narrowing perceptual sensitivity to the native language in infancy: Exogenous influences on developmental timing. *Behavioral Sciences*, *3*(1), 120–132. https://doi.org/10.3390/bs3010120

Else-Quest, N. M., Higgins, A., Allison, C., & Morton, L. C. (2012). Gender differences in self-conscious emotional experience: A meta-analysis. *Psychological Bulletin*, *138*(5), 947–981. https://doi.org/10.1037/a0027930

Else-Quest, N. M., & Hyde, J. S. (2018). *The psychology of women and gender*. SAGE.

Else-Quest, N. M., & Morse, E. (2015). Ethnic variations in parental ethnic socialization and adolescent ethnic identity: A longitudinal study. *Cultural Diversity and Ethnic Minority Psychology*, *21*(1), 54–64. https://doi.org/10.1037/a0037820

Eltanamly, H., Leijten, P., Jak, S., & Overbeek, G. (2021). Parenting in times of war: A meta-analysis and qualitative synthesis of war exposure, parenting, and child adjustment. *Trauma, Violence, and Abuse, 22*(1), 147–160. https://doi.org/10.1177/1524838019833001

Ely, D. M., & Driscoll, A. K. (2021). Infant Mortality in the United States, 2019: Data From the Period Linked Birth/Infant Death File. *National Vital Statistics Reports, 70*(14), 1–18. https://doi.org/10.15620/cdc:111053

Ely, D. M., & Hoyert, D. L. (2018). Differences between rural and urban areas in mortality rates for the leading causes of infant death: United States, 2013–2015. *NCHS Data Brief*, (No 300), 300. https://www.cdc.gov/nchs/products/databriefs/db300.htm

Eme, R. (2020). Life course persistent antisocial behavior silver anniversary. *Aggression and Violent Behavior, 50*, 101344. https://doi.org/10.1016/j.avb.2019.101344

Emeruwa, U. N., Ona, S., Shaman, J. L., Turitz, A., Wright, J. D., Gyamfi-Bannerman, C., & Melamed, A. (2020). Associations between built environment, neighborhood socioeconomic status, and SARS-CoV-2 infection among pregnant women in New York City. *JAMA, 324*(4), 390–392. https://doi.org/10.1001/jama.2020.11370

Emmanuel, M., & Bokor, B. R. (2017). *Tanner stages. StatPearls*. http://www.ncbi.nlm.nih.gov/pubmed/29262142

Emond, J. A., Tantum, L. K., Gilbert-Diamond, D., Kim, S. J., Lansigan, R. K., & Neelon, S. B. (2018). Household chaos and screen media use among preschool-aged children: A cross-sectional study. *BMC Public Health, 18*(1), 1210. https://doi.org/10.1186/s12889-018-6113-2

Endendijk, J. J., Groeneveld, M. G., Bakermans-Kranenburg, M. J., & Mesman, J. (2016). Gender-differentiated parenting revisited: Meta-analysis reveals very few differences in parental control of boys and girls. *PLoS ONE, 11*(7), e0159193. https://doi.org/10.1371/journal.pone.0159193

Endendijk, J. J., Groeneveld, M. G., van der Pol, L. D., van Berkel, S. R., Hallers-Haalboom, E. T., Bakermans-Kranenburg, M. J., & Mesman, J. (2017). Gender differences in child aggression: Relations with gender-differentiated parenting and parents' gender-role stereotypes. *Child Development, 88*(1), 299–316. https://doi.org/10.1111/cdev.12589

Enge, A., Kapoor, S., Kieslinger, A.-S., & Skeide, M. A. (2023). A meta-analysis of mental rotation in the first years of life. *Developmental Science, 26*(6), e13381. https://doi.org/10.1111/desc.13381

Engel, M. L., & Gunnar, M. R. (2020). The development of stress reactivity and regulation during human development. In A. Clow & N. Smyth (Eds.), *International Review of Neurobiology* (Vol. 150, pp. 41–76). https://doi.org/10.1016/bs.irn.2019.11.003

Engel, M. L., & Gunnar, M. R. (2020). The development of stress reactivity and regulation during human development. In A. Clow & N. Smyth (Eds.), *International Review of Neurobiology* (Vol. 150). https://doi.org/10.1016/bs.irn.2019.11.003

Engels, M. C., Spilt, J., Denies, K., & Verschueren, K. (2021). The role of affective teacher-student relationships in adolescents' school engagement and achievement trajectories. *Learning and Instruction, 75*, 101485. https://doi.org/10.1016/j.learninstruc.2021.101485

Engler, A. D., Sarpong, K. O., Van Horne, B. S., Greeley, C. S., & Keefe, R. J. (2022). A systematic review of mental health disorders of children in foster care. *Trauma, Violence, & Abuse, 23*(1), 255–264. https://doi.org/10.1177/1524838020941197

Englund, K., & Behne, D. (2006). Changes in infant directed speech in the first six months. *Infant and Child Development: An International Journal of Research and Practice, 15*(2), 139–160. https://doi.org/10.1002/icd.445

Ennouri, K., & Bloch, H. (1996). Visual control of hand approach movements in newborns. *British Journal of Developmental Psychology, 14*(3), 327–338. https://doi.org/10.1111/j.2044-835X.1996.tb00709.x

Enright, R. D., Bjerstedt, Å., Enright, W. F., Levy, V. M., Jr, Lapsley., K, D., Buss, R. R., Harwell, M., & Zindler, Monica. (1984). Distributive justice development: Cross-cultural, contextual, and longitudinal evaluations. *Child Development, 55*(5), 1737–1751. https://doi.org/10.1111/1467-8624.ep7304494

Erchick, D. J., Agarwal, S., Kaysin, A., Gibson, D. G., & Labrique, A. B. (2022). Changes in prenatal care and vaccine willingness among pregnant women during the COVID-19 pandemic. *BMC Pregnancy and Childbirth, 22*(1), 1–9. https://doi.org/10.1186/S12884-022-04882-X/TABLES/4

Erck Lambert, A. B., Shapiro-Mendoza, C. K., Parks, S. E., Cottengim, C., Faulkner, M., & Hauck, F. R. (2024). Characteristics of sudden unexpected infant deaths on shared and nonshared sleep surfaces. *Pediatrics, 153*(3), e2023061984. https://doi.org/10.1542/peds.2023-061984

Erdley, C. A., & Day, H. J. (2016). Friendship in childhood and adolescence. In M. Hojjat & A. Moyer (Eds.), *The psychology of friendship* (pp. 3–20). Oxford University Press. https://doi.org/10.1093/acprof:oso/9780190222024.003.0001

Ericsson, K. A., & Moxley, J. H. (2013). Experts' superior memory: From accumulation of chunks to building memory skills that mediate improved performance and learning. In T. J. Perfect & D. S. Lindsay (Eds.), *The SAGE handbook of applied memory* (pp. 404–420). SAGE.

Erikson, E. H. (1950). *Childhood and society*. Norton.

Erikson, E. H. (1959). *Identity and the life cycle* (Vol. 64). Norton.

Erol, R. Y., & Orth, U. (2011). Self-esteem development from age 14 to 30 years: A longitudinal study. *Journal of Personality and Social Psychology, 101*(3), 607–619. https://doi.org/10.1037/a0024299

Ersan, C. (2020). Physical aggression, relational aggression and anger in preschool children: The mediating role of emotion regulation. *Journal of General Psychology, 147*(1), 18–42. https://doi.org/10.1080/00221309.2019.1609897

Ertekin Pinar, S., & Ozbek, H. (2022). Paternal depression and attachment levels of first-time fathers in Turkey. *Perspectives in Psychiatric Care, 58*(3), 1082–1088. https://doi.org/10.1111/ppc.12905

Ervin, J., Scovelle, A., Churchill, B., Maheen, H., & King, T. (2023). Gender identity and sexual orientation: A glossary. *Journal of Epidemiology & Community Health, 77*(5), 344–348. https://doi.org/10.1136/jech-2022-220009

Esakky, P., & Moley, K. H. (2016). Paternal smoking and germ cell death: A mechanistic link to the effects of cigarette smoke on spermatogenesis and possible long-term sequelae in offspring. *Molecular and Cellular Endocrinology, 435*, 85–93. https://doi.org/10.1016/J.MCE.2016.07.015

Esnaola, I., Sesé, A., Antonio-Agirre, I., & Azpiazu, L. (2020). The development of multiple self-concept dimensions during adolescence. *Journal of Research on Adolescence, 30*(S1), 100–114. https://doi.org/10.1111/jora.12451

Esoh, K., & Wonkam, A. (2021). Evolutionary history of sickle-cell mutation: Implications for global genetic medicine. *Human Molecular Genetics, 30*(R1), R119–R128. https://doi.org/10.1093/hmg/ddab004

Espinoza, G., & Juvonen, J. (2011). Perceptions of the school social context across the transition to middle school: Heightened sensitivity among Latino students? *Journal of Educational Psychology*, *103*(3), 749–758. https://doi.org/10.1037/a0023811

Esteban-Cornejo, I., Tejero-Gonzalez, C. M., Sallis, J. F., & Veiga, O. L. (2015). Physical activity and cognition in adolescents: A systematic review. *Journal of Science and Medicine in Sport*, *18*(5), 534–539. https://doi.org/10.1016/J.JSAMS.2014.07.007

Estes, K. G., & Hurley, K. (2013). Infant-directed prosody helps infants map sounds to meanings. *Infancy*, *18*(5), 797–824. https://doi.org/10.1111/infa.12006

Esteve-Gilbert, N., & Prieto, P. (2013). Prosody signals the emergence of intentional communication in the first year of life: Evidence from Catalan-babbling infants. *Journal of Child Language*, *40*(5), 919–944. https://doi.org/10.1017/S0305000912000359

Estrada, S., Gee, D. G., Bozic, I., Cinguina, M., Joormann, J., & Baskin-Sommers, A. (2023). Individual and environmental correlates of childhood maltreatment and exposure to community violence: Utilizing a latent profile and a multilevel meta-analytic approach. *Psychological Medicine*, *53*(1), 189–205. https://doi.org/10.1017/S0033291721001380

Etaugh, C., & Liss, M. B. (1992). Home, school, and playroom: Training grounds for adult gender roles. *Sex Roles*, *26*(3), 129–147. https://doi.org/10.1007/BF00289754

Ethier, K. A., Kann, L., & McManus, T. (2018). Sexual intercourse among high school students—29 states and United States overall, 2005–2015. *Morbidity and Mortality Weekly Report*, *66*(5152), 1393–1397. https://doi.org/10.15585/mmwr.mm665152a1

Ettinger, K., & Cohen, A. (2020). Patterns of multitasking behaviours of adolescents in digital environments. *Education and Information Technologies*, *25*(1), 623–645. https://doi.org/10.1007/s10639-019-09982-4

Evans, D. W., Milanak, M. E., Medeiros, B., & Ross, J. L. (2002). Magical beliefs and rituals in young children. *Child Psychiatry and Human Development*, *33*, 43–58.

Evans, G. W., & Kim, P. (2013). Childhood poverty, chronic stress, self-regulation, and coping. *Child Development Perspectives*, *7*(1), 43–48. https://doi.org/10.1111/cdep.12013

Evans, S. W., Owens, J. S., Wymbs, B. T., & Ray, A. R. (2018). Evidence-based psychosocial treatments for children and adolescents with attention deficit/hyperactivity disorder. *Journal of Clinical Child & Adolescent Psychology*, *47*(2), 157–198. https://doi.org/10.1080/15374416.2017.1390757

Evans-Lacko, S., Takizawa, R., Brimblecombe, N., King, D., Knapp, M., Maughan, B., & Arseneault, L. (2017). Childhood bullying victimization is associated with use of mental health services over five decades: A longitudinal nationally representative cohort study. *Psychological Medicine*, *47*(1), 127–135. https://doi.org/10.1017/S0033291716001719

Eves, R., Mendonça, M., Bartmann, P., & Wolke, D. (2020). Small for gestational age—Cognitive performance from infancy to adulthood: An observational study. *BJOG*, *127*(13). https://doi.org/10.1111/1471-0528.16341

Eyler, A. A., Schmidt, L., Kepper, M., Mazzucca, S., Gilbert, A., & Beck, A. (2021). Parent perceptions of changes in child physical activity during COVID-19 stay-at-home orders. *Frontiers in Public Health*, *9*, 637151. https://doi.org/10.3389/fpubh.2021.637151

Eyuboglu, M., Eyuboglu, D., Pala, S. C., Oktar, D., Demirtas, Z., Arslantas, D., & Unsal, A. (2021). Traditional school bullying and cyberbullying: Prevalence, the effect on mental health problems and self-harm behavior. *Psychiatry Research*, *297*, 113730. https://doi.org/10.1016/j.psychres.2021.113730

Fadjukoff, P., Pulkkinen, L., & Kokko, K. (2016). Identity formation in adulthood: A longitudinal study from age 27 to 50. *Identity*, *16*(1), 8–23. https://doi.org/10.1080/15283488.2015.1121820

Fadus, M. C., Ginsburg, K. R., Sobowale, K., Halliday-Boykins, C. A., Bryant, B. E., Gray, K. M., & Squeglia, L. M. (2020). Unconscious bias and the diagnosis of disruptive behavior disorders and ADHD in African American and Hispanic youth. *Academic Psychiatry*, *44*(1), 95–102. https://doi.org/10.1007/s40596-019-01127-6

Fagan, J. F. (2011). Intelligence in infancy. In R. J. Sternberg & S. B. Kaufman (Eds.), *The Cambridge handbook of intelligence* (pp. 130–142). Cambridge University Press.

Fagard, J., Spelke, E., & von Hofsten, C. (2009). Reaching and grasping a moving object in 6-, 8-, and 10-month-old infants: Laterality and performance. *Infant Behavior & Development*, *32*(2), 137–146. https://doi.org/10.1016/j.infbeh.2008.12.002

Fallah, H., & Rademaker, M. (2022). Isotretinoin for acne vulgaris–an update on adverse effects and laboratory monitoring. *Journal of Dermatological Treatment*, *33*(5). https://doi.org/10.1080/09546634.2021.1967269

Family Equality. (n.d.). *Average adoption costs in the United States*. Retrieved February 16, 2024, from https://www.familyequality.org/resources/average-adoption-costs-in-the-united-states/

Fandakova, Y., & Hartley, C. A. (2020). Mechanisms of learning and plasticity in childhood and adolescence. *Developmental Cognitive Neuroscience*, *42*, 100764. https://doi.org/10.1016/j.dcn.2020.100764

Fang, K., Mu, M., Liu, K., & He, Y. (2019). Screen time and childhood overweight/obesity: A systematic review and meta-analysis. *Child: Care, Health and Development*, *45*(5). https://doi.org/10.1111/cch.12701

Fantz, R. L. (1961). The origin of form perception. *Scientific American*, *204*, 66–72.

Farago, F., Martin, C. L., Granger, K. L., Santos, C. E., & Miller, C. F. (2022). Teachers' gender-role attitudes and gendered classroom practices. *Sex Roles*, *87*(9), 471–486. https://doi.org/10.1007/s11199-022-01331-z

Faraone, S. V., Bellgrove, M. A., Brikell, I., Cortese, S., Hartman, C. A., Hollis, C., Newcorn, J. H., Philipsen, A., Polanczyk, G. V., Rubia, K., Sibley, M. H., & Buitelaar, J. K. (2024). Attention-deficit/hyperactivity disorder. *Nature Reviews Disease Primers*, *10*(11). https://doi.org/10.1038/s41572-024-00495-0

Farber, D. A., & Beteleva, T. G. (2011). Development of the brain's organization of working memory in young schoolchildren. *Human Physiology*, *37*(1), 1–13. https://doi.org/10.1134/s0362119710061015

Farhi, A., Glasser, S., & Lerner-Geva, L. (2019). Health and development of children born following assisted reproductive technology treatments. In O. Taubman. – Ben-Ari (Ed.), *Pathways and barriers to parenthood: Existential concerns regarding fertility, pregnancy, and early parenthood* (pp. 101–111). Springer International. https://doi.org/10.1007/978-3-030-24864-2_6

Farooq, M. A., Parkinson, K. N., Adamson, A. J., Pearce, M. S., Reilly, J. K., Hughes, A. R., Janssen, X., Basterfield, L., & Reilly, J. J. (2018). Timing of the decline in physical activity in childhood and adolescence: Gateshead millennium cohort study. *British Journal of Sports Medicine*, *52*, 1002–1006. https://doi.org/10.1136/bjsports-2016-096933

Farr, R. H. (2017). Does parental sexual orientation matter? A longitudinal follow-up of adoptive families with school-age children. *Developmental Psychology*, *53*(2), 252–264. https://doi.org/10.1037/dev0000228

Farr, R. H., Bruun, S. T., & Patterson, C. J. (2019). Longitudinal associations between coparenting and child adjustment among lesbian, gay, and heterosexual adoptive parent families. *Developmental Psychology*, 55, 2547–2560. https://doi.org/10.1037/dev0000828

Farr, R. H., & Grotevant, H. D. (2019). Adoption. In B. H. Fiese, M. Celano, K. Deater-Deckard, E. N. Jouriles, & M. A. Whisman (Eds.), *APA handbook of contemporary family psychology: Foundations, methods, and contemporary issues across the lifespan* (Vol. 1, pp. 725–741). American Psychological Association. https://doi.org/10.1037/0000099-040

Farrell, A. D., Thompson, E. L., & Mehari, K. R. (2017). Dimensions of peer influences and their relationship to adolescents' aggression, other problem behaviors and prosocial behavior. *Journal of Youth and Adolescence*, 46, 1351–1369. https://doi.org/10.1007/s10964-016-0601-4

Farroni, T., Menon, E., Rigato, S., & Johnson, M. H. (2007). The perception of facial expressions in newborns. *European Journal of Developmental Psychology*, 4(1), 2–13. https://doi.org/10.1080/17405620601046832

Farrow, J., Wasik, B. A., & Hindman, A. H. (2020). Exploring the unique contributions of teachers' syntax to preschoolers' and kindergarteners' vocabulary learning. *Early Childhood Research Quarterly*, 51, 178–190. https://doi.org/10.1016/j.ecresq.2019.08.005

Farruggia, S. P., Germo, G. R., & Solomon, B. J. (2018). Foster care. In R. J. R. Levesque (Ed.), *Encyclopedia of Adolescence* (pp. 1469–1486). Springer International. https://doi.org/10.1007/978-3-319-33228-4_299

Farver, J. A. M., Xu, Y., Eppe, S., Fernandez, A., & Schwartz, D. (2005). Community violence, family conflict, and preschoolers' socioemotional functioning. *Developmental Psychology*, 41, 160–170. https://doi.org/10.1037/0012-1649.41.1.160

Fast, A. A., & Olson, K. R. (2018). Gender development in transgender preschool children. *Child Development*, 89(2), 620–637. https://doi.org/10.1111/cdev.12758

Fatollahzade, M., Parvizi, S., Kashaki, M., Haghani, H., & Alinejad-Naeini, M. (2020). The effect of gentle human touch during endotracheal suctioning on procedural pain response in preterm infant admitted to neonatal intensive care units: A randomized controlled crossover study. *Journal of Maternal-Fetal & Neonatal Medicine*, 35(7), 1370–1376. https://doi.org/10.1080/14767058.2020.1755649

Fauser, B. C. J. M., Devroey, P., Diedrich, K., Balaban, B., Bonduelle, M., Delemarre-van de Waal, H. A., Estella, C., Ezcurra, D., Geraedts, J. P. M., Howles, C. M., Lerner-Geva, L., Serna, J., & Wells, D. (2014). Health outcomes of children born after IVF/ICSI: A review of current expert opinion and literature. *Reproductive BioMedicine Online*, 28(2), 162–182. https://doi.org/10.1016/J.RBMO.2013.10.013

Federal Interagency Forum on Child and Family Statistics. (2017). *America's children: Key national indicators of well-being, 2017*. U.S. Department of Health and Human Services. https://www.childstats.gov/americaschildren/index.asp

Federal Interagency Forum on Child and Family Statistics. (2021). *Introduction*. Key National Indicators of Well-Being. 2021 https://www.childstats.gov/americaschildren/index.asp

Federal Interagency Forum on Child and Family Statistics. (2023). *Sexual activity*. Key National Indicators of Well-Being. 2023 https://www.childstats.gov/americaschildren/beh4.asp

Federico, M. J., McFarlane, A. E., Szefler, S. J., & Abrams, E. M. (2020). The impact of social determinants of health on children with asthma. *Journal of Allergy and Clinical Immunology: In Practice*, 8(6). https://doi.org/10.1016/j.jaip.2020.03.028

Fedewa, A. L., Black, W. W., & Ahn, S. (2014). Children and adolescents with same-gender parents: A meta-analytic approach in assessing outcomes. *Journal of GLBT Family Studies*, 11(1), 1–34. https://doi.org/10.1080/1550428X.2013.869486

Feeney, B. C., & Monin, J. K. (2016). Divorce through the lens of attachment theory. In J. Shaver & P. R. Cassidy (Eds.), *Handbook of Attachment: Theory, Research, and Clinical Applications* (pp. 941–965).

Fehr, K. K., Boog, K. E., & Leraas, B. C. (2020). Play behaviors: Definition and typology. In S. Hupp & J. D. Jewell (Eds.), *The encyclopedia of child and adolescent development* (pp. 1–10). Wiley. https://doi.org/10.1002/9781119171492.wecad272

Feinberg, M. E., Mogle, J. A., Lee, J.-K., Tornello, S. L., Hostetler, M. L., Cifelli, J. A., Bai, S., & Hotez, E. (2022). Impact of the COVID-19 pandemic on parent, child, and family functioning. *Family Process*, 61(1), 361–374. https://doi.org/10.1111/famp.12649

Feinberg, M. E., Solmeyer, A. R., & McHale, S. M. (2012). The third rail of family systems: Sibling relationships, mental and behavioral health, and preventive intervention in childhood and adolescence. *Clinical Child and Family Psychology Review*, 15(1), 43–57. https://doi.org/10.1007/s10567-011-0104-5

Feldman, M. A., King, C. K., Vitale, S., Denhardt, B., Stroup, S., Reese, J., & Stromberg, S. (2023). The impact of COVID-19 on adolescents with eating disorders: Increased need for medical stabilization and decreased access to care. *International Journal of Eating Disorders*, 56(1), 257–262. https://doi.org/10.1002/eat.23788

Feldman, R., Dollberg, D., & Nadam, R. (2011). The expression and regulation of anger in toddlers: Relations to maternal behavior and mental representations. *Infant Behavior & Development*, 34(2), 310–320. https://doi.org/10.1016/j.infbeh.2011.02.001

Felmlee, D., McMillan, C., Inara Rodis, P., & Osgood, D. W. (2018). Falling behind: Lingering costs of the high school transition for youth friendships and grades. *Sociology of Education*, 91(2), 159–182. https://doi.org/10.1177/0038040718762136

Fen, X. (2024). Perceptual development. In *The ECPH Encyclopedia of Psychology* (pp. 1–2). Springer Nature. https://doi.org/10.1007/978-981-99-6000-2_340-1

Ferguson, C. J. (2013a). Television violence. In C. J. Ferguson (Ed.), *Adolescents, crime, and the media: A critical analysis* (pp. 83–103). Springer. https://doi.org/10.1007/978-1-4614-6741-0_6

Ferguson, C. J. (2013b). Violent video games and the Supreme Court: Lessons for the scientific community in the wake of Brown v. Entertainment Merchants Association. *American Psychologist*, 68(2), 57–74. https://doi.org/10.1037/a0030597

Ferguson, C. J. (2015). Do angry birds make for angry children? A meta-analysis of video game influences on children's and adolescents' aggression, mental health, prosocial behavior, and academic performance. *Perspectives on Psychological Science*, 10(5), 646–666. https://doi.org/10.1177/1745691615592234

Ferguson, G. M., Hafen, C. A., & Laursen, B. (2010). Adolescent psychological and academic adjustment as a function of discrepancies between actual and ideal self-perceptions. *Journal of Youth and Adolescence*, 39(12), 1485–1497. https://doi.org/10.1007/s10964-009-9461-5

Ferguson, S., Brass, N. R., Medina, M. A., & Ryan, A. M. (2022). The role of school friendship stability, instability, and network size in early adolescents' social adjustment. *Developmental Psychology, 58*, 950–962. https://doi.org/10.1037/dev0001328

Fergusson, D. M., Boden, J. M., Horwood, L. J., Miller, A. L., & Kenned., M. A. (2011). MAOA, abuse exposure and antisocial behaviour: 30-year longitudinal study. *British Journal of Psychiatry, 198*(6), 457–463. https://doi.org/10.1192/bjp.bp.110.086991

Ferjan Ramírez, N. (2022). Fathers' infant-directed speech and its effects on child language development. *Language and Linguistics Compass, 16*(1), e12448. https://doi.org/10.1111/LNC3.12448

Ferjan Ramírez, N., Ramírez, R. R., Clarke, M., Taulu, S., & Kuhl, P. K. (2017). Speech discrimination in 11-month-old bilingual and monolingual infants: A magnetoencephalography study. *Developmental Science, 20*(1), e12427. https://doi.org/10.1111/desc.12427

Fernald, A., Marchman, V. A., & Weisleder, A. (2013). SES differences in language processing skill and vocabulary are evident at 18 months. *Developmental Science, 16*(2), 234–248. https://doi.org/10.1111/desc.12019

Fernald, A., & Morikawa, H. (1993). Common themes and cultural variations in Japanese and American mothers' speech to infants. *Child Development, 64*(3), 657–674. https://doi.org/10.1111/j.1467-8624.1993.tb02933.x

Fernandes, D. M., Oliveira, C. R., Guerguis, S., Eisenberg, R., Choi, J., Kim, M., Abdelhemid, A., Agha, R., Agarwal, S., Aschner, J. L., Avner, J. R., Ballance, C., Bock, J., Bhavsar, S. M., Campbell, M., Clouser, K. N., Gesner, M., Goldman, D. L., Hammerschlag, M. R., & …; Herold, B. C. (2021). Severe acute respiratory syndrome coronavirus 2 clinical syndromes and predictors of disease severity in hospitalized children and youth. *Journal of Pediatrics, 230*, 23–31.e10. https://doi.org/10.1016/j.jpeds.2020.11.016

Fernández, de Gamarra-Oca., L, Ojeda., N, Gómez-Gastiasoro., A, Peña., J, Ibarretxe-Bilbao., N, García-Guerrero., A, M., Loureiro, B., & Zubiaurre-Elorza, L. (2021). Long-term neurodevelopmental outcomes after moderate and late preterm birth: A systematic review. *Journal of Pediatrics, 237*, 168–176.e11. https://doi.org/10.1016/j.jpeds.2021.06.004

Fernández-Zabala, A., Ramos-Díaz, E., Rodríguez-Fernández, A., & Núñez, J. L. (2020). Sociometric popularity, perceived peer support, and self-concept in adolescence. *Frontiers in Psychology, 11*, 594007. https://www.frontiersin.org/articles/10.3389/fpsyg.2020.594007

Fernyhough, C., & Borghi, A. M. (2023). Inner speech as language process and cognitive tool. *Trends in Cognitive Sciences, 27*(12), 1180–1193. https://doi.org/10.1016/j.tics.2023.08.014

Ferrara, A. M., Mullins, C. A., Ellner, S., & Van Meter, P. (2023). Early child maltreatment and reading processes, abilities, and achievement: A systematic review. *Child Abuse & Neglect, 142*, 105857. https://doi.org/10.1016/j.chiabu.2022.105857

Ferrari, V., Stefanucci, S., Ferrari, M., Ciofi, D., Stagi, S., Milanesi, A., Cecchi, R., Fiore, R., Pierattelli, M., Pittari, A. M., Chiccoli, A., Becherucci, P., Cova, A., Guidotti, T., Balzer, E., Citino, G. S. G., Bagni, P., Guarnieri, M., Pecchioli, R., & …; Gabbrielli, M. (2022). Retrospective longitudinal analysis of the effects of postnatal weight gain on the timing and tempo of puberty and menarche in a cohort of Italian girls. *Italian Journal of Pediatrics, 48*(1). https://doi.org/10.1186/s13052-022-01222-9

Ferreira Pinto, R., & Xu, Y. (2021). A computational theory of child overextension. *Cognition, 206*, 104472. https://doi.org/10.1016/j.cognition.2020.104472

Ferschmann, L., Vijayakumar, N., Grydeland, H., Overbye, K., Sederevicius, D., Due-Tønnessen, P., Fjell, A. M., Walhovd, K. B., Pfeifer, J. H., & Tamnes, C. K. (2019). Prosocial behavior relates to the rate and timing of cortical thinning from adolescence to young adulthood. *Developmental Cognitive Neuroscience, 40*, 100734. https://doi.org/10.1016/J.DCN.2019.100734

Feugé, É. A., Cyr, C., Cossette, L., & Julien, D. (2020). Adoptive gay fathers' sensitivity and child attachment and behavior problems. *Attachment & Human Development, 22*(3), 247–268. https://doi.org/10.1080/14616734.2018.1557224

Field, N. H., Choukas-Bradley, S., Giletta, M., Telzer, E. H., Cohen, G. L., & Prinstein, M. J. (2024). Why adolescents conform to high-status peers: Associations among conformity, identity alignment, and self-esteem. *Child Development, 95*(3), 879–894. https://doi.org/10.1111/cdev.14038

Fields-Olivieri, M. A., Cole, P. M., & Roben, C. K. P. (2020). Toddler emotion expressions and emotional traits: Associations with parent-toddler verbal conversation. *Infant Behavior and Development, 61*, 101474. https://doi.org/10.1016/j.infbeh.2020.101474

Figueiredo, B., Dias, C. C., Pinto, T. M., & Field, T. (2016). Infant sleep-wake behaviors at two weeks, three and six months. *Infant Behavior and Development, 44*, 169–178. https://doi.org/10.1016/J.INFBEH.2016.06.011

Filipović, K. (2018). Gender representation in children's books: Case of an early childhood setting. *Journal of Research in Childhood Education, 32*(3), 310–325. https://doi.org/10.1080/02568543.2018.1464086

Filippello, P., Buzzai, C., Costa, S., Orecchio, S., & Sorrenti, L. (2020). Teaching style and academic achievement: The mediating role of learned helplessness and mastery orientation. *Psychology in the Schools, 57*(1), 5–16. https://doi.org/10.1002/PITS.22315

Filippova, E., & Astington, J. W. (2008). Further development in social reasoning revealed in discourse irony understanding. *Child Development, 79*(1), 126–138. https://doi.org/10.1111/j.1467-8624.2007.01115.x

Finch, J. E. (2019). Do schools promote executive functions? Differential working memory growth across school-year and summer months. *AERA Open, 5*(2), 233285841984844. https://doi.org/10.1177/2332858419848443

Finegold, D. N. (2021). *Overview of genetics—special subjects—Merck manuals professional edition*. Merck Manual. https://www.merckmanuals.com/professional/special-subjects/general-principles-of-medical-genetics/overview-of-genetics

Fink, E., Patalay, P., Sharpe, H., & Wolpert, M. (2018). Child- and school-level predictors of children's bullying behavior: A multilevel analysis in 648 primary schools. *Journal of Educational Psychology, 110*(1), 17–26. https://doi.org/10.1037/edu0000204

Finkelhor, D., Ormrod, R. K., & Turner, H. A. (2009). The developmental epidemiology of childhood victimization. *Journal of Interpersonal Violence, 24*(5), 711–731. https://doi.org/10.1177/0886260508317185

Finn, A. S., Minas, J. E., Leonard, J. A., Mackey, A. P., Salvatore, J., Goetz, C., West, M. R., Gabrieli, C. F. O., & Gabrieli, J. D. E. (2017). Functional brain organization of working memory in adolescents varies in relation to family income and academic achievement. *Developmental Science, 20*(5), e12450. https://doi.org/10.1111/desc.12450

Fiorilli, C., Grimaldi Capitello, T., Barni, D., Buonomo, I., & Gentile, S. (2019). Predicting adolescent depression: The interrelated roles of self-esteem and interpersonal stressors. *Frontiers in Psychology, 10*(MAR), 565. https://doi.org/10.3389/fpsyg.2019.00565

Fischer, U., Suggate, S. P., Schmirl, J., & Stoeger, H. (2018). Counting on fine motor skills: Links between preschool finger dexterity and numerical skills. *Developmental Science, 21*(4), e12623. https://doi.org/10.1111/desc.12623

Fischer, U., Suggate, S. P., & Stoeger, H. (2020). The implicit contribution of fine motor skills to mathematical insight in early childhood. *Frontiers in Psychology, 11*, 1143. https://doi.org/10.3389/fpsyg.2020.01143

Fish, J. N. (2020). Future directions in understanding and addressing mental health among LGBTQ youth. *Journal of Clinical Child & Adolescent Psychology, 49*(6), 943–956. https://doi.org/10.1080/15374416.2020.1815207

Fish, J. N., Bishop, M. D., & Russell, S. T. (2023). Age trends in bias-based bullying and mental health by sexual orientation and gender identity. *Prevention Science, 24*(6), 1142–1151. https://doi.org/10.1007/s11121-023-01530-4

Fish, R. E. (2019). Standing out and sorting in: Exploring the role of racial composition in racial disparities in special education. *American Educational Research Journal, 56*(6), 2573–2608. https://doi.org/10.3102/0002831219847966

Fisher, A., & Kloos, H. (2016). Development of selective sustained attention: The role of executive functions. In J. A. Griffin, P. McCardle, & L. S. Freund (Eds.), *Executive function in preschool-age children: Integrating measurement, neurodevelopment, and translational research* (pp. 215–237). American Psychological Association. https://doi.org/10.1037/14797-010

Fisher, A. V. (2019). Selective sustained attention: A developmental foundation for cognition. *Current Opinion in Psychology, 29*, 248–253. https://doi.org/10.1016/j.copsyc.2019.06.002

Fisher, C. B., Busch-Rossnagel, Nancy A. Jopp., S, D., & Brown, J. (2013). Applied developmental science: Contributions and challenges for the 21st century. In I. B. Weiner (Ed.), *Handbook of psychology* (Vol. 6, pp. 517–546). Wiley.

Fisher, S. E. (2017). Evolution of language: Lessons from the genome. *Psychonomic Bulletin & Review, 24*(1), 34–40. https://doi.org/10.3758/s13423-016-1112-8

Fiske, A., & Holmboe, K. (2019). Neural substrates of early executive function development. *Developmental Review, 52*, 42–62. https://doi.org/10.1016/j.dr.2019.100866

Fite, P. J., Hendrickson, M., Rubens, S. L., Gabrielli, J., & Evans, S. (2013). The role of peer rejection in the link between reactive aggression and academic performance. *Child & Youth Care Forum, 42*(3), 193–205. https://doi.org/10.1007/s10566-013-9199-9

Fitneva, S. A., & Matsui, T. (2015). The emergence and development of language across cultures. In L. A. Jensen (Ed.), *The Oxford handbook of human development and culture: An interdisciplinary perspective*. Oxford University Press. https://doi.org/10.1093/oxfordhb/9780199948550.013.8

Fitzpatrick, M., & McPherson, B. (2010). Coloring within the lines: Gender stereotypes in contemporary coloring books. *Sex Roles, 62*, 127–137. https://doi.org/10.1007/s11199-009-9703-8

Fitzsimmons, P., Leddy, D., Johnson, L., Biggam, S., & Locke, S. (2013). The moon challenge. *Science and Children, 51*(1), 36–41. https://doi.org/10.2505/4/sc13_051_01_36

Fivush, R. (2011). The development of autobiographical memory. *Annual Review of Psychology, 62*, 559–582. https://doi.org/10.1146/annurev.psych.121208.131702

Fivush, R. (2019). Sociocultural developmental approaches to autobiographical memory. *Applied Cognitive Psychology, 33*(4), 489–497. https://doi.org/10.1002/acp.3512

Fivush, R., Hudson, J., & Nelson, K. (1983). Children's long-term memory for a novel event: An exploratory study. *Merrill-Palmer Quarterly, 30*, 303–316.

Fivush, R., & Zaman, W. (2014). Gender, subjective perspective, and autobiographical consciousness. In J. Bauer & R. Fivush (Eds.), *The Wiley handbook on the development of children's memory* (pp. 586–604). https://psycnet.apa.org/record/2013-26762-025

Flaherty, S. C., & Sadler, L. S. (2022). Parenting stress among adolescent mothers: An integrative literature review. *Western Journal of Nursing Research, 44*(7), 701–719. https://doi.org/10.1177/01939459211014241

Flanagan, D. P., & Alfonso, V. C. (2017). *Essentials of WISC-V assessment*. Wiley.

Flannery, K. M., & Smith, R. L. (2017). The effects of age, gender, and gender role ideology on adolescents' social perspective-taking ability and tendency in friendships. *Journal of Social and Personal Relationships, 34*(5), 617–635. https://doi.org/10.1177/0265407516650942

Flannery, K. M., & Smith, R. L. (2021). Breaking up (with a friend) is hard to do: An examination of friendship dissolution among early adolescents. *Journal of Early Adolescence, 41*(9), 1368–1393. https://doi.org/10.1177/02724316211002266

Flaudias, V., Iceta, S., Zerhouni, O., Rodgers, R. F., Billieux, J., Llorca, P. M., Boudesseul, J., Chazeron, I. D. E., Romo, L., Maurage, P., Samalin, L., Begue, L., Naassila, M., Brousse, G., & Guillaume, S. (2020). COVID-19 pandemic lockdown and problematic eating behaviors in a student population. *Journal of Behavioral Addictions, 9*(3), 826–835. https://doi.org/10.1556/2006.2020.00053

Flavell, J. H. (1993). The development of children's understanding of false belief and the appearance-reality distinction. *International Journal of Psychology, 28*, 595–604. https://doi.org/10.1080/00207599308246944

Flavell, J. H. (1999). Cognitive development: Children's knowledge about the mind. *Annual Review of Psychology, 50*, 21–45. https://doi.org/10.1146/annurev.psych.50.1.21

Flavell, J. H., Everett, B. H., Croft, K., & Flavell, E. R. (1981). Young children's knowledge about visual perception: Further evidence for the level 1-level 2 distinction. *Developmental Psychology, 17*, 99–103. https://doi.org/10.1037/0012-1649.17.1.99

Flavell, J. H., Flavell, E. R., & Green, F. L. (2001). Development of children's understanding of connections between thinking and feeling. *Psychological Science, 12*(5), 430–432. https://doi.org/10.1111/1467-9280.00379

Flavell, J. H., Green, F. L., & Flavell, E. R. (1986). Development of knowledge about the appearance-reality distinction. *Monographs of the Society for Research in Child Development, 51*(1), i–1–v.87.

Flavell, J. H., Green, F. L., & Flavell, E. R. (1995). Young children's knowledge about thinking. *Monographs of the Society for Research in Child Development*. https://doi.org/10.2307/1166124 *60*(1, Serial No. 243 i, iii, v–vi, 1–113

Flieller, A. (1999). Comparison of the development of formal thought in adolescent cohorts aged 10 to 15 years (1967–1996 and 1972–1993). *Developmental Psychology, 35*(4), 1048–1058. https://doi.org/10.1037//0012-1649.35.4.1048

Flint, J., Greenspan, R. J., & Kendler, K. S. (2020). *How genes influence behavior* (2nd ed.). Oxford University Press.

Floccia, C., Christophe, A., & Bertoncini, J. (1997). High-amplitude sucking and newborns: The quest for underlying mechanisms. *Journal of Experimental Child Psychology*, *64*, 175-198.

Floccia, C., Christophe, A., & Bertoncini, J. (1997). High-amplitude sucking and newborns: The quest for underlying mechanisms. *Journal of Experimental Child Psychology*, *64*, 175-198. https://doi.org/10.1006/jecp.1996.2349

Flor, L. S., Friedman, J., Spencer, C. N., Cagney, J., Arrieta, A., Herbert, M. E., Stein, C., Mullany, E. C., Hon, J., Patwardhan, V., Barber, R. M., Collins, J. K., Hay, S. I., Lim, S. S., Lozano, R., Mokdad, A. H., Murray, C. J. L., Reiner, R. C., Sorensen, R. J. D., & &#hillip1; Gakidou, E. (2022). Quantifying the effects of the COVID-19 pandemic on gender equality on health, social, and economic indicators: A comprehensive review of data from March, 2020, to September, 2021. *Lancet*, *399*(10344), 2381-2397. https://doi.org/10.1016/S0140-6736(22)00008-3

Floyd, S., & Goldberg, A. E. (2021). Children make use of relationships across meanings in word learning. *Journal of Experimental Psychology: Learning Memory and Cognition*, *47*(1), 29. https://doi.org/10.1037/xlm0000821

Flynn, J. R. (1987). Massive IQ gains in 14 nations: What IQ tests really measure. *Psychological Bulletin of the World Health Organization*, *101*, 171-191.

Flynn, J. R. (1998). IQ gains over time: Toward finding the causes. In I. U. Neisser (Ed.), *The rising curve: Long-term gains in IQ and related measures* (pp. 25-66). American Psychological Association.

Flynn, J. R. (2020). Secular changes in intelligence: The "Flynn effect.". In *The Cambridge handbook of intelligence* (2nd ed., pp. 940-963). Cambridge University Press. https://doi.org/10.1017/9781108770422.040

Flynn, J. R., & Sternberg, R. J. (2019). Environment and intelligence. In R. J. Sternberg (Ed.), *Human intelligence: An introduction*. Cambridge University Press. https://www.cambridge.org/us/academic/subjects/psychology/psychology-general-interest/human-intelligence-introduction?format=PB&isbn=9781108703864

Flynn, J. R., & Weiss, L. G. (2007). American IQ gains from 1932 to 2002: The WISC subtests and educational progress. *International Journal of Testing*, *7*(2), 209-224. https://doi.org/10.1080/15305050701193587

Fogel, A. (2007). *Infancy: Infant, family, and society*. Sloan Educational.

Fombouchet, Y., Pineau, S., Perchec, C., Lucenet, J., & Lannegrand, L. (2023). The development of emotion regulation in adolescence: What do we know and where to go next? *Social Development*, *32*(4), 1227-1242. https://doi.org/10.1111/sode.12684

Fons Van de Vijver, Lawrence Weiss., & Donald, Saklofske. (2019). Cross cultural issues in children's intelligence: An international perspective. In L. Weiss, D. Saklofske, J. Holdnack, & A. Prifitera (Eds.), *WISC-V: Clinical use and interpretation*. Academic Press. https://www.elsevier.com/books/wisc-v/weiss/978-0-12-815744-2

Font, S. A., & Berger, L. M. (2014). Child maltreatment and children's developmental trajectories in early to middle childhood. *Child Development*, *86*(2), 536-556. https://doi.org/10.1111/cdev.12322

Fontanellaz-Castiglione, C. E., Markovic, A., & Tarokh, L. (2020). Sleep and the adolescent brain. *Current Opinion in Physiology*, *15*, 167-171. https://doi.org/10.1016/j.cophys.2020.01.008

Foran, H. M., Eckford, R. D., Sinclair, R. R., & Wright, K. M. (2017). Child mental health symptoms following parental deployment: The impact of parental posttraumatic stress disorder symptoms, marital distress, and general aggression. *SAGE Open*, *7*(3), 215824401772048. https://doi.org/10.1177/2158244017720484

Forbringer, L. (2020). Special education. In S. Hupp & J. D. Jewell (Eds.), *The encyclopedia of child and adolescent development* (pp. 1-12). Wiley. https://doi.org/10.1002/9781119171492.wecad379

Ford, D. Y., Collins, K. H., Grantham, T. C., & Moore, J. L. (2021). Equity-based gifted and talented education to increase the recruitment and retention of Black and other underrepresented students. In R. J. Sternberg & D. Ambrose (Eds.), *Conceptions of giftedness and talent* (pp. 141-161). Springer International. https://doi.org/10.1007/978-3-030-56869-6_9

Forestell, C. A. (2016). The development of flavor perception and acceptance: The roles of nature and nurture. *Nestle Nutrition Institute Workshop Series*, *85*, 135-143. https://doi.org/10.1159/000439504

Forestell, C. A. (2017). Flavor perception and preference development in human infants. *Annals of Nutrition and Metabolism*, *70*(3), 17-25. https://doi.org/10.1159/000478759

Forsberg, A., Adams, E. J., & Cowan, N. (2023). Why does visual working memory ability improve with age: More objects, more feature detail, or both? A registered report. *Developmental Science*, *26*(2), e13283. https://doi.org/10.1111/desc.13283

Forsberg, A., Blume, C. L., & Cowan, N. (2021). The development of metacognitive accuracy in working memory across childhood. *Developmental Psychology*, *57*(8), 1297-1317. https://doi.org/10.1037/dev0001213

Forsberg, A., Guitard, D., Adams, E. J., Pattanakul, D., & Cowan, N. (2022). Children's long-term retention is directly constrained by their working memory capacity limitations. *Developmental Science*, *25*(2), e13164. https://doi.org/10.1111/desc.13164

Fortea, J., Zaman, S. H., Hartley, S., Rafii, M. S., Head, E., & Carmona-Iragui, M. (2021). Alzheimer's disease associated with Down syndrome: A genetic form of dementia. *Lancet Neurology*, *20*(11). https://doi.org/10.1016/S1474-4422(21)00245-3

Fortenberry, J. D. (2013). Puberty and adolescent sexuality. *Hormones and Behavior*, *64*(2), 280-287. https://doi.org/10.1016/j.yhbeh.2013.03.007

Fosco, G. M., Sloan, C. J., Fang, S., & Feinberg, M. E. (2022). Family vulnerability and disruption during the COVID-19 pandemic: Prospective pathways to child maladjustment. *Journal of Child Psychology and Psychiatry, and Allied Disciplines*, *63*(1), 47-57. https://doi.org/10.1111/jcpp.13458

Fowler-Finn, K. D., & Boutwell, B. (2019). Using variation in heritability estimates as a test of G x E in behavioral research: A brief research note. *Behavior Genetics*, *49*(3), 340-346. https://doi.org/10.1007/s10519-019-09948-9

Fraga, L. R., Vianna, F. S. L., Del Campo, M., Sanseverino, M. T. V., & Schuler-Faccini, L. (2022). Editorial: Teratogenesis: Experimental models, mechanisms and clinical findings in humans. *Frontiers in Genetics*, *1*(3). https://doi.org/10.3389/FGENE.2022.901400

Frahsek, S., Mack, W., Mack, C., Pfalz-Blezinger, C., & Knopf, M. (2010). Assessing different aspects of pretend play within a play setting: Towards a standardized assessment of pretend play in young children. *British Journal of Developmental Psychology*, *28*(2), 331-345. https://doi.org/10.1348/026151009x413666

Fraley, R. C., & Shaver, P. R. (2021). Attachment theory and its place in contemporary personality theory and research. In *Handbook of personality: Theory and research*, 4th ed (pp. 642-666). The Guilford Press.

Franchak, J. M. (2020). The ecology of infants' perceptual-motor exploration. *Current Opinion in Psychology*, *3*(2). https://doi.org/10.1016/j.copsyc.2019.06.035

Franchini, M., Smith, I. M., Sacrey, L., Duku, E., Brian, J., Bryson, S. E., Vaillancourt, T., Armstrong, V., Szatmari, P., Roberts, W., Roncadin, C., & Zwaigenbaum, L. (2023). Continuity of trajectories of autism symptom severity from infancy to childhood. *Journal of Child Psychology and Psychiatry*, 64(6), 895–906. https://doi.org/10.1111/jcpp.13744

Francis, F., & Cappello, S. (2021). Neuronal migration and disorders – an update. *Current Opinion in Neurobiology*, 6(6). https://doi.org/10.1016/j.conb.2020.10.002

Frangou, S., Modabbernia, A., Williams, S. C. R., Papachristou, E., Doucet, G. E., Agartz, I., Aghajani, M., Akudjedu, T. N., Albajes-Eizagirre, A., Alnæs, D., Alpert, K. I., Andersson, M., Andreasen, N. C., Andreassen, O. A., Asherson, P., Banaschewski, T., Bargallo, N., Baumeister, S., Baur-Streubel, R., & &#hillip1; Dima, D. (2022). Cortical thickness across the lifespan: Data from 17,075 healthy individuals aged 3–90 years. *Human Brain Mapping*, 43(1), 431–451. https://doi.org/10.1002/hbm.25364

Franić, S., Dolan, C. V., Broxholme, J., Hu, H., Zemojtel, T., Davies, G. E., Nelson, K. A., Ehli, E. A., Pool, R., Hottenga, J.-J., Ropers, H.-H., & Boomsma, D. I. (2015). Mendelian and polygenic inheritance of intelligence: A common set of causal genes? Using next-generation sequencing to examine the effects of 168 intellectual disability genes on normal-range intelligence. *Intelligence*, 49, 10–22. https://doi.org/10.1016/j.intell.2014.12.001

Frankenhuis, W. E., & Tiokhin, L. (2018). Bridging evolutionary biology and developmental psychology: Toward an enduring theoretical infrastructure. *Child Development*, 89, 2303–2306. https://doi.org/10.1111/cdev.13021

Franz, A. P., Bolat, G. U., Bolat, H., Matijasevich, A., Santos, I. S., Silveira, R. C., Procianoy, R. S., Rohde, L. A., & Moreira-Maia, C. R. (2018). Attention-deficit/hyperactivity disorder and very preterm/very low birth weight: A meta-analysis. *Pediatrics*, 141(1), 20171645. https://doi.org/10.1542/peds.2017-1645

Frausel, R., & Burroughs, N. (2023). *Changes in children's household broadband access, 2019–2021*. Public Policy Associates. https://ppa1.wpenginepowered.com/wp-content/uploads/2023/02/Changes-in-Childrens-Household-Broadband-Access.pdf

Frawley, T. J. (2008). Gender schema and prejudicial recall: How children misremember, fabricate, and distort gendered picture book information. *Journal of Research in Childhood Education*, 22(3), 291–303. http://dx.doi.org/10.1080/02568540809594628

Frederickson, N., Petrides, K. V., & Simmonds, E. (2012). Trait emotional intelligence as a predictor of socioemotional outcomes in early adolescence. *Personality and Individual Differences*, 52(3), 323–328. https://doi.org/10.1016/j.paid.2011.10.034

Frederiksen, L. E., Ernst, A., Brix, N., Braskhøj Lauridsen, L. L., Roos, L., Ramlau-Hansen, C. H., & Ekelund, C. K. (2018). Risk of Adverse Pregnancy Outcomes at Advanced Maternal Age. *Obstetrics & Gynecology*, 131(3), 457–463. https://doi.org/10.1097/AOG.0000000000002504

Freeman, N. (2007). Preschoolers' perceptions of gender appropriate toys and their parents' beliefs about genderized behaviors: Miscommunication, mixed messages, or hidden truths? *Early Childhood Education Journal*, 34(5), 357–366. https://doi.org/10.1007/s10643-006-0123-x

Freilinger, P., Kliegel, D., Hänig, S., Oehl-Jaschkowitz, B., Henn, W., & Meyer, J. (2018). Behavioral and psychological features in girls and women with triple-X syndrome. *American Journal of Medical Genetics Part A*, 176(11), 2284–2291. https://doi.org/10.1002/AJMG.A.40477

French, D. C., & Cheung, H. S. (2018). Peer relationships. In J. E. Lansford & P. Banati (Eds.), *Handbook of adolescent development research and its impact on global policy* (pp. 130–149). Oxford University Press. https://doi.org/10.1093/oso/9780190847128.003.0007

French, D. C., Purwono, U., & Rodkin, P. C. (2012). Religiosity of adolescents and their friends and network associates: Homophily and associations with antisocial behavior. *Journal of Research on Adolescence*, 22(2), 326–332. https://doi.org/10.1111/j.1532-7795.2012.00778.x

Frenzel, A. C., Goetz, T., & Stockinger, K. (2023). Emotions and Emotion Regulation. In P. A. Schutz & K. R. Muis (Eds.), *Handbook of Educational Psychology* (4th ed.). Routledge.

Frick, A., Chavaillaz, A., Mäntylä, T., & Kubik, V. (2022). Development of multitasking abilities in middle childhood. *Learning and Instruction*, 77, 101540. https://doi.org/10.1016/j.learninstruc.2021.101540

Frick, A. P. (2021). Advanced maternal age and adverse pregnancy outcomes. *Best Practice & Research Clinical Obstetrics & Gynaecology*, 70, 92–100. https://doi.org/10.1016/J.BPOBGYN.2020.07.005

Friederici, A. D. (2017). Evolution of the neural language network. *Psychonomic Bulletin & Review*, 24(1), 41–47. https://doi.org/10.3758/s13423-016-1090-x

Friedlmeier, W., Çorapçi, F., & Benga, O. (2015). Early emotional development in cultural perspective. In L. A. Jensen (Ed.), *The Oxford handbook of human development and culture* (pp. 127–148). Oxford University Press. https://doi.org/10.1093/oxfordhb/9780199948550.013.9

Friedlmeier, W., Çorapçi, F., & Cole, P. M. (2011). Emotion socialization in cross-cultural perspective. *Social and Personality Psychology Compass*, 5(7), 410–427. https://doi.org/10.1111/j.1751-9004.2011.00362.x

Friedman, J. L., Somers, C. L., & Mangus, L. (2019). The role of peers and siblings in adolescent sexual decisions. *Families in Society*, 100(4), 433–441. https://doi.org/10.1177/1044389419872845

Friedman, J., York, H., Mokdad, A. H., & Gakidou, E. (2021). U.S. children "learning online" during COVID-19 without the Internet or a computer: Visualizing the gradient by race/ethnicity and parental educational attainment. *Socius*, 7, 2378023121992607. https://doi.org/10.1177/2378023121992607

Friedman, N. P., Banich, M. T., & Keller, M. C. (2021). Twin studies to GWAS: There and back again. *Trends in Cognitive Sciences*, 25(10). https://doi.org/10.1016/j.tics.2021.06.007

Friedman-Krauss, A. H., Barnett, W. S., Garver, K. A., Hodges, K. S., Weisenfeld, G., Gardiner, B. A., & Jost, T. M. (2022). *The state of preschool yearbook 2021*. National Institute for Early Education Research. https://nieer.org/state-preschool-yearbooks-yearbook2021

Friedman-Krauss, A. H., Barnett, W. S., Hodges, K. S., Garver, K. A., Jost, T. M., Weisenfeld, G., & Duer, J. (2024). *The state of preschool 2023: State preschool yearbook*. National Institute for Early Education Research. https://nieer.org/yearbook/2023

Friel, C. P., Duran, A. T., Shechter, A., & Diaz, K. M. (2020). U.S. Children meeting physical activity, screen time, and sleep guidelines. *American Journal of Preventive Medicine*, 59(4), 513–521. https://doi.org/10.1016/j.amepre.2020.05.007

Frodi, A. M., Lamb, M. E., Hwang, C.-P., & Frodi, M. (1983). Father-mother infant interaction in traditional and nontraditional Swedish families: A longitudinal study. *Alternative Lifestyles*, 5(3), 142–163. https://doi.org/10.1007/bf01091325

Froggatt, S., Covey, J., & Reissland, N. (2020). Infant neurobehavioural consequences of prenatal cigarette exposure: A systematic review and meta-analysis. *Acta Paediatrica*, *109*(6), 1112–1124. https://doi.org/10.1111/apa.15132

Froggatt, S., Reissland, N., & Covey, J. (2020). The effects of prenatal cigarette and e-cigarette exposure on infant neurobehaviour: A comparison to a control group. *EClinicalMedicine*, *2*(8). https://doi.org/10.1016/j.eclinm.2020.100602

Frost, A., Hoyt, L. T., Chung, A. L., & Adam, E. K. (2015). Daily life with depressive symptoms: Gender differences in adolescents' everyday emotional experiences. *Journal of Adolescence*, *43*, 132–141. https://doi.org/10.1016/j.adolescence.2015.06.001

Frost, J. L., Wortham, S. C., & Reifel, S. C. (2012). *Play and child development*. Pearson. https://www.pearson.com/us/higher-education/program/Frost-Play-and-Child-Development-4th-Edition/PGM141867.html

Fry, C. M., Telzer, E. H., & Rogers, C. R. (2021). Siblings as buffers: Social problems and internalizing and externalizing behaviors across early adolescence. *Journal of Family Psychology*, *35*(7), 939–949. https://doi.org/10.1037/fam0000876

Fryer, K., Munoz, M. C., Rahangdale, L., & Stuebe, A. M. (2021). Multiparous Black and Latinx women face more barriers to prenatal care than White women. *Journal of Racial and Ethnic Health Disparities*, *8*, 80–87. https://doi.org/10.1007/s40615-020-00759-x

Fryer, K., Santos, H. P., Pedersen, C., & Stuebe, A. M. (2018). The Hispanic paradox: Socioeconomic factors and race/ethnicity in breastfeeding outcomes. *Breastfeeding Medicine*, *13*(3), 174–180. https://doi.org/10.1089/bfm.2017.0157

Fuchs, L. S., Malone, A. S., Schumacher, R. F., Namkung, J., & Wang, A. (2017). Fraction intervention for students with mathematics difficulties: Lessons learned from five randomized controlled trials. *Journal of Learning Disabilities*, *50*(6), 631–639. https://doi.org/10.1177/0022219416677249

Fuemmeler, B. F., Glasgow, T. E., Schechter, J. C., Maguire, R., Sheng, Y., Bidopia, T., Barsell, D. J., Ksinan, A., Zhang, J., Lin, Y., Hoyo, C., Murphy, S., Qin, J., Wang, X., & Kollins, S. (2023). Prenatal and Childhood Smoke Exposure Associations with Cognition, Language, and Attention-Deficit/Hyperactivity Disorder. *Journal of Pediatrics*, *256*, 77-84.e1. https://doi.org/10.1016/j.jpeds.2022.11.041

Fuertes, M., Antunes, S., Martelo, I., & Dionisio, F. (2022). The impact of low birthweight in infant patterns of regulatory behavior, mother-infant quality of interaction, and attachment. *Early Human Development*, *172*, 105633. https://doi.org/10.1016/j.earlhumdev.2022.105633

Fuertes, M., Martelo, I., Almeida, R., Gonçalves, J. L., & Barbosa, M. (2024). Attachment and mother-infant interactions in dyads with infants born full-term, moderate-to-late preterm, and very-to-extreme preterm. *Early Human Development*, *189*, 105943. https://doi.org/10.1016/j.earlhumdev.2024.105943

Fuhrmann, D., Knoll, L. J., & Blakemore, S.-J. (2015). Adolescence as a sensitive period of brain development. *Trends in Cognitive Sciences*, *19*(10), 558–566. https://doi.org/10.1016/j.tics.2015.07.008

Fujiyama, H., Kamo, Y., & Schafer, M. (2021). Peer effects of friend and extracurricular activity networks on students' academic performance. *Social Science Research*, *97*, 102560. https://doi.org/10.1016/j.ssresearch.2021.102560

Fuligni, A. J., Arruda, E. H., Krull, J. L., & Gonzales, N. A. (2018). Adolescent sleep duration, variability, and peak levels of achievement and mental health. *Child Development*, *89*(2), e18–e28. https://doi.org/10.1111/cdev.12729

Fuligni, A. J., & Tsai, K. M. (2015). Developmental flexibility in the age of globalization: Autonomy and identity development among immigrant adolescents. *Annual Review of Psychology*, *66*(1), 411–431. https://doi.org/10.1146/annurev-psych-010814-015111

Fung, W. kai., Chung, K. K. hoa., & Cheng, R. W. yi. (2019). Gender differences in social mastery Motivation and its relationships to vocabulary knowledge, behavioral self-regulation, and socioemotional skills. *Early Education and Development*, *30*(2), 280–293. https://doi.org/10.1080/10409289.2018.1544004

Furr, R. M. (2021). *Psychometrics: An introduction*. SAGE.

G, Lucas-Thompson, R., Seiter, N. S., & Lunkenheimer, E. S. (2020). Interparental conflict, attention to angry interpersonal interactions, and adolescent anxiety. *Family Relations*, *69*(5), 1041–1054. https://doi.org/10.1111/fare.12505

Gabbard, C. P. (2021). *Lifelong motor development*. Wolters Kluwer.

Gabbe, S. G., Niebyl, Jennifer., Simpson, Joe., Landon, Mark., Galan, Henry., Jauniaux, Eric., Driscoll, Deborah., Berghella, Vincenzo., & William, Grobman. (2016). *Obstetrics: Normal and problem pregnancies*. Elsevier.

Gabriel, M. A. M., Alonso, C. R. P., Bértolo, J. D. L. C., Carbonero, S. C., Maestro, M. L., Pumarega, M. M., Díaz, C. A., & Pablos, D. L. (2009). Age of sitting unsupported and independent walking in very low birth weight preterm infants with normal motor development at 2 years. *Acta Paediatrica*, *98*(11), 1815–1821. https://doi.org/10.1111/j.1651-2227.2009.01475.x

Gabrielli, J., Traore, A., Stoolmiller, M., Bergamini, E., & Sargent, J. D. (2016). Industry television ratings for violence, sex, and substance use. *Pediatrics*, *138*(3), e20160487. https://doi.org/10.1542/peds.2016-0487

Gaches, S. (2021). Can I share your ideas with the world? Young children's consent in the research process. *Journal of Childhood Studies*, *46*(2), 20–33. https://doi.org/10.18357/jcs462202119925

Gaffney, H., Ttofi, M. M., & Farrington, D. P. (2021). What works in anti-bullying programs? Analysis of effective intervention components. *Journal of School Psychology*, *85*, 37–56. https://doi.org/10.1016/J.JSP.2020.12.002

Gagnon, S. G., Huelsman, T. J., Reichard, A. E., Kidder-Ashley, P., Griggs, M. S., Struby, J., & Bollinger, J. (2013). Help me play! Parental behaviors, child temperament, and preschool peer play. *Journal of Child and Family Studies*, *23*(5), 872–884. https://doi.org/10.1007/s10826-013-9743-0

Gaillard, A., Fehring, D. J., & Rossell, S. L. (2021). A systematic review and meta-analysis of behavioural sex differences in executive control. *European Journal of Neuroscience*, *53*(2), 519–542. https://doi.org/10.1111/ejn.14946

Gaillard, V., Barrouillet, P., Jarrold, C., & Camos, V. (2011). Developmental differences in working memory: Where do they come from? *Journal of Experimental Child Psychology*, *110*(3), 469–479. https://doi.org/10.1016/j.jecp.2011.05.004

Galatzer-Levy, I. R., Mazursky, H., Mancini, A. D., & Bonanno, G. A. (2011). What we don't expect when expecting: Evidence for heterogeneity in subjective well-being in response to parenthood. *Journal of Family Psychology*, *25*(3), 384–392. https://doi.org/10.1037/a0023759

Galiana-Simal, A., Vela-Romero, M., Romero-Vela, V. M., Oliver-Tercero, N., García-Olmo, V., Benito-Castellanos, P. J., Muñoz-Martinez, V., & Beato-Fernandez, L. (2020). Sensory processing disorder: Key points of a frequent alteration in neurodevelopmental disorders. *Cogent*

Medicine, 7(1), 1736829. https://doi.org/10.1080/2331205x.2020.1736829

Galkin, F., Kovalchuk, O., Koldasbayeva, D., Zhavoronkov, A., & Bischof, E. (2023). Stress, diet, exercise: Common environmental factors and their impact on epigenetic age. *Ageing Research Reviews, 88*, 101956. https://doi.org/10.1016/j.arr.2023.101956

Gallagher, A. (2008). *Developing thinking with four and five year old pupils: The impact of a cognitive acceleration programme through early science skill development.* [Master's thesis Dublin City University]. https://doras.dcu.ie/2357/1/Andrea_Gallagher_thesis.pdf

Gallagher, A. M., Updegraff, K. A., Padilla, J., & McHale, S. M. (2018). Longitudinal associations between sibling relational aggression and adolescent adjustment. *Journal of Youth and Adolescence, 47*(10), 2100–2113. https://doi.org/10.1007/s10964-018-0871-0

Gallegos, A., Dudovitz, R., Biely, C., Chung, P. J., Coker, T. R., Barnert, E., Guerrero, A. D., Szilagyi, P. G., & Nelson, B. B. (2021). Racial disparities in developmental delay diagnosis and services received in early childhood. *Academic Pediatrics, 21*(7), 1230–1238. https://doi.org/10.1016/j.acap.2021.05.008

Gallegos, M. L., & Segrin, C. (2021). Family connections and the Latino health paradox: Exploring the mediating role of loneliness in the relationships between the Latina/o cultural value of familism and health. *Health Communication, 37*(9), 1204–1214. https://doi.org/10.1080/10410236.2021.1909244

Galler, J. R., Bringas-Vega, M. L., Tang, Q., Rabinowitz, A. G., Musa, K. I., Chai, W. J., Omar, H., Abdul Rahman, M. R., Abd Hamid, A. I., Abdullah, J. M., & Valdés-Sosa, P. A. (2021). Neurodevelopmental effects of childhood malnutrition: A neuroimaging perspective. *NeuroImage, 231*, 117828. https://doi.org/10.1016/j.neuroimage.2021.117828

Galler, J. R., Bryce, C. P., Waber, D., Hock, R. S., Exner, N., Eaglesfield, D., Fitzmaurice, G., & Harrison, R. (2010). Early childhood malnutrition predicts depressive symptoms at ages 11–17. *Journal of Child Psychology & Psychiatry, 51*(7), 789–798. https://doi.org/10.1111/j.1469-7610.2010.02208.x

Galliher, R. V., Jones, M. D., & Dahl, A. (2011). Concurrent and longitudinal effects of ethnic identity and experiences of discrimination on psychosocial adjustment of Navajo adolescents. *Developmental Psychology, 47*(2), 509–526. https://doi.org/10.1037/a0021061

Galliher, R. V., McLean, K. C., & Syed, M. (2017). An integrated developmental model for studying identity content in context. *Developmental Psychology, 53*(11), 2011–2022. https://doi.org/10.1037/dev0000299

Galloway, J. C., & Thelen, E. (2004). Feet first: Object exploration in young infants. *Infant Behavior and Development, 27*(1), 107–112. https://doi.org/10.1016/j.infbeh.2003.06.001

Galván, A. (2020). The unrested adolescent brain. *Child Development Perspectives, 13*(3), 141–146. https://doi.org/10.1111/cdep.12332

Gámez, P. B., Palermo, F., Perry, J. S., & Galindo, M. (2023). Spanish-English bilingual toddlers' vocabulary skills: The role of caregiver language input and warmth. *Developmental Science, 26*(2), e13308. https://doi.org/10.1111/desc.13308

Gaml-Sørensen, A., Brix, N., Ernst, A., Lunddorf, L. L. H., & Ramlau-Hansen, C. H. (2021). Father absence in pregnancy or during childhood and pubertal development in girls and boys: A population-based cohort study. *Child Development, 92*(4), 1494–1508. https://doi.org/10.1111/cdev.13488

Gampe, A., Wermelinger, S., & Daum, M. M. (2019). Bilingual children adapt to the needs of their communication partners, monolinguals do not. *Child Development, 90*(1), 98–107. https://doi.org/10.1111/cdev.13190

Ganong, L., & Coleman, M. (2017). Siblings, half-siblings, and stepsiblings. In L. G. Coleman (Ed.), *Stepfamily relationships.* Springer. https://doi.org/10.1007/978-1-4899-7702-1_10

Ganong, L., Coleman, M., & Russell, L. T. (2015). Children in diverse families. In M. H. Bornstein & T. Leventhal (Eds.), *Handbook of child psychology and developmental science* (pp. 1–42). John Wiley & Sons. https://doi.org/10.1002/9781118963418.childpsy404

Ganong, L., Coleman, M., Sanner, C., & Berkley, S. (2022). Summary and synthesis of research on what works in stepfamily childrearing. *Family Relations, 71*(3), 935–952. https://doi.org/10.1111/fare.12674

Ganong, L., Sanner, C., Berkley, S., & Coleman, M. (2022). Effective coparenting in stepfamilies: Empirical evidence of what works. *Family Relations, 71*(3), 918–934. https://doi.org/10.1111/fare.12607

Gardiner, H. W., & Kosmitzki, C. (2018). *Lives across cultures: Cross-cultural human development.* Pearson.

Gardner, H. (2017). Taking a multiple intelligences (MI) perspective. *Behavioral and Brain Sciences, 40*, e203. https://doi.org/10.1017/S0140525X16001631

Gardner, H., Kornhaber, M., & Chen, J.-Q. (2018). The theory of multiple intelligences. In R. J. Sternberg (Ed.), *The nature of human intelligence* (pp. 116–129). Cambridge University Press. https://doi.org/10.1017/9781316817049.009

Gardon, L., Picciolini, O., Squarza, C., Frigerio, A., Giannì, M. L., Gangi, S., Fumagalli, M., & Mosca, F. (2019). Neurodevelopmental outcome and adaptive behaviour in extremely low birth weight infants at 2 years of corrected age. *Early Human Development, 128*, 81–85. https://doi.org/10.1016/j.earlhumdev.2018.12.013

Garenne, M. (2020). Trends in age at menarche and adult height in selected African countries (1950–1980). *Annals of Human Biology, 47*(1), 25–31. https://doi.org/10.1080/03014460.2020.1716994

Gariepy, G., Danna, S., Gobiņa, I., Rasmussen, M., Gaspar de Matos, M., Tynjälä, J., Janssen, I., Kalman, M., Villeruša, A., Husarova, D., Brooks, F., Elgar, F. J., Klavina-Makrecka, S., Šmigelskas, K., Gaspar, T., & Schnohr, C. (2020). How are adolescents sleeping? Adolescent sleep patterns and sociodemographic differences in 24 European and North American countries. *Journal of Adolescent Health, 66*(6), S81–S88. https://doi.org/10.1016/j.jadohealth.2020.03.013

Garrido-Miguel, M., Cavero-Redondo, I., Álvarez-Bueno, C., Rodríguez-Artalejo, F., Moreno, L. A., Ruiz, J. R., Ahrens, W., & Martínez-Vizcaíno, V. (2019). Prevalence and trends of overweight and obesity in European children from 1999 to 2016: A systematic review and meta-analysis. *JAMA Pediatrics, 173*(10), 192430. https://doi.org/10.1001/jamapediatrics.2019.2430

Gartstein, M. A., Kirchhoff, C. M., & Lowe, M. E. (2024). Individual differences in temperament: A developmental perspective. In J. D. Osofsky, H. E. Fitzgerald, M. Keren, & K. Puura (Eds.), *WAIMH handbook of infant and early childhood mental health: Biopsychosocial factors* (Vol. 1, pp. 31–48). Springer International. https://doi.org/10.1007/978-3-031-48627-2_3

Gartstein, M. A., Putnam, S. P., Aron, E. N., & Rothbart, M. K. (2016). S. Maltzman & Ed (Eds.), *Temperament and personality* (Vol. 1). Oxford University Press. https://doi.org/10.1093/oxfordhb/9780199739134.013.2

Gaskins, S. (2014). Children's play as cultural activity. In E. Brooker, M. Blaise, & S. Edwards (Eds.), *SAGE handbook of play and learning in early childhood* (pp. 31–42). SAGE. https://doi.org/10.4135/9781473907850

Gaskins, S., & Paradise, R. (2010). Learning through observation in daily life. In D. F. Lancy, J. Bock, & S. Gaskins (Eds.), *The anthropology of learning in childhood* (pp. 85–117). AltaMira Press. https://psycnet.apa.org/record/2010-03678-005

Gasser, U. E., & Hatten, M. E. (1990). Central nervous system neurons migrate on astroglial fibers from heterotypic brain regions in vitro. *Proceedings of the National Academy of Sciences of the United States of America, 87*(12), 4543–4547. https://doi.org/10.1073/pnas.87.12.4543

Gates, G. J. (2011). *How many people are lesbian, gay, bisexual and transgender?* The Williams Institute. https://escholarship.org/uc/item/09h684x2

Gath, M. E. (2022). Parents and adolescents in stepfamilies: Longitudinal links to physical health, psychological distress, and stress. *Journal of Child and Family Studies, 31*(1), 17–28. https://doi.org/10.1007/s10826-021-02078-z

Gaultney, J. F., & Gingras, J. L. (2005). Fetal rate of behavioral inhibition and preference for novelty during infancy. *Early Human Development, 81*(4), 379–386.

Gauvain, M., Perez, S., Gauvain, M., & Perez, S. (2015). Cognitive development and culture. In L. S. Liben & U. Müller (Eds.), *Handbook of child psychology and developmental science* (pp. 1–43). John Wiley & Sons. https://doi.org/10.1002/9781118963418.childpsy220

Gavand, K. A., Cain, K. L., Conway, T. L., Saelens, B. E., Frank, L. D., Kerr, J., Glanz, K., & Sallis, J. F. (2019). Associations between neighborhood recreation environments and adolescent physical activity. *Journal of Physical Activity and Health, 16*(10), 880–885. https://doi.org/10.1123/jpah.2018-0556

Gawlik, K. S., Melnyk, B. M., & Tan, A. (2018). An epidemiological study of population health reveals social smoking as a major cardiovascular risk factor. *American Journal of Health Promotion, 32*(5), 1221–1227. https://doi.org/10.1177/0890117117706420

Gayatri, M., & Irawaty, D. K. (2022). Family resilience during COVID-19 pandemic: A literature review. *Family Journal, 30*(2), 132–138. https://doi.org/10.1177/10664807211023875

Gaylord-Harden, N. K., Dickson, D., & Pierre, C. (2016). Profiles of community violence exposure among African American youth: An examination of desensitization to violence using latent class analysis. *Journal of Interpersonal Violence, 31*(11), 2077–2101. https://doi.org/10.1177/0886260515572474

Ge, X., Natsuaki, M. N., Neiderhiser, J. M., & Reiss, D. (2009). The longitudinal effects of stressful life events on adolescent depression are buffered by parent-child closeness. *Development and Psychopathology, 21*(2), 621–635. https://doi.org/10.1017/s0954579409000339

Geary, D. C. (2021). Now you see them, and now you don't: An evolutionarily informed model of environmental influences on human sex differences. *Neuroscience & Biobehavioral Reviews, 125*, 26–32. https://doi.org/10.1016/j.neubiorev.2021.02.020

Geary, D. C., Hoard, M. K., Nugent, L., & Ünal, Z. E. (2023). Sex differences in developmental pathways to mathematical competence. *Journal of Educational Psychology, 115*, 212–228. https://doi.org/10.1037/edu0000763

Gee, D. G. (2022). When do sensitive periods emerge later in development? *Trends in Cognitive Sciences, 26*(2), 97–98. https://doi.org/10.1016/j.tics.2021.12.001

Gee, D. G., & Cohodes, E. M. (2021). Influences of caregiving on development: A sensitive period for biological embedding of predictability and safety cues. *Current Directions in Psychological Science, 30*(5), 376–383. https://doi.org/10.1177/09637214211015673

Geeraert, B. L., Lebel, R. M., & Lebel, C. (2019). A multiparametric analysis of white matter maturation during late childhood and adolescence. *Human Brain Mapping, 40*(15), 4345–4356. https://doi.org/10.1002/hbm.24706

Geilhufe, B., Tripp, O., Silverstein, S., Birchfield, L., & Raimondo, M. (2021). Gender-affirmative eating disorder care: Clinical considerations for transgender and gender expansive children and youth. *Pediatric Annals, 50*(9), e371–e378. https://doi.org/10.3928/19382359-20210820-01

Gellman, M. D (Ed.). (2020). Positron emission tomography (PET). In *Encyclopedia of behavioral medicine*. Springer. https://doi.org/10.1007/978-3-030-39903-0_301463_1720)

Genovese, G., Spinelli, M., Lauro, L. J. R., Aureli, T., Castelletti, G., & Fasolo, M. (2020). Infant-directed speech as a simplified but not simple register: A longitudinal study of lexical and syntactic features. *Journal of Child Language, 47*(1), 22–44. https://doi.org/10.1017/S0305000919000643

Gentile, D. A., Bender, P. K., & Anderson, C. A. (2017). Violent video game effects on salivary cortisol, arousal, and aggressive thoughts in children. *Computers in Human Behavior, 70*, 39–43. https://doi.org/10.1016/J.CHB.2016.12.045

Georgas, J., Weiss, L. G., van de Vijver, F. J. R., & Saklofske, D. H. (2003). Cross-cultural psychology, intelligence, and cognitive processes. In J. Georgas, L. G. Weiss, F. J. Van. de Vijver, & D. H. Saklofske (Eds.), *Culture and children's intelligence: Cross-cultural analysis of the WISC-III* (pp. 23–37). Academic Press.

Gerber, J. P. (2020). Social comparison theory. In Virgil. Zeigler-Hill & K. Shackelford. Todd (Eds.), *Encyclopedia of personality and individual differences* (pp. 5004–5011). Springer. https://doi.org/10.1007/978-3-319-24612-3_1182

Gerdts, J. V. (2021). Perceptual development. In F. R. Volkmar (Ed.), *Encyclopedia of autism spectrum disorders* (pp. 3414–3423). Springer International. https://doi.org/10.1007/978-3-319-91280-6_745

Gerhardt, C. (2016). Only children. In C. L. Shehan (Ed.), *Encyclopedia of family studies* (pp. 1–3). John Wiley & Sons. https://doi.org/10.1002/9781119085621.wbefs042

Gerlach, J., Fößel, J. M., Vierhaus, M., Sann, A., Eickhorst, A., Zimmermann, P., & Spangler, G. (2022). Family risk and early attachment development: The differential role of parental sensitivity. *Infant Mental Health Journal, 43*(2), 340–356. https://doi.org/10.1002/imhj.21964

Gershoff, E. T., Goodman, G. S., Miller-Perrin, C. L., Holden, G. W., Jackson, Y., & Kazdin, A. E. (2018). The strength of the causal evidence against physical punishment of children and its implications for parents, psychologists, and policymakers. *American Psychologist, 73*(5), 626–638. https://doi.org/10.1037/amp0000327

Gerstenberg, A. (2020). 8. Pragmatic development in the (middle and) later stages of life. In K. P. Schneider & E. Ifantidou (Eds.), *Developmental and clinical pragmatics* (pp. 209–234). De Gruyter Mouton. https://doi.org/10.1515/9783110431056-008

Gervain, J. (2022). Development of speech perception. In L. Holt. Lori, E. Peelle. Jonathan, B. Coffin. Allison, N. Popper. Arthur, & R. Fay. Richard (Eds.), *Speech perception* (pp. 201–226). Springer. https://doi.org/10.1007/978-3-030-81542-4_8

Gest, S. D., Davidson, A. J., Rulison, K. L., Moody, J., & Welsh, J. A. (2007). Features of groups and status hierarchies in girls' and boys' early adolescent peer networks. *New Directions for Child & Adolescent Development*, 43–60. https://doi.org/10.1002/cd.200 *2007*(118)

Gesterling, L., & Bradford, H. (2022). Cannabis use in pregnancy: A state of the science review. *Journal of Midwifery and Women's Health*, *67*(3). https://doi.org/10.1111/jmwh.13293

Gettler, L. T., Kuo, P. X., Sarma, M. S., Trumble, B. C., Burke Lefever, J. E., & Braungart-Rieker, J. M. (2021). Fathers' oxytocin responses to first holding their newborns: Interactions with testosterone reactivity to predict later parenting behavior and father-infant bonds. *Developmental Psychobiology*, *63*(5), 1384–1398. https://doi.org/10.1002/dev.22121

Gettler, L. T., & McKenna, J. J. (2011). Evolutionary perspectives on mother-infant sleep proximity and breastfeeding in a laboratory setting. *American Journal of Physical Anthropology*, *144*(3), 454–462. https://doi.org/10.1002/ajpa.21426

Ghai, M., & Kader, F. (2022). A review on epigenetic inheritance of experiences in humans. *Biochemical Genetics*, *60*(4). https://doi.org/10.1007/s10528-021-10155-7

Ghassabian, A., Sundaram, R., Bell, E., Bello, S. C., Kus, C., & Yeung, E. (2016). Gross Motor Milestones and Subsequent Development. *Pediatrics*, *138*(1), e20154372. https://doi.org/10.1542/peds.2015-4372

Ghavami, N., Katsiaficas, D., & Rogers, L. O. (2016). Toward an intersectional approach in developmental science: The role of race, gender, sexual orientation, and immigrant status. *Advances in Child Development and Behavior*, *50*, 31–73. https://doi.org/10.1016/BS.acdb.2015.12.001

Ghetti, S., & Fandakova, Y. (2020). Neural development of memory and metamemory in childhood and adolescence: Toward an integrative model of the development of episodic recollection. Annual. *Review of Developmental Psychology*, *2*, 365–388. doi:10.1146/annurev-devpsych-060320-085634

Ghio, M., Cara, C., & Tettamanti, M. (2021). The prenatal brain readiness for speech processing: A review on foetal development of auditory and primordial language networks. *Neuroscience & Biobehavioral Reviews*, *128*, 709–719. https://doi.org/10.1016/j.neubiorev.2021.07.009

Ghio, M., Cara, C., & Tettamanti, M. (2021). The prenatal brain readiness for speech processing: A review on foetal development of auditory and primordial language networks. *Neuroscience & Biobehavioral Reviews*, *128*, 709–719. https://doi.org/10.1016/J.NEUBIOREV.2021.07.009

Ghosh, A., Coakley, R. C., Mascenik, T., Rowell, T. R., Davis, E. S., Rogers, K., Webster, M. J., Dang, H., Herring, L. E., Sassano, M. F., Livraghi-Butrico, A., Van Buren, S. K., Graves, L. M., Herman, M. A., Randell, S. H., Alexis, N. E., & Tarran, R. (2018). Chronic e-cigarette exposure alters the human bronchial epithelial proteome. *American Journal of Respiratory and Critical Care Medicine*, *198*(1), 67–76. https://doi.org/10.1164/rccm.201710-2033OC

Ghosh, R., & Tabrizi, S. J. (2018). Huntington disease. In D. H. Geschwind, H. L. Paulson, & C. Klein (Eds.), *Handbook of clinical neurology* (Vol. 147, pp. 255–278). Elsevier B.V. https://doi.org/10.1016/B978-0-444-63233-3.00017-8

Gialluisi, A., Andlauer, T. F. M., Mirza-Schreiber, N., Moll, K., Becker, J., Hoffmann, P., Ludwig, K. U., Czamara, D., Pourcain, B. S., Honbolygó, F., Tóth, D., Csépe, V., Huguet, G., Chaix, Y., Iannuzzi, S., Demonet, J. F., Morris, A. P., Hulslander, J., Willcutt, E. G., & &#hillip1; Schulte-Körne, G. (2021). Genome-wide association study reveals new insights into the heritability and genetic correlates of developmental dyslexia. *Molecular Psychiatry*, *26*(7), 3004–3017. https://doi.org/10.1038/s41380-020-00898-x

Giangrande, E. J., Beam, C. R., Finkel, D., Davis, D. W., & Turkheimer, E. (2022). Genetically informed, multilevel analysis of the Flynn Effect across four decades and three WISC versions. *Child Development*, *93*(1), e47–e58. https://doi.org/10.1111/cdev.13675

Giannakopoulos, G., & Kolaitis, G. (2021). Sleep problems in children and adolescents following traumatic life events. *World Journal of Psychiatry*, *11*(2). https://doi.org/10.5498/wjp.v11.i2.27

Giardino, A. P., Giardino, E. R., & Isaac, R. (2022). Child maltreatment and disabilities: Increased risk? In R. D. Krugman & J. E. Korbin (Eds.), *Handbook of child maltreatment* (pp. 307–325). Springer International. https://doi.org/10.1007/978-3-030-82479-2_15

Gibb, R. (2020). Brain development. In O. Braddick (Ed.), *Oxford research encyclopedia of psychology*. Oxford University Press. https://doi.org/10.1093/acrefore/9780190236557.013.785

Gibbs, J. C., Basinger, K. S., Grime, R. L., & Snarey, J. R. (2007). Moral judgment development across cultures: Revisiting Kohlberg's universality claims. *Developmental Review*, *27*(4), 443–500. https://doi.org/10.1016/j.dr.2007.04.001

Gibson, E. J., & Pick, A. D. (2000). *An ecological approach to perceptual learning and development*. Oxford University Press. http://psycnet.apa.org/psycinfo/2001-18056-000

Gibson, E. J., & Walk, R. D. (1960). The "visual cliff.". *Scientific American*, *202*(4), 64–71. doi:10.1038/scientificamerican0460-64

Gibson, J. (1979). *The ecological approach to visual perception*. Houghton, Mifflin and Company. http://psycnet.apa.org/psycinfo/2003-00063-000

Giddens, N. T., Juneau, P., Manza, P., Wiers, C. E., & Volkow, N. D. (2022). Disparities in sleep duration among American children: Effects of race and ethnicity, income, age, and sex. *Proceedings of the National Academy of Sciences of the United States of America*, *119*(30), e2120009119. https://doi.org/10.1073/pnas.2120009119

Giedd, J. N. (2018). A ripe time for adolescent research. *Journal of Research on Adolescence*, *28*(1), 157–159. https://doi.org/10.1111/jora.12378

Giedd, J. N., Lalonde, F. M., Celano, M. J., White, S. L., Wallace, G. L., Lee, N. R., & Lenroot, R. K. (2009). Anatomical brain magnetic resonance imaging of typically developing children and adolescents. *Journal of the American Academy of Child and Adolescent Psychiatry*, *48*(5), 465–470. https://doi.org/10.1097/CHI.0b013e31819f215

Giff, S. T., Renshaw, K. D., & Allen, E. S. (2019). Post-deployment parenting in military couples: Associations with service members' PTSD symptoms. *Journal of Family Psychology*, *33*(2), 166–175. https://doi.org/10.1037/fam0000477

Gigliotti, F., Esposito, D., Basile, C., Cesario, S., & Bruni, O. (2022). Sleep terrors—A parental nightmare. *Pediatric Pulmonology*, *57*(8), 1869–1878. https://doi.org/10.1002/ppul.25304

Gill, P., Lende, M., & Van Hook, J. W. (2022). *Twin births*. StatPearls.

Gilligan, C. (1982). In *a different voice: Psychological theory and women's development*. Harvard University Press.

Gilligan, C., & Attanucci, J. (1988). Two moral orientations: Gender differences and similarities. *Merrill-Palmer Quarterly*, *34*(3), 223–237.

Gilmore, J. H., Knickmeyer, R. C., & Gao, W. (2018). Imaging structural and functional brain development in early childhood. *Nature Reviews Neuroscience*, *19*(3),

123-137. https://doi.org/10.1038/nrn.2018.1

Giménez-Dasí, M., Pons, F., & Bender, P. K. (2016). Imaginary companions, theory of mind and emotion understanding in young children. *European Early Childhood Education Research Journal*, *24*(2), 186-197. https://doi.org/10.1080/1350293X.2014.919778

Giofrè, D., Mammarella, I. C., & Cornoldi, C. (2013). The structure of working memory and how it relates to intelligence in children. *Intelligence*, *41*(5), 396-406. https://doi.org/10.1016/j.intell.2013.06.006

Gioia, K. A., & Tobin, R. M. (2010). Role of sociodramatic play in promoting self-regulation. In C. E. Schaefer (Ed.), *Play therapy for preschool children* (pp. 181-198). American Psychological Association. https://doi.org/10.1037/12060-009

Giordano, K., Palmieri, C. S., LaTourette, R., Godoy, K. M., Denicola, G., Paulino, H., & Kosecki, O. (2024). Face masks and emotion literacy in preschool children: Implications during the COVID-19 pandemic. *Early Childhood Education Journal*, *52*(1), 21-29. https://doi.org/10.1007/s10643-022-01400-8

Girelli, L. (2023). What does gender has to do with math? Complex questions require complex answers. *Journal of Neuroscience Research*, *101*(5), 679-688. https://doi.org/10.1002/jnr.25056

Gjersoe, N. L., Hall, E. L., & Hood, B. (2015). Children attribute mental lives to toys when they are emotionally attached to them. *Cognitive Development*, *34*, 28-38. https://doi.org/10.1016/j.cogdev.2014.12.002

Glashouwer, K. A., van der Veer, R. M. L., Adipatria, F., de Jong, P. J., & Vocks, S. (2019). The role of body image disturbance in the onset, maintenance, and relapse of anorexia nervosa: A systematic review. *Clinical Psychology Review*, *74*, 101771. https://doi.org/10.1016/j.cpr.2019.101771

Glass, L., Moore, E. M., & Mattson, S. N. (2023). Current considerations for fetal alcohol spectrum disorders: Identification to intervention. *Current Opinion in Psychiatry*, *36*(3), 249-256. https://doi.org/10.1097/YCO.0000000000000862

Gleason, T. R. (2017). The psychological significance of play with imaginary companions in early childhood. *Learning & Behavior*, *45*(4), 432-440. https://doi.org/10.3758/s13420-017-0284-z

Gleason, T. R., & Kalpidou, M. (2014). Imaginary companions and young children's coping and competence. *Social Development*, *23*(4), 820-839. https://doi.org/10.1111/sode.12078

Glenn, C. R., Kleiman, E. M., Kellerman, J., Pollak, O., Cha, C. B., Esposito, E. C., Porter, A. C., Wyman, P. A., & Boatman, A. E. (2020). Annual research review: A meta-analytic review of worldwide suicide rates in adolescents. *Journal of Child Psychology and Psychiatry*, *61*(3), 294-308. https://doi.org/10.1111/jcpp.13106

Glenwright, M., & Pexman, P. (2010). Development of children's ability to distinguish sarcasm and verbal irony. *Journal of Child Language*, *37*(2), 429-451. https://doi.org/10.1017/S0305000909009520

Glick, I., Kadish, E., & Rottenstreich, M. (2021). Management of pregnancy in women of advanced maternal age: Improving outcomes for mother and baby. *International Journal of Women's Health*, *1*(3). https://doi.org/10.2147/IJWH.S283216

Glover, V., & Capron, L. (2017). Prenatal parenting. *Current Opinion in Psychology*, *15*, 66-70. https://doi.org/10.1016/j.copsyc.2017.02.007

Goddings, A.-L., Beltz, A., Peper, J. S., Crone, E. A., & Braams, B. R. (2019). Understanding the role of puberty in structural and functional development of the adolescent brain. *Journal of Research on Adolescence*, *29*(1), 32-53. https://doi.org/10.1111/jora.12408

Godfrey, E. B., & Burson, E. (2018). Interrogating the intersections: How intersectional perspectives can inform developmental scholarship on critical consciousness. *New Directions for Child and Adolescent Development*, 17-38. https://doi.org/10.1002/cad.20246 *2018*(161)

Goeke-Morey, M. C., & Cummings, E. M. (2017). Religiosity and parenting: Recent directions in process-oriented research. *Current Opinion in Psychology*, *15*, 7-12. https://doi.org/10.1016/j.copsyc.2017.02.006

Goforth, A. N., Pham, A. V., & Oka, E. R. (2015). Parent-child conflict, acculturation gap, acculturative stress, and behavior problems in Arab American adolescents. *Journal of Cross-Cultural Psychology*, *46*(6), 821-836. https://doi.org/10.1177/0022022115585140

Gölcük, M., & Berument, S. K. (2021). The relationship between negative parenting and child and maternal temperament. *Current Psychology*, *40*(7), 3596-3608. https://doi.org/10.1007/s12144-019-00307-9

Goldberg, A. E., Downing, J. B., & Moyer, A. M. (2012). Why parenthood, and why now?: Gay men's motivations for pursuing parenthood. *Family Relations*, *61*(1), 157-174. https://doi.org/10.1111%2Fj.1741-3729.2011.00687.x

Golden, A. R., Griffin, C. B., Metzger, I. W., & Cooper, S. M. (2018). School racial climate and academic outcomes in African American adolescents: The protective role of peers. *Journal of Black Psychology*, *44*(1), 47-73. https://doi.org/10.1177/0095798417736685

Golden, J. C., & Jacoby, J. W. (2018). Playing princess: Preschool girls' interpretations of gender stereotypes in Disney princess media. *Sex Roles*, *79*(5-6), 299-313. https://doi.org/10.1007/s11199-017-0773-8

Goldfarb, E. S., & Lieberman, L. D. (2021). Three decades of research: The case for comprehensive sex education. *Journal of Adolescent Health*, *68*(1), 13-27. https://doi.org/10.1016/j.jadohealth.2020.07.036

Goldschmidt, L., Langa, M., Alexander, D., & Canham, H. (2022). A review of Kohlberg's theory and its applicability in the South African context through the lens of early childhood development and violence. In O. N. Saracho & R. Evans (Eds.), *The influence of theorists and pioneers on early childhood education*. Routledge.

Goldsmith, H. H., Buss, A. H., Plomin, R., Rothbart, M. K., Thomas, A., Chess, S., & al, et. (1987). Roundtable: What is temperament? Four approaches. *Child Development*, *58*, 505-529. https://doi.org/10.2307/1130527

Goldstein, S. E., Boxer, P., & Rudolph, E. (2015). Middle school transition stress: Links with academic performance, motivation, and school experiences. *Contemporary School Psychology*, *19*(1), 21-29. https://doi.org/10.1007/s40688-014-0044-4

Goldstein, T. R., & Lerner, M. D. (2018). Dramatic pretend play games uniquely improve emotional control in young children. *Developmental Science*, *21*(4), e12603. https://doi.org/10.1111/desc.12603

Goleman, D. (1996). Emotional intelligence: Why it can matter more than IQ. *Learning*, *24*(6), 49-50.

Goleman, D., & Boyatzis, R. (2017). Emotional intelligence has 12 elements. Which do you need to work on. *Harvard Business Review*, *84*(2), 1-5.

Golinkoff, R. M., Hoff, E., Rowe, M. L., S Tamis-LeMonda, C., & Hirsh-Pasek, K. (2019). Language matters: Denying the existence of the 30-million-word gap has serious consequences. *Child Development*, *90*(3), 985-992. https://doi.org/10.1111/cdev.13128

Gollub, E. L., Green, J., Richardson, L., Kaplan, I., & Shervington, D. (2019). Indirect violence exposure and mental health symptoms among an urban public-school population: Prevalence and correlates. *PLoS ONE*, *14*(11), e0224499. https://doi.org/10.1371/journal.pone.0224499

Golombok, S. (2013). Families created by reproductive donation: Issues and research. *Child Development Perspectives*, *7*(1), 61–65. https://doi.org/10.1111/cdep.12015

Golombok, S. (2017). Parenting in new family forms. *Current Opinion in Psychology*, *15*, 76–80. https://doi.org/10.1016/j.copsyc.2017.02.004

Golombok, S., Ilioi, E., Blake, L., Roman, G., & Jadva, V. (2017). A longitudinal study of families formed through reproductive donation: Parent-adolescent relationships and adolescent adjustment at age 14. *Developmental Psychology*, *53*(10), 1966–1977. https://doi.org/10.1037/dev0000372

Gomes, J. do A., Olstad, E. W., Kowalski, T. W., Gervin, K., Vianna, F. S. L., Schüler-Faccini, L., & Nordeng, H. M. E. (2021). Genetic susceptibility to drug teratogenicity: A systematic literature review. *Frontiers in Genetics*, *12*, 531. https://doi.org/10.3389/FGENE.2021.645555/BIBTEX

Gómez-Ortiz, O., Romera, E. M., & Ortega-Ruiz, R. (2016). Parenting styles and bullying. The mediating role of parental psychological aggression and physical punishment. *Child Abuse & Neglect*, *51*, 132–143. https://doi.org/10.1016/j.chiabu.2015.10.025

Gómez-Roig, M. D., Pascal, R., Cahuana, M. J., Garciá-Algar, O., Sebastiani, G., Andreu-Fernández, V., Martínez, L., Rodríguez, G., Iglesia, I., Ortiz-Arrabal, O., Mesa, M. D., Cabero, M. J., Guerra, L., Llurba, E., Domínguez, C., Zanini, M. J., Foraster, M., Larqué, E., Cabañas, F., & &#hillip1; Vento, M. (2021). Environmental exposure during pregnancy: Influence on prenatal development and early life: A comprehensive review. *Fetal Diagnosis and Therapy*, *48*(4), 245–257. https://doi.org/10.1159/000514884

Gonçalves, J. L., Fuertes, M., Alves, M. J., Antunes, S., Almeida, A. R., Casimiro, R., & Santos, M. (2020). Maternal pre and perinatal experiences with their full-term, preterm and very preterm newborns. *BMC Pregnancy and Childbirth*, *20*(1), 276. https://doi.org/10.1186/s12884-020-02934-8

Göncü, A., & Gauvain, M. (2012). Sociocultural approaches to educational psychology: Theory, research, and application. In J. Harris, K. R. Graham, S. Urdan, T. McCormick, C. B. Sinatra, & G. M. Sweller (Eds.), *APA educational psychology handbook: Theories, constructs, and critical issues* (Vol. 1, pp. 125–154). American Psychological Association. https://doi.org/10.1037/13273-006

Gong, L., Parikh, S., Rosenthal, P. J., & Greenhouse, B. (2013). Biochemical and immunological mechanisms by which sickle cell trait protects against malaria. *Malaria Journal*, *12*, 317. https://doi.org/10.1186/1475-2875-12-317

Gonzales-Backen, M. A., Meca, A., Lorenzo-Blanco, E. I., Des Rosiers, S. E., Córdova, D., Soto, D. W., Á, Cano, M., Oshri, A., Zamboanga, B. L., Baezconde-Garbanati, L., Schwartz, S. J., Szapocznik, J., & Unger, J. B. (2018). Examining the temporal order of ethnic identity and perceived discrimination among Hispanic immigrant adolescents. *Developmental Psychology*, *54*(5), 929–937. https://doi.org/10.1037/dev0000465

Gonzalez, D. C., Ory, J., Blachman-Braun, R., Nackeeran, S., Best, J. C., & Ramasamy, R. (2022). Advanced paternal age and sperm DNA fragmentation: A systematic review. *World Journal of Men's Health*, *40*(1), 104–115. https://doi.org/10.5534/WJMH.200195

González-Fernández, F. T., Delgado-García, G., Coll, J. S., Silva, A. F., Nobari, H., & Clemente, F. M. (2023). Relationship between cognitive functioning and physical fitness in regard to age and sex. *BMC Pediatrics*, *23*(1), 204. https://doi.org/10.1186/s12887-023-04028-8

Goodarzi, M. O. (2018). Genetics of obesity: What genetic association studies have taught us about the biology of obesity and its complications. *Lancet Diabetes & Endocrinology*, *6*(3), 223–236. https://doi.org/10.1016/S2213-8587(17)30200-0

Goodman, M. A., & Dyer, W. J. (2020). From parent to child: Family factors that influence faith transmission. *Psychology of Religion and Spirituality*, *12*, 178–190. https://doi.org/10.1037/rel0000283

Goodman-Scott, E., & Lambert, S. F. (2015). Professional counseling for children with sensory processing disorder. *Professional Counselor*, *5*(2), 273–292. https://doi.org/10.15241/egs.5.2.273

Goodnow, J. J., & Lawrence, J. A. (2015). Children and Cultural Context. In M. H. Bornstein & T. Leventhal (Eds.), *Handbook of Child Psychology and Developmental Science* (Vol. 4;, pp. 1–41). John Wiley & Sons. https://doi.org/10.1002/9781118963418.childpsy419

Goodvin, R., Meyer, S., Thompson, R. A., & Hayes, R. (2008). Self-understanding in early childhood: Associations with child attachment security and maternal negative affect. *Attachment & Human Development*, *10*(4), 433–450. https://doi.org/10.1080/14616730802461466

Goodvin, R., Thompson, R. A., & Winer, A. C. (2015). The individual child: Temperament, emotion, self, and personality. In M. Bornstein & M. Lamb (Eds.), *Developmental Psychology: An Advanced Textbook* (pp. 491–533). Psychology Press.

Goodwin, G. P., & Johnson-Laird, P. N. (2008). Transitive and pseudo-transitive inferences. *Cognition*, *108*(2), 320–352. https://doi.org/10.1016/j.cognition.2008.02.010

Goodwyn, S. W., & Acredolo, L. P. (1998). Encouraging symbolic gestures: A new perspective on the relationship between gesture and speech. *New Directions for Child and Adolescent Development*, 61–73. https://doi.org/10.1002/cd.23219987905 1998(79)

Goossens, L. (2001). Global versus domain-specific statuses in identity research: A comparison of two self-report measures. *Journal of Adolescence*, *24*(6), 681–699. https://doi.org/10.1006/jado.2001.0438

Gopnik, A., & Choi, S. (1995). *Beyond names for things: Children's acquisition of verbs*. Erlbaum.

Gori, M., Schiatti, L., & Amadeo, M. B. (2021). Masking Emotions: Face Masks Impair How We Read Emotions. *Frontiers in Psychology*, *1*(2). https://www.frontiersin.org/articles/10.3389/fpsyg.2021.669432

Gorry, D. (2023). Consequences of teenage childbearing on child outcomes in the United States. *Journal of Policy Analysis and Management*, *42*(1), 225–254. https://doi.org/10.1002/pam.22454

Gorter, J. W., Stewart, D., Smith, M. W., King, G., Wright, M., Nguyen, T., Freeman, M., & Swinton, M. (2014). Pathways toward positive psychosocial outcomes and mental health for youth with disabilities: A knowledge synthesis of developmental trajectories. *Canadian Journal of Community Mental Health*, *33*(1), 45–61. https://doi.org/10.7870/cjcmh-2014-005

Gosdin, L. K., Deputy, N. P., Kim, S. Y., Dang, E. P., & Denny, C. H. (2022). Alcohol consumption and binge drinking during pregnancy among adults aged 18–49 years—United States, 2018–2020. *Morbidity and Mortality Weekly Report*, *71*(1), 10–13. https://doi.org/10.15585/mmwr.mm7101a2

Gosselin, V., Leone, M., & Laberge, S. (2020). Socioeconomic and gender-based disparities in the motor competence of school-age children. *Journal of Sports*

Sciences, 39(3), 341–350. https://doi.org/10.1080/02640414.2020.1822585

Gottlieb, G. (2007). Probabilistic epigenesis. Developmental Science, 10(1), 1–11. https://doi.org/10.1111/j.1467-7687.2007.00556.x

Gottschalk, L. (2003). Same-sex sexuality and childhood gender non-conformity: A spurious connection. Journal of Gender Studies, 12(1), 35–50. https://doi.org/10.1080/0958923032000067808

Gottschling, J., Hahn, E., Beam, C. R., Spinath, F. M., Carroll, S., & Turkheimer, E. (2019). Socioeconomic status amplifies genetic effects in middle childhood in a large German twin sample. Intelligence, 72, 20–27. https://doi.org/10.1016/j.intell.2018.11.006

Gould, J. F., Hunt, E., Roberts, R. M., Louise, J., Collins, C. T., & Makrides, M. (2019). Can the Bayley scales of infant development at 18 months predict child behaviour at 7 years? Journal of Paediatrics and Child Health, 55(1), 74–81. https://doi.org/10.1111/jpc.14163

Gourley, L., Wind, C., Henninger, E. M., & Chinitz, S. (2013). Sensory processing difficulties, behavioral problems, and parental stress in a clinical population of young children. Journal of Child and Family Studies, 22(7), 912–921. https://doi.org/10.1007/s10826-012-9650-9

Gower, A. L., Forster, M., Gloppen, K., Johnson, A. Z., Eisenberg, M. E., Connett, J. E., & Borowsky, I. W. (2018). School practices to foster LGBT-supportive climate: Associations with adolescent bullying involvement. Prevention Science, 19(6), 813–821. https://doi.org/10.1007/s11121-017-0847-4

Gower, A. L., Lingras, K. A., Mathieson, L. C., Kawabata, Y., & Crick, N. R. (2014). The role of preschool relational and physical aggression in the transition to kindergarten: Links with social-psychological adjustment. Early Education and Development, 25(5), 619–640. https://doi.org/10.1080/10409289.2014.844058

Gracia, R., Pamias, M., Mortier, P., Alonso, J., Pérez, V., & Palao, D. (2021). Is the COVID-19 pandemic a risk factor for suicide attempts in adolescent girls? Journal of Affective Disorders, 29(2). https://doi.org/10.1016/j.jad.2021.05.044

Grady, J. S., & Karraker, K. (2017). Mother and child temperament as interacting correlates of parenting sense of competence in toddlerhood. Infant and Child Development, 26(4), e1997. https://doi.org/10.1002/icd.1997

Graf, M., Tuly, R., Gallagher, M., Sullivan, J., & Jena, A. B. (2022). Value of a cure for sickle cell disease in reducing economic disparities. American Journal of Hematology, 97(8), E289–E291. https://doi.org/10.1002/ajh.26617

Graham, N., Schultz, L., Mitra, S., & Mont, D. (2017). Disability in middle childhood and adolescence. In D. A. P. Bundy, N. de Silva, S. Horton, D. T. Jamison, & G. C. Patton (Eds.), Disease control priorities: Child and adolescent health and development (3rd ed., Vol. 8, pp. 221–238). The World Bank. https://doi.org/10.1596/978-1-4648-0423-6_ch17

Graham, S., Kogachi, K., & Morales-Chicas, J. (2022). Do I fit in: Race/ethnicity and feelings of belonging in school. Educational Psychology Review, 34(4), 2015–2042. https://doi.org/10.1007/s10648-022-09709-x

Graham, S., Munniksma, A., & Juvonen, J. (2014). Psychosocial benefits of cross-ethnic friendships in urban middle schools. Child Development, 85(2), 469–483. https://doi.org/10.1111/cdev.12159

Granat, A., Gadassi, R., Gilboa-Schechtman, E., & Feldman, R. (2017). Maternal depression and anxiety, social synchrony, and infant regulation of negative and positive emotions. Emotion, 17(1), 11–27. https://doi.org/10.1037/emo0000204

Grande, G., Graziani, A., Mambro, A. D., Selice, R., & Ferlin, A. (2023). Osteoporosis and bone metabolism in patients with Klinefelter syndrome. Endocrine Connections, 12(8). https://doi.org/10.1530/EC-23-0058

Grandy, C., Donnan, J., Bishop, L., Vidyasankar, A., & Blackmore, A. (2022). An update on perinatal cannabis use. Journal of Obstetrics and Gynaecology Canada, 44(3). https://doi.org/10.1016/j.jogc.2021.10.009

Granqvist, P. (2002). Attachment and religiosity in adolescence: Cross-sectional and longitudinal evaluations. Personality and Social Psychology Bulletin, 28(2), 260–270. https://doi.org/10.1177/0146167202282011

Granqvist, P., Sroufe, L. A., Dozier, M., Hesse, E., Steele, M., van Ijzendoorn, M., Solomon, J., Schuengel, C., Fearon, P., Bakermans-Kranenburg, M., Steele, H., Cassidy, J., Carlson, E., Madigan, S., Jacobvitz, D., Foster, S., Behrens, K., Rifkin-Graboi, A., Gribneau, N., & &#hillip1; Duschinsky, R. (2017). Disorganized attachment in infancy: A review of the phenomenon and its implications for clinicians and policy-makers. Attachment & Human Development, 19(6), 534–558. https://doi.org/10.1080/14616734.2017.1354040

Grant, K. S., Conover, E., & Chambers, C. D. (2020). Update on the developmental consequences of cannabis use during pregnancy and lactation. Birth Defects Research, 112(15). https://doi.org/10.1002/bdr2.1766

Grant, T., Croce, E., & Matsui, E. C. (2022). Asthma and the social determinants of health. Annals of Allergy, Asthma and Immunology, 128(1). https://doi.org/10.1016/j.anai.2021.10.002

Grassetti, S. N., Hubbard, J. A., Docimo, M. A., Bookhout, M. K., Swift, L. E., & Gawrysiak, M. J. (2020). Parental advice to preadolescent bystanders about how to intervene during bullying differs by form of bullying. Social Development, 29(1), 290–302. https://doi.org/10.1111/sode.12397

Grassetti, S. N., Hubbard, J. A., Smith, M. A., Bookhout, M. K., Swift, L. E., & Gawrysiak, M. J. (2018). Caregivers' advice and children's bystander behaviors during bullying incidents. Journal of Clinical Child & Adolescent Psychology, 47, S329–S340. https://doi.org/10.1080/15374416.2017.1295381

Gravholt, C. H., Chang, S., Wallentin, M., Fedder, J., Moore, P., & Skakkebæk, A. (2018). Klinefelter syndrome: Integrating genetics, neuropsychology, and endocrinology. Endocrine Reviews, 39(4), 389–423. https://doi.org/10.1210/er.2017-00212

Gravholt, C. H., Viuff, M., Just, J., Sandahl, K., Brun, S., van der Velden, J., Andersen, N. H., & Skakkebaek, A. (2023). The changing face of Turner syndrome. Endocrine Reviews, 44(1), 33–69. https://doi.org/10.1210/ENDREV/BNAC016

Gray, C., & MacBlain, S. (2015). Learning theories in childhood. SAGE.

Gray, K. M., & Squeglia, L. M. (2018). Research review: What have we learned about adolescent substance use? Journal of Child Psychology and Psychiatry and Allied Disciplines, 59(6), 618–627. https://doi.org/10.1111/jcpp.12783

Green, A. E., DeChants, J. P., Price, M. N., & Davis, C. K. (2022). Association of gender-affirming hormone therapy with depression, thoughts of suicide, and attempted suicide among transgender and nonbinary youth. Journal of Adolescent Health, 70(4), 643–649. https://doi.org/10.1016/j.jadohealth.2021.10.036

Green, J., Fowler, C., Petty, J., & Whiting, L. (2021). The transition home of extremely premature babies: An integrative review. Journal of Neonatal Nursing, 27(1), 26–32. https://doi.org/10.1016/j.jnn.2020.09.011

Greene, R. M., & Pisano, M. M. (2019). Developmental toxicity of e-cigarette aerosols. *Birth Defects Research*, *111*(17), 1294-1301. https://doi.org/10.1002/bdr2.1571

Gregg, A. R., Gross, S. J., Best, R. G., Monaghan, K. G., Bajaj, K., Skotko, B. G., Thompson, B. H., & Watson, M. S. (2013). ACMG statement on noninvasive prenatal screening for fetal aneuploidy. *Genetics in Medicine*, *15*(5), 395-398. https://doi.org/10.1038/gim.2013.29

Gregorová, K., Eldar, E., Deserno, L., & Reiter, A. M. F. (2024). A cognitive-computational account of mood swings in adolescence. *Trends in Cognitive Sciences*, *28*(4), 290-303. https://doi.org/10.1016/j.tics.2024.02.006

Greitemeyer, T. (2022). The dark and bright side of video game consumption: Effects of violent and prosocial video games. *Current Opinion in Psychology*, *46*, 101326. https://doi.org/10.1016/j.copsyc.2022.101326

Gremmen, M. C., Berger, C., Ryan, A. M., Steglich, C. E. G., Veenstra, R., & Dijkstra, J. K. (2019). Adolescents' friendships, academic achievement, and risk behaviors: Same-behavior and cross-behavior selection and influence processes. *Child Development*, *90*(2), e192-e211. https://doi.org/10.1111/cdev.13045

Gremmen, M. C., Dijkstra, J. K., Steglich, C., & Veenstra, R. (2017). First selection, then influence: Developmental differences in friendship dynamics regarding academic achievement. *Developmental Psychology*, *53*(7), 1356-1370. https://doi.org/10.1037/dev0000314

Grewen, K., Burchinal, M., Vachet, C., Gouttard, S., Gilmore, J. H., Lin, W., Johns, J., Elam, M., & Gerig, G. (2014). Prenatal cocaine effects on brain structure in early infancy. *NeuroImage*, *101*, 114-123. https://doi.org/10.1016/J.NEUROIMAGE.2014.06.070

Griffith, A. K. (2022). Parental burnout and child maltreatment during the COVID-19 pandemic. *Journal of Family Violence*, *37*(5), 725-731. https://doi.org/10.1007/s10896-020-00172-2

Griffiths, A. (2023). *School enrollment rates of 3- and 4-year-olds returned to pre-pandemic levels in 2022*. https://www.census.gov/library/stories/2023/11/preschool-enrollment-rebounds.html

Grigg-Damberger, M. M., & Wolfe, K. M. (2017). Infants sleep for brain. *Journal of Clinical Sleep Medicine*, *13*(11), 1233-1234. https://doi.org/10.5664/jcsm.6786

Grigorenko, E. L., Compton, D. L., Fuchs, L. S., Wagner, R. K., Willcutt, E. G., & Fletcher, J. M. (2020). Understanding, educating, and supporting children with specific learning disabilities: 50 years of science and practice. *American Psychologist*, *75*(1), 37-51. https://doi.org/10.1037/amp0000452

Grimm, J., Stemmler, M., Golub, Y., Schwenke, E., Goecke, T. W., Fasching, P. A., Beckmann, M. W., Kratz, O., Moll, G. H., Kornhuber, J., & Eichler, A. (2021). The association between prenatal alcohol consumption and preschool child stress system disturbance. *Developmental Psychobiology*, *63*(4), 687-697. https://doi.org/10.1002/DEV.22038

Grissom, N. M., & Reyes, T. M. (2018). Let's call the whole thing off: Evaluating gender and sex differences in executive function. *Neuropsychopharmacology*, *44*(1), 86-96. https://doi.org/10.1038/s41386-018-0179-5

Grogan-Kaylor, A., Castillo, B., Pace, G. T., Ward, K. P., Ma, J., Lee, S. J., & Knauer, H. (2021). Global perspectives on physical and nonphysical discipline: A Bayesian multilevel analysis. *International Journal of Behavioral Development*, *45*(3), 216-225. https://doi.org/10.1177/0165025420981642

Grogan-Kaylor, A., Ma, J., & Graham-Bermann, S. A. (2018). The case against physical punishment. *Current Opinion in Psychology*, *19*, 22-27. https://doi.org/10.1016/j.copsyc.2017.03.022

Groh, A. M., Fearon, R. M. P., van IJzendoorn, M. H., Bakermans-Kranenburg, M. J., & Roisman, G. I. (2017). Attachment in the early life course: Meta-analytic evidence for its role in socioemotional development. *Child Development Perspectives*, *11*(1), 70-76. https://doi.org/10.1111/cdep.12213

Groh, A. M., & Narayan, A. J. (2019). Infant attachment insecurity and baseline physiological activity and physiological reactivity to interpersonal stress: A meta-analytic review. *Child Development*, *90*(3), 679-693. https://doi.org/10.1111/cdev.13205

Grolleman, J. F., Gravesteijn, C., & Hoffenaar, P. J. (2023). Trajectories of change in parental self-esteem and emotion regulation from pregnancy until 4 years postpartum. *Journal of Child and Family Studies*, *32*(4), 1088-1101. https://doi.org/10.1007/s10826-022-02306-0

Grosse Wiesmann, C., Friederici, A. D., Singer, T., & Steinbeis, N. (2017). Implicit and explicit false belief development in preschool children. *Developmental Science*, *20*(5), e12445. https://doi.org/10.1111/desc.12445

Grossman, A. H., Park, J. Y., & Russell, S. T. (2016). Transgender youth and suicidal behaviors: Applying the interpersonal psychological theory of suicide. *Journal of Gay & Lesbian Mental Health*, *20*(4), 329-349. https://doi.org/10.1080/19359705.2016.1207581

Grossmann, K. E., Spangler, G., Suess, G., & Unzner, L. (1985). Maternal sensitivity and newborns' orientation responses as related to quality of attachment in Northern Germany. Growing points of attachment theory and research. I. Bretherton & E. Waters (Eds.), *Monographs of the Society for Research in Child Development*, 233-256. *50*(1-2, Serial No. 209)

Groulx, T., Bagshawe, M., Giesbrecht, G., Tomfohr-Madsen, L., Hetherington, E., & Lebel, C. A. (2021). Prenatal care disruptions and associations with maternal mental health during the COVID-19 pandemic. *Frontiers in Global Women's Health*, *2*, 20. https://doi.org/10.3389/FGWH.2021.648428

Grover, M. M., & Jenkins, T. G. (2020). Transgenerational epigenetics: A window into paternal health influences on offspring. *Urologic Clinics of North America*, *47*(2), 219-225. https://doi.org/10.1016/j.ucl.2019.12.010

Grueneisen, S., & Warneken, F. (2022). The development of prosocial behavior—From sympathy to strategy. *Current Opinion in Psychology*, *43*, 323-328. https://doi.org/10.1016/j.copsyc.2021.08.005

Gruenenfelder-Steiger, A. E., Harris, M. A., & Fend, H. A. (2016). Subjective and objective peer approval evaluations and self-esteem development: A test of reciprocal, prospective, and long-term effects. *Developmental Psychology*, *52*(10), 1563-1577. https://doi.org/10.1037/dev0000147

Grünebaum, A., Dudenhausen, J., & Chervenak, F. A. (2023). Covid and pregnancy in the United States – an update as of August 2022. *Journal of Perinatal Medicine*, *51*(1), 34-38. https://doi.org/10.1515/jpm-2022-0361

Gruzieva, O., Merid, S. K., Koppelman, G. H., & Melén, E. (2021). An update on the epigenetics of asthma. *Current Opinion in Allergy and Clinical Immunology*, *21*(2). https://doi.org/10.1097/ACI.0000000000000723

Grzanka, P. R. (2020). From buzzword to critical psychology: An invitation to take intersectionality seriously. *Women and Therapy*, *43*(3-4), 244-261. https://doi.org/10.1080/02703149.2020.1729473

Guan, X., Sun, C., Hwang, G., Xue, K., & Wang, Z. (2024). Applying game-based learning in primary education: A systematic review of journal publications from 2010 to 2020. *Interactive Learning Environments*, 32(2), 534–556. https://doi.org/10.1080/10494820.2022.2091611

Gubbels, J., van der Put, C. E., Stams, G.-J. J. M., & Assink, M. (2021). Effective components of school-based prevention programs for child abuse: A meta-analytic review. *Clinical Child and Family Psychology Review*, 24(3), 553–578. https://doi.org/10.1007/s10567-021-00353-5

Guellai, B., Somogyi, E., Esseily, R., & Chopin, A. (2022). Effects of screen exposure on young children's cognitive development: A review. *Frontiers in Psychology*, 13, 923370. https://doi.org/10.3389/fpsyg.2022.923370

Guevara, H. (2022). *Report demonstrates inequitable access to Head Start services*. First Five Years Fund. https://www.ffyf.org/resources/2022/12/report-inequitable-access-to-head-start-services/

Guido, V., Alessandro, P., & Francesca, G. (2021). Child psychological adjustment to war and displacement: A discriminant analysis of resilience and trauma in Syrian refugee children. *Journal of Child and Family Studies*, 30(10), 2575–2588. https://doi.org/10.1007/S10826-021-02067-2

Guimond, S., Chatard, A., & Lorenzi-Cioldi, F. (2013). The social psychology of gender across cultures. In M. K. Ryan (Ed.), *The SAGE handbook of gender and psychology* (pp. 216–233). SAGE. https://doi.org/10.4135/9781446269930.n14

Guldner, S., Sarvasmaa, A. S., Lemaître, H., Massicotte, J., Vulser, H., Miranda, R., Bezivin-Frère, P., Filippi, I., Penttilä, J., Banaschewski, T., Barker, G. J., Bokde, A. L., Bromberg, U., Büchel, C., Conrod, P. J., Desrivières, S., Flor, H., Frouin, V., Gallinat, J., & &#hillip1; Martinot, J.-L. (2023). Longitudinal associations between adolescent catch-up sleep, white-matter maturation and internalizing problems. *Developmental Cognitive Neuroscience*, 5(9). https://www.sciencedirect.com/science/article/pii/S1878929322001360

Gülgöz, S., DeMeules, M., Gelman, S. A., & Olson, K. R. (2019). Gender essentialism in transgender and cisgender children. *PLoS ONE*, 14(11), e0224321. https://doi.org/10.1371/journal.pone.0224321

Gülgöz, S., Edwards, D. L., & Olson, K. R. (2022). Between a boy and a girl: Measuring gender identity on a continuum. *Social Development*, 31(3), 916–929. https://doi.org/10.1111/sode.12587

Gunn, J. K. L., Rosales, C. B., Center, K. E., Nuñez, A., Gibson, S. J., Christ, C., & Ehiri, J. E. (2016). Prenatal exposure to cannabis and maternal and child health outcomes: A systematic review and meta-analysis. *BMJ Open*, 6(4), e009986. https://doi.org/10.1136/bmjopen-2015-009986

Gunnerud, H. L., Braak, ten., D, Reikerås., L, E. K., Donolato, E., & Melby-Lervåg, M. (2020). Is bilingualism related to a cognitive advantage in children? A systematic review and meta-analysis. *Psychological Bulletin*, 146, 1059–1083. https://doi.org/10.1037/bul0000301

Günther, V., Alkatout, I., Vollmer, C., Maass, N., Strauss, A., & Voigt, M. (2021). Impact of nicotine and maternal BMI on fetal birth weight. *BMC Pregnancy and Childbirth*, 21(1), 1–6. https://doi.org/10.1186/S12884-021-03593-Z/FIGURES/2

Guo, L., Yang, L., Liu, Z., & Song, T. (2005). An experimental research on the formation of primary school pupils' self-confidence. *Psychological Science (China)*, 28(5), 1068–1071.

Guo, M., O'Connor Duffany, K., Shebl, F. M., Santilli, A., & Keene, D. E. (2018). The effects of length of residence and exposure to violence on perceptions of neighborhood safety in an urban sample. *Journal of Urban Health*, 95(2), 245–254. https://doi.org/10.1007/s11524-018-0229-7

Guo, Y., Leu, S.-Y., Barnard, K. E., Thompson, E. A., & Spieker, S. J. (2015). An examination of changes in emotion co-regulation among mother and child dyads during the strange situation. *Infant and Child Development*, 24(3), 256–273. https://doi.org/10.1002/icd.1917

Gur, R. E., Moore, T. M., Rosen, A. F. G., Barzilay, R., Roalf, D. R., Calkins, M. E., Ruparel, K., Scott, J. C., Almasy, L., Satterthwaite, T. D., Shinohara, R. T., & Gur, R. C. (2019). Burden of environmental adversity associated with psychopathology, maturation, and brain behavior parameters in youths. *JAMA Psychiatry*, 76(9), 966–975. https://doi.org/10.1001/jamapsychiatry.2019.0943

Guralnick, M. J. (2017). Early intervention for children with intellectual disabilities: An update. *Journal of Applied Research in Intellectual Disabilities*, 30(2), 211–229. https://doi.org/10.1111/jar.12233

Gurley, J. R. (2011). Crime, Adolescence. In S. Goldstein & J. A. Naglieri (Eds.), *Encyclopedia of child behavior and development* (pp. 431–433). Springer. https://doi.org/10.1007/978-0-387-79061-9_727

Güroglu, B., Bos, W. van den., & Crone, E. A. (2014). Sharing and giving across adolescence: An experimental study examining the development of prosocial behavior. *Frontiers in Psychology*, 5, 291. https://doi.org/10.3389/fpsyg.2014.00291

Guttmacher Institute. (2020). *Substance use during pregnancy*. https://www.guttmacher.org/state-policy/explore/substance-use-during-pregnancy

Guyer, A. E., Beard, S. J., & Venticinque, J. S. (2023). Brain development during adolescence and early adulthood. In *APA handbook of adolescent and young adult development* (pp. 21–37). American Psychological Association. https://doi.org/10.1037/0000298-002

Gyurkovics, M., Stafford, T., & Levita, L. (2020). Cognitive control across adolescence: Dynamic adjustments and mind-wandering. *Journal of Experimental Psychology: General*, 149(6), 1017–1031. https://doi.org/10.1037/xge0000698

Habermas, T., Negele, A., & Mayer, F. B. (2010). "Honey, you're jumping about"—Mothers' scaffolding of their children's and adolescents' life narration. *Cognitive Development*, 25(4), 339–351. https://doi.org/10.1016/j.cogdev.2010.08.004

Habib, A., Harris, L., Pollick, F., & Melville, C. (2019). A meta-analysis of working memory in individuals with autism spectrum disorders. *PLoS ONE*, 14(4), e0216198. https://doi.org/10.1371/journal.pone.0216198

Hadders-Algra, M. (2022). Human face and gaze perception is highly context specific and involves bottom-up and top-down neural processing. *Neuroscience and Biobehavioral Reviews*, 13(2). https://doi.org/10.1016/j.neubiorev.2021.11.042

Haden, C. A., & Fivush, F. (1996). Contextual variation in maternal conversational styles. *Merrill-Palmer Quarterly*, 42, 200–227.

Háden, G. P., Mády, K., Török, M., & Winkler, I. (2020). Newborn infants differently process adult directed and infant directed speech. *International Journal of Psychophysiology*, 147, 107–112. https://doi.org/10.1016/j.ijpsycho.2019.10.011

Hadley, P. A., Rispoli, M., Fitzgerald, C., & Bahnsen, A. (2011). Predictors of morphosyntactic growth in typically developing toddlers: Contributions of parent input and child sex. *Journal of Speech Language and Hearing Research*, 54(2), 549–566. https://doi.org/10.1044/1092-4388(2010/09-0216

Hage, C., Gan, H. W., Ibba, A., Patti, G., Dattani, M., Loche, S., Maghnie, M., & Salvatori, R. (2021). Advances in differential diagnosis and management of growth hormone deficiency in children. *Nature Reviews Endocrinology, 17*(10), 608–624. https://doi.org/10.1038/s41574-021-00539-5

Hagerman, R. J., & Hagerman, P. J. (2022). Fragile X syndrome: Lessons learned and what new treatment avenues are on the horizon. *Annual Review of Pharmacology and Toxicology, 62*, 365–381. https://doi.org/10.1146/Annurev-Pharmtox-052120-090147

Häggman-Laitila, A., Salokekkilä, P., & Karki, S. (2019). Young people's preparedness for adult life and coping after foster care: A systematic review of perceptions and experiences in the transition period. *Child & Youth Care Forum, 48*(5), 633–661. https://doi.org/10.1007/s10566-019-09499-4

Hahn-Holbrook, J., Holbrook, C., & Bering, J. (2010). Snakes, spiders, strangers: How the evolved fear of strangers may misdirect efforts to protect children from harm. In J. M. Lampinen & K. Sexton-Radek (Eds.), *Protecting Children from Violence: Evidence Based Interventions*. Psychology Press. https://digitalcommons.chapman.edu/psychology_books/4

Haier, R. J. (2023). *The neuroscience of intelligence* (2nd ed.). Cambridge University Press.

Haimovitz, K., & Dweck, C. S. (2016). Parents' views of failure predict children's fixed and growth intelligence mind-sets. *Psychological Science, 27*(6), 859–869. https://doi.org/10.1177/0956797616639727

Haimovitz, K., & Dweck, C. S. (2017). The origins of children's growth and fixed mindsets: New research and a new proposal. *Child Development, 88*(6), 1849–1859. https://doi.org/10.1111/cdev.12955

Haines, E. L., Deaux, K., & Lofaro, N. (2016). The times they are a-changing... or are they not? A comparison of gender stereotypes, 1983–2014. *Psychology of Women Quarterly, 40*(3), 353–363. https://doi.org/10.1177/0361684316634081

Hair, N. L., Hanson, J. L., Wolfe, B. L., Pollak, S. D., & Knight, R. T. (2015). Association of child poverty, brain development, and academic achievement. *JAMA Pediatrics, 169*(9), 822–829. https://doi.org/10.1001/jamapediatrics.2015.1475

Hajal, N. J., & Paley, B. (2020). Parental emotion and emotion regulation: A critical target of study for research and intervention to promote child emotion socialization. *Developmental Psychology, 56*(3), 403. https://doi.org/10.1037/dev0000864

Halberstadt, A. G., & Lozada, F. T. (2011). Emotion development in infancy through the lens of culture. *Emotion Review, 3*(2), 158–168. https://doi.org/10.1177/1754073910387946

Hale, A. E., Chertow, S. Y., Weng, Y., Tabuenca, A., & Aye, T. (2021). Perceptions of support among transgender and gender-expansive adolescents and their parents. *Journal of Adolescent Health, 68*(6), 1075–1081. https://doi.org/10.1016/j.jadohealth.2020.11.021

Halevi, G., Djalovski, A., Vengrober, A., & Feldman, R. (2016). Risk and resilience trajectories in war-exposed children across the first decade of life. *Journal of Child Psychology and Psychiatry, 57*(10), 1183–1193. https://doi.org/10.1111/jcpp.12622

Halford, G. S., & Andrews, G. (2011). Information-processing models of cognitive development. In U. Goswami (Ed.), *The Wiley-Blackwell handbook of childhood cognitive development* (2nd ed., pp. 697–721). Wiley.

Halim, M. L. D. (2016). Princesses and superheroes: Social-cognitive influences on early gender rigidity. *Child Development Perspectives, 10*(3), 155–160. https://doi.org/10.1111/cdep.12176

Halim, M. L. D., Ruble, D. N., Tamis-LeMonda, C. S., Shrout, P. E., & Amodio, D. M. (2017). Gender attitudes in early childhood: Behavioral consequences and cognitive antecedents. *Child Development, 88*(3), 882–899. https://doi.org/10.1111/cdev.12642

Halim, M. L. D., Ruble, D., Tamis-LeMonda, C., & Shrout, P. E. (2013). Rigidity in gender-typed behaviors in early childhood: A longitudinal study of ethnic minority children. *Child Development, 84*(4), 1269–1284. https://doi.org/10.1111/cdev.12057

Hall, C. M., Bierman, K. L., & Jacobson, L. N. (2022). Latent profiles of students at social-emotional risk: Heterogeneity among peer-rejected students in early elementary school. *Journal of Emotional and Behavioral Disorders, 30*(4), 260–272. https://doi.org/10.1177/10634266211051405

Hall, G. Stanley. (1904). *Adolescence*. Appleton.

Hall, R., Taylor, J., Hewitt, C. E., Heathcote, C., Jarvis, S. W., Langton, T., & Fraser, L. (2024). Impact of social transition in relation to gender for children and adolescents: A systematic review. *Archives of Disease in Childhood*. https://doi.org/10.1136/archdischild-2023-326112 Advance online publication

Hall, S. P. (2018). Identity status. In J. R. Levesque. Roger (Ed.), *Encyclopedia of adolescence* (pp. 1836–1844). Springer. https://doi.org/10.1007/978-3-319-33228-4_212

Hall, S. P., & Brassard, M. R. (2008). Relational support as a predictor of identity status in an ethnically diverse early adolescent sample. *Journal of Early Adolescence, 28*(1), 92–114. https://doi.org/10.1177/0272431607308668

Hall, W. J., Dawes, H. C., & Plocek, N. (2021). Sexual orientation identity development milestones among lesbian, gay, bisexual, and queer people: A systematic review and meta-analysis. *Frontiers in Psychology, 12*, 753954. https://www.frontiersin.org/journals/psychology/articles/10.3389/fpsyg.2021.753954

Halliday, L., Nelson, S. M., & Kearns, R. J. (2022). Epidural analgesia in labor: A narrative review. *International Journal of Gynecology & Obstetrics, 159*(2), 356–364. https://doi.org/10.1002/IJGO.14175

Halliday, S., Gregory, T., Taylor, A., Digenis, C., & Turnbull, D. (2021). The impact of bullying victimization in early adolescence on subsequent psychosocial and academic outcomes across the adolescent period: A systematic review. *Journal of School Violence, 20*(3), 351–373. https://doi.org/10.1080/15388220.2021.1913598

Halpern, H. P., & Perry-Jenkins, M. (2016). Parents' gender ideology and gendered behavior as predictors of children's gender-role attitudes: A longitudinal exploration. *Sex Roles, 74*(11–12), 527–542. https://doi.org/10.1007/s11199-015-0539-0

Hamidullah, S., Thorpe, H. H. A., Frie, J. A., Mccurdy, R. D., & Khokhar, J. Y. (2020). Adolescent substance use and the brain: Behavioral, cognitive and neuroimaging correlates. *Frontiers in Human Neuroscience, 14*, 298. https://doi.org/10.3389/fnhum.2020.00298

Hamilton, B. E., Martin, J. A., Osterman, M. J. K., & Rossen, L. M. (2019). Births: Provisional data for 2018. In *Vital Statistics Rapid Release*. National Center for Health Statistics. 7

Hamilton, J. L., Nesi, J., & Choukas-Bradley, S. (2022). Reexamining social media and socioemotional well-being among adolescents through the lens of the COVID-19 pandemic: A theoretical review and directions for future research:. *Perspectives on Psychological Science, 17*, 662–679. https://doi.org/10.1177/17456916211014189

Hamilton, M., Ross, A., Blaser, E., & Kaldy, Z. (2022). Proactive interference and the development of working memory. *WIREs Cognitive Science, 13*(3), e1593. https://doi.org/10.1002/wcs.1593

Hamlat, E. J., Laraia, B., Bleil, M. E., Deardorff, J., Tomiyama, A. J., Mujahid, M., Shields, G. S., Brownell, K., Slavich, G. M.,

& Epel, E. S. (2022). Effects of Early Life Adversity on Pubertal Timing and Tempo in Black and White Girls: The National Growth and Health Study. *Psychosomatic Medicine*, *84*(3), 297–305. https://doi.org/10.1097/PSY.0000000000001048

Hamlat, E. J., McCormick, K. C., Young, J. F., & Hankin, B. L. (2020). Early pubertal timing predicts onset and recurrence of depressive episodes in boys and girls. *Journal of Child Psychology and Psychiatry*, *61*(11), 1266–1274. https://doi.org/10.1111/JCPP.13198

Hamlat, E. J., Prather, A. A., Horvath, S., Belsky, J., & Epel, E. S. (2021). Early life adversity, pubertal timing, and epigenetic age acceleration in adulthood. *Developmental Psychobiology*, *63*(5), 890–902. https://doi.org/10.1002/dev.22085

Hamlat, E. J., Snyder, H. R., Young, J. F., & Hankin, B. L. (2019). Pubertal timing as a transdiagnostic risk for psychopathology in youth. *Clinical Psychological Science*, *7*(3), 411–429. https://doi.org/10.1177/2167702618810518

Hamlin, J. K. (2013). Moral judgment and action in preverbal infants and toddlers: Evidence for an innate moral core. *Current Directions in Psychological Science*, *22*(3), 186–193. https://doi.org/10.1177/0963721412470687

Hamlin, J. K. (2014). The origins of human morality: Complex socio-moral evaluations by preverbal infants. In J. Decety & Y. Christen (Eds.), *New frontiers in social neuroscience* (pp. 165–188). Springer International. https://doi.org/10.1007/978-3-319-02904-7_10

Hammond, C. J., Chaney, A., Hendrickson, B., & Sharma, P. (2020). Cannabis use among U.S. adolescents in the era of marijuana legalization: A review of changing use patterns, comorbidity, and health correlates. *International Review of Psychiatry*, *32*(3), 221–234. https://doi.org/10.1080/09540261.2020.1713056

Hammond, S. I., & Carpendale, J. I. M. (2015). Helping children help: The relation between maternal scaffolding and children's early help. *Social Development*, *24*(2), 367–383. https://doi.org/10.1111/sode.12104

Han, C., & Hong, Y. C. (2019). Fetal and childhood malnutrition during the Korean War and metabolic syndrome in adulthood. *Nutrition*, *62*, 186–193. https://doi.org/10.1016/j.nut.2019.01.003

Han, D., & Adolph, K. E. (2021). The impact of errors in infant development: Falling like a baby. *Developmental Science*, *24*(5). https://doi.org/10.1111/desc.13069

Han, G., & Son, H. (2022). A systematic review of socio-ecological factors influencing current e-cigarette use among adolescents and young adults. *Addictive Behaviors*, *135*, 107425. https://doi.org/10.1016/J.ADDBEH.2022.107425

Han, J., Schwartz, A. E., & Elbel, B. (2020). Does proximity to fast food cause childhood obesity? Evidence from public housing. *Regional Science and Urban Economics*, *84*, 103565. https://doi.org/10.1016/j.regsciurbeco.2020.103565

Hanania, R., & Smith, L. B. (2010). Selective attention and attention switching: Towards a unified developmental approach. *Developmental Science*, *13*(4), 622–635. https://doi.org/10.1111/j.1467-7687.2009.00921.x

Handen, B. L. (2020). The search for biomarkers of Alzheimer's disease in down syndrome. *American Journal on Intellectual and Developmental Disabilities*, *25*(2), 97–99. https://doi.org/10.1352/1944-7558-125.2.97

Hanley, J. R., Cortis, C., Budd, M.-J., & Nozari, N. (2016). Did I say dog or cat? A study of semantic error detection and correction in children. *Journal of Experimental Child Psychology*, *142*, 36–47. https://doi.org/10.1016/j.jecp.2015.09.008

Hans, S. L. (2024). Adolescent mothers of young children. In J. D. Osofsky, H. E. Fitzgerald, M. Keren, & K. Puura (Eds.), *WAIMH handbook of infant and early childhood mental health: Biopsychosocial factors* (Vol. 1, pp. 351–371). Springer International. https://doi.org/10.1007/978-3-031-48627-2_21

Hansen, A., Turpyn, C. C., Mauro, K., Thompson, J. C., & Chaplin, T. M. (2019). Adolescent brain response to reward is associated with a bias toward immediate reward. *Developmental Neuropsychology*, *44*(5), 417–428. https://doi.org/10.1080/87565641.2019.1636798

Hansen, J. E., & Broekhuizen, M. L. (2021). Quality of the language-learning environment and vocabulary development in early childhood. *Scandinavian Journal of Educational Research*, *65*(2), 302–317. https://doi.org/10.1080/00313831.2019.1705894

Hansen, M. B., & Markman, E. M. (2009). Children's use of mutual exclusivity to learn labels for parts of objects. *Developmental Psychology*, *45*(2), 592–596. https://doi.org/10.1037/a0014838

Harden, K. P. (2021). "Reports of my death were greatly exaggerated": Behavior genetics in the postgenomic era. *Annual Review of Psychology*, *7*(2). https://doi.org/10.1146/annurev-psych-052220-103822

Harden, K. P. (2021). "Reports of my death were greatly exaggerated": Behavior genetics in the postgenomic era. *Annual Review of Psychology*, *72*, 37–60. https://doi.org/10.1146/annurev-psych-052220-103822

Hardie, J. H., Pearce, L. D., & Denton, M. L. (2016). The dynamics and correlates of religious service attendance in adolescence. *Youth and Society*, *48*(2), 151–175. https://doi.org/10.1177/0044118X13483777

Harding, J. F., Hughes, D. L., & Way, N. (2017). Racial/ethnic differences in mothers' socialization goals for their adolescents. *Cultural Diversity and Ethnic Minority Psychology*, *23*(2), 281–290. https://doi.org/10.1037/cdp0000116

Hardy, S. A., Baldwin, C. R., Herd, T., & Kim-Spoon, J. (2020). Dynamic associations between religiousness and self-regulation across adolescence into young adulthood. *Developmental Psychology*, *56*(1), 180–197. https://doi.org/10.1037/dev0000841

Hardy, S. A., & King, P. E. (2019). Processes of religious and spiritual influence in adolescence: Introduction to a special section. *Journal of Research on Adolescence*, *29*(2), 244–253. https://doi.org/10.1111/jora.12509

Hardy, S. A., Nelson, J. M., Frandsen, S. B., Cazzell, A. R., & Goodman, M. A. (2022). Adolescent religious motivation: A self-determination theory approach. *International Journal for the Psychology of Religion*, *32*(1), 16–30. https://doi.org/10.1080/10508619.2020.1844968

Harlow, H. F. (1958). The nature of love. *American Psychologist*, *13*(12), 673–685. https://doi.org/10.1037/h0047884

Harlow, H. F., & Zimmerman, R. (1959). Affectional responses in the infant monkey. *Science*, *130*, 421–432.

Harper, J. M., Padilla-Walker, L. M., & Jensen, A. C. (2016). Do siblings matter independent of both parents and friends? Sympathy as a mediator between sibling relationship quality and adolescent outcomes. *Journal of Research on Adolescence*, *26*(1), 101–114. https://doi.org/10.1111/jora.12174

Harries, M. D., Paglia, H. A., Redden, S. A., & Grant, J. E.-M. (2018). Age at first sexual activity: Clinical and cognitive associations. *Annals of Clinical Psychiatry*, *30*(2), 102–112.

Harriman, A. E., & Lukosius, P. A. (1982). On why Wayne Dennis found Hopi infants retarded in age at onset of walking.

Perceptual and Motor Skills, 55(1), 79–86. https://doi.org/10.2466/pms.1982.55.1.79

Harrington, E. M., Trevino, S. D., Lopez, S., & Giuliani, N. R. (2020). Emotion regulation in early childhood: Implications for socioemotional and academic components of school readiness. Emotion, 20(1), 48–53. https://doi.org/10.1037/emo0000667

Harris, K., & Yudin, M. H. (2020). HIV infection in pregnant women: A 2020 update. Prenatal Diagnosis, 40(13), 1715–1721. https://doi.org/10.1002/pd.5769

Harris, M. A., Gruenenfelder-Steiger, A. E., Ferrer, E., Donnellan, M. B., Allemand, M., Fend, H., Conger, R. D., & Trzesniewski, K. H. (2015). Do parents foster self-esteem? Testing the prospective impact of parent closeness on adolescent self-esteem. Child Development, 86(4), 995–1013. https://doi.org/10.1111/cdev.12356

Harris, M. A., & Orth, U. (2020). The link between self-esteem and social relationships: A meta-analysis of longitudinal studies. Journal of Personality and Social Psychology, 119(6), 1459–1477. https://doi.org/10.1037/pspp0000265

Harris, N. (2020). Artificial insemination: Procedures, costs, and success rates. Parents. https://www.parents.com/getting-pregnant/infertility/treatments/artificial-insemination-procedures-costs-and-success-rates/

Harris, R. A., Chen, D., & Santos, H. P. (2022). Which roads lead to depression in Latinas? A network analysis of prenatal depressive symptoms, discrimination, acculturative stress, and low birth weight. Research in Nursing and Health, 45(3). https://doi.org/10.1002/nur.22210

Harris, W. A. (2022). Zero to birth: How the human brain is built. Princeton University Press. https://press.princeton.edu/books/hardcover/9780691211312/zero-to-birth

Harrison, D., & Bueno, M. (2023). Translating evidence: Pain treatment in newborns, infants, and toddlers during needle-related procedures. Pain Reports, 8(2), e1064. https://doi.org/10.1097/PR9.0000000000001064

Harrison, L. (2017). Brown bodies, white babies: The politics of cross-racial surrogacy. NYU Press. https://nyupress.org/9781479894864/brown-bodies-white-babies/

Hart, B., & Risley, T. R. (1995). Meaningful differences in the everyday experience of young American children. Paul H. Brookes.

Hart, J. R., Coates, E. E., & Smith-Bynum, M. A. (2019). Parenting style and parent-adolescent relationship quality in African American mother-adolescent dyads. Parenting, 19(4), 318–340. https://doi.org/10.1080/15295192.2019.1642085

Hartanto, A., Yang, H., & Yang, S. (2018). Bilingualism positively predicts mathematical competence: Evidence from two large-scale studies. Learning and Individual Differences, 61, 216–227. https://doi.org/10.1016/j.lindif.2017.12.007

Harter, S. (2012a). Emerging self-processes during childhood and adolescence. In M. R. Leary & J. P. Tangney (Eds.), Handbook of self and identity (pp. 680–715).

Harter, S. (2012b). The construction of the self: Developmental and sociocultural foundations. Guilford.

Hartley, K., Ryan, P., Brokamp, C., & Gillespie, G. L. (2020). Effect of greenness on asthma in children: A systematic review. Public Health Nursing, 37(3), 453–460. https://doi.org/10.1111/phn.12701

Hartman, S., Eilertsen, E. M., Ystrom, E., Belsky, J., & Gjerde, L. C. (2020). Does prenatal stress amplify effects of postnatal maternal depressive and anxiety symptoms on child problem behavior? Developmental Psychology, 56(1), 128–137. https://doi.org/10.1037/dev0000850

Hartwig, T. S., Ambye, L., Sørensen, S., & Jørgensen, F. S. (2017). Discordant non-invasive prenatal testing (NIPT)—A systematic review. Prenatal Diagnosis, 37(6), 527–539. https://doi.org/10.1002/pd.5049

Haslam, D., Poniman, C., Filus, A., Sumargi, A., & Boediman, L. (2020). Parenting style, child emotion regulation and behavioral problems: The moderating role of cultural values in Australia and Indonesia. Marriage and Family Review, 56(4), 320–342. https://doi.org/10.1080/01494929.2020.1712573

Hassinger-Das, B., Brennan, S., Dore, R. A., Golinkoff, R. M., & Hirsh-Pasek, K. (2020). Children and screens. Annual Review of Developmental Psychology, 2(1), 69–92. https://doi.org/10.1146/annurev-devpsych-060320-095612

Hatchel, T., Valido, A., De Pedro, K. T., Huang, Y., & Espelage, D. L. (2019). Minority stress among transgender adolescents: The role of peer victimization, school belonging, and ethnicity. Journal of Child and Family Studies, 28, 2467–2476. https://doi.org/10.1007/s10826-018-1168-3

Hatzis, D., Dawe, S., Harnett, P., & Barlow, J. (2017). Quality of caregiving in mothers with illicit substance use: A systematic review and meta-analysis. Substance Abuse: Research and Treatment, 11, 1178221817694038. https://doi.org/10.1177/1178221817694038

Hauck, J. D. (2020). Language Evolution. In J. Stanlaw (Ed.), The international encyclopedia of linguistic anthropology (pp. 1–23). John Wiley & Sons. https://doi.org/10.1002/9781118786093.iela0124

Hauser, M. D., Yang, C., Berwick, R. C., Tattersall, I., Ryan, M. J., Watumull, J., Chomsky, N., & Lewontin, R. C. (2014). The mystery of language evolution. Frontiers in Psychology, 5, 401. https://doi.org/10.3389/fpsyg.2014.00401

Hawes, D. J., & Tully, L. A. (2020). Parent discipline and socialization in middle childhood. In S. Hupp & J. D. Jewell (Eds.), The encyclopedia of child and adolescent development (pp. 1–10). Wiley. https://doi.org/10.1002/9781119171492.wecad236

Hawk, L. W., Fosco, W. D., Colder, C. R., Waxmonsky, J. G., Pelham, W. E., & Rosch, K. S. (2018). How do stimulant treatments for ADHD work? Evidence for mediation by improved cognition. Journal of Child Psychology and Psychiatry, 59, 1271–1281. https://doi.org/10.1111/jcpp.12917

Hay, D. F. (2016). The early development of human aggression. Child Development Perspectives, 11(2), 102–106. https://doi.org/10.1111/cdep.12220

Hay, D. F., Hurst, S.-L., Waters, C. S., & Chadwick, A. (2011). Infants' use of force to defend toys: The origins of instrumental aggression. Infancy, 16(5), 471–489. https://doi.org/10.1111/j.1532-7078.2011.00069.x

Hayek, J., Schneider, F., Lahoud, N., Tueni, M., & Vries, H. de. (2022). Authoritative parenting stimulates academic achievement, also partly via self-efficacy and intention towards getting good grades. PLoS ONE, 17(3), e0265595. https://doi.org/10.1371/journal.pone.0265595

Hayes, S., Delker, E., & Bandoli, G. (2023). The prevalence of cannabis use reported among pregnant individuals in the United States is increasing, 2002–2020. Journal of Perinatology, 43(3), Article 3. https://doi.org/10.1038/s41372-022-01550-y

Hayne, H., Boniface, J., & Barr, R. (2000). The development of declarative memory in human infants: Age-related changes in deffered imitation. Behavioral Neuroscience, 114(1), 77–83. https://doi.org/10.1037/0735-7044.114.1.77

Hayslip, B., & Blumenthal, H. (2016). Grandparenthood: A developmental perspective. In M. H. Meyer & E. Daniele (Eds.), Gerontology: Changes, challenges, and solutions (pp. 271–298). Praeger.

Hayslip, B., Fruhauf, C. A., & Dolbin-MacNab, M. L. (2017). Grandparents raising grandchildren: What have we learned over the past decade? *Gerontologist, 57*(6), 1196. https://doi.org/10.1093/geront/gnx124

Hazel, C. E., Walls, N. E., & Pomerantz, L. (2019). Gender and sexual minority students' engagement with school: The impacts of grades, reeling unsafe, and gay/straight alliances. *Contemporary School Psychology, 23*, 432–443. https://doi.org/10.1007/s40688-018-0199-5

Hazel, W. N., Black, R., Smock, R. C., Sear, R., & Tomkins, J. L. (2020). An age-dependent ovulatory strategy explains the evolution of dizygotic twinning in humans. *Nature Ecology and Evolution, 4*(7), 987–992. https://doi.org/10.1038/s41559-020-1173-y

Hazer, L., & Gredebäck, G. (2023). The effects of war, displacement, and trauma on child development. *Humanities and Social Sciences Communications, 10*(1), 1–19. https://doi.org/10.1057/s41599-023-02438-8

He, M., Walle, E. A., & Campos, J. J. (2015). A cross-national investigation of the relationship between infant walking and language development. *Infancy, 20*(3), 283–305. https://doi.org/10.1111/infa.12071

He, Y., Chen, J., Zhu, L.-H., Hua, L.-L., & Ke, F.-F. (2020). Maternal smoking during pregnancy and ADHD. *Journal of Attention Disorders, 24*, 1637–1647. https://doi.org/10.1177/1087054717696766

Heaman, M. I., Sword, W., Elliott, L., Moffatt, M., Helewa, M. E., Morris, H., Gregory, P., Tjaden, L., Cook, C., Chalmers, B., Mangiaterra, V., Porter, R., D'Ascoli, P., Alexander, G., Petersen, D., Kogan, M., Heaman, M., Green, C., Newburn-Cook, C., & &#hillip1; Brown, J. (2015). Barriers and facilitators related to use of prenatal care by inner-city women: Perceptions of health care providers. *BMC Pregnancy and Childbirth, 15*(1), 2. https://doi.org/10.1186/s12884-015-0431-5

Heath, S. B. (1989). Oral and literate tradition among black Americans living in poverty. *American Psychologist, 44*(2), 367–373. https://doi.org/10.1037/0003-066X.44.2.367

Heatly, M. C., & Votruba-Drzal, E. (2019). Developmental precursors of engagement and motivation in fifth grade: Linkages with parent- and teacher-child relationships. *Journal of Applied Developmental Psychology, 60*, 144–156. https://doi.org/10.1016/j.appdev.2018.09.003

Heffer, T., Good, M., Daly, O., MacDonell, E., & Willoughby, T. (2019). The longitudinal association between social-media use and depressive symptoms among adolescents and young adults: An empirical reply to Twenge et al. *Clinical Psychological Science, 7*(3), 462–470. https://doi.org/10.1177/2167702618812727 2018

Hegde, A., & Mitra, R. (2020). Environment and early life: Decisive factors for stress-resilience and vulnerability. In A. Clow & N. Smyth (Eds.), *Stress and Brain Health: Across the Life Course* (Vol. 150, pp. 155–185). https://doi.org/10.1016/bs.irn.2019.12.002

Heilmann, A., Mehay, A., Watt, R. G., Kelly, Y., Durrant, J. E., van Turnhout, J., & Gershoff, E. T. (2021). Physical punishment and child outcomes: A narrative review of prospective studies. *Lancet, 398*(10297), 355–364. https://doi.org/10.1016/S0140-6736(21)00582-1

Heimann, M., & Meltzoff, A. N. (1996). Deferred imitation in 9- and 14-month-old infants: A longitudinal study of a Swedish sample. *British Journal of Developmental Psychology, 14*(1), 55–64. https://doi.org/10.1111/j.2044-835X.1996.tb00693.x

Heine, S. J., & Hamamura, T. (2007). search of East Asian self-enhancement. *Personality and Social Psychology Review, 11*(1), 4–27. https://doi.org/10.1177/1088868306294587

Heinrich, J. (2011). Influence of indoor factors in dwellings on the development of childhood asthma. *International Journal of Hygiene & Environmental Health, 214*(1), 1–25. https://doi.org/10.1016/j.ijheh.2010.08.009

Helm, A. F., McCormick, S. A., Deater-Deckard, K., Smith, C. L., Calkins, S. D., & Bell, M. A. (2020). Parenting and children's executive function stability across the transition to school. *Infant and Child Development, 29*(1), e2171. https://doi.org/10.1002/icd.2171

Helms, J. E. (1992). Why is there no study of cultural equivalence in standardized cognitive ability testing? *American Psychologist, 47*(9), 1083–1101. https://doi.org/10.1037/0003-066X.47.9.1083

Helms, S. W., Choukas-Bradley, S., Widman, L., Giletta, M., Cohen, G. L., & Prinstein, M. J. (2014). Adolescents misperceive and are influenced by high-status peers' health risk, deviant, and adaptive behavior. *Developmental Psychology, 50*(12), 2697–2714. https://doi.org/10.1037/a0038178

Helms, S. W., Gallagher, M., Calhoun, C. D., Choukas-Bradley, S., Dawson, G. C., & Prinstein, M. J. (2015). Intrinsic religiosity buffers the longitudinal effects of peer victimization on adolescent depressive symptoms. *Journal of Clinical Child and Adolescent Psychology, 44*(3), 471–479. https://doi.org/10.1080/15374416.2013.865195

Helwig, C. C., & Prencipe, A. (1999). Children's judgments of flags and flag-burning. *Child Development, 70*(1), 132–143. https://doi.org/10.1111/1467-8624.00010

Hendriks, S., Grady, C., Wasserman, D., Wendler, D., Bianchi, D. W., & Berkman, B. E. (2022). A new ethical framework for assessing the unique challenges of fetal therapy trials. *American Journal of Bioethics, 22*(3), 45–61. https://doi.org/10.1080/15265161.2020.1867932

Hendry, A., Johnson, M. H., & Holmboe, K. (2019). Early development of visual attention: Change, stability, and longitudinal associations. *Annual Review of Developmental Psychology, 1*(1), 251–275. https://doi.org/10.1146/annurev-devpsych-121318-085114

Hennefield, L., & Markson, L. (2022). The development of optimistic expectations in young children. *Cognitive Development, 63*, 101201. https://doi.org/10.1016/j.cogdev.2022.101201

Henriques, J., Jauniaux, E., de Maisieres, A. T., & Gélat, P. (2022). Sound before birth: Foetal hearing and the auditory environment of the womb. In J. L. Drever & A. Hugill (Eds.), *Aural diversity* (pp. 27–41). Routledge.

Henry, D. A., Cortés, L. B., & Votruba-Drzal, E. (2020). Black-white achievement gaps differ by family socioeconomic status from early childhood through early adolescence. *Journal of Educational Psychology, 112*, 1471–1489. https://doi.org/10.1037/edu0000439

Hensch, T. K. (2022). Factors that initiate and terminate critical periods. In A. A. Benasich & U. Ribary (Eds.), *Emergent brain dynamics prebirth to adolescence* (pp. 69–80). MIT Press. https://direct.mit.edu/books/edited-volume/3660/chapter/122055/Factors-that-Initiate-and-Terminate-Critical

Hensums, M., Brummelman, E., Larsen, H., van den Bos, W., & Overbeek, G. (2023). Social goals and gains of adolescent bullying and aggression: A meta-analysis. *Developmental Review, 68*, 101073. https://doi.org/10.1016/j.dr.2023.101073

Hensums, M., de Mooij, B., Kuijper, S. C., Cross, D., DeSmet, A., Garandeau, C. F., Joronen, K., Leadbeater, B., Menesini, E., Palladino, B. E., Salmivalli, C., Solomontos-Kountouri, O., Veenstra, R., Fekkes, M., Overbeek, G., & BIRC. (2023). The Anti-Bullying Interventions Research Consortium. What works for whom in school-based anti-bullying interventions? An individual participant data meta-analysis.

Prevention Science, 24(8), 1435–1446. https://doi.org/10.1007/s11121-022-01387-z

Hepach, R., Engelmann, J. M., Herrmann, E., Gerdemann, S. C., & Tomasello, M. (2023). Evidence for a developmental shift in the motivation underlying helping in early childhood. *Developmental Science, 26*(1), e13253. https://doi.org/10.1111/desc.13253

Hepach, R., Vaish, A., & Tomasello, M. (2012). Young children are intrinsically motivated to see others helped. *Psychological Science, 23*(9), 967–972. https://doi.org/10.1177/0956797612440571

Hepper, P. (2015). Behavior during the prenatal period: Adaptive for development and survival. *Child Development Perspectives, 9*(1), 38–43. https://doi.org/10.1111/cdep.12104

Herati, A. S., Zhelyazkova, B. H., Butler, P. R., & Lamb, D. J. (2017). Age-related alterations in the genetics and genomics of the male germ line. *Fertility and Sterility, 107*(2), 319–323. https://doi.org/10.1016/j.fertnstert.2016.12.021

Herbert, J., Eckerman, C. O., Goldstein, R. F., & Stanton, M. E. (2004). Contrasts in classical eyeblink conditioning as a function of premature birth. *Infancy, 5*(3), 367–383.

Herculano-Houzel, S. (2020). Remarkable, but not special: What human brains are made of. In J. H. Kaas (Ed.), *Evolutionary neuroscience* (2nd ed., pp. 803–813). Academic Press. https://doi.org/10.1016/B978-0-12-820584-6.00033-7

Herd, T., & Kim-Spoon, J. (2021). A systematic review of associations between adverse peer experiences and emotion regulation in adolescence. *Clinical Child and Family Psychology Review, 24*(1), 141–163. https://doi.org/10.1007/S10567-020-00337-X

Herd, T., King-Casas, B., & Kim-Spoon, J. (2020). Developmental changes in emotion regulation during adolescence: Associations with socioeconomic risk and family emotional context. *Journal of Youth and Adolescence, 49*(7), 1545–1557. https://doi.org/10.1007/S10964-020-01193-2

Hernández, M. M., Conger, R. D., Robins, R. W., Bacher, K. B., & Widaman, K. F. (2014). Cultural socialization and ethnic pride among Mexican-origin adolescents during the transition to middle school. *Child Development, 85*(2), 695–708. https://doi.org/10.1111/cdev.12167

Hernandez-Pavon, J. C., Sosa, M., Lutter, W. J., Maier, M., & Wakai, R. T. (2008). *Auditory evoked responses in neonates by MEG.*

AIP Conference Proceedings, 1032(1 (pp. 114–117). https://doi.org/10.1063/1.2979244

Herpertz-Dahlmann, B., Dempfle, A., Konrad, K., Klasen, F., Ravens-Sieberer, U., & the, BELLA Study Group. (2015). Eating disorder symptoms do not just disappear: The implications of adolescent eating-disordered behaviour for body weight and mental health in young adulthood. *European Child & Adolescent Psychiatry, 24*(6), 675–684. https://doi.org/10.1007/s00787-014-0610-3

Herrera-Gómez, A., Luna-Bertos, E. D., Ramos-Torrecillas, J., Ocaña-Peinad., F. M., García-Martínez, O., & Ruiz, C. (2017). The effect of epidural analgesia alone and in association with other variables on the risk of cesarean section. *Biological Research for Nursing, 19*(4), 393–398. https://doi.org/10.1177/1099800417706023

Herts, J., & Levine, S. C. (2020, March 31). Gender and math development. *Oxford research encyclopedia of education.* Oxford University Press. https://doi.org/10.1093/acrefore/9780190264093.013.1186

Herts, J., & Levine, S. C. (2020). Gender and math development. In *Oxford research encyclopedia of education.* Oxford University Press. https://doi.org/10.1093/acrefore/9780190264093.013.1186

Herzberg, M. P., & Gunnar, M. R. (2020). Early life stress and brain function: Activity and connectivity associated with processing emotion and reward. *NeuroImage, 209,* 116493. https://doi.org/10.1016/j.neuroimage.2019.116493

Hetherington, E. M., Reiss, D., & Plomin, R (Eds.). (2013). Separate social world of siblings: The impact of nonshared environment on development. Routledge. https://doi.org/10.4324/9780203773192

Heward, W. L. (2018). *Exceptional children: an introduction to special education.* Pearson. https://www.pearson.com/us/higher-education/program/Heward-Exceptional-Children-An-Introduction-to-Special-Education-Plus-Revel-Access-Card-Package-11th-Edition/PGM2019655.html

Hewitt, L., Kerr, E., Stanley, R. M., & Okely, A. D. (2020). Tummy time and infant health outcomes: A systematic review. *Pediatrics, 145*(6), e20192168. https://doi.org/10.1542/peds.2019-2168

Hewlett, B. (2008). Fathers and infants among Aka pygmies. In R. A. LeVine & R. S. New (Eds.), *Anthropology and child development: A cross-cultural reader* (pp. 84–99). Blackwell.

Hewlett, B. S., Lamb, M. E., Shannon, D., Leyendecker, B., & Scholmerich, A. (1998). Culture and early infancy among central African foragers and farmers. *Developmental Psychology, 34,* 653–661. https://doi.org/10.1037/0012-1649.34.4.653

Hewlett, B. S., & MacFarlan, S. J. (2010). Fathers, roles in hunter-gatherer and other small-scale cultures. In M. E. Lamb (Ed.), *The role of the father in child development* (pp. 413–434). Wiley.

Heyes, C. (2014). False belief in infancy: A fresh look. *Developmental Science, 17*(5), 647–659. https://doi.org/10.1111/desc.12148

Heynen, E., Hoogsteder, L., van Vugt, E., Schalkwijk, F., Stams, G.-J., & Assink, M. (2024). Effectiveness of moral developmental interventions for youth engaged in delinquent behavior: A meta-analysis. *International Journal of Offender Therapy and Comparative Criminology.* https://doi.org/10.1177/0306624X231172648

Hiatt, C., Laursen, B., Mooney, K. S., & Rubin, K. H. (2015). Forms of friendship: A person-centered assessment of the quality, stability, and outcomes of different types of adolescent friends. *Personality and Individual Differences, 77,* 149–155. https://doi.org/10.1016/j.paid.2014.12.051

Hiatt, C., Laursen, B., Stattin, H., & Kerr, M. (2017). Best friend influence over adolescent problem behaviors: Socialized by the satisfied. *Journal of Clinical Child & Adolescent Psychology, 46*(5), 695–708. https://doi.org/10.1080/15374416.2015.1050723

Hiatt, R. A., Stewart, S. L., Deardorff, J., Danial, E., Abdiwahab, E., Pinney, S. M., Teitelbaum, S. L., Windham, G. C., Wolff, M. S., Kushi, L. H., & Biro, F. M. (2021). Childhood socioeconomic status and menarche: A prospective study. *Journal of Adolescent Health, 69*(1), 33–40. https://doi.org/10.1016/j.jadohealth.2021.02.003

Hibiya-Motegi, R., Nakayama, M., Matsuoka, R., Takeda, J., Nojiri, S., Itakura, A., Koike, T., & Ikeda, K. (2020). Use of sound-elicited fetal heart rate accelerations to assess fetal hearing in the second and third trimester. *International Journal of Pediatric Otorhinolaryngology, 133,* 110001. https://doi.org/10.1016/j.ijporl.2020.110001

Hildebrand, L., Posid, T., Moss-Racusin, C. A., Hymes, L., & Cordes, S. (2023). Does my daughter like math? Relations between parent and child math attitudes and beliefs. *Developmental Science, 26*(1), e13243. https://doi.org/10.1111/desc.13243

Hilger, K., Winter, N. R., Leenings, R., Sassenhagen, J., Hahn, T., Basten, U.,

& Fiebach, C. J. (2020). Predicting intelligence from brain gray matter volume. *Brain Structure and Function, 225*(7), 2111–2129. https://doi.org/10.1007/s00429-020-02113-7

Hill, M. S., & Wagovich, S. A. (2020). Word learning from context in school-age children: Relations with language ability and executive function. *Journal of Child Language, 47*(5), 1006–1029. https://doi.org/10.1017/S0305000919000989

Hillman, C., Logan, N., & Shigeta, T. (2019). A review of acute physical activity effects on brain and cognition in children. *Translational Journal of the American College of Sports Medicine, 4*(17), 132. https://doi.org/10.1249/TJX.0000000000000101

Hilton, C. B., Moser, C. J., Bertolo, M., Lee-Rubin, H., Amir, D., Bainbridge, C. M., Simson, J., Knox, D., Glowacki, L., Alemu, E., Galbarczyk, A., Jasienska, G., Ross, C. T., Neff, M. B., Martin, A., Cirelli, L. K., Trehub, S. E., Song, J., Kim, M., & &#hillip1; Mehr, S. A. (2022). Acoustic regularities in infant-directed speech and song across cultures. *Nature Human Behaviour, 6*(11), 1545–1556. https://doi.org/10.1038/s41562-022-01410-x

Hilton, M., Twomey, K. E., & Westermann, G. (2019). Taking their eye off the ball: How shyness affects children's attention during word learning. *Journal of Experimental Child Psychology, 183*, 134–145. https://doi.org/10.1016/j.jecp.2019.01.023

Hindman, A. H., Skibbe, L. E., & Foster, T. D. (2014). Exploring the variety of parental talk during shared book reading and its contributions to preschool language and literacy: Evidence from the early childhood longitudinal study-birth cohort. *Reading and Writing, 27*(2), 287–313. https://doi.org/10.1007/s11145-013-9445-4

Hindman, A. H., & Wasik, B. A. (2015). Building vocabulary in two languages: An examination of Spanish-speaking dual language learners in Head Start. *Early Childhood Research Quarterly, 31*, 19–33. https://doi.org/10.1016/j.ecresq.2014.12.006

Hindman, A. H., Wasik, B. A., & Snell, E. K. (2016). Closing the 30 million word gap: Next steps in designing research to inform practice. *Child Development Perspectives, 10*(2), 134–139. https://doi.org/10.1111/cdep.12177

Hinduja, S., & Patchin, J. W. (2022). Bullying and cyberbullying offending among US youth: The influence of six parenting dimensions. *Journal of Child and Family Studies, 31*(5), 1454–1473. https://doi.org/10.1007/s10826-021-02208-7

Hines, C. T., Markowitz, A. J., & Johnson, A. D. (2021). Food insecurity: What are its effects, why, and what can policy do about it? *Policy Insights from the Behavioral and Brain Sciences, 8*(2), 127–135. https://doi.org/10.1177/23727322211032250

Hines, C. T., Padilla, C. M., & Ryan, R. M. (2020). The effect of birth weight on child development prior to school entry. *Child Development, 91*(3), 724–732. https://doi.org/10.1111/cdev.13355

Hines, C. T., Steimle, S., & Ryan, R. (2024). Associations between daily food insecurity and parent and child well-being. *Developmental Psychology, 60*(5), 809–839. https://doi.org/10.1037/dev0001667

Hines, M. (2015). Gendered development. In M. Lewis (Ed.), *Handbook of child psychology and developmental science* (pp. 1–46). John Wiley & Sons. https://doi.org/10.1002/9781118963418.childpsy320

Hirota, T., & King, B. H. (2023). Autism Spectrum Disorder: A Review. *JAMA, 329*(2), 157–168. https://doi.org/10.1001/jama.2022.23661

Hisle-Gorman, E., & Susi, A. (2021). The impact of parental injury on children's mental health diagnoses and classes of psychotropic medication by child age. *Military Medicine, 186*(Suppl_1), 222–229. https://doi.org/10.1093/milmed/usaa466

Hithersay, R., Hamburg, S., Knight, B., & Strydom, A. (2017). Cognitive decline and dementia in Down syndrome. *Current Opinion in Psychiatry, 30*(2), 102–107. https://doi.org/10.1097/YCO.0000000000000307

Hladik, J., & Hrbackova, K. (2021). Peer-rejected students: An analysis of their self-regulatory mechanisms. *Children and Youth Services Review, 126*, 106030. https://doi.org/10.1016/j.childyouth.2021.106030

Hoch, H. E., Houin, P. R., & Stillwell, P. C. (2019). Asthma in children: A brief review for primary care providers. *Pediatric Annals, 48*(3), e103–e109. https://doi.org/10.3928/19382359-20190219-01

Hoch, J. E., O'Grady, S. M., & Adolph, K. E. (2019). It's the journey, not the destination: Locomotor exploration in infants. *Developmental Science, 22*(2). https://doi.org/10.1111/desc.12740

Hoch, J. E., Rachwani, J., & Adolph, K. E. (2020). Where infants go: Real-time dynamics of locomotor exploration in crawling and walking infants. *Child Development, 91*(3), 1001–1020. https://doi.org/10.1111/cdev.13250

Hock, A., Oberst, L., Jubran, R., White, H., Heck, A., & Bhatt, R. S. (2017). Integrated emotion processing in infancy: Matching of faces and bodies. *Infancy, 22*(5), 608–625. https://doi.org/10.1111/infa.12177

Hodel, A. S. (2018). Rapid infant prefrontal cortex development and sensitivity to early environmental experience. *Developmental Review, 48*, 113–144. https://doi.org/10.1016/J.DR.2018.02.003

Hodges, H., Fealko, C., & Soares, N. (2020). Autism spectrum disorder: Definition, epidemiology, causes, and clinical evaluation. *Translational Pediatrics, 9*(S1), S55–S65. https://doi.org/10.21037/tp.2019.09.09

Hodges-Simeon, C. R., Gurven, M., Cárdenas, R. A., & Gaulin, S. J. C. (2013). Voice change as a new measure of male pubertal timing: A study among Bolivian adolescents. *Annals of Human Biology, 40*(3), 209–219. https://doi.org/10.3109/03014460.2012.759622

Hoeben, E. M., Meldrum, R. C., Walker, D., & Young, J. T. N. (2016). The role of peer delinquency and unstructured socializing in explaining delinquency and substance use: A state-of-the-art review. *Journal of Criminal Justice, 47*, 108–122. https://doi.org/10.1016/j.jcrimjus.2016.08.001

Hoehl, S., Fairhurst, M., & Schirmer, A. (2021). Interactional synchrony: Signals, mechanisms and benefits. *Social Cognitive and Affective Neuroscience, 16*(1–2), 5–18. https://doi.org/10.1093/scan/nsaa024

Hoerr, J. J., Heard, A. M., Baker, M. M., Fogel, J., Glassgow, A. E., Kling, W. C., Clark, M. D., & Ronayne, J. P. (2018). Substance-exposed newborn infants and public health law: Differences in addressing the legal mandate to report. *Child Abuse and Neglect, 81*, 206–213. https://doi.org/10.1016/j.chiabu.2018.04.021

Hoeve, M., Dubas, J. S., Gerris, J. R. M., van der Laan, P. H., & Smeenk, W. (2011). Maternal and paternal parenting styles: Unique and combined links to adolescent and early adult delinquency. *Journal of Adolescence, 34*(5), 813–827. https://doi.org/10.1016/j.adolescence.2011.02.004

Hofer, C., Eisenberg, N., Spinrad, T. L., Morris, A. S., Gershoff, E., Valiente, C., Kupfer, A., & Eggum, N. D. (2013). Mother-adolescent conflict: Stability, change, and relations with externalizing and internalizing behavior problems. *Social Development, 22*(2), 259–279. https://doi.org/10.1111/sode.12012

Hoff, E. (2016). Language development. In M. H. Bornstein & M. E. Lamb (Eds.), *Developmental science: An advanced textbook*. Psychology Press.

Hoff, E. (2020). Lessons from the study of input effects on bilingual development.

International Journal of Bilingualism, 24(1), 82–88. https://doi.org/10.1177/1367006918768370

Hoff, E., Core, C., Place, S., Rumiche, R., Señor, M., & Parra, M. (2012). Dual language exposure and early bilingual development. *Journal of Child Language, 39*(1), 1–27. https://doi.org/10.1017/S0305000910000759

Hoff, E., Højen, A., & Bleses, D. (2022). Social contexts and language development: Past, present and future. In J. Law, S. Reilly, & S. McKean (Eds.), *Language development: Individual differences in a social context* (pp. 23–40). https://doi.org/10.1017/9781108643719.003

Hoff, E., & Naigles, L. (2002). How children use input to acquire a lexicon. *Child Development, 73*(2), 418–433. https://doi.org/10.1111/1467-8624.00415

Hoff, E., Rumiche, R., Burridge, A., Ribot, K. M., & Welsh, S. N. (2014). Expressive vocabulary development in children from bilingual and monolingual homes: A longitudinal study from two to four years. *Early Childhood Research Quarterly, 29*(4), 433–444. https://doi.org/10.1016/j.ecresq.2014.04.012

Hoffman, M. L. (1970). Conscience, personality, and socialization technique. *Human Development, 13*, 90–126. https://doi.org/10.1159/000270884

Hoffman, M. L. (2007). The origins of empathic morality in toddlerhood. In C. A. Brownell & C. B. Kopp (Eds.), *Socioemotional development in the toddler years: Transitions and transformations* (pp. 132–145). Guilford Press.

Hoffmann, J., & Russ, S. (2012). Pretend play, creativity, and emotion regulation in children. *Psychology of Aesthetics, Creativity, and the Arts, 6*(2), 175–184. https://doi.org/10.1037/a0026299

Hofman, D. L., Champ, C. L., Lawton, C. L., Henderson, M., & Dye, L. (2018). A systematic review of cognitive functioning in early treated adults with phenylketonuria. *Orphanet Journal of Rare Diseases, 13*(1), 1–19. https://doi.org/10.1186/s13023-018-0893-4

Hofmann, V., & Müller, C. M. (2018). Avoiding antisocial behavior among adolescents: The positive influence of classmates' prosocial behavior. *Journal of Adolescence, 68*, 136–145. https://doi.org/10.1016/j.adolescence.2018.07.013

Hoggatt, K. J., Flores, M., Solorio, R., Wilhelm, M., & Ritz, B. (2012). The "Latina Epidemiologic Paradox" revisited: The role of birthplace and acculturation in predicting infant low birth weight for Latinas in Los Angeles, CA. *Journal of Immigrant and Minority Health, 14*(5), 875–884. https://doi.org/10.1007/s10903-011-9556-4

Höhle, B., Bijeljac-Babic, R., & Nazzi, T. (2020). Variability and stability in early language acquisition: Comparing monolingual and bilingual infants' speech perception and word recognition. *Bilingualism, 23*(1), 56–71. https://doi.org/10.1017/S1366728919000348

Hollenstein, T., & Lougheed, J. P. (2013). Beyond storm and stress: Typicality, transactions, timing, and temperament to account for adolescent change. *American Psychologist, 68*(6), 444–454. https://doi.org/10.1037/a0033586

Holler, S., Köstinger, G., Martin, K. A. C., Schuhknecht, G. F. P., & Stratford, K. J. (2021). Structure and function of a neocortical synapse. *Nature, 591*(7848), 111–116. https://doi.org/10.1038/s41586-020-03134-2

Holliday, K. (2014, October 21). *China to ease 1-child rule further, but do people care?* CNBC News. http://www.cnbc.com/id/102104640#

Holloway, K., & Varner, F. (2021). Parenting despite discrimination: Does racial identity matter? *Cultural Diversity and Ethnic Minority Psychology, 27*(4), 781–795. https://doi.org/10.1037/cdp0000452

Holmes, C., Brieant, A., King-Casas, B., & Kim-Spoon, J. (2019). How is religiousness associated with adolescent risk-taking? The roles of emotion regulation and executive function. *Journal of Research on Adolescence, 29*(2), 334–344. https://doi.org/10.1111/jora.12438

Holz, N. E., Berhe, O., Sacu, S., Schwarz, E., Tesarz, J., Heim, C. M., & Tost, H. (2023). Early Social Adversity, Altered brain functional connectivity, and mental health. *Biological Psychiatry, 93*(5), 430–441. https://doi.org/10.1016/j.biopsych.2022.10.019

Homola, W., & Zimmer, M. (2019). Safety of amniocentesis in normal pregnancies and pregnancies considered high-risk due to fetal genetic anomalies – an observational study. *Clinical and Experimental Obstetrics and Gynecology, 46*(3), 403–407. https://doi.org/10.12891/ceog4713.2019

Hong, S., Hardi, F., & Maguire-Jack, K. (2023). The moderating role of neighborhood social cohesion on the relationship between early mother-child attachment security and adolescent social skills: Brief report. *Journal of Social and Personal Relationships, 40*(1), 277–287. https://doi.org/10.1177/02654075221118096

Honomichl, R. D., & Zhe, C. (2011). Relations as rules: The role of attention in the dimensional change card sort task. *Developmental Psychology, 47*(1), 50–60. https://doi.org/10.1037/a0021025

Hood, W., Bradley, G. L., & Ferguson, S. (2017). Mediated effects of perceived discrimination on adolescent academic achievement: A test of four models. *Journal of Adolescence, 54*, 82–93. https://doi.org/10.1016/j.adolescence.2016.11.011

Hopkins, B. (1991). Facilitating early motor development: An intercultural study of West Indian mothers and their infants living in Britain. In J. K. Nugent, B. M. Lester, & T. B. Brazelton (Eds.), *The cultural context of infancy: Multicultural and interdisciplinary approaches to parent-infant relations* (Vol. 2). Ablex.

Hopkins, B., & Westra, T. (1989). Maternal expectations of their infants' development: Some cultural differences. *Developmental Medicine and Child Neurology, 31*(3), 384–390.

Hopkins, B., & Westra, T. (1990). Motor development, maternal expectations, and the role of handling. *Infant Behavior and Development, 13*(1), 117–122.

Hopkins, S., & Richardson, L. (2021). Gender identity: From biological essentialism binaries to a nonbinary gender spectrum. In W. L. Filho, A. M. Azul, L. Brandli, A. L. Salvia, & T. Wal (Eds.), *Gender equality* (pp. 534–543). Springer. https://doi.org/10.1007/978-3-319-95687-9_87

Hopmeyer, A., & Medovoy, T. (2017). Emerging adults' self-identified peer crowd affiliations, risk behavior, and social-emotional adjustment in college. *Emerging Adulthood, 5*(2), 143–148. https://doi.org/10.1177/2167696816665055

Horányi, D., É, Babay, L., Győrffy, B., & Nagy, G. R. (2018). Longer oral contraception history as a possible preventive factor against fetal trisomy 21 in advanced maternal age pregnancies. *Orvosi Hetilap, 159*(28), 1146–1152. https://doi.org/10.1556/650.2018.31094

Horger, M. N., DeMasi, A., Allia, A. M., Scher, A., & Berger, S. E. (2023). The unique contributions of day and night sleep to infant motor problem solving. *Journal of Experimental Child Psychology, 226*, 105536. https://doi.org/10.1016/j.jecp.2022.105536

Horn, S. S., Bayen, U. J., & Michalkiewicz, M. (2021). The development of clustering in episodic memory: A cognitive-modeling approach. *Child Development, 92*(1), 239–257. https://doi.org/10.1111/cdev.13407

Hornberger, L. L., & Lane, M. A. (2021). Identification and management of eating disorders in children and adolescents. *Pediatrics, 147*(1), e2020040279. https://doi.org/10.1542/peds.2020-040279

Horne, R. S. C. (2019). Sudden infant death syndrome: Current perspectives. *Internal Medicine Journal, 49*(4), 433–438. https://doi.org/10.1111/imj.14248

Hornfeck, F., Bovenschen, I., Heene, S., Zimmermann, J., Zwönitzer, A., & Kindler, H. (2019). Emotional and behavior problems in adopted children – The role of early adversities and adoptive parents' regulation and behavior. *Child Abuse and Neglect, 98*, 104221. https://doi.org/10.1016/j.chiabu.2019.104221

Horowitz, S. H., Rawe, J., & Whittaker, M. C. (2017). *The state of learning disabilities: Understanding the 1 in 5*. National Center for Learning Disabilities.

Horton, C. (2023). "Euphoria": Trans children and experiences of prepubertal social transition. *Family Relations, 72*(4), 1890–1907. https://doi.org/10.1111/fare.12764

Horvath, G., Knopik, V. S., & Marceau, K. (2020). Polygenic influences on pubertal timing and tempo and depressive symptoms in boys and girls. *Journal of Research on Adolescence, 30*(1), 78–94. https://doi.org/10.1111/jora.12502

Hospodar, C. M., Hoch, J. E., Lee, D. K., Shrout, P. E., & Adolph, K. E. (2021). Practice and proficiency: Factors that facilitate infant walking skill. *Developmental Psychobiology, 63*(7). https://doi.org/10.1002/dev.22187

Hossain, Z., Field, T., Pickens, J., Malphurs, J., & Del Valle, C. (1997). Fathers' caregiving in low-income African-American and Hispanic-American families. *Early Development & Parenting, 6*(2), 73–82, 2<73::AID-EDP145>3.0.CO;2-O. https://doi.org/10.1002/(SICI)1099-0917(199706)6:

Hossain, Z., Roopnarine, J. L., Ismail, R., Hashmi, S. I., & Sombuling, A. (2007). Fathers' and mothers' reports of involvement in caring for infants in Kadazan families in Sabah, Malaysia. *Fathering: A journal of theory, research, & practice about men as fathers, 5*(1), 58–72. https://doi.org/10.3149/fth.0501.58

Houdé, O., Pineau, A., Leroux, G., Poirel, N., Perchey, G., Lanoë, C., Lubin, A., Turbelin, M.-R., Rossi, S., Simon, G., Delcroix, N., Lamberton, F., Vigneau, M., Wisniewski, G., Vicet, J.-R., & Mazoyer, B. (2011). Functional magnetic resonance imaging study of Piaget's conservation-of-number task in preschool and school-age children: A neo-Piagetian approach. *Journal of Experimental Child Psychology, 110*(3), 332–346. https://doi.org/10.1016/j.jecp.2011.04.008

Houghton, S., Lawrence, D., Hunter, S. C., Rosenberg, M., Zadow, C., Wood, L., & Shilton, T. (2018). Reciprocal relationships between trajectories of depressive symptoms and screen media use during adolescence. *Journal of Youth and Adolescence, 47*(11), 2453–2467. https://doi.org/10.1007/s10964-018-0901-y

Houtrow, A. J., Larson, K., Olson, L. M., Newacheck, P. W., & Halfon, N. (2014). Changing trends of childhood disability, 2001–2011. *Pediatrics, 134*(3), 530–538. https://doi.org/10.1542/peds.2014-0594

Howe, M. L. (2015). Memory development. In L. S. Liben & U. Mueller (Eds.), *Handbook of child psychology and developmental science* (pp. 1–47). John Wiley & Sons. https://doi.org/10.1002/9781118963418.childpsy206

Howe, M. L. (2019). Unravelling the nature of early (autobiographical) memory. *Memory, 27*(1), 115–121. https://doi.org/10.1080/09658211.2019.1537140

Howe, M. L. (2022). Early childhood memories are not repressed: Either they were never formed or were quickly forgotten. *Topics in Cognitive Science*. https://doi.org/10.1111/tops.12636 Advance online publication

Howe, N., Paine, A. L., Ross, H. S., & Recchia, H. (2022). Sibling relations in early and middle childhood. In P. K. Smith & C. H. Hart (Eds.), *The Wiley-Blackwell handbook of childhood social development* (pp. 443–458). John Wiley & Sons. https://doi.org/10.1002/9781119679028.ch24

Howell, B. R., McMurray, M. S., Guzman, D. B., Nair, G., Shi, Y., McCormack, K. M., Hu, X., Styner, M. A., & Sanchez, M. M. (2017). Maternal buffering beyond glucocorticoids: Impact of early life stress on corticolimbic circuits that control infant responses to novelty. *Social Neuroscience, 12*(1), 50–64. https://doi.org/10.1080/17470919.2016.1200481

Hoyt, L. T., Niu, L., Pachucki, M. C., & Chaku, N. (2020). Timing of puberty in boys and girls: Implications for population health. *SSM - Population Health, 10*, 100549. https://doi.org/10.1016/j.ssmph.2020.100549

Hrapczynski, K. M., & Leslie, L. A. (2019a). Do preparation for bias and cultural socialization protect against discrimination for transracially adopted adolescents? *Adoption Quarterly, 22*(2), 116–134. https://doi.org/10.1080/10926755.2019.1579136

Hrapczynski, K. M., & Leslie, L. A. (2019b). Engagement in racial socialization among transracial adoptive families with White parents. *Family Relations, 67*(3), 354–367. https://doi.org/10.1111/fare.12316

Hu, T., Jin, F., & Deng, H. (2024). Association between gender nonconformity and victimization: A meta-analysis. *Current Psychology, 43*(1), 281–299. https://doi.org/10.1007/s12144-023-04269-x

Hu, Y., Xu, Y., & Tornello, S. L. (2016). Stability of self-reported same-sex and both-sex attraction from adolescence to young adulthood. *Archives of Sexual Behavior, 45*(3), 651–659. https://doi.org/10.1007/s10508-015-0541-1

Hua, L. L. (2023). Interventions supporting and empowering pregnant and parenting adolescents. In J.-V. P. Wittenberg, D. F. Becker, & L. T. Flaherty (Eds.), *Adolescent pregnancy and parenting: Reducing stigma and improving outcomes* (pp. 83–100). Springer International. https://doi.org/10.1007/978-3-031-42502-8_7

Huber, E., Corrigan, N. M., Yarnykh, V. L., Ramírez, N. F., & Kuhl, P. K. (2023). Language experience during infancy predicts white matter myelination at age 2 years. *Journal of Neuroscience, 43*(9), 1590–1599. https://doi.org/10.1523/JNEUROSCI.1043-22.2023

Hubert, J. N., & Demars, J. (2022). Genomic imprinting in the new omics era: A model for systems-level approaches. *Frontiers in Genetics, 1*(3). https://doi.org/10.3389/fgene.2022.838534

Huelke, D. F. (1998). An overview of anatomical considerations of infants and children in the adult world of automobile safety design. *Annual Proceedings / Association for the Advancement of Automotive Medicine, 42*, 93–113.

Huesmann, L. R. (2007). The impact of electronic media violence: Scientific theory and research. *Journal of Adolescent Health, 41*(6 Suppl 1), S6–13. https://doi.org/10.1016/j.jadohealth.2007.09.005

Huesmann, L. R., Dubow, E. F., Boxer, P., Landau, S. F., Gvirsman, S. D., Shikaki, K., Abelson, R. P., Atran, S., Barber, B. K., Barber, B. K., Berkowitz, L., Boxer, P., Sloan-Power, E., Boxer, P., Sloan-Power, E., Mercado, I., Schappell, A., Bushman, B. J., Huesmann, L. R., & &#hillip1; Sapolsky, R. M. (2016). Children's exposure to violent political conflict stimulates aggression at peers by increasing emotional distress, aggressive script rehearsal, and normative beliefs favoring aggression. *Development and Psychopathology, 36*(7), 1–12. https://doi.org/10.1017/S0954579416001115

Huesmann, L. R., Lagerspetz, K., & Eron, L. D. (1984). Intervening variables in the TV violence-aggression relation: Evidence from two countries. *Developmental Psychology, 20*(5), 746–775. https://doi.org/10.1037/0012-1649.20.5.746

Huesmann, L. R., Moise-Titus, J., Podolski, C.-L., & Eron, L. D. (2003). Longitudinal relations between children's exposure to TV violence and their aggressive and violent behavior in young adulthood: 1977–1992. *Developmental Psychology, 39*(2), 201–221.

Huesmann, L. Rowell., & Eron, L. D. (1986). *Television and the aggressive child: A cross national comparison*. Routledge.

Huey, M., Hiatt, C., Laursen, B., Burk, W. J., & Rubin, K. (2017). Mother-adolescent conflict types and adolescent adjustment: A person-oriented analysis. *Journal of Family Psychology, 31*(4), 504–512. https://doi.org/10.1037/fam0000294

Huey, M., Laursen, B., Kaniušonytė, G., Malinauskienė, O., & Žukauskienė, R. (2020). Self-esteem mediates longitudinal associations from adolescent perceptions of parenting to adjustment. *Journal of Abnormal Child Psychology, 48*(3), 331–341. https://doi.org/10.1007/s10802-019-00599-2

Hughes, A. N. (2021). Glial cells promote myelin formation and elimination. *Frontiers in Cell and Developmental Biology, 9*, 661486. https://www.frontiersin.org/articles/10.3389/fcell.2021.661486

Hughes, C. H., & Devine, R. T. (2015). A social perspective on theory of mind. In M. E. Lamb (Ed.), *Handbook of child psychology and developmental science* (pp. 1–46). John Wiley & Sons. https://doi.org/10.1002/9781118963418.childpsy314

Hughes, C. H., & Ensor, R. (2007). Executive function and theory of mind: Predictive relations from ages 2 to 4. *Developmental Psychology, 43*(6), 1447–1459. https://doi.org/10.1037/0012-1649.43.6.1447

Hughes, C., McHarg, G., & White, N. (2018). Sibling influences on prosocial behavior. *Current Opinion in Psychology, 20*, 96–101. https://doi.org/10.1016/j.copsyc.2017.08.015

Hughes, D., Del Toro, J., Harding, J. F., Way, N., & Rarick, J. R. D. (2016). Trajectories of discrimination across adolescence: Associations with academic, psychological, and behavioral outcomes. *Child Development, 87*(5), 1337–1351. https://doi.org/10.1111/cdev.12591

Hughes, D., Hagelskamp, C., Way, N., & Foust, M. D. (2009). The role of mothers' and adolescents' perceptions of ethnic-racial socialization in shaping ethnic-racial identity among early adolescent boys and Girls. *Journal of Youth & Adolescence, 38*(5), 605–626. https://doi.org/10.1007/s10964-009-9399-7

Hughes, D. L., Del Toro, J., & Way, N. (2017). Interrelations among dimensions of ethnic-racial identity during adolescence. *Developmental Psychology, 53*(11), 2139–2153. https://doi.org/10.1037/dev0000401

Hui, K., Angelotta, C., & Fisher, C. E. (2017). Criminalizing substance use in pregnancy: Misplaced priorities. *Addiction, 112*(7), 1123–1125. https://doi.org/10.1111/add.13776

Huijsmans, T., Eichelsheim, V. I., Weerman, F., Branje, S. J. T., & Meeus, W. (2019). The role of siblings in adolescent delinquency next to parents, school, and peers: Do gender and age matter? *Journal of Developmental and Life-Course Criminology, 5*(2), 220–242. https://doi.org/10.1007/s40865-018-0094-9

Huijsmans, T., Nivette, A. E., Eisner, M., & Ribeaud, D. (2021). Social influences, peer delinquency, and low self-control: An examination of time-varying and reciprocal effects on delinquency over adolescence. *European Journal of Criminology, 18*(2), 192–212. https://doi.org/10.1177/1477370819838720

Hull, C. (2020). Prediction signals in the cerebellum: Beyond supervised motor learning. *eLife*. https://doi.org/10.7554/eLife.54073 9

Hull, J. V., Dokovna, L. B., Jacokes, Z. J., Torgerson, C. M., Irimia, A., & Van Horn, J. D. (2017). Resting-state functional connectivity in autism spectrum disorders: A review. *Frontiers in Psychiatry, 7*, 205. https://doi.org/10.3389/fpsyt.2016.00205

Hulme, C., Snowling, M. J., West, G., Lervåg, A., & Melby-Lervåg, M. (2020). Children's language skills can be improved: Lessons from psychological science for educational policy. *Current Directions in Psychological Science, 29*(4), 372–377. https://doi.org/10.1177/0963721420923684

Humphreys, K. L., King, L. S., Guyon-Harris, K. L., & Zeanah, C. H. (2022). Caregiver regulation: A modifiable target promoting resilience to early adverse experiences. *Psychological Trauma: Theory, Research, Practice, and Policy, 14*(S1), S63–S71. https://doi.org/10.1037/tra0001111

Humphreys, K. L., & Salo, V. C. (2020). Expectable environments in early life. *Current Opinion in Behavioral Sciences, 36*, 115–119. https://doi.org/10.1016/j.cobeha.2020.09.004

Hung, C. O.-Y., & Loh, E. K.-Y. (2021). Examining the contribution of cognitive flexibility to metalinguistic skills and reading comprehension. *Educational Psychology, 41*(6), 712–729. https://doi.org/10.1080/01443410.2020.1734187

Hunnius, S., & Geuze, R. H. (2004). Developmental changes in visual scanning of dynamic faces and abstract stimuli in infants: A longitudinal study. *Infancy, 6*(2), 231–255.

Huntsinger, C. S., Jose, P. E., & Larson, S. L. (1998). Do parent practices to encourage academic competence influence the social adjustment of young European American and Chinese American children? *Developmental Psychology, 34*, 747–756. https://doi.org/10.1037//0012-1649.34.4.747

Huppert, E., Cowell, J. M., Cheng, Y., Contreras-Ibáñez, C., Gomez-Sicard, N., L, Gonzalez-Gadea, M., Huepe, D., Ibanez, A., Lee, K., Mahasneh, R., Malcolm-Smith, S., Salas, N., Selcuk, B., Tungodden, B., Wong, A., Zhou, X., & Decety, J. (2019). The development of children's preferences for equality and equity across 13 individualistic and collectivist cultures. *Developmental Science, 22*(2), e12729. https://doi.org/10.1111/desc.12729

Hurst, J. L., Widman, L., Maheux, A. J., Evans-Paulson, R., Brasileiro, J., & Lipsey, N. (2022). Parent-child communication and adolescent sexual decision making: An application of family communication patterns theory. *Journal of Family Psychology, 36*(3), 449–457. https://doi.org/10.1037/fam0000916

Husky, M. M., Delbasty, E., Bitfoi, A., Carta, M. G., Goelitz, D., Koç, C., Lesinskiene, S., Mihova, Z., Otten, R., & Kovess-Masfety, V. (2020). Bullying involvement and self-reported mental health in elementary school children across Europe. *Child Abuse and Neglect, 107*, 104601. https://doi.org/10.1016/j.chiabu.2020.104601

Huston, A. C. (2008). From research to policy and back. *Child Development, 79*(1), 1–12. https://doi.org/10.1111/j.1467-8624.2007.01107.x

Hutaff-Lee, C., Bennett, E., Howell, S., & Tartaglia, N. (2019). Clinical developmental, neuropsychological, and social-emotional features of Turner syndrome. *American Journal of Medical Genetics, Part C: Seminars in Medical Genetics, 181*(1), 126–134. https://doi.org/10.1002/ajmg.c.31687

Hutchison, J. E., Lyons, I. M., & Ansari, D. (2019). More similar than different: Gender differences in children's basic numerical skills are the exception not the rule. *Child*

Development, 90(1), e66–e79. https://doi.org/10.1111/cdev.13044

Hutson, E., Kelly, S., & Militello, L. K. (2018). Systematic review of cyberbullying interventions for youth and parents with implications for evidence-based practice. Worldviews on Evidence-Based Nursing, 15(1), 72–79. https://doi.org/10.1111/wvn.12257

Huttenlocher, J., Levine, S., & Vevea, J. (1998). Environmental input and cognitive growth: A study using time-period comparisons. Child Development, 69(4), 1012–1029. https://doi.org/10.1111/j.1467-8624.1998.tb06158.x

Huttenlocher, J., Vasilyeva, M., Cymerman, E., & Levine, S. (2002). Language input and child syntax. Cognitive Psychology, 45(3), 337–374. https://doi.org/10.1016/S0010-0285(02)00500-5

Huttenlocher, J., Waterfall, H., Vasilyeva, M., Vevea, J., & Hedges, L. V. (2010). Sources of variability in children's language growth. Cognitive Psychology, 61(4), 343–365. https://doi.org/10.1016/j.cogpsych.2010.08.002

Huynh, H. T., Demeter, N. E., Burke, R. V., & Upperman, J. S. (2017). The role of adult perceptions and supervision behavior in preventing child injury. Journal of Community Health, 42(4), 649–655. https://doi.org/10.1007/s10900-016-0300-9

Hwang, H. G., Debnath, R., Meyer, M., Salo, V. C., Fox, N. A., & Woodward, A. (2021). Neighborhood racial demographics predict infants' neural responses to people of different races. Developmental Science, 24(4). https://doi.org/10.1111/desc.13070

Hwang, N. Y., Reyes, M., & Eccles, J. S. (2019). Who holds a fixed mindset and whom does it harm in mathematics? Youth and Society, 51(2), 247–267. https://doi.org/10.1177/0044118X16670058

Hyde, D. C. (2023). Cognitive neuroscience: An abstract sense of number in the infant brain. Current Biology, 33(10), R400–R402. https://doi.org/10.1016/j.cub.2023.03.079

Hyde, J., & DeLamater, J. (2020). Understanding human sexuality. McGraw Hill. https://www.mheducation.com/highered/product/understanding-human-sexuality-hyde-delamater/M9781260500233.html

Hyde, K. L., Lerch, J., Norton, A., Forgeard, M., Winner, E., Evans, A. C., & Schlaug, Gottfried. (2009). Musical Training Shapes Structural Brain Development. Journal of Neuroscience, 29(10), 3019–3025.

Hyde, L. W., Gard, A. M., Tomlinson, R. C., Burt, S. A., Mitchell, C., & Monk, C. S. (2020). An ecological approach to understanding the developing brain: Examples linking poverty, parenting, neighborhoods, and the brain. American Psychologist, 75(9), 1245–1259. https://doi.org/10.1037/amp0000741

Hyde, L. W., Gard, A. M., Tomlinson, R. C., Suarez, G. L., & Westerman, H. B. (2022). Parents, neighborhoods, and the developing brain. Child Development Perspectives, 16(3), 148–156. https://doi.org/10.1111/CDEP.12453

Hymel, S., & Swearer, S. M. (2015). Four decades of research on school bullying: An introduction. American Psychologist, 70(4), 293–299. https://doi.org/10.1037/a0038928

Hysing, M., Askeland, K. G., La Greca, A. M., Solberg, M. E., Breivik, K., & Sivertsen, B. (2019). Bullying involvement in adolescence: Implications for sleep, mental health, and academic outcomes. Journal of Interpersonal Violence, 36(17–18), NP8992–NP9014. https://doi.org/10.1177/0886260519853409

Ibbotson, P., & Tomasello, M. (2016). Evidence rebuts Chomsky's theory of language learning. Scientific American, 315(5), 70–75. https://doi.org/10.1038/scientificamerican1116-70

Icenogle, G., & Cauffman, E. (2021). Adolescent decision making: A decade in review. Journal of Research on Adolescence, 31(4), 1006–1022. https://doi.org/10.1111/JORA.12608

Icenogle, G., Steinberg, L., Duell, N., Chein, J., Chang, L., Chaudhary, N., Di Giunta, L., Dodge, K. A., Fanti, K. A., Lansford, J. E., Oburu, P., Pastorelli, C., Skinner, A. T., Sorbring, E., Tapanya, S., Tirado, L. M. U., Alampay, L. P., Al-Hassan, S. M., Takash, H. M. S., & Bacchini, D. (2019). Adolescents' cognitive capacity reaches adult levels prior to their psychosocial maturity: Evidence for a "maturity gap" in a multinational, cross-sectional sample. Law and Human Behavior, 43(1), 69–85. https://doi.org/10.1037/lhb0000315

Ilmarinen, V.-J., Vainikainen, M.-P., Verkasalo, M. J., & Lönnqvist, J.-E. (2017). Homophilous friendship assortment based on personality traits and cognitive ability in middle childhood: The moderating effect of peer network size. European Journal of Personality, 31(3), 208–219. https://doi.org/10.1002/per.2095

Ilyas, M., Mir, A., Efthymiou, S., & Houlden, H. (2020). The genetics of intellectual disability: Advancing technology and gene editing. F1000Research, 9, 22. https://doi.org/10.12688/f1000research.16315.1

Im, D., Sirivolu, S., Shah, S., & Berry, J. L. (2023). Genetic counseling. In Özdek. Ş, A. Berrocal, & U. Spandau (Eds.), Pediatric vitreoretinal surgery (pp. 893–909). Springer International. https://doi.org/10.1007/978-3-031-14506-3_60

Imrie, S., & Golombok, S. (2020). Impact of new family forms on parenting and child development. Annual Review of Developmental Psychology, 2(1), 295–316. https://doi.org/10.1146/annurev-devpsych-070220-122704

Imuta, K., Henry, J. D., Slaughter, V., Selcuk, B., & Ruffman, T. (2016). Theory of mind and prosocial behavior in childhood: A meta-analytic review. Developmental Psychology, 52(8), 1192–1205. https://doi.org/10.1037/dev0000140

Ingoglia, S., Liga, F., Coco, A. L., & Inguglia, C. (2021). Informant discrepancies in perceived parental psychological control, adolescent autonomy, and relatedness psychological needs. Journal of Applied Developmental Psychology, 77, 101333. https://doi.org/10.1016/j.appdev.2021.101333

Inhelder, B., & Piaget, J. (1958). The growth of logical thinking: From childhood to adolescence. Basic Books. https://doi.org/10.1037/10034-000

Inhelder, B., & Piaget, J. (1964). The early growth of logic in the child: Classification and seriation. Harper & Row.

Iruka, I. U., Gardner-Neblett, N., Telfer, N. A., Ibekwe-Okafor, N., Curenton, S. M., Sims, J., Sansbury, A. B., & Neblett, E. W. (2022). Effects of racism on child development: Advancing antiracist developmental science. Annual Review of Developmental Psychology, 4(1), 109–132. https://doi.org/10.1146/annurev-devpsych-121020-031339

Isaacs, E. B., Fischl, B. R., Quinn, B. T., Chong, W. K., Gadian, D. G., & Lucas, A. (2010). Impact of breast milk on intelligence quotient, brain size, and white matter development. Pediatric Research, 67(4), 357–362.

Isen, J., Tuvblad, C., Younan, D., Ericson, M., Raine, A., & Baker, L. A. (2022). Developmental trajectories of delinquent and aggressive behavior: Evidence for differential heritability. Child Psychiatry & Human Development, 53(2), 199–211. https://doi.org/10.1007/S10578-020-01119-W

Iskandar, B. J., & Finnell, R. H. (2022). Spina bifida. New England Journal of Medicine, 387(5), 444–450. https://doi.org/10.1056/NEJMra2116032

Islamiah, N., Breinholst, S., Walczak, M. A., & Esbjørn, B. H. (2023). The role of fathers in children's emotion regulation development: A systematic review. Infant and Child

Development, 32(2), e2397. https://doi.org/10.1002/icd.2397

Isojima, T., & Yokoya, S. (2023). Growth in girls with Turner syndrome. *Frontiers in Endocrinology*, *1*(3). https://www.frontiersin.org/journals/endocrinology/articles/10.3389/fendo.2022.1068128

Issard, C., Tsuji, S., & Cristia, A. (2023). Infants' preference for speech is stable across the first year of life: Meta-analytic evidence. *Infancy*, *28*(3), 550–568. https://doi.org/10.1111/infa.12529

Iverson, J. M. (2021). Developmental variability and developmental cascades: Lessons from motor and language development in infancy. *Current Directions in Psychological Science*, *30*(3). https://doi.org/10.1177/0963721421993822

Iyengar, U., Snowden, N., Asarnow, J. R., Moran, P., Tranah, T., & Ougrin, D. (2018). A further look at therapeutic interventions for suicide attempts and self-harm in adolescents: An updated systematic review of randomized controlled trials. *Frontiers in Psychiatry*, *9*, 583. https://doi.org/10.3389/fpsyt.2018.00583

Izard, C. E., Woodburn, E. M., & Finlon, K. J. (2010). Extending emotion science to the study of discrete emotions in infants. *Emotion Review*, *2*(2), 134–136. https://doi.org/10.1177/1754073909355003

Jackson, D. B., Testa, A., & Turney, K. (2022). Unpacking the connection between parental incarceration and parenting stress: The mediating role of child health and health care strains. *Journal of Criminal Justice*, *81*, 101918. https://doi.org/10.1016/j.jcrimjus.2022.101918

Jackson, E. F., Bussey, K., & Myers, E. (2021). Encouraging gender conformity or sanctioning nonconformity? Felt pressure from parents, peers, and the self. *Journal of Youth and Adolescence*, *50*(4), 613–627. https://doi.org/10.1007/s10964-020-01387-8

Jadva, V., Guasp, A., Bradlow, J. H., Bower-Brown, S., & Foley, S. (2021). Predictors of self-harm and suicide in LGBT youth: The role of gender, socio-economic status, bullying and school experience. *Journal of Public Health*, *45*(1), 102–108. https://doi.org/10.1093/pubmed/fdab383

Jadva, V., Imrie, S., & Golombok, S. (2015). Surrogate mothers 10 years on: A longitudinal study of psychological well-being and relationships with the parents and child. *Human Reproduction*, *30*(2), 373–379. https://doi.org/10.1093/humrep/deu339

Jaeger, E. L. (2016). Negotiating complexity: A bioecological systems perspective on literacy development. *Human Development*, *59*(4), 163–187. https://doi.org/10.1159/000448743

Jaekel, J., Baumann, N., Bartmann, P., & Wolke, D. (2018). Mood and anxiety disorders in very preterm/very low–birth weight individuals from 6 to 26 years. *Journal of Child Psychology and Psychiatry*, *59*(1), 88–95. https://doi.org/10.1111/jcpp.12787

Jaekel, J., Pluess, M., Belsky, J., & Wolke, D. (2015). Effects of maternal sensitivity on low birth weight children's academic achievement: A test of differential susceptibility versus diathesis stress. *Journal of Child Psychology and Psychiatry*, *56*(6), 693–701. https://doi.org/10.1111/jcpp.12331

Jafari, A., Naghshi, S., Shahinfar, H., Salehi, S. O., Kiany, F., Askari, M., Surkan, P. J., & Azadbakh, L. (2022). Relationship between maternal caffeine and coffee intake and pregnancy loss: A grading of recommendations assessment, development, and evaluation-assessed, dose-response meta-analysis of observational studies. *Frontiers in Nutrition*, *9*, 886224.

Jaffee, S., & Hyde, J. S. (2000). Gender differences in moral orientation: A meta-analysis. *Psychological Bulletin*, *126*(5), 703–726. https://doi.org/10.1037/0033-2909.126.5.703

Jagers, R. J., Bingham, K., & Hans, S. L. (1996). Socialization and social judgments among inner-city African-American kindergartners. *Child Development*, *67*, 140–150. https://doi.org/10.2307/1131692

Jaggy, A.-K., Kalkusch, I., Bossi, C. B., Weiss, B., Sticca, F., & Perren, S. (2023). The impact of social pretend play on preschoolers' social development: Results of an experimental study. *Early Childhood Research Quarterly*, *64*, 13–25. https://doi.org/10.1016/j.ecresq.2023.01.012

Jahromi, L. B., & Stifter, C. A. (2007). Individual differences in the contribution of maternal soothing to infant distress reduction. *Infancy*, *11*(3), 255–269. https://doi.org/10.1080/15250000701310371

Jambon, M., & Smetana, J. G. (2014). Moral complexity in middle childhood: Children's evaluations of necessary harm. *Developmental Psychology*, *50*(1), 22–33. https://doi.org/10.1037/a0032992

James, J. E. (2021). Maternal caffeine consumption and pregnancy outcomes: A narrative review with implications for advice to mothers and mothers-to-be. *BMJ Evidence-Based Medicine*, *26*(3), 114–115. https://doi.org/10.1136/bmjebm-2020-111432

James, W. (1890). *Principles of psychology*. Henry Holt.

Jäncke, L., Liem, F., & Merillat, S. (2021). Are language skills related to structural features in Broca's and Wernicke's area? *European Journal of Neuroscience*, *53*(4), 1124–1135. https://doi.org/10.1111/ejn.15038

Janusek, L. W., Tell, D., & Mathews, H. L. (2019). Epigenetic perpetuation of the impact of early life stress on behavior. *Current Opinion in Behavioral Sciences*, *28*, 1–7. https://doi.org/10.1016/j.cobeha.2019.01.004

Jaramillo, N., Buhi, E. R., Elder, J. P., & Corliss, H. L. (2017). Associations between sex education and contraceptive use among heterosexually active, adolescent males in the United States. *Journal of Adolescent Health*, *60*(5), 534–540. https://doi.org/10.1016/j.jadohealth.2016.11.025

Jarvis, J. A., Otero, C., Poff, J. M., Dufur, M. J., & Pribesh, S. L. (2023). Family structure and child behavior in the United Kingdom. *Journal of Child and Family Studies*, *32*(1), 160–179. https://doi.org/10.1007/s10826-021-02159-z

Javadi, A. H., Schmidt, D. H. K., & Smolka, M. N. (2014). Differential representation of feedback and decision in adolescents and adults. *Neuropsychologia*, *56*, 280–288. https://doi.org/10.1016/j.neuropsychologia.2014.01.021

Jaxon, J., Lei, R. F., Shachnai, R., Chestnut, E. K., & Cimpian, A. (2019). The acquisition of gender stereotypes about intellectual ability: Intersections with race. *Journal of Social Issues*, *75*(4), 1192–1215. https://doi.org/10.1111/josi.12352

Jebeile, H., Kelly, A. S., O'Malley, G., & Baur, L. A. (2022). Obesity in children and adolescents: Epidemiology, causes, assessment, and management. *The Lancet Diabetes and Endocrinology*, *10*(5). https://doi.org/10.1016/S2213-8587(22)00047-X

Jelenkovic, A., Sund, R., Hur, Y.-M., Yokoyama, Y., Hjelmborg, J. v. B., Möller, S., Honda, C., Magnusson, P. K. E., Pedersen, N. L., Ooki, S., Aaltonen, S., Stazi, M. A., Fagnani, C., D'Ippolito, C., Freitas, D. L., Maia, J. A., Ji, F., Ning, F., Pang, Z., & &#hillip1; Silventoinen, K. (2016). Genetic and environmental influences on height from infancy to early adulthood: An individual-based pooled analysis of 45 twin cohorts. *Scientific Reports*, *6*(1), 28496. https://doi.org/10.1038/srep28496

Jenkins, J. M., & Foster, E. M. (2014). The effects of breastfeeding exclusivity on early childhood outcomes. *American Journal of Public Health*, *104*, S128–S135. https://doi.org/10.2105/AJPH.2013.301713

Jenkins, L. N., Bogart, S., & Miskimon, K. (2021). Contextual characteristics in relation to student intervention in bullying. *Journal of Prevention and Health Promotion*, 3(1), 97–119. https://doi.org/10.1177/26320770211063630

Jennings, K. D., Sandberg, I., Kelley, S. A., Valdes, L., Yaggi, K., Abrew, A., & Macey-Kalcevic, M. (2008). Understanding of self and maternal warmth predict later self-regulation in toddlers. *International Journal of Behavioral Development*, 32(2), 108–118. https://doi.org/10.1177/0165025407087209

Jennings, S., Mellish, L., Tasker, F., Lamb, M., & Golombok, S. (2014). Why adoption? Gay, lesbian, and heterosexual adoptive parents' reproductive experiences and reasons for adoption. *Adoption Quarterly*, 17(3), 205–226. https://doi.org/10.1080/10926755.2014.891549

Jensen, A. C., Killoren, S. E., Campione-Barr, N., Padilla, J., & Chen, B.-B. (2023). Sibling relationships in adolescence and young adulthood in multiple contexts: A critical review. *Journal of Social and Personal Relationships*, 40(2), 384–419. https://doi.org/10.1177/02654075221104188

Jespersen, K., Kroger, J., & Martinussen, M. (2013). Identity status and moral reasoning: A meta-analysis. *Identity*, 13(3), 266–280. https://doi.org/10.1080/15283488.2013.799472

Jewell, J. A., & Brown, C. S. (2014). Relations among gender typicality, peer relations, and mental health during early adolescence. *Social Development*, 23(1), 137–156. https://doi.org/10.1111/sode.12042

Jewell, J. D., Krohn, E. J., Scott, V. G., Carlton, M., & Meinz, E. (2008). The differential impact of mothers' and fathers' discipline on preschool children's home and classroom behavior. *North American Journal of Psychology*, 10(1), 173–188.

Jha, A. K., Baliga, S., Kumar, H. H., Rangnekar, A., & Baliga, B. S. (2015). Is there a preventive role for vernix caseosa?: An invitro study. *Journal of Clinical and Diagnostic Research*, 9(11), SC13–SC16. https://doi.org/10.7860/JCDR/2015/14740.6784

Jhuremalani, A., Tadros, E., & Goody, A. (2022). Stereo-atypical: An investigation into the explicit and implicit gender stereotypes in primary school-aged children. *Early Childhood Education Journal*, 51, 1115–1129. https://doi.org/10.1007/s10643-022-01355-w

Jia, G., & Aaronson, D. (2003). A longitudinal study of Chinese children and adolescents learning English in the United States. *Applied Psycholinguistics*, 24(1), 131–161. https://doi.org/10.1017/S0142716403000079

Jiang, H., Gallier, S., Feng, L., Han, J., & Liu, W. (2022). Development of the digestive system in early infancy and nutritional management of digestive problems in breastfed and formula-fed infants. *Food & Function*, 13(3), 1062–1077. https://doi.org/10.1039/D1FO03223B

Jiang, Y., Lau, C., & Tan, C. Y. (2024). Socioeconomic Status and Children's English Language and Literacy Outcomes: The Mediating Role of Home Literacy Environment. *Early Education and Development*, 35(3), 588–614. https://doi.org/10.1080/10409289.2023.2186089

Jiao, C., & Cui, M. (2024). Indulgent parenting, self-control, self-efficacy, and adolescents' fear of missing out. *Current Psychology*, 43(3), 2186–2195. https://doi.org/10.1007/s12144-023-04450-2

Jin, M. K., Jacobvitz, D., Hazen, N., & Jung, S. H. (2012). Maternal sensitivity and infant attachment security in Korea: Cross-cultural validation of the strange situation. *Attachment & Human Development*, 14(1), 33–44. https://doi.org/10.1080/14616734.2012.636656

Jing, W., Liu, J., Ma, Q., Zhang, S., Li, Y., & Liu, M. (2022). Fertility intentions to have a second or third child under China's three-child policy: A national cross-sectional study. *Human Reproduction*, 37(8), 1907–1918. https://doi.org/10.1093/humrep/deac101

Jipson, J. L., Gülgöz, S., & Gelman, S. A. (2016). Parent-child conversations regarding the ontological status of a robotic dog. *Cognitive Development*, 39, 21–35. https://doi.org/10.1016/j.cogdev.2016.03.001

Johansen, E. R., Nielsen, H. S., & Verner, M. (2020). Long-term consequences of early parenthood. *Journal of Marriage and Family*, 82(4), 1286–1303. https://doi.org/10.1111/jomf.12634

Johansson, S., & Englund, G. (2021). Cyberbullying and its relationship with physical, verbal, and relational bullying: A structural equation modelling approach. *Educational Psychology*, 41(3), 320–337. https://doi.org/10.1080/01443410.2020.1769033

Johns, M. M., Beltran, O., Armstrong, H. L., Jayne, P. E., & Barrios, L. C. (2018). Protective factors among transgender and gender variant youth: A systematic review by socioecological level. *Journal of Primary Prevention*, 39(3), 263–301. https://doi.org/10.1007/s10935-018-0508-9

Johns, M. M., Lowry, R., Andrzejewski, J., Barrios, L. C., Demissie, Z., McManus, T., Rasberry, C. N., Robin, L., & Underwood, J. M. (2019). Transgender identity and experiences of violence victimization, substance use, suicide risk, and sexual risk behaviors among high school students—19 states and large urban school districts, 2017. *Morbidity and Mortality Weekly Report*, 68(3), 67. http://doi.org/10.15585/mmwr.mm6803a3

Johnson, A. D., Partika, A., Martin, A., Horm, D., Phillips, D. A., & the, Tulsa SEED Study Team. (2023). A deeper dive, a wider pool: Preschool benefits sustain to first grade on a broader set of outcomes. *Child Development*, 94(5), 1298–1318. https://doi.org/10.1111/cdev.13928

Johnson, A. Z., Sieving, R. E., Pettingell, S. L., & McRee, A.-L. (2015). The roles of partner communication and relationship status in adolescent contraceptive use. *Journal of Pediatric Health Care*, 29(1), 61–69. https://doi.org/10.1016/j.pedhc.2014.06.008

Johnson, D., Policelli, J., Li, M., Dharamsi, A., Hu, Q., Sheridan, M. A., McLaughlin, K. A., & Wade, M. (2021). Associations of early-life threat and deprivation with executive functioning in childhood and adolescence: A systematic review and meta-analysis. *JAMA Pediatrics*, 175(11), e212511. https://doi.org/10.1001/jamapediatrics.2021.2511

Johnson, K. C., LeBlanc, A. J., Sterzing, P. R., Deardorff, J., Antin, T., & Bockting, W. O. (2020). adolescents' perceptions and experiences of their parents' supportive and rejecting behaviors. *Journal of Counseling Psychology*, 67(2), 156–170. https://doi.org/10.1037/cou0000419

Johnson, K., Caskey, M., Rand, K., Tucker, R., & Vohr, B. (2014). Gender differences in adult-infant communication in the first months of life. *Pediatrics*, 134(6), e1603–e1610. https://doi.org/10.1542/peds.2013-4289

Johnston, J. C. (2005). Teaching gestural signs to infants to advance child development: A review of the evidence. *First Language*, 25(2), 235–251. https://doi.org/10.1177/0142723705050340

Johnston, M., Warton, C., Pertile, M. D., Taylor-Sands, M., Delatycki, M. B., Hui, L., Savulescu, J., & Mills, C. (2022). Ethical issues associated with prenatal screening using non-invasive prenatal testing for sex chromosome aneuploidy. *Prenatal Diagnosis*, 43(2), 226–234. https://doi.org/10.1002/PD.6217

Jonas, W., Atkinson, L., Steiner, M., Meaney, M. J., Wazana, A., & Fleming, A. S.

(2015). Breastfeeding and maternal sensitivity predict early infant temperament. *Acta Paediatrica*, 104(7), 678–686. https://doi.org/10.1111/apa.12987

Jones, D. C., Abbey, B. B., & Cumberland, A. (1998). The development of display rule knowledge: Linkages with family expressiveness and social competence. *Child Development*, 69(4), 1209–1222. https://doi.org/10.1111/j.1467-8624.1998.tb06168.x

Jones, D., Innerd, A., Giles, E. L., & Azevedo, L. B. (2020). Association between fundamental motor skills and physical activity in the early years: A systematic review and meta-analysis. *Journal of Sport and Health Science*, 9(6), 542–552. https://doi.org/10.1016/j.jshs.2020.03.001

Jones, E. J. H., & Herbert, J. S. (2006). Exploring memory in infancy: Deferred imitation and the development of declarative memory. *Infant and Child Development*, 15, 195–205. https://doi.org/10.1002/icd.436

Jones, E. P., & Mistry, J. (2019). The sociocultural process of child development. In Jones. Elizabeth Pufall & Jayanthi. Mistry (Eds.), *The Wiley handbook of early childhood care and education* (pp. 59–77). John Wiley & Sons. https://doi.org/10.1002/9781119148104.CH3

Jones, J. D., Fraley, R. C., Ehrlich, K. B., Stern, J. A., Lejuez, C. W., Shaver, P. R., & Cassidy, J. (2018). Stability of attachment style in adolescence: An empirical test of alternative developmental processes. *Child Development*, 89(3), 871–880. https://doi.org/10.1111/cdev.12775

Jones, J. H., Call, T. A., Wolford, S. N., & McWey, L. M. (2021). Parental stress and child outcomes: The mediating role of family conflict. *Journal of Child and Family Studies*, 30(3), 746–756. https://doi.org/10.1007/S10826-021-01904-8

Jones, K. M., Power, M. L., Queenan, J. T., & Schulkin, J. (2015). Racial and ethnic disparities in breastfeeding. *Breastfeeding Medicine*, 10(4), 186–196. https://doi.org/10.1089/bfm.2014.0152

Jones, N. F., Bishop, A. J., & Finchum, T. (2022). Considering the relevance of childhood religious experiences through centenarian oral histories. *International Journal of Aging and Human Development*, 94(1), 93–111. https://doi.org/10.1177/00914150211050883

Jones, T. M., & Montero, F. (2021, December 19). *Chorionic villus sampling*. StatPearls. https://doi.org/10.1016/B978-0-323-44548-1.00113-3

Jones, W., & Klin, A. (2013). Attention to eyes is present but in decline in 2–6-month-old infants later diagnosed with autism. *Nature*, 504(7480), 427–431. https://doi.org/10.1038/nature12715

Jonsson, B., Wiklund-Hörnqvist, C., Nyroos, M., & Börjesson, A. (2014). Self-reported memory strategies and their relationship to immediate and delayed text recall and working memory capacity. *Education Inquiry*, 5, 22850. https://doi.org/10.3402/edui.v5.22850

Joo, M. (2010). Long-term effects of Head Start on academic and school outcomes of children in persistent poverty: Girls vs. Boys. *Children & Youth Services Review*, 32(6), 807–814. https://doi.org/10.1016/j.childyouth.2010.01.018

Jordan, J. W., Stalgaitis, C. A., Charles, J., Madden, P. A., Radhakrishnan, A. G., & Saggese, D. (2019). Peer crowd identification and adolescent health behaviors: Results from a statewide representative study. *Health Education and Behavior*, 46(1), 40–52. https://doi.org/10.1177/1090198118759148

Jordan, P., & Hernandez-Reif, M. (2009). Reexamination of young children's racial attitudes and skin tone preferences. *Journal of Black Psychology*, 35(3), 388–403. https://doi.org/10.1177/0095798409333621

Joseph, N. T., Stanhope, K. K., Badell, M. L., Horton, J. P., Boulet, S. L., & Jamieson, D. J. (2020). Sociodemographic predictors of SARS-CoV-2 infection in obstetric patients. *Emerging Infectious Diseases*, 26(11), 2786–2788. https://doi.org/10.3201/eid2611.203091

Joseph, S. P., Borrell, L. N., Lovinsky-Desir, S., Maroko, A. R., & Li, S. (2022). Bullying and lifetime asthma among children and adolescents in the United States. *Annals of Epidemiology*, 69, 41–47. https://doi.org/10.1016/j.annepidem.2022.02.001

Joseph, V. A., Martínez-Alés, G., Olfson, M., Shaman, J., Gould, M. S., & Keyes, K. M. (2022). Temporal Trends in Suicide Methods Among Adolescents in the US. *JAMA Network Open*, 5(10), e2236049–e2236049. doi:10.1001/jamanetworkopen.2022.36049

Joshi, D. S., & Lebrun-Harris, L. A. (2022). Child health status and health care use in grandparent- versus parent-led households. *Pediatrics*, 150(3), e2021055291. https://doi.org/10.1542/peds.2021-055291

Jouhki, M.-R., Suominen, T., & Åstedt-Kurki, P. (2017). Giving birth on our own terms-Women's experience of childbirth at home. *Midwifery*, 53, 35–41. https://doi.org/10.1016/j.midw.2017.07.008

Juett, J., & Kuipers, B. (2019). Learning and acting in peripersonal space: Moving, reaching, and grasping. *Frontiers in Neurorobotics*, 13, 4. https://doi.org/10.3389/fnbot.2019.00004

Jugert, P., Leszczensky, L., & Pink, S. (2020). Differential influence of same- and cross-ethnic friends on ethnic-racial identity development in early adolescence. *Child Development*, 91(3), 949–963. https://doi.org/10.1111/cdev.13240

Jugl, I., Bender, D., & Lösel, F. (2021). Do sports programs prevent crime and reduce reoffending? A systematic review and meta-analysis on the effectiveness of sports programs. *Journal of Quantitative Criminology*, 39, 333–384. https://doi.org/10.1007/s10940-021-09536-3

Jullien, S. (2021). Sudden infant death syndrome prevention. *BMC Pediatrics*, 21(1), 1–9. https://doi.org/10.1186/s12887-021-02536-z

Juraska, J. M. (2024). The last stage of development: The restructuring and plasticity of the cortex during adolescence especially at puberty. *Developmental Psychobiology*, 66(2), e22468. https://doi.org/10.1002/dev.22468

Juruena, M. F., Eror, F., Cleare, A. J., & Young, A. H. (2020). The role of early life stress in HPA axis and anxiety. In Y.-K. Kim (Ed.), *Anxiety Disorders Rethinking and Understanding Recent Discoveries* (pp. 141–153). Springer. https://doi.org/10.1007/978-981-32-9705-0_9

Jusienė, R., Rakickienė, L., Breidokienė, R., & Laurinaitytė, I. (2020). Executive function and screen-based media use in preschool children. *Infant and Child Development*, 29(1), e2173. https://doi.org/10.1002/icd.2173

Juvonen, J., & Graham, S. (2014). Bullying in schools: The power of bullies and the plight of victims. *Annual Review of Psychology*, 65, 159–185. https://doi.org/10.1146/annurev-psych-010213-115030

Juvonen, J., Kogachi, K., & Graham, S. (2018). When and how do students benefit from ethnic diversity in middle school? *Child Development*, 89(4), 1268–1282. https://doi.org/10.1111/cdev.12834

K, Memmott-Elison, M., Holmgren, H. G., M, Padilla-Walker, L., & Hawkins, A. J. (2020). Associations between prosocial behavior, externalizing behaviors, and internalizing symptoms during adolescence: A meta-analysis. *Journal of Adolescence*, 80(1), 98–114. https://doi.org/10.1016/j.adolescence.2020.01.012

Kabátek, J., & Perales, F. (2021). Academic achievement of children in same- and different-sex-parented families: A population-level analysis of linked administrative data from the Netherlands. *Demography*, *58*(2), 393–418. https://doi.org/10.1215/00703370-8994569

Kaestle, C. E. (2019). Sexual orientation trajectories based on sexual attractions, partners, and identity: A longitudinal investigation from adolescence through young adulthood using a U.S. representative sample. *Journal of Sex Research*, *56*(7), 811–826. https://doi.org/10.1080/00224499.2019.1577351

Kaestle, C. E., Allen, K. R., Wesche, R., & Grafsky, E. L. (2021). Adolescent sexual development: A family perspective. *Journal of Sex Research*, *58*(7), 874–890. https://doi.org/10.1080/00224499.2021.1924605

Kagan, J. (2013). Temperamental contributions to inhibited and uninhibited profiles. In P. D. Zelazo (Ed.), *The Oxford handbook of developmental psychology* (Vol. 2, pp. 142–165). Oxford University Press. https://doi.org/10.1093/oxfordhb/9780199958474.013.0007

Kagan, J., Arcus, D., Snidman, N., Feng, W., Handler, J., & Greene, S. (1994). Reactivity in infants: A cross national comparison. *Developmental Psychology*, *30*, 342–345. https://doi.org/10.1037/0012-1649.30.3.342

Kågesten, A., Gibbs, S., Blum, R. W., Moreau, C., Chandra-Mouli, V., Herbert, A., & Amin, A. (2016). Understanding factors that shape gender attitudes in early adolescence globally: A mixed-methods systematic review. *PLoS ONE*, *11*(6), e0157805. https://doi.org/10.1371/journal.pone.0157805

Kahn, N. F., & Halpern, C. T. (2019). Is developmental change in gender-typed behavior associated with adult sexual orientation? *Developmental Psychology*, *55*(4), 855–865. https://doi.org/10.1037/dev0000662

Kaiser, L., Allen, L., & American, Dietetic Association. (2008). Position of the American Dietetic Association: Nutrition and lifestyle for a healthy pregnancy outcome. *Journal of the American Dietetic Association*, *108*(3), 553–561. https://doi.org/10.1016/j.jada.2008.01.030

Kalashnikova, M., & Carreiras, M. (2022). Input quality and speech perception development in bilingual infants' first year of life. *Child Development*, *93*(1), e32–e46. https://doi.org/10.1111/cdev.13686

Kalashnikova, M., Mattock, K., & Monaghan, P. (2016). Flexible use of mutual exclusivity in word learning. *Language Learning and Development*, *12*(1), 79–91. https://doi.org/10.1080/15475441.2015.1023443

Kalat, J. W. (2024). *Biological psychology*. Cengage.

Kaldy, Z., & Blaser, E. (2020). Putting effort into infant cognition. *Current Directions in Psychological Science*, *29*(2), 180–185. https://doi.org/10.1177/0963721420903015

Kalisher, A., Gosciak, J., & Spielfogel, J. (2020). *The Multiethnic Placement Act 25 years later*. https://aspe.hhs.gov/sites/default/files/migrated_legacy_files/197691/MEPA-Data-report.pdf

Kam, J. A., Gasiorek, J., Pines, R., & Fazio, K. S. (2018). Latina/o adolescents' family undocumented-status disclosures directed at school counselors: A latent transition analysis. *Journal of Counseling Psychology*, *65*(3), 267–279. https://doi.org/10.1037/cou0000259

Kaminen-Ahola, N. (2020). Fetal alcohol spectrum disorders: Genetic and epigenetic mechanisms. *Prenatal Diagnosis*, *40*, 1185–1192. https://doi.org/10.1002/pd.5731

Kamper-DeMarco, K. E., & Ostrov, J. M. (2017). Prospective associations between peer victimization and social-psychological adjustment problems in early childhood. *Aggressive Behavior*, *43*(5), 471–482. https://doi.org/10.1002/ab.21705

Kampis, D., Grosse Wiesmann, C., Koop, S., & Southgate, V. (2022). Understanding the self in relation to others: Infants spontaneously map another's face to their own at 16–26 months. *Developmental Science*, *25*(3), e13197. https://doi.org/10.1111/desc.13197

Kan, P. F., & Kohnert, K. (2008). Fast mapping by bilingual preschool children. *Journal of Child Language*, *35*(3), 495–514. https://doi.org/10.1017/S0305000907008604

Kana, R. K., Maximo, J. O., Williams, D. L., Keller, T. A., Schipul, S. E., Cherkassky, V. L., Minshew, N. J., Just, M. A., Gallagher, H., Frith, C., Barch, D., Burgess, G., Harms, M., Petersen, S., Schlaggar, B., Corbetta, M., Overwalle, F., Dufour, N., Redcay, E., & &#hillip1; Müller, R. (2015). Aberrant functioning of the theory-of-mind network in children and adolescents with autism. *Molecular Autism*, *6*(1), 59. https://doi.org/10.1186/s13229-015-0052-x

Kancherla, V. (2023). Neural tube defects: A review of global prevalence, causes, and primary prevention. *Child's Nervous System*, *39*(7), 1703–1710. https://doi.org/10.1007/s00381-023-05910-7

Kang, H.-K. (2014). Influence of culture and community perceptions on birth and perinatal care of immigrant women: Doulas' perspective. *Journal of Perinatal Education*, *23*(1), 25–32. https://doi.org/10.1891/1058-1243.23.1.25

Kanka, M. H., Wagner, P., Buchmann, M., & Spiel, C. (2019). Gender-stereotyped preferences in childhood and early adolescence: A comparison of cross-sectional and longitudinal data. *European Journal of Developmental Psychology*, *16*(2), 198–214. https://doi.org/10.1080/17405629.2017.1365703

Kann, L., McManus, T., Harris, W. A., Shanklin, S. L., Flint, K. H., Queen, B., Lowry, R., Chyen, D., Whittle, L., Thornton, J., Lim, C., Bradford, D., Yamakawa, Y., Leon, M., Brener, N., & Ethier, K. A. (2018). Youth risk behavior surveillance—United States, 2017. *MMWR Surveillance Summaries*, *67*(8), 1–114. https://doi.org/10.15585/mmwr.ss6708A1

Kantor, L., & Levitz, N. (2017). Parents' views on sex education in schools: How much do Democrats and Republicans agree? *PLoS ONE*, *12*(7), e0180250. https://doi.org/10.1371/journal.pone.0180250

Kapasi, A., & Pei, J. (2022). Mindset theory and school psychology. *Canadian Journal of School Psychology*, *37*(1), 57–74. https://doi.org/10.1177/08295735211053961

Kapetanovic, S., Boele, S., & Skoog, T. (2019). Parent-adolescent communication and adolescent delinquency: Unraveling within-family processes from between-family differences. *Journal of Youth and Adolescence*, *48*(9), 1707–1723. https://doi.org/10.1007/s10964-019-01043-w

Kapetanovic, S., Rothenberg, W. A., Lansford, J. E., Bornstein, M. H., Chang, L., Deater-Deckard, K., Di Giunta, L., Dodge, K. A., Gurdal, S., Malone, P. S., Oburu, P., Pastorelli, C., Skinner, A. T., Sorbring, E., Steinberg, L., Tapanya, S., Uribe Tirado, L. M., Yotanyamaneewong, S., Peña Alampay, L., & &#hillip1; Bacchini, D. (2020). Cross-cultural examination of links between parent-adolescent communication and adolescent psychological problems in 12 cultural groups. *Journal of Youth and Adolescence*, *49*(6), 1225–1244. https://doi.org/10.1007/s10964-020-01212-2

Kapetanovic, S., & Skoog, T. (2021). The role of the family's emotional climate in the links between parent-adolescent communication and adolescent psychosocial functioning. *Journal of Abnormal Child Psychology*, *49*(2), 141–154. https://doi.org/10.1007/s10802-020-00705-9

Kaplan, H., & Dove, H. (1987). Infant development among the Ache of eastern Paraguay. *Developmental Psychology, 23*(2), 190–198.

Karasik, L. B., & Robinson, S. R. (2022). Milestones or millstones: How standard assessments mask cultural variation and misinform policies aimed at early childhood development. *Policy Insights from the Behavioral and Brain Sciences, 9*(1). https://doi.org/10.1177/23727322211068546

Karasik, L. B., Tamis-LeMonda, C. S., Adolph, K. E., & Bornstein, M. H. (2015). Places and postures: A cross-cultural comparison of sitting in 5-month-olds. *Journal of Cross-Cultural Psychology, 46*(8), 1023–1038. https://doi.org/10.1177/0022022115593803

Karim, A., Qaisar, R., & Hussain, M. A. (2021). Growth and socio-economic status, influence on the age at menarche in school going girls. *Journal of Adolescence, 86*, 40–53. https://doi.org/10.1016/j.adolescence.2020.12.001

Karltorp, E., Eklöf, M., Östlund, E., Asp, F., Tideholm, B., & Löfkvist, U. (2020). Cochlear implants before 9 months of age led to more natural spoken language development without increased surgical risks. *Acta Paediatrica, 109*(2), 332–341. https://doi.org/10.1111/apa.14954

Kärnä, A., Voeten, M., Poskiparta, E., & Salmivalli, C. (2010). Vulnerable children in varying classroom contexts: Bystanders' behaviors moderate the effects of risk factors on victimization. *Merrill-Palmer Quarterly: Journal of Developmental Psychology, 56*(3), 261–282. http://doi.org/10.1353/mpq.0.0052

Karoly, H. C., Ross, J. M., Ellingson, J. M., & Feldstein Ewing, S. W. (2020). Exploring cannabis and alcohol co-use in adolescents: A narrative review of the evidence. *Journal of Dual Diagnosis, 16*(1), 58–74. https://doi.org/10.1080/15504263.2019.1660020

Kärtner, J., Borke, J., Maasmeier, K., Keller, H., & Kleis, A. (2011). Sociocultural influences on the development of self-recognition and self-regulation in Costa Rican and Mexican toddlers. *Journal of Cognitive Education and Psychology, 10*(1), 96–112. https://doi.org/10.1891/1945-8959.10.1.96

Kärtner, J., Giner Torréns, M., & Schuhmacher, N. (2021). Parental structuring during shared chores and the development of helping across the second year. *Social Development, 30*(2), 374–395. https://doi.org/10.1111/SODE.12490

Kärtner, J., Keller, H., Chaudhary, N., & Yovsi, R. D. (2012). The development of mirror self-recognition in different sociocultural contexts. *Monographs of the Society for Research in Child Development, 77*(4), i–101.

Kärtner, J., Schuhmacher, N., & Giner Torréns, M. (2020). Culture and early social-cognitive development. In S. Hunnius & M. Meyer (Eds.), *Progress in brain research* (Vol. 254, pp. 225–246). Elsevier. https://doi.org/10.1016/bs.pbr.2020.06.011

Katsantonis, I., McLellan, R., & Marquez, J. (2023). Development of subjective well-being and its relationship with self-esteem in early adolescence. *British Journal of Developmental Psychology, 41*(2), 157–171. https://doi.org/10.1111/bjdp.12436

Katz, A. N. (2017). Psycholinguistic approaches to metaphor acquisition and use. In E. Semino & Z. Demjén (Eds.), *The Routledge handbook of metaphor and language* (pp. 472–485). Routledge.

Katz, J. C., & Buchholz, E. S. (1999). "I did it myself": The necessity of solo play for preschoolers. *Early Child Development and Care, 155*(1), 39–50. https://doi.org/10.1080/0030443991550104

Katz, V. S., Moran, M. B., & Gonzalez, C. (2018). Connecting with technology in lower-income US families. *New Media & Society, 20*(7), 2509–2533. https://doi.org/10.1177/1461444817726319

Kaufman, E. A., & Wiese, D. L. (2012). Skin-tone preferences and self-representation in Hispanic children. *Early Child Development and Care, 182*(2), 277–290. https://doi.org/10.1080/03004430.2011.556250

Kaufman, J. C., Kaufman, S. B., & A, Plucker, J. (2013). Contemporary theories of intelligence. In D. Reisberg (Ed.), *Oxford handbook of cognitive psychology* (pp. 811–822).

Kaufman, J. C., Plucker, J. A., & Russell, C. M. (2012). Identifying and assessing creativity as a component of giftedness. *Journal of Psychoeducational Assessment, 30*(1), 60–73. https://doi.org/10.1177/0734282911428196

Kaufman, T. M. L., Laninga-Wijnen, L., & Lodder, G. M. A. (2022). Are victims of bullying primarily social outcasts? Person-group dissimilarities in relational, socio-behavioral, and physical characteristics as predictors of victimization. *Child Development*. https://doi.org/10.1111/cdev.13772

Kaufmann, L., Mazzocco, M. M., Dowker, A., von Aster, M., Göbel, S. M., Grabner, R. H., Henik, A., Jordan, N. C., Karmiloff-Smith, A. D., Kucian, K., Rubinsten, O., Szucs, D., Shalev, R., & Nuerk, H.-C. (2013). Dyscalculia from a developmental and differential perspective. *Frontiers in Psychology, 4*, 516. https://doi.org/10.3389/fpsyg.2013.00516

Kaufmann, W. E., Kidd, S. A., Andrews, H. F., Budimirovic, D. B., Esler, A., Haas-Givler, B., Stackhouse, T., Riley, C., Peacock, G., Sherman, S. L., Brown, W. T., & Berry-Kravis, E. (2017). Autism spectrum disorder in fragile X syndrome: Cooccurring conditions and current treatment. *Pediatrics, 139*(Suppl 3), S194–S206. https://doi.org/10.1542/peds.2016-1159F

Kaur, G., Begum, R., Thota, S., & Batra, S. (2019). A systematic review of smoking-related epigenetic alterations. *Archives of Toxicology, 93*(10), 2715–2740. https://doi.org/10.1007/s00204-019-02562-y

Kaushanskaya, M., & Crespo, K. (2019). Does exposure to code-switching influence language performance in bilingual children? *Child Development, 90*(3), 708–718. https://doi.org/10.1111/cdev.13235

Kavanagh, P. L., Fasipe, T. A., & Wun, T. (2022). Sickle Cell Disease: A Review. *JAMA, 328*(1), 57–68. https://doi.org/10.1001/jama.2022.10233

Kavšek, M. (2004). Predicting later IQ from infant visual habituation and dishabituation: A meta-analysis. *Journal of Applied Developmental Psychology, 25*(3), 369–393. https://doi.org/10.1016/j.appdev.2004.04.006

Kavšek, M. (2013). The comparator model of infant visual habituation and dishabituation: Recent insights. *Developmental Psychobiology, 55*(8), 793–808. https://doi.org/10.1002/dev.21081

Kavšek, M., & Bornstein, M. H. (2010). Visual habituation and dishabituation in preterm infants: A review and meta-analysis. *Research in Developmental Disabilities, 31*(5), 951–975. https://doi.org/10.1016/j.ridd.2010.04.016

Kawabata, Y., & Crick, N. R. (2011). The significance of cross-racial/ethnic friendships: Associations with peer victimization, peer support, sociometric status, and classroom diversity. *Developmental Psychology, 47*(6), 1763–1775. https://doi.org/10.1037/a0025399

Kawai, N. (2010). Towards a new study on associative learning in human fetuses: Fetal associative learning in primates. *Infant & Child Development, 19*(1), 55–59. https://doi.org/10.1002/icd.654

Kawakami, K., Takai-Kawakami, K., Kawakami, F., Tomonaga, M., Suzuki, M., & Shimizu, Y. (2008). Roots of smile: A preterm neonates' study. *Infant Behavior &*

Development, 31(3), 518–522. https://doi.org/10.1016/j.infbeh.2008.03.002

Kaye, M., Williams, E., Anderson, A., Arredondo, F., Pike, J., & Mak, W. (2022). A case series to examine the perinatal outcomes of infants conceived by intravaginal culture (IVC). *Journal of Assisted Reproduction and Genetics*, 39(1367–1371.

Kayed, N. S., Farstad, H., & van der Meer, A. L. H. (2008). Preterm infants' timing strategies to optical collisions. *Early Human Development*, 84(6), 381–388. https://doi.org/10.1016/j.earlhumdev.2007.10.006

Kazi, S., & Galanaki, E. (2020). Piagetian theory of cognitive development. In S. Hupp & J. D. Jewell (Eds.), *The encyclopedia of child and adolescent development* (pp. 1–11). Wiley. https://doi.org/10.1002/9781119171492.wecad364

Kearns, S., Kroll, T., O'Shea, D., & Neff, K. (2021). Experiences of transgender and non-binary youth accessing gender-affirming care: A systematic review and meta-ethnography. *PLoS ONE*, 16(9), e0257194. https://doi.org/10.1371/journal.pone.0257194

Keating, D. P. (2012). Cognitive and brain development in adolescence. *Enfance*, 3, 267–279. https://doi.org/10.4074/S0013754512003035

Keene, P. A., deBettencourt, M. T., Awh, E., & Vogel, E. K. (2022). Pupillometry signatures of sustained attention and working memory. *Attention, Perception, & Psychophysics*, 84(8), 2472–2482. https://doi.org/10.3758/s13414-022-02557-5

Keizer, R., Helmerhorst, K. O. W., & van Rijn-van Gelderen, L. (2019). Perceived quality of the mother-adolescent and father-adolescent attachment relationship and adolescents' self-esteem. *Journal of Youth and Adolescence*, 48(6), 1203–1217. https://doi.org/10.1007/s10964-019-01007-0

Keizer, R., Helmerhorst, K. O. W., & van Rijn-van Gelderen, L. (2019). Perceived quality of the mother-adolescent and father-adolescent attachment relationship and adolescents' self-esteem. *Journal of Youth and Adolescence*. https://doi.org/10.1007/s10964-019-01007-0

Keller, H. (2003). Socialization for competence: Cultural models of infancy. *Human Development*, 46(5), 288–311. https://doi.org/10.1159/000071937

Keller, H. (2017). Culture and development: A systematic relationship. *Perspectives on Psychological Science*, 12(5), 833–840. https://doi.org/10.1177/1745691617704097

Keller, H. (2018). Parenting and socioemotional development in infancy and early childhood. *Developmental Review*, 50, 31–41. https://doi.org/10.1016/j.dr.2018.03.001

Keller, H. (2019). The role of emotions in socialization processes across cultures. Implications for theory and practice. In D. Matsumoto & H. Hwang (Eds.), *Oxford handbook of culture and psychology*. Oxford University Press.

Keller, H., Kärtner, J., Borke, J., Yovsi, R., & Kleis, A. (2005). Parenting styles and the development of the categorical self: A longitudinal study on mirror self-recognition in Cameroonian Nso and German families. *International Journal of Behavioral Development*, 29(6), 496–504. https://doi.org/10.1080/01650250500147485

Kelley, B., Weyer, M., McCann, M., & Broom, S. (2020). *50-state comparison: State K–3 policies*. Education Commission of the States. https://www.ecs.org/kindergarten-policies/

Kelly, Y., Zilanawala, A., Sacker, A., Hiatt, R., & Viner, R. (2017). Early puberty in 11-year-old girls: Millennium Cohort Study findings. *Archives of Disease in Childhood*, 102(3), 232–237. https://doi.org/10.1136/archdischild-2016-310475

Kenned., S., & Fitch, C. A. (2012). Measuring cohabitation and family structure in the United States: Assessing the impact of new data from the Current Population Survey. *Demography*, 49(4), 1479–1498. https://doi.org/10.1007/s13524-012-0126-8

Kenny, M. C., Wurtele, S. K., & Vázquez, A. L. (2020). Childhood sexual abuse. In S. Hupp & J. D. Jewell (Eds.), *The encyclopedia of child and adolescent development* (pp. 1–12). Wiley. https://doi.org/10.1002/9781119171492.wecad232

Kent, C., Cordier, R., Joosten, A., Wilkes-Gillan, S., Bundy, A., & Speyer, R. (2020). A systematic review and meta-analysis of interventions to improve play skills in children with autism spectrum disorder. *Review Journal of Autism and Developmental Disorders*, 7(1), 91–118. https://doi.org/10.1007/s40489-019-00181-y

Kenward, B., & Dahl, M. (2011). Preschoolers distribute scarce resources according to the moral valence of recipients' previous actions. *Developmental Psychology*, 47(4), 1054–1064. https://doi.org/10.1037/a0023869

Kenward, B., Folke, S., Holmberg, J., Johansson, A., & Gredebäck, G. (2009). Goal directedness and decision making in infants. *Developmental Psychology*, 45(3), 809–819. https://doi.org/10.1037/a0014076

Kesmodel, U. S., Nygaard, S. S., Mortensen, E. L., Bertrand, J., Denny, C. H., Glidewell, A., & Astley Hemingway, S. (2019). Are low-to-moderate average alcohol consumption and isolated episodes of binge drinking in early pregnancy associated with facial features related to fetal alcohol syndrome in 5-year-old children? *Alcoholism: Clinical and Experimental Research*, 43(6), acer.14047. https://doi.org/10.1111/acer.14047

Keywan, C., Poduri, A. H., Goldstein, R. D., & Holm, I. A. (2021). Genetic factors underlying sudden infant death syndrome. *Application of Clinical Genetics*, 14, 61. https://doi.org/10.2147/TACG.S239478

Khalsa, S. S., Portnoff, L. C., McCurdy-McKinnon, D., & Feusner, J. D. (2017). What happens after treatment? A systematic review of relapse, remission, and recovery in anorexia nervosa. *Journal of Eating Disorders*, 5(1), 1–12. https://doi.org/10.1186/s40337-017-0145-3

Khan, F., Fraley, R. C., Young, J. F., & Hankin, B. L. (2020). Developmental trajectories of attachment and depressive symptoms in children and adolescents. *Attachment & Human Development*, 22(4), 392–408. https://doi.org/10.1080/14616734.2019.1624790

Khundrakpam, B. S., Lewis, J. D., Reid, A., Karama, S., Zhao, L., Chouinard-Decorte, F., & Evans, A. C. (2017). Imaging structural covariance in the development of intelligence. *NeuroImage*, 144, 227–240. https://doi.org/10.1016/j.neuroimage.2016.08.041

Khurana, A., Bleakley, A., Ellithorpe, M. E., Hennessy, M., Jamieson, P. E., & Weitz, I. (2019). Media violence exposure and aggression in adolescents: A risk and resilience perspective. *Aggressive Behavior*, 45(1), 70–81. https://doi.org/10.1002/ab.21798

Kia, H., MacKinnon, K. R., Abramovich, A., & Bonato, S. (2021). Peer support as a protective factor against suicide in trans populations: A scoping review. *Social Science & Medicine*, 279, 114026. https://doi.org/10.1016/j.socscimed.2021.114026

Kiani, A. K., Paolacci, S., Scanzano, P., Michelini, S., Capodicasa, N., D'agruma, L., Notarangelo, A., Tonini, G., Piccinelli, D., Farshid, K. R., Petralia, P., Fulcheri, E., Buffelli, F., Chiurazzi, P., Terranova, C., Plotti, F., Angioli, R., Castori, M., Pös, O., & &#hillip1; Bertelli, M. (2020). Prenatal genetic diagnosis: Fetal therapy as a possible solution to a positive test. *Acta Biomedica*, 9(1). https://doi.org/10.23750/abm.v91i13-S.10534

Kibbe, M. M. (2015). Varieties of visual working memory representation in infancy and beyond. *Current Directions in Psychological Science, 24*(6), 433–439. https://doi.org/10.1177/0963721415605831

Kibbe, M. M., & Leslie, A. M. (2019). Conceptually rich, perceptually sparse: Object representations in 6-month-old infants' working memory. *Psychological Science, 30*(3), 362–375. https://doi.org/10.1177/0956797618817754

Kidd, K. M., Sequeira, G. M., Katz-Wise, S. L., Fechter-Leggett, M., Gandy, M., Herring, N., Miller, E., & Dowshen, N. L. (2023). "Difficult to find, stressful to navigate": Parents' experiences accessing affirming care for gender-diverse youth. *LGBT Health, 10*(7), 496–504. https://doi.org/10.1089/lgbt.2021.0468

Kidger, J., Araya, R., Donovan, J., & Gunnell, D. (2012). The effect of the school environment on the emotional health of adolescents: A systematic review. *Pediatrics, 129*(5), 925–949. https://doi.org/10.1542/peds.2011-2248

Kienbaum, J., & Mairhofer, S. (2022). Need, effort, or integration? The development of intuitive distributive justice decisions in children, adolescents, and adults. *Social Development, 31*(3), 603–618. https://doi.org/10.1111/sode.12563

Killen, M., & Dahl, A. (2021). Moral reasoning enables developmental and societal change. *Perspectives on Psychological Science, 16*(6), 1209–1225. https://doi.org/10.1177/1745691620964076

Killen, M., McGlothlin, H., & Lee-Kim, J. (2002). Between individuals and culture: Individuals' evaluations of exclusion from social groups. In H. Keller, Y. Poortinga, & A. Schoelmerich (Eds.), *Between biology and culture: Perspectives on ontogenetic development* (pp. 159–190). Cambridge University Press.

Killen, M., & Smetana, J. G. (2015). Origins and development of morality. In M. Lamb (Ed.), *Handbook of child psychology and developmental science* (pp. 1–49). John Wiley & Sons. https://doi.org/10.1002/9781118963418.childpsy317

Killen, M., Yee, K. M., & Ruck, M. D. (2021). Social and racial justice as fundamental goals for the field of human development. *Human Development, 65*(5–6), 257–269. https://doi.org/10.1159/000519698

Kim, B.-R., & Teti, D. M. (2014). Maternal emotional availability during infant bedtime: An ecological framework. *Journal of Family Psychology, 28*(1), 1–11. https://doi.org/10.1037/a0035157

Kim, H., Drake, B., & Jonson-Reid, M. (2018). An examination of class-based visibility bias in national child maltreatment reporting. *Children and Youth Services Review, 85*, 165–173. https://doi.org/10.1016/j.childyouth.2017.12.019

Kim, J.-S., & Böckenholt, U. (2000). Modeling stage-sequential change in ordered categorical responses. *Psychological Methods, 5*(3), 380–400.

Kim, J.-Y., Minnes, S., Min, M. O., Kim, S. K., Lang, A., Weishampel, P., Short, E. j., Powers, G., & Singer, L. T. (2022). Self-reported mental health outcomes in prenatally cocaine exposed adolescents at 17 years of age. *Neurotoxicology and Teratology, 94*, 107132.

Kim, K., Yaffe, K., Rehkopf, D. H., Zheng, Y., Nannini, D. R., Perak, A. M., Nagata, J. M., Miller, G. E., Zhang, K., Lloyd-Jones, D. M., Joyce, B. T., & Hou, L. (2023). Association of adverse childhood experiences with accelerated epigenetic aging in midlife. *JAMA Network Open, 6*(6), e2317987. https://doi.org/10.1001/jamanetworkopen.2023.17987

Kim, L., Whitaker, M., O'Halloran, A., Kambhampati, A., Chai, S. J., Reingold, A., Armistead, I., Kawasaki, B., Meek, J., Yousey-Hindes, K., Anderson, E. J., Openo, K. P., Weigel, A., Ryan, P., Monroe, M. L., Fox, K., Kim, S., Lynfield, R., Bye, E., & &#hillip1; Wortham, J. (2020). Hospitalization rates and characteristics of children aged <18 years hospitalized with laboratory-confirmed COVID-19—COVID-NET, 14 States, March 1–July 25, 2020. *Morbidity and Mortality Weekly Report, 69*(32), 1081–1088. http://dx.doi.org/10.15585/mmwr.mm6932e3

Kim, M. (2016). A meta-analysis of the effects of enrichment programs on gifted students. *Gifted Child Quarterly, 60*(2), 102–116. https://doi.org/10.1177/0016986216630607

Kim, S., Fleisher, B., & Sun, J. Y. (2017). The long-term health effects of fetal malnutrition: Evidence from the 1959–1961 China Great Leap Forward Famine. *Health Economics, 26*(10), 1264–1277. https://doi.org/10.1002/hec.3397

Kim, Y., Cubbin, C., & Oh, S. (2019). A systematic review of neighbourhood economic context on child obesity and obesity-related behaviours. *Obesity Reviews, 20*(3), 420–431. https://doi.org/10.1111/OBR.12792

Kim-Spoon, J., McCullough, M. E., Bickel, W. K., Farley, J. P., & Longo, G. S. (2015). Longitudinal associations among religiousness, delay discounting, and substance use initiation in early adolescence. *Journal of Research on Adolescence, 25*(1), 36–43. https://doi.org/10.1111/jora.12104

Kimball, M. M. (1986). Television and sex-role attitudes. In T. M. Williams (Ed.), *The impact of television: A natural experiment in three communities* (pp. 265–301). Academic Press.

King, P. E., Hardy, S. A., & Noe, S. (2021). Developmental perspectives on adolescent religious and spiritual development. *Adolescent Research Review, 6*(3), 253–264. https://doi.org/10.1007/s40894-021-00159-0

King, P. E., Roeser, R. W., King, P. E., & Roeser, R. W. (2009). Religion and spirituality in adolescent development. In R. M. Lerner & L. Steinberg (Eds.), *Handbook of adolescent psychology*. John Wiley & Sons. https://doi.org/10.1002/9780470479193.adlpsy001014

King, R. B., & Trinidad, J. E. (2021). Growth mindset predicts achievement only among rich students: Examining the interplay between mindset and socioeconomic status. *Social Psychology of Education, 24*(3), 635–652. https://doi.org/10.1007/s11218-021-09616-z

King, T. L., Scovelle, A. J., Meehl, A., Milner, A. J., & Priest, N. (2021). Gender stereotypes and biases in early childhood: A systematic review. *Australasian Journal of Early Childhood, 46*(2), 112–125. https://doi.org/10.1177/1836939121999849

Király, I., Takács, S., Kaldy, Z., & Blaser, E. (2017). Preschoolers have better long-term memory for rhyming text than adults. *Developmental Science, 20*(3), e12398. https://doi.org/10.1111/desc.12398

Kirk, E., Donnelly, S., Furman, R., Warmington, M., Glanvillee, J., & Eggleston, A. (2022). The relationship between infant pointing and language development: A meta-analytic review. *Developmental Review, 64*, 101023. https://doi.org/10.1016/j.dr.2022.101023

Kirk, E., Howlett, N., Pine, K. J., & Fletcher, B. C. (2013). To sign or not to sign? The impact of encouraging infants to gesture on infant language and maternal mind-mindedness. *Child Development, 84*(2), 574–590. https://doi.org/10.1111/j.1467-8624.2012.01874.x

Kirkorian, H. L., Wartella, E. A., & Anderson, D. R. (2008). Media and young children's learning. *Future of Children, 18*(1), 39–61. https://doi.org/10.1353/foc.0.0002

Kisilevsky, B. S. (2016). Fetal auditory processing: Implications for language development? In N. Reissland & B. S. Kisilevsky (Eds.), *Fetal development* (pp. 133–152).

Springer International. https://doi.org/10.1007/978-3-319-22023-9_8

Kisilevsky, B. S., & Hains, S. M. (2011). Onset and maturation of fetal heart rate response to the mother's voice over late gestation. *Developmental Science*, *14*, 214–223. https://doi.org/doi: 10.1111/j.1467-7687.2010.00970.x

Kitts, J. A., & Leal, D. F. (2021). What is(n't) a friend? Dimensions of the friendship concept among adolescents. *Social Networks*, *66*, 161–170. https://doi.org/10.1016/j.socnet.2021.01.004

Kiuru, N., Wang, M.-T., Salmela-Aro, K., Kannas, L., Ahonen, T., & Hirvonen, R. (2020). Associations between adolescents' interpersonal relationships, school well-being, and academic achievement during educational transitions. *Journal of Youth and Adolescence*, *49*(5), 1057–1072. https://doi.org/10.1007/s10964-019-01184-y

Kjeldsen, A., Janson, H., Stoolmiller, M., Torgersen, L., & Mathiesen, K. S. (2014). Externalising behaviour from infancy to mid-adolescence: Latent profiles and early predictors. *Journal of Applied Developmental Psychology*, *35*(1), 25–34. https://doi.org/10.1016/j.appdev.2013.11.003

Kjellstrand, J., Yu, G., Eddy, J. M., & Clark, M. (2020). Children with incarcerated parents and developmental trajectories of internalizing problems across adolescence. *American Journal of Criminal Justice*, *45*(1), 48–69. https://doi.org/10.1007/s12103-019-09494-4

Klaczynski, P. A., Felmban, W. S., & Kole, J. (2020). Gender intensification and gender generalization biases in pre-adolescents, adolescents, and emerging adults. *British Journal of Developmental Psychology*, *38*(3), 415–433. https://doi.org/10.1111/bjdp.12326

Klahr, A. M., Thomas, K. M., Hopwood, C. J., Klump, K. L., & Burt, S. A. (2013). Evocative gene-environment correlation in the mother-child relationship: A twin study of interpersonal processes. *Development and Psychopathology*, *25*(01), 105–118. https://doi.org/10.1017/S0954579412000934

Klahr, D. (1985). Solving problems with ambiguous subgoal ordering: Preschoolers' performance. *Child Development*, *56*, 940–952.

Klahr, D., & Wallace, J. G. (2022). *Cognitive development: An information-processing view*. Routledge.

Klein, K. O., Rosenfield, R. L., Santen, R. J., Gawlik, A. M., Backeljauw, P., Gravholt, C. H., Sas, T. C. J., & Mauras, N. (2020). Estrogen replacement in Turner syndrome. In Y. Fechner. Patricia (Ed.), *Turner syndrome* (pp. 93–122). Springer International. https://doi.org/10.1007/978-3-030-34150-3_5

Kleiser Polk, M., & Mayeux, L. (2023). Associations between peer-perceived and self-perceived gender typicality and peer status in early adolescence. *Journal of Early Adolescence*, *43*(3), 320–341. https://doi.org/10.1177/02724316221105604

Klemfuss, J. Z., & Olaguez, A. P. (2018). Individual differences in children's suggestibility: An updated review. *Journal of Child Sexual Abuse*, *29*(2), 158–182. https://doi.org/10.1080/10538712.2018.1508108

Kliegman, R. M., & Geme, J, St. (2025). *Nelson textbook of pediatrics* (22nd ed.). Elsevier.

Klimstra, T. A., Kuppens, P., Luyckx, K., Branje, S., Hale, W. W., Oosterwegel, A., Koot, H. M., & Meeus, W. H. J. (2016). Daily dynamics of adolescent mood and identity. *Journal of Research on Adolescence*, *26*(3), 459–473. https://doi.org/10.1111/jora.12205

Knafo, A., & Jaffee, S. R. (2013). Gene-environment correlation in developmental psychopathology. *Development and Psychopathology*, *25*(01), 1–6. https://doi.org/10.1017/S0954579412000855

Knafo-Noam, A., Uzefovsky, F., Israel, S., Davidov, M., & Zahn-Waxler, C. (2015). The prosocial personality and its facets: Genetic and environmental architecture of mother-reported behavior of 7-year-old twins. *Frontiers in Psychology*, *6*, 112. https://doi.org/10.3389/fpsyg.2015.00112

Knoop, M. S., de Groot, E. R., & Dudink, J. (2021). Current ideas about the roles of rapid eye movement and non–rapid eye movement sleep in brain development. *Acta Paediatrica*, *110*(1), 36–44. https://doi.org/10.1111/APA.15485

Knox, P. L., Fagley, N. S., & Miller, P. M. (2004). Care and justice moral orientation among African American college students. *Journal of Adult Development*, *11*(1), 41–45. https://doi.org/10.1023/B:JADE.0000012526.73211.cd

Ko, J. Y., Coy, K. C., Haight, S. C., Haegerich, T. M., Williams, L., Cox, S., Njai, R., & Grant, A. M. (2020). Characteristics of marijuana use during pregnancy—eight states, pregnancy risk assessment monitoring system, 2017. *Morbidity and Mortality Weekly Report*, *69*(32), 1058–1063. http://dx.doi.org/10.15585/mmwr.mm6932a2

Kobak, R., Abbott, C., Zisk, A., & Bounoua, N. (2017). Adapting to the changing needs of adolescents: Parenting practices and challenges to sensitive attunement. *Current Opinion in Psychology*, *15*, 137–142. https://doi.org/10.1016/j.copsyc.2017.02.018

Kobaş, M., Kızıldere, E., Doğan, I., Aktan-Erciyes, A., Demir-Lira, E., Akman, İ., & Göksun, T. (2023). Motor skills, language development, and visual processing in preterm and full-term infants. *Current Psychology*, *42*, 12463–12475. https://doi.org/10.1007/s12144-021-02658-8

Kobayashi, T., Good, C., Mamiya, K., Skinner, R., & Garcia-Rill, E. (2004). Development of REM sleep drive and clinical implications. *Journal of Applied Physiology*, *96*(2), 735–746.

Koevoet, D., Strauch, C., Van der Stigchel, S., Mathôt, S., & Naber, M. (2024). Revealing visual working memory operations with pupillometry: Encoding, maintenance, and prioritization. *WIREs Cognitive Science*, *15*(2), e1668. https://doi.org/10.1002/wcs.1668

Kohlberg, L. (1966). A cognitive-developmental analysis of children's sex-role concepts and attitudes. In E. E. Maccoby (Ed.), *The development of sex differences* (pp. 82–173). Stanford University Press.

Kohlberg, L. (1969). Stage and sequence: The cognitive-developmental approach to socialization. In D. A. Goslin (Ed.), *Handbook of Socialization* (pp. 347–480). Rand McNally.

Kohlberg, L. (1976). Moral stages and moralization: The cognitive developmental approach. In T. Lickona (Ed.), *Moral development and moral behavior: Theory, research, and social issues* (pp. 31–53). Holt, Rinehart & Winston.

Kohlberg, L. (1981). *Essays on moral development*. Harper & Row.

Kohlberg, L., Levine, C., & Hewer, A. (1983). Moral stages: A current formulation and a response to critics. *Contributions to Human Development*, *10*, 174.

Kohlberg, L., & Ryncarz, R. A. (1990). Beyond justice reasoning: Moral development and consideration of a seventh stage. In C. N. Alexander & E. J. Langer (Eds.), *Higher stages of human development: Perspectives on adult growth* (pp. 191–207). Oxford University Press.

Kohlhoff, J., Eapen, V., Dadds, M., Khan, F., Silove, D., & Barnett, B. (2017). Oxytocin in the postnatal period: Associations with attachment and maternal caregiving. *Comprehensive Psychiatry*, *76*, 56–68. https://doi.org/10.1016/j.comppsych.2017.03.010

Kohlhoff, J., Karlov, L., Dadds, M., Barnett, B., Silove, D., & Eapen, V. (2022). The contributions of maternal oxytocin and maternal sensitivity to infant attachment security. *Attachment and Human Development*, 24(4), 525–540. https://doi.org/10.1080/14616734.2021.2018472

Kojima, H. (1986). Becoming nurturant in Japan: Past and present. In A. Fogel & G. F. Melson (Eds.), *Origins of nurturance: Developmental, biological, and cultural perspectives on caregiving* (pp. 359–376). Erlbaum.

Kokoç, M. (2021). The mediating role of attention control in the link between multitasking with social media and academic performances among adolescents. *Scandinavian Journal of Psychology*, 62(4), 493–501. https://doi.org/10.1111/sjop.12731

Kolb, B. (2020). Brain development during early childhood. In D. Güngör (Ed.), *The encyclopedia of child and adolescent development* (pp. 1–14). Wiley. https://doi.org/10.1002/9781119171492.wecad015

Kolb, B. (2022). Sensitive periods for recovery from early brain injury. In S. L. Andersen (Ed.), *Sensitive periods of brain development and preventive interventions* (pp. 189–212). Springer International. https://doi.org/10.1007/7854_2021_296

Kolb, B., Mychasiuk, R., & Gibb, R. (2014). Brain development, experience, and behavior. *Pediatric Blood & Cancer*, 61(10), 1720–1723. https://doi.org/10.1002/pbc.24908

Kolb, B., Whishaw, I. Q., & Teskey, G. (2023). *An introduction to brain and behavior* (7th ed.). Macmillan Learning.

Koletić, G. (2017). Longitudinal associations between the use of sexually explicit material and adolescents' attitudes and behaviors: A narrative review of studies. *Journal of Adolescence*, 57, 119–133. https://doi.org/10.1016/j.adolescence.2017.04.006

Koletić, G., Jurković, L., Tafro, A., Milas, G., Landripet, I., & Štulhofer, A. (2023). A meta-analytic exploration of associations between religious service attendance and sexual risk taking in adolescence and emerging adulthood. *Journal of Health Psychology*, 28(12), 1103–1116. https://doi.org/10.1177/13591053231164542

Kolk, S. M., & Rakic, P. (2022). Development of prefrontal cortex. *Neuropsychopharmacology*, 47(1), 41–57. https://doi.org/10.1038/s41386-021-01137-9

Kolling, T., Goertz, C., Stefanie, F., & Knopf, M. (2010). Memory development throughout the second year: Overall developmental pattern, individual differences, and developmental trajectories. *Infant Behavior & Development*, 33(2), 159–167. https://doi.org/10.1016/j.infbeh.2009.12.007

Kondracki, A. J. (2019). Prevalence and patterns of cigarette smoking before and during early and late pregnancy according to maternal characteristics: The first national data based on the 2003 birth certificate revision, United States, 2016. *Reproductive Health*, 16(1), 142. https://doi.org/10.1186/s12978-019-0807-5

Konijn, C., Admiraal, S., Baart, J., van Rooij, F., Stams, G.-J., Colonnesi, C., Lindauer, R., & Assink, M. (2019). Foster care placement instability: A meta-analytic review. *Children and Youth Services Review*, 96, 483–499. https://doi.org/10.1016/j.childyouth.2018.12.002

Konkel, L. (2018). The brain before birth: Using fMRI to explore the secrets of fetal neurodevelopment. *Environmental Health Perspectives*, 126(11), 112001. https://doi.org/10.1289/EHP2268

Korlat, S., Foerst, N. M., Schultes, M.-T., Schober, B., Spiel, C., & Kollmayer, M. (2021). Gender role identity and gender intensification: Agency and communion in adolescents' spontaneous self-descriptions. *European Journal of Developmental Psychology*, 19(1), 64–88. https://doi.org/10.1080/17405629.2020.1865143

Kornafel, T., Paremski, A. C., & Prosser, L. A. (2023). Unweighting infants reveals hidden motor skills. *Developmental Science*, 26(2), e13279. https://doi.org/10.1111/desc.13279

Kornbluh, M., & Neal, J. W. (2016). Examining the many dimensions of children's popularity. *Journal of Social and Personal Relationships*, 33(1), 62–80. https://doi.org/10.1177/0265407514562562

Kornienko, O., Santos, C. E., Martin, C. L., & Granger, K. L. (2016). Peer influence on gender identity development in adolescence. *Developmental Psychology*, 52(10), 1578–1592. https://doi.org/10.1037/dev0000200

Korotchikova, I., Stevenson, N. J., Livingstone, V., Ryan, C. A., & Boylan, G. B. (2016). Sleep–wake cycle of the healthy term newborn infant in the immediate postnatal period. *Clinical Neurophysiology*, 127(4), 2095–2101. https://doi.org/10.1016/j.clinph.2015.12.015

Korous, K. M., Causadias, J. M., Bradley, R. H., Luthar, S. S., & Levy, R. (2022). A Systematic Overview of Meta-Analyses on Socioeconomic Status, Cognitive Ability, and Achievement: The Need to Focus on Specific Pathways. *Psychological Reports*, 125(1), 55–97. https://doi.org/10.1177/0033294120984127

Kosakowska-Berezecka, N., Sawicki, A., Celikkol, G., Bosson, J. K., Van Laar, C., Van Rossum, A., Best, D., Jurek, P., Besta, T., Olech, M., & Glick, P. (2024). Does culture moderate gender stereotypes? Individualism predicts communal (but not agentic) prescriptions for men across 62 nations. *Social Psychological and Personality Science*, 19485506231221913. https://doi.org/10.1177/19485506231221913

Kosciw, J. G., Greytak, E. A., Zongrone, A. D., Caitlin Clark, M. M., & Truong, N. L. (2018). *The 2017 National School Climate Survey*. GLSEN.

Koşkulu-Sancar, S., van, de Weijer-Bergsma., E, Mulder., H, & Blom, E. (2023). Examining the role of parents and teachers in executive function development in early and middle childhood: A systematic review. *Developmental Review*, 67, 101063. https://doi.org/10.1016/j.dr.2022.101063

Kostelnik, M. J., Soderman, A. Keil., Whiren, A. Phipps., & Rupiper, M. Q. (2015). *Developmentally appropriate curriculum: Best practices in early childhood education*. Pearson.

Köster, M., & Hepach, R. (2024). Preverbal infants' understanding of social norms. *Scientific Reports*, 14(1), Article 1. https://doi.org/10.1038/s41598-024-53110-3

Köster, M., Kayhan, E., Langeloh, M., & Hoehl, S. (2020). Making sense of the world: Infant learning from a predictive processing perspective. *Perspectives on Psychological Science*, 15(3), 562–571. https://doi.org/10.1177/1745691619895071

Kothari, C. L., Romph, C., Bautista, T., & Lenz, D. (2017). Perinatal periods of risk analysis: Disentangling race and socioeconomic status to inform a black infant mortality community action initiative. *Maternal and Child Health Journal*, 21(1), 49–58. https://doi.org/10.1007/s10995-017-2383-z

Kotsou, I., Mikolajczak, M., Heeren, A., Grégoire, J., & Leys, C. (2019). Improving emotional intelligence: A systematic review of existing work and future challenges. *Emotion Review*, 11(2), 151–165. https://doi.org/10.1177/1754073917735902

Kovacs, K., & Conway, A. R. A. (2019). A unified cognitive/differential approach to human intelligence: Implications for IQ testing. *Journal of Applied Research in Memory and Cognition*, 8(3), 255–272. https://doi.org/10.1016/j.jarmac.2019.05.003

Kozhimannil, K. B., Dowd, W. N., Ali, M. M., Novak, P., & Chen, J. (2019). Substance use disorder treatment admissions and state-level prenatal substance use policies: Evidence from a national treatment database. *Addictive Behaviors*, 90, 272–277. https://doi.org/10.1016/j.addbeh.2018.11.019

Kozhimannil, K. B., Hardeman, R. R., Alarid-Escudero, F., Vogelsang, C. A.,

Blauer-Peterson, C., & Howell, E. A. (2016). Modeling the cost-effectiveness of doula care associated with reductions in preterm birth and cesarean delivery. *Birth*, *43*(1), 20–27. https://doi.org/10.1111/birt.12218

Krahé, B. (2012). Report of the Media Violence Commission. *Aggressive Behavior*, *38*(5), 335–341. https://doi.org/10.1002/ab.21443

Kramer, J., & Arnold, C. K. (2020). Siblings, overview. In F. Maggino (Ed.), *Encyclopedia of quality of life and well-being research* (pp. 1–3). Springer International. https://doi.org/10.1007/978-3-319-69909-7_2701-2

Kramer, L. (2014). Learning emotional understanding and emotion regulation through sibling interaction. *Early Education and Development*, *25*(2), 160–184. https://doi.org/10.1080/10409289.2014.838824

Kramer, L., Conger, K. J., Rogers, C. R., & Ravindran, N. (2018). Siblings. In B. H. Fiese, M. Celano, K. Deater-Deckard, E. N. Jouriles, & M. A. Whisman (Eds.), *APA handbook of contemporary family psychology: Foundations, methods, and contemporary issues across the lifespan* (Vol. 1, pp. 521–538). American Psychological Association. https://doi.org/10.1037/0000099-029

Krammer, I., Schrank, B., Pollak, I., Stiehl, K. A. M., Nater, U. M., & Woodcock, K. A. (2023). Early adolescents' perspectives on factors that facilitate and hinder friendship development with peers at the time of school transition. *Journal of School Psychology*, *98*, 113–132. https://doi.org/10.1016/j.jsp.2023.03.001

Kranzler, J. H., & Floyd, R. G. (2020). *Assessing intelligence in children and adolescents: A practical guide for evidence-based assessment*. Rowman & Littlefield.

Krassner, A. M., Gartstein, M. A., Park, C., Ł, Dragan, W., Lecannelier, F., & Putnam, S. P. (2017). East–west, collectivist-individualist: A cross-cultural examination of temperament in toddlers from Chile, Poland, South Korea, and the U.S. *European Journal of Developmental Psychology*, *14*(4), 449–464. https://doi.org/10.1080/17405629.2016.1236722

Krauss, S., Orth, U., & Robins, R. W. (2020). Family environment and self-esteem development: A longitudinal study from age 10 to 16. *Journal of Personality and Social Psychology*, *119*(2), 457–478. https://doi.org/10.1037/pspp0000263

Kravitz, E., Suh, M., Russell, M., Ojeda, A., Levison, J., & McKinney, J. (2021). Screening for substance use disorders during pregnancy: A decision at the intersection of racial and reproductive justice. *American Journal of Perinatology*. https://doi.org/10.1055/s-0041-1739433

Kray, J., Kreis, B. K., & Lorenz, C. (2021). Age differences in decision making under known risk: The role of working memory and impulsivity. *Developmental Psychology*, *57*(2), 241–252. https://doi.org/10.1037/dev0001132

Kressley-Mba, R. A., Lurg, S., & Knopf, M. (2005). Testing for deferred imitation of 2- and 3-step action sequences with 6-month-olds. *Infant Behavior & Development*, *28*(1), 82–86. https://doi.org/10.1016/j.infbeh.2004.07.003

Kretch, K. S., & Adolph, K. E. (2017). The organization of exploratory behaviors in infant locomotor planning. *Developmental Science*, *20*(4), e12421. https://doi.org/10.1111/desc.12421

Kretch, K. S., Franchak, J. M., & Adolph, K. E. (2014). Crawling and walking infants see the world differently. *Child Development*, *85*(4), 1503–1518. https://doi.org/10.1111/cdev.12206

Kretch, K. S., Koziol, N. A., Marcinowski, E. C., Kane, A. E., Inamdar, K., Brown, E. D., Bovaird, J. A., Harbourne, R. T., Hsu, L. Y., Lobo, M. A., & Dusing, S. C. (2022). Infant posture and caregiver-provided cognitive opportunities in typically developing infants and infants with motor delay. *Developmental Psychobiology*, *64*(1), e22233. https://doi.org/10.1002/dev.22233

Kretch, K. S., Marcinowski, E. C., Hsu, L.-Y., Koziol, N. A., Harbourne, R. T., Lobo, M. A., & Dusing, S. C. (2023). Opportunities for learning and social interaction in infant sitting: Effects of sitting support, sitting skill, and gross motor delay. *Developmental Science*, *26*(3), e13318. https://doi.org/10.1111/desc.13318

Kretsch, N., Mendle, J., Cance, J. D., & Harden, K. P. (2016). Peer group similarity in perceptions of pubertal timing. *Journal of Youth and Adolescence*, *45*(8), 1696–1710. https://doi.org/10.1007/s10964-015-0275-3

Kretschmer, T., Veenstra, R., Deković, M., & Oldehinkel, A. J. (2017). Bullying development across adolescence, its antecedents, outcomes, and gender-specific patterns. *Development and Psychopathology*, *29*(3), 941–955. https://doi.org/10.1017/S0954579416000596

Kriegbaum, K., Becker, N., & Spinath, B. (2018). The relative importance of intelligence and motivation as predictors of school achievement: A meta-analysis. *Educational Research Review*, *25*, 120–148. https://doi.org/10.1016/j.edurev.2018.10.001

Kringelbach, M. L., Stark, E. A., Alexander, C., Bornstein, M. H., & Stein, A. (2016). On cuteness: Unlocking the parental brain and beyond. *Trends in Cognitive Sciences*, *20*(7), 545–558. https://doi.org/10.1016/j.tics.2016.05.003

Kroese, J., Bernasco, W., Liefbroer, A. C., & Rouwendal, J. (2020). Growing up in single-parent families and the criminal involvement of adolescents: A systematic review. *Psychology, Crime & Law*, *27*(1), 61–75. https://doi.org/10.1080/1068316X.2020.1774589

Kroger, J. (2015). Identity development through adulthood: The move toward "wholeness.". In K. C. McLean & M. Syed (Eds.), *The Oxford handbook of identity development* (pp. 65–80). Oxford University Press.

Kroger, J., & Marcia, J. E. (2011). The identity statuses: Origins, meanings, and interpretations. In J. Schwartz. Seth, Koen. Luyckx, & L. Vignoles. Vivian (Eds.), *Handbook of identity theory and research* (pp. 31–53). Springer New York. https://doi.org/10.1007/978-1-4419-7988-9_2

Kroger, J., Martinussen, M., & Marcia, J. E. (2010). Identity status change during adolescence and young adulthood: A meta-analysis. *Journal of Adolescence*, *33*(5), 683–698. https://doi.org/10.1016/j.adolescence.2009.11.002

Krogstad, J. M., Passel, J. S., & Noe-Bustamante, L. (2023). *Key facts about U.S. Latinos for National Hispanic Heritage Month*. Pew Research Center. https://www.pewresearch.org/fact-tank/2022/09/23/key-facts-about-u-s-latinos-for-national-hispanic-heritage-month/

Kromm, H., Färber, M., & Holodynski, M. (2015). Felt or false smiles? Volitional regulation of emotional expression in 4-, 6-, and 8-year-old children. *Child Development*, *86*(2), 579–597. https://doi.org/10.1111/cdev.12315

Kronenberger, W., & Pisoni, D. (2018). Neurocognitive functioning in deaf children with cochlear implants. In H. Knoors & M. Marschark (Eds.), *Evidence-based practices in deaf education* (pp. 363–398). Oxford Scholarship.

Kroon, E., Kuhns, L., & Cousijn, J. (2021). The short-term and long-term effects of cannabis on cognition: Recent advances in the field. *Current Opinion in Psychology*, *38*, 49–55. https://doi.org/10.1016/j.copsyc.2020.07.005

Krstić, N., & Običan, S. G. (2020). Current landscape of prenatal genetic screening and testing. *Birth Defects Research*, *112*(4),

321–331. https://doi.org/10.1002/bdr2.1598

Krüger, M., Bartels, W., & Krist, H. (2019). Illuminating the Dark Ages: Pupil dilation as a measure of expectancy violation across the life span. *Child Development*, *91*(6), 2221–2236. https://doi.org/10.1111/cdev.13354

Kruithof, P., & Ban, S. (2021). A brief overview of fetal alcohol syndrome for health professionals. *British Journal of Nursing*, *30*(15), 890–893. https://doi.org/10.12968/BJON.2021.30.15.890

Kubota, M., Chevalier, N., & Sorace, A. (2020). Losing access to the second language and its effect on executive function development in childhood: The case of "returnees.". *Journal of Neurolinguistics*, *55*, 100906. https://doi.org/10.1016/j.jneuroling.2020.100906

Kucharský, Š., Zaharieva, M., Raijmakers, M., & Visser, I. (2024). Habituation, part II. Rethinking the habituation paradigm. *Infant and Child Development*, *33*(1), e2383. https://doi.org/10.1002/icd.2383

Kucian, K., & von Aster, M. (2015). Developmental dyscalculia. *European Journal of Pediatrics*, *174*(1), 1–13. https://doi.org/10.1007/s00431-014-2455-7

Kucker, S. C., McMurray, B., & Samuelson, L. K. (2015). Slowing down fast mapping: Redefining the dynamics of word learning. *Child Development Perspectives*, *9*(2), 74–78. https://doi.org/10.1111/cdep.12110

Kuhl, P. K. (2015). Baby talk. *Scientific American*, *313*(5), 64–69. https://doi.org/10.1038/scientificamerican1115-64

Kuhl, P. K. (2016). Language and the social brain: The power of surprise in science. In R. J. Sternberg, S. T. Fiske, & D. J. Foss (Eds.), *Scientists making a difference: One hundred eminent behavioral and brain scientists talk about their most important contributions* (pp. 206–209). Cambridge University Press.

Kuhl, P. K. (2021). Infant speech perception. In *Minnesota symposia on child psychology* (pp. 113–158). John Wiley & Sons. https://doi.org/10.1002/9781119684527.ch5

Kuhl, P. K., Stevens, E., Hayashi, A., Deguchi, T., Kiritani, S., & Iverson, P. (2006). Infants show a facilitation effect for native language phonetic perception between 6 and 12 months. *Developmental Science*, *9*(2), F13–F21. https://doi.org/10.1111/j.1467-7687.2006.00468.x

Kuhl, P. K., Tsao, F.-M., & Liu, H.-M. (2003). Foreign-language experience in infancy: Effects of short-term exposure and social interaction on phonetic learning. *Proceedings of the National Academy of Sciences of the United States of America*, *100*(15), 9096–1101. https://doi.org/10.1073/pnas.1532872100

Kuhlman, K. R., Straka, K., Mousavi, Z., Tran, M.-L., & Rodgers, E. (2021). Predictors of adolescent resilience during the COVID-19 pandemic: Cognitive reappraisal and humor. *Journal of Adolescent Health*, *69*(5), 729–736. https://doi.org/10.1016/j.jadohealth.2021.07.006

Kuhlmeier, V., Dunfield, K., & O'Neill, A. (2014). Selectivity in early prosocial behavior. *Frontiers in Psychology*, *5*, 836. https://doi.org/10.3389/fpsyg.2014.00836

Kuhn, D. (2012). The development of causal reasoning. *Wiley Interdisciplinary Reviews: Cognitive Science*, *3*(3), 327–335. https://doi.org/10.1002/wcs.1160

Kuhn, D. (2013). Reasoning. In P. D. Zelazo (Ed.), *The Oxford handbook of developmental psychology* (Vol. 1, pp. 744–764). Oxford University Press. https://doi.org/10.1093/oxfordhb/9780199958450.013.0026

Kuhn, D. (2020). Why is reconciling divergent views a challenge? *Current Directions in Psychological Science*, *29*(1), 27–32. https://doi.org/10.1177/0963721419885996

Kuhn, D., Pease, M., & Wirkala, C. (2009). Coordinating the effects of multiple variables: A skill fundamental to scientific thinking. *Journal of Experimental Child Psychology*, *103*(3), 268–284. https://doi.org/10.1016/j.jecp.2009.01.009

Kumar, S., & Kelly, A. S. (2017). Review of childhood obesity: From epidemiology, etiology, and comorbidities to clinical assessment and treatment. *Mayo Clinic Proceedings*, *92*(2), 251–265. https://doi.org/10.1016/j.mayocp.2016.09.017

Kumar, V. L., & Goldstein, M. A. (2020). Cyberbullying and adolescents. *Current Pediatrics Reports*, 8(3), 86–92. https://doi.org/10.1007/s40124-020-00217-6

Kung, K. T. F., Louie, K., Spencer, D., & Hines, M. (2024). Prenatal androgen exposure and sex-typical play behaviour: A meta-analysis of classic congenital adrenal hyperplasia studies. *Neuroscience & Biobehavioral Reviews*, *159*, 105616. https://doi.org/10.1016/j.neubiorev.2024.105616

Kuo, Y.-L., Liao, H.-F., Chen, P.-C., Hsieh, W.-S., & Hwang, A.-W. (2008). The influence of wakeful prone positioning on motor development during the early life. *Journal of Developmental and Behavioral Pediatrics*, *29*(5), 367–376. https://doi.org/10.1097/DBP.0b013e3181856d54

Kurtz, M. P. (2023). Prenatal diagnoses and intervention. *Urologic Clinics*, *50*(3), 351–359. https://doi.org/10.1016/j.ucl.2023.04.006

Kurtz-Costes, B., Copping, K. E., Rowley, S. J., & Kinlaw, C. R. (2014). Gender and age differences in awareness and endorsement of gender stereotypes about academic abilities. *European Journal of Psychology of Education*, *29*(4), 603–618. https://doi.org/10.1007/s10212-014-0216-7

Kuther, T. L., & Burnell, K. (2019). A life span developmental perspective on psychosocial development in midlife. *Adultspan Journal*, *18*(1), 27–39. https://doi.org/10.1002/adsp.12067

Kuzyk, O., Friend, M., Severdija, V., Zesiger, P., & Poulin-Dubois, D. (2020). Are there cognitive benefits of code-switching in bilingual children? A longitudinal study. *Bilingualism: Language and Cognition*, *23*(3), 542–553. https://doi.org/10.1017/S1366728918001207

Kwak, Y., Payne, J. W., Cohen, A. L., & Huettel, S. A. (2015). The rational adolescent: Strategic information processing during decision making revealed by eye tracking. *Cognitive Development*, *36*, 20–30. https://doi.org/10.1016/j.cogdev.2015.08.001

Kwan, M. Y. W., Ceccacci, A., Paolucci, N., & Rebar, A. (2020). Physical activity and internalizing symptoms during the transition from adolescence to emerging adulthood: A systematic review of prospective and longitudinal studies. *Adolescent Research Review*, *6*(1), 75–89. https://doi.org/10.1007/S40894-020-00132-3

Kyere, E., & Huguley, J. P. (2020). Exploring the process by which positive racial identity develops and influences academic performance in Black youth: Implications for social work. *Journal of Ethnic and Cultural Diversity in Social Work*, *29*(4), 286–304. https://doi.org/10.1080/15313204.2018.1555502

Kyvelidou, A., & Stergiou, N. (2018). Visual and somatosensory contributions to infant sitting postural control. *Somatosensory & Motor Research*. https://doi.org/10.1080/08990220.2018.1551203 *35*(3-4

La Rooy, D., Lamb, M. E., & Pipe, M. E. (2011). Repeated interviewing: A critical evaluation of the risks and potential benefits. In K. Kuehnle & M. Connell (Eds.), *The evaluation of child sexual abuse allegations: A comprehensive guide to assessment and testimony* (pp. 327–361). Wiley-Blackwell.

Labella, M. H., & Masten, A. S. (2018). Family influences on the development of aggression and violence. *Current Opinion in Psychology*, *19*, 11–16. https://doi.org/10.1016/j.copsyc.2017.03.028

Labouvie-Vief, G. (2006). Emerging structures of adult thought. In J. J. Arnett & J. L. Tanner (Eds.), *Emerging adults in America: Coming of age in the 21st century* (pp. 59–84). American Psychological Association. https://doi.org/10.1037/11381-003

Labouvie-Vief, G. (2015). *Integrating emotions and cognition throughout the lifespan*. Springer. https://doi.org/10.1007/978-3-319-09822-7

Ladd, G. W., & Kochenderfer-Ladd, B. (2016). Research in educational psychology: Social exclusion in school. In P. Riva & J. Eck (Eds.), *Social Exclusion* (pp. 109–132). Springer International. https://doi.org/10.1007/978-3-319-33033-4_6

Lærum, A. M. W., Reitan, S. K., Evensen, K. A. I., Lydersen, S., Brubakk, A. M., Skranes, J., & Indredavik, M. S. (2019). Psychiatric symptoms and risk factors in adults born preterm with very low birthweight or born small for gestational age at term. *BMC Psychiatry*, 19(1). https://doi.org/10.1186/s12888-019-2202-8

Lafontaine, M. P., Knoth, I. S., & Lippé, S. (2020). Learning abilities. In A. Gallagher, C. Bulteau, D. Cohen, & J. L. Michaud (Eds.), *Handbook of clinical neurology* (Vol. 173, pp. 241–254). Elsevier. https://doi.org/10.1016/B978-0-444-64150-2.00021-6

LaFontana, K. M., & Cillessen, A. H. N. (2010). Developmental changes in the priority of perceived status in childhood and adolescence. *Social Development*, 19(1), 130–147. https://doi.org/10.1111/j.1467-9507.2008.00522.x

Lagattuta, K. H., Kramer, H. J., Kenned., K., Hjortsvang, K., Goldfarb, D., & Tashjian, S. (2015). Chapter six – Beyond Sally's missing marble: Further development in children's understanding of mind and emotion in middle childhood. *Advances in Child Development and Behavior*, 48, 185–217. https://doi.org/10.1016/bs.acdb.2014.11.005

Laible, D., Davis, A., Karahuta, E., & Van Norden, C. (2020). Does corporal punishment erode the quality of the mother-child interaction in early childhood? *Social Development*, 29(3), 674–688. https://doi.org/10.1111/sode.12427

Laible, D., McGinley, M., Carlo, G., Augustine, M., & Murphy, T. (2014). Does engaging in prosocial behavior make children see the world through rose-colored glasses? *Developmental Psychology*, 50(3), 872–880. https://psycnet.apa.org/doi/10.1037/a0033905

Laing, C., & Bergelson, E. (2020). From babble to words: Infants' early productions match words and objects in their environment. *Cognitive Psychology*, 122, 101308. https://doi.org/10.1016/j.cogpsych.2020.101308

Laith, R., & Vaillancourt, T. (2022). The temporal sequence of bullying victimization, academic achievement, and school attendance: A review of the literature. *Aggression and Violent Behavior*, 64, 101722. https://doi.org/10.1016/j.avb.2022.101722

Lakhani, N., Kulkarni, K., Barwel, J., Vasudevan, P., & Dorkins, H. (2023). *Clinical genetics and genomics at a glance*. Wiley.

Lam, C. B., Stanik, C., & McHale, S. M. (2017). The development and correlates of gender role attitudes in African American youth. *British Journal of Developmental Psychology*, 35, 406–419. https://doi.org/10.1111/bjdp.12182

Lam, T. K., Vartanian, O., & Hollands, J. G. (2022). The brain under cognitive workload: Neural networks underlying multitasking performance in the multi-attribute task battery. *Neuropsychologia*, 174, 108350. https://doi.org/10.1016/j.neuropsychologia.2022.108350

Lamari-Fisher, A., & Bond, M. A. (2021). Protective factors in preventing delinquency: Caregiver support, caregiver monitoring, and school engagement. *Journal of Community Psychology*, 49(7), 2818–2837. https://doi.org/10.1002/jcop.22554

Lamaze, F. (1956). *Painless childbirth: Psychoprophylactic method*. Contemporary Books.

Lamb, M. E. (2012). Mothers, fathers, families, and circumstances: Factors affecting children's adjustment. *Applied Developmental Science*, 16(2), 98–111. https://doi.org/10.1080/10888691.2012.667344

Lamb, M. E., & Lewis, C. (2015). The role of parent-child relationships in child development. In M. H. Bornstein & M. E. Lamb (Eds.), *Developmental science: An advanced textbook* (7th ed., pp. 469–517). Psychology Press.

Lambie, J. A., & Lindberg, A. (2016). The role of maternal emotional validation and invalidation on children's emotional awareness. *Merrill-Palmer Quarterly*, 62(2), 129–157. https://doi.org/10.13110/merrpalmquar1982.62.2.0129

Lampl, M., & Johnson, M. L. (2011). Infant growth in length follows prolonged sleep and increased naps. *Sleep*, 34(5), 641–650. https://doi.org/10.1093/sleep/34.5.641

Lampl, M., Johnson, M. L., & Frongillo, E. A. (2001). Mixed distribution analysis identifies saltation and stasis growth. *Annals of Human Biology*, 28(4), 403–411.

The Lancet. (2020). The plight of essential workers during the COVID-19 pandemic. *Lancet*, 395(10237), 1587. https://doi.org/10.1016/S0140-6736(20)31200-9

Landor, A., Simons, L. G., Simons, R. L., Brody, G. H., & Gibbons, F. X. (2011). The role of religiosity in the relationship between parents, peers, and adolescent risky sexual behavior. *Journal of Youth and Adolescence*, 40(3), 296–309. https://doi.org/10.1007/s10964-010-9598-2

Langfur, S. (2013). The You-I event: On the genesis of self-awareness. *Phenomenology and the Cognitive Sciences*, 12(4), 769–790. https://doi.org/10.1007/s11097-012-9282-y

Lannoy, S., Pfefferbaum, A., Berre, A. P. L., Thompson, W. K., Brumback, T., Schulte, T., Pohl, K. M., De Bellis, M. D., Nooner, K. B., Baker, F. C., Prouty, D., Colrain, I. M., Nagel, B. J., Brown, S. A., Clark, D. B., Tapert, S. F., Sullivan, E. V., & Müller-Oehring, E. M. (2022). Growth trajectories of cognitive and motor control in adolescence: How much is development and how much is practice? *Neuropsychology*, 36(1), 44–54. https://doi.org/10.1037/neu0000771

Lansford, J. E. (2014). Parents' aggression toward children and children's own aggression. In H. Selin (Ed.), *Parenting across cultures* (Vol. 7, pp. 445–458). Springer Netherlands. https://doi.org/10.1007/978-94-007-7503-9

Lansford, J. E., Costanzo, P. R., Grimes, C., Putallaz, M., Miller, S., & Malone, P. S. (2009). Social network centrality and leadership status: Links with problem behaviors and tests of gender differences. *Merrill-Palmer Quarterly*, 55(1), 1–25. https://doi.org/10.1353/mpq.0.0014

Lansford, J. E., Deater-Deckard, K., Dodge, K. A., Bates, J. E., & Pettit, G. S. (2004). Ethnic differences in the link between physical discipline and later adolescent externalizing behaviors. *Journal of Child Psychology & Psychiatry*, 45(4), 801–812. https://doi.org/10.1111/j.1469-7610.2004.00273.x

Lansford, J. E., Zietz, S., Bornstein, M. H., Deater-Deckard, K., Di Giunta, L., Dodge, K. A., Gurdal, S., Liu, Q., Long, Q., Malone, P. S., Oburu, P., Pastorelli, C., Skinner, A. T., Sorbring, E., Steinberg, L., Tapanya, S., Uribe Tirado, L. M., Yotanyamaneewong, S., Alampay, L. P., & &#hillip1; Chang, L. (2020). Opportunities and peer support for aggression and delinquency during adolescence in nine countries. *New Directions for Child and Adolescent Development*, 73–88. https://doi.org/10.1002/cad.20361 *2020*(172)

Lansu, T. A. M. (2023). How popularity goal and popularity status are related to observed and peer-nominated aggressive and prosocial behaviors in elementary school students. *Journal of Experimental Child Psychology*, *227*, 105590. https://doi.org/10.1016/j.jecp.2022.105590

Lappé, M., & Jeffries Hein, R. (2021). You are what your mother endured: Intergenerational epigenetics, early caregiving, and the temporal embedding of adversity. *Medical Anthropology Quarterly*, *35*(4), 458–475. https://doi.org/10.1111/MAQ.12683

Larion, S., Warsof, S., Maher, K., Peleg, D., & Abuhamad, A. (2016). Success of universal carrier screening for fetal diagnosis of genetic disease. *Obstetrics & Gynecology*, *127*, 128. https://doi.org/10.1097/01.AOG.0000483518.67531.79

Larsen, J. T., To, Y. M., & Fireman, G. (2007). Children's understanding and experience of mixed emotions. *Psychological Science*, *18*(2), 186–191. https://doi.org/10.1111/j.1467-9280.2007.01870.x

Larsen, K. L., & Jordan, S. S. (2020). Organized chaos: Daily routines link household chaos and child behavior problems. *Journal of Child and Family Studies*, *29*(4), 1094–1107. https://doi.org/10.1007/s10826-019-01645-9

Larson, R., & Csikszentmihalyi, M. (2014). The experience sampling method. In M. Csikszentmihalyi (Ed.), *Flow and the foundations of positive psychology* (pp. 21–34). Springer Netherlands. http://link.springer.com/chapter/10.1007/978-94-017-9088-8_3

Larson, R., Csikszentmihalyi, M., & Graef, R. (2014). Mood variability and the psychosocial adjustment of adolescents. In M. Csikszentmihalyi (Ed.), *Applications of flow in human development and education* (pp. 285–304). Springer Netherlands. http://link.springer.com/chapter/10.1007/978-94-017-9094-9_15

Larson, R., & Ham, M. (1993). Stress and 'storm and stress' in early adolescence: The relationship of negative events with. *Developmental Psychology*, *29*(1), 130–140. https://psycnet.apa.org/doi/10.1037/0012-1649.29.1.130

Larson, R. W., Moneta, G., Richards, M. H., & Wilson, S. (2002). Continuity, stability, and change in daily emotional experience across adolescence. *Child Development*, *73*(4), 1151–1165. https://doi.org/10.1111/1467-8624.00464

Larson, R. W., Wilson, S., Brown, B. B., Furstenberg, J. F. F., & Verma, S. (2002). Changes in adolescents' interpersonal experiences: Are they being prepared for adult relationships in the twenty-first century? *Journal of Research on Adolescence*, *12*, 31–68. https://doi.org/10.1111/1532-7795.00024

Larzelere, R. E., Gunnoe, M. L., Ferguson, C. J., & Roberts, M. W. (2019). The insufficiency of the evidence used to categorically oppose spanking and its implications for families and psychological science: Comment on Gershoff et al. *American Psychologist*, *74*(4), 497–499. https://doi.org/10.1037/amp0000461 2018

Last, B. S., Lawson, G. M., Breiner, K., Steinberg, L., & Farah, M. J. (2018). Childhood socioeconomic status and executive function in childhood and beyond. *PLoS ONE*, *13*(8), e0202964. https://doi.org/10.1371/journal.pone.0202964

Laubach, Z. M., Bozack, A., Aris, I. M., Slopen, N., Tiemeier, H., Hivert, M.-F., Cardenas, A., & Perng, W. (2024). Maternal prenatal social experiences and offspring epigenetic age acceleration from birth to mid-childhood. *Annals of Epidemiology*, *90*, 28–34. https://doi.org/10.1016/j.annepidem.2023.10.003

Laube, C., van den Bos, W., & Fandakova, Y. (2020). The relationship between pubertal hormones and brain plasticity: Implications for cognitive training in adolescence. *Developmental Cognitive Neuroscience*, *42*, 100753. https://doi.org/10.1016/j.dcn.2020.100753

Laurent, G., Hecht, H. K., Ensink, K., & Borelli, J. L. (2018). Emotional understanding, aggression, and social functioning among preschoolers. *American Journal of Orthopsychiatry*, *90*(1), 9–21. https://doi.org/10.1037/ort0000377

Laurent, H. K., Harold, G. T., Leve, L., Shelton, K. H., & Van Goozen, S. H. M. (2016). Understanding the unfolding of stress regulation in infants. *Development and Psychopathology*, *28*(4pt2), 1431–1440. https://doi.org/10.1017/S0954579416000171

Laureys, F., De Waelle, S., Barendse, M. T., Lenoir, M., & Deconinck, F. J. A. (2022). The factor structure of executive function in childhood and adolescence. *Intelligence*, *90*, 101600. https://doi.org/10.1016/j.intell.2021.101600

Laursen, B. (2017). Making and keeping friends: The importance of being similar. *Child Development Perspectives*, *11*(4), 282–289. https://doi.org/10.1111/cdep.12246

Laursen, B., Altman, R. L., Bukowski, W. M., & Wei, L. (2020). Being fun: An overlooked indicator of childhood social status. *Journal of Personality*, *88*(5), 993–1006. https://doi.org/10.1111/jopy.12546

Laursen, B., & Faur, S. (2022). What does it mean to be susceptible to influence? A brief primer on peer conformity and developmental changes that affect it. *International Journal of Behavioral Development*, *46*(3), 222–237. https://doi.org/10.1177/01650254221084103

Laursen, B., & Veenstra, R. (2023). defense of peer influence: The unheralded benefits of conformity. *Child Development Perspectives*, *17*(1), 74–80. https://doi.org/10.1111/cdep.12477

Lautarescu, A., Craig, M. C., & Glover, V. (2020). Prenatal stress: Effects on fetal and child brain development. In A. Clow & N. Smyth (Eds.), *International review of neurobiology* (Vol. 150, pp. 17–40). Elsevier. https://doi.org/10.1016/bs.irn.2019.11.002

Lavi, I., Katz, L. F., Ozer, E. J., & Gross, J. J. (2019). Emotion reactivity and regulation in maltreated children: A meta-analysis. *Child Development*, *90*(5), 1503–1524. https://doi.org/10.1111/cdev.13272

Lavrič, M., & Naterer, A. (2020). The power of authoritative parenting: A cross-national study of effects of exposure to different parenting styles on life satisfaction. *Children and Youth Services Review*, *116*, 105274. https://doi.org/10.1016/j.childyouth.2020.105274

Lawrence, A., & Choe, D. E. (2021). Mobile media and young children's cognitive skills: A review. *Academic Pediatrics*, *21*(6), 996–1000. https://doi.org/10.1016/J.ACAP.2021.01.007

Lawrence, J., Haszard, J. J., Taylor, B., Galland, B., Gray, A., Sayers, R., Hanna, M., & Taylor, R. (2021). A longitudinal study of parental discipline up to 5 years. *Journal of Family Studies*, *27*(4), 589–606. https://doi.org/10.1080/13229400.2019.1665570

Lawrence, K. C., & Adebowale, T. A. (2023). Adolescence dropout risk predictors: Family structure, mental health, and self-esteem. *Journal of Community Psychology*, *51*(1), 120–136. https://doi.org/10.1002/jcop.22884

Lawson, G. M., Hook, C. J., & Farah, M. J. (2018). A meta-analysis of the relationship between socioeconomic status and executive function performance among children. *Developmental Science*, *21*(2), e12529. https://doi.org/10.1111/desc.12529

Layton, A. M. (2023). Isotretinoin. In S. H. Wakelin, H. I. Maibach, & C. B. Archer (Eds.), *Handbook of systemic drug treatment in dermatology* (3rd ed.). CRC Press.

Layton, E., Dollahite, D. C., & Hardy, S. A. (2011). Anchors of religious commitment in adolescents. *Journal of Adolescent*

Research, 26(3), 381–413. https://doi.org/10.1177/0743558410391260

Lazarides, R., Fauth, B., Gaspard, H., & Göllner, R. (2021). Teacher self-efficacy and enthusiasm: Relations to changes in student-perceived teaching quality at the beginning of secondary education. *Learning and Instruction*, 73, 101435. https://doi.org/10.1016/j.learninstruc.2020.101435

Le Bas, G. A., Youssef, G. J., Macdonald, J. A., Rossen, L., Teague, S. J., Kothe, E. J., McIntosh, J. E., Olsson, C. A., & Hutchinson, D. M. (2020). The role of antenatal and postnatal maternal bonding in infant development: A systematic review and meta-analysis. *Social Development*, 29(1), 3–20. https://doi.org/10.1111/sode.12392

Le Grange, D., Eckhardt, S., Dalle Grave, R., Crosby, R. D., Peterson, C. B., Keery, H., Lesser, J., & Martell, C. (2022). Enhanced cognitive-behavior therapy and family-based treatment for adolescents with an eating disorder: A non-randomized effectiveness trial. *Psychological Medicine*, 52(13), 2520–2530. https://doi.org/10.1017/S0033291720004407

Lea, R. G., Davis, S. K., Mahoney, B., & Qualter, P. (2019). Does emotional intelligence buffer the effects of acute stress? A systematic review. *Frontiers in Psychology*, 10, 810. https://doi.org/10.3389%2Ffpsyg.2019.00810

Leahey, E., & Guo, G. (2001). Gender differences in mathematical trajectories. *Social Forces*, 80(2), 713–732. https://doi.org/10.1353/sof.2001.0102

Leaper, C. (2022). Origins and consequences of childhood gender segregation: Toward an integrative developmental systems model. In D. P. VanderLaan & W. I. Wong (Eds.), *Gender and sexuality development: Contemporary theory and research* (pp. 159–205). Springer International. https://doi.org/10.1007/978-3-030-84273-4_6

Lease, M., Kwon, K., Lovelace, M., & Huang, H. C. (2020). Peer influence in elementary school: The importance of assessing the likeability of popular children. *Journal of Genetic Psychology*, 181(2-3), 95–110. https://doi.org/10.1080/00221325.2020.1730744

Lebel, C., & Deoni, S. (2018). The development of brain white matter microstructure. *NeuroImage*, 182, 207–218. https://doi.org/10.1016/j.neuroimage.2017.12.097

Lebrun-Harris, L. A., Sherman, L. J., & Miller, B. (2020). State-level prevalence of bullying victimization among children and adolescents, national survey of children's health, 2016–2017. *Public Health Reports*, 135(3), 303–309. https://doi.org/10.1177/0033354920912713

Lecce, S., Bianco, F., & Ronchi, L. (2020). Executive function in the school context: The role of peer relationships. *Infant and Child Development*, 29(1), e2151. https://doi.org/10.1002/icd.2151

Lecce, S., Demicheli, P., Zocchi, S., & Palladino, P. (2015). The origins of children's metamemory: The role of theory of mind. *Journal of Experimental Child Psychology*, 131, 56–72. https://doi.org/10.1016/j.jecp.2014.11.005

Lecce, S., & Devine, R. T. (2022). Theory of mind at school: Academic outcomes and the influence of the school context. *Infant and Child Development*, 31(1), e2274. https://doi.org/10.1002/icd.2274

Lederberg, A. R., Schick, B., & Spencer, P. E. (2013). Language and literacy development of deaf and hard-of-hearing children: Successes and challenges. *Developmental Psychology*, 49(1), 15–30. https://doi.org/10.1037/a0029558

Lee, C. G., Seo, D.-C., Torabi, M. R., Lohrmann, D. K., & Song, T. M. (2018). Longitudinal trajectory of the relationship between self-esteem and substance use from adolescence to young adulthood. *Journal of School Health*, 88(1), 9–14. https://doi.org/10.1111/josh.12574

Lee, D. B., & Neblett, E. W. (2019). Religious development in African American adolescents: Growth patterns that offer protection. *Child Development*, 90(1), 245–259. https://doi.org/10.1111/cdev.12896

Lee, E. H., Zhou, Q., Eisenberg, N., & Wang, Y. (2013). Bidirectional relations between temperament and parenting styles in Chinese children. *International Journal of Behavioral Development*, 37(1), 57–67. https://doi.org/10.1177/0165025412460795

Lee, H., & Galloway, J. C. (2012). Early intensive postural and movement training advances head control in very young infants. *Physical therapy*, 92(7), 935–947. https://doi.org/10.2522/ptj.20110196

Lee, J. J., Saraiya, N., & Kuzniewicz, M. W. (2023). Prenatal opioid exposure and neurodevelopmental outcomes. *Journal of Neurosurgical Anesthesiology*, 35(1), 142. https://doi.org/10.1097/ANA.0000000000000876

Lee, J., & Kim, J. H. (2021). Endocrine comorbidities of pediatric obesity. *Clinical and Experimental Pediatrics*, 64(12), 619–627. https://doi.org/10.3345/CEP.2021.00213

Lee, N.-C., Chien, Y.-H., & Hwu, W.-L. (2017). A review of biomarkers for Alzheimer's disease in Down syndrome. *Neurology and Therapy*, 6(S1), 69–81. https://doi.org/10.1007/s40120-017-0071-y

Lee, S. J., Bora, S., Austin, N. C., Westerman, A., & Henderson, J. M. T. (2020). Neurodevelopmental outcomes of children born to opioid-dependent mothers: A systematic review and meta-analysis. *Academic Pediatrics*, 20(3), 308–318. https://doi.org/10.1016/j.acap.2019.11.005

Lee, S. M., Daniels, M. H., & Kissinger, D. B. (2006). Parental influences on adolescent adjustment: Parenting styles versus parenting practices. *Family Journal*, 14, 253–259. http://dx.doi.org/10.1177/1066480706287654

Lee, W. K., & Joo, Y. S. (2024). COVID-19 stress, marital conflict, social capital, and parenting of preschoolers. *Family Relations*, 73(3), 1518–1535. https://doi.org/10.1111/fare.13000

Lee, Y.-E., Brophy-Herb, H. E., Vallotton, C. D., Griffore, R. J., Carlson, J. S., & Robinson, J. L. (2016). Do young children's representations of discipline and empathy moderate the effects of punishment on emotion regulation? *Social Development*, 25(1), 120–138. https://doi.org/10.1111/sode.12141

Leenders, I., & Brugman, D. D. (2005). Moral/non-moral domain shift in young adolescents in relation to delinquent behaviour. *British Journal of Developmental Psychology*, 23(1), 65–79. https://doi.org/10.1348/026151004X20676

Lees, B., Mewton, L., Jacobus, J., Valadez, E. A., Stapinski, L. A., Teesson, M., Tapert, S. F., & Squeglia, L. M. (2020). Association of prenatal alcohol exposure with psychological, behavioral, and neurodevelopmental outcomes in children from the adolescent brain cognitive development study. *American Journal of Psychiatry*, 177(11), 1060–1072. https://doi.org/10.1176/appi.ajp.2020.20010086

Legare, C. H., Clegg, J. M., & Wen, N. J. (2018). Evolutionary developmental psychology: 2017 redux. *Child Development*, 89, 2282–2287. https://doi.org/10.1111/cdev.13018

Legare, C. H., Wen, N. J., Herrmann, P. A., & Whitehouse, H. (2015). Imitative flexibility and the development of cultural learning. *Cognition*, 142, 351–361. https://doi.org/10.1016/j.cognition.2015.05.020

Legoff, L., D'Cruz, S. C., Tevosian, S., Primig, M., & Smagulova, F. (2019). Transgenerational inheritance of environmentally induced epigenetic alterations during mammalian development. *Cells*, 8(12), 1559. https://doi.org/10.3390/cells8121559

Lehman, D. R., & Nisbett, R. E. (1990). A longitudinal study of the effects of undergraduate training on reasoning. *Developmental Psychology*, *26*, 952–960.

Leidman, E., Duca, L. M., Omura, J. D., Proia, K., Stephens, J. W., & Sauber-Schatz, E. K. (2021). COVID-19 trends among persons aged 0–24 years—United States, March 1–December 12, 2020. *Morbidity and Mortality Weekly Report*, *70*(3), 88–94. http://dx.doi.org/10.15585/mmwr.mm7003e1

Leloux-Opmeer, H., Kuiper, C., Swaab, H., & Scholte, E. (2016). Characteristics of children in foster care, family-style group care, and residential care: A scoping review. *Journal of Child and Family Studies*, *25*(8), 2357–2371. https://doi.org/10.1007/s10826-016-0418-5

Lemery-Chalfant, K., Kao, K., Swann, G., & Goldsmith, H. H. (2013). Childhood temperament: Passive gene–environment correlation, gene–environment interaction, and the hidden importance of the family environment. *Development and Psychopathology*, *25*(01), 51–63. https://doi.org/10.1017/S0954579412000892

Lenehan, S. M., Boylan, G. B., Livingstone, V., Fogarty, L., Twomey, D. M., Nikolovski, J., Irvine, A. D., Kiely, M., Kenny, L. C., Hourihane, J. O. B., & Murray, D. M. (2020). The impact of short-term predominate breastfeeding on cognitive outcome at 5 years. *Acta Paediatrica*, *109*(5), 982–988. https://doi.org/10.1111/apa.15014

Lenhart, A. (2015). *Social media and teen friendships*. Pew Research Center. https://www.pewinternet.org/2015/08/06/chapter-4-social-media-and-friendships/

Léonard, C., Billet, M., Willems, S., & Geurten, M. (2023). Relation between parental conversational style and preschoolers' recognition memory: The role of metacognition. *Journal of Applied Research in Memory and Cognition*, *12*(4), 597–606. https://doi.org/10.1037/mac0000097

Leone, T., & Brown, L. J. (2020). Timing and determinants of age at menarche in low-income and middle-income countries. *BMJ Global Health*, *5*(12), e003689. https://doi.org/10.1136/bmjgh-2020-003689

Lerkkanen, M.-K., Kiuru, N., Pakarinen, E., Poikkeus, A.-M., Rasku-Puttonen, H., Siekkinen, M., & Nurmi, J.-E. (2016). Child-centered versus teacher-directed teaching practices: Associations with the development of academic skills in the first grade at school. *Early Childhood Research Quarterly*, *36*, 145–156. https://doi.org/10.1016/j.ecresq.2015.12.023

Lerner, R. M. (2012). Developmental science: Past, present, and future. *International Journal of Developmental Science*, *6*(1–2), 29–36. https://doi.org/10.3233/dev-2012-12102

Lerner, R. M., Agans, J. P., DeSouza, L. M., & Hershberg, R. M. (2014). Developmental science in 2025: A predictive review. *Research in Human Development*, *11*(4), 255–272. https://doi.org/10.1080/15427609.2014.967046

Lerner, R. M., Johnson, S. K., & Buckingham, M. H. (2015). Relational developmental systems-based theories and the study of children and families: Lerner and Spanier (1978) revisited. *Journal of Family Theory & Review*, *7*(2), 83–104. https://doi.org/10.1111/jftr.12067

Lessard, L. M., & Juvonen, J. (2018). Losing and gaining friends: Does friendship instability compromise academic functioning in middle school? *Journal of School Psychology*, *69*, 143–153. https://doi.org/10.1016/j.jsp.2018.05.003

Lessard, L. M., Kogachi, K., & Juvonen, J. (2019). Quality and stability of cross-ethnic friendships: Effects of classroom diversity and out-of-school contact. *Journal of Youth and Adolescence*, *48*(3), 554–566. https://doi.org/10.1007/s10964-018-0964-9

Lessard, L. M., Puhl, R. M., & Watson, R. J. (2020). Gay-straight alliances: A mechanism of health risk reduction among lesbian, gay, bisexual, transgender, and questioning adolescents. *American Journal of Preventive Medicine*, *59*(2), 196–203. https://doi.org/10.1016/j.amepre.2020.02.020

Leung, E. (2020). Gender schemas. In V. Zeigler-Hill & T. K. Shackelford (Eds.), *Encyclopedia of personality and individual differences* (pp. 1743–1746). Springer International. https://doi.org/10.1007/978-3-319-24612-3_667

Lévesque, S., Bisson, V., Charton, L., & Fernet, M. (2020). Parenting and relational well-being during the transition to parenthood: Challenges for first-time parents. *Journal of Child and Family Studies*, *29*(7), 1938–1956. https://doi.org/10.1007/s10826-020-01727-z

Levickis, P., Eadie, P., Mensah, F., McKean, C., Bavin, E. L., & Reilly, S. (2023). Associations between responsive parental behaviours in infancy and toddlerhood, and language outcomes at age 7 years in a population-based sample. *International Journal of Language & Communication Disorders*, *58*(4), 1098–1112. https://doi.org/10.1111/1460-6984.12846

Levine, D., Pace, A., Luo, R., Hirsh-Pasek, K., Michnick Golinkoff, R., de Villiers, J., Iglesias, A., & Sweig Wilson, M. (2020). Evaluating socioeconomic gaps in preschoolers' vocabulary, syntax and language process skills with the Quick Interactive Language Screener (QUILS). *Early Childhood Research Quarterly*, *50*, 114–128. https://doi.org/10.1016/J.ECRESQ.2018.11.006

Levine, D., Strother-Garcia, K., Golinkoff, R. M., & Hirsh-Pasek, K. (2016). Language development in the first year of life. *Otology & Neurotology*, *37*(2), e56–e62. https://doi.org/10.1097/MAO.0000000000000908

Levine, L. E. (1983). Mine: Self-definition in 2-year-old boys. *Developmental Psychology*, *19*, 544–549. https://doi.org/10.1037//0012-1649.19.4.544

Levine, T. A., & Woodward, L. J. (2018). Early inhibitory control and working memory abilities of children prenatally exposed to methadone. *Early Human Development*, *116*, 68–75. https://doi.org/10.1016/j.earlhumdev.2017.11.010

Levitt, A. G., Aydelott Utman, J. G., Jakobson, R., Menn, L., Oller, D. K., & STARK, R. E. (1992). From babbling towards the sound systems of English and French: A longitudinal two-case study. *Journal of Child Language*, *19*(1), 19–49. https://doi.org/10.1017/S0305000900013611

Lew-Williams, C., Ferguson, B., Abu-Zhaya, R., & Seidl, A. (2019). Social touch interacts with infants' learning of auditory patterns. *Developmental Cognitive Neuroscience*, *35*, 66–74. https://doi.org/10.1016/j.dcn.2017.09.006

Lewis, K. M., Holloway, S. D., Bavarian, N., Silverthorn, N., Dubois, D. L., Flay, B. R., & Siebert, C. F. (2021). Effects of positive action in elementary school on student behavioral and social-emotional outcomes. *Elementary School Journal*, *121*(4), 635–655. https://doi.org/10.1086/714065

Lewis, M. (2011). Inside and outside: The relation between emotional states and expressions. *Emotion Review*, *3*(2), 189–196. https://doi.org/10.1177/1754073910387947

Lewis, M. (2016). Self-conscious emotions: Embarrassment, pride, shame, guilt, and hubris. In L. F. Barrett, M. Lewis, & J. M. Haviland-Jones (Eds.), *Handbook of emotions* (p. 928).

Lewis, M. (2019). The self-conscious emotions and the role of shame in psychopathology. In V. LoBue, K. Pérez-Edgar, & K. A. Buss (Eds.), *Handbook of emotional development* (pp. 311–350). Springer International. https://doi.org/10.1007/978-3-030-17332-6_13

Lewis, M., & Carmody, D. P. (2008). Self-representation and brain development. *Developmental Psychology, 44*(5), 1329–1334. https://doi.org/10.1037/a0012681

Lewis, M., Cristiano, V., Lake, B. M., Kwan, T., & Frank, M. C. (2020). The role of developmental change and linguistic experience in the mutual exclusivity effect. *Cognition, 198*, 104191. https://doi.org/10.1016/j.cognition.2020.104191

Lewis, M., & Minar, N. J. (2022). Self-recognition and emotional knowledge. *European Journal of Developmental Psychology, 19*(3), 319–342. https://doi.org/10.1080/17405629.2021.1890578

Lewis, M., Ramsay, D. S., & Kawakami, K. (1993). Differences between Japanese infants and Caucasian American infants in behavioral and cortisol response to inoculation. *Child Development, 64*(6), 1722–1731. https://doi.org/10.1111/j.1467-8624.1993.tb04209.x

Lewis, M., Takai-Kawakami, K., Kawakami, K., & Sullivan, M. W. (2010). Cultural differences in emotional responses to success and failure. *International Journal of Behavioral Development, 34*(1), 53–61. https://doi.org/10.1177/0165025409348559

Lewis, R. (2024). *Human genetics*. McGraw-Hill.

Lewis, R. B., Wheeler, J. J., & Carter, S. L. (2017). *Teaching students with special needs in general education classrooms*. Pearson.

Lewis, T. L. (2018). Vision. In M. H. Bornstein (Ed.), *The SAGE encyclopedia of lifespan human development* (pp. 2209–2301). SAGE.

Lewkowicz, D. J., & Bremner, A. J. (2020). Chapter 4—The development of multisensory processes for perceiving the environment and the self. In K. Sathian & V. S. Ramachandran (Eds.), *Multisensory perception* (pp. 89–112). Academic Press. https://doi.org/10.1016/B978-0-12-812492-5.00004-8

Lewkowicz, D. J., Leo, I., & Simion, F. (2010). Intersensory perception at birth: Newborns match nonhuman primate faces and voices. *Infancy, 15*(1), 46–60. https://doi.org/10.1111/j.1532-7078.2009.00005.x

Li, D., Chan, V. F., Virgili, G., Piyasena, P., Negash, H., Whitestone, N., O'Connor, S., Xiao, B., Clarke, M., Cherwek, D. H., Singh, M. K., She, X., Wang, H., Boswell, M., Prakalapakorn, S. G., Patnaik, J. L., & Congdon, N. (2022). Impact of vision impairment and ocular morbidity and their treatment on depression and anxiety in children: A systematic review. *Ophthalmology, 129*(10), 1152–1170. https://doi.org/10.1016/j.ophtha.2022.05.020

Li, D., Li, W., & Zhu, X. (2024). The association between authoritarian parenting style and peer interactions among Chinese children aged 3–6: An analysis of heterogeneity effects. *Frontiers in Psychology, 14*, 1290911. https://doi.org/10.3389/fpsyg.2023.1290911

Li, Db., Yao, J., Sun, L., Wu, B., Li, X., Liu, Sl., Hou, Jm., Liu, Hl., Sui, Jf., & Wu, Gy. (2019). Reevaluating the ability of cerebellum in associative motor learning. *Scientific Reports, 9*(1). https://doi.org/10.1038/s41598-019-42413-5

Li, G., & Davis, J. T. M. (2020). Sexual experimentation in heterosexual, bisexual, lesbian/gay, and questioning adolescents from ages 11 to 15. *Journal of Research on Adolescence, 30*(2), 423–439. https://doi.org/10.1111/jora.12535

Li, G., Kung, K. T. F., & Hines, M. (2017). Childhood gender-typed behavior and adolescent sexual orientation: A longitudinal population-based study. *Developmental Psychology, 53*(4), 764–777. https://doi.org/10.1037/dev0000281

Li, J. J., Berk, M. S., & Lee, S. S. (2013). Differential susceptibility in longitudinal models of gene-environment interaction for adolescent depression. *Development and Psychopathology, 25*(4 Pt 1), 991–1003. https://doi.org/10.1017/S0954579413000321

Li, M., Cai, M., Zhong, H., & Liu, H. (2021). Comparisons of academic achievements of one-only children vs. Children with siblings in China. *Current Psychology, 40*(11), 5658–5671. https://doi.org/10.1007/s12144-020-01263-5

Li, M., Fu, X., Xie, W., Guo, W., Li, B., Cui, R., & Yang, W. (2020). Effect of early life stress on the epigenetic profiles in depression. *Frontiers in Cell and Developmental Biology, 8*, 867. https://doi.org/10.3389/fcell.2020.00867

Li, Q., Liu, P., Yan, N., & Feng, T. (2020). Executive function training improves emotional competence for preschool children: The roles of inhibition control and working memory. *Frontiers in Psychology, 11*, 347. https://doi.org/10.3389/fpsyg.2020.00347

Li, R., Perrine, C. G., Anstey, E. H., Chen, J., Macgowan, C. A., & Elam-Evans, L. D. (2019). Breastfeeding trends by race/ethnicity among US children born from 2009 to 2015. *JAMA Pediatrics, 173*(12), e193319–e193319. doi:10.1001/jamapediatrics.2019.3319

Li, Y., Li, Y., Chen, G., & Yang, J. (2024). Being an only child and children's prosocial behaviors: Evidence from rural China and the role of parenting styles. *Humanities and Social Sciences Communications, 11*(1), 1–14. https://doi.org/10.1057/s41599-024-03078-2

Liao, H.-F., Jozsa, K., Wang, P.-J., Blasco, P., & Morgan, G. (2021). Understanding and supporting mastery motivation in everyday activities: A focus on early childhood intervention. *Journal of Psychological and Educational Research, 29*, 150–173.

Liberman, Z. (2022). Infants' learning from distinct negative emotions. *Emotion, 23*(3), 764–775. https://doi.org/10.1037/emo0001131

Libertus, K., Joh, A. S., & Needham, A. W. (2016). Motor training at 3 months affects object exploration 12 months later. *Developmental Science, 19*(6), 1058–1066. https://doi.org/10.1111/desc.12370

Libertus, K., & Needham, A. (2010). Teach to reach: The effects of active vs. Passive reaching experiences on action and perception. *Vision Research, 50*(24), 2750–2757. https://doi.org/10.1016/j.visres.2010.09.001

Libertus, M. E., Starr, A., & Brannon, E. M. (2014). Number trumps area for 7-month-old infants. *Developmental Psychology, 50*(1), 108–12. https://doi.org/10.1037/a0032986

Lickenbrock, D. M., & Braungart-Rieker, J. M. (2015). Examining antecedents of infant attachment security with mothers and fathers: An ecological systems perspective. *Infant Behavior and Development, 39*, 173–187. https://doi.org/10.1016/j.infbeh.2015.03.003

Lickliter, R., & Witherington, D. C. (2017). Towards a truly developmental epigenetics. *Human Development, 60*(2–3), 124–138. https://doi.org/10.1159/000477996

Lieberman, L. J., Lepore, M., Lepore-Stevens, M., & Ball, L. (2019). Physical education for children with visual impairment or blindness. *Journal of Physical Education, Recreation & Dance, 90*(1), 30–38. https://doi.org/10.1080/07303084.2018.1535340

Lieneman, C. C., & McNeil, C. B. (2023). *Time-out in child behavior management*. Hogrefe.

Lieven, E., & Stoll, S. (2010). Language. In M. H. Bornstein (Ed.), *Handbook of cultural developmental science* (pp. 143–160). Psychology Press.

Likar, I. P., Jere, K. S., Možina, T., Verdenik, I., & Tul, N. (2020). Pregnancy loss after amniocentesis and chorionic villus sampling: Cohort study. *Zdravstveno Varstvo*,

60(1). https://doi.org/10.2478/sjph-2021-0005

Lillard, A. S. (2015). The development of play. In R. M. Lerner (Ed.), *Handbook of child psychology and developmental science* (pp. 1–44). John Wiley & Sons. https://doi.org/10.1002/9781118963418.childpsy211

Lillard, A. S. (2021). Montessori as an alternative early childhood education. *Early Child Development and Care*, *191*, 1196–1206. https://doi.org/10.1080/03004430.2020.1832998

Lillevoll, K. R., Kroger, J., & Martinussen, M. (2013). Identity status and anxiety: A meta-analysis. *Identity*, *13*(3), 214–227. https://doi.org/10.1080/15283488.2013.799432

Lin, S., Falbo, T., Qu, W., Wang, Y., & Feng, X. (2021). Chinese only children and loneliness: Stereotypes and realities. *American Journal of Orthopsychiatry*, *91*(4), 531–544. https://doi.org/10.1037/ort0000554

Lin, S., Wang, L., Zhou, W., Kitsantas, P., Wen, X., & Xue, H. (2023). E-cigarette use during pregnancy and its association with adverse birth outcomes in the US. *Preventive Medicine*, *166*, 107375. https://doi.org/10.1016/J.YPMED.2022.107375

Lin, Y., Stavans, M., & Baillargeon, R. (2022). Infants' physical reasoning and the cognitive architecture that supports it. In O. Houdé & G. Borst (Eds.), *The Cambridge handbook of cognitive development*. Cambridge University Press.

Lin, Y., Xu, J., Huang, J., Jia, Y., Zhang, J., Yan, C., & Zhang, J. (2017). Effects of prenatal and postnatal maternal emotional stress on toddlers' cognitive and temperamental development. *Journal of Affective Disorders*, *207*, 9–17. https://doi.org/10.1016/j.jad.2016.09.010

Lindberg, L. D., Firestein, L., & Beavin, C. (2021). Trends in U.S. adolescent sexual behavior and contraceptive use, 2006–2019. *Contraception: X*, *3*, 100064. https://doi.org/10.1016/j.conx.2021.100064

Lindell, A. K., & Campione-Barr, N. (2017). Relative power in sibling relationships across adolescence. *New Directions for Child and Adolescent Development*, 49–66. https://doi.org/10.1002/cad.20201 *2017*(156)

Linderkamp, O., & Linderkamp-Skoruppa, D. B. (2021). Prenatal structural brain development: Genetic and environmental determinants. In K. Evertz, L. Janus, & R. Linder (Eds.), *Handbook of prenatal and perinatal psychology: Integrating research and practice* (pp. 19–32). Springer International. https://doi.org/10.1007/978-3-030-41716-1_3

Lindsay, A. C., Greaney, M. L., Wallington, S. F., Mesa, T., & Salas, C. F. (2017). A review of early influences on physical activity and sedentary behaviors of preschool-age children in high-income countries. *Journal for Specialists in Pediatric Nursing*, *22*(3), e12182. https://doi.org/10.1111/jspn.12182

Lindsey, E. W., & Colwell, M. J. (2013). Pretend and physical play: Links to preschoolers' affective social competence. *Merrill-Palmer Quarterly*, *59*(3), 330–360. https://doi.org/10.1353/mpq.2013.0015

Linebarger, D. L., & Vaala, S. E. (2010). Screen media and language development in infants and toddlers: An ecological perspective. *Developmental Review*, *30*(2), 176–202. https://doi.org/10.1016/j.dr.2010.03.006

Lionetti, F., Palladino, B. E., Moses Passini, C., Casonato, M., Hamzallari, O., Ranta, M., Dellagiulia, A., & Keijsers, L. (2019). The development of parental monitoring during adolescence: A meta-analysis. *European Journal of Developmental Psychology*, *16*(5), 552–580. https://doi.org/10.1080/17405629.2018.1476233

Lipsitt, L. P., & Kaye, H. (1964). Conditioned sucking in the human newborn. *Psychonomic Science*, *1*, 29–30.

Lisdahl, K. M., Gilbart, E. R., Wright, N. E., & Shollenbarger, S. (2013). Dare to delay? The impacts of adolescent alcohol and marijuana use onset on cognition, brain structure, and function. *Frontiers in Psychiatry*, *4*, 53. https://doi.org/10.3389/fpsyt.2013.00053

Lisonkova, S., Ukah, U. V., John, S., Yearwood, L., Muraca, G. M., Razaz, N., Sabr, Y., Yong, P. J., & Bedaiwy, M. A. (2022). Racial and ethnic disparities in the perinatal health of infants conceived by ART. *Pediatrics*, *150*(5), e2021055855. https://doi.org/10.1542/peds.2021-055855

Litovsky, R. Y., & Ashmead, D. H. (1997). Developmental of binaural and spatial hearing in infants and children. In R. H. Gilkey & T. R. Anderson (Eds.), *Binaural and special hearing in real and virtual environments* (pp. 571–592). Erlbaum.

Little, A. H., Lipsitt, L. P., & Rovee-Collier, C. K. (1984). Classical conditioning and retention of the infants eyelid response: Effects of age and interstimulus interval. *Journal of Experimental Child Psychology*, *37*, 512–524.

Little, L. M., Dean, E., Tomchek, S., & Dunn, W. (2018). Sensory processing patterns in autism, attention deficit hyperactivity disorder, and typical development. *Physical and Occupational Therapy in Pediatrics*, *38*(3). https://doi.org/10.1080/01942638.2017.1390809

Littschwager, J. C., & Markman, E. M. (1994). Sixteen- and 24-month-olds' use of mutual exclusivity as a default assumption in second-label learning. *Developmental Psychology*, *30*, 955–968. https://doi.org/10.1037/0012-1649.30.6.955

Liu, B., Xu, G., Sun, Y., Qiu, X., Ryckman, K. K., Yu, Y., Snetselaar, L. G., & Bao, W. (2020). Maternal cigarette smoking before and during pregnancy and the risk of preterm birth: A dose–response analysis of 25 million mother–infant pairs. *PLoS Medicine*, *17*(8), e1003158. https://doi.org/10.1371/journal.pmed.1003158

Liu, C., Huang, L., Huang, S., Wei, L., Cao, D., Zan, G., Tan, Y., Wang, S., Yang, M., Tian, L., Tang, W., He, C., Shen, C., Luo, B., Zhu, M., Liang, T., Pang, B., Li, M., Mo, Z., & Yang, X. (2022). Association of both prenatal and early childhood multiple metals exposure with neurodevelopment in infant: A prospective cohort study. *Environmental Research*, *205*, 112450. https://doi.org/10.1016/j.envres.2021.112450

Liu, C., & Rahman, M. N. A. (2022). Relationships between parenting style and sibling conflicts: A meta-analysis. *Frontiers in Psychology*, *13*, 936253. https://www.frontiersin.org/journals/psychology/articles/10.3389/fpsyg.2022.936253

Liu, C., Zheng, Y., Ganiban, J. M., & Saudino, K. J. (2023). Genetic and environmental influences on temperament development across the preschool period. *Journal of Child Psychology and Psychiatry*, *64*(1), 59–70. https://doi.org/10.1111/jcpp.13667

Liu, J., Riesch, S., Tien, J., Lipman, T., Pinto-Martin, J., & O'Sullivan, A. (2022). Screen media overuse and associated physical, cognitive, and emotional/behavioral outcomes in children and adolescents: An integrative review. *Journal of Pediatric Health Care*, *36*(2), 99–109. https://doi.org/10.1016/j.pedhc.2021.06.003

Liu, M.-R., & Chen, K.-L. (2020). Development of theory of mind (ToM) and its relation to their everyday performance of social communication and interaction in school-age children. *American Journal of Occupational Therapy*, 7411515398p1. https://doi.org/10.5014/ajot.2020.74S1-PO5125 74(4_Suppl_1

Liu, N., Vigod, S., Farrugia, M., Urquia, M., & Ray, J. (2018). Intergenerational teen pregnancy: A population-based cohort study. *International Journal of Obstetrics & Gynaecology*, *125*(13), 1766–1774. https://doi.org/10.1111/1471-0528.15297

Liu, S. R., & Glynn, L. M. (2022). The contribution of racism-related stress and adversity to disparities in birth outcomes: Evidence and research recommendations. *F&S Reports*, 3(2), 5–13. https://doi.org/10.1016/j.xfre.2021.10.003

Liu, W., Guo, S., Qiu, G., & Zhang, S. X. (2021). Corporal punishment and adolescent aggression: An examination of multiple intervening mechanisms and the moderating effects of parental responsiveness and demandingness. *Child Abuse & Neglect*, 115, 105027. https://doi.org/10.1016/j.chiabu.2021.105027

Liu, X., Rosa-Lugo, L. I., Cosby, J. L., & Pritchett, C. V. (2021). Racial and insurance inequalities in access to early pediatric cochlear implantation. *Otolaryngology-Head and Neck Surgery*, 164(3), 667–674. https://doi.org/10.1177/0194599820953381

Liu, Y., & Jiang, Q. (2021). Who benefits from being an only child? A study of parent-child relationship among Chinese junior high school students. *Frontiers in Psychology*, 11, 608995. https://doi.org/10.3389/fpsyg.2020.608995

Liu, Y., Kaaya, S., Chai, J., McCoy, D. C., Surkan, P. J., Black, M. M., Sutter-Dallay, A.-L., Verdoux, H., & Smith-Fawzi, M. C. (2017). Maternal depressive symptoms and early childhood cognitive development: A meta-analysis. *Psychological Medicine*, 47(4), 680–689. https://doi.org/10.1017/S003329171600283X

Llorca, A., Richaud, M. C., & Malonda, E. (2017). Parenting, peer relationships, academic self-efficacy, and academic achievement: Direct and mediating effects. *Frontiers in Psychology*, 8, 2120. https://doi.org/10.3389/fpsyg.2017.02120

Lloyd, B. J., Coller, R., & Miller, L. T. (2019). *BRS pediatrics*. Wolters Kluwer.

Lo, J. H.-Y., Fu, G., Lee, K., & Cameron, C. A. (2020). Development of moral reasoning in situational and cultural contexts. *Journal of Moral Education*, 49(2), 177–193. https://doi.org/10.1080/03057240.2018.1563881

Lo, J. O., Hedges, J. C., & Girardi, G. (2022). Impact of cannabinoids on pregnancy, reproductive health, and offspring outcomes. *American Journal of Obstetrics and Gynecology*, 227(4), 571–581. https://doi.org/10.1016/j.ajog.2022.05.056

Lobel, A., Engels, R. C. M. E., Stone, L. L., Burk, W. J., & Granic, I. (2017). Video gaming and children's psychosocial wellbeing: A longitudinal study. *Journal of Youth and Adolescence*, 46(4), 884–897. https://doi.org/10.1007/s10964-017-0646-z

Lobo, M. A., & Galloway, J. C. (2012). Enhanced handling and positioning in early infancy advances development throughout the first year. *Child Development*, 83(4), 1290–1302. https://doi.org/10.1111/j.1467-8624.2012.01772.x

LoBraico, E. J., Brinberg, M., Ram, N., & Fosco, G. M. (2020). Exploring processes in day-to-day parent-adolescent conflict and angry mood: Evidence for circular causality. *Family Process*, 59(4), 1706–1721. https://doi.org/10.1111/famp.12506

Lobstein, T., Jackson-Leach, R., Moodie, M. L., Hall, K. D., Gortmaker, S. L., Swinburn, B. A., James, W. P. T., Wang, Y., & McPherson, K. (2015). Child and adolescent obesity: Part of a bigger picture. *Lancet (London, England)*, 385(9986), 2510–2520. https://doi.org/10.1016/S0140-6736(14)61746-3

LoBue, V., & Adolph, K. E. (2019). Fear in infancy: Lessons from snakes, spiders, heights, and strangers. *Developmental Psychology*, 55(9), 1889–1907. https://doi.org/10.1037/dev0000675

LoBue, V., Kim, E., & Delgado, M. (2019). Fear in development. In V. LoBue, K. Pérez-Edgar, & K. A. Buss (Eds.), *Handbook of emotional development* (pp. 257–282). Springer International. https://doi.org/10.1007/978-3-030-17332-6_11

LoBue, V., Nishida, T., Chiong, C., DeLoache, J. S., & Haidt, J. (2011). When getting something good is bad: Even three-year-olds react to inequality. *Social Development*, 20(1), 154–170. https://doi.org/10.1111/j.1467-9507.2009.00560.x

Lockenhoff, C. E., Chan, W., McCrae, R. R., De Fruyt, F., Jussim, L., De Bolle, M., Costa, P. T., Sutin, A. R., Realo, A., Allik, J., Nakazato, K., Shimonaka, Y., H ebi, kova., M, Graf., S, Yik., M, Fickova., E, Brunner-Sciarra., M., Leibovich de Figueora, N, Schmidt, V., & &#hillip1; Terracciano, A. (2014). Gender stereotypes of personality: Universal and accurate? *Journal of Cross-Cultural Psychology*, 45(5), 675–694. https://doi.org/10.1177/0022022113520075

Lockl, K., & Schneider, Wolfgang. (2007). Knowledge about the mind: Links between theory of mind and later metamemory. *Child Development*, 78(1), 148–167. https://doi.org/10.1111/j.1467-8624.2007.00990.x

Lohaus, A., Keller, H., Lamm, B., Teubert, M., Fassbender, I., Freitag, C., Goertz, C., Graf, F., Kolling, T., Spangler, S., Vierhaus, M., Knopf, M., & Schwarzer, G. (2011). Infant development in two cultural contexts: Cameroonian Nso farmer and German middle-class infants. *Journal of Reproductive and Infant Psychology*, 29(2), 148–161. https://doi.org/10.1080/02646838.2011.558074

Lohman, D. F. (2011). *Cognitive abilities test, form 7 (CogAT7)*. Riverside.

Lohman, D. F., & Gambrell, J. L. (2012). Using nonverbal tests to help identify academically talented children. *Journal of Psychoeducational Assessment*, 30, 25–44. https://doi.org/10.1177/0734282911428194

Lohmann, H., & Tomasello, M. (2003). The role of language in the development of false belief understanding: A training study. *Child Development*, 74(4), 1130–1144. https://doi.org/10.1111/1467-8624.00597

Lomax, A. (2021). Assessment of gestational age and newborn reflexes. In A. Lomax (Ed.), *Examination of the newborn an evidence-based guide*. Wiley-Blackwell.

Lonas, L. (2021, September 30). Americans overestimate number of undocumented Latinos: Poll [Text]. *The Hill* https://thehill.com/latino/574783-americans-overestimate-number-of-undocumented-latino spoll/

Long, B. L., Sanchez, A., Kraus, A. M., Agrawal, K., & Frank, M. C. (2022). Automated detections reveal the social information in the changing infant view. *Child Development*, 93(1), 101–116. https://doi.org/10.1111/cdev.13648

Long, X., & Lebel, C. (2022). Evaluation of brain alterations and behavior in children with low levels of prenatal alcohol exposure. *JAMA Network Open*, 5(4), e225972. https://doi.org/10.1001/jamanetworkopen.2022.5972

Loock, C., Elliott, E., & Social, L. C. (2020). Fetal alcohol spectrum disorder. In A. L. Begun & M. M. Murray (Eds.), *The Routledge handbook of social work and addictive behaviors*. Routledge.

Loos, R. J. F., & Yeo, G. S. H. (2022). The genetics of obesity: From discovery to biology. *Nature Reviews Genetics*, 23(2). https://doi.org/10.1038/s41576-021-00414-z

LoParo, D., Fonseca, A. C., Matos, A. P., & Craighead, W. E. (2023). A developmental cascade analysis of peer rejection, depression, anxiety, and externalizing problems from childhood through young adulthood. *Research on Child and Adolescent Psychopathology*, 51(9), 1303–1314. https://doi.org/10.1007/s10802-023-01053-0

Lope-Piedrafita, S. (2018). Diffusion tensor imaging (DTI). In María Luisa. García Martín & Larrubia. Pilar López (Eds.), *Methods in molecular biology* (Vol. 1718, pp. 103–116). Humana Press. https://doi.org/10.1007/978-1-4939-7531-0_7

Lopez, A. B., Huynh, V. W., & Fuligni, A. J. (2011). A longitudinal study of religious identity and participation during adolescence. *Child Development*, *82*(4), 1297–1309. https://doi.org/10.1111/j.1467-8624.2011.01609.x

Lopez, L. D., Walle, E. A., Pretzer, G. M., & Warlaumont, A. S. (2020). Adult responses to infant prelinguistic vocalizations are associated with infant vocabulary: A home observation study. *PLoS ONE*, *15*(11), e0242232. https://doi.org/10.1371/journal.pone.0242232

López-Fernández, F. J., Mezquita, L., Etkin, P., Griffiths, M. D., Ortet, G., & Ibáñez, M. I. (2021). The role of violent video game exposure, personality, and deviant peers in aggressive behaviors among adolescents: A two-wave longitudinal study. *Cyberpsychology, Behavior, and Social Networking*, *24*(1), 32–40. https://doi.org/10.1089/cyber.2020.0030

Lopez-Tamayo, R., LaVome Robinson, W., Lambert, S. F., Jason, L. A., & Ialongo, N. S. (2016). Parental monitoring, association with externalized behavior, and academic outcomes in urban African-American youth: A moderated mediation analysis. *American Journal of Community Psychology*, *57*(3–4), 366–379. https://doi.org/10.1002/ajcp.12056

Lord, C., Brugha, T. S., Charman, T., Cusack, J., Dumas, G., Frazier, T., Jones, E. J. H., Jones, R. M., Pickles, A., State, M. W., Taylor, J. L., & Veenstra-VanderWeele, J. (2020). Autism spectrum disorder. *Nature Reviews Disease Primers*, *6*(1), 1–23. https://doi.org/10.1038/s41572-019-0138-4

Lord, C., Charman, T., Havdahl, A., Carbone, P., Anagnostou, E., Boyd, B., Carr, T., de Vries, P. J., Dissanayake, C., Divan, G., Freitag, C. M., Gotelli, M. M., Kasari, C., Knapp, M., Mundy, P., Plank, A., Scahill, L., Servili, C., Shattuck, P., & &#hillip1; McCauley, J. B. (2022). The Lancet Commission on the future of care and clinical research in autism. *Lancet*, *399*(10321), 271–334. https://doi.org/10.1016/S0140-6736(21)01541-5

Lorenz, K. (1952). *King Solomon's ring*. Crowell.

Lorenzetti, V., Hoch, E., & Hall, W. (2020). Adolescent cannabis use, cognition, brain health and educational outcomes: A review of the evidence. *European Neuropsychopharmacology*, *36*, 169–180. https://doi.org/10.1016/j.euroneuro.2020.03.012

Loso, H. M., Locke Dube, S., Chaarani, B., Ivanova, M., Garavan, H., Johns, M. M., & Potter, A. S. (2023). Associations between gender nonconformity, school environments, family conflict, and emotional and behavioral health among children ages 10–11. *Journal of Adolescent Health*, *72*(6), 869–876. https://doi.org/10.1016/j.jadohealth.2023.02.008

Lottero-Leconte, R., Isidro Alonso, C. A., Castellano, L., & Perez Martinez, S. (2017). Mechanisms of the sperm guidance, an essential aid for meeting the oocyte. *Translational Cancer Research*, *6*(2), S427–S430. https://doi.org/10.21037/12829

Louie, P., Upenieks, L., Erving, C. L., & Thomas Tobin, C. S. (2022). Do racial differences in coping resources explain the Black-White paradox in mental health? A test of multiple mechanisms. *Journal of Health and Social Behavior*, *63*(1), 55–70. https://doi.org/10.1177/00221465211041031

Louie, P., & Wheaton, B. (2019). The Black-White paradox revisited: Understanding the role of counterbalancing mechanisms during adolescence. *Journal of Health and Social Behavior*, *60*(2), 169–187. https://doi.org/10.1177/0022146519845069

Louis-Jacques, A., & Stuebe, A. (2018). Long-term maternal benefits of breastfeeding: Longer durations of breastfeeding are associated with improved health outcomes for mothers and should be supported by ob/gyns. *Contemporary OB/GYN*, *63*(7), 26–30.

Loussert, L., Vidal, F., Parant, O., Hamdi, S. M., Vayssiere, C., & Guerby, P. (2020). Aspirin for prevention of preeclampsia and fetal growth restriction. *Prenatal Diagnosis*, *40*(5), 519–527. https://doi.org/10.1002/pd.5645

Lovell, M. E., Akhurst, J., Padgett, C., Garry, M. I., & Matthews, A. (2020). Cognitive outcomes associated with long-term, regular, recreational cannabis use in adults: A meta-analysis. *Experimental and Clinical Psychopharmacology*, *28*(4), 471–494. https://doi.org/10.1037/pha0000326

Lowe, C. J., Cho, I., Goldsmith, S. F., & Morton, J. B. (2021). The bilingual advantage in children's executive functioning is not related to language status: A meta-analytic review. *Psychological Science*, *32*(7), 1115–1146. https://doi.org/10.1177/0956797621993108

Lozoff, B., Wolf, A. W., & Davis, N. S. (1984). Cosleeping in urban families with young children in the United States. *Pediatrics*, *74*, 171–182.

Lu, W. (2019). Adolescent depression: National trends, risk factors, and healthcare disparities. *American Journal of Health Behavior*, *43*(1), 181–194. https://doi.org/10.5993/AJHB.43.1.15

Lu, Y., Ma, M., Chen, G., & Zhou, X. (2020). Can abacus course eradicate developmental dyscalculia. *Psychology in the Schools*, *58*(2), 235–251. https://doi.org/10.1002/pits.22441

Luby, J. L., Constantino, J. N., & Barch, D. M. (2022). Poverty and developing brain. *Cerebrum*, MC9224364.

Lucassen, P. J., Fitzsimons, C. P., Salta, E., & Maletic-Savatic, M. (2020). Adult neurogenesis, human after all (again): Classic, optimized, and future approaches. *Behavioural Brain Research*, *381*, 112458. https://doi.org/10.1016/j.bbr.2019.112458

Lucca, K., Horton, R., & Sommerville, J. A. (2019). Keep trying!: Parental language predicts infants' persistence. *Cognition*, *193*, 104025. https://doi.org/10.1016/j.cognition.2019.104025

Luckey, A. J., & Fabes, R. A. (2005). Understanding nonsocial play in early childhood. *Early Childhood Education Journal*, *33*(2), 67–72. https://doi.org/10.1007/s10643-006-0054-6

Ludvigsson, J. F. (2020). Systematic review of COVID-19 in children shows milder cases and a better prognosis than adults. *Acta Paediatrica*, *109*(6), 1088–1095. https://doi.org/10.1111/APA.15270

Luijten, C. C., van de Bongardt, D., & Nieboer, A. P. (2023). Adolescents' friendship quality and over-time development of well-being: The explanatory role of self-esteem. *Journal of Adolescence*, *95*(5), 1057–1069. https://doi.org/10.1002/jad.12175

Luk, M. S. K., Hui, C., Tsang, S. K. M., Fung, Y. L., & Chan, C. H. Y. (2023). Physical and psychosocial impacts of parental incarceration on children and adolescents: A systematic review differentiating age of exposure. *Adolescent Research Review*, *8*(2), 159–178. https://doi.org/10.1007/s40894-022-00182-9

Lüke, C., Leinweber, J., & Ritterfeld, U. (2019). Walking, pointing, talking-the predictive value of early walking and pointing behavior for later language skills. *Journal of Child Language*, *46*(6), 1228–1237. https://doi.org/10.1017/S0305000919000394

Luo, R., Pace, A., Levine, D., Iglesias, A., de Villiers, J., Golinkoff, R. M., Wilson, M. S., & Hirsh-Pasek, K. (2021). Home literacy environment and existing knowledge mediate the link between socioeconomic status and language learning skills in dual language learners. *Early Childhood Research Quarterly*, *55*, 1–14. https://doi.org/10.1016/J.ECRESQ.2020.10.007

Luo, Y., Weibman, D., Halperin, J. M., & Li, X. (2019). A review of heterogeneity in attention deficit/hyperactivity disorder (ADHD). *Frontiers in Human Neuroscience*, *13*, 42. https://doi.org/10.3389/fnhum.2019.00042

Lussier, A. A., Hawrilenko, M., Wang, M., Choi, K. W., Cerutti, J., Zhu, Y., & Dunn, E. C. (2021). Genetic susceptibility for major depressive disorder associates with trajectories of depressive symptoms across childhood and adolescence. *Journal of Child Psychology and Psychiatry*, *62*, 895–904. https://doi.org/10.1111/jcpp.13342

Lut, I., Woodman, J., Armitage, A., Ingram, E., Harron, K., & Hardelid, P. (2021). Health outcomes, healthcare use and development in children born into or growing up in single-parent households: A systematic review study protocol. *BMJ Open*, *11*(2), e043361. https://doi.org/10.1136/bmjopen-2020-043361

Luthar, S. S., & Ciciolla, L. (2016). What it feels like to be a mother: Variations by children's developmental stages. *Developmental Psychology*, *52*(1), 143–154. https://doi.org/10.1037/dev0000062

Luthar, S. S., Crossman, E. J., Small, P. J., Luthar, S. S., Crossman, E. J., & Small, P. J. (2015). Resilience and Adversity. In R. M. Lerner (Ed.), *Handbook of child psychology and developmental science* (pp. 1–40). John Wiley & Sons. https://doi.org/10.1002/9781118963418.childpsy307

Luttikhuizen dos Santos, E. S., de Kieviet, J. F., Königs, M., van Elburg, R. M., & Oosterlaan, J. (2013). Predictive value of the Bayley Scales of Infant Development on development of very preterm/very low birth weight children: A meta-analysis. *Early Human Development*, *89*(7), 487–496. https://doi.org/10.1016/j.earlhumdev.2013.03.008

Luyckx, K., Teppers, E., Klimstra, T. A., & Rassart, J. (2014). Identity processes and personality traits and types in adolescence: Directionality of effects and developmental trajectories. *Developmental Psychology*, *50*(8), 2144–2153. https://doi.org/10.1037/a0037256

Lynch, J. L., & Gibbs, B. G. (2017). Birth weight and early cognitive skills: Can parenting offset the link? *Maternal and Child Health Journal*, *21*(1), 156–167. https://doi.org/10.1007/s10995-016-2104-z

Lynch, K. (2016). Gene-environment correlation. In V. Zeigler-Hill & T. K. Shackelford (Eds.), *Encyclopedia of personality and individual differences* (pp. 1–4). Springer International. https://doi.org/10.1007/978-3-319-28099-8_1470-1

Lynn, R. (2013). Who discovered the Flynn effect? A review of early studies of the secular increase of intelligence. *Intelligence*, *41*(6), 765–769. https://doi.org/10.1016/j.intell.2013.03.008

Lyons-Ruth, K., & Jacobvitz, D. (2016). Attachment disorganization from infancy to adulthood: Neurobiological correlates, parenting contexts, and pathways to disorder. In J. Cassidy & P. R. Shaver (Eds.), *Handbook of attachment: Theory, research, and clinical applications* (pp. 667–695).

Ma, J., Lee, S. J., & Grogan-Kaylor, A. (2021). Adverse childhood experiences and spanking have similar associations with early behavior problems. *Journal of Pediatrics*, *235*, 170–177. https://doi.org/10.1016/j.jpeds.2021.01.072

Ma, T. L., Zarrett, N., Simpkins, S., Vandell, D. L., & Jiang, S. (2020). Brief report: Patterns of prosocial behaviors in middle childhood predicting peer relations during early adolescence. *Journal of Adolescence*, *78*, 1–8. https://doi.org/10.1016/j.adolescence.2019.11.004

MacCann, C., Jiang, Y., Brown, L. E. R., Double, K. S., Bucich, M., & Minbashian, A. (2019). Emotional intelligence predicts academic performance: A meta-analysis. *Psychological Bulletin*, *44*(1), 25–31. https://doi.org/10.1037/bul0000219

MacConnell, A., & Daehler, M. W. (2004). The development of representational insight: Beyond the model/room paradigm. *Cognitive Development*, *19*(3), 345–362. https://doi.org/10.1016/j.cogdev.2004.03.002

MacGowan, T. L., & Schmidt, L. A. (2021). Helping as prosocial practice: Longitudinal relations among children's shyness, helping behavior, and empathic response. *Journal of Experimental Child Psychology*, *209*, 105154. https://doi.org/10.1016/j.jecp.2021.105154

Mackey, K., Ayers, C. K., Kondo, K. K., Saha, S., Advani, S. M., Young, S., Spencer, H., Rusek, M., Anderson, J., Veazie, S., Smith, M., & Kansagara, D. (2021). Racial and ethnic disparities in COVID-19-related infections, hospitalizations, and deaths. *Annals of Internal Medicine*, *174*(3), 362–373. https://doi.org/10.7326/M20-6306

Mackie, G., Lambert, K., & Patlamazoglou, L. (2021). The mental health of transgender young people in secondary schools: A scoping review. *School Mental Health*, *13*(1), 13–27. https://doi.org/10.1007/S12310-020-09403-9

Mackintosh, J. N. (2011). *IQ and human intelligence*. Oxford University Press.

MacNeill, L. A., & Pérez-Edgar, K. (2020). Temperament and emotion. In S. Hupp & J. D. Jewell (Eds.), *The encyclopedia of child and adolescent development* (pp. 1–12). Wiley. https://doi.org/10.1002/9781119171492.wecad180

MacPhee, D., & Prendergast, S. (2019). Room for improvement: Girls' and boys' home environments are still gendered. *Sex Roles*, *80*(5–6), 332–346. https://doi.org/10.1007/s11199-018-0936-2

MacPhee, D., Prendergast, S., Albrecht, E., Walker, A. K., & Miller-Heyl, J. (2018). The child-rearing environment and children's mastery motivation as contributors to school readiness. *Journal of Applied Developmental Psychology*, *56*, 1–12. https://doi.org/10.1016/j.appdev.2018.01.002

Macswan, J., Thompson, M. S., Rolstad, K., McAlister, K., & Lobo, G. (2017). Three theories of the effects of language education programs: An empirical evaluation of bilingual and English-only policies. *Annual Review of Applied Linguistics*, *37*, 218–240. https://doi.org/10.1017/S0267190517000137

MacWhinney, B. (2015). Language development. In L. S. Liben & Ulrich. Müller (Eds.), *Handbook of child psychology and developmental science* (pp. 296–338). John Wiley & Sons. https://doi.org/10.1002/9781118963418.childpsy208

Madigan, S., Fearon, R. M. P., van IJzendoorn, M. H., Duschinsky, R., Schuengel, C., Bakermans-Kranenburg, M. J., Ly, A., Cooke, J. E., Deneault, A.-A., Oosterman, M., & Verhage, M. L. (2023). The first 20,000 strange situation procedures: A meta-analytic review. *Psychological Bulletin*, *149*(1–2), 99–132. https://doi.org/10.1037/bul0000388

Madigan, S., McArthur, B. A., Anhorn, C., Eirich, R., & Christakis, D. A. (2020). Associations between screen use and child language skills: A systematic review and meta-analysis. *JAMA Pediatrics*, *174*(7), 665–675. https://doi.org/10.1001/jamapediatrics.2020.0327

Madjar, N., & Cohen-Malayev, M. (2016). Perceived school climate across the transition from elementary to middle school. *School Psychology Quarterly*, *31*(2), 270–288. https://doi.org/10.1037/spq0000129

Madore, K. P., & Wagner, A. D. (2019). Multicosts of multitasking. *Cerebrum: The Dana Forum on Brain Science*, cer-04-19. *2019*

Madsen, H. B., & Kim, J. H. (2016). Ontogeny of memory: An update on 40 years of work on infantile amnesia. *Behavioural Brain Research*, *298*, 4–14. https://doi.org/10.1016/j.bbr.2015.07.030

Madsen, K. M., Peters-Sanders, L. A., Kelley, E. S., Barker, R. M., Seven, Y., Olsen, W. L., Soto-Boykin, X., & Goldstein, H. (2022).

Optimizing vocabulary instruction for preschool children. *Journal of Early Intervention*, *10538151221116596*. https://doi.org/10.1177/10538151221116596

Magro, S. W., Utesch, T., Dreiskämper, D., & Wagner, J. (2019). Self-esteem development in middle childhood: Support for sociometer theory. *International Journal of Behavioral Development*, *43*(2), 118–127. https://doi.org/10.1177/0165025418802462

Maheux, A. J., Evans, R., Widman, L., Nesi, J., Prinstein, M. J., & Choukas-Bradley, S. (2020). Popular peer norms and adolescent sexting behavior. *Journal of Adolescence*, *78*, 62–66. https://doi.org/10.1016/j.adolescence.2019.12.002

Mahmood, L., Flores-Barrantes, P., Moreno, L. A., Manios, Y., & Gonzalez-Gil, E. M. (2021). The influence of parental dietary behaviors and practices on children's eating habits. *Nutrients*, *13*(4), 1138. https://doi.org/10.3390/NU13041138/S1

Mai, C. T., Isenburg, J. L., Canfield, M. A., Meyer, R. E., Correa, A., Alverson, C. J., Lupo, P. J., Riehle-Colarusso, T., Cho, S. J., Aggarwal, D., & Kirby, R. S. (2019). National population-based estimates for major birth defects, 2010–2014. *Birth Defects Research*, *111*(18), 1420–1435. https://doi.org/10.1002/bdr2.1589

Main, M., & Solomon, J. (1986). Discovery of an insecure, disorganized/disoriented attachment pattern: Procedures, findings, and implications for the classification of behavior. In M. Yogman & T. B. Brazelton (Eds.), *Affective development in infancy* (pp. 95–124). Ablex.

Mak, E., Nichiporuk Vanni, N., Yang, X., Lara, M., Zhou, Q., & Uchikoshi, Y. (2023). Parental perceptions of bilingualism and home language vocabulary: Young bilingual children from low-income immigrant Mexican American and Chinese American families. *Frontiers in Psychology*, *14*, 1059298. https://doi.org/10.3389/fpsyg.2023.1059298

Mäkelä, T. E., Peltola, M. J., Nieminen, P., Paavonen, E. J., Saarenpää-Heikkilä, O., Paunio, T., & Kylliäinen, A. (2018). Night awakening in infancy: Developmental stability and longitudinal associations with psychomotor development. *Developmental Psychology*, *54*(7), 1208–1218. https://doi.org/10.1037/dev0000503

Malagoli, C., & Usai, M. C. (2018). The effects of gender and age on inhibition and working memory organization in 14- to 19-year-old adolescents and young adults. *Cognitive Development*, *45*, 10–23. https://doi.org/10.1016/j.cogdev.2017.10.005

Malatesta, C. Z., & Haviland, J. M. (1982). Learning display rules: The socialization of emotion expression in infancy. *Child Development*, *53*(4), 991–1003.

Malave, L., Dijk, M. T. van., & Anacker, C. (2022). Early life adversity shapes neural circuit function during sensitive postnatal developmental periods. *Translational Psychiatry*, *12*, 306.

Malik-Moraleda, S., Ayyash, D., Gallée, J., Affourtit, J., Hoffmann, M., Mineroff, Z., Jouravlev, O., & Fedorenko, E. (2022). An investigation across 45 languages and 12 language families reveals a universal language network. *Nature Neuroscience*, *25*(8), 1014–1019. https://doi.org/10.1038/s41593-022-01114-5

Malm, K., & Welti, K. (2010). Exploring motivations to adopt. *Adoption Quarterly*, *13*(3–4), 185–208. https://doi.org/10.1080/10926755.2010.524872

Malti, T., & Dys, S. P. (2018). From being nice to being kind: Development of prosocial behaviors. *Current Opinion in Psychology*, *20*, 45–49. https://doi.org/10.1016/j.copsyc.2017.07.036

Malti, T., Keller, M., & Buchmann, M. (2013). Do moral choices make us feel good? The development of adolescents' emotions following moral decision making. *Journal of Research on Adolescence*, *23*(2), 389–397. https://doi.org/10.1111/jora.12005

Mamluk, L., Edwards, H. B., Savović, J., Leach, V., Jones, T., Moore, T. H. M., Ijaz, S., Lewis, S. J., Donovan, J. L., Lawlor, D., Smith, G. D., Fraser, A., & Zuccolo, L. (2017). Low alcohol consumption and pregnancy and childhood outcomes: Time to change guidelines indicating apparently "safe" levels of alcohol during pregnancy? A systematic review and meta-analyses. *BMJ Open*, *7*(7), e015410. https://doi.org/10.1136/bmjopen-2016-015410

Mammen, M., & Paulus, M. (2023). The communicative nature of moral development: A theoretical framework on the emergence of moral reasoning in social interactions. *Cognitive Development*, *66*, 101336. https://doi.org/10.1016/j.cogdev.2023.101336

Mancilla-Martinez, J., Hwang, J. K., Oh, M. H., & Mcclain, J. B. (2020). Early elementary grade dual language learners from Spanish-speaking homes struggling with English reading comprehension: The dormant role of language skills. *Journal of Educational Psychology*, *112*(5), 880–894. https://doi.org/10.1037/edu0000402

Manczak, E. M., Scott, S. R., & Millwood, S. N. (2021). Accelerated epigenetic aging at birth interacts with parenting hostility to predict child temperament and subsequent psychological symptoms. *Development and Psychopathology*, *35*(1), 109–118. https://doi.org/10.1017/S0954579421000614

Mandel, D. R., Jusczyk, P. W., & Pisoni, D. B. (1995). Infants' recognition of the sound patterns of their own names. *Psychological Science*, *6*(5), 314–317. https://doi.org/10.1111/j.1467-9280.1995.tb00517.x

Mandler, J. M. (2004). *The foundations of mind: Origins of conceptual thought*. Oxford University Press.

Manganelli, S., Cavicchiolo, E., Lucidi, F., Galli, F., Cozzolino, M., Chirico, A., & Alivernini, F. (2021). Differences and similarities in adolescents' academic motivation across socioeconomic and immigrant backgrounds. *Personality and Individual Differences*, *182*, 111077. https://doi.org/10.1016/j.paid.2021.111077

Mangelsdorf, S. C. (1992). Developmental changes in infant-stranger interaction. *Infant Behavior & Development*, *15*(2), 191–208. https://doi.org/10.1016/0163-6383(92)80023-n

Mani, N., & Ackermann, L. (2018). Why do children learn the words they do? *Child Development Perspectives*, *12*(4), 253–257. https://doi.org/10.1111/cdep.12295

Manning, W. D. (2015). Cohabitation and child wellbeing. *Future of Children*, *25*(2), 51–66. https://doi.org/10.1353/foc.2015.0012

Manoach, D. S., Schlaug, G., Siewert, B., Darby, D. G., Bly, B. M., Benfield, A., Edelman, R. R., & Warach, S. (1997). Prefrontal cortex fMRI signal changes are correlated with working memory load. *NeuroReport*, *8*(2), 545–549. https://doi.org/10.1097/00001756-199701200-00033

Manotas, M. C., González, D. M., Céspedes, C., Forero, C., & Moreno, A. P. R. (2022). Genetic and epigenetic control of puberty. *Sexual Development*, *16*(1). https://doi.org/10.1159/000519039

Manotas, M. C., González, D. M., Céspedes, C., Forero, C., & Moreno, A. P. R. (2022). Genetic and epigenetic control of puberty. *Sexual Development*, *16*(1), 1–10. https://doi.org/10.1159/000519039

Månsson, J., Stjernqvist, K., Serenius, F., Ådén, U., & Källén, K. (2019). Agreement between Bayley-III measurements and WISC-IV measurements in typically developing children. *Journal of Psychoeducational Assessment*, *37*(5), 603–616. https://doi.org/10.1177/0734282918781431

Manuck, S. B., & McCaffery, J. M. (2014). Gene-environment interaction. *Annual Review of Psychology*, 65, 41–70.

Many Babies Consortium. (2020). Quantifying sources of variability in infancy research using the infant-directed-speech preference. *Advances in Methods and Practices in Psychological Science*, 3(1), 24–52. https://doi.org/10.1177/2515245919900809

Marceau, K., Nair, N., Rogers, M. L., & Jackson, K. M. (2020). Lability in parent- and child-based sources of parental monitoring is differentially associated with adolescent substance use. *Prevention Science*, 21(4), 568–579. https://doi.org/10.1007/s11121-020-01094-7

Marceau, K., Ram, N., & Susman, E. J. (2015). Development and lability in the parent-child relationship during adolescence: Associations with pubertal timing and tempo. *Journal of Research on Adolescence*, 25(3), 474–489. https://doi.org/10.1111/jora.12139

Marcellus, L., & Badry, D. (2023). Infants, children, and youth in foster care with prenatal substance exposure: A synthesis of two scoping reviews. *International Journal of Developmental Disabilities*, 69(2), 265–290. https://doi.org/10.1080/20473869.2021.1945890

Marchand, G., Masoud, A. T., Govindan, M., Ware, K., King, A., Ruther, S., Brazil, G., Ulibarri, H., Parise, J., Arroyo, A., Coriell, C., Goetz, S., Karrys, A., & Sainz, K. (2022). Birth outcomes of neonates exposed to marijuana in utero: A systematic review and meta-analysis. *JAMA Network Open*, 5(1), e2145653. https://doi.org/10.1001/jamanetworkopen.2021.45653

Marcia, J. E. (1966). Development and validation of ego-identity status. *Journal of Personality and Social Psychology*, 3(5), 551–558.

Marcinowski, E. C., Tripathi, T., Hsu, L. Y., McCoy, Westcott., S, & Dusing, S. C. (2019). Sitting skill and the emergence of arms-free sitting affects the frequency of object looking and exploration. *Developmental Psychobiology*, 61(7), 1035–1047. https://doi.org/10.1002/dev.21854

Marcone, R., Affuso, G., & Borrone, A. (2020). Parenting styles and children's internalizing-externalizing behavior: The mediating role of behavioral regulation. *Current Psychology*, 39(1), 13–24. https://doi.org/10.1007/s12144-017-9757-7

Marcovitch, S., Clearfield, M. W., Swingler, M., Calkins, S. D., & Bell, M. A. (2016). Attentional predictors of 5-month-olds' performance on a looking A-not-B task. *Infant and Child Development*, 25(4), 233–246. https://doi.org/10.1002/icd.1931

Margolis, A., Bansal, R., Hao, X., Algermissen, M., Erickson, C., Klahr, K. W., Naglieri, J. A., & Peterson, B. S. (2013). Using IQ discrepancy scores to examine the neural correlates of specific cognitive abilities. *Journal of Neuroscience*, 33(35), 14135–14145. https://doi.org/10.1523/JNEUROSCI.0775-13.2013

Margoni, F., & Surian, L. (2020). Conceptual continuity in the development of intent-based moral judgment. *Journal of Experimental Child Psychology*, 194, 104812. https://doi.org/10.1016/j.jecp.2020.104812

Margoni, F., Surian, L., & Baillargeon, R. (2023). The violation-of-expectation paradigm: A conceptual overview. *Psychological Review*, 131(3), 716–748. https://doi.org/10.1037/rev0000450

Mariani Wigley, I. L. C., Mascheroni, E., Bonichini, S., & Montirosso, R. (2022). Epigenetic protection: Maternal touch and DNA-methylation in early life. *Current Opinion in Behavioral Sciences*, 43, 111–117. https://doi.org/10.1016/j.cobeha.2021.09.004

Mariani Wigley, I. L. C., Mascheroni, E., Peruzzo, D., Giorda, R., Bonichini, S., & Montirosso, R. (2021). Neuroimaging and DNA Methylation: An Innovative Approach to Study the Effects of Early Life Stress on Developmental Plasticity. *Frontiers in Psychology*, 1(2). https://doi.org/10.3389/fpsyg.2021.672786

Marin, M. M., Rapisardi, G., & Tani, F. (2015). Two-day-old newborn infants recognise their mother by her axillary odour. *Acta Paediatrica*, 104(3), 237–240. https://doi.org/10.1111/apa.12905

Marinellie, S. A., & Kneile, L. A. (2012). Acquiring knowledge of derived nominals and derived adjectives in context. *Language Speech and Hearing Services in Schools*, 43(1), 53–65. https://doi.org/10.1044/0161-1461(2011/10-0053

Marino, J. L., Lin, A., Davies, C., Kang, M., Bista, S., & Skinner, S. R. (2023). Childhood and adolescence gender role nonconformity and gender and sexuality diversity in young adulthood. *JAMA Pediatrics*, 177(11), 1176–1186. https://doi.org/10.1001/jamapediatrics.2023.3873

Mariz, C., Cruz, O. S., & Moreira, D. (2022). The influence of environmental and genetic factors on the development of psychopathy: A systematic review. *Aggression and Violent Behavior*, 62, 101715. https://doi.org/10.1016/j.avb.2021.101715

Markant, J., & Scott, L. S. (2018). Attention and perceptual learning interact in the development of the other-race effect. *Current Directions in Psychological Science*, 27(3), 163–169. https://doi.org/10.1177/0963721418769884

Markiewicz, D., & Doyle, A. B. (2016). Best friends. In R. Levesque (Ed.), *Encyclopedia of adolescence* (pp. 1–8). Springer. https://doi.org/10.1007/978-3-319-32132-5_314-2

Markman, E. M., & Wachtel, G. F. (1988). Children's use of mutual exclusivity to constrain the meaning of words. *Cognitive Psychology*, 20(2), 121–157. https://doi.org/10.1016/0010-0285(88)90017-5

Markowitz, A. J., Bassok, D., & Hamre, B. (2018). Leveraging developmental insights to improve early childhood education. *Child Development Perspectives*, 12(2), 87–92. https://doi.org/10.1111/cdep.12266

Marks, P. E. L. (2017). Introduction to the Special Issue: 20th-century origins and 21st-century developments of peer nomination methodology. *New Directions for Child and Adolescent Development*, 7–19. https://doi.org/10.1002/cad.20205 2017(157)

Markus, H. R., & Hamedani, M. G. (2020). People are culturally shaped shapers: The psychological science of culture and culture change. In D. Cohen & S. Kitayama (Eds.), *The handbook of cultural psychology* (pp. 11–52).

Markus, H. R., & Kitayama, S. (1991). Culture and the self: Implications for cognition, emotion, and motivation. *Psychological Review*, 98(2), 224–253. https://doi.org/10.1037/0033-295X.98.2.224

Markus, H. R., & Kitayama, S. (2010). Cultures and selves: A cycle of mutual constitution. *Perspectives on Psychological Science*, 5(4), 420–430. https://doi.org/10.1177/1745691610375557

Marley, C. L., Pollard, T. M., Barton, R. A., & Street, S. E. (2022). A systematic review of sex differences in rough and tumble play across non-human mammals. *Behavioral Ecology and Sociobiology*, 76(12), 158. https://doi.org/10.1007/s00265-022-03260-z

Marlier, L., & Schaal, B. (2005). Human newborns prefer human milk: Conspecific milk odor is attractive without postnatal exposure. *Child Development*, 76(1), 155–168.

Marotz, L. R. (2015). *Health, safety, and nutrition for the young child*. Cengage. https://www.cengage.com/c/health-safety-and-nutrition-for-the-young-child-9e-marotz/9781285427331

Marozio, L., Picardo, E., Filippini, C., Mainolfi, E., Berchialla, P., Cavallo, F., Tancredi,

A., & Benedetto, C. (2019). Maternal age over 40 years and pregnancy outcome: A hospital-based survey. *Journal of Maternal-Fetal and Neonatal Medicine, 32*(10), 1602–1608. https://doi.org/10.1080/14767058.2017.1410793

Marraccini, M. E., Hamm, J. V., & Farmer, T. W. (2022). Changes in African American and Latinx students' perceived ethnic-racial discrimination during the middle school transition year. *Journal of Early Adolescence, 42*(3), 327–358. https://doi.org/10.1177/02724316211036745

Marsh, S., Dobson, R., & Maddison, R. (2020). The relationship between household chaos and child, parent, and family outcomes: A systematic scoping review. *BMC Public Health, 20*(1), 1–27. https://doi.org/10.1186/s12889-020-08587-8

Marshall, E. J. (2014). Adolescent alcohol use: Risks and consequences. *Alcohol and Alcoholism (Oxford, Oxfordshire), 49*(2), 160–164. https://doi.org/10.1093/alcalc/agt180

Marshall, S. L., Parker, P. D., Ciarrochi, J., & Heaven, P. C. L. (2014). Is self-esteem a cause or consequence of social support? A 4-year longitudinal study. *Child Development, 85*(3), 1275–1291. https://doi.org/10.1111/cdev.12176

Marti, Eduardo., & Rodríguez, Cintia. (2012). *After Piaget*. Transaction.

Martin, C. L., Andrews, N. C. Z., England, D. E., Zosuls, K., & Ruble, D. N. (2017). A dual identity approach for conceptualizing and measuring children's gender identity. *Child Development, 88*(1), 167–182. https://doi.org/10.1111/cdev.12568

Martin, C. L., Kornienko, O., Schaefer, D. R., Hanish, L. D., Fabes, R. A., & Goble, P. (2013). The role of sex of peers and gender-typed activities in young children's peer affiliative networks: A longitudinal analysis of selection and influence. *Child Development, 84*(3), 921–937. https://doi.org/10.1111/cdev.12032

Martin, C. L., & Ruble, D. N. (2010). Patterns of gender development. *Annual Review of Psychology, 61*, 353–381. https://doi.org/10.1146/annurev.psych.093008.100511

Martin, J. A. (2023). Births in the United States, 2022. *NCHS Data Brief, 47*(7). https://www.cdc.gov/nchs/data/databriefs/db477.pdf

Martin, J. A., Hamilton, B. E., M, J, K., Osterman., & Driscoll, A. K. (2021). Births: Final data for 2019. *National Vital Statistics Reports, 70*(2). https://doi.org/10.15620/CDC:100472

Martin, J. A., Hamilton, B. E., Osterman, M. J., Driscoll, A. K., & Drake, P. (2018). Births: Final data for 2016. *National Vital Statistics Reports, 67*(1). https://stacks.cdc.gov/view/cdc/51199

Martin, J. A., Hamilton, B. E., Osterman, M. J. K., Curtin, S. C., & Mathews, T. J. (2013). Births: Final data for 2012. *National Vital Statistics Reports, 62*(9).

Martin, J. A., & Osterman, M. J. K. (2023). Changes in prenatal care utilization: United States, 2019-2021. *National Vital Statistics Reports, 72*(4), 1–14.

Martin-Ordas, G. (2018). "First, I will get the marbles." Children's foresight abilities in a modified spoon task. *Cognitive Development, 45*, 152–161. https://doi.org/10.1016/j.cogdev.2017.07.001

Martin-Storey, A. (2016). Gender, sexuality, and gender nonconformity: Understanding variation in functioning. *Child Development Perspectives, 10*(4), 257–262. https://doi.org/10.1111/cdep.12194

Martinez, G. M. (2020). Trends and patterns in menarche in the United States: 1995 through 2013–2017. *National Health Statistics Reports, 146*, 1–12.

Martins, N., & Riddle, K. (2022). Reassessing the risks: An updated content analysis of violence on U.S. children's primetime television. *Journal of Children and Media, 16*(3), 368–386. https://doi.org/10.1080/17482798.2021.1985548

Martinson, M. L., & Reichman, N. E. (2016). Socioeconomic inequalities in low birth weight in the United States, the United Kingdom, Canada, and Australia. *American Journal of Public Health, 106*(4), 748–754. https://doi.org/10.2105/ajph.2015.303007

Martzog, P., Stoeger, H., & Suggate, S. (2019). Relations between preschool children's fine motor skills and general cognitive abilities. *Journal of Cognition and Development, 20*(4), 443–465. https://doi.org/10.1080/15248372.2019.1607862

Marx, R. A., & Kettrey, H. H. (2016). Gay-straight alliances are associated with lower levels of school-based victimization of LGBTQ+ youth: A systematic review and meta-analysis. *Journal of Youth and Adolescence, 45*(7), 1269–1282. https://doi.org/10.1007/s10964-016-0501-7

Mascaro, J. S., Rentscher, K. E., Hackett, P. D., Mehl, M. R., & Rilling, J. K. (2017). Child gender influences paternal behavior, language, and brain function. *Behavioral Neuroscience, 131*, 262–273. https://doi.org/10.1037/bne0000199

Masche, J. G. (2010). Explanation of normative declines in parents' knowledge about their adolescent children. *Journal of Adolescence, 33*(2), 271–284. https://doi.org/10.1016/j.adolescence.2009.08.002

Masek, L. R., Ramirez, A. G., McMillan, B. T. M., Hirsh-Pasek, K., & Golinkoff, R. M. (2021). Beyond counting words: A paradigm shift for the study of language acquisition. *Child Development Perspectives, 15*(4), 274–280. https://doi.org/10.1111/cdep.12425

Masi, A., DeMayo, M. M., Glozier, N., & Guastella, A. J. (2017). An overview of autism spectrum disorder, heterogeneity and treatment options. *Neuroscience Bulletin, 33*(2), 183–193. https://doi.org/10.1007/s12264-017-0100-y

Mason, G. M., & Spencer, R. M. C. (2022). Sleep and memory in infancy and childhood. *Annual Review of Developmental Psychology, 4*(1), 89–108. https://doi.org/10.1146/annurev-devpsych-121020-033411

Mason, L., & Otero, M. (2021). Just How Effective is Direct Instruction? *Perspectives on Behavior Science, 44*(2), 225–244. https://doi.org/10.1007/s40614-021-00295-x

Mason, M., Mennis, J., Russell, M., Moore, M., & Brown, A. (2019). Adolescent depression and substance use: The protective role of prosocial peer behavior. *Journal of Abnormal Child Psychology, 47*(6), 1065–1074. https://doi.org/10.1007/s10802-018-0501-z

Masonbrink, A. R., & Hurley, E. (2020). Advocating for children during the COVID-19 school closures. *Pediatrics, 146*(3), e20201440. https://doi.org/10.1542/PEDS.2020-1440

Masselli, G., Vaccaro Notte, M. R., Zacharzewska-Gondek, A., Laghi, F., Manganaro, L., & Brunelli, R. (2020). Fetal MRI of CNS abnormalities. *Clinical Radiology*. https://doi.org/10.1016/j.crad.2020.03.035

Masten, A. S., Cicchetti, D., Masten, A. S., & Cicchetti, D. (2016). Resilience in development: Progress and transformation. In D. Cicchetti (Ed.), *Developmental psychopathology* (pp. 1–63). John Wiley & Sons. https://doi.org/10.1002/9781119125556.devpsy406

Masten, A. S., Lucke, C. M., Nelson, K. M., & Stallworthy, I. C. (2021). Resilience in development and psychopathology: Multisystem perspectives. *Annual Review of Clinical Psychology, 17*, 521–549. https://doi.org/10.1146/annurev-clinpsy-081219-120307

Masten, A. S., Narayan, A. J., & Wright, M. O. (2023). Resilience processes in development: Multisystem integration emerging from four waves of research. In S. Goldstein & R. B. Brooks (Eds.), *Handbook of* resilience in children (pp. 19–46). Springer International. https://doi.org/10.1007/978-3-031-14728-9_2

Master, A. (2021). Gender stereotypes influence children's STEM motivation. *Child Development Perspectives*, *15*(3), 203–210. https://doi.org/10.1111/cdep.12424

Mastropieri, M. A., & Scruggs, T. E. (2017). *The inclusive classroom: Strategies for effective differentiated instruction.* Pearson. https://books.google.com/books/about/The_Inclusive_Classroom.html?id=-9ZRMQAACAAJ

Matarma, T., Lagström, H., Löyttyniemi, E., & Koski, P. (2020). Motor skills of 5-year-old children: Gender differences and activity and family correlates. *Perceptual and Motor Skills*, *127*(2), 367–385. https://doi.org/10.1177/0031512519900732

Mathews, C. J., Medina, M. A., Bañales, J., Pinetta, B. J., Marchand, A. D., Agi, A. C., Miller, S. M., Hoffman, A. J., Diemer, M. A., & Rivas-Drake, D. (2020). Mapping the intersections of adolescents' ethnic-racial identity and critical consciousness. *Adolescent Research Review*, *5*(4), 363–379. https://doi.org/10.1007/s40894-019-00122-0

Mathews, T. J., & Hamilton, B. E. (2002). Mean age of mother, 1970–2000. National Vital Statistics Reports: From the Centers for Disease Control and Prevention, National Center for Health Statistics. *National Vital Statistics System*, *51*(1), 1–13.

Mathewson-Chapman, M., & Chapman, H. J. (2020). One Health and veterans' post-deployment health. *Clinical Teacher*, *18*, 24–31. https://doi.org/10.1111/tct.13244

Mattingly, V., & Kraiger, K. (2019). Can emotional intelligence be trained? A meta-analytical investigation. *Human Resource Management Review*, *29*(2), 140–155. https://doi.org/10.1016/j.hrmr.2018.03.002

Matuschka, L. K., Scott, J. G., Campbell, M. A., Lawrence, D., Zubrick, S. R., Bartlett, J., & Thomas, H. J. (2022). Correlates of help-seeking behaviour in adolescents who experience bullying victimisation. *International Journal of Bullying Prevention*, *4*(2), 99–114. https://doi.org/10.1007/s42380-021-00090-x

Mauger, C., Lancelot, C., Roy, A., Coutant, R., Cantisano, N., & Le Gall, D. (2018). Executive functions in children and adolescents with Turner syndrome: A systematic review and meta-analysis. *Neuropsychology Review*, *28*(2), 188–215. https://doi.org/10.1007/S11065-018-9372-X

Maule, J., Skelton, A. E., & Franklin, A. (2023). The development of color perception and cognition. *Annual Review of Psychology*, *74*(1), 87–111. https://doi.org/10.1146/annurev-psych-032720-040512

Maunder, R., & Monks, C. P. (2019). Friendships in middle childhood: Links to peer and school identification, and general self-worth. *British Journal of Developmental Psychology*, *37*(2), 211–229. https://doi.org/10.1111/bjdp.12268

Maurer, D. (2017). Critical periods re-examined: Evidence from children treated for dense cataracts. *Cognitive Development*, *42*, 27–36. https://doi.org/10.1016/j.cogdev.2017.02.006

Mavroveli, S., Petrides, K. V., Rieffe, C., & Bakker, F. (2007). Trait emotional intelligence, psychological well-being and peer-rated social competence in adolescence. *British Journal of Developmental Psychology*, *25*(2), 263–275. https://doi.org/10.1348/026151006X118577

May, L., Gervain, J., Carreiras, M., & Werker, J. F. (2018). The specificity of the neural response to speech at birth. *Developmental Science*, *21*(3), e12564. https://doi.org/10.1111/desc.12564

Mayer, A., & Träuble, B. (2015). The weird world of cross-cultural false-belief research: A true-and false-belief study among Samoan children based on commands. *Journal of Cognition and Development*, *16*(4), 650–665. https://doi.org/10.1080/15248372.2014.926273

Mayne, S. L., Hannan, C., Davis, M., Young, J. F., Kelly, M. K., Powell, M., Dalembert, G., McPeak, K. E., Jenssen, B. P., & Fiks, A. G. (2021). COVID-19 and adolescent depression and suicide risk screening outcomes. *Pediatrics*, *148*(3), e2021051507. https://doi.org/10.1542/peds.2021-051507

Maziarz, L. N., Dake, J. A., & Glassman, T. (2020). Sex education, condom access, and contraceptive referral in U.S. high schools. *Journal of School Nursing*, *36*(5), 325–329. https://doi.org/10.1177/1059840519872785

Mazrekaj, D., & De Witte, K. (2023). The impact of school closures on learning and mental health of children: Lessons from the COVID-19 pandemic. *Perspectives on Psychological Science*, *17456916231181108*. https://doi.org/10.1177/17456916231181108 Advance online publication

Mazrekaj, D., De Witte, K., & Cabus, S. (2020). School outcomes of children raised by same-sex parents: Evidence from administrative panel data. *American Sociological Review*, *85*(5), 830–856. https://doi.org/10.1177/0003122420957249

Mazul, M. C., Salm Ward, T. C., & Ngui, E. M. (2017). Anatomy of good prenatal care: Perspectives of low income African-American women on barriers and facilitators to prenatal care. *Journal of Racial and Ethnic Health Disparities*, *4*(1), 79–86. https://doi.org/10.1007/s40615-015-0204-x

McAdams, D. P., & Zapata-Gietl, C. (2015). Three strands of identity development across the human life course. In K. C. McLean & M. Syed (Eds.), *The Oxford handbook of identity development* (pp. 81–96). Oxford University Press. https://doi.org/10.1093/oxfordhb/9780199936564.013.006

McAlister, A. R., & Peterson, C. C. (2013). Siblings, theory of mind, and executive functioning in children aged 3–6 years: New longitudinal evidence. *Child Development*, *84*(4), 1442–1458. https://doi.org/10.1111/cdev.12043

McAnally, H. M., Forsyth, B. J., Taylor, M., & Reese, E. (2020). Imaginary companions in childhood: What can prospective longitudinal research tell us about their fate by adolescence? *Journal of Creative Behavior*, *55*(1), 276–283. https://doi.org/10.1002/jocb.468

McCaskey, U., von Aster, M., O'Gorman, R., & Kucian, K. (2020). Persistent differences in brain structure in developmental dyscalculia: A longitudinal morphometry study. *Frontiers in Human Neuroscience*, *14*, 272. https://doi.org/10.3389/fnhum.2020.00272

Mcclain, M.-C., & Pfeiffer, S. (2012). Identification of gifted students in the United States today: A look at state definitions, policies, and practices. *Journal of Applied School Psychology*, *28*(1), 59–88. https://doi.org/10.1080/15377903.2012.643757

McCleery, J. P., Akshoomoff, N., Dobkins, K. R., & Carver, L. J. (2009). Atypical face versus object processing and hemispheric asymmetries in 10-month-old infants at risk for autism. *Biological Psychiatry*, *66*(10), 950–957. https://doi.org/10.1016/j.biopsych.2009.07.031

McClelland, M. M., & Cameron, C. E. (2011). Self-regulation and academic achievement in elementary school children. *New Directions for Child and Adolescent Development*, 29–44. https://doi.org/10.1002/cd.302 *2011*(133)

McClelland, M. M., John Geldhof, G., Cameron, C. E., Wanless, S. B., McClelland, M. M., John Geldhof, G., Cameron, C. E., & Wanless, S. B. (2015). Development and self-regulation. In *Handbook of child psychology and developmental science* (pp. 1–43). John Wiley & Sons. https://doi.org/10.1002/9781118963418.childpsy114

McClure, R., Kegler, S., Davey, T., & Clay, F. (2015). Contextual determinants of childhood injury: A systematic review of studies with multilevel analytic methods. *American Journal of Public Health, 105*(12), e37–e43. https://doi.org/10.2105/AJPH.2015.302883

McConaughy, S. H., & Whitcomb, S. A. (2022). *Clinical interviews for children and adolescents: Assessment to Intervention.* Guilford.

McConnachie, A. L., Ayed, N., Jadva, V., Lamb, M., Tasker, F., & Golombok, S. (2020). Father-child attachment in adoptive gay father families. *Attachment and Human Development, 22*(1), 110–123. https://doi.org/10.1080/14616734.2019.1589067

McConnell, E. A., Birkett, M., & Mustanski, B. (2016). Families matter: Social support and mental health trajectories among lesbian, gay, bisexual, and transgender youth. *Journal of Adolescent Health, 59*(6), 674–680. https://doi.org/10.1016/j.jadohealth.2016.07.026

McCord, J. (1996). Unintended consequences of punishment. *Pediatrics, 98*(4), 832–834. https://doi.org/10.1542/peds.98.4.832

McCourt, A. D., White, S. A., Bandara, S., Schall, T., Goodman, D. J., Patel, E., & McGinty, E. E. (2022). Development and implementation of state and federal child welfare laws related to drug use in pregnancy. *Milbank Quarterly, 100*(4), 1076–1120. https://doi.org/10.1111/1468-0009.12591

McCoy, D. C. (2022). Building a model of cultural universality with specificity for global early childhood development. *Child Development Perspectives, 16*(1). https://doi.org/10.1111/cdep.12438

McCoy, S. S., Dimler, L. M., Samuels, D. V., & Natsuaki, M. N. (2019). Adolescent Susceptibility to deviant peer pressure: Does gender matter? *Adolescent Research Review, 4*(1), 59–71. https://doi.org/10.1007/s40894-017-0071-2

McCrea, K. T., Richards, M., Quimby, D., Scott, D., Davis, L., Hart, S., Thomas, A., & Hopson, S. (2019). Understanding violence and developing resilience with African American youth in high-poverty, high-crime communities. *Children and Youth Services Review, 99*, 296–307. https://doi.org/10.1016/j.childyouth.2018.12.018

McDade, R. S., Vidourek, R. A., Biradar, K. S., King, K. A., & Merianos, A. A. (2020). Impact of parental communication on African American adolescent sexual behavior: A mini literature review. *Sexuality & Culture, 24*(5), 1579–1593. https://doi.org/10.1007/s12119-019-09678-4

McDevitt, T. M., & Ormrod, J. Ellis. (2016). *Child development and education.* Pearson.

McDonald, K. L., & Asher, S. R. (2018). Peer acceptance, peer rejection, and popularity: Social-cognitive and behavioral perspectives. In W. M. Bukowski, B. Laursen, & K. H. Rubi (Eds.), *Handbook of peer interactions, relationships, and groups* (pp. 429–446). https://psycnet.apa.org/record/2018-00748-022

McDonell, J. R. (2014). Neighborhood characteristics and children's safety. In A. C. Michalos (Ed.), *Encyclopedia of quality of life and well-being research* (pp. 4314–4318). Springer Netherlands. https://doi.org/10.1007/978-94-007-0753-5_3773

McDougall, P., & Vaillancourt, T. (2015). Long-term adult outcomes of peer victimization in childhood and adolescence: Pathways to adjustment and maladjustment. *American Psychologist, 70*(4), 300–310. https://doi.org/10.1037/a0039174

McDowell, N. (2023). A review of the literature to inform the development of a practice framework for supporting children with cerebral visual impairment (CVI). *International Journal of Inclusive Education, 27*(6), 718–738. https://doi.org/10.1080/13603116.2020.1867381

McEwen, F. S., Popham, C., Moghames, P., Smeeth, D., de Villiers, B., Saab, D., Karam, G., Fayyad, J., Karam, E., & Pluess, M. (2022). Cohort profile: Biological pathways of risk and resilience in Syrian refugee children (BIOPATH). *Social Psychiatry and Psychiatric Epidemiology, 57*(4), 873–883. https://doi.org/10.1007/S00127-022-02228-8

McGlade, M. S., Saha, S., & Dahlstrom, M. E. (2004). The Latina paradox: An opportunity for restructuring prenatal care delivery. *American Journal of Public Health, 94*(12), 2062–2065.

McGowan, P. O., & Matthews, S. G. (2018). Prenatal stress, glucocorticoids, and developmental programming of the stress response. *Endocrinology, 159*(1), 69–82. https://doi.org/10.1210/en.2017-00896

McGue, M., & Christensen, K. (2013). Growing old but not growing apart: Twin similarity in the latter half of the lifespan. *Behavior Genetics, 43*(1), 1–12. https://doi.org/10.1007/s10519-012-9559-5

McHale, S. M., Crouter, A. C., & Whiteman, S. D. (2003). The family contexts of gender development in childhood and adolescence. *Social Development, 12*(1), 125–148. https://doi.org/10.1111/1467-9507.00225

McHale, S. M., Updegraff, K. A., & Whiteman, S. D. (2012). Sibling relationships and influences in childhood and adolescence. *Journal of Marriage and the Family, 74*(5), 913–930. https://doi.org/10.1111/j.1741-3737.2012.01011.x

McHarg, G., Ribner, A. D., Devine, R. T., & Hughes, C. (2020). Screen time and executive function in toddlerhood: A longitudinal study. *Frontiers in Psychology, 11*, 570392. https://www.frontiersin.org/articles/10.3389/fpsyg.2020.570392

McHenry, M. S., McAteer, C. I., Oyungu, E., McDonald, B. C., Bosma, C. B., Mpofu, P. B., Deathe, A. R., & Vreeman, R. C. (2018). Neurodevelopment in young children born to HIV-infected mothers: A meta-analysis. *Pediatrics, 141*(2), e20172888. https://doi.org/10.1542/peds.2017-2888

McIlvain, G., Clements, R. G., Magoon, E. M., Spielberg, J. M., Telzer, E. H., & Johnson, C. L. (2020). Viscoelasticity of reward and control systems in adolescent risk taking. *NeuroImage, 215*, 116850. https://doi.org/10.1016/j.neuroimage.2020.116850

McIntosh, J. E., Opie, J., Greenwood, C. J., Booth, A., Tan, E., Painter, F., Messer, M., Macdonald, J. A., Letcher, P., Olsson, C. A., ATPG3 MAC, Lab., & Consortium. (2024). Infant and preschool attachment, continuity and relationship to caregiving sensitivity: Findings from a new population-based Australian cohort. *Journal of Child Psychology and Psychiatry, 65*(1), 64–76. https://doi.org/10.1111/jcpp.13865

McKenna, J. J., & Volpe, L. E. (2007). Sleeping with baby: An internet-based sampling of parental experiences, choices, perceptions, and interpretations in a Western industrialized context. *Infant and Child Development, 16*(4), 359–385. https://doi.org/10.1002/icd.525

McKinney, C., & Renk, K. (2011). A multivariate model of parent-adolescent relationship variables in early adolescence. *Child Psychiatry and Human Development, 42*(4), 442–462. https://doi.org/10.1007/s10578-011-0228-3

McKone, E., Wan, L., Pidcock, M., Crookes, K., Reynolds, K., Dawel, A., Kidd, E., & Fiorentini, C. (2019). A critical period for faces: Other-race face recognition is improved by childhood but not adult social contact. *Scientific Reports, 9*(1). https://doi.org/10.1038/s41598-019-49202-0

McKown, C., & Strambler, M. J. (2009). Developmental antecedents and social and academic consequences of stereotype-consciousness in middle childhood. *Child Development, 80*(6), 1643–1659. https://doi.org/10.1111/j.1467-8624.2009.01359.x

McKown, C., & Weinstein, R. S. (2003). The development and consequences of stereotype consciousness in middle childhood. *Child Development*, 74(2), 498–515. https://doi.org/10.1111/1467-8624.7402012

McKusick-Nathans Institute of Genetic Medicine. (2020). *OMIM - Online Mendelian Inheritance in Man*. Johns Hopkins University School of Medicine. http://www.omim.org/about

McLean, K. C., Syed, M., & Shucard, H. (2016). Bringing identity content to the fore. *Emerging Adulthood*, 4(5), 356–364. https://doi.org/10.1177/2167696815626820

McLean, K. C., Syed, M., Way, N., & Rogers, O. (2015). "[T]hey say Black men won't make it, but I know I'm gonna make it.". In K. C. McLean & M. Syed (Eds.), *The Oxford handbook of identity development* (pp. 269–287). Oxford University Press. https://doi.org/10.1093/oxfordhb/9780199936564.013.032

McLoughlin, C. S. (2005). The coming-of-age of China's single-child policy. *Psychology in the Schools*, 42(3), 305–313. https://doi.org/10.1002/pits.20081

McLoyd, V. C., Hardaway, C. R., & Jocson, R. M. (2019). African American parenting. In M. H. Bornstein (Ed.), *Handbook of parenting: Social conditions and applied parenting* (3rd ed., Vol. 4, pp. 57–107). Routledge.

McLoyd, V. C., & Smith, J. (2002). Physical discipline and behavior problems in African American, European American, and Hispanic children: Emotional support as a moderator. *Journal of Marriage and Family*, 64, 40–53. https://doi.org/10.1111/j.1741-3737.2002.00040.x

McMahan True, M., Pisani, L., & Oumar, F. (2001). Infant–Mother Attachment among the Dogon of Mali. *Child Development*, 72(5), 1451–1466. https://doi.org/10.1111/1467-8624.00359

McMahon, E. M., Corcoran, P., O'Regan, G., Keeley, H., Cannon, M., Carli, V., Wasserman, C., Hadlaczky, G., Sarchiapone, M., Apter, A., Balazs, J., Balint, M., Bobes, J., Brunner, R., Cozman, D., Haring, C., Iosue, M., Kaess, M., Kahn, J.-P., & &#hillip1; Wasserman, D. (2017). Physical activity in European adolescents and associations with anxiety, depression and well-being. *European Child & Adolescent Psychiatry*, 26(1), 111–122. https://doi.org/10.1007/s00787-016-0875-9

McNamara, H. C., Kane, S. C., Craig, J. M., Short, R. V., & Umstad, M. P. (2016). A review of the mechanisms and evidence for typical and atypical twinning. *American Journal of Obstetrics and Gynecology*, 214(2), 172–191. https://doi.org/10.1016/j.ajog.2015.10.930

McPartland, J. C., Lerner, M. D., Bhat, A., Clarkson, T., Jack, A., Koohsari, S., Matuskey, D., McQuaid, G. A., Su, W.-C., & Trevisan, D. A. (2021). Looking back at the next 40 years of ASD neuroscience research. *Journal of Autism and Developmental Disorders*, 51(12), 4333–4353. https://doi.org/10.1007/s10803-021-05095-5

McRae, C. S., Overall, N. C., Henderson, A. M. E., Low, R. S. T., & Chang, V. T. (2021). Parents' distress and poor parenting during a COVID-19 lockdown: The buffering effects of partner support and cooperative coparenting. *Developmental Psychology*, 57, 1623–1632. https://doi.org/10.1037/dev0001207

McWhirter, E. H., Garcia, E. A., & Bines, D. (2018). Discrimination and other education barriers, school connectedness, and thoughts of dropping out among Latina/o students. *Journal of Career Development*, 45(4), 330–344. https://doi.org/10.1177/0894845317696807

Meca, A., Gonzales-Backen, M., Davis, R., Rodil, J., Soto, D., & Unger, J. B. (2020). Discrimination and ethnic identity: Establishing directionality among Latino/a youth. *Developmental Psychology*, 56, 982–992. https://doi.org/10.1037/dev0000908

Mechler, K., Banaschewski, T., Hohmann, S., & Häge, A. (2022). Evidence-based pharmacological treatment options for ADHD in children and adolescents. *Pharmacology & Therapeutics*, 230, 107940. https://doi.org/10.1016/j.pharmthera.2021.107940

Meehan, C. L., & Hawks, S. (2013). Cooperative breeding and attachment among the Aka Foragers. In N. Quinn & J. M. Mageo (Eds.), *Attachment reconsidered* (pp. 85–113). Palgrave Macmillan. https://doi.org/10.1057/9781137386724_4

Meeus, W. (2023). Fifty years of longitudinal research into identity development in adolescence and early adulthood: An overview. In L. J. Crockett, G. Carlo, & J. E. Schulenberg (Eds.), *APA handbook of adolescent and young adult development* (pp. 139–157). American Psychological Association. https://doi.org/10.1037/0000298-009

Meeus, W. H. J. (2011). The study of adolescent identity formation 2000–2010: A review of longitudinal research. *Journal of Research on Adolescence*, 21(1), 75–94. https://doi.org/10.1111/j.1532-7795.2010.00716.x

Meeus, W. H. J. (2016). Adolescent psychosocial development: A review of longitudinal models and research. *Developmental Psychology*, 52(12), 1969–1993. https://doi.org/10.1037/dev0000243

Meeus, W. H. J., & de Wied, M. (2007). Relationships with parents and identity in adolescence: A review of 25 years of research. In M. Watzlawik & A. Born (Eds.), *Capturing identity: Quantitative and qualitative methods* (pp. 131–147). University Press of America.

Mehl, M. R. (2017). The electronically activated recorder (EAR). *Current Directions in Psychological Science*, 26(2), 184–190. https://doi.org/10.1177/0963721416680611

Mehta, C. M., Arnett, J. J., Palmer, C. G., & Nelson, L. J. (2020). Established adulthood: A new conception of ages 30 to 45. *American Psychologist*, 75, 431–444. https://doi.org/10.1037/amp0000600

Mehta, P. K. (2016). Pregnancy with chicken pox. In A. Gandhi, N. Malhotra, J. Malhotra, N. Gupta, & N. M. Bora (Eds.), *Principles of Critical Care in Obstetrics* (pp. 21–30). Springer India. https://doi.org/10.1007/978-81-322-2686-4_4

Mehus, C. J., & Patrick, M. E. (2021). Prevalence of spanking in US national samples of 35-year-old parents from 1993 to 2017. *JAMA Pediatrics*, 175(1), 92–94. https://doi.org/10.1001/jamapediatrics.2020.2197

Meier, A., Musick, K., Fischer, J., & Flood, S. (2018). Mothers' and fathers' well-being in parenting across the arch of child development. *Journal of Marriage and Family*, 80(4), 992–1004. https://doi.org/10.1111/jomf.12491

Meinhofer, A., Witman, A., Maclean, J. C., & Bao, Y. (2022). Prenatal substance use policies and newborn health. *Health Economics*, 31(7), 1452–1467. https://doi.org/10.1002/hec.4518

Meinzen-Derr, J., Wiley, S., Grove, W., Altaye, M., Gaffney, M., Satterfield-Nash, A., Folger, A. T., Peacock, G., & Boyle, C. (2020). Kindergarten readiness in children who are deaf or hard of hearing who received early intervention. *Pediatrics*, 146(4), e20200557. https://doi.org/10.1542/peds.2020-0557

Meisel, J. M. (1989). Early differentiation of languages in bilingual children. In K. Hyltenstam & L. K. Obler (Eds.), *Bilingualism across the lifespan: Aspects of acquisition, maturity and loss* (pp. 13–40). Cambridge University Press,.

Meléndez, L. (2005). Parental beliefs and practices around early self-regulation: The impact of culture and immigration. *Infants & Young Children*, 18(2), 136–146.

Melisse, B., de Beurs, E., & van Furth, E. F. (2020). Eating disorders in the Arab world:

A literature review. *Journal of Eating Disorders*, *8*(59). https://doi.org/10.1186/s40337-020-00336-x

Melogno, S., Pinto, M. A., & Lauriola, M. (2022). Becoming the metalinguistic mind: The development of metalinguistic abilities in children from 5 to 7. *Children*, *9*(4), 550. https://doi.org/10.3390/children9040550

Meltzoff, A. N. (1990). Towards a developmental cognitive science. The implications of cross-modal matching and imitation for the development of representation and memory in infancy. *Annals of the New York Academy of Sciences*, *608*, 1–37. https://doi.org/10.1111/j.1749-6632.1990.tb48889.x

Meltzoff, A. N. (2007). 'Like me': A foundation for social cognition. *Developmental Science*, *10*(1), 126–134. https://doi.org/10.1111/j.1467-7687.2007.00574.x

Meltzoff, A. N., & Moore, M. K. (1994). Imitation, memory, and the representation of persons. *Infant Behavior & Development*, *17*(1), 83–99. https://doi.org/10.1016/0163-6383(94)90024-8

Memmert, D. (2014). Inattentional blindness to unexpected events in 8–15-year-olds. *Cognitive Development*, *32*, 103–109. https://doi.org/10.1016/j.cogdev.2014.09.002

Memmott-Elison, M. K., & Toseeb, U. (2022). Prosocial behavior and psychopathology: An 11-year longitudinal study of inter- and intraindividual reciprocal relations across childhood and adolescence. *Development and Psychopathology*, *34*(4), 1–15. https://doi.org/10.1017/S0954579422000657

Mencarini, L. (2023). Gender-role beliefs. In F. Maggino (Ed.), *Encyclopedia of quality of life and well-being research* (pp. 2719–2720). Springer International. https://doi.org/10.1007/978-3-031-17299-1_1140

Mendez, M., Durtschi, J., Neppl, T. K., & Stith, S. M. (2016). Corporal punishment and externalizing behaviors in toddlers: The moderating role of positive and harsh parenting. *Journal of Family Psychology*, *30*(8), 887–895. https://doi.org/10.1037/fam0000187

Mendle, J. (2014). Beyond pubertal timing: New directions for studying individual differences in development. *Current Directions in Psychological Science*, *23*(3), 215–219. https://doi.org/10.1177/0963721414530144

Mendoza, A. N., Fruhauf, C. A., & MacPhee, D. (2020). Grandparent caregivers' resilience: Stress, support, and coping predict life satisfaction. *International Journal of Aging and Human Development*, *91*(1), 3–20. https://doi.org/10.1177/0091415019843459

Menesini, E., & Salmivalli, C. (2017). Bullying in schools: The state of knowledge and effective interventions. *Psychology, Health & Medicine*, *22*(sup1), 240–253. https://doi.org/10.1080/13548506.2017.1279740

Mennella, J. A., & Beauchamp, G. K. (2002). Flavor experiences during formula feeding are related to preferences during childhood. *Early Human Development*, *68*(2), 71–82.

Menon, M. (2011). Does felt gender compatibility mediate influences of self-perceived gender nonconformity on early adolescents' psychosocial adjustment? *Child Development*, *82*(4), 1152–1162. https://doi.org/10.1111/j.1467-8624.2011.01601.x

Mercer, N., Crocetti, E., Branje, S., van Lier, P., & Meeus, W. (2017). Linking delinquency and personal identity formation across adolescence: Examining between- and within-person associations. *Developmental Psychology*, *53*(11), 2182–2194. https://doi.org/10.1037/dev0000351

Merhar, S. L., Kline, J. E., Braimah, A., Kline-Fath, B. M., Tkach, J. A., Altaye, M., He, L., & Parikh, N. A. (2020). Prenatal opioid exposure is associated with smaller brain volumes in multiple regions. *Pediatric Research*, *90*(2), 397–402. https://doi.org/10.1038/s41390-020-01265-w

Merlo, C. L. (2020). Dietary and physical activity behaviors among high school students—youth risk behavior survey, United States, 2019. *MMWR Supplements*, *6*(9). https://doi.org/10.15585/mmwr.su6901a8

Mermelshtine, R. (2017). Parent-child learning interactions: A review of the literature on scaffolding. *British Journal of Educational Psychology*, *87*(2), 241–254. https://doi.org/10.1111/bjep.12147

Merrin, G. J., Davis, J. P., Berry, D., & Espelage, D. L. (2019). Developmental changes in deviant and violent behaviors from early to late adolescence: Associations with parental monitoring and peer deviance. *Psychology of Violence*, *9*(2), 196–208. https://doi.org/10.1037/vio0000207

Meruelo, A. D., Castro, N., Cota, C. I., & Tapert, S. F. (2017). Cannabis and alcohol use, and the developing brain. *Behavioural Brain Research*, *325*(Pt A), 44–50. https://doi.org/10.1016/j.bbr.2017.02.025

Mesman, E., Vreeker, A., & Hillegers, M. (2021). Resilience and mental health in children and adolescents: An update of the recent literature and future directions. *Current Opinion in Psychiatry*, *34*(6). https://doi.org/10.1097/YCO.0000000000000741

Mesman, J., Basweti, N., & Misati, J. (2018). Sensitive infant caregiving among the rural Gusii in Kenya. *Attachment & Human Development*, 1–9. https://doi.org/10.1080/14616734.2018.1454053

Mesman, J., van IJzendoorn, M. H., & Sagi-Schwartz, A. (2016). Cross-cultural patterns of attachment: Universal and contextual dimensions. In J. Cassidy & P. R. Shaver (Eds.), *Handbook of attachment: Theory, research, and clinical applications* (3rd ed., pp. 852–876).

Messinger, D., & Fogel, A. (2007). The interactive development of social smiling. In R. V. Kail (Ed.), *Advances in child development and behavior* (Vol. 35, pp. 327–366). Elsevier Academic Press.

Messinger, D., Mitsven, S. G., Ahn, Y. A., Prince, E. B., Sun, L., & Rivero-Fernández, C. (2019). Happiness and Joy. In V. LoBue, K. Pérez-Edgar, & K. A. Buss (Eds.), *Handbook of emotional development* (pp. 171–198). Springer International. https://doi.org/10.1007/978-3-030-17332-6_8

Metcalf, B. S., Hosking, J., Jeffery, A. N., Henley, W. E., & Wilkin, T. J. (2015). Exploring the adolescent fall in physical activity: A 10-yr cohort study (EarlyBird 41). *Medicine and Science in Sports and Exercise*, *47*(10), 2084–2092. https://doi.org/10.1249/MSS.0000000000000644

Metcalfe, R. E., Muentner, L. D., Reino, C., Schweer-Collins, M. L., Kjellstrand, J. M., & Eddy, J. M. (2023). Witnessing parental arrest as a predictor of child internalizing and externalizing symptoms during and after parental incarceration. *Journal of Child & Adolescent Trauma*, *16*(2), 329–338. https://doi.org/10.1007/s40653-022-00490-1

Meter, D. J., & Card, N. A. (2016). Stability of children's and adolescents' friendships: A meta-analytic review. *Merrill-Palmer Quarterly*, *62*(3), 252–284. https://doi.org/10.13110/merrpalmquar1982.62.3.0252

Meyer, S., & Schlesier, J. (2022). The development of students' achievement emotions after transition to secondary school: A multilevel growth curve modelling approach. *European Journal of Psychology of Education*, *37*(1), 141–161. https://doi.org/10.1007/s10212-021-00533-5

Michalek, J., Lisi, M., Binetti, N., Ozkaya, S., Hadfield, K., Dajani, R., & Mareschal, I. (2022). War-related trauma linked to increased sustained attention to threat in children. *Child Development*, *93*(4), 900–909. https://doi.org/10.1111/CDEV.13739

Michikyan, M., & Suárez-Orozco, C. (2016). Adolescent media and social media use. *Journal of Adolescent Research*, *31*(4), 411–414. https://doi.org/10.1177/0743558416643801

Miconi, D., Moscardino, U., Ronconi, L., & Altoè, G. (2017). Perceived parenting, self-esteem, and depressive symptoms in immigrant and non-immigrant adolescents in Italy: A multigroup path analysis. *Journal of Child and Family Studies*, 26(2), 345–356. https://doi.org/10.1007/s10826-016-0562-y

Midgley, C., Anderman, E., & Hicks, L. (1995). Differences between elementary and middle school teachers and students: A goal theory approach. *Journal of Early Adolescence*, 15(1), 90–113. https://doi.org/10.1177/0272431695015001006

Miech, R. A., Johnston, L. D., Patrick, M. E., O'Malley, P. M., & Bachman, J. G. (2024). *Monitoring the Future national survey results on drug use, 1975–2023: Overview and detailed results for secondary school students*. Institute for Social Research, University of Michigan. https://monitoringthefuture.org/wp-content/uploads/2024/01/mtfoverview2024.pdf

Miech, R. A., Johnston, L. D., Patrick, M. E., O'Malley, P. M., Bachman, J. G., & Schulenberg, J. E. (2023). *Monitoring the Future national survey results on drug use, 1975–2022: Secondary school students. Monitoring the Future Monograph Series*. Institute for Social Research, University of Michigan. http://monitoringthefuture.org/results/publications/monographs

Miedema, E., Le Mat, M. L. J., & Hague, F. (2020). But is it comprehensive? Unpacking the 'comprehensive' in comprehensive sexuality education. *Health Education Journal*, 79(7), 747–762. https://doi.org/10.1177/0017896920915960

Mielke, G. I., Brown, W. J., Nunes, B. P., Silva, I. C. M., & Hallal, P. C. (2017). Socioeconomic correlates of sedentary behavior in adolescents: Systematic review and meta-analysis. *Sports Medicine*, 47(1), 61–75. https://doi.org/10.1007/s40279-016-0555-4

Miesen, A. I. R. van der., Steensma, T. D., Vries, A. L. C. de., Bos, H., & Popma, A. (2020). Psychological functioning in transgender adolescents before and after gender-affirmative care compared with cisgender general population peers. *Journal of Adolescent Health*, 66(6), 699–704. https://doi.org/10.1016/j.jadohealth.2019.12.018

Miething, A., Almquist, Y. B., Edling, C., Rydgren, J., & Rostila, M. (2017). Friendship trust and psychological well-being from late adolescence to early adulthood: A structural equation modelling approach. *Scandinavian Journal of Public Health*, 45(3), 244–252. https://doi.org/10.1177/1403494816680784

Mihalec-Adkins, B. P., & Shlafer, R. (2022). The role of policy in shaping and addressing the consequences of parental incarceration for child development in the United States. *Social Policy Report*, 35(3), 1–24. https://doi.org/10.1002/sop2.25

Milevsky, A. (2016). Parenting styles. In R. Levesque (Ed.), *Encyclopedia of adolescence* (pp. 1–6). Springer International. https://doi.org/10.1007/978-3-319-32132-5_38-2

Milevsky, A. (2022). Relationships in transition: Maternal and paternal parenting styles and change in sibling dynamics during adolescence. *European Journal of Developmental Psychology*, 19(1), 89–109. https://doi.org/10.1080/17405629.2020.1865144

Miller, C. F., Trautner, H. M., & Ruble, D. N. (2006). The role of gender stereotypes in children's preferences and behavior. In L. Balter & C. S. Tamis-LeMonda (Eds.), *Child psychology: A handbook of contemporary issues* (2nd ed., pp. 293–323). Psychology Press.

Miller, C. F., Wheeler, L. A., & Woods, B. (2024). A multidimensional examination of children's endorsement of gender stereotypes. *Social Development*, 33(2), e12725. https://doi.org/10.1111/sode.12725

Miller, D. J. (2024). Sperm in the mammalian female reproductive tract: Surfing through the tract to try to beat the odds. *Annual Review of Animal Biosciences*, 12(1), 301–319. https://doi.org/10.1146/annurev-animal-021022-040629

Miller, J. G. (2018). Physiological mechanisms of prosociality. *Current Opinion in Psychology*, 20, 50–54. https://doi.org/10.1016/j.copsyc.2017.08.018

Miller, J. G., Englebrecht, J., Wang, Z., & Tsudaka, G. (2020). Toward greater cultural sensitivity in developmental psychology. *Applied Developmental Science*, 1–13. https://doi.org/10.1080/10888691.2020.1789348

Miller, J. G., & Hastings, P. D. (2020). Prosocial behaviors in children. In Stephen. Hupp & D. Jewell. Jeremy (Eds.), *The Encyclopedia of child and adolescent development* (pp. 1–10). Wiley. https://doi.org/10.1002/9781119171492.wecad277

Miller, J. M., Fan, Y., Sherwood, N. E., Osypuk, T., & French, S. (2020). Are low income children more physically active when they live in homes with bigger yards? A longitudinal analysis of the NET-Works Study. *Health and Place*, 63, 102330. https://doi.org/10.1016/j.healthplace.2020.102330

Miller, K. E., Koppenol-Gonzalez, G. V., Arnous, M., Tossyeh, F., Chen, A., Nahas, N., & Jordans, M. J. D. (2020). Supporting Syrian families displaced by armed conflict: A pilot randomized controlled trial of the Caregiver Support Intervention. *Child Abuse & Neglect*, 106, 104512. https://doi.org/10.1016/j.chiabu.2020.104512

Miller, L., Nielsen, D. M., Schoen, S. A., & Brett-Green, B. A. (2009). Perspectives on sensory processing disorder: A call for translational research. *Frontiers in Integrative Neuroscience*, 3, 22. https://doi.org/10.3389/neuro.07.022.2009

Miller, P. H. (2016). *Theories of developmental psychology*. Worth.

Miller, P. H. (2016). *Theories of developmental psychology* (6th ed.).

Miller, P. J., & Fung, H. (2012). I. Introduction. How socialization happens on the ground: Narrative practices as alternate socializing pathways in Taiwanese and European-American families. P. J. Miller, H. Fung, S. Lin, E. C-H. Chen, & B. R Boldt (Eds.), *Monographs of the Society for Research in Child Development*, 77(1), 1–14. https://doi.org/10.1111/j.1540-5834.2011.00642.x

Miller, P. J., Wang, S. hua., Sandel, T., & Cho, G. E. (2002). Self-esteem as folk theory: A comparison of European American and Taiwanese mothers' beliefs. *Parenting*, 2(3), 209–239. https://doi.org/10.1207/S15327922PAR0203_02

Miller, S., McCulloch, S., & Jarrold, C. (2015). The development of memory maintenance strategies: Training cumulative rehearsal and interactive imagery in children aged between 5 and 9. *Frontiers in Psychology*, 6, 524. https://doi.org/10.3389/fpsyg.2015.00524

Miller-Jacobs, C., Operario, D., & Hughto, J. M. W. (2023). State-level policies and health outcomes in U.S. transgender adolescents: Findings from the 2019 Youth Risk Behavior Survey. *LGBT Health*. https://doi.org/10.1089/lgbt.2022.0247

Mills, K. L., Goddings, A.-L., Herting, M. M., Meuwese, R., Blakemore, S.-J., Crone, E. A., Dahl, R. E., Güroğlu, B., Raznahan, A., Sowell, E. R., & Tamnes, C. K. (2016). Structural brain development between childhood and adulthood: Convergence across four longitudinal samples. *NeuroImage*, 141, 273–281. https://doi.org/10.1016/j.neuroimage.2016.07.044

Mills, K. L., & Tamnes, C. K. (2024). Longitudinal structural and functional brain development in childhood and adolescence. In K. Cohen Kadosh (Ed.), *Oxford handbook of developmental cognitive neuroscience* (pp. 75–98). Oxford University Press. https://doi.org/10.1093/oxfordhb/9780198827474.013.4

Mims, L. C., & Williams, J. L. (2020). "They told me what I was before I could tell them what I was": Black girls' ethnic-racial identity development within multiple worlds. *Journal of Adolescent Research, 35*(6), 754–779. https://doi.org/10.1177/0743558 420913483

Min, M. O., Albert, J. M., Minnes, S., Kim, J.-Y., Kim, S.-K., & Singer, L. T. (2023). Prenatal cocaine exposure and self-reported behavioral adjustments from ages 12 to 21: Environmental pathways. *Psychological Medicine*, 1–11. https://doi.org/10.1017/S00 33291723002404

Min, M. O., Minnes, S., Kim, S.-K., Kim, J.-Y., & Singer, L, T. (2023). Prenatal cocaine exposure and substance use disorder in emerging adulthood at age 21. *Drug and Alcohol Dependence, 242*, 109736.

Minnis, A. M., Browne, E. N., Chavez, M., McGlone, L., Raymond-Flesch, M., & Auerswald, C. (2022). Early sexual debut and neighborhood social environment in Latinx youth. *Pediatrics, 149*(3), e2021050861. https://doi.org/10.1542/peds.2021-050861

Mirabolfathi, V., Schweizer, S., Moradi, A. R., & Jobson, L. (2020). Affective working memory capacity in refugee adolescents. *Psychological Trauma: Theory, Research, Practice, and Policy, 14*(6), 983–988. https://doi.org/10.1037/tra0000552

Miranda-Mendizábal, A., Castellví, P., Parés-Badell, O., Almenara, J., Alonso, I., Blasco, M. J., Cebrià, A., Gabilondo, A., Gili, M., Lagares, C., Piqueras, J. A., Roca, M., Rodríguez-Marín, J., Rodríguez, T., Soto-Sanz, V., Vilagut, G., & Alonso, J. (2017). Sexual orientation and suicidal behaviour in adolescents and young adults: Systematic review and meta-analysis. *British Journal of Psychiatry, 211*, 77–87. doi:10.1192/bjp.bp.116.196345

Mireault, G. C., & Reddy, V. (2020). Making sense of infants' differential responses to incongruity. *Human Development, 64*(2), 1–9. https://doi.org/10.1159/000509980

Mirkovic, B., Chagraoui, A., Gerardin, P., & Cohen, D. (2020). Epigenetics and attention-deficit/hyperactivity disorder: New perspectives? *Frontiers in Psychiatry, 11*, 579. https://doi.org/10.3389/fpsyt.202 0.00579

Misailidi, P. (2006). Young children's display rule knowledge: Understanding the distinction between apparent and real emotions and the motives underlying the use of display rules. *Social Behavior and Personality: An International Journal, 34*(10), 1285–1296. https://doi.org/10.2224/sbp.20 06.34.10.1285

Mistry, J., Li, J., Yoshikawa, H., Tseng, V., Tirrell, J., Kiang, L., Mistry, R., & Wang, Y. (2016). An integrated conceptual framework for the development of Asian American children and youth. *Child Development, 87*(4), 1014–1032. https://doi.org/10.1111/cdev.12577

Mistry, R. S., Benner, A. D., & Kimura, A. M. (2022). COVID-19 and children's social development. In P. K. Smith & C. H. Hart (Eds.), *The Wiley-Blackwell handbook of childhood social development* (3rd ed., pp. 224–238). Wiley.

Mitchell, E. A. (2009). Risk factors for SIDS. *BMJ, 339*, 873–874. https://doi.org/10.1136/bmj.b3466

Mithun, M. (2019). Tense and aspect in morphology. In M. Aronoff (Ed.), *Oxford research encyclopedia of linguistics*. Oxford University Press. https://doi.org/10.1093/ACREFORE/9780199384655.013.548

Mix, K. S., Huttenlocher, J., & Levine, S. C. (2002). Multiple cues for quantification in infancy: Is number one of them? *Psychological Bulletin, 128*(2), 278–294.

M.K, K., & Choi, J. (2020). *Associations between breastfeeding and cognitive function in children from early childhood to school age: A prospective birth cohort study*, https://doi.org/10.21203/RS.3.RS-16984/V2

Modzelewska, D., Bellocco, R., Elfvin, A., Brantsæter, A. L., Meltzer, H. M., Jacobsson, B., & Sengpiel, V. (2019). Caffeine exposure during pregnancy, small for gestational age birth and neonatal outcome—Results from the Norwegian Mother and Child Cohort Study. *BMC Pregnancy and Childbirth, 19*(1), 80. https://doi.org/10.1186/s12884-019-2215-9

Moen, P., & Wethington, E. (1999). Midlife development in a life course context. In S. L. Willis & J. D. Reid (Eds.), *Life in the middle: Psychological and social development in middle age* (pp. 3–23). Academic Pres.

Moffitt, T. E. (2017). Adolescence-limited and life-course-persistent antisocial behavior: A developmental taxonomy. In K. M. Beaver (Ed.), *The termination of criminal careers* (pp. 405–432). Taylor and Francis. https://doi.org/10.4324/9781315096278-3

Mohanty, J. (2015). Ethnic identity and psychological well-being of international transracial adoptees: A curvilinear relationship. Adoptees' ethnic identity within family and social contexts. E. E. Pinderhughes & R. Rosnati (Eds.), *New Directions for Child and Adolescent Development, 150*, 33–45. https://doi.org/10.1002/cad.20117

Moilanen, K. L., Rasmussen, K. E., & Padilla-Walker, L. M. (2015). Bidirectional associations between self-regulation and parenting styles in early adolescence. *Journal of Research on Adolescence, 25*(2), 246–262. https://doi.org/10.1111/jora.12 125

Mojahed, S., Reyhanizadeh, F., Tabatabaei, R. S., & Dehghani, A. (2021). Evaluation of the effect of education on perceived stress of mother candidates for amniocentesis. *Journal of Education and Health Promotion, 10*(1), 267. https://doi.org/10.4103/jehp.jeh p_785_20

Molina, R. L., Tsai, T. C., Dai, D., Soto, M., Rosenthal, N., Orav, E. J., & Figueroa, J. F. (2022). Comparison of pregnancy and birth outcomes before vs during the COVID-19 pandemic. *JAMA Network Open, 5*(8), e2226531.

Molitor, A., & Hsu, H.-C. (2019). Child development across cultures. In K. Keith (Ed.), *Cross-cultural psychology* (pp. 153–189). John Wiley & Sons. https://doi.org/10. 1002/9781119519348.ch8

Molnar, B. E., Goerge, R. M., Gilsanz, P., Hill, A., Subramanian, S. V., Holton, J. K., Duncan, D. T., Beatriz, E. D., & Beardslee, W. R. (2016). Neighborhood-level social processes and substantiated cases of child maltreatment. *Child Abuse & Neglect, 51*, 41–53. https://doi.org/10.1016/j.chiabu.20 15.11.007

Molnar, B. E., Scoglio, A. A. J., & Beardslee, W. R. (2022). Community-level prevention of child maltreatment. In R. D. Krugman & J. E. Korbin (Eds.), *Handbook of child maltreatment* (pp. 459–477). Springer International. https://doi.org/10.1007/97 8-3-030-82479-2_23

Monden, C., Pison, G., & Smits, J. (2021). Twin peaks: More twinning in humans than ever before. *Human Reproduction (Oxford. https://doi.org/10.1093/humrep/deab029 England), 36*(6)

Mondschein, E. R., Adolph, K. E., & Tamis-LeMonda, C. S. (2000). Gender bias in mothers' expectations about infant crawling. *Journal of Experimental Child Psychology, 77*(4), 304–316. https://doi.org/10.1006 /jecp.2000.2597

Monroe, P., Campbell, J. A., Harris, M., & Egede, L. E. (2023). Racial/ethnic differences in social determinants of health and health outcomes among adolescents and youth ages 10–24 years old: A scoping review. *BMC Public Health, 23*(1), 410. https://doi.org/10.1186/s12889-023-15274-x

Monsrud, M.-B., Rydland, V., Geva, E., Thurmann-Moe, A. C., & Halaas Lyster, S.-A. (2022). The advantages of jointly considering first and second language vocabulary skills among emergent bilingual children. *International Journal of Bilingual Education and Bilingualism, 25*(1), 42–58. https://doi.org/10.1080/13670050.2019.1624685

Montgomery, J., & Jordan, N. A. (2018). Racial-ethnic socialization and transracial adoptee outcomes: A systematic research synthesis. *Child and Adolescent Social Work Journal, 35*(5), 439–458. https://doi.org/10.1007/s10560-018-0541-9

Montgomery, J., Srivastava, S., London-Johnson, A., Ferrill, J., & Iheanacho, E. C. (2020). Cultural activities in transracially adoptive families. *Journal of Ethnic and Cultural Diversity in Social Work, 30*(5), 430–444. https://doi.org/10.1080/15313204.2020.1730288

Montirosso, R., & McGlone, F. (2020). The body comes first. Embodied reparation and the co-creation of infant bodily-self. *Neuroscience and Biobehavioral Reviews, 113*, 77–87. https://doi.org/10.1016/j.neubiorev.2020.03.003

Montoya-Williams, D., Williamson, V. G., Cardel, M., Fuentes-Afflick, E., Maldonado-Molina, M., & Thompson, L. (2021). The Hispanic/Latinx perinatal paradox in the United States: A scoping review and recommendations to guide future research. *Journal of Immigrant and Minority Health, 23*(5), 1078–1091. https://doi.org/10.1007/S10903-020-01117-z

Moon, C., Cooper, R. P., & Fifer, W. P. (1993). Two-day-old infants prefer their native language. *Infant Behavior and Development, 16*, 495–500.

Moon, C., Cooper, R. P., & Fifer, W. P. (1993). Two-day-old infants prefer their native language. *Infant Behavior and Development, 16*, 495–500. https://psycnet.apa.org/doi/10.1016/0163-6383(93)80007-U

Moon, R. Y. (2016b). & Task Force on Sudden Infant Death Syndrome. SIDS and other sleep-related infant deaths: Updated 2016 recommendations for a safe infant sleeping environment. *Pediatrics, 138*(5), e20162938. https://doi.org/10.1542/peds.2016-2938

Moon, R. Y., Carlin, R. F., & Hand, I. (2022). & Task Force on Sudden Infant Death Syndrome and the Committee on Fetus and Newborn. Sleep-related infant deaths: Updated 2022 recommendations for reducing infant deaths in the sleep environment. *Pediatrics, 150*(1), e2022057990. https://doi.org/10.1542/peds.2022-057990

Moon, R. Y., & Task, Force on Sudden Infant Death Syndrome. (2016a). SIDS and other sleep-related infant deaths: Evidence base for 2016 updated recommendations for a safe infant sleeping environment. *Pediatrics, 138*(5), e20162940. https://doi.org/10.1542/peds.2016-2940

Moore, C., Angelopoulos, M., & Bennett, P. (1999). Word learning in the context of referential and salience cues. *Developmental Psychology, 35*(1), 60–68. https://doi.org/10.1037/0012-1649.35.1.60

Moore, C., Dailey, S., Garrison, H., Amatuni, A., & Bergelson, E. (2019). Point, walk, talk: Links between three early milestones, from observation and parental report. *Developmental Psychology, 55*(8), 1579–1593. https://doi.org/10.1037/dev0000738

Moore, D. S. (2017). Behavioral epigenetics. *Wiley Interdisciplinary Reviews: Systems Biology and Medicine, 9*(1), e1333. https://doi.org/10.1002/wsbm.1333

Moore, J. S. B., & Smith, M. (2018). Children's levels of contingent self-esteem and social and emotional outcomes. *Educational Psychology in Practice, 34*(2), 113–130. https://doi.org/10.1080/02667363.2017.1411786

Moore, K. L., Persaud, T. V. N., & Torchia, M. G. (2021). *Before we are born: Essentials of embryology and birth defects* (10th ed.). Elsevier. https://www.us.elsevierhealth.com/before-we-are-born-9780323608497.html

Moore, R., Vitale, D., & Stawinoga, N. (2018). *The digital divide and educational equity: A look at students with very limited access to electronic devices at home*. ACT Center for Equity in Learning.

Moore, S. E., Norman, R. E., Suetani, S., Thomas, H. J., Sly, P. D., & Scott, J. G. (2017). Consequences of bullying victimization in childhood and adolescence: A systematic review and meta-analysis. *World Journal of Psychiatry, 7*(1), 60–76. https://doi.org/10.5498/wjp.v7.i1.60

Moore, S. R., Harden, K. P., & Mendle, J. (2014). Pubertal timing and adolescent sexual behavior in girls. *Developmental Psychology, 50*(6), 1734–1745. https://doi.org/10.1037/a0036027

Moran-Lev, H., Farhi, A., Bauer, S., Nehama, H., Yerushalmy-Feler, A., Mandel, D., & Lubetzky, R. (2021). Association of socioeconomic factors and infant nutrition decisions: Breastfeeding and type of formula. *Breastfeeding Medicine, 16*(7), 553–557. https://doi.org/10.1089/bfm.2020.0398

Morawska, A. (2020). The effects of gendered parenting on child development outcomes: A systematic review. *Clinical Child and Family Psychology Review, 23*(4), 553–576. https://doi.org/10.1007/s10567-020-00321-5

Morawska, A., Dittman, C. K., & Rusby, J. C. (2019). Promoting self-regulation in young children: The role of parenting interventions. *Clinical Child and Family Psychology Review, 22*(1), 43–51. https://doi.org/10.1007/s10567-019-00281-5

Morawska, A., & Sanders, M. (2011). Parental use of time out revisited: A useful or harmful parenting strategy? *Journal of Child & Family Studies, 20*(1), 1–8. https://doi.org/10.1007/s10826-010-9371-x

Morelli, G. (2015). The evolution of attachment theory and cultures of human attachment in infancy and early childhood. In L. A. Jensen (Ed.), *The Oxford handbook of human development and culture* (pp. 149–164). Oxford University Press. https://doi.org/10.1093/oxfordhb/9780199948550.013.10

Morelli, G., Rogoff, B., Oppenheim, D., & Goldsmith, D. (1992). Cultural variation in infants' sleeping arrangements: Questions of independence. *Developmental Psychology, 28*, 604–613.

Moreno, M. A., & Uhls, Y. T. (2019). Applying an affordances approach and a developmental lens to approach adolescent social media use. *Digital Health, 5*, 2055207619826678. https://doi.org/10.1177/2055207619826678

Moreno, O., Janssen, T., Cox, M. J., Colby, S., & Jackson, K. M. (2017). Parent-adolescent relationships in Hispanic versus Caucasian families: Associations with alcohol and marijuana use onset. *Addictive Behaviors, 74*, 74–81. https://doi.org/10.1016/j.addbeh.2017.05.029

Morey, C. C., Mareva, S., Lelonkiewicz, J. R., & Chevalier, N. (2018). Gaze-based rehearsal in children under 7: A developmental investigation of eye movements during a serial spatial memory task. *Developmental Science, 21*(3), e12559. https://doi.org/10.1111/desc.12559

Morgan, C., Forti, M. D., & Fisher, H. L. (2020). Gene-environment interaction. In J. Das-Munshi, T. Ford, M. Hotopf, M. Prince, & R. Stewart (Eds.), *Practical psychiatric epidemiology* (pp. 343–358).

Morgan, G., Curtin, M., & Botting, N. (2021). The interplay between early social interaction, language and executive function development in deaf and hearing infants. *Infant Behavior and Development, 64*, 101591. https://doi.org/10.1016/j.infbeh.2021.101591

Morgan, P. L., Farkas, G., Hillemeier, M. M., & Maczuga, S. (2017). Replicated evidence of racial and ethnic disparities in disability identification in U.S. schools. *Educational Researcher*, *46*(6), 305–322. https://doi.org/10.3102/0013189X17726282

Mori, A., & Cigala, A. (2016). Perspective taking: Training procedures in developmentally typical preschoolers. Different intervention methods and their effectiveness. *Educational Psychology Review*, *28*(2), 267–294. https://doi.org/10.1007/s10648-015-9306-6

Moriguchi, Y. (2014). The early development of executive function and its relation to social interaction: A brief review. *Frontiers in Psychology*, *5*, 388. https://doi.org/10.3389/fpsyg.2014.00388

Moriguchi, Y. (2020). Functional magnetic resonance imaging (fMRI). In M. D. Gellman (Ed.), *Encyclopedia of behavioral medicine* (pp. 905–907). Springer International. https://doi.org/10.1007/978-3-030-39903-0_402

Morimoto, Y., Imamura, A., Yamamoto, N., Kanegae, S., Ozawa, H., & Iwanaga, R. (2021). Atypical sensory characteristics in autism spectrum disorders. In A. M. Grabrucker (Ed.), *Autism spectrum disorders* (pp. 55–66). https://www.ncbi.nlm.nih.gov/books/NBK573615/

Morley, D., Till, K., Ogilvie, P., & Turner, G. (2015). Influences of gender and socioeconomic status on the motor proficiency of children in the UK. *Human Movement Science*, *44*, 150–156. https://doi.org/10.1016/j.humov.2015.08.022

Morley, J. E. (2016). *Protein-energy undernutrition (PEU). Merck Manual*. http://www.merckmanuals.com/professional/nutritional-disorders/undernutrition/protein-energy-undernutrition-peu

Morneau-Vaillancourt, G., Dionne, G., Brendgen, M., Vitaro, F., Feng, B., Henry, J., Forget-Dubois, N., Tremblay, R., & Boivin, M. (2019). The genetic and environmental etiology of shyness through childhood. *Behavior Genetics*, *49*(4), 376–385. https://doi.org/10.1007/s10519-019-09955-w

Morokuma, S., Fukushima, K., Kawai, N., Tomonaga, M., Satoh, S., & Nakano, H. (2004). Fetal habituation correlates with functional brain development. *Behavioural Brain Research*, *153*(2), 459–463. https://doi.org/10.1016/j.bbr.2004.01.002

Morris, A. R., Turner, A., Gilbertson, C. H., Corner, G., Mendez, A. J., & Saxbe, D. E. (2021). Physical touch during father-infant interactions is associated with paternal oxytocin levels. *Infant Behavior and Development*, *64*, 101613. https://doi.org/10.1016/j.infbeh.2021.101613

Morris, A. S., Squeglia, L. M., Jacobus, J., & Silk, J. S. (2018). Adolescent brain development: Implications for understanding risk and resilience processes through neuroimaging research. *Journal of Research on Adolescence*, *28*(1), 4–9. https://doi.org/10.1111/jora.12379

Morris, G., Baker-Ward, L., & Bauer, P. J. (2010). What remains of that day: The survival of children's autobiographical memories across time. *Applied Cognitive Psychology*, *24*(4), 527–544. https://doi.org/10.1002/acp.1567

Morris, L. A., Tishelman, A. C., Kremen, J., & Ross, R. A. (2020). Depression in Turner syndrome: A systematic review. *Archives of Sexual Behavior*, *49*(2), 769–786. https://doi.org/10.1007/s10508-019-01549-1

Morris, T., Gomez, A., Naiman-Sessions, M., & Morton, C. H. (2018). Paradox lost on the U.S.-Mexico border: U.S. Latinas and cesarean rates. *BMC Pregnancy and Childbirth*, *18*(1), 82. https://doi.org/10.1186/s12884-018-1701-9

Morrison, M., & Drake, B. (2023). Foster children in care due to parental incarceration: A national longitudinal study. *Children and Youth Services Review*, *144*, 106708. https://doi.org/10.1016/j.childyouth.2022.106708

Moses, L. J., Coon, J. A., & Wusinich, N. (2000). Young children's understanding of desire formation. *Developmental Psychology*, *36*(1), 77–90. https://doi.org/10.1037/0012-1649.36.1.77

Moses-Payne, M. E., Habicht, J., Bowler, A., Steinbeis, N., & Hauser, T. U. (2021). I know better! Emerging metacognition allows adolescents to ignore false advice. *Developmental Science*, *24*(5), e13101. https://doi.org/10.1111/desc.13101

Mosher, S. W. (2006). China's one-child policy: Twenty-five years later. *Human Life Review*, *32*(1), 76–101.

Moshman, D. (2021). Adolescent reasoning and rationality. In D. Fasko & F. Fair (Eds.), *Critical thinking and reasoning* (pp. 99–113). Brill. https://doi.org/10.1163/9789004444591_007

Moslimani, M. (2022). *Around four-in-ten Latinos in U.S. worry that they or someone close to them could be deported*. Pew Research Center. https://www.pewresearch.org/fact-tank/2022/02/14/around-four-in-ten-latinos-in-u-s-worry-that-they-or-someone-close-to-them-could-be-deported/

Moulin-Stożek, D., & James, M. W. (2022). Religion and social development in childhood. In *The Wiley-Blackwell handbook of childhood social development* (pp. 405–421). John Wiley & Sons. https://doi.org/10.1002/9781119679028.ch22

Movalled, K., Sani, A., Nikniaz, L., & Ghojazadeh, M. (2023). The impact of sound stimulations during pregnancy on fetal learning: A systematic review. *BMC Pediatrics*, *23*(1), 183. https://doi.org/10.1186/s12887-023-03990-7

Movement Advancement Project. (2018). *Foster and adoption laws*. http://www.lgbtmap.org/equality-maps/foster_and_adoption_laws

Mowery, T. M., Kotak, V. C., & Sanes, D. H. (2016). The onset of visual experience gates auditory cortex critical periods. *Nature Communications*, *7*, 10416. https://doi.org/10.1038/ncomms10416

Mpofu, E., & Vijver, F. J. R. van de. (2000). Taxonomic structure in early to middle childhood: A longitudinal study with Zimbabwean schoolchildren. *International Journal of Behavioral Development*, *24*(2), 204–212. https://doi.org/10.1080/016502500383331

Mrick, S. E., & Mrtorell, G. A. (2011). Sticks and stones may break my bones: Protective factors for the effects of perceived discrimination on social competence in adolescence. *Personal Relationships*, *18*(3), 487–501. https://doi.org/10.1111/j.1475-6811.2010.01320.x

Mu, S., Wu, H., Zhang, J., & Chang, C. (2022). Structural brain changes and associated symptoms of ADHD subtypes in children. *Cerebral Cortex*, *32*(6), 1152–1158. https://doi.org/10.1093/cercor/bhab276

Mueller, I., Shakiba, N., Brown, M. A., Crowel, S. E., & Conradt, E. (2021). Epigenetic effects of prenatal stress. In A. Wazana, E. Székely, & T. F. Oberlander (Eds.), *Prenatal stress and child development*. Springer. https://doi.org/10.1007/978-3-030-60159-1_5

Mueller, I., & Tronick, E. (2019). Early life exposure to violence: Developmental consequences on brain and behavior. *Frontiers in Behavioral Neuroscience*, *13*, 156. https://doi.org/10.3389/fnbeh.2019.00156

Mueller, V., & Sepulveda, A. (2014). Parental perception of a baby sign workshop on stress and parent–child interaction. *Early Child Development and Care*, *184*(3), 450–468. https://doi.org/10.1080/03004430.2013.797899

Muenks, K., Wigfield, A., & Eccles, J. S. (2018). I can do this! The development and calibration of children's expectations for success and competence beliefs.

Developmental Review, 48, 24–39. https://doi.org/10.1016/j.dr.2018.04.001

Muennig, P., Robertson, D., Johnson, G., Campbell, F., Pungello, E. P., & Neidell, M. (2011). The effect of an early education program on adult health: The Carolina Abecedarian Project randomized controlled trial. American Journal of Public Health, 101(3), 512–516. https://doi.org/10.2105/AJPH.2010.200063

Muenssinger, J., Matuz, T., Schleger, F., Kiefer-Schmidt, I., Goelz, R., Wacker-Gussmann, A., Birbaumer, N., & Preissl, H. (2013). Auditory habituation in the fetus and neonate: An fMEG study. Developmental Science, 16(2), 287–295. https://doi.org/10.1111/desc.12025

Muentner, L., Shlafer, R. J., Heard-Garris, N., & Jackson, D. B. (2023). Parental incarceration in the United States: 2016–2021. Pediatrics, 152(6), e2023062420. https://doi.org/10.1542/peds.2023-062420

Mulder, H., Oudgenoeg-Paz, O., Verhagen, J., van der Ham, I. J. M., & Van der Stigchel, S. (2022). Infant walking experience is related to the development of selective attention. Journal of Experimental Child Psychology, 220, 105425. https://doi.org/10.1016/j.jecp.2022.105425

Mulholland, E., Dahlberg, D., & McDowell, L. (2020). A two-front war: Exploring military families' battle with parental deployment. Journal of Pediatric Nursing, 54, 34–41. https://doi.org/10.1016/j.pedn.2020.05.019

Müller-Oehring, E. M., Kwon, D., Nagel, B. J., Sullivan, E. V., Chu, W., Rohlfing, T., Prouty, D., Nichols, B. N., Poline, J.-B., Tapert, S. F., Brown, S. A., Cummins, K., Brumback, T., Colrain, I. M., Baker, F. C., De Bellis, M. D., Voyvodic, J. T., Clark, D. B., Pfefferbaum, A., & Pohl, K. M. (2018). Influences of age, sex, and moderate alcohol drinking on the intrinsic functional architecture of adolescent brains. Cerebral Cortex, 28(3), 1049–1063. https://doi.org/10.1093/cercor/bhx014

Mulligan, S., Douglas, S., & Armstrong, C. (2021). Characteristics of idiopathic sensory processing disorder in young children. Frontiers in Integrative Neuroscience, 15, 647928. https://doi.org/10.3389/fnint.2021.647928

Mulvey, N., & Jenkins, L. (2021). Language skills as predictors of social skills and behaviors in preschool children. Contemporary School Psychology, 25(4), 503–514. https://doi.org/10.1007/s40688-020-00281-1

Mulvihill, A., Matthews, N., Dux, P. E., & Carroll, A. (2023). Task difficulty and private speech in typically developing and at-risk preschool children. Journal of Child Language, 50(2), 464–491. https://doi.org/10.1017/S0305000921000945

Mummert, A., Schoen, M., & Lampl, M. (2018). Growth and life course health development. In N. Halfon, C. B. Forrest, R. M. Lerner, & E. M. Faustman (Eds.), Handbook of life course health development (pp. 405–429). Springer International. https://doi.org/10.1007/978-3-319-47143-3_17

Muncer, G., Higham, P. A., Gosling, C. J., Cortese, S., Wood-Downie, H., & Hadwin, J. A. (2021). A meta-analysis investigating the association between metacognition and math performance in adolescence. Educational Psychology Review, 34, 301–334. https://doi.org/10.1007/s10648-021-09620-x

Murnan, A. W., Keim, S. A., Yeates, K. O., Boone, K. M., Sheppard, K. W., & Klebanoff, M. A. (2021). Behavioral and cognitive differences in early childhood related to prenatal marijuana exposure. Journal of Applied Developmental Psychology, 77, 101348. https://doi.org/10.1016/j.appdev.2021.101348

Murray, J. S. (2019). War and conflict: Addressing the psychosocial needs of child refugees. Journal of Early Childhood Teacher Education, 40(1), 3–18. https://doi.org/10.1080/10901027.2019.1569184

Murray, P. G., Dattani, M. T., & Clayton, P. E. (2016). Controversies in the diagnosis and management of growth hormone deficiency in childhood and adolescence. Archives of Disease in Childhood, 101(1), 96–100. https://doi.org/10.1136/archdischild-2014-307228

Murray-Close, D., Nelson, D. A., Ostrov, J. M., Casas, J. F., & Crick, N. R. (2016). Relational aggression: A developmental psychopathology perspective. In D. Cicchetti (Ed.), Developmental psychopathology (pp. 1–63). John Wiley & Sons. https://doi.org/10.1002/9781119125556.devpsy413

Murry, V. M., Brody, G. H., Simons, R. L., Cutrona, C. E., & Gibbons, F. X. (2008). Disentangling ethnicity and context as predictors of parenting within rural African American families. Applied Developmental Science, 12(4), 202–210. https://doi.org/10.1080/10888690802388144

Murthy, V. H. (2017). E-cigarette use among youth and young adults. JAMA Pediatrics, 171(3), 209–210. https://doi.org/10.1001/jamapediatrics.2016.4662

Myers, N. A., & Perlmutter, M. (2014). Memory in the years from two to five. In P. A. Ornstein (Ed.), Memory development in children (pp. 191–218). Psychology Press.

Myrhaug, H. T., Brurberg, K. G., Hov, L., & Markestad, T. (2019). Survival and impairment of extremely premature infants: A meta-analysis. Pediatrics, 143(2), 20180933. https://doi.org/10.1542/peds.2018-0933

Nabors, L. (2022). Resilience in children and families. In L. Nabors (Ed.), Resilient children (pp. 7–21). Springer. https://doi.org/10.1007/978-3-030-81728-2_2

Nagata, J. M., Cortez, C. A., Dooley, E. E., Iyer, P., Ganson, K. T., & Pettee Gabriel, K. (2022). Moderate-to-vigorous intensity physical activity among adolescents in the USA during the COVID-19 pandemic. Preventive Medicine Reports, 25, 101685. https://doi.org/10.1016/j.pmedr.2021.101685

Nagata, J. M., Ganson, K. T., & Austin, S. B. (2020). Emerging trends in eating disorders among sexual and gender minorities. Current Opinion in Psychiatry, 33(6). https://doi.org/10.1097/YCO.0000000000000645

Nagata, J. M., Trompeter, N., Singh, G., Ganson, K. T., Testa, A., Jackson, D. B., Assari, S., Murray, S. B., Bibbins-Domingo, K., & Baker, F. C. (2022). Social epidemiology of early adolescent cyberbullying in the United States. Academic Pediatrics, 22(8), 1287–1293. https://doi.org/10.1016/j.acap.2022.07.003

Nakano, T., Watanabe, H., Homae, F., & Taga, G. (2009). Prefrontal cortical involvement in young infants' analysis of novelty. Cerebral Cortex, 19(2), 455–463. https://doi.org/10.1093/cercor/bhn096

Nallet, C., & Gervain, J. (2021). Neurodevelopmental preparedness for language in the neonatal brain. Annual Review of Developmental Psychology, 3(1), 41–58. https://doi.org/10.1146/annurev-devpsych-050620-025732

Náñez, J. E., Sr, & Yonas, A. (1994). Effects of luminance and texture motion on infant defensive reactions to optical collision. Infant Behavior and Development, 17, 165–174.

Narita, Z., DeVylder, J., Yamasaki, S., Ando, S., Endo, K., Miyashita, M., Yamaguchi, S., Usami, S., Stanyon, D., Knowles, G., Hiraiwa-Hasegawa, M., Furukawa, T. A., Kasai, K., & Nishida, A. (2024). Uncovering associations between gender nonconformity, psychosocial factors, and mental health in adolescents: A birth cohort study. Psychological Medicine, 54(5), 921–930. https://doi.org/10.1017/S0033291723002623

Nasir, N. S., McKinney de Royston, M., O'Connor, K., & Wischnia, S. (2017). Knowing about racial stereotypes versus believing them. Urban Education, 52(4), 491–524. https://doi.org/10.1177/0042085916672290

Nasiri, S., Dolatian, M., Tehrani, F. R., Majd, H. A., Bagheri, A., & Malekifar, P. (2020). Factors related to the age at menarche in Iran: A systematic review and meta-analysis. *International Journal of Pediatrics, 8*(9), 12091–12104. https://doi.org/10.22038/ijp.2020.49222.3939

Natale, V., & Rajagopalan, A. (2014). Worldwide variation in human growth and the World Health Organization growth standards: A systematic review. *BMJ Open, 4*(1), e003735. https://doi.org/10.1136/bmjopen-2013-003735

National Association for Down Syndrome. (2020). *Facts about Down syndrome*. https://www.nads.org/resources/facts-about-down-syndrome/

National Association of College and Employers. (2022). *The attributes employers want to see on college students' resumes*. https://www.naceweb.org/about-us/press/the-attributes-employers-want-to-see-on-college-students-resumes/

National Center for Education Statistics. (2024). *Table 318.10. Degrees conferred by postsecondary institutions, by level of degree and sex of student: Selected academic years, 1869–70 through 2031–32*. https://nces.ed.gov/programs/digest/d22/tables/dt22_318.10.asp?current=yes

National Center for Health Statistics. (2015). *National marriage and divorce rate trends*. National Center for Health Statistics.

National Center for Health Statistics. (2022). *Leading causes of death and number of deaths, by age: United States, 1980 and 2019*. Health, United States. 2020

National Center for Health Statistics. (2024, March 13). *FastStats: Marriage and divorce*. https://www.cdc.gov/nchs/fastats/marriage-divorce.htm

National Center for Hearing Assessment and Management. (2019). *Early hearing detection and intervention components*. https://www.infanthearing.org/index.html

National Coalition for Women and Girls in Education. (2022). *Title IX At 50: A Report by the National Coalition for Women and Girls in Education*. https://ncwge.org/index.html

National Institute of Mental Health. (2019). *Major depression*. https://www.nimh.nih.gov/health/statistics/major-depression.shtml

National Middle School Association. (2003). *This we believe: Successful schools for young adolescents*.

National Science Foundation. (2018). *Science and Engineering Indicators*.

Natsuaki, M. N., Shaw, D. S., Neiderhiser, J. M., Ganiban, J. M., Harold, G. T., Reiss, D., & Leve, L. D. (2014). Raised by depressed parents: Is it an environmental risk? *Clinical Child and Family Psychology Review, 17*(4), 357–367. https://doi.org/10.1007/s10567-014-0169-z

Natu, V. S., Rosenke, M., Wu, H., Querdasi, F. R., Kular, H., Lopez-Alvarez, N., Grotheer, M., Berman, S., Mezer, A. A., & Grill-Spector, K. (2021). Infants' cortex undergoes microstructural growth coupled with myelination during development. *Communications Biology, 4*(1), 1191. https://doi.org/10.1038/s42003-021-02706-w

Natu, V. S., Rosenke, M., Wu, H., Querdasi, F. R., Kular, H., Lopez-Alvarez, N., Grotheer, M., Berman, S., Mezer, A. A., & Grill-Spector, K. (2021). Infants' cortex undergoes microstructural growth coupled with myelination during development. *Communications Biology, 4*, 1191. https://doi.org/10.1038/s42003-021-02706-w

Nazzari, S., Fearon, P., Rice, F., Dottori, N., Ciceri, F., Molteni, M., & Frigerio, A. (2019). Beyond the HPA-axis: Exploring maternal prenatal influences on birth outcomes and stress reactivity. *Psychoneuroendocrinology, 101*, 253–262. https://doi.org/10.1016/j.psyneuen.2018.11.018

NCD Risk Factor Collaboration. (2016). A century of trends in adult human height. *eLife, 5*, e13410. https://doi.org/10.7554/eLife.13410

Ncube, C. N., Enquobahrie, D. A., Albert, S. M., Herrick, A. L., & Burke, J. G. (2016). Association of neighborhood context with offspring risk of preterm birth and low birthweight: A systematic review and meta-analysis of population-based studies. *Social Science & Medicine, 153*, 156–164. https://doi.org/10.1016/j.socscimed.2016.02.014

Neff, E. P. (2019). CRISPR goes prenatal. *Lab Animal, 48*(6), 164. https://doi.org/10.1038/s41684-019-0319-5

Neisser, U. (1993). *The perceived self: Ecological and interpersonal sources of self-knowledge*. Cambridge University Press.

Neisser, U., Boodoo, G., Bouchard, T. J., Jr, Boykin., W, A., Brody, N., Ceci, S. J., Halpern, D. F., Loehlin, J. C., Perloff, R., Sternberg, R. J., & Urbina, S. (1996). Intelligence: Knowns and unknowns. *American Psychologist, 51*(2), 77–101. https://doi.org/10.1037/0003-066X.51.2.77

Nellore, J., Tippabathani, J. K., Narayan, A. S., Sunkar, S., Nachiyar, C. V., Renugadevi, K., & Namasivayam, S. K. R. (2022). Early life nutrition, epigenetics, and programming of later life. In *Handbook of nutraceuticals and natural products* (pp. 301–362). John Wiley & Sons. https://doi.org/10.1002/9781119746843.ch15

Nelson, C. A., & Gabard-Durnam, L. J. (2020). Early adversity and critical periods: Neurodevelopmental consequences of violating the expectable environment. *Trends in Neurosciences, 43*(3), 133–143. https://doi.org/10.1016/j.tins.2020.01.002

Nelson, C. A., Sullivan, E., & Engelstad, A.-M. (2024). Annual research review: Early intervention viewed through the lens of developmental neuroscience. *Journal of Child Psychology and Psychiatry*. https://onlinelibrary.wiley.com/doi/abs/10.1111/jcpp.13858

Nelson, C. A., Zeanah, C. H., & Fox, N. A. (2019). How early experience shapes human development: The case of psychosocial deprivation. *Neural Plasticity, 1676285*. https://doi.org/10.1155/2019/1676285 *2019*

Nelson, L. H., White, K. R., & Grewe, J. (2012). Evidence for website claims about the benefits of teaching sign language to infants and toddlers with normal hearing. *Infant and Child Development, 21*(5), 474–502. https://doi.org/10.1002/icd.1748

Nelson, R. M., & DeBacker, T. K. (2008). Achievement motivation in adolescents: The role of peer climate and best friends. *Journal of Experimental Education, 76*(2), 170–189. https://doi.org/10.3200/JEXE.76.2.170-190

Nelson, S. C., Syed, M., Tran, A. G. T. T., Hu, A. W., & Lee, R. M. (2018). Pathways to ethnic-racial identity development and psychological adjustment: The differential associations of cultural socialization by parents and peers. *Developmental Psychology, 54*(11), 2166–2180. https://doi.org/10.1037/dev0000597

Nencheva, M. L., & Lew-Williams, C. (2022). Understanding why infant-directed speech supports learning: A dynamic attention perspective. *Developmental Review, 66*, 101047. https://doi.org/10.1016/j.dr.2022.101047

Nese, R. N. T., Horner, R. H., Dickey, C. R., Stiller, B., & Tomlanovich, A. (2014). Decreasing bullying behaviors in middle school: Expect respect. *School Psychology Quarterly, 29*(3), 272–286. https://doi.org/10.1037/spq0000070

Neshat, H., Jebreili, M., Seyyedrasouli, A., Ghojazade, M., Hosseini, M. B., & Hamishehkar, H. (2016). Effects of breast milk and vanilla odors on premature neonate's heart rate and blood oxygen saturation during and after venipuncture. *Pediatrics &*

Neonatology, 57(3), 225–231. https://doi.org/10.1016/j.pedneo.2015.09.004

Nesi, J., Choukas-Bradley, S., & Prinstein, M. J. (2018). Transformation of adolescent peer relations in the social media context: Part 2—Application to peer group processes and future directions for research. Clinical Child and Family Psychology Review, 21(3), 295–319. https://doi.org/10.1007/s10567-018-0262-9

Nesi, J., Choukas-Bradley, S., & Prinstein, M. J. (2018). Transformation of adolescent peer relations in the social media context: Part 1-A theoretical framework and application to dyadic peer relationships. Clinical Child and Family Psychology Review, 21(3), 267–294. https://doi.org/10.1007/s10567-018-0261-x

Ness, I. J. (2023). Zone of proximal development. In V. P. Glăveanu (Ed.), The Palgrave encyclopedia of the possible (pp. 1781–1786). Springer International. https://doi.org/10.1007/978-3-030-90913-0_60

Neubauer, A. C., & Fink, A. (2009). Intelligence and neural efficiency. Neuroscience & Biobehavioral Reviews, 33(7), 1004–1023. https://doi.org/10.1016/j.neubiorev.2009.04.001

Neuburger, S., Ruthsatz, V., Jansen, P., & Quaiser-Pohl, C. (2015). Can girls think spatially? Influence of implicit gender stereotype activation and rotational axis on fourth graders' mental-rotation performance. Learning and Individual Differences, 37, 169–175. https://doi.org/10.1016/j.lindif.2014.09.003

Neveu, A., Gangopadhyay, I., Ellis Weismer, S., & Kaushanskaya, M. (2022). Immersion in dual-language programs does not impede children's native language processing. International Journal of Bilingualism, 27(5), 815–841. https://doi.org/10.1177/13670069221122679

Neville, R. D., Lakes, K. D., Hopkins, W. G., Tarantino, G., Draper, C. E., Beck, R., & Madigan, S. (2022). Global changes in child and adolescent physical activity during the COVID-19 Pandemic: A systematic review and meta-analysis. JAMA Pediatrics, 176(9), 886–894. https://doi.org/10.1001/jamapediatrics.2022.2313

Newcombe, N., & Huttenlocher, J. (1992). Children's early ability to solve perspective-taking problems. Developmental Psychology, 28, 635–643. https://doi.org/10.1037/0012-1649.28.4.635

Newcombe, N. S. (2020). The puzzle of spatial sex differences: Current status and prerequisites to solutions. Child Development Perspectives, 14(4), 251–257. https://doi.org/10.1111/cdep.12389

Newell, B. R., & Shanks, D. R. (2014). Unconscious influences on decision making: A critical review. Behavioral and Brain Sciences, 37(1), 1–19. https://doi.org/10.1017/S0140525X12003214

Newland, R. P., Parade, S. H., Dickstein, S., & Seifer, R. (2016). The association between maternal depression and sensitivity: Child-directed effects on parenting during infancy. Infant Behavior and Development, 45, 47–50. https://doi.org/10.1016/j.infbeh.2016.09.001

Newton, E., & Jenvey, V. (2011). Play and theory of mind: Associations with social competence in young children. Early Child Development & Care, 181(6), 761–773. https://doi.org/10.1080/03004430.2010.486898

Newton, E. K., Laible, D., Carlo, G., Steele, J. S., & McGinley, M. (2014). Do sensitive parents foster kind children, or vice versa? Bidirectional influences between children's prosocial behavior and parental sensitivity. Developmental Psychology, 50(6), 1808–1816. https://doi.org/10.1037/a0036495

Ng, K., Cooper, J., McHale, F., Clifford, J., & Woods, C. (2020). Barriers and facilitators to changes in adolescent physical activity during COVID-19. BMJ Open Sport & Exercise Medicine, 6(1), e000919. https://doi.org/10.1136/bmjsem-2020-000919

Nguyen, T., Li, G. E., Chen, H., Cranfield, C. G., McGrath, K. C., & Gorrie, C. A. (2018). Maternal e-cigarette exposure results in cognitive and epigenetic alterations in offspring in a mouse model. Chemical Research in Toxicology, 31(7), 601–611. https://doi.org/10.1021/acs.chemrestox.8b00084

Nguyen, V. H., & Harley, K. G. (2022). Prenatal cannabis use and infant birth outcomes in the pregnancy risk assessment monitoring system. Journal of Pediatrics, 240, 87–93. https://doi.org/10.1016/j.jpeds.2021.08.088

Nguyen-Louie, T. T., Brumback, T., Worley, M. J., Colrain, I. M., Matt, G. E., Squeglia, L. M., & Tapert, S. F. (2018). Effects of sleep on substance use in adolescents: A longitudinal perspective. Addiction Biology, 23(2), 750–760. https://doi.org/10.1111/adb.12519

Nicoladis, E., & Laurent, A. (2020). When knowing only one word for "car" leads to weak application of mutual exclusivity. Cognition, 196, 104087. https://doi.org/10.1016/j.cognition.2019.104087

Nicolaides, N. C., Kanaka-Gantenbein, C., & Pervanidou, P. (2024). Developmental neuroendocrinology of early-life stress: Impact on child development and behavior. Current Neuropharmacology, 22(3), 461–474. https://doi.org/10.2174/1570159X21666230810162344

Niebaum, J., & Munakata, Y. (2020). Deciding what to do: Developments in children's spontaneous monitoring of cognitive demands. Child Development Perspectives, 14(4), 202–207. https://doi.org/10.1111/cdep.12383

Nielsen, A. N., Kaplan, S., Meyer, D., Alexopoulos, D., Kenley, J. K., Smyser, T. A., Wakschlag, L. S., Norton, E. S., Raghuraman, N., Warner, B. B., Shimony, J. S., Luby, J. L., Neil, J. J., Petersen, S. E., Barch, D. M., Rogers, C. E., Sylvester, C. M., & Smyser, C. D. (2023). Maturation of large-scale brain systems over the first month of life. Cerebral Cortex, 33(6), 2788–2803. https://doi.org/10.1093/cercor/bhac242

Nielson, M. G., Martin, C. L., England, D. E., Hanish, L. D., Santos, C. E., Delay, D., Updegraff, K. A., & Rogers, A. A. (2024). Patterns of gender development across intersections of age, gender, and ethnicity-race. Archives of Sexual Behavior, 53, 1793–1812. https://doi.org/10.1007/s10508-024-02824-6

Nielson, M. G., Schroeder, K. M., Martin, C. L., & Cook, R. E. (2020). Investigating the relation between gender typicality and pressure to conform to gender norms. Sex Roles, 83(9), 523–535. https://doi.org/10.1007/s11199-020-01136-y

Nieto, M., Ros, L., Ricarte, J. J., & Latorre, J. M. (2018). The role of executive functions in accessing specific autobiographical memories in 3- to 6-year-olds. Early Childhood Research Quarterly, 43, 23–32. https://doi.org/10.1016/j.ecresq.2017.11.004

Nigg, J. T., Sibley, M. H., Thapar, A., & Karalunas, S. L. (2020). Development of ADHD: Etiology, heterogeneity, and early life course. Annual Review of Developmental Psychology, 2(2), 559–583. https://doi.org/10.1146/annurev-devpsych-060320-093413

Nikolaus, M., & Fourtassi, A. (2023). Communicative feedback in language acquisition. New Ideas in Psychology, 68, 100985. https://doi.org/10.1016/j.newideapsych.2022.100985

Nilsen, E. S., & Bacso, S. A. (2017). Cognitive and behavioural predictors of adolescents' communicative perspective-taking and social relationships. Journal of Adolescence, 56, 52–63. https://doi.org/10.1016/j.adolescence.2017.01.004

Ninio, A. (2014). Pragmatic development. In P. J. Brooks & V. Kempe (Eds.), Encyclopedia of language development. SAGE. https://doi.org/10.4135/9781483346441.n153

Nisbett, R. E., Aronson, J., Blair, C., Dickens, W., Flynn, J., Halpern, D. F., & Turkheimer, E. (2013). Intelligence: New findings and theoretical developments. *American Psychologist*, *67*(2), 130–159. https://doi.org/10.1037/a0026699

Nishijima, K., Yoned., M., Hirai, T., Takakuwa, K., & Enomoto, T. (2019). Biology of the vernix caseosa: A review. *Journal of Obstetrics and Gynaecology Research*, *45*(11), 2145–2149. https://doi.org/10.1111/jog.14103

Nishina, A., Lewis, J. A., Bellmore, A., & Witkow, M. R. (2019). Ethnic diversity and inclusive school environments. *Educational Psychologist*, *54*(4), 306–321. https://doi.org/10.1080/00461520.2019.1633923

Nishiyori, R., Bisconti, S., Meehan, S. K., & Ulrich, B. D. (2016). Developmental changes in motor cortex activity as infants develop functional motor skills. *Developmental Psychobiology*, *58*(6), 773–783. https://doi.org/10.1002/dev.21418

Nixon, E., Hadfield, K., Nixon, E., & Hadfield, K. (2016). Blended families. In C. L. Shehan (Ed.), *Encyclopedia of family studies* (pp. 1–5). John Wiley & Sons. https://doi.org/10.1002/9781119085621.wbefs207

Nobes, G., & Pawson, C. (2003). Children's understanding of social rules and social status. *Merrill-Palmer Quarterly*, *49*, 77–99.

Noble, K. G., & Giebler, M. A. (2020). The neuroscience of socioeconomic inequality. *Current Opinion in Behavioral Sciences*, *36*, 23–28. https://doi.org/10.1016/j.cobeha.2020.05.007

Noble, K. G., Houston, S. M., Brito, N. H., Bartsch, H., Kan, E., Kuperman, J. M., Akshoomoff, N., Amaral, D. G., Bloss, C. S., Libiger, O., Schork, N. J., Murray, S. S., Casey, B. J., Chang, L., Ernst, T. M., Frazier, J. A., Gruen, J. R., Kenned., D. N., Van Zijl, P., & &#hillip1; Sowell, E. R. (2015). Family income, parental education and brain structure in children and adolescents. *Nature Neuroscience*, *18*(5), 773–778. https://doi.org/10.1038/nn.3983

Nocentini, A., Fiorentini, G., Di Paola, L., & Menesini, E. (2019). Parents, family characteristics and bullying behavior: A systematic review. *Aggression and Violent Behavior*, *45*, 41–50. https://doi.org/10.1016/j.avb.2018.07.010

Nogueira Avelar e, Silva., R., van de Bongardt, D, Baams, L., & Raat, H. (2018). Bidirectional associations between adolescents' sexual behaviors and psychological well-being. *Journal of Adolescent Health*, *62*(1), 63–71. https://doi.org/10.1016/j.jadohealth.2017.08.008

Noh, J. Y. (2020). Children's developing understanding of merit in a distributive justice context. *Journal of Child and Family Studies*, *29*(5), 1484–1492. https://doi.org/10.1007/s10826-019-01606-2

Nomaguchi, K., & Milkie, M. A. (2020). Parenthood and well-being: A decade in review. *Journal of Marriage and Family*, *82*(1), 198–223. https://doi.org/10.1111/jomf.12646

Nomaguchi, K., & Milkie, M. A. (2023). Trends in the parenthood gap in health and well-being among U.S. women from 1996 to 2018. *Socius*, *9*, 23780231221145067. https://doi.org/10.1177/23780231221145067

Nook, E. C., Vidal Bustamante, C. M., Cho, H. Y., & Somerville, L. H. (2020). Use of linguistic distancing and cognitive reappraisal strategies during emotion regulation in children, adolescents, and young adults. *Emotion*, *20*, 525–540. https://doi.org/10.1037/emo0000570

Norbom, L. B., Ferschmann, L., Parker, N., Agartz, I., Andreassen, O. A., Paus, T., Westlye, L. T., & Tamnes, C. K. (2021). New insights into the dynamic development of the cerebral cortex in childhood and adolescence: Integrating macro- and microstructural MRI findings. *Progress in Neurobiology*, *204*, 102109. https://doi.org/10.1016/j.pneurobio.2021.102109

Norholt, H. (2020). Revisiting the roots of attachment: A review of the biological and psychological effects of maternal skin-to-skin contact and carrying of full-term infants. *Infant Behavior and Development*, *60*, 101441. https://doi.org/10.1016/j.infbeh.2020.101441

Norris, C. J. (2021). The negativity bias, revisited: Evidence from neuroscience measures and an individual differences approach. *Social Neuroscience*, *16*(1), 68–82. https://doi.org/10.1080/17470919.2019.1696225

Nowicki, P., Kemppainen, J., Maskill, L., & Cassidy, J. (2019). The role of obesity in pediatric orthopedics. *JAAOS: Global Research and Reviews*, *3*(5), e036. https://doi.org/10.5435/jaaosglobal-d-19-00036

Nugent, A. C., Ballard, E. D., Park, L. T., & Zarate, C. A. (2019). Research on the pathophysiology, treatment, and prevention of suicide: Practical and ethical issues. *BMC Psychiatry*, *19*(1), 1–12. https://doi.org/10.1186/S12888-019-2301-6

Nugent, B. M., & McCarthy, M. M. (2011). Epigenetic underpinnings of developmental sex differences in the brain. *Neuroendocrinology*, *93*(3), 150–158. https://doi.org/10.1159/000325264

Nugent, J. K. (2013). The Competent Newborn and the Neonatal Behavioral Assessment Scale: T. Berry Brazelton's legacy. *Journal of Child and Adolescent Psychiatric Nursing*, *26*(3), 173–179. https://doi.org/10.1111/jcap.12043

Nuñez, M., Beal, S. J., & Jacquez, F. (2022). Resilience factors in youth transitioning out of foster care: A systematic review. *Psychological Trauma: Theory, Research, Practice, and Policy*, *14*, S72–S81. https://doi.org/10.1037/tra0001096

Nuttall, A. K., Valentino, K., Comas, M., McNeill, A. T., & Stey, P. C. (2014). Autobiographical memory specificity among preschool-aged children. *Developmental Psychology*, *50*, 1963–1972. https://doi.org/10.1037/a0036988

Nygaard, E., Slinning, K., Moe, V., Due-Tønnessen, P., Fjell, A., & Walhovd, K. B. (2018). Neuroanatomical characteristics of youths with prenatal opioid and poly-drug exposure. *Neurotoxicology and Teratology*, *68*, 13–26. https://doi.org/10.1016/j.ntt.2018.04.004

Nyiti, R. M. (1982). The validity of "cultural differences explanations" for cross-cultural variation in the rate of Piagetian cognitive development. In H. W. Stevenson & D. A. Wagner (Eds.), *Cultural perspectives on child development* (pp. 146–166). W. H. Freeman.

Oakes, L. M. (2010). Using habituation of looking time to assess mental processes in infancy. *Journal of Cognition & Development*, *11*(3), 255–268. https://doi.org/10.1080/15248371003699977

Oakes, L. M., & Rakison, D. H. (2020). *Developmental cascades: Building the infant mind*. Oxford University Press.

Obeidallah, D. A., Brennan, R. T., Brooks-Gunn, J., & Earls, F. (2004). Links between pubertal timing and neighborhood contexts: Implications for girls' violent behavior. *Journal of the American Academy of Child and Adolescent Psychiatry*, *43*(12), 1460–1468.

Oberauer, K. (2019). Working memory and attention – A conceptual analysis and review. *Journal of Cognition*, *2*(1), 1–23. https://doi.org/10.5334/joc.58

Ochs, E., & Schieffein, B. (1984). Language acquisition and socialization: Three developmental stories and their implications. In R. A. Shweder & R. A. LeVine (Eds.), *Culture theory: Essays on mind, self, and emotion* (pp. 276–320). Cambridge University Press.

O'Connell, A. E., Guseh, S., Lapteva, L., Cummings, C. L., Wilkins-Haug, L., Chan,

J., Peranteau, W. H., Almeida-Porada, G., & Kourembanas, S. (2020). Gene and stem cell therapies for fetal care: A review. *JAMA Pediatrics*, *174*(10). https://doi.org/10.1001/jamapediatrics.2020.1519

O'Connor, K. E. (2021). Psychosocial adjustment across aggressor/victim subgroups: A systematic review and critical evaluation of theory. *Clinical Child and Family Psychology Review*, *24*(3), 500–528. https://doi.org/10.1007/s10567-021-00347-3

Oddi, K. B., Murdock, K. W., Vadnais, S., Bridgett, D. J., & Gartstein, M. A. (2013). Maternal and infant temperament characteristics as contributors to parenting stress in the first year postpartum. *Infant and Child Development*, *22*(6), 553–579. https://doi.org/10.1002/icd.1813

Odgers, C. L., & Jensen, M. R. (2020). Annual research review: Adolescent mental health in the digital age: facts, fears, and future directions. *Journal of Child Psychology and Psychiatry*, *61*(3), 336–348. https://doi.org/10.1111/jcpp.13190

Odgers, C. L., Schueller, S. M., & Ito, M. (2020). Screen time, social media use, and adolescent development. *Annual Review of Developmental Psychology*, *2*(1), 485–502. https://doi.org/10.1146/annurev-devpsych-121318-084815

Odgers, C. L., Schueller, S. M., & Ito, M. (2020). Screen time, social media use, and adolescent development. *Annual Review of Developmental Psychology*, *2*(1). https://doi.org/10.1146/annurev-devpsych-121318-084815

Odibo, A. O. (2015). Amniocentesis, chorionic villus sampling, and fetal blood sampling. In A. Milunsky & J. M. Milunsky (Eds.), *Genetic disorders and the fetus* (pp. 68–97). John Wiley & Sons. https://doi.org/10.1002/9781118981559.ch2

O'Donnell, K. J., & Meaney, M. J. (2020). Epigenetics, Development, and Psychopathology. *Annual Review of Clinical Psychology*, *16*(1), 327–350. https://doi.org/10.1146/annurev-clinpsy-050718-095530

Office for National Statistics. (2015). *What are the top causes of death by age and gender?* http://visual.ons.gov.uk/what-are-the-top-causes-of-death-by-age-and-gender/

Office of the Administration for Children & Families, & U.S. Department of Health & Human Services. (n.d.). *Trends in foster care and adoption: FY 2012–2021*. Retrieved March 23, 2023, from https://www.acf.hhs.gov/cb/report/trends-foster-care-adoption

Ogren, M., & Johnson, S. P. (2020). Factors facilitating early emotion understanding development: Contributions to individual differences. *Human Development*, *64*(3), 108–118. https://doi.org/10.1159/000511628

Ohlsson, C., Bygdell, M., Celind, J., Sondén, A., Tidblad, A., Sävendahl, L., & Kindblom, J. M. (2019). Secular trends in pubertal growth acceleration in Swedish boys born from 1947 to 1996. *JAMA Pediatrics*, *173*(9), 860–865. https://doi.org/10.1001/jamapediatrics.2019.2315

Ohta, H. (2019). Growth spurts of the bone from infancy to puberty. *Clinical Calcium*, *29*(1), 9–17. https://doi.org/clica1901917

Ojodu, J., Hulihan, M. M., Pope, S. N., & Grant, A. M. (2014). Incidence of sickle cell trait—United States, 2010. *Morbidity and Mortality Weekly Report*, *63*(49), 1155–1158.

Okagaki, L., & Sternberg, R. J. (1993). Parental beliefs and children's school performance. *Child Development*, *64*, 36–56. https://doi.org/10.1111/j.1467-8624.1993.tb02894.x

Okanda, M., Taniguchi, K., Wang, Y., & Itakura, S. (2021). Preschoolers' and adults' animism tendencies toward a humanoid robot. *Computers in Human Behavior*, *118*, 106688. https://doi.org/10.1016/j.chb.2021.106688

O'Keefe, P., & Rodgers, J. L. (2020). The Flynn effect can become embedded in tests: How cross-sectional age norms can corrupt longitudinal research. *Intelligence*, *82*, 101481. https://doi.org/10.1016/j.intell.2020.101481

Olsavsky, A. L., Berrigan, M. N., Schoppe-Sullivan, S. J., Brown, G. L., & Kamp Dush, C. M. (2020). Paternal stimulation and father-infant attachment. *Attachment and Human Development*, *22*(1), 15–26. https://doi.org/10.1080/14616734.2019.1589057

Olsavsky, A. L., Grannis, C., Bricker, J., Chelvakumar, G., Indyk, J. A., Leibowitz, S. F., Mattson, W. I., Nelson, E. E., Stanek, C. J., & Nahata, L. (2023). Associations among gender-affirming hormonal interventions, social support, and transgender adolescents' mental health. *Journal of Adolescent Health*, *72*(6), 860–868. https://doi.org/10.1016/j.jadohealth.2023.01.031

Olson, K. R. (2016). Prepubescent transgender children: What we do and do not know. *Journal of the American Academy of Child & Adolescent Psychiatry*, *55*(3), 155-156.e3. https://doi.org/10.1016/j.jaac.2015.11.015

Olson, K. R., Durwood, L., DeMeules, M., & McLaughlin, K. A. (2016). Mental health of transgender children who are supported in their identities. *Pediatrics*, *137*(3), e20153223. https://doi.org/10.1542/peds.2015-3223

Olson, K. R., Durwood, L., Horton, R., Gallagher, N. M., & Devor, A. (2022). Gender identity 5 years after social transition. *Pediatrics*, *150*(2), e2021056082. https://doi.org/10.1542/peds.2021-056082

Olson, K. R., & Enright, E. A. (2018). Do transgender children (gender) stereotype less than their peers and siblings? *Developmental Science*, *21*(4), e12606. https://doi.org/10.1111/desc.12606

Olson, K. R., & Gülgöz, S. (2018). Early findings from the TransYouth project: Gender development in transgender children. *Child Development Perspectives*, *12*(2), 93–97. https://doi.org/10.1111/cdep.12268

Olson, K. R., Key, A. C., & Eaton, N. R. (2015). Gender cognition in transgender children. *Psychological Science*, *26*(4), 467–474. https://doi.org/10.1177/0956797614568156

Olson, S. L., Lansford, J. E., Evans, E. M., Blumstein, K. P., & Ip, K. I. (2019). Parents' ethnotheories of maladaptive behavior in young children. *Child Development Perspectives*, *13*(3), 153–158. https://doi.org/10.1111/cdep.12330

Olsson, M., & Martiny, S. E. (2018). Does exposure to counterstereotypical role models influence girls' and women's gender stereotypes and career choices? A review of social psychological research. *Frontiers in Psychology*, *9*, 2264. https://doi.org/10.3389/fpsyg.2018.02264

Olweus, D. (2013). School bullying: Development and some important challenges. *Annual Review of Clinical Psychology*, *9*(1), 751–780. https://doi.org/10.1146/annurev-clinpsy-050212-185516

Olweus, D., & Limber, S. P. (2010). Bullying in school: Evaluation and dissemination of the Olweus bullying prevention program. *American Journal of Orthopsychiatry*, *80*(1), 124–134. https://doi.org/10.1111/j.1939-0025.2010.01015.x

O'Neal, C. W., & Mancini, J. A. (2021). Military families' stressful reintegration, family climate, and their adolescents' psychosocial health. *Journal of Marriage and Family*, *83*(2), 375–393. https://doi.org/10.1111/jomf.12711

Onetti, W., Fernández-García, J. C., & Castillo-Rodríguez, A. (2019). Transition to middle school: Self-concept changes. *PLoS ONE*, *14*(2), e0212640. https://doi.org/10.1371/journal.pone.0212640

Ono, Y., Zhang, X., Noah, J. A., Dravida, S., & Hirsch, J. (2022). Bidirectional connectivity between Broca's area and Wernicke's area during interactive verbal communication. *Brain Connectivity*, *12*(3), 210–222. https://doi.org/10.1089/brain.2020.0790

Opendak, M., & Sullivan, R. M. (2019). Unique infant neurobiology produces distinctive trauma processing. *Developmental Cognitive Neuroscience*, *36*, 100637. https://doi.org/10.1016/j.dcn.2019.100637

Opie, J. E., McIntosh, J. E., Esler, T. B., Duschinsky, R., George, C., Schore, A., Kothe, E. J., Tan, E. S., Greenwood, C. J., & Olsson, C. A. (2021). Early childhood attachment stability and change: A meta-analysis. *Attachment and Human Development*, *23*(6), 897–930. https://doi.org/10.1080/14616734.2020.1800769

Oppenheim, G. M., Griffin, Z., Peña, E. D., & Bedore, L. M. (2020). Longitudinal evidence for simultaneous bilingual language development with shifting language dominance, and how to explain it. *Language Learning*, *70*(S2), 20–44. https://doi.org/10.1111/lang.12398

Orben, A. (2020). Teenagers, screens and social media: A narrative review of reviews and key studies. *Social Psychiatry and Psychiatric Epidemiology*, *55*(4), 407–414. https://doi.org/10.1007/s00127-019-01825-4

Orena, A. J., Byers-Heinlein, K., & Polka, L. (2020). What do bilingual infants actually hear? Evaluating measures of language input to bilingual-learning 10-month-olds. *Developmental Science*, *23*(2), e12901. https://doi.org/10.1111/desc.12901

Orihuela, C. A., Mrug, S., Davies, S., Elliott, M. N., Tortolero Emery, S., Peskin, M. F., Reisner, S., & Schuster, M. A. (2020). Neighborhood disorder, family functioning, and risky sexual behaviors in adolescence. *Journal of Youth and Adolescence*, *49*(5), 991–1004. https://doi.org/10.1007/s10964-020-01211-3

Orkin, M., May, S., & Wolf, M. (2017). How parental support during homework contributes to helpless behaviors among struggling readers. *Reading Psychology*, *38*(5), 506–541. https://doi.org/10.1080/02702711.2017.1299822

Orth, U. (2017). The lifespan development of self-esteem. In J. Specht (Ed.), *Personality development across the lifespan* (pp. 181–195). Elsevier. https://doi.org/10.1016/B978-0-12-804674-6.00012-0

Orth, U., Dapp, L. C., Erol, R. Y., Krauss, S., & Luciano, E. C. (2020). Development of domain-specific self-evaluations: A meta-analysis of longitudinal studies. *Journal of Personality and Social Psychology*, *120*(1), 145–172. https://doi.org/10.1037/pspp0000378

Orth, U., Erol, R. Y., & Luciano, E. C. (2018). Development of self-esteem from age 4 to 94 years: A meta-analysis of longitudinal studies. *Psychological Bulletin*, *144*(10), 1045–1080. https://doi.org/10.1037/bul0000161

Orth, U., & Robins, R. W. (2019). Development of self-esteem across the lifespan. In D. P. McAdams, R. L. Shiner, & J. L. Tackett (Eds.), *Handbook of personality development* (pp. 328–344). https://psycnet.apa.org/record/2018-63285-019

Orth, U., & Robins, R. W. (2022). Is high self-esteem beneficial? Revisiting a classic question. *American Psychologist*, *77*(1), 5–17. https://doi.org/10.1037/amp0000922

Ortiz, F. A. (2020). Self-actualization in the Latino/Hispanic culture. *Journal of Humanistic Psychology*, *60*(3), 418–435. https://doi.org/10.1177/0022167817741785

Ose Askvik, E., van der Weel, F. R. (Ruud, & van der Meer, A. L. H. (2020). The importance of cursive handwriting over typewriting for learning in the classroom: A high-density EEG study of 12-year-old children and young adults. *Frontiers in Psychology*, *11*, 1810. https://doi.org/10.3389/fpsyg.2020.01810

Osgood, D. W., Ragan, D. T., Dole, J. L., & Kreager, D. A. (2022). Similarity of friends versus nonfriends in adolescence: Developmental patterns and ecological influences. *Developmental Psychology*, *58*, 1386–1401. https://doi.org/10.1037/dev0001359

O'Shaughnessy, R. (2023). Individual and cultural differences in attachment. In R. O'Shaughnessy, K. Berry, R. Dallos, & K. Bateson (Eds.), *Attachment theory* (pp. 15–34). Routledge.

Osher, D., Cantor, P., Berg, J., Steyer, L., & Rose, T. (2020). Drivers of human development: How relationships and context shape learning and development. In *The Science of Learning and Development*. Routledge.

Osher, D., Kidron, Y., Brackett, M., Dymnicki, A., Jones, S., & Weissberg, R. P. (2016). Advancing the science and practice of social and emotional learning. *Review of Research in Education*, *40*(1), 644–681. https://doi.org/10.3102/0091732X16673595

Osinubi, A., Lewis-de los, Angeles., P, C., Poitevien, P., & Topor, L. S. (2022). Are Black girls exhibiting puberty earlier? Examining implications of race-based guidelines. *Pediatrics*, *150*(2), e2021055595. https://doi.org/10.1542/peds.2021-055595

Osinubi, A(Ade)., Lewis-de los, Angeles., P, C., Poitevien, P., & Topor, L. S. (2022). Are black girls exhibiting puberty earlier? Examining implications of race-based guidelines. *Pediatrics*, *150*(2), e2021055595. https://doi.org/10.1542/peds.2021-055595

Ostatnikova, D., Lakatošová, S., Babková, J., Hodosy, J., & Celec, P. (2020). Testosterone and the brain: From cognition to autism. *Physiological Research*, *69*(Suppl 3), S403–S419.

Osterhaus, C., & Koerber, S. (2021). Childhood: A longitudinal study from age 5 to 10 years. *Child Development*, *92*(5), 1872–1888. https://doi.org/10.1111/cdev.13627

Osterman, M. J. K., Hamilton, B. E., Martin, J. A., Driscoll, A. K., & Valenzuela, C. P. (2022). Births: Final data for 2020. *National Vital Statistics Reports*, *70*(17). https://doi.org/10.15620/CDC:112078

Osterman, M. J. K., Hamilton, B. E., Martin, J. A., Driscoll, A. K., & Valenzuela, C. P. (2022). Births: Final data for 2020. *National Vital Statistics Reports*, *70*(17). https://doi.org/10.15620/cdc:112078

Osterman, M. J. K., Hamilton, B. E., Martin, J. A., Driscoll, A. K., & Valenzuela, C. P. (2023). Births: Final data for 2021. National Vital Statistics Reports: From the Centers for Disease Control and Prevention. *National Center for Health Statistics, National Vital Statistics System*, *72*(1), 1–53.

Osterman, M. J. K., Hamilton, B. E., Martin, J. A., Driscoll, A. K., & Valenzuela, C. P. (2023). Births: Final data for 2021. National Vital Statistics Reports: From the Centers for Disease Control and Prevention. *National Center for Health Statistics, National Vital Statistics System*, *72*(1), 1–53. https://doi.org/10.15620/cdc:122047

Osterman, M. J. K., Hamilton, B. E., Martin, J. A., Driscoll, A. K., & Valenzuela, C. P. (2023). Births: Final data for 2021. *National Vital Statistics Reports*, *72*(1), 1–53.

Ostrov, J. M., & Godleski, S. A. (2010). Toward an integrated gender-linked model of aggression subtypes in early and middle childhood. *Psychological Review*, *117*(1), 233–242. https://doi.org/10.1037/a0018070

O'Sullivan, A., & Monk, C. (2020). Maternal and environmental influences on perinatal and infant development. *Future of Children*, *30*(2), 11–34.

Oswald, T. K., Rumbold, A. R., Kedzior, S. G. E., & Moore, V. M. (2020). Psychological impacts of "screen time" and "green time" for children and adolescents: A systematic scoping review. *PLoS ONE*, *15*(9), e0237725.

https://doi.org/10.1371/journal.pone.0237725

Otgaar, H., Howe, M. L., Merckelbach, H., & Muris, P. (2018). Who is the better eyewitness? Adults and children. *Current Directions in Psychological Science*, 27(5), 378–385. https://doi.org/10.1177/0963721418770998

Otter, M., Campforts, B. C. M., Stumpel, C. T. R. M., Amelsvoort, T. A. M. J. van., & Drukker, M. (2023). Triple X syndrome: Psychiatric disorders and impaired social functioning as a risk factor. *European Psychiatry*, 66(1), e7. https://doi.org/10.1192/j.eurpsy.2022.2355

Otto, A. K., Jary, J. M., Sturza, J., Miller, C. A., Prohaska, N., Bravender, T., & Van Huysse, J. (2021). Medical admissions among adolescents with eating disorders during the COVID-19 pandemic. *Pediatrics*, 148(4), e2021052201. https://doi.org/10.1542/peds.2021-052201

Owen, J. P., Marco, E. J., Desai, S., Fourie, E., Harris, J., Hill, S. S., Arnett, A. B., & Mukherjee, P. (2013). Abnormal white matter microstructure in children with sensory processing disorders. *NeuroImage: Clinical*, 2, 844–853. https://doi.org/10.1016/J.NICL.2013.06.009

Owen, K., & Barnes, C. (2021). The development of categorization in early childhood: A review. *Early Child Development and Care*, 191(1), 13–20. https://doi.org/10.1080/03004430.2019.1608193

Owens, J. A., Dearth-Wesley, T., Herman, A. N., Oakes, J. M., & Whitaker, R. C. (2017). A quasi-experimental study of the impact of school start time changes on adolescent sleep. *Sleep Health*, 3(6), 437–443. https://doi.org/10.1016/j.sleh.2017.09.001

Owens, R. E. (2020). *Language development: An introduction*. Pearson.

Owotomo, O., & Maslowsky, J. (2021). Adolescent e-cigarette users at highest risk of cigarette smoking intention. *American Journal of Health Behavior*, 45(4), 711–722. https://doi.org/10.5993/AJHB.45.4.10

Owusu, P., & Obuo Addo, A. (2023). Alikoto: Mathematics instruction and cultural games in Ghana. *Cogent Education*, 10(1), 2207045. https://doi.org/10.1080/2331186X.2023.2207045

Ozen Tunay, Z., Ustunyurt, Z., & Idil, A. (2021). Causes of severe visual impairment in infants and methods of management. *Eye*, 35(4), Article 4. https://doi.org/10.1038/s41433-020-1101-z

Öztürk, R., & Güneri, S. E. (2020). Symptoms experiences and attitudes towards menstruation among adolescent girls. *Journal of Obstetrics and Gynaecology*. https://doi.org/10.1080/01443615.2020.1789962

Pace, A., Luo, R., Levine, D., Iglesias, A., Villiers, J., Golinkoff, R. M., Wilson, M. S., & Hirsh-Pasek, K. (2021). Within and across language predictors of word learning processes in dual language learners. *Child Development*, 91, 35–53. https://doi.org/10.1111/cdev.13418

Pace, C. S., Muzi, S., & Madera, F. (2022). Emotional-behavioral problems, attachment and verbal skills in late-adopted adolescents: The role of pre-adoption adversities and adoption variables. *Child Abuse and Neglect*, 13(0). https://doi.org/10.1016/j.chiabu.2021.105188

Pace, C. S., Muzi, S., & Madera, F. (2022). Emotional-behavioral problems, attachment and verbal skills in late-adopted adolescents: The role of pre-adoption adversities and adoption variables. *Child Abuse and Neglect*, 130, 105188. https://doi.org/10.1016/j.chiabu.2021.105188

Packer, M. J., & Cole, M. (2020). Culture and human development. In O. Braddick (Ed.), *Oxford research encyclopedia of psychology*. Oxford University Press. https://doi.org/10.1093/acrefore/9780190236557.013.581

Padgett, J. K., & Tremblay, P. F. (2020). Gender differences in aggression. In *The Wiley encyclopedia of personality and individual differences* (pp. 173–177). John Wiley & Sons. https://doi.org/10.1002/9781119547174.ch206

Padiath, Q. S. (2023). *Overview of genetics*. Merck Manuals Professional Edition. https://www.merckmanuals.com/professional/special-subjects/general-principles-of-medical-genetics/overview-of-genetics

Padilla-Walker, L. M., Carlo, G., & Memmott-Elison, M. K. (2018). Longitudinal change in adolescents' prosocial behavior toward strangers, friends, and family. *Journal of Research on Adolescence*, 28(3), 698–710. https://doi.org/10.1111/jora.12362

Padilla-Walker, L. M., & Christensen, K. J. (2011). Empathy and self-regulation as mediators between parenting and adolescents' prosocial behavior toward strangers, friends, and family. *Journal of Research on Adolescence*, 21(3), 545–551. https://doi.org/10.1111/j.1532-7795.2010.00695.x

Padilla-Walker, L. M., Dyer, W. J., Yorgason, J. B., Fraser, A. M., & Coyne, S. M. (2015). Adolescents' prosocial behavior toward family, friends, and strangers: A person-centered approach. *Journal of Research on Adolescence*, 25(1), 135–150. https://doi.org/10.1111/jora.12102

Padilla-Walker, L. M., & Memmott-Elison, M. K. (2020). Family and moral development. In L. A. Jensen (Ed.), *The Oxford handbook of moral development: An interdisciplinary perspective* (p. 461).

Padilla-Walker, L. M., Memmott-Elison, M. K., & Coyne, S. M. (2018). Associations between prosocial and problem behavior from early to late adolescence. *Journal of Youth and Adolescence*, 47(5), 961–975. https://doi.org/10.1007/s10964-017-0736-y

Padilla-Walker, L. M., Millett, M. A., & Memmott-Elison, M. K. (2020). Can helping others strengthen teens? Character strengths as mediators between prosocial behavior and adolescents' internalizing symptoms. *Journal of Adolescence*, 79, 70–80. https://doi.org/10.1016/j.adolescence.2020.01.001

Pagani, L. S., Bernard, J., & Fitzpatrick, C. (2023). Prospective associations between preschool exposure to violent televiewing and psychosocial and academic risks in early adolescent boys and girls. *Journal of Developmental & Behavioral Pediatrics*, 44(1), e1–e11. https://doi.org/10.1097/DBP.0000000000001135

Page, J., Cock, M. L., Murray, L., Eadie, T., Niklas, F., Scull, J., & Sparling, J. (2019). An Abecedarian approach with Aboriginal families and their young children in Australia: Playgroup participation and developmental outcomes. *International Journal of Early Childhood*, 51(2), 233–250. https://doi.org/10.1007/s13158-019-00246-3

Pages, R., Protzko, J., & Bailey, D. H. (2022). The breadth of impacts from the Abecedarian Project early intervention on cognitive skills. *Journal of Research on Educational Effectiveness*, 15(2), 243–262. https://doi.org/10.1080/19345747.2021.1969711

Paine, A. L., Perra, O., Anthony, R., & Shelton, K. H. (2021). Charting the trajectories of adopted children's emotional and behavioral problems: The impact of early adversity and postadoptive parental warmth. *Development and Psychopathology*, 33(3). https://doi.org/10.1017/S0954579420000231

Paine, A. L., Perra, O., Anthony, R., & Shelton, K. H. (2021). Charting the trajectories of adopted children's emotional and behavioral problems: The impact of early adversity and postadoptive parental warmth. *Development and Psychopathology*, 33(3), 922–936. https://doi.org/10.1017/S0954579420000231

Palacios, J., & Brodzinsky, D. (2010). Review: Adoption research: Trends, topics, outcomes. *International Journal of Behavioral Development*, 34(3), 270–284. https://doi.org/10.1177/0165025410362837

Palomero-Gallagher, N., & Amunts, K. (2022). A short review on emotion processing: A lateralized network of neuronal networks. *Brain Structure and Function*, *227*(2), 673–684. https://doi.org/10.1007/S00429-021-02331-7

Pampati, S., Andrzejewski, J., Sheremenko, G., Johns, M., Lesesne, C. A., & Rasberry, C. N. (2020). School climate among transgender high school students: An exploration of school connectedness, perceived safety, bullying, and absenteeism. *Journal of School Nursing*, *36*(4), 293–303. https://doi.org/10.1177/1059840518818259

Panagiotakopoulos, L., Chulani, V., Koyama, A., Childress, K., Forcier, M., Grimsby, G., & Greenberg, K. (2020). The effect of early puberty suppression on treatment options and outcomes in transgender patients. *Nature Reviews Urology*, *17*(11), 626–636. https://doi.org/10.1038/s41585-020-0372-2

Panchal, U., Salazar de Pablo, G., Franco, M., Moreno, C., Parellada, M., Arango, C., & Fusar-Poli, P. (2021). The impact of COVID-19 lockdown on child and adolescent mental health: Systematic review. *European Child and Adolescent Psychiatry*, *32*, 1151–1177. https://doi.org/10.1007/s00787-021-01856-w

Pandita, A., Panghal, A., Gupta, G., Verma, A., Pillai, A., Singh, A., & Naranje, K. (2018). Is kangaroo mother care effective in alleviating vaccination associated pain in early infantile period? A RCT. *Early Human Development*, *127*, 69–73. https://doi.org/10.1016/j.earlhumdev.2018.10.001

Pantell, R. H. (2017). & Committee on Psychosocial Aspects of Child and Family Health. The child witness in the courtroom. *Pediatrics*, *139*(3), e20164008. https://doi.org/10.1542/peds.2016-4008

Papadimitriou, A. (2016). The evolution of the age at menarche from prehistorical to modern times. *Journal of Pediatric and Adolescent Gynecology*, *29*(6), 527–530. https://doi.org/10.1016/j.jpag.2015.12.002

Papageorgiou, K. a., Smith, T. J., Wu, R., Johnson, M. H., Kirkham, N. Z., & Ronald, A. (2014). Individual differences in infant fixation duration relate to attention and behavioral control in childhood. *Psychological Science*, *25*(7), 1371–1379. https://doi.org/10.1177/0956797614531295

Papousek, H. (1967). Conditioning during early postnatal development. In Y. Brackbill & G. G. Thompson (Eds.), *Behavior in infancy and early childhood* (pp. 268–284). Free Press.

Pappas, K. B., Migeon, C. J., Pappas, K. B., & Migeon, C. J. (2017). Sex chromosome abnormalities. In D. N. Cooper (Ed.), *eLS* (pp. 1–9). John Wiley & Sons. https://doi.org/10.1002/9780470015902.a0005943.pub2

Paquette, N., Lassonde, M., Vannasing, P., Tremblay, J., González-Frankenberger, B., Florea, O., Béland, R., Lepore, F., & Gallagher, A. (2015). Developmental patterns of expressive language hemispheric lateralization in children, adolescents and adults using functional near-infrared spectroscopy. *Neuropsychologia*, *68*, 117–125. https://doi.org/10.1016/j.neuropsychologia.2015.01.007

Parent, N. (2023). Basic need satisfaction through social media engagement: A developmental framework for understanding adolescent social media use. *Human Development*, *67*(1), 1–17. https://doi.org/10.1159/000529449

Pariseau, E. M., Chevalier, L., Long, K. A., Clapham, R., Edwards-Leeper, L., & Tishelman, A. C. (2019). The relationship between family acceptance-rejection and transgender youth psychosocial functioning. *Clinical Practice in Pediatric Psychology*, *7*(3), 267–277. https://doi.org/10.1037/cpp0000291

Park, C. J., Yelland, G. W., Taffe, J. R., & Gray, K. M. (2012). Brief report: The relationship between language skills, adaptive behavior, and emotional and behavior problems in pre-schoolers with autism. *Journal of Autism and Developmental Disorders*, *42*(12), 2761–2766. https://doi.org/10.1007/s10803-012-1534-8

Park, N. (2011). Military children and families: Strengths and challenges during peace and war. *American Psychologist*, *66*(1), 65–72. https://doi.org/10.1037/a0021249

Parker, L. L., & Harriger, J. A. (2020). Eating disorders and disordered eating behaviors in the LGBT population: A review of the literature. *Journal of Eating Disorders*, *8*(51). https://doi.org/10.1186/s40337-020-00327-y

Parks, S. E., Erck Lambert, A. B., & Shapiro-Mendoza, C. K. (2017). Racial and ethnic trends in sudden unexpected infant deaths: United States, 1995–2013. *Pediatrics*, *139*(6), e20163844.

Paro, R., Grossniklaus, U., Santoro, R., & Wutz, A. (2021). *Introduction to epigenetics*. Springer. http://www.ncbi.nlm.nih.gov/books/NBK585706/

Parra, M., Hoff, E., & Core, C. (2011). Relations among language exposure, phonological memory, and language development in Spanish–English bilingually developing 2-year-olds. *Journal of Experimental Child Psychology*, *108*(1), 113–125. https://doi.org/10.1016/j.jecp.2010.07.011

Parten, M. (1932). Social participation among preschool children. *Journal of Abnormal and Social Psychology*, *27*, 243–269. https://doi.org/10.1037/h0074524

Partridge, S., Balayla, J., Holcroft, C., & Abenhaim, H. (2012). Inadequate prenatal care utilization and risks of infant mortality and poor birth outcome: A retrospective analysis of 28,729,765 U.S. deliveries over 8 Years. *American Journal of Perinatology*, *29*(10), 787–794. https://doi.org/10.1055/s-0032-1316439

Pascal, A., Govaert, P., Oostra, A., Naulaers, G., Ortibus, E., & Van den Broeck, C. (2018). Neurodevelopmental outcome in very preterm and very-low-birthweight infants born over the past decade: A meta-analytic review. *Developmental Medicine and Child Neurology*, *60*(4), 342–355. https://doi.org/10.1111/dmcn.13675

Pascalis, O., Dechonen, S., Morton, J., Duruelle, C., & Grenet, F. (1995). Mother's face recognition in neonates: A replication and an extension. *Infant Behavior and Development*, *18*, 79–85.

Pascalis, O., Fort, M., & Quinn, P. C. (2020). Development of face processing: Are there critical or sensitive periods? *Current Opinion in Behavioral Sciences*, *36*, 7–12. https://doi.org/10.1016/j.cobeha.2020.05.005

Pasco, M. C., White, R. M. B., & Seaton, E. K. (2021). A systematic review of neighborhood ethnic-racial compositions on cultural developmental processes and experiences in adolescence. *Adolescent Research Review*, *6*(2), 229–246. https://doi.org/10.1007/s40894-021-00152-7

Pascoe, J. M., Wood, D. L., Duffee, J. H., & Kuo, A. (2016). Mediators and adverse effects of child poverty in the United States. *Pediatrics*, *137*(4), e20160340. https://doi.org/10.1542/peds.2016-0340

Passel, J. S., Lopez, M. H., & Cohn, D. (2022). *U.S. Hispanic population continued its geographic spread in the 2010s*. Pew Research Center. https://www.pewresearch.org/fact-tank/2022/02/03/u-s-hispanic-population-continued-its-geographic-spread-in-the-2010s/

Passolunghi, M. C., Rueda Ferreira, T. I., & Tomasetto, C. (2014). Math-gender stereotypes and math-related beliefs in childhood and early adolescence. *Learning and Individual Differences*, *34*, 70–76. https://doi.org/10.1016/j.lindif.2014.05.005

Pasterski, V., & Bibonas, D. (2022). Biological approaches to studying gender development. In D. P. VanderLaan & W. I. Wong (Eds.), *Gender and sexuality development: Contemporary theory and research* (pp. 73–99). Springer International. https://doi.org/10.1007/978-3-030-84273-4_3

Patel, D. R., Cabral, M. D., Ho, A., & Merrick, J. (2020). A clinical primer on intellectual disability. *Translational Pediatrics, 9*(Suppl 1), S23. https://doi.org/10.21037/TP.2020.02.02

Patel, S., Gaylord, S., & Fagen, J. (2013). Generalization of deferred imitation in 6-, 9-, and 12-month-old infants using visual and auditory contexts. *Infant Behavior and Development, 36*(1), 25–31. https://doi.org/10.1016/j.infbeh.2012.09.006

Patenaude, Y., Pugash, D., Lim, K., Morin, L., Lim, K., Bly, S., Butt, K., Cargill, Y., Davies, G., Denis, N., Hazlitt, G., Morin, L., Naud, K., Ouellet, A., & Salem, S. (2014). The use of magnetic resonance imaging in the obstetric patient. *Journal of Obstetrics and Gynaecology Canada, 36*(4), 349–355. https://doi.org/10.1016/S1701-2163(15)30612-5

Patterson, C. J. (2017). Parents' sexual orientation and children's development. *Child Development Perspectives, 11*(1), 45–49. https://doi.org/10.1111/cdep.12207

Patterson, M. M., & Vannoy, M. R. (2023). Gender beliefs, gender stereotypes, and gender identity development. In P. W. St J. Watson, C. M. Rubbie-Davies, & B. Ertl (Eds.), *The Routledge international handbook of gender beliefs, stereotype threat, and teacher expectations*. Routledge.

Pätzold, W., & Liszkowski, U. (2020). Pupillometric VoE paradigm reveals that 18- but not 10-month-olds spontaneously represent occluded objects (but not empty sets). *PLoS ONE, 15*(4), e0230913. https://doi.org/10.1371/journal.pone.0230913

Paul, S. E., Hatoum, A. S., Fine, J. D., Johnson, E. C., Hansen, I., Karcher, N. R., Moreau, A. L., Bondy, E., Qu, Y., Carter, E. B., Rogers, C. E., Agrawal, A., Barch, D. M., & Bogdan, R. (2021). Associations between prenatal cannabis exposure and childhood outcomes: Results from the ABCD study. *JAMA Psychiatry, 78*(1), 64–76. https://doi.org/10.1001/jamapsychiatry.2020.2902

Paul Victor, C. G., & Treschuk, J. V. (2020). Critical literature review on the definition clarity of the concept of faith, religion, and spirituality. *Journal of Holistic Nursing, 38*(1), 107–113. https://doi.org/10.1177/0898010119895368

Pauletti, R. E., Cooper, P. J., & Perry, D. G. (2014). Influences of gender identity on children's maltreatment of gender-nonconforming peers: A person x target analysis of aggression. *Journal of Personality and Social Psychology, 106*(5), 843–866. https://doi.org/10.1037/a0036037

Pauletti, R. E., Menon, M., Cooper, P. J., Aults, C. D., & Perry, D. G. (2017). Psychological androgyny and children's mental health: A new look with new measures. *Sex Roles, 76*(11–12), 705–718. https://doi.org/10.1007/s11199-016-0627-9

Pauletto, M., Grassi, M., Passolunghi, M. C., & Penolazzi, B. (2021). Psychological well-being in childhood: The role of trait emotional intelligence, regulatory emotional self-efficacy, coping and general intelligence. *Clinical Child Psychology and Psychiatry, 26*(4), 1284–1297. https://doi.org/10.1177/13591045211040681

Paulus, M. (2014). The emergence of prosocial behavior: Why do infants and toddlers help, comfort, and share? *Child Development Perspectives, 8*(2), 77–81. https://doi.org/10.1111/cdep.12066

Paulus, M., & Moore, C. (2014). The development of recipient-dependent sharing behavior and sharing expectations in preschool children. *Developmental Psychology, 50*(3), 914–921. https://doi.org/10.1037/a0034169

Paulus, M., Nöth, A., & Wörle, M. (2018). Preschoolers' resource allocations align with their normative judgments. *Journal of Experimental Child Psychology, 175*, 117–126. https://doi.org/10.1016/j.jecp.2018.05.001

Paulussen-Hoogeboom, M. C., Stams, G. J. J. M., Hermanns, J. M. A., & Peetsma, T. T. D. (2007). Child negative emotionality and parenting from infancy to preschool: A meta-analytic review. *Developmental Psychology, 43*(2), 438–453. https://doi.org/10.1037/0012-1649.43.2.438

Payne, V. G., & D. (Larry D, Isaacs, L. (2020). *Human motor development: A lifespan approach* (10th ed.). Routledge.

Payne, V. G., & Isaacs, L. D. (2020). *Human motor development: A lifespan approach*. Routledge.

Payne, V. G., & Isaacs, L. D. (2025). *Human motor development: A lifespan approach* (11th ed.). Routledge.

Pazol, K., Whiteman, M. K., Folger, S. G., Kourtis, A. P., Marchbanks, P. A., & Jamieson, D. J. (2015). Sporadic contraceptive use and nonuse: Age-specific prevalence and associated factors. *American Journal of Obstetrics and Gynecology, 212*(3), 324.e1–8. https://doi.org/10.1016/j.ajog.2014.10.004

Pearman, F. A., & McGee, E. O. (2022). Antiblackness and racial disproportionality in gifted education. *Exceptional Children, 88*(4), 359–380. https://doi.org/10.1177/00144029211073523

Pedersen, E. R., Osilla, K. C., Miles, J. N. V., Tucker, J. S., Ewing, B. A., Shih, R. A., & D'Amico, E. J. (2017). The role of perceived injunctive alcohol norms in adolescent drinking behavior. *Addictive Behaviors, 67*, 1–7. https://doi.org/10.1016/j.addbeh.2016.11.022

Pederson, C. A., Khazvand, S., Clifton, R. L., Carroll, P. A., Carson, I., Harvey, J., Barnes-Najor, J., & Zapolski, T. C. B. (2022). The relationship between neighborhood safety and adolescent substance use: The role of self-esteem and social support. *Journal of Child and Family Studies, 31*(11), 3234–3246. https://doi.org/10.1007/s10826-022-02452-5

Pei, R., Lauharatanahirun, N., Cascio, C. N., O'Donnell, M. B., Shope, J. T., Simons-Morton, B. G., Vettel, J. M., & Falk, E. B. (2020). Neural processes during adolescent risky decision making are associated with conformity to peer influence. *Developmental Cognitive Neuroscience, 44*, 100794. https://doi.org/10.1016/j.dcn.2020.100794

Peiro, J. L., & Scorletti, F. (2019). Fetoscopy: The minimally invasive fetal surgery. In C. Esposito, F. Becmeur, H. Steyaert, & P. Szavay (Eds.), *ESPES manual of pediatric minimally invasive surgery* (pp. 549–560). Springer International. https://doi.org/10.1007/978-3-030-00964-9_76

Pellegrini, A. D., & Roseth, C. J. (2006). Relational aggression and relationships in preschoolers: A discussion of methods, gender differences, and function. *Journal of Applied Developmental Psychology, 27*(3), 269–276. http://dx.doi.org/10.1016/j.appdev.2006.02.007

Pellicano, E., & den Houting, J. (2022). Annual research review: Shifting from 'normal science' to neurodiversity in autism science. *Journal of Child Psychology and Psychiatry, 63*(4), 381–396. https://doi.org/10.1111/jcpp.13534

Pellis, S. M., Pellis, V. C., Ham, J. R., & Stark, R. A. (2023). Play fighting and the development of the social brain: The rat's tale. *Neuroscience & Biobehavioral Reviews, 145*, 105037. https://doi.org/10.1016/j.neubiorev.2023.105037

Peltz, J., Zhang, L., Sasser, J., Oshri, A., & Doane, L. D. (2024). The influence of pubertal development on early adolescent sleep and changes in family functioning. *Journal of Youth and Adolescence, 53*(2), 459–471. https://doi.org/10.1007/s10964-023-01882-8

Pemberton Roben, C. K., Bass, A. J., Moore, G. A., Murray-Kolb, L., Tan, P. Z.,

Gilmore, R. O., Buss, K. A., Cole, P. M., & Teti, L. O. (2012). Let me go: The influences of crawling experience and temperament on the development of anger expression. *Infancy*, *17*(5), 558–577. https://doi.org/10.1111/j.1532-7078.2011.00092.x

Peng, P., & Kievit, R. A. (2020). The development of academic achievement and cognitive abilities: A bidirectional perspective. *Child Development Perspectives*, *14*(1), 15–20. https://doi.org/10.1111/cdep.12352

Peranteau, W. H., & Flake, A. W. (2020). The future of in utero gene therapy. *Molecular Diagnosis and Therapy*, *24*(2), 135–142. https://doi.org/10.1007/s40291-020-00445-y

Perera, B. P. U., Faulk, C., Svoboda, L. K., Goodrich, J. M., & Dolinoy, D. C. (2020). The role of environmental exposures and the epigenome in health and disease. *Environmental and Molecular Mutagenesis*, *61*(1), 176–192. https://doi.org/10.1002/em.22311

Perez, J., & Feigenson, L. (2022). Violations of expectation trigger infants to search for explanations. *Cognition*, *21*(8). https://doi.org/10.1016/j.cognition.2021.104942

Perez, J., & Feigenson, L. (2022). Violations of expectation trigger infants to search for explanations. *Cognition*, *218*, 104942. https://doi.org/10.1016/j.cognition.2021.104942

Pérez-Escamilla, R. (2022). What will it take to improve breastfeeding outcomes in the United States without leaving anyone behind? *American Journal of Public Health*, *112*, S766–S769. https://doi.org/10.2105/AJPH.2022.307057

Pérez-Escamilla, R., Martinez, J. L., & Segura-Pérez, S. (2016). Impact of the Baby-friendly Hospital Initiative on breastfeeding and child health outcomes: A systematic review. *Maternal and Child Nutrition*, *12*(3), 402–417. https://doi.org/10.1111/mcn.12294

Pérez-González, A., Guilera, G., Pereda, N., & Jarne, A. (2017). Protective factors promoting resilience in the relation between child sexual victimization and internalizing and externalizing symptoms. *Child Abuse & Neglect*, *72*, 393–403. https://doi.org/10.1016/j.chiabu.2017.09.006

Perhamus, G. R., & Ostrov, J. M. (2020). Emotions and cognitions in early childhood aggression: The role of irritability and hostile attribution biases. *Research on Child and Adolescent Psychopathology*, *49*(1), 63–75. https://doi.org/10.1007/S10802-020-00707-7

Perlman, S. B., Huppert, T. J., & Luna, B. (2016). Functional near-infrared spectroscopy evidence for development of prefrontal engagement in working memory in early through middle childhood. *Cerebral Cortex*, *26*(6), 2790–2799. https://doi.org/10.1093/cercor/bhv139

Perone, S., Almy, B., & Zelazo, P. D. (2018). Toward an understanding of the neural basis of executive function development. In R. Gibb & B. Kolb (Eds.), *The neurobiology of brain and behavioral development* (pp. 291–314). Elsevier. https://doi.org/10.1016/B978-0-12-804036-2.00011-X

Perone, S., Simmering, V. R., & Buss, A. T. (2021). A dynamical reconceptualization of executive-function development. *Perspectives on Psychological Science*, *16*(6). https://doi.org/10.1177/1745691620966792

Perry, D. G., Pauletti, R. E., & Cooper, P. J. (2019). Gender identity in childhood: A review of the literature. *International Journal of Behavioral Development*, *43*(4), 289–304. https://doi.org/10.1177/0165025418811129

Perry, L. K. (2015). To have and to hold: Looking vs. touching in the study of categorization. *Frontiers in Psychology*, *6*, 178. https://doi.org/10.3389/fpsyg.2015.00178

Perszyk, D. R., Lei, R. F., Bodenhausen, G. V., Richeson, J. A., & Waxman, S. R. (2019). Bias at the intersection of race and gender: Evidence from preschool-aged children. *Developmental Science*, *22*(3), e12788. https://doi.org/10.1111/desc.12788

Pesu, L., Viljaranta, J., & Aunola, K. (2016). The role of parents' and teachers' beliefs in children's self-concept development. *Journal of Applied Developmental Psychology*, 63–71. https://doi.org/10.1016/j.appdev.2016.03.001 44(May–June

Peter, J., & Valkenburg, P. M. (2009). Adolescents' exposure to sexually explicit Internet material and notions of women as sex objects: Assessing causality and underlying processes. *Journal of Communication*, *59*(3), 407–433. https://doi.org/10.1111/j.1460-2466.2009.01422.x

Petersen, I. T., Lindhiem, O., LeBeau, B., Bates, J. E., Pettit, G. S., Lansford, J. E., & Dodge, K. A. (2018). Development of internalizing problems from adolescence to emerging adulthood: Accounting for heterotypic continuity with vertical scaling. *Developmental Psychology*, *54*(3), 586–599. https://doi.org/10.1037/dev0000449

Petersen, J. (2018). Gender difference in verbal performance: A meta-analysis of United States State performance assessments. *Educational Psychology Review*, *30*(4), 1269–1281. https://doi.org/10.1007/s10648-018-9450-x

Peterson, C., Warren, K. L., & Short, M. M. (2011). Infantile amnesia across the years: A 2-year follow-up of children's earliest memories. *Child Development*, *82*(4), 1092–1105. https://doi.org/10.1111/j.1467-8624.2011.01597.x

Peterson, K. C., Peterson, M., & Carducci, B. J. (2020). Stanford-Binet Intelligence Scale. In B. J. Carducci, C. S. Nave, & B. J. Carducci (Eds.), *The Wiley encyclopedia of personality and individual differences: Models and theories* (pp. 451–455). Wiley.

Peterson, R. L., & Pennington, B. F. (2012). Developmental dyslexia. *Lancet*, *379*(9830), 1997–2007. https://doi.org/10.1016/S0140-6736(12)60198-6

Petitpierre, G., Luisier, A. C., & Bensafi, M. (2021). Eating behavior in autism: Senses as a window towards food acceptance. *Current Opinion in Food Science*, *4*(1). https://doi.org/10.1016/j.cofs.2021.04.015

Petrides, K. V., Mikolajczak, M., Mavroveli, S., Sanchez-Ruiz, M.-J., Furnham, A., & Perez-Gonzalez, J.-C. (2016). Developments in trait emotional intelligence research. *Emotion Review*, *8*(4), 335–341. https://doi.org/10.1177/1754073916650493

Petursdottir, A. I., & Mellor, J. R. (2017). Reinforcement contingencies in language acquisition. *Policy Insights From the Behavioral and Brain Sciences*, *4*(1), 25–32. https://doi.org/10.1177/2372732216686083

Peverill, M., Dirks, M. A., Narvaja, T., Herts, K. L., Comer, J. S., & McLaughlin, K. A. (2021). Socioeconomic status and child psychopathology in the United States: A meta-analysis of population-based studies. *Clinical Psychology Review*, *83*, 101933. https://doi.org/10.1016/j.cpr.2020.101933

Peviani, K. M., Brieant, A., Holmes, C. J., King-Casas, B., & Kim-Spoon, J. (2019). Religious social support protects against social risks for adolescent substance use. *Journal of Research on Adolescence*, *30*(2), 361–371. https://doi.org/10.1111/jora.12529

Pew Research Center. (2015). *Parenting in America: The American Family Today*. http://www.pewsocialtrends.org/2015/12/17/1-the-american-family-today/

Pew Research Center. (2020, September 10). *U.S. teens take after their parents religiously, attend services together and enjoy family rituals. Pew Research Center's Religion & Public Life Project*. https://www.pewresearch.org/religion/2020/09/10/u-s-teens-take-after-their-parents-religiously-attend-services-together-and-enjoy-family-rituals/

Pexman, P. M. (2022). Persuasive language development: The case of irony and humour in children's language. In J. Fahnestock & R. A. Harris (Eds.), *The

Routledge handbook of language and persuasion. Routledge.

Peyre, H., Hoertel, N., Bernard, J. Y., Rouffignac, C., Forhan, A., Taine, M., Heude, B., & Ramus, F. (2019). Sex differences in psychomotor development during the preschool period: A longitudinal study of the effects of environmental factors and of emotional, behavioral, and social functioning. *Journal of Experimental Child Psychology*, *178*, 369–384. https://doi.org/10.1016/j.jecp.2018.09.002

Pham, H. T., DiLalla, L. F., Corley, R. P., Dorn, L. D., & Berenbaum, S. A. (2022). Family environmental antecedents of pubertal timing in girls and boys: A review and open questions. *Hormones and Behavior*, *138*, 105101. https://doi.org/10.1016/j.yhbeh.2021.105101

Phillips, D., Gormley, W., & Anderson, S. (2016). The effects of Tulsa's CAP Head Start program on middle-school academic outcomes and progress. *Developmental Psychology*, *52*(8), 1247–1261. https://doi.org/10.1037/dev0000151

Phillips, K., & Power, M. (2018). Emotion regulation. In R. J. R. Levesque (Ed.), *Encyclopedia of adolescence* (pp. 1157–1165). Springer. https://doi.org/10.1007/978-3-319-33228-4_22

Phinney, J. S. (1989). Stages of ethnic identity development in minority group adolescents. *Journal of Early Adolescence*, *9*(1–2), 34–49. https://doi.org/10.1177/0272431689091004

Phinney, J. S., & Chavira, V. (1992). Ethnic identity and self-esteem: An exploratory longitudinal study. *Journal of Adolescence*, *15*(3), 271–281. https://doi.org/10.1016/0140-1971(92)90030-9

Phinney, J. S., & Ong, A. D. (2007). Conceptualization and measurement of ethnic identity: Current status and future directions. *Journal of Counseling Psychology*, *54*(3), 271–281. https://doi.org/10.1037/0022-067.54.3.271

Piaget, J. (1929). *The child's conception of the world*. Routledge & Kegan Paul.

Piaget, J. (1932). *The moral judgment of the child*. Harcourt Brace.

Piaget, J. (1952). *The origins of intelligence in children*. International Universities Press. (Original work published in 1936

Piaget, J. (1962). Play, dreams, and imitation in childhood. *Norton*, 2<189::AID-PITS2310030222>3.0.CO;2-Z. https://doi.org/10.1002/1520-6807(196604)3:

Piaget, J. (1962). Play, dreams, and imitation in childhood. (paper). *Psychology in the Schools*, *3*(2), 189–189, 296 p. $1.85. 2<189::AID-PITS2310030222>3.0.CO;2-Z. W. W. Norton. (The Norton Library. https://doi.org/10.1002/1520-6807(196604)3: 1962

Piaget, J. (1972). Intellectual evolution from adolescence to adulthood. *Human Development*, *51*(1), 40–47. https://doi.org/10.1159/000112531

Piaget, J., & Inhelder, B. (1967). *The child's conception of space*. Norton.

Piantadosi, S. T., & Cantlon, J. F. (2017). True numerical cognition in the wild. *Psychological Science*, *28*(4), 462–469. https://doi.org/10.1177/0956797616686862

Piccolo, L. R., Merz, E. C., & Noble, K. G. (2018). School climate is associated with cortical thickness and executive function in children and adolescents. *Developmental Science*, *22*(1), e12719. https://doi.org/10.1111/desc.12719

Piekarski, D. J., Colich, N. L., & Ho, T. C. (2023). The effects of puberty and sex on adolescent white matter development: A systematic review. *Developmental Cognitive Neuroscience*, *60*, 101214. https://doi.org/10.1016/j.dcn.2023.101214

Pierrehumbert, B., Nicole, A., Muller-Nix, C., Forcada-Guex, M., & Ansermet, F. (2003). Parental post-traumatic reactions after premature birth: Implications for sleeping and eating problems in the infant. *Archives of Disease in Childhood - Fetal and Neonatal Edition*, *88*(5), F400–F404. https://doi.org/10.1136/fn.88.5.F400

Pieters, S., Burk, W. J., Van der Vorst, H., Dahl, R. E., Wiers, R. W., & Engels, R. C. M. E. (2015). Prospective relationships between sleep problems and substance use, internalizing and externalizing problems. *Journal of Youth and Adolescence*, *44*(2), 379–388. https://doi.org/10.1007/s10964-014-0213-9

Pietschnig, J., Penke, L., Wicherts, J. M., Zeiler, M., & Voracek, M. (2015). Meta-analysis of associations between human brain volume and intelligence differences: How strong are they and what do they mean? *Neuroscience & Biobehavioral Reviews*, *57*, 411–432. https://doi.org/10.1016/j.neubiorev.2015.09.017

Pietschnig, J., & Voracek, M. (2015). One century of global IQ gains: A formal meta-analysis of the Flynn effect (1909–2013). *Perspectives on Psychological Science*, *10*, 282–306. https://doi.org/10.1177/1745691615577701

Pillow, B. H. (2008). Development of children's understanding of cognitive activities. *Journal of Genetic Psychology*, *169*(4), 297–321.

Pinel, C., Prainsack, B., & McKevitt, C. (2018). Markers as mediators: A review and synthesis of epigenetics literature. *BioSocieties*, *13*(1), 276–303. https://doi.org/10.1057/s41292-017-0068-x

Pinquart, M. (2017). Associations of parenting dimensions and styles with externalizing problems of children and adolescents: An updated meta-analysis. *Developmental Psychology*, *53*(5), 873–932. https://doi.org/10.1037/dev0000295

Pinquart, M. (2021). Cultural differences in the association of harsh parenting with internalizing and externalizing symptoms: A meta-analysis. *Journal of Child and Family Studies*, *30*(12), 2938–2951. https://doi.org/10.1007/s10826-021-02113-z

Pinquart, M., & Fischer, A. (2022). Associations of parenting styles with moral reasoning in children and adolescents: A meta-analysis. *Journal of Moral Education*, *51*(4), 463–476. https://doi.org/10.1080/03057240.2021.1933401

Pinquart, M., & Gerke, D. C. (2019). Associations of parenting styles with self-esteem in children and adolescents: A meta-analysis. *Journal of Child and Family Studies*, *28*(8), 2017–2035. https://doi.org/10.1007/s10826-019-01417-5

Piotrowski, J. T., Lapierre, M. A., & Linebarger, D. L. (2013). Investigating correlates of self-regulation in early childhood with a representative sample of English-speaking American families. *Journal of Child and Family Studies*, *22*(3), 423–436. https://doi.org/10.1007/s10826-012-9595-z

Pipe, S. W., Gonen-Yaacovi, G., & Segurado, O. G. (2022). Hemophilia A gene therapy: Current and next-generation approaches. *Expert Opinion on Biological Therapy*, *22*(9), 1099–1115. https://doi.org/10.1080/14712598.2022.2002842

Piras, G. N., Bozzola, M., Bianchin, L., Bernasconi, S., Bona, G., Lorenzoni, G., Buzi, F., Rigon, F., Tonini, G., De Sanctis, V., & Perissinotto, E. (2020). The levelling-off of the secular trend of age at menarche among Italian girls. *Heliyon*, *6*(6), e04222. https://doi.org/10.1016/j.heliyon.2020.e04222

Pirchio, S., Passiatore, Y., Panno, A., Maricchiolo, F., & Carrus, G. (2018). A chip off the old block: Parents' subtle ethnic prejudice predicts children's implicit prejudice. *Frontiers in Psychology*, *9*, 1–9. https://doi.org/10.3389/fpsyg.2018.00110

Pison, G., Monden, C., & Smits, J. (2015). Twinning rates in developed countries: Trends and explanations. *Population and Development Review*, *41*(4), 629–649. https://doi.org/10.1111/j.1728-4457.2015.00088.x

Pittman, J. F., Keiley, M. K., Kerpelman, J. L., & Vaughn, B. E. (2011). Attachment, identity, and intimacy: Parallels between Bowlby's and Erikson's paradigms. *Journal of Family Theory & Review*, *3*(1), 32–46. https://doi.org/10.1111/j.1756-2589.2010.00079.x

Pivnick, L. K., Gordon, R. A., & Crosnoe, R. (2020). Crowd sourcing: Do peer crowd prototypes match reality? *Social Psychology Quarterly*, *83*(3), 272–293. https://doi.org/10.1177/0190272520936228

Pizzol, D., Tudor, F., Racalbuto, V., Bertoldo, A., Veronese, N., & Smith, L. (2021). Systematic review and meta-analysis found that malnutrition was associated with poor cognitive development. *Acta Paediatrica*, *110*(10), 2704–2710. https://doi.org/10.1111/APA.15964

Plaisier, X. S., & Konijn, E. A. (2013). Rejected by peers—Attracted to antisocial media content: Rejection-based anger impairs moral judgment among adolescents. *Developmental Psychology*, *49*(6), 1165–1173. https://doi.org/10.1037/a0029399

Planalp, E. M., & Goldsmith, H. H. (2020). Observed profiles of infant temperament: Stability, heritability, and associations with parenting. *Child Development*, *91*(3), e563–e580. https://doi.org/10.1111/cdev.13277

Planalp, E. M., Van Hulle, C., Lemery-Chalfant, K., & Goldsmith, H. H. (2017). Genetic and environmental contributions to the development of positive affect in infancy. *Emotion*, *17*(3), 412–420. https://doi.org/10.1037/emo0000238

Platt, J. M., Keyes, K. M., McLaughlin, K. A., & Kaufman, A. S. (2019). The Flynn effect for fluid IQ may not generalize to all ages or ability levels: A population-based study of 10,000 US adolescents. *Intelligence*, *77*, 101385. https://doi.org/10.1016/j.intell.2019.101385

Plebanek, D. J., & Sloutsky, V. M. (2019). Selective attention, filtering, and the development of working memory. *Developmental Science*, *22*(1), e12727. https://doi.org/10.1111/desc.12727

Plomin, R. (2019). *Blueprint: How DNA makes us who we are*. MIT Press.

Plomin, R. D., & Deary, I. J. (2015). Genetics and intelligence differences: Five special findings. *Molecular Psychiatry*, *20*(1), 98–108. https://doi.org/10.1038/mp.2014.105

Plomin, R. D., DeFries, J. C., Knopik, V. S., & Neiderhiser, J. M. (2016). Top 10 replicated findings from behavioral genetics. *Perspectives on Psychological Science*, *11*(1), 3–23. https://doi.org/10.1177/1745691615617439

Plomin, R. D., & Von Stumm, S. (2018). The new genetics of intelligence. *Nature Reviews Genetics*, *19*(3), 148–159. https://doi.org/10.1038/nrg.2017.104

Plomin, R., & Spinath, F. M. (2004). Intelligence: Genetics, genes, and genomics. *Journal of Personality & Social Psychology*, *86*(1), 112–129. https://doi.org/10.1037/0022-3514.86.1.112

Poehlmann, J., Schwichtenberg, A. J. M., Shlafer, R. J., Hahn, E., Bianchi, J.-P., & Warner, R. (2011). Emerging self-regulation in toddlers born preterm or low birth weight: Differential susceptibility to parenting? *Development & Psychopathology*, *23*(1), 177–193. https://doi.org/10.1017/s0954579410000726

Poehlmann-Tynan, J., & Turney, K. (2020). A developmental perspective on children with incarcerated parents. *Child Development Perspectives*, *15*(1), 3–11. https://doi.org/10.1111/cdep.12392

Poirel, N., Borst, G. G., Simon, G., Rossi, S., Cassotti, M., Pineau, A., Houdé, O., Hevia, M. D. de., Girelli, L., Vallar, G., Fias, W., Brysbaert, M., Geypens, F., D'Ydewalle, G., Walsh, V., Dehaene, S., Brannon, E., Houdé, O., Pineau, A., & &#hillip1; Jouvent, R. (2012). Number conservation is related to children's prefrontal inhibitory control: An fMRI study of a Piagetian task. *PLoS ONE*, *7*(7), e40802. https://doi.org/10.1371/journal.pone.0040802

Polanin, J. R., Espelage, D. L., Grotpeter, J. K., Ingram, K., Michaelson, L., Spinney, E., Valido, A., Sheikh, A. E., Torgal, C., & Robinson, L. (2022). A systematic review and meta-analysis of interventions to decrease cyberbullying perpetration and victimization. *Prevention Science*, *23*(3), 439–454. https://doi.org/10.1007/s11121-021-01259-y

Pollmann-Schult, M. (2014). Parenthood and life satisfaction: Why don't children make people happy? *Journal of Marriage and Family*, *76*(2), 319–336. https://doi.org/10.1111/jomf.12095

Pons, F., Harris, P. L., & de Rosnay, M. (2004). Emotion comprehension between 3 and 11 years: Developmental periods and hierarchical organization. *European Journal of Developmental Psychology*, *1*(2), 127–152. https://doi.org/10.1080/17405620344000022

Poole, D. A., & White, L. T. (1991). Effects of question repetition on the eyewitness testimony of children and adults. *Developmental Psychology*, *27*, 975–986.

Poole, D. A., & White, L. T. (1993). Two years later: Effects of question repetition and retention interval on the eyewitness testimony of children and adults. *Developmental Psychology*, *29*, 844–853. https://doi.org/10.1037/0012-1649.29.5.844

Poornima, S., Daram, S., Devaki, R. K., & Qurratulain, H. (2020). Chromosomal abnormalities in couples with primary and secondary infertility: Genetic counseling for assisted reproductive techniques (ART). *Journal of Reproduction and Infertility*, *21*(4). https://doi.org/10.18502/jri.v21i4.4331

Popat, A., & Tarrant, C. (2023). Exploring adolescents' perspectives on social media and mental health and well-being – A qualitative literature review. *Clinical Child Psychology and Psychiatry*, *28*(1), 323–337. https://doi.org/10.1177/13591045221092884

Popova, S., Charness, M. E., Burd, L., Crawford, A., Hoyme, H. E., Mukherjee, R. A. S., Riley, E. P., & Elliott, E. J. (2023). Fetal alcohol spectrum disorders. *Nature Reviews Disease Primers*, *9*(1), Article 1. https://doi.org/10.1038/s41572-023-00420-x

Poppen, P. (1974). Sex differences in moral judgment. *Personality and Social Psychology Bulletin*, *1*(1), 313–315. https://doi.org/10.1177/014616727400100106

Posadas, D. M., & Carthew, R. W. (2014). MicroRNAs and their roles in developmental canalization. *Current Opinion in Genetics & Development*, *27*, 1–6. https://doi.org/10.1016/j.gde.2014.03.005

Poteat, V. P., Watson, R. J., & Fish, J. N. (2021). Teacher support moderates associations among sexual orientation identity outness, victimization, and academic performance among LGBQ+youth. *Journal of Youth and Adolescence*, *50*(8), 1634–1648. https://doi.org/10.1007/s10964-021-01455-7

Potegal, M., Robison, S., Anderson, F., Jordan, C., & Shapiro, E. (2007). Sequence and priming in 15 month-olds' reactions to brief arm restraint: Evidence for a hierarchy of anger responses. *Aggressive Behavior*, *33*(6), 508–518. https://doi.org/10.1002/ab.20207

Potmesilova, P., & Potmesil, M. (2021). Temperament and school readiness – A literature review. *Frontiers in Psychology*, *12*, 599411. https://doi.org/10.3389/fpsyg.2021.599411

Potter, D. (2010). Psychosocial well-being and the relationship between divorce and children's academic achievement. *Journal of Marriage & Family*, *72*(4), 933–946. https://doi.org/10.1111/j.1741-3737.2010.00740.x

Poulin, F., & Chan, A. (2010). Friendship stability and change in childhood and adolescence. *Developmental Review, 30*(3), 257–272. https://doi.org/10.1016/j.dr.2009.01.001

Powell, K. M., Rahm-Knigge, R. L., & Conner, B. T. (2020). Resilience protective factors checklist (RPFC): Buffering childhood adversity and promoting positive outcomes. *Psychological Reports, 124*(4), 1437–1461. https://doi.org/10.1177/0033294120950288

Powell, S. D. (2019). *Your introduction to education: Explorations in teaching*. Pearson, 0.00. https://bookshelf.vitalsource.com/#/books/9780134737027/cfi/1!/4/4@0:

Power, F. C., Higgins, A., & Kohlberg, L. (1989). *Lawrence Kohlberg's approach to moral education*. Columbia University Press.

Power, L., & McKinney, C. (2013). Emerging adult perceptions of parental religiosity and parenting practices: Relationships with emerging adult religiosity and psychological adjustment. *Psychology of Religion and Spirituality, 5*(2), 99–109. https://doi.org/10.1037/a0030046

Powers, M. E., Takagishi, J., & Committee, on Adolescence. (2021). Care of adolescent parents and their children. *Pediatrics, 147*(5), e2021050919. https://doi.org/10.1542/peds.2021-050919

Powlishta, K. K., Serbin, L. A., & Moller, L. C. (1993). The stability of individual differences in gender typing: Implications for understanding gender segregation. *Sex Roles, 29*(11), 723–737. https://doi.org/10.1007/BF00289214

Pozzoli, T., Gini, G., & Vieno, A. (2012). The role of individual correlates and class norms in defending and passive bystanding behavior in bullying: A multilevel analysis. *Child Development, 83*(6), 1917–1931. https://doi.org/10.1111/j.1467-8624.2012.01831.x

Prabaharan, N., & Spadafora, N. (2020). Rejected children. In T. K. Shackelford & V. A. Weekes-Shackelford (Eds.), *Encyclopedia of evolutionary psychological science* (pp. 1–4). Springer International. https://doi.org/10.1007/978-3-319-16999-6_181-1

Prady, S. L., Kiernan, K., Fairley, L., Wilson, S., & Wright, J. (2014). Self-reported maternal parenting style and confidence and infant temperament in a multi-ethnic community: Results from the born in Bradford cohort. *Journal of Child Health Care, 18*(1), 31–46. https://doi.org/10.1177/1367493512473855

Prechtl, H. F. R. (1974). The behavioural states of the newborn infant (a review). *Brain Research, 76*(2), 185–212. https://doi.org/10.1016/0006-8993(74)90454-5

Preckel, F., Niepel, C., Schneider, M., & Brunner, M. (2013). Self-concept in adolescence: A longitudinal study on reciprocal effects of self-perceptions in academic and social domains. *Journal of Adolescence, 36*(6), 1165–1175. https://doi.org/10.1016/j.adolescence.2013.09.001

Prenoveau, J. M., Craske, M. G., West, V., Giannakakis, A., Zioga, M., Lehtonen, A., Davies, B., Netsi, E., Cardy, J., Cooper, P., Murray, L., & Stein, A. (2017). Maternal postnatal depression and anxiety and their association with child emotional negativity and behavior problems at two years. *Developmental Psychology, 53*(1), 50–62. https://doi.org/10.1037/dev0000221

Prentza, A. (2021). Metalinguistic awareness and written production in primary school: A differentiated teaching approach. *European Journal of Language Studies, 8*(1), 14–23.

Prescott, J. (2020). Development of food preferences. In H. L. Meiselman (Ed.), *Handbook of eating and drinking: Interdisciplinary perspectives* (pp. 199–217). Springer International. https://doi.org/10.1007/978-3-030-14504-0_24

Previc, F. H. (1991). A general theory concerning the prenatal origins of cerebral lateralization in humans. *Psychological Review, 98*(3), 299–334. https://doi.org/10.1037/0033-295x.98.3.299

Prewett, S. L., Bergin, D. A., & Huang, F. L. (2019). Student and teacher perceptions on student-teacher relationship quality: A middle school perspective. *School Psychology International, 40*(1), 66–87. https://doi.org/10.1177/0143034318807743

Price-Feeney, M., Green, A. E., & Dorison, S. (2020). Understanding the mental health of transgender and nonbinary youth. *Journal of Adolescent Health, 66*(6), 684–690. https://doi.org/10.1016/j.jadohealth.2019.11.314

Price-Williams, D., Gordon, W., & Ramirez, M. (1969). Skill and conservation: A study of pottery-making children. *Developmental Psychology*, 769. https://doi.org/10.1037/H0028264 1(6, Pt. 1

Priess, H. A., & Lindberg, S. M. (2018). Gender intensification. In R. J. R. Levesque (Ed.), *Encyclopedia of adolescence* (pp. 1135–1142). Springer New York. https://doi.org/10.1007/978-1-4419-1695-2_391

Prime, H., Wade, M., & Browne, D. T. (2020). Risk and resilience in family well-being during the COVID-19 pandemic. *American Psychologist, 75*, 631–643. https://doi.org/10.1037/amp0000660

Principe, G. F., & London, K. (2022). How parents can shape what children remember: Implications for the testimony of young witnesses. *Journal of Applied Research in Memory and Cognition, 11*, 289–302. https://doi.org/10.1037/mac0000059

Pritzl, K., Milavetz, Z., Cuthrell, H., Muentner, L., & Poehlmann-Tynan, J. (2022). Young children's contact with their parents in jail and child behavior problems. *Journal of Offender Rehabilitation, 61*(2), 88–105. https://doi.org/10.1080/10509674.2021.2018381

Privado, J., de Urturi, C. S., Dávila, J., López, C., Burgaleta, M., Román, F. J., Escorial, S., & Colom, R. (2014). White matter integrity predicts individual differences in (fluid) intelligence through working memory. *Personality and Individual Differences, 60*, S77. https://doi.org/10.1016/j.paid.2013.07.347

Provasi, J. (2019). Parent-Preterm Infant Interaction. In G. Apter, E. Devouche, & M. Gratier (Eds.), *Early interaction and developmental psychopathology* (pp. 123–149). Springer International. https://doi.org/10.1007/978-3-030-04769-6_7

Provenzi, L., Brambilla, M., Scotto di Minico, G., Montirosso, R., & Borgatti, R. (2020). Maternal caregiving and DNA methylation in human infants and children: Systematic review. *Genes, Brain and Behavior, 19*(3), e12616. https://doi.org/10.1111/gbb.12616

Przybylski, A. K., & Weinstein, N. (2019). Digital screen time limits and young children's psychological well-being: Evidence from a population-based study. *Child Development, 90*(1), e56–e65. https://doi.org/10.1111/cdev.13007

Puckett, J. A., Cleary, P., Rossman, K., Mustanski, B., & Newcomb, M. E. (2018). Barriers to gender-affirming care for transgender and gender nonconforming individuals. *Sexuality Research and Social Policy, 15*(1), 48–59. https://doi.org/10.1007/s13178-017-0295-8

Pulice-Farrow, L., Cusack, C. E., & Galupo, M. P. (2020). "Certain parts of my body don't belong to ne": Trans individuals' descriptions of body-specific gender dysphoria. *Sexuality Research and Social Policy, 17*(4), 654–667. https://doi.org/10.1007/s13178-019-00423-y

Pulkkinen, L., Fadjukoff, P., & Pitkänen, T. (2020). Persistent offenders and adolescence-limited offenders: Differences in life-courses. *Criminal Behaviour and Mental*

Health, 30(4), 196–209. https://doi.org/10.1002/cbm.2157

Puls, H. T., Anderst, J. D., Bettenhausen, J. L., Clark, N., Krager, M., Markham, J. L., & Hall, M. (2019). Newborn risk factors for subsequent physical abuse hospitalizations. Pediatrics, 143(2). https://doi.org/10.1542/peds.2018-2108

Putnick, D. L., Bornstein, M. H., Lansford, J. E., Chang, L., Deater-Deckard, K., Di Giunta, L., Dodge, K. A., Malone, P. S., Oburu, P., Pastorelli, C., Skinner, A. T., Sorbring, E., Tapanya, S., Tirado, L. M. U., Zelli, A., Alampay, L. P., Al-Hassan, S. M., Bacchini, D., & Bombi, A. S. (2018). Parental acceptance-rejection and child prosocial behavior: Developmental transactions across the transition to adolescence in nine countries, mothers and fathers, and girls and boys. Developmental Psychology, 54(10), 1881–1890. https://doi.org/10.1037/dev0000565

Putnick, D. L., Hahn, C.-S., Hendricks, C., & Bornstein, M. H. (2020). Developmental stability of scholastic, social, athletic, and physical appearance self-concepts from preschool to early adulthood. Journal of Child Psychology and Psychiatry, 61(1), 95–103. https://doi.org/10.1111/jcpp.13107

Pyra, E., & Schwarz, W. (2019). Puberty: Normal, delayed, and precocious. In A. Grossman, C. Follin, C. Yedinak, & S. Llahana (Eds.), Advanced practice in endocrinology nursing (pp. 63–84). Springer International. https://doi.org/10.1007/978-3-319-99817-6_4

Qian, J., Chen, Q., Ward, S. M., Duan, E., & Zhang, Y. (2020). Impacts of caffeine during pregnancy. Trends in Endocrinology and Metabolism, 31(3), 218–227. https://doi.org/10.1016/j.tem.2019.11.004

Qiao, J., Dai, L. J., Zhang, Q., & Ouyang, Y. Q. (2020). A meta-analysis of the association between breastfeeding and early childhood obesity. Journal of Pediatric Nursing, 53, 57–66. https://doi.org/10.1016/j.pedn.2020.04.024

Qiu, X., Yu, J., Li, T., Cheng, N., & Zhu, L. (2017). Children's inequity aversion in procedural justice context: A comparison of advantageous and disadvantageous inequity. Frontiers in Psychology, 8, 1855. https://doi.org/10.3389/fpsyg.2017.01855

Quam, C., & Roberts, T. (2023). Language Development. In Oxford Research Encyclopedia of Psychology. https://doi.org/10.1093/acrefore/9780190236557.013.57

Quarmley, M., Feldman, J., Grossman, H., Clarkson, T., Moyer, A., & Jarcho, J. M. (2022). Testing effects of social rejection on aggressive and prosocial behavior: A meta-analysis. Aggressive Behavior, 48(6), 529–545. https://doi.org/10.1002/ab.22026

Quinn, M., & Hennessy, E. (2010). Peer relationships across the preschool to school transition. Early Education & Development, 21(6), 825–842. https://doi.org/10.1080/10409280903329013

Quinn, P. C. (2016). Establishing cognitive organization in infancy. In L. Balter & C. S. Tamis-LeMonda (Eds.), Child psychology: A handbook of contemporary issues (3rd ed., pp. 79–104). Psychology Press.

Quinn, P. C., Balas, B. J., & Pascalis, O. (2021). Reorganization in the representation of face-race categories from 6 to 9 months of age: Behavioral and computational evidence. Vision Research, 179, 34–41. https://doi.org/10.1016/j.visres.2020.11.006

Quinn, P. C., Doran, M. M., Reiss, J. E., & Hoffman, J. E. (2010). Neural markers of subordinate-level categorization in 6- to 7-month-old infants. Developmental Science, 13(3), 499–507. https://doi.org/10.1111/j.1467-7687.2009.00903.x

Quinn, P. C., Eimas, P. D., & Rosenkrantz, S. L. (1993). Evidence for representations of perceptual similar natural categories by 3 and 4 month old infants. Perception, 22(4), 463–475. https://doi.org/10.1068/p220463 Article information

Quinn, P. C., Lee, K., & Pascalis, O. (2018). Perception of face race by infants: Five developmental changes. Child Development Perspectives, 12(3), 204–209. https://doi.org/10.1111/cdep.12286

Quinn, P. C., Lee, K., & Pascalis, O. (2019). Face processing in infancy and beyond: The case of social categories. Annual Review of Psychology, 70(1), 165–189. https://doi.org/10.1146/annurev-psych-010418-102753

Quinn, P. C., Yahr, J., Kuhn, A., Slater, A. M., & Pascalis, O. (2002). Representation of the gender of human faces by infants: A preference for female. Perception, 31(9), 1109–1121. https://doi.org/10.1068/p3331

Quiñones-Camacho, L. E., & Davis, E. L. (2020). Children's awareness of the context-appropriate nature of emotion regulation strategies across emotions. Cognition and Emotion, 34(5), 977–985. https://doi.org/10.1080/02699931.2019.1687426

Quintana, S. M. (1998). Children's developmental understanding of ethnicity and race. Applied and Preventive Psychology, 7(1), 27–45. https://doi.org/10.1016/S0962-1849(98)80020-6

Quiroga, M. A., Diaz, A., Román, F. J., Privado, J., & Colom, R. (2019). Intelligence and video games: Beyond "brain-games.". Intelligence, 75, 85–94. https://doi.org/10.1016/j.intell.2019.05.001

Rabbitt, M. P., Hales, L. J., Burke, M. P., & Coleman-Jensen, A (Eds.). (2023). https://doi.org/10.22004/ag.econ.338945 Household food security in the United States in 2022

Raby, K. L., Steele, R. D., Carlson, E. A., & Sroufe, L. A. (2015). Continuities and changes in infant attachment patterns across two generations. Attachment & Human Development, 17(4), 414–428. https://doi.org/10.1080/14616734.2015.1067824

Racy, F., Morin, A., & Duhnych, C. (2020). Using a thought listing procedure to construct the general inner speech questionnaire: An ecological approach. Journal of Constructivist Psychology, 33(4), 385–405. https://doi.org/10.1080/10720537.2019.1633572

Radvansky, G. A. (2017). Human memory. Routledge. https://doi.org/10.4324/9781315542768

Raffington, L., Belsky, D. W., Kothari, M., Malanchini, M., Tucker-Drob, E. M., & Harden, K. P. (2021). Socioeconomic disadvantage and the pace of biological aging in children. Pediatrics, 147(6). https://doi.org/10.1542/peds.2020-024406

Raffington, L., Tanksley, P. T., Sabhlok, A., Vinnik, L., Mallard, T., King, L. S., Goosby, B., Harden, K. P., & Tucker-Drob, E. M. (2023). Socially Stratified Epigenetic Profiles Are Associated With Cognitive Functioning in Children and Adolescents. Psychological Science, 34(2), 170–185. https://doi.org/10.1177/09567976221122760

Rafiee, F., Rezvani Habibabadi, R., Motaghi, M., Yousem, D. M., & Yousem, I. J. (2022). Brain MRI in autism spectrum disorder: Narrative review and recent advances. Journal of Magnetic Resonance Imaging, 55(6), 1613–1624. https://doi.org/10.1002/jmri.27949

Raftery, J. N., Grolnick, W. S., & Flamm, E. S. (2012). Families as facilitators of student engagement: Toward a home-school partnership model. In S. L. Christenson, A. L. Reschly, & C. Wylie (Eds.), Handbook of research on student engagement (pp. 343–364). Springer. https://doi.org/10.1007/978-1-4614-2018-7_16

Ragelienė, T. (2016). Links of adolescents identity development and relationship with peers: A systematic literature review. Journal of the Canadian Academy of Child and Adolescent Psychiatry, 25(2), 97–105.

Raifman, J., Charlton, B. M., Arrington-Sanders, R., Chan, P. A., Rusley, J., Mayer, K. H., Stein, M. D., Austin, S. B., & McConnell, M. (2020). Sexual orientation and suicide attempt disparities among US adolescents: 2009-2017. *Pediatrics*, *145*(3), e20191658. https://doi.org/10.1542/peds.2019-1658

Rainwater-Lovett, K., Luzuriaga, K., & Persaud, D. (2015). Very early combination antiretroviral therapy in infants: Prospects for cure. *Current Opinion in HIV and AIDS*, *10*(1), 4–11. https://doi.org/10.1097/COH.0000000000000127

Rajendran, K., Kruszewski, E., & Halperin, J. M. (2016). Parenting style influences bullying: A longitudinal study comparing children with and without behavioral problems. *Journal of Child Psychology and Psychiatry*, *57*(2), 188-195. https://doi.org/10.1111/jcpp.12433

Rakesh, D., & Whittle, S. (2021). Socioeconomic status and the developing brain – A systematic review of neuroimaging findings in youth. *Neuroscience & Biobehavioral Reviews*, *130*, 379-407. https://doi.org/10.1016/j.neubiorev.2021.08.027

Rakison, D. H., & Butterworth, G. E. (1998). Infants' use of object parts in early categorization. *Developmental Psychology*, *34*(1), 49–62. https://doi.org/10.1037/0012-1649.34.1.49

Rakoczy, H. (2022). Foundations of theory of mind and its development in early childhood. *Nature Reviews Psychology*, *1*(4), 223–235. https://doi.org/10.1038/s44159-022-00037-z

Rakoczy, H., Warneken, F., & Tomasello, M. (2007). "This way!" "No! That way!"—3-year olds know that two people can have mutually incompatible desires. *Cognitive Development*, *22*(1), 47–68. https://doi.org/10.1016/j.cogdev.2006.08.002

Raley, J. A., Fisher, W. M., Halder, R., & Shanmugan, K. (2013). Child custody and homosexual/bisexual parents: A survey of judges. *Journal of Child Custody*, *10*(1), 54–67. https://doi.org/10.1080/15379418.2013.781843

Raley, R. K., & Sweeney, M. M. (2020). Divorce, repartnering, and stepfamilies: A decade in review. *Journal of Marriage and Family*, *82*(1), 81–99. https://doi.org/10.1111/jomf.12651

Ramat, P. (2021). Morphological units: Words. In R. Lieber (Ed.), *Oxford research encyclopedia of linguistics*. Oxford University Press. https://doi.org/10.1093/acrefore/9780199384655.013.543

Rambaran, J. A., Hopmeyer, A., Schwartz, D., Steglich, C., Badaly, D., & Veenstra, R. (2017). Academic functioning and peer influences: A short-term longitudinal study of network-behavior dynamics in middle adolescence. *Child Development*, *88*(2), 523–543. https://doi.org/10.1111/cdev.12611

Ramchand, R., Gordon, J. A., & Pearson, J. L. (2021). Trends in suicide rates by race and ethnicity in the United States. *JAMA Network Open*, *4*(5), e2111563. doi:10.1001/jamanetworkopen.2021.11563

Ramey, C. T., & Ramey, S. L. (1998). Prevention of intellectual disabilities: Early interventions to improve cognitive development. *Preventive Medicine*, *27*, 224–232.

Ramírez, N. F., & Kuhl, P. K. (2016). *Bilingual language learning in children*. University of Washington.

Ramírez, P. C. (2020). Secondary dual language learners and emerging pedagogies. In C. J. Faltis & P. C. Ramírez (Eds.), *Dual language education in the US: Rethinking pedagogy, curricula, and teacher education to support dual language learning for all* (pp. 127-137). Taylor & Francis.

Ramos, G. G. F., Mengai, A. C. S., Daltro, C. A. T., Cutrim, P. T., Zlotnik, E., & Beck, A. P. A. (2021). Systematic review: Puberty suppression with GnRH analogues in adolescents with gender incongruity. *Journal of Endocrinological Investigation*, *44*(6), 1151–1158. https://doi.org/10.1007/s40618-020-01449-5

Ramraj, C., Pulver, A., O'Campo, P., Urquia, M. L., Hildebrand, V., & Siddiqi, A. (2020). A Scoping review of socioeconomic inequalities in distributions of birth outcomes: Through a conceptual and methodological lens. *Maternal and Child Health Journal*, *24*(2), 144-152. https://doi.org/10.1007/s10995-019-02838-w

Ramsaran, A. I., Schlichting, M. L., & Frankland, P. W. (2019). The ontogeny of memory persistence and specificity. *Developmental Cognitive Neuroscience*, *36*, 100591. https://doi.org/10.1016/j.dcn.2018.09.002

Ramsdell, H. L., Oller, D. K., Buder, E. H., Ethington, C. A., & Chorna, L. (2012). Identification of prelinguistic phonological categories. *Journal of Speech, Language, and Hearing Research*, *55*(6), 1626-1639. https://doi.org/10.1044/1092-4388(2012/11-0250

Ranjbar, A., Shirzadfard Jahromi, M., Boujarzadeh, B., Roozbeh, N., Mehrnoush, V., & Darsareh, F. (2023). Pregnancy, childbirth and neonatal outcomes associated with adolescent pregnancy. *Gynecology and Obstetrics Clinical Medicine*, *3*(2), 100–105. https://doi.org/10.1016/j.gocm.2023.02.002

Rapin, I., Shalev, R. S., Manor, O., Kerem, B., al, et., Molko, N., Cachia, A., Riviere, D., al, et., Docherty, S. J., Davis, O. S., Kovas, Y., al, et., Krapohl, E., Rimfeld, K., Shakeshaft, N. G., al, et., Kaufmann, L., Mazzocco, M. M., & &#hillip1; Honda, M. (2016). Dyscalculia and the calculating brain. *Pediatric Neurology*, *61*, 11–20. https://doi.org/10.1016/j.pediatrneurol.2016.02.007

Rapoport, E., Muthiah, N., Keim, S. A., & Adesman, A. (2020). Family well-being in grandparent-versus parent-headed households. *Pediatrics*, *146*(3), e20200115. https://doi.org/10.1542/peds.2020-0115

Rasmussen, S. A., & Jamieson, D. J. (2022). COVID-19 vaccination during pregnancy—two for the price of one. *New England Journal of Medicine*, *387*(2), 178–179. https://doi.org/10.1056/NEJMe2206730

Rattaz, V., Puglisi, N., Tissot, H., & Favez, N. (2022). Associations between parent–infant interactions, cortisol and vagal regulation in infants, and socioemotional outcomes: A systematic review. *Infant Behavior and Development*, *67*, 101687. https://doi.org/10.1016/j.infbeh.2022.101687

Raval, V. V., & Walker, B. L. (2019). Unpacking 'culture': Caregiver socialization of emotion and child functioning in diverse families. *Developmental Review*, *51*, 146-174. https://doi.org/10.1016/j.dr.2018.11.001

Ravitsky, V., Roy, M. C., Haidar, H., Henneman, L., Marshall, J., Newson, A. J., Ngan, O. M. Y., & Nov-Klaiman, T. (2021). The emergence and global spread of noninvasive prenatal testing. *Annual Review of Genomics and Human Genetics*, *2*(2). https://doi.org/10.1146/annurev-genom-083118-015053

Rayburn, A. D., McWey, L. M., & Gonzales-Backen, M. A. (2021). Living under the shadows: Experiences of Latino immigrant families at risk for deportation. *Family Relations*, *70*(2), 359–373. https://doi.org/10.1111/fare.12534

Reale, C., Invernizzi, F., Panteghini, C., & Garavaglia, B. (2023). Genetics, sex, and gender. *Journal of Neuroscience Research*, *101*(5), 553–562. https://doi.org/10.1002/jnr.24945

Ream, G. L., & Savin-Williams, R. C. (2006). Religious development in adolescence. In G. R. Adams & M. Berzonsky (Eds.), *Blackwell handbook of adolescence* (pp. 50–59). https://doi.org/10.1002/9780470756607.ch3

Rebbe, R., Mienko, J. A., Brown, E., & Rowhani-Rahbar, A. (2019a). Child protection reports and removals of infants diagnosed with prenatal substance exposure. *Child Abuse and Neglect*, *88*, 28–36. https://doi.org/10.1016/j.chiabu.2018.11.001

Rebbe, R., Mienko, J. A., Brown, E., & Rowhani-Rahbar, A. (2019b). Hospital variation in child protection reports of substance exposed infants. *Journal of Pediatrics*, 208, 141–147.e2. https://doi.org/10.1016/j.jpeds.2018.12.065

Rebbe, R., Sattler, K. M., & Mienko, J. A. (2022). The association of race, ethnicity, and poverty with child maltreatment reporting. *Pediatrics*, 150(2), e2021053346. https://doi.org/10.1542/peds.2021-053346

Redick, T. S., Unsworth, N., Kelly, A. J., & Engle, R. W. (2012). Faster, smarter? Working memory capacity and perceptual speed in relation to fluid intelligence. *Journal of Cognitive Psychology*, 24(7), 844–854. https://doi.org/10.1080/20445911.2012.704359

Rees, C. A., Monuteaux, M. C., Raphael, J. L., & Michelson, K. A. (2020). Disparities in pediatric mortality by neighborhood income in United States emergency departments. *Journal of Pediatrics*, 219, 209–215.e3. https://doi.org/10.1016/j.jpeds.2019.09.016

Regan, A. K., Bombard, J. M., O'Hegarty, M. M., Smith, R. A., & Tong, V. T. (2021). Adverse birth outcomes associated with prepregnancy and prenatal electronic cigarette use. *Obstetrics and Gynecology*, 138(1), 85–94. https://doi.org/10.1097/aog.0000000000004432

Regan, A. K., & Pereira, G. (2021). Patterns of combustible and electronic cigarette use during pregnancy and associated pregnancy outcomes. *Scientific Reports*, 11(1), 1–9. https://doi.org/10.1038/s41598-021-92930-5

Reh, R. K., Hensch, T. K., & Werker, J. F. (2021). Distributional learning of speech sound categories is gated by sensitive periods. *Cognition*, 213, 104653. https://doi.org/10.1016/j.cognition.2021.104653

Rehani, M. M., & Nacouzi, D. (2020). Higher patient doses through x-ray imaging procedures. *Physica Medica*, 79, 80–86. https://doi.org/10.1016/j.ejmp.2020.10.017

Reid, C. N., Fryer, K., Cabral, N., & Marshall, J. (2021). Health care system barriers and facilitators to early prenatal care among diverse women in Florida. *Birth*, 48(3). https://doi.org/10.1111/birt.12551

Reid, V. M., & Dunn, K. (2021). The fetal origins of human psychological development. *Current Directions in Psychological Science*, 30(2), 144–150. https://doi.org/10.1177/0963721420984419

Reigal, R. E., Moral-Campillo, L., Morillo-Baro, J. P., Juárez-Ruiz de Mier, R., Hernández-Mendo, A., & Morales-Sánchez, V. (2020). Physical exercise, fitness, cognitive functioning, and psychosocial variables in an adolescent sample. *International Journal of Environmental Research and Public Health*, 17(3), 1100. https://doi.org/10.3390/ijerph17031100

Reilly, J. J. (2007). Childhood obesity: An overview. *Children and Society*, 21(5), 390–396. https://doi.org/10.1111/j.1099-0860.2007.00092.x

Reis, L. F., Surkan, P. J., Atkins, K., Garcia-Cerde, R., & Sanchez, Z. M. (2023). Risk factors for early sexual intercourse in adolescence: A systematic review of cohort studies. *Child Psychiatry & Human Development*. https://doi.org/10.1007/s10578-023-01519-8

Reis, O., & Youniss, J. (2004). Patterns in Identity Change and Development in Relationships With Mothers and Friends. *Journal of Adolescent Research*, 19(1), 31–44.

Reiss, F., Meyrose, A.-K., Otto, C., Lampert, T., Klasen, F., & Ravens-Sieberer, U. (2019). Socioeconomic status, stressful life situations and mental health problems in children and adolescents: Results of the German BELLA cohort-study. *PLoS ONE*, 14(3), e0213700. https://doi.org/10.1371/journal.pone.0213700

Reissland, N., Francis, B., & Mason, J. (2013). Can healthy fetuses show facial expressions of "pain" or "distress"? *PLoS ONE*, 8(6), e65530. https://doi.org/10.1371/journal.pone.0065530

Reiter, E. O., & Lee, P. A. (2001). Have the onset and tempo of puberty changed? *Archives of Pediatrics & Adolescent Medicine*, 155(9), 988–989. https://doi.org/10.1001/archpedi.155.9.988

Reitsema, A. M., Jeronimus, B. F., van Dijk, M., & de Jonge, P. (2021). Emotion dynamics in children and adolescents: A meta-analytic and descriptive review. *Emotion*, 22(2), 374–396. https://doi.org/10.1037/emo0000970

Rekow, D., Leleu, A., Poncet, F., Damon, F., Rossion, B., Durand, K., Schaal, B., & Baudouin, J. Y. (2020). Categorization of objects and faces in the infant brain and its sensitivity to maternal odor: Further evidence for the role of intersensory congruency in perceptual development. *Cognitive Development*, 55, 100930. https://doi.org/10.1016/j.cogdev.2020.100930

Relji, G., Ferring, D., & Martin, R. (2015). A meta-analysis on the effectiveness of bilingual programs in Europe. *Review of Educational Research*, 85(1), 92–128. https://doi.org/10.3102/0034654314548514

Remer, J., Croteau-Chonka, E., Dean, D. C., D'Arpino, S., Dirks, H., Whiley, D., & Deoni, S. C. L. (2017). Quantifying cortical development in typically developing toddlers and young children, 1–6 years of age. *NeuroImage*, 153, 246–261. https://doi.org/10.1016/j.neuroimage.2017.04.010

Remien, K., & Kanchan, T. (2022, November 15). *Parental consent*. StatPearls. https://doi.org/10.4135/9781452240121.n263

Remon, D., Loevenbruck, H., Deudon, M., Girardie, O., Bouyer, K., Pascalis, O., & Thorpe, S. (2020). 24-month-olds and over remember novel object names after a single learning event. *Journal of Experimental Child Psychology*, 196, 104859. https://doi.org/10.1016/j.jecp.2020.104859

Renfrew, M. J., McFadden, A., Bastos, M. H., Campbell, J., Channon, A. A., Cheung, N. F., Silva, D. R. A. D., Downe, S., Kenned., H. P., Malata, A., McCormick, F., Wick, L., & Declercq, E. (2014). Midwifery and quality care: Findings from a new evidence-informed framework for maternal and newborn care. *Lancet*, 384(9948), 1129–1145. https://doi.org/10.1016/S0140-6736(14)60789-3

Rennels, J. L., & Kayl, A. J. (2017). How experience affects infants' facial categorization. In H. Cohen & C. Lefebvre (Eds.), *Handbook of categorization in cognitive science* (pp. 637–652). Elsevier. https://doi.org/10.1016/B978-0-08-101107-2.00026-9

Renzulli, J. S. (2020). Reflections on my work: The identification and development of creative/productive giftedness. In D. Y. Dai & R. J. Sternberg (Eds.), *Scientific inquiry into human potential*. Routledge.

Reschke, P. J., Fraser, A. M., Picket, J., Workman, K., Lehnardt, H., Stockdale, L. A., Padilla-Walker, L. M., Cox, K., Holmgren, H. G., Hagen, S., Summers, K., Clifford, B. N., Essig, L. W., & Coyne, S. M. (2023). Variability in infant helping and sharing behaviors across the second and third years of life: Differential roles of target and socialization. *Developmental Psychology*, 59, 524–537. https://doi.org/10.1037/dev0001441

Rew, L., Young, C. C., Monge, M., & Bogucka, R. (2021). Review: Puberty blockers for transgender and gender diverse youth—A critical review of the literature. *Child and Adolescent Mental Health*, 26(1), 3–14. https://doi.org/10.1111/CAMH.12437

Rey-Mermet, A., Gade, M., Souza, A. S., von Bastian, C. C., & Oberauer, K. (2019). Is executive control related to working memory capacity and fluid intelligence? *Journal of Experimental Psychology: General*, 148(8), 1335–1372. https://doi.org/10.1037/xge0000593

Reyes, L. M., Jaekel, J., Bartmann, P., & Wolke, D. (2021). Peer relationship trajectories in very preterm and term individuals from childhood to early adulthood. *Journal of Developmental & Behavioral Pediatrics*, *42*(8), 621–630. https://doi.org/10.1097/DBP.0000000000000949

Reyes, L. M., Jaekel, J., Kreppner, J., Wolke, D., & Sonuga-Barke, E. (2019). A comparison of the effects of preterm birth and institutional deprivation on child temperament. *Development and Psychopathology*, *32*(4), 1–10. https://doi.org/10.1017/s0954579419001457

Reyna, V. F., & Rivers, S. E. (2008). Current theories of risk and rational decision making. *Developmental Review*, *28*(1), 1–11. https://doi.org/10.1016/j.dr.2008.01.002

Reynolds, G. D., & Romano, A. C. (2016). The development of attention systems and working memory in infancy. *Frontiers in Systems Neuroscience*, *10*, 15. https://doi.org/10.3389/fnsys.2016.00015

Reynolds, M., Hajovsky, D., & Caemmerer, J. M. (2022). The sexes do not differ in general intelligence, but they do in some specifics. *Elsevier*, *92*, 101651.

Reynolds, M. R., Niileksela, C. R., Gignac, G. E., & Sevillano, C. N. (2022). Working memory capacity development through childhood: A longitudinal analysis. *Developmental Psychology*, *58*, 1254–1263. https://doi.org/10.1037/dev0001360

Rezaeiyeh, R. D., Mehrara, A., Pour, A. M. A., Fallahi, J., & Forouhari, S. (2022). Impact of various parameters as predictors of the success rate of in vitro fertilization. *International Journal of Fertility & Sterility*, *16*(2), 76. https://doi.org/10.22074/IJFS.2021.531672.1134

Ribner, A. D., & McHarg, G. (2021). Screens across the pond: Findings from longitudinal screen time research in the US and UK. *Infant Behavior and Development*, *63*, 101551. https://doi.org/10.1016/j.infbeh.2021.101551

Ricciardi, C., Manfra, L., Hartman, S., Bleiker, C., Dineheart, L., & Winsler, A. (2021). School readiness skills at age four predict academic achievement through 5th grade. *Early Childhood Research Quarterly*, *57*, 110–120. https://doi.org/10.1016/J.ECRESQ.2021.05.006

Richards, J. E. (1997). Effects of attention on infant's preference for briefly exposed visual stimuli in the paired-comparison recognition-memory paradigm. *Developmental Psychology*, *32*, 22–31.

Richards, J. E. (2010). The development of attention to simple and complex visual stimuli in infants: Behavioral and psychophysiological measures. *Developmental Review*, *30*(2), 203–219. https://doi.org/10.1016/j.dr.2010.03.005

Richards, M. H., & Larson, R. (1993). Pubertal development and the daily subjective states of young adolescents. *Journal of Research on Adolescence*, *3*(2), 145–169. https://doi.org/10.1207/s15327795jra0302_3

Richards, T. L., Grabowski, T. J., Boord, P., Yagle, K., Askren, M., Mestre, Z., Robinson, P., Welker, O., Gulliford, D., Nagy, W., & Berninger, V. (2015). Contrasting brain patterns of writing-related DTI parameters, fMRI connectivity, and DTI-fMRI connectivity correlations in children with and without dysgraphia or dyslexia. *NeuroImage: Clinical*, *8*, 408–421. https://doi.org/10.1016/J.NICL.2015.03.018

Richardson, K., & Norgate, S. H. (2015). Does IQ really predict job performance? *Applied Developmental Science*, *19*(3), 153–169. https://doi.org/10.1080/10888691.2014.983635

Richlan, F. (2019). The functional neuroanatomy of letter-speech sound integration and its relation to brain abnormalities in developmental dyslexia. *Frontiers in Human Neuroscience*, *13*, 21. https://doi.org/10.3389/fnhum.2019.00021

Richmond, A. D., Laursen, B., & Stattin, H. (2019). Homophily in delinquent behavior: The rise and fall of friend similarity across adolescence. *International Journal of Behavioral Development*, *43*(1), 67–73. https://doi.org/10.1177/0165025418767058

Rickard, I. J., Frankenhuis, W. E., & Nettle, D. (2014). Why are childhood family factors associated with timing of maturation? A role for internal prediction. *Perspectives on Psychological Science*, *9*(1), 3–15. https://doi.org/10.1177/1745691613513467

Riddle, K., & Martins, N. (2022). A content analysis of American primetime television: A 20-year update of the national television violence studies. *Journal of Communication*, *72*(1), 33–58. https://doi.org/10.1093/joc/jqab043

Rideout, V. J., & Katz, V. S. (2016). *Opportunity for all? Technology and learning in lower-income families*. Joan Ganz Cooney Center at Sesame Workshop https://eric.ed.gov/?id=ED574416

Rideout, V. J., Peebles, A., Mann, S., & Robb, M. B. (2022). *Common Sense census: Media use by tweens and teens, 2021*. Common Sense.

Rideout, V. J., & Robb, M. B. (2020). *The Common Sense Census: Media use by kids age zero to eight, 2020*. Common Sense.

Rideout, V. J., & Robb, M. B. (2021). *The role of media during the pandemic: Connection, creativity, and learning for tweens and teens*. Common Sense. https://www.commonsensemedia.org/sites/default/files/research/report/8-18-role-of-media-research-report-final-web.pdf

Rider, G. N., McMorris, B. J., Gower, A. L., Coleman, E., & Eisenberg, M. E. (2018). Health and care utilization of transgender and gender nonconforming youth: A population-based study. *Pediatrics*, *141*(3), e20171683. https://doi.org/10.1542/peds.2017-1683

Riediger, M., & Bellingtier, J. A. (2022). Emotion regulation across the life span. In D. Dukes, A. C. Samson, & E. A. Walle (Eds.), *The Oxford handbook of emotional development* (pp. 93–109). Oxford University Press. https://doi.org/10.1093/oxfordhb/9780198855903.001.0001

Rigato, S., De Sepulveda, R., Richardson, E., & Filippetti, M. L. (2024). This is me! Neural correlates of self-recognition in 6- to 8-month-old infants. *Child Development*, *95*, 1797–1810. https://doi.org/10.1111/cdev.14102

Riggins, T., & Bauer, P. J. (2022). A developmental cognitive neuroscience approach to the study of memory. In M. L. Courage & N. Cowan (Eds.), *The development of memory in infancy and childhood* (3rd ed., pp. 1–30). Psychology Press.

Riggins, T., Canad., K. L., & Botdorf, M. (2020). Empirical evidence supporting neural contributions to episodic memory development in early childhood: Implications for childhood amnesia. *Child Development Perspectives*, *14*(1), 41–48. https://doi.org/10.1111/cdep.12353

Rigney, J., & Wang, S. (2015). Delineating the boundaries of infants' spatial categories: The case of containment. *Journal of Cognition and Development*, *16*(3), 420–441. https://doi.org/10.1080/15248372.2013.848868

Rindermann, H., & Thompson, J. (2013). Ability rise in NAEP and narrowing ethnic gaps? *Intelligence*, *41*(6), 821–831. https://doi.org/10.1016/j.intell.2013.06.016

Rind et al. Lilienfeld, S. O. (2002). When worlds collide. Social science, politics, and the. Child sexual abuse meta-analysis. *American Psychologist*, *57*(3), 176–188. 1998

Risi, A., Pickard, J. A., & Bird, A. L. (2021). The implications of parent mental health and wellbeing for parent-child attachment:

A systematic review. *PLoS ONE*, *16*(12), e0260891. https://doi.org/10.1371/journal.pone.0260891

Ristic, J., & Enns, J. T. (2015a). Attentional development. In L. S. Liben & U. Muller (Eds.), *Handbook of child psychology and developmental science* (pp. 1–45). John Wiley & Sons. https://doi.org/10.1002/9781118963418.childpsy205

Ristic, J., & Enns, J. T. (2015b). The changing face of attentional development. *Current Directions in Psychological Science*, *24*(1), 24–31. https://doi.org/10.1177/0963721414551165

Ristori, J., & Steensma, T. D. (2016). Gender dysphoria in childhood. *International Review of Psychiatry*, *28*(1), 13–20. https://doi.org/10.3109/09540261.2015.1115754

Ritchie, K., Bora, S., & Woodward, L. J. (2018). Peer relationship outcomes of school-age children born very preterm. *Journal of Pediatrics*, *201*, 238–244. https://doi.org/10.1016/j.jpeds.2018.05.034

Ritz, B. R., Chatterjee, N., Garcia-Closas, M., Gauderman, W. J., Pierce, B. L., Kraft, P., Tanner, C. M., Mechanic, L. E., & McAllister, K. (2017). Lessons learned from past gene-environment interaction successes. *American Journal of Epidemiology*, *186*(7), 778–786. https://doi.org/10.1093/aje/kwx230

Riva, D. (2023). Sex and gender difference in cognitive and behavioral studies in developmental age: An introduction. *Journal of Neuroscience Research*, *101*(5), 543–552. https://doi.org/10.1002/jnr.24970

Rivas-Drake, D., Lozada, F. T., Pinetta, B. J., & Jagers, R. J. (2020). School-based social-emotional learning and ethnic-racial identity among African American and Latino adolescents. *Youth & Society*, *52*(7), 1331–1354. https://doi.org/10.1177/0044118X20939736

Rivas-Drake, D., Seaton, E. K., Markstrom, C., Quintana, S., Syed, M., Lee, R. M., Schwartz, S. J., Umaña-Taylor, A. J., French, S., & Yip, T. (2014). Ethnic and racial identity in adolescence: Implications for psychosocial, academic, and health outcomes. *Child Development*, *85*(1), 40–57. https://doi.org/10.1111/cdev.12200

Rivas-Drake, D., Umaña-Taylor, A. J., Schaefer, D. R., & Medina, M. (2017). Ethnic-racial identity and friendships in early adolescence. *Child Development*, *88*(3), 710–724. https://doi.org/10.1111/cdev.12790

Roa, J., & Tena-Sempere, M. (2014). Connecting metabolism and reproduction: Roles of central energy sensors and key molecular mediators. *Molecular and Cellular Endocrinology*, *397*(1–2), 4–14. https://doi.org/10.1016/j.mce.2014.09.027

Robbins, E., Starr, S., & Rochat, P. (2016). Fairness and distributive justice by 3- to 5-year-old Tibetan children. *Journal of Cross-Cultural Psychology*, *47*(3), 333–340. https://doi.org/10.1177/0022022115620487

Robbins, J. (2005). Contexts, collaboration, and cultural tools: A sociocultural perspective on researching children's thinking. *Contemporary Issues in Early Childhood*, *6*(2), 140–149. https://doi.org/10.2304/ciec.2005.6.2.4

Roberge, S., Bujold, E., & Nicolaides, K. H. (2017). Aspirin for the prevention of preterm and term preeclampsia: Systematic review and meta-analysis. *American Journal of Obstetrics and Gynecology*, *218*(3), 287–293. https://doi.org/10.1016/j.ajog.2017.11.561

Roberts, A. L., Rosario, M., Slopen, N., Calzo, J. P., & Austin, S. B. (2013). Childhood gender nonconformity, bullying victimization, and depressive symptoms across adolescence and early adulthood: An 11-year longitudinal study. *Journal of the American Academy of Child and Adolescent Psychiatry*, *52*(2), 143–152. https://doi.org/10.1016/j.jaac.2012.11.006

Roberts, G., Quach, J., Mensah, F., Gathercole, S., Gold, L., Anderson, P., Spencer-Smith, M., & Wake, M. (2015). Schooling duration rather than chronological age predicts working memory between 6 and 7 years. *Journal of Developmental & Behavioral Pediatrics*, *36*(2), 68–74. https://doi.org/10.1097/dbp.0000000000000121

Roberts, S. C. M., & Nuru-Jeter, A. (2012). Universal screening for alcohol and drug use and racial disparities in child protective services reporting. *Journal of Behavioral Health Services & Research*, *39*(1), 3–16. https://doi.org/10.1007/s11414-011-9247-x

Roberts, S. O., & Gelman, S. A. (2017). Now you see race, now you don't: Verbal cues influence children's racial stability judgments. *Cognitive Development*, *43*, 129–141. https://doi.org/10.1016/j.cogdev.2017.03.003

Robinson, E., Daly, M., & Sutin, A. (2020). Association of parental identification of child overweight and mental health problems during childhood. *International Journal of Obesity*, *44*(9), 1928–1935. https://doi.org/10.1038/s41366-020-0587-6

Robinson, J. B., Burns, B. M., & Davis, D. Winders. (2009). Maternal scaffolding and attention regulation in children living in poverty. *Journal of Applied Developmental Psychology*, *30*(2), 82–91. https://doi.org/10.1016/j.appdev.2008.10.013

Robinson, K., Fial, A., & Hanson, L. (2019). Racism, bias, and discrimination as modifiable barriers to breastfeeding for African American women: A scoping review of the literature. *Journal of Midwifery & Women's Health*, *64*(6), 734–742. https://doi.org/10.1111/jmwh.13058

Robinson, T. N., Banda, J. A., Hale, L., Lu, A. S., Fleming-Milici, F., Calvert, S. L., & Wartella, E. (2017). Screen media exposure and obesity in children and adolescents. *Pediatrics*, *140*(Suppl 2), S97–S101. https://doi.org/10.1542/peds.2016-1758K

Roby, A. C., & Kidd, E. (2008). The referential communication skills of children with imaginary companions. *Developmental Science*, *11*(4), 531–540. https://doi.org/10.1111/j.1467-7687.2008.00699.x

Rochat, P. (1998). Self-perception and action in infancy. *Experimental Brain Research*, *123*(1–2), 102–109. https://doi.org/10.1007/s002210050550

Rochat, P. (2010). Emerging self-concept. In J. G. Bremner & T. D. Wachs (Eds.), *The Wiley-Blackwell handbook of infant development* (pp. 320–344). Wiley-Blackwell. https://doi.org/10.1002/9781444327564.ch10

Rochat, P. (2013). Self-conceptualizing in development. In P. D. Zelazo (Ed.), *The Oxford handbook of developmental psychology Self and other* (Vol. 2, pp. 378–396). Oxford University Press. https://doi.org/10.1093/oxfordhb/9780199958474.013.0015

Rochat, P. (2018). The ontogeny of human self-consciousness. *Current Directions in Psychological Science*, *27*(5), 345–350. https://doi.org/10.1177/0963721418760236

Rochat, P. (2019). Self-unity as ground zero of learning and development. *Frontiers in Psychology*, *10*(MAR), 414. https://doi.org/10.3389/FPSYG.2019.00414

Rochat, P. (2023). The evolution of developmental theories since Piaget: A metaview. *Perspectives on Psychological Science*. https://doi.org/10.1177/17456916231186611

Rochat, P., Broesch, T., & Jayne, K. (2012). Social awareness and early self-recognition. *Consciousness and Cognition*, *21*(3), 1491–1497. https://doi.org/10.1016/j.concog.2012.04.007

Rochat, P., Dias, M. D. G., Guo Liping, G., Broesch, T., Passos-Ferreira, C., Winning, A., & Berg, B. (2009). Fairness in distributive justice by 3- and 5-year-olds across seven cultures. *Journal of Cross-Cultural Psychology*, *40*(3), 416–442. https://doi.org/10.1177/0022022109332844

Roche, L., Tones, M., Cross, M., Bellgard, M., & Heussler, H. (2022). An overview of the adaptive behaviour profile in young children with Angelman syndrome: Insights from the Global Angelman Syndrome Registry. *Advances in Neurodevelopmental Disorders*, *6*, 442–455. https://doi.org/10.1007/s41252-022-00278-2

Rock, P. F., Cole, D. J., Houshyar, S., Lythcott, M., & Prinstein, M. J. (2011). Peer status in an ethnic context: Associations with African American adolescents' ethnic identity. *Journal of Applied Developmental Psychology*, *32*(4), 163–169. https://doi.org/10.1016/j.appdev.2011.03.002

Röder, B., Kekunnaya, R., & Guerreiro, M. J. S. (2021). Neural mechanisms of visual sensitive periods in humans. *Neuroscience and Biobehavioral Reviews*, *12*(0). https://doi.org/10.1016/j.neubiorev.2020.10.030

Rodprasert, W., JormaTopparia, & Virtanen, H. E. (2023). Environmental toxicants and male fertility. *Best Practice & Research Clinical Obstetrics & Gynaecology*, 102298. https://doi.org/10.1016/j.bpobgyn.2022.102298

Rodriguez, S. (2017). "People hide, but I'm here. I count:" Examining undocumented youth identity formation in an urban community-school. *Educational Studies*, *53*(5), 468–491. https://doi.org/10.1080/00131946.2017.1322970

Rodríguez-Meirinhos, A., Vansteenkiste, M., Soenens, B., Oliva, A., Brenning, K., & Antolín-Suárez, L. (2020). When is parental monitoring effective? A person-centered analysis of the role of autonomy-supportive and psychologically controlling parenting in referred and non-referred adolescents. *Journal of Youth and Adolescence*, *49*(1), 352–368. https://doi.org/10.1007/s10964-019-01151-7

Rodway, C., Tham, S. G., Turnbull, P., Kapur, N., & Appleby, L. (2020). Suicide in children and young people: Can it happen without warning? *Journal of Affective Disorders*, *275*(1), 307–310. https://doi.org/10.1016/j.jad.2020.06.069

Roe, J. (2019). Social-emotional aspects of visual impairment: A practitioner's perspective. In *The Routledge Handbook of Visual Impairment*. Routledge.

Rogers, A. A., DeLay, D., & Martin, C. L. (2017). Traditional masculinity during the middle school transition: Associations with depressive symptoms and academic engagement. *Journal of Youth and Adolescence*, *46*(4), 709–724. https://doi.org/10.1007/s10964-016-0545-8

Rogers, C. R., Chen, X., Kwon, S.-J., McElwain, N. L., & Telzer, E. H. (2022). The role of early attachment and parental presence in adolescent behavioral and neurobiological regulation. *Developmental Cognitive Neuroscience*, *53*, 101046. https://doi.org/10.1016/j.dcn.2021.101046

Rogler, L. H. (2002). Historical generations and psychology: The case of the Great Depression and World War II. *American Psychologist*, *57*, 1013–1023.

Rogoff, B. (2003). *The cultural nature of human development*. Oxford University Press.

Rogoff, B. (2014). Learning by observing and pitching in to family and community endeavors: An orientation. *Human Development*, *57*(2–3), 69–81. https://doi.org/10.1159/000356757

Rogoff, B. (2016). Culture and participation: A paradigm shift. *Current Opinion in Psychology*, *8*, 182–189. https://doi.org/10.1016/j.copsyc.2015.12.002

Rogoff, B., Callanan, M., Gutiérrez, K. D., & Erickson, F. (2016). The organization of informal learning. *Review of Research in Education*, *40*(1), 356–401. https://doi.org/10.3102/0091732X16680994

Rogoff, B., & Chavajay, P. (1995). What's become of research on the cultural basis of cognitive development? *American Psychologist*, *50*(10), 859–877. https://doi.org/10.1037/0003-066X.50.10.859

Rogoff, B., Dahl, A., & Callanan, M. (2018). The importance of understanding children's lived experience. *Developmental Review*, *50*, 5–15. https://doi.org/10.1016/j.dr.2018.05.006

Rogoff, B., Moore, L. C., Correa-Chavez, M., & Dexter, A. L. (2014). Children develop cultural repertoires through engaging in everyday routines and practices. In J. Grusec & P. Hastings (Eds.), *Handbook of socialization: Theory and research* (pp. 472–498).

Rogoff, B., & Waddell, K. J. (1982). Memory for information organized in a scene by children from two cultures. *Child Development*, *53*(5), 1224–1228. https://doi.org/10.2307/1129009

Rolls, E. T. (2017). Evolution of the emotional brain. In S. Watanabe, M. A. Hofman, & T. Shimizu (Eds.), *Evolution of the brain, cognition, and emotion in vertebrates* (pp. 251–272). Springer Japan. https://doi.org/10.1007/978-4-431-56559-8_12

Romani, C., Olson, A., Aitkenhead, L., Baker, L., Patel, D., Spronsen, F. V., MacDonald, A., Wegberg, A. van., & Huijbregts, S. (2022). Meta-analyses of cognitive functions in early-treated adults with phenylketonuria. *Neuroscience & Biobehavioral Reviews*, *43*, 104925. https://doi.org/10.1016/J.NEUBIOREV.2022.104925

Romani, C., Palermo, L., MacDonald, A., Limback, E., Hall, S. K., & Geberhiwot, T. (2017). The impact of phenylalanine levels on cognitive outcomes in adults with phenylketonuria: Effects across tasks and developmental stages. *Neuropsychology*, *31*(3), 242–254. https://doi.org/10.1037/neu0000336

Rome, S. H., & Raskin, M. (2019). Transitioning out of foster care: The first 12 months. *Youth & Society*, *51*(4), 529–547. https://doi.org/10.1177/0044118X17694968

Romera, E. M., Bravo, A., Ortega-Ruiz, R., & Veenstra, R. (2019). Differences in perceived popularity and social preference between bullying roles and class norms. *PLoS ONE*, *14*(10), e0223499. https://doi.org/10.1371/journal.pone.0223499

Romero, A. J., Edwards, L. M., Fryberg, S. A., & Orduña, M. (2014). Resilience to discrimination stress across ethnic identity stages of development. *Journal of Applied Social Psychology*, *44*(1), 1–11. https://doi.org/10.1111/jasp.12192

Romm, K. F., & Metzger, A. (2021). Profiles of parenting behaviors: Associations with adolescents' problematic outcomes. *Journal of Child and Family Studies*, *30*(4), 941–954. https://doi.org/10.1007/s10826-021-01920-8

Roncero, C., Valriberas-Herrero, I., Mezzatesta-Gava, M., Villegas, J. L., Aguilar, L., & Grau-López, L. (2020). Cannabis use during pregnancy and its relationship with fetal developmental outcomes and psychiatric disorders. A systematic review. *Reproductive Health*, *17*(1), 1–9. https://doi.org/10.1186/S12978-020-0880-9

Roopnarine, J. L., Talukder, E., Jain, D., Joshi, P., & Srivastav, P. (1992). Personal well-being, kinship tie, and mother-infant and father-infant interactions in single-wage and dual-wage families in New Delhi, India. *Journal of Marriage & Family*, *54*(2), 293–301.

Roos, L. E., Salisbury, M., Penner-Goeke, L., Cameron, E. E., Protudjer, J. L. P., Giuliano, R., Afifi, T. O., & Reynolds, K. (2021). Supporting families to protect child health: Parenting quality and household needs during the COVID-19 pandemic. *PLoS ONE*, *16*(5), e0251720. https://doi.org/10.1371/journal.pone.0251720

Rose, A. J., Borowski, S. K., Spiekerman, A., & Smith, R. L. (2022). Children's friendships. In *The Wiley-Blackwell handbook of childhood social development* (pp. 487–502). John Wiley & Sons. https://doi.org/10.1002/9781119679028.ch26

Rose, J., Roman, N., Mwaba, K., & Ismail, K. (2018). The relationship between parenting and internalizing behaviours of children: A systematic review. *Early Child Development and Care*, *188*(10), 1468–1486. https://doi.org/10.1080/03004430.2016.1269762

Rose, S. A., Feldman, J. F., Jankowski, J. J., & Van Rossem, R. (2012). Information processing from infancy to 11 years: Continuities and prediction of IQ. *Intelligence*, *40*(5), 445–457. https://doi.org/10.1016/j.intell.2012.05.007

Rose, T., McDonald, A., Von Mach, T., Witherspoon, D. P., & Lambert, S. (2019). Patterns of social connectedness and psychosocial wellbeing among African American and Caribbean Black adolescents. *Journal of Youth and Adolescence*, *48*(11), 2271–2291. https://doi.org/10.1007/s10964-019-01135-7

Rose-Greenland, F., & Smock, P. J. (2013). Living together unmarried: What do we know about cohabiting families? In G. W. Peterson & K. R. Bush (Eds.), *Handbook of marriage and the family* (pp. 255–273). Springer.

Rosenthal, S. M. (2021). Challenges in the care of transgender and gender-diverse youth: An endocrinologist's view. *Nature Reviews Endocrinology*, *17*(10), 581–591. https://doi.org/10.1038/s41574-021-00535-9

Rosiak-Gill, A., Gill, K., Jakubik, J., Fraczek, M., Patorski, L., Gaczarzewicz, D., Kurzawa, R., Kurpisz, M., & Piasecka, M. (2019). Age-related changes in human sperm DNA integrity. *Aging*, *11*(15), 5399–5411. https://doi.org/10.18632/aging.102120

Ross, E. S. (2017). Flavor and taste development in the first years of life. *Nestle Nutrition Institute Workshop Series*, *87*, 49–58. https://doi.org/10.1159/000448937

Ross, J., Hutchison, J., & Cunningham, S. J. (2020). The me in memory: The role of the self in autobiographical memory development. *Child Development*, *91*(2), e299–e314. https://doi.org/10.1111/cdev.13211

Ross, J., Yilmaz, M., Dale, R., Cassidy, R., Yildirim, I., & Suzanne Zeedyk, M. (2017). Cultural differences in self-recognition: The early development of autonomous and related selves? *Developmental Science*, *20*(3), e12387. https://doi.org/10.1111/desc.12387

Ross-Sheehy, S., & Eschman, B. (2019). Assessing visual STM in infants and adults: Eye movements and pupil dynamics reflect memory maintenance. *Visual Cognition*, *27*(1), 78–92. https://doi.org/10.1080/13506285.2019.1600089

Rosselli, M., Ermini, E., Tosi, B., Boddi, M., Stefani, L., Toncelli, L., & Modesti, P. A. (2020). Gender differences in barriers to physical activity among adolescents. *Nutrition, Metabolism and Cardiovascular Diseases*, *30*(9), 1582–1589. https://doi.org/10.1016/j.numecd.2020.05.005

Rote, W. M., & Smetana, J. G. (2016). Beliefs about parents' right to know: Domain differences and associations with change in concealment. *Journal of Research on Adolescence*, *26*, 334–344. https://doi.org/10.1111/jora.12194

Rote, W. M., Smetana, J. G., & Feliscar, L. (2020). Longitudinal associations between adolescent information management and mother-teen relationship quality: Between-versus within-family differences. *Developmental Psychology*, *56*(10), 1935–1947. https://doi.org/10.1037/dev0000947

Rothbart, M. K. (2011). *Becoming who we are: Temperament and personality in development*. Guilford.

Rothbart, M. K., & Bates, J. E. (2007). Temperament. In N. Eisenberg (Ed.), *Handbook of child psychology* (pp. 207–212). John Wiley & Sons. https://doi.org/10.1002/9780470147658.chpsy0303

Rothbart, M. K., & Posner, M. I. (2022). Individual differences in temperament and the efficiency of brain networks. *Current Opinion in Behavioral Sciences*, *43*, 242–248. https://doi.org/10.1016/J.COBEHA.2021.11.001

Rothbaum, F., Weisz, J., Pott, M., Miyake, K., & Morelli, G. (2000). Attachment and culture: Security in the United States and Japan. *American Psychologist*, *55*, 1093–1104. https://doi.org/10.1037//0003-066x.55.10.1093

Rothe, E. M., Fortuna, L. R., Tobon, A. L., Postlethwaite, A., Sanchez-Lacay, J. A., & Anglero, Y. L. (2021). Structural inequities and the impact of COVID-19 on Latinx children: Implications for child and adolescent mental health practice. *Journal of the American Academy of Child and Adolescent Psychiatry*, *60*(6), 669–671. https://doi.org/10.1016/j.jaac.2021.02.013

Rotstein, M., Stolar, O., Uliel, S., Mandel, D., Mani, A., Dollberg, S., Reifen, R., Steiner, J. E., Harel, S., & Leitner, Y. (2015). Facial expression in response to smell and taste stimuli in small and appropriate for gestational age newborns. *Journal of Child Neurology*, *30*(11), 1466–1471. https://doi.org/10.1177/0883073815570153

Rovee-Collier, C. K., & Bhatt, R. S. (1993). Evidence of long-term memory in infancy. *Annals of Child Development*, *9*, 1–45.

Rowe, M. L. (2012). A longitudinal investigation of the role of quantity and quality of child-directed speech in vocabulary development. *Child Development*, *83*(5), 1762–1774. https://doi.org/10.1111/j.1467-8624.2012.01805.x

Rowe, M. L. (2018). Understanding socioeconomic differences in parents' speech to children. *Child Development Perspectives*, *12*(2), 122–127. https://doi.org/10.1111/cdep.12271

Rowe, M. L., Wei, R., & Salo, V. C. (2022). Early gesture predicts later language development. In *Gesture in language: Development across the lifespan* (pp. 93–111). American Psychological Association. https://doi.org/10.1037/0000269-004

Rowe, M. L., & Weisleder, A. (2020). Language development in context. *Annual Review of Developmental Psychology*, *2*(1), 201–223. https://doi.org/10.1146/annurev-devpsych-042220-121816

Ruba, A. L., & Repacholi, B. M. (2020). Do preverbal infants understand discrete facial expressions of emotion? *Emotion Review*, *12*(4), 235–250. https://doi.org/10.1177/1754073919871098

Rubin, J. D., Gülgöz, S., Alonso, D., & Olson, K. R. (2020). Transgender and cisgender children's stereotypes and beliefs about others' stereotypes. *Social Psychological and Personality Science*, *11*(5), 638–646. https://doi.org/10.1177/1948550619879911

Rubin, K. H., Bukowski, W. M., & Bowker, J. C. (2015). Children in peer groups. In M. H. Bornstein & T. Leventhal (Eds.), *Handbook of child psychology and developmental science* (pp. 1–48). John Wiley & Sons. https://doi.org/10.1002/9781118963418.childpsy405

Rubin, K. H., & Chronis-Tuscano, A. (2021). Perspectives on Social Withdrawal in Childhood: Past, Present, and Prospects. *Child Development Perspectives*, *15*(3), 160–167. https://doi.org/10.1111/cdep.12417

Rubin, K. H., Coplan, R. J., & Bowker, J. C. (2009). Social withdrawal in childhood. *Annual Review of Psychology*, *60*(1), 141–171. https://doi.org/10.1146/annurev.psych.60.110707.163642

Rubin, K. H., Hastings, P., Chen, X., Stewart, S., & McNichol, K. (1998). Interpersonal and maternal correlates of aggression, conflict, and externalizing problems in toddlers. *Child Development*, *69*, 1614–1629. https://doi.org/10.2307/1132135

Rubin, K. H., Wojslawowicz, J. C., Rose-Krasnor, L., Booth-LaForce, C., & Burgess, K. B. (2006). The best friendships of shy/

withdrawn children: Prevalence, stability, and relationship quality. *Journal of Abnormal Child Psychology, 34*(2), 143–157. https://doi.org/10.1007/s10802-005-9017-4

Rubio-Fernández, P. (2019). Publication standards in infancy research: Three ways to make violation-of-expectation studies more reliable. *Infant Behavior and Development, 54*, 177–188. https://doi.org/10.1016/j.infbeh.2018.09.009

Rudolph, K. D., & Dodson, J. F. (2022). Gender differences in friendship values: Intensification at adolescence. *Journal of Early Adolescence, 42*(4), 586–607. https://doi.org/10.1177/02724316211051948

Rudolph, K. D., Troop-Gordon, W., Lambert, S. F., & Natsuaki, M. N. (2014). Long-term consequences of pubertal timing for youth depression: Identifying personal and contextual pathways of risk. *Development and Psychopathology, 26*(4pt2), 1423–1444.

Rueda, M. R. (2013). Development of attention. In K. Ochsner & S. M. Kosslyn (Eds.), *The Oxford handbook of cognitive neuroscience* (Vol. 1, p. 656). Oxford University Press.

Rueda, M. R., & Conejero, A. (2020). Chapter 23—Developing attention and self-regulation in infancy and childhood. In J. Rubenstein, P. Rakic, B. Chen, & K. Y. Kwan (Eds.), *Neural circuit and cognitive development* (2nd ed., pp. 505–522). Academic Press. https://doi.org/10.1016/B978-0-12-814411-4.00023-8

Rueger, S. Y., Chen, P., Jenkins, L. N., & Choe, H. J. (2014). Effects of perceived support from mothers, fathers, and teachers on depressive symptoms during the transition to middle school. *Journal of Youth and Adolescence, 43*(4), 655–670. https://doi.org/10.1007/s10964-013-0039-x

Ruff, S. C., Durtschi, J. A., & Day, R. D. (2018). Family subsystems predicting adolescents' perceptions of sibling relationship quality over time. *Journal of Marital and Family Therapy, 44*(3), 527–542. https://doi.org/10.1111/jmft.12265

Ruffman, T. (2023). Belief it or not: How children construct a theory of mind. *Child Development Perspectives, 17*(2), 106–112. https://doi.org/10.1111/cdep.12483

Ruiz, J. M., Hamann, H. A., Mehl, M. R., & OConnor, M.-F. (2016). The Hispanic health paradox: From epidemiological phenomenon to contribution opportunities for psychological science. *Group Processes & Intergroup Relations, 19*(4), 462–476. https://doi.org/10.1177/1368430216638540

Russ, S. W. (2022). Play. In V. P. Glăveanu (Ed.), *The Palgrave encyclopedia of the possible* (pp. 1008–1014). Springer International. https://doi.org/10.1007/978-3-030-90913-0_124

Russell, D. H., Hoq, M., Coghill, D., & Pang, K. C. (2022). Prevalence of mental health problems in transgender children aged 9 to 10 years in the US, 2018. *JAMA Network Open, 5*(7), e2223389. https://doi.org/10.1001/jamanetworkopen.2022.23389

Russell, D. W., & Russell, C. A. (2019). The evolution of mental health outcomes across a combat deployment cycle: A longitudinal study of the Guam Army National Guard. *PLoS ONE, 14*(10), e0223855. https://doi.org/10.1371/journal.pone.0223855

Russell, S. T., Pollitt, A. M., Li, G., & Grossman, A. H. (2018). Chosen name use is linked to reduced depressive symptoms, suicidal ideation, and suicidal behavior among transgender youth. *Journal of Adolescent Health, 63*(4), 503–505. https://doi.org/10.1016/j.jadohealth.2018.02.003

Rutledge, S. A., Cohen-Vogel, L., Osborne-Lampkin, L., & Roberts, R. L. (2015). Understanding effective high schools: Evidence for personalization for academic and social emotional learning. *American Educational Research Journal, 52*(6), 1060–1092. https://doi.org/10.3102/0002831215602328

Rutter, M. (2023). Resilience: Some conceptual considerations. In V. E. Cree & T. McCulloch (Eds.), *Social work* (2nd ed., pp. 122–127). Routledge.

Ruzgis, P., & Grigorenko, E. L. (1994). Cultural meaning systems, intelligence, and personality. In R. J. Sternberg & P. Ruzgis (Eds.), *Personality and intelligence* (pp. 248–270). Cambridge University Press.

Ryan, C., Russell, S. T., Huebner, D., Diaz, R., & Sanchez, J. (2010). Family acceptance in adolescence and the health of LGBT young adults. *Journal of Child and Adolescent Psychiatric Nursing, 23*(4), 205–213. https://doi.org/10.1111/j.1744-6171.2010.00246.x

Ryan, J. P., Jacob, B. A., Gross, M., Perron, B. E., Moore, A., & Ferguson, S. (2018). Early Exposure to Child Maltreatment and Academic Outcomes. *Child Maltreatment, 23*(4), 365–375. https://doi.org/10.1177/1077559518786815

Ryan, R. M., Claessens, A., & Markowitz, A. J. (2015). Associations between family structure change and child behavior problems: The moderating effect of family income. *Child Development, 86*, 112–127. https://doi.org/10.1111/cdev.12283

Rydell, A.-M. (2016). Violent media exposure, aggression and CU traits in adolescence: Testing the selection and socialization hypotheses. *Journal of Adolescence, 52*, 95–102. https://doi.org/10.1016/j.adolescence.2016.07.009

Rytting, E., Waltz, J., & Ahmed, M. S. (2022). Fetal drug therapy. In D. Mattison & L.-A. Halbert (Eds.), *Clinical pharmacology during pregnancy* (pp. 61–78). Academic Press. https://doi.org/10.1016/B978-0-12-818902-3.00007-5

Saarni, C. (2000). Emotional competence: A developmental perspective. In R. Bar-On & J. D. A. Parker (Eds.), *The Handbook of emotional intelligence: Theory, development, assessment, and application at home, school, and in the workplace* (pp. 68–69). Jossey-Bass.

Saarni, C., Mumme, D. L., & Campos, J. J. (1998). Emotional development: Action, communication, and understanding. In N. Eisenberg & W. Damon (Eds.), *Handbook of child psychology* (Vol. 3, pp. 237–309). John Wiley & Sons.

Sabbagh, M. A., Xu, F., Carlson, S. M., Moses, L. J., & Lee, K. (2006). The development of executive functioning and theory of mind. *Psychological Science, 17*(1), 74–81.

Sackett, P. R., Lievens, F., Van Iddekinge, C. H., & Kuncel, N. R. (2017). Individual differences and their measurement: A review of 100 years of research. *Journal of Applied Psychology, 102*(3), 254–273. https://doi.org/10.1037/APL0000151

Sadler, K. (2017). Pubertal development. In M. A. Goldstein (Ed.), *The MassGeneral Hospital for Children Adolescent Medicine Handbook* (pp. 19–26). Springer International. https://doi.org/10.1007/978-3-319-45778-9_3

Sadler, T. L. (2023). *Langman's medical embryology*. Lippincott Williams & Wilkins.

Saengkaew, T., & Howard, S. R. (2022). Genetics of pubertal delay. *Clinical Endocrinology, 97*(4). https://doi.org/10.1111/cen.14606

Saewyc, E. M. (2011). Research on adolescent sexual orientation: Development, health disparities, stigma, and resilience. *Journal of Research on Adolescence, 21*(1), 256–272. https://doi.org/10.1111/j.1532-7795.2010.00727.x

Safer, J. D., & Chan, K. J. (2019). Review of medical, socioeconomic, and systemic barriers to transgender care. In L. Poretsky & W. C. Hembree (Eds.), *Transgender medicine* (pp. 25–38). Humana Press. https://doi.org/10.1007/978-3-030-05683-4_2

Safer, J. D., & Tangpricha, V. (2019). Care of transgender persons. *New England Journal* of Medicine, 381(25), 2451–2460. https://doi.org/10.1056/nejmcp1903650

Saffran, J. R. (2020). Statistical language learning in infancy. *Child Development Perspectives*, 14(1), 49–54. https://doi.org/10.1111/cdep.12355

Sagi, A., IJzendoorn, Van., H, M., & Koren-Karie, N. (1991). Primary appraisal of the strange situation: A cross-cultural analysis of preseparation episodes. *Developmental Psychology*, 27(4), 587–596. https://doi.org/10.1037/0012-1649.27.4.587

Sagi, A., Lamb, M. E., Lewkowicz, K. S., Shoham, R., Dvir, R., & Estes, D. (1985). Security of infant-mother, -father, and -metapelet attachments among Kibbutz-reared Israeli children. *Monographs of the Society for Research in Child Development*, 50(1–2), 257–275. https://doi.org/10.1111/1540-5834.ep11890146

Sahlan, R. N., Saunders, J. F., Mond, J. M., & Fitzsimmons-Craft, E. E. (2021). Eating disorder symptoms among adolescent boys and girls in Iran. *International Journal of Eating Disorders*, 54(1), 19–23. https://doi.org/10.1002/eat.23420

Sai, F. Z. (2005). The role of the mother's voice in developing mother's face preference: Evidence for intermodal perception at birth. *Infant & Child Development*, 14, 29–50.

Saint, S. E., Hammond, B. R., O'Brien, K. J., & Frick, J. E. (2017). Developmental trends in infant temporal processing speed. *Vision Research*, 138, 71–77. https://doi.org/10.1016/j.visres.2017.07.004

Sakkalou, E., Sakki, H., O'reilly, M. A., Salt, A. T., & Dale, N. J. (2018). Parenting stress, anxiety, and depression in mothers with visually impaired infants: A cross-sectional and longitudinal cohort analysis. *Developmental Medicine & Child Neurology*, 60(3), 290–298. https://doi.org/10.1111/dmcn.13633

Sala, M. N., Pons, F., & Molina, P. (2014). Emotion regulation strategies in preschool children. *British Journal of Developmental Psychology*, 32(4), 440–453. https://doi.org/10.1111/bjdp.12055

Salapatek, P. (1973). Pattern perception in early infancy. In L. B. Cohen & P. Salapatek (Eds.), *Infant perception: From sensation to cognition* (Vol. 1, pp. 133–248). Academic Press.

Salary.com. (n.d.). *Neuropsychology technician salary in the United States*. Retrieved March 31, 2023, from https://www.salary.com/research/salary/hiring/neuropsychology-technician-salary

Salary.com. (n.d.a). *Board certified behavior analyst salary*. Retrieved May 17, 2024, from https://www.salary.com/research/salary/alternate/board-certified-behavior-analyst-salary

Salary.com. (n.d.b). *Child life specialist salary*. Retrieved July 19, 2024, from https://www.salary.com/research/salary/benchmark/child-life-specialist-salary

Salcedo-Arellano, M. J., Dufour, B., McLennan, Y., Martinez-Cerdeno, V., & Hagerman, R. (2020). Fragile X syndrome and associated disorders: Clinical aspects and pathology. *Neurobiology of Disease*, 136, 104740. https://doi.org/10.1016/j.nbd.2020.104740

Saleem, F. T., & Byrd, C. M. (2021). Unpacking school ethnic-racial socialization: A new conceptual model. *Journal of Social Issues*, 77(4), 1106–1125. https://doi.org/10.1111/josi.12498

Saleem, M., Anderson, C. A., & Gentile, D. A. (2012). Effects of prosocial, neutral, and violent video games on children's helpful and hurtful behaviors. *Aggressive Behavior*, 38(4), 281–287. https://doi.org/10.1002/ab.21428

Salend, S. J. (2015). *Creating inclusive classrooms: Effective, differentiated and reflective practices*. Pearson College.

Salisch, M. von., Voltmer, K., Miller-Slough, R., Chin, J.-C., & Denham, S. (2022). Emotions and Social Development in Childhood. In P. K. Smith & C. H. Hart (Eds.), *The Wiley-Blackwell handbook of childhood social development* (3rd ed., pp. 631–650). Wiley.

Salmivalli, C. (2014). Participant roles in bullying: How can peer bystanders be utilized in interventions? *Theory Into Practice*, 53(4), 286–292. https://doi.org/10.1080/00405841.2014.947222

Salo, V. C., Rowe, M. L., & Reeb-Sutherland, B. C. (2018). Exploring infant gesture and joint attention as related constructs and as predictors of later language. *Infancy*, 23(3), 432–452. https://doi.org/10.1111/infa.12229

Salomon, L. J., Sotiriadis, A., Wulff, C. B., Odibo, A., & Akolekar, R. (2019). Risk of miscarriage following amniocentesis or chorionic villus sampling: Systematic review of literature and updated meta-analysis. *Ultrasound in Obstetrics & Gynecology*, 54(4), 442–451. https://doi.org/10.1002/uog.20353

Salovey, P., & Mayer, J. D. (1989). Emotional intelligence. *Imagination, Cognition and Personality*, 9(3), 185–211. https://doi.org/10.2190/DUGG-P24E-52WK-6CDG

Salter, M. D. (1940). *An evaluation of adjustment based upon the concept of security*. University of Toronto Press.

Saltz, J. B. (2019). Gene-environment correlation in humans: Lessons from psychology for quantitative genetics. *Journal of Heredity*, 110(4), 455–466. https://doi.org/10.1093/jhered/esz027

Salvadori, E. A., Colonnesi, C., Elsammak, L., Oort, F. J., & Messinger, D. S. (2022). Beyond the familial: The development of emotional communication with mothers, fathers, and strangers. *Infancy*, 27(4), 836–862. https://doi.org/10.1111/infa.12467

Salzwedel, A., Chen, G., Chen, Y., Grewen, K., & Gao, W. (2020). Functional dissection of prenatal drug effects on baby brain and behavioral development. *Human Brain Mapping*, 41(17), 4789–4803. https://doi.org/10.1002/hbm.25158

Samdan, G., Kiel, N., Petermann, F., Rothenfußer, S., Zierul, C., & Reinelt, T. (2020). The relationship between parental behavior and infant regulation: A systematic review. *Developmental Review*, 57, 100923. https://doi.org/10.1016/j.dr.2020.100923

Sameroff, A. J., Seifer, R., Baldwin, A., & Baldwin, C. (1993). Stability of intelligence from preschool to adolescence: The influence of social and family risk factors. *Child Development*, 64(1), 80–97. https://doi.org/10.1111/j.1467-8624.1993.tb02896.x

Samour, P. Queen., & King, K. (2013). *Essentials of pediatric nutrition*. Jones & Bartlett Learning.

Samudra, P. G., Wong, K. M., & Neuman, S. B. (2022). Can small changes matter? Reducing cognitive load in educational media supports low-income preschoolers' vocabulary learning. *Journal of Educational Psychology*, 114, 1277–1291. https://doi.org/10.1037/edu0000742

Samuels, R. (2019). Nativism. In S. Robins, J. Symons, & P. Calvo (Eds.), *The Routledge companion to philosophy of psychology* (2nd ed., pp. 332–335). Routledge.

Samuelson, L. K. (2021). Toward a precision science of word learning: Understanding individual vocabulary pathways. *Child Development Perspectives*, 15(2). https://doi.org/10.1111/cdep.12408

Samuelson, L. K., & McMurray, B. (2017). What does it take to learn a word? *Wiley Interdisciplinary Reviews: Cognitive Science*, 8(1–2), e1421. https://doi.org/10.1002/wcs.1421

Samura, O. (2020). Update on noninvasive prenatal testing: A review based on current worldwide research. *Journal of Obstetrics* and Gynaecology Research, 46(8), 1246–1254. https://doi.org/10.1111/jog.14268

Sanchez, D., Whittaker, T. A., Hamilton, E., & Arango, S. (2017). Familial ethnic socialization, gender role attitudes, and ethnic identity development in Mexican-origin early adolescents. Cultural Diversity and Ethnic Minority Psychology, 23(3), 335–347. https://doi.org/10.1037/cdp0000142

Sánchez-Queija, I., Oliva, A., & Parra, Á. (2017). Stability, change, and determinants of self-esteem during adolescence and emerging adulthood. Journal of Social and Personal Relationships, 34(8), 1277–1294. https://doi.org/10.1177/0265407516674831

Sanchez-Ruiz, M.-J., Mavroveli, S., & Poullis, J. (2013). Trait emotional intelligence and its links to university performance: An examination. Personality and Individual Differences, 54(5), 658–662. https://doi.org/10.1016/j.paid.2012.11.013

Sanchez-Vaznaugh, E. V., Braveman, P. A., Egerter, S., Marchi, K. S., Heck, K., & Curtis, M. (2016). Latina birth outcomes in California: Not so paradoxical. Maternal and Child Health Journal, 20(9), 1849–1860. https://doi.org/10.1007/s10995-016-1988-y

Sanchis-Sanchis, A., Grau, M. D., Moliner, A. R., & Morales-Murillo, C. P. (2020). Effects of age and gender in emotion regulation of children and adolescents. Frontiers in Psychology, 11, 946. https://doi.org/10.3389/fpsyg.2020.00946

Sanders, J. O., Qiu, X., Lu, X., Duren, D. L., Liu, R. W., Dang, D., Menendez, M. E., Hans, S. D., Weber, D. R., & Cooperman, D. R. (2017). The uniform pattern of growth and skeletal maturation during the human adolescent growth spurt. Scientific Reports, 7(1), 16705. https://doi.org/10.1038/s41598-017-16996-w

Sanders, M. R., & Kirby, J. N. (2014). A public-health approach to improving parenting and promoting children's well-being. Child Development Perspectives, 8(4), 250–257. https://doi.org/10.1111/cdep.12086

Sann, C., & Streri, A. (2007). Perception of object shape and texture in human newborns: Evidence from cross-modal transfer tasks. Developmental Science, 10(3), 399–410. https://doi.org/10.1111/j.1467-7687.2007.00593.x

Santelli, J., Kantor, L. M., Grilo, S. A., Speizer, I. S., Lindberg, L. D., Heitel, J., Schalet, A. T., Lyon, M. E., Mason-Jones, A. J., McGovern, T., Heck, C. J., Rogers, J., & Ott, M. A. (2017). Abstinence-only-until-marriage: An updated review of U.S. policies and programs and their impact. Journal of Adolescent Health, 61(3), 273–280. https://doi.org/10.1016/j.jadohealth.2017.05.031

Santoro, J. D., Pagarkar, D., Chu, D. T., Rosso, M., Paulsen, K. C., Levitt, P., & Rafii, M. S. (2021). Neurologic complications of Down syndrome: A systematic review. Journal of Neurology, 268(12). https://doi.org/10.1007/s00415-020-10179-w

Santos, C. E., & Toomey, R. B. (2018). Integrating an intersectionality lens in theory and research in developmental science. New Directions for Child and Adolescent Development, 7–15. https://doi.org/10.1002/cad.20245 2018(161)

Santos, R. M. S., Mendes, C. G., Marques Miranda, D., & Romano-Silva, M. A. (2022). The association between screen time and attention in children: A systematic review. Https://Doi.Org/10.1080/87565641.2022.2064863, 47(4), 175–192. https://doi.org/10.1080/87565641.2022.2064863

Sapp, F., Lee, K., & Muir, D. (2000). Three-year-olds' difficulty with the appearance-reality distinction: Is it real or is it apparent? Developmental Psychology, 36, 547–560.

Saraiya, A., Garakani, A., & Billick, S. B. (2013). Mental health approaches to child victims of acts of terrorism. The Psychiatric Quarterly, 84(1), 115–124. https://doi.org/10.1007/s11126-012-9232-4

Sarman, I. (2018). Review shows that early foetal alcohol exposure may cause adverse effects even when the mother consumes low levels. Acta Paediatrica, 107(6), 938–941. https://doi.org/10.1111/apa.14221

Sarmiento, I. G., Olson, C., Yeo, G., Chen, Y. A., Toma, C. L., Brown, B. B., Bellmore, A., & Mares, M.-L. (2020). How does social media use relate to adolescents' internalizing symptoms? Conclusions from a systematic narrative review. Adolescent Research Review, 5(4), 381–404. https://doi.org/10.1007/s40894-018-0095-2

Sato, W., & Uono, S. (2019). The atypical social brain network in autism. Current Opinion in Neurology, 32(4), 617–621. https://doi.org/10.1097/WCO.0000000000000713

Sattari, M., Serwint, J. R., & Levine, D. M. (2019). Maternal implications of breastfeeding: A review for the internist. American Journal of Medicine, 132(8), 912–920. https://doi.org/10.1016/j.amjmed.2019.02.021

Sattler, J. M. (2014). Foundations of behavioral, social and clinical assessment of children. Jerome M. Sattler.

Sauce, B., & Matzel, L. D. (2018). The paradox of intelligence: Heritability and malleability coexist in hidden gene-environment interplay. Psychological Bulletin, 144(1), 26–47. https://doi.org/10.1037/bul0000131

Saudino, K. J., & Micalizzi, L. (2015). Emerging trends in behavioral genetic studies of child temperament. Child Development Perspectives, 9(3), 144–148. https://doi.org/10.1111/cdep.12123

Savin-Williams, R. C. (2021). Bi: Bisexual, pansexual, fluid, and nonbinary youth. NYU Press.

Savina, E. (2020). Self-regulation in preschool and early elementary classrooms: Why it is important and how to promote it. Early Childhood Education Journal, 49(3), 1–9. https://doi.org/10.1007/s10643-020-01094-w

Saxe, G. B. (2005). Practices of quantification from a socio-cultural perspective. In Cognitive Developmental Change: Theories, Models and Measurement. https://doi.org/10.1017/CBO9780511489938.009

Saxton, M. (1997). The contrast theory of negative input. Journal of Child Language, 24, 139–161. https://doi.org/10.1017/S030500099600298X

Sayfan, L., & Lagattuta, K. H. (2009). Scaring the monster away: What children know about managing fears of real and imaginary creatures. Child Development, 80(6), 1756–1774. https://doi.org/10.1111/j.1467-8624.2009.01366.x

Scarr, S. (1992). Developmental theories for the 1990s: Development and individual differences. Child Development, 63(1), 1–19. https://doi.org/10.1111/1467-8624.ep9203091721

Scarr, S., & McCartney, K. (1983). How people make their own environments: A theory of genotype environment effects. Child Development, 54(2), 424. https://doi.org/10.1111/1467-8624.ep8877295

Schaal, B. (2017). Infants and children making sense of scents. In A. Buettner (Ed.), Springer handbook of odor (pp. 107–108). Springer International. https://doi.org/10.1007/978-3-319-26932-0_43

Schaffhuser, K., Allemand, M., & Schwarz, B. (2017). The development of self-representations during the transition to early adolescence: The role of gender, puberty, and school transition. Journal of Early Adolescence, 37(6), 774–804. https://doi.org/10.1177/0272431615624841

Schaik, S. D. M., Mavridis, C., Harkness, S., De Looze, M., Blom, M. J. M., & Super, C. M. (2020). Getting the baby on a schedule: Dutch and American mothers' ethnotheories and the establishment of diurnal rhythms in early infancy. In S. Harkness & C. M. Super (Eds.), Cross-cultural research on parents: Applications to the care and education of children. New directions for child and adolescent development (Vol. 170, pp. 13–41). https://doi.org/10.1002/cad.20336

Schalock, R., Luckasson, R., & Tassee, M. (2021). *Intellectual disability: Definition, diagnosis, classification, and systems of supports*. American Association on Intellectual and Developmental Disabilities. https://www.aaidd.org/publications/bookstore-home/product-listing/intellectual-disability-definition-diagnosis-classification-and-systems-of-supports-12th-edition

Schapira, R., & Aram, D. (2020). Shared book reading at home and preschoolers' socio-emotional competence. *Early Education and Development*, 31(6), 819–837. https://doi.org/10.1080/10409289.2019.1692624

Scharping, T. (2019). Abolishing the one-child policy: Stages, issues and the political process. *Journal of Contemporary China*, 28(117), 327–347. https://doi.org/10.1080/10670564.2018.1542217

Scheffler, C., Bogin, B., & Hermanussen, M. (2021). Catch-up growth is a better indicator of undernutrition than thresholds for stunting. *Public Health Nutrition*, 24(1), 52–61. https://doi.org/10.1017/S1368980020003067

Schenck-Fontaine, A., & Gassman-Pines, A. (2020). Income inequality and child maltreatment risk during economic recession. *Children and Youth Services Review*, 112, 104926. https://doi.org/10.1016/j.childyouth.2020.104926

Schlesinger, M. A., Hassinger-Das, B., Zosh, J. M., Sawyer, J., Evans, N., & Hirsh-Pasek, K. (2020). Cognitive behavioral science behind the value of play: Leveraging everyday experiences to promote play, learning, and positive interactions. *Journal of Infant, Child, and Adolescent Psychotherapy*, 19(2), 202–216. https://doi.org/10.1080/15289168.2020.1755084

Schlinger, H. D. (2022). The impact of B. F. Skinner's science of operant learning on early childhood research, theory, treatment, and care. In Evans. R & O. N. Saracho (Eds.), *The influence of theorists and pioneers on early childhood education* (pp. 101–118). Routledge.

Schmidt, A., Kramer, A. C., Brose, A., Schmiedek, F., & Neubauer, A. B. (2021). Distance learning, parent–child interactions, and affective well-being of parents and children during the COVID-19 pandemic: A daily diary study. *Developmental Psychology*, 57, 1719–1734. https://doi.org/10.1037/dev0001232

Schmitt, J. E., Raznahan, A., Clasen, L. S., Wallace, G. L., Pritikin, J. N., Lee, N. R., Giedd, J. N., & Neale, M. C. (2019). The dynamic associations between cortical thickness and general intelligence are genetically mediated. *Cerebral Cortex*, 29(11), 4743–4752. https://doi.org/10.1093/cercor/bhz007

Schmitt, L., Shaffer, R., Hessl, D., & Erickson, C. (2019). Executive function in fragile X syndrome: A systematic review. *Brain Sciences*, 9(1), 15. https://doi.org/10.3390/brainsci9010015

Schneider, J. L., & Iverson, J. M. (2022). Cascades in action: How the transition to walking shapes caregiver communication during everyday interactions. *Developmental Psychology*, 58(1). https://doi.org/10.1037/dev0001280

Schneider, J. L., & Iverson, J. M. (2023). Equifinality in infancy: The many paths to walking. *Developmental Psychobiology*, 65(2), e22370. https://doi.org/10.1002/dev.22370

Schneider, J., Sandoz, V., Equey, L., Williams-Smith, J., Horsch, A., & Bickle Graz, M. (2022). The Role of Face Masks in the Recognition of Emotions by Preschool Children. *JAMA Pediatrics*, 176(1), 96–98. https://doi.org/10.1001/jamapediatrics.2021.4556

Schneider, M., & Hirsch, J. S. (2020). Comprehensive sexuality education as a primary prevention strategy for sexual violence perpetration. *Trauma, Violence, & Abuse*, 21(3), 439–455. https://doi.org/10.1177/1524838018772855

Schneider, S. (2020). Associations between childhood exposure to community violence, child maltreatment and school outcomes. *Child Abuse & Neglect*, 104, 104473. https://doi.org/10.1016/j.chiabu.2020.104473

Schneider, T. (2020). Asthma and academic performance among children and youth in North America: A systematic review. *Journal of School Health*, 90(4), 319–342. https://doi.org/10.1111/josh.12877

Schneider, W., & Bjorklund, D. F. (1992). Expertise, aptitude, and strategic remembering. *Child Development*, 63(2), 461–473. https://doi.org/10.1111/j.1467-8624.1992.tb01640.x

Schneider, W., & Niklas, F. (2017). Intelligence and verbal short-term memory/working memory: Their interrelationships from childhood to young adulthood and their impact on academic achievement. *Journal of Intelligence*, 5(2), 26. https://doi.org/10.3390/jintelligence5020026

Schneider, W., & Ornstein, P. A. (2015). The development of children's memory. *Child Development Perspectives*, 9(3), 190–195. https://doi.org/10.1111/cdep.12129

Schneider, W., & Pressley, M. (2013). *Memory development between two and twenty*. Erlbaum.

Schneider, W., Tibken, C., & Richter, T. (2022). The development of metacognitive knowledge from childhood to young adulthood: Major trends and educational implications. In J. J. Lockman (Ed.), *Advances in child development and behavior* (Vol. 63, pp. 273–307). JAI. https://doi.org/10.1016/bs.acdb.2022.04.006

Schnitker, S. A., Medenwaldt, J. M., & Williams, E. G. (2021). Religiosity in adolescence. *Current Opinion in Psychology*, 40, 155–159. https://doi.org/10.1016/j.copsyc.2020.09.012

Schnur, E., & Belanger, S. (2000). What works in Head Start. In M. P. Kluger, G. Alexander, & P. A. Curtis (Eds.), *What works in child welfare* (pp. 277–284). Child Welfare League of America.

Schoemaker, N. K., Wentholt, W. G. M., Goemans, A., Vermeer, H. J., Juffer, F., & Alink, L. R. A. (2020). A meta-analytic review of parenting interventions in foster care and adoption. *Development and Psychopathology*, 32(3), 1–24. https://doi.org/10.1017/s0954579419000798

Schonert-Reichl, K. A. (1999). Relations of peer acceptance, friendship adjustment, and social behavior to moral reasoning during early adolescence. *Journal of Early Adolescence*, 19(2), 249–279. https://doi.org/10.1177/0272431699019002006

Schønning, V., Hjetland, G. J., Aarø, L. E., & Skogen, J. C. (2020). Social media use and mental health and well-being among adolescents – A scoping review. *Frontiers in Psychology*, 1(1). https://www.frontiersin.org/articles/10.3389/fpsyg.2020.01949

Schoppmann, J., Schneider, S., & Seehagen, S. (2019). Wait and see: Observational learning of distraction as an emotion regulation strategy in 22-month-old toddlers. *Journal of Abnormal Child Psychology*, 47(5), 851–863. https://doi.org/10.1007/s10802-018-0486-7

Schreiber, J. (1977). Birth, the family and the community: A southern Italian example. *Birth and the Family Journal*, 4, 153–157.

Schroeder, K. M., & Liben, L. S. (2020). Felt pressure to conform to cultural gender roles: Correlates and consequences. *Sex Roles*, 84, 125–138. https://doi.org/10.1007/s11199-020-01155-9

Schubert, A. L., & Frischkorn, G. T. (2020). Neurocognitive psychometrics of intelligence: How measurement advancements

Schuetze, P., Godleski, S., & Sassaman, J. (2021). Prenatal exposure to opioids: Associations between the caregiving environment and externalizing behaviors. *Neurotoxicology and Teratology*, *87*, 107019. https://doi.org/10.1016/j.ntt.2021.107019

Schuhmacher, N., Köster, M., & Kärtner, J. (2019). Modeling prosocial behavior increases helping in 16-month-olds. *Child Development*, *90*(5), 1789–1801. https://doi.org/10.1111/cdev.13054

Schuldiner, O., & Yaron, A. (2015). Mechanisms of developmental neurite pruning. *Cellular and Molecular Life Sciences*, *72*(1), 101–119. https://doi.org/10.1007/s00018-014-1729-6

Schulenberg, J. E., Johnston, L. D., O'malley, P. M., Bachman, J. G., Miech, R. A., & Patrick, M. E. (2021). *Monitoring the Future national survey results on drug use, 1975–2019: Volume II, College students and adults ages 19–60*. Institute for Social Research, The University of Michigan.

Schumacher, A. M., Miller, A. L., Watamura, S. E., Kurth, S., Lassonde, J. M., & LeBourgeois, M. K. (2017). Sleep moderates the association between response inhibition and self-regulation in early childhood. *Journal of Clinical Child and Adolescent Psychology*, *46*(2), 222–235. https://doi.org/10.1080/15374416.2016.1204921

Schumm, W., & Crawford, D. (2019). Scientific consensus on whether LGBTQ parents are more likely (or not) to have LGBTQ children: An analysis of 72 social science reviews of the literature published between 2001 and 2017. *Journal of International Women's Studies*, *20*(7), Article 1. https://vc.bridgew.edu/jiws/vol20/iss7/1

Schutte, N. S., Malouff, J. M., & Thorsteinsson, E. B. (2013). Increasing emotional intelligence through training: Current status and future directions. *International Journal of Emotional Education*, *5*(1), 56–72.

Schwab, J. F., & Lew-Williams, C. (2016). Language learning, socioeconomic status, and child-directed speech. *Wiley Interdisciplinary Reviews: Cognitive Science*, *7*(4), 264–275. https://doi.org/10.1002/wcs.1393

Schwartz, B. L. (2018). *Memory*. SAGE. https://us.sagepub.com/en-us/nam/memory/book248685

Schwartz, D., Lansford, J. E., Dodge, K. A., Pettit, G. S., & Bates, J. E. (2015). Peer victimization during middle childhood as a lead indicator of internalizing problems and diagnostic outcomes in late adolescence. *Journal of Clinical Child and Adolescent Psychology*, *44*(3), 393–404. https://doi.org/10.1080/15374416.2014.881293

Schwartz, F., Epinat-Duclos, J., Léone, J., Poisson, A., & Prado, J. (2020). Neural representations of transitive relations predict current and future math calculation skills in children. *Neuropsychologia*, *141*, 107410. https://doi.org/10.1016/j.neuropsychologia.2020.107410

Schwartz, L., Caixàs, A., Dimitropoulos, A., Dykens, E., Duis, J., Einfeld, S., Gallagher, L., Holland, A., Rice, L., Roof, E., Salehi, P., Strong, T., Taylor, B., & Woodcock, K. (2021). Behavioral features in Prader-Willi syndrome (PWS): Consensus paper from the International PWS Clinical Trial Consortium. *Journal of Neurodevelopmental Disorders*, *13*(1). https://doi.org/10.1186/s11689-021-09373-2

Schwartz, N. L., Patel, B. A., Garland, T., & Horner, A. M. (2018). Effects of selective breeding for high voluntary wheel-running behavior on femoral nutrient canal size and abundance in house mice. *Journal of Anatomy*, *233*(2), 193–203. https://doi.org/10.1111/joa.12830

Schwartz, P. D., Maynard, A. M., & Uzelac, S. M. (2008). Adolescent egocentrism: A contemporary view. *Adolescence*, *43*(171), 441–448.

Schwartz, S. J. (2001). The evolution of Eriksonian and neo-Eriksonian identity theory and research: A review and integration. *Identity*, *1*(1), 7–58.

Schwartz, S. J., Luyckx, K., & Crocetti, E. (2015). What have we learned since Schwartz (2001)? In K. C. McLean & M. Syed (Eds.), *The Oxford handbook of identity development* (pp. 539–561). Oxford University Press. https://doi.org/10.1093/oxfordhb/9780199936564.013.028

Schwartz, S. J., Zamboanga, B. L., Luyckx, K., Meca, A., & Ritchie, R. A. (2013). Identity in emerging adulthood: Reviewing the field and looking forward. *Emerging Adulthood*, *1*(2), 96–113. https://doi.org/10.1177/2167696813479781

Schwartz-Mette, R. A., Shankman, J., Dueweke, A. R., Borowski, S., & Rose, A. J. (2020). Relations of friendship experiences with depressive symptoms and loneliness in childhood and adolescence: A meta-analytic review. *Psychological Bulletin*, *146*(8), 664–700. https://doi.org/10.1037/bul0000239

Schwarzfischer, P., Gruszfeld, D., Socha, P., Luque, V., Closa-Monasterolo, R., Rousseaux, D., Moretti, M., ReDionigi, A., Verduci, E., Koletzko, B., & Grote, V. (2020). Effects of screen time and playing outside on anthropometric measures in preschool aged children. *PLoS ONE*, *15*(3), e0229708. https://doi.org/10.1371/journal.pone.0229708

Schwebel, D. C. (2019). Why "accidents" are not accidental: Using psychological science to understand and prevent unintentional child injuries. *American Psychologist*, *74*(9), 1137–1147. https://doi.org/10.1037/amp0000487

Schweinhart, L. J., Montie, J., Iang, Z., Barnett, W. S., Belfield, C. R., & Nores, M. (2005). *Lifetime effects: The High/Scope Perry Preschool study through age 40*. High/Scope Press.

Scott, E., & Panksepp, J. (2003). Rough-and-tumble play in human children. *Aggressive Behavior*, *29*(6), 539–551. https://doi.org/10.1002/ab.10062

Scott, L. S., Pascalis, O., & Nelson, C. A. (2007). A domain-general theory of the development of perceptual discrimination. *Current Directions in Psychological Science*, *16*(4), 197–201. https://doi.org/10.1111/j.1467-8721.2007.00503.x

Seaton, E. K., Yip, T., Morgan-Lopez, A., & Sellers, R. M. (2012). Racial discrimination and racial socialization as predictors of African American adolescents' racial identity development using latent transition analysis. *Developmental Psychology*, *48*(2), 448–458. https://doi.org/10.1037/a0025328

Sebastian-Galles, N., & Santolin, C. (2020). Bilingual acquisition: The early steps. *Annual Review of Developmental Psychology*, *2*(1), 47–68. https://doi.org/10.1146/annurev-devpsych-013119-023724

Sedgh, G., Finer, L. B., Bankole, A., Eilers, M. A., & Singh, S. (2015). Adolescent pregnancy, birth, and abortion rates across countries: Levels and recent trends. *Journal of Adolescent Health*, *56*(2), 223–230. https://doi.org/10.1016/j.jadohealth.2014.09.007

Seehagen, S., Schneider, S., Sommer, K., La Rocca, L., & Konrad, C. (2021). State-dependent memory in infants. *Child Development*, *92*(2), 578–585. https://doi.org/10.1111/cdev.13444

Seelman, K. L., Forge, N., Walls, N. E., & Bridges, N. (2015). School engagement among LGBTQ high school students: The roles of safe adults and gay-straight alliance characteristics. *Children and Youth Services Review*, *57*, 19–29. https://doi.org/10.1016/j.childyouth.2015.07.021

[Note: entry before Schuetze begins mid-sentence:] unveiled the role of mental speed in intelligence differences. *Current Directions in Psychological Science*, *29*(2), 140–146. https://doi.org/10.1177/0963721419896365

Segal, J., & Newman, R. S. (2015). Infant preferences for structural and prosodic properties of infant-directed speech in the second year of life. *Infancy, 20*(3), 339–351. https://doi.org/10.1111/infa.12077

Sege, R. D., & Siegel, B. S. (2018). Effective discipline to raise healthy children. *Pediatrics, 142*(6), e20183112. https://doi.org/10.1542/peds.2018-3112

Sehmi, R., Rushton, A., Pickles, A., Grant, M., & Maughan, B. (2020). Infant domestic adoption: Outcomes at mid-life. *Journal of Child Psychology and Psychiatry, 61*(7), 789–797. https://doi.org/10.1111/jcpp.13178

Seifer, R., Dickstein, S., Parade, S., Hayden, L. C., Magee, K. D., & Schiller, M. (2014). Mothers' appraisal of goodness of fit and children's social development. *International Journal of Behavioral Development, 38*(1), 86–97. https://doi.org/10.1177/0165025413507172

Seiler, N. K. (2016). Alcohol and pregnancy: CDC's health advice and the legal rights of pregnant women. *Public Health Reports, 131*(4), 623–627. https://doi.org/10.1177/0033354916662222

Selezneva, E., & Wetzel, N. (2022). The impact of probabilistic cues on sound-related pupil dilation and ERP responses in 7–9-year-old children. *Auditory Perception & Cognition*. https://doi.org/10.1080/25742442.2022.2048592 5(1–2

Selkie, E., Adkins, V., Masters, E., Bajpai, A., & Shumer, D. (2020). Transgender adolescents' uses of social media for social support. *Journal of Adolescent Health, 66*(3), 275–280. https://doi.org/10.1016/j.jadohealth.2019.08.011

Selman, R. L. (1980). *The growth of interpersonal understanding*. Academic Press.

Selph, S. S., Bougatsos, C., Dana, T., Grusing, S., & Chou, R. (2019). Screening for HIV infection in pregnant women: Updated evidence report and systematic review for the US Preventive Services Task Force. *JAMA, 321*(23), 2349–2360. https://doi.org/10.1001/jama.2019.2593

Sember, V., Jurak, G., Morrison, S. A., & Starc, G. (2020). Children's physical activity, academic performance, and cognitive functioning: A systematic review and meta-analysis. *Frontiers in Public Health, 8*, 307. https://doi.org/10.3389/fpubh.2020.00307

Semega, J., Kollar, M., Shrider, E. A., & Creamter, J. (2020). *Income and poverty in the United States: 2019*. Census. https://www.census.gov/library/publications/2020/demo/p60-270.html

Semeraro, C., Coppola, G., Cassibba, R., & Lucangeli, D. (2019). Teaching of cursive writing in the first year of primary school: Effect on reading and writing skills. *PLoS ONE, 14*(2), e0209978. https://doi.org/10.1371/journal.pone.0209978

Senzaki, S., Shimizu, Y., & Calma-Birling, D. (2021). The development of temperament and maternal perception of child: A cross-cultural examination in the United States and Japan. *Personality and Individual Differences, 170*, 110407. https://doi.org/10.1016/j.paid.2020.110407

Seo, E., & Lee, Y. (2021). Stereotype threat in high school classrooms: How it links to teacher mindset climate, mathematics anxiety, and achievement. *Journal of Youth and Adolescence, 50*(7), 1410–1423. https://doi.org/10.1007/s10964-021-01435-x

Seo, S., Yang, J. Y., & McDonald, K. L. (2023). Yearning for popularity: How are popularity goals and self-perceived popularity related to aggression and victimization? *Journal of Early Adolescence, 43*(9), 1105–1128. https://doi.org/10.1177/02724316221149414

Serafini, G., Aguglia, A., Amerio, A., Canepa, G., Adavastro, G., Conigliaro, C., Nebbia, J., Franchi, L., Flouri, E., & Amore, M. (2023). The relationship between bullying victimization and perpetration and non-suicidal self-injury: A systematic review. *Child Psychiatry & Human Development, 54*(1), 154–175. https://doi.org/10.1007/s10578-021-01231-5

Serpell, R. (1974). Aspects of intelligence in a developing country. *African Social Research, 17*, 578–596.

Serpell, R., & Jere-Folotiya, J. (2008). Developmental assessment, cultural context, gender, and schooling in Zambia. *International Journal of Psychology, 43*(2), 88–96.

Serpell, R., & Simatende, B. (2016). Contextual responsiveness: An enduring challenge for educational assessment in Africa. *Journal of Intelligence, 4*(1), 3. https://doi.org/10.3390/jintelligence4010003

Serra, R., Kiekens, G., Vanderlinden, J., Vrieze, E., Auerbach, R. P., Benjet, C., Claes, L., Cuijpers, P., Demyttenaere, K., Ebert, D. D., Tarsitani, L., Green, J. G., Kessler, R. C., Nock, M. K., Mortier, P., & Bruffaerts, R. (2020). Binge eating and purging in first-year college students: Prevalence, psychiatric comorbidity, and academic performance. *International Journal of Eating Disorders, 53*(3). https://doi.org/10.1002/eat.23211

Servant, M., Cassey, P., Woodman, G. F., & Logan, G. D. (2018). Neural bases of automaticity. *Journal of Experimental Psychology: Learning, Memory, and Cognition, 44*(3), 440–464. https://doi.org/10.1037/xlm0000454

Shablack, H., & Lindquist, K. A. (2019). The Role of Language in Emotional Development. In V. LoBue, K. Pérez-Edgar, & K. A. Buss (Eds.), *Handbook of emotional development* (pp. 451–478). Springer International. https://doi.org/10.1007/978-3-030-17332-6_18

Shaffer, D. R. (2002). *Developmental psychology: Childhood and adolescence* (6th ed.). Wadsworth/Thomson.

Shah, K., DeRemigis, A., Hageman, J. R., Sriram, S., & Waggoner, D. (2017). Unique characteristics of the X chromosome and related disorders. *NeoReviews, 18*(4), e209–e216. https://doi.org/10.1542/neo.18-4-e209

Shah-Kulkarni, S., Lee, S., Jeong, K. S., Hong, Y.-C., Park, H., Ha, M., Kim, Y., & Ha, E.-H. (2020). Prenatal exposure to mixtures of heavy metals and neurodevelopment in infants at 6 months. *Environmental Research, 182*, 109122. https://doi.org/10.1016/j.envres.2020.109122

Shahaeian, A., Peterson, C. C., Slaughter, V., & Wellman, H. M. (2011). Culture and the sequence of steps in theory of mind development. *Developmental Psychology, 47*(5), 1239–1247. https://doi.org/10.1037/a0023899

Shahbazian, N., Barati, M., Arian, P., & Saadati, N. (2012). Comparison of complications of chorionic villus sampling and amniocentesis. *International Journal of Fertility & Sterility, 5*(4), 241–244.

Shain, B. N. (2019). Increases in rates of suicide and suicide attempts among black adolescents. *Pediatrics, 144*(5), e20191912. https://doi.org/10.1542/peds.2019-1912

Shankar, P., Chung, R., & Frank, D. A. (2017). Association of food insecurity with children's behavioral, emotional, and academic outcomes: A systematic review. *Journal of Developmental and Behavioral Pediatrics, 38*(2), 135–150. https://doi.org/10.1097/DBP.0000000000000383

Shannon, K. A., Scerif, G., & Raver, C. C. (2021). Using a multidimensional model of attention to predict low-income preschoolers' early academic skills across time. *Developmental Science, 24*, e13025. https://doi.org/10.1111/desc.13025

Sharma, D., Farahbakhsh, N., Sharma, S., Sharma, P., & Sharma, A. (2019). Role of kangaroo mother care in growth and breast feeding rates in very low birth weight (VLBW) neonates: A systematic review. *Journal of Maternal-Fetal and Neonatal Medicine*, *32*(1), 129–142. https://doi.org/10.1080/14767058.2017.1304535

Shayer, M., Demetriou, A., & Pervez, M. (1988). The structure and scaling of concrete operational thought: Three studies in four countries. *Genetic, Social, and General Psychology Monographs*, *114*(3), 307–375.

Shaywitz, B. A., & Shaywitz, S. E. (2020). The American experience: Towards a 21st century definition of dyslexia. *Oxford Review of Education*, *46*(4), 454–471. https://doi.org/10.1080/03054985.2020.1793545

Shaywitz, S. E., Shaywitz, J. E., & Shaywitz, B. A. (2021). Dyslexia in the 21st century. *Current Opinion in Psychiatry*, *34*(2), 80–86. https://doi.org/10.1097/YCO.0000000000000670

Shea, J. D. (1985). Studies of cognitive development in Papua New Guinea. *International Journal of Psychology*, *20*(1), 33–61. https://doi.org/10.1002/j.1464-066X.1985.tb00013.x

Shearer, C. B. (2020). A resting state functional connectivity analysis of human intelligence: Broad theoretical and practical implications for multiple intelligences theory. *Psychology and Neuroscience*, *13*(2), 127–148. https://doi.org/10.1037/pne0000200

Shearer, C. B., & Karanian, J. M. (2017). The neuroscience of intelligence: Empirical support for the theory of multiple intelligences? *Trends in Neuroscience and Education*, *6*, 211–223. https://doi.org/10.1016/j.tine.2017.02.002

Sheehan, K. J., Ferguson, B., Msall, C., & Uttal, D. H. (2020). Forgetting and symbolic insight: Delay improves children's use of a novel symbol. *Journal of Experimental Child Psychology*, *192*, 104744. https://doi.org/10.1016/j.jecp.2019.104744

Shelton, J. (2023). Gender identity and gender expression. In C. Franklin (Ed.), *Encyclopedia of social work*. Oxford University Press. https://doi.org/10.1093/acrefore/9780199975839.013.1324

Shen, Y., Lee, H., Choi, Y., Hu, Y., & Kim, K. (2022). Ethnic-racial socialization, ethnic-racial identity, and depressive symptoms in Korean adolescents in the United States and China. *Journal of Youth and Adolescence*, *51*(2), 377–392. https://doi.org/10.1007/s10964-021-01523-y

Sheng, L., Yang, B., Story, M., Wu, W., Xi, X., Zhou, Y., Wen, Y., Wang, H., & Liu, Q. (2022). Emotional and behavioral changes and related factors of firstborn school-aged compared to same age only children. *Frontiers in Public Health*, *10*, 822761. https://doi.org/10.3389/fpubh.2022.822761

Shenouda, J., Barrett, E., Davidow, A. L., Sidwell, K., Lescott, C., Halperin, W., Silenzio, V. M. B., & Zahorodny, W. (2023). Prevalence and Disparities in the Detection of Autism Without Intellectual Disability. *Pediatrics*, *151*(2), e2022056594. https://doi.org/10.1542/peds.2022-056594

Shi, B., & Xie, H. (2012). Popular and non-popular subtypes of physically aggressive preadolescents: Continuity of aggression and peer mechanisms during the transition to middle school. *Merrill-Palmer Quarterly*, *58*(4), 530–553. https://doi.org/10.1353/mpq.2012.0025

Shi, D., Ma, N., Liu, Y., Dang, J., Zhong, P., Cai, S., Hu, P., Ma, J., Song, Y., & Lau, P. W. (2023). Secular trend and urban–rural disparity for age at spermarche among Chinese Han boys from 1995 to 2019. *Acta Paediatrica*, *112*(13), 529–536.

Shim, S.-S., Malone, F., Canick, J., Ball, R., Nyberg, D., Comstock, C., Bukowski, R., Norwitz, E., Levy, B., Brambati, B., Guercilena, S., Bonacchi, I., Oldrini, A., Lanzani, A., Piceni, L., South, S., Chen, Z., Brothman, A., Hsu, L., & …Abuhamad, A. (2014). Chorionic villus sampling. *Journal of Genetic Medicine*, *11*(2), 43–48. https://doi.org/10.5734/JGM.2014.11.2.43

Shimizu, M., Gillis, B. T., Buckhalt, J. A., & El-Sheikh, M. (2020). Linear and nonlinear associations between sleep and adjustment in adolescence. *Behavioral Sleep Medicine*, *18*(5), 690–704. https://doi.org/10.1080/15402002.2019.1665049

Shinskey, J. L. (2012). Disappearing décalage: Object search in light and dark at 6 Months. *Infancy*, *17*(3), 272–294. https://doi.org/10.1111/j.1532-7078.2011.00078.x

Shipman, K. L., & Zeman, J. (2001). Socialization of children's emotion regulation in mother–child dyads: A developmental psychopathology perspective. *Development and Psychopathology*, *13*(2), 317–336. https://doi.org/10.1017/S0954579401002073

Shirazi, T. N., & Rosinger, A. Y. (2021). Reproductive health disparities in the USA: Self-reported race/ethnicity predicts age of menarche and live birth ratios, but not infertility. *Journal of Racial and Ethnic Health Disparities*, *8*(1), 33–46. https://doi.org/10.1007/s40615-020-00752-4

Shorer, M., & Leibovich, L. (2022). Young children's emotional stress reactions during the COVID-19 outbreak and their associations with parental emotion regulation and parental playfulness. *Early Child Development and Care*, *192*(6). https://doi.org/10.1080/03004430.2020.1806830

Shpiegel, S., Aparicio, E. M., Smith, R., Grinnell-Davis, C., & King, B. (2022). Early fatherhood and socioeconomic outcomes among young men transitioning from foster care in the United States. *Children and Youth Services Review*, *133*, 106346. https://doi.org/10.1016/j.childyouth.2021.106346

Shubert, J., Wray-Lake, L., & McKay, B. (2020). Looking ahead and working hard: How school experiences foster adolescents' future orientation and perseverance. *Journal of Research on Adolescence*, *30*(4), 989–1007. https://doi.org/10.1111/jora.12575

Shuffrey, L. C., Myers, M. M., Isler, J. R., Lucchini, M., Sania, A., Pini, N., Nugent, J. D., Condon, C., Ochoa, T., Brink, L., Plessis, du., C, Odendaal., J, H., Nelson, M. E., Friedrich, C., Angal, J., Elliott, A. J., Groenewald, C., Burd, L., & Fifer, W. P. (2020). Association between prenatal exposure to alcohol and tobacco and neonatal brain activity: Results from the safe passage study. *JAMA Network Open*, *3*(5), e204714. https://doi.org/10.1001/jamanetworkopen.2020.4714

Shulman, E. P., & Cauffman, E. (2013). Reward-biased risk appraisal and its relation to juvenile versus adult crime. *Law and Human Behavior*, *37*(6), 412–423. https://doi.org/10.1037/lhb0000033

Shulman, E. P., Smith, A. R., Silva, K., Icenogle, G., Duell, N., Chein, J., & Steinberg, L. (2016). The dual systems model: Review, reappraisal, and reaffirmation. *Developmental Cognitive Neuroscience*, *17*, 103–117. https://doi.org/10.1016/j.dcn.2015.12.010

Shutts, K., Kenward, B., Falk, H., Ivegran, A., & Fawcett, C. (2017). Early preschool environments and gender: Effects of gender pedagogy in Sweden. *Journal of Experimental Child Psychology*, *162*, 1–17. https://doi.org/10.1016/j.jecp.2017.04.014

Shwe, H. I., & Markman, E. M. (1997). Young children's appreciation of the mental impact of their communicative signals. *Developmental Psychology*, *33*(4), 630–636. https://doi.org/10.1037/0012-1649.33.4.630

Sicard-Cras, I., Rioualen, S., Pellae, E., Misery, L., Sizun, J., & Roué, J. M. (2022). A review of the characteristics, mechanisms and clinical significance of habituation in foetuses and newborn infants. *Acta Paediactrica*, *111*(2), 245–258. https://doi.org/10.1111/apa.16115

Sicard-Cras, I., Rioualen, S., Pellae, E., Misery, L., Sizun, J., & Roué, J. M. (2022). A review of the characteristics, mechanisms and clinical significance of habituation in foetuses and newborn infants. *Acta*

Paediactrica, *111*(2). https://doi.org/10.1111/apa.16115

Sieber, F., & Zmyj, N. (2022). Stability and structure of infant and toddler temperament in two longitudinal studies in Germany. *Infant Behavior and Development*, *67*, 101714. https://doi.org/10.1016/j.infbeh.2022.101714

Siegler, R. S. (2016). How does change occur? In R. Sternberg, S. Fiske, & D. Foss (Eds.), *Scientists making a difference: One hundred eminent behavioral and brain scientists talk about their most important contributions* (pp. 223–227). Cambridge University Press.

Siegler, R. S. (2016). Continuity and change in the field of cognitive development and in the perspectives of one cognitive developmentalist. *Child Development Perspectives*, *10*(2), 128–133. https://doi.org/10.1111/cdep.12173

Siekerman, K., Barbu-Roth, M., Anderson, D. I., Donnelly, A., Goffinet, F., & Teulier, C. (2015). Treadmill stimulation improves newborn stepping. *Developmental Psychobiology*, *57*(2), 247–254. https://doi.org/10.1002/dev.21270

Sierens, S., Van Avermaet, P., Van Houtte, M., & Agirdag, O. (2020). Does pre-schooling contribute to equity in education? Participation in universal pre-school and fourth-grade academic achievement:. *European Educational Research Journal*, *19*(6), 564–586. https://doi.org/10.1177/1474904120925981

Signorella, M., & Liben, L. S. (1984). Recall and reconstruction of gender-related pictures: Effects of attitude, task difficulty, and age. *Child Development*, *55*, 393–405.

Silinskas, G., & Kikas, E. (2022). Patterns of children's relationships with parents and teachers in grade 1: Links to task persistence and performance. *Frontiers in Psychology*, *13*, 836472. https://doi.org/10.3389/fpsyg.2022.836472

Silke, C., Brady, B., Boylan, C., & Dolan, P. (2018). Factors influencing the development of empathy and pro-social behaviour among adolescents: A systematic review. *Children and Youth Services Review*, *94*, 421–436. https://doi.org/10.1016/j.childyouth.2018.07.027

Sills, J., Rowse, G., & Emerson, L.-M. (2016). The role of collaboration in the cognitive development of young children: A systematic review. *Child: Care, Health and Development*, *42*(3), 313–324. https://doi.org/10.1111/cch.12330

Silva, K., Ford, C. A., & Miller, V. A. (2020). Daily parent-teen conflict and parent and adolescent well-being: The moderating role of daily and person-level warmth. *Journal of Youth and Adolescence*, *49*(8), 1601–1616. https://doi.org/10.1007/s10964-020-01251-9

Silva, M., Strasser, K., & Cain, K. (2014). Early narrative skills in Chilean preschool: Questions scaffold the production of coherent narratives. *Early Childhood Research Quarterly*, *29*(2), 205–213. https://doi.org/10.1016/j.ecresq.2014.02.002

Silva, R. L., & Alves, S. G. (2020). Contemporary theories of gender identity. In B. J. Carducci, C. S. Nave, J. S. Mio, & R. E. Riggio (Eds.), *The Wiley encyclopedia of personality and individual differences* (pp. 215–219). Wiley. https://doi.org/10.1002/9781118970843.ch36

Silva-Santos, S., Santos, A., Duncan, M., Vale, S., & Mota, J. (2019). Association between moderate and vigorous physical activity and gross motor coordination in preschool children. *Journal of Motor Learning and Development*, *7*(2), 273–285. https://doi.org/10.1123/jmld.2017-0056

Silveira, F., Shafer, K., Dufur, M. J., & Roberson, M. (2021). Ethnicity and parental discipline practices: A cross-national comparison. *Journal of Marriage and Family*, *83*(3), 644–666. https://doi.org/10.1111/jomf.12715

Silventoinen, K., Jelenkovic, A., Palviainen, T., Dunkel, L., & Kaprio, J. (2022). The association between puberty timing and body mass index in a longitudinal setting: The contribution of genetic factors. *Behavior Genetics*, *52*(3), 186–194. https://doi.org/10.1007/s10519-022-10100-3

Silvers, J. A. (2020). Extinction learning and cognitive reappraisal: Windows into the neurodevelopment of emotion regulation. *Child Development Perspectives*, *14*(3), 178–184. https://doi.org/10.1111/cdep.12372

Silvers, J. A. (2022). Adolescence as a pivotal period for emotion regulation development. *Current Opinion in Psychology*, *44*, 258–263. https://doi.org/10.1016/j.copsyc.2021.09.023

Silvers, J. A., & Guassi Moreira, J. F. (2019). Capacity and tendency: A neuroscientific framework for the study of emotion regulation. *Neuroscience Letters*, *693*, 35–39. https://doi.org/10.1016/j.neulet.2017.09.017

Sim, A., Fazel, M., Bowes, L., & Gardner, F. (2018). Pathways linking war and displacement to parenting and child adjustment: A qualitative study with Syrian refugees in Lebanon. *Social Science & Medicine*, *200*, 19–26. https://doi.org/10.1016/j.socscimed.2018.01.009

Sim, Z. L., & Xu, F. (2019). Another look at looking time: Surprise as rational statistical inference. *Topics in Cognitive Science*, *11*(1), 154–163. https://doi.org/10.1111/tops.12393

Simard, D., & Gutiérrez, X. (2018). The study of metalinguistic constructs in second language acquisition research. In P. Garrett & J. M. Cots (Eds.), *The Routledge handbook of language awareness*. Routledge. https://www.routledge.com/The-Routledge-Handbook-of-Language-Awareness/Garrett-Cots/p/book/9781138937048

Simmering, V. R. (2016). Working memory capacity in context: Modeling dynamic processes of behavior, memory, and development. *Monographs of the Society for Research in Child Development*, *81*(3), 7–24. https://doi.org/10.1111/mono.12249

Simmonds, M., Llewellyn, A., Owen, C. G., & Woolacott, N. (2016). Predicting adult obesity from childhood obesity: A systematic review and meta-analysis. *Obesity Reviews*, *17*(2), 95–107. https://doi.org/10.1111/obr.12334

Simmons, K. (2015). *Sub-Saharan Africa makes progress against poverty but has long way to go*. Pew Research Center. http://www.pewresearch.org/fact-tank/2015/09/24/sub-saharan-africa-makes-progress-against-poverty-but-has-long-way-to-go/

Simmons, S. C., Grecco, G. G., Atwood, B. K., & Nugent, F. S. (2023). Effects of prenatal opioid exposure on synaptic adaptations and behaviors across development. *Neuropharmacology*, *222*, 109312. https://doi.org/10.1016/j.neuropharm.2022.109312

Simon, C. (2021). The role of race and ethnicity in parental ethnic-racial socialization: A scoping review of research. *Journal of Child and Family Studies*, *30*(1), 182–195. https://doi.org/10.1007/s10826-020-01854-7

Simon, K. A., & Farr, R. H. (2022). Identity-based socialization and adopted children's outcomes in lesbian, gay, and heterosexual parent families. *Applied Developmental Science*, *26*(1), 155–175. https://doi.org/10.1080/10888691.2020.1748030

Simon, R. W., & Caputo, J. (2019). The costs and benefits of parenthood for mental and physical health in the United States: The importance of parenting stage. *Society and Mental Health*, *9*(3), 296–315. https://doi.org/10.1177/2156869318786760

Simons, L., Schrager, S. M., Clark, L. F., Belzer, M., & Olson, J. (2013). Parental support and mental health among transgender adolescents. *Journal of Adolescent Health*, *53*(6), 791–793. https://doi.org/10.1016/j.jadohealth.2013.07.019

Simons, S. S. H., Cillessen, A. H. N., & de Weerth, C. (2017). Cortisol stress responses and children's behavioral functioning at school. *Developmental Psychobiology*, *59*(2), 217–224. https://doi.org/10.1002/dev.21484

Simpkins, S. D., Delgado, M. Y., Price, C. D., Quach, A., & Starbuck, E. (2013). Socioeconomic status, ethnicity, culture, and immigration: Examining the potential mechanisms underlying Mexican-origin adolescents' organized activity participation. *Developmental Psychology*, *49*(4), 706–721. https://doi.org/10.1037/a0028399

Singh, C. (2020). Rubella in pregnancy. *Journal of Fetal Medicine*, *7*(1), 37–41. https://doi.org/10.1007/s40556-019-00238-2

Singh, G. K., & Yu, S. M. (2019). Infant Mortality in the United States, 1915-2017: Large social inequalities have persisted for over a century. *International Journal of Maternal and Child Health and AIDS (IJMA)*, *8*(1), 19–31. https://doi.org/10.21106/ijma.271

Singh, L. (2021). Evidence for an early novelty orientation in bilingual learners. *Child Development Perspectives*, *15*(2), 110–116. https://doi.org/10.1111/cdep.12407

Singh, L., Fu, C. S. L., Tay, Z. W., & Golinkoff, R. M. (2018). Novel word learning in bilingual and monolingual infants: Evidence for a bilingual advantage. *Child Development*, *89*(3), e183–e198. https://doi.org/10.1111/cdev.12747

Singh, L., Phneah, K. T., Wijayaratne, D. C., Lee, K., & Quinn, P. C. (2022). Effects of interracial experience on the race preferences of infants. *Journal of Experimental Child Psychology*, *21*(6). https://doi.org/10.1016/j.jecp.2021.105352

Singh, L., Rajendra, S. J., & Mazuka, R. (2022). Diversity and representation in studies of infant perceptual narrowing. *Child Development Perspectives*, *16*(4), 191–199.

Singh, N., & Singh, S. (2020). Determination of age at menarche and its association with socio-economic status and physical activity: A study among Tibetan adolescent girls of Kangra District, Himachal Pradesh, India. *Online Journal of Health Allied Sciences*, *19*(1), 2. https://www.ojhas.org/issue73/2020-1-2.html

Singletary, B., Schmeer, K. K., Purtell, K. M., Sayers, R. C., Justice, L. M., Lin, T.-J., & Jiang, H. (2022). Understanding family life during the COVID-19 shutdown. *Family Relations*, *71*(2), 475–493. https://doi.org/10.1111/fare.12655

Singleton, N. Capone., & Shulman, B. B. (2020). *Language development: Foundations, processes, and clinical applications*. Jones & Bartlett Learning.

Sipsma, H. L., Rabinowitz, M. R., Young, D., Phillipi, C., Larson, I. A., & Kair, L. R. (2019). Exposure to hospital breastfeeding support by maternal race and ethnicity: A pilot study. *Journal of Midwifery and Women's Health*, *64*(6), 743–748. https://doi.org/10.1111/jmwh.13048

Sirois, S., & Jackson, I. R. (2012). Pupil dilation and object permanence in infants. *Infancy*, *17*(1), 61–78. https://doi.org/10.1111/j.1532-7078.2011.00096.x

Sirugo, G., Williams, S. M., & Tishkoff, S. A. (2019). The missing diversity in human genetic studies. *Cell*, *177*(1), 26–31. https://doi.org/10.1016/j.cell.2019.02.048

Skakkebæk, A., Wallentin, M., & Gravholt, C. H. (2021). Klinefelter syndrome or testicular dysgenesis: Genetics, endocrinology, and neuropsychology. In D. F. Swaab, R. M. Buijs, P. J. Lucassen, A. Salehi, & F. Kreier (Eds.), *Handbook of clinical neurology* (Vol. 181, pp. 445–462). Elsevier. https://doi.org/10.1016/B978-0-12-820683-6.00032-4

Skaugset, L. M., Farrell, S., Carney, M., Wolff, M., Santen, S. A., Perry, M., & Cico, S. J. (2016). Can you multitask? Evidence and limitations of task switching and multitasking in emergency medicine. *Annals of Emergency Medicine*, *68*(2), 189–195. https://doi.org/10.1016/j.annemergmed.2015.10.003

Skelton, A. E., Maule, J., & Franklin, A. (2022). Infant color perception: Insight into perceptual development. *Child Development Perspectives*, *16*(2). https://doi.org/10.1111/cdep.12447

Skinner, B. F. (1957). *Verbal behavior*. Appleton-Century-Crofts.

Skinner, E. A., Graham, J. P., Brule, H., Rickert, N., & Kindermann, T. A. (2020). "I get knocked down but I get up again": Integrative frameworks for studying the development of motivational resilience in school. *International Journal of Behavioral Development*, *44*(4), 290–300. https://doi.org/10.1177/0165025420924122

Skinner, O. D., & McHale, S. M. (2016). Parent-adolescent conflict in African American families. *Journal of Youth and Adolescence*, *45*(10), 2080–2093. https://doi.org/10.1007/s10964-016-0514-2

Skoog, T., & Bayram Özdemir, S. (2016). Explaining why early-maturing girls are more exposed to sexual harassment in early adolescence. *Journal of Early Adolescence*, *36*(4), 490–509. https://doi.org/10.1177/0272431614568198

Skoog, T., & Kapetanovic, S. (2021). The role of relational support in the longitudinal links between adolescent sexual harassment victimization and psychological health. *Development and Psychopathology*, *33*(4), 1368–1380. https://doi.org/10.1017/S0954579420000565

Sladek, M. R., Umaña-Taylor, A. J., Hardesty, J. L., Aguilar, G., Bates, D., Bayless, S. D., Gomez, E., Hur, C. K., Ison, A., Jones, S., Luo, H., Satterthwaite-Freiman, M., & Vázquez, M. A. (2022). "So, like, it's all a mix of one": Intersecting contexts of adolescents' ethnic-racial socialization. *Child Development*, *93*(5), 1284–1303. https://doi.org/10.1111/cdev.13756

Slater, A., Rose, D., & Morison, V. (1984). New-born infants' perception of similarities and differences between two- and three-dimensional stimuli. *British Journal of Developmental Psychology*, *3*, 211–220.

Slaughter, V., Imuta, K., Peterson, C. C., & Henry, J. D. (2015). Meta-analysis of theory of mind and peer popularity in the preschool and early school years. *Child Development*, *86*(4), 1159–1174. https://doi.org/10.1111/cdev.12372

Slaughter, V., & Perez-Zapata, D. (2014). Cultural variations in the development of mind reading. *Child Development Perspectives*, *8*(4), 237–241. https://doi.org/10.1111/cdep.12091

Slaughter, V., Peterson, C. C., & Mackintosh, Emily. (2007). Mind what mother says: Narrative input and theory of mind in typical children and those on the autism spectrum. *Child Development*, *78*(3), 839–858. https://doi.org/10.1111/j.1467-8624.2007.01036.x

Slawinski, B. L., Klump, K. L., & Alexandra Burt, S. (2019). No sex differences in the origins of covariation between social and physical aggression. *Psychological Medicine*, *49*(15), 2515–2523. https://doi.org/10.1017/S0033291718003392

Slicker, G., & Hustedt, J. T. (2019). Children's school readiness in socioeconomically diverse pre-K classrooms. *Early Child Development and Care*, *190*, 2366–2379. https://doi.org/10.1080/03004430.2019.1582527

Śliwerski, A., Kossakowska, K., Jarecka, K., Świtalska, J., & Bielawska-Batorowicz, E. (2020). The effect of maternal depression on infant attachment: A systematic review. *International Journal of Environmental Research and Public Health*, *17*(8), 2675. https://doi.org/10.3390/ijerph17082675

Slobodin, O., & Masalha, R. (2020). Challenges in ADHD care for ethnic minority children: A review of the current literature. *Transcultural Psychiatry*, *57*(3), 468–483. https://doi.org/10.1177/1363461520902885

Slobodskaya, H. R., Gartstein, M. A., Nakagawa, A., & Putnam, S. P. (2013). Early temperament in Japan, the United States, and Russia. *Journal of Cross-Cultural Psychology*, *44*(3), 438–460. https://doi.org/10.1177/0022022112453316

Smetana, J. G. (2011). Parenting beliefs, parenting, and parent-adolescent communication in African American families. In H. E. Fitzgerald, N. E. Hill, & T. Mann (Eds.), *African American families. African American children's mental health: Development and context* (pp. 173–197). ABC-CLIO.

Smetana, J. G. (2013). Moral development. In P. D. Zelazo (Ed.), *The Oxford handbook of developmental psychology* (Vol. 1). *Body and mind*. Oxford University Press. https://doi.org/10.1093/oxfordhb/9780199958450.013.0029

Smetana, J. G., & Ball, C. L. (2019). Heterogeneity in children's developing moral judgments about different types of harm. *Developmental Psychology*, *55*(6), 1150–1163. https://doi.org/10.1037/dev0000718

Smetana, J. G., Jambon, M., & Ball, C. L. (2018). Normative changes and individual differences in early moral judgments: A constructivist developmental perspective. *Human Development*, *61*(4–5), 264–280. https://doi.org/10.1159/000492803

Smetana, J. G., Jambon, Marc., & Courtney, Ball. (2014). The social domain approach to children's moral and social judgments. In M. Killen & J. G. Smetana (Eds.), *Handbook of moral development* (pp. 23–44). Psychology Press. https://doi.org/10.4324/9780203581957

Smetana, J. G., & Rote, W. M. (2019). Adolescent-parent relationships: Progress, processes, and prospects. *Annual Review of Developmental Psychology*, *1*(1), 41–68. https://doi.org/10.1146/annurev-devpsych-121318-084903

Smetana, J. G., & Yoo, H. N. (2023). Development and variations in moral and social-conventional judgments: A social domain theory approach. In M. Killen & J. G. Smetana (Eds.), *Handbook of moral (development*(3rd ed., pp. 19–36). Routledge.

Smink, F. R. E., van Hoeken, D., & Hoek, H. W. (2013). Epidemiology, course, and outcome of eating disorders. *Current Opinion in Psychiatry*, *26*(6), 543–548. https://doi.org/10.1097/YCO.0b013e328365a24f

Smith, A. R., Steinberg, L., Strang, N., & Chein, J. (2015). Age differences in the impact of peers on adolescents' and adults' neural response to reward. *Developmental Cognitive Neuroscience*, *11*, 75–82. https://doi.org/10.1016/j.dcn.2014.08.010

Smith, B., Rogers, S. L., Blissett, J., & Ludlow, A. K. (2020). The relationship between sensory sensitivity, food fussiness and food preferences in children with neurodevelopmental disorders. *Appetite*, *15*(0). https://doi.org/10.1016/j.appet.2020.104643

Smith, C. D., & Smith Lee, J. R. (2019). Advancing social justice and affirming humanity in developmental science research with African American boys and young men. *Applied Developmental Science*, *24*(3), 208–214. https://doi.org/10.1080/10888691.2019.1630277

Smith, C. E., Blake, P. R., & Harris, P. L. (2013). I should but I won't: Why young children endorse norms of fair sharing but do not follow them. *PLoS ONE*, *8*(3), e59510. https://doi.org/10.1371/journal.pone.0059510

Smith, C. E., & Warneken, F. (2016). Children's reasoning about distributive and retributive justice across development. *Developmental Psychology*, *52*(4), 613–628. https://doi.org/10.1037/a0040069

Smith, C., & Snell, P. (2009). *Souls in transition: The religious and spiritual lives of emerging adults*. Oxford University Press.

Smith, D. S., & Juvonen, J. (2017). Do I fit in? Psychosocial ramifications of low gender typicality in early adolescence. *Journal of Adolescence*, *60*, 161–170. https://doi.org/10.1016/j.adolescence.2017.07.014

Smith, G. C., Dolbin-MacNab, M., Infurna, F. J., Crowley, D. M., Castro, S., Musil, C., & Webster, B. (2024). Self-reported adverse childhood experiences and risk for internalizing and externalizing difficulties among adolescent custodial grandchildren. *Journal of Child and Family Studies*, *33*(3), 982–997. https://doi.org/10.1007/s10826-024-02803-4

Smith, L., van Jaarsveld, C. H. M., Llewellyn, C. H., Fildes, A., López Sánchez, G. F., Wardle, J., & Fisher, A. (2017). Genetic and environmental influences on developmental milestones and movement: Results from the Gemini cohort study. *Research Quarterly for Exercise and Sport*, *88*(4), 401–407. https://doi.org/10.1080/02701367.2017.1373268

Smith, M., Manduchi, B., Burke, É., Carroll, R., McCallion, P., & McCarron, M. (2020). Communication difficulties in adults with intellectual disability: Results from a national cross-sectional study. *Research in Developmental Disabilities*, *97*, 103557. https://doi.org/10.1016/J.RIDD.2019.103557

Smith, N. C., & Nicholson, H. L. (2022). Perceived discrimination and mental health among African American and Caribbean Black adolescents: Ethnic differences in processes and effects. *Ethnicity and Health*, *27*(3), 687–704. https://doi.org/10.1080/13557858.2020.1814998

Smith, P. K., & StGeorge, J. M. (2023). Play fighting (rough-and-tumble play) in children: Developmental and evolutionary perspectives. *International Journal of Play*, *12*(1), 113–126. https://doi.org/10.1080/21594937.2022.2152185

Smith, P. S. (2019). From research to reform: Improving the experiences of the children and families of incarcerated parents in Europe. In J. M. Eddy & J. Poehlmann-Tynan (Eds.), *Handbook on children with incarcerated parents: Research, policy, and practice* (pp. 267–277). Springer International. https://doi.org/10.1007/978-3-030-16707-3_18

Smith, S., Ferguson, C., & Beaver, K. (2018). A longitudinal analysis of shooter games and their relationship with conduct disorder and self-reported delinquency. *International Journal of Law and Psychiatry*, *58*, 48–53. https://doi.org/10.1016/j.ijlp.2018.02.008

SmithBattle, L., Bekaert, S., Phengnum, W., & Schneider, J. (2024). Untangling risky discourse with evidence: A scoping review of outcomes for teen mothers' offspring. *Children and Youth Services Review*, *161*, 107609. https://doi.org/10.1016/j.childyouth.2024.107609

SmithBattle, L., & Flick, L. H. (2023). A narrative review of teen mothers' long-term outcomes: What birth cohort studies tell us. *Longitudinal and Life Course Studies*, *14*(3), 313–338. https://doi.org/10.1332/175795921X16643247963616

Smock, P. J., & Schwartz, C. R. (2020). The demography of families: A review of patterns and change. *Journal of Marriage and Family*, *82*(1), 9–34. https://doi.org/10.1111/jomf.12612

Smolucha, L., & Smolucha, F. (2022). Vygotsky's theory in-play: Early childhood education. In *The influence of theorists and pioneers on early childhood education*. Routledge.

Snider, J. B., Clements, A., & Vazsonyi, A. T. (2004). Late adolescent perceptions of parent religiosity and parenting processes. *Family process*, *43*(4), 489–502. https://doi.org/10.1111/j.1545-5300.2004.00036.x

Snowling, M. J. (2013). Early identification and interventions for dyslexia: A contemporary view. *Journal of Research in Special Educational Needs*, *13*(1), 7–14. https://doi.org/10.1111/j.1471-3802.2012.01262.x

Snowling, M. J., Hulme, C., & Nation, K. (2020). Defining and understanding dyslexia: Past, present and future. *Oxford Review of Education*, *46*(4), 501–513. https://doi.org/10.1080/03054985.2020.1765756

Society for Research in Child Development. (2021). *Ethical principles and standards for developmental scientists*. https://www.srcd.org/about-us/ethical-principles-and-standards-developmental-scientists

Söderström-Anttila, V., Wennerholm, U.-B., Loft, A., Pinborg, A., Aittomäki, K., Romundstad, L. B., & Bergh, C. (2015). Surrogacy: Outcomes for surrogate mothers, children and the resulting families—A systematic review. *Human Reproduction Update*, *22*(2), dmv046. https://doi.org/10.1093/humupd/dmv046

Sodian, B., Kristen-Antonow, S., & Kloo, D. (2020). How does children's theory of mind become explicit? A review of longitudinal findings. *Child Development Perspectives*, *14*(3), 171–177. https://doi.org/10.1111/cdep.12381

Soenens, B., Vansteenkiste, M., & Beyers, W. (2019). Parenting adolescents. In M. H. Bornstein (Ed.), *Handbook of parenting: Social conditions and applied parenting* (3rd ed., Vol. 4, pp. 111–167). Routledge. https://doi.org/10.4324/9780429440847-4

Softness, K. A., Trussler, J. T., & Carrasquillo, R. J. (2020). Advanced sperm testing. *Current Opinion in Urology*, *30*(3), 290–295. https://doi.org/10.1097/MOU.0000000000000761

Solebo, A. L., Teoh, L., & Rahi, J. (2017). Epidemiology of blindness in children. *Archives of Disease in Childhood*, *102*(9), 853–857. https://doi.org/10.1136/archdischild-2016-310532

Soliman, A., De Sanctis, V., Alaaraj, N., Ahmed, S., Alyafei, F., Hamed, N., & Soliman, N. (2021). Early and long-term consequences of nutritional stunting: From childhood to adulthood. *Acta Biomedica*, *92*(1). https://doi.org/10.23750/abm.v92i1.11346

Solmeyer, A. R., McHale, S. M., & Crouter, A. C. (2014). Longitudinal associations between sibling relationship qualities and risky behavior across adolescence. *Developmental Psychology*, *50*(2), 600–610. https://doi.org/10.1037/a0033207

Soltani, S., Salari-Moghaddam, A., Saneei, P., Askari, M., Larijani, B., Azadbakht, L., & Esmaillzadeh, A. (2022). Maternal caffeine consumption during pregnancy and risk of low birth weight: A dose–response meta-analysis of cohort studies. *Critical Reviews in Food Science and Nutrition*, *63*(2), 224–233. https://doi.org/10.1080/10408398.2021.1945532

Soneji, S., & Beltrán-Sánchez, H. (2019). Association of maternal cigarette smoking and smoking cessation with preterm birth. *JAMA Network Open*, *2*(4), e192514. https://doi.org/10.1001/jamanetworkopen.2019.2514

Song, J., Bong, M., Lee, K., & Kim, S. I. (2015). Longitudinal investigation into the role of perceived social support in adolescents' academic motivation and achievement. *Journal of Educational Psychology*, *107*(3), 821–841. https://doi.org/10.1037/edu0000016

Song, J., Kim, S. I., & Bong, M. (2020). Controllability attribution as a mediator in the effect of mindset on achievement goal adoption following failure. *Frontiers in Psychology*, *10*, 2943. https://doi.org/10.3389/fpsyg.2019.02943

Song, Y., Barger, M. M., & Bub, K. L. (2022). The association between parents' growth mindset and children's persistence and academic skills. *Frontiers in Education*, *6*, 791652. https://www.frontiersin.org/articles/10.3389/feduc.2021.791652

Song, Y., Broekhuizen, M., & Dubas, J. S. (2022). A three-wave study on the development of prosocial behaviours across toddlerhood: The role of socialization. *Infant and Child Development*, *31*(2), e2289. https://doi.org/10.1002/icd.2289

Sonuga-Barke, E. J. S., Becker, S. P., Bölte, S., Castellanos, F. X., Franke, B., Newcorn, J. H., Nigg, J. T., Rohde, L. A., & Simonoff, E. (2023). Annual research review: Perspectives on progress in ADHD science – from characterization to cause. *Journal of Child Psychology and Psychiatry*, *64*(4), 506–532. https://doi.org/10.1111/jcpp.13696

Sonuga-Barke, E. J. S., Hanć, T., Stehli, A., Trampush, J. W., Kenned., M., Kreppner, J., Rutter, M., & Swanson, J. M. (2022). Severe deprivation in early childhood leads to permanent growth stunting: Longitudinal analysis of height trajectories from childhood-to-adulthood. *Child Abuse and Neglect*, *123*, 105427. https://doi.org/10.1016/j.chiabu.2021.105427

Sood, B., & Fuentes, R. W. C. (2022). *Jacobs syndrome*. StatPearls. https://www.ncbi.nlm.nih.gov/books/NBK557699/

Sorbara, J. C., Chiniara, L. N., Thompson, S., & Palmert, M. R. (2020). Mental health and timing of gender-affirming care. *Pediatrics*, *146*(4), e20193600. https://doi.org/10.1542/peds.2019-3600

Sørensen, K., Mouritsen, A., Aksglaede, L., Hagen, C. P., Mogensen, S. S., & Juul, A. (2012). Recent secular trends in pubertal timing: Implications for evaluation and diagnosis of precocious puberty. *Hormone Research in Paediatrics*, *77*(3), 137–145. https://doi.org/10.1159/000336325

Sorenson Duncan, T., & Paradis, J. (2020). Home language environment and children's second language acquisition: The special status of input from older siblings. *Journal of Child Language*, *47*(5), 982–1005. https://doi.org/10.1017/S0305000919000977

Sosa-Hernandez, L., Sack, L., Seddon, J. A., Bailey, K., & Thomassin, K. (2020). Mother and father repertoires of emotion socialization practices in middle childhood. *Journal of Applied Developmental Psychology*, *69*, 101159. https://doi.org/10.1016/j.appdev.2020.101159

Sosnowska, J., Kuppens, P., De Fruyt, F., & Hofmans, J. (2020). New directions in the conceptualization and assessment of personality—A dynamic systems approach. *European Journal of Personality*, *34*(6), 988–998. https://doi.org/10.1002/PER.2233

Soto-Heras, S., Sakkas, D., & Miller, D. J. (2023). Sperm selection by the oviduct: Perspectives for male fertility and assisted reproductive technologies. *Biology of Reproduction*, *108*(4), 538–552. https://doi.org/10.1093/biolre/ioac224

Sparapani, N., Connor, C. M. D., McLean, L., Wood, T., Toste, J., & Day, S. (2018). Direct and reciprocal effects among social skills, vocabulary, and reading comprehension in first grade. *Contemporary Educational Psychology*, *53*, 159–167. https://doi.org/10.1016/j.cedpsych.2018.03.003

Sparling, J., & Meunier, K. (2019). Abecedarian: An early childhood education approach that has a rich history and a vibrant present. *International Journal of Early Childhood*, *51*(2), 207–216. https://doi.org/10.1007/s13158-019-00247-2

Spear, L. P. (2018). Effects of adolescent alcohol consumption on the brain and behaviour. *Nature Reviews Neuroscience*, *19*(4), 197–214. https://doi.org/10.1038/nrn.2018.10

Spearman, C. (1904). "General intelligence," Objectively determined and measured. *American Journal of Psychology*, *15*(2), 201–292. https://doi.org/10.2307/1412107

Spelke, E. S. (2016). Core knowledge and conceptual change: A perspective on social cognition. In D. Barner & A. S. Baron (Eds.), *Core knowledge and conceptual change* (pp. 279–300). Oxford University Press. https://doi.org/10.1093/acprof:oso/9780190467630.003.0016

Spelke, E. S. (2022). *What babies know: Core knowledge and composition* (Vol. 1). Oxford University Press.

Spencer, D., Pasterski, V., Neufeld, S. A. S., Glover, V., O'Connor, T. G., Hindmarsh, P. C., Hughes, I. A., Acerini, C. L., & Hines, M. (2021). Prenatal androgen exposure and children's gender-typed behavior and toy and playmate preferences. *Hormones and Behavior*, *127*, 104889. https://doi.org/10.1016/j.yhbeh.2020.104889

Spencer, J. P. (2020). The development of working memory. *Current Directions in Psychological Science*, *29*(6), 545–553. https://doi.org/10.1177/0963721420959835

Spencer, J. P., Vereijken, B., Diedrich, F. J., & Thelen, E. (2000). Posture and the emergence of manual skills. *Developmental Science*, *3*(2), 216–217.

Spencer, M. B., & Markstrom-Adams, C. (1990). Identity processes among racial and ethnic minority children in America. *Child Development*, *61*(2), 290–310. https://doi.org/10.1111/j.1467-8624.1990.tb02780.x

Spencer, M. B., Swanson, D. P., & Harpalani, V. (2015). Development of the self. In M. E. Lamb (Ed.), *Handbook of child psychology and developmental science* (pp. 1–44). John Wiley & Sons. https://doi.org/10.1002/9781118963418.childpsy318

Spencer, S. J., Logel, C., & Davies, P. G. (2016). Stereotype threat. *Annual Review of Psychology*, *67*(1), 415–437. https://doi.org/10.1146/annurev-psych-073115-103235

Sperry, D. E., Sperry, L. L., & Miller, P. J. (2019). Reexamining the verbal environments of children from different socioeconomic backgrounds. *Child Development*, *90*(4), 1303–1318. https://doi.org/10.1111/cdev.13072

Spettigue, W., Obeid, N., Erbach, M., Feder, S., Finner, N., Harrison, M. E., Isserlin, L., Robinson, A., & Norris, M. L. (2021). The impact of COVID-19 on adolescents with eating disorders: A cohort study. *Journal of Eating Disorders*, *9*(65). https://doi.org/10.1186/s40337-021-00419-3

Speyer, L. G., Hang, Y., Hall, H. A., & Murray, A. L. (2022). The role of harsh parenting practices in early- to middle-childhood socioemotional development: An examination in the Millennium Cohort Study. *Child Development*, *93*(5), 1304–1317. https://doi.org/10.1111/cdev.13761

Spiegel, C., & Halberda, J. (2011). Rapid fast-mapping abilities in 2-year-olds. *Journal of Experimental Child Psychology*, *109*(1), 132–140. https://doi.org/10.1016/j.jecp.2010.10.013

Spiegel, J. A., Goodrich, J. M., Morris, B. M., Osborne, C. M., & Lonigan, C. J. (2021). Relations between executive functions and academic outcomes in elementary school children: A meta-analysis. *Psychological Bulletin*, *147*(4), 329–351. https://doi.org/10.1037/bul0000322

Spielberg, J. M., Olino, T. M., Forbes, E. E., & Dahl, R. E. (2014). Exciting fear in adolescence: Does pubertal development alter threat processing? *Developmental Cognitive Neuroscience*, *8*, 86–95. https://doi.org/10.1016/j.dcn.2014.01.004

Spinelli, A., Buoncristiano, M., Kovacs, V. A., Yngve, A., Spiroski, I., Obreja, G., Starc, G., Pérez, N., Rito, A. I., Kunešová, M., Sant'Angelo, V. F., Meisfjord, J., Bergh, I. H., Kelleher, C., Yardim, N., Pudule, I., Petrauskiene, A., Duleva, V., Sjöberg, A., & &#hillip;; Breda, J. (2019). Prevalence of severe obesity among primary school children in 21 European countries. *Obesity Facts*, *12*(2), 244–258. https://doi.org/10.1159/000500436

Spinelli, M., & Mesman, J. (2018). The regulation of infant negative emotions: The role of maternal sensitivity and infant-directed speech prosody. *Infancy*, *23*(4), 502–518. https://doi.org/10.1111/infa.12237

Spinner, L., Tenenbaum, H. R., Cameron, L., & Wallinheimo, A.-S. (2021). A school-based intervention to reduce gender-stereotyping. *School Psychology International*, *42*(4), 422–449. https://doi.org/10.1177/01430343211009944

Spinrad, T. L., & Gal, D. E. (2018). Fostering prosocial behavior and empathy in young children. *Current Opinion in Psychology*, *20*, 40–44. https://doi.org/10.1016/j.copsyc.2017.08.004

Spivey, L. A., Huebner, D. M., & Diamond, L. M. (2018). Parent responses to childhood gender nonconformity: Effects of parent and child characteristics. *Psychology of Sexual Orientation and Gender Diversity*, *5*(3), 360–370. https://doi.org/10.1037/sgd0000279

Spriet, C., Abassi, E., Hochmann, J. R., & Papeo, L. (2022). Visual object categorization in infancy. *Proceedings of the National Academy of Sciences of the United States of America*, *119*(8), e2105866119. https://doi.org/10.1073/pnas.2105866119

Sravanti, L., & Sagar Kommu, J. V. (2020). Gender intensification in adolescence. *Journal of Psychosexual Health*, *2*(2), 190–191. https://doi.org/10.1177/2631831820924593

Srivastava, A., Winn, J., Senese, J., & Goldbach, J. T. (2022). Sexual orientation change among adolescents and young adults: A systematic review. *Archives of Sexual Behavior*, *51*(7), 3361–3376. https://doi.org/10.1007/s10508-022-02394-5

Sroufe, L. A. (1977). Wariness of strangers and the study of infant development. *Child Development*, *48*(3), 731–746. https://doi.org/10.2307/1128323

Sroufe, L. A. (1997). Psychopathology as an outcome of development. *Development and Psychopathology*, *7*, 323–336. https://doi.org/10.1017/S0954579497002046

Sroufe, L. A., & Waters, E. (1976). The ontogenesis of smiling and laughter: A perspective on the organization of development in infancy. *Psychological Review*, *83*(3), 173–189. https://doi.org/10.1037/0033-295x.83.3.173

Stacks, A. M., Oshio, T., Gerard, J., & Roe, J. (2009). The moderating effect of parental warmth on the association between spanking and child aggression: A longitudinal approach. *Infant & Child Development*, *18*(2), 178–194. https://doi.org/10.1002/icd.596

Stahl, A. E., & Feigenson, L. (2019). Violations of core knowledge shape early learning. *Topics in Cognitive Science*, *11*(1), 136–153. https://doi.org/10.1111/tops.12389

Stahl, A. E., & Kibbe, M. M. (2022). Great expectations: The construct validity of the violation-of-expectation method for studying infant cognition. *Infant and Child Development*, *31*(6), e2359. https://doi.org/10.1002/icd.2359

Stalgaitis, C. A., Navarro, M. A., Wagner, D. E., & Walker, M. W. (2020). Who uses tobacco products? Using peer crowd segmentation to identify youth at risk for cigarettes, cigar products, hookah, and e-cigarettes. *Substance Use and Misuse*, *55*(7), 1045–1053. https://doi.org/10.1080/10826084.2020.1722698

Stalgaitis, C. A., Wagner, D. E., Djakaria, M., & Jordan, J. W. (2019). Understanding adversity and peer crowds to prevent youth health risks. *American Journal of Health Behavior*, *43*(4), 767–780. https://doi.org/10.5993/AJHB.43.4.10

Stams, G.-J. J. M., Juffer, F., & van IJzendoorn, M. H. (2002). Maternal sensitivity, infant attachment, and temperament in early childhood predict adjustment in middle childhood: The case of adopted children and their biologically unrelated parents. *Developmental Psychology*, *38*(5),

806–821. https://doi.org/10.1037/0012-16 49.38.5.806

Stanley, A. Y., Durham, C. O., Sterrett, J. J., & Wallace, J. B. (2019). Safety of over-the-counter medications in pregnancy. *American Journal of Maternal/Child Nursing, 44*(4), 196–205. https://doi.org/10.1097/NMC.000 0000000000537

Stapel, J. C., van, Wijk., I., Bekkering, H., & Hunnius, S. (2017). Eighteen-month-old infants show distinct electrophysiological responses to their own faces. *Developmental Science, 20*(5), e12437. https://doi.org/10 .1111/desc.12437

Statistics Canada. (2015). *The 10 leading causes of death, 2011.* http://www.statcan. gc.ca/pub/82-625-x/2014001/article/1189 6-eng.htm

Stearns, M., & McKinney, C. (2019). Connection between parent and child religiosity: A meta-analysis examining parent and child gender. *Journal of Family Psychology, 33*(6), 704–710. https://doi.org/10.1037/FA M0000550

Steele, C. M., & Aronson, J. (1995). Stereotype threat and the intellectual test performance of African Americans. *Journal of Personality and Social Psychology, 69*(5), 797–811. https://doi.org/10.1037/0022-35 14.69.5.797

Steensma, T. D., Kreukels, B. P. C., de Vries, A. L. C., & Cohen-Kettenis, P. T. (2013). Gender identity development in adolescence. *Hormones and Behavior, 64*(2), 288–297. https://doi.org/10.1016/j.yhbeh.2 013.02.020

Stein, A. D., Wang, M., Martorell, R., Norris, S. A., Adair, L. S., Bas, I., Sachdev, H. S., Bhargava, S. K., Fall, C. H. D., Gigante, D. P., & Victora, C. G. (2010). Growth patterns in early childhood and final attained stature: Data from five birth cohorts from low- and middle-income countries. *American Journal of Human Biology, 22*(3), 353–359. ht tps://doi.org/10.1002/ajhb.20998

Stein, G. L., Cheah, C. S. L., Oh, W., & Witherspoon, D. P. (2023). Developmental science in the twenty-first century: Eschewing segregated science and integrating cultural and racial processes into research. In D. P. Witherspoon & G. L. Stein (Eds.), *Diversity and developmental science: Bridging the gaps between research, practice, and policy* (pp. 1–18). Springer. https:// doi.org/10.1007/978-3-031-23163-6_1

Stein, Y., Hwang, S., Liu, C. L., Diop, H., & Wymore, E. (2020). The association of concomitant maternal marijuana use on health outcomes for opioid exposed newborns in Massachusetts, 2003–2009. *Journal of Pediatrics, 218*, 238–242. https:// doi.org/10.1016/j.jpeds.2019.10.071

Steinberg, L. (2001). We know some things: Parent-adolescent relationships in retrospect and prospect. *Journal of Research on Adolescence, 11*(1), 1–19. https://doi.org/10. 1111/1532-7795.00001

Steinberg, L. (2013). Does recent research on adolescent brain development inform the mature minor doctrine? *Journal of Medicine and Philosophy, 38*, 256–267. https: //doi.org/10.1093/jmp/jht017

Steinberg, L., Icenogle, G., Shulman, E. P., Breiner, K., Chein, J., Bacchini, D., Chang, L., Chaudhary, N., Giunta, L. D., Dodge, K. A., Fanti, K. A., Lansford, J. E., Malone, P. S., Oburu, P., Pastorelli, C., Skinner, A. T., Sorbring, E., Tapanya, S., Tirado, L. M. U. ... S, H. M. (2018). Around the world, adolescence is a time of heightened sensation seeking and immature self-regulation. *Developmental Science, 21*(2), e12532. https: //doi.org/10.1111/desc.12532

Steinberg, L., & Monahan, K. C. (2007). Age differences in resistance to peer influence. *Developmental Psychology, 43*(6), 1531–1543. https://doi.org/10.1037/0012-1 649.43.6.1531

Steiner, J. E. (1979). Human facial expressions in response to taste and smell stimulations. In L. P. Lipsitt & H. W. Reese (Eds.), *Advances in child development: Vol 13* (pp. 257–295). Academic Press.

Steinmayr, R., Weidinger, A. F., Schwinger, M., & Spinath, B. (2019). The importance of students' motivation for their academic achievement – replicating and extending previous findings. *Frontiers in Psychology, 10*, 1730. https://doi.org/10.3389/fpsyg.20 19.01730

Stenberg, G. (2017). Does contingency in adults' responding influence 12-month-old infants' social referencing? *Infant Behavior and Development, 46*, 67–79. https://doi.org/ 10.1016/j.infbeh.2016.11.013

Stephens, K. K., Fresch, R. J., Degrandis, M., & DeFranco, E. (2020). The Association of Maternal Education on prenatal care sufficiency [39J]. *Obstetrics & Gynecology, 135*, 113. https://doi.org/10.1097/01.aog.00 00664392.22912.83

Stephenson, J. (2005). Fetal ultrasound safety. *JAMA, 293*(3), 286.

Stern, J. A., & Cassidy, J. (2018). Empathy from infancy to adolescence: An attachment perspective on the development of individual differences. *Developmental Review, 47*, 1–22. https://doi.org/10.1016/J. DR.2017.09.002

Sternberg, R. J. (1985). *Beyond IQ: A triarchic theory of human intelligence.* Cambridge University Press.

Sternberg, R. J. (2011). The theory of successful intelligence. In R. J. Sternberg & S. B. Kaufman (Eds.), *The Cambridge handbook of intelligence* (pp. 504–527). Cambridge University Press.

Sternberg, R. J. (2018). The triarchic theory of successful intelligence. In D. P. Flanagan & E. M. McDonough (Eds.), *Contemporary intellectual assessment: Theories, tests, and issues* (pp. 174–194). https://psycnet.ap a.org/record/2018-36604-005

Sternberg, R. J. (2020). The nature of intelligence and its development in childhood. In *The nature of intelligence and its development in childhood.* Cambridge University Press. https://doi.org/10.1017/97811088 66217

Sternberg, R. J. (2021). *Adaptive intelligence.* Cambridge University Press.

Sternberg, R. J., & Ambrose, D. (2021). Uniform points of agreement in diverse viewpoints on giftedness and talent. In R. J. Sternberg & D. Ambrose (Eds.), *Conceptions of giftedness and talent* (pp. 513–525). Springer International. https://doi.org/10.1 007/978-3-030-56869-6_28

Sternberg, R. J., & Grigorenko, E. L. (2008). Ability testing across cultures. In L. A. Suzuki & J. G. Ponterotto (Eds.), *Handbook of multicultural assessment: Clinical, psychological, and educational applications* (pp. 449–470). Jossey-Bass.

Sternberg, R. J., Grigorenko, E. L., & Bundy, D. A. (2001). The predictive value of IQ. *Merrill-Palmer Quarterly, 47*, 1–41.

Stevens, E. N., Lovejoy, M. C., & Pittman, L. D. (2014). Understanding the relationship between actual:ideal discrepancies and depressive symptoms: A developmental examination. *Journal of Adolescence, 37*(5), 612–621. https://doi.org/10.1016/j.adolesc ence.2014.04.013

Stevens, J., Gomez-Lobo, V., & Pine-Twaddell, E. (2015). Insurance coverage of puberty blocker therapies for transgender youth. *Pediatrics, 136*(6), 1029–1031. https:/ /doi.org/10.1542/peds.2015-2849

Stewart, J. L., Spivey, L. A., Widman, L., Choukas-Bradley, S., & Prinstein, M. J. (2019). Developmental patterns of sexual identity, romantic attraction, and sexual behavior among adolescents over three years. *Journal of Adolescence, 77*(1), 90–97. https://doi.org/10.1016/j.adolescence.20 19.10.006

StGeorge, J., & Fletcher, R. (2020). Rough-and-tumble play. In S. Hupp & J. D. Jewell

(Eds.), *The encyclopedia of child and adolescent development* (pp. 1–14). Wiley. https://doi.org/10.1002/9781119171492.wecad276

Stidham-Hall, K., Moreau, C., & Trussell, J. (2012). Patterns and correlates of parental and formal sexual and reproductive health communication for adolescent women in the United States, 2002–2008. *Journal of Adolescent Health: Official Publication of the Society for Adolescent Medicine, 50*(4), 410–413. https://doi.org/10.1016/j.jadohealth.2011.06.007

Stierman, B., Afful, J., Carroll, M. D., Chen, T. C., Davy, O., Fink, S., Fryar, C. D., Gu, Q., Hales, C. M., Hughes, J. P., Ostchega, Y., Storandt, R. J., & Akinbami, L. J. (2021). National Health and Nutrition Examination Survey 2017–March 2020 prepandemic data files—development of files and prevalence estimates for selected health outcomes. *National Health Statistics Reports*. https://doi.org/10.15620/cdc:106273 *2021*(158)

Stifter, C., & Augustine, M. (2019). Emotion regulation. In V. LoBue, K. Pérez-Edgar, & K. A. Buss (Eds.), *Handbook of emotional development* (pp. 405–430). Springer International. https://doi.org/10.1007/978-3-030-17332-6_16

Stipek, D., Gralinski, J. H., & Kopp, C. B. (1990). Self-concept development in the toddler years. *Developmental Psychology, 26*(6), 972–977. https://doi.org/10.1037/0012-1649.26.6.972

Stockdale, L., Holmgren, H. G., Porter, C. L., Clifford, B. N., & Coyne, S. (2022). Varying trajectories of infant television viewing over the first four years of life: Relations to language development and executive functions. *Journal of Applied Developmental Psychology, 80*, 101418. https://doi.org/10.1016/j.appdev.2022.101418

Stone, M. M., Blumberg, F. C., Blair, C., & Cancelli, A. A. (2016). The "EF" in deficiency: Examining the linkages between executive function and the utilization deficiency observed in preschoolers. *Journal of Experimental Child Psychology, 152*, 367–375. https://doi.org/10.1016/j.jecp.2016.07.003

Stout, W., Karahuta, E., Laible, D., & Brandone, A. C. (2021). A longitudinal study of the differential social-cognitive foundations of early prosocial behaviors. *Infancy, 26*(2), 271–290. https://doi.org/10.1111/infa.12381

Strathearn, L., Jian, L., Fonagy, P., & Montague, P. R. (2008). What's in a smile? Maternal brain responses to infant facial cues. *Pediatrics, 122*(1), 40–51. https://doi.org/10.1542/peds.2007-1566

Strelau, J. (2020). Temperament. In V. Zeigler-Hill & T. K. Shackelford (Eds.), *Encyclopedia of personality and individual differences* (pp. 5388–5407). Springer International. https://doi.org/10.1007/978-3-319-24612-3_446

Streri, A., & de Hevia, M. D. (2023). How do human newborns come to understand the multimodal environment? *Psychonomic Bulletin & Review, 30*(4), 1171–1186. https://doi.org/10.3758/s13423-023-02260-y

Streri, A., Hevia, M., Izard, V., & Coubart, A. (2013). What do we know about neonatal cognition? *Behavioral Sciences, 3*(1), 154–169. https://doi.org/10.3390/bs3010154

Stubbs, A., Baidawi, S., & Mendes, P. (2023). Young people transitioning from out-of-home care: Their experience of informal support. A scoping review. *Children and Youth Services Review, 144*, 106735. https://doi.org/10.1016/j.childyouth.2022.106735

Sturdivant, T. D., & Alanis, I. (2021). "I'm gonna cook my baby in a pot": Young Black girls' racial preferences and play behavior. *Early Childhood Education Journal, 49*(3), 473–482. https://doi.org/10.1007/s10643-020-01095-9

Su, Y., & Zheng, L. (2023). Stability and change in asexuality: Relationship between sexual/romantic attraction and sexual desire. *Journal of Sex Research, 60*(2), 231–241. https://doi.org/10.1080/00224499.2022.2045889

Suárez, M. I., Stackhouse, E. W., Keese, J., & Thompson, C. G. (2023). A meta-analysis examining the relationship between parents' sexual orientation and children's developmental outcomes. *Journal of Family Studies, 29*(4), 1584–1605. https://doi.org/10.1080/13229400.2022.2060121

Suárez-Orozco, C. (2017). Conferring disadvantage. *Journal of Developmental & Behavioral Pediatrics, 38*(6), 424–428. https://doi.org/10.1097/DBP.0000000000000462

Suarez-Rivera, C., Smith, L. B., & Yu, C. (2019). Multimodal parent behaviors within joint attention support sustained attention in infants. *Developmental Psychology, 55*(1), 96–109. https://doi.org/10.1037/dev0000628

Subrahmanyam, K., & Greenfield, P. M. (1996). Effect of video game practice on spatial skills in girls and boys. In P. M. Greenfield & R. R. Cocking (Eds.), *Interacting with video* (pp. 95–114). Ablex.

Sučević, J., Althaus, N., & Plunkett, K. (2021). The role of labels and motions in infant category learning. *Journal of Experimental Child Psychology, 205*, 105062. https://doi.org/10.1016/j.jecp.2020.105062

Sugden, N. A., Mohamed-Ali, M. I., & Moulson, M. C. (2014). I spy with my little eye: Typical, daily exposure to faces documented from a first-person infant perspective. *Developmental Psychobiology, 56*(2), 249–261. https://doi.org/10.1002/dev.21183

Suggate, S., Pufke, E., & Stoeger, H. (2019). Children's fine motor skills in kindergarten predict reading in grade 1. *Early Childhood Research Quarterly, 47*, 248–258. https://doi.org/10.1016/j.ecresq.2018.12.015

Suizzo, M.-A., Jackson, K. M., & Nauman, C. (2023). Low-income adolescents' future goals and current achievement: Parents as sources of resilience during the transition to middle school. *Journal of Early Adolescence, 43*(6), 815–838. https://doi.org/10.1177/02724316221126414

Sullivan, J., Moss-Racusin, C., Lopez, M., & Williams, K. (2018). Backlash against gender stereotype-violating preschool children. *PLoS ONE, 13*(4), e0195503. https://doi.org/10.1371/journal.pone.0195503

Sullivan, J., Wilton, L., & Apfelbaum, E. P. (2021). Adults delay conversations about race because they underestimate children's processing of race. *Journal of Experimental Psychology: General, 150*, 395–400. https://doi.org/10.1037/xge0000851

Sullivan, J., Wilton, L., & Apfelbaum, E. P. (2022). How age and race affect the frequency, timing, and content of conversations about race with children. *Child Development, 93*(3), 633–652. https://doi.org/10.1111/cdev.13787

Sullivan, M. W., Carmody, D. P., & Lewis, M. (2010). How neglect and punitiveness influence emotion knowledge. *Child Psychiatry and Human Development, 41*(3), 285–298. https://doi.org/10.1007/s10578-009-0168-3

Sullivan, M. W., & Lewis, M. (2003). Contextual determinants of anger and other negative expressions in young infants. *Developmental Psychology, 39*(4), 693–705. https://doi.org/10.1037/0012-1649.39.4.693

Sullivan-Pyke, C. S., Senapati, S., Mainigi, M. A., & Barnhart, K. T. (2017). vitro fertilization and adverse obstetric and perinatal outcomes. *Seminars in Perinatology, 41*(6), 345–353. https://doi.org/10.1053/j.semperi.2017.07.001

Sumter, S. R., Bokhorst, C. L., & Westenberg, P. M. (2018). Resistance and conformity. In R. J. R. Levesque (Ed.), *Encyclopedia of adolescence* (pp. 3149–3160). Springer International. https://doi.org/10.1007/978-3-319-33228-4_327

Sun, Y., Mensah, F. K., Azzopardi, P., Patton, G. C., & Wake, M. (2017). Childhood social disadvantage and pubertal timing: A national birth cohort from Australia. *Pediatrics*, *139*(6), e20164099. https://doi.org/10.1542/peds.2016-4099

Sunderam, S., Kissin, D. M., Zhang, Y., Folger, S. G., Boulet, S. L., Warner, L., Callaghan, W. M., & Barfield, W. D. (2019). Assisted reproductive technology surveillance—United States, 2016. *Morbidity and Mortality Weekly Report. Surveillance Summaries*, *68*(4), 1–23. https://doi.org/10.15585/mmwr.ss6804a1

Sundqvist, A., Nordqvist, E., Koch, F. S., & Heimann, M. (2016). Early declarative memory predicts productive language: A longitudinal study of deferred imitation and communication at 9 and 16 months. *Journal of Experimental Child Psychology*, *151*, 109–119. https://doi.org/10.1016/j.jecp.2016.01.015

Suni, E. (2021). *How much sleep do we really need? Sleep Foundation*. https://www.sleepfoundation.org/how-sleep-works/how-much-sleep-do-we-really-need

Supanitayanon, S., Trairatvorakul, P., & Chonchaiya, W. (2020). Screen media exposure in the first 2 years of life and preschool cognitive development: A longitudinal study. *Pediatric Research*, *88*(6), 894–902. https://doi.org/10.1038/s41390-020-0831-8

Super, C. M. (1981). Cross-cultural research on infancy. In H. C. Triandis & A. Heron (Eds.), *Handbook of cross-cultural psychology: Developmental psychology* (Vol. 4). Allyn & Bacon.

Super, C. M., & Harkness, S. (1982). The infant's niche in rural Kenya and metropolitan America. In L. L. Adler (Ed.), *Cross-cultural research at issue* (pp. 247–255). Academic Press.

Super, C. M., & Harkness, S. (2010). Culture and infancy. In J. G. Bremner & T. D. Wachs (Eds.), *The Wiley-Blackwell handbook of infant development* (pp. 623–649). Wiley-Blackwell. https://doi.org/10.1002/9781444327564.ch21

Super, C. M., & Harkness, S. (2015). Charting infant development. In L. A. Jensen (Ed.), *The Oxford handbook of human development and culture*. Oxford University Press. https://doi.org/10.1093/oxfordhb/9780199948550.013.6

Superbia-Guimarães, L., & Cowan, N. (2023). Disentangling processing and storage accounts of working memory development in childhood. *Developmental Review*, *69*, 101089. https://doi.org/10.1016/j.dr.2023.101089

Susperreguy, M. I., Davis-Kean, P. E., Duckworth, K., & Chen, M. (2018). Self-concept predicts academic achievement across levels of the achievement distribution: Domain specificity for math and reading. *Child Development*, *89*(6), 2196–2214. https://doi.org/10.1111/cdev.12924

Sussman, S., Pokhrel, P., Ashmore, R. D., & Brown, B. B. (2007). Adolescent peer group identification and characteristics: A review of the literature. *Addictive Behaviors*, *32*, 1602–1627. https://doi.org/10.1016/j.addbeh.2006.11.018

Sutton, A., Langenkamp, A. G., Muller, C., & Schiller, K. S. (2018). Who gets ahead and who falls behind during the transition to high school? Academic performance at the intersection of race/ethnicity and gender. *Social Problems*, *65*(2), 154–173. https://doi.org/10.1093/socpro/spx044

Suurland, J., van der Heijden, K. B., Smaling, H. J. A., Huijbregts, S. C. J., van Goozen, S. H. M., & Swaab, H. (2017). Infant autonomic nervous system response and recovery: Associations with maternal risk status and infant emotion regulation. *Development and Psychopathology*, *29*(3), 759–773. https://doi.org/10.1017/S0954579416000456

Svetlova, M., Nichols, S. R., & Brownell, C. A. (2010). Toddlers prosocial behavior: From instrumental to empathic to altruistic helping. *Child Development*, *81*(6), 1814–1827. https://doi.org/10.1111/j.1467-8624.2010.01512.x

Swartz, J. R., Weissman, D. G., Ferrer, E., Beard, S. J., Fassbender, C., Robins, R. W., Hastings, P. D., & Guyer, A. E. (2020). Reward-related brain activity prospectively predicts increases in alcohol use in adolescents. *Journal of the American Academy of Child and Adolescent Psychiatry*, *59*(3), 391–400. https://doi.org/10.1016/j.jaac.2019.05.022

Swearer, S. M., & Hymel, S. (2015). Understanding the psychology of bullying: Moving toward a social-ecological diathesis-stress model. *American Psychologist*, *70*(4), 344–353. https://doi.org/10.1037/a0038929

Swit, C. S., Harty, S. C., & Pascoe, S. (2024). Relational and physical aggression in preschool-age children: Associations with teacher, parent, sibling, and peer relationship quality. *Aggressive Behavior*, *50*(1), e22115. https://doi.org/10.1002/ab.22115

Syed, M., Azmitia, M., & Phinney, J. S. (2007). Stability and change in ethnic identity among Latino emerging adults in two contexts. *Identity*, *7*(2), 155–178. https://doi.org/10.1080/15283480701326117

Syed, M., & Juan, M. J. D. (2012). Birds of an ethnic feather? Ethnic identity homophily among college-age friends. *Journal of Adolescence*, *35*(6), 1505–1514. https://doi.org/10.1016/j.adolescence.2011.10.012

Syvertsen, J. L., Toneff, H., Howard, H., Spadola, C., Madden, D., & Clapp, J. (2021). Conceptualizing stigma in contexts of pregnancy and opioid misuse: A qualitative study with women and healthcare providers in Ohio. *Drug and Alcohol Dependence*, *222*, 108677. https://doi.org/10.1016/j.drugalcdep.2021.108677

Szpak, M., & Białecka-Pikul, M. (2020). Links between attachment and theory of mind in childhood: Meta-analytic review. *Social Development*, *29*(3), 653–673. https://doi.org/10.1111/sode.12432

Taber, K. S. (2020). *Mediated learning leading development—the social development theory of Lev Vygotsky* (pp. 277–291). Springer. https://doi.org/10.1007/978-3-030-43620-9_19

Tait, A. R., & Geisser, M. E. (2017). Development of a consensus operational definition of child assent for research. *BMC Medical Ethics*, *18*(1), 41. https://doi.org/10.1186/s12910-017-0199-4

Takács, L., Smolík, F., Kaźmierczak, M., & Putnam, S. P. (2020). Early infant temperament shapes the nature of mother-infant bonding in the first postpartum year. *Infant Behavior and Development*, *58*, 101428. https://doi.org/10.1016/j.infbeh.2020.101428

Takács, L., Smolík, F., & Putnam, S. (2019). Assessing longitudinal pathways between maternal depressive symptoms, parenting self-esteem and infant temperament. *PLoS ONE*, *14*(8), e0220633. https://doi.org/10.1371/journal.pone.0220633

Takahashi, K. (1990). Are the key assumptions of the "strange situation" procedure universal? A view from Japanese research. *Human Development*, *33*(1), 23–30. https://doi.org/10.1159/000276500

Takahashi, K. H. (2019). Multiple modes of canalization: Links between genetic, environmental canalizations and developmental stability, and their trait-specificity. In V. Debat & A. L. Rouzic (Eds.), *Seminars in cell and developmental biology* (Vol. 88, pp. 14–20). Elsevier. https://doi.org/10.1016/j.semcdb.2018.05.018

Takeuchi, H., Taki, Y., Nouchi, R., Yokoyama, R., Kotozaki, Y., Nakagawa, S., Sekiguchi, A., Iizuka, K., Hanawa, S., Araki, T., Miyauchi, C. M., Sakaki, K., Sassa, Y., Nozawa, T., Ikeda, S., Yokota, S., Daniele, M., & Kawashima, R. (2018). General intelligence is associated with working memory-related brain activity: New evidence from a large sample study. *Brain Structure and Function, 223*(9), 4243–4258. https://doi.org/10.1007/S00429-018-1747-5

Talleyrand, R. M., & Vojtech, J. T.-G. (2018). Potential stressors of undocumented Latinx youth: Implications and recommendations for school counselors. *Professional School Counseling, 22*(1). https://doi.org/10.1177/2156759x19847168

Tamariz, M., & Kirby, S. (2016). The cultural evolution of language. *Current Opinion in Psychology, 8*, 37–43. https://doi.org/10.1016/j.copsyc.2015.09.003

Tamis-Lemonda, C., & Bornstein, M. (2015). Infant word learning in biopsychosocial perspective. In S. Calkins (Ed.), *Handbook of infant development: A biopsychosocial perspective.* https://nyuscholars.nyu.edu/en/publications/infant-word-learning-in-biopsychosocial-perspective

Tamis-LeMonda, C. S., & Bornstein, M. H. (1989). Habituation and maternal encouragement of attention in infancy as predictors of toddler language, play, and representational competence. *Child Development, 60*, 738–751. https://doi.org/10.1111/j.1467-8624.1989.tb02754.x

Tamis-LeMonda, C. S., Bornstein, M. H., & Baumwell, L. (2001). Maternal responsiveness and children's achievement of language milestones. *Child Development, 72*(3), 748–767. https://doi.org/10.1111/1467-8624.00313

Tamis-LeMonda, C. S., Bornstein, M. H., Cyphers, L., Toda, S., & Ogino, M. (1992). Language and play at one year: A comparison of toddlers and mothers in the United States and Japan. *International Journal of Behavioral Development, 15*(1), 19–42. https://doi.org/10.1177/016502549201500102

Tamis-LeMonda, C. S., Briggs, R. D., McClowry, S. G., & Snow, D. L. (2009). Maternal control and sensitivity, child gender, and maternal education in relation to children's behavioral outcomes in African American families. *Journal of Applied Developmental Psychology, 30*(3), 321–331. https://doi.org/10.1016/j.appdev.2008.12.018

Tamis-LeMonda, C. S., Kuchirko, Y., & Song, L. (2014). Why is infant language learning facilitated by parental responsiveness? *Current Directions in Psychological Science, 23*(2), 121–126. https://doi.org/10.1177/0963721414522813

Tamnes, C., & Mills, K. (2020). Imaging structural brain development in childhood and adolescence. In D. Poeppel, G. Mangun, & M. Gazzaniga (Eds.), *The cognitive neurosciences VI* (pp. 17–25). MIT.

Tamnes, C., & Mills, K. (2020). Imaging structural brain development in childhood and adolescence. In D. Poeppel, G. Mangun, & M. Gazzaniga (Eds.), *The cognitive neurosciences* (6th ed., pp. 17–25). MIT Press.

Tamnes, C., & Mills, K. (2020). Imaging structural brain development in childhood and adolescence. In D. Poeppel, G. Mangun, & M. Gazzaniga (Eds.), *The Cognitive Neurosciences VI* (pp. 17–25). MIT.

Tan, E., & Hamlin, J. K. (2024). Toddlers' affective responses to sociomoral scenes: Insights from physiological measures. *Journal of Experimental Child Psychology, 237*, 105757. https://doi.org/10.1016/j.jecp.2023.105757

Tan, E. S., McIntosh, J. E., Kothe, E. J., Opie, J. E., & Olsson, C. A. (2018). Couple relationship quality and offspring attachment security: A systematic review with meta-analysis. *Attachment & Human Development, 20*(4), 349–377. https://doi.org/10.1080/14616734.2017.1401651

Tan, R., Yang, Y., Huang, T., Lin, X., & Gao, H. (2023). Parent–child attachment and mental health in young adolescents: A moderated mediation analysis. *Frontiers in Psychology, 14*, 1298485. https://doi.org/10.3389/fpsyg.2023.1298485

Tan, T. X., Kim, E. S., Baggerly, J., Mahoney, E. E., & Rice, J. (2017). Beyond adoption status: Post-adoptive parental involvement and children's reading and math performance from kindergarten to first grade. *American Journal of Orthopsychiatry, 87*(3), 337–346. https://doi.org/10.1037/ort0000216

Tan, W. C., & Sin, D. D. (2018). What are the long-term effects of smoked marijuana on lung health? *CMAJ, 190*(42), e1243–e1244. https://doi.org/10.1503/cmaj.181307

Taneri, B., Asilmaz, E., Delikurt, T., Savas, P., & Targen, S. (2020). *Human genetics and genomics: A practical guide.* Wiley.

Tankersley, A. P., Grafsky, E. L., Dike, J., & Jones, R. T. (2021). Risk and resilience factors for mental health among transgender and gender nonconforming (TGNC) youth: A systematic review. *Clinical Child and Family Psychology Review, 24*(2), 183–206. https://doi.org/10.1007/S10567-021-00344-6

Tanner, A., & Dounavi, K. (2021). The emergence of autism symptoms prior to 18 months of age: A systematic literature review. *Journal of Autism and Developmental Disorders, 51*(3), 973–993. https://doi.org/10.1007/s10803-020-04618-w

Tanner, J. M. (1990). *Foetus into man: Physical growth from conception to maturity.* Harvard University Press.

Tannock, M. (2011). Observing young children's rough-and-tumble play. *Australasian Journal of Early Childhood, 36*(2), 13–20. https://doi.org/10.1177/183693911103600203

Tao, B., Yang, P., Wang, C., Du, W., Shen, P., Wu, Y., Ding, X., Chen, S., Wu, S., & Li, Y. (2021). Fetal exposure to the Great Chinese Famine and risk of ischemic stroke in midlife. *European Journal of Neurology, 28*(4), 1244–1252. https://doi.org/10.1111/ene.14661

Tappin, D., Mitchell, E. A., Carpenter, J., Hauck, F., & Allan, L. (2023). Bed-sharing is a risk for sudden unexpected death in infancy. *Archives of Disease in Childhood, 108*(2), 79–80. https://doi.org/10.1136/archdischild-2021-322480

Taran, N., Farah, R., DiFrancesco, M., Altaye, M., Vannest, J., Holland, S., Rosch, K., Schlaggar, B. L., & Horowitz-Kraus, T. (2022). The role of visual attention in dyslexia: Behavioral and neurobiological evidence. *Human Brain Mapping, 43*(5), 1720–1737. https://doi.org/10.1002/hbm.25753

Tardif, T., Fletcher, P., Liang, W., Zhang, Z., Kaciroti, N., & Marchman, V. A. (2008). Baby's first 10 words. *Developmental Psychology, 44*(4), 929–938. https://doi.org/10.1037/0012-1649.44.4.929

Tardif, T., Shatz, M., & Naigles, L. (1997). Caregiver speech and children's use of nouns versus verbs: A comparison of English, Italian, and Mandarin. *Journal of Child Language, 24*, 535–565. https://doi.org/10.1017/S030500099700319X

Tarokh, L., Short, M., Crowley, S. J., Fontanellaz-Castiglione, C. E. G., & Carskadon, M. A. (2019). Sleep and circadian rhythms in adolescence. *Current Sleep Medicine Reports, 5*(4), 181–192. https://doi.org/10.1007/s40675-019-00155-w

Tarry, H., & Emler, N. (2007). Attitude, values and moral reasoning as predictors of delinquency. *British Journal of Developmental Psychology, 25*(2), 169–183. https://doi.org/10.1348/026151006x113671

Tarullo, A. R., Isler, J. R., Condon, C., Violaris, K., Balsam, P. D., & Fifer, W. P. (2016). Neonatal eyelid conditioning during sleep. *Developmental Psychobiology, 58*(7), 875–882. https://doi.org/10.1002/dev.21424

Tashjian, S. M., & Galván, A. (2020). Neural recruitment related to threat perception differs as a function of adolescent sleep.

Developmental Science, *23*(5), e12933. https://doi.org/10.1111/DESC.12933

Taumoepeau, M. (2015). From talk to thought. *Journal of Cross-Cultural Psychology*, *46*(9), 1169–1190. https://doi.org/10.1177/0022022115604393

Taumoepeau, M. (2016). Maternal expansions of child language relate to growth in children's vocabulary. *Language Learning and Development*, *12*(4), 429–446. https://doi.org/10.1080/15475441.2016.1158112

Taussig, H. N., Bender, K., Bennett, R., Combs, K. M., Fireman, O., & Wertheimer, R. (2020). Mentoring for teens with child welfare involvement: Permanency outcomes from a randomized controlled trial of the fostering healthy futures for teens program. *Child Welfare*, *97*(5), 1–24.

Taylor, A. W., Nesheim, S. R., Zhang, X., Song, R., FitzHarris, L. F., Lampe, M. A., Weidle, P. J., & Sweeney, P. (2017). Estimated perinatal HIV infection among infants born in the United States, 2002–2013. *JAMA Pediatrics*, *171*(5), 435–442. https://doi.org/10.1001/jamapediatrics.2016.5053

Taylor, D. (2020). *Fifteen percent of same-sex couples have children in their household*. America Counts: Stories Behind the Numbers. U.S. Census Bureau https://www.census.gov/library/stories/2020/09/fifteen-percent-of-same-sex-couples-have-children-in-their-household.html

Taylor, K., & Kan, P. F. (2021). The impact of older siblings on vocabulary learning in bilingual children. *International Journal of Bilingual Education and Bilingualism*, *24*(6), 804–821. https://doi.org/10.1080/13670050.2018.1518969

Taylor, M. (1999). *Imaginary companions and the children who create them*. Oxford University Press.

Taylor, M., Shawber, A. B., & Mannering, A. M. (2009). Children's imaginary companions: What is it like to have an invisible friend? In K. D. Markman, W. M. P. Klein, & J. A. Suhr (Eds.), *Handbook of imagination and mental simulation* (pp. 211–224). Psychology Press.

Taylor, Z. E., Eisenberg, N., Spinrad, T. L., Eggum, N. D., & Sulik, M. J. (2013). The relations of ego-resiliency and emotion socialization to the development of empathy and prosocial behavior across early childhood. *Emotion*, *13*(5), 822–831. https://doi.org/10.1037/a0032894

te Nijenhuis, J. (2013). The Flynn effect, group differences, and g loadings. *Personality and Individual Differences*, *55*(3), 224–228. https://doi.org/10.1016/j.paid.2011.12.023

Tebbi, C. K. (2022). Sickle cell disease, a review. *Hemato*, *3*(2), Article 2. https://doi.org/10.3390/hemato3020024

Tecwyn, E. C., Thorpe, S. K. S., & Chappell, J. (2014). Development of planning in 4- to 10-year-old children: Reducing inhibitory demands does not improve performance. *Journal of Experimental Child Psychology*, *125*(1), 85–101. https://doi.org/10.1016/J.JECP.2014.02.006

Tenenbaum, H. R., & Leaper, C. (2003). Parent-child conversations about science: The socialization of gender inequities? *Developmental Psychology*, *39*(1), 34–47. https://doi.org/10.1037/0012-1649.39.1.34

Teoh, P. J., & Maheshwari, A. (2014). Low-cost in vitro fertilization: Current insights. *International Journal of Women's Health*, *6*, 817–827. https://doi.org/10.2147/IJWH.S51288

Terán, L., Yan, K., & Aubrey, J. S. (2020). "But first let me take a selfie": U.S. adolescent girls' selfie activities, self-objectification, imaginary audience beliefs, and appearance concerns. *Journal of Children and Media*, *14*(3), 343–360. https://doi.org/10.1080/17482798.2019.1697319

Terman, L. M. (1917). *The Stanford revision and extension of the Binet-Simon scale for measuring intelligence*. Warwick & York.

Tevlin, C. (2021). Sex differences in aggression. In T. K. Shackelford & V. A. Weekes-Shackelford (Eds.), *Encyclopedia of evolutionary psychological science* (pp. 7072–7085). Springer. https://doi.org/10.1007/978-3-319-19650-3_1671

Thamban, T., Agarwaal, V., & Khosla, S. (2020). Role of genomic imprinting in mammalian development. *Journal of Biosciences*, *45*(1), 1–21. https://doi.org/10.1007/s12038-019-9984-1

Thelen, E. (1995). Motor development: A new synthesis. *American Psychologist*, *50*(2), 79–95. https://doi.org/10.1037/0003-066X.50.2.79

Thelen, E. (2000). Motor development as foundation and future of developmental psychology. *International Journal of Behavioral Development*, *24*(4), 385–397.

Theodora, M., Antsaklis, A., Antsaklis, P., Blanas, K., Daskalakis, G., Sindos, M., Mesogitis, S., & Papantoniou, N. (2016). Fetal loss following second trimester amniocentesis. Who is at greater risk? How to counsel pregnant women? *Journal of Maternal-Fetal & Neonatal Medicine*, *29*(4), 590–595. https://doi.org/10.3109/14767058.2015.1012061

Theodoraki, T. E., McGeown, S. P., Rhodes, S. M., & MacPherson, S. E. (2020). Developmental changes in executive functions during adolescence: A study of inhibition, shifting, and working memory. *British Journal of Developmental Psychology*, *38*(1), 74–89. https://doi.org/10.1111/bjdp.12307

Theurel, A., & Gentaz, E. (2018). The regulation of emotions in adolescents: Age differences and emotion-specific patterns. *PLoS ONE*, *13*(6), e0195501. https://doi.org/10.1371/journal.pone.0195501

Thiel, F., Eberhard-Gran, M., & Garthus-Niegel, S. (2021). The impact of perinatal life stress on infant temperament and child development: A 2-year follow-up cohort study. *Journal of Developmental & Behavioral Pediatrics*, *42*(4), 299–306. https://doi.org/10.1097/DBP.0000000000000887

Thoma, B. C., Salk, R. H., Choukas-Bradley, S., Goldstein, T. R., Levine, M. D., & Marshal, M. P. (2019). Suicidality disparities between transgender and cisgender adolescents. *Pediatrics*, *144*(5), e20191183. https://doi.org/10.1542/peds.2019-1183

Thomaes, S., Poorthuis, A., & Nelemans, S. (2011). Self-esteem. In M. Bradford Brown & M. J. Prinstein (Eds.), *Encyclopedia of adolescence* (pp. 316–324). Academic Press. https://doi.org/10.1016/B978-0-12-373951-3.00037-5

Thoman, E. B., & Ingersoll, E. W. (1993). Learning in premature infants. *Developmental Psychology*, *28*, 692–700.

Thomas, A., & Chess, S. (1977). *Temperament and development*. Brunner/Mazel.

Thomas, A., Chess, S., & Birch, H. G. (1970). The origin of personality. *Scientific American*, *223*(2), 102–109. https://doi.org/10.1038/scientificamerican0870-102

Thomas, J. C., Letourneau, N., Campbell, T. S., Tomfohr-Madsen, L., & Giesbrecht, G. F. (2017). Developmental origins of infant emotion regulation: Mediation by temperamental negativity and moderation by maternal sensitivity. *Developmental Psychology*, *53*(4), 611–628. https://doi.org/10.1037/dev0000279

Thomas, R., Wheeler, L. A., Delgado, M. Y., Nair, R. L., & Coulter, K. M. (2022). Latinx adolescents' academic self-efficacy: Explaining longitudinal links between ethnic–racial identity and educational adjustment. *Cultural Diversity and Ethnic Minority Psychology*, *28*, 29–38. https://doi.org/10.1037/cdp0000488

Thompson, A. E., & Voyer, D. (2014). Sex differences in the ability to recognise non-verbal displays of emotion: A meta-analysis. *Cognition and Emotion*, *28*(7),

1164–1195. https://doi.org/10.1080/02699931.2013.875889

Thompson, A. L. (2021). What is normal, healthy growth? Global health, human biology, and parental perspectives. *American Journal of Human Biology*, *33*(5). https://doi.org/10.1002/ajhb.23597

Thompson, J., & Stanković-Ramirez, Z. (2021). What early childhood educators know about developmentally appropriate practice. *Phi Delta Kappan*, *103*(2), 20–23. https://doi.org/10.1177/00317217211051138

Thompson, R. A. (2011). Emotion and emotion regulation: Two sides of the developing coin. *Emotion Review*, *3*(1), 53–61. https://doi.org/10.1177/1754073910380969

Thompson, R. A. (2013). Attachment theory and research: Précis and prospect. In P. D. Zelazo (Ed.), *The Oxford handbook of developmental psychology* (Vol. 2, pp. 191–216). Oxford University Press. https://doi.org/10.1093/oxfordhb/9780199958474.013.0009

Thompson, R. A. (2016). Early attachment and later development: Reframing the questions. In J. Cassidy & P. R. Shaver (Eds.), *Handbook of attachment* (pp. 330–347).

Thompson, R. A., & Goodvin, R. (2007). Taming the tempest in the teapot: Emotion regulation in toddlers. In C. A. Brownell & C. B. Kopp (Eds.), *Transitions in early socioemotional development: The toddler years* (pp. 320–341).

Thompson, R. A., & Limber, S. (1991). "Social anxiety" in infancy: Stranger wariness and separation distress. In H. Leitenberg (Ed.), *Handbook of social and evaluation anxiety* (pp. 85–137). Plenum.

Thompson, R. A., & Newton, E. K. (2013). Baby altruists? Examining the complexity of prosocial motivation in young children. *Infancy*, *18*(1), 120–133. https://doi.org/10.1111/j.1532-7078.2012.00139.x

Thompson, R. A., Simpson, J. A., & Berlin, L. J. (2022). Taking perspective on attachment theory and research: Nine fundamental questions. *Attachment & Human Development*, *24*(5), 543–560. https://doi.org/10.1080/14616734.2022.2030132

Thompson, R. A., & Virmani, E. A. (2010). Self and personality. In M. H. Bornstein (Ed.), *Handbook of cultural developmental science* (pp. 195–207). Psychology Press.

Thompson, S. F., Zalewski, M., Kiff, C. J., Moran, L., Cortes, R., & Lengua, L. J. (2020). An empirical test of the model of socialization of emotion: Maternal and child contributors to preschoolers' emotion knowledge and adjustment. *Developmental Psychology*, *56*(3), 418–430. https://doi.org/10.1037/dev0000860

Thornberg, R., Thornberg, U. B., Alamaa, R., & Daud, N. (2016). Children's conceptions of bullying and repeated conventional transgressions: Moral, conventional, structuring and personal-choice reasoning. *Educational Psychology*, *36*(1), 95–111. https://doi.org/10.1080/01443410.2014.915929

Thurman, S. L., & Corbetta, D. (2017). Spatial exploration and changes in infant–mother dyads around transitions in infant locomotion. *Developmental Psychology*, *53*(7), 1207–1221. https://doi.org/10.1037/dev0000328

Thurstone, L. L., & Thurstone, T. G. (1941). Factorial studies of intelligence. *Psychometric Monographs*, *2*, 94–94.

Tierney, K., & Cai, Y. (2019). Assisted reproductive technology use in the United States: A population assessment. *Fertility and Sterility*, *112*(6), 1136–1143.e4. https://doi.org/10.1016/j.fertnstert.2019.07.1323

Timeo, S., Farroni, T., & Maass, A. (2017). Race and color: Two sides of one story? Development of biases in categorical perception. *Child Development*, *88*(1), 83–102. https://doi.org/10.1111/cdev.12564

Tinggaard, J., Mieritz, M. G., Sørensen, K., Mouritsen, A., Hagen, C. P., Aksglaede, L., Wohlfahrt-Veje, C., & Juul, A. (2012). The physiology and timing of male puberty. *Current Opinion in Endocrinology, Diabetes, and Obesity*, *19*(3), 197–203. https://doi.org/10.1097/MED.0b013e3283535614

Tistarelli, N., Fagnani, C., Troianiello, M., Stazi, M. A., & Adriani, W. (2020). The nature and nurture of ADHD and its comorbidities: A narrative review on twin studies. *Neuroscience and Biobehavioral Reviews*, *109*, 63–77. https://doi.org/10.1016/j.neubiorev.2019.12.017

Titz, C., & Karbach, J. (2014). Working memory and executive functions: Effects of training on academic achievement. *Psychological Research*, *78*(6), 852–868. https://doi.org/10.1007/s00426-013-0537-1

Titzmann, P. F., Brenick, A., & Silbereisen, R. K. (2015). Friendships fighting prejudice: A longitudinal Perspective on Adolescents' Cross-Group Friendships with Immigrants. *Journal of Youth and Adolescence*, *44*(6), 1318–1431. https://doi.org/10.1007/s10964-015-0256-6

Todd, B. K., Fischer, R. A., Di Costa, S., Roestorf, A., Harbour, K., Hardiman, P., & Barry, J. A. (2018). Sex differences in children's toy preferences: A systematic review, meta-regression, and meta-analysis. *Infant and Child Development*, *27*(2), e2064. https://doi.org/10.1002/icd.2064

Toft, D. J. (2018). *Growth hormone therapy: The most common growth hormone deficiency treatment*. Endocrineweb. https://www.endocrineweb.com/conditions/growth-disorders/growth-hormone-therapy

Tomalski, P., Marczuk, K., Pisula, E., Malinowska, A., Kawa, R., & Niedźwiecka, A. (2017). Chaotic home environment is associated with reduced infant processing speed under high task demands. *Infant Behavior and Development*, *48*, 124–133. https://doi.org/10.1016/j.infbeh.2017.04.007

Tomasello, M. (2012). A usage-based approach to child language acquisition. *Proceedings of the Annual Meeting of the Berkeley Linguistics Society*, *26*(1), 305–319. https://doi.org/10.3765/bls.v26i1.1123

Tomasello, M. (2018). How children come to understand false beliefs: A shared intentionality account. *Proceedings of the National Academy of Sciences*, *115*(34), 8491–8498. https://doi.org/10.1073/PNAS.1804761115

Tomasi, D., & Volkow, N. D. (2021). Associations of family income with cognition and brain structure in USA children: Prevention implications. *Molecular Psychiatry*, *26*(11), 6619–6629. https://doi.org/10.1038/s41380-021-01130-0

Tomaz Barbosa, R. R., Monteiro, K. S., Maciel, Cavalcanti., Á, C., Silva, da., P, F. E., Jales, L. M., Santino, T. A., do Amaral, C. T., & de Mendonça, K. M. P. P. (2021). Relationship between anxiety symptoms, clinical control and quality of life of children with asthma: A cross-sectional study. *Pediatric Pulmonology*, *56*(7), 1906–1914. https://doi.org/10.1002/ppul.25377

Tomlinson, R. C., Burt, S. A., Waller, R., Jonides, J., Miller, A. L., Gearhardt, A. N., Peltier, S. J., Klump, K. L., Lumeng, J. C., & Hyde, L. W. (2020). Neighborhood poverty predicts altered neural and behavioral response inhibition. *NeuroImage*, *209*, 116536. https://doi.org/10.1016/j.neuroimage.2020.116536

Tomova, A. (2016). Body weight and puberty. In P. Kumanov & A. Agarwal (Eds.), *Puberty* (pp. 95–108). Springer International. https://doi.org/10.1007/978-3-319-32122-6_7

Tomova, L., Andrews, J. L., & Blakemore, S.-J. (2021). The importance of belonging and the avoidance of social risk taking in adolescence. *Developmental Review*, *61*, 100981. https://doi.org/10.1016/j.dr.2021.100981

Tompkins, V., & Villaruel, E. (2021). Parent discipline and pre-schoolers' social skills. *Early Child Development and Care, 192*(3), 410–424. https://doi.org/10.1080/03004430.2020.1763978

Tønnessen, E., Svendsen, I. S., Olsen, I. C., Guttormsen, A., & Haugen, T. (2015). Performance development in adolescent track and field athletes according to age, sex and sport discipline. *PLoS ONE, 10*(6), e0129014. https://doi.org/10.1371/journal.pone.0129014

Tooley, U. A., Bassett, D. S., & Mackey, A. P. (2021). Environmental influences on the pace of brain development. *Nature Reviews Neuroscience, 22*(6), 372–384. https://doi.org/10.1038/s41583-021-00457-5

Toomey, R. B., Card, N. A., & Casper, D. M. (2014). Peers' perceptions of gender nonconformity: Associations with overt and relational peer victimization and aggression in early adolescence. *Journal of Early Adolescence, 34*(4), 463–485. https://doi.org/10.1177/0272431613495446

Toomey, R. B., Syvertsen, A. K., & Shramko, M. (2018). Transgender adolescent suicide behavior. *Pediatrics, 142*(4), e20174218. https://doi.org/10.1542/peds.2017-4218

Toseeb, U., McChesney, G., Dantchev, S., & Wolke, D. (2020). Precursors of sibling bullying in middle childhood: Evidence from a UK-based longitudinal cohort study. *Child Abuse & Neglect, 108*, 104633. https://doi.org/10.1016/j.chiabu.2020.104633

Touyz, S., Lacey, H., & Hay, P. (2020). Eating disorders in the time of COVID-19. *Journal of Eating Disorders, 8*(1), 1–3. https://doi.org/10.1186/S40337-020-00295-3

Tovar, M., Rosillo, M., & Spaniardi, A. (2023). Social media's influence on identity formation and self expression. In A. Spaniardi & J. M. Avari (Eds.), *Teens, screens, and social connection: An evidence-based guide to key problems and solutions* (pp. 49–61). Springer International. https://doi.org/10.1007/978-3-031-24804-7_4

Traboulsi, H., Cherian, M., Abou Rjeili, M., Preteroti, M., Bourbeau, J., Smith, B. M., Eidelman, D. H., & Baglole, C. J. (2020). Inhalation Toxicology of Vaping Products and Implications for Pulmonary Health. *International Journal of Molecular Sciences, 21*(10), 3495. https://doi.org/10.3390/ijms21103495

Tracy, J. L., & Weidman, A. C. (2021). The self-conscious and social emotions: A personality and social functionalist account. In O. P. John & R. W. Robins (Eds.), *Handbook of personality: Theory and research* (pp. 504–522).

Tramutola, A., Lanzillotta, C., Di Domenico, F., Head, E., Butterfield, D. A., Perluigi, M., & Barone, E. (2020). Brain insulin resistance triggers early onset Alzheimer disease in Down syndrome. *Neurobiology of Disease, 137*, 104772. https://doi.org/10.1016/j.nbd.2020.104772

Tratner, A. E., Sela, Y., Lopes, G. S., Shackelford, T. K., McDonald, M. M., Weekes-Shackelford, V. A., & Abed, M. G. (2020). Childhood religious experiences with peers and primary caregivers: Associations with individual differences in adult religiosity. *Personality and Individual Differences, 158*, 109802. https://doi.org/10.1016/j.paid.2019.109802

Traub, F., & Boynton-Jarrett, R. (2017). Modifiable resilience factors to childhood adversity for clinical pediatric practice. *Pediatrics, 139*(5), e20162569. https://doi.org/10.1542/peds.2016-2569

Trawick-Smith, J., & Dziurgot, T. (2011). 'Good-fit' teacher-child play interactions and the subsequent autonomous play of preschool children. *Early Childhood Research Quarterly, 26*(1), 110–123. https://doi.org/10.1016/j.ecresq.2010.04.005

Tremblay, L., & Larivière, M. (2020). Predictors of puberty onset. In S. Hupp & J. D. Jewell (Eds.), *The encyclopedia of child and adolescent development* (pp. 1–10). Wiley. https://doi.org/10.1002/9781119171492.wecad352

Tremblay, M., Baydala, L., Khan, M., Currie, C., Morley, K., Burkholder, C., Davidson, R., & Stillar, A. (2020). Primary substance use prevention programs for children and youth: A systematic review. *Pediatrics, 146*(3). https://doi.org/10.1542/peds.2019-2747

Tremblay, R. E., Nagin, D. S., Séguin, J. R., Zoccolillo, M., Zelazo, P. D., Boivin, M., Pérusse, D., & Japel, Christa. (2004). Physical aggression during early childhood: Trajectories and predictors. *Pediatrics, 114*(1), e43–e50.

Trettien, A. W. (1990). Creeping and walking. *American Journal of Psychology, 12*, 1–57.

Trinh, S. L., Lee, J., Halpern, C. T., & Moody, J. (2019). Our buddies, ourselves: The role of sexual homophily in adolescent friendship networks. *Child Development, 90*(1), e132–e147. https://doi.org/10.1111/cdev.13052

Trionfi, G., & Reese, E. (2009). A good story: Children with imaginary companions create richer narratives. *Child Development, 80*(4), 1301–1313. https://doi.org/10.1111/j.1467-8624.2009.01333.x

Tristão, R. M., Lauand, L., Costa, K. S. F., Brant, L. A., Fernandes, G. M., Costa, K. N., Spilski, J., & Lachmann, T. (2021). Olfactory sensory and perceptual evaluation in newborn infants: A systematic review. *Developmental Psychobiology, 63*(7). https://doi.org/10.1002/dev.22201

Troche, S. J., Thomas, P., Tadin, D., & Rammsayer, T. H. (2018). On the relationship between spatial suppression, speed of information processing, and psychometric intelligence. *Intelligence, 67*, 11–18. https://doi.org/10.1016/j.intell.2017.12.002

Tronick, E. Z., Morelli, G. A., & Ivey, P. K. (1992). The Efe forager infant and toddler's pattern of social relationships: Multiple and simultaneous. *Developmental Psychology, 28*, 568–577. https://doi.org/10.1037/0012-1649.28.4.568

Troop-Gordon, W., MacDonald, A. P., & Corbitt-Hall, D. J. (2019). Children's peer beliefs, friendlessness, and friendship quality: Reciprocal influences and contributions to internalizing symptoms. *Developmental Psychology, 55*(11), 2428–2439. https://doi.org/10.1037/dev0000812

Trosman, I., & Ivanenko, A. (2021). Classification and epidemiology of sleep disorders in children and adolescents. *Child and Adolescent Psychiatric Clinics of North America, 30*(1). https://doi.org/10.1016/j.chc.2020.08.002

Trost, K., Eichas, K., Ferrer-Wreder, L., & Galanti, M. R. (2020). The study of family context: Examining its role for identity coherence and adolescent adjustment for Swedish adolescents. *Journal of Early Adolescence, 40*(2), 165–196. https://doi.org/10.1177/0272431619833479

Troutman, B. (2015). Viewing parent-child interactions through the lens of behaviorism. In B. Troutman (Ed.), *Integrating behaviorism and attachment theory in parent coaching* (pp. 3–20). Springer. https://doi.org/10.1007/978-3-319-15239-4_1

Trucco, E. M. (2020). A review of psychosocial factors linked to adolescent substance use. *Pharmacology Biochemistry and Behavior, 196*, 172969. https://doi.org/10.1016/j.pbb.2020.172969

Tsai, M. C., Wang, Y. C. L., & Chan, H. Y. (2023). Pubertal progression and its relationship to psychological and behavioral outcomes among adolescent boys. *Development and Psychopathology, 35*(4), 1891–1900. doi:10.1017/S0954579422000554

Tsamantioti, E. S., & Hashmi, M. F. (2024). *Teratogenic medications*. StatPearls. http://www.ncbi.nlm.nih.gov/books/nbk553086/

Tsao, Y.-L. (2020). Gender issues in young children's literature. *Reading Improvement*, *57*(1), 16–21.

Tsuji, S., Fiévét, A.-C., & Cristia, A. (2021). Toddler word learning from contingent screens with and without human presence. *Infant Behavior and Development*, *63*, 101553. https://doi.org/10.1016/j.infbeh.2021.101553

Tu, K., Shen, C., Luo, Y., Mo, Y., Jian, L., Mei, X., Zhang, Q., Jin, L., & Qin, H. (2024). The relationships between screen exposure, parent-child interactions and comprehension in 8-month-old infants: The mediating role of shared viewing and parent-child conversation. *PLoS ONE*, *19*(1), e0296356. https://doi.org/10.1371/journal.pone.0296356

Tucker, C. J., Finkelhor, D., & Turner, H. (2019). Patterns of sibling victimization as predictors of peer victimization in childhood and adolescence. *Journal of Family Violence*, *34*, 745–755. https://doi.org/10.1007/s10896-018-0021-1

Tucker, C. J., Updegraff, K., & Baril, M. E. (2010). Who's the boss? Patterns of control in adolescents' sibling relationships. *Family Relations*, *59*(5), 520–532. https://doi.org/10.1111/j.1741-3729.2010.00620.x

Tudge, J. R. H., Merçon-Vargas, E. A., & Payir, A. (2022). Urie Bronfenbrenner's bioecological theory: Its development, core concepts, and critical issues. In K. Adamsons, A. L. Few-Demo, C. Proulx, & K. Roy (Eds.), *Sourcebook of family theories and methodologies: A dynamic approach* (pp. 235–254). Springer. https://doi.org/10.1007/978-3-030-92002-9_16

Tudge, J. R. H., Payir, A., Merçon-Vargas, E., Cao, H., Liang, Y., Li, J., & O'Brien, L. (2016). Still misused after all these years? A reevaluation of the uses of Bronfenbrenner's bioecological theory of human development. *Journal of Family Theory & Review*, *8*(4), 427–445. https://doi.org/10.1111/jftr.12165

Tullius, J. M., De Kroon, M. L. A., Almansa, J., & Reijneveld, S. A. (2022). Adolescents' mental health problems increase after parental divorce, not before, and persist until adulthood: A longitudinal TRAILS study. *European Child & Adolescent Psychiatry*, *31*(6), 969–978. https://doi.org/10.1007/s00787-020-01715-0

Tulving, E. (2002). Episodic memory: From mind to brain. *Annual Review of Psychology*, *53*, 1–25. https://doi.org/10.1146/annurev.psych.53.100901.135114

Tunau, K., Adamu, A., Hassan, M., Ahmed, Y., & Ekele, B. (2012). Age at menarche among school girls in Sokoto, Northern Nigeria. *Annals of African Medicine*, *11*(2), 103–107.

Turban, J. L., Kraschel, K. L., & Cohen, I. G. (2021). Legislation to criminalize gender-affirming medical care for transgender youth. *JAMA*, *325*(22), 2251–2252. https://doi.org/10.1001/jama.2021.7764

Turecki, G., & Meaney, M. J. (2016). Effects of the social environment and stress on glucocorticoid receptor gene methylation: A systematic review. *Biological Psychiatry*, *79*(2), 87–96. https://doi.org/10.1016/j.biopsych.2014.11.022

Turfkruyer, M., & Verhasselt, V. (2015). Breast milk and its impact on maturation of the neonatal immune system. *Current Opinion in Infectious Diseases*, *28*(3), 199–206. https://doi.org/10.1097/QCO.0000000000000165

Turiel, E. (1998). The development of morality. In N. Eisenberg (Ed.), *Handbook of child Psychology* (Vol. 3, pp. 863–932). Wiley.

Turiel, E., & Nucci, L. (2017). Moral development in context. In A. Dick & U. Muller (Eds.), *Advancing developmental science: Philosophy, theory, and method* (pp. 107–121). Routledge.

Turk-Browne, N. B., Scholl, B. J., & Chun, M. M. (2008). Babies and brains: Habituation in infant cognition and functional neuroimaging. *Frontiers in Human Neuroscience*, *2*, 16. https://doi.org/10.3389/neuro.09.016.2008

Turkheimer, E. (2019). Genetics and human agency: The philosophy of behavior genetics introduction to the special issue. *Behavior Genetics*, *49*(2), 123–127. https://doi.org/10.1007/s10519-019-09952-z

Turnbull, K., & Justice, L. M. (2016). *Language development from theory to practice*. Pearson.

Turner, J. H. (2014). J. E. Stets & J. H. Turner (Eds.), *The evolution of human emotions Handbook of the sociology of emotions* (Vol. II, pp. 11–31). Springer. https://doi.org/10.1007/978-94-017-9130-4_2

Turney, K., & Goodsell, R. (2018). Parental incarceration and children's wellbeing. *Future of Children*, *28*(1), 147–164.

Turocy, J., Adashi, E. Y., & Egli, D. (2021). Heritable human genome editing: Research progress, ethical considerations, and hurdles to clinical practice. *Cell*, *184*(6). https://doi.org/10.1016/j.cell.2021.02.036

Twenge, J. M., Haidt, J., Joiner, T. E., & Campbell, W. K. (2020). Underestimating digital media harm. *Nature Human Behaviour*, *4*(4), 346–348. https://doi.org/10.1038/s41562-020-0839-4

Twum-Antwi, A., Jefferies, P., & Ungar, M. (2020). Promoting child and youth resilience by strengthening home and school environments: A literature review. *International Journal of School and Educational Psychology*, *8*(2), 78–89. https://doi.org/10.1080/21683603.2019.1660284

Tyrrell, E., & Prasad, V. (2021). Risk and prevention of unintentional injuries in children and young people with attention-deficit/hyperactivity disorder. *Paediatrics and Child Health*, *31*(10), 371–375. https://doi.org/10.1016/J.PAED.2021.07.001

Uddin, M., Jansen, S., & Telzer, E. H. (2017). Adolescent depression linked to socioeconomic status? Molecular approaches for revealing premorbid risk factors. *BioEssays*, *39*(3), 1600194. https://doi.org/10.1002/bies.201600194

Uhl, E. R., Camilletti, C. R., Scullin, M. H., & Wood, J. M. (2016). Under pressure: Individual differences in children's suggestibility in response to intense social influence. *Social Development*, *25*(2), 422–434. https://doi.org/10.1111/sode.12156

Uhler, K. M., Anderson, S. R., Yoshinaga-Itano, C., Walker, K. A., & Hunter, S. (2022). Speech discrimination in infancy predicts language outcomes at 30 months for both children with normal hearing and those with hearing differences. *Journal of Clinical Medicine*, *11*(19), 5821. https://doi.org/10.3390/jcm11195821

Uhls, Y. T., Ellison, N. B., & Subrahmanyam, K. (2017). Benefits and costs of social media in adolescence. *Pediatrics*, *140*(Suppl 2), S67–S70. https://doi.org/10.1542/peds.2016-1758E

UK Department of Health. (2005). *Reduce the risk of cot death: An easy guide*.

Umaña-Taylor, A. J. (2016a). A post-racial society in which ethnic-racial discrimination still exists and has significant consequences for youths' adjustment. *Current Directions in Psychological Science*, *25*(2), 111–118. https://doi.org/10.1177/0963721415627858

Umaña-Taylor, A. J. (2016b). Ethnic-racial identity conceptualization, development, and youth adjustment. In L. Balter & C. S. Tamis-LeMonda (Eds.), *Child psychology: A handbook of contemporary issues* (pp. 305–328). Routledge. https://doi.org/10.4324/9781315764931

Umaña-Taylor, A. J., Alfaro, E. C., Bámaca, M. Y., & Guimond, A. B. (2009). The central role of familial ethnic socialization in Latino adolescents' cultural orientation.

Journal of Marriage & Family, 71(1), 46–60. https://doi.org/10.1111/j.1741-3737.2008.00579.x

Umaña-Taylor, A. J., & Hill, N. E. (2020). Ethnic-racial socialization in the family: A decade's advance on precursors and outcomes. *Journal of Marriage and Family, 82*(1), 244–271. https://doi.org/10.1111/jomf.12622

Umaña-Taylor, A. J., Quintana, S. M., Lee, R. M., Cross, W. E., Rivas-Drake, D., Schwartz, S. J., Syed, M., Yip, T., & Seaton, E. (2014). Ethnic and racial identity during adolescence and into young adulthood: An integrated conceptualization. *Child Development, 85*(1), 21–39. https://doi.org/10.1111/cdev.12196

Umaña-Taylor, A. J., & Rivas-Drake, D. (2021). Ethnic-racial identity and adolescents' positive development in the context of ethnic-racial marginalization: Unpacking risk and resilience. *Human Development, 65*(5–6), 293–310. https://doi.org/10.1159/000519631

Umer, A., Lilly, C., Hamilton, C., Baldwin, A., Breyel, J., Tolliver, A., Mullins, C., John, C., & Maxwell, S. (2020). Prevalence of alcohol use in late pregnancy. *Pediatric Research, 88*(2), 312–319. https://doi.org/10.1038/s41390-019-0731-y

UNICEF, WHO, & World Bank. (2021). *UNICEF-WHO-The World Bank: Joint child malnutrition estimates – levels and trends – 2021 edition—UNICEF Data*. https://data.unicef.org/resources/jme-report-2021/

Updegraff, K. A., & Perez-Brena, N. J. (2023). Studying families as systems in adolescence and early adulthood. In L. J. Crockett, G. Carlo, & J. E. Schulenberg (Eds.), *APA handbook of adolescent and young adult development* (pp. 177–192). American Psychological Association. https://doi.org/10.1037/0000298-011

Ursache, A., & Noble, K. G. (2016). Neurocognitive development in socioeconomic context: Multiple mechanisms and implications for measuring socioeconomic status. *Psychophysiology, 53*(1), 71–82. https://doi.org/10.1111/psyp.12547

U.S. Bureau of Labor Statistics. (2022). *Labor force participation of mothers and fathers little changed in 2021, remains lower than in 2019. The Economics Daily*. https://www.bls.gov/opub/ted/2022/labor-force-participation-of-mothers-and-fathers-little-changed-in-2021-remains-lower-than-in-2019.htm

U.S. Bureau of Labor Statistics. (2024). *2023 Occupational outlook handbook*. https://www.bls.gov/ooh/

U.S. Census Bureau. (2022). *Same-sex couples are more likely to adopt or foster children*. https://www.census.gov/library/stories/2020/09/fifteen-percent-of-same-sex-couples-have-children-in-their-household.html

U.S. Census Bureau. (2023, April 10). *National Siblings Day:. 2023* https://www.census.gov/newsroom/stories/siblings.html

U.S. Census Bureau. (2024). *Southern states had higher than average share of adults Age 30 and over who lived with grandchildren in 2021*. https://www.census.gov/library/stories/2024/03/grandparents-living-with-grandchildren.html

U.S. Department of Education. (2023). *Table 226.10. Number, percentage distribution, and SAT mean scores of high school seniors taking the SAT, by sex, race/ethnicity, first language learned, and highest level of parental education: Selected years, 2017 through 2022 [Data table]*. Digest of Education Statistics.; National Center for Education Statistics. https://nces.ed.gov/programs/digest/d22/tables/dt22_226.10.asp

U.S. Department of Health and Human Services. (2018a). *Child Maltreatment. 2016* https://www.acf.hhs.gov/cb/resource/child-maltreatment-2016

U.S. Department of Health and Human Services. (2018b). *Physical activity guidelines for Americans*.

U.S. Department of Health and Human Services. (2019). *United States adolescent mental health facts*. https://www.hhs.gov/ash/oah/facts-and-stats/national-and-state-data-sheets/adolescent-mental-health-fact-sheets/united-states/index.html

U.S. Department of Health and Human Services. (2024). *Child maltreatment 2022*. https://www.acf.hhs.gov/cb/report/child-maltreatment-2022

U.S. Department of Health and Human Services & Administration for Children and Families. (2010). *Head Start impact study: Final report*. https://www.acf.hhs.gov/opre/report/head-start-impact-study-final-report

U.S. Department of Labor. (2023). *Civilian labor force by sex*. https://www.dol.gov/agencies/wb/data/lfp/civilianlfbysex

U.S. Food and Drug Administration. (2010). *iPLEDGE information*. https://www.fda.gov/drugs/postmarket-drug-safety-information-patients-and-providers/ipledge-risk-evaluation-and-mitigation-strategy-rems

U.S. Preventive Services Task Force. (2023). Folic acid supplementation to prevent neural tube defects: US Preventive Services Task Force reaffirmation recommendation statement. *JAMA, 330*(5), 454–459. https://doi.org/10.1001/jama.2023.12876

Ustun, B., Covey, J., & Reissland, N. (2023). Chemosensory continuity from prenatal to postnatal life in humans: A systematic review and meta-analysis. *PLoS ONE, 18*(3), e0283314. https://doi.org/10.1371/journal.pone.0283314

Uyoga, S., Macharia, A. W., Ndila, C. M., Nyutu, G., Shebe, M., Awuondo, K. O., Mturi, N., Peshu, N., Tsofa, B., Scott, J. A. G., Maitland, K., & Williams, T. N. (2019). The indirect health effects of malaria estimated from health advantages of the sickle cell trait. *Nature Communications, 10*(1), 1–7. https://doi.org/10.1038/s41467-019-08775-0

Vaivada, T., Akseer, N., Akseer, S., Somaskandan, A., Stefopulos, M., & Bhutta, Z. A. (2020). Stunting in childhood: An overview of global burden, trends, determinants, and drivers of decline. *American Journal of Clinical Nutrition, 112*(Suppl 2), 777S–791S. https://doi.org/10.1093/ajcn/nqaa159

Valadi, S., & Gabbard, C. (2020). The effect of affordances in the home environment on children's fine- and gross motor skills. *Early Child Development and Care, 190*(8). https://doi.org/10.1080/03004430.2018.1526791

Valiente, C., Swanson, J., DeLay, D., Fraser, A. M., & Parker, J. H. (2020). Emotion-related socialization in the classroom: Considering the roles of teachers, peers, and the classroom context. *Developmental Psychology, 56*(3), 578–594. https://doi.org/10.1037/dev0000863

Valkenborghs, S. R., Noetel, M., Hillman, C. H., Nilsson, M., Smith, J. J., Ortega, F. B., & Lubans, D. R. (2019). The impact of physical activity on brain structure and function in youth: A systematic review. *Pediatrics, 144*(4), 20184032. https://doi.org/10.1542/peds.2018-4032

Valkenburg, P. M., Meier, A., & Beyens, I. (2022). Social media use and its impact on adolescent mental health: An umbrella review of the evidence. *Current Opinion in Psychology, 44*, 58–68. https://doi.org/10.1016/j.copsyc.2021.08.017

Valle, J., Baker, J. R., Madrigal, D., Ferrerosa, J., & Paulukonis, S. (2022). Sickle cell disease among Latinx in California. *PLOS ONE*. https://doi.org/10.1371/journal.pone.0276653

Vallotton, C. D., Decker, K. B., Kwon, A., Wang, W., & Chang, T. (2017). Quantity and quality of gestural input: Caregivers' sensitivity predicts caregiver-infant bidirectional communication through gestures.

Infancy, 22(1), 56–77. https://doi.org/10.1111/infa.12155

Vally, Z., & El Hichami, F. (2020). Knowledge about parenting as a predictor of behavioral discipline practices between mothers and fathers. *Psychological Studies, 65*(1), 40–50. https://doi.org/10.1007/s12646-019-00497-z

van den Berg, L., & Gredebäck, G. (2021). The sticky mittens paradigm: A critical appraisal of current results and explanations. *Developmental Science, 24*(5), e13036. https://doi.org/10.1111/desc.13036

van den Berg, L., Libertus, K., Nyström, P., Gottwald, J. M., Licht, V., & Gredebäck, G. (2022). A pre-registered sticky mittens study: Active training does not increase reaching and grasping in a Swedish context. *Child Development, 93*(6), e656–e671. https://doi.org/10.1111/cdev.13835

van den Berg, Y. H. M., Deutz, M. H. F., Smeekens, S., & Cillessen, A. H. N. (2017). Developmental pathways to preference and popularity in middle childhood. *Child Development, 88*(5), 1629–1641. https://doi.org/10.1111/cdev.12706

van den Heuvel, M. I., Hect, J. L., Smarr, B. L., Qawasmeh, T., Kriegsfeld, L. J., Barcelona, J., Hijazi, K. E., & Thomason, M. E. (2021). Maternal stress during pregnancy alters fetal cortico-cerebellar connectivity in utero and increases child sleep problems after birth. *Scientific Reports, 11*(1). https://doi.org/10.1038/s41598-021-81681-y

Van der Graaff, J., Carlo, G., Crocetti, E., Koot, H. M., & Branje, S. (2018). Prosocial behavior in adolescence: Gender differences in development and links with empathy. *Journal of Youth and Adolescence, 47*(5), 1086–1099. https://doi.org/10.1007/s10964-017-0786-1

van der Ploeg, R., Steglich, C., & Veenstra, R. (2020). The way bullying works: How new ties facilitate the mutual reinforcement of status and bullying in elementary schools. *Social Networks, 60*, 71–82. https://doi.org/10.1016/j.socnet.2018.12.006

van der Schuur, W. A., Baumgartner, S. E., Sumter, S. R., & Valkenburg, P. M. (2015). The consequences of media multitasking for youth: A review. *Computers in Human Behavior, 53*, 204–215. https://doi.org/10.1016/j.chb.2015.06.035

van der Schuur, W. A., Baumgartner, S. E., Sumter, S. R., & Valkenburg, P. M. (2020). Exploring the long-term relationship between academic-media multitasking and adolescents' academic achievement. *New Media & Society, 22*, 140–158. https://doi.org/10.1177/1461444819861956

van der Stel, M., & Veenman, M. V. J. (2013). Metacognitive skills and intellectual ability of young adolescents: A longitudinal study from a developmental perspective. *European Journal of Psychology of Education, 29*(1), 117–137. https://doi.org/10.1007/s10212-013-0190-5

van der Wilt, F., van der Veen, C., van Kruistum, C., & van Oers, B. (2019). Why do children become rejected by their peers? A review of studies into the relationship between oral communicative competence and sociometric status in childhood. *Educational Psychology Review, 31*(3), 699–724. https://doi.org/10.1007/s10648-019-09479-z

Van de Vondervoort, J. W., & Hamlin, J. K. (2016). Evidence for intuitive morality: Preverbal infants make sociomoral evaluations. *Child Development Perspectives, 10*(3), 143–148. https://doi.org/10.1111/cdep.12175

van Dijk, A., Poorthuis, A. M. G., & Malti, T. (2017). Psychological processes in young bullies versus bully-victims. *Aggressive Behavior, 43*(5), 430–439. https://doi.org/10.1002/ab.21701

Van Dijk, M. P. A., Branje, S., Keijsers, L., Hawk, S. T., Hale, W. W., & Meeus, W. H. J. (2014). Self-concept clarity across adolescence: Longitudinal associations with open communication with parents and internalizing symptoms. *Journal of Youth and Adolescence, 43*(11), 1861–1876. https://doi.org/10.1007/s10964-013-0055-x

van Dijk, R., van der Valk, I. E., Buist, K. L., Branje, S., & Deković, M. (2022). Longitudinal associations between sibling relationship quality and child adjustment after divorce. *Journal of Marriage and Family, 84*(2), 393–414. https://doi.org/10.1111/jomf.12808

van Dijken, M. W., Stams, G. J. J. M., & de Winter, M. (2016). Can community-based interventions prevent child maltreatment? *Children and Youth Services Review, 61*, 149–158. https://doi.org/10.1016/j.childyouth.2015.12.007

van Dommelen, P., Koledova, E., & Wit, J. M. (2018). Effect of adherence to growth hormone treatment on 0–2 year catch-up growth in children with growth hormone deficiency. *PLoS ONE, 13*(10), e0206009. https://doi.org/10.1371/journal.pone.0206009

van Duijvenvoorde, A. C. K., Peters, S., Braams, B. R., & Crone, E. A. (2016). What motivates adolescents? Neural responses to rewards and their influence on adolescents' risk taking, learning, and cognitive control. *Neuroscience & Biobehavioral Reviews, 70*, 135–147. https://doi.org/10.1016/j.neubiorev.2016.06.037

van Duijvenvoorde, A. C. K., van Hoorn, J., & Blankenstein, N. E. (2022). Risks and rewards in adolescent decision-making. *Current Opinion in Psychology, 48*, 101457. https://doi.org/10.1016/j.copsyc.2022.101457

van Eeden, A. E., van Hoeken, D., & Hoek, H. W. (2021). Incidence, prevalence and mortality of anorexia nervosa and bulimia nervosa. *Current Opinion in Psychiatry, 34*(6), 515–524. https://doi.org/10.1097/yco.0000000000000739

Van Eldik, W. M., de Haan, A. D., Parry, L. Q., Davies, P. T., Luijk, M. P. C. M., Arends, L. R., & Prinzie, P. (2020). The interparental relationship: Meta-analytic associations with children's maladjustment and responses to interparental conflict. *Psychological Bulletin, 146*(7), 553–594. https://doi.org/10.1037/bul0000233

van Hell, J. G.. (2022). Code-switching. In A. Godfroid & H. Hopp (Eds.), *The Routledge handbook of second language acquisition and psycholinguistics*. Routledge.

van Heteren, C. F., Boekkooi, P. F., Jongsma, H. W., & Nijhuis, J. G. (2000). Fetal learning and memory. *Lancet, 356*, 1169–1170.

van Hoogdalem, A.-G., Singer, E., Eek, A., & Heesbeen, D. (2013). Friendship in young children: Construction of a behavioural sociometric method. *Journal of Early Childhood Research, 11*(3), 236–247. https://doi.org/10.1177/1476718X13488337

Van Hoorn, J., Crone, E. A., & Van Leijenhorst, L. (2017). Hanging out with the right crowd: Peer influence on risk-taking behavior in adolescence. *Journal of Research on Adolescence, 27*(1), 189–200. https://doi.org/10.1111/jora.12265

van Hoorn, J., van Dijk, E., Meuwese, R., Rieffe, C., & Crone, E. A. (2016). Peer influence on prosocial behavior in adolescence. *Journal of Research on Adolescence, 26*(1), 90–100. https://doi.org/10.1111/jora.12173

Van Ijzendoorn, M. H., & Kroonenberg, P. M. (1988). Cross-cultural patterns of attachment: A meta-analysis of the strange situation. *Child Development, 59*(1), 147–156. https://doi.org/10.2307/1130396

van Lieshout, R. J., McGowan, P. O., de Vega, W. C., Savoy, C. D., Morrison, K. M., Saigal, S., Mathewson, K. J., & Schmidt, L. A. (2021). Extremely low birth weight and accelerated biological aging. *Pediatrics, 147*(6). https://doi.org/10.1542/peds.2020-001230

Van Ryzin, M. J., Carlson, E. A., & Sroufe, L. A. (2011). Attachment discontinuity in a high-risk sample. *Attachment & Human Development, 13*(4), 381–401. https://doi.org/10.1080/14616734.2011.584403

van Scheppingen, M. A., Denissen, J. J. A., & Bleidorn, W. (2018). Stability and change in self-control during the transition to parenthood. *European Journal of Personality, 32*(6), 690–704. https://doi.org/10.1002/per.2172

van Sluijs, E. M. F., Ekelund, U., Crochemore-Silva, I., Guthold, R., Ha, A., Lubans, D., Oyeyemi, A. L., Ding, D., & Katzmarzyk, P. T. (2021). Physical activity behaviours in adolescence: Current evidence and opportunities for intervention. *Lancet, 398*(10298), 429–442. https://doi.org/10.1016/S0140-6736(21)01259-9

van Spronsen, F. J., Blau, N., Harding, C., Burlina, A., Longo, N., & Bosch, A. M. (2021). Phenylketonuria. *Nature Reviews Disease Primers, 7*(36). https://doi.org/10.1038/s41572-021-00267-0

van 't Hof., M, Tisseur., Berckelear-Onnes, C., van., I., van Nieuwenhuyzen, A, Daniels, A. M., Deen, M., Hoek, H. W., & Ester, W. A. (2021). Age at autism spectrum disorder diagnosis: A systematic review and meta-analysis from 2012 to 2019. *Autism: The International Journal of Research and Practice, 25*(4), 862–873. https://doi.org/10.1177/1362361320971107

van Tetering, M., van der Donk, M., de Groot, R. H. M., & Jolles, J. (2019). Sex differences in the performance of 7–12 year olds on a mental rotation task and the relation with arithmetic performance. *Frontiers in Psychology, 10*, 107. https://doi.org/10.3389/fpsyg.2019.00107

Van Winkle, Z., & Leopold, T. (2021). Family size and economic wellbeing following divorce: The United States in comparative perspective. *Social Science Research, 96*, 102541. https://doi.org/10.1016/j.ssresearch.2021.102541

Vance, S. R., Jr Boyer., B, C., Glidden, D. V., & Sevelius, J. (2021). Mental health and psychosocial risk and protective factors among Black and Latinx transgender youth compared with peers. *JAMA Network Open, 4*(3), e213256. https://doi.org/10.1001/jamanetworkopen.2021.3256

Vandenbroucke, A. R. E., Sligte, I. G., Barrett, A. B., Seth, A. K., Fahrenfort, J. J., & Lamme, V. A. F. (2014). Accurate metacognition for visual sensory memory representations. *Psychological Science, 25*(4), 861–873. https://doi.org/10.1177/0956797613516146

Vandermaas-Peeler, M., Massey, K., & Kendall, A. (2016). Parent guidance of young children's scientific and mathematical reasoning in a science museum. *Early Childhood Education Journal, 44*(3), 217–224. https://doi.org/10.1007/s10643-015-0714-5

Vandierendonck, A. (2016). A working memory system with distributed executive control. *Perspectives on Psychological Science, 11*(1), 74–100. https://doi.org/10.1177/1745691615596790

Vanhalst, J., Luyckx, K., Scholte, R. H. J., Engels, R. C. M. E., & Goossens, L. (2013). Low self-esteem as a risk factor for loneliness in adolescence: Perceived—but not actual—social acceptance as an underlying mechanism. *Journal of Abnormal Child Psychology, 41*(7), 1067–1081. https://doi.org/10.1007/s10802-013-9751-y

Vannasing, P., Florea, O., González-Frankenberger, B., Tremblay, J., Paquette, N., Safi, D., Wallois, F., Lepore, F., Béland, R., Lassonde, M., & Gallagher, A. (2016). Distinct hemispheric specializations for native and non-native languages in one-day-old newborns identified by fNIRS. *Neuropsychologia, 84*, 63–69. https://doi.org/10.1016/j.neuropsychologia.2016.01.038

Vannucci, A., & McCauley Ohannessian, C. (2019). Social media use subgroups differentially predict psychosocial well-being during early adolescence. *Journal of Youth and Adolescence, 48*(8), 1469–1493. https://doi.org/10.1007/s10964-019-01060-9

Vargesson, N. (2022). Chapter 22—Thalidomide. In R. C. Gupta (Ed.), *Reproductive and developmental toxicology* (3rd ed., pp. 423–437). Academic Press. https://doi.org/10.1016/B978-0-323-89773-0.00022-9

Vargesson, N., & Stephens, T. (2021). Thalidomide: History, withdrawal, renaissance, and safety concerns. *Expert Opinion on Drug Safety, 20*(12), 1455–1457. https://doi.org/10.1080/14740338.2021.1991307

Varnum, M. E. W., & Grossmann, I. (2017). Cultural change: The how and the why. *Perspectives on Psychological Science, 12*(6), 956–972. https://doi.org/10.1177/1745691617699971

Vasc, D., & Lillard, A. (2020). Pretend and sociodramatic play. In S. Hupp & J. D. Jewell (Eds.), *The encyclopedia of child and adolescent development* (pp. 1–9). Wiley. https://doi.org/10.1002/9781119171492.wecad274

Vasilenko, S. A. (2022). Sexual behavior and health from adolescence to adulthood: Illustrative examples of 25 years of research from add health. *Journal of Adolescent Health, 71*(6S), S24–S31. https://doi.org/10.1016/j.jadohealth.2022.08.014

Vasileva, M., Schilpzand, E. J., Mangelsdorf, S. N., Conroy, R., Barrett, A., Jowett, H., Bressan, S., Babl, F. E., Anderson, V., Mehl, M. R., & Alisic, E. (2022). Children's daily life after potentially traumatic injury: A naturalistic observation study. *Traumatology, 28*(1), 129–137. https://doi.org/10.1037/trm0000301

Vasileva, O., & Balyasnikova, N. (2019). (Re)Introducing Vygotsky's thought: From historical overview to contemporary psychology. *Frontiers in Psychology, 10*, 1515. https://www.frontiersin.org/articles/10.3389/fpsyg.2019.01515

Vasilopoulos, F., Jeffrey, H., Wu, Y., & Dumontheil, I. (2023). Multi-level meta-analysis of physical activity interventions during childhood: Effects of physical activity on cognition and academic achievement. *Educational Psychology Review, 35*(2), 59. https://doi.org/10.1007/s10648-023-09760-2

Vaughan, E. P., Speck, J. S., Frick, P. J., Robertson, E. L., Ray, J. V., Thornton, L. C., Wall Myers, T. D., Steinberg, L., & Cauffman, E. (2022). Longitudinal associations of parental monitoring and delinquent peer affiliation: The potential influence of parental solicitation and monitoring rules. *Journal of Adolescence, 94*(4), 656–666. https://doi.org/10.1002/jad.12054

Vazquez, C. E., & Cubbin, C. (2020). Socioeconomic status and childhood obesity: A review of literature from the past decade to inform intervention research. *Current Obesity Reports, 9*(4), 562–570. https://doi.org/10.1007/s13679-020-00400-2

Veer, I. M., Luyten, H., Mulder, H., van Tuijl, C., & Sleegers, P. J. C. (2017). Selective attention relates to the development of executive functions in 2.5- to 3-year-olds: A longitudinal study. *Early Childhood Research Quarterly, 41*, 84–94. https://doi.org/10.1016/j.ecresq.2017.06.005

Veiga, G., O'Connor, R., Neto, C., & Rieffe, C. (2022). Rough-and-tumble play and the regulation of aggression in preschoolers. *Early Child Development and Care, 192*(6), 980–992. https://doi.org/10.1080/03004430.2020.1828396

Veiga, R. V., Schuler-Faccini, L., França, G. V. A., Andrade, R. F. S., Teixeira, M. G., Costa, L. C., Paixão, E. S., Costa, M. da C. N., Barreto, M. L., Oliveira, J. F., Oliveira, W. K., Cardim, L. L., & Rodrigues, M. S. (2021). Classification algorithm for congenital Zika syndrome: Characterizations, diagnosis and validation. *Scientific Reports, 11*(1), 1–7. https://doi.org/10.1038/s41598-021-86361-5

Veldman, S. L. C., Jones, R. A., Chandler, P., Robinson, L. E., & Okely, A. D. (2020). Prevalence and risk factors of gross motor delay in pre-schoolers. *Journal of Paediatrics and Child Health*, 56(4), 571–576. https://doi.org/10.1111/JPC.14684

Veldman, S. L. C., Santos, R., Jones, R. A., Sousa-Sá, E., & Okely, A. D. (2019). Associations between gross motor skills and cognitive development in toddlers. *Early Human Development*, 132, 39–44. https://doi.org/10.1016/j.earlhumdev.2019.04.005

Vélez-Agosto, N. M., Soto-Crespo, J. G., Vizcarrondo-Oppenheimer, M., Vega-Molina, S., & García Coll, C. (2017). Bronfenbrenner's bioecological theory revision: Moving culture from the macro into the micro. *Perspectives on Psychological Science*, 12(5), 900–910. https://doi.org/10.1177/1745691617704397

Venta, A., & Abate, A. (2021). Insecure attachment and related difficulties. In P. Fonagy, C. Sharp, J. M. Fletcher, & A. Venta (Eds.), *Developmental psychopathology*. Wiley. https://doi.org/10.1002/9781118686089.ch4

Ventura, A. K., & Worobey, J. (2013). Early influences on the development of food preferences. *Current Biology*, 23(9), R401–R408. https://doi.org/10.1016/J.CUB.2013.02.037

Verbeek, M., van de Bongardt, D., Reitz, E., & Deković, M. (2020). A warm nest or 'the talk'? Exploring and explaining relations between general and sexuality-specific parenting and adolescent sexual emotions. *Journal of Adolescent Health*, 66(2), 210–216. https://doi.org/10.1016/j.jadohealth.2019.08.015

Vereijken, B., & Thelen, E. (1997). Training infant treadmill stepping: The role of individual pattern stability. *Developmental Psychobiology*, 30, 89–102.

Vergauwe, E., Besch, V., Latrèche, C., & Langerock, N. (2021). The use of attention to maintain information in working memory: A developmental investigation of spontaneous refreshing in school-aged children. *Developmental Science*, 24(5), e13104. https://doi.org/10.1111/desc.13104

Verhage, M. L., Oosterman, M., & Schuengel, C. (2013). Parenting self-efficacy predicts perceptions of infant negative temperament characteristics, not vice versa. *Journal of Family Psychology*, 27(5), 844–849. https://doi.org/10.1037/a0034263

Verhoef, E., Shapland, C. Y., Fisher, S. E., Dale, P. S., & St Pourcain, B. (2021). The developmental origins of genetic factors influencing language and literacy: Associations with early-childhood vocabulary. *Journal of Child Psychology and Psychiatry*, 62(6), 728–738. https://doi.org/10.1111/jcpp.13327

Veríssimo, M., Santos, J., J, A., Fernandes, C., Shin, N., & Vaughn, B. E. (2014). Associations between attachment security and social competence in preschool children. *Merrill-Palmer Quarterly*, 60(1), 80–99. https://doi.org/10.13110/merrpalmquar1982.60.1.0080

Verkooijen, K. T., de Vries, N. K., & Nielsen, G. A. (2007). Youth crowds and substance use: The impact of perceived group norm and multiple group identification. *Psychology of Addictive Behaviors*, 21(1), 55–61. https://doi.org/10.1037/0893-164x.21.1.55

Vermeulen, M. C. M., Heijden, K. B., Kocevska, D., Treur, J. L., Huppertz, C., Beijsterveldt, C. E. M., Boomsma, D. I., Swaab, H., Someren, E. J. W., & Bartels, M. (2021). Associations of sleep with psychological problems and well-being in adolescence: Causality or common genetic predispositions? *Journal of Child Psychology and Psychiatry*, 62(1), 28–39. https://doi.org/10.1111/jcpp.13238

Vernon-Feagans, L., Bratsch-Hines, M., Reynolds, E., & Willoughby, M. (2020). How early maternal language input varies by race and education and predicts later child language. *Child Development*, 91(4), 1098–1115. https://doi.org/10.1111/cdev.13281

Véronneau, M. H., Vitaro, F., Brendgen, M., Dishion, T. J., & Tremblay, R. E. (2010). Transactional analysis of the reciprocal links between peer experiences and academic achievement from middle childhood to early adolescence. *Developmental Psychology*, 46(4), 773–790. https://doi.org/10.1037/a0019816

Verschueren, K. (2020). Attachment, self-esteem, and socio-emotional adjustment: There is more than just the mother. *Attachment and Human Development*, 22(1), 105–109. https://doi.org/10.1080/14616734.2019.1589066

Vial, A., van der Put, C., Stams, G. J. J. M., Kossakowski, J., & Assink, M. (2020). Exploring the interrelatedness of risk factors for child maltreatment: A network approach. *Child Abuse and Neglect*, 107, 104622. https://doi.org/10.1016/j.chiabu.2020.104622

Victora, C. G., Bahl, R., Barros, A. J. D., França, G. V. A., Horton, S., Krasevec, J., Murch, S., Sankar, M. J., Walker, N., & Rollins, N. C. (2016). Breastfeeding in the 21st century: Epidemiology, mechanisms, and lifelong effect. *Lancet*, 387(10017), 475–490. https://doi.org/10.1016/S0140-6736(15)01024-7

Victora, M. D., Victora, C. G., & Barros, F. C. (1990). Cross-cultural differences in developmental rates: A comparison between British and Brazilian children. *Child: Care, Health and Development*, 16(3), 151–164. https://doi.org/10.1111/j.1365-2214.1990.tb00647.x

Vijayakumar, N., Youssef, G., Allen, N. B., Anderson, V., Efron, D., Mundy, L., Patton, G., Simmons, J. G., Silk, T., & Whittle, S. (2021). The effects of puberty and its hormones on subcortical brain development. *Comprehensive Psychoneuroendocrinology*, 7, 100074. https://doi.org/10.1016/j.cpnec.2021.100074

Vijayakumar, N., Youssef, G. J., Allen, N. B., Anderson, V., Efron, D., Hazell, P., Mundy, L., Nicholson, J. M., Patton, G., Seal, M. L., Simmons, J. G., Whittle, S., & Silk, T. (2021). A longitudinal analysis of puberty-related cortical development. *NeuroImage*, 228, 117684. https://doi.org/10.1016/j.neuroimage.2020.117684

Villanueva, L., Prado-Gascó, V., & Montoya-Castilla, I. (2022). Longitudinal analysis of subjective well-being in preadolescents: The role of emotional intelligence, self-esteem and perceived stress. *Journal of Health Psychology*, 27(2), 278–291. https://doi.org/10.1177/1359105320951605

Villar, J., Ariff, S., Gunier, R. B., Thiruvengadam, R., Rauch, S., Kholin, A., Roggero, P., Prefumo, F., do Vale, M. S., Cardona-Perez, J. A., Maiz, N., Cetin, I., Savasi, V., Deruelle, P., Easter, S. R., Sichitiu, J., Soto Conti, C. P., Ernawati, E., Mhatre, M., & &#hillip1; Papageorghiou, A. T. (2021). Maternal and neonatal morbidity and mortality among pregnant women with and without COVID-19 infection: The INTERCOVID Multinational Cohort Study. *JAMA Pediatrics*, 175(8), 817–826. https://doi.org/10.1001/jamapediatrics.2021.1050

Villela, D., Che, H., Van Ghelue, M., Dehaspe, L., Brison, N., Van Den Bogaert, K., Devriendt, K., Lewi, L., Bayindir, B., & Vermeesch, J. R. (2019). Fetal sex determination in twin pregnancies using non-invasive prenatal testing. *Npj Genomic Medicine*, 4(1), 1–6. https://doi.org/10.1038/s41525-019-0089-4

Vinden, P. (1996). Junín Quechua children's understanding of mind. *Child Development*, 67(4), 1707–1716. https://doi.org/10.1111/j.1467-8624.1996.tb01822.x

Vink, J., & Quinn, M. (2018a). Amniocentesis. In Joshua. Copel, M. E. D'Alton, H. Feltovich, E. Gratacos, A. O. Odibo, L. Platt, & B. Tutschek (Eds.), *Obstetric imaging: Fetal diagnosis and care* (pp. 473–475.e1). Elsevier. https://doi.org/10.1016/B978-0-323-44548-1.00111-X

Vink, J., & Quinn, M. (2018b). Chorionic Villus Sampling. In J. Copel, M. E. D'Alton, H. Feltovich, E. Gratacos, A. O. Odibo, L. Platt, & B. Tutschek (Eds.), *Obstetric imaging: Fetal diagnosis and care* (pp. 479–481.e1). Elsevier. https://doi.org/10.1016/B978-0-323-44548-1.00113-3

Vishkin, A., Bigman, Y., & Tamir, M. (2014). Religion, emotion regulation, and well-being. In C. Kim-Prieto (Ed.), *Religion and spirituality across cultures* (pp. 247–269). Springer. https://doi.org/10.1007/978-94-017-8950-9_13

Vision and Eye Health Surveillance System study group. Flaxman, A. D., Wittenborn, J. S., Robalik, T., Gulia, R., Gerzoff, R. B., Lundeen, E. A., Saaddine, J., & Rein, D. B. (2021). Prevalence of visual acuity loss or blindness in the US: A Bayesian meta-analysis. *JAMA Ophthalmology*, 139(7), 717–723. https://doi.org/10.1001/jamaophthalmol.2021.0527

Vismara, L., Sechi, C., Neri, M., Paoletti, A., & Lucarelli, L. (2021). Maternal perinatal depression, anxiety, fear of birth, and perception of infants' negative affectivity at three months. *Journal of Reproductive and Infant Psychology*, 39(5), 532–543. https://doi.org/10.1080/02646838.2020.1843612

Visscher, M., & Narendran, V. (2014). Vernix caseosa: Formation and functions. *Newborn and Infant Nursing Reviews*, 14(4), 142–146. https://doi.org/10.1053/j.nainr.2014.10.005

Vissers, C. Th. W. M., Tomas, E., & Law, J. (2020). The emergence of inner speech and its measurement in atypically developing children. *Frontiers in Psychology*, 11, 279. https://doi.org/10.3389/fpsyg.2020.00279

Vissers, L. E. L. M., Gilissen, C., & Veltman, J. A. (2016). Genetic studies in intellectual disability and related disorders. *Nature Reviews Genetics*, 17(1), 9–18. https://doi.org/10.1038/nrg3999

Viteri, O., Soto, E., Bahado-Singh, R., Christensen, C., Chauhan, S., & Sibai, B. (2015). Fetal anomalies and long-term effects associated with substance abuse in pregnancy: A literature review. *American Journal of Perinatology*, 32(05), 405–416. https://doi.org/10.1055/s-0034-1393932

Vo-Jutabha, E. D., Dinh, K. T., McHale, J. P., & Valsiner, J. (2009). A qualitative analysis of Vietnamese adolescent identity exploration within and outside an ethnic enclave. *Journal of Youth and Adolescence*, 38(5), 672–690. https://doi.org/10.1007/s10964-008-9365-9

Volkmar, F. R (Ed.). (2021). Angelman/Prader-Willi locus. In *Encyclopedia of Autism Spectrum Disorders* (pp. 202–202). Springer International. https://doi.org/10.1007/978-3-319-91280-6_300107

Vollmer, B., & Edmonds, C. J. (2019). School age neurological and cognitive outcomes of fetal growth retardation or small for gestational age birth weight. *Frontiers in Endocrinology*, 10(MAR), 186. https://doi.org/10.3389/FENDO.2019.00186/BIBTEX

von Bartheld, C. S., Bahney, J., & Herculano-Houzel, S. (2016). The search for true numbers of neurons and glial cells in the human brain: A review of 150 years of cell counting. *Journal of Comparative Neurology*, 524(18), 3865–3895. https://doi.org/10.1002/cne.24040

von Hofsten, C., Kochukhova, O., & Rosander, K. (2007). Predictive tracking over occlusions by 4-month-old infants. *Developmental Science*, 10(5), 625–640. https://doi.org/10.1111/j.1467-7687.2006.00604.x

von Hofsten, C., & Rönnqvist, L. (1993). The structuring of neonatal arm movements. *Child Development*, 64(4), 1046–1057.

Von Holle, A., North, K. E., Gahagan, S., Burrows, R. A., Blanco, E., Lozoff, B., Howard, A. G., Justice, A., Graff, M., & Voruganti, V. S. (2020). Sociodemographic predictors of early postnatal growth: Evidence from a Chilean infancy cohort. *BMJ Open*, 10(6), 33695. https://doi.org/10.1136/bmjopen-2019-033695

von Lüpke, H. (2021). Epigenetics. In K. Evertz, L. Janus, & R. Linder (Eds.), *Handbook of prenatal and perinatal psychology: Integrating research and practice* (pp. 149–154). Springer International. https://doi.org/10.1007/978-3-030-41716-1_9

von Soest, T., Wichstrøm, L., & Kvalem, I. L. (2016). The development of global and domain-specific self-esteem from age 13 to 31. *Journal of Personality and Social Psychology*, 110(4), 592–608. https://doi.org/10.1037/pspp0000060

von Stumm, S. (2017). Socioeconomic status amplifies the achievement gap throughout compulsory education independent of intelligence. *Intelligence*, 60, 57–62. https://doi.org/10.1016/j.intell.2016.11.006

von Stumm, S., & Plomin, R. (2021). Using DNA to predict intelligence. *Intelligence*, 86, 101530. https://doi.org/10.1016/j.intell.2021.101530

Vonk, J., Jett, S. E., Tomeny, T. S., Mercer, S. H., & Cwikla, J. (2020). Young children's theory of mind predicts more sharing with friends over time. *Child Development*, 91(1), 63–77. https://doi.org/10.1111/cdev.13112

Voorhies, W., Dajani, D. R., Vij, S. G., Shankar, S., Turan, T. O., & Uddin, L. Q. (2018). Aberrant functional connectivity of inhibitory control networks in children with autism spectrum disorder. *Autism Research*, 11(11), 1468–1478. https://doi.org/10.1002/aur.2014

Vorgias, D., & Bernstein, B. (2022). *Fetal alcohol syndrome*. StatPearls. https://www.ncbi.nlm.nih.gov/books/NBK448178/

Vosylis, R., Erentaitė, R., & Crocetti, E. (2018). Global versus domain-specific identity processes. *Emerging Adulthood*, 6(1), 32–41. https://doi.org/10.1177/2167696817694698

Vosylis, R., Erentaitė, R., & Klimstra, T. (2021). The material context of adolescent identity formation: A family economic stress approach. *Identity*, 21, 200–218. https://doi.org/10.1080/15283488.2020.1836491

Vouloumanos, A., Hauser, M. D., Werker, J. F., & Martin, A. (2010). The tuning of human neonates' preference for speech. *Child Development*, 81(2), 517–527. https://doi.org/10.1111/j.1467-8624.2009.01412.x

Vozzola, E. C., & Senland, A. K. (2022). *Moral development: Theory and applications*. Routledge.

Vrabič, N., Juroš, B., & Tekavčič Pompe, M. (2021). Automated visual acuity evaluation based on preferential looking technique and controlled with remote eye tracking. *Ophthalmic Research*, 64(3). https://doi.org/10.1159/000512395

Vuoksimaa, E., Rose, R. J., Pulkkinen, L., Palviainen, T., Rimfeld, K., Lundström, S., Bartels, M., van Beijsterveldt, C., Hendriks, A., de Zeeuw, E. L., Plomin, R., Lichtenstein, P., Boomsma, D. I., & Kaprio, J. (2021). Higher aggression is related to poorer academic performance in compulsory education. *Journal of Child Psychology and Psychiatry*, 62(3), 327–338. https://doi.org/10.1111/jcpp.13273

Vuong, Q. C., & Geangu, E. (2023). The development of emotion processing of body expressions from infancy to early childhood: A meta-analysis. *Frontiers in Cognition*, 2, 1155031. https://www.frontiersin.org/articles/10.3389/fcogn.2023.1155031

Vygotsky, L. S. (1962). *Thought and language*. MIT Press.

Vygotsky, L. S. (1978). *Mind in society: The development of higher psychological processes*. Harvard University Press.

Vygotsky, L. S. (1978). M. Cole, V. Jolm-Steiner, S. Scribner, & E. Souberman (Eds.), *Mind in society: The development of higher psychological processes*. Harvard University Press.

Vygotsky, L. S. (1978). *Mind in society: The development of higher psychological processes.* Harvard University Press.

Vygotsky, L. S., & Minick, N. (1987). T. N. Minick (Ed.), *Thinking and speech.* Plenum Press.

Waasdorp, T. E., & Bradshaw, C. P. (2011). Examining student responses to frequent bullying: A latent class approach. *Journal of Educational Psychology, 103*(2), 336–352. https://doi.org/10.1037/a0022747

Wagner, M. F., Milner, J. S., McCarthy, R. J., Crouch, J. L., McCanne, T. R., & Skowronski, J. J. (2015). Facial emotion recognition accuracy and child physical abuse: An experiment and a meta-analysis. *Psychology of Violence, 5*(2), 154–162. https://doi.org/10.1037/a0036014

Wagner, R. S. (2022). Recognizing sleep disorders in visually impaired children. *Journal of Pediatric Ophthalmology & Strabismus, 59*(2), 72–72. https://doi.org/10.3928/01913913-20220202-01

Wagnsson, S., Lindwall, M., & Gustafsson, H. (2014). Participation in organized sport and self-esteem across adolescence: The mediating role of perceived sport competence. *Journal of Sport & Exercise Psychology, 36*(6), 584–594. https://doi.org/10.1123/jsep.2013-0137

Waid, J. D., Tanana, M. J., Vanderloo, M. J., Voit, R., & Kothari, B. H. (2020). The role of siblings in the development of externalizing behaviors during childhood and adolescence: A scoping review. *Journal of Family Social Work, 23*(4), 318–337. https://doi.org/10.1080/10522158.2020.1799893

Waldfogel, J., Craigie, T.-A., & Brooks-Gunn, J. (2010). Fragile families and child wellbeing. *Future of Children, 20*(2), 87–112. https://doi.org/10.1353/foc.2010.0002

Waldman, I. D., Tackett, J. L., Van Hulle, C. A., Applegate, B., Pardini, D., Frick, P. J., & Lahey, B. B. (2011). Child and adolescent conduct disorder substantially shares genetic influences with three socioemotional dispositions. *Journal of Abnormal Psychology, 120*(1), 57–70. https://doi.org/10.1037/a0021351

Walk, R. D. (1968). Monocular compared to binocular depth perception in human infants. *Science, 162,* 473–475.

Walle, E. A., Reschke, P. J., & Knothe, J. M. (2017). Social referencing: Defining and delineating a basic process of emotion. *Emotion Review, 9*(3), 245–252. https://doi.org/10.1177/1754073916669594

Wallentin, M. (2020). Chapter 6—Gender differences in language are small but matter for disorders. In R. Lanzenberger, G. S. Kranz, & I. Savic (Eds.), *Handbook of clinical neurology* (Vol. 175, pp. 81–102). Elsevier. https://doi.org/10.1016/B978-0-444-64123-6.00007-2

Walsh, A., & Leaper, C. (2019). A content analysis of gender representations in preschool children's television. *Mass Communication and Society, 23*(3), 331–355. https://doi.org/10.1080/15205436.2019.1664593

Walsh, J. J., Christoffel, D. J., & Malenka, R. C. (2023). Neural circuits regulating prosocial behaviors. *Neuropsychopharmacology, 48*(1), 79–89. https://doi.org/10.1038/s41386-022-01348-8

Walters, G. D. (2021). School-age bullying victimization and perpetration: A meta-analysis of prospective studies and research. *Trauma, Violence, & Abuse, 22*(5), 1129–1139. https://doi.org/10.1177/1524838020906513

Walters, G. D., & Espelage, D. L. (2022). Mediating the pathway from bullying victimization to bullying perpetration with hostility, peer delinquency, and pro-bullying attitudes: Transforming victims into aggressors. *Psychology of Violence, 13*(3), 194–204. https://doi.org/10.1037/vio0000435

Walton, M., Dewey, D., & Lebel, C. (2018). Brain white matter structure and language ability in preschool-aged children. *Brain and Language, 176,* 19–25. https://doi.org/10.1016/j.bandl.2017.10.008

Wamakima, B. W., McKinney, S., Bookman, L., Gompers, A., Hacker, M. R., & Farid, H. (2023). Postmenopausal vaginal and cervical cancer risk related to in utero diethylstilbestrol exposure. *Journal of Lower Genital Tract Disease, 27*(1), 35. https://doi.org/10.1097/LGT.0000000000000713

Wang, D., Kato, N., Inaba, Y., Tango, T., Yoshida, Y., Kusaka, Y., Deguchi, Y., Tomita, F., & Zhang, Q. (2000). Physical and personality traits of preschool children in Fuzhou, China: Only child vs sibling. *Child: Care, Health & Development, 26*(1), 49–60.

Wang, F., Christ, S. L., Mills-Koonce, W. R., Garrett-Peters, P., & Cox, M. J. (2013). Association between maternal sensitivity and externalizing behavior from preschool to preadolescence. *Journal of Applied Developmental Psychology, 34*(2), 89–100. https://doi.org/10.1016/j.appdev.2012.11.003

Wang, M. T., Henry, D. A., Smith, L. V., Huguley, J. P., & Guo, J. (2020). Parental ethnic-racial socialization practices and children of color's psychosocial and behavioral adjustment: A systematic review and meta-analysis. *American Psychologist, 75*(1), 1–22. https://doi.org/10.1037/AMP0000464

Wang, M., Wang, J., Deng, X., & Chen, W. (2019). Why are empathic children more liked by peers? The mediating roles of prosocial and aggressive behaviors. *Personality and Individual Differences, 144,* 19–23. https://doi.org/10.1016/j.paid.2019.02.029

Wang, M.-T., Degol, J. L., & Amemiya, J. L. (2019). Older siblings as academic socialization agents for younger siblings: Developmental pathways across adolescence. *Journal of Youth and Adolescence, 48,* 1218–1233. https://doi.org/10.1007/s10964-019-01005-2

Wang, M.-T., Dishion, T. J., Stormshak, E. A., & Willett, J. B. (2011). Trajectories of family management practices and early adolescent behavioral outcomes. *Developmental Psychology, 47*(5), 1324–1341. https://doi.org/10.1037/a0024026

Wang, M.-T., Henry, D. A., Del Toro, J., Scanlon, C. L., & Schall, J. D. (2021). COVID-19 employment status, dyadic family relationships, and child psychological well-being. *Journal of Adolescent Health, 69*(5), 705–712. https://doi.org/10.1016/j.jadohealth.2021.07.016

Wang, M.-T., & Hofkens, T. L. (2020). Beyond classroom academics: A school-wide and multi-contextual perspective on student engagement in school. *Adolescent Research Review, 5,* 419–433. https://doi.org/10.1007/s40894-019-00115-z

Wang, Q. (2004). The emergence of cultural self-constructs: Autobiographical memory and self-description in European American and Chinese children. *Developmental Psychology, 40*(1), 3–15. https://psycnet.apa.org/doi/10.1037/0012-1649.40.1.3

Wang, Q. (2021). Cultural pathways and outcomes of autobiographical memory development. *Child Development Perspectives, 15*(3), 196–202. https://doi.org/10.1111/cdep.12423

Wang, Q., Zheng, S.-X., Ni, Y.-F., Lu, Y.-Y., Zhang, B., Lian, Q.-Q., & Hu, M.-P. (2018). The effect of labor epidural analgesia on maternal–fetal outcomes: A retrospective cohort study. *Archives of Gynecology and Obstetrics, 298*(1), 89–96. https://doi.org/10.1007/s00404-018-4777-6

Wang, W., Spinrad, T. L., & Eisenberg, N. (2023). The development and prediction of young children's behavioral mastery motivation. *Early Childhood Research Quarterly, 62,* 239–250. https://doi.org/10.1016/j.ecresq.2022.09.001

Wang, X., Bernas, R., & Eberhard, Philippe. (2008). Responding to children's everyday transgressions in Chinese working-class families. *Journal of Moral Education, 37*(1),

55–79. https://doi.org/10.1080/03057240701803684

Wang, X., Huebner, E. S., & Tian, L. (2023). Longitudinal relations among perceived parental warmth, self-esteem and social behaviours from middle childhood to early adolescence in China: Disentangling between- and within-person associations. *British Journal of Psychology*, 114(4), 969–990. https://doi.org/10.1111/bjop.12672

Wang, Y. (2021). Daily ethnic/racial context in peer groups: Frequency, structure, and implications for adolescent outcomes. *Child Development*, 92(2), 650–661. https://doi.org/10.1111/cdev.13509

Wang, Y., Chen, X., Wang, A., Jordan, L. P., & Lu, S. (2024). Research review: Grandparental care and child mental health – a systematic review and meta-analysis. *Journal of Child Psychology and Psychiatry*, 65(4), 568–586. https://doi.org/10.1111/jcpp.13943

Wang, Y., Huebner, E. S., & Tian, L. (2021). Parent-child cohesion, self-esteem, and academic achievement: The longitudinal relations among elementary school students. *Learning and Instruction*, 73, 101467. https://doi.org/10.1016/j.learninstruc.2021.101467

Wang, Y., & Lim, H. (2012). The global childhood obesity epidemic and the association between socio-economic status and childhood obesity. *International Review of Psychiatry*, 24(3), 176–188. https://doi.org/10.3109/09540261.2012.688195

Wang, Y., & Lin, S. (2023). Peer ethnic/racial socialization in adolescence: Current knowledge and future directions. *Infant and Child Development*, 32(6), e2409. https://doi.org/10.1002/icd.2409

Wang, Y., Palonen, T., Hurme, T. R., & Kinos, J. (2019). Do you want to play with me today? Friendship stability among preschool children. *European Early Childhood Education Research Journal*, 27(2), 170–184. https://doi.org/10.1080/1350293X.2019.1579545

Wang, Y., Shafto, C. L., & Houston, D. M. (2018). Attention to speech and spoken language development in deaf children with cochlear implants: A 10-year longitudinal study. *Developmental Science*, 21(6), e12677. https://doi.org/10.1111/desc.12677

Wang, Y., Shi, H., Chen, L., Zheng, D., Long, X., Zhang, Y., Wang, H., Shi, Y., Zhao, Y., Wei, Y., & Qiao, J. (2021). Absolute risk of adverse obstetric outcomes among twin pregnancies after in vitro fertilization by maternal age. *JAMA Network Open*, 4(9), e2123634–e2123634. https://doi.org/10.1001/JAMANETWORKOPEN.2021.23634

Wang, Y., Zhang, Y., Liu, L., Cui, J., Wang, J., Shum, D. H. K., van Amelsvoort, T., & Chan, R. C. K. (2017). A meta-analysis of working memory impairments in autism spectrum disorders. *Neuropsychology Review*, 27(1), 46–61. https://doi.org/10.1007/s11065-016-9336-y

Wang, Y., Zhang, Y., & Wadsworth, H. (2023). Family and peer ethnic-racial socialization in adolescents' everyday life: A daily transactional model with ethnic-racial identity and discrimination. *Child Development*, 94(6), 1566–1580. https://doi.org/10.1111/cdev.13937

Wängqvist, M., Carlsson, J., van der Lee, M., & Frisén, A. (2016). Identity development and romantic relationships in the late twenties. *Identity*, 16(1), 24–44. https://doi.org/10.1080/15283488.2015.1121819

Wantchekon, K. A., & Umaña-Taylor, A. J. (2021). Relating profiles of ethnic-racial identity process and content to the academic and psychological adjustment of Black and Latinx adolescents. *Journal of Youth and Adolescence*, 50(7), 1333–1352. https://doi.org/10.1007/s10964-021-01451-x

Ward, K. P., Lee, S. J., Limb, G. E., & Grogan-Kaylor, A. C. (2021). Physical punishment and child externalizing behavior: Comparing American Indian, White, and African American children. *Journal of Interpersonal Violence*, 36(17–18), NP9885–NP9907. https://doi.org/10.1177/0886260519861678

Ward, L. M., & Grower, P. (2020). Media and the development of gender role stereotypes. *Annual Review of Developmental Psychology*, 2(1), 177–199. https://doi.org/10.1146/annurev-devpsych-051120-010630

Ware, R. E., de Montalembert, M., Tshilolo, L., & Abboud, M. R. (2017). Sickle cell disease. *The Lancet*, 390(10091), 311–323.

Warne, R. T. (2015). Test review: Cognitive abilities test, form 7 (CogAT7). *Journal of Psychoeducational Assessment*, 33(2), 188–192. https://doi.org/10.1177/0734282914548324

Warneken, F., Lohse, K., Melis, A. P., & Tomasello, M. (2011). Young children share the spoils after collaboration. *Psychological Science*, 22(2), 267–273. https://doi.org/10.1177/0956797610395392

Warner, T. D. (2018). Adolescent sexual risk taking: The distribution of youth behaviors and perceived peer attitudes across neighborhood contexts. *Journal of Adolescent Health*, 62(2), 226–233. https://doi.org/10.1016/j.jadohealth.2017.09.007

Wasik, B. A., Hindman, A. H., & Snell, E. K. (2016). Book reading and vocabulary development: A systematic review. *Early Childhood Research Quarterly*, 37, 39–57. https://doi.org/10.1016/j.ecresq.2016.04.003

Wass, R., & Golding, C. (2014). Sharpening a tool for teaching: The zone of proximal development. *Teaching in Higher Education*, 19(6), 671–684. https://doi.org/10.1080/13562517.2014.901958

Wass, S. V., Clackson, K., Georgieva, S. D., Brightman, L., Nutbrown, R., & Leong, V. (2018). Infants' visual sustained attention is higher during joint play than solo play: Is this due to increased endogenous attention control or exogenous stimulus capture? *Developmental Science*, 21(6), e12667. https://doi.org/10.1111/desc.12667

Wasserberg, M. J. (2014). Stereotype threat effects on African American children in an urban elementary school. *Journal of Experimental Education*, 82(4), 502–517. https://doi.org/10.1080/00220973.2013.876224

Wasserman, J. D. (2018). A history of intelligence assessment: The unfinished tapestry. In D. P. Flanagan & E. M. McDonough (Eds.), *Contemporary intellectual assessment: Theories, tests, and issues* (pp. 3–55). https://psycnet.apa.org/record/2018-36604-001

Waterhouse, L. (2006). Multiple intelligences, the Mozart effect, and emotional intelligence: A critical review. *Educational Psychologist*, 41(4), 207–225. https://doi.org/10.1207/s15326985ep4104_1

Waterland, R. A., & Jirtle, R. L. (2003). Transposable elements: Targets for early nutritional effects on epigenetic gene regulation. *Molecular and Cellular Biology*, 23(15), 5293–5300. https://doi.org/10.1128/MCB.23.15.5293-5300.2003

Waters, S. F., West, T. V., Karnilowicz, H. R., & Mendes, W. B. (2017). Affect contagion between mothers and infants: Examining valence and touch. *Journal of Experimental Psychology: General*, 146(7), 1043–1051. https://doi.org/10.1037/xge0000322

Waters, S. F., West, T. V., & Mendes, W. B. (2014). Stress contagion: Physiological covariation between mothers and infants. *Psychological Science*, 25(4), 934–942. https://doi.org/10.1177/0956797613518352

Watkins, M. W., Canivez, G. L., Dombrowski, S. C., McGill, R. J., Pritchard, A. E., Holingue, C. B., & Jacobson, L. A. (2022). Long-term stability of Wechsler Intelligence Scale for Children–fifth edition scores in a clinical sample. *Applied Neuropsychology: Child*, 11(3), 422–428. https://doi.org/10.1080/21622965.2021.1875827

Watkins, M. W., & Smith, L. G. (2013). Long-term stability of the Wechsler intelligence scale for children—Fourth edition. *Psychological Assessment, 25*(2), 477–483. https://doi.org/10.1037/a0031653

Watson, A., Dumuid, D., Maher, C., Fraysse, F., Mauch, C., Tomkinson, G. R., Ferguson, T., & Olds, T. (2023). Parenting styles and their associations with children's body composition, activity patterns, fitness, diet, health, and academic achievement. *Childhood Obesity, 19*(5), 316–331. https://doi.org/10.1089/chi.2022.0054

Watson, J. (1925). *Behaviorism*. Norton.

Watson, J. B., & Raynor, R. (1920). Conditioned emotional reactions. *Journal of Experimental Psychology, 3*, 1–14. https://psycnet.apa.org/doi/10.1037/h0069608

Watson, R. J., Grossman, A. H., & Russell, S. T. (2019). Sources of social support and mental health among LGB youth. *Youth & Society, 51*(1), 30–48. https://doi.org/10.1177/0044118X16660110

Watts, A. W., Mason, S. M., Loth, K., Larson, N., & Neumark-Sztainer, D. (2016). Socioeconomic differences in overweight and weight-related behaviors across adolescence and young adulthood: 10-year longitudinal findings from Project EAT. *Preventive Medicine, 87*, 194–199. https://doi.org/10.1016/j.ypmed.2016.03.007

Watts, L. L., Hamza, E. A., Bedewy, D. A., & Moustafa, A. A. (2024). A meta-analysis study on peer influence and adolescent substance use. *Current Psychology, 43*(5), 3866–3881. https://doi.org/10.1007/s12144-023-04944-z

Wautier, A., Tournaire, M., Devouche, E., Epelboin, S., Pouly, J.-L., & Levadou, A. (2020). Genital tract and reproductive characteristics in daughters of women and men prenatally exposed to diethylstilbestrol (DES). *Therapies, 75*(5), 439–448. https://doi.org/10.1016/j.therap.2019.10.004

Waxman, S., Fu, X., Arunachalam, S., Leddon, E., Geraghty, K., & Song, H. (2013). Are nouns learned before verbs? Infants provide insight into a long-standing debate. *Child Development Perspectives, 7*(3), 155–159. https://doi.org/10.1111/cdep.12032

Waxman, S. R. (2021). Racial awareness and bias begin early: Developmental entry points, challenges, and a call to action. *Perspectives on Psychological Science, 16*, 893–902. https://doi.org/10.1177/17456916211026968

Weaver, J., Crespi, S., Tosetti, M., & Morrone, M. (2015). Map of visual activity in the infant brain sheds light on neural development. *PLoS Biology, 13*(9), e1002261. https://doi.org/10.1371/journal.pbio.1002261

Weaver, J. M., & Schofield, T. J. (2015). Mediation and moderation of divorce effects on children's behavior problems. *Journal of Family Psychology, 29*(1), 39–48. https://doi.org/10.1037/fam0000043

Webb, R., & Ayers, S. (2015). Cognitive biases in processing infant emotion by women with depression, anxiety and post-traumatic stress disorder in pregnancy or after birth: A systematic review. *Cognition and Emotion, 29*(7), 1278–1294. https://doi.org/10.1080/02699931.2014.977849

Weber, A., Miskle, B., Lynch, A., Arndt, S., & Acion, L. (2021). Substance use in pregnancy: Identifying stigma and improving care. *Substance Abuse and Rehabilitation, 12*, 105–121. https://doi.org/10.2147/sar.S319180

Webster, G. D., Graber, J. A., Gesselman, A. N., Crosier, B. S., & Schember, T. O. (2014). A life history theory of father absence and menarche: A meta-analysis. *Evolutionary Psychology, 12*(2), 147470491401200. https://doi.org/10.1177/147470491401200202

Webster, S., Morris, G., & Kevelighan, E. (2018). *Essential human development*. Wiley.

Wechsler, D. (1944). *The measurement of adult intelligence*. Williams & Wilkins.

Wechsler, D. (2014). *Wechsler intelligence scale for children* (5th ed.). NCS Pearson.

Wedderburn, C. J., Evans, C., Yeung, S., Gibb, D. M., Donald, K. A., & Prendergast, A. J. (2019). Growth and neurodevelopment of HIV-exposed uninfected children: A conceptual framework. *Current HIV/AIDS Reports, 16*(6), 501–513. https://doi.org/10.1007/s11904-019-00459-0

Wei, S. Q., Bilodeau-Bertrand, M., Liu, S., & Auger, N. (2021). The impact of COVID-19 on pregnancy outcomes: A systematic review and meta-analysis. *CMAJ, 193*(16), E540–E548. https://doi.org/10.1503/cmaj.202604

Weider, S., Lærum, A. M. W., Evensen, K. A. I., Reitan, S. K., Lydersen, S., Brubakk, A. M., Skranes, J., & Indredavik, M. S. (2023). Neurocognitive function and associations with mental health in adults born preterm with very low birthweight or small for gestational age at term. *Frontiers in Psychology, 13*, 1078232. https://www.frontiersin.org/journals/psychology/articles/10.3389/fpsyg.2022.1078232

Weil, L. G., Fleming, S. M., Dumontheil, I., Kilford, E. J., Weil, R. S., Rees, G., Dolan, R. J., & Blakemore, S.-J. (2013). The development of metacognitive ability in adolescence. *Consciousness and Cognition, 22*(1), 264–271. https://doi.org/10.1016/j.concog.2013.01.004

Weimer, A. A., Warnell, K. R., Ettekal, I., Cartwright, K. B., Guajardo, N. R., & Liew, J. (2021). Correlates and antecedents of theory of mind development during middle childhood and adolescence: An integrated model. *Developmental Review, 59*, 100945. https://doi.org/10.1016/j.dr.2020.100945

Weinberg, M. K., Tronick, E. Z., Cohn, J. F., & Olson, K. L. (1999). Gender differences in emotional expressivity and self-regulation during early infancy. *Developmental Psychology, 35*(1), 175–188. https://doi.org/10.1037/0012-1649.35.1.175

Weinfield, N. S., Sroufe, L. A., Egeland, B., & Carlson, E. (2008). Individual differences in infant-caregiver attachment: Conceptual and empirical aspects of security. In J. Cassidy & P. R. Shaver (Eds.), *Handbook of attachment: Theory, research, and clinical applications* (pp. 78–101). Guilford Press.

Weis, R., & Toolis, E. E. (2010). Parenting across cultural contexts in the USA: Assessing parenting behaviour in an ethnically and socioeconomically diverse sample. *Early Child Development & Care, 180*(7), 849–867. https://doi.org/10.1080/03004430802472083

Weisgram, E. S. (2016). The cognitive construction of gender stereotypes: Evidence for the dual pathways model of gender differentiation. *Sex Roles, 75*(7–8), 301–313. https://doi.org/10.1007/s11199-016-0624-z

Weisgram, E. S. (2022). Gender, toys, and play: How gendered early experiences shape later development. In D. P. VanderLaan & W. I. Wong (Eds.), *Gender and sexuality development: Contemporary theory and research* (pp. 207–232). Springer International. https://doi.org/10.1007/978-3-030-84273-4_7

Weisleder, A., & Fernald, A. (2013). Talking to children matters: Early language experience strengthens processing and builds vocabulary. *Psychological Science, 24*(11), 2143–2152. https://doi.org/10.1177/0956797613488145

Weisleder, P. (2020). Helping them decide: A scoping review of interventions used to help minors understand the concept and process of assent. *Frontiers in Pediatrics, 8*, 25. https://doi.org/10.3389/fped.2020.00025

Weisner, M. L., Harris, M. S., Mitsova, D., & Liu, W. (2023). Drinking water disparities and aluminum concentrations: Assessing socio-spatial dimensions across an urban landscape. *Social Sciences & Humanities Open, 8*(1), 100536. https://doi.org/10.1016/j.ssaho.2023.100536

Weiss, L. G., Saklofske, D. H., Holdnack, J. A., & Prifitera, A. (2016). *WISC-V assessment and interpretation: Scientist-practitioner perspectives*. Elsevier Academic Press. https://psycnet.apa.org/record/2015-26909-000

Weissberg, R. P. (2019). Promoting the social and emotional learning of millions of school children. *Perspectives on Psychological Science*, *14*(1), 65–69. https://doi.org/10.1177/1745691618817756

Weisz, A. N., & Black, B. M. (2002). Gender and moral reasoning: African American youth respond to dating dilemmas. *Journal of Human Behavior in the Social Environment*, *5*(1), 35–52. https://doi.org/10.1300/J137v05n01_03

Wellman, H. M. (2017). The development of theory of mind: Historical reflections. *Child Development Perspectives*, *11*(3), 207–214. https://doi.org/10.1111/cdep.12236

Wellman, H. M., & Banerjee, M. (1991). Mind and emotion: Children's understanding of the emotional consequences of beliefs and desires. *British Journal of Developmental Psychology*, *9*, 191–214. https://doi.org/10.1111/j.2044-835X.1991.tb00871.x

Wellman, H. M., Fang, F., & Peterson, C. C. (2011). Sequential progressions in a theory-of-mind scale: Longitudinal perspectives. *Child Development*, *82*(3), 780–792. https://doi.org/10.1111/j.1467-8624.2011.01583.x

Welsh, J. A., Bierman, K. L., Nix, R. L., & Heinrichs, B. N. (2020). Sustained effects of a school readiness intervention: 5th grade outcomes of the Head Start REDI program. *Early Childhood Research Quarterly*, *53*, 151–160. https://doi.org/10.1016/j.ecresq.2020.03.009

Welshman, J. (2010). From Head Start to sure start: Reflections on policy transfer. *Children & Society*, *24*(2), 89–99. https://doi.org/10.1111/j.1099-0860.2008.00201.x

Wen, T., Arditi, B., D'Alton, M. E., & Friedman, A. M. (2021). 570 Maternal education disparities among prenatal care trends in a national sample. *American Journal of Obstetrics & Gynecology*, *224*(2), S361. https://doi.org/10.1016/j.ajog.2020.12.591

Wenger, Y. (2018). *Baltimore tries to close digital divide with free tablets, internet*. Government Technology. https://www.govtech.com/network/Baltimore-Tries-to-Close-Digital-Divide-with-Free-Tablets-Internet.html

Wentzel, K. R. (2014). Prosocial behavior and peer relations in adolescence. In G. C. Laura M. Padilla-Walker (Ed.), *Prosocial development: A multidimensional approach* (pp. 178–200). Oxford Univ Press.

Wentzel, K. R. (2014). Prosocial behavior and peer relations in adolescence. In L. M. Padilla-Walker & G. Carlo (Eds.), *Prosocial development: A multidimensional approach* (pp. 178–200). Oxford University Press. https://doi.org/10.1093/acprof:oso/9780199964772.003.0009

Wentzel, K. R., Jablansky, S., & Scalise, N. R. (2021). Peer social acceptance and academic achievement: A meta-analytic study. *Journal of Educational Psychology*, *113*(1), 157–180. https://doi.org/10.1037/EDU0000468

Werker, J. (2012). Perceptual foundations of bilingual acquisition in infancy. *Annals of the New York Academy of Sciences*, 50–61. https://doi.org/10.1111/j.1749-6632.2012.06484.x *1251*(1)

Werner, E. E. (2012). Children and war: Risk, resilience, and recovery. *Development and Psychopathology*, *24*(02), 553–558. https://doi.org/10.1017/S0954579412000156

Werner, H., Albrecht, J. N., Widmer, N., Janisch, D., Huber, R., & Jenni, O. G. (2022). Adolescents' preference for later school start times. *Journal of Sleep Research*, *31*(1), e13401. https://doi.org/10.1111/JSR.13401

Wertsch, J. V. (1998). *Mind as action*. Oxford University Press.

Werwach, A., Mürbe, D., Schaadt, G., & Männel, C. (2021). Infants' vocalizations at 6 months predict their productive vocabulary at one year. *Infant Behavior and Development*, *64*, 101588. https://doi.org/10.1016/j.infbeh.2021.101588

West, D., Luys, E., Gypen, L., Van Holen, F., & Vanderfaeillie, J. (2023). Behavior problems in foster care, systematic review of associated factors. *Children and Youth Services Review*, *155*, 107240. https://doi.org/10.1016/j.childyouth.2023.107240

West, K. L., & Iverson, J. M. (2021). Communication changes when infants begin to walk. *Developmental Science*, *24*(5). https://doi.org/10.1111/desc.13102

West, K. L., Saleh, A. N., Adolph, K. E., & Tamis-LeMonda, C. S. (2023). "Go, go, go!" Mothers' verbs align with infants' locomotion. *Developmental Science*, *26*(6), e13397. https://doi.org/10.1111/desc.13397

Westen, D. (1998). The scientific legacy of Sigmund Freud: Toward a psychodynamically informed psychological science. *Psychological Bulletin*, *124*, 333–371.

Westrick-Payne, K. K., & Wiborg, C. E. (2021). *Children's family structure. Family Profiles, FP-21-26*. National Center for Family & Marriage Research. 2021 https://www.bgsu.edu/ncfmr/resources/data/family-profiles/payne-wiborg-children-family-structure-2021-fp-21-26.html

Weymouth, B. B., Buehler, C., Zhou, N., & Henson, R. A. (2016). A meta-analysis of parent-adolescent conflict: Disagreement, hostility, and youth maladjustment. *Journal of Family Theory & Review*, *8*(1), 95–112. https://doi.org/10.1111/jftr.12126

Whaley, G. L., & Pfefferbaum, B. (2023). Parental challenges during the COVID-19 pandemic: Psychological outcomes and risk and protective factors. *Current Psychiatry Reports*, *25*(4), 165–174. https://doi.org/10.1007/s11920-023-01412-0

White, A. E., Moeller, J., Ivcevic, Z., Brackett, M. A., & Stern, R. (2018). LGBTQ adolescents' positive and negative emotions and experiences in U.S. high schools. *Sex Roles*, *79*(9–10), 594–608. https://doi.org/10.1007/s11199-017-0885-1

White, E. E., Baden, A. L., Ferguson, A. L., & Smith, L. (2022). The intersection of race and adoption: Experiences of transracial and international adoptees with microaggressions. *Journal of Family Psychology*, *36*, 1318–1328. https://doi.org/10.1037/fam0000922

White, H., Chroust, A., Heck, A., Jubran, R., Galati, A., & Bhatt, R. S. (2019). Categorical perception of facial emotions in infancy. *Infancy*, *24*(2), 139–161. https://doi.org/10.1111/infa.12275

Whitehouse, A. J. O., Robinson, M., Li, J., & Oddy, W. H. (2011). Duration of breast feeding and language ability in middle childhood. *Paediatric & Perinatal Epidemiology*, *25*(1), 44–52. https://doi.org/10.1111/j.1365-3016.2010.01161.x

Whiteman, S. D., Jensen, A. C., & McHale, S. M. (2017). Sibling influences on risky behaviors from adolescence to young adulthood: Vertical socialization or bidirectional effects? *New Directions for Child and Adolescent Development*, 67–85. https://doi.org/10.1002/cad.20197 *2017*(156)

Whitley, D. M., & Fuller-Thomson, E. (2018). Latino solo grandparents raising grandchildren. *Hispanic Health Care International*, *16*(1), 11–19. https://doi.org/10.1177/1540415318757219

Whittington, J. R., Simmons, P. M., Phillips, A. M., Gammill, S. K., Cen, R., Magann, E. F., & Cardenas, V. M. (2018). The use of electronic cigarettes in pregnancy. *Obstetrical & Gynecological Survey*, *73*(9), 544–549. https://doi.org/10.1097/OGX.0000000000000595

Wickens, C. D., & Carswell, C. M. (2021). Information processing. In G. Salvendy & W. Karwowski (Eds.), *Handbook of human factors and ergonomics* (pp. 114–158). John Wiley & Sons. https://doi.org/10.1002/9781119636113.CH5

Wickens, C. D., & Carswell, C. M. (2021). Information processing. In Gavriel. Salvendy & Waldemar. Karwowski (Eds.), *Handbook of human factors and ergonomics* (pp. 114–158). John Wiley & Sons. https://doi.org/10.1002/9781119636113.CH5

Widom, C. S. (2014). Longterm consequences of childhood maltreatment. In J. E. Korbin & R. D. Krugman (Eds.), *Handbook of child maltreatment* (Vol. 2, pp. 225–247). Springer Netherlands. https://doi.org/10.1007/978-94-007-7208-3

Widom, C. S. (2022). Longterm consequences of childhood maltreatment. In R. D. Krugman & J. E. Korbin (Eds.), *Handbook of child maltreatment* (pp. 371–395). Springer International. https://doi.org/10.1007/978-3-030-82479-2_18

Wiedeman, A. M., Black, J. A., Dolle, A. L., Finney, E. J., & Coker, K. L. (2015). Factors influencing the impact of aggressive and violent media on children and adolescents. *Aggression and Violent Behavior*, 25, 191–198. https://doi.org/10.1016/J.AVB.2015.04.008

Wiertsema, M., Vrijen, C., van der Ploeg, R., Sentse, M., & Kretschmer, T. (2023). Bullying perpetration and social status in the peer group: A meta-analysis. *Journal of Adolescence*, 95(1), 34–55. https://doi.org/10.1002/jad.12109

Wigby, K., D'Epagnier, C., Howell, S., Reicks, A., Wilson, R., Cordeiro, L., & Tartaglia, N. (2016). Expanding the phenotype of triple X syndrome: A comparison of prenatal versus postnatal diagnosis. *American Journal of Medical Genetics Part A*, 170(11), 2870–2881. https://doi.org/10.1002/ajmg.a.37688

Wigfield, A., Eccles, J. S., Fredricks, J. A., Simpkins, S., Roeser, R. W., & Schiefele, U. (2015). Development of achievement motivation and engagement. In M. Lamb (Ed.), *Handbook of child psychology and developmental science* (pp. 1–44). John Wiley & Sons. https://doi.org/10.1002/9781118963418.childpsy316

Wigfield, A., Faust, L. T., Cambria, J., & Eccles, J. S. (2019). Motivation in education. In R. M. Ryan (Ed.), *The Oxford handbook of human motivation* (2nd ed., pp. 443–461). Oxford University Press.

Wigfield, A., Muenks, K., & Eccles, J. S. (2021). Achievement motivation: What we know and where we are going. *Annual Review of Developmental Psychology*, 3(1), 87–111. https://doi.org/10.1146/annurev-devpsych-050720-103500

Wigfield, A., Muenks, K., & Rosenzweig, E. Q. (2015). Children's achievement motivation in school. In C. M. Rubie-Davies, J. M. Stephens, & P. Watson (Eds.), *International handbook of social psychology of the classroom* (1st ed., pp. 9–20). Routledge. https://doi.org/10.4324/9781315716923

Wiglesworth, A., Rey, L. F., Fetter, A. K., Prairie Chicken, M. L., Azarani, M., Davis, A. R., Young, A. R., Riegelman, A., & Gone, J. P. (2022). Attempted suicide in American Indian and Alaska Native populations: A systematic review of research on protective factors. *Clinical Psychology: Science and Practice*, 29, 205–218. https://doi.org/10.1037/cps0000085

Wigmore-Sykes, M., Ferris, M., & Singh, S. (2021). Contemporary beliefs surrounding the menarche: A pilot study of adolescent girls at a school in middle England. *Education for Primary Care*, 23, 59–60. https://doi.org/10.1080/14739879.2020.1836678

Wiik, K. L., & Gunnar, M. R. (2009). Development and social regulation of stress neurobiology in human development. In J. Quas & R. Fivush (Eds.), *Emotion in memory and development* (pp. 256–277). Oxford University Press. https://doi.org/10.1093/acprof:oso/9780195326932.003.0010

Wilbur, M. B., Little, S., & Szymanski, L. M. (2015). Is home birth safe? *New England Journal of Medicine*, 373(27), 2683–2685. https://doi.org/10.1056/NEJMclde1513623

Wildeman, C., Goldman, A. W., & Turney, K. (2018). Parental incarceration and child health in the United States. *Epidemiologic Reviews*, 40(1), 146–156. https://doi.org/10.1093/epirev/mxx013

Wiley, M. O. L. (2017). Adoption research, practice, and societal trends: Ten years of progress. *American Psychologist*, 72(9), 985–995. https://doi.org/10.1037/amp0000218

Wilkinson, P. O., Trzaskowski, M., Haworth, C. M. A., & Eley, T. C. (2013). The role of gene-environment correlations and interactions in middle childhood depressive symptoms. *Development and Psychopathology*, 25(01), 93–104. https://doi.org/10.1017/S0954579412000922

Williams, A., & Steele, J. R. (2019). Examining children's implicit racial attitudes using exemplar and category-based measures. *Child Development*, 90(3), e322–e338. https://doi.org/10.1111/cdev.12991

Williams, C. D., Byrd, C. M., Quintana, S. M., Anicama, C., Kiang, L., Umaña-Taylor, A. J., Calzada, E. J., Pabón Gautier, M., Ejesi, K., Tuitt, N. R., Martinez-Fuentes, S., White, L., Marks, A., Rogers, L. O., & Whitesell, N. (2020). A lifespan model of ethnic-racial identity. *Research in Human Development*, 17(2–3), 99–129. https://doi.org/10.1080/15427609.2020.1831882

Williamson, A. A., Gould, R., Leichman, E. S., Walters, R. M., & Mindell, J. A. (2021). Socioeconomic disadvantage and sleep in early childhood: Real-world data from a mobile health application. *Sleep Health*, 7(2), 143–152. https://doi.org/10.1016/j.sleh.2021.01.002

Williamson, A. A., Mindell, J. A., Hiscock, H., & Quach, J. (2020). Longitudinal sleep problem trajectories are associated with multiple impairments in child well-being. *Journal of Child Psychology and Psychiatry*, 61(10), 1092–1103. https://doi.org/10.1111/jcpp.13303

Williamson, V., Stevelink, S. A. M., Da Silva, E., & Fear, N. T. (2018). A systematic review of wellbeing in children: A comparison of military and civilian families. *Child and Adolescent Psychiatry and Mental Health*, 12(1), 1–11. https://doi.org/10.1186/s13034-018-0252-1

Willis-Owen, S. A. G., Cookson, W. O. C., & Moffatt, M. F. (2018). The genetics and genomics of asthma. *Annual Review of Genomics and Human Genetics*, 19(1), 223–246. https://doi.org/10.1146/annurev-genom-083117-021651

Wimer, C., Fox, L., Garfinkel, I., Kaushal, N., Nam, J. H., & Waldfogel, J. (2021). Trends in the economic wellbeing of unmarried-parent families with children: New estimates using an improved measure of poverty. *Population Research and Policy* Review, 1253–1276. https://doi.org/10.1007/S11113-021-09673-4 6, 40(6

Winne, P. H. (2021). Cognition, metacognition, and self-regulated learning. In G. Noblit (Ed.), *Oxford research encyclopedia of education*. Oxford University Press. https://doi.org/10.1093/acrefore/9780190264093.013.1528

Winnebeck, E. C., Vuori-Brodowski, M. T., Biller, A. M., Molenda, C., Fischer, D., Zerbini, G., & Roenneberg, T. (2020). Later school start times in a flexible system improve teenage sleep. *Sleep*, 43(6), 1–17. https://doi.org/10.1093/sleep/zsz307

Winsler, A., Fernyhough, C., & Montero, I. (2009). *Private speech, executive functioning, and the development of verbal self-regulation*. Cambridge University Press.

Winters, A. M. (2020). Theoretical foundations: Delinquency risk factors and services aimed at reducing ongoing offending.

Child and Adolescent Social Work Journal, 37(3), 263-269. https://doi.org/10.1007/s10560-020-00655-7

Wiradhany, W., & Koerts, J. (2021). Everyday functioning-related cognitive correlates of media multitasking: A mini meta-analysis. *Media Psychology, 24*(2), 276-303. https://doi.org/10.1080/15213269.2019.1685393

Witherington, D. C., & Lickliter, R. (2016). Integrating development and evolution in psychological science: Evolutionary developmental psychology, developmental systems, and explanatory pluralism. *Human Development, 59*(4), 200-234. https://doi.org/10.1159/000450715

Withers, P. J., Bouman, C., Carmignato, S., Cnudde, V., Grimaldi, D., Hagen, C. K., Maire, E., Manley, M., Du Plessis, A., & Stock, S. R. (2021). X-ray computed tomography. *Nature Reviews Methods Primers, 1*(1), 18. https://doi.org/10.1038/S43586-021-00015-4

Wittig, S. M. O., & Rodriguez, C. M. (2019). Emerging behavior problems: Bidirectional relations between maternal and paternal parenting styles with infant temperament. *Developmental Psychology, 55*(6), 1199-1210. https://doi.org/10.1037/dev0000707

Wohlfahrt-Veje, C., Mouritsen, A., Hagen, C. P., Tinggaard, J., Mieritz, M. G., Boas, M., Petersen, J. H., Skakkebæk, N. E., & Main, K. M. (2016). (Vol. *101*, pp. 2667-2674). https://doi.org/10.1210/jc.2016-1073

Wojciak, A. S., McWey, L. M., & Waid, J. (2018). Sibling relationships of youth in foster care: A predictor of resilience. *Children and Youth Services Review, 84*, 247-254. https://doi.org/10.1016/j.childyouth.2017.11.030

Wojslawowicz Bowker, J. C., Rubin, K. H., Burgess, K. B., Booth-Laforce, C., & Rose-Krasnor, L. (2006). Behavioral characteristics associated with stable and fluid best friendship patterns in middle childhood. *Merrill-Palmer Quarterly, 52*(4), 671-693. https://psycnet.apa.org/doi/10.1353/mpq.2006.0000

Wolfe, K., & Ralls, F. M. (2019). Rapid eye movement sleep and neuronal development. *Current Opinion in Pulmonary Medicine, 25*(6), 555-560. https://doi.org/10.1097/mcp.0000000000000622

Wolff, P. H. (1966). The causes, controls and organization of behavior in the neonate. *Psychological Issues Monograph Series, 5*(1), 1-105.

Wolke, D., Eryigit-Madzwamuse, S., & Gutbrod, T. (2014). Very preterm/very low birthweight infants' attachment: Infant and maternal characteristics. *Archives of Disease in Childhood. Fetal and Neonatal Edition, 99*(1), F70-F755. https://doi.org/10.1136/archdischild-2013-303788

Wong, K. K.-Y., & Buda, M. (2020). Gender differences in personality, evolutionary perspective on. In *The Wiley encyclopedia of personality and individual differences* (pp. 209-214). John Wiley & Sons. https://doi.org/10.1002/9781119547143.ch35

Wong, T. K. Y., Konishi, C., & Kong, X. (2021). Parenting and prosocial behaviors: A meta-analysis. *Social Development, 30*(2), 343-373. https://doi.org/10.1111/sode.12481

Wong, T. K. Y., Konishi, C., & Kong, X. (2021). Parenting and prosocial behaviors: A meta-analysis. *Social Development, 30*, 343-373. https://doi.org/10.1111/sode.12481

Wood, M. A., Bukowski, W. M., & Lis, E. (2016). The digital self: How social media serves as a setting that shapes youth's emotional experiences. *Adolescent Research Review, 1*(2), 163-173. https://doi.org/10.1007/s40894-015-0014-8

Woodhouse, S. S., Scott, J. R., Hepworth, A. D., & Cassidy, J. (2020). Secure base provision: A new approach to examining links between maternal caregiving and infant attachment. *Child Development, 91*(1), e249-e265. https://doi.org/10.1111/cdev.13224

Woodward, A. L., Markman, E. M., & Fitzsimmons, C. M. (1994). Rapid word learning in 13- and 18-month-olds. *Developmental Psychology, 30*, 553-556. https://doi.org/10.1037/0012-1649.30.4.553

Woolley, J. D., & E Ghossainy, M. (2013). Revisiting the fantasy-reality distinction: Children as naïve skeptics. *Child Development, 84*(5), 1496-1510. https://doi.org/10.1111/cdev.12081

Woolverton, G. A., & Marks, A. K. (2023). "I just check 'other'": Evidence to support expanding the measurement inclusivity and equity of ethnicity/race and cultural identifications of U.S. adolescents. *Cultural Diversity and Ethnic Minority Psychology, 29*, 64-73. https://doi.org/10.1037/cdp0000360

World Health Organization. (2009). *BMI classification*. http://apps.who.int/bmi/index.jsp?introPage=intro_3.html

Worrell, F. C., & Dixson, D. D. (2022). Achieving equity in gifted education: Ideas and issues. *Gifted Child Quarterly, 66*(2), 79-81. https://doi.org/10.1177/00169862211068551

Worrell, F. C., Subotnik, R. F., Olszewski-Kubilius, P., & Dixson, D. D. (2019). Gifted students. *Annual Review of Psychology, 70*(1), 551-576. https://doi.org/10.1146/annurev-psych-010418-102846

Wouldes, T. A., & Lester, B. M. (2023). Opioid, methamphetamine, and polysubstance use: Perinatal outcomes for the mother and infant. *Frontiers in Pediatrics, 11*, 1305508. https://doi.org/10.3389/fped.2023.1305508

Wozniak, J. R., Riley, E. P., & Charness, M. E. (2019). Clinical presentation, diagnosis, and management of fetal alcohol spectrum disorder. *Lancet Neurology, 18*(8), 760-770. https://doi.org/10.1016/S1474-4422(19)30150-4

Wright, A. J. (2020). Equivalence of remote, digital administration and traditional, in-person administration of the Wechsler intelligence scale for children, fifth edition (WISC-V). *Psychological Assessment, 32*(9), 809-817. https://doi.org/10.1037/pas0000939

Wright, A. W., Austin, M., Booth, C., & Kliewer, W. (2016). Exposure to community violence and physical health outcomes in youth: A systematic review. *Journal of Pediatric Psychology, 42*(4), 364-378. https://doi.org/10.1093/jpepsy/jsw088

Wright, B. C., & Smailes, J. (2015). Factors and processes in children's transitive deductions. *Journal of Cognitive Psychology, 27*(8), 967-978. https://doi.org/10.1080/20445911.2015.1063641

Wright, B., Hargate, R., Garside, M., Carr, G., Wakefield, T., Swanwick, R., Noon, I., & Simpson, P. (2021). A systematic scoping review of early interventions for parents of deaf infants. *BMC Pediatrics, 21*(1), 1-13. https://doi.org/10.1186/S12887-021-02893-9

Wright, K. M., Riviere, L. A., Merrill, J. C., & Cabrera, O. A. (2013). Resilience in military families: A review of programs and empirical evidence. In R. R. Sinclair & T. W. Britt (Eds.), *Building psychological resilience in military personnel: Theory and practice* (pp. 167-191). American Psychological Association. https://doi.org/10.1037/14190-008

Wright, N., Hill, J., Sharp, H., & Pickles, A. (2021). Impact of COVID-19 on young adolescent mental health: Comparison of depression, anxiety and behaviour problems in 12 year olds immediately before and during the pandemic in a UK birth cohort. https://doi.org/10.2139/SSRN.3717557

Wu, Y., & Jobson, L. (2019). Maternal reminiscing and child autobiographical memory elaboration: A meta-analytic review.

Developmental Psychology, 55, 2505–2521. https://doi.org/10.1037/dev0000821

Wu, Y., Schulz, L. E., Frank, M. C., & Gweon, H. (2021). Emotion as information in early social learning. Current Directions in Psychological Science, 30(6), 468–475. https://doi.org/10.1177/09637214211040779

Wühl, E. (2019). Hypertension in childhood obesity. Acta Paediatrica, International Journal of Paediatrics, 108(1), 37–43. https://doi.org/10.1111/apa.14551

Wylie, B. J., Hauptman, M., Hacker, M. R., & Hawkins, S. S. (2021). Understanding rising electronic cigarette use. Obstetrics and Gynecology, 137(3), 521–527. https://doi.org/10.1097/aog.0000000000004282

Wysman, L., Scoboria, A., Gawrylowicz, J., & Memon, A. (2014). The cognitive interview buffers the effects of subsequent repeated questioning in the absence of negative feedback. Behavioral Sciences & the Law, 32(2), 207–219. https://doi.org/10.1002/bsl.2115

Xaverius, P., Alman, C., Holtz, L., & Yarber, L. (2016). Risk factors associated with very low birth weight in a large urban area, stratified by adequacy of prenatal care. Maternal and Child Health Journal, 20(3), 623–629. https://doi.org/10.1007/s10995-015-1861-4

Xiao, E., Shen, J., & Harris, P. (2022). Children with siblings differ from only children in their sharing behaviour. Early Child Development and Care, 192(7), 1007–1019. https://doi.org/10.1080/03004430.2020.1829610

Xiao, S. X., Cook, R. E., Martin, C. L., & Nielson, M. G. (2019). Characteristics of preschool gender enforcers and peers who associate with them. Sex Roles, 81(11–12), 671–685. https://doi.org/10.1007/s11199-019-01026-y

Xiao, S. X., Hashi, E. C., Korous, K. M., & Eisenberg, N. (2019). Gender differences across multiple types of prosocial behavior in adolescence: A meta-analysis of the prosocial tendency measure-revised (PTM-R). Journal of Adolescence, 77, 41–58. https://doi.org/10.1016/j.adolescence.2019.09.003

Xiao, S. X., Hoffer, A. L., Benoit, R. L., Scrofani, S., & Martin, C. L. (2023). Parents matter: Accepting parents have less anxious gender expansive children. Sex Roles, 89(9), 459–474. https://doi.org/10.1007/s11199-023-01387-5

Xiao, S. X., Hoffer, A., Martin, C. L., & Jenkins, D. L. (2022). Early adolescents' gender typicality and depressive symptoms: The moderating role of parental acceptance. Journal of Early Adolescence, 42(6), 822–840. https://doi.org/10.1177/02724316221078832

Xiao-na, H., Hui-shan, W., Li-jin, Z., & Xi-cheng, L. (2010). Co-sleeping and children's sleep in China. Biological Rhythm Research, 41(3), 169–181. https://doi.org/10.1080/09291011003687940

Xie, D., Yang, W., Fang, J., Li, H., Xiong, L., Kong, F., Wang, A., Liu, Z., & Wang, H. (2021). Chromosomal abnormality: Prevalence, prenatal diagnosis and associated anomalies based on a provincial-wide birth defects monitoring system. Journal of Obstetrics and Gynaecology Research, 47(3), 865–872. https://doi.org/10.1111/jog.14569

Xu, J., Hardy, L. L., Guo, C. Z., & Garnett, S. P. (2018). The trends and prevalence of obesity and morbid obesity among Australian school-aged children, 1985-2014. Journal of Paediatrics and Child Health, 54(8), 907–912. https://doi.org/10.1111/jpc.13922

Xu, J. Z., & Thein, S. L. (2019). The carrier state for sickle cell disease is not completely harmless. Haematologica, 104(6), 1106–1111. https://doi.org/10.3324/haematol.2018.206060

Xu, Q., Chodorow, M., & Valian, V. (2023). How infants' utterances grow: A probabilistic account of early language development. Cognition, 230, 105275. https://doi.org/10.1016/j.cognition.2022.105275

Xu, Y., Farver, J. A. M., Zhang, Z., Zeng, Q., Yu, L., & Cai, B. (2005). Mainland Chinese parenting styles and parent-child interaction. International Journal of Behavioral Development, 29(6), 524–531. https://doi.org/10.1177/01650250500147121

Xu, Y., Norton, S., & Rahman, Q. (2021). Childhood gender nonconformity and the stability of self-reported sexual orientation from adolescence to young adulthood in a birth cohort. Developmental Psychology, 57(4), 557–569. https://doi.org/10.1037/dev0001164

Xu, Y., Wang, Y., McCarthy, L. P., Harrison, T., & Doherty, H. (2022). Mental/behavioural health and educational outcomes of grandchildren raised by custodial grandparents: A mixed methods systematic review. Health & Social Care in the Community, 30(6), 2096–2127. https://doi.org/10.1111/hsc.13876

Yager, Z., Diedrichs, P. C., Ricciardelli, L. A., & Halliwell, E. (2013). What works in secondary schools? A systematic review of classroom-based body image programs. Body Image, 10(3), 271–281. https://doi.org/10.1016/j.bodyim.2013.04.001

Yamamoto, H., Sato, A., & Itakura, S. (2020). Transition from crawling to walking changes gaze communication space in everyday infant-parent interaction. Frontiers in Psychology, 10, 2987. https://doi.org/10.3389/fpsyg.2019.02987

Yang, B., Ostbye, T., Huang, X., Li, Y., Fang, B., Wang, H., & Liu, Q. (2021). Maternal age at menarche and pubertal timing in boys and girls: A cohort study from Chongqing, China. Journal of Adolescent Health, 68(3), 508–516. https://doi.org/10.1016/j.jadohealth.2020.06.036

Yang, C., Crain, S., Berwick, R. C., Chomsky, N., & Bolhuis, J. J. (2017). The growth of language: Universal grammar, experience, and principles of computation. Neuroscience & Biobehavioral Reviews, 81, 103–119. https://doi.org/10.1016/j.neubiorev.2016.12.023

Yang, J. (2007). The one-child policy and school attendance in China. Comparative Education Review, 51(4), 471–495. https://doi.org/10.1086/520858

Yang, L., Wang, H., Yang, L., Zhao, M., Guo, Y., Bovet, P., & Xi, B. (2022). Maternal cigarette smoking before or during pregnancy increases the risk of birth congenital anomalies: A population-based retrospective cohort study of 12 million mother-infant pairs. BMC Medicine, 20(1), 1–17. https://doi.org/10.1186/S12916-021-02196-X/TABLES/6

Yang, M.-Y., & Maguire-Jack, K. (2018). Individual and cumulative risks for child abuse and neglect. Family Relations, 67(2), 287–301. https://doi.org/10.1111/fare.12310

Yang, S., & Sternberg, R. J. (1997). Conceptions of intelligence in ancient Chinese philosophy. Journal of Theoretical and Philosophical Psychology, 17(2), 101–119. https://doi.org/10.1037/h0091164

Yang, W., Jin, S., Duan, W., Yu, H., Ping, L., Shen, Z., Cheng, Y., Xu, X., & Zhou, C. (2023). The effects of childhood maltreatment on cortical thickness and gray matter volume: A coordinate-based meta-analysis. Psychological Medicine, 53(5), 1681–1699. https://doi.org/10.1017/S0033291723000661

Yaoying, X., & Xu, Y. (2010). Children's social play sequence: Parten's classic theory revisited. Early Child Development and Care, 180(4), 489–498. https://doi.org/10.1080/03004430802090430

Yard, E., Radhakrishnan, L., Ballesteros, M. F., Sheppard, M., Gates, A., Stein, Z., Hartnett, K., Kite-Powell, A., Rodgers, L., Adjemian, J., Ehlman, D. C., Holland, K., Idaikkadar, N., Ivey-Stephenson, A.,

Martinez, P., Law, R., & ScD, D. M. S. (2021). Emergency department visits for suspected suicide attempts among persons aged 12–25 years before and during the COVID-19 pandemic—United States. *Morbidity and Mortality Weekly Report*, 70(24), 888–894. https://doi.org/10.15585/mmwr.mm7024e1 January 2019–May 2021

Yau, J. C., & Reich, S. M. (2018). "It's just a lot of work": Adolescents' self-presentation norms and practices on Facebook and Instagram. *Journal of Research on Adolescence*, 29(1), 196–209. https://doi.org/10.1111/jora.12376

Yau, J., & Smetana, J. G. (2003). Conceptions of moral, social-conventional, and personal events among Chinese preschoolers in Hong Kong. *Child Development*, 74(3), 647–658. https://doi.org/10.1111/1467-8624.00560

Yavorsky, J. E., Qian, Y., & Sargent, A. C. (2021). The gendered pandemic: The implications of COVID-19 for work and family. *Sociology Compass*, 15(6), e12881. https://doi.org/10.1111/SOC4.12881

Yavuz, H. M., Colasante, T., & Malti, T. (2022). Parental warmth predicts more child pro-social behaviour in children with better emotion regulation. *British Journal of Developmental Psychology*, 40(4), 539–556. https://doi.org/10.1111/bjdp.12425

Ye, Z., Wu, D., He, X., Ma, Q., Peng, J., Mao, G., Feng, L., & Tong, Y. (2023). Meta-analysis of the relationship between bullying and depressive symptoms in children and adolescents. *BMC Psychiatry*, 23(1), 215. https://doi.org/10.1186/s12888-023-04681-4

Yeager, D. S., Dahl, R. E., & Dweck, C. S. (2018). Why interventions to influence adolescent behavior often fail but could succeed. *Perspectives on Psychological Science*, 13(1), 101–122. https://doi.org/10.1177/1745691617722620

Yeager, D. S., & Dweck, C. S. (2020). What can be learned from growth mindset controversies? *American Psychologist*, 75(9), 1269–1284. https://doi.org/10.1037/amp0000794

Yelinek, J., & Grady, J. S. (2019). 'Show me your mad faces!' Preschool teachers' emotion talk in the classroom. *Early Child Development and Care*, 189(7), 1063–1071. https://doi.org/10.1080/03004430.2017.1363740

Yeoh, S. L., Eastwood, J., Wright, I. M., Morton, R., Melhuish, E., Ward, M., & Oei, J. L. (2019). Cognitive and motor outcomes of children with prenatal opioid exposure: A systematic review and meta-analysis. *JAMA Network Open*, 2(7), e197025. https://doi.org/10.1001/jamanetworkopen.2019.7025

Yi, C., Wang, Q., Qu, Y., Niu, J., Oliver, B. G., & Chen, H. (2022). In-utero exposure to air pollution and early-life neural development and cognition. *Ecotoxicology and Environmental Safety*, 238, 113589. https://doi.org/10.1016/j.ecoenv.2022.113589

Yildiz, M. (2020). Conflicting nature of social-pragmatic cues with mutual exclusivity regarding three-year-olds' label-referent mappings. *Psychology of Language and Communication*, 24(1), 124–141. https://doi.org/10.2478/plc-2020-0008

Yip, S. W., Lichenstein, S. D., Liang, Q., Chaarani, B., Dager, A., Pearlson, G., Banaschewski, T., Bokde, A. L. W., Desrivières, S., Flor, H., Grigis, A., Gowland, P., Heinz, A., Brühl, R., Martinot, J.-L., Martinot, M.-L. P., Artiges, E., Nees, F., Orfanos, D. P., & &#hillip1; Garavan, H. (2023). Brain networks and adolescent alcohol use. *JAMA Psychiatry*, 80(11), 1131–1141. https://doi.org/10.1001/jamapsychiatry.2023.2949

Yip, T. (2014). Ethnic identity in everyday life: The influence of identity development status. *Child Development*, 85(1), 205–219. https://doi.org/10.1111/cdev.12107

Yip, T. (2018). Ethnic/racial identity—a double-edged sword? Associations with discrimination and psychological outcomes. *Current Directions in Psychological Science*, 27(3), 170–175. https://doi.org/10.1177/0963721417739348

Yip, T., Cham, H., Wang, Y., & Xie, M. (2022). Applying stress and coping models to ethnic/racial identity, discrimination, and adjustment among diverse adolescents. *Developmental Psychology*, 58, 176–192. https://doi.org/10.1037/dev0001283

Yoakum, C. S., & Yerkes, R. M. (1920). *Army mental tests*. Holt.

Yoo, H. N., & Smetana, J. G. (2022). Distinctions between moral and conventional judgments from early to middle childhood: A meta-analysis of social domain theory research. *Developmental Psychology*, 58, 874–889. https://doi.org/10.1037/dev0001330

Yoon, E., Adams, K., Clawson, A., Chang, H., Surya, S., & Jérémie-Brink, G. (2017). East Asian adolescents' ethnic identity development and cultural integration: A qualitative investigation. *Journal of Counseling Psychology*, 64(1), 65–79. https://doi.org/10.1037/cou0000181

York, C. (2020). Behavior genetics and twin studies. In K. Floyd & R. Weber (Eds.), *The handbook of communication science and biology*. Routledge.

Yoshinaga-Itano, C., Sedey, A. L., Mason, C. A., Wiggin, M., & Chung, W. (2020). Early intervention, parent talk, and pragmatic language in children with hearing loss. *Pediatrics*, 146(Supplement_3), S270–S277. https://doi.org/10.1542/peds.2020-0242F

Young, A. W. (2021). Face perception. In *Oxford research encyclopedia of psychology*. https://doi.org/10.1093/acrefore/9780190236557.013.844

Young, G. (2016). Lateralization and specialization of the brain. In G. Young (Ed.), *Unifying causality and psychology* (pp. 177–200). Springer International. https://doi.org/10.1007/978-3-319-24094-7_8

Young, N. A. E. (2021). Childhood disability in the United States: 2019. *American Community Survey Briefs*, ACSBR-006. https://www.census.gov/content/dam/Census/library/publications/2021/acs/acsbr-006.pdf

Yousefi, M., Karmaus, W., Zhang, H., Roberts, G., Matthews, S., Clayton, B., & Arshad, S. H. (2013). Relationships between age of puberty onset and height at age 18 years in girls and boys. *World Journal of Pediatrics*, 9(3), 230–238. https://doi.org/10.1007/s12519-013-0399-z

Yu, C., & Smith, L. B. (2016). The social origins of sustained attention in one-year-old human infants. *Current Biology*, 26(9), 1235–1240. https://doi.org/10.1016/j.cub.2016.03.026

Yu, X. (2023). Less is more: A critical role of synapse pruning in neural circuit wiring. *Nature Reviews Neuroscience*, 24(2), Article 2. https://doi.org/10.1038/s41583-022-00665-7

Yue, X., & Zhang, Q. (2023). The association between peer rejection and aggression types: A meta-analysis. *Child Abuse & Neglect*, 135, 105974. https://doi.org/10.1016/j.chiabu.2022.105974

Yuen, W. S., Chan, G., Bruno, R., Clare, P., Mattick, R., Aiken, A., Boland, V., McBride, N., McCambridge, J., Slade, T., Kypri, K., Horwood, J., Hutchinson, D., Najman, J., De Torres, C., & Peacock, A. (2020). Adolescent alcohol use trajectories: Risk factors and adult outcomes. *Pediatrics*, 146(4), e20200440. https://doi.org/10.1542/peds.2020-0440

Yule, K., Houston, J., & Grych, J. (2019). Resilience in children exposed to violence: A meta-analysis of protective factors across ecological contexts. *Clinical Child and Family Psychology Review*, 22(3),

406–431. https://doi.org/10.1007/s10567-019-00293-1

Yunger, J. L., Carver, P. R., & Perry, D. G. (2004). Does gender identity influence children's psychological well-being? *Developmental Psychology*, *40*(4), 572–582. https://doi.org/10.1037/0012-1649.40.4.572

Zablotsky, B., & Black, L. I. (2020). Prevalence of children aged 3–17 years with developmental disabilities, by urbanicity: United States, 2015–2018. *National Health Statistics Reports*, *13*(9). https://www.cdc.gov/nchs/products/index.htm

Zablotsky, B., Black, L. I., Maenner, M. J., Schieve, L. A., Danielson, M. L., Bitsko, R. H., Blumberg, S. J., Kogan, M. D., & Boyle, C. A. (2019). Prevalence and trends of developmental disabilities among children in the United States: 2009–2017. *Pediatrics*, *144*(4), e20190811. https://doi.org/10.1542/peds.2019-0811

Zablotsky, B., Bramlett, M. D., & Blumberg, S. J. (2020). The co-occurrence of autism spectrum disorder in children with ADHD. *Journal of Attention Disorders*, *24*(1), 94–103. https://doi.org/10.1177/1087054717713638

Zadeh, S. (2020). Single motherhood via sperm donation: Empirical insights from a longitudinal study of solo mother families in the UK. In K. Beier, C. Brügge, P. Thorn, & C. Wiesemann (Eds.), *Assistierte reproduktion mit hilfe dritter* (pp. 389–399). Springer Berlin Heidelberg. https://doi.org/10.1007/978-3-662-60298-0_25

Zagel, A. L., Cutler, G. J., Linabery, A. M., Spaulding, A. B., & Kharbanda, A. B. (2019). Unintentional injuries in primary and secondary schools in the United States, 2001–2013. *Journal of school health*, *89*(1), 38–47. https://doi.org/10.1111/josh.12711

Zahn-Waxler, C., Friedman, R. J., Cole, P. M., Mizuta, I., & Hiruma, N. (1996). Japanese and United States preschool children's responses to conflict and distress. *Child Development*, *67*, 2462–2477. https://doi.org/10.2307/1131634

Zaitchik, D., Iqbal, Y., & Carey, S. (2014). The effect of executive function on biological reasoning in young children: An individual differences study. *Child Development*, *85*(1), 160–175. https://doi.org/10.1111/cdev.12145

Zajac, L., Bookhout, M. K., Hubbard, J. A., Carlson, E. A., & Dozier, M. (2020). Attachment disorganization in infancy: A developmental precursor to maladaptive social information processing at age 8. *Child Development*, *91*(1), 145–162. https://doi.org/10.1111/cdev.13140

Zajączkowska, M., & Abbot-Smith, K. (2020). "Sure I'll help—I've just been sitting around doing nothing at school all day": Cognitive flexibility and child irony interpretation. *Journal of Experimental Child Psychology*, *199*, 104942. https://doi.org/10.1016/j.jecp.2020.104942

Zambrano, P. L., Perez-Brena, N. J., Duncan, J. C., Bishop, N. J., Toews, M. L., & Barnett, M. A. (2023). Mother-father and parent-grandmother coparenting conflict and caregiver involvement in adolescent parent families. *Journal of Social and Personal Relationships*, *41*(6), 1370–1392. https://doi.org/10.1177/02654075231221832

Zammit, M., & Atkinson, S. (2017). The relations between 'babysigning', child vocabulary and maternal mind-mindedness. *Early Child Development and Care*, *187*(12), 1887–1895. https://doi.org/10.1080/03004430.2016.1193502

Zanobetti, A., Ryan, P. H., Coull, B., Brokamp, C., Datta, S., Blossom, J., Lothrop, N., Miller, R. L., Beamer, P. I., Visness, C. M., Andrews, H., Bacharier, L. B., Hartert, T., Johnson, C. C., Ownby, D., Hershey, G. K. K., Joseph, C., Yiqiang, S., Mendonça, E. A., & &#hillip1; Liu, Z. (2022). Childhood asthma incidence, early and persistent wheeze, and neighborhood socioeconomic factors in the ECHO/CREW Consortium. *JAMA Pediatrics*, *176*(8), 759–767. https://doi.org/10.1001/jamapediatrics.2022.1446

Zee, M., Rudasill, K. M., & Bosman, R. J. (2021). A cross-lagged study of students' motivation, academic achievement, and relationships with teachers from kindergarten to 6th grade. *Journal of Educational Psychology*, *113*, 1208–1226. https://doi.org/10.1037/edu0000574

Zelazo, N. A., Zelazo, P. R. D. R., Cohen, K. M., & Zelazo, P. D. (1993). Specificity of practice effects on elementary neuromotor patterns. *Developmental Psychology*, *29*(4), 686–691. https://doi.org/10.1037/0012-1649.29.4.686

Zelazo, P. D., Reznick, J. S., & Spinazzola, J. (1998). Representational flexibility and response control in a multistep, multilocation search task. *Developmental Psychology*, *34*(2), 203–214. https://doi.org/10.1037/0012-1649.34.2.203

Zelazo, P. R. (1983). The development of walking: New findings on old assumptions. *Journal of Motor Behavior*, *2*, 99–137. https://doi.org/10.1080/00222895.1983.10735292

Zelekha, Y., & Yaakobi, E. (2020). Intergenerational attachment orientations: Gender differences and environmental contribution. *PLoS ONE*, *15*(7), e0233906. https://doi.org/10.1371/journal.pone.0233906

Zell, E., Strickhouser, J. E., Sedikides, C., & Alicke, M. D. (2019). The better-than-average effect in comparative self-evaluation: A comprehensive review and meta-analysis. *Psychological Bulletin*, *146*(2), 118–149. https://doi.org/10.1037/BUL0000218

Zeman, J., Cassano, M., & Adrian, M. C. (2013). Socialization influences on children's and adolescents' emotional self-regulation processes. In K. C. Barrett, N. A. Fox, G. A. Morgan, & D. J. Fidler (Eds.), *Handbook of self-regulatory processes in development* (pp. 79–107). Psychology Press. https://doi.org/10.4324/9780203080719.ch5

Zeman, J., & Garber, J. (1996). Display rules for anger, sadness, and pain: It depends on who is watching. *Child Development*, *67*(3), 957–973. https://doi.org/10.1111/j.1467-8624.1996.tb01776.x

Zemp, M., & Bodenmann, G. (2018). Family structure and the nature of couple relationships: Relationship distress, separation, divorce, and repartnering. In M. R. Sanders & A. Morawska (Eds.), *Handbook of parenting and child development across the lifespan* (pp. 415–440). Springer International. https://doi.org/10.1007/978-3-319-94598-9_18

Zettersten, M., & Saffran, J. R. (2021). Sampling to learn words: Adults and children sample words that reduce referential ambiguity. *Developmental Science*, *24*(3), e13064. https://doi.org/10.1111/DESC.13064

Zettl, M., Akin, Z., Back, S., Taubner, S., Goth, K., Zehetmair, C., Nikendei, C., & Bertsch, K. (2022). Identity development and maladaptive personality traits in young refugees and first- and second-generation migrants. *Frontiers in Psychiatry*, *12*, 798152. https://www.frontiersin.org/articles/10.3389/fpsyt.2021.798152

Zgodic, A., McLain, A. C., Eberth, J. M., Federico, A., Bradshaw, J., & Flory, K. (2023). County-level prevalence estimates of ADHD in children in the United States. *Annals of Epidemiology*, *79*, 56–64. https://doi.org/10.1016/j.annepidem.2023.01.006

Zhai, S., Liang, Y., Lu, C., & He, J. (2024). Influence of parenting styles on children's development of externalizing behaviors: The role of resting respiratory sinus arrhythmia. *International Journal of Behavioral Development*, *48*(2), 156–165. https://doi.org/10.1177/01650254231222434

Zhang, F., & Emberson, L. L. (2020). Using pupillometry to investigate predictive processes in infancy. *Infancy, 25*(6), 758–780. https://doi.org/10.1111/infa.12358

Zhang, F., Gervain, J., & Roeyers, H. (2022). Developmental changes in the brain response to speech during the first year of life: A near-infrared spectroscopy study of Dutch-learning infants. *Infant Behavior and Development, 67*, 101724. https://doi.org/10.1016/j.infbeh.2022.101724

Zhang, F., & Roeyers, H. (2019). Exploring brain functions in autism spectrum disorder: A systematic review on functional near-infrared spectroscopy (fNIRS) studies. *International Journal of Psychophysiology, 137*, 41–53. https://doi.org/10.1016/j.ijpsycho.2019.01.003

Zhang, Q., Goodman, M., Adams, N., Corneil, T., Hashemi, L., Kreukels, B., Motmans, J., Snyder, R., & Coleman, E. (2020). Epidemiological considerations in transgender health: A systematic review with focus on higher quality data. *International Journal of Transgender Health, 21*(2), 125–137. https://doi.org/10.1080/26895269.2020.1753136

Zhang, V. H., Elmlinger, S. L., & Goldstein, M. H. (2024). Developmental cascades of vocal turn-taking connect prelinguistic vocalizing with early language. *Infant Behavior and Development, 75*, 101945. https://doi.org/10.1016/j.infbeh.2024.101945

Zhang, W., & Wang, Z. (2023). Parenting styles and adolescents' problem behaviors: The mediating effect of adolescents' self-control. *Psychological Reports, 126*(6), 2979–2999. https://doi.org/10.1177/00332941221105216

Zhang, X., Liu, X., Xi, Q., Zhu, H., Li, L., Liu, R., Yu, Y., & Pang, M. G. (2020). Reproductive outcomes of 3 infertile males with XYY syndrome: Retrospective case series and literature review. *Medicine, 99*(9). https://doi.org/10.1097/MD.0000000000019375

Zhao, T. C., Boorom, O., Kuhl, P. K., & Gordon, R. (2021). Infants' neural speech discrimination predicts individual differences in grammar ability at 6 years of age and their risk of developing speech-language disorders. *Developmental Cognitive Neuroscience, 48*, 100949. https://doi.org/10.1016/j.dcn.2021.100949

Zhao, W., Li, B., Shanks, D. R., Zhao, W., Zheng, J., Hu, X., Su, N., Fan, T., Yin, Y., Luo, L., & Yang, C. (2022). When judging what you know changes what you really know: Soliciting metamemory judgments reactively enhances children's learning. *Child Development, 93*(2), 405–417. https://doi.org/10.1111/cdev.13689

Zhao, X., & Kushnir, T. (2019). How U.S. and Chinese children talk about personal, moral and conventional choices. *Cognitive Development, 52*, 100804. https://doi.org/10.1016/j.cogdev.2019.100804

Zielinski, R., Ackerson, K., & Kane Low, L. (2015). Planned home birth: Benefits, risks, and opportunities. *International Journal of Women's Health, 7*, 361–377. https://doi.org/10.2147/IJWH.S55561

Zigler, E., & Styfco, S. J. (2004). Moving Head Start to the states: One experiment too many. *Applied Developmental Science, 8*(1), 51–55. http://dx.doi.org/10.1207/S1532480XADS0801_7

Zill, N. (2015). *The paradox of adoption*. Institute for Family Studies. https://ifstudies.org/blog/the-paradox-of-adoption/

Zimlich, R. (2019). LGBT teens and suicide risk: How you can help. *Contemporary Pediatrics, 36*(3). https://www.contemporarypediatrics.com/view/lgbt-teens-and-suicide-risk-how-you-can-help

Zimmer, M., & Desch, L. (2012). Sensory integration therapies for children with developmental and behavioral disorders. *Pediatrics, 129*(6), 1186–1189. https://doi.org/10.1542/PEDS.2012-087

Zimmer-Gembeck, M. J., & Skinner, E. A. (2016). The development of coping: Implications for psychopathology and resilience. In D. Cicchetti (Ed.), *Developmental psychopathology* (pp. 1–61). John Wiley & Sons. https://doi.org/10.1002/9781119125556.devpsy410

Zimmer-Gembeck, M. J., Webb, H. J., Farrell, L. J., & Waters, A. M. (2018). Girls' and boys' trajectories of appearance anxiety from age 10 to 15 years are associated with earlier maturation and appearance-related teasing. *Development and Psychopathology, 30*(01), 337–350. https://doi.org/10.1017/S0954579417000657

Zimmer-Gembeck, M. J., Webb, H. J., Pepping, C. A., Swan, K., Merlo, O., Skinner, E. A., Avdagic, E., & Dunbar, M. (2017). Is parent-child attachment a correlate of children's emotion regulation and coping? *International Journal of Behavioral Development, 41*(1), 74–93. https://doi.org/10.1177/0165025415618276

Ziporyn, T. D., Owens, J. A., Wahlstrom, K. L., Wolfson, A. R., Troxel, W. M., Saletin, J. M., Rubens, S. L., Pelayo, R., Payne, P. A., Hale, L., Keller, I., & Carskadon, M. A. (2022). Adolescent sleep health and school start times: Setting the research agenda for California and beyond. A research summit summary. *Sleep Health, 8*(1). https://doi.org/10.1016/j.sleh.2021.10.008

ZipRecruiter. (2023, (2023, March). *Salary: Postpartum doula. United States*. ZipRecruiter. https://www.ziprecruiter.com/Salaries/Postpartum-Doula-Salary

Zondervan-Zwijnenburg, M., Dobbelaar, S., van der Meulen, M., & Achterberg, M. (2022). Longitudinal associations between prosocial behavior and behavioral problems across childhood: A robust random-intercept cross-lagged panel model. *Developmental Psychology, 58*, 1139–1155. https://doi.org/10.1037/dev0001346

Zosh, J. M., Brinster, M., & Halberda, J. (2013). Optimal contrast: Competition between two referents improves word learning. *Applied Developmental Science, 17*(1), 20–28. https://doi.org/10.1080/10888691.2013.748420

Zosuls, K. M., Andrews, N. C. Z., Martin, C. L., England, D. E., & Field, R. D. (2016). Developmental changes in the link between gender typicality and peer victimization and exclusion. *Sex Roles, 75*(5–6), 243–256. https://doi.org/10.1007/s11199-016-0608-z

Zosuls, K. M., Ruble, D. N., Tamis-LeMonda, C. S., Shrout, P. E., Bornstein, M. H., & Greulich, F. K. (2009). The acquisition of gender labels in infancy: Implications for gender-typed play. *Developmental Psychology, 45*(3), 688–701. https://doi.org/10.1037/a0014053

Zsiga, E. C. (2024). *The sounds of language: An introduction to phonetics and phonology* (2nd ed.). John Wiley & Sons.

Zucker, K. J. (2017). Epidemiology of gender dysphoria and transgender identity. *Sexual Health, 14*(5), 404–411. https://doi.org/10.1071/SH17067

Zufferey, S. (2020). 2. Pragmatic development in a first language: An overview. In *2. Pragmatic development in a first language: An overview* (pp. 33–60). De Gruyter Mouton. https://doi.org/10.1515/9783110431056-002

Zuk, J., Yu, X., Sanfilippo, J., Figuccio, M. J., Dunstan, J., Carruthers, C., Sideridis, G., Turesky, T. K., Gagoski, B., Grant, P. E., & Gaab, N. (2021). White matter in infancy is prospectively associated with language outcomes in kindergarten. *Developmental Cognitive Neuroscience, 50*, 100973. https://doi.org/10.1016/j.dcn.2021.100973

Zwir, I., Arned., J., Del-Val, C., Pulkki-Råback, L., Konte, B., Yang, S. S., Romero-Zaliz, R., Hintsanen, M., Cloninger, K.

M., Garcia, D., Svrakic, D. M., Rozsa, S., Martinez, M., Lyytikäinen, L.-P., Giegling, I., Kähönen, M., Hernandez-Cuervo, H., Seppälä, I., Raitoharju, E., & &#hillip1; Cloninger, C. R. (2020). Uncovering the complex genetics of human temperament. *Molecular Psychiatry*, *25*(10), 2275–2294. https://doi.org/10.1038/s41380-018-0264-5

Zych, I., Farrington, D. P., Llorent, V. J., & Ttofi, M. M. (2017). *Protecting children against bullying and its consequences*. Springer International. https://doi.org/10.1007/978-3-319-53028-4

Zycha, I., Ortega-Ruiza, R., & Del Rey, R. (2015). Systematic review of theoretical studies on bullying and cyberbullying: Facts, knowledge, prevention, and intervention. *Aggression and Violent Behavior*, *23*, 1–21. https://doi.org/10.1016/j.avb.2015.10.001

AUTHOR INDEX

A

Aaronson, D., 272
Abacan, M. A., 54
Abate, A., 311
Abbot-Smith, K., 271
Abbott, R., 111
Aboud, F. E., 332
Abraham, L. M., 276
Abramowicz, J. S., 57
Abrego, L. J., 425
Acar, E., 152
Achterberg, M., 355
Acker, J., 147
Ackerman, D. J., 442
Ackermann, L., 267
Acredolo, L. P., 265
Adames, H. Y., 425
Adashi, E. Y., 55
Addabbo, M., 292
Adebowale, T. A., 326
Aderibigbe, O., 139
Adolph, K. E., 20, 63, 115–116, 121–123, 127–128, 130–131, 179, 293–294, 299
Aertsen, M., 58
Afful, J., 154
Affuso, G., 340
Afshordi, N., 436
Ager, A., 457
Aggarwal, S., 366
Agnew-Blais, J. C., 210
Agorastos, A., 454
Agrawal, A., 80
Aguiar, N. R., 434
Ahmad, F. B., 93
Ahmad, M. A., 59
Ahmed, A., 181
Ahn, R. R., 250
Aikins, D., 424
Aikins, J. W., 424
Ainsworth, M. D. S., 310–311
Akhtar, F., 51, 85
Akhtar, S., 217
Akinbami, L. J., 154
Akolekar, R., 57–58
Aksglaede, L., 148
al'Absi, M., 454
Alanis, I., 332
Alarcon-Rubio, D., 198
Alberry, M. S., 58
Alberts, A., 195
Aldao, A., 375
Alderson-Day, B., 198
Alexander, K., 152
Alfalahi, M., 159
Alfonso, V. C., 242
Ali, N., 411
Ali-Saleh Darawshy, N., 456
Alisic, E., 23
Allen, K., 214, 387
Allen, L. R., 214, 387
Allen, S. E. M., 271
Alley, K. M., 448
Almeida, J., 94
Al-Namlah, A. S., 198
Alvarenga, P., 277, 279
Alvarez, C., 245, 325
Alves, S. G., 377
Al-Yagon, M., 456
Amato, P. R., 420
Ambrose, D., 253
Amir, D., 8
Amodia-Bidakowska, A., 312
Amor, H., 86
Ampaabeng, S. K., 140
Amso, D., 208, 216
Amunts, K., 291
Anaele, B. I., 426
Anderson, D. I., 115
Anderson, D. M., 160
Anderson, M., 444, 452
Anderson, N. J., 268
Anderson, S., 442
Anderson, V. A., 111
Anderson-Yockel, J., 279
Andersson, U., 221
Andescavage, N. N., 76
Andrews, G., 16
Andrews, J. L., 227, 356, 363
Andrews, K., 215
Andruski, J. E., 262
Angley, M., 393
Ansari, D., 182
Antheunis, M. L., 452
Anthony, C. J., 420
Antonarakis, S. E., 51
Antonoplis, S., 245
Antshel, K. M., 210
Apfelbaum, E. P., 333
Apgar, V., 93
Arabiat, D., 444
Arakelyan, S., 457
Aral, T., 334
Aram, D., 295
Arbeau, K. A., 432–433
Archer, L., 340
Ardila, A., 226–227
Arditi, B., 97
Arditi-Babchuk, H., 97
Arditti, J. A., 424, 457
Argabright, S. T., 147
Ari-Even Roth, D., 108
Armah, A., 434–435
Armstrong-Carter, E., 48, 63, 65
Armstrong-Heimsoth, A., 455
Arnett, J. J., 296, 327
Arnold, C. K., 406
Arnold, S. H., 332
Aronson, J., 246
Arseneault, L., 361–362
Arterberry, M. E., 128, 223
Arthur, A. E., 377
Artman, L., 190
Asarnow, J. R., 163, 457
Asch, A., 56
Asher, S. R., 437–438
Ashman, S. B., 305
Ashmead, D. H., 128
Ask, H., 60
Aslaner, D. M., 80
Aslin, R. N., 125
Asperholm, M., 374
Assink, M., 155
Astington, J. W., 224, 271
Astley Hemingway, S. J., 78
Ati, N. A. L., 162
Atkins, D. N., 82
Atkinson, A. L., 213
Atkinson, R. C., 205
Atkinson, S., 265
Atske, S., 452
Attanucci, J., 350
Aubrey, J. S., 380
Augustine, M., 297–300
Austin, A. E., 82, 156
Avagliano, L., 84
Avalos, L. A., 87
Aviles, A. I., 426
Axelsson, E., 263
Axelsson, J., 86
Ayers, S., 312
Aytuglu, H. A., 313
Azagba, S., 80
Azmitia, M., 32
Azpiazu Izaguirre, L., 302
Azuine, R. E., 81

B

Baams, L., 148, 391
Babore, A., 327
Baccassino, F., 253
Bachman, J. G., 160, 325
Backes, C. H., 76
Backschneider, A. G., 187
Bacso, S. A., 194
Baddeley, A., 205–206, 221
Badihian, N., 85
Badry, D., 454
Baer, R. J., 87
Baert, S., 420
Bagci, S. C., 436
Baglivio, M. T., 363
Bagni, C., 51
Bagwell, C. L., 437

Bai, S., 404
Baiao, R., 65
Baiden, P., 455
Bailen, N. H., 296
Bailey, B. A., 81
Bailey, M. J., 443
Baillargeon, R., 179–180
Bajanowski, T., 151
Baker, J. M., 52
Baker, S., 297–298
Bakermans-Kranenburg, M. J., 65, 312
Balakrishnan, A., 323
Balas, B. J., 583
Balenzano, C., 421
Ball, C. L., 351
Ball, H. L., 142
Ball, J. W., 139
Baltes, P. B., 7, 404
Balyasnikova, N., 196, 199
Balzer, B. W. R., 296
Ban, S., 79
Bandoli, G., 77
Bandura, A., 14–15, 378, 380
Banerjee, M., 224
Banneyer, K. N., 425
Banny, A., 155
Banse, R., 384
Banuazizi, A., 358–359
Banyai, F., 452
Barac, R., 272
Barbosa-Mendez, S., 81
Barbot, B., 30
Bard, K. A., 321
Barel, E., 374
Barendse, M. E. A., 148
Bargh, J. A., 11
Barnard-Brak, L., 253
Barnes, C., 222–223
Barnes, J., 312
Barnett, A. P., 391
Barnett, E. R., 82
Barnett, L. M., 117
Barnett, S. M., 237
Barone, L., 422
Barr, R., 182, 217, 298, 449
Barrett, K. C., 337
Barrow, B. H., 365
Barry, C. -J. S., 60
Barry, C. M., 365
Barry, C. T., 326
Barry, E. S., 142
Bartram, S. C., 93
Bassano, D., 277
Bastaits, K., 420
Basten, U., 235
Bater, L. R., 210
Bates, E., 264, 322
Bates, J. E., 303
Bateson, P., 20
Bathelt, J., 235
Batini, F., 295
Baudat, S., 416
Baudry, C., 393
Bauer, P. J., 217–219
Bauer, T., 126
Baumeister, R. F., 326

Baumrind, D., 409–412
Baus, C., 272
Bax, A. C., 252–253
Bayet, L., 126
Bayley, N., 240–241
Bayram Ozdemir, S., 148
Bazinet, A. D., 81
Beal, M. A., 86
Beatty, W. W., 376
Beauchamp, G. K., 129
Beaujean, A. A., 242
Beauregard, J. L., 139
Becerra-Culqui, T. A., 387
Becht, A. I., 328
Beebe, B., 291, 311
Beelmann, A., 362
Begun, A. L., 351
Behne, D., 277
Behrend, D. A., 267
Behrens, K. Y., 311
Beier, J. S., 356
Beitsch, R., 56
Belanger, S., 443
Belcher, B. R., 149
Bell, M. A., 181–182, 294, 299
Bellingtier, J. A., 299
Bellows, L. L., 117
Belsky, J., 147
Beltran-Sanchez, H., 80
Bem, S. L., 377–378, 382
Bender, K., 455
Bendezu, J. J., 416
Beneke, M. R., 332
Benga, O., 519
Benigno, J. P., 198
Benitez-Burraco, A., 275
Benner, A. D., 427, 447
Benson, J. E., 224
Benson, P. L., 364
Berardi, N., 109
Berčnik, S., 443
Berenbaum, S. A., 144, 376
Bergelson, E., 258, 262–263, 278
Berger, L. M., 155
Berger, S. E., 123
Berger, T., 145
Berk, L. E., 198, 432
Berkowitz, M. W., 351
Bernanke, J., 210
Bernard, K., 311
Bernard, S., 225
Bernecker, K., 338
Bernier, A., 110
Berninger, V. W., 250
Bernstein, B., 79
Bernstein, D. M., 224
Bertenthal, B. I., 127
Berument, S. K., 304
Berwick, R. C., 274–275
Best, D. L., 312, 372
Best, P., 452
Best, R. M., 270
Betancourt, L. M., 214
Beteleva, T. G., 213
Bethlehem, R. a. I., 114
Beuriat, P. A., 119

Beyens, I., 406
Bhatia, N., 373
Bhatia, S., 373
Bhatt, R. S., 217
Bhattacharya, N., 387
Białecka-Pikul, M., 225
Bialik, K., 408
Bialystok, E., 269, 272
Bian, L., 377
Bianchi, E., 72
Bibbins-Domingo, K., 84
Bibonas, D., 376
Bick, J., 109
Biddle, S. J. H., 142, 149
Bierman, K. L., 438
Bigelow, A. E., 321
Bigler, R. S., 381
Birch, S. A. J., 224
Bird, R. J., 52
Birkeland, M. S., 327, 455
Birkinshaw, S., 366
Birner, B. J., 260
Birney, D. P., 16, 194
Biro, F. M., 146
Biro, S., 293
Bisiacchi, P., 108
Bitsko, R. H., 248
Bjorklund, D. F., 8, 20, 182, 205–206, 213, 220, 243, 292
Black, B. M., 350
Black, L. I., 247, 252
Black, S. E., 81
Blackburn, J., 151
Blair, C., 454
Blake, A. J., 57, 421
Blake, M. J., 149
Blakeney, E. L., 87
Blakeslee, J. E., 455
Blanche, S., 84
Blandon, A. Y., 438
Blankenship, T. L., 208
Blaser, E., 212
Blasi, C. H., 20
Blass, E. M., 99
Blau, N., 49
Bleah, D. A., 298
Blehar, M. C., 476
Bloch, H., 117
Block, J., 386
Bloomfield, F. H., 129
Blumberg, M. S., 96
Blumenthal, H., 423
Boateng, T., 79
Bockenholt, U., 29
Bodenmann, G., 420–421
Bodrova, E., 198
Bogaerts, A., 331
Bogan, E., 427
Bogartz, R. S., 180
Boggess, T., 81
Boguszewski, M. C. S., 138
Bohannon, J. N., 276
Bohman, A., 436
Bokhari, S. R. A., 51
Bokor, B. R., 144–146
Boldt, L. J., 313, 315

Bond, M. A., 363
Bondi, D., 117
Bonifacio, J. H., 388
Bonomi, M., 52
Boom, J. J., 349–350
Boonk, L., 447
Boonzaaijer, M., 119
Booth, J. M., 363
Booth, M. Z., 444, 447
Booth-LaForce, C., 313
Bordogna, A. L., 393
Borges, E., 86
Borghi, A. M., 198
Borich, G. D., 442
Bornstein, M. H., 9, 98, 128, 223, 235, 241, 262, 277, 292, 293, 298, 299, 304, 307, 308, 410, 414
Bos, H. M. W., 417
Bosch-Bayard, J., 106, 140
Boseovski, J. J., 324
Bostwick, K. C. P., 339
Boterberg, S., 251
Botto, S. V., 322
Bouchard, D., 274
Boundy, E. O., 94
Boutakidis, I. P., 335
Boutwell, B. B., 436
Bowen, M., 404
Bower, B., 223
Bowker, J. C., 437, 438
Bowlby, J., 20, 307, 316
Boyatzis, C. J., 365
Boysson-Bardies, B. D., 262
Bradshaw, D., 424
Brajša-Žganec, A., 405
Bralten, J., 60
Branco, S. F., 422
Brand, R. J., 293
Brandel, M., 405
Brandes, N., 65
Brandl, J. L., 321
Brandt, J. S., 86
Branje, S., 328–331, 365, 384, 415
Braun, M., 86
Braun, S. S., 383
Braungart-Rieker, J. M., 291
Braveman, P. A., 94
Bravo, A., 436
Brazelton, T. B., 92
Brazzelli, E., 259
Brechwald, W. A., 441
Breiner, K., 227
Bremner, J. G., 182
Bretas, R. V., 275
Bretherton, I., 310, 316
Breton, C. V., 66
Breuer, J., 451
Breuner, C. C., 394
Brickell, T. A., 424
Briley, D. A., 62–63, 65
Brinums, M., 226
Brittian, A. S., 337
Brix, N., 147
Brocklehurst, P., 92
Broderick, A. V., 419
Brodie, N., 83, 457

Brodzinsky, D., 57, 422
Broesch, T., 276, 298, 321
Bronfenbrenner, U., 17, 18
Brooker, R., 45, 293
Brooks, R., 293
Brooks, S. J., 149
Brooks-Gunn, J., 146, 279
Brown, A., 32, 57, 421
Brown, C. S., 147, 313, 373, 379
Brown, C., 30
Brown, D. A., 220
Brown, G. L., 147, 312, 313, 373, 379
Brown, H. R., 32, 421
Brown, S. L., 220, 420
Brownell, C. A., 356
Brugman, D., 350–351
Brummelman, E., 324–325, 340–341, 360
Bruns, A., 424
Bryant, B. R., 250
Bryant, G. A., 276
Bubac, C. M., 60
Bucci, R., 148
Buhler, J. L., 7
Buhler-Wassmann, A. C., 299
Bui, L., 157
Buist, K. L., 315–316, 406
Bull, M. J., 51
Bullo, A., 361
Bullock, A., 321
Bullock, M., 321
Burack, J. A., 252
Burchinal, M., 447
Burden, P. R., 442, 448
Burgdorf, J., 434
Burger, C., 362
Burkhardt, J., 451
Burkhardt-Reed, M. M., 265
Burkitt, E., 111
Burnell, K., 405
Burns, E. C., 448
Burroughs, N., 444
Burrus, B. B., 392
Burson, E., 33
Burton, L. M., 416
Busch, A. S., 145–147
Busching, R., 357
Bushman, B. J., 451
Busnelli, A., 46
Buss, A. H., 302
Bussey, K., 378, 380
Bustamante, A. S., 443
Butler, G., 52
Butler, M. G., 48
Butterworth, G. E., 223
Butts, S. F., 54
Butwick, A. J., 91
Byers-Heinlein, K., 266, 276
Bygdell, M., 147
Byrd, A. L., 65, 65, 336
Byrd, C. M., 336
Byrd, D. M., 442, 448
Byrnes, J. P., 374

C

Cabral, M. D. I., 210

Cabrera, C., 155
Cabrera, L., 128
Cabrera, N. J., 312–313
Caceres, V., 54
Cafiero, R., 112
Cahan, S., 190
Cai, Y., 54
Cain, M. S., 211
Cainelli, E., 108
Caldas, S. J., 142
Calkins, S. D., 291, 379
Callaghan, T., 224
Calvert, S. L., 450
Calzo, J. P., 391
Camacho, A., 360–361
Cameron, C. E., 118, 302
Cameron-Faulkner, T., 265
Camerota, M., 95
Camos, V., 221
Campbell, C. E., 113
Campbell, F. A., 113, 443
Campbell, K., 159
Campione-Barr, N., 407
Camras, L. A., 292, 294
Camur, Z., 129
Cancian, M., 418
Candy, T. R., 125
Canevello, A., 377
Canning, E. A., 339
Cantlon, J. F., 182
Cao, H., 159, 420
Caporaso, J. S., 214
Cappello, S., 105
Capron, L., 86
Caputo, J., 405
Card, N. A., 437
Carey, A. L., 23
Carey, S., 179
Carlberg, C., 66
Carlo, G., 349, 355–356
Carlson, B. M., 73–77
Carlson, D. L., 392
Carlson, L., 423
Carlson, S. M., 186, 221
Carlsson, J., 331
Carmody, D. P., 322
Carone, N., 56
Carpendale, J. I. M., 226, 356
Carr, R. C., 443
Carreiras, M., 266
Carroll, J. B., 235
Carroll, J. J., 82
Carroll, S. L., 363
Carson, A. S., 358
Carson, S. A., 54
Carswell, C. M., 16, 204, 206
Carter, C. S., 356
Carter, C., 433
Carter, R., 148
Carthew, R. W., 62
Caruso, D. R., 238
Carvalho, M., 360
Carver, K., 383
Casale, D., 140
Case, R., 190
Casey, B. J., 227

Casey, K., 380
Cashon, C. H., 223
Caspi, A., 65
Cassano, M., 300
Cassiano, R. G. M., 304
Cassibba, R., 314
Cassidy, J., 312, 353
Castaldi, E., 250
Castner, J., 422
Castro, D. C., 272
Castro, V. L., 295
Cattelan, S., 72
Cauce, A. M., 413
Cauffman, E., 227
Cautilli, J., 99, 120, 125
Cavanagh, S. E., 419
Cavas, B., 237
Cavas, P., 237
Ceballo, R., 455
Cebioğlu, S., 321
Ceci, S. J., 221
Cecil, C. A. M., 155
Cederbaum, J. A., 393
Celeghin, A., 291
Cetincelik, M., 263
Chad-Friedman, E., 110, 410
Chaibal, S., 119
Chakravorty, S., 48
Challamel, M.-J., 294
Chambers, A. M., 142
Chambers, C. D., 77
Chan, A., 437
Chan, K. J., 388
Chan, S. Y., 110
Chan, W., 58
Chandler, M. J., 226
Chandra Handa, M., 254
Chang, C.-Y., 436
Chang, D. S., 81
Chang, S. M., 94
Chang, Y.-S., 250
Chao, R. K., 352, 414
Chaplin, T. M., 375
Chapman, H. J., 425
Charles, E., 93
Charness, M. E., 78
Chasan-Taber, L., 89
Chatkin, J., 153
Chattopadhyaya, B., 111
Chatziparasidis, G., 153
Chauhan, S., 444
Chavajay, P., 196, 220
Chavez, D. V., 357
Chavez-Duenas, N. Y., 425
Chavira, V., 334
Chemin, A., 118
Chen, C., 266
Chen, D. R., 154
Chen, D., 388
Chen, E., 153
Chen, F. R., 148
Chen, K.-L., 271
Chen, L.-W., 92
Chen, S. H., 272
Chen, W. Y., 304, 306, 456
Chen, X., 326, 408, 413

Chen, Y., 151, 235
Cheng, C., 213
Cheng, S., 361
Cheng, W., 143, 249
Cheng, Z. H., 159
Chervonsky, E., 301
Chess, S., 302–304
Chester, M., 295
Cheung, H. S., 437
Cheung, P., 182
Chevalier, N., 107
Chiang, K. V., 138
Chiang, S.-C., 404
Chiari, C., 347, 349
Chilaka, V. N., 84
Chiocca, E. M., 412
Chladkova, K., 261
Chmait, R. H., 84
Choe, D. E., 413, 449
Choi, J. K., 162
Choi, J., 123, 139
Choi, S., 277
Chokron, S., 128
Chomsky, N., 274–275
Chong, I., 130
Chou, B., 75
Chow, J. C., 270
Christ, S. E., 49
Christensen, K. J., 355
Christensen, K., 64
Christiansen, M. H., 275
Christodoulou, J., 182
Chronis-Tuscano, A., 438
Chu, J. T. W., 80
Chun, M. M., 180
Chung, A., 154
Chung, P. J., 250
Cicchetti, D., 94, 155, 321
Ciciolla, L., 405
Cigala, A., 187
Cillessen, A. H. N., 438
Cimpian, A., 324
Cirulli, F., 86
Cisneros-Franco, J. M., 109–110
Clark, E. V., 270–271
Clark, K. A., 249
Clayborne, Z. M., 85, 161
Clearfield, M. W., 299
Clerkin, E. M., 263
Clifford, A., 127
Cliffordson, C., 246
Coe, J. L., 313
Coelho, V. A., 446–447
Coe-Odess, S. J., 296, 301
Coffey, C., 161
Coffino, J. A., 159
Cohen, A. O., 227
Cohen, A., 211
Cohen, J. R., 236
Cohen, L. B., 223
Cohen-Malayev, M., 448
Cohodes, E. M., 297, 454
Cole, E., 266
Cole, M., 7
Cole, P. M., 300
Cole, W. G., 121, 130–131

Coleman, M., 420–421
Coleman-Jensen, A., 141
Colwell, M. J., 295
Combs-Orme, T., 312
Comunian, A. L., 350
Conejero, A., 209
Conlon, J. L., 78
Connolly, J., 440
Conradt, E., 81, 82, 85
Conte, S., 16, 126
Conway, A. R. A., 235
Cook, R. E., 378, 382
Cooke, J. E., 311, 315
Cooley, J. L., 361, 439
Coome, L. A., 434
Cooper, A. R., 56
Cooper, S. M., 32, 447
Copeland, W. E., 148
Coplan, R. J., 432–433, 438
Corbetta, D., 122, 299
Corby, B. C., 382
Core, C., 269
Cornell, D., 362
Corpus, J. H., 340
Corrigall, K. A., 63
Corrigan, N. M., 275
Corsi, D. J., 81
Cosbey, J., 251
Costa, P. A., 421
Costello, M. A., 437
Cote, S. L., 266
Cottini, M., 222, 226
Coubart, A., 182
Coughlin, C., 219
Coulombe, B. R., 325
Courage, M. L., 208, 216, 218, 321, 449
Covey, J., 80
Covington, L. B., 143
Cowan, N., 212–213, 219, 221
Cox, C. M., 54
Cox, C. R., 276
Coyle, E. F., 380
Coyle, S., 406
Coyle, T. R., 234
Coyne, S. M., 380, 451, 453
Crago, M. B., 271
Craig, W., 360, 440
Crain, W. C., 179
Cramm, H., 424–425
Crane, T., 11–12, 14, 16–17
Crasta, J. E., 251
Crawford, A. D., 81
Crawford, D., 417
Creech, S. K., 425
Crenshaw, K., 32
Crespo, K., 272
Crespo, L. M., 300
Cresswell, L., 393
Crick, N. R., 437
Crissman, H. P., 385
Critz, C., 251
Crocetti, E., 331, 331
Crockenberg, S. C., 297
Crone, E. A., 194, 213–214, 221, 355
Cropper, R., 152
Crosnoe, R., 446

Cross, C. P., 375
Cross, J. R., 440
Crowell, J. A., 297, 299
Csikszentmihalyi, M., 296
Cuartas, J., 156, 414
Cuba Bustinza, C., 361
Cubbin, C., 149
Cuellar, J., 414
Cuevas, K., 181–182, 217, 321
Cui, M., 410
Cummings, E. M., 365, 366
Cunitz, K., 424
Cunningham, C., 94
Curby, T. W., 295
Curenton, S. M., 332
Curley, J. P., 86
Cutuli, J. J., 457–458
Cvencek, D., 323, 326, 377
Cyrus, E., 161

D

D'Esposito, M., 236
d'Oiron, R., 51
D'Souza, H., 122
Dąbrowska, E., 274
Dacre Pool, L., 239
Dadds, M. R., 412
Daehler, M. W., 185
Dagan, O., 312–313, 315
Dagli, A. I., 48
Dahl, A., 127, 346, 351, 353–354, 356–357
Dahl, M., 351
Dai, K., 408
Dailey, S., 258, 278
Dale, N., 128
Dale, P. S., 268
Daley, C. E., 245
Daley, T. C., 244
Dallagiovanna, C., 46
Dalle Grave, R., 159
Damon, W., 354
Daniel, S. K., 301–302
Daniels, H., 17, 196
Daniels, M., 61
Danielson, M. L., 248
Daoud, R., 444
Das, J. K., 144
Dasen, P. R., 191
Dasgupta, N., 323, 375
Dash, G. F., 65
Daspe, M., 440
Datta, S., 159
Davidov, M., 306
Davidson, A. J., 383
Davidson, C., 214
Davidson, R. D., 420
Davies, P., 420
Davinson, K., 217, 321
Davis, J. P., 455
Davis, J. T. M., 378, 391
Davis, P. E., 435
Davis-Kean, P. E., 325, 340
Davy, O., 154
Dawson, G., 305
Dawson, T. L., 349

Day, H. J., 437, 440
Day, J., 86
Day, R. D., 365
De Beritto, T. V., 96–97
de Faria, O., 107, 112
De France, K., 301
De Genna, N., 392
de Haan, B., 424
de Hevia, M. D., 129
De Houwer, A., 266
de Jonge, A., 92
De Lange, J., 162
De Los, Reyes., 416
de Maat, D. A., 454
De Maio, F., 94
de Moor, E. L., 329
de Morais, M. L., 347, 349
de Onis, M., 140–141
De Paepe, M., 46
De Rosnay, M., 294
de Villiers, J. G., 268
de Villiers, P. A., 268
de Vries, E. E., 379
de Vries, R., 185
de Waal, F. B. M., 376
de Wied, M., 330
De Witte, K., 7
Deak, G. O., 187
Deakin, J., 157
Deary, I. J., 234, 245
Deater-Deckard, K., 63
Deaton, A. E., 87
DeBacker, T. K., 341
DeCamp, W., 451
Declercq, E. R., 91
Dediu, D., 275
Deep, N. L., 266
Defoe, I. N., 407
Dehaene-Lambertz, G., 262, 275
Del Rosario, C., 241
Del Toro, J., 337
DeLamater, J., 373
Deleau, Michel., 225
DelGiudice, M., 21
Della Longa, L., 130
Delsing, M. J. M. H., 440
Demars, J., 48
deMayo, B. E., 385
Demissie, Z., 392
Dempsey, J., 456
den Houting, J., 248
Deneault, A.-A., 313
Deneault, J., 189, 301
Denison, S., 183
Denissen, J. J. A., 325
Dennis, M. G., 119
Dennis, T. A., 358
Dennis, W., 119
Deoni, S., 107, 112
Desch, L., 251
Desjardins, T., 415
Devera, J. L., 84
Devine, R. T., 224–225, 406
DeVito, E. E., 80
Devlin, B., 61
DeVoe, E. R., 424

DeVries, R., 347
Dewan, M. C., 84
Di Cesare, M., 153
Di Cristo, G., 111
Di Giorgio, E., 182
Diamond, A., 119
Diamond, L. M., 373, 385
Diaz-Strong, D. X., 425
Dickerson, A., 215
DiClemente, C. M., 455
Dieke, A. C., 55
Diener, M., 92
Dimler, L. M., 148, 410
Dimond, D., 107
Dinehart, L., 118
Ding, G., 153
Dinkel, D., 378
Dismukes, A., 305
Dixson, D. D., 254
Dixson, H. G. W., 225
Do, K. T., 356
Dobbs, A. R., 213
Dodson, J. F., 437
Doebel, S., 212–213
Doenyas, C., 224
Doherty, M. J., 185
Dohla, D., 250
Dolbin-MacNab, M. L., 422
Doley, R., 423
Dollahite, D. C., 365
Dollar, J. M., 291, 379
Domina, T., 445
Dominguez-Folgueras, M., 373
Domitrovich, C. E., 363
Donaldson, S. K., 295
Donaldson, T., 79
Dondi, M., 320
Dong, S., 304–306
Donkelaar, ten. J. H., 84
Donnelly, S., 268
Donovan, T., 125
Doodson, L., 421
Dorn, A. van., 412
dos Santos, J. F., 81, 241
Dotterer, A. M., 447
Doughty, S. E., 407
Douglass, S., 334, 447
Dounavi, K., 249
Dove, H., 120
Dowdall, N., 279
Dowe, K. N., 208
Downey, D. B., 407
Doyle, A. B., 436
Dozier, M., 311
Draganova, R., 96
Drake, B., 424
Drapeau, S., 420
Driscoll, A. K., 86, 150–151
Drollette, E. S., 142
Drozd, F., 57, 421
Drubina, B., 361
Dryburgh, N. S. J., 437
Du, Y., 373
Dubois, J., 111
Duchesne, S., 446
Dudovitz, R. N., 323

Duell, N., 114, 228
Duer, J., 444
Dugre, J. R., 359
Duke, S.-A., 296
Dumontheil, I., 114
Duncan, G. J., 443
Dunn, J., 406, 444
Dunn, K., 181
Dur, Ş., 129
Durante, F., 246
Duriez, B., 365
Durik, A., 91
Durrance, C. P., 82
Durwood, L., 387
Dussias, P. E., 25
Dutton, G. N., 128
Duyme, M., 245
Dweck, C. S., 338–341
Dwyer, P., 248
Dyer, S., 433
Dyer, W. J., 365
Dykstra, V. W., 416
Dys, S. P., 355
Dyson, M. W., 304
Dziewolska, H., 99, 120, 124–125
Dziurgot, T., 197

E

E Ghossainy, M., 187
Eagly, A. H., 373
Eales, L., 426
Easterbrooks, M. A., 293
Eather, N., 142
Ebeh, D. N., 54
Eccles, J. S., 337, 340, 446–448
Eckert-Lind, C., 147
Edelson, S. M., 114, 227
Edmonds, C. J., 93
Edwards, C. P., 435
Efron, D., 112
Egan, S. K., 382, 384
Egbert, A. H., 159
Eggen, P., 16
Egli, D., 55
Ehli, S., 292
Ehrensaft, D., 387
Einspieler, C., 75
Eirich, R., 449
Eisbach, A. O., 224
Eisenberg, N., 299, 300, 353, 355–356, 358
Eisenberg, S. L., 268
Eisner, M. P., 359–360, 450
El Hichami, F., 413
El Mallah, S., 355
Elder, G. H., 7, 9
Elenbaas, L., 32, 355, 436–437
Elhusseini, S., 356
Eliot, L., 375
Elkind, D., 194–195
Ellett, M. L., 298
Ellis, B. J., 457
Ellis, C. T., 208
Ellis, K. J., 138
Ellis, W. E., 439
Ellwood-Lowe, M. E., 279

Else-Quest, N. M., 334, 375
Eltanamly, H., 456
Ely, D. M., 150–151
Emberson, L. L., 180
Eme, R., 363
Emler, N., 351
Emmanuel, M., 144–146
Enge, A., 374
Engel, M. L., 110, 305
Engels, M. C., 448
Engler, A. D., 454
Englund, G., 360
Englund, K., 277
Ennouri, K., 117
Enright, E. A., 386
Enright, R. D., 354
Ensor, R., 224
Erchick, D. J., 87
Erck Lambert, A. B., 151
Erdley, C. A., 437, 440
Erdoğan, C., 129
Ericsson, K. A., 220
Erikson, E. H., 11–12, 327–328
Erol, R. Y., 325–326
Eron, L. D., 450
Ersan, C., 360
Ertekin Pinar, S., 311
Ervin, J., 391
Esakky, P., 86
Eschman, B., 212
Esnaola, I., 323, 325
Esoh, K., 53
Espelage, D. L., 361
Espinoza, G., 447
Esposito, G., 298
Esteban-Cornejo, I., 148
Estes, K. G., 276
Esteve-Gilbert, N., 262
Estrada, S., 455
Etaugh, C., 379
Ethier, K. A., 389
Ettinger, K., 211
Evans, D. W., 25
Evans, G. W., 215
Evans, S. W., 210
Evans-Lacko, S., 362
Eves, R., 93
Eyler, A. A., 142
Eyuboglu, M., 360, 362

F

Fabes, R. A., 433
Fadjukoff, P., 330
Fadus, M. C., 253
Fagan, J. F., 235
Fagard, J., 117
Fallah, H., 79
Fandakova, Y., 111, 226
Fang, K., 154
Fantz, R. L., 124–125
Farago, F., 380
Farber, D. A., 213
Farhi, A., 56
Farooq, M. A., 149, 154
Farr, R. H., 57, 417–418, 421

Farrell, A. D., 357, 441
Farroni, T., 292
Farrow, J., 268
Farruggia, S. P., 454–455
Farver, J. A. M., 455–456
Fast, A. A., 386
Fatollahzade, M., 129
Faur, S., 441
Federico, M. J., 153
Fedewa, A. L., 417
Feeney, B. C., 313, 387
Fehr, K. K., 433–434
Feigenson, L., 183
Feinberg, M. E., 406, 426
Feldman, M. A., 159
Feldman, R., 297–298
Feldstein, S., 484
Felmlee, D., 446
Fen, X., 124–125
Ferguson, C. J., 451
Ferguson, G. M., 323
Ferguson, S., 438
Fergusson, D. M., 65
Ferjan Ramirez, N., 265, 276
Fernald, A., 275, 277–278
Fernandes, D. M., 427
Fernandez-Zabala, A., 323
Fernyhough, C., 198
Ferrara, A. M., 155
Ferrari, V., 146
Ferreira Pinto, R., 264
Ferschmann, L., 356
Feuge, E. A., 313
Field, N. H., 441
Fields-Olivieri, M. A., 291
Figueiredo, B., 142
Filipović, K., 380
Filippello, P., 340
Filippova, E., 271
Finch, J. E., 214
Finegold, D. N., 44, 48
Fink, A., 236
Fink, E., 362
Finkelhor, D., 360
Finn, A. S., 215
Finnell, R. H., 84
Fiorilli, C., 326
Fischer, A., 349
Fischer, U., 118
Fish, J. N., 391
Fish, R. E., 253
Fisher, A., 208
Fisher, P. A., 275
Fisher, S. E., 275
Fiske, A., 213
Fiske, S. T., 246
Fitch, C. A., 419
Fite, P. J., 438–439
Fitneva, S. A., 261, 276
Fitzpatrick, M., 380
Fitzsimmons, P., 191
Fivush, F., 219
Fivush, R., 219
Flaherty, S. C., 393
Flake, A. W., 59
Flanagan, D. P., 242

Flannery, K. M., 194, 437
Flaudias, V., 159
Flavell, J. H., 185, 187, 223–224, 226, 294
Flaxman, A. D., 128
Fletcher, R., 434
Flexer, C. Ann, 266
Flick, L. H., 393
Flieller, A., 193
Flint, J., 48, 64
Floccia, C., 99, 124
Flor, L. S., 373
Floyd, R. G., 243
Floyd, S., 270
Flynn, J. R., 244–245
Fogel, A., 92
Fogel, J., 291
Foli, K. J., 422
Fombouchet, Y., 301
Fomby, P., 419
Fons Van de Vijver, 243
Font, S. A., 155
Fontanellaz-Castiglione, C. E., 149
Foran, H. M., 424–425
Forbringer, L., 445
Forcada-Guex, M., 580
Ford, D. Y., 254
Forestell, C. A., 129
Forsberg, A., 213, 216, 226
Fortea, J., 52
Fortenberry, J. D., 392
Fosco, G. M., 426
Foster, E. M., 139
Fourtassi, A., 274
Fowler-Finn, K. D., 60, 64–65
Fraley, R. C., 307
Franchak, J. M., 63, 116, 123, 130, 299
Franchini, M., 249
Francis, F., 105
Franić, S., 244
Frankenhuis, W. E., 21
Frausel, R., 444
Frawley, T. J., 378
Frederickson, N., 239
Freeman, N., 379
French, D. C., 366, 437
Frenzel, A. C., 301
Frick, A., 85, 211
Friederici, A. D., 274–275
Friedlmeier, W., 300–301, 306
Friedman, J. L., 60, 392, 445
Friedman, J., 60, 445
Friedman, N. P., 60, 445
Friedman-Krauss, A. H., 443–444
Friel, C. P., 149
Frischkorn, G. T., 235
Frodi, A. M., 312
Froggatt, S., 80
Frost, A., 296
Frost, J. L., 434
Fry, C. M., 406
Fryar, C. D., 154
Fryer, K., 87, 139
Fuchs, L. S., 250
Fuemmeler, B. F., 80
Fuentes, R. W. C., 52
Fuertes, M., 94, 311

Fuhrmann, D., 112
Fujiyama, H., 341
Fulcher, M., 380
Fuligni, A. J., 149, 194, 415
Fuller-Thomson, E., 423
Fung, H., 413
Fung, W. kai, 338
Furr, R. M., 234

G

Gabard-Durnam, L. J., 77, 109–110
Gabbard, C., 116, 123
Gabbe, S. G., 91, 92
Gabriel, M. A. M., 139
Gabrielli, J., 450
Gaches, S., 32
Gaffney, H., 362
Gagnon, S. G., 410
Gaillard, A., 375
Gaillard, V., 221
Gakidou, E., 445
Gal, D. E., 356
Galanaki, E., 192, 194
Galatzer-Levy, I. R., 404
Galiana-Simal, A., 250–251
Galkin, F., 87
Gallagher, A. M., 407
Gallagher, A., 187
Gallegos, A., 253
Gallegos, M. L., 88
Galler, J. R., 140
Galliher, R. V., 328, 336
Galloway, J. C., 115, 119
Galvan, A., 149
Gambrell, J. L., 240
Gamez, P. B., 266
Gampe, A., 269
Ganong, L., 420–421
Gao, W., 106
Garber, J., 300
Gardiner, H. W., 92, 190, 306, 314
Gardner, H., 237–238
Gardon, L., 94
Garenne, M., 146
Garfinkel, I., 619
Gariepy, G., 149
Garrido-Miguel, M., 153
Gartrell, N., 417
Gartstein, M. A., 302, 304
Garver, K. A., 444
Gaskins, S., 196, 435
Gasser, U. E., 105
Gassman-Pines, A., 155
Gates, G. J., 385
Gath, M. E., 420
Gaultney, J. F., 98
Gauvain, M., 190, 199
Gavand, K. A., 149
Gawlik, K. S., 161
Gayatri, M., 426
Gaylord-Harden, N. K., 455
Ge, X., 162
Geangu, E., 293
Geary, D. C., 374, 376
Gee, D. G., 112, 297, 454

Geeraert, B. L., 112
Geilhufe, B., 159
Geisser, M. E., 31
Gellman, M. D., 26, 207
Gelman, S. A., 332
Geme, J, St., 137–138, 140
Gentaz, E., 301
Gentile, D. A., 27
Georgas, J., 243
Gerard, J. M., 446–447
Gerber, J. P., 324
Gerdts, J. V., 129
Gerhardt, C., 407
Gerke, D. C., 327
Gerlach, J., 311
Gershoff, E. T., 412
Gerstenberg, A., 260
Gervain, J., 261, 275
Gest, S. D., 440
Gesterling, L., 80
Gettler, L. T., 143, 308, 312
Geurten, M., 226
Geuze, R. H., 125
Ghai, M., 66
Ghassabian, A., 116
Ghavami, N., 32
Ghetti, S., 226
Ghio, M., 96, 128
Ghosh, R., 49, 161
Giangrande, E. J., 244
Giannakopoulos, G., 143
Giardino, A. P., 155
Gibb, R., 16
Gibbs, B. G., 95
Gibbs, J. C., 350
Gibson, E. J., 127, 130
Gibson, J., 130
Giddens, N. T., 143
Giebler, M. A., 214
Giedd, J. N., 112
Gielen, U. P., 350
Giff, S. T., 425
Gigliotti, F., 143
Gill, P., 45–46
Gilligan, C., 350
Gilmore, J. H., 106–107, 111
Gimenez-Dasi, M., 435
Gingras, J. L., 98
Giofre, D., 235
Gioia, K. A., 434
Giordano, K., 295
Girelli, L., 374
Gjersoe, N. L., 187
Glashouwer, K. A., 158
Glass, L., 79
Gleason, T. R., 435
Glenn, C. R., 162
Glenwright, M., 271
Glick, I., 85
Glover, V., 86
Glynn, L. M., 85
Goddings, A.-L., 112, 114
Godfrey, E. B., 33
Godleski, S. A., 359, 375
Goeke-Morey, M. C., 365–366
Goforth, A. N., 415

Golcuk, M., 304
Goldberg, A. E., 270
Goldberg, A., 421
Golden, A. R., 447
Golden, J. C., 380
Goldfarb, E. S., 394
Golding, C., 198
Goldschmidt, L., 350
Goldsmith, H. H., 302
Goldstein, M. A., 362
Goldstein, S. E., 446
Goldstein, T. R., 433
Goleman, D., 238
Golinkoff, R. M., 277–278
Gollub, E. L., 455
Golombok, S., 56, 417–419
Gomez-Roig, M. D., 81
Goncalves, J. L., 311
Goncu, A., 199
Gong, L., 53
Gonzales, R. G., 425
Gonzales-Backen, M. A., 337
Gonzalez, D. C., 86
Good, K., 340
Goodarzi, M. O., 154
Goodman, M. A., 365
Goodman-Scott, E., 250–251
Goodnow, J. J., 190
Goodsell, R., 424
Goodvin, R., 292, 294–295, 299–300, 304–305, 324
Goodwin, G. P., 188
Goodwyn, S. W., 265
Goossens, L., 329
Gopnik, A., 277
Gordon, J. A., 162
Gori, M., 295
Gorry, D., 393
Gorter, J. W., 252
Gosdin, L. K., 79
Gosselin, V., 117
Gottlieb, G., 62
Gottschalk, L., 383
Gottschling, J., 245
Gould, J. F., 241
Gourley, L., 251
Gower, A. L., 360, 392
Gracia, R., 163
Grady, J. S., 295, 305
Graf, M., 53
Graham, N., 247
Graham, S., 326, 360–361, 437, 447
Granat, A., 312
Grande, G., 52
Grandy, C., 81
Granqvist, P., 311, 313, 366
Grant, K. S., 81
Grant, T., 153
Grassetti, S. N., 362
Gravholt, C. H., 52
Gray, C., 187
Gray, K. M., 161
Gredeback, G., 120, 456
Green, A. E., 388
Green, J., 9
Greene, R. M., 80

Greenfield, P. M., 246
Greenwald, A. G., 326
Gregg, A. R., 58
Gregorova, K., 296
Gregory, C. A., 141
Greitemeyer, T., 451
Gremmen, M. C., 341, 440, 447
Grewen, K., 81
Griffith, A. K., 155
Griffiths, A., 443
Grigg-Damberger, M. M., 96–97
Grigorenko, E. L., 237, 249
Grimm, J., 79
Grissom, N. M., 374
Grogan-Kaylor, A., 411
Groh, A. M., 311, 315
Grolleman, J. F., 405
Grosse Wiesmann, C., 224
Grossman, A. H., 162
Grossmann, I., 19
Grossmann, K. E., 314
Grotevant, H. D., 57, 421
Groulx, T., 87
Grover, M. M., 66
Grower, P., 380
Grueneisen, S., 353–354
Gruenenfelder-Steiger, A. E., 327
Grunebaum, A., 84
Gruzieva, O., 153
Grzanka, P. R., 33
Gu, Q., 154
Guan, X., 444
Guassi Moreira, J. F., 301
Gubbels, J., 156
Guellai, B., 449
Guevara, H., 443
Guido, V., 457
Guimond, S., 372
Guldner, S., 149
Gulgoz, S., 382, 386
Guneri, S. E., 147
Gunn, J. K. L., 80
Gunnar, M. R., 110, 305, 454
Gunnerud, H. L., 272
Gunther, V., 80
Guo, G., 374
Guo, L., 408
Guo, M., 456
Guo, Y., 199, 311
Gur, R. E., 214
Guralnick, M. J., 252
Gurley, J. R., 363
Guroğlu, B., 355
Gustafsson, J.-E., 246
Gutierrez, X., 270
Guyer, A. E., 112–114
Gyurkovics, M., 214

H

Habermas, T., 219
Habib, A., 249
Hadders-Algra, M., 126
Haden, C. A., 219
Haden, G. P., 276
Hadley, P. A., 275

Haebig, E., 276
Hage, C., 138
Hagen, C. P., 146
Hagerman, R. J., 51
Haggman-Laitila, A., 455
Hahn-Holbrook, J., 293
Haier, R. J., 235
Haimovitz, K., 339–340
Haines, E. L., 373
Hains, S. M., 96
Hair, N. L., 214
Hajal, N. J., 299
Halberda, J., 263
Halberstadt, A. G., 294, 298
Hale, A. E., 387
Hales, C. M., 154
Halevi, G., 456
Halford, G. S., 16
Halim, M. L. D., 377
Hall, C. M., 438
Hall, G., 296
Hall, R., 386
Hall, S. P., 328, 330
Hall, W. J., 391
Halliday, L., 91
Halliday, S., 362
Halpern, C. T., 383
Halpern, H. P., 386
Ham, M., 296
Hamamura, T., 326
Hamedani, M. G., 17
Hamidullah, S., 114, 160
Hamilton, B. E., 86–87
Hamilton, J. L., 220, 452
Hamilton, M., 220, 452
Hamlat, E. J., 147–148
Hamlin, J. K., 353
Hammond, C. J., 160–161
Hammond, S. I., 356
Han, C., 83
Han, D., 123
Han, G., 161
Han, J., 154
Hanania, R., 210
Handen, B. L., 52
Hanley, J. R., 270
Hans, S. L., 393
Hansen, A., 114
Hansen, J. E., 268
Hansen, M. B., 267
Harden, K. P., 59, 62, 64, 244
Hardie, J. H., 365
Harding, J. F., 334
Hardy, S. A., 366
Harkness, S., 120, 143, 237, 306
Harley, K. G., 80
Harlow, H. F., 307–308
Harper, J. M., 357
Harries, M. D., 389
Harriger, J. A., 159
Harriman, A. E., 119
Harrington, E. M., 301
Harris, K., 84
Harris, M. A., 326–327
Harris, N., 55
Harris, R. A., 85

Harris, W. A., 105
Harrison, D., 129
Harrison, L., 56
Hart, B., 278
Hart, J. R., 411, 415
Hart, S. L., 20, 292
Hartanto, A., 531
Hartley, C. A., 111
Hartley, K., 153
Hartman, S., 85
Hartwig, T. S., 58
Hashmi, M. F., 79
Haslam, D., 414
Hassinger-Das, B., 30
Hastings, P. D., 355–356
Hatchel, T., 387
Hatten, M. E., 105
Hatzis, D., 82
Hauck, J. D., 275
Hauser, M. D., 275
Haviland, J. M., 300
Hawes, D. J., 411
Hawk, L. W., 210
Hawks, S., 293
Hay, D. F., 359–360
Hayek, J., 340
Hayes, S., 80
Hayne, H., 182
Haynes, W. O., 279
Hayslip, B., 422–423
Hazel, C. E., 387
Hazel, W. N., 46
Hazell, P., 112
Hazer, L., 456
He, M., 6, 116
He, Y., 80
Heaman, M. I., 87
Heath, S. B., 245
Heatly, M. C., 340
Heffer, T., 452
Hegde, A., 454
Heilmann, A., 412
Heim, S., 250
Heimann, M., 182
Hein, S., 85
Heine, S. J., 326
Heinrich, J., 153
Helms, J. E., 245
Helms, S. W., 366, 440
Helwig, C. C., 352
Hendriks, S., 59
Hendry, A., 207–208
Hennefield, L., 324
Hennessy, E., 433
Henriques, J., 261
Henry, D. A., 245
Hensch, T. K., 109
Hensums, M., 360, 362
Hepper, P., 75, 96–97
Herati, A. S., 86
Herbert, J. S., 182
Herbert, J., 99
Herculano-Houzel, S., 107
Herd, T., 296, 301
Hernandez, M. M., 335
Hernandez-Pavon, J. C., 128

Hernandez-Reif, M., 332
Heron, A., 191
Herpertz-Dahlmann, B., 159
Herrera-Gomez, A., 91
Herts, J., 246, 374
Herzberg, M. P., 454
Hetherington, E. M., 61
Hevia, M. D. de, 129
Heward, W. L., 445–446
Hewitt, L., 119
Hewlett, B. S., 312
Hewlett, B., 112
Heyes, C., 180
Heynen, E., 351
Hiatt, C., 392, 437, 441
Hiatt, R. A., 147
Hibel, L. C., 299
Hibiya-Motegi, R., 96
Hildebrand, L., 374
Hilger, K., 235
Hill, M. S., 270
Hill, N. E., 334–335
Hillman, C., 142
Hilton, M., 263
Hindman, A. H., 269, 279
Hinduja, S., 361
Hines, C. T., 94, 142, 378
Hines, M., 374, 379
Hirota, T., 248
Hirsch, J. S., 393
Hisle-Gorman, E., 424
Hithersay, R., 52
Hladik, J., 438
Hoch, H. E., 123, 153
Hoch, J. E., 115–116, 121, 123, 128, 179
Hock, A., 292
Hodel, A. S., 109
Hodges, H., 248
Hodges-Simeon, C. R., 145
Hoeben, E. M., 363
Hoehl, S., 311
Hoerr, J. J., 82
Hoeve, M., 410–411
Hofer, C., 415
Hoff, E., 261, 269–270, 272, 275
Hoffman, M. L., 348, 353
Hoffmann, J., 295
Hofkens, T. L., 448
Hofman, D. L., 49
Hofmann, V., 441
Hoggatt, K. J., 89
Hohle, B., 266
Hollenstein, T., 296, 301
Holler, S., 105
Holloway, K., 334
Holmboe, K., 213
Holmes, C., 366
Holz, N. E., 110
Homola, W., 57
Hong, S., 315
Hong, Y. C., 83
Honomichl, R. D., 210
Hood, W., 336
Hopkins, B., 8, 120
Hopkins, S., 391
Hopmeyer, A., 440

Horanyi, D., 85
Horger, M. N., 142
Horn, S. S., 219
Hornberger, L. L., 159
Horne, R. S. C., 152
Hornfeck, F., 57, 421
Horowitz, S. H., 249–250
Horton, C., 386
Horvath, G., 146
Hospodar, C. M., 122–123
Hossain, Z., 312
Houde, O., 189
Houghton, S., 452
Houtrow, A. J., 247
Howard, S. R., 146
Howe, M. L., 216–218
Howe, N., 406
Howell, B. R., 454
Hoyert, D. L., 150
Hoyt, L. T., 148
Hrbackova, K., 438
Hsu, H.-C., 191
Hu, T., 384
Hu, Y., 391
Hua, L. L., 393
Huber, E., 275
Hubert, J. N., 48
Huelke, D. F., 137
Huesmann, L. R., 450, 456
Huey, M., 327, 415
Hughes, A. N., 107
Hughes, C. H., 224–225, 406
Hughes, C., 357
Hughes, D., 333–336
Hughes, J. P., 154
Huguley, J. P., 334
Hui, K., 82
Huijsmans, T., 363, 407
Hull, C., 119
Hull, J. V., 248
Hulme, C., 279
Humphreys, K. L., 109, 457
Hung, C. O.-Y., 271
Hunnius, S., 125
Hunt, C., 301
Huntsinger, C. S., 414
Huppert, E., 358
Hurley, E., 445
Hurley, K., 276
Hurren, B. J., 52
Hurst, J. L., 392
Husky, M. M., 361
Hustedt, J. T., 443
Huston, A. C., 443
Hutaff-Lee, C., 52
Hutchison, J. E., 374
Hutson, E., 362
Huttenlocher, J., 187, 245, 368, 275
Huynh, H. T., 152
Hwang, H. G., 332
Hwang, N. Y., 339
Hyde, D. C., 182
Hyde, J. S., 350
Hyde, J., 373
Hyde, K. L., 111
Hyde, L. W., 110–111

Hymel, S., 360-361
Hysing, M., 362

I

Ibbotson, P., 274
Icenogle, G., 227
Ilmarinen, V.-J., 436
Ilyas, M., 252
Im, D., 54
Imrie, S., 417-419
Imuta, K., 353
Ingersoll, E. W., 99, 125
Ingoglia, S., 416
Inhelder, B., 184, 189, 192
Irawaty, D. K., 426
Iriki, A., 491
Iruka, I. U., 32
Isaacs, E. B., 139
Isaacs, L. D., 8, 97, 116-119, 144
Isen, J., 60
Iskandar, B. J., 84
Islamiah, N., 299
Isojima, T., 52
Issard, C., 128
Ivanenko, A., 143
Iverson, J. M., 6, 116
Iyengar, U., 163
Izard, C. E., 290-291

J

Jackson, D. B., 424
Jackson, E. F., 383-384
Jackson, I. R., 180
Jacobvitz, D., 313
Jacoby, J. W., 380
Jadva, V., 56, 162
Jaeger, E. L., 19
Jaekel, J., 93, 95
Jafari, A., 79
Jaffee, S., 63, 350
Jagers, R. J., 413
Jaggy, A.-K., 433
Jahanfar, S., 54
Jahromi, L. B., 298
Jambon, M., 351
James, J. E., 79
James, M. W., 364
James, W., 222
Jamieson, D. J., 84
Jancke, L., 275
Janicki, D. L., 365
Janusek, L. W., 454
Jaramillo, N., 392
Jarrett, R. L., 416
Jarvis, J. A., 419
Javadi, A. H., 227
Jaxon, J., 246
Jebeile, H., 154
Jeffries Hein, R., 85
Jelenkovic, A., 59, 62
Jenkins, J. M., 139
Jenkins, L. N., 362
Jenkins, L., 259
Jenkins, T. G., 66
Jennings, S., 421

Jensen, A. C., 407
Jensen, M. R., 452
Jenvey, V., 434
Jere-Folotiya, J., 237
Jespersen, K., 331
Jewell, J. A., 384
Jewell, J. D., 410
Jha, A. K., 91, 95
Jhuremalani, A., 377
Jia, G., 272
Jiang, H., 139
Jiang, Q., 407
Jiang, Y., 245
Jiao, C., 410
Jin, M. K., 314
Jing, W., 408
Jipson, J. L., 187
Jirtle, R. L., 66
Job, V., 338
Jobson, L., 219
Johansen, E. R., 393
Johansson, S., 360
Johns, M. M., 385, 387
Johnson, A. D., 443
Johnson, A. Z., 392
Johnson, D., 214
Johnson, E. I., 424, 457
Johnson, K. C., 387
Johnson, K., 378
Johnson, M. L., 10
Johnson, S. P., 295
Johnson-Laird, P. N., 188
Johnston, J. C., 265
Johnston, M., 58
Jones, D. C., 300
Jones, D., 116
Jones, E. J. H., 182
Jones, E. P., 7
Jones, J. D., 316
Jones, J. H., 419
Jones, K. M., 139
Jones, N. F., 365
Jones, T., 58
Jones, W., 249
Jonsson, B., 219
Joo, M., 443
Joo, Y. S., 552
Jordan, J. W., 440
Jordan, N. A., 422
Jordan, P., 332
Jordan, S. S., 210, 450
Joseph, N. T., 84
Joseph, V. A., 162
Joshi, D. S., 422-423
Jost, T. M., 444
Juan, M. J. D., 336
Juett, J., 117
Jugert, P., 336
Jugl, I., 363
Jullien, S., 151-152
Juraska, J. M., 112
Juruena, M. F., 454
Jusienė, R., 449
Justice, L. M., 268, 271
Juul, A., 148
Juvonen, J., 360-361, 384, 437, 447

K

Kabatek, J., 417
Kader, F., 66
Kaestle, C. E., 391-392
Kagan, J., 306, 309
Kagesten, A., 373, 384
Kahn, N. F., 383
Kalashnikova, M., 266-267
Kalat, J. W., 105, 109
Kaldy, Z., 212
Kalisher, A., 422
Kallen, A. N., 54
Kalpidou, M., 435
Kam, J. A., 425
Kaminen-Ahola, N., 78
Kamper-DeMarco, K. E., 23
Kampis, D., 321
Kan, P. F., 263, 272
Kana, R. K., 249
Kancherla, V., 84
Kang, H.-K., 92
Kanka, M. H., 377
Kantar, A., 153
Kantor, L., 393
Kapasi, A., 338-339
Kapetanovic, S., 363, 391, 416
Kaplan, H., 120
Karanian, J. M., 238
Karasik, L. B., 123
Karbach, J., 219
Karim, A., 147
Karltorp, E., 266
Karna, A., 362
Karoly, H. C., 161
Karraker, K., 305
Kartner, J., 196, 321, 356
Katsantonis, I., 326
Katz, A. N., 270
Katz, J. C., 433
Katz, V. S., 444
Kaufman, E. A., 332
Kaufman, J. C., 237, 253
Kaufman, T. M. L., 361, 391
Kaufmann, L., 249-250
Kaur, G., 80
Kaushanskaya, M., 272
Kavanagh, P. L., 53
Kavšek, M., 98, 235
Kawabata, Y., 437
Kawai, N., 99
Kawakami, K., 291
Kaye, H., 99
Kaye, M., 56
Kayed, N. S., 127
Kayl, A. J., 126
Kazi, S., 192, 194
Kearns, S., 388
Keating, D. P., 194, 221
Keene, P. A., 212
Keller, H., 8, 120, 314, 321
Kelley, B., 442
Kelly, A. S., 155
Kelly, Y., 147
Kempe, V., 264
Kenny, M. C., 155
Kenward, B., 338, 351

Kesmodel, U. S., 79
Kettrey, H. H., 387
Keywan, C., 151
Khan, F., 315
Khundrakpam, B. S., 235
Khurana, A., 450
Kia, H., 387
Kiani, A. K., 59
Kibbe, M. M., 180, 212–213
Kidd, E., 268, 435
Kidd, K. M., 388
Kidger, J., 448
Kienbaum, J., 354–355
Kievit, R. A., 214
Kikas, E., 340
Killen, M., 32, 346, 351–352
Kim, B.-R., 304
Kim, H., 155
Kim, J. H., 154, 218
Kim, J.-S., 29
Kim, J.-Y., 81
Kim, K., 67
Kim, L., 153
Kim, M., 254
Kim, P., 215
Kim, S., 83
Kim, Y., 154
Kimball, M. M., 380
Kim-Spoon, J., 301, 366
King, B. H., 248
King, K., 139
King, P. E., 364, 366, 377
King, R. B., 340
King, T., 364, 377
Kiraly, I., 220
Kirby, J. N., 420
Kirby, S., 275
Kirk, E., 265
Kirkham, N., 208, 216
Kirkorian, H. L., 449
Kisilevsky, B. S., 96, 128
Kitayama, S., 7, 326
Kitts, J. A., 437
Kiuru, N., 448
Kjeldsen, A., 360
Kjellstrand, J., 424
Klaczynski, P. A., 384
Klahr, A. M., 63
Klahr, D., 16
Klein, K. O., 52
Kleiser Polk, M., 384–385
Klemfuss, J. Z., 221
Kliegman, R. M., 137–138, 140
Klimstra, T. A., 329, 331
Klin, A., 249
Kloos, H., 208
Knafo, A., 63
Knafo-Noam, A., 356
Kneile, L. A., 263
Knickmeyer, R. C., 106
Knoop, M. S., 142
Knox, P. L., 350
Ko, J. Y., 80
Kobak, R., 415
Kobayashi, T., 96
Kochenderfer-Ladd, B., 439

Koerber, S., 224
Koerts, J., 211
Koevoet, D., 212
Kogan, M. D., 248
Kohlberg, L., 347, 349–350, 376–378
Kohlhoff, J., 308
Kohnert, K., 263
Kojima, H., 306
Kokoc, M., 211
Kolaitis, G., 143
Kolb, B., 105–106, 108, 110–111
Koletić, G., 366, 380
Kolk, S. M., 106–107, 111
Kolling, T., 182
Kondracki, A. J., 80
Konijn, E. A., 450–451
Konje, J. C., 84
Konkel, L., 105
Korlat, S., 385
Kornafel, T., 122
Kornbluh, M., 438
Kornienko, O., 383
Korotchikova, I., 96
Korous, K. M., 245
Kosciw, J. G., 387
Kosmitzki, C., 92, 190, 306, 314
Kostelnik, M. J., 442
Koster, M., 25, 183
Kothari, C. L., 150
Kotsou, I., 239
Kovacs, K., 235
Kozhimannil, K. B., 82, 92
Krahe, B., 357, 450
Kraiger, K., 239
Kramer, J., 406
Kramer, L., 295, 357
Krammer, I., 437
Kranzler, J. H., 243
Krassner, A. M., 306
Krauss, S., 325
Kravitz, E., 82
Kray, J., 214
Kressley-Mba, R. A., 182
Kretch, K. S., 115–116, 122–123, 130–131
Kretsch, N., 146
Kretschmer, T., 362
Kriegbaum, K., 245–246
Kringelbach, M. L., 307
Kroese, J., 418
Kroger, J., 328–331
Kromm, H., 300
Kronenberger, W., 266
Kroon, E., 161
Kroonenberg, P. M., 314
Krstić, N., 57
Kruger, M., 180
Kruithof, P., 79
Kubota, M., 272
Kucharsky, Š., 124, 208
Kucian, K., 250
Kucker, S. C., 267
Kuhl, P. K., 261–262, 266
Kuhlman, K. R., 301
Kuhlmeier, V., 354
Kuhn, D., 192–194, 227
Kuipers, B., 117

Kulkarni, K., 81
Kumar, S., 155
Kumar, V. L., 362
Kung, K. T. F., 376
Kuo, Y.-L., 119
Kurtz, M. P., 59
Kurtz-Costes, B., 377
Kushnir, T., 624
Kuther, T. L., 405
Kuzyk, O., 269
Kwak, Y., 227
Kwan, M. Y. W., 149
Kyere, E., 334
Kyvelidou, A., 115

L

La Rooy, D., 221
Labella, M. H., 450, 457
Labouvie-Vief, G., 194, 365
Ladd, G. W., 439
Lærum, A. M. W., 93
Lafontaine, M. P., 223
LaFontana, K. M., 438
Lagattuta, K. H., 294
Laible, D., 412, 438
Laing, C., 262
Laith, R., 362
Lakhani, N., 46, 48
Lam, C. B., 385
Lam, T. K., 211
Lamari-Fisher, A., 363
Lamaze, F., 91
Lamb, M. E., 220, 309–310, 313, 418, 420
Lambert, S. F., 250–251
Lambie, J. A., 379
Lampl, M., 9–10, 138
Landers-Potts, M., 434–435
Landor, A., 366
Lane, M. A., 159
Langfur, S., 321
Lannoy, S., 206
Lansford, J. E., 363, 414, 438–439
Lansu, T. A. M., 438
Lappe, M., 85
Larion, S., 54
Lariviere, M., 147
Larkina, M., 219
Larsen, J. T., 295
Larsen, K. L., 450
Larson, R. W., 296
Larson, R., 296
Larzelere, R. E., 412
Last, B. S., 215
Lau, B. K., 128
Laubach, Z. M., 86
Laube, C., 112
Lauer, J., 374
Laurent, A., 269
Laurent, G., 295
Laurent, H. K., 454
Laureys, F., 214
Laursen, B., 415, 436–438, 440–441
Lautarescu, A., 85
Lavi, I., 155
Lavrič, M., 411

Lawrence, A., 449
Lawrence, J., 412–413
Lawrence, K. C., 326
Lawson, G. M., 215
Layton, A. M., 79
Layton, E., 365
Lazarides, R., 446
Le Bas, G. A., 304
Le Grange, D., 159
Lea, R. G., 239
Leadbeater, B. J., 415
Leahey, E., 374
Leal, D. F., 437
Leaper, C., 379–380
Lease, M., 438
Lebel, C., 79, 107, 112
Lebrun-Harris, L. A., 360, 422–423
Lecce, S., 214, 224, 226
Lederberg, A. R., 266
Lee, C. G., 326
Lee, D. B., 366
Lee, E. H., 414
Lee, H., 119, 424
Lee, J. J., 82
Lee, J., 154
Lee, N.-C., 52
Lee, P. A., 296
Lee, S. J., 82–83
Lee, S. M., 323
Lee, W. K., 426
Lee, Y., 246, 456
Lee, Y.-E., 414
Leenders, I., 351
Leerkes, E. M., 297
Lees, B., 79
Legare, C. H., 21, 196
Legette, K. B., 336
Legoff, L., 66
Lehman, D. R., 193
Leibovich, L., 30
Leloux-Opmeer, H., 454
Lemery-Chalfant, K., 303
Lenehan, S. M., 139
Lenhard, W., 451
Lenhart, A., 452–453
Leonard, C., 226, 228
Leone, T., 147
Leong, D. J., 198
Leopold, T., 420
Lerkkanen, M.-K., 442
Lerner, M. D., 433
Lerner, R. M., 9, 19, 30, 404
Leslie, A. M., 212
Lessard, L. M., 392, 436–437
Lester, B. M., 82
Leung, E., 378, 382
Levesque, S., 404
Levickis, P., 277
Levine, D., 266, 275
Levine, L. E., 322
Levine, S. C., 374
Levine, T. A., 81
Levitt, A. G., 262
Levitz, N., 393
Lewis, C., 309–310, 313
Lewis, K. M., 295

Lewis, M., 267–268, 292, 306, 322–323
Lewis, R. B., 446
Lewis, R., 44
Lewis, T. L., 125–127
Lewkowicz, D. J., 129
Lew-Williams, C., 130, 276, 278–279
Li, D., 128, 410
Li, Db., 119
Li, G., 383
Li, J. J., 65
Li, M., 162, 407
Li, Q., 214
Li, R., 119, 139
Li, Y., 407
Liao, H.-F., 338
Liben, L. S., 378, 383
Liberman, Z., 293, 436
Libertus, K., 119–120
Libertus, M. E., 183
Lickenbrock, D. M., 312–313
Lickliter, R., 8, 20, 67
Lieberman, L. D., 394
Lieneman, C. C., 412
Lieven, E., 277
Likar, I. P., 57–58
Lillard, A., 433–434
Lillevoll, K. R., 433, 442
Lim, H., 149
Limber, S. P., 362
Limber, S., 293
Limeri, L. B., 339
Lin, S., 80, 335, 407
Lin, Y., 85, 182
Lindberg, A., 379
Lindberg, L. D., 392
Lindberg, S. M., 384–385
Lindell, A. K., 407
Linderkamp, O., 105
Linderkamp-Skoruppa, D. B., 105
Lindquist, K. A., 294
Lindsay, A. C., 142
Lindsey, E. W., 295
Linebarger, D. L., 449
Lionetti, F., 416
Lipsitt, L. P., 555
Lisdahl, K. M., 161
Lisonkova, S., 54
Liss, M. B., 379
Liszkowski, U., 578
Litovsky, R. Y., 128
Little, A. H., 99
Little, L. M., 251
Littschwager, J. C., 269
Liu, B., 80
Liu, C., 81, 302, 406
Liu, J., 449
Liu, M.-R., 271
Liu, N., 393
Liu, S. R., 85
Liu, W., 363
Liu, X., 266
Liu, Y., 312, 407
Llorca, A., 410
Lloyd, B. J., 138
Lo, J. H.-Y., 350
Lo, J. O., 81

Lobel, A., 451
Lobo, M. A., 119
LoBraico, E. J., 415
Lobstein, T., 155
LoBue, V., 293–294, 354
Lockl, K., 223
Loh, E. K.-Y., 271
Lohaus, A., 120
Lohman, D. F., 240
Lohmann, H., 225
Lomax, A., 97
London, K., 221
Long, B. L., 115
Long, X., 79
Loock, C., 79
Loos, R. J. F., 60, 154
LoParo, D., 439
Lope-Piedrafita, S., 26
Lopez, A. B., 365
Lopez, L. D., 262
Lopez-Fernandez, F. J., 451
Lopez-Tamayo, R., 416
Lord, C., 248–249
Lorenz, K., 20
Lorenzetti, V., 161
Loso, H. M., 384
Lottero-Leconte, R., 72
Lougheed, J. P., 296
Louie, P., 149, 325–326
Louis-Jacques, A., 139
Loussert, L., 79
Lovell, M. E., 161
Lowe, C. J., 272
Lozada, F. T., 298
Lozoff, B., 143
Lu, H. H., 154
Lu, W., 162
Lu, Y., 250
Luby, J. L., 110–111
Lucas, R., 139
Lucassen, P. J., 105
Lucas-Thompson, R., 415
Lucca, K., 338
Luckey, A. J., 433
Ludvigsson, J. F., 153
Luijten, C. C., 437
Luk, M. S. K., 424
Luke, C., 6
Lukosius, P. A., 119
Luo, R., 277
Luo, Y., 210
Lussier, A. A., 162
Lut, I., 418
Luthar, S. S., 405, 457
Lutkenhaus, P., 321
Luttikhuizen dos Santos, E. S., 241
Luyckx, K., 330
Lynch, J. L., 95
Lynch, K., 63
Lynn, R., 244
Lyons-Ruth, K., 313

M

M.K, K., 139
Ma, J., 412

Ma, T. L., 355
MacBlain, S., 187
MacCann, C., 239
MacConnell, A., 185
MacFarlan, S. J., 312
MacGowan, T. L., 356
Mackey, K., 426
Mackie, G., 387
Mackintosh, J. N., 246
MacNeill, L. A., 304
MacPhee, D., 338, 379
Macswan, J., 272
MacWhinney, B., 263, 268
Madigan, S., 310–314, 449
Madjar, N., 448
Madore, K. P., 211
Madsen, H. B., 218
Madsen, K. M., 268
Maenner, M. J., 248
Magnuson, K., 443
Magro, S. W., 325
Maguire-Jack, K., 155
Maheshwari, A., 56
Maheux, A. J., 440
Mahmood, L., 139
Mai, C. T., 76
Main, M., 310
Mairhofer, S., 354–355
Mak, E., 269
Makela, T. E., 142
Malagoli, C., 214
Malatesta, C. Z., 300
Malave, L., 109–110
Malik-Moraleda, S., 275
Malm, K., 421
Malti, T., 350, 355, 359–360, 450
Mamluk, L., 80
Mammen, M., 349
Mancilla-Martinez, J., 272
Mancini, J. A., 424
Manczak, E. M., 67
Mandel, D. R., 261
Mandler, J. M., 223
Manfra, L., 118
Manganelli, S., 340
Mangelsdorf, S. C., 294
Mani, A., 263, 267
Manning, W. D., 419
Manoach, D. S., 190
Manotas, M. C., 9, 146
Mansson, J., 241
Manuck, S. B., 62, 65
Marceau, K., 405, 416
Marcellus, L., 454
Marchand, G., 80
Marcia, J. E., 328–329
Marcinowski, E. C., 115
Marcone, R., 410
Marcovitch, S., 182
Margolis, A., 235
Margoni, F., 179, 182, 351
Mariani Wigley, I. L. C., 67, 454
Marin, M. M., 129
Marinellie, S. A., 263
Marino, J. L., 383
Mariz, C., 65

Markant, J., 126
Markiewicz, D., 436
Markman, E. M., 265, 267, 269
Markowitz, A. J., 442
Marks, A. K., 333
Marks, P. E. L., 438
Markson, L., 324
Markstrom-Adams, C., 332
Markus, H. R., 7, 17, 326
Marley, C. L., 434
Marlier, L., 129
Marmor, R., 56
Marotz, L. R., 139
Marraccini, M. E., 447
Marsh, S., 215
Marshall, E. J., 161
Marshall, S. L., 327
Marti, Eduardo, 194
Martin, C. L., 377, 378, 382
Martin, J. A., 45, 76, 87, 92, 392
Martin, M., 420
Martinez, G. M., 146
Martin-Ordas, G., 213
Martins, N., 450
Martinson, M. L., 94
Martin-Storey, A., 383
Martiny, S. E., 381
Martzog, P., 118
Marx, R. A., 387
Masalha, R., 253
Mascaro, J. S., 379
Masche, J. G., 416
Masek, L. R., 278
Masi, A., 248
Maslowsky, J., 161
Mason, G. M., 142
Mason, L., 442
Mason, M., 161
Masonbrink, A. R., 445
Masten, A. S., 450, 457–458
Mastropieri, M. A., 446
Matarma, T., 373
Mathews, C. J., 32
Mathews, T. J., 405
Mathewson-Chapman, M., 425
Matsui, T., 261, 276
Matthews, S. G., 85
Mattingly, V., 239
Matuschka, L. K., 361
Matzel, L. D., 245
Mauger, C., 52
Maule, J., 127
Maunder, R., 437
Maurer, D., 109
Mavroveli, S., 239
May, L., 128
Mayer, A., 225
Mayer, J. D., 238
Mayeux, L., 384–385
Mayne, S. L., 163
Maziarz, L. N., 392
Mazrekaj, D., 7, 417
Mazul, M. C., 87
Mazzocco, M. M., 250
McAdams, D. P., 329–330
McAlister, A. R., 225

McAnally, H. M., 434
McAuliffe, K., 8
McCaffery, J. M., 62, 65
McCarthy, M. M., 376
McCartney, K., 63
McCaskey, U., 250
McCauley Ohannessian, C., 452
Mcclain, M.-C., 253
McCleery, J. P., 249
McClelland, M. M., 301
McClure, R., 152
McConaughy, S. H., 24
McConnachie, A. L., 313
McConnell, E. A., 391
McCord, J., 412
McCourt, A. D., 82
McCoy, D. C., 7
McCoy, S. S., 440
McCrea, K. T., 157, 363
McDade, R. S., 392
McDevitt, T. M., 191
McDonald, K. L., 438
McDonell, J. R., 153
McDougall, P., 362
McDowell, N., 128
McEwen, F. S., 456
McGee, E. O., 254
McGlade, M. S., 88
McGlone, F., 320
McGowan, P. O., 85
McGue, M., 61, 64
McHale, S. M., 379, 406–407, 415
McHarg, G., 449
McHenry, M. S., 84
McIlvain, G., 113, 227
McIntosh, J. E., 313
McKeever, N., 391
McKenna, J. J., 142–143
McKinney, C., 364, 411
McKone, E., 126
McKown, C., 246
McLean, K. C., 330, 336
McLoughlin, C. S., 407
McLoyd, V. C., 414
McMahan True, M., 315
McMahon, E. M., 148
McMurray, B., 264
McNamara, H. C., 46
McNeil, C. B., 412
McPartland, J. C., 248
McPherson, B., 380
McRae, C. S., 426
McWhirter, E. H., 336
Meaney, M. J., 66–67, 454
Meca, A., 337
Mechler, K., 210
Medovoy, T., 440
Meehan, C. L., 293
Meeus, W. H. J., 328–330, 415
Meeus, W., 327
Mehl, M. R., 23
Mehlum, L., 163
Mehta, C. M., 408
Mehta, P. K., 84
Mehus, C. J., 412–413
Meier, A., 405

Meinhofer, A., 82
Meinzen-Derr, J., 266
Meisel, J. M., 269
Melendez, L., 298
Melisse, B., 159
Mellor, J. R., 274
Melogno, S., 270
Meltzoff, A. N., 182, 293, 320
Memmert, D., 210
Memmott-Elison, M. K., 352, 355
Mencarini, L., 372
Mendez, M., 412
Mendle, J., 144
Mendoza, A. N., 423
Menesini, E., 360–361
Mennella, J. A., 129
Menon, M., 382
Mercer, N., 331
Merhar, S. L., 81
Merlo, C. L., 149
Mermelshtine, R., 196
Merrin, G. J., 416
Meruelo, A. D., 161
Mesman, E., 457
Mesman, J., 298, 314
Messinger, D., 291
Metcalf, B. S., 149
Metcalfe, R. E., 424
Meter, D. J., 437
Metzger, A., 415
Meunier, K., 443
Meuwese, R., 358
Meyer, D. R., 418
Meyer, S., 446
Micalizzi, L., 302
Michalek, J., 456
Michikyan, M., 453
Miconi, D., 327
Midgley, C., 447
Miech, R. A., 25, 160–161
Miedema, E., 393
Mielke, G. I., 149
Miesen, A. I. R., 388
Miething, A., 437
Mihalec-Adkins, B. P., 424
Miklikowska, M., 436
Milevsky, A., 410–411
Milkie, M. A., 405
Miller, C. F., 377, 378
Miller, D. J., 72
Miller, J. G., 8, 350, 355–356
Miller, J. M., 142
Miller, K. E., 457
Miller, K., 25
Miller, L., 250
Miller, P. H., 9, 11, 17, 182, 274
Miller, P. J., 413
Miller, S., 219
Miller-Jacobs, C., 385, 388
Mills, K., 111, 112, 113, 206, 296, 363
Mims, L. C., 337
Min, M. O., 81, 83
Minar, N. J., 292, 322
Minick, N., 198
Minnes, S., 81
Minnis, A. M., 389

Mirabolfathi, V., 214
Mireault, G. C., 180
Mirkovic, B., 210
Misailidi, P., 300
Mistry, J., 7, 19
Mistry, R. S., 7
Mitchell, E. A., 143
Mithun, M., 259
Mitra, D., 327
Mitra, R., 454
Mix, K. S., 183
Modzelewska, D., 79
Moen, P., 405
Moffitt, T. E., 363
Mogensen, S. S., 148
Mohanty, J., 422
Moilanen, K. L., 410
Mojahed, S., 57
Mokdad, A. H., 445
Moley, K. H., 86
Molina, R. L., 87
Molitor, A., 191
Molnar, B. E., 156
Molnar, F., 66
Monahan, K. C., 440–441
Monden, C., 46
Moneta, G., 296, 433
Monin, J. K., 313
Monk, C., 313
Monks, C. P., 437
Monroe, P., 334
Monsrud, M.-B., 269
Montero, F., 58
Montgomery, J., 422
Montirosso, R., 320
Moon, C., 96, 99, 124
Moon, R. Y., 143, 151–152
Moore, C., 263, 354
Moore, D. S., 84
Moore, J. S. B., 324
Moore, K. L., 72, 75–76
Moore, M. K., 182
Moore, R., 444
Moore, S. E., 362
Moore, S. R., 148
Moran-Lev, H., 139
Morawska, A., 298, 312, 378–379, 412
Morelli, G., 143, 315
Moreno, M. A., 452
Moreno, O., 415
Morey, C. C., 219
Morgan, C., 62
Morgan, G., 266, 337
Morgan, P. L., 253
Mori, A., 187
Moriguchi, Y., 26, 197
Morikawa, H., 277
Morimoto, Y., 248
Morley, D., 117, 421
Morley, J. E., 140
Morneau-Vaillancourt, G., 60
Morokuma, S., 98
Morris, A. R., 308, 312
Morris, A. S., 112
Morris, G., 219
Morris, L. A., 52

Morris, P. A., 17–19
Morris, T., 89, 112
Morrison, C. M., 424
Morse, E., 334
Mortelmans, D., 420
Moses, L. J., 224
Moses-Payne, M. E., 227
Mosher, S. W., 408
Moshman, D., 192, 194
Moslimani, M., 425
Moulin-Stoz-ek, D., 364
Mouritsen, A., 148
Movalled, K., 261
Mowery, T. M., 109
Moxley, J. H., 220
Mpofu, E., 190
Mrick, S. E., 336
Mrtorell, G. A., 336
Mu, S., 210
Mueller, I., 85, 454
Mueller, V., 265
Muenks, K., 339–340
Muennig, P., 443
Muentner, L., 424
Mulder, H., 208
Mulholland, E., 424
Muller, C. M., 441
Muller-Oehring, E. M., 160
Mulligan, S., 250
Mulvey, N., 259
Mulvihill, A., 198
Mummert, A., 140
Munakata, Y., 210, 213, 226
Muncer, G., 227
Mundy, L., 112
Munholland, K., 310, 316
Murnan, A. W., 81
Murray, J. S., 456–457
Murray, P. G., 138
Murray-Close, D., 360
Murry, V. M., 414
Murthy, V. H., 161
Myers, A., 205, 213, 243
Myers, N. A., 219
Myrhaug, H. T., 77

N

Nabors, L., 457
Nacouzi, D., 26
Nagata, J. M., 149, 159, 360
Naigles, L., 275
Nakano, H., 98
Nakano, T., 98
Nallet, C., 261, 275
Nanez, J. E., 127
Narayan, A. J., 311
Narendran, V., 91
Narita, Z., 384
Nasir, N. S., 247
Nasiri, S., 147
Natale, V., 138
Naterer, A., 411
Natsuaki, M. N., 148, 162
Natu, V. S., 106, 107, 206
Nazzari, S., 85

Ncube, C. N., 94
Neal, J. W., 438
Neblett, E. W., 366
Needham, A. W., 119
Neff, E. P., 59
Neisser, U., 245, 246, 320
Nellore, J., 87
Nelson, C. A., 77, 109, 110
Nelson, L. H., 265
Nelson, R. M., 341
Nelson, S. C., 320, 335, 336
Nencheva, M. L., 276
Nese, R. N. T., 362
Neshat, H., 95, 101, 129
Nesi, J., 362, 453
Neubauer, A. C., 236
Neveu, A., 272
Neville, R. D., 142
Newcombe, N. S., 374
Newcombe, N., 187
Newell, B. R., 25
Newland, R. P., 312
Newman, R. S., 277
Newton, E. K., 353, 356
Newton, E., 434
Ng, K., 149
Nguyen, T., 80
Nguyen, V. H., 80
Nguyen-Louie, T. T., 149
Nicholson, H. L., 326
Nicoladis, E., 269
Nicolaides, N. C., 454
Niebaum, J., 210, 213, 226
Nielsen, A. N., 106
Nielson, M. G., 383, 384
Nieto, M., 219
Nigg, J. T., 210
Nikitin, J., 7, 492
Niklas, F., 235
Nikolaus, M., 274
Nilsen, E. S., 194
Nilsen, W., 194
Ninio, A., 271
Nisbett, R. E., 193, 245, 246
Nishijima, K., 95
Nishina, A., 447
Nishiyori, R., 119
Nixon, E., 420
Noam, A., 274
Nobes, G., 347
Noble, K. G., 214
Nocentini, A., 361
Nogueira Avelar e, Silva. R., 389
Noh, J. Y., 359
Nomaguchi, K., 405
Nook, E. C., 301
Norbom, L. B., 111
Norgate, S. H., 246
Norholt, H., 312
Norris, C. J., 293
Nowicki, P., 154
Nucci, L., 351
Nugent, A. C., 163
Nugent, B. M., 376
Nugent, J. K., 93
Nunez, M., 455

Nuru-Jeter, A., 82
Nuttall, A. K., 219
Nygaard, S. S., 81
Nyiti, R. M., 190

O

O'Connell, A. E., 59
O'Connell, L. M., 422
O'Connor, K. E., 361
O'Connor, T., 63
O'Donnell, K. J., 66, 67
O'Keefe, P., 244
O'Neal, C. W., 424
O'Shaughnessy, R., 314
O'Sullivan, A., 313
Oakes, L. M., 179, 223
Obeid, N., 147
Oberauer, K., 205
Običan, S. G., 57
Obuo Addo, A., 435
Ochs, E., 277
Oddi, K. B., 305
Odgers, C. L., 30, 452
Odibo, A. O., 57
Ogren, M., 295
Ohlsson, C., 147
Ohta, H., 138
Ojodu, J., 48
Okagaki, L., 237
Okanda, M., 187
Olaguez, A. P., 221
Olsavsky, A. L., 312, 313, 387, 388
Olson, K. R., 382, 386
Olson, S. L., 413
Olsson, M., 381
Olweus, D., 360, 362
Onetti, W., 325
Ong, A. D., 331, 333, 334
Ono, Y., 275
Onwuegbuzie, A. J., 245
Opendak, M., 312
Opie, J. E., 313
Oppenheim, G. M., 272
Orben, A., 452
Orena, A. J., 265
Orihuela, C. A., 389
Orkin, M., 340
Ormrod, J. Ellis., 191
Ornstein, P. A., 219, 226
Orth, U., 324–327
Ortiz, F. A., 326
Ose Askvik, E., 118
Osgood, D. W., 436
Osher, D., 7, 363
Osinubi, A., 146, 389
Ostatnikova, D., 376
Ostchega, Y., 154
Osterhaus, C., 224
Osterman, M. J. K., 46, 85–88, 91, 93, 94, 392, 405
Ostrov, J. M., 23, 359, 375
Oswald, T. K., 449
Otero, M., 442
Otgaar, H., 221
Otter, M., 52

Otto, C., 159
Owen, J. P., 250
Owen, K., 222, 223
Owens, J. A., 149
Owens, R. E., 259, 262–265, 267, 268, 271
Owotomo, O., 161
Owusu, P., 435
Ozbek, H., 311
Ozen Tunay, Z., 128
Öztürk, R., 576

P

Pace, A., 269
Pace, C. S., 57, 421
Packer, M. J., 7
Padgett, J. K., 375
Padiath, Q. S., 45
Padilla-Walker, L. M., 352, 355, 356
Pagani, L. S., 450
Page, J., 443
Pages, R., 443
Pahlke, E., 381
Paillereau, N., 261
Paine, A. L., 57, 421
Palacios, J., 421
Paley, B., 299
Palomero-Gallagher, N., 291
Pampati, S., 387
Panagiotakopoulos, L., 388
Panchal, U., 163
Pandita, A., 129
Panksepp, J., 373
Pantell, R. H., 220
Papadimitriou, A., 147
Papageorgiou, K. a., 303
Papousek, H., 99
Pappas, K. B., 52
Paquette, N., 275
Paradis, J., 272
Paradise, R., 196
Parent, N., 452
Pariseau, E. M., 387
Park, C. J., 268
Parker, N., 424
Parks, S. E., 151
Paro, R., 66
Parra, M., 269
Parten, M., 433
Partridge, S., 87
Pascal, A., 93
Pascalis, O., 126, 129
Pasco, M. C., 334
Pascoe, J. M., 215
Passel, J. S., 425
Passolunghi, M. C., 377
Pasterski, V., 376
Patchin, J. W., 361
Patel, D. R., 251, 252
Patel, S., 182
Patenaude, Y., 58
Patrick, M. E., 412
Patterson, C. J., 417
Patterson, M. M., 376, 377, 384
Patton, G. C., 161
Patzold, W., 180

Paul Victor, C. G., 364
Paul, S. E., 81
Pauletti, R. E., 382, 383
Pauletto, M., 239
Paulus, M., 349, 353–355
Paulussen-Hoogeboom, M. C., 305
Pawson, C., 347
Payne, V. G., 8, 97, 116–119, 144
Pazol, K., 392
Pearman, F. A., 254
Pearson, J. L., 162
Pedersen, E. R., 161
Peebles, R., 159
Pei, J., 338, 339, 441
Peiro, J. L., 59
Pellegrini, A. D., 359
Pellicano, E., 248
Pellis, S. M., 434
Peltz, J., 405
Peng, P., 214
Pennington, B. F., 249
Perales, F., 417
Peranteau, W. H., 59
Pereira, G., 80
Perera, B. P. U., 86
Perez, J., 183, 221
Perez-Brena, N. J., 404, 407
Perez-Escamilla, R., 138, 139
Perez-Gonzalez, A., 457
Perez-Zapata, D., 225, 226
Perhamus, G. R., 359
Perlman, S. B., 111, 213
Perlmutter, M., 219
Perner, J., 185
Perone, S., 20, 213
Perry, D. G., 223, 382–385
Perry-Jenkins, M., 386
Perszyk, D. R., 332
Pesu, L., 322
Peter, J., 380
Petersen, I. T., 161
Petersen, J., 374
Peterson, C., 218, 225
Peterson, K. C., 242
Peterson, R. L., 249
Petitpierre, G., 139
Petrides, K. V., 239
Petursdottir, A. I., 274
Peverill, M., 418
Peviani, K. M., 366
Pexman, P., 271
Peyre, H., 373, 374
Pfefferbaum, B., 426
Pfeiffer, S., 253
Pham, H. T., 147
Phillips, D., 442, 443
Phillips, K., 296, 301
Phinney, J. S., 331, 333, 334
Phneah, K. T., 126
Piaget, J., 15–17, 24, 34, 128, 174–177, 179, 181–184, 187, 189, 190, 192, 196, 199, 346–348, 432, 442
Piantadosi, S. T., 182
Piccolo, L. R., 215
Pick, A. D., 130
Piekarski, D. J., 112

Pierrehumbert, B., 94
Pietschnig, J., 235, 244
Pillow, B. H., 226
Pinel, C., 66
Pinnelli, S., 253
Pinquart, M., 327, 349, 410, 411, 447
Piotrowski, J. T., 410
Pipe, S. W., 51
Piras, G. N., 147
Pirchio, S., 332
Pisano, M. M., 80
Pison, G., 46
Pisoni, D., 266
Pittman, J. F., 330
Pivnick, L. K., 440
Pizzol, D., 140
Plaisier, X. S., 450, 451
Planalp, E. M., 302, 304
Platt, J. M., 244
Plebanek, D. J., 213
Plomin, R. D., 64, 65, 245
Plomin, R., 46, 59–61, 244, 302
Poehlmann, J., 304
Poehlmann-Tynan, J., 423, 424
Poirel, N., 189
Polanin, J. R., 362
Pollmann-Schult, M., 405
Pons, F., 294, 299
Poole, D. A., 221
Poornima, S., 54
Popat, A., 452
Popli, G. K., 215
Popova, S., 79, 80
Poppen, P., 350
Posadas, D. M., 62
Posner, J., 302, 303
Poteat, V. P., 387
Potegal, M., 292
Potmesil, M., 304
Potmesilova, P., 304
Potter, D., 420
Potvin, S., 359
Poulin, F., 437
Powell, K. M., 457, 458
Powell, S. D., 442
Power, F. C., 349
Power, L., 364
Power, M., 296, 301
Powers, M. E., 391
Powlishta, K. K., 379
Pozzoli, T., 362
Prabaharan, N., 438, 439
Prady, S. L., 305
Prasad, V., 152
Prechtl, H. F. R., 96
Preckel, F., 325
Prencipe, A., 352
Prendergast, S., 379
Prenoveau, J. M., 312
Prentza, A., 271
Prescott, J., 129
Pressley, M., 226
Previc, F. H., 108
Prewett, S. L., 448
Price-Feeney, M., 387
Price-Williams, D., 190

Priess, H. A., 384, 385
Prime, H., 426
Principe, G. F., 221
Prinstein, M. J., 441
Pritzl, K., 424
Privado, J., 235
Proctor, R. W., 130
Progovac, L., 275
Prosser, L. A., 122
Provasi, J., 94
Provenzi, L., 67, 454
Przybylski, A. K., 449
Puckett, J. A., 388
Pulice-Farrow, L., 386
Pulkkinen, L., 363
Puls, H. T., 94
Putnick, D. L., 323, 356, 410, 411
Puzio, A. R., 372
Pyra, E., 148

Q

Qiao, J., 79, 139
Qiu, X., 354
Qualter, P., 239
Quam, C., 262
Quarmley, M., 438
Quinn, M., 57, 433
Quinn, P. C., 126, 222, 223, 332, 376
Quinones-Camacho, L. E., 300
Quintana, S. M., 332
Quiroga, M. A., 247

R

Rabbitt, M. P., 141
Raby, K. L., 313
Racy, F., 198
Rademaker, M., 79
Radvansky, G. A., 205, 206
Raffington, L., 67
Rafiee, F., 248
Raftery, J. N., 340
Ragelienė, T., 330
Rahman, M. N. A., 406
Rahm-Knigge, R. L., 458
Rainwater-Lovett, K., 84
Rajagopalan, A., 138
Rajendra, S. J., 126
Rajendran, K., 361
Rakesh, D., 214
Rakic, P., 106, 107, 111
Rakison, D. H., 179, 223
Rakoczy, H., 224
Raley, J. A., 417
Raley, R. K., 420
Ralls, F. M., 97
Ramat, P., 259
Rambaran, J. A., 341, 448
Ramchand, R., 162
Ramey, C. T., 443
Ramey, S. L., 443
Ramirez, N. F., 266
Ramirez, P. C., 272
Ramos, G. G. F., 388
Ramraj, C., 94

Ramsaran, A. I., 218
Ramsdell, H. L., 262
Ranjbar, A., 393
Rapin, I., 250
Rapoport, E., 422, 423
Raskin, M., 455
Rasmussen, S. A., 84
Rattaz, V., 298, 299
Raval, V. V., 298
Ravitsky, V., 58
Raynor, R., 99
Reale, C., 376
Ream, G. L., 365, 366
Rebbe, R., 82, 155
Reddy, V., 180
Redick, T. S., 235
Rees, C. A., 152
Regan, A. K., 80
Reh, R. K., 261
Rehani, M. M., 26
Reich, S. M., 195
Reichman, N. E., 94
Reid, C. N., 87
Reid, V. M., 125
Reilly, J. J., 154
Reilly, M. S., 142
Reis, L. F., 392
Reis, O., 330
Reiss, F., 418
Reissland, N., 80, 129
Reiter, E. O., 296
Reitsema, A. M., 296
Rekow, D., 223
Relji, G., 272
Remer, J., 106
Remon, D., 263
Renfrew, M. J., 91
Renk, K., 411
Renkert, L. E., 312
Rennels, J. L., 126
Renzulli, J. S., 253
Repacholi, B. M., 292, 293
Reschke, P. J., 353, 356
Rew, L., 388
Reyes, L. M., 93, 304, 374
Reyes, T. M., 93, 304
Rey-Mermet, A., 235
Reyna, V. F., 114, 227
Reynolds, G. D., 207
Reynolds, M. R., 213
Reynolds, M., 374
Rezaeiyeh, R. D., 54
Ribner, A. D., 449
Ricard, M., 189, 301
Ricciardi, C., 443
Richards, J. E., 98, 208
Richards, J., 16
Richards, M. H., 296, 455
Richards, T. L., 250
Richardson, K., 246
Richardson, L., 391
Richlan, F., 249
Richmond, A. D., 436
Rickard, I. J., 147
Riddle, K., 450
Rideout, V. J., 444, 449, 450, 452

Rider, G. N., 388
Riediger, M., 299
Rieffe, C., 358
Rigato, S., 321
Riggins, T., 217, 218
Rigney, J., 223
Rindermann, H., 245
Risher, W. C., 81
Risi, A., 313
Risley, T. R., 278
Ristori, J., 386
Ritchie, K., 93
Ritz, B. R., 62
Riva, D., 373
Rivas-Drake, D., 331, 334, 336, 337, 425
Rivers, S. E., 227
Roa, J., 147
Robb, M. B., 449, 450
Robbins, E., 358
Robbins, J., 196
Roben, C. K. P., 299
Roberge, S., 79
Roberts, A. L., 380
Roberts, G., 214
Roberts, L., 380
Roberts, R. L., 214
Roberts, S. C. M., 82
Roberts, S. O., 332
Roberts, T., 262
Robins, R. W., 324, 326
Robinson, E., 154
Robinson, J. B., 197
Robinson, K., 139
Robinson, S. R., 115, 123
Robinson, T. N., 154
Roby, A. C., 435
Rochat, P., 174, 179, 320–322, 324, 358
Roche, L., 48
Rock, P. F., 336
Roder, B., 109
Rodgers, J. L., 244
Rodprasert, W., 86
Rodriguez, C., 194, 304
Rodriguez, S., 425
Rodriguez-Meirinhos, A., 416
Rodway, C., 163
Roe, J., 128
Roeder, K., 61
Roeser, R. W., 446–448
Roeyers, H., 248
Rogers, A. A., 384
Rogers, C. R., 315
Rogler, L. H., 7
Rogoff, B., 17, 190, 196, 197, 220
Rolls, E. T., 291
Romani, C., 49
Romano, A. C., 207
Rome, S. H., 455
Romera, E. M., 438
Romero, A. J., 333
Romm, K. F., 415
Roncero, C., 81
Ronnqvist, L., 117
Roopnarine, J. L., 312
Roos, L. E., 426
Rose, A. J., 379–380

Rose, J., 410
Rose, S. A., 235
Rose, T., 326
Rose-Greenland, F., 419
Rosenthal, S. M., 388
Roseth, C. J., 359
Rosiak-Gill, A., 86
Rosinger, A. Y., 55
Ross, E. S., 129, 321
Ross, J., 218
Rosselli, M., 373
Ross-Sheehy, S., 212
Rote, W. M., 415, 416
Rothbart, M. K., 302, 303
Rothbaum, F., 306, 314
Rothe, E. M., 163
Rotstein, M., 95, 101
Rovee-Collier, C. K., 217
Rowe, M. L., 264, 265, 277, 278
Rožman Krivec, L., 443
Ruba, A. L., 292, 293
Rubin, J. D., 386
Rubin, K. H., 305, 413, 433, 437, 438
Rubio-Fernandez, P., 181
Ruble, D. N., 146, 377
Rudolph, K. D., 148, 437
Rueda, M. R., 207, 209, 213
Rueger, S. Y., 162
Ruel, J., 489
Ruff, S. C., 406
Ruffman, T., 181, 226
Ruiz, J. M., 88
Rule, B. G., 213
Russ, S. W., 432, 433
Russ, S., 295
Russell, D. H., 387
Russell, D. W., 425
Russell, S. T., 387, 421
Rutter, M., 457
Ruzgis, P., 237
Ryan, A. M., 155, 250, 386, 418, 421
Ryan, C., 386
Ryan, J. P., 155
Ryan, R. M., 418, 421
Rydell, A.-M., 451
Ryncarz, R. A., 349
Rytting, E., 59

S

Saarni, C., 293, 301
Sabbagh, M. A., 224
Sackett, P. R., 240, 243
Sadler, K., 144
Sadler, L. S., 393
Sadler, T. L., 44, 53, 57, 72, 75
Saengkaew, T., 146
Saewyc, E. M., 391
Safer, J. D., 385, 388
Saffran, J. R., 183, 261, 270
Sagar Kommu, J. V., 385
Sagi, A., 313–315
Sagi-Schwartz, A., 312, 313, 315
Sahlan, R. N., 159
Sai, F. Z., 129
Saint, S. E., 206

Sakkalou, E., 128
Sala, M. N., 300
Salapatek, P., 126
Salazar-Juarez, A., 81
Salcedo-Arellano, M. J., 50, 51
Saleem, F. T., 336
Saleem, M., 451
Salend, S. J., 446
Salmivalli, C., 360–362
Salo, V. C., 23, 109
Salomon, L. J., 58
Salovey, P., 238
Salter, M. D., 309
Saltz, J. B., 63
Salvadori, E. A., 293
Salzwedel, A., 82
Samdan, G., 298
Sameroff, A. J., 243
Samour, P. Queen, 139
Samudra, P. G., 268
Samuels, R., 274
Samuelson, L. K., 9, 264
Samura, O., 58
Sanchez, D., 335
Sanchez-Queija, I., 327
Sanchez-Ruiz, M.-J., 239
Sanchez-Vaznaugh, E. V., 89
Sanchis-Sanchis, A., 301
Sanders, J. O., 144
Sanders, M. R., 420
Sanders, M., 412
Sann, C., 129
Sanner, C., 421
Santelli, J., 393
Santolin, C., 265
Santoro, J. D., 51
Santos, C. E., 32
Santos, R. M. S., 449
Sapp, F., 186, 187
Saraiya, A., 455, 456
Sarman, I., 80
Sarmiento, I. G., 452
Sato, W., 249
Sattari, M., 139
Sattler, J. M., 242
Sauce, B., 245
Saudino, K. J., 302
Savina, E., 214, 220
Savin-Williams, R. C., 365, 366, 391
Saxe, G. B., 190
Saxton, M., 275
Sayfan, L., 294
Scarr, S., 63, 245
Schaal, B., 129
Schaffhuser, K., 325
Schaik, S. D. M., 142
Schalock, R., 251, 252
Schapira, R., 295
Scharping, T., 408
Scheffler, C., 140
Schellenberg, E. G., 63
Schenck-Fontaine, A., 155
Schieffein, B., 277
Schieve, L. A., 248
Schlesier, J., 446
Schlinger, H. D., 124

Schmidt, L. A., 304, 306, 356, 426
Schmitt, J. E., 51
Schmitt, L., 235
Schneider, J. L., 116, 226, 295, 393, 455
Schneider, M., 153
Schneider, W., 219, 220, 223, 226, 235
Schnitker, S. A., 366
Schnur, E., 443
Schober, B., 547
Schoemaker, N. K., 57, 421
Schofield, T. J., 420
Scholl, B. J., 180
Schonert-Reichl, K. A., 350
Schoppmann, J., 298
Schreiber, J., 92
Schroeder, K. M., 383
Schubert, A. L., 235
Schuhmacher, N., 353, 356
Schuldiner, O., 106
Schulenberg, J. E., 160
Schumacher, A. M., 143
Schumm, W., 417
Schutte, N. S., 239
Schwab, J. F., 278, 279
Schwartz, B. L., 218, 219
Schwartz, C. R., 419
Schwartz, F., 188
Schwartz, L., 48
Schwartz, N. L., 60
Schwartz, P. D., 195
Schwartz, S. J., 330, 439
Schwartz-Mette, R. A., 437
Schwarzfischer, P., 449
Schwebel, D. C., 153
Schweinhart, L. J., 443
Scorletti, F., 59
Scott, E., 373
Scott, L. S., 126
Scruggs, T. E., 446
Seaton, E. K., 335
Sebastian-Galles, N., 265
Sedgh, G., 392
Sedikides, C., 324, 325, 340, 341
Seehagen, S., 182, 217
Seelman, K. L., 387
Segal, J., 277
Sege, R. D., 412
Segrin, C., 88
Sehmi, R., 57, 421
Seifer, R., 304, 311
Seiler, N. K., 82
Selezneva, E., 25
Selkie, E., 387
Selman, R. L., 194
Selph, S. S., 84
Sember, V., 142
Semega, J., 150
Semeraro, C., 118
Senland, A. K., 346, 349
Senor, M., 269
Senzaki, S., 306
Seo, E., 246
Seo, S., 438
Sepulveda, A., 265
Serafini, G., 361
Serpell, R., 237, 247

Serra, R., 159
Servant, M., 206
Shablack, H., 294
Shaffer, D. R., 126
Shah, K., 50
Shahaeian, A., 225
Shahbazian, N., 58
Shah-Kulkarni, S., 81
Shain, B. N., 162
Shankar, P., 142
Shanks, D. R., 25
Shannon, K. A., 210
Sharma, D., 94
Shaver, P. R., 307
Shaw, D. S., 363
Shayer, M., 190
Shaywitz, B. A., 249
Shaywitz, S. E., 249
Shea, J. D., 190
Shearer, C. B., 238
Sheehan, K. J., 185
Shelton, J., 372
Shen, Y., 334
Sheng, L., 407
Shenouda, J., 249
Sheya, A., 217
Shi, B., 438
Shi, D., 147
Shiffrin, R. M., 205
Shim, S.-S., 58
Shimizu, M., 149
Shimizu, Y., 149
Shinskey, J. L., 181
Shipman, K. L., 300
Shirazi, T. N., 55
Shlafer, R., 424
Shorer, M., 30
Shpiegel, S., 393
Shubert, J., 446
Shuffrey, L. C., 80
Shulman, B. B., 259, 260
Shulman, E. P., 113, 227
Shutts, K., 380–381
Shwe, H. I., 265
Sicard-Cras, I., 98, 208
Siegel, B. S., 412
Siegler, R. S., 9, 204–206
Siekerman, K., 9, 119
Sierens, S., 443
Signorella, M., 378
Silinskas, G., 340
Silke, C., 357
Sills, J., 197
Silva, K., 415
Silva, M., 197
Silva, R. L., 377, 378
Silva, R., 389
Silva-Santos, S., 116
Silveira, F., 414
Silventoinen, K., 146
Silvers, J. A., 301
Sim, A., 456
Sim, Z. L., 183
Simard, D., 270
Simatende, B., 247
Simmering, V. R., 212

Simmonds, M., 154
Simmons, S. C., 81, 140
Simon, C., 334
Simon, K. A., 417
Simon, R. W., 405
Simons, L., 386
Simons, S. S. H., 25
Simpkins, S. D., 340
Sin, D. D., 161
Singh, A., 141
Singh, C., 84
Singh, G. K., 150
Singh, L., 126, 266, 269
Singh, N., 147
Singh, S., 147
Singletary, B., 426
Singleton, N., 259, 260
Sipsma, H. L., 139
Sirois, S., 180
Sirugo, G., 65
Skakkebaek, A., 52
Skaugset, L. M., 211
Skelton, A. E., 126
Skinner, B. F., 14, 273
Skinner, E. A., 340
Skinner, O. D., 299, 415
Skoog, T., 148, 391
Skranes, J., 550
Sladek, M. R., 334
Slater, A., 127
Slaughter, V., 224–226, 438
Slicker, G., 443
Śliwerski, A., 312
Slobodin, O., 253
Slobodskaya, H. R., 306
Sloutsky, V. M., 213
Smailes, J., 188
Smetana, J. G., 346, 350–352, 415, 416
Smink, F. R. E., 159
Smith Lee, J. R., 32
Smith, A. R., 227
Smith, B., 139
Smith, C. D., 32
Smith, C. E., 208, 243, 354, 355
Smith, C., 366
Smith, D. S., 194, 384
Smith, G. C., 422
Smith, J., 414
Smith, L. B., 209, 210, 263
Smith, L. G., 243
Smith, L., 119
Smith, M., 252, 324
Smith, N. C., 326
Smith, P. K., 373, 434
Smith, P. S., 424
Smith, R. L., 437
Smith, S., 451
SmithBattle, L., 393
Smock, P. J., 419
Smolucha, F., 198
Smolucha, L., 198
Snapp-Childs, W., 122
Snell, P., 366
Snider, J. B., 366
Snowling, M. J., 249
Snyder, K., 378

Soderstrom-Anttila, V., 56
Sodian, B., 225
Soenens, B., 405
Softness, K. A., 54
Solebo, A. L., 128
Soliman, A., 140
Solmeyer, A. R., 407
Solomon, J., 310
Soltani, S., 79
Son, H., 161
Soneji, S., 80
Song, J., 339–341
Song, Y., 340, 353, 354
Sonuga-Barke, E. J. S., 140, 210
Sood, B., 52
Sorbara, J. C., 388
Sorenson Duncan, T., 272
Sosa-Hernandez, L., 300
Sosnowska, J., 20
Soto-Heras, S., 72
Spadafora, N., 438, 439
Sparapani, N., 270
Sparling, J., 443
Spear, L. P., 160, 161
Spearman, C., 234
Spelke, E. S., 182, 262
Spencer, D., 376
Spencer, J. P., 117, 122, 213
Spencer, M. B., 330–332
Spencer, R. M. C., 142
Spencer, S. J., 246
Sperry, D. E., 278
Spettigue, W., 159
Speyer, L. G., 300
Spiegel, C., 214
Spiegel, J. A., 263
Spielberg, J. M., 114
Spinath, F. M., 61
Spinelli, A., 153
Spinelli, M., 298
Spinner, L., 381
Spinrad, T. L., 356
Spivey, L. A., 386
Spriet, C., 223
Squeglia, L. M., 161
Sravanti, L., 385
Srivastava, A., 391
Sroufe, L. A., 291, 293
Stacks, A. M., 414
Staff, J., 148
Stahl, A. E., 180, 183
Stalgaitis, C. A., 440
Stallworthy, I. C., 458
Stams, G. -J. J. M., 277
Stanković-Ramirez, Z., 442
Stanley, A. Y., 79
Stanowicz, L., 276
Stapel, J. C., 321
Stearns, M., 364
Steele, C. M., 246
Steele, J. R., 332
Steensma, T. D., 384, 386
Stein, A. D., 140
Stein, G. L., 32
Stein, Y., 82
Steinbeis, N., 213

Steinberg, L., 114, 195, 227, 228, 405, 440, 441
Steiner, J. E., 129
Steinmayr, R., 339
Stenberg, G., 293
Stephens, K. K., 87
Stephens, T., 79
Stephenson, J., 57
Stergiou, N., 115
Stern, J. A., 353
Sternberg, R. J., 16, 194, 234, 236, 237, 243, 245, 246, 253
Stevens, E. N., 323
Stevens, J., 388
Stewart, J. L., 391
StGeorge, J. M., 373, 434
Stidham-Hall, K., 146
Stierman, B., 154
Stifter, C., 297–300
Stipek, D., 322
Stockdale, L., 449, 451
Stoll, S., 277
Stone, M. M., 219, 220
Storandt, R. J., 154
Stout, J. G., 375
Stout, W., 353
Strambler, M. J., 246
Strathearn, L., 308
Strelau, J., 302, 304, 305
Streri, A., 129, 217
Stubbs, A., 455
Stuebe, A., 139
Sturdivant, T. D., 332
Styfco, S. J., 443
Su, Y., 391
Suarez, M. I., 417
Suarez-Orozco, C., 425, 453
Suarez-Rivera, C., 208, 209
Subrahmanyam, K., 246
Sučević, J., 223
Sugden, N. A., 126
Suggate, S., 118
Suizzo, M.-A., 447
Sullivan, J., 332–334, 379
Sullivan, M. W., 290, 410
Sullivan, R. M., 312
Sullivan-Pyke, C. S., 56
Sumter, S. R., 440
Sun, Y., 147
Sunderam, S., 56
Sundqvist, A., 217
Suni, E., 142, 143
Supanitayanon, S., 449
Super, C. M., 8, 120, 143, 237, 306
Superbia-Guimaraes, L., 213
Surian, L., 351
Susi, A., 424
Susperreguy, M. I., 323
Sussman, S., 440
Sutton, A., 447
Svetlova, M., 353
Swartz, J. R., 227
Swearer, S. M., 360, 361
Sweeney, M. M., 420
Swingley, D., 262
Swit, C. S., 375

Syed, M., 334, 336
Syvertsen, J. L., 81
Szpak, M., 225
Szucs, D., 325

T

Taber, K. S., 89, 198, 199
Tabrizi, S. J., 49
Tait, A. R., 31
Takacs, L., 304, 305
Takahashi, K., 62, 315
Takahira, S., 374
Takeuchi, H., 236
Talleyrand, R. M., 425
Tamariz, M., 275
Tamis-LeMonda, C. S., 98, 123, 277, 414
Tamnes, C. K., 113, 363
Tamnes, C., 112, 206, 296
Tan, C. M., 140
Tan, E. S., 313
Tan, E., 353
Tan, R., 315
Tan, T. X., 421
Tan, W. C., 161
Taneri, B., 44, 53
Tangpricha, V., 385
Tankersley, A. P., 387
Tanner, A., 249
Tanner, J. M., 147
Tannock, M., 434
Tao, B., 83
Tappin, D., 151
Taran, N., 249
Tardif, T., 277
Tarokh, L., 149
Tarrant, C., 452
Tarry, H., 351
Tarullo, A. R., 99
Tashjian, S. M., 149
Tasker, F., 421
Taumoepeau, M., 225, 276
Taussig, H. N., 455
Taylor, A. W., 84
Taylor, D., 417
Taylor, K., 272
Taylor, M., 434, 435
Taylor, Z. E., 356
te Nijenhuis, J., 244
Tebbi, C. K., 53
Tecwyn, E. C., 213
Tena-Sempere, M., 147
Tenenbaum, H. R., 379
Teoh, P. J., 56
Teran, L., 195
Terman, L. M., 242
Teti, D. M., 304
Tevlin, C., 375
Thamban, T., 48
Thatcher, J. Y., 365
Thein, S. L., 48
Thelen, E., 20, 115, 119, 121
Theodora, M., 58
Theodoraki, T. E., 210, 214, 215
Theule, J., 312
Theurel, A., 301

Thoma, B. C., 387
Thomaes, S., 325
Thoman, E. B., 99, 125
Thomas, A., 302–304
Thomas, J. C., 298
Thomas, R., 336
Thompson, A. E., 375
Thompson, A. L., 62, 442
Thompson, J., 245
Thompson, R. A., 293, 299, 300, 307, 310, 313, 315, 322, 323, 353
Thompson, S. F., 295, 415
Thornberg, R., 351
Thurman, S. L., 299
Thurstone, L. L., 234
Thurstone, T. G., 234
Tierney, K., 54
Timeo, S., 332
Tinggaard, J., 144
Tiokhin, L., 21
Tistarelli, N., 210
Titz, C., 219
Titzmann, P. F., 437
Tobin, R. M., 434
Todd, B. K., 379
Toft, D. J., 138
Tomalski, P., 215
Tomasello, M., 187, 225, 274
Tomaz Barbosa, R. R., 153
Tomlinson, R. C., 111
Tomova, A., 146
Tomova, L., 227
Tompkins, V., 413
Tooley, U. A., 110, 214, 215
Toolis, E. E., 414
Toomey, R. B., 32, 162, 385
Toseeb, U., 355
Toth, S. L., 94
Touyz, S., 159
Tovar, M., 453
Traboulsi, H., 161
Tracy, J. L., 292
Tramutola, A., 52
Traub, F., 457
Trauble, B., 225
Trawick-Smith, J., 197
Tremblay, L., 147
Tremblay, M., 161, 375
Tremblay, R. E., 359
Treschuk, J. V., 364
Trettien, A. W., 120
Trinh, S. L., 436
Trinidad, J. E., 340
Trionfi, G., 435
Tristao, R. M., 129
Troche, S. J., 235
Tronick, E. Z., 293
Tronick, E., 454
Troop-Gordon, W., 437
Trosman, I., 143
Trost, K., 330
Troutman, B., 14
Trucco, E. M., 161
Tsai, K. M., 415
Tsai, M. C., 148
Tsamantioti, E. S., 79

Tsao, Y.-L., 380
Tsuji, S., 268
Tu, K., 449
Tucker, C. J., 406, 407
Tudge, J. R. H., 19
Tullius, J. M., 420
Tully, L. A., 411, 412
Tulving, E., 216
Tunau, K., 146
Turban, J. L., 386
Turecki, G., 454
Turfkruyer, M., 139
Turiel, E., 351, 352
Turk-Browne, N. B., 180
Turkheimer, E., 65
Turnbull, K., 268, 271
Turner, J. H., 291
Turney, K., 423, 424
Turocy, J., 55, 59
Twenge, J. M., 452
Twum-Antwi, A., 457
Tyrrell, E., 152
Tzischinsky, O., 374

U

Uddin, M., 162
Uhl, E. R., 221
Uhls, Y. T., 452, 453
Umana-Taylor, A. J., 331, 332, 334–337
Umer, A., 79
Uono, S., 249
Updegraff, K. A., 404, 407
Usai, M. C., 214
Ustun, B., 129

V

Vaala, S. E., 449
Vaillancourt, T., 362
Vaivada, T., 140
Valadi, S., 123
Valenzuela, C. P., 86
Valiente, C., 295
Valkenborghs, S. R., 149
Valkenburg, P. M., 380, 452
Valle, J., 48
Vallotton, C. D., 265
Vally, Z., 413
van 't, Hof., 249
Van de Vondervoort, J. W., 353
van den Berg, L., 120
van den Berg, Y. H. M., 438
van den Heuvel, M. I., 85
Van der Graaff, J., 355
van der Ploeg, R., 360
van der Schuur, W. A., 211
van der Stel, M., 226, 227
Van der Straeten, G., 420
van Dijk, A., 361
van Dijk, E., 358
van Dijk, R., 406
van Dommelen, P., 138
van Duijvenvoorde, A. C. K., 114
van Eeden, A. E., 159
Van Eldik, W. M., 420

van Hell, J. G., 272
van Heteren, C. F., 98
van Hoogdalem, A.-G., 433
Van Hoorn, J., 441
van IJzendoorn, M. H., 65, 312
Van Ryzin, M. J., 313
van Scheppingen, M. A., 405
Van Winkle, Z., 420
Vance, S. R., 387
Vandenbroucke, A. R. E., 205
Vandermaas-Peeler, M., 197
Vandierendonck, A., 206
Vanhalst, J., 327
Vannasing, P., 275
Vannoy, M. R., 376, 377, 384
Vannucci, A., 452
Vargesson, N., 79
Varner, F., 334
Varnum, M. E. W., 19
Vasc, D., 433, 434
Vasilenko, S. A., 389–391
Vasileva, M., 23
Vasileva, O., 196, 199
Vasilopoulos, F., 142
Vaughan, E. P., 363
Vazquez, C. E., 149
Veenman, M. V. J., 226, 227
Veenstra, R., 440, 441
Veiga, G., 434
Veiga, R. V., 84
Veldman, S. L. C., 116, 117
Vennemann, M., 151
Venta, A., 311
Ventura, A. K., 95
Verbeek, M., 392
Vereijken, B., 119
Vergauwe, E., 210
Vergeer, I., 142
Verhage, M. L., 305
Verhasselt, V., 139
Verhoef, E., 275
Verissimo, M., 315
Verkooijen, K. T., 440
Vermande, M., 406
Vermeulen, M. C. M., 149
Vernon-Feagans, L., 279
Veronneau, M. H., 447
Verschueren, K., 324, 325
Victora, C. G., 139
Victora, M. D., 117
Vijayakumar, N., 112
Vijver, F. J. R., 190
Villanueva, L., 239
Villaruel, E., 413
Villela, D., 58
Vinden, P., 225
Virmani, E. A., 322, 323
Vishkin, A., 366
Vismara, L., 312
Visscher, M., 91
Vissers, C., 198
Vissers, L. E. L. M., 252
Viteri, O., 83
Vohs, K. D., 326
Vojtech, J. T.-G., 425
Vo-Jutabha, E. D., 335

Volkmar, F. R., 48
Vollmer, B., 93
Volpe, L. E., 142
von Aster, M., 250
von Hofsten, C., 117, 181
Von Holle, A., 139
von Lupke, H., 66
von Soest, T., 325
Von Stumm, S., 64
Vonk, J., 353
Voorhies, W., 249
Voracek, M., 244
Vorgias, D., 79
Vosylis, R., 330
Votruba-Drzal, E., 340
Vouloumanos, A., 96
Voyer, D., 375
Vozzola, E. C., 346, 349
Vrabič, N., 124
Vuoksimaa, E., 360
Vuong, Q. C., 293
Vygotsky, L. S., 17, 195–199, 201, 218, 432, 434

W

Waasdorp, T. E., 361
Wachtel, G. F., 267
Waddell, K. J., 220
Wagner, A. D., 211
Wagner, M. F., 155
Wagner, R. S., 128
Wagnsson, S., 325
Wagovich, S. A., 270
Waid, J. D., 407
Waldfogel, J., 418
Waldman, I. D., 356
Walk, R. D., 127
Walker, B. L., 298
Wallace, J. G., 16
Wallbridge, B., 356
Walle, E. A., 292
Wallentin, M., 374
Walsh, A., 380
Walsh, J. J., 356
Walters, G. D., 361
Walton, M., 108
Wamakima, B. W., 78
Wang, D., 408
Wang, F., 360
Wang, M. T., 334–335, 407, 416, 427, 448
Wang, M., 438
Wang, Q., 91, 220, 323
Wang, S., 223
Wang, W., 338
Wang, X., 325, 352
Wang, Y., 56, 149, 249, 266, 324, 335–336, 423, 433
Wang, Z., 410
Wangqvist, M., 330
Wantchekon, K. A., 334
Warburton, W., 451
Ward, K. P., 412, 414
Ward, L. M., 380
Ware, R. E., 48
Warne, R. T., 240
Warneken, F., 353–355

Warner, T. D., 390
Warreyn, P., 251
Wasik, B. A., 269–270
Wass, R., 198
Wass, S. V., 208
Wasserberg, M. J., 246
Wasserman, J. D., 239, 241–242
Waterhouse, L., 237
Waterland, R. A., 66
Waters, E., 291
Waters, S. F., 293, 298
Watkins, M. W., 243
Watson, A., 410
Watson, J., 13, 99
Watson, R. J., 391
Watts, A. W., 149
Watts, L. L., 441
Wautier, A., 78
Waxman, S., 126, 263, 332
Weaver, J., 125, 420
Webb, R., 312
Weber, A., 82
Webster, B., 147
Webster, S., 75, 84
Wechsler, D., 242
Wedderburn, C. J., 84
Weeks, M. S., 437
Wei, S. Q., 84
Weidman, A. C., 292
Weil, L. G., 226
Weimer, A. A., 294
Weinberg, M. K., 375
Weinfield, N. S., 311
Weingarten, J., 437
Weinstein, E., 453
Weinstein, N., 449
Weinstein, R. S., 246
Weis, R., 414
Weisenfeld, G., 444
Weisgram, E. S., 377–380
Weisleder, A., 275, 277–278
Weisleder, P., 31–32
Weisner, M. L., 245
Weiss, L. G., 244, 247
Weissberg, R. P., 363
Weisz, A. N., 350
Wellman, H. M., 223–225, 294
Wellons, J. C., 84
Welsh, J. A., 443
Welshman, J., 443
Welti, K., 421
Wen, T., 87
Wenger, Y., 444
Wentzel, K. R., 341, 355, 437, 441
Werker, J., 269
Werner, E. E., 456
Werner, H., 149
Wertsch, J. V., 199
Werwach, A., 262
West, D., 6, 454
West, K. L., 6, 116
Westen, D., 11
Westerman, M. A., 295
Westra, T., 8, 120
Westrick-Payne, K. K., 418
Wethington, E., 405

Wetzel, N., 25
Weymouth, B. B., 415
Whaley, G. L., 426
Wheaton, B., 325
Whitcomb, S. A., 24
White, A. E., 391
White, E. E., 422
White, H., 292
White, L. T., 221
Whitehouse, A. J. O., 139
Whiteman, S. D., 407
Whitley, D. M., 423
Whittington, J. R., 80
Whittle, S., 214
Wiborg, C. E., 418, 420
Wickens, C. D., 16, 204, 206
Widom, C. S., 155–156
Wiedeman, A. M., 450–451
Wiertsema, M., 360
Wiese, D. L., 332
Wigby, K., 52
Wigfield, A., 337–338, 340–341
Wiglesworth, A., 157
Wigmore-Sykes, M., 146
Wiik, K. L., 305
Wilbur, M. B., 91
Wildeman, C., 424
Wiley, M. O. L., 57, 421–422
Wilkinson, P. O., 63
Williams, A., 332
Williams, C. D., 332
Williams, J. L., 337
Williams, T. N., 48
Williamson, A. A., 143
Williamson, V., 424
Willis-Owen, S. A. G., 153
Wilson, S., 296
Wilton, L., 333
Wimer, C., 418
Winne, P. H., 16
Winnebeck, E. C., 149
Winsler, A., 198, 432
Winters, A. M., 363
Wiradhany, W., 211
Witherington, D. C., 8, 20, 67
Withers, P. J., 26
Wittig, S. M. O., 304
Wohlfahrt-Veje, C., 146
Wojciak, A. S., 406
Wolf, B. J., 250
Wolfe, K., 96–97
Wolff, P. H., 96
Wolke, D., 94
Wong, K. K.-Y., 376
Wong, T. K. Y., 356, 410–411
Wonkam, A., 53
Wood, M. A., 453
Woodhouse, N., 242
Woodhouse, S. S., 311–312
Woodward, A. L., 263
Woodward, L. J., 81
Woolley, J. D., 187
Woolverton, G. A., 333
Worobey, J., 95
Worrell, F. C., 253–254
Wouldes, T. A., 82

Wozniak, J. R., 79
Wright, A. J., 243
Wright, A. W., 455
Wright, B. C., 188
Wright, B., 266
Wright, G. J., 72
Wright, K. M., 424
Wright, N., 163
Wu, Y., 219, 293
Wuhl, E., 154
Wylie, B. J., 80
Wysman, L., 221

X

Xaverius, P., 87
Xiao, E., 406
Xiao, S. X., 355, 380, 382
Xiao-na, H., 143
Xie, D., 85
Xie, H., 438
Xu, F., 183
Xu, J. Z., 48
Xu, J., 153
Xu, Q., 264
Xu, Y., 264, 383, 414, 422, 433

Y

Yaakobi, E., 313
Yager, Z., 448
Yamamoto, H., 116
Yang, B., 146
Yang, C., 274
Yang, J., 407
Yang, L., 80
Yang, M.-Y., 155
Yang, S., 237
Yang, W., 155
Yaoying, X., 433
Yaron, A., 106
Yates, T. M., 325
Yau, J. C., 195
Yau, J., 352
Yavorsky, J. E., 373
Yavuz, H. M., 356
Ye, Z., 361
Yeager, D. S., 338–341, 363
Yelinek, J., 295
Yeo, G. S. H., 60, 154
Yeoh, S. L., 81
Yerkes, R. M., 239
Yi, C., 81
Yildiz, M., 268
Yip, S. W., 114
Yip, T., 333–334, 337
Yoakum, C. S., 239
Yokoya, S., 52
Yonas, A., 127
Yoo, H. N., 351
Yoon, E., 335
York, C., 60, 64
York, H., 445
Yoshinaga-Itano, C., 266
Young, A. W., 126
Young, G., 108
Young, N. A. E., 247

Youniss, J., 330
Yousefi, M., 144
Youssef, G., 112
Yu, C., 106, 111, 208, 209
Yu, S. M., 150
Yudin, M. H., 64
Yue, X., 360
Yuen, W. S., 161
Yule, K., 456
Yunger, J. L., 383

Z

Zablotsky, B., 210, 247–248, 252
Zadeh, S., 418
Zagel, A. L., 152
Zahn-Waxler, C., 413
Zaitchik, D., 187
Zajac, L., 311
Zajączkowska, M., 271
Zaman, W., 219
Zambrano, P. L., 393
Zammit, M., 265
Zan, B., 347
Zanobetti, A., 153
Zapata-Gietl, C., 329–330
Zarbatany, L., 439, 441
Zee, M., 448
Zelazo, N. A., 119
Zelazo, P. D., 181
Zelazo, P. R., 119
Zelekha, Y., 313
Zell, E., 324
Zeman, J., 300
Zemp, M., 420–421
Zettersten, M., 270
Zettl, M., 330
Zgodic, A., 210
Zhai, S., 410
Zhang, F., 128, 180, 248
Zhang, Q., 360, 385
Zhang, V. H., 262
Zhang, W., 410
Zhang, X., 52
Zhao, T. C., 262
Zhao, W., 228
Zhao, X., 352
Zhe, C., 210
Zheng, L., 391
Zielinski, R., 92
Zigler, E., 443
Zill, N., 421
Zimlich, R., 162
Zimmer, M., 57, 251
Zimmer-Gembeck, M. J., 148, 299, 311
Zimmerman, R., 307
Ziporyn, T. D., 149
Zondervan-Zwijnenburg, M., 355
Zosh, J. M., 267
Zosuls, K. M., 377, 380, 382, 384
Zsiga, E. C., 259
Zucker, K. J., 385
Zufferey, S., 260
Zuk, J., 275
Zukin, R. S., 51
Zych, I., 360
Zycha, I., 360

SUBJECT INDEX

A

Academic achievement
    parents, 447
    peers, 447–448
    schools, 448
    teachers, 448
Accommodation, 175, 175 (figure)
Accreditation Council for Genetic Counseling, 167
Achievement motivation, 337–341
    achievement attributions, 338
    contextual influences on, 339–341
    helpless orientation, 339, 339 (table)
    learning goals, 338–339
    mastery motivation, 337–338
    mastery orientation, 339, 339 (table)
    mindset, 338
    parents, 339–340
    peers, 341
    performance goals, 338–339
    teachers, 340–341
Acquired immune deficiency syndrome (AIDS), 84
Active child, 9
Active gene-environment correlation, 63
Active learning, 222
Activity and coordination, motor skills, 116
Adolescence (about 11 to about 18 years), 5
Adolescent egocentrism, 194–195
Adolescent growth spurt, 144
Adoption, 56–57
    adoptive families, 420–421
    behavior studies, 60
Affordances, 130
Age of viability, 76
Aggression, 359–363
    aggressive-rejected children, 438
    bullying, 360–363
    bullying intervention, 362–363
    bully-victims, 361–362
    children who are bullied, 361–362
    children who bully, 360–361
    cyberbullying, 360, 362
    delinquency, 363
    instrumental aggression, 359
    physical aggression, 359–360, 375
    reactive aggression, 361
    relational aggression, 359
    sex differences in, 375
    traditional bullying, 360
The American Academy of Pediatrics, 143, 151, 251
The American Association on Intellectual and Developmental Disabilities, 252
The American College of Obstetricians and Gynecologists, 54, 91
The American Midwifery Certification Board, 167
Amniocentesis, 57
Amnion, 75, 89
Ampe (game), 435
Analytical intelligence, 236
Androgynous, 382
Anencephaly, 84
Anesthetics, 91
Angelman syndrome, 48
Animism, 184, 187
Anorexia nervosa, 158
Antisocial behavior, 359–360; See also Aggression
Apgar scale, 92, 93 (table)
Appearance-reality distinction, 185
Applied behavior analyst, 398
Applied developmental science, 30
Applied intelligence, 236
Artificial insemination, 55
Assimilation, 175, 175 (figure)
Assisted reproductive technology (ART), 54–56
    artificial insemination, 55
    surrogacy, 56
    in vitro fertilization, 55–56
Associative play, 433
Asthma, 153
Attachment, 307–316
    caregiver depression, 311–312
    in childhood and adolescence, 315–316
    cultural variations in, 313–315, 314 (figure)
    ethological theory of attachment (see Ethological theory of attachment, Bowlby's)
    father-infant attachment, 312–313
    influences on, 311–313
    insecure-avoidant attachment, 310, 313
    insecure-disorganized attachment, 310–311
    insecure-resistant attachment, 310
    internal working model, 310–311
    secure base, 310–311
    security of attachment, 309–310
    sensitive caregiving, 311
    stability on, 313
    Strange Situation and (Ainsworth), 309–310, 309 (table), 313–315
Attention, 207–212
    ADHD, 210
    adolescence, 210–211
    attentional control, 210
    childhood, 209–210
    developmental changes, 210
    implications for education and parenting, 211–212
    infancy, 207–209
    types of, 207
Attention-deficit/hyperactivity disorder (ADHD), 210, 251–253
Audiologist, 168–169
Authoritarian parenting style, 409–410
Authoritative parenting style, 411
Autism spectrum disorders (ASD), 248–249, 252
Autobiographical memory, 216, 218–219
Automaticity, 206
Autonomous morality, 347
Autonomy, 31
Axon, 105

B

Babbling, 262
Baby signing programs, 265
Back to Sleep campaign, 151
Bandura, Albert, 14–15
Bayley Scales of Infant Development III (BSID-III), 240–241
Behavior genetics, 59–61, 61 (table)
    heritability and personal characteristics, 60–61
    nonshared environment, 61
    research methods, 60
Behaviorism, 13
Behaviorist and social learning theories, 13–15
Bilingual language learning, 268–269, 269 (figure), 271–272
Binet-Simon test, 241
Binge eating disorder, 158–159
Bioecological systems theory, 17–19, 19 (figure), 199
Blastocyst, 74
Body growth
    body proportions throughout life, 137 (figure)
    breastfeeding, 138–139
    cephalocaudal and proximodistal development, 137 (figure)
    in childhood, 138
    childhood food preferences, 139
    growth norms, 137
    in infancy, 137–138
    malnutrition, 139–142
    and maturation in adolescence (see Puberty)
    nutrition and growth, 138–139
    patterns of growth, 136
    physical activity, 142
    sleep (see sleep)

Body mass index (BMI), 154
Brain development, 104–114, 213, 296
    adolescence, 112–114
    cerebral cortex, 107
    childhood, 111–112
    experience-dependent brain development, 109–111
    experience-expectant brain development, 109
    infancy, 109–111
    lateralization, 108
    and malnutrition, 140–142, 141 (figure)
    myelination, 107
    neurogenesis, 105
    neurons, 104–105
    synaptogenesis and pruning, 106, 106 (figure)
Brain, human, 113 (figure)
Brazelton Neonatal Behavioral Assessment Scale (NBAS), 93
Breastfeeding, 138–139
Broca's area, 275
Bulimia nervosa, 158
Bully-victims, 361

C

Caffeine, 79
Canalization, 62
Careers in child development, 36–39, 36 (table)
    applied behavior analyst, 398
    audiologist, 168–169
    child development career fields, 37–39
    child life specialist, 397
    clinical psychologist, 398–399
    cognitive development, 282–285
    counseling psychologist, 398–399
    developmental psychologist, 284–285
    doula (caregiver), 167
    early childhood educator, 282
    elementary education, 282–283
    English as a Second Language (ESL) teacher, 283–284
    genetic counselor, 166–167
    intervention research, 399
    marriage and family therapists, 462–463
    middle school teacher/high school teacher, 283
    midwife, 167
    neuropsychological technician, 284
    occupational therapist/occupational therapy assistant, 169–170
    pediatric and neonatal nurse, 167–168
    physical therapist/physical therapy assistant, 169
    physician and pediatrician, 168
    preschool and child care center director, 461
    recreation worker, 461
    school counselor, 462
    school psychologist, 462
    social worker, 396–397
    socioemotional development, 396–399
    special education, 283
    speech-language pathologists, 284
    substance abuse counselors, 397
    toy and media research, 463
    transferable skills, 36–37
    user design and usability, 463
Caregiver depression, 311–312
Care orientation, 350
Carolina Abecedarian Project, 443
Carroll, John, 235
Categorical self, 322
Categorization, 222–223
Cell-free fetal DNA, 58
Centers for Disease Control and Prevention, 154, 391
Centration, 185
Cephalocaudal pattern of development, 115
Cerebellum, 119
Cerebral cortex, 107, 107 (figure)
Certified Critical Care Registered Nurse Neonatal Exam, 168
Certified Pediatric Nurse Examination, 168
Child abuse/maltreatment, 155–156, 156 (table)
Child assent, 31–32
Child behavior specialists, 398
Childbirth
    breech position, 91
    cesarean delivery (C-section), 91
    cultural childbirth practices, 92
    doula (caregiver), 92
    home birth, 91–92
    labor, 89, 90 (figure)
    low birth weight and preterm infants, 93–95
    medication during delivery, 91
    midwife, 91
    natural childbirth, 91
    newborn health screening, 92–93
Child directed speech, SES and, 278
Childhood amnesia, 217–218
Child life specialist, 397
Children's play
    and cognitive development, 432–433
    culture and play, 435–436
    imaginary companions, 434–435
    rough-and-tumble play, 434
    social development and early friendships, 433
    sociodramatic play, 433–434
Chorionic villus sampling (CVS), 57–58
Chromosomal abnormalities, 51–54, 75, 85
    down syndrome, 51–52
    sex chromosome abnormalities, 52, 53 (table)
Chromosomes, 44–45, 45 (figure)
Chronic poverty, 214–215
Chronic stressors, 147
Chronosystem, 18
Cigarette and e-cigarette, use of, 80, 161
Cisgender, 385
Classical conditioning, 13–14
Class inclusion, 189
Cleavage, 73
Cliques, 439–440
Code-switching, 272
Cognitive development, 6, 17, 130
    assimilation and accommodation, 174–175, 175 (figure)
    cognitive-developmental theory, 15–16, 376–377
    equilibration, 175–176
    stages of, 16 (table)
Cognitive equilibration, 175–176
Cognitive operations, 184
Cognitive schemas, 15
Cognitive theories, 15–17
Cohort, 7
Common Core in the United States, 118
Community violence, 455–456
Computerized tomography (CT), 26
Concealment, 301
Conceptual skills, 251
Concrete operational reasoning (in middle childhood), 188–191
    characteristics of, 188–189
    classification, 188
    class inclusion, 189
    conservation, 189–190
    and education, 191
    familiarity and contextual demands, 190–191
    schooling and language, 190
    seriation, 188–189
    transitive inference, 188
Conditioned stimulus, 98
Congenital abnormalities, 84
Congenital Zika syndrome, 84
Constructivist classroom, 442
Context, 6–7
    and opportunities for movement, 116–117
Contextual influences on intelligence, 244–247
    group differences and majority culture, 245–246
    reducing cultural bias in IQ tests, 246–247
    socioeconomic status of IQ, 245
    sociohistorical context and IQ, 244
    stereotypes and IQ, 246
Contextual influences on language development, 276–279
    exposure to infant-directed speech (see Infant-directed speech)
    SES and child directed speech, 278–279
    SES and language development, 277, 278 (figure)
    socioeconomic status, 277–279
Continuous change, 9, 10 (figure)
Control group, 28
Conventional moral reasoning, 347
Cooing, 262
Cooperative play, 433
Core knowledge theory, 182–183
Corporal punishment, 411–412
Corpus callosum, 108
Correlational research, 27
Cortex, 107
Cortical visual impairment (CVI), 128

Subject Index **651**

Co-sleeping, 143
COVID-19 pandemic, 7, 30, 84, 149
   and challenges for families, 426–427
   and children, 153–154
   children's access to computer and Internet, 445, 445 (figure)
   decline of prenatal care during, 87
   depression and suicide, 163
   and gender, 373
   masks and emotion recognition of children, 295
   and preschool enrollment, 443, 444 (figure)
   social media use, 452
   women infected with Covid during pregnancy, 84
Crawling, motor development, 116, 120
Creative intelligence, 236
Crossing over process, 45
Cross-sectional research study, 28
Crowds, 440
Crowning, 89
Cultural context, 7–8
Culture, 7–8, 18–19, 237, 245–246
   cultural differences in infant-directed speech, 276–277
   cultural differences in temperament, 306
   cultural socialization, 300–301
   cultural variations in attachment, 313–315, 314 (figure)
   and moral reasoning, 350, 352
   prosocial behavior, 358–359
Cyberbullying, 360, 362

D

Darwin, Charles, 20
Debriefing, 31
Deferred imitation tasks, 182, 217
Delinquency, 363
Dendrites, 104–105
Deoxyribonucleic acid (DNA), 44, 86
Dependent variable, 27
Depression, 161–163
Development, 4, 8
   continuities and discontinuities in, 9, 10 (figure)
   influence of biology and environment in, 8–9
   self influence of children in, 9
Developmental disabilities, 247, 248 (figure)
Developmental domains (types of development), 6, 6 (figure)
Developmental dyscalculia, 249–250
Developmental dysgraphia, 250
Developmental dyslexia, 249
Developmentally appropriate practice, 442
Developmental period, 5
Developmental psychologist, 284–285
Developmental science, 1
Developmental shifts in gene-environment correlation, 63–64
Diagnostic and Statistical Manual of Mental Disorders (DSM), 251
Diffusion tensor imaging (DTI), 26

Digital technology, children's access to, 444–445, 445 (figure)
Direct instruction, 442
Discontinuous change, 9, 10 (figure)
Disequilibrium, 175
Dishabituation, 208
Distributive justice, 354
Divided attention, 207
Dizygotic (DZ) twins, 45–46, 56, 60, 119; *See also* Monozygotic (MZ) twins
Doctor of Physical Therapy degree (DPT), 169
Dominant-recessive disorders, 49–50, 50 (table)
Dominant-recessive inheritance, 46–47, 47 (figure)
Doula (caregiver), 92, 167
Down syndrome, 51–52
Dual-language learning (dual-language immersion), 272
Dynamic systems theory, 19–20, 121–123, 121 (figure)
   goal-directed behavior, 122–123
   physical maturation and integrated abilities, 122
   social and cultural context, 123
   unweighting infants to discover motor skills, 122 (figure)
Dyslexia, 52

E

Early auditory deprivation, 266
Early childhood (about 2 to about 6 years), 5
Early childhood education interventions, 443
Early childhood educator, 282
Early-life stress, 453–454
Eating disorders, 158–159
   anorexia nervosa, 158
   binge eating disorder, 158–159
   bulimia nervosa, 158
   influences and treatment, 159
   prevalence of, 159
E-cigarettes (vaping), 80, 161
Ectoderm, 74
Education
   attention and, 211–212
   concrete operational reasoning and, 190–191
   long-term memory and, 221–222
   preoperational reasoning and, 187
   thinking skills and, 228
   working memory and, 215–216
Egocentrism, 184, 187
   adolescent egocentrism, 194–195
Electroencephalography (EEG), 25
Electronically activated voice recorder (EAR), 23
Embryo, 74
Embryonic disk, 74
Emotional experience, 290–296
   of adolescents, 296
   of children, 294–295
   emotional competence, 294
   of infants, 290–294

   masks and emotion recognition, 295
   milestones in emotional development, 291 (table)
   negative emotions, 291, 312
   positive emotions, 296
   primary emotions, 290–291
   recognizing others' emotions, 292–293
   self-conscious emotions, 292
   social interaction and emotional understanding, 295
   social smile, 291
   stranger wariness/stranger anxiety, 293–294
   understanding others' emotions, 294–295
Emotional intelligence, 238–239
Emotional regulation, 297–302, 360
   adolescence, 301–302
   caregiver sensitivity, 298
   childhood, 299–301
   cultural socialization, 300–301
   dynamic caregiver-infant interactions, 299
   emotional display rules, 300
   infancy, 297–299
   managing emotions, 297
   strategies, 299–300
Empathy, 353
Endoderm, 74
English as a Second Language (ESL) teacher, 283–284
Epigenetics, 66–67
   processes in animals, 66
   processes in people, 66–67
Episodic memory, 216, 219
Equilibration, 175–176
Erikson, Erik, 11–12
Ethnic-racial identity, 331–337
   achievement status, 334
   adolescence, 333–334
   childhood, 332–333
   discrimination and, 336–337
   ethnic socialization, 334–336
   exploration status, 333
   infancy, 332
   influences on, 334–336
   parent-child conversations about race, 333 (figure)
   parents, 334–335
   peers, 335–336
   perceived pressure, 335
   teachers and schools, 336
   unexamined status, 333
Ethological theory of attachment, Bowlby's, 307–310
   attachment in the makings (2 through 6-7 months), 309
   clear-cut attachments (7 to 24 months), 309
   infants' signals and adults' responses, 307–308
   phases of attachment, 308–310
   pre-attachment (birth to 2 months), 308–309
   reciprocal relationships (24 to 30 months onward), 309

Ethology, 20
Event sampling method, 296
Evocative gene-environment correlation, 63
Evolutionary developmental theory, 20–21
Executive function, 51–52, 81, 107, 110–111, 206, 213–214, 220, 224
    poverty and, 214–215
Exosystem, 18
Experience-dependent brain development, 109–110
Experience-expectant brain development, 109
Experimental groups/test groups, 28
Experimental Research, 27–28
Expressive vocabulary, 268
Externality effect, 125, 126 (figure)

F

False belief tasks, 224
Families, challenges for, 423–427
    COVID-19 and, 426–427
    family system, 426
    migrant families, 425–426
    parental deployment, 424–425
    parental incarceration, 423–424
    racial disparities, 426–427
Family constellations, 416–423
    adoption and child outcomes, 421–422
    adoptive families, 420–421
    blended families, 420–421
    cohabiting families, 419
    divorced and divorcing families, 419–420
    family structure of minor children by race/ethnicity, 418 (figure)
    grandparent-headed families, 422–423
    one-parent families/single parent, 418–419
    same-sex parented families, 417–418, 417 (figure)
    transracial adoption, 422
Family systems theory, 404–408, 426
    adolescence, 406–407
    adoptive families, 421–422
    changing child, 404–405
    changing parent, 405
    childhood, 406
    one-child policy in china, 407–408
    only children, 407–408
    reciprocal interaction, 404
    siblings, 406–407
Fast mapping process, 263
Father-infant attachment, 312–313
Felt other-gender typicality, 382
Felt same-gender typicality, 382
Fertilization, 72–73
Fetal alcohol spectrum disorders, 79
Fetal alcohol syndrome (FAS), 79
Fetal MRI, 58
Fetoscopy, 59
Fetus, 75
Fine motor development, 117–118
Food insecurity, 141 (figure)
Food preferences, childhood, 139
Formal operational reasoning (in adolescence), 192–195
    adolescent egocentrism, 194–195
    characteristics of, 192
    evaluation of, 192–194
    limited use of, 193–194
    opportunities to apply, 192–193
    pendulum task, 193 (figure)
    perspective taking, 194
    social cognition, 194–195
    variability in, 194
Foster care, 454–455
Fragile X syndrome, 50–51
Fraternal twins. *See* Dizygotic (DZ) twins
Freud, Sigmund, 11, 307
Friendship
    children's and adolescents', 436–437
    qualities, 437
    stability, 437–438
Functional magnetic resonance imaging (fMRI), 26, 308, 356

G

Gametes, 44
Gender
    cognitive abilities, 374–375
    gender constancy, 377
    gender identity, 372, 377
    gender stability, 377
    gender stereotypes, 372–373
    mental rotation, 374, 374 (figure)
    and moral reasoning, 350
    physical abilities, 373
    sex differences, 373–375
    socioemotional abilities, similarities and differences, 375
Gender identity, 372, 377
    in adolescence, 384–385
    androgynous, 382
    in childhood and adolescence, 382–385
    dimensions of, 382–384
    felt other-gender typicality, 382
    felt pressure to conform to gender roles, 383
    felt same-gender typicality, 382
    gender contentedness, 382–383
    gender intensification, 384–385
    transgender (*see* Transgender identity)
Gender typing, 375–381
    autonomy support, 379
    biological explanations, 376
    cognitive explanations, 376–378
    contextual explanations, 378–380
    evolution, 376
    gendered interactions, 378–379
    gendered toys and play, 379
    gender-neutral preschool, 381
    gender schema theory, 377–378
    genes, 376
    hormones, 376
    media, 380
    parents, 378–379
    peers, 379–380
    reducing gender stereotyping, 380–381
    and sexual orientation, 383–384
    theories of, 381 (table)
Gene-environment interactions, 61–65
    gene-environment correlation, 63–64, 64 (figure)
    over life span, 65 (figure)
    range of reaction, 62–63, 62 (figure)
Gene therapy, 59
Genetic counseling, 54
Genetic counselor, 166–167
Genetic disorders, 49–51
    dominant-recessive disorders, 49
    prenatal treatment of, 59
    X-linked disorders, 50–51
Genetic inheritance, patterns of, 46–48, 48 (table)
    dominant-recessive inheritance, 46–47, 47 (figure), 47 (table)
    genomic imprinting, 48
    incomplete dominance of genes, 48
    polygenic inheritance, 48
Genetics, 44–46
    cell reproduction, 44–45
    genes shared by twins, 45–46
    sex determination, 45, 46 (figure)
Genomic imprinting, 48
Glial cells, 105, 105 (figure)
Goal-directed behavior, 122–123
Goodness of fit, 304
Grammar, 260, 270–271
Grandparent-headed families, 422–423
Gray matter, 111, 113 (figure). *See also* White matter
Gross motor development, 114
Growth hormone deficiency, 138
Growth stunting, 140
Guided participation (apprenticeship in thinking), 196

H

Habituation, 97–98, 98 (figure), 223, 235
Health of adolescent, threat to, 157–164
    alcohol and substance use, 159–161, 160 (figure)
    cigarette and e-cigarette use, 161
    depression and suicide (*see* Suicide, depression and)
    eating disorders (*see* eating disorders)
    injuries and mortality, 157, 158 (figure)
Health of infants and children, threat to, 150–156
    asthma, 153
    child abuse/maltreatment, 155–156, 156 (table)
    childhood, 152–153
    COVID-19 pandemic, 153–154
    infancy, 150–152
    injuries and mortality, 150–152
    obesity, 153–155, 154 (figure)
    physical activity, 154
    race and SES differences, 150–151

sudden infant death syndrome (SIDS), 151–152, 152 (figure)
   supervision and intervention, 152
   unintentional injuries, 152
Hearing loss in infancy, 266
Helpless orientation, 339, 339 (table)
Hemisphere, 108 (figure)
Hemispheric dominance, 108
Hemophilia, 51
Heredity, 154
Heteronomous morality, 347
Holophrases, 262
Homework gap, 444
Homicide, 157
Hormone oxytocin, 308
Household stress, 147
Human brain, 113 (figure)
Huntington's disease, 49
Hypothesis, 11
Hypothetical-deductive reasoning, 192

I

Ideal self, 323
Identical twins. *See* Monozygotic (MZ) twins
Identity, 327–331
   domains of, 329–330
   identity achievement, 327
   identity diffusion, 328, 330–331
   identity foreclosed, 328, 330
   identity status, 328–329, 329 (figure)
   influences on identity development, 330
   occupational identity, 330
   outcomes associated with identity development, 331
   psychosocial moratorium, 327–328
Imaginary audience, 195
Imaginary companions, 434–435
Immersion, 271
Implantation, 74
Inclusion, 446
Incomplete dominance of genes, 48
Independent variable, 27–28
Individualized education plan (IEP), 445
Inductive discipline, 412–413
Infancy and toddlerhood (birth to about 2 years), 5, 136
Infant amnesia, 217–218
Infant-directed speech, 276–277
   changes in, 277
   cultural differences in, 276–277
Information processing theory, 16–17, 204–207, 205 (figure)
   assumptions, 204–205
   attention, 205
   central executive, 205
   and intelligence, 235
   long-term memory, 206
   mental stores, 205–206
   processing speed, 206
   sensory memory, 205
   working memory, 205–206
Informed consent, 31

Inherited chromosomes, 45
Insecure-avoidant attachment, 310
Insecure-disorganized attachment, 310–311
Insecure-resistant attachment, 310
Instrumental aggression, 359
Instrumental assistance, 353
Intellectual disability (ID), 251–252
Intelligence, 234–239
   adaptive behavior scale, 240
   analytical intelligence, 236
   applied intelligence, 236
   Bayley Scales of Infant Development III (BSID-III), 240–241
   block design test, 241 (figure)
   cognitive scale, 240
   contextual influences on (*see* Contextual influences on intelligence)
   creative intelligence, 236
   emotional intelligence, 238–239
   group administered tests, 239–240
   individually administered tests, 240–243
   information processing and, 235
   intelligence quotient (IQ) score, 242–243
   language scale, 240
   mental age, 242
   motor scale measures, 240
   multiple intelligence theory, 237–238, 238 (figure)
   neurological development and, 235–236
   psychometric approach, 234–235
   social-emotional scale, 240
   socioeconomic status and IQ, 245
   sociohistorical context and IQ, 244
   stability and change in childhood and adolescence, 243
   Stanford-Binet 5, 242
   Stanford-Binet test, 241–242
   triarchic theory of intelligence, 236–237, 236 (figure)
   Weschler tests, 242–243, 243 (table)
Intelligence quotient (IQ), 242
   socioeconomic status and, 245
   sociohistorical context and, 244
Interactionist theory, 274–276
   biological influences, 275
   environmental influences, 275–276
Intermodal perception, 129–130
Internal working model, 310–311
International Statistical Classification of Diseases, 251
Intersectionality and development, 32–33
Intravaginal culture (IVC), 56
In vitro fertilization, 55–56
Irreversibility, 185–186
Isotretinoin, 79

J

Jacob's syndrome, 52
Joint attention, 208, 209 (figure)
Justice, 31
Justice orientation, 350

K

Kangaroo care, 94
Klinefelter syndrome, 52
Kwashiorkor, 140

L

Lamaze method of childbirth, 91
Language
   components of, 259–260
   and development, 258–259
   holophrases, 262
   language acquisition, 262
   morphology, 259
   phonology, 259
   pragmatics, 260, 271
   productive language, 262
   receptive language, 262
   semantics, 260
   syntax, 259–260
Language acquisition device (LAD), 274
Language development
   babbling, 262
   in bilingual infants, 265–266
   bilingual language learning, 268–269, 269 (figure), 271–272
   in childhood and adolescence, 267–272
   contextual influences on (*see* Contextual influences on language development)
   cooing, 262
   in deaf infants, 266
   early childhood, 267–269
   early preferences for speech sounds, 261–262
   explanations for, 273–279
   first words, 262–263
   grammar, 260, 270–271
   in infancy and toddlerhood, 261–266
   infant gesture, 265
   interactionist theory (*see* Interactionist theory)
   learning theory, 273–274
   learning words, 263–264, 264 (figure)
   in monolingual infants, 265
   nativist theory, 274
   prelinguistic communication, 262
   putting words together, 262–265
   school-age children and adolescents, 270–272
   syntax and pragmatics, 268
   theories of, 273 (table)
   in trilingual infants, 266
   two-word utterances, 264–265
   vocabulary, 267–268, 270
Lanugo, 75, 95
Lateralization, 108
Latina paradox, 87–89
Learning goals, 338
Learning theory, 13, 273–274
LGBTQ+ youth, 159, 162
Licensed clinical social workers (LCSW), 397

Limbic system, 112
Logical extension, 267
Longitudinal research study, 28–29
Long-term memory, 206, 216–222
    adolescence, 221
    autobiographical memory, 216, 218–219
    childhood, 218–221
    childhood amnesia, 217–218
    deferred imitation tasks, 217
    elaboration, 219
    episodic memory, 216, 219
    implications for education and parenting, 221–222
    infancy, 217–218
    knowledge and experience, 220
    memory strategies, 219–220, 222
    memory suggestibility, 220–221
    organization, 219
    recall in infancy, 218 (figure)
    rehearsal, 219
    semantic memory, 216
Low birth weight infants, 93–95
    caring for, 94–95
    characteristics of, 93–94
    race, SES, and, 94

M

Macrosystem, 18
Malaria, 53
Malnutrition, 139–142
    and brain development, 140–142, 141 (figure)
    food insecurity, 141 (figure)
    growth stunting, 140
    kwashiorkor, 140
    marasmus, 140
Mandated reporters, 156
Marasmus, 140
Marriage and family therapists, 462–463
Mastery motivation, 337–338
Mastery orientation, 339, 339 (table)
Maturation in adolescence, body growth. *See* Puberty
Media multitasking, 211–212
Media violence, 450
    television, 450–451
    video games, 451
Medical gender transition, 388
Meiosis, 44–45
Memory strategies, 219–220, 222
Memory suggestibility, 220–221
Menarche, 146
Menstruation, 146
Mental age, 242
Mental rotation, 374, 374 (figure)
Mesoderm, 74
Mesosystem, 18
Metacognition, 207, 226
Metalinguistic awareness, 270
Metamemory, 226
Microsystem, 18
Middle childhood (about 6 to about 11 years), 5
Migrant families, 425–426

Mirror recognition, 321–322
Mitosis, 44
Monitoring, parental, 416
Monitoring the Future Study, 25
Monoamine oxidase A (MAOA), 65
Monozygotic (MZ) twins, 46, 56, 60, 119; *See also* Dizygotic (DZ) twins
Montessori schools, 442
Morality of constraint, 347
Morality of cooperation, 347
Moral reasoning, 346–352
    autonomous morality, 347
    and behavior, 350–351
    care orientation, 350
    conventional moral reasoning, 347, 352
    culture, 352
    developmental changes in, 349
    gender and, 350
    heteronomous morality, 347
    influences on, 349–350
    justice orientation, 350
    moral issues, 351–352
    older children, 351–352
    personal issues, 351
    postconventional moral reasoning, 347–348
    preconventional reasoning, 347, 349
    reasoning about justice theory, Kohlberg's, 347–350, 348 (table)
    reasoning about rules theory, Piaget's, 346–347, 348 (table)
    social conventions/social customs, 351
    young children, 351
Morpheme, 259
Morphology, 259
Mortality
    adolescent mortality rates, 157, 158 (figure)
    infant mortality rates, 150–152, 151 (figure)
    Sudden infant death syndrome (SIDS), 151–152, 152 (figure)
Motor development, 114–118
    biological influences on, 119
    childhood, 116–118
    cultural styles of interaction and, 120–121
    as dynamic system, 118–123
    dynamic systems theory (*see* Dynamic systems theory)
    fine motor development, 117–118
    gross motor development, 114
    infancy, 115–117, 115 (figure), 120
    practice and, 119–120
Multiple intelligence theory, 237–238, 238 (figure)
Mutations, 53
Mutual exclusivity assumption, 267
Mutual perspective taking, 194
Myelination, 107, 112, 275

N

National Board for Certification of Occupational Therapy exam, 170

National Physical Therapy Examination, 169
Native-language discrimination, 261
Nativist theory, 274
Nature-nurture debate, 8–9
Negative emotions, 291, 312
Neighborhood violence, 455–456
Neonatal intensive care units (NICUs), 168
Neonatal nurses, 168
Neonate, 72
Neural transmission, 104 (table)
Neural tube, 75
Neurodevelopmental conditions, 247–254
    autism spectrum disorders (ASD), 248–249
    context and disability, 252–253
    giftedness, 253–254
    intellectual disability (ID), 251–252
    sensory processing disorder (SPD), 250–251
    specific learning disorders (SLD), 249–250
Neurodiversity, 248
Neurogenesis, 105
Neurological development and intelligence, 235–236
Neurons, 104, 104 (figure)
    motor neurons, 105
    sensory neurons, 105
Neuropsychological technician, 284
Neurotransmitters, 104–105
Neutral stimulus, 14, 98–99
Newborn, 95–99
    classical conditioning, 98–99
    early learning capacities, 97–98
    habituation, 97–98, 98 (figure)
    newborn health screening, 92–93
    operant conditioning, 14, 99, 124
    perceptual capacities, 95–96
    reflexes, 97, 97 (table)
    states of arousal, 96–97, 96 (table)
New York Longitudinal Study, 302
Niche picking, 63
Nicotine, 161
Nightmares, 143
Nonabusive spanking, 412
Noninvasive prenatal testing (NIPT), 58
Nonshared environment, 61
Nonsocial activity, 433
North American Registry of Midwives, 167
Nurse-midwife practice, 167

O

Obesity, childhood, 153–155, 154 (figure)
Object permanence in infants, 177, 180 (figure)
Observational learning, 15
Occupational therapist/occupational therapy assistant, 169–170
One-child policy in China, 407–408
One-parent families/single parent, 418–419
Ontogenetic development, 18
Operant conditioning, 14, 99, 124
Ossification, 138
Overextension, 264

Overregulation errors, 268
Over-the-counter (OTC) drugs, 79

P

Parallel play, 433
Parenting, 408–416
    attention, 211–212
    authoritarian parenting style, 409–410
    authoritative parenting style, 411
    conflict, 415
    cross cultural comparisons, 413–414
    culture, context and, 413–414
    discipline, 411–413
    long-term memory, 221–222
    nonphysical punishment, 412
    North American children, 414
    parent-adolescent relationships, 414–416
    parental monitoring, 416
    parenting styles, 409–411, 409 (figure)
    permissive parenting style, 410
    physical punishment, 411–412
    thinking skills and, 228
    time out, 412
    uninvolved parenting style, 410
    working memory, 215–216
Passive gene-environment correlation, 63
Pavlov, Ivan, 13–14
Pediatricians, 168
Pediatric nurses, 167–168
Peer acceptance, 438
Peer influence, 441, 441 (figure)
Peer rejection, 438
Peer relationships
    cliques and crowds, 439–440
    friendship, 436–438
    peer acceptance, popularity, and rejection, 438–439, 439 (table)
    peer conformity, 440–441
Peer victimization, 360
Perception, 124
Perceptual narrowing, 126
Performance goals, 338
Period of the zygote, 73–74
Periods of development, 5
Permissive parenting style, 410
Perry Preschool Project, 443
Personal fable, 195
Phenomes, 259
Phenotype, 46
Phenylketonuria (PKU), 49
Phonology, 259
Physical activity
    in adolescents, 148–149
    in childhood, 142
The Physical Activity Guidelines for Americans, 142
Physical aggression, 359–360, 375
Physical and mental disabilities, children with, 155
Physical bullying, 360
Physical development, 6, 18, 130
Physical therapist/physical therapy assistant, 169

Piaget's theory
    concrete operational reasoning (see Concrete operational reasoning)
    formal operational reasoning (see Formal operational reasoning)
    preoperational reasoning (see Preoperational reasoning)
    reasoning about rules, 346–347
    sensorimotor reasoning (see Sensorimotor reasoning)
Placenta, 75
Plasticity, 111
Polygenic inheritance, 48
Popular (popularity), 438
Positive emotions, 296, 354
Positron emission tomography (PET), 26
Postconventional moral reasoning, 347–348
Postnatal stress, 85
Posttraumatic stress disorder (PTSD), 155
Posture/postural skills, 115
Poverty, child development, 110, 150
    chronic poverty, 214–215
    and executive function, 214–215
Practical skills, 251
Prader-Willi syndrome, 48
Pragmatics, 260, 271
Preconventional reasoning, 347, 349
Prefrontal cortex, 107, 113–114, 213, 296
Prelinguistic communication, 262
Prenatal care, 87–89, 150
    barriers to, 87
    race, ethnicity and, 87–89, 88 (figure)
Prenatal development, 76 (figure), 136
    conception, 5, 72–73
    embryonic period (3 to 8 Weeks), 74–75
    fetal period (9 Weeks to Birth), 75–77
    germinal period (0 to 2 Weeks), 73–74, 73 (figure)
    paternal characteristics and, 86–87
    racial disparities in addressing maternal substance use, 82
    teratogens (see Teratogens)
    teratology (see Teratology, principles of)
Prenatal diagnosis, 57–58, 58 (table)
Prenatal environment, 83–86
    maternal age, 85, 86 (figure)
    maternal emotional well-being, 85
    maternal illness, 84
    maternal nutrition, 83–4
Prenatal stress, 85
Prenatal treatment of genetic disorders, 59
Preoperational reasoning (in early childhood), 183–187
    animism, 184, 187
    appearance vs. reality, 185 (figure), 187
    centration, 185
    characteristics of, 184–186, 186 (table)
    conservation/conservation problems, 185, 186 (figure)
    and education, 187
    egocentrism, 184, 187
    irreversibility, 185–186
    reversibility, 187
    three-mountains task, 184 (figure)

    underestimating young children (Piaget's test), 186–187
Preterm infants, 93–95, 119, 304
Primary emotions, 290–291
Primary sex characteristics, 145–146
Private speech, 198
Productive language, 262
Project Head Start, 443
Prosocial behavior, 353–359
    and adjustment, 355
    in adolescence, 355
    biological influences, 356
    cultural context, 358–359
    developmental changes, 354–355
    distributive justice, 354
    family influences, 356–357, 357 (figure)
    helping, 353–354
    influences on, 355–359
    instrumental assistance, 353
    peer influences, 357, 358 (figure)
    sharing, 354–355
Protective factors, 457
Proximodistal development, 136
Pruning, 112
Psychoanalytic theories of development, 11–12, 12–13 (table)
Psychometric approach, 234–235
Psychosexual theory, 11
Psychosocial moratorium, 327–328
Psychosocial theory, 11–12, 12 (table)
Puberty, 112, 144–149, 373
    adolescent growth spurt, 144
    biological and contextual factors on pubertal timing, 146–147
    genetics, 146
    menarche, 146
    menstruation, 146
    physical activity, 148–149
    primary sex characteristics, 145–146
    pubertal timing and socioemotional development, 147–148
    puberty suppressors, 388
    secondary sex characteristics, 145
    secular trend, 147, 148 (figure)
    sequence of physical changes with, 145 (figure)
    and sleep patterns, 149
    stress, 147
    weight and nutrition, 146–147
Punishment, 14
    corporal punishment, 411–412
    nonphysical punishment, 412
    physical punishment, 411–412
Pupillometry, 180

R

Race/racism
    context and disability, 252–253
    racial differences in low birth weight, 94
    racial disparities, 82, 426–427
    self-esteem, 325–326, 326 (figure)
    and socioeconomic intersections and language development, 279
Random assignment, 28

Rapid eye movement (REM) sleep, 96–97, 142
Reactive aggression, 361
Real self, 323
Reasoning about justice theory, Kohlberg's, 347–348
Receptive language, 262
Reciprocal determinism, 14–15, 15 (figure)
Reciprocal interaction, 404
Recognition memory, 217
Recreation workers, 461
Rehearsal, 219
Reinforcement, 14
Relational aggression, 359
Religiosity, 364
    and adjustment, 366
    in adolescence, 364–365
    in childhood, 364
    religious socialization, 365–367
Representational play, 432
Reproductive system of female, 73 (figure)
Research ethics, 31–32
Research in child development
    case study, 27
    comparing research designs, 30 (table)
    correlational research, 27
    cross-sectional research study, 28
    data collection methods, 23–26, 26 (table)
    developmental research designs, 28–30, 29 (figure)
    experimental Research, 27–28
    longitudinal research study, 28–29
    naturalistic observation, 23
    open-ended interview, 24
    physiological measures, 25–26
    questionnaires, 25
    research designs, 27–28
    scientific method, 22–23
    self-report measures, 24
    sequential research, 29
    structured interview, 24–25
    structured observation, 24
Resilience, 457; *See also* Risk and resilience
Reward sensitivity, 114
Risk and resilience
    characteristics, 457, 458 (table)
    exposure to early life stress, 453–454
    foster care, 454–455
    neighborhood and community violence, 455–456
    war and terror, 456–457
Risk factors, 457; *See also* Risk and resilience
Rothbart, Mary, 303
Roughand-tumble play, 434
Rubella (German measles), 84

S

Same-sex parented families, 417–418, 417 (figure)
Scaffolding, 196–197
School
    academic achievement, influences on, 447–448
    children's access to digital technology, 444–445, 445 (figure)
    early childhood education interventions, 443
    educating children with special needs, 445–446
    educational approaches, 442
    transitions, 446–447
School counselors, 462
School psychologists, 462
Screen media use
    in childhood and adolescence, 449–450
    in infancy, 449
    media violence, 450–451
    social media and adolescent development, 452–453
Secondary sex characteristics, 145
Secular trend, 147, 148 (figure)
Secure base, 310–311
Security of attachment, 309–310
Selective attention, 207
Selective breeding studies, 60
Self-awareness, 320–321
Self-concept, 320–323
    adolescence, 323
    categorical self, 322
    childhood, 322–323
    emerging, 322–323
    ideal self, 323
    infancy, 320–322
    mirror recognition, 321–322
    real self, 323
    self-awareness, 320–321
    self-recognition, 321–322
Self-conscious emotions, 292
Self-esteem, 324–327
    and adjustment, 326
    adolescence, 325–327
    contextual influences on, 326–327
    early childhood, 324
    middle childhood, 324–325
    racial and ethnic differences, 325–326, 326 (figure)
    shifts in, 325
    social comparison, 324
Self-recognition, 321–322
Semantic memory, 216
Semantics, 260
Sensation, 124
Sensitive caregiving, 311
Sensitive parenting, 95
Sensitive period, 109
Sensorimotor reasoning (in infancy), 174–183
    A-not-B error tasks, 181, 181 (figure)
    cognitive development, 174–176
    coordination of secondary circular reactions (8 to 12 months), 177, 179 (table)
    deferred imitation tasks, 182
    mental representation (18 to 24 months), 176, 178, 179 (table), 182
    object permanence in infants, 177, 180 (figure)
    primary circular reactions (1 to 4 months), 176, 178 (figure), 179 (table)
    reflexes (birth to 1 month), 176, 179 (table)
    secondary circular reactions (4 to 8 months), 176, 178 (figure), 179 (table)
    simple tasks, 181
    tertiary circular reactions (12 to 18 months), 177, 178 (figure), 179 (table)
    underestimating infants (Piaget's test), 179–182
    violation-of-expectation task, 179–182
Sensory and perceptual development, 124–131
    hearing, 128
    infant-context interactions and perceptual development, 130–131
    intermodal perception, 129–130
    methods for studying infant perception, 124–125
    smell and taste, 129
    touch, 128–129
    vision (*see* Vision)
Sensory deprivation, 266
Sensory integration therapy, 251
Sensory memory, 205
Sensory neurons, 105
Sensory neurons have
Sensory processing disorder (SPD), 250–251
Separation anxiety/separation protest, 309
Sequential research, 29
Sequential touching tasks, 223
Seriation, 188–189
Sex, 372
Sex chromosomes, 45
    sex chromosome abnormalities, 52, 53 (table)
Sexual activity in adolescence, 389–394
    adolescent pregnancy, 392–393
    contraceptive use, 392
    ethnic differences in sexual initiation, 390 (figure)
    lesbian, gay, and bisexual adolescents, 390–392
    outcomes of adolescent pregnancy, 393
    parents, peers, and adolescent sexual activity, 392
    prevalence of, 389–390, 390 (figure)
    supports for adolescent parents, 393
Sexuality education, 393–394
Sexual orientation, 390
Shared environment, 61
Sickle cell anemia, 48–49, 53
Simon, Theodore, 241
Sleep
    childhood, 143
    co-sleeping, 143
    cultural variations, 142–143
    infancy, 142–143

nightmares and sleep terrors, 143
poor sleep, 143
puberty and sleep patterns, 149
REM sleep and development, 142
Sleeper effects, 78
Sleep terrors, 143
Small for date, 93
Social category, 32
Social cognition in adolescence, 194–195
Social cognitive theory, 14–15
Social comparison, 324
Social input, 261
Social media
adolescents' views of, 452
and development, 452–453
effects of, 452
Social policy, 5
Social referencing, 292–293
Social skills, 251
Social smile, 291
Social workers, 396–397
Societal perspective taking, 194
Sociocultural theory, 17, 195–199
cultural tools, 196
evaluation of, 198–199
guided participation and scaffolding, 196–197
private speech, 198
zone of proximal development, 197–198, 197 (figure)
Sociodramatic play, 433–434
Socio-economic status (SES), 139, 147, 150–155, 157, 214–215, 245–246, 330
and child directed speech, 278
context and disability, 252–253
and language development, 277–279, 278 (figure)
Socioemotional development, 6, 305
effects of child maltreatment, 155
and puberty, 147–148
Sociohistorical context, 7
Spanking, 411–412, 413 (figure)
Spearman, Charles, 234
Special education, 283
Specific learning disorders (SLD), 249–250
Speech discrimination, 261
Speech-language pathologists, 284
Spina bifida, 84
Spirituality, 364
Stanford-Binet test, 241–242
Stepfamilies/reconstituted families, 420–421
Stereotypes and IQ, 246
Stereotype threat, 246
Stranger wariness/stranger anxiety, 293–294
Strange Situation, 309–310, 309 (table), 313–315
Substance abuse counselors, 397
Sudden infant death syndrome (SIDS), 151–152, 152 (figure)
Suicide, depression and, 157, 161–163
during COVID-19 pandemic, 163
risk factors for, 162
suicide prevention, 163
suicide rate for boys (ages 15-24), 162 (figure)
warning signs, 164 (table)
Surrogacy, 56
Sustained attention, 207
Synapse, 105
Synaptic pruning, 106, 112
Synaptogenesis, 106, 106 (figure), 111
Syntax, 259–260
and pragmatics, 268
Systems theories, 17–20

T

Telegraphic speech, 264
Television violence, 450–451
Temperament, 302–306
caregiver temperament and expectations, 305
characteristics of, 302–303
context and goodness of fit, 304–305
cultural differences in, 306
difficult temperament, 303
dimensions of temperament, 303
easy temperament, 303
experience and goodness of fit, 305
infant temperament, 304–305
slow-to-warm up temperament, 303
styles of, 302–304
Teratogens, 77–78, 252
alcohol, 79–80
cigarette and e-cigarette use, 80
cocaine, 81
environmental hazards, 81
marijuana/cannabis, 80–81
opioids, 81
prescription and nonprescription drugs, 79
teratogen-context interactions, 82–83
Teratology, principles of, 77–78
complicated effects, 78
critical periods, 77, 78 (figure)
dose, 77–78
individual differences, 78
Testosterone, 145
Thalidomide, 79
Theories of development, 11
behaviorist and social learning theories, 13–15
cognitive theories, 15–17
comparing theories of development, 21–22 (table)
ethology and evolutionary developmental theory, 20–21
psychoanalytic, 11–12, 12–13 (table)
systems theories, 17–20
Theory of mind, 223–224
Thinking skills, 222–228
adolescence, 226–228
categorization, 222–223
childhood, 223–226
cognitive skills and false-belief understanding, 224
context and culture, 224
cultural variations, 225
decision making, 227–228
false belief tasks, 224
habituation tasks, 223
implications for education and parenting, 228
infancy, 222–223
metacognition, 223–227
sequential touching tasks, 223
theory of mind, 223–224
thoughts and beliefs, 225–226
Toy and media research, 463
Traditional bullying, 360
Transgender identity, 385–388
adjustment, 387
adolescence, 386–388
childhood, 386
gender-affirming health care, 388
gender affirming support, 387
medical gender transition, 388
puberty suppressors, 388
Transitions, school
connections with teachers, 446–447
racial and ethnic differences, 447
Transitive inference, 188
Transracial adoption, 422
Triarchic theory of intelligence, 236–237, 236 (figure)
Triple X syndrome, 52
Turner syndrome, 52
Twins, 45–46
behavior studies, 60
dizygotic (DZ) twins, 45–46, 56, 60, 119
monozygotic (MZ) twins, 46, 56, 60, 119

U

Ultrasound, 57
Unconditioned stimulus, 98–99
Underextension, 264
Unintentional injuries, 152
Uninvolved parenting style, 410
U.S. Individuals with Disabilities Education Improvement Act, 445

V

Vaping (e-cigarettes), 161
Vernix caseosa, 75, 95
Video games, media violence, 451
Violation-of-expectation method, 179–182
Vision, 125–128
color vision, 126–127
depth perception, 127–128
externality effect, 125, 126 (figure)
face perception, 126, 126 (figure)
newborn visual processing, 125
visual acuity in infancy, 125 (figure)
visual cliff, 127, 127 (figure)
visual impairment, 128
Visual acuity, 125, 125 (figure)
Vocabulary, 267–268, 269 (figure), 270
Vocabulary spurt, 264

W

Walking, motor development, 116, 123
War and terrorism, 456–457
Wechsler Adult Intelligence Scale (WAIS), 242
Wechsler Intelligence Scale for Children (WISC-V), 242
Wechsler Preschool and Primary Scale of Intelligence (WPPSI), 242
Wernicke's area, 275
Weschler tests, 242–243, 243 (table)
White matter, 112, 113 (figure). *See also* Gray matter
Withdrawn-rejected children, 438
Working memory, 205–206, 212–216, 235
    adolescence, 214
    childhood, 213–214
    delayed response tasks, 212
    implications for education and parenting, 215–216
    infancy, 212–213
    inhibitory control, 213–214
    planning, 213
    storage component of, 213
    visual working memory, 213
    workspace of, 213

X

X-linked disorders, 50–51, 51 (table)

Y

Youth Risk Behavior Survey, 391

Z

Zone of proximal development, 197–198, 197 (figure)
Zygote, 45